THE CAMBRIDGE HISTORY OF

THE PACIFIC OCEAN

*

VOLUME II

The Pacific Ocean since 1800

Volume II of *The Cambridge History of the Pacific Ocean* focuses on the latest era of Pacific history, examining the period from 1800 to the present day. This volume discusses advances and emerging trends in the historiography of the colonial era, before outlining the main themes of the twentieth century when the idea of a Pacific-centred century emerged. It concludes by exploring how history and the past inform preparations for the emerging challenges of the future. These essays emphasize the importance of understanding how the post-colonial period shaped the modern Pacific and its historians.

ANNE PEREZ HATTORI is Professor of History at the University of Guam.

JANE SAMSON is Professor of History at the University of Alberta.

THE CAMBRIDGE HISTORY OF
THE PACIFIC OCEAN

General Editor

PAUL D'ARCY, *Australian National University*

These volumes present a comprehensive survey of the history of the Pacific Ocean, an area making up around one third of the Earth's surface, from initial human colonization to the present day. Reflecting a wide range of cultural and disciplinary perspectives, this two-volume work details different ways of telling and viewing history in a Pacific world of exceptionally diverse cultural traditions, over time spans that require multidisciplinary and multicultural collaborative perspectives. The central importance of nations touched by the Pacific in contemporary world affairs cannot be understood without recourse to the deep history of interactions on and across the Pacific. In reflecting the diversity and dynamism of the societies of this blue hemisphere, these volumes seek to enhance world histories and broaden readers' perspectives on forms of historical knowledge and expression. Volume I explores the history of the Pacific Ocean pre-1800 and Volume II examines the period from 1800 to the present day.

Volume I: The Pacific Ocean to 1800

EDITED BY RYAN TUCKER JONES AND MATT K. MATSUDA

Volume II: The Pacific Ocean since 1800

EDITED BY ANNE PEREZ HATTORI AND JANE SAMSON

THE CAMBRIDGE HISTORY OF
THE PACIFIC OCEAN

*

VOLUME II
The Pacific Ocean since 1800

*

Edited by
ANNE PEREZ HATTORI
University of Guam

JANE SAMSON
University of Alberta

*

General Editor
PAUL D'ARCY

CAMBRIDGE
UNIVERSITY PRESS

Shaftesbury Road, Cambridge CB2 8EA, United Kingdom

One Liberty Plaza, 20th Floor, New York, NY 10006, USA

477 Williamstown Road, Port Melbourne, VIC 3207, Australia

314–321, 3rd Floor, Plot 3, Splendor Forum, Jasola District Centre, New Delhi – 110025, India

103 Penang Road, #05–06/07, Visioncrest Commercial, Singapore 238467

Cambridge University Press is part of Cambridge University Press & Assessment, a department of the University of Cambridge.

We share the University's mission to contribute to society through the pursuit of education, learning and research at the highest international levels of excellence.

www.cambridge.org
Information on this title: www.cambridge.org/9781316510407
DOI: 10.1017/9781108226875

© Cambridge University Press 2023

This publication is in copyright. Subject to statutory exception and to the provisions of relevant collective licensing agreements, no reproduction of any part may take place without the written permission of Cambridge University Press & Assessment.

First published 2023

Printed in the United Kingdom by TJ Books Limited, Padstow Cornwall

A catalogue record for this publication is available from the British Library.

Library of Congress Cataloging-in-Publication Data
NAMES: Jones, Ryan Tucker, editor. | Matsuda, Matt K., editor.
TITLE: The Cambridge history of the Pacific Ocean / edited by Ryan Tucker Jones, University of Oregon, and Matt Matsuda, Rutgers University, New Jersey.
DESCRIPTION: Cambridge, United Kingdom; New York, NY: Cambridge University Press, 2022– | Includes bibliographical references and index. | Contents: v. 1. The Pacific Ocean to 1800 – v. 2 The Pacific Ocean since 1800
IDENTIFIERS: LCCN 2021038598 | ISBN 9781108423939 (v. 1 ; hardback) | ISBN 9781316510407 (v. 2 ; hardback) | ISBN 9781108539227 (2 volume set ; hardback)
SUBJECTS: LCSH: Pacific Area–History. | Pacific Ocean–History. | BISAC: HISTORY / World
CLASSIFICATION: LCC DU28.3 ,C36 2022 | DDC 909/.09823–DC23
LC record available at https://lccn.loc.gov/2021038598

Two Volume Set ISBN 978-1-108-53922-7 Hardback
Volume I ISBN 978-1-108-42393-9 Hardback
Volume II ISBN 978-1-316-51040-7 Hardback

Cambridge University Press & Assessment has no responsibility for the persistence or accuracy of URLs for external or third-party internet websites referred to in this publication and does not guarantee that any content on such websites is, or will remain, accurate or appropriate.

Contents

List of Figures   *xi*
List of Tables   *xiv*
List of Contributors to Volume II   *xv*

General Editor's Introduction   *1*
PAUL D'ARCY

Preface to Volume II   *15*
ANNE PEREZ HATTORI AND JANE SAMSON

PART VII
RETHINKING THE PACIFIC

32 · Climate Change, Rising Seas, and Endangered Island Nations   *25*
HILDA HEINE AND KATHY JETIÑIL-KIJINER

33 · Authority, Identity, and Place in the Pacific Ocean and Its Hinterlands,
c. 1200 to c. 2000   *33*
LEWIS MAYO

34 · Europe's Other? Academic Discourse on the Pacific as a Cultural
Space   *70*
ANNA JOHNSTON

35 · The Phantom Empire: Japan in Oceania and Oceania in Japan from the
1890s Onward   *98*
GREG DVORAK

CONTENTS

36 · Blue Continent to Blue Pacific *132*
JANE SAMSON

PART VIII
APPROACHES, SOURCES, AND SUBALTERN
HISTORIES OF THE MODERN PACIFIC

37 · Archives and Community Memory in the Pacific *167*
OPETA ALEFAIO AND NICHOLAS HALTER

38 · Missing in Action: Women's Under-representation and Decolonizing the
Archival Experience *191*
SAFUA AKELI AMAAMA

39 · Rethinking Gender and Identity in Asia and the Pacific *206*
ANGELA WANHALLA

40 · Fifty Years of the Hawaiian Nation: Integrations of Resistance, Language,
and the Love of Our Land *233*
JONATHAN KAY KAMAKAWIWOʻOLE OSORIO

41 · Pacific Literature and History *246*
ALICE TE PUNGA SOMERVILLE

42 · Film and Pacific History *266*
ALEXANDER MAWYER

43 · The Visual and Performing Arts of the Pacific: A Historical
Overview *286*
ADRIENNE L. KAEPPLER

PART IX
CULTURE CONTACT AND THE IMPACT OF
PRE-COLONIAL EUROPEAN INFLUENCES

44 · The Pacific in the Age of Revolutions *315*
SUJIT SIVASUNDARAM

45 · Disease in Pacific History: 'The Fatal Impact'? *335*
VICKI LUKER

viii

Contents

46 · The Culture Concept and Christian Missions in the Pacific   *349*
HELEN GARDNER

47 · Trading Nature in the Pacific: Ecological Exchange prior to 1900   *369*
DAVID IGLER

48 · Seaborne Ethnography to the Science of Race, 1521–1850   *389*
BRONWEN DOUGLAS

PART X
THE COLONIAL ERA IN THE PACIFIC

49 · Political Developments in the Pacific Islands in the Nineteenth
Century CE   *423*
LORENZ GONSCHOR

50 · Timorese Islanders and the Portuguese Empire in the Indonesian
Archipelago   *450*
RICARDO ROQUE

51 · Pacific Bodies and Personal Space Redefined, 1850–1960   *490*
JACQUELINE LECKIE

52 · The Pacific in the Age of Steam, Undersea Cables, and Wireless
Telegraphy, 1860–1930   *514*
FRANCES STEEL

53 · Latin America's Pacific Ambitions, 1571–2022   *539*
EDWARD MELILLO

PART XI
THE PACIFIC CENTURY?

54 · The USA and the Pacific since 1800: Manifestly Facing West   *563*
DAVID HANLON

55 · World War II and the Pacific   *588*
JUDITH A. BENNETT AND LIN POYER

CONTENTS

56 · The Nuclear Pacific: From Hiroshima to Fukushima, 1945–2018 614
BARBARA ROSE JOHNSTON

57 · Shrinking the Pacific since 1945: Containerships, Jets, and Internet 634
PETER J. RIMMER AND HOWARD W. DICK

58 · China and the Pacific since 1949 664
FEI SHENG AND PAUL D'ARCY

59 · Pacific Island Nations since Independence 683
STEPHANIE LAWSON

PART XII

PACIFIC FUTURES

60 · Ancestral Voices of the Sea: Hearing the Past to Lead the Future 707
TĒVITA O. KA'ILI

61 · Defining the Contours of the Lagoon: Political Strategies towards Post-Nouméa Accord Political Futures in New Caledonia 729
ANTHONY TUTUGORO

62 · New Pacific Voyages since Independence: 1960 Onwards 752
ROANNIE NG SHIU AND ROCHELLE BAILEY

63 · Creating Sustainable Pacific Environments during the Anthropocene: The Lessons of Pacific History 776
TAMATOA BAMBRIDGE AND GONZAGA PUAS

64 · Concluding Reflection: 'Choppy Waters' 802
ANNE PEREZ HATTORI

References to Volume II 805
Index 888

Figures

	Political and cultural divisions of the contemporary Pacific.	xvii
34.1	'Les Sauvages de la Mer Pacifique', wallpaper design by Jean Gabriel Charvet.	71
34.2	Tupaia's map: chart of the Society Islands.	88
35.1	Map of Inner and Outer Nanyō.	105
35.2	Ishiwata Tatsunosuke was an employee of Nanyō Takushoku Kaisha (Nantaku) Phosphate Mining Division in Ebon Atoll, Marshall Islands. Photo courtesy of Minami Lemae family.	110
35.3	Postcards of *Kanaka* and *Chamoro* produced during the 1930s. Personal collection of the author.	112
35.4	'Yume no Hawai [Hawai'i Dreaming]: *Aloha Oe* Ukulele', by Kimura Ryōko, 2017. Photo courtesy of the artist.	125
37.1	Beqa villagers' traditional fish drive, 1947. NAF Facebook post, G533. Courtesy of the National Archives of Fiji.	187
43.1	Exhibit case of Fijian ivory ornaments acquired by Anatole von Hugel, Sir Arthur Gordon, and Alfred Maudsley. University Museum of Archaeology and Anthropology, Cambridge.	290
43.2	Four men wearing Semese masks, Kerema, Papua New Guinea, 1 March 1911. The Joseph N. Field South Pacific Expedition. Photo © The Field Museum, Image No. cSA37933, Cat. No. 142119, photographer A.B. Lewis.	295
43.3	Back of sacred or tamburan house (built 1551), Wakde, Papua New Guinea, 1 May 1911. The Joseph N. Field South Pacific Expedition, photo © The Field Museum, Image No. cSA37418, photographer A.B. Lewis.	296
43.4	Masks from Melanesia, with a focus on New Britain and New Ireland. In the former exhibition in the Museum am Rothenbaum – Kulturen und Künste der Welt, Hamburg, Germany, © MARKK, Brigitte Saal.	296
43.5	Engraving of a kava ceremony inside a ceremonial house in Tonga, after a drawing by John Webber from the Atlas to Cook's Third Voyage, Smithsonian Institution Libraries. Photograph James DiLoreto.	297
43.6	Māori storehouse (*pataka*), late nineteenth/early twentieth century, as mounted in 1984 for the Hall of Peoples of the Pacific, American Museum of Natural History, New York. Purchase, T.E. Donne, 1909, (80.0/2897).	300

LIST OF FIGURES

43.7 Fijian wooden sculptures from the US Exploring Expedition, 1840. Magnificent Voyagers exhibit, National Museum of Natural History, Washington, DC, 1985. — 302

43.8 Rapa Nui barkcloth sculptures. Gift of the Heirs of David Kimball, 1899. © President and Fellows of Harvard College, Peabody Museum of Archaeology and Ethnology, left PM 99-12-70/53543, right PM 99-12-70/53542. — 303

43.9 Dress worn by the chief mourner at a funeral ceremony in Tahiti. Collected during Cook's second voyage. British Museum (Oc.Tah.78). — 304

43.10 Presentation of fine mats (*'ie tōga*) at the death of distinguished elder Fa'animo. Falealupo village, Sāmoa. Photograph J.W. Love, 1974. — 305

43.11 Micronesian exhibit of weaving and important objects, 1970s. National Museum of Natural History, Washington, DC. — 306

43.12 Presentation of a large Tongan barkcloth to Sinaitakala Fakafonua for a ceremony in honour of her marriage the following day to the Tongan Crown Prince. Photograph Linny Folau, Vava'u Press. — 308

43.13 Hawaiian feathered cape and helmet as mounted in 1971 for the Hall of Peoples of the Pacific, American Museum of Natural History, New York. Cape, gift of George S. Bowdoin, 1908 (80.0/784); helmet, history unknown before 1907 (80.0/671). — 309

43.14 Hawaiian drum, *pahu*. Oldman collection, Canterbury Museum, New Zealand (E150.1185). — 311

43.15 Hawaiian hula performances. Photographs Pelehonuamea Harman at Pu'u Huluhulu, Hawai'i. — 312

48.1 Anon., 'Ladrones', in [Sino-Spanish (Boxer) Codex, Boxer mss. II, LMC 2444, fols. 1v–2r, Lilly Library, Indiana University, Bloomington, IN, https://iucat.iu.edu/catalog/8843094.] — 393

48.2 E. Bowen, 'A map of the discoveries made by Captn. Willm. Dampier in the Roebuck in 1699', in J. Harris, *Navigantium atque Itinerantium Bibliotheca* ... (1744), vol. 1, facing p. 125, National Library of Australia, Canberra, http://nla.gov.au/nla.obj-163902730. — 397

48.3 S. Leroy, [Îles des Papous: Divers portraits de naturels vus sur l'île Rawak], watercolour (n.d.). PIC Solander Box A42 #T223 NK6063/A, National Library of Australia, Canberra, http://nla.gov.au/nla.obj-134723809. — 408

48.4 L.-A. de Sainson, 'Vanikoro: vue du village de Nama', lithograph, detail, in J. Dumont d'Urville, *Atlas, Voyage de la corvette l'Astrolabe* ... (1833), plate 183, PIC vol. 578 #U1892 NK3340, National Library of Australia, Canberra, http://nla.gov.au/nla.obj-135844356. — 412

48.5 A. Tardieu, 'Carte générale de l'Océanie', in J. Dumont d'Urville, *Atlas, Voyage de la corvette l'Astrolabe* ... (1833), [map 1], MAP NK 2456/73, National Library of Australia, Canberra, http://nla.gov.au/nla.obj-230622715. — 413

48.6 L.A. Bisson, 'Orion (Papouas) ... Mélanésie'; 'Liké-liké ... Archipel Viti'; 'Taha-Tahala ... (Polynésie)'; 'Faustino-Tchargualoff ... (Micronésie)', in [P.-M. A. Dumoutier], *Atlas anthropologique, Voyage au pôle sud et dans l'Océanie* ... (1846), plates 11, 5, 13, 10. Photograph by B. Douglas. — 416

49.1 Networks of institutional transfer. — 432

xii

List of Figures

50.1 Exhibition of a deteriorated ancient lulik monarchic flag by ritual keepers from the sacred houses of Afaloicai to Portuguese colonial authorities in 1957. Photographer Victor Santa. IICT Photography Collection. ULisboa-IICT-MAT26678. Courtesy of Museu Nacional de História Natural e da Ciência, Lisbon. 479

51.1 Examining a schoolboy of Bucalevu School during the yaws campaign, 1955. Neg. #6557, National Archives of Fiji. 507

52.1 Stranding of the steamship *Macgregor* in Kadavu Passage, Fiji, 18 May 1874. IAN18/05/74/85, State Library of Victoria. 519

52.2 Fanning Island – sports day. c5487, Overseas Telecommunications Commission photographic collection. National Archives of Australia. 531

52.3 'Plan of Radiotelegraphy in the Pacific' in *Linking Australia and New Zealand with the Pacific Islands by Radiotelegraphy*. National Library of Australia. 535

53.1 A Chifa (Chinese-Peruvian restaurant) in Lima's Barrio Chino. Photograph by the author. 548

53.2 A map published by Chile's Ministry of Education showing a depiction of *Chile tricontinental* (Tricontinental Chile). Ministerio de Educación, Gobierno de Chile, 'Unidad de currículum y evaluación: Chile tricontinental', https://curriculumnacional.mineduc.cl/614/articles-29379_recurso_jpg.jpg. 557

53.3 Rano Raraku *mo'ai* on the lower slopes of Rapa Nui's Terevaka Volcano. Photograph in the public domain. 558

55.1 World War II, the Pacific War 1937–42. Map drawn by Les O'Neill. 591

55.2 Two-pronged offensives by the Allies. Map drawn by Les O'Neill. 594

55.3 World War II counteroffensives, 1943–5. Map drawn by Les O'Neill. 595

56.1 The Nuclear Pacific. 615

57.1 Principal international airlines in the Pacific, June 1941. S.B. Smith, *Air Transport in the Pacific Area* (New York: International Institute of Pacific Relations, 1942). 640

57.2 Container ports with the world's top-100 located in the Pacific, 2015. 647

57.3 Top passenger airport pairs in international traffic, 2015. 652

57.4 Outgoing flows and strength of connections between countries in terms of Millions of Telecommunications Minutes (MiTT), 2015. Based on data provided by TeleGeography on eleven countries. Personal communication, 2018. 656

57.5 The network of networks. 658

57.6 Gateway regions, gateways, and sub-gateways in the Pacific. 659

57.7 Geologistics map of the Pacific. 661

62.1 Participation rates of RSE and SWP. Source: R. Bailey, *Health Care Management in Australia's and New Zealand's Seasonal Workers Schemes*, DPA Working Paper Series 2020/2 (Canberra: ANU, 2020). 769

Tables

49.1 Chronology of Oceanian constitutions.	427
49.2 Treaties of Pacific states, 1800–1900.	437
49.3 Timeline of colonial claims up to 1901.	442
57.1 Moving goods, people, and information.	636
57.2 Throughput of the Pacific's major container port ranges, 1975, 1990, and 2010.	644
57.3 Containerized trade on major east–west trade routes, 1999, 2005, and 2015.	645
57.4 Top-three countries in the world container port traffic league at five-yearly intervals, 1995–2010.	645
57.5 World's top-five container ports, 1995, 2005, and 2015.	646
57.6 Main and feeder services offered by the top twenty-five container liner operators between East Asia and other trade zones, 2014.	648
57.7 Aircraft operated by Qantas Empire Airways Ltd and Qantas Airways Ltd on Australia–North America route, 1954–2008.	649
57.8 Time taken to traverse the Pacific by mode, 1900–30 and 2015.	660
62.1 Selected Pacific Islands and Territories populations census data at home and abroad.	758
62.2 Pacific national university institutions.	762
63.1 Environmental zones in the Mortlock Islands, FSM.	782

Contributors to Volume II

SAFUA AKELE AMAAMA is Head of the History and Pacific Cultures Department at Te Papa Tongarewa, Museum of New Zealand, Wellington.

OPETA ALEFAIO is a Records Manager at the University of the South Pacific and former Director of The National Archives of Fiji.

ROCHELLE BAILEY is Research Fellow in the Department of Pacific Affairs at the Australian National University.

TAMATOA BAMBRIDGE is Director of Research at the French National Centre for Scientific Research's Centre of Island Research and Environmental Observatory / Directeur de Recherche, Centre National de la Recherche Scientifique (CNRS), Centre de Recherche Insulaire et Observatoire de l'Environnement (CRIOBE), Papetoai, Mo'orea, Polynésie Française

JUDY BENNETT is Emeritus Professor of History at the University of Otago / Te Whare Wānanga o Otāgo.

PAUL D'ARCY is an Associate Professor in the Department of Pacific Affairs at the Australian National University.

HOWARD W. DICK is Emeritus Professor of Economic History at the University of Melbourne.

BRONWEN DOUGLAS is Honorary Professor in the School of Archaeology and Anthropology at the Australian National University.

GREG DVORAK is Professor of International Cultural Studies at Waseda University, Tokyo.

HELEN GARDNER is Associate Professor of History at Deakin University.

LORENZ GONSCHOR is Senior Lecturer in English at the University of French Polynesia / L'université de la Polynésie française, Puna'aui'a, Tahiti.

NICHOLAS HALTER is Lecturer in History at the University of the South Pacific.

DAVID HANLON is Emeritus Professor of History at the University of Hawai'i at Mānoa.

ANNE PEREZ HATTORI is Professor of History, CHamoru Studies and Micronesian Studies at the University of Guam / Unibetsedåt Guåhan.

HILDA HEINE is former President of the Republic of the Marshall Islands, Majuro.

DAVID IGLER is Professor of History at University of California, Irvine.

KATHY JETÑIL KIJINER is cofounder of the Marshall Islands environmental not-for-profit organisation Jo-Jikum, and a doctoral candidate in anthropology at the Australian National University.

LIST OF CONTRIBUTORS TO VOLUME II

ANNA JOHNSTON is Associate Professor in Literature in the School of Communication and Arts at the University of Queensland.

BARBARA ROSE JOHNSTON is Senior Fellow at the Center for Political Ecology, Santa Cruz, California, and Adjunct Professor of Anthropology at Michigan State University.

THE LATE ADRIENNE KAEPPLER was Curator of Oceanic Ethnography, Department of Anthropology, at the National Museum of Natural History, Smithsonian Institution, Washington DC.

TĒVITA KAʻILI is Professor of Anthropology and Dean of the Faculty of Culture, Language and Performing Arts at Brigham Young University, Hawaiʻi.

STEPHANIE LAWSON is Professor of Politics and International Relations at Macquarie University; Honorary Professor in Pacific Affairs, Australian National University; and Senior Research Associate, Faculty of Humanities, University of Johannesburg.

JACQUELINE LECKIE is Associate Professor and Adjunct Research Fellow at the Victoria University of Wellington/Te Herenga Waka and Conjoint Associate Professor, University of Newcastle, Australia.

VICKI LUKER is Visiting Fellow in the Department of Pacific Affairs at the Australian National University.

ALEXANDER MAWYER is Associate Professor of Anthropology at the University of Hawaiʻi at Mānoa

LEWIS MAYO is Associate Professor at The Asia Institute at the University of Melbourne.

EDWARD D. MELILLO is William R. Kenan Jr Professor of History and Environmental Studies at Amherst College, Massachusetts.

ROANNIE NG SHIU is Pacific Health Research Program Manager, Office of the Associate Dean (Pacific), Faculty of Medicine & Health Science, University of Auckland// Waipapa Taumata Rau.

JONATHAN KAY KAMAKAWIWOʻOLE OSORIO is Dean of the Hawaiʻinuiākea School of Hawaiian Knowledge and Professor of History at the University of Hawaiʻi at Mānoa

LYN POYER is Professor of Cultural Anthropology at the University of Wyoming.

GONZAGA PUAS is Director of the Micronesian Institute for Research and Development.

PETER RIMMER is Emeritus Professor of Human Geography at the Australian National University.

RICARDO ROQUE is Research Fellow at the Institute of Social Sciences, University of Lisbon/ Instituto de Ciências Sociais, Lisboa, Portugal

JANE SAMSON is Professor of History at the University of Alberta, Edmonton.

FEI SHENG is Deputy Director of the National Center for Oceanian Studies and Associate Professor of History at Sun Yat-Sen University.

SUJIT SIVASUNDARAM is Professor of World History at the University of Cambridge and Fellow in History at Gonville and Caius College, Cambridge.

FRANCES STEEL is Senior Lecturer in History at the University of Otago/Te Whare Wānanga o Otāgo.

ALICE TE PUNGA SOMERVILLE holds a joint appointment in the University of British Columbia's Department of English Language and Literatures and the Institute for Critical Indigenous Studies.

ANTHONY TUTUGORO is a PhD candidate at the Université de la Polynésie française, Punaʻauiʻa /Université de la Nouvelle-Calédonie, Nouméa.

ANGELA WANHALLA (Ngāi Te Ruahikihiki, Ngāi Tahu, Pākehā) is a professor in the History Programme at the University of Otago/Te Whare Wānanga o Otāgo.

xvi

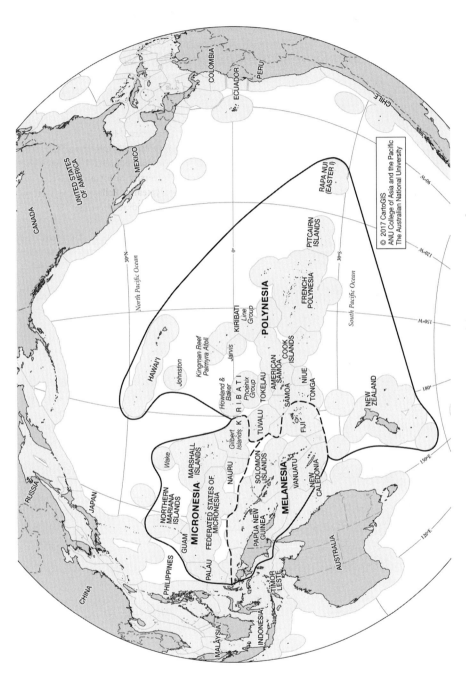

Political and cultural divisions of the contemporary Pacific.

General Editor's Introduction

PAUL D'ARCY

There has never been a more appropriate time for a comprehensive history of the Pacific Ocean as we attempt in this collection. The dramatic rise of East Asian economies in the decades after World War II has given rise to one of the most rapid realignments of global economic and political influences in world history. Energy resources and raw materials flow into East Asia from Australia, South America, Central Asia, Southeast Asia, and the Indian Ocean world to fuel the new workshop of the world in the People's Republic of China. China has become the fulcrum point of the global economy in what has been deemed to be the Pacific Century.[1] The massive flow of trade goods across the Pacific Ocean between the United States and China lies at the heart of this Pacific-centred realignment, accompanied by increasing tensions over rival spheres of influence in the Pacific between these two superpowers. Recent maritime confrontations in the Pacific have largely been analysed by international relations experts and legal scholars with limited reference to the rich but fragmented history of cultural exchanges across and within the Pacific Ocean.

Momentum towards conceptualizing the Pacific Ocean in its entirety as a zone of interaction has mounted since the 1980s. The classic work on Pacific Ocean history remains O.H.K. Spate's visionary three-volume *The Pacific since Magellan* written in the 1970s and 1980s.[2] Books on Pacific Island navigation and cultural encounters with European explorers in the Pacific, especially those involving Captain Cook, continue to sell well since emerging

---

[1] See for example R. Elegant, *Pacific Destiny: The Rise of the East* (London: Hamish Hamilton, 1990) and the masterful overview of academic literature on this concept by Akira Iriye, 'A Pacific century?', in D. Armitage and A. Bashford (eds.), *Pacific Histories: Ocean, Land, People* (Basingstoke: Palgrave Macmillan, 2014), 97–118.
[2] O.H.K. Spate, *The Pacific since Magellan*, 3 vols. (Canberra: ANU Press, 1979–88).

as a genre in the 1960s.[3] These works target university and general public audiences. The 1990s produced Simon Winchester's popular histories of the rise of the Pacific to global prominence, Walter McDougall's history of the North Pacific, *Let the Sea Make a Noise*, Arif Dirlik's article-length attempt to conceptualize the Pacific as a zone of interaction in the early 1990s, and John McNeill's astute environmental perspectives on the interaction between technology, transport, and trade in the history of resource use in the Pacific.[4] Ron Crocombe's 2007 *Asia in the Pacific Islands*, Matt Matsuda's *Pacific Worlds* in 2012, and a host of other special issues and edited collections have closely explored the increasing interactions between the societies of the Pacific's western rim and the rest of the Pacific. There has also been a growing number of studies of the maritime dimension of many Asian societies.[5]

The few Pacific-wide histories that have been attempted focus on the region's integration into a wider global economy which is seen as beginning when Europeans began to move into the Pacific. The modern concept of a Pacific community is essentially based on the modern economic relationship between East Asia and North America. It is a relationship with little legacy of pre-existing cultural or historical ties, and one that has only been made possible by communications and transport revolutions in the last two centuries. Prior to this phase the Pacific is generally viewed as a prohibitive void rather than an avenue for movement. Pre-European Pacific peoples are

---

[3] There are too many books written on Cook to cite all. Among the more notable are J.C. Beaglehole (ed.), *The Journals of Captain James Cook on his Voyages of Discovery*, 4 vols. (Cambridge: Cambridge University Press, 1955, 1961, 1967), and N. Thomas, *Cook: The Extraordinary Voyages of Captain James Cook* (New York: Walker, 2003).

[4] See S. Winchester, *The Pacific* (London: Hutchinson, 1991) and his updated version *Pacific: Ocean of the Future* (London: William Collins, 2015); W.A. McDougall, *Let the Sea Make a Noise: Four Hundred Years of Cataclysm, Conquest, War and Folly in the North Pacific* (New York: Avon Books, 1993); A. Dirlik, 'The Asia-Pacific idea: reality and representation in the invention of a regional structure', *Journal of World History* 3:1 (1992), 55–79. For an overview of the concept, see J. McNeill, 'Of rats and men: a synoptic environmental history of the island Pacific', *Journal of World History* 5:3 (1994), 299–349.

[5] R. Crocombe, *Asia in the Pacific Islands: Replacing the West* (Suva: Institute of Pacific Studies, 2007) and M.K. Matsuda, *Pacific Worlds: A History of Seas, Peoples, and Cultures* (Cambridge: Cambridge University Press, 2012). On maritime Southeast Asia see especially Chapters 9 (Cynthia Neri Zayas and Paul D'Arcy), 17 (Hsiao-chun Hung), 25 (Leonard Y. Andaya), 30 (Xing Hang), 31 (Jennifer L. Gaynor) and 50 (Ricardo Roque). See also J. Warren, *The Sulu Zone: The World Capitalist Economy and the Historical Imagination* (Amsterdam: VU Press, 1998). For East Asia see Chapters 17 (Hsiao-chun Hung), 23 (Kent Deng), 24 (Ronald C. Po), 29 (Dahpon Ho), 30 (Xing Hang), 35 (Greg Dvorak), and 58 (Fei Sheng and Paul D'Arcy). For the Americas see Chapters 16 (Jon M. Erlandson), 21 (José Miguel Ramírez-Aliaga), 26 (Madonna L. Moss), 27 (Andrea Ballesteros Danel and Antonio Jaramillo Arango), 28 (Rainer F. Buschmann and David Monzano Cosano), 53 (Edward Melillo), and 54 (David Hanlon).

usually considered to have conducted localized interactions only, with a resultant consciousness that was at best regional rather than pan-Pacific.[6] Such pan-Pacific passages were dominated by European vessels. European encounters with the South Pacific began in 1567 when Magellan sailed westward across Oceania from South America. Other Spanish voyages of discovery followed in his wake. A series of violent encounters and the decimation of colonies in Melanesia from malaria soon ended Spain's South Pacific engagement. Henceforth, the Spanish focused on Micronesia and the trans-Pacific galleon trade carrying goods between the colonial ports of Manila and Acapulco. Their route bypassed most inhabited islands in the Pacific, while former links between Guam and the Caroline Islands diminished with the violent establishment of Spanish rule in the Marianas and the subsequent loss of seafaring capacity within the island chain.[7] European contact with the Pacific became more sustained from the late 1760s onwards as voyages of exploration by a number of European nations gradually mapped Australasia and Oceania, most famously and comprehensively through the three expeditions of Captain James Cook from 1768 to 1779. Focusing solely on the flow of traffic between the Pacific's terrestrial margins overlooks numerous more localized seafaring interactions and as well as interactions with the sea that were part of daily life for many Pacific inhabitants.

Most Pacific Island history has focused on inter-cultural relations between Pacific Islanders and Europeans over the last two and a half centuries.[8] Pacific historians have largely focused on the impact of Western products, peoples, and ideas on Pacific Islanders, with increasing emphasis placed on presenting Pacific Islanders as rational, active agents in this process. The majority of Pacific Islanders' millennia of history was recorded and conveyed orally, which has meant that much Pacific history has become multidisciplinary to

---

[6] Dirlik, 'The Asia-Pacific idea', 64. Dirlik grossly underestimated the degree of Indigenous interactions in the pre-European Pacific. Subsequent studies since 1992 continue to expand the extent of Indigenous navigational knowledge and seaborne exchanges among Pacific peoples as is detailed in Volume I's Part iv: The Initial Colonization of the Pacific and Part V: The Evolution of Pacific Communities.

[7] See O.H.K. Spate, *The Pacific since Magellan*, vol. 1, *The Spanish Lake* (Canberra: ANU Press, 1979). Pan-Pacific exchanges in this collection are discussed in Chapters 2 (David Christian), 16 (Jon M. Erlandson), 33 (Lewis Mayo), 36 (Jane Samson), 47 (David Igler), 52 (Frances Steel), and 57 (Peter Rimmer and Howard Dick).

[8] See D. Munro and B. Lal (eds.), *Texts and Contexts: Reflections in Pacific Islands Historiography* (Honolulu: University of Hawai'i Press, 2006). The terms Pacific Islander and Islander are used here interchangeably to refer to Pacific Islanders in general, while the terms European and Western are used interchangeably to refer to influences and people emanating from Europe and the Americas after European colonization.

incorporate non-literate sources such as oral traditions, linguistic patterns, and material remains. For this reason, Pacific history cannot be viewed in isolation, but must be seen as part of a larger body of work produced by their Pacific-focused colleagues in anthropology, archaeology, linguistics, and geography. This has enhanced rather than diluted the nature of Pacific history. The coastal peoples of the Pacific Rim were also orientated towards the sea, and shared many of the experiences Pacific Islanders encountered as well as made distinct by local context.

There has recently been mounting academic interest in ocean history, as demonstrated by the above-cited ocean history forum in the world's top-ranked history journal, the *American Historical Review* in 2006, and new ocean history series launched by Cambridge University Press.[9] The Pacific as a region is also experiencing renewed academic interest, with Palgrave launching a new Pacific History series edited by Matt Matsuda and Bronwen Douglas. Matsuda's book *Pacific Worlds* received critical acclaim and in 2014 Atlantic World specialist, Harvard's David Armitage co-edited *Pacific Histories: Ocean, Land, People* with Alison Bashford. Anthropologist Nicholas Thomas was jointly awarded the Wolfson History Prize for his 2010 general history of Pacific peoples in the era of European contact and colonial rule, *Islanders: The Pacific in the Age of Empire.*[10]

The Pacific's maritime histories of and by its coastal inhabitants are particularly relevant to historians of other ocean spaces seeking to conceptualize their field in terms more of histories of the sea than of histories across the sea. Calls have mounted recently to balance essentially continental, Eurocentric outlooks emphasizing the flow of goods and people across the sea as measures of cultural and regional coherence with more oceanic ones, where the sea is not merely a time passage for people between terrestrial stages of historical actions but also one rich in spaces of historical enactment, and cultural meaning and memory. As Stanford University geographer Kären Wigen noted in her introduction to the *American Historical Review* forum on oceans in history, 'No longer outside time, the sea is being given a history, even as the history of the world is being retold from the perspective of the sea.'[11]

---

[9] A discussion of the 2006 *American Historical Review* Ocean Forum follows. See note 11. This two-volume work is part of the Cambridge Ocean History Series edited by D. Armitage, A. Bashford, and S. Sivasundaram, see www.cambridge.org/core/series/cambridge-oceanic-histories.

[10] Armitage and Bashford (eds.), *Pacific Histories*. N. Thomas, *Islanders: The Pacific in the Age of Empire* (New Haven: Yale University Press, 2010).

[11] K. Wigen, 'Introduction', Oceans of History Forum, *American Historical Review* 111:3 (2006), 717–21, para. 1, and A. Games, 'Atlantic history: definitions, challenges, and opportunities', *American Historical Review* 111:3 (2006), 741–57, paras. 10, 17–19.

General Editor's Introduction

Many Pacific coastal peoples remain more closely linked to local maritime environments for their subsistence and identity than peoples in most other parts of the globe who have grown less dependent on local seas because of their central place in the global economy their overseas expansion helped create. These features combine to produce populated seas that are, even today, used intensively, culturally mapped in intimate detail, and imbued with history.[12] This redefining of the sea as sea peoples in the region define it – as a series of differentiated and distinct sea spaces – has major implications for other environmental histories of the sea where sea spaces still largely remain voids occasionally punctuated by islands between continental margins and largely conceptualized as a passage of time. Others have begun to argue for the need to incorporate the sea into our vision in ways that go beyond merely tracing the highways of sea travel between islands. Archaeologist and accomplished sailor Geoff Irwin notes that: 'Most prehistorians have concentrated on the evidence for intervals of time between islands but it could help our explanations to give more consideration to the intervening space – which is ocean – and the changing social and environmental circumstances of the islands and people in it.'[13]

The actions and policies of national governments and international organizations are also reflecting mounting environmental concerns about the Pacific Ocean. This trend is also feeding back into tertiary education with the rising popularity of programmes focused on sustainable development and environmental issues. The World Bank mobilized these concerns in 2012 and announced a massive programme specifically focused on sustainable ocean policies for the Pacific Ocean to be supported by a number of partners from the Global Partnership for Oceans (GPO). The GPO is a coalition of more than 120 countries and organizations, including the World Bank.[14] *National Geographic* has focused on Pacific Islander reef and lagoon rehabilitation and the massive floating garbage vortices in the northern Pacific from East Asia and North America.[15] Blue economies have become the focus of much future

---

[12] P. D'Arcy (ed.), *Peoples of the Pacific: The History of Oceania to 1870* (Aldershot: Ashgate, 2008), xix–xlv.

[13] G. Irwin, *The Prehistoric Exploration and Colonisation of the Pacific* (Cambridge: Cambridge University Press, 1992), 136.

[14] World Bank, 'World Bank announces proposed package of support for World's largest ocean', 31 August 2012, www.worldbank.org/en/news/press-release/2012/08/31/world-bank-announces-proposed-package-of-support-for-worlds-largest-ocean0.

[15] T. Eichenseher, 'Bridging Western science and Polynesian tradition', *National Geographic News*, 25 February 2011, http://news.nationalgeographic.com/news/2011/02/110223-biodiversity-cultural-tradition-moorea-indigenous-knowledge/, and M. Simon, 'Trash islands', *Earth Times*, 15 December 2012, www.earthtimes.org/pollution/trash-islands/2253/.

planning for Pacific Island and Pacific Rim nations since 2010. The blue economy refers to the rapid development of sustainable marine economies, generally in conjunction with sustainable terrestrial, low-carbon green economies. This has become a global research priority in recent years as the threat of climate change accelerates – prompting, for example, an extended Economist Intelligence Unit discussion section in *The Economist* in 2015 for the World Ocean Summit, and becoming a research priority for Pacific regional institutions and most Pacific governments.[16] In May 2015, the Pacific Islands Forum Secretariat Secretary-General, Dame Meg Taylor, became the world's first politically endorsed ocean advocate as Commissioner of the Pacific Ocean Alliance. This history collection arose within this context of long and deep cultural connections to the Pacific Ocean and mounting academic and political interest.

This history of the Pacific Ocean brings together for the first time the extensive corpus of studies on the interaction of Pacific Island and Pacific Rim societies with the ocean and with each other from humankind's initial maritime explorations until the present day. It offers a unified perspective on three great phases of Pacific Ocean history. The first is the colonization of the Pacific Rim and islands by land and sea and the establishment of diverse civilizations that interacted with the neighbours to varying degrees according to fluid internal dynamics and external influences. The diverse maritime cultures that resulted demonstrated much greater resilience and continuity than is generally acknowledged in most world history texts during the next phase when European explorers and conquerors transformed the Pacific into their desired vision, albeit restricted by the limits of their resources at these most distant of their imperial endeavours. The last phase since the dropping of atomic bombs on Hiroshima and Nagasaki has seen the decolonization and increasing assertiveness of Pacific communities in regional forums and on the world stage. Hidden and neglected histories are being discovered and created to legitimize and frame these societies' preferred role on the world stage.

The need to address the Pacific lacuna in world history has now become vital as the economies of the Asian Pacific Rim rapidly expand and become the main engine of increasingly inter-related world trade networks and harmful industrial pollutants driving climate change. Many of the world's

---

[16] The Economist Intelligence Unit, 'The Blue Economy: growth, opportunity and a sustainable ocean economy', An Economist Intelligence Unit briefing paper for the World Ocean Summit, 2015, https://eiuperspectives.economist.com/sites/default/files/images/Blue%20Economy_briefing%20paper_WOS2015.pdf.

General Editor's Introduction

worst polluters and the first nations to perhaps disappear under the sea because of climate-change induced sea level rises are located in the Pacific. The *Cambridge History of the Pacific Ocean* anticipates the shifting tectonics of global economics, demography, and political ecology, and provides a *longue durée* viewpoint to understand the mounting tensions and emerging environmental and political conflicts over Pacific Ocean spaces, and their resources and freedom of passage. The Pacific Century cannot be understood without the deep history of interactions on and across the Pacific which this study provides. In reflecting the neglected diversity and dynamism of the societies of this blue hemisphere, it acts as a major corrective to world histories too long framed in terms of Western triumphalism.

Colonial history and historiography divided sea worlds into worlds perceived to be discrete, restricted, and controlled spaces unified by the language of the colonizer. Such perceived spaces impose colonial order on maritime environments that have always resisted attempts to control and master them by human communities, and upon independent seafaring peoples who have always dwelt beyond the power of the state, or existed at its margins. They represent seascapes of desire by the powerful rather than reflections of reality. It follows that attempts to map and narrate the range and vision of maritime peoples before their domination and marginalization by land-based, numerically or militarily superior peoples offer a way of decolonizing their history. Part of this decolonizing involves a form of subaltern history whereby the centrality of sea, forever present in the worldview of maritime peoples, is restored to its former central place. A number of chapters demonstrate that Pacific Islanders, Amerindian and Inuit peoples, Malay peoples of Southeast Asia, Japanese, Korean, and Chinese all have long and enduring associations with the sea. Many of these associations have been marginalized or understated in world history, much to their detriment in current global forums on ocean governance. The definition and use of the Pacific's ocean spaces has always been contested between cultures. These long and diverse histories are all the more relevant today as the Asia-Pacific region rises to dominate the world economy and the Pacific Ocean becomes the next battleground for overfishing, industrial pollution, and climatic degradation from industrial pollution. The fact that the Pacific Ocean contains almost 50 per cent of the Earth's water surfaces also makes it a vital carbon sink in the battle to contain global warming, warming generated, in part, by the booming economies of its Asian and American shores.

The contributors represent diverse perspectives as one would expect from a work encompassing an ocean that makes up so much of the Earth's surface.

This collection has seventy-seven contributors drawn from twenty-three nations and four Pacific territories seeking greater self-government, spread across multiple disciplines and non-academic reservoirs of knowledge. This work differs in focus and composition from its predecessor *The Cambridge History of the Pacific Islanders* edited by Donald Denoon with Stewart Firth, Jocelyn Linnekin, and Malama Meleisea in 1997. That work was the first general edited history of the entire Pacific Islands region. It was a major advance in Pacific Studies and captured the diversity of our sub-discipline with great coherence. It was a much smaller work than this current collection, consisting of twenty contributors and focused solely on the Pacific Islands, including Aotearoa New Zealand.[17] Australia and the Pacific Rim were only covered as colonial powers or when elements of various Pacific diasporas touched upon their shores.

Much has changed in the intervening twenty-six years. Chinese influence has increased dramatically across the Pacific, while academic research has revealed far greater historical links between the Pacific Rim and island Pacific than previously acknowledged in East Asia, Southeast Asia, and South America. At the same time, Pacific Island nations and scholars have demonstrated an increasing confidence and assertiveness on the global stage to write their own histories on their own terms and to advocate Pacific Islander solutions for both their own and global problems, most notably climate-change mitigation and ocean conservation. The global advocacy of prominent Pacific Island women such as Dame Meg Taylor, President Hilda Heine of the Republic of the Marshall Islands, and her daughter Kathy Jetñil-Kijiner has been notable in this regard. Lastly, this work is a history of the Pacific Ocean and not just the Pacific Islands in the previous Cambridge collection. This adjusted focus represents another decolonizing methodology for peoples not bounded by shorelines as continental peoples tend to conceive oceans, but rather connected by oceans as the iconic Pacific Island scholar Epeli Hau'ofa reminded us with his reconceptualization of the Pacific as a 'Sea of Islands'.[18]

The sheer size of the Pacific and centrality of the many diverse nations, cultures, and regions discussed in these two volumes to world history means

---

[17] Aotearoa New Zealand is the current (2022) preferred government name acknowledging the long Indigenous past. Chapters in both volumes generally refer to periods before European colonization as either Aotearoa or Aotearoa New Zealand, and after European colonization as New Zealand or Aotearoa New Zealand. The exception is the use of New Zealand in volume I as both a geographical and a cultural entity. We have also sought to accommodate author preferences as much as possible.

[18] E. Hau'ofa, 'Our Sea of Islands', *Contemporary Pacific* 6:1 (1994), 147–61. First published in V. Naidu, E. Waddell, and E. Hau'ofa (eds.), *A New Oceania: Rediscovering Our Sea of Islands* (Suva: School of Social and Economic Development, The University of the South Pacific, 1993).

that contributors have been drawn from different parts of the world and academic lineages, legacies, and traditions to engage in a truly representative exchange in this work. The depth and breadth of this coverage requires that this project must involve experts from a variety of human and natural sciences, and Indigenous knowledge holders with much longer whakapapa (genealogy) drawn from beyond universities. The editors early on decided that the collection had to be truly multidisciplinary and multifaceted to be comprehensive. For this reason, thematic and methodological chapters sit alongside and engage with each other and more chronologically orientated chapters. These diverse traditions involve a number of means of expression such as oral traditions, poetry, navigational lore, and chants evoking elements of the natural world and ancestral spirits, as well as historical linguistics, archival studies, archaeology, genetics, geology, botany, marine science, art history, literary analysis, and visual media history. Prominent Pacific Indigenous voices on the global stage are to the fore – we open Volume I with a traditional mihi to Te Moana Nui a Kiwa from Māori writer and film maker Witi Ihimaera, while Volume II begins with a reflection on Pacific futures from President Hilda Heine and poet and environmental advocate Kathy Jetñil-Kijiner. Contributors are balanced between established authorities and young scholars and leaders of the future, including traditional Yapese navigators and Gumbaynggirr Aboriginal community ocean educators. Without this diversity of approaches, only a fraction of the history conveyed in these volumes would have been able to be presented.

The format of this collection facilitated the presentation of diverse approaches. Publishing a two-volume collection totalling 600,000 words both as a standard library reference work and in electronic format to enable specific chapter downloads means that chapters could cover overlapping material with different approaches. Chapters are grouped in related themes or distinct eras in the history of the Pacific Ocean. While each chapter is designed to be self-contained for online audiences, many also refer to relevant chapters and related illustrations elsewhere in the collection to alert readers wishing to pursue particular research interests and passions further. The online version provides a one-paragraph summary and key words for each chapter to aid in online thematic searches. Chapter groupings and chapters sharing related themes are outlined below, as well as in the table of contents, and in the volume editors' introductions that follow this general, thematic introduction. Our editorial policy has broadly favoured giving diverse voices and modes of expression as much leeway as possible rather than imposing uniform formatting on all chapters in keeping with the decolonizing nature of much Asia-Pacific scholarship and the Eurocentric nature of much maritime scholarship in particular. The region's diversity and the series' wider global audience persuaded us to opt for a standardized CE (Common Era) – BCE (Before the Common Era) dating format rather than the more culturally neutral BP (Before the Present) format because the latter is still largely restricted to scientific literature and almost totally absent from historical discourse. To refer to Captain Cook's death as occurring 241 BP rather than in 1779 or the settlement of Hawai'i occurring 1020 BP rather than 1000 CE still requires a mental conversion for most readers that also hinders a sense of comparative timelines with other events in world or Pacific history. We have also opted to standardize Asian, Pacific, and European name formatting for authors in footnotes and bibliography, but not in running text where we reflect the fluid preferences in referring to East Asian authors by either surname/family name first or last. Historical figures noted in text and footnotes are referred to by their most commonly used name form or names, as in Mao Zedong (last name, first name) for example. Forename and surname are clarified in the accompanying footnotes where the first initial of the forename is followed by the full surname. Finally, bibliography entries are presented surname first followed by a comma and the first initial of the forename. We have used authors' preferred vernacular language protocols and spelling, including phonetic symbols, at the time of going to press in 2022.

Chapters are divided into twelve parts, evenly split between Volumes I and II. The emphasis on the diverse cultural traditions of the sea in the Pacific means that European explorers only appear in Part VI of Volume I. Both volumes start with lead essays which seek to push the boundaries and challenge orthodoxies in Pacific history and its methodologies. Each contains another part on particular methodologies or sources that distinguished Pacific historical practice. Volume I also has parts discussing diverse concepts of the Pacific environment and its impact on human history, the early exploration and colonization of the Pacific, the evolution of Indigenous maritime cultures after colonization, and finally the disruptive arrival of Europeans. The last four parts of Volume II detail advances and emerging trends in the historiography of culture contact and the colonial era respectively, before outlining the main themes of the twentieth century when the idea of a Pacific-centred century emerged, before ending with a part on how history and the past inform preparations for the emerging challenges of the future policymakers and implementors.

All scholarship is a collective enterprise, and especially so for such a large project covering approximately 40 per cent of the globe when Pacific Rim nation land territory is also included. Little wonder then that this project took

General Editor's Introduction

over five years to conceptualize and assemble. While I am the project coordinator as general editor, the project would not have been possible without the intellectual complementarity, coherence, and collegiality of our project's five-person editorial team: Anne Perez Hattori (University of Guam), Paul D'Arcy (Australian National University), Jane Samson (University of Alberta), Matt Matsuda (Rutgers University), and Ryan Tucker Jones (University of Oregon). We have worked together incredibly well and resolved every one of the many problems that have arisen on this long journey quickly, effectively, and with considerable empathy, humour, and understanding. I do not recall a single disagreement between us, despite robust but focused debate on many potentially troubling, unexpected issues. Each one of my four academic editorial colleagues has added wonderful dimensions to the original conceptualization that have enhanced the project beyond my wildest expectations. All of us have endured personal stresses beyond the general stress academics across the globe face from increasing workloads, deteriorating conditions, and the erosion of academic values under creeping managerialism. However, I usually only found this out through third parties rather than direct complaints, and it has never undermined the editorial team's commitment to the project. This collection would not have been published without their support, inspiration, and editorial acumen. Warm thanks are also due to all contributors who believed in this project, delivered stunningly comprehensive yet innovative chapters, and stuck with us throughout this protracted and disrupted process. Thank you all.

Each member of the editorial team brings different and highly complementary backgrounds and academic engagements to the study of Pacific history. Anne, Jane, Matt, and Ryan briefly outline their backgrounds and interests in their respective volume introductions. Being raised in Aotearoa New Zealand to first-generation migrants from the English seaport of Liverpool made me value environmental conservation. My parents were founding members of the New Zealand Values Party from which evolved the New Zealand Green Party. My native Otago's rugged coastline instilled a fascination with Pacific peoples' ease in and with the ocean and respect for nature compared to the more sanguine and fatalistic attitudes of seafarers from my North Atlantic heritage. While majoring in history at Otago University, I also did honours in geography and anthropology/archaeology to broaden my environmental interests, specializing in the Pacific Islands. When a dream job as a researcher for TVNZ's Natural History Unit's Seven Seas project fell through because of funding problems I carried on with sea research in my PhD. My first book, *The People of the Sea*, arose from this fascination. My PhD introduced me to Hawai'i, Micronesia, and Tahiti, which all figure prominently in my research. I have also published on the hidden histories of Chinese, Filipino, and Latin American engagement with the Pacific Ocean. I have been based in the ANU's Department of Pacific Affairs for most of this project, where community impact and empowerment are major priorities in all our teaching and research. This focus has reinforced a pervasive theme in this collection – the relevance of past experiences to current and future challenges. The current generation of Pacific students are the best in my thirty years of teaching. They will write or rewrite the histories of their communities, instilling more local voices and perspectives.

This project is part of a series launched by Professor David Armitage of Harvard University on ocean-centred regional histories. David has been a role model and mentor since we first met, and has provided total support and intellectual inspiration throughout this long process. David's fellow series editors, Alison Bashford and Sujit Sivasundaram, are equally inspiring and open-minded scholars, with Sujit also providing a chapter in Volume II. Cambridge University Press has invested significant resources into this project and been a delight to deal with from start to finish. Our commissioning editor Lucy Rhymer, project editors Emily Plater, Emily Sharp, Lisa Carter, and Elizabeth Hanlon, as well as project administrative assistant Santosh Laxmi Kota, have been professional, kind, and personable, and flexible to our many requests. The Press has been especially responsive to contributors extending approaches into intellectual frontiers to reflect the cultural diversity in forms of recording and recounting history and identity. The Press's independent copyeditor, Frances Brown, has done an exceptional job in detecting and correcting inconsistencies across this massive collection. We would also like to thank Auriol Griffith-Jones for the excellent indexes. The Press's production team headed by Natasha Whelan have also been models of professionalism, as well as endlessly patient and helpful. There is good reason for Cambridge University Press's global reputation for quality and intellectual integrity.

Special mention must be made of the staff of the Australian National University College of Asia and the Pacific's CartoGIS map makers, Kay Dancey, Jenny Sheehan, and especially Karina Pelling, who made most of the maps shown in this collection. All have become dear friends over the years, and I remain in awe of their cartographic genius which I consider world best practice. Nothing is ever a problem for them, and their technical proficiency and professionalism is always masked by a warm, can-do attitude.

We give far too little recognition to our editors, cartographers, and the other production staff so vital for academic publications to flourish and be accessible and affordable. They face the same and often worse financial pressures and constraints academics face, and yet I have never met staff involved in production who are anything less than consummate professionals, and warm, engaging colleagues committed to this vital aspect of scholarship and learning. The partnership between production and academic staff is at the heart of creativity and representation. My deepest thanks go out to you all.

In 2015, I was adopted into the Langachu subclan of the Sor clan of seafarers and fisherfolk who inhabit the atolls of the Mortlock Islands of Micronesia. My fellow kinsman Gonzaga (Zag) Puas and I have been asked to write the long history of the Sor clan, which is still largely recorded only in oral traditions.[19] Langachu means connecting people, which is the purpose of our clan history and also of this general history of the Pacific's many shores and metuol (sea-paths) beyond our home island of Lekinoich, this island municipality home to part of the Sor diaspora.

As I was writing this introduction, Zag informed me that the body of our friend and mentor Peter Sitan had been found washed ashore on the distant atoll of Pingelap after he had gone missing at sea while out fishing by himself off Pohnpei. Peter was a guardian of the sea par excellence, earning a living from its bounty, but also working tirelessly to provide his nation of Federated States of Micronesia (FSM) with the Pacific Islands' first commercially successful domestic tuna fleet. The more viable locally controlled fleets there are, the more sustainable and locally profitable the fishery can become.[20] The alternative is earning limited income off fishing licence fees from Distant Water Fishing Nation (DWFN) vessels and no income from illegal and unregulated vessels. While Peter was missing at sea, the FSM President was introducing a national policy to increase marine protected areas within its Exclusive Economic Zone (EEZ) by a further 30 per cent despite the centrality of tuna fishing to national income. The bill's introduction was made possible by the success of Peter's sustainable fishing initiatives. It was only fitting that the sea returned his body to his family and kin.

Ole la lon kinamwe atongach

Rest well beloved guardian

---

[19] See Chapter 63 in this collection by Tamatoa Bambridge and Gonzaga Puas on sustainable development.

[20] See P. Sitan, 'The development of the Federated States of Micronesia (FSM) tuna management regime', in G. Puas and N. Halter (eds.), Special Issue on 'Micronesia in Focus', *Tamkang Journal of International Affairs* 19:2 (2015), 125–66.

Preface to Volume II

ANNE PEREZ HATTORI AND JANE SAMSON

Anne Hattori was in attendance when Tongan scholar Epeli Hauʻofa delivered a speech that would become his profound and seminal essay, 'Our Sea of Islands'. Attending the conference with other Pacific Island graduate students, she recalls that it shook them from their insularity and sense of smallness. It reminded them of their historic interconnectedness, fluidity, and dynamism. Yet she also understood that Pacific Islanders, in general, have a strongly centred sense of place. They are grounded in their individual villages and specific islands. This is most clearly demonstrated in the Micronesian navigational concept of *etak*, the navigational practice of positioning one's home island as the reference point from which all other movement is located, thus requiring you to know your precise point of origin before undertaking any voyage. Read metaphorically, *etak* engrains in Islanders the consciousness that they must know their homeland well before moving forward in a reliable and safe manner.

The contributions to this second volume of *The Cambridge History of the Pacific Ocean* bring all of us into the latest era of Pacific historiography, one in which scholars of Oceania acknowledge the foundational nature of this region's maritime environment. They also recognize both the opportunities and the costs of the ebb and flow of migration, economic power, and geopolitics in the Pacific world. In these post-colonial days we are particularly aware of the ways in which colonization, formal or not, has shaped both the modern history of the Pacific and also its historians. This volume's first five chapters in Part VII introduce readers to broad perspectives in Pacific History, beginning most trenchantly with contributions from a mother and daughter, Dr Hilda Heine, past President of the Republic of the Marshall Islands, and Kathy Jetñil-Kijiner, a renowned environmental activist and poet. Their powerful, personalized pieces draw attention to the local and global stakes associated with global warming, biodiversity, and continued struggles for survival that face Pacific peoples. In Chapter 33, Lewis Mayo offers a trans-oceanic perspective to demonstrate the linkages between parts of the Pacific that might otherwise be overlooked. With an eye on Bolivia in the Americas, Banaba in Oceania, and Haizhou in Eurasia, this chapter explores a history of relationships between authority, identity, and place as they interact with histories of minerals such as phosphates and nitrates. Anna Johnston's contribution in Chapter 34 examines academic discourse on the Pacific, connecting art, writing, and history-making since the 1800s to demonstrate that archival encounters between Oceania and Europe continue to serve as an active site of both contestation and creativity in the Pacific, as well as beyond. In Chapter 35, Greg Dvorak immerses readers in a long history of networks and memories between Japan and Oceania. Drawing on a diverse range of literary, artistic, and historical sources, he examines ways in which World War II informs Japanese memories of the Pacific as 'virtual cemeteries haunted by the phantoms of loved ones', while Islanders continue to sense and even perpetuate elements of imperial Japan in the present. Wrapping up this section of conceptual essays, in Chapter 36 Jane Samson makes creative use of kaleidoscopic imagery to show the many faces of Oceania in the historical imagination, as well as to suggest the possibilities of new celebrations of Indigenous voices and agency.

Part VIII moves on to examine 'Approaches, Sources, and Subaltern Histories of the Modern Pacific'; engaging in particular with some of the ways in which colonial archives have shaped Pacific scholarship and have narrowly delineated the bounds of Pacific history. As in Part I, these chapters range widely over the latest developments in history-writing and the recovery of new sources. It was especially important for us to include scholars whose work disrupts longstanding perceptions about the Pacific as someone else's space: an extension of Asia-Pacific; a scramble of European-dominated colonies; or an 'American Lake'. Anne notes how World War II left such a powerful mark on the Chamorro psyche that the entire twentieth century is demarcated in history books as either 'Pre-War', 'War', or 'Post-War', as if those living in 1900 knew this event was coming their way. This precise centring of Guam's history around World War II sets up a focus on the global powers who chose Pacific islands for their battlefields. It consequently relegates Islanders to the sidelines, as props who simply are not major players on the world stage, and, for that matter, not even central figures on their own islands. Written this way, historiography is configured to glorify the USA as Guam's teacher, benevolent colonial ruler, role model, and, ultimately, saviour.

Addressing the weighty presence of the colonizer within the available array of sources, Pacific archivists have contributed two significant pieces to this collection. In Chapter 37, Opeta Alefaio and Nicholas Halter consider the ways in which archives, despite being generally understood in Oceania as repositories reflecting colonial domination, must work in sustained ways to gain the trust of Islanders. Their engaging essay shares the outcomes of several community engagement projects that have sparked community conversations about Fijian culture and history, in the process becoming instrumental in nurturing Fijian society. In Chapter 38, Safua Akeli Amaama similarly identifies some of the shortcomings of Pacific archival collections, specifically as they tend to represent a body of privileged knowledge, often reflecting colonial interests. Yet the chapter asserts the potential of archives to create spaces for new voices to be heard, including the histories of women and other under-represented sectors of society.

Understandings of gender and race form the centre of Angela Wanhalla's wide-ranging inquiry into mixed-race families and their complex identities in the age of empire. In Chapter 39, she surveys a history of interracial relationships in particular locations across the Pacific and Asia, and colonial understandings about race mixing. Focusing on family testimonies, this chapter destabilizes colonial ideas about identity that revolved around race and blood, in the process highlighting some of the gendered dimensions of colonialism.

Jon Kamakawiwoʻole Osorio's contribution in Chapter 40 provides a deep genealogy of Hawaiian historical literature, particularly considering an 'intellectual liberation' since the 1980s. Osorio weaves together a large body of innovative and bold scholarship concerning Hawaiian language, culture, land, artistic traditions, and more, in the process linking this historiography to issues of Hawaiian resistance to colonialism, cultural revitalization, and environmental care. He poignantly demonstrates the breadth and depth of what Hawaiian scholars have collectively contributed, not only to their nation's historiography, but also to broader questions of knowledge, epistemology, and the ways in which we do and do not empower students to think critically about colonialism in its past and present forms.

In Chapter 41, Alice Te Punga Somerville examines the relationship between history and literature in the Pacific, noting that 'Ours is a sea of writing'. Focusing on the works of Albert Wendt, Chantal Spitz, Ron and Marjorie Crocombe, and Vernice Wineers, the chapter considers ways in which texts by Indigenous Islanders 'respond to, reflect on, and produce the vast Pacific we call home'. From literature, this volume moves to film in Pacific History with an essay by Alexander Mawyer. In Chapter 42, he provides an overview of film about and by Islanders to discuss ways in which Pacific film reflects shifting 'beliefs, values, and understandings of filmmakers and their communities' while also presenting opportunities for contemporary Islanders to reform, revise, and respond to older representations. In Chapter 43, the late Adrienne Kaeppler provides a substantial overview of Pacific art forms from architecture and sculpture to music and dance; from textiles and clothing to body art and ornamentation. She addresses concerns about definitions of art, discusses some changes over time, identifies some exemplary works found in museums around the world, and provides examples of traditional arts in contemporary contexts.

The chapters in Part IX address 'Culture Contact and the Impact of Pre-colonial European Influences'. In Chapter 44, Sujit Sivasundaram recontextualizes the so-called 'age of revolution', typically understood as a Euro-American era transitioning to modernity, as instead a Pacific concept of conflict and contestation. He examines social and cultural changes in Tasmania to show ways in which the Pacific could 'remake, resist, and contribute to the making of the global'. Another major impact of pre-colonial cultural contact took the form of disease, and Vicki Luker's Chapter 45 examines the half-century old 'Fatal Impact' debate. This chapter maps out the contours and controversies surrounding the history of disease and its effects on Islands and Islanders, as well as issues concerning agency, colonialism, and Pacific historiography. Attention to Christian missionization follows in Chapter 46, with Helen Gardner providing an intellectual geneaology of the concept of 'culture', particularly as a concept wielded by missionaries to Oceania. She articulates the evolution of the culture concept in the West alongside Christian missionary deployment of the concept to represent the customs and societies in which they worked.

From philosophies, diseases, and missions, the focus shifts to ecological exchanges and their impact on Island societies. David Igler's Chapter 47 examines environmental change in the Pacific that occurred through the introduction of biota, often intentionally transported by humans as they moved across the ocean. This contribution reminds readers that invasive species have been a part of Pacific History for centuries, and thus a 'broad lens and lengthy timeframe' can elucidate the complexity of natural and human interactions. This section ends with Bronwen Douglas's erudite contribution on the science of race. In Chapter 48, she charts the transformation of 'anthropology' to 'raciology' after 1800 through an investigation of 'seaborne ethnography', those accounts by European voyagers of their fleeting encounters with Pacific Islanders, as well as the writings of travelling naturalists and European-based scientists. The chapter demonstrates ways in which observations of Pacific peoples were deployed to explain racial differences among humans.

The power of colonialism to shape and to distort is astonishing. For Anne, having grown up in what she describes as 'thick colonial brainwashing' that nearly divorced her from her own history, this recognition is particularly welcome. For Jane, it was also welcome, but for very different reasons. Born on an island in the Pacific Ocean – Vancouver Island – Jane is not a Pacific Islander. She understands the importance of *etak* but, unlike Anne, she is the descendant of colonial settlers. Everything about determining her point of origin, her island home, is problematic. Vancouver Island's First Nations are related through ancient kinship, trade, and cultural ties to the other Indigenous peoples of neighbouring islands and the coastlands of what is now referred to as Canada's west coast and the northwestern coast of the United States. But for whom is it the 'west coast' or 'northwest coast'? These geographical descriptors are continental, drawn from the baseline of the North American land mass. Jane must surely be from the northeastern Pacific coast, but such terminology was not used as she was growing up and is rarely used today. She comes from what she calls 'the rimworld', but whose rim? The continent's or the ocean's? From where exactly did her own canoe set out?

Today's Guam touts itself as 'Where America's day begins', a catchy slogan that makes its political affiliation crystal clear. For air travellers to Guam and other Pacific islands, the ocean can be erased, an apparently empty space glimpsed through the clouds from 40,000 feet. It is an obstacle creating annoyingly long flights from one continental centre to another. As essays in Part X, 'The Colonial Era in the Pacific' make clear, for too long the main reference point for Pacific history lay elsewhere, in distant Spain or Britain, in Asian trading centres, or in the Cold War priorities of the United States. To forget this is to impose what Jane calls 'rimbound' histories and identities on the region. This section begins in the Pacific Islands where some Indigenous leaders remained in charge while most of the islands were divided up between the colonial powers as the nineteenth-century 'scramble for the Pacific'. Nevertheless, as Lorenz Gonschor emphasizes in Chapter 49, Pacific Islanders transformed and adapted the colonial modernity that accompanied European or American rule, creating independent Indigenous states, and challenging Eurocentric narratives that describe the loss of Indigenous authority as inevitable. The following chapter by Ricardo Roque brings a neglected Pacific colony – Timor – into focus as the site of experimentation, with national flags symbolizing Indigenous identity and authority. Roque's approach brings welcome attention to the importance of objects in history, demonstrating how flags could be powerful anti-colonial objects. Under the official Portuguese flag (or the Union Jack, or the Stars and Stripes in other cases) flew other flags of deeper significance to the local population.

The colonial era in the Pacific impacted islanders in ways far beyond the politics of empire, and in Chapter 51 Jacqueline Leckie engages with the intersections of race and gender in her examination of bodies, disease, and colonial medicine in the Pacific islands. Here we see the power of colonialism invading the most intimate spaces of human life, classifying, separating, medicating, and sometimes incarcerating Pacific bodies identified as diseased, either physically or mentally. In Chapter 52, Frances Steel argues that only after the age of steam was the Pacific fully 'globalized'. Earlier global connections were significant, but the dramatic alteration of time and space, enabled by modern communications technology, meant that coast-to-coast connections became routine, and islands too often considered peripheral, like Hawai'i, became central to the technological systems dependent on their port facilities and re-transmission stations.

Edward Melillo explains in Chapter 53 that Pacific ambitions were not confined to the so-called 'great powers'. In his wide-ranging study of Latin American involvement, he notes how much conflict between Latin American nations revolved around access to Pacific ports, noting that 'dictators, revolutionaries, pundits, and policymakers throughout the Americas have anchored their aspirations to diverse transpacific visions'. Speaking of anchors, the age of empire had a technological impact on the Pacific world, especially through steamships and telegraph cables.

Our volume's section on 'The Pacific Century?' features a question mark for this and many other reasons. Even as Pacific nations and peoples achieved political independence after World War II, powerful forces remained in place from the colonial era, and from emerging regional powers like China. The section opens with a penetrating examination of the United States and its outsized influence on the Pacific world, including and transcending formal colonial rule. In Chapter 54 David Hanlon provides a wide-ranging overview of ways in which 'the region has been a consistent theatre of American desire, ambition, profit, and power'. Unlike most histories that situate the United States' budding interest in the Pacific in the late nineteenth century, Hanlon takes readers back to the 1700s, providing rich insight into what has become a long series of powerful interventions.

It is clear how deep was the impact made by World War II, as Judith Bennett and Lin Poyer show in Chapter 55. Pacific Islanders sometimes experienced unprecedented prosperity behind the lines, while others saw their communities and livelihoods devastated by battles not of their making. Evidence from oral history has helped to bring Island women's experiences into focus by documenting, for example, the generational impact of the children of foreign servicemen. Women were also a central focus for both community activism and intergenerational tragedy as their bodies, and those of their children, reflected the impact of the nuclear age. In Chapter 56 Barbara Rose Johnston shows how 'the Pacific has been a figurative and literal ground zero for nuclear diplomacy, popular resistance, and continuing debates about human rights, international law, economic and political power, and the environment'.

Peter Rimmer and Howard Dick carry the technological focus through to the era of container shipping, air travel, and the internet. They make a particularly important point in Chapter 57, namely that talk of a 'Pacific Century' is questionable because 'The greatest shrinkage [in time and space] can be seen across the narrow neck of the North Pacific, a route that in the 1850s scarcely existed yet is now the world's leading trade route in terms of value and frequency in all three modes.' Because the southern Pacific lags so far behind, 'Terms such as "Pacific Century" therefore conflate too much of the vast Pacific into a single proposition'.

Chapter 58 by Fei Sheng and Paul D'Arcy also addresses Pacific-centred empires, in this case the rising influence of China. Here they present a story of two eras. The first, before 1978, centred on rebuilding and restructuring following the Communist victory in China's civil war. After 1978, China turned outward to exploit Pacific resources and exercise growing influence in its geopolitics. Finally, in Chapter 59, Stephanie Lawson's review of recent Pacific Islands political history reveals how political independence came relatively late compared with decolonization in Africa and Asia. Today, island polities struggle with 'the tensions between modern representative democracy and traditional political and social practices'.

Turning to the final section, on 'Pacific Futures', our authors consider the struggle for agency and identity in a globalized world. In Chapter 60, Tongan Tēvita Ka'ili gifts us with a poem of his own composition honouring the ancestral figures Tangaloa, Māui, and Hina, before discussing how traditional Indigenous patterns of respectful sustainability are, in fact, our collective future in terms of caring for Pacific ecosystems and human thriving. Anthony Tutugoro notes in Chapter 61 that flying the flag of the Front de Libération Nationale Kanak et Socialiste (FLNKS) has been a mechanism for amplifying Indigenous Kanak voices after the defeat of the latest independence referendum in 2018. However, many peoples live in New Caledonia: immigration from other Pacific islands and France has reduced Kanaks to a minority in their own land. Tutugoro surveys the complex political and social landscape in which most voters prefer increased autonomy under French rule. In an elegant counterpoint, Roannie Ng Shiu and Rochelle Bailey review the accelerating diaspora of Pacific peoples since decolonization in Chapter 62, making the point that, as in the past, the recent flows of Pacific migration have been multidirectional, featuring journeys made for complex reasons: 'a Pacific ethnoscape of transnational communities is not merely an abstract reconceptualization but an actualisation of the lived experiences of Pacific communities across the globe'.

This final section of the volume, and of the series, includes essays that show how deeply the future depends on understanding the past. We do not mean this in the conventional Western sense of 'learning lessons from history', but rather in the Indigenous sense as expressed by 'Ōkusitino Māhina, who explains that in the Tongan theory of time and space 'people are thought to walk forward into the past and walk backward into the future, both taking place in the present, where the past and future are constantly mediated in the ever-transforming present'.[1] These goals are then assessed in a broad survey of the Anthropocene by Tamatoa Bambridge and Gonzago Puas in Chapter 63, with an eye to the role of Pacific history in shaping its future environmental sustainability.

This volume set sail with the goal of unsettling traditional Eurocentric reference points in Pacific history, building instead on more recent post-colonial and Pacific-centred scholarship. We present readers with a host of islands, littoral zones, and canoe wakes in which new spaces and places of belonging have been negotiated for millennia. After all, these Pacific currents allowed our own two canoes to meet up, thousands of miles away from our home islands, on the welcoming swells of deep Pacific histories. Out there, far from continental centres of gravity, is a profound hospitality. As fellow historians of the Pacific, Anne and Jane discovered many common interests and activisms, and forged a friendship, amid the Pacific's depth of maritime interaction and human creativity. Initial reactions to this project voiced the concern that voices and perspectives from the Pacific Islands would be drowned by the larger Asian and American nations that border our ocean. Yet the scholars in this volume have not allowed that to happen. Global events that link Oceania to both the East and the West receive their due attention, but not to the detriment of the peoples of our sea. Insightful essays trace the place of the Pacific within US and Japanese histories, yet without losing the centrality of Oceania in the narrative. They ground themselves in the region that is our home, rather than relegating the Pacific to some prop of American or Asian manipulation.

The tide has clearly turned as historians write with a new sense of centre, and as historians, archivists, and others work ardently to integrate Indigenous epistemologies into their life work. Across this volume there permeates the quintessence of Pacific esteem and entrenchment, a palpable respect for our ocean, pride in our Pacific heritage, and our responsibility to protect it as well as we can into a future that will be at least as turbulent as was our past.

---

[1] 'Ō. Māhina, 'Tā, vā, and moana: temporality, spatiality, and indigeneity', *Pacific Studies* 33:2 (2010), 168–202, at 170.

PART VII

★

RETHINKING THE PACIFIC

32

Climate Change, Rising Seas, and Endangered Island Nations

HILDA HEINE AND KATHY JETÑIL-KIJINER

In this chapter, an Indigenous mother and daughter dynamic duo share their thoughts and fears, as well as their experiences and insights, as people from Micronesian atolls whose lands face destruction due to rising sea levels associated with global warming. Dr Hilda Heine served as President of the Republic of the Marshall Islands, a position that followed a long list of 'firsts', including being the first Indigenous Marshallese to earn a doctorate degree and the first female president of any Micronesian government. Her career began in the classroom, and even as a Head of State she used her vocation and talents to further the world's knowledge of the Marshall Islands, Micronesia, and the wider Pacific, particularly highlighting environmental issues that threaten her people's future.

President Heine's contribution comes in the form of a keynote speech, delivered as Head of State at an academic conference, again speaking to her unique blending of politics and education. This venue was the conference of the Society for Advancement of Chicanos/Hispanics & Native Americans in Science (SACNAS), held in Honolulu, Hawai'i in 2019. This speech addresses key issues that informed her entire career in education and politics – Marshall Islanders' indelible ties to their land, the centrality of land to their culture and identity, and the reality of facing the rising tides that threaten to engulf their low-lying atolls. The SACNAS speech speaks especially to young Indigenous scientists, as well as all advocates of Indigenous knowledge. It issues a clarion call from mothers to their children to take tangible action that will assist in combatting the impact of climate change. It calls on modern Islanders to fuse traditional and modern scientific knowledge in ways that will protect Oceania's lands and seas.

A generation removed yet just as passionately committed to her nation's and region's future, President Heine's daughter, Kathy Jetñil-Kijiner, has likewise dedicated her life to the survival of the Marshall Islands and to the wellbeing of Oceania's people. Self-described as a poet, performance artist, and educator, Kathy gained international notice with the performance of 'Dear Matafele Peinam' at the opening of the 2014 United Nations Climate Summit, held in New York. Her electrifying performances have been featured by media including CNN, Democracy Now, Mother Jones, Nobel Women's Initiative, the Huffington Post, NBC News, and National Geographic.[1] The Pacific Community, an organization representing the independent nations of Oceania, has recognized her as one of '70 Inspiring Pacific Women',[2] and she has received similar accolades including 2017 Impact Hero of the Year by Earth Company, and *Vogue* magazine's list of thirteen Climate Warriors in 2015.[3] In addition to founding and running Jo-Jikum, a nonprofit organization dedicated to Marshallese youth and environmental issues, Kathy also serves as the Climate Envoy for the Marshall Islands Ministry of Environment.

Both mother and daughter have become recognized voices and activist leaders in the pursuit of climate change reform. The works featured here can only scratch the surface of their profound and ongoing contributions to safeguard the future for all Pacific peoples.

Living, Breathing Experiments

SACNAS Remarks, H.E. Hilda C. Heine, EdD, President of the Republic of the Marshall Islands, 31 October – 2 November 2019

Iokwe kom aolep, I have just greeted you in the usual way in my language, Kajin-Majol or the Marshallese language and I have just said, 'You are all rainbows.'[4]

Like Aloha is for Hawai'i, '*Iokwe*' is the Marshallese greeting. Literally, it means: 'You are a rainbow.'

The rainbow is a long-standing symbol of hope and recovery, especially after the storm. For us, living on small strips of land in a large expanse of ocean barely higher than the high tide, the rainbow can be the most beautiful thing in the world. And our greeting to one another says, 'You are beautiful, there is hope, we will recover, especially after the storm.'

My story today is based on what I often see as a potential 'fault line', in my understanding of modern science. On one hand I am a Marshallese woman

---

[1] 'Official bio', www.kathyjetnilkijiner.com/author-bio/.
[2] 'Kathy Jetnil-Kijiner', www.spc.int/sdp/70-inspiring-pacific-women/kathy-jetnil-kijiner.
[3] 'Kathy Jetnil-Kijner', https://hawaii.edu/cpis/alumni-and-friends/alumni-spotlight/kathy-jetnil-kijiner-2/.
[4] www.sacnas.org/what-we-do/conference/2019-sacnas/. SACNAS is the Society for Advancement of Chicanos/Hispanics & Native Americans in Science.

grounded in *manit* in Majol or my culture and Kajin Majol, my language. On the other, I am a graduate of the academy, the modern academy where I learned to hone my English and research skills as I wrote for the highest of academic awards, a doctoral degree, as part of the education system we inherited post-1946.

The fault line, as I often experience it, is the place where traditional or cultural knowledge and modern science meet. I am not a scientist, or 'an expert who studies or works in one of the sciences' like a nuclear or forensic scientist.

Yet, here I am at the SACNAS 2019 Conference, delivering the keynote address. Reflecting on that thought, it is perhaps not such an anomaly that I stand before you today at this STEM-based gathering,[5] because we Marshallese intimately understand the systematic study of the physical world. We are also the only country in the world where the impacts of both the climate crises and the US nuclear weapons testing programme are intersecting to further threaten our way of life.

All of my life I have identified as Marshallese, as part of the Ri-Majol system where behaviour is culturally prescribed through a structure or framework of beliefs passed down from one generation to the next as part of our oral culture. While some of this information has been written down or recorded in various multimedia formats, much is still done mainly through storytelling or *bwebwenato*. We have informed ourselves over time based on our own systematic ways of understanding natural and not so natural phenomena.

Marshall Islands, known to us as *Aelon Kein Ad*, is comprised of twenty-nine low-lying coral atolls and five solitary low coral islands no more than a few feet above the sea level. Our atolls and islands total 70 square miles in land area surrounded by 750,000 square miles of the Pacific Ocean. A total of 1,225 individual islands and islets make up the Ratak or Sunrise chain in the east, and the Ralik or Sunset chain in the west. The atolls, built over millions of years by living coral organisms, are now threatened by rise in sea level temperatures and acidifications. We are located in the central-western Pacific, four hours away by plane from Honolulu. Our marine environment is extremely rich in productivity, diversity, and complexity.

We have a strong dependence on our natural resources and biodiversity – not only for food and income, but our relationship with these islands forms the basis of our culture and society. Land is livelihood, and for us as Marshallese it is simply and overwhelmingly about survival. Take a look at a map of the Marshall Islands and you will see what I mean.

One of our conservationists four years ago said:

I don't think my grandchildren will be able to sail. How will your children know how to make *bwiro*, preserved breadfruit, if we're migrating to the

---

[5] Acronym for Science, Technology, Engineering, and Mathematics.

United States or even to other places around the world? How can our children learn how to sail with the stars, or even fish, or even weave mats? The language will be there but language itself doesn't come with culture. *Manit* . . . doesn't come with speaking the language. You got to learn ways to survive, learn how to sail [with] the stars, weave mats, make food, live in the harshest conditions that the world can give you.

Land and subsistence are the cornerstones of Marshallese culture. To lose the land is to lose the basis of social order, the traditional power structure, life-giving provisions for sustenance. Our value system, based primarily on respect and reciprocity at the different levels of the traditional hierarchy, would be non-existent without our land. Our identities are intricately tied to our land, so much so that the RMI Government owns less than 1 per cent of land. Our culture and livelihood as a people are intricately connected to our ancestral lands.

We are accomplished seafarers, navigators, and fishermen. The many fishing methods devised and used demonstrate a deep understanding of sea life, ranging from the simple hook and line to nets, traps, spears, clubs, rope, and coconut fronds. Some methods were used only for specific types of fish, in specific areas or seasons. Some methods involved the participation of many people, and some were practised by the individual.

Many traditional fishing practices remain in use today, but many are being lost along with the in-depth understanding of the sea and its creatures. Moreover, fish and other marine creatures remain important subsistence foods, the catching and sharing of which revive culture and community. We have, over thousands of years, lived in harmony with our large ocean environments.

Today I share with you all two continuing and momentous experiences in my encounters with the world of modern science using the definition I have just shared. Both experiences are part of the historical fabric of the Marshall Islands. The first, more commonly known as climate change, has in my lifetime, considerably altered our terrestrial and marine environments. The second centres on a US scientific experiment in 1954 codenamed Castle Bravo.

Climate change is a grim reality for the Republic of the Marshall Islands – the clock is ticking for the critically vulnerable countries among us. We share a similar fate to other low-lying island states, like Kiribati, Tuvalu, and the Maldives. Among these easily overlooked countries with small susceptible populations, we are the definition of the popular expression: 'sink or swim'.

Our children and grandchildren, from very early ages, continue to play in our front and backyards which are usually marine playgrounds, not terrestrial. As I watch them play, many thoughts cross my mind. I wonder whether they know about the plants and creatures of the sea, about our relationships with our natural environment as I knew them growing up, our rationale for using or not using certain plants for medicinal purposes or post-natal bathing practices for women who had just given birth to help the healing process; our own scientific system based on observation, experience, and experimentation over thousands of years.

We are testaments of the scientific process, human experiments, guinea pigs used to test the effects of radiation between 1946 and 1958. The biggest of the sixty-seven nuclear bombs tested in our islands as part of Secret Project 4.1 was detonated on Bikini Atoll on March 1, 1954. In preparation for the test, the people of Bikini Atoll were moved in 1946 to other atolls and islands in the RMI. The Castle Bravo explosion in 1954, which was equivalent to dropping 1.6 Hiroshima bombs daily for twelve years, vaporized entire islands and left a huge crater a mile wide. One hundred miles away on Rongelap Atoll, people saw a bright flash and radioactive ash they called 'snow' rained down on them, immediately causing vomiting, headaches, and stomach discomfort.

We are still trying to work out exactly what effects these blasts had on our land, our people, our lagoons and ocean, our plants, our fish, our everything, even though we have no Marshallese scientists.

The US Cold War legacy rests inside the Runit Dome, or the 'Tomb' as the locals call it, on Runit Island in Enewetak Atoll in the Marshall Islands. This bulky legacy of years of US nuclear testing, constructed in 1979, stores around 111,000 cubic yards of collected radioactive waste left over from twelve years of nuclear tests conducted in the Marshall Islands.

According to a 2013 report by the US Department of Energy, soil around the Dome is already more contaminated than its contents, which is probably true given the dumping of radioactive materials into the lagoon. The Dome is cracked in certain sections and, as sea level rises, radioactive waste is starting to leach out of the crater into the ocean. The intersection between the nuclear legacy and climate change speaks volumes about our vulnerability despite our attempts to remain resilient following in the footsteps of our ancestors.

Even as scientists hypothesized, tested, and analysed and even as our cultural heritage continues to be adversely threatened by accelerated soil erosion, sea level rise, salt water intrusion into wells, declining fish populations and coral bleaching, we are applying our traditional knowledge in much the same way that modern science operates.

We are reinterpreting 'vulnerability' and 'adaptability' in terms of Marshallese traditional knowledge within the *Reimaanlok* (looking ahead) process. With the *Reimaanlok*, our eight-step Conservation Area Management Planning Framework, we are assisting atoll communities in the Marshall Islands to think globally and act locally. *Reimaanlok* employs community-based tools and approaches to articulate local objectives that translate to national, regional, and international goals.

In 2004, Parties to the Convention on Biological Diversity committed to have effectively conserved at least 10 per cent of marine and coastal ecological regions globally by 2010. In Micronesia, we went further. We have pledged to effectively conserve 30 per cent of nearshore marine and 20 per cent of terrestrial resources. In this endeavour, our strength lies directly in the partnerships we make. We continue to combine local knowledge in recognition of our own practices to protect biodiversity with the scientific expertise of international partners.

But even as we rise to the challenges of the pledges we have made, including our commitments to the Paris Agreement, we fear that nature threatens to sink us. We fear that our fellow men and women will not adjust their destructive behaviours in a timely fashion. We fear that the world will not notice if we sink.

The time has come for the global community to seek viable and effective solutions to the climate crises, and to do so with unrestrained speed. It is my hope the global community can summon the leadership needed to urgently increase its ambition to get us on a pathway consistent with the Paris Agreement and to avoid the worst impacts of climate change.

At the last Pacific Islands Forum countries meeting in Tuvalu, I joined fellow Pacific Island Forum leaders in affirming that the climate crises remain the single greatest threat to our regional security. Last month, our Parliament, the Nitijela, approved a resolution declaring a national climate crisis, highlighting the special circumstances we face as a low-lying coral atoll nation. We are also developing a landmark National Adaptation Plan, which we called 'National Survival Plan', to shore up our own future, including possibly raising some of our islands.

That is why I am so committed to sharing as many stakeholders as possible – especially female champions, leaders of colours and diverse STEM students and professionals – with a shared desire to protect our common vital resources.

Summary

So, where, on the continuum of scientific research are my reflections of our Marshallese history, located? In a sentence, in our responsibility as researchers in science.

There are differences in terms of expectations of research processes in Indigenous research as opposed to other academic research. Mainstream and Indigenous viewpoints will collide at times, but both perspectives need to understand the value of an ethical framework. Moreover, if an ethical framework for Indigenous research is constructed for everyone to use, the cultural mandate must be robust for it to be considered legitimate. This is the case even if resources are provided from national agencies.

Our challenge, as Indigenous researchers in science is to continue interrogating the limits of existing methodologies because we need to create new ones that will be inclusive of our traditional frameworks and ethos. 'Our lands and territories are at the core of our existence – we are the land and the land is us; we have a distinct spiritual and material relationship with our lands and territories and they are inextricably linked to our survival. Once our lands and territories are devastated, we threaten the continuity of our traditional cultures and our existence as Indigenous people. Many of us share the belief that: 'we walk to the future in the footprints of our ancestors' (Kimberley Declaration 2002). If the footprints are destroyed, then we have no future.

We, as Marshallese, have a holistic view of our world as part of our Indigenous culture. This view includes nature's provision of clean water and access to traditional food and herbs within a prescribed, hierarchical, social organization of authority in relation to resources. The scientific result of any research must recognize this cultural perspective, otherwise it will be purely based upon a Western, scientific view of Indigenous peoples and our traditional knowledge and will not be representative of our story. All interventions and intrusions in modern Marshallese society like the atomic bomb tests and the effects of climate change as we live them are points on the Marshallese storyline that began with our first ancestors.

New Zealand prime minister Jacinda Ardern said in her recent address at the 74th Session of the UN General Assembly, 'there is no changing a nation's history, but we can choose how it defines us'.

As modern-day Marshallese, we are largely Christians, and we are constantly reminded that God gave Noah the sign of the rainbow that He would never flood the world again. Despite our faith, we experience our world differently. We are proud of our advocacy efforts around the climate crises threatening our very existence. Institutes such as those convened by SACNAS prepare the youth of today to assume the responsibilities and leadership potential of our nations, especially in light of the impacts we face due to climate change and ongoing adverse medical conditions due to radioactive exposure.

We continue to develop initiatives to mitigate the critical challenges facing us in relation to climate change even as the king tides on one hand inundate our homes and droughts at other times of the year threaten crucial food and water supplies.

Adapting to the now more frequent droughts, we have built water catchments to enable safe supply of water for at least four months in each of our outer island communities. We have built seawalls to safeguard our homes, graveyards, and other infrastructures. If we don't do it, who will?

Resources being redirected to combat the impacts of climate change are very much needed in other critical and fundamental areas of education and health.

Combining the strength of our traditional knowledge with modern scientific expertise, our children will be a force to be reckoned with. Our resilient island warriors will champion the protection of our lands and seas, and openly admonish any endeavour to do otherwise. They will channel the advocating, outspoken spirits of our role models such as Dwight Heine, Tony DeBrum, or Darlene Keju Johnson and they will devise community specific strategies to move forward as a small island–large ocean nation utilizing traditional local knowledge in the face of a changing climate. They will tell you that you are a rainbow. You are beautiful. And they will swim, because we have done so for thousands of years!

Nice Voice
When my daughter whines I tell her –
Say what you want in a nice voice.

My nice voice is reserved for meetings with a view, my palm outstretched saying here. Are our problems. Legacies rolling out like multicoloured marbles. *Don't focus so much on the 'doom and gloom'* they keep saying. We don't want to depress. Everyone. This is only our survival. *We rely heavily on foreign aid* I am instructed to say. I am instructed to point out the need for funds to build islands, move families from weto to weto, my mouth a shovel to spade the concrete with but I am just pointing out neediness. So needy. These small. Underdeveloped countries. I feel myself shrinking in the back of the taxi when a diplomat compliments me. How brave for admitting it so openly. The allure of global negotiations dulls. Like the back of a worn spoon.

I lose myself easily in a kemem. Kemem defined as feast. As celebration. A baby's breath endures their first year so we pack hundreds of close bodies under tents, lined up for plates I pass to my cousin, assembly line style. Plastic gloved hands pluck out barbeque chicken, fried fish, scoop potato salad, droplets of bōb and mā. Someone yells for another container of jajimi. The speaker warbles a keyboarded song. A child inevitably cries. Mine dances in the middle of the party. The MC shouts *Boke ajiri ne nejim jen maan.* The children are obstructing our view. Someone wheels a grandma onto the dance floor, the dance begin now here

is a nice celebration

of survival.

Kathy Jetñil-Kijiner

33

Authority, Identity, and Place in the Pacific Ocean and Its Hinterlands, c. 1200 to c. 2000

LEWIS MAYO

The history of the Pacific Ocean is sometimes imagined as an alternative to continentally defined histories, such as those of the Americas and those of Eurasia. With the island world at its heart, the Pacific is seen as having a history that is fundamentally oceanic in character.[1] This history is understood as involving a plurality of places, identities, and systems of authority that are at once independent and interlinked. It is often thought that it is with the advent of industrial modernity in the nineteenth century that this oceanic plurality acquires the character of an integrated whole, a process that entails the subordination of previously autonomous societies to the homogenizing effect of external power, above all to that of colonial empire.[2]

Rather than seeking to overturn this account of the history of the Pacific Ocean, this chapter extends and qualifies it. By considering phenomena in the island world in tandem with those on the Pacific coast of the Americas and in eastern Eurasia, and by considering the history of the industrial era in light of longer-term developments, a sense of the interconnections between different

---

[1] The most influential modern articulations of this vision are those of Epeli Hauʻofa. The core collection of his writing is *We Are the Ocean: Selected Works* (Honolulu: University of Hawaiʻi Press, 2008). Historical works which seek to build on this model include P. D'Arcy's *The People of the Sea: Environment, Identity, and History in Oceania* (Honolulu: University of Hawaiʻi Press, 2006) and M.K. Matsuda's *Pacific Worlds: A History of Seas, Peoples and Cultures* (Cambridge: Cambridge University Press, 2012).

[2] An example of a work which takes the nineteenth century as a critical divide is K. Sugihara, 'The economy since 1800', in D. Armitage and A. Bashford (eds.), *Pacific Histories: Ocean, Land, People* (Basingstoke: Palgrave Macmillan, 2014), 166–90. The salience of the period between the late eighteenth and early nineteenth centuries is emphasized in D. Igler, *The Great Ocean: Pacific Worlds from Captain Cook to the Gold Rush* (Oxford: Oxford University Press, 2013). The significance of the nineteenth-century colonial period is also stressed in N. Thomas, *Islanders: The Pacific in the Age of Empire* (New Haven: Yale University Press, 2010), although the author emphasizes the dynamism of the response of Pacific Islanders to foreign influences in this era.

spaces and times in the Pacific Ocean and its hinterlands is sought without sacrificing a sense of the specificity of particular localities. As an example of what this kind of history might look like, the chapter presents an account of the historical interactions between authority, identity, minerals, and war in three different places: the state of Bolivia; the island of Banaba in the Republic of Kiribati; and the district of Haizhou in the port city of Lianyungang in the People's Republic of China. The history of these places is presented in the context of an analysis of wider historical developments in the Pacific world and beyond it in the period between the twelfth and thirteenth centuries and the present.

Introduction

Histories – in the twin sense of happenings in the past and narratives of and inquiries into the past – can be seen as involving three interlocking domains. First of all, there are those forms of history that involve concrete entities and processes, such as landscapes and environments or the phonological and grammatical transformations of languages; and secondly, there are those involving disputation and struggle, particularly between individuals and groups who exert power and individuals and groups who experience power as something which others exert upon them; and thirdly, there are those forms of history that involve domains of imaginative engagement and projection and of symbolic construction. In the case of the histories of those things we call institutions, all three dimensions are involved – institutions are concrete entites whose existence is difficut to deny; they are also sites and foci of contestation and rivalry; and they are at the same time entities that are imagined and which structure acts of imagining.

We can therefore see a history of the Pacific Ocean as simultaneously involving three things. There is a concrete, physical entity – the Pacific Ocean that people can see, hear, and feel, and which they live by and travel across. There is also an object of dispute and struggle, a zone of physical and symbolic contest. Finally there is something which is both a focus for imaginative action and a site in which imaginative actions take place. This threefold history is also a matter of institutions. Institutions extend from languages, to art systems, to structures of ownership of and association with landscapes and seascapes, to modes of livelihood, to familal, religious, and political structures. Institutions are at once objects of perceptions and entities that structure perceptions. Families, businesses, religious groupings, states: these are things that people depict to themselves at the same time as being things that organize and shape people's perceptions. Institutions are also things that people commit themselves to defending or to overthrowing. This is particularly evident in what is said about institutions in the history of people who in one sense or another live around the Pacific. In the nineteenth and twentieth centuries, revolutionary processes, which coincided with and often arose from state-building, affected a great many of the regions around the Pacific. Many of the Pacific Rim state-focused identities that we can recognize in the present – such as those of Filipinos, Indonesians, Chinese, Mexicans, and Nicaraguans – are the products of nineteenth- and twentieth-century revolutions that sought to overthrow and remake the institutional structures found in the spatially bounded territories that we call empires and nation-states.

At one level the construct of a Pacific Ocean history is an ideological one: it is something which reflects the agendas of political interest groups, of which navies and economic cooperation organizations are key examples;[3] it is also a construct which is deployed by those seeking to challenge existing power structures – trans-Pacific alliances of Indigenous groups, or of opponents of environmental degradation, or of writers and artists who are marginalized by the publishing, museum curatorship, and art marketing structures that centre on the North Atlantic, and who see in the shared experience of living around an ocean a possibility for a fluid and flexible way of imagining oneself that is also rooted in a strong sense of place and belonging.[4] It can be suggested that the linkages and differences between the imagination of the Pacific by naval high commands or by banking corporations and the imagination of the Pacific by Indigenous activists and by poets and artists[5] oblige us to adopt a mode of historical narration that moves between what would be found in studies of the history of military technology or in economic geography and what would be found in literary analysis and art criticism.

---

[3] See A. Woodside, 'The Asia-Pacific idea as a mobilization myth', in A. Dirlik (ed.), *What Is in a Rim? Critical Perspectives on the Pacific Region Idea*, 2nd edn (Lanham: Rowman & Littlefield, 1998), 37–52; C.L. Connery, 'Pacific Rim discourse: the U.S. global imaginary in the late Cold War years', *boundary 2* 21:1 (1994), 30–56, and the discussion in M. Jolly, 'Imagining Oceania: indigenous and foreign representations of a Sea of Islands', *Contemporary Pacific* 19:2 (2007), 508–45.
[4] Few scholars have written on these issues with the range and versatility of the late Teresia Teaiwa: see K. Teaiwa, A. Henderson, and T. Wesley-Smith, 'Teresia K. Teaiwa: a bibliography', *Journal of Pacific History* 53:1 (2018), 103–7.
[5] See the different uses of the Asia-Pacific concept by the Daniel K. Inouye Center for Asia-Pacific Security Studies, located in Camp Smith in Hawai'i, the location of the Headquarters of the United States Indo-Pacific Command, and by the Asia-Pacific Triennial of Contemporary Art, held in the Queensland Art Gallery & Gallery of Modern Art in Brisbane.

Between these two poles are the ways of looking at the past that arise in disputes, in which contesting approaches to what are purportedly common experiences are placed in opposition to each other. Because struggles over places and claims made on them are of pivotal importance across the Pacific, from Taiwan to Papua New Guinea to Australia, to French Polynesia to the United States to Ecuador, Peru, Bolivia, and Chile, dispute and conflict are critical aspects of the experience and depiction of places. This is most evident in contexts where an incoming population significantly challenges, massively outnumbers, and to one extent or another subordinates the Indigenous population, as is the case in Hawai'i, Australia, Aotearoa New Zealand, New Caledonia, and Guam. In such settings, representations of the past are frequently tied to conflicts that are legal and political; history spills over into the law courts and into the domain of electoral politics. Historically orientated political and legal disputes are also present in places where Pacific Island people are either formally or substantively sovereign, at least in terms of having ownership of the land – Sāmoa and Fiji are clear examples of this. These contests and disputes are, of course, framed by structures of authority, in particular the authority structures of the modern state and the legal institutions that are part of the everyday exercise of modern forms of state power. These disputes are also framed by – and often help to create identities for – those who see themselves as the rightful owners of places, but who experience dispossesson, defining their identities in terms of that history of alienation. Equally, those who have moved to another place because of some kind of alienation or dispossesion in their homeland understand and express their identity in terms of a history of movement and displacement that was not a matter of choice. Furthermore, there are those for whom the act of moving – of acquiring affiliation to a new place and of settling there – is a matter of pride and even of celebration.

Chronologies and Geographies

By the end of the 1200s, Hawai'i, Rapa Nui/Easter Island, and Aotearoa New Zealand, which constitute the northernmost, easternmost, and southermost peripheries of what scholars refer to as Remote Oceania, were all clearly established as Polynesian places. The languages, cultures, identities, and systems of authority in those places, although isolated from each other and focused on their own internal concerns, were part of a network of related structures, such that when the present-day Polynesian inhabitants of those places encounter one another they can articulate a sense of cultural commonality,[6] a sense of commonality which is all the more precious because in all three places Polynesian cultural and political systems have been subordinated to structures such as those of the Americas and, beyond that, of the eastern periphery of the North Atlantic: Hawai'i and Rapa Nui are politically part of nation-states located on the American continent (the United States of America and Chile respectively) and Aotearoa New Zealand is a sovereign nation which has strong cultural links to the United Kingdom of Great Britain, and whose head of state is also the English monarch.

Native Hawaiians, Rapa Nui people, and Māori people in Aotearoa New Zealand thus have a twofold historical identity: they are at once the peoples Indigenous to the northernmost, easternmost, and southernmost parts of the pre-modern Polynesian settlement zone and they are also the Polynesians who are the most directly and profoundly affected by the cultures and power structures of settler peoples – speakers of Spanish and English – whose ultimate homeland is in western Eurasia. We can argue that the strong sense contemporary Polynesian intellectuals have of the Pacific Ocean being what creates their common identity[7] – something that is shared by Micronesians and by many people in Melanesia as well – has extra force in Hawai'i, Rapa Nui, and Aotearoa New Zealand for two reasons. One is that these three places are geographically distant from other parts of Polynesia and thus had perhaps the most autonomous histories in the Polynesian cultural zone in the period prior to the eighteenth and nineteenth centuries, and the other is that they are the places most subjected to influences from the Americas and Eurasia in the period since the 1800s, and are thus the place in which Polynesians in the present are the least autonomous.

For many people, both Indigenous and non-Indigenous, the modern history of Hawai'i, Rapa Nui, and Aotearoa New Zealand is one defined by the assault on Indigenous lifeways and the loss of political and cultural autonomy

---

[6] See for example, L. Kame'eleihiwa, 'Hawai'i-nui-akea cousins: ancestral gods and bodies of knowledge are treasures for the descendants', *Te Kaharoa* 2:1 (2009), 42–63, and C. Spiller, H. Barclay-Kerr, and J. Panoho, *Wayfinding Leadership: Groundbreaking Wisdom for Developing Leaders* (Wellington: Huia Publishers, 2015). For a discussion of the wider connection between Māori and the Pacific, see A.Te Punga Somerville, *Once Were Pacific: Māori Connections to Oceania* (Minneapolis: University of Minnesota Press, 2012).
[7] An early articulation of this in print is that by the Samoan writer Albert Wendt, 'Towards a new Oceania', *Mana Review: A South Pacific Journal of Language and Literature* 1:1 (1976), 49–60. Wendt's views are echoed and expanded upon by Hau'ofa in 'Our Sea of Islands' and 'We are the Ocean' (see *We Are the Ocean: Selected Works* (Honolulu: University of Hawai'i Press, 2008), 27–40 and 41–59). The native Hawaiian scholar Haunani-Kay Trask states: 'Hawaiians are not Americans. Nor are we Asians or Europeans. We are not from the Pacific Rim, nor are we immigrants to the Pacific. We are the children of Papa – earth mother – and Wākea – sky father – who created the sacred lands of Hawai'i Nei'; H.-K. Trask, 'Coalition building between natives and non-natives', *Stanford Law Review* 43:6 (1991), 1197–1213, at 1197.

resulting from the colonization of these lands by people of European background. A closely related narrative is that the post-eighteenth-century histories of these three places are ones of essentially isolated island societies being brought into contact with a modern world system centred on the North Atlantic. These accounts often leave out the question of how Pacific Island societies engaged with external influences that did not originate in the North Atlantic – above all influences from the Americas and Asia. As Chilean citizens, Rapa Nui people are part of a nation-state which not only historically asserts its American separateness from Spain and Europe but also contains key communities who see themselves as being not of European origin, but rather as Indigenous to the Americas, the Mapuche people of the southern Pacific coast of Chile being among the most prominent.[8] Equally, New Zealanders or Hawai'i residents who would consider themselves as of Asian background have personal and collective histories that are also not 'European', and this is true for many people in the Oceanic world, from Fiji to New Caledonia to Guam.

A history of authority, identity, and place in the Pacific Ocean that moves beyond the older focus on the Pacific Islander–European dichotomy[9] and examines the history of Oceania from this wider range of cultural contexts will hopefully provide a more faithful representation of these complexities, and scholars of Oceania have been moving in this direction for some time. At the same time, there will be people who see themselves as being in some sense or another defined by having a place in the Pacific but who may feel almost no connection to the Oceanic world. Persons from British Columbia may see themselves as having a Pacific identity that contrasts them with Canadians from the Atlantic rim; Colombians from the Pacific coast may define themselves in contrast to Caribbean or Andean Colombians; Queenslanders may define themselves with reference to the Pacific in contrast to Western Australians or South Australians, and people from

---

[8] R. Delsing, *Articulating Rapa Nui: Polynesian Cultural Politics in a Latin American Nation-State* (Honolulu: University of Hawai'i Press, 2015); M. Makihara, 'Linguistic syncretism and language ideologies: transforming sociolinguistic hierarchy on Rapa Nui (Easter Island)', *American Anthropologist* 106: 3 (2004), 529–40; F.W. Young '"I Hē Koe? Placing Rapa Nui', *Contemporary Pacific* 24:1 (2012), 1–30; F.W. Young, 'Unsettling the boundaries of Latin America: Rapa Nui and the refusal of Chilean settler colonialism', *Settler Colonial Studies* (2020), doi:10.1080/2201473X.2020.1823751; J. Crow, *The Mapuche in Modern Chile: A Cultural History* (Gainesville: University Press of Florida, 2013).

[9] See, for example, B. Smith, *European Vision and the South Pacific*, 3rd edn (Oxford: Oxford University Press, 1989); K.R. Howe, *Where the Waves Fall: A New South Sea Islands History from First Settlement to Colonial Rule* (Honolulu: University of Hawai'i Press, 1984); and J. Gascoigne, *Encountering the Pacific in the Age of Enlightenment* (Cambridge: Cambridge University Press, 2014).

Vladivostok may invoke the Pacific to differentiate themselves from Russians who live around the Baltic or the Black Sea or in western Siberia.

It is obvious that in each of these cases dramatically different forms of Pacific identity, different relationships to place, and different relationships to structures of authority are involved. Many would argue that because of these differences a history of identity, authority, and place that takes the Pacific Ocean as its subject is fundamentally ill-conceived. It would be better, such critics might suggest, to produce either a history that was fully global or one that was more restricted in its geographic scope. A further critique would be levelled at the decision to take the period between the twelfth and thirteenth centuries and the present as the unit of inquiry; if the Pacific only gets the name by which it is now known in the early 1500s and arguably only becomes a zone in which there is direct interaction between all of its parts in the late eighteenth century, there is little justification for starting with an earlier period. Finally, it might also be objected that a Pacific Ocean history is already large enough in its scope, and to add in the ambiguous category of 'hinterlands' (a category deployed in this chapter) dilutes the focus of the analysis to the point where it may be almost meaningless.

If we agree that historical inquiry concerns concrete processes and structures (such as those involving the environment, population, and technologies), contestation and dispute and acts of imaginative creation and projection, along with the interplay between these domains, and is also both an interrogation of institutions and a product of institutions, we can suggest that the interaction zone that we call the Pacific Ocean is as legitimate an object of historical analysis as any other. But we can also argue that because the Pacific is not a centralized or unified entity, and because it is subject to multiple definitions, it would be wrong to present the history of that space as if it could be given a single or homogenous representation. Yet rather than simply offering an account of how the Pacific has been imagined or represented, which would place us firmly in the domain of cultural and intellectual history, we can suggest that it is best to try to create a dialogue between the history of the places that are spread across the Pacific and in which and from which different kinds of Pacific identities are created, a dialogue that entails examination of the structures of authority which exist in and help to create those places and those identities.

The present chapter can be seen as an example of an 'associative history'; it is an example of how history can be narrated by means of association rather than by attempts to define unities and divisions. This involves not simply the creation of associations within the narrative of the past that this text provides – associations that reflect the imaginative work of the author and are the products of the author's interests – but also the associations between places that result from actual contacts and connections forged by voyages and journeys, and by acts of conquest and transplantation. We can also think of an associative history of the Pacific as an attempt to do justice to historical entities that may otherwise be seen as ephemeral; a friendship group in a linguistically and ethnically diverse high school in an early twenty-first-century Pacific Rim city with a large immigrant population will involve connections between people and their histories that may be difficult to map using conventional forms of historical narration. The same can be said of groups of people meeting in public hospitals or in prisons or in immigration detention or at expensive resorts or on cruise ships or in the offices of multinational companies, or in a multiplicity of other 'contact zones' around the contemporary Pacific. While economists, anthropologists, cultural theorists, and writers have written extensively about such sites of contact, historians seem much more cautious about addressing them, regarding them as being either too complex or too historically shallow to be meaningfully analysed. Historians fear producing the narrative equivalent of a food court, in which the juxtapositions of cultures and their histories is the result of proximities that are more-or-less arbitrary.

There are two possible ways of thinking past these concerns. One is that food-court-style juxtapositions of hitherto widely separated cultural and historical experiences are now common and we need historical accounts that help people to see the lines of connection that have brought them together, while also narrating the antagonisms and solidarities to which such intersections give rise. Another is that historical inquiry needs to do justice both to the coherence and regularity in human experience and to the arbitrary and the haphazard. A good analogy for this is the logs prized for canoe building in pre-industrial Micronesian societies that washed up on the beaches of Micronesian islands with limited natural vegetation, having been borne by currents across the Pacific from as far away as North America or Papua New Guinea. Such logs represented connections between widely separated geographical zones, and, once they had been worked into sailing vessels, had a vital role in the life and the histories of the societies in which they were used.[10] The long-term history of Pacific Ocean cultures is marked by precisely this process of long-

---

[10] See D. Alessio and A. Kelen, 'Waan Aelōñ in Majōl: canoes of the Marshall Islands', in A.L. Loeak, V.C. Kiluwe, and L. Crowl (eds.), *Life in the Republic of the Marshall Islands* (Suva: Suva: Institute of Pacific Studies, University of the South Pacific, 2004), 192–225, at 202. On driftwood and related materials, see D.H.R. Spennemann, *Gifts from the Waves: A Case of Marine Transport of Obsidian to Nadikdik Atoll and the Occurrence of Other Drift Materials in the Marshall Islands* (Albury: Charles Sturt University, The Johnstone Centre of Parks, Recreation and Heritage, 1995), 40–7.

distance movement and local refashioning of the cultures and peoples who arrive as a result of the historical analogue of ocean currents propelling logs across the sea, forces that combine macro regularities and macro patterns with happenstance. We can argue that the 'associative histories' that this chapter presents are attempts to produce on the page a representation of this particuar form of historical reality.

Timeframes

This chapter proceeds from the assumption that we can see the beginnings of the modern Pacific in the twelfth to thirteenth centuries for three reasons. One, as stated above, is that it is in the thirteenth century that Polynesian migration reaches its known limits using the sailing technologies that it had developed under its own auspices.[11] This is also the period when, it can be argued, the political structures that are the foundation for present-day Fiji, Tonga, and Sāmoa, and also those of the hierarchical societies of the eastern Carolines (Kosrae and Pohnpei) come into being.[12] Another is that the Mongol conquests in East and Southeast Asia which reach their apogee in the 1200s mark the point at which we can see an interlocking system of regional cultural and political entities that extend from Siberia to the eastern part of Indonesia.[13]

[11] K.R. Howe (ed.), *Vaka Moana: Voyages of the Ancestors: The Discovery and Settlement of the Pacific* (Auckland: David Bateman, 2006) and A. Anderson, *The First Migration: Māori Origins 3000BC–AD1450* (Auckland: Bridget Williams Books, 2016) present these developments for the general reader. T.L. Hunt and C. Lipo, 'The archaeology of Rapa Nui (Easter Island)', in E.E. Cochrane and T.L. Hunt (eds.), *The Oxford Handbook of Prehistoric Oceania* (Oxford: Oxford University Press, 2018), 416–49, and A. Anderson, 'The prehistory of South Polynesia', in Cochrane and Hunt (eds.), *The Oxford Handbook of Prehistoric Oceania*, 396–415, sum up the current views of archaeologists.

[12] I.C. Campbell, *Classical Tongan Kingship* (Nukuʻalofa: ʻAtenisi University, 1989); A.M. Tuimalealiʻifano, *O Tama a ʻĀiga: The Politics of Succession to Sāmoa's Paramount Titles* (Suva: Institute of Pacific Studies, University of the South Pacific, 2006); M. Spriggs and D. Scarr (eds.), *Aubrey Parke, Degei's Descendants: Spirits, Place and People in Pre-cession Fiji* (Canberra: ANU Press, 2014); D. Hanlon, *Upon a Stone Altar: A History of the Island of Pohnpei to 1890* (Honolulu: University of Hawaiʻi Press, 1988); D. Hanlon, 'Histories of the before: Lelu, Nan Madol, and deep time', in E. Hermann (ed.), *Changing Contexts, Shifting Meanings: Transformations of Cultural Traditions in Oceania* (Honolulu: University of Hawaiʻi Press in association with the Honolulu Academy of Arts, 2011), 41–55.

[13] A recent overall treatment of this period is T. May, *The Mongol Conquests in World History* (London: Reaktion, 2012). For a discussion of broad developments in Southeast Asia in this period, see chapters 2, 3, and 5 of A. Reid, *A History of Southeast Asia: Critical Crossroads* (Chichester: Wiley-Blackwell, 2015). For the broader China-Southeast Asia maritime context, see B.K.L. So, *Prosperity, Region and Institutions in Maritime China: The South Fukien Pattern, 946–1368* (Cambridge, MA: Harvard University Press, 2001), O.W. Wolters, *Early Indonesian Commerce: A Study of the Origins of Srivijaya* (Ithaca, NY: Cornell University Press, 1967), and O.W. Wolters, *The Fall of Srivijaya in Malay History* (Ithaca, NY: Cornell University Press, 1970).

The third reason is that the foundations for the Aztec and Inca polities which form the basis for the nation-state complexes that we now call Mexico and Guatemala and, in the south, Ecuador, Peru, Bolivia, and Chile, take rough shape in the twelfth and thirteenth centuries.[14] These three different zones, in the Pacific, in the Americas, and in East and Southeast Asia, together form a lattice of separate but internally interlinked societies and cultures, which have in the centuries between the 1200s and the present come to constitute core parts of the network that makes up the Pacific system. In the 1300s and 1400s in each of these spaces we can see the formation of a steadily intensifying set of processes of cultural articulation. In some contexts this cultural articulation involves increasing centralization and concentration of populations and of power; in others, such as in the Eastern Polynesian linguistic zone, this cultural articulation involves separate centres of development, as settlements evolve in isolation from the sites from which their populations originated. In the Southeast Asian border zones adjoining the Pacific, the conversion of polities to Islam (which we might see as a long-term effect of the increasing presence of Muslims in the Chinese cultural zone as a product of the extensive use by the Mongols of Persians and other Muslim groups as administrators) helps to bring the western edge of the Pacific into contact with the Indian Ocean world. It is in the 1300s and 1400s that the Aztec and Inca imperial states take their true shape and consolidate their territorial authority.[15]

These structures in the Americas are brought into connection with East and Southeast Asia in the 1500s when they are annexed by the Spanish, at the same time that Iberians establish footholds in East and Southeast Asia – of

On the Song dynasty maritime order, see A. Schottenhammer, 'China's emergence as a maritime power', in J.W. Chaffee and D. Twitchett (eds.), *The Cambridge History of China*, vol. v, part 2, *Sung China, 960–1279* (Cambridge: Cambridge University Press, 2015), 437–525. On the Southern Song and Yuan periods, see J.-p. Lo, *China as a Sea Power, 1127–1368: A Preliminary Survey of the Maritime Expansion and Naval Exploits of the Chinese People during the Southern Song and Yuan Periods*, ed. B.A. Elleman (Hong Kong: Hong Kong University Press, 2012).

[14] Scholars of Aztec history refer to the period from 1150 to 1350 as the early Aztec period; see M. Hodge, 'Archaeological views of Aztec culture', *Journal of Archaeological Research* 6:3 (1998), 195–238, at 198. Scholars of Inca history refer to the period from 1100 to 1400 as the late intermediate period; see B.S. Bauer and R.A. Covey, 'Processes of state formation in the Inca heartland (Cuzco, Peru)', *American Anthropologist* 104:3 (2002), 846–64, at 846.

[15] See M. Rostworowski de Diez Canseco, *History of the Inca Realm* (Cambridge: Cambridge University Press, 1999); T.N. D'Altroy, *The Incas* (Oxford: Blackwell, 2002); F. Berdan, *The Aztecs of Central Mexico: An Imperial Society*, 2nd edn (Belmont, CA: Wadsworth Cengage, 2005); S. Schroeder, *Tlacaelel Remembered: Mastermind of the Aztec Empire* (Norman: University of Oklahoma Press, 2016). A comparative treatment of Aztec and Inca imperial formation by archaeologists is G.W. Conrad and A.A. Demarest, *Religion and Empire: The Dynamics of Aztec and Inca Expansionism* (Cambridge: Cambridge University Press, 1984).

which the Spanish presence in what is now the central Philippines and the Portuguese presence in Macao are perhaps the most important.[16] In this structure, a line of coastal and overland interconnection joined the territories of the Ming Dynasty (a state strongly concerned with problems of its maritime border, but still engaged with it) to Japan, Korea, and the Northeast Asian zones between Mongolia and the Pacific and to insular and mainland Southeast Asia, and, eastwards across the Pacific to the Americas.[17] The 1600s, which saw political consolidation in Japan, a crisis in the Ming territory that led to the overthrow of the dynasty by Manchu conquerors from Northeast Asia, and the foundation of the Qing Dynasty, which by the mid-1700s had created the largest unified political unit in human history, were characterized by the consolidation of the Spanish imperial structure in the Americas, and continued interaction across the Pacific.[18] In insular Southeast Asia, Muslim polities competed with the Dutch and with the Spanish, a rivalry that moved back and forth into the eighteenth century.[19] With the Qing conquest of Taiwan in the late seventeenth century (the Qing defeated the forces of the Zheng family, who were nominally loyal to the defeated Ming dynasty; the Zheng state had replaced a Dutch colonial polity based in southern Taiwan, which, along with a Spanish presence in north Taiwan, had sought to use Taiwan as a base for participation in the East Asian trade network that extended from Japan to Vietnam), a period

---

[16] The classic study focused on the Pacific is O.H.K. Spate, *The Spanish Lake* (Canberra: ANU Press, 2004 [1979]). More recent work tends to situate the developments in the Pacific in this period in the wider context of global history – see A. Giraldez, *The Age of Trade: The Manila Galleons and the Dawn of the Global Economy* (Lanham: Rowman & Littlefield, 2015) and J.L. Gasch-Tomás, *The Atlantic World and the Manila Galleons: Circulation, Market, and Consumption of Asian Goods in the Spanish Empire, 1565–1650* (Leiden: Brill, 2019). Recent monographs on the social and cultural dimensions of early modern trans-Pacific exchanges between Asia and the Spanish Americas include R. Padrón, *The Indies of the Setting Sun: How Early Modern Spain Mapped the Far East as the Transpacific West* (Chicago: University of Chicago Press, 2020) and T. Seijas, *Asian Slaves in Colonial Mexico: From Chinos to Indians* (Cambridge: Cambridge University Press, 2014).

[17] See K. Li., *The Ming Maritime Trade Policy in Transition* (Wiesbaden: Harrassowitz, 2010).

[18] L.A. Struve, *The Qing Formation in World-Historical Time* (Cambridge, MA: Harvard University Asia Center, 2004); C. Totman, *Early Modern Japan* (Berkeley: University of California Press, 1993); P. Crossley, *The Manchus* (Cambridge, MA: Blackwell, 1997); F. Wakeman Jr, *The Great Enterprise: The Manchu Reconstruction of Imperial Order in Seventeenth-Century China* (Berkeley: University of California Press, 1985).

[19] J.L. Gaynor, *Intertidal History in Island Southeast Asia: Submerged Genealogy and the Legacy of Coastal Capture* (Ithaca, NY: Cornell University Press, 2016); A. Reid, *Southeast Asia in the Age of Commerce, 1450–1680*, 2 vols. (New Haven: Yale University Press, 1988–93); also, area-specific studies such as L. Andaya, *The World of Maluku: Eastern Indonesia in the Early Modern Period* (Honolulu: University of Hawai'i Press, 1993) and L. Andaya, *The Heritage of Arung Palakka: A History of South Sulawesi (Celebes) in the Seventeenth Century* (The Hague: Nijhoff, 1981).

of economic expansion in East and Southeast Asia that was centred on Fujian province was initiated, lasting until the late eighteenth century.[20] In the years between the early 1600s and the 1780s, other parts of the Pacific, including southeastern Australia and Aotearoa New Zealand, were brought into direct connection with the larger web of links that spanned the whole ocean from the Americas to the China coast. Between the 1770s and the 1840s, we can argue, the various zones of local interaction around the Pacific from the Arctic to the southern peripheries of Polynesia in the cold seas at the southern tip of New Zealand, and in the areas from northern Australia to the north and south of Papua New Guinea into the insular zone that extends from Fiji-Tonga and Sāmoa to the Solomon Islands, Vanuatu and New Caledonia, were brought into sustained connection with each other.[21] The rebellion of the Spanish colonies in the Americas in the early nineteenth century produced a network of new republican states dominated by Spanish-speaking creole elites along the Pacific coast from Mexico stretching down through Central America to Colombia, Ecuador, Peru, Bolivia, and Chile.[22] The rebellions that brought these new states into existence were followed by massive upheavals in the territory of the Qing, inspired in part by religious commitments. The Taiping uprising of the mid-nineteenth century, often described as the largest civil war in human history, was affiliated to a Christian-derived millenarian movement that was dedicated to the replacement of the Qing state by a 'Kingdom of Great Peace'; large-scale Muslim rebellions broke out in north China and in Inner Asia after

---

[20] On the conquest of Taiwan and its subsequent transformation see J.R. Shepherd, *Statecraft and Political Economy on the Taiwan Frontier, 1600–1800* (Stanford: Stanford University Press, 1993); T. Andrade, *Commerce, Culture, and Conflict: Taiwan under European Rule, 1624–1662* (New Haven: Yale University Press, 2000) and T. Andrade, *How Taiwan Became Chinese: Dutch, Spanish, and Han Colonization in the Seventeenth Century* (New York: Columbia University Press, 2008). For the trade system that emerged in this era see, C.-k. Ng, *Trade and Society: The Amoy Network on the China Coast 1683–1735*, 2nd edn (Singapore: NUS Press, 2015) and G. Zhao, *The Qing Opening to the Ocean: Chinese Maritime Policy, 1684–1757* (Honolulu: University of Hawai'i Press, 2013)

[21] For an overview of the whole Pacific in this period, see chapter 14 of Matsuda's *Pacific Worlds*. Monographs focused on this period include, K.R. Howe, *Where the Waves Fall: A New South Sea Islands History from First Settlement to Colonial Rule* (Honolulu: University of Hawai'i Press, 1984) and Igler, *The Great Ocean.*

[22] J. Lynch's *The Spanish American Revolutions, 1808–1826*, 2nd edn (New York: Norton, 1986) retains its power as an account of the emergence of these societies. Other overviews of Latin American independence include J.E. Rodríguez O., *The Independence of Spanish America* (Cambridge: Cambridge University Press, 1998); J.C. Hasteen, *Americanos: Latin America's Struggle for Independence* (Oxford: Oxford University Press, 2008); and R. Graham, *Independence in Latin America: Contrasts and Comparisons*, 3rd edn (Austin: University of Texas Press, 2013).

the Taiping upheaval.[23] English-speaking settling and colonizing states were established in Australia-New Zealand and on the Pacific coast of the Americas in this period; gold rushes in California and later in Australia, New Zealand, and Canada brought great influxes of new people into these societies; racial antagonisms were built up as core features of these new Pacific places, with English-speaking whites constructing themselves as rightful owners of these spaces, displacing Indigenous populations and opposing permanent settlement by Asian migrants.[24] Plantation societies emerged in the tropical zones in the Pacific at this time, societies creating cultural and economic structures that in many respects reduplicated what had been established in the commercial agricultural systems of Southeast Asia and in the Americas.[25] The long-term effect of the expansion of these structures in the nineteenth century was the subordination of Pacific Islanders to the economic and political power of Europeans and white Americans, with Asian migrants occupying complex middle positions in those places where they were imported as labourers, but where they also pursued economic opportunities.[26] The later parts of the

[23] On the Taiping Rebellion see T.H. Reilly, *The Taiping Heavenly Kingdom: Rebellion and the Blasphemy of Empire* (Seattle: University of Washington Press, 2004); J. Spence, *God's Chinese Son: The Chinese Heavenly Kingdom of Hong Xiuquan* (Hammersmith: Flamingo, 1997); and R.G. Wagner, *Reenacting the Heavenly Vision: The Role of Religion in the Taiping Rebellion* (Berkeley: University of California, 1982). On Muslim rebellions see D.G. Atwill, *Chinese Sultanate: Islam, Ethnicity, and the Panthay Rebellion in Southwest China, 1856–1873* (Stanford: Stanford University Press, 2005) and H. Kim, *Holy War in China: The Muslim Rebellion and State in Chinese Central Asia, 1864–1877* (Stanford: Stanford University Press, 2004).
[24] A key overview is J. Belich, *Replenishing the Earth: The Settler Revolution and the Rise of the Anglo-World* (Oxford: Oxford University Press, 2009). Some classic works include: K. Starr, *Americans and the California Dream, 1850–1915* (Oxford: Oxford University Press, 1973); A. Atkinson, *The Europeans in Australia*, vol. 1, *The Beginning* (Oxford: Oxford University Press, 1997); and J. Belich, *Making Peoples: A History of the New Zealanders from Polynesian Settlement to the End of the Nineteenth Century* (Honolulu: University of Hawai'i Press, 1996). A. Perry, *On the Edge of Empire: Gender, Race, and the Making of British Columbia, 1849–1871* (Toronto: University of Toronto Press, 2001) and M. Lake, *Progressive New World: How Settler Colonialism and Transpacific Exchange Shaped American Reform* (Cambridge, MA: Harvard University Press, 2019) stress the importance of race and gender in the formation of these societies and their ideologies. On white settler societies and Asian migration see A.M. McKeown, *Melancholy Order: Asian Migration and the Globalization of Borders* (New York: Columbia University Press, 2008).
[25] See B.V. Lal, D. Munro and E.D. Beechert (eds.), *Plantation Workers: Resistance and Accommodation* (Honolulu: University of Hawai'i Press, 1993); R. Takaki, *Pau Hana: Plantation Life and Labor in Hawaii, 1835–1920* (Honolulu: University of Hawai'i Press, 1983); B.V. Lal, *Girmitiyas: The Origins of the Fiji Indians* (Lautoka: Fiji Institute of Applied Studies, 2004); D. Shineberg, *The People Trade: Pacific Island Laborers and New Caledonia, 1865–1930* (Honolulu: University of Hawai'i Press, 1999).
[26] The history of Hawai'i in the nineteenth and twentieth centuries is a key instance of these developments; see L. Kame'eleihiwa, *Native Land and Foreign Desires: Ko Hawai'i Āina a me Nā Koi Pu'umake a ka Po'e Haole* (Honolulu: Bishop Museum Press, 1992); J.K.K. Osorio, *Dismembering Lāhui: A History of the Hawaiian Nation to 1887* (Honolulu: University of Hawai'i

nineteenth century saw the emergence of the United States as an imperial power in the Pacific, with Americans overthrowing the Hawaiian kingdom in the 1890s and taking over old Spanish colonies in the western Pacific following the Philippine Revolution against Spain, a revolution which resulted not in the full independence of the Philippines but in annexation by the United States.[27] The Qing state experienced a series of crises in the late nineteenth century which both stemmed from and led to the establishment of zones of control by industrial imperial powers. Japan, which had built up an industrial economy and a military system based on industrial structures, defeated the Qing in a war in 1894 which led to Japan's annexation of Taiwan, marking the beginning of Japan's rise as an industrial empire.[28] By 1900 almost everywhere in the Pacific outside of the territories of the Latin American republics was part of some kind of imperial structure.[29] The first major displacement of an imperial entity in this period – if we discount the Philippine Revolution against Spain – was the overthrow of the Qing state in Mongolia and China in 1911.[30] Revolution also occurred in Mexico – a non-imperial state – in this period, but it was arguably with the Bolshevik revolution of 1917 that a serious challenge to the imperial

Press, 2002); and S.E. Merry, *Colonizing Hawai'i: The Cultural Power of Law* (Princeton: Princeton University Press, 2000).

[27] P.A. Kramer, *The Blood of Government: Race, Empire, the United States, & the Philippines* (Chapel Hill: University of North Carolina Press, 2006); L. Thompson, *Imperial Archipelago: Representation and Rule in the Insular Territories under U.S. Dominion after 1898* (Honolulu: University of Hawai'i Press, 2010); E. San Juan Jr, *U.S. Imperialism and Revolution in the Philippines* (New York: Palgrave Macmillan, 2007); N.K. Silva, *Aloha Betrayed: Native Hawaiian Resistance to American Colonialism* (Durham, NC: Duke University Press, 2004).

[28] See W.G. Beasley, *Japanese Imperialism 1894–1945* (Oxford: Clarendon Press, 1987); R.H. Myers and M.R. Peattie (eds.), *The Japanese Colonial Empire, 1895–1945* (Princeton: Princeton University Press, 1984); P. Duus, *The Abacus and the Sword: The Japanese Penetration of Korea, 1895–1910* (Berkeley: University of California Press, 1995); L.T.S. Ching, *Becoming 'Japanese': Colonial Taiwan and the Politics of Identity Formation* (Berkeley: University of California Press, 2001); M. Peattie, *Nan'yō: The Rise and Fall of the Japanese in Micronesia, 1885–1945* (Honolulu: University of Hawai'i Press, 1988); R.T. Tierney, *Tropics of Savagery: The Culture of Japanese Empire in Comparative Frame* (Berkeley: University of California Press, 2010).

[29] K. van Dijk, *Pacific Strife: The Great Powers and Their Political and Economic Rivalries in Asia and the Western Pacific 1870–1914* (Amsterdam: Amsterdam University Press, 2015); D. Scarr, *Fragments of Empire: A History of the Western Pacific High Commission, 1877–1914* (Canberra: ANU Press, 1967); J. Dunmore, *Visions and Realities: France in the Pacific, 1695–1995* (Waikanae: Heritage Press, 1997); P.J. Hempenstall, *Pacific Islanders under German Rule: A Study in the Meaning of Colonial Resistance* (Canberra: ANU Press, 1978).

[30] Book-length studies of the Chinese Revolution include: P. Zarrow, *China in War and Revolution 1895–1949* (New York: RoutledgeCurzon, 2005); D. Lary, *China's Republic* (Cambridge: Cambridge University Press, 2007); J.K. Fairbank, *The Great Chinese Revolution, 1800–1985* (New York: HarperPerennial, 1987); J.D. Spence, *Gate of Heavenly Peace: The Chinese and Their Revolution, 1895–1980* (New York: Viking, 1981).

order in the Pacific Rim outside of the Latin American zone was mounted.[31] On the surface, empire appeared strong in this period, particularly in the Oceanic realm. German colonial possesssions around the Pacific had been seized in 1914 by Britain and the British Dominions (Australia and New Zealand) and by Japan. With Germany's defeat in 1918, the wider Pacific zone developed into a zone of contest between the rival imperial forces of the United States, Japan, and the British (and the British dominions – including Canada), with the Dutch and French imperial states occupying secondary positions. Ideologies and institutions that had their origin in the political economy structures of the nineteenth century – ideologies of liberalism and conservativism and of race and evolutionary pictures of human development – were in many ways the dominant frameworks across the Pacific in this period, with their effects being strongly evident in colonial and settler states.[32] However, as noted, this was also a period in which these ideologies and stuctures began to be subject to challenge by radical frameworks which questioned divisions of class, and sometimes of race and gender as well.

[31] See A. Knight, *The Mexican Revolution* (Cambridge: Cambridge University Press, 1986). Examples of the wider effects of revolutionary ideologies across the Pacific in this era include: J. Nery, *Revolutionary Spirit: José Rizal in Southeast Asia* (Singapore: Institute of Southeast Asian Studies, 2011); C. Christie, *Ideology and Revolution in Southeast Asia 1900–1980* (Richmond: Curzon, 2001); A. Belogurova, *The Nanyang Revolution: The Comintern and Chinese Networks in Southeast Asia 1890–1957* (Cambridge: Cambridge University Press, 2018); A. Pantsov, *The Bolsheviks and the Chinese Revolution 1919–1927* (Honolulu: University of Hawai'i Press, 2000); M.A. Navarro-Génie, *Augusto 'César' Sandino: Messiah of Light and Truth* (Syracuse: Syracuse University Press, 2002); I. García-Bryce, *Haya de la Torre and the Pursuit of Power in Twentieth-Century Peru and Latin America* (Chapel Hill: University of North Carolina Press, 2018).
[32] Struggles between groups designated as liberals and conservatives were a central feature of nineteenth-century politics in Latin American republics – see F.S. Weaver, 'Reform and (counter)revolution in post-independence Guatemala: liberalism, conservatism, and post-modem controversies', *Latin American Perspectives* 26:2 (1999), 129–58. On intersections between liberalism and race in nineteenth-century South America, see B. Larson, *Trials of Nation Making: Liberalism, Race, and Ethnicity in the Andes, 1810–1910* (Cambridge: Cambridge University Press, 2004). For conservatism and liberalism in British Columbia in the years after World War I, see R.K. Burkinshaw, *Pilgrims in Lotus Land: Conservative Protestantism in British Columbia, 1917–1981* (Montreal: McGill-Queen's University Press, 1995) and J. Murton, *Creating a Modern Countryside: Liberalism and Land Resettlement in British Columbia* (Vancouver: UBC Press, 2007). For conservatism in California in the 1930s see, K.S. Olmsted, *Right Out of California: The 1930s and the Big Business Roots of Modern Conservatism* (New York: The New Press, 2015). For liberalism and conservatism in Japan in this period, see G.A. Hoston, 'The state, modernity, and the fate of liberalism in prewar Japan', *Journal of Asian Studies* 51:2 (1992), 287–316, and C.W.A. Szpilman, 'Conservatism and conservative reaction', in S. Saaler and C.W.A. Szpilman (eds.), *Routledge Handbook of Modern Japanese History* (London: Routledge, 2017). In Australia the category 'liberal' contains elements that would affiliate it with values that would be labelled 'conservative' in a number of other Pacific Rim countries; see J. Brett, *Australian Liberals and the Moral Middle Class: From Alfred Deakin to John Howard* (Cambridge: Cambridge University Press, 2003). In all these places, liberal and conservative ideologies were powerfully connected with ideas about race and about social development.

The revolutionary struggles in China in the 1920s and 1930s, and Japan's incursions into the territories of the Chinese Republic, were a central focus for these ideological contests, but their effects were also felt in the colonial territories in Southeast Asia, and in the Spanish- and English-speaking nation-states of the Pacific Rim (in which ideas of equality and of progress were key elements in the ways in which these states depicted themselves to internal and external constituencies, ideas that often sat uneasily beside the internal racial and ethnic inequalities that characterized these polities) and in colonized places in the Pacific. The outbreak of war between Japan, the United States, Britian, and the British Dominions in the Pacific in 1941 is seen by almost all observers as marking a critical juncture in the Pacific system, precipitating major structural changes in almost every society in the Pacific Ocean and its hinterlands (the Latin American countries being the most prominent exceptions).[33] The war brought Pacific Island peoples into far more direct contact with the structures of industrial empire – Japanese and Anglo-American – than had been the case in the years prior to 1941, particularly through the ferocious fighting in the Solomon Islands, Papua New Guinea, and Micronesia.[34] While Japan's defeat meant that American power was virtually unchallenged across the Pacific world in the years between 1945 and the early twenty-first century, when Chinese economic, political, and military influence began to be felt in Oceania and around the Pacific rim in signficant ways, we can argue that the success of revolutionary movements in China in 1949 and in Southeast Asia between the expulsion of the Dutch and the French from Southeast Asia in the 1940s and 1950s and the defeat of American-backed regimes in Vietnam, Laos, and Cambodia in 1975 signified a continued questioning of the systems of authority and the models of identity promoted by the power structures of the United States.[35] (It is worth

---

[33] Of the many studies of the subject, B. Cumings's *Parallax Visions: Making Sense of American–East Asian Relations* (Durham, NC: Duke University Press, 2002) is distinguished for the acuity of its analysis. See also J.W. Dower, *War without Mercy: Race and Power in the Pacific War* (New York: Pantheon Books, 1986); K. Gotō, *Tensions of Empire: Japan and Southeast Asia in the Colonial and Postcolonial World*, ed. and with an intro. by P.H. Kratoska (Athens: Ohio University Press, 2003); T. Fujitani, G.M. White, and L. Yoneyama (eds.), *Perilous Memories: The Asia-Pacific War (s)* (Durham, NC: Duke University Press, 2001).

[34] G.M. White and L. Lindstrom (eds.), *The Pacific Theater: Island Representations of World War II*, Pacific Islands Monograph Series 8 (Honolulu: University of Hawai'i Press, 1989); G.M. White (ed.), *Remembering the Pacific War*, Occasional Paper 36, Center for Pacific Islands Studies School of Hawaiian, Asian & Pacific Studies (Honolulu: University of Hawai'i Press, 1991); A.A. Kwai, *Solomon Islanders in World War II: An Indigenous Perspective* (Canberra: ANU Press, 2017).

[35] See for example, A. Reid, *Imperial Alchemy: Nationalism and Political Identity in Southeast Asia* (Cambridge: Cambridge University Press, 2010); A.C. Guan, *Southeast Asia's Cold War: An Interpretive History* (Honolulu: University of Hawai'i Press, 2018); C. Bayly and T. Harper, *Forgotten Wars: Freedom and Revolution in Southeast Asia* (Cambridge, MA: Belknap Press, 2007).

pointing out that a good deal of the late twentieth- and early twenty-first-century scholarly work on the modern history of the Pacific that has been published in English in the United States and in countries that are its allies is characterized by a critique of imperialism and colonialism and their effects on societies across and around the Pacific.) A key irony of the historical process of Anglophone cultural influence coming to be felt across the Pacific Ocean in the course of the twentieth century is that that cultural expansion, which often appears like a homogenizing juggernaut that wipes out what is in its path, provides the concrete foundation for thinking and writing comparatively and critically about the internal variety and diversity of Pacific Ocean historical experience.

Two broad themes dominate what is written about the history of the Pacific Ocean over the last 100 years – the theme of colonization and decolonization (including whether or not decolonization has actually taken place) and the theme of economic development with its twin aspects of producing great improvements in human material circumstances (measured above all in increased life expectancies) and of devastating local and regional ecologies, natural and cultural.[36] One problem with the focus on these two themes to the exclusion of other historical phenomena is that they lead to a narrative in which European influences are placed on centrestage – whether those influences be cast in the role of heroes or villains. Another problem is that both colonizaton (and settlement and empire) and economic development are wrongly construed as things that are uniquely or distinctively European, with the implication that Pacific histories are simply adjuncts to European histories; Pacific places, and the identities and systems of authority that are found in and around the Pacific, end up being discussed in terms of how they do or do not resemble European ones. While much of the discussion of how to decolonize the historiography of the Pacific concerns precisely this problem, the discourse is arguably still framed by the idea that the core processes in the history of the Pacific Ocean and the lands that surround it are those that were initiated by the arrival of Europeans in the region, either in the thirteenth century, when the first European eyewitness accounts of East Asia were produced by visitors to the Mongol empire in

---

[36] For an example of scholarship focused on colonialism, see T. Banivanua-Mar, *Decolonisation and the Pacific: Indigenous Globalisation and the Ends of Empire* (Cambridge: Cambridge University Press, 2016); for an example of the economic growth approach, see E. Jones, L. Frost, and C. White, *Coming Full Circle: An Economic History of the Pacific Rim* (Oxford: Oxford University Press, 1993); for an example of the environmental change approach, see D.S. Garden, *Australia, New Zealand, and the Pacific: An Environmental History* (Santa Barbara, CA: ABC-CLIO, 2005).

China, or in the sixteenth century, when Iberian seafarers arrived in the Pacific and the Indian Oceans.

This chapter endorses the view that it is possible to write histories of the Pacific that are not focused on Europeans and their influences, and attempts to present one picture of what this might look like. It adopts the unusual and perhaps improper strategy of not defining its core terms – identity, authority, place, ocean, and hinterland – at the outset, but rather chooses to let a narrative unfold so that readers may explore these concepts for themselves through the histories of the Oceanic places and those in the Americas and Asia which border the Pacific that it selects. It is hoped that by not defining the organizing concepts at the outset, a picture of the past appropriate to the 'uncentred' nature of the Pacific Ocean can be constructed. Through this approach readers can hopefully find bases for assembling their own pictures of Pacific pasts.

Oceans and Hinterlands: Nitrates, Phosphates, Wars, and Identities in Bolivia, Banaba and Haizhou

Bolivia: Nitrates, War, and Identity

In modern discourses about Bolivian identity the idea that Bolivia has been cut off from the Pacific since the 1880s has great prominence.[37] A long line of Bolivian politicians has laid claim to authority on the grounds that they are committed to restoring the Pacific territories, territories ceded to Chile after the latter's victory over Bolivia and its ally Peru in a war that arguably still stands as the most signifcant military conflict between the nations on the west coast of South America – the War of the Pacific.[38]

To be Bolivian, these nationalist discourses argue, is to yearn for a Pacific Ocean from which the country has been cut off by the machinations of an unscrupulous neighbouring power (Chile). Rightfully a Pacific nation, Bolivian nationalists assert, Bolivia has been forced to become a landlocked

---

[37] See, for example, the discussions by L. Perrier Bruslé, 'La Bolivie, sa mer perdue et la construction nationale', *Annales de Géographie* 689:1 (2013), 47–72; trans as 'Bolivia: its lost coastline and nation-building', www.cairn-int.info/article-E_AG_689_0047–bolivia-its-lost-coast line-and-nation-bu.htm; by R. Llanos Mansilla of the 'landlocked' condition of Bolivia in 'La mediterraneidad de Bolivia', *Agenda Internacional* 11:21 (2004), 11–26; and by J.L. Otero and P.R. Pardo, 'El imaginario social marítimo Boliviano: una explicación social de la política exterior de Bolivia hacia Chile', *Diálogo Andino* 57 (2018) 111–20.

[38] Studies include B. Farcau, *The Ten Cents War: Chile, Peru, and Bolivia in the War of the Pacific, 1879–1884* (London: Praeger, 2000) and W.F. Sater, *Andean Tragedy: Fighting the War of the Pacific, 1879–1884* (Lincoln: University of Nebraska Press, 2007).

Andean hinterland state, whose economic and political difficulties can be attributed in part to its lack of a direct connection to the Pacific. For Chileans and Peruvians, the War of the Pacific and the Pacific Ocean play a different role in the public construction of national identity from that which they perform in Bolivia. Peruvians see in the bravery and chivalry of the naval commander Miguel Grau Seminario, who died in the battle of Angamos in 1879, a symbol of Peru's claim to be a significant Pacific Ocean power. The Chilean naval officer Arturo Prat, who died when his ship the *Esmerelda* was sunk by Grau's vessel in the battle of Iquique, has a comparable position in heroic narratives of Chilean identity. Prat's patriotic devotion to his homeland has long been invoked by nationalists in Chile.[39]

The War of the Pacific arose from conflict over the mineral resources of the Atacama desert regions of what was at that stage Bolivian territory on the Pacific coast, resources which Chilean companies and their international affiliates were keen to exploit. In the nineteenth century the demands of the global industrial economy for guano, which could be used for fertilizer production, and for nitrates, which could be used for the manufacture of both fertilizers and explosives, transformed an arid zone hitherto quite marginal to the economies and societies of South America into a zone of active contest between competing nation-states. For the early twenty-first-century inhabitants of the northern Chilean city of Antofagasta, the key urban centre in the old Bolivian lands on the Pacific coast, a sense of their own place and its culture is built primarily on the basis of how this area was transformed by the economic development brought by Chilean control.[40] In regional perspective, the prosperity of Antofagasta and the areas that surround it is the outcome of Chile's connections with the modern industrial order, connections, Chilean nationalists would suggest, that lay at the heart of Chilean military success in the War of the Pacific.[41]

Indeed, some might see the War of the Pacific as representative of the overall transformation of the Pacific Ocean world by the forces of industial empire in the middle of the nineteenth century. Such observers might argue

[39] W.F. Sater, *The Heroic Image in Chile: Arturo Prat, Secular Saint* (Berkeley: University of California Press, 1973); G. Arosemena Garland, *El Almirante Miguel Grau* (Lima: Banco de Crédito del Perú, 1979).
[40] See, for example, J.A. González Pizarro, *La pampa salitrera en Antofagasta: la vida cotidiana durante los ciclos Shanks y Guggenheim en el desierto de Atacama* (Antofagasta: Corporación Pro Antofagasta, 2003) and J.L. Panadés Vargas and J.A. González Pizarro, *Antofagasta, historia de mi ciudad* (Antofagasta: Corporación Pro Antofagasta, 1998).
[41] On the racial ideologies used in Chile to justify and explain the War of the Pacific, see E. Beckman, 'The creolization of imperial reason: Chilean state racism in the War of the Pacific', *Journal of Latin American Cultural Studies* 18:1 (2009), 73–90.

that this was a period in which the modern nation-states in the Pacific, from Canada to China, from Fiji to the Philippines, and from Nicaragua to Nauru to New Zealand, acquired the substance of their contemporary identities. In this view, independent Pacific societies, such as those of the Marquesas, the Marshall Islands, Vanuatu, Wallis, and Futuna, were annexed by Atlantic Rim colonial powers. 'Old' Pacific Ocean powers, this viewpoint would argue, such as the Spanish Empire and the Qing Dynasty, proved unable to cope with these changes, and yielded to anti-imperial revolution. The modern republican nation-states in China and the Philippines are the long-term products of this process of the late nineteenth-century collapse of the empires that had been the dominant forces in the Pacific world between the sixteenth and eighteenth centuries – that of Spain in the Americas and in Southeast Asia, and that of the Qing in East Asia. In this new world, concepts, experiences, and practices of place, identity, and authority across the Pacific would be shaped above all by industrial structures and the worldviews associated with them.

The above-mentioned narrative seems to suggest that those nineteenth-century Pacific Rim countries such as Chile or Japan or the United States of America that were able to build effective navies and armies and were able to structure their economies to fit in with the logic of the system of global industrial production centred on the east coast of the North Atlantic could, with the seizure of the territory of weaker states, attain a position of at least regional dominance. The long-term outcome of these post-1850 geopolitical and economic changes across the region, it would be argued, was the mid-twentieth-century military conflict between Japan and the United States for supremacy in the Pacific. The 1942 Battle of Midway, the crucial confrontation in the twentieth-century Pacific War between the Japanese and US navies, was, this view would hold, simply the logical extension of the 1879 naval confrontations between Peru and Chile in the War of the Pacific that gave rise to the cults of Miguel Grau and Arturo Prat and the nationally orientated systems of identity and authority with which they are connected. The *Huascar*, Grau's ship that was captured by the Chileans in the battle in which he was killed, is preserved as a museum ship in the way that the Japanese battleship *Mikasa* (which saw action in the Russo-Japanese War) and the USS *Iowa* or the USS *Missouri* are kept – these vessels provide a concrete focus for national identity narratives that are linked to histories of naval warfare.

On the surface, the military systems that took shape around the Pacific in the nineteenth century, and which, in the twentieth century, brought the whole of the Pacific into their orbit, represent a decisive break with the forms of authority and the types of identity which had been in existence in earlier centuries. The demands for resources that followed the emergence of the industrial system brought localized systems of authority and local systems of organizing and experiencing place into contact with much larger structures of power that were centred in distant places. The armed forces personnel who were involved in the struggle between Japan and the United States and its allies in the Pacific War were subjected to regimes of military discipline that were closely aligned to the systems of control and regimentation that prevailed in factories and in the industrial economy more broadly. The encounter between those who had been moulded by these forms of power and people in different parts of the Pacific whose lives had not been subjected to them has been a major theme in narratives of modern Pacific history.[42] The meetings between Pacific Islanders and Japanese and Allied military personnel during World War II or between the agents of modern industrial enterprises and people adhering to what are considered traditional (that is, non-industrial) lifestyles have been depicted in popular representations as encounters between different worlds, one understood as traditional (and very often as 'primitive') and the other as modern. We can even argue that the Pacific Ocean has often been seen as the site par excellence in world history of contact betweent these polarized and opposing forms of identity. The testing of nuclear weapons in Micronesia, in French Polynesia, and in the Australian desert – that is, in places where Indigenous people maintain lifestyles very far removed from those of people living in the industrial centres – stands as one of the most extreme examples of the contrast between the structures of industrial military power and those of the non-industrial world.[43]

The contrast between industrial military power and the forms of authority, identity, and modes for organizing and conceptualizing places that it engenders, and the lifeways and worldviews that the industrial power system seems to sweep aside or render insignificant obliges us to treat the worlds of the Pacific Ocean and the lands that border it as being defined by radical asymmetries between places and their histories. A history of modern Yokohama or San Diego, it seems, cannot be meaningfully discussed alongside a history of the Bismarck Archipelago or even that of the Visayas unless we place in the

---

[42] See White and Lindstrom, *The Pacific Theater*.
[43] N. Maclellan, 'The nuclear age in the Pacific Islands', *Contemporary Pacific* 17:2 (2005), 363–72; T.K. Teaiwa, 'Bikinis and other s/pacific n/oceans', *Contemporary Pacific* 6:1 (1994), 87–109; repr. in S. Shigematsu and K.L. Camacho (eds.), *Militarized Currents: Toward a Decolonized Future in Asia and the Pacific* (Minneapolis: University of Minnesota Press, 2010), 15–31; J. Dibblin, *Day of Two Suns: US Nuclear Testing and the Pacific Islanders* (New York: New Amsterdam, 1990).

foreground the disparities in power and wealth that separate the two zones. Not to emphasize these disparities runs the risk of playing down the inequalities between places that the industrial order creates and relies upon. A proper history of the Pacific, it follows, must chronicle and explain these inequalities and their emergence. Such an account would see the structures of industrial warfare and of the industrial economy as fundamental to the creation of power imbalances between different parts of the Pacific. As the forms of authority that are generated by industrial military power and by industrial economic activity gain in strength, two broad types of identity and two broad types of places are brought into being, one affiliated to that power system and one opposed to it. For those who see the core strand in the history of the Pacific in the course of the last century or so as being the emergence of an industrial structure in East Asia and on the Pacific coast of North America (with the persistent claim that the Pacific is poised to replace the Atlantic as the oceanic centre of the world economy), the major contrast in the moden Pacific is between the places which have linked themselves successfully to the industrial order and those which have not.

In this framework, Bolivian anger about the loss of its Pacific coastline can be read as an expression of a sense that Bolivia has become what economic geographers refer to as a hinterland – a place that has a subordinated status in relation to a port zone which is the focus of commercial activity and wealth accumulation. The image of Bolivia as a land of Andean peasants cut off from the world of maritime trade is one constituent of the way in which Bolivian identity is constructed, both by Bolivians themselves and by non-Bolivians. This image, we can suggest, is built up in symbolic opposition to a concept of the Pacific as a space of economic development driven by industrial progress. This picture of the Pacific – a Pacific from which Bolivia is seen to be excluded – has been widely promoted by planning elites from countries across the region in the last few decades, echoing narratives that were deployed in the modernization discourses of states around the Pacific from the mid-nineteenth century onwards, discourses that were promoted with great energy by the governments of Japan and the United States in the twentieth century and which have been driven forward more recently by China and by other industrializing and industrialized countries in Asia, the Americas, and Oceania.[44]

For many English-speaking historians of the Pacific, the way in which Bolivians frame an identity that is thought of as defined in part by its

---

[44] Dirlik, *What is in a Rim?*

exclusion from the Pacific as a result of the military successes of Chile in 1879 and the early 1880s may seem to be of little consequence. What it points to, however, is how a sense of connection to the Pacific as an oceanic space that may be strongly accented in one location is ignored in another. A history of steel ships and of the forms of naval power with which they are connected – a history that extends from the late nineteenth century to the present – provides a reference point for thinking about the shared histories of Jeju, Okinawa, Guam, and Subic Bay, but it is not clear that this narrative of Pacific historical experience will be of great interest to people in Vanuatu and New Caledonia. Equally, a friendship group in a high school in Auckland that includes Koreans, Indo-Fijians, Samoans, Pākehā, Somalis, and Filipinos may have little interest in an account of identity in the Pacific that focuses on how Mexicans in coastal Nayarit or Jalisco articulate a sense of place that is Pacific-focused and which is different from the identities of Mexicans in landlocked Durango or of people in Yucatán on Mexico's Caribbean coast. The struggles of some Mexicans to articulate a sense of connection with the Pacific as a counterweight to a dominant account of Mexican identity that is Mexico-centric (in the sense of being preoccupied with an Aztec and post-Aztec historical story whose centre is Mexico City and whose key historical rivals are either the United States or the Spanish – and, perhaps, Guatemalans and Central American countries more broadly) will perhaps seem almost completely incomprehensible to people in Tuvalu or Kiribati, even though common ground may perhaps be found in the sense of shared subordination to the industrial power of the USA and its allies.

Banaba: Phosphates, Identity, and War

Latin American historians often use the name 'The Guano and Saltpeter War' for the War of the Pacific. This name permits us to pair the history of an identity formed by a loss of place in the Pacific in the case of Bolivia with the histories of place, identity, and loss – and their links to war – in Banaba (also known as Ocean Island) whose modern history has been dominated by the mining of phosphates used for fertilizer. Banaba's phosphates do not in fact derive from guano; they emerge rather from much older excretion of phosphates by living organisms, deposits pushed up from the sea floor by processes of geological uplift.[45] However, as scholars of Pacific

---

[45] The key work which has linked the phosphate histories of the Pacific coast of South America with Banaba is G.T. Cushman's *Guano and the Opening of the Pacific World: A Global Ecological History* (Cambridge: Cambridge University Press, 2013).

environmental history have observed, there is an interlocking history here. It is one in which the world of minerals and the living organic worlds of humans and the animals and plants with which they interact overlap and intermingle.

Banaban historians, and non-Banabans who are observers of Banaban culture and society, convey a powerful sense of a place and an identity that have persisted despite the destruction of the Banaban environment by phosphate mining, and the displacement of most of the Banaban population to Rabi in Fiji.[46] For some Banabans the history of the destruction of their home place by phosphate mining is indissolubly linked with the profound transformations of Banaban systems of culture and authority by outside forces that pre-date the arrival of the forces of the global industrial economy; an earlier phase of transformation, in these historical accounts, begins with the arrival of people from the larger Kiribati world who help to initiate the replacement of the Banaban language by Gilbertese, which, these accounts contend, was different from the original language of the island.[47] Banaban authority structures and ways of life were reworked by these Gilbertese influences, which, it is intimated, are a precursor to the later incursions of the phosphate mining forces. This narrative carries the implication that where Banabans may have originally possessed the capacity to resist foreign influences politically, and even militarily, these capacities for practical resistance were slowly undercut by external power. With the relocation of the bulk of the Banaban population to Fiji, a further layer of cultural modification was added, such that contemporary Banaban culture is perceived as entailing a complex relationship between the sense of an enduring core of Banaban identity and mutliple experiences of displacement.[48]

What is enduring through all this, it seems, is amongst other things a sense of Banaban identity created by the relationship between people and islands and

---

[46] Key works include K. Teaiwa, *Consuming Ocean Island: Stories of People and Phosphate from Banaba* (Bloomington: Indiana University Press, 2014) and R.K. Sigrah and S.M. King, *Te Rii ni Banaba* (Suva: Institute of Pacific Studies, University of the South Pacific, 2001).

[47] Sigrah and King, *Te Rii ni Banaba*, 13–23.

[48] Teaiwa, *Consuming Ocean Island* and Sigrah and King, *Te Rii ni Banaba*. See also J. Shennan and M.C. Tekenimatang (eds.), *One and a Half Pacific Islands/Teuana ao Teiterana n aba n te Betebeke: Stories the Banaban People Tell of Themselves/I-Banaba aika a Karakin oin Rongorongoia* (Wellington: Victoria University Press, 2005); E. Hermann, 'Emotions and the relevance of the past: historicity and ethnicity among the Banabans of Fiji', *History and Anthropology* 16:3 (2005), 275–91; W. Kempf and E. Hermann, 'Reconfigurations of place and ethnicity: positionings, performances and politics of relocated Banabans in Fiji', *Oceania* 75:4 (2005), 368–86; and W. Kempf, '"Songs cannot die": ritual composing and the politics of emplacement among the Banabans resettled on Rabi Island in Fiji', *Journal of the Polynesian Society* 112:1 (2003), 33–64.

thus by the relationship between land and oceans, with those islands forming the ground not only for the cultural and historical distinctiveness of Banaba but also for the structures of authority which shape the places (in the sense of physical locations that are endowed with social meaning) in which Banabans live. These ideas about Banaban distinctiveness are moulded by an intimate experience with the two different modern nation-states with which Banabans are strongly connected – Kiribati and Fiji. In this respect, Banaban history may be seen as exemplifying a pattern seen throughout the Pacific, that of a cultural entity possessing a strong sense of place, identity, and a set of authority relations which structure communal life, but which is subsumed into the structures of one or more larger political entities that limit its autonomy.

For some observers of the histories of Pacific Ocean societies, particularly those such as Vanuatu and Papua New Guinea which are characterized by very high levels of linguistic diversity – the highest in the world when measured by the number of languages relative to the overall population of the state – this sense of a patchwork of places and communities that are to some extent or other autonomous leads to a situation of inherent structural tension, in which neither true independence nor true cultural and political integration is ever achieved. Such critical accounts suggest that these societies are simply the artificial products of European colonial power, fated never to unite fully nor to separate into workable political units.[49] What is notable, however, is that many people from within these societies do not seem to endorse these critiques. There has been strong resistance from Pacific Island scholars to the idea that the forms of identity and authority characteristic of contemporary Pacific societies are in some sense or another 'inauthentic' or 'dysfunctional'.[50] At the same time, there is also a strong sense that colonial power had a disruptive and corrosive effect on Indigenous lifeways, and that much of the modern history of Pacific Ocean societies entails a struggle to preserve or revive the identities, places, and systems of authority that colonial power assailed. This is most clear in cases such as Hawai'i and Aotearoa New Zealand where Pacific Islanders are minorities in places in which they had previously been majorities (which are often also places in which Pacific Island people are most exposed to the cultural institutions of industrial society, of which modern standardized education is a key part).[51]

---

[49] See the outline of the 'failed state' image of the Pacific in in R.J. May, 'Weak states, collapsed states, broken backed states, kleptocracies: general concepts and Pacific realities', *New Pacific Review* 2:1 (2003), 35–58.
[50] See T.K. Teaiwa, 'On analogies: rethinking the Pacific in a global context', *Contemporary Pacific* 18:1 (2006), 71–87.

In English-language scholarship on the history of the Pacific Islands, the narration of the contrast and conflict between Indigenous culture and the culture of those who arrived in the Pacific as newcomers in the wake of contact with Europeans (starting in the sixteenth and seventeenth centuries in parts of the western Pacific and accelerating in the speed and intensity of its impact in the nineteenth and twentieth centuries) is often the central focus of the narrative. Over the last few decades, scholars have attempted to find an alternative model to narratives that centre on European influences. Pacific Island scholars with strong connections to Indigenous traditions of historical knowledge have not found it particularly difficult to move beyond an account of the past that deals primarily with the acts and thoughts of Europeans (and of the descendants of Europeans born and raised in Pacific lands, people who lead lives that in many respects are very similar to those of people in the ancestral lands of the Europeans in the North Atlantic).[52] For other Indigenous Pacific scholars, the struggle against the disruptive power of European colonial knowledge systems seems definitive: the proper job of historians, such scholars would suggest, is to chronicle this disruption as part of a politics of resistance to the power of the modern state, whose structures are the product of European imperialism.[53] Yet there are also those who strongly emphasize the disruptive effects of European colonial influence (and how these effects are felt in the purportedly post-colonial present) who advance narratives of Pacific systems of identity and authority that can be broadly characterized as being affiliated to state-strengthening nationalism.

The official cultures of contemporary Tonga, Fiji, and Sāmoa evince an intense sense of pride in traditional cultures, cultures that are often presented as being essentially conservative in their social values; piety, hierarchy, respect, and formality are depicted in official representations as the defining qualities of these societies.[54] Defenders and opponents of these depictions of

---

[51] See L.T. Smith, *Decolonizing Methodologies: Research and Indigenous Peoples*, 2nd edn (London: Zed Books, 2012); H.-K. Trask, *From a Native Daughter: Colonialism and Sovereignty in Hawaii*, rev. edn (Honolulu: University of Hawai'i Press, 1999 [1983]).

[52] Examples of historians focused on Pacific knowledge traditions include K.K. Uriam, *In Their Own Words: History and Society in Gilbertese Oral Tradition* (Canberra: Journal of Pacific History, 1995) and 'O. Māhina, 'The Tongan traditional history tala-e-fonua: a vernacular ecology-centred historico-cultural concept', PhD thesis, Australian National University, Canberra, 1992.

[53] See Smith, *Decolonizing Methodologies*; H.-K. Trask, 'Natives and anthropologists: the colonial struggle', *Contemporary Pacific* 3:1 (1991), 159–67; H.-K. Trask, 'Politics in the Pacific Islands: imperialism and native self-determination', *Amerasia Journal* 16:1 (1990), 1–19.

[54] For a critical view of conservative official nationalism in Fiji, Tonga, and Sāmoa, see S. Lawson, *Tradition versus Democracy in the South Pacific: Fiji, Tonga and Western Samoa* (Cambridge: Cambridge University Press, 1996). For a critical overview of different approaches,

Pacific culture disagree on the extent to which these representations of the past are inventions of the colonial era.[55] For some Pacific Islanders in places like Hawai'i dominated by populations of immigrants from Europe or Asia who arrived between the nineteenth century and the present, the fact that Tonga, Fiji, and Sāmoa are sovereign entities, in which, on the surface at least, Pacific Island identities, languages, and systems of authority are at the fore, is something to be praised.[56] For critics, the visions of culture that are promoted by conservative interests in these countries are primarily ways in which local elites silence their critics and deny full citizenship to those who in one sense or another are deemed to be 'foreign', the clearest example of which is the Indo-Fijian population.[57]

Memories of place, and their relationship both to claims to authority and to the articulation of identity, are thus in sharp focus in written accounts of Banaban history and culture. This, we can argue, is not simply a result of the multiple experiences of displacement which have shaped modern Banaban history. The centrality of movement in shaping the history of the Oceanic cultural world means that political life, and above all the parts of political life that relate to land, is intimately related to questions of when and how a particular group is held to have arrived in a given location. These relationships are dynamic rather than fixed; instead of an unchanging order, there is a constant reworking of group connections to locality. Political claims can be lodged and challenged on the basis of whether or not the claimant is an original or early inhabitant of a place. Banaba's distinctiveness in the wider Gilbertese cultural and linguistic world with which Banabans are in dialogue rests in part in claims to a distinctive relationship to the island, and, critically, to being unaffected by some of the waves of settlement that affected other parts of Kiribati.[58] As noted above, in its most dramatic forms, these claims

---

see S. Ratuva, 'Reconceptualising contemporary Pacific Island states: towards a syncretic approach', *New Pacific Review* 2:1 (2003), 246–62.

[55] The best-known presentation of the idea of an invented tradition in the Pacific is R.M. Keesing's 'Creating the past: custom and identity in the Pacific', *Contemporary Pacific* 1:1–2 (1989), 19–42. Keesing's arguments were strongly criticized by Haunani-Kay Trask (Trask, 'Natives and anthropologists'). See the evaluation of these arguments in Ratuva, 'Reconceptualising contemporary Pacific Island states'.

[56] This is one implication of the arguments of Haunani-Kay Trask. See Trask, 'Natives and anthropologists', 159.

[57] See, for example, Lawson, *Tradition versus Democracy in the South Pacific*.

[58] Kambati Uriam notes that Banaba, along with the islands of Butaritari and Makin in the northern Gilberts, was unaffected by the wars of Kaitu and Uakeia from the island of Beru, which transformed culture in the rest of Kiribati. See Uriam, *In Their Own Words*, 17, 70. Uriam dates the wars to the sixteenth century.

about distinctiveness entail the argument that Banabans have a different ethnic origin from people in the rest of Kiribati; scholars of Kiribati history have argued that the religious traditions of pre-Christian Banaba represent a cultural stratum that is either separate from the larger Kiribati cultural configuration or something which survived in Banaba when it was lost elsewhere as a result of the arrival of newcomers from other parts of the island world.[59]

The destruction of Banaba by phosphate mining adds another, tragic, dimension to the authority–identity–place relationship – that of an identity framed by the destruction of a homeland by industrial processes. As scholars of Banaban identity and historians of the environment have observed, the destruction of Banaban landscapes and the creation of identities in which mourning that destruction plays a central role are the practical foundation of the lush pastoral landscapes that define the place–identity–authority structures of Pacific Rim settler societies such as Australia and New Zealand.[60] The lands of meat and milk that settlers of European background created for themselves, lands in which material abundance – marked above all by access to animal protein – correlated with identities that emphasized the possibilities for individual and collective social advancement that were afforded by societies which were lauded as being unencumbered by the hierarchies associated with hereditary nobility, were dependent on chemical fertilizer inputs that were procured by transforming Banaba and places like it into barren wastelands.

One complex result of the destruction of Banaba, which is seen by many in the present as presaging the destruction of Gilbertese spaces through global sea level rise, is that Banaban historical experience has a global visibility greater than that of many other Pacific Island societies.[61] Banaban history has become emblematic of the wider processes of environmental and sociopolitical change that have threatened and are threatening the survival of places and cultures across the Pacific. Between the late twentieth century

---

[59] The key issue is that Banaba is held to have been initially unaffected by the group of 'Samoans', emigrants from the Gilberts who had settled in 'Sāmoa' and returned to the islands bringing a new culture with them. See Uriam, *In Their Own Words*, 62. According to Uriam, Banaba oral tradition is not affected by the dominant Gilbertese culture associated with the Karongoa myth and history tradition imported from 'Sāmoa' (*In Their Own Words*, 78).

[60] K. Teaiwa, 'Banaban Island: paying the price for other peoples' development', *Indigenous Affairs* 1 (2000), 38–45.

[61] J.B. Edwards, 'Phosphate mining and the relocation of the Banabans to northern Fiji in 1945: lessons for climate change-forced displacement', *Journal de la Société des Océanistes* 138–9 (2014), 121–36.

and the present, the government of Kiribati has been one of the most active in the world in drawing attention to the consequences of sea level rise, which calls the very existence of Kiribati into question. The industrial processes which rendered Banaba a place in which the majority of Banabans could not live have gone on to endanger the state of which Banaba is now a part. Banaba was the first place in the Gilbertese cultural realm to experience the effects of industrial structures which, by the early twenty-first century, had produced environmental changes that threaten to sink Kiribati beneath the waves. Early twentieth-century phosphate mining on Banaba – something whose precondition was the establishment of British colonial rule in the Central and Western Pacific in the late nineteenth century – physically implanted the technologies, economic structures, and personnel (managers, engineers, labourers, and others) of the industrial system in the Gilbertese cultural world.[62]

There was a dramatic acceleration in this direct engagement with the forces of industrial empire during World War II, when Banaba and other parts of the Gilbertese island zone were the foci of conflict between Japan and the United States and its allies. The occupation of Banaba by Japanese forces is generally recalled as having initiated a major deterioration in the condition of Banaban people, not simply because of the harshness of the conditions on the island when it was under Japanese rule, but also because it was a critical point in the displacement of the Banaban population; although arrangements for the transfer of the people of Banaba to Rabi in Fiji had been made before the war, it was the disruption wrought by the Japanese occupation that led to the removal of the overwhelming majority of Banaba's inhabitants from the island.[63] Japan's interest in Banaba, like that of the British whom they ousted, was driven by the need for phosphate fertilizers for food production, a need that was intensified by the war effort. However, for many outside observers the key emblem of the effects of industrial war on Kiribati is the 1943 battle of Tarawa, remnants of which – the wrecks of fortifications, tanks, and other war materiel – can still be seen on the island. The ferocity of this battle is frequently commented upon, and the intensity of the power struggle between the Japanese and the Americans seems to push I Kiribati experience to the sidelines, something which stands as a kind of synecdoche of the processes of Pacific history in the industrial era, in which

---

[62] A picture of this world, given by one of the proponents of phosphate mining, can be found in A.F. Ellis, *Ocean Island and Nauru* (Sydney: Angus and Robertson, 1936).
[63] Sigrah and King, *Te Rii ni Banaba*, 261–96.

Pacific Islanders end up cast as bystanders or spectators observing a historical drama involving political actors from the edges of the Pacific region.

From this angle, in the case of Kiribati, the global industrial order shows its two contrasting faces: on the one hand, there is industry as a mechanism that multiplies the productive power of human labour (represented by the huge increases in agricultural output that result from the use of chemical fertilizers); on the other hand, there is industry as a mechanism which multiplies the destructive power of human weaponry (represented by the still-visible war relics on Tarawa, a battle which was part of a larger conflict that culminated in the atomic bombing of Hiroshima and Nagasaki, one of the great symbols of the capacity of industrial systems to produce mass death). The history of the Pacific Ocean seems here to involve the pulverizing, obliterating force of massive power structures on societies which have almost no capacity to resist them, with industrial war-making serving as the ultimate symbol of this destructiveness. But an account of the history of authority, identity, and place in the Pacific cannot simply treat the experiences of places like Banaba as mere adjuncts to a story of great power rivalry. It is clear from what is written and said about Banaba that things that are outside of the industrial order are central to Banaban narratives of their culture. This is not simply a matter of an enduring tradition or of one that is constructed in retrospect as a way of resisting the dominant order in the present. It is a contest over the past, including contestation over connections to place and over the forms of authority that those connections to place entail, that gives Banaban identities their reality and their substance.[64] This contestation can be glimpsed in the written record which both reflects and is a component of the texture of community life. The unwillingness of Pacific Island societies to have their histories subsumed into those of ostensibly historically more influential political and economic entities – and great powers in particular – is one of the most striking features of the modern history of the Pacific Islands, something which, we can argue, is not simply a response to the effects of colonial and neo-colonial power, but is rather something much older, and which gives the authority–place–identity nexus its distinctive force in the Oceanic world.[65]

---

[64] Sigrah and King's *Te Rii ni Banaba* presents the claim to primacy lodged by the Te Aka clan; other Banaban perspectives can be found in Shennan and Tekenimatang, *One and a Half Islands*, and in Teaiwa, *Consuming Ocean Island*.

[65] A powerful discussion of these issues is D.W. Gegeo, 'Cultural rupture and indigeneity: the challenge of (re)visioning "place" in the Pacific', *Contemporary Pacific* 13:2 (2001), 467–507.

Authority, Identity, and Place

Haizhou: Phosphates, Nitrates, Identity, and War

For a brief moment during World War II the Japanese empire controlled the phosphates both of Banaba and in the Jinping mine in Haizhou, an area that is now a district in the city of Lianyungang, located in the northern part of Jiangsu province and one of the key ports in the People's Republic of China. Present-day accounts of the Jinping mine generally position it within the larger narrative of China's industrialization, above all the industrialization authored by the post-1949 government of the Chinese Communist Party.[66] The mine was actually established in the decade after the overthrow of the Qing dynasty in 1911, and its history is thus roughly contemporary with the history of phosphate mining in Banaba. An historical narrative whose central focus was phosphates would be able to plot a story of trans-Pacific linkages between zones of phosphate production that would see the Jinping mine as part of a story of the political economy of minerals in the Pacific, one in which state actors ranged from imperial structures such as those of Japan, Britain, and the US to republican regimes such as those in Bolivia, Peru, and the Republic of China. It would not be difficult to map the nationalist identities and ideologies that surrounded phosphate extraction on the Pacific coast of South America to those in the post-Qing Chinese republics. Such a narrative would see sovereign control over phosphates and other minerals as framed by the wider project of imagining nations and the citizens who constituted these nations. Externally orientated antagonism to foreign forces – and above all those of the industrial empires – which kept these republics in subordinated positions was coupled with the internally orien-tated attempt to incorporate economic and cultural hinterlands into polities centred on ports, a process that was strongly linked to that of attempting to integrate marginalized internal populations into the frameworks of nationally defined citizenhood.

This mapping of the identity, authority, and place relationships connected with the Jinping mine is one that divides the Pacific Rim histories of the nineteenth and twentieth centuries from the histories of earlier periods. In this account, the mining of phosphates is co-eval with the emergence of post-dynastic structures of power and post-dynastic forms of identity, something that would be strongly identified with the confrontation between Chinese

---

[66] A recent short overview of the mine's history in the form of personal reminiscences is X. Zhang, 'Jiyi zhong de Jinping linkuang', *Lianyunggang shi zhi* 1 (2014), 41–3. A volume of essays devoted to the history of the mine is A. Ni (ed.), *Jinping linkuang lunwenji* (Lianyungang: Lianyungang shi Jinping linkuang, 1999), 1381.

cultural systems and maritime industrial imperialism in the years after the First Opium War in the early 1840s. According to this paradigm, in the nineteenth century new forces coming from the sea disrupt a dynastic cultural order which has lasted for around two millennia and which is essentially continental in its orientation; it is a paradigm which has much in common with the old narrative of the disruption of the inland polities of the Incas and the Aztecs by the expansive maritime-orientated Iberian empires – an essentially inward-looking state is challenged and overthrown by outward-looking forces.[67] The limitations of this paradigm are obvious, yet it is currently politically dominant. In the orthodox story of Chinese nationalism, the crisis of the modern era is one in which foreign aggression humiliates a great civilization. In the orthodox story of modern liberalism, the story of the Chinese world in the nineteenth century is one in which closed markets become open, unleashing an economic dynamism which, in the twenty-first century, is the driving force in global growth. The Jinping phosphate mine presents problems to neither of these narratives. In the Chinese nationalist paradigm it is a symbol of the resurgence of the Chinese nation, a resurgence which is attributed to the deployment of the energies of a united populace in the cause of state-strengthening industrialization, something which has restored China's international influence. In the liberal paradigm, the phosphate mine at Jinping is a symbol of the embrace of modern industry and commerce by a society historically dominated by the conservatism of agricultural empire; this paradigm has a long pedigree, manifested in the belief of some of the eighteenth-century founders of the United States of America that the ultimate purpose of the projected westward expansion of their nation was to liberate China's trade.[68]

The problem with the nationalist and liberal paradigms is that the model of history on which they depend is based on a divide between the period constituted by the era between the nineteenth century and the present and the period constituted by the centuries running up to the nineteenth century. It is a divide that is common in the broader historiography of the Pacific Ocean: in Latin America, it is constituted by the divide between the colonial

---

[67] The contrast between a dominant continental tradition and a minor maritime tradition is articulated by J.K. Fairbank in 'Maritime and continental in China's history', in J.K. Fairbank (ed.), *The Cambridge History of China*, vol. xii, *Republican China, 1912–1949*, part 1 (Cambridge: Cambridge University Press, 1983), 1–27. Fairbank does not see the maritime and continental contrast as one between dynamism and stagnation.

[68] J.G.A. Pocock, *The Machiavellian Moment: Florentine Thought and the Atlantic Republican Tradition* (Princeton: Princeton University Press, 2003), 542.

era and that of the independent republics; in the history of the Pacific coast of the USA and Canada, it is the divide between the era of Anglophone white settlement and what precedes it; in the history of Oceania it is the divide between the era of Anglophone and Francophone colonization and the pre-colonial era; in the history of Southeast Asia, it is the divide between the old empires and kingdoms, including those in the Dutch East Indies, and the Iberian empires in the Philippines and East Timor and Macao, while in Japan, Korea, and the Russian Far East it is the divide between the era of the early modern polities and the polities of the age of steam, of which mid-nineteenth-century Russia and post-Tokugawa Japan are pre-eminent examples.

The horse-riding cowboy and the steam-powered battleship – a vessel that is a fusion of guns and steel liberated from the natural constraints imposed on earlier sailing craft by the wind – are some of the great symbols of this sense of a historical divide between the nineteenth century and what precedes it. In this narrative, power over horses and other large quadrupeds, firearms, and minerals (especially over the fossil residue connected with long-dead prehistoric organisms, key examples being coal, petroleum, and phosphates that are not derived from guano deposited in historic times), together with modern forms of political and social organization – modern business enterprises, modern armies and navies, and modern systems of banking and public administration – produces a massive increase in the capacity to shape and reshape human and natural worlds. The Australian sheep station, the Soviet tractor factory, the Canadian salmon canning plant, the Hong Kong apartment complex, the Patagonian cattle ranch, the Japanese civil service building and the Fiji sugar plantation – these entities provide contexts and stimuli for the processes of revolutionary industrialization in which the post-Qing Chinese republics have engaged, of which the Jinping phosphate mine in Haizhou is both a product and a symbol. The preceding paragraphs have set forth a story of food, weapons, tools, and the geographies, institutions, ceremonies, and languages in which they are embedded and which they create. It is essentially a story about the idea of modernization. It is a story, moreover, in which the ultimate source of modernization in the Pacific is exogenous – it originates in the North Atlantic and makes its way by one route or another into the Pacific. As stated above, the ideologies of both orthodox Chinese nationalism and orthodox modern liberalism endorse the basic outlines of this story. However, if an account of authority and identity and place in Bolivia and Banaba involves more than the question of how those locations have experienced the power structures of industrial modernity (symbolized by competition for minerals and by industrial war), the same should apply to Haizhou. In addition, when acknowledging the massive transformative effect of modern industrial technologies like phosphate fertilizers, and the massive environmental, economic, and demographic effects that they have on the Pacific and the lands that surround it, the wider social and material histories from which these technologies emerge need to be acknowledged.

The cowboy-and-steamship narrative of industrial modernity has two effects. On the one hand, it divides societies in the Pacific between those either driving forward these innovations, or able to ally themselves with them, and those societies left behind or overwhelmed by them. On the other hand, it treats the changes taking place in the nineteenth and twentieth centuries as being without precedent. If Haizhou is portrayed as a place in which, after a painful initial period, the structures and technologies of industrial modernity were mastered, allowing it to escape the fate of Bolivia and Banaba, its story is one of 'success' rather than of 'failure'. At the same time, the question of what relationship there is between the history of Haizhou in the period between the nineteenth century and the present and the history of Haizhou prior to the age of industrial empire goes unasked.

Although the ideologies of Chinese nationalism and of modern liberalism both focus on the idea of the nineteenth century as the critical juncture in Chinese history (and, as already stated, in the wider history of the Pacific), academic historical scholarship produced between the first quarter of the twentieth century and the present has in different ways called this account of the Chinese past into question. A key part of this has been to focus on the aspects of the imperial-era Chinese system that can in one sense or another be thought of as modern. One key element in this questioning is the idea that the selection of government officials on the basis of their achievements in standardized examinations is a major break with aristocratic systems of social pre-eminence that are based on the claims of birth or of military prowess.[69] Between the time of the Northern Song Dynasty (960–1126) and the last years of the Qing, the use of educational accomplishment as a key criterion for membership in the political and social elites of the dynastic states created a set of identity and authority structures which can be meaningfully described as 'post-feudal'.[70] This post-feudal social order was one in which the standing of elite men and of leading families was subject to centralized testing of its

---

[69] See A. Woodside, *Lost Modernities: China, Vietnam, Korea, and the Hazards of World History* (Cambridge, MA: Harvard University Press, 2006).
[70] Woodside, *Lost Modernities*, 52–5.

knowledge and its literary skills. Contemporary with the rise of this elite was the rise of a commercialized economy in which market structures and market values played a decisive role. An expansionist mercantile structure not only spread across the territories which the Chinese dynastic states controlled, it pushed out into neighbouring regions, into Central Asia and in the maritime zone in East and Southeast Asia.

When the Spanish conquest of the Americas brought the western and eastern coasts of the Pacific into direct contact in the sixteenth century, it was in a historical conjuncture in which East and Southeast Asian maritime trade systems formed an interlinked network that had been in existence for more than a millennium. This maritime network was juxtaposed with an agrarian Chinese cultural zone and the various cultures and polities of Inner Eurasia, cultures and polities in which control of horses, sheep, and other pastoral animals played a central role. These Inner Eurasian societies are often portrayed as having been in an antagonistic relationship with the Chinese cultural realm, an antagonism which is a mirror image of the picture of the Chinese world as being an essentially inward-looking entity hostile to the sea, until jolted out of this 'insularity' by the upheavals of the nineteenth century. This picture is inadequate for the very simple reason that the polities that were present in the centuries that this chapter discusses had a combined presence in the Inner Eurasian zone and in the maritime world. In other words, there is a linked history in which oceanic and continental structures interact. The world of the Chinese examination elites and that of the commercial culture with which those elites co-existed, the world of the Inner Asian pastoral and forest polities and societies, and the world of the seas form a triangulated historical whole.

Haizhou's own history is emblematic of these realities. In the twelfth century it was a frontier town, one of the southernmost outposts of the territory of the Jin Dynasty (1126–1234), whose founders, the Jurchens (a Tungusic-speaking people from the Northeast Asian Forest and Steppe zone who were the ancestors of the Manchus who founded the Qing Dynasty in the late sixteenth and early seveneteenth centuries), had driven the Song Dynasty out of north China in the 1120s.[71] In wars between the Song and the Jin, Haizhou was part of a zone of military confrontation in which both powers used naval and land forces in which there were some of the

---

[71] H. Franke, 'The Chin Dynasty', in H. Franke and D. Twitchett (eds.), *The Cambridge History of China*, vol. VI, *Alien Regimes and Border States* (Cambridge: Cambridge University Press, 1994), 215–320; F.W. Mote, *Imperial China, 900–1800* (Cambridge, MA: Harvard University Press, 1999), 193–221.

oldest recorded large-scale deployments of gunpowder-based weapons in battles both at sea and on land.[72] With the Mongol conquest of both the Jin and the Song in the thirteenth century, Haizhou and the wider coastal zone to which it belonged were absorbed into an imperial state whose point of origin was in the horse-riding nomadic pastoral region in Inner Eurasia. Mongolian maritime expansion has been perceived as the progenitor of the early Ming era voyages of Zheng He in Southeast Asia and the Indian Ocean. Indeed, Zheng He's patron, the Yongle emperor, is seen by some as seeking to restore Mongolian power structures and institutions, not only in the Inner Eurasian zone, but also in the maritime world. Historians of the Ming, and of the Qing Dynasty which overthrew it, use the term 'gunpowder empire' to describe these states, seeing them as having been similar to other Eurasian imperial states, not only those of the Ottomans, the Mughals, and the Saffavids, but also those of the Spanish, the Portuguese, and other European maritime powers of the early modern era. It is tempting to see the relationship between gunpowder, ships, and horses in these early modern empires as prefiguring the cowboy-and-steamship structures that are held to have radically restructured the Pacific world in the nineteenth century, structures that seem in this light less like breaks with the past than an outgrowth of it.

If Haizhou's recent history is tied up with the replacement of the horse as a key factor in the history of Eurasian warfare through the rise of a minerals-based industrial system in which firearms and navies are more important than cavalry – something that eclipses the power of the Inner Asian empires, such that Mongolia and other land-locked polities become hinterlands which are dependent on the coastal states – its earlier history is one in which the interplay between minerals, ships, and horses is more dynamic. Phosphates, which permit a massive increase in the productivity of land, including pastoral land, and nitrates, which, as fertilizers, perform the same historical functions as phosphates, and which, as constituents of explosives, permit a massive increase in the destructive power of weapons, thus form two threads in the story of Haizhou as a place, threads through which we can map its changing relationship to the wider history of the Pacific Ocean and its hinterlands.

This chapter has used three different sites – Bolivia in the Americas, Banaba in Oceania, and Haizhou in Eurasia – to chart an associative history of relationships between authority, identity, and place that interacts with stories

---

[72] See Schottenhammer, 'China's emergence as a maritime power', 457; Lo, *China as a Sea Power*, chapter 5.

of minerals (phosphates and nitrates) and war in the Pacific Ocean and its hinterlands between the twelfth century and the present. What it has set forth is only one way in which that history can be configured, and its method is 'associative', constructing connections between zones that have on the surface only remote links to each other. What emerges from this method is a set of linkages that may not be visible at first glance. These linkages might appear to some sceptical readers as nothing more than artefacts of the writer's whim. But the act of creating these linkages makes it possible to see patterns of similarity between historical experiences in different parts of the Pacific Ocean that might not have appeared had conventional boundaries been adhered to. At the very least, we can argue that what this associative history offers us is a picture that is faithful to the fact that an idea of 'the Pacific Ocean' has had powerful symbolic and real effects in different places and at different times, but which shows that there is no clear single account of what that idea means (even though it would be wrong to suggest that this idea is devoid of content). Associative history represents one way in which the distinctive quality of Pacific Ocean history can be set forth, one in which the Pacific is understood as simultaneously a material reality, an object of contest, and an imaginative projection.

34

Europe's Other? Academic Discourse on the Pacific as a Cultural Space

ANNA JOHNSTON

Twenty-first-century gallery audiences in Italy, New Zealand, and Australia have experienced the immersive digital video work *Pursuit of Venus (Infected)*, 2015–17, by Māori artist Lisa Reihana.[1] The work both re-animates and re-stages an 1802 French wallpaper design that featured key scenes from eighteenth-century Pacific and exploration history, drawn from the voyage accounts of Captain James Cook and others (Figure 34.1). In Enlightenment salons – and afterwards in selected museums – historical audiences found themselves surrounded by tableaux of cross-cultural encounter and exchange. Curiosity, titillation, and aesthetics were combined in the wall-paper, as they are in Reihana's video art. Viewers were immersed into the Pacific world in both the wallpaper and the video, while the contemporary visual technologies also reminded viewers of their distance from it. Exotic, erotic, scientific, historic – the modes of engagement are intellectual and affective, for both Enlightenment and contemporary viewers.

Significantly, Reihana's work engages Pacific people as performers and interpreters of their own histories, rather than as static illustrations of Europe's encounter with its Pacific 'others'. Māori, Islander, and Aboriginal performers activate the stories of the past with their bodies, their music, and their dance. We see Tupaia, the famous Raiaitean navigator; we see Tahitian women as active participants in the politics of beach crossings; we see the gentleman naturalist Joseph Banks attempting a seduction; we see Sydney Parkinson, Banks's natural history illustrator, beating off flies from the fish he attempts to sketch. We hear the music of the Pacific and the maritime British, we faintly perceive voices in both Pacific and European languages striving to communicate across cultural divides, and we imaginatively sketch in narrative arcs to explain the short sequences of action featured in the

---

[1] See stills and a link to a short, five-minute version of the film, www.inpursuitofvenus.com/.

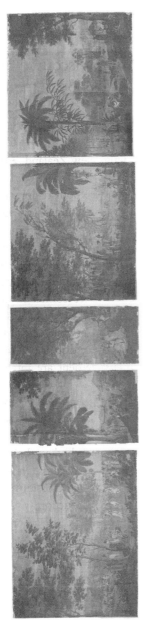

Figure 34.1 'Les Sauvages de la Mer Pacifique', wallpaper designed by Jean Gabriel Charvet and printed by Joseph Dufour, 1802.

camera's multi-channel projection of a moving panoramic scene. We cannot smell the bodies – dancing, fighting, being tattooed, being flogged, being seduced, being unwrapped – but it is easy to imagine that we can. The multiplicity of the staged micro-narratives is such that the viewer cannot comprehend each one as it passes, but the audience instead imagines a set of experiential narratives to make meaning from the rich moving tapestry. Both in 1802 and in 2017, these Pacific scenes are cultural spaces that viewers are invited to enter; to imagine themselves into. It is a vision that attempts to explain Europe's others, and the European self.

This chapter examines how the Pacific entered European discourses and intellectual traditions to ask what meanings the Pacific held in European intellectual history and academic discourse. It argues first that the Pacific was a paradigmatic site at which Europe encountered its other: the region and its peoples were constructed in ways that emphasized their alterity and savagery, especially as Europe's own developmental discourse depended upon a teleology from pre-modern times to the Enlightenment. Yet the other is always a category that allows the definition of one's self, and in Pacific encounters (like many others) Europeans found similarity and connection alongside difference and incomprehension. Read in this light, the Pacific is also a potent contact zone of mutual encounter and exchange, one that sustains oceanic people and influences visiting Europeans.[2] It is a littoral zone where mutual understanding and incomprehension proceed together; where boundaries are marked, transgressed, and remade with regularity, sometimes intentionally, sometimes by accident; and where archives and textual sources can reveal subtle and shifting negotiations by individuals forging new lives for themselves and their communities. At the same time, the modern period emerged, roughly and unevenly, shot through with power and ideology, alongside exceptionally inventive thought, technology, and cultural adaptation.

This chapter encompasses a wide survey of the place of the Pacific in academic discourse, beginning with its role in voyage literature and insisting on the generative connection between the archives of Pacific encounter and the art, writing, and history making of the twentieth and twenty-first centuries. It argues that this imperial archive cannot be foreclosed as simply a troubled repository of European prejudice and Pacific stereotyping (although such evidence is easily found) when it continues to provoke new forms of

---

[2] M.L. Pratt, *Imperial Eyes: Travel Writing and Transculturation* (London: Routledge, 1992).

meaning in cultural, historical, and artistic spheres. Instead, the archive of Pacific encounter with Europe is an active site of contact, contestation, and creativity that continues to shape our view of both the past and the future.

European Visions of the Pacific

The Pacific has been a paradigmatic site of European encounters with its others since early European voyages of exploration, and especially since the culturally, scientifically, and territorially transformative voyages of the eighteenth century. European voyages to the Pacific were motivated primarily by territorial ambitions and trade, but in seeking passages through the dense cultural space of the Pacific Ocean travellers found much more than shipping routes. Encountering Pacific peoples and their societies, European voyagers were required to consider different ways of *organizing society*, of understanding the relationship between *humans and their natural environment*, and new forms of *subjectivity and identity*. Coinciding with transformative changes sweeping Europe during the Enlightenment, voyagers' encounters with Islanders, and the knowledge they brought back from the Pacific, were foundational in influencing some of the key aspects of Europe's understanding of itself, and its Pacific others.

European travellers interpreted social organization in the Pacific most easily in terms that mirrored their home culture. Island cultures such as those in Hawai'i and Polynesia – where society was predominately organized through a distinctive hierarchy of inheritance through leading families – were familiar to Europeans accustomed to royalty and dynastic privilege, even though their social organization was distinctive, and based upon dense networks of reciprocity. European confidence in negotiating relationships between the British state and Pacific polities was based on identifying leaders such as the Kamehameha family in Hawai'i and the Pomare dynasty in Tahiti, from Cook's voyages onwards. The terms of those relationships were not neutral, especially as stadial theories of civilization developed across the eighteenth and nineteenth centuries, yet the capacity of voyagers to describe the organization of some Pacific societies in terms familiar to Europeans rendered those islands amenable to European ideas of diplomacy, exchange, and trade at the level of elite governmentality. Pacific cultures whose social organization was less intelligible to visitors – across islands that came to be labelled 'Melanesia', as well as in Australia and Terra del Fuego, to name a few examples – fared poorly in the European recognition of sovereignty and statehood. Such island encounters were often marked by a violent response to European voyagers and, if some form of engagement was possible, Europeans characterized these societies as chaotic and unpredictable, lacking in (recognizable) order and social structure, and inherently savage as opposed to European civility. Micronesia remains less prominent in the scholarship on Pacific encounters, despite a long tradition of European engagement with the region beginning in the 1500s, in part because the Spanish saw voyage accounts as critical territorial intelligence and kept them secret.[3] Yet from the late 1820s, many European commentators, including Dumont d'Urville, linked Polynesians and Micronesians as superior Pacific 'races', to the detriment of Melanesians.[4] Voyagers' evaluations of Pacific polities lay beneath early ethnographic and later anthropological science that profoundly influenced global thought, although they were shifting and contingent in their initial construction.

Pacific environments were attractive to European voyagers, and the relationship between island peoples and their natural world proved fascinating to European philosophers and readers. As Enlightenment thought questioned the role of religion as the main structuring principle of society, the Pacific seemed to reveal to Europeans an Edenic environment that pre-dated the Fall, and showed what a society might be like that was liberated from the Christian regulation of morality, mores, and identity. This shaped how some Europeans represented and experienced gender and sexuality (discussed below) but it also fundamentally influenced their understanding of the natural world in the Pacific. The unique flora and fauna of the Pacific revealed yawning chasms in European knowledge – species whose place in the emerging taxonomies of scientific classification was unknown – in ways that challenged the universalist ambitions of such systems. So too the relationship between Pacific Islanders and their environments was distinctive and often challenging. Navigation by stars and currents, accommodative small-scale agriculture, the mobility of

---

[3] Work specifically on the region is rich, particularly given the vibrant cosmopolitan cultures of places such as Pohnpei in the Caroline Islands since the 1840s (now Micronesia), but limited to specific fields, including Pacific linguistics. For a historical overview that pays attention to Portuguese and Spanish engagement with Micronesia, see B. Douglas, *Science, Voyages, and Encounters in Oceania, 1511–1850* (New York: Palgrave Macmillan, 2014), especially Part I. For a deep history of the Federated States of Micronesia that seeks to link the region's pre-colonial history with its current political situation, see D. Hanlon, 'A different historiography for "a handful of chickpeas flung over the sea": approaching the Federated States of Micronesia's deeper past', in W. Anderson, M. Johnson, and B. Brookes (eds.), *Pacific Futures: Past and Present* (Honolulu: University of Hawai'i Press, 2018), 81–104.

[4] See B. Douglas, 'In the event: indigenous countersigns and the ethnohistory of voyaging', in M. Jolly, S. Tcherkéoff, and D. Tryon (eds.), *Oceanic Encounters: Exchange, Desire, Violence* (Canberra: ANU Press, 2009), 175–98.

species across island archipelagoes, and close relationships between people and the natural world all proved intriguing, challenging, and at times incomprehensible to European observers.

Pacific forms of identity and affiliation, too, appealed to some Europeans and alienated others. Hierarchical relations between royal elites and ordinary folk were comprehensible to Romantic and Enlightenment thinkers, and to more conservative commentators. Freedom from European norms was favourably assessed in accordance with a Romantic idealization of exotic peoples and societies. In Rousseau's *The Social Contract* (1762), the family is the base unit of social organization, and the chief of the tribe the natural extension of the patriarch: Rousseau placed an idealized state of nature as the basis of 'Primitive Societies', and built his philosophical model of individual freedom within civil society from there.[5] The role of religious elites such as the *'arioi* was more complex: their social mobility and esoteric and at times exotic ritual practices troubled many accounts of Pacific society. Banks was famously titillated by the same ritualistic sexual performances that disconcerted Cook during their 1770 voyage.[6] In 1789, William Bligh was so disconcerted that he halted an *'arioi* performance which he had requested.[7] Sacred *'arioi* knowledge dedicated to the worship of 'Oro remained impervious to European curiosity and was thus rendered problematic by travellers who were otherwise charmed by seemingly easy intimacy between Pacific peoples and visitors. Despite declaring Tahiti the 'Paradise of the World' during his detailed study of local customs during the visit of the *Bounty*, Bligh was increasingly influenced by Dissenting missionaries on his return to England, and came to attribute sexual opportunism as a leading cause of his crew's mutiny.[8] Intimate encounters initiated by both men and women, in an atmosphere free from the Christian ethics that governed the lives of many sailors and their captains, certainly rendered the Pacific an erotic paradise in the eyes of many. Different orderings of sexuality and gender intrigued Europeans also experiencing the growing regulation and classification of forms of sexual identity. Friendships and sexual liaisons brought captains and their crew into close personal contact with

---

[5] Remarkably, even a 2019 edition of *The Social Contract* uses the abstract idea of 'an Islander' to explain the relationship between individual and collective good: J.-J. Rousseau, *On the Social Contract* (1762), ed. and intro. David Wootton, 2nd edn (Indianapolis: Hackett, 2019), xxi.

[6] See G. Dening, *Performances* (Carlton South: Melbourne University Press, 1996): and in a popular vein P. Fara, *Sex, Botany and Empire: The Story of Carl Linnaeus and Joseph Banks* (London: Icon Books, 2003).

[7] On Bligh and the *'arioi*, see A. Salmond, *Bligh: William Bligh in the South Seas* (Berkeley: University of California Press, 2011), 188.

[8] See Salmond, *Bligh*, 395–6.

Islanders and enhanced their intimate knowledge of both familiarity and difference. Less immediately obvious to the travellers were the mutual obligations engendered by such exchanges, often only evident when they transgressed Islander expectations.

European Print and Visual Cultures of the Pacific

All of these fascinating, perplexing, titillating, curiosity- and horror-provoking elements of European encounter in the Pacific emerged in a rich print and visual culture that grew exponentially from the exploration period onwards. Of course, it built upon older speculative accounts of the Pacific and particularly the southern hemisphere. Classical manuscripts inspired beautiful global maps that illustrated some of the most important early printed books of the late 1400s and 1500s. Later, real and fictional travellers – Marco Polo, Sir John Mandeville, Francisco Alvares, Henry Melville, Gabriel de Foigny – allowed European readers to imagine the world beyond known boundaries. Although dubiously authoritative, such accounts nonetheless provoked a fascination with southern hemisphere peoples and landscapes, as a corollary of emergent European narratives of self-discovery that sought to understand the balance between nature, geography, and the human condition.[9] Following the English voyages of the eighteenth century in particular, published voyage accounts proliferated and information about the Pacific based on first-hand observation became more available.

The English also sought to control the publication of voyage accounts with strict instructions issued for the return of all officers' journals on each state-sponsored voyage, which were seen as the intellectual property of the Admiralty, to be edited, combined, and published as the authorized account. James Cook's first voyage provides an illustrative example. Aware of his heavy and damaged vessel, Cook signalled to a British man-of-war in St Helena harbour in May 1771, knowing that it could travel faster and would arrive in England before the *Endeavour*. Cook writes: 'Captain Elliot himself came on board, and I delivered to him a letter for the Admiralty, with a box, containing the common log books of the ship, and the journals of some of the officers.'[10] With this act, Cook placed the raw material for the official

---

[9] On the Australian component of this tradition, see A. Johnston, 'Australian travel writing', in N. Das and T. Youngs (eds.), *The Cambridge History of Travel Writing* (Cambridge: Cambridge University Press, 2019), 267–82.

[10] Derived from J. Hawkesworth (ed.), *An Account of the Voyages Undertaken by Order of His Present Majesty for Making Discoveries in the Southern Hemisphere. . .* 3 vols. (London: W. Strahan & T. Cadell, 1773), vols. II–III, 798–9.

account in the hands of the British Admiralty, as was regulated, and hence both inaugurated but did not individually author the rich and ongoing print culture that emerged from the *Endeavour* voyage. The texts arrived before the ship and its crew. The official account authorized by the Admiralty was John Hawkesworth's *An Account of the Voyages* (1773), which combined both Cook's and Banks's accounts with editorial commentary. It was a publishing triumph.[11] Voyage accounts 'were studded with images and descriptions that took root in the English folk memory. They are there in the original books and in their various reprints, abridgments and serializations, in ballads, plays and engravings.'[12] Voyage accounts were widely read, highly influential, and disseminated throughout British culture; the knowledge they produced about exotic cultures and climates was absorbed into domestic British culture and spread throughout Europe. Cook's voyage account was a defining moment of the role of the Pacific in intellectual discourse about Europe and its others.

Voyages of exploration and printing technologies flourished simultaneously, and increased literacy throughout the eighteenth and nineteenth centuries ensured new and avid readers of voyages and travels. So too popularizations of exotic accounts made knowledge about the Pacific available in accessible ways to broad audiences, even if their literacy was not high. Innovations in reproduction ensured a market for print at a variety of price points, from broadsides to collectors' editions. Visual culture enthusiastically engaged with Pacific subjects. Engravings of scenes from exploration accounts were pored over, and reproduced for purchase by enthusiasts. New techniques responded to the challenges of a visually literate market. The panoramic wallpaper 'Les Sauvages de la Mer Pacifique', 1804–6 (that would later inspire Reihana) was a twenty-panel work featuring the people, places, and encounters of Europeans in the Pacific, inspired by Cook's journals and reflecting the revolutionary Enlightenment spirit of France in its educative messages about equality, popular knowledge, and nature[13] (see Figure 34.1). Designed by Jean Gabriel Charvet and printed by Joseph Dufour, at 2 metres high and more than 10 metres long, it was significant

---

[11] Hawkesworth (ed.), *An Account of the Voyages*.

[12] G. Williams, *The Great South Sea: English Voyages and Encounters, 1570-1750* (New Haven: Yale University Press, 1997), xiv.

[13] The full version in colour held by Te Papa Museum is available here: https://collections .tepapa.govt.nz/object/1495632. The National Gallery of Australia has high-quality, restored sections and a detailed account of the wallpaper production and restoration processes here: https://nga.gov.au/conservation/paper/lessauv.cfm.

in both its size and its technological ambition, even if the images are more decorative than accurate. Nicholas Thomas describes it: 'A luminous evocation of voluptuous foliage, human variety, refined performance, remarkable ritual garb and regalia, it is also evidently fantastic, an overt romanticisation reducing the power, presence and complexity of Pacific life to enticing decoration'.[14] Increasingly, serious artists undertook commissions or created new work related to the heroes of European expansion: Cook and Banks were the subject of many portraits. Benjamin West's well-known portrait of Banks (1771–2) – wrapped in Pacific *tapa* (barkcloth) and surrounded by the collections of his voyages – exemplifies Banks's self-construction as an expert on cross-cultural knowledge. The Pacific travellers who accompanied them back to the northern hemisphere were also the subject of both high and low cultural representations. The Raiatean Mai/Omai, who arrived in London in 1774 from Cook's second voyage, was fêted by Banks at British society's leading events. Mai's portrait was made by a variety of leading artists, including Joshua Reynolds; a popular pantomime was staged about him; he featured in society belles-lettres and philosophical meditations; and his visit inspired various ephemeral broadsides and ballads.[15]

Throughout the nineteenth century, alongside these elite, popular, and often scandalous representations of European encounters with the Pacific, another body of literature about the Pacific emerged that sought to serve as a moral corrective to visions of a licentious Pacific. Missionary societies operated in the region from 1796 when the London Missionary Society (LMS) sent its inaugural overseas representatives to Polynesia. LMS director George Haweis was directly influenced by Cook's voyage accounts, advised by Bligh, and partly enabled by Banks's later role as President of the Royal Society and influential role within government bodies (missionaries made good botanical collectors as part of Banks's vast global network, and the Tahitian missions bore a mutually beneficial relationship with the Australian colonies, in which Banks took a personal interest).[16] The Pacific was seen as a field ripe for evangelical harvest: missions aimed for Christian reform of many of the aspects of society, religion, and self that were attractive to Europeans seeking a prelapsarian, sexually liberated, edenic landscape. Missionaries wrote prolifically about Pacific cultures and peoples – foregrounding

---

[14] N. Thomas, 'Lisa Reihana: encounters in Oceania', *Artlink* 37.2 (2017), 22–6, at 22.

[15] K. Fullagar, *The Savage Visit* (Berkeley: University of California Press, 2012).

[16] On Banks's sceptical but pragmatic relationship with evangelical missionaries, see J. Gascoigne, *Joseph Banks and the English Enlightenment: Useful Knowledge and Polite Culture* (Cambridge: Cambridge University Press, 1995).

paganism, violence, and the plight of women and children – and their accounts created a market for morally improving literature about exotic locales.[17] Once population-wide conversions to Christianity began in the 1810s, missionary writing deployed the Pacific as an exemplary mission field, the prototype for global evangelical reform. Yet missionary experience in the Pacific also provided extraordinarily detailed accounts of Pacific peoples, cultures, and environments. From John Williams's *A Narrative of Missionary Enterprises in the South Sea Islands* (1837) onwards, natural history, language, and thick descriptions of Island cultures emerged from observers who otherwise sought to implant European culture as part of an evangelical 'civilization' mission.[18] By the mid to late nineteenth century, missionary ethnography eventually merged into the new science of anthropology. As long-resident fieldwork observers, missionaries provided immense amounts of information about the Pacific that was synthesized, theorized, and formally authorized by armchair commentators, either by way of individual relationships to procure data and specimens or through access to published missionary accounts.[19] Although anthropology would later disavow much missionary knowledge in its own attempts to establish its academic and methodological credentials, evangelical science underpinned much of the knowledge about the Pacific in human, natural, biological, marine, and earth sciences.[20]

In both elite and vernacular European sources, then, the Pacific generated a crucial body of knowledge during the Enlightenment and modern periods. The Pacific entered European intellectual history alongside its place in imperial history; its natural productions contributed to the emergence of robust systems of classification of flora and fauna; its artefacts influenced the emergence of modern religious and philosophical thought, as well as studies of material culture; and writing about Pacific peoples influenced the development of theories of race and culture. European interest in Pacific topics

---

[17] See A. Johnston, *Missionary Writing and Empire, 1800–1860* (Cambridge: Cambridge University Press, 2003), part 3.

[18] J. Williams, *A Narrative of Missionary Enterprises in the South Sea Islands: With Remarks upon the Natural History of the Islands, Origin, Languages, Traditions, and Usages of the Inhabitants*, 7th edn (London: J. Snow, 1838 [1837]); C. Herbert, *Culture and Anomie: Ethnographic Imagination in the Nineteenth Century* (Chicago: University of Chicago Press, 1991); R. Edmond, *Representing the South Pacific: Colonial Discourse from Cook to Gauguin* (Cambridge: Cambridge University Press, 1997).

[19] J. Samson, *Race and Redemption: British Missionaries Encounter Pacific Peoples, 1797–1920* (Grand Rapids, MI: Eerdmans, 2017).

[20] S. Sivasundaram, *Nature and Godly Empire: Science and Evangelical Mission in the Pacific, 1795–1850* (Cambridge: Cambridge University Press, 2005).

was specialized and technical, but it was also popular. Enthusiasts and collectors participated in a market for Pacific texts and artefacts – mirroring the trade between museums and collectors – that rewarded careful study and deep knowledge: even if that deep knowledge was more often based on European sources rather than lived experience or engagement with Pacific peoples and cultures.

Academic Discourse on Pacific Texts

Colonial discourse theory provided twentieth-century scholars with tools to analyse these classic texts of cross-cultural encounter and to identify the 'othering' processes at play, particularly in relation to race, gender, and sexuality. If Orientalism as a theoretical and intellectual term encapsulates the comprehensive engagement by Europeans with Eastern art, culture, peoples, and knowledge, then we might posit 'Pacificism' as its (awkward) corollary.[21] The key tenets of Orientalism replay fairly neatly in the Pacific context: 'Pacificism' is a way that Europeans came to terms with the region based on its special place in European experience and imagination; the Pacific is the source of a rich and long tradition of images of the other; and expertise in the Pacific produced discursive forms typified by particular vocabulary, imagery, and scholarship, supported by institutions and colonial bureaucracies.[22] Academic traditions upheld ontological and epistemological distinctions between the Pacific and Europe, and in the popular imagination this distinction was shaped by writers, artists, political and philosophical commentators, and imperial administrators into a truism of cultural difference, if not alterity. So too, knowledge of the Pacific in these terms enabled its conceptual management by Europeans. Although formal annexation of Pacific colonies emerged only in the mid to late nineteenth century – considerably later than Said's case studies – much of the attitude to and discourse about the Pacific was indubitably imperial from the exploration voyages onwards.

It is commonplace to find evidence of imperial ideologies in texts of Pacific encounter. Using the three, indicative, broad areas of European interest in the Pacific – social organization; the natural world; and Pacific subjectivities – we can identify classic imperial tropes at work. Greg Dening's classic account of Captain Samuel Wallis's 1767 act of claiming Tahiti for King George III

---

[21] E.W. Said, *Orientalism* (New York: Vintage, 1979).   [22] Said, *Orientalism*, 1.

reveals the failures of understanding that dogged early encounters. As Wallis and his crew on the *Dolphin* sought to read the social world of the beach, the sea, and the shoreline, they made some assumptions about hierarchy and social order, and missed many other signs, to tragic ends. The Europeans were shocked by being pelted with pebbles by thousands of Islanders in canoes streaming out from the shore. A double-hulled vessel held a man wrapped in red *tapa* cloth – the island's king, Wallis and his men assumed – although perplexingly there were also women in the canoes who flaunted their nakedness, jeering at the sailors. In Dening's terms, the naval laws of the *Dolphin* were strict and incapable of shifting their rules of engagement: 'on the edge of this battle, the Natives were other. Their otherness was nowhere so marked as in the wanton antics of the women who stood on the prows of most of the canoes.'[23] Superior weaponry and excessive force meant that the Europeans' attack on the canoes was lethal: 'The *realpolitick* of discovery and possession meant the Native was not owed the ordinary etiquettes of war.'[24] Here – as later when Cook himself was killed by Islanders – imperial tropes of savagery, disorder, and immorality combined in on-the-spot responses and then later representations that fundamentally misunderstood both the nature of Pacific society and the terms of cross-cultural engagement. Acts of violence often took place when tabu or protocol were transgressed: but imperial ways of seeing blinded the visitors to rules of engagement other than their own.[25] Europeans in the Pacific regularly misidentified leaders and misread their influence. Understanding Pacific polities was profoundly challenging, and often only became legible through the kinds of engagement undertaken by those castaways and missionaries who committed themselves to residence in an island society for long periods, and rarely by transient voyagers.[26]

Imperial science could similarly confound potential communication between Europeans and Islanders about the natural world and its resources. Cook's voyages were exemplary of the ways that scientific activities of mapping, charting, collecting, and classifying were tied to imperial geopolitical aims.[27] Regulating relations between imperial centres and their

---

[23] Dening, *Performances*, 137.   [24] Dening, *Performances*, 137.
[25] N. Thomas, *Islanders: The Age of Empire in the Pacific* (New Haven: Yale University Press, 2010), 53.
[26] Thomas, *Islanders*, 45.
[27] J. Gascoigne, *Science in the Service of Empire: Joseph Banks, the British State, and the Uses of Science in the Age of Revolution* (Cambridge: Cambridge University Press, 1998); P. Smethurst, *Travel Writing and the Natural World, 1768–1840* (Basingstoke: Palgrave, 2013).

peripheries was undertaken as much through botany as through trade and economic policy; travelling scientists such as Daniel Solander, Johann Reinhold and Georg Forster, Alexander von Humboldt, and Charles Darwin sent key strategic information back to imperial centres along with their scientific observations.[28] Kew Gardens – one of Banks's key projects on his return from the Pacific – and its collection and dispersal of botanical material was an exemplary scientific centre through which the intellectual class sought to identify natural laws of science and then extend those to organize human societies, as part of its global geopolitical ambitions.[29] Trade routes and relations set up for natural resources also extended to human populations.[30] Various kinds of scientific knowledge about nature underpinned the development of a global consciousness based in mercantile capitalism and imperialism, and set the terms for relations of extraction, consumption, and exploitation that continue to entrench global disadvantage in the present.

Imperial thought also shaped European readings of Pacific individuals and identities, and dogged representations of cross-cultural encounters. Recognition of Polynesian social hierarchies did not prevent the English from mocking what some saw as savage derivations of morality. Purea, presented to English readers as the 'Queen of Tahiti', was relentlessly satirized for her sexuality, her tattooed body, and her liaison with Joseph Banks in Tahiti. Purea 'entered the English imagination not as the Other but as a setting for an argument about morality and corruption', Dening argued.[31] Yet placed within a tradition of imperial representations of Indigenous women and their sexuality – Pocohontas in early colonial America, Sarah Baartman in the Cape Colony, and Truganini of Van Diemen's Land, to name only a few – we can identify narrative tropes that indubitably position such women both as others and as intimate interlocutors of imperial fantasies of race, possession, and control.[32] Purea's staging of a scene of public sexual intercourse for Cook's sailors at Point Venus in

---

[28] Smethurst, *Travel Writing*, 10.

[29] R. Drayton, *Nature's Government: Science, Imperial Britain, and the 'Improvement' of the World* (New Haven: Yale University Press, 2000).

[30] T. Banivanua-Mar, *Violence and Colonial Dialogue: The Australian-Pacific Indentured Labor Trade* (Honolulu: University of Hawai'i Press, 2006).

[31] Dening, *Performances*, 152.

[32] On Baartman, see most recently N. Gordon-Chipembere (ed.), *Representation and Black Womanhood: The Legacy of Sarah Baartman* (New York: Palgrave Macmillan, 2011). On Truganini, see most recently C. Pybus, *Truganini: Journey through the Apocalypse* (Sydney: Allen & Unwin, 2020).

1769 exemplified European visions of the Pacific as a licentious paradise. In Hawkesworth's hands, this scene became paradigmatic for both the allure and the otherness of the Pacific, here focalized through women's bodies. Yet as Nicholas Thomas suggests, the absence of similar public sexual performances in the fulsome archives of missionaries and later ethnographers indicates that this Tahitian theatre of otherness was much more likely to have been about European visitors and their desires. When European satirists and philosophers utilized this performance to question European morals, they did so in terms that rendered Tahitians unconvincingly naive: 'They could credit Tahitians with innocence, happiness and sensuality, but not with critical intelligence. They had no idea that mere savages might be satirists too.'[33] Play, satire, affect, and strategy accompanied many intimate encounters with Europeans that Pacific peoples initiated.

Imperial commentators repeatedly misread those encounters as motivated only by European agency and intentions, and for the display of various imperial virtues: masculinity, morality, and martial prowess, for example. As Lee Wallace notes, paying attention to other kinds of sexual encounters in Pacific texts reveals the region as a place where 'the known limits of masculinity come undone'.[34] Bligh's 1789 experience with Tahitian *māhū* (boys and men in same-sex relations) inaugurated a long tradition whereby male–male relationships in the Pacific caught the imperial attention, and troubled their assumptions about gender and sexuality. Related to but incommensurate with the British Navy's concern with and management of male desire on board their ships, same-sex sexualities complicate the ways that heterosexual fantasies imagined Pacific women as other to European men, and their intimate acts as a corollary of imperial conquest.[35] Even when European voyagers sought to cultivate cross-cultural relationships seemingly less freighted with power – such as the realm of friendship – what they were offered by Pacific peoples was connections such as *taio* in Tahiti, which in some ways fitted the contours of European friendship, but also exceeded and failed those expectations in subtle and complex ways.[36] Relationships that imperial texts represented as warmly

---

[33] Thomas, *Islanders*, 159.

[34] L. Wallace, *Sexual Encounters: Pacific Texts, Modern Sexualities* (Ithaca, NY: Cornell University Press, 2003), 13.

[35] Wallace, *Sexual Encounters*, 20–1.

[36] V. Smith, *Intimate Strangers: Friendship, Exchange, and Pacific Encounters* (Cambridge: Cambridge University Press, 2010); V. Smith, 'Banks, Tupaia, and Mai: cross-cultural exchanges and friendship in the Pacific', *Parergon* 26.2 (2009), 139–60.

fraternal – but which also often carried connotations of deception, treachery, or exploitation when relations soured – were perhaps only newly invented on the beach of cross-cultural encounter. Understandings of Pacific notions of kinship, reciprocity, and obligation were slow to emerge when voyagers experienced only short-term, intense exposure to Pacific people, however those encounters (perhaps unrepresentative and certainly unreliably narrated) lived on in textual forms that profoundly shaped European visions of and intellectual paradigms about the Pacific.

Despite the persuasiveness of colonial discourse analysis – its identification of power and ideology, particularly in the fields of race, gender, and class – Pacific texts have always exceeded that theoretical paradigm. There are forms of encounter, kinds of evidence, and complex, unsettled accounts that cannot be neatly accounted for simply by identifying imperial hegemony. Jane Samson, analysing British missionary encounters with Pacific peoples, identifies the paradox of 'othering and brothering' embodied by Christian missionaries. That is, missionaries from the eighteenth century onwards worked simultaneously with fixed ideas about savagery and paganism, alongside seemingly contradictory assumptions that Pacific 'others' were in fact mutable, complex, and commensurate with Europeans as part of a shared, religiously inspired, human-ness: 'brothers'.[37] Of course missionary activity was entangled with colonialism, contributing to Westernization that was destructive of traditional cultures, paternalism that denied Pacific people agency, and practices such as child removal and assimilation that profoundly damaged individuals, families, and societies. But as Samson and others have teased out, individual evangelists were also involved in engaging deeply with and seeking to preserve Pacific languages and cultural knowledge, in advocating for rights to self-determination and sovereignty, and in their propagation of the Christian message, so introducing a powerful theological and rhetorical tool that was adopted and adapted by Indigenous and Pacific peoples to diverse and potent ends, including decolonization.[38] Positioning missionaries as unquestioning agents of imperial power and their Pacific converts as misled dupes is neither intellectually convincing nor respectful of human motivations and complexity.

A rich tradition and an increasing volume of academic scholarship analyses Pacific texts of encounter as moments of exchange, of mutual comprehension and incomprehension, of exploration of boundaries that were not immutable

---

[37] Samson, *Race and Redemption*, 5.   [38] Samson, *Race and Redemption*, 7.

in the historical period, and are not so now.[39] Such scholarship does not render power obsolete but rather seeks to account for more subtle and shifting negotiations by historical agents, on both sides of Dening's beach, than totalizing colonial discourse theories might allow. In this field, many aspects of encounter continue to make new meanings from the texts and the Pacific-European archive, in innovative ways that enable us to see the past differently.

Seeing the Pacific Otherwise

A key shift in late twentieth-century academic discourse about the Pacific was the widespread adoption of the Pacific scholar Epeli Hau'ofa's notion of the 'Sea of Islands', a subtle but far-reaching reformulation of European visions of the Pacific as small and isolated 'islands in the sea'.[40] Hau'ofa explicitly rejected the imperial geography that emerged from exploration voyages, and the perspective of 'continental men' who imagined small land masses in large (if not empty) oceans, who later positioned individual island communities within colonial boundaries that 'confined ocean peoples to tiny spaces'.[41] Suggesting that the descriptor 'Oceania' rather than 'Pacific' better captures the ambitious world-making tendencies of Pacific peoples from ancient ancestors onwards, Hau'ofa attempted to shift the (academic and lived) terms of engagement:

> 'Oceania' connotes a sea of islands with their inhabitants. The world of our ancestors was a large sea full of places to explore, to make their homes in, to breed generations of seafarers like themselves ... Theirs was a large world in which peoples and cultures moved and mingled unhindered by boundaries of the kind erected much later by imperial powers.[42]

Hau'ofa's poetic mode (he was a creative writer as well as an anthropologist) and utopian address (he sought to empower a new generation of Pacific students) resonated with global interest in post-colonial writing and activism

---

[39] Exchange is a recurring motif in Pacific scholarship: see N. Thomas, *Entangled Objects: Exchange, Material Culture, and Colonialism in the Pacific* (Cambridge, MA: Harvard University Press, 1991); N. Thomas, *Colonialism's Culture: Anthropology, Travel and Government* (Carlton: Melbourne University Press, 1994); J. Lamb, V. Smith, and N. Thomas (eds.), *Exploration and Exchange: A South Seas Anthology* (Chicago: University of Chicago Press, 2000).
[40] E. Hau'ofa, 'Our Sea of Islands', in E. Waddell, V. Naidu, and E. Hau'ofa (eds.), *A New Oceania: Rediscovering Our Sea of Islands* (Suva: School of Social and Economic Development, University of the South Pacific in association with Beake House, 1993), 2–16. This essay exists in several forms, including two keynote addresses at University of Hawai'i in 1993; an article in *The Contemporary Pacific* (Spring 1994); and later republished in various locations.
[41] Hau'ofa, 'Our Sea of Islands', 7.   [42] Hau'ofa, 'Our Sea of Islands', 8.

in the 1990s, immediately creating a 'trans-Pacific currency' for his ideas, as Teresia Teaiwa wryly noted.[43] Although based initially in social and economic development studies at the University of the South Pacific in Fiji, which employed Hau'ofa and his colleagues who popularized the core tenets of this renovated and future-orientated view of the Pacific, these ideas have gone on to influence a range of scholarship in many fields, including historians who compellingly reread the Pacific past along these lines.

Of course, like Pacific interlocutors during the voyaging period, Hau'ofa was closely engaged with new ideas emerging regionally and globally during the same period. The conversation between his 'Oceanic' ideas and those emerging in area studies, decolonization, and historical, literary and cultural studies is explicit both in Hau'ofa's writing and for those scholars engaged in cognate questions. Oskar Spate had noted in 1979 that 'there was not, and could not be, any concept "Pacific" until the limits and lineaments of the Ocean were set', and this, like the denotation of geopolitical spaces of islands and Pacific rims, was 'basically a Euro-American creation, though built on an indigenous substructure'.[44] Hau'ofa himself noted that key terms of his argument had come about in correspondence with the ethnogeographer Eric Waddell.[45] The book-length set of responses to Hau'ofa's coinage included an inserted commentary from R.G. Ward and J.W. Webb's *The Settlement of Polynesia* (1973) that the western Pacific Islander navigator, as opposed to 'continental men' on European ships, would expect that 'islands would rise over the horizon to meet him'.[46] Dening's emphasis on history telling as both poetic and performative had considerable affinities with Hau'ofa's interdisciplinary project. For Dening, this was usually a historical projection back into the eighteenth century where the metaphor of 'islands and beaches' offered ways to understand the oceanic world of the Pacific, 'where islands are everywhere and beaches must be crossed to enter them or leave them, to make them or change them'.[47] The idea of a highly mobile, oceanic world of trade, exchange, and travel had long historical roots in the Pacific, which Hau'ofa reactivated for new pedagogical, creative, and scholarly audiences.[48]

---

[43] T. Teaiwa, 'Review of *A New Oceania: Rediscovering Our Sea of Islands*, edited by Eric Waddell, Vijay Naidu, and Epeli Hau'ofa', *Contemporary Pacific* 8 (1996), 214–17, at 214.
[44] O.H.K. Spate, *The Spanish Lake* (Canberra: ANU Press, 2004 [1979]), ix.
[45] Hau'ofa, 'Our Sea of Islands', note 3, 16.   [46] Waddell et al. (eds.), *A New Oceania*, 17.
[47] Dening reflected upon his development of ideas of poetics and performance in *Performances* (1996) but his methodology was evident in *Islands and Beaches: Discourse on a Silent Land, Marquesas 1774–1880* (Chicago: The Dorsey Press, 1980), 3.
[48] On the *longue durée* of 'the new Oceania', see E. Hau'ofa, 'A new Oceania: an interview with Epeli Hau'ofa by Juniper Ellis', *Antipodes* 15:1 (2001), 22–5.

The rise of spatial approaches in history, anthropology, and geography enabled Pacific scholarship to produce new visions of the pre-colonial region, the period of European voyages and intense and inaugural cross-cultural encounters, and the rich, multicultural late colonial and modern period.[49] (While this section focuses on humanities scholarship, Reihana's panoramic videoart evidences the parallel processes in visual art, to which I return at the end of the chapter.) Thinking about mobility enabled scholars to see European ships and their onboard culture as equally important in the voyaging as in the arrival. The ship – Michel Foucault's 'heterotopia par excellence', as a 'floating piece of space' that is both self-contained and the physical portal for contact with other worlds – became a potent and multivalent analytical tool for spatial thinking.[50] In Dening's re-vision of Pacific contact, Europeans 'came in islands of their own ships or they made islands of their own in mission stations and forts'.[51] Ships on Cook's Pacific voyages were not only vehicles of transport. The *Endeavour* conjoined Cook's primary purposes of geographical exploration with the 'floating laboratory' of innovative botanical inquiry, funded and undertaken by Banks.[52] Such ships and their global voyages prefigured a significant shift in European knowledge production, whereby first-hand observation could authoritatively verify (or dismiss) phenomena speculated about by European philosophers. Cook's ships were 'scientific instruments ... [that] mediated the complex interplay between representation and reality that lies at the heart of eighteenth-century geography'.[53] That interplay was complex and cross-cultural from the moment of its creation. As scholars have re-evaluated the role of Pacific travellers on board European ships as energetic participants in these innovative experiments in cartography and voyaging, the ship has emerged as a cross-cultural site of knowledge production (for Tupaia's map, see Figure 34.2 below).

[49] Most influentially, spatial and network models have been advanced by T. Ballantyne, *Orientalism and Race: Aryanism and the British Empire* (Basingstoke: Palgrave, 2002) and A. Lester, *Imperial Networks: Creating Identities in Nineteenth-Century South Africa and Britain* (London: Routledge, 2001).

[50] M. Foucault and Jay Miskowiec, 'Of other spaces', *Diacritics* 16:1 (1986), 22–7, at 27.

[51] Dening, *Islands and Beaches*, 18.

[52] J.D. Hooker (ed.), *Journal of the Right Hon. Sir Joseph Banks* ... (London: Macmillan, 1896), cited xxxix. See a longer version of this argument in A. Johnston, 'Exhibiting the Enlightenment: Joseph Banks's *Florilegium* and colonial knowledge production', *Journal of Australian Studies* 43:1 (2019), 118–32.

[53] R. Sorrenson, 'The ship as a scientific instrument in the eighteenth century', in T. Ballantyne (ed.), *Science, Empire and the European Exploration of the Pacific* (Aldershot: Ashgate, 2004 [1996]), 123–236.

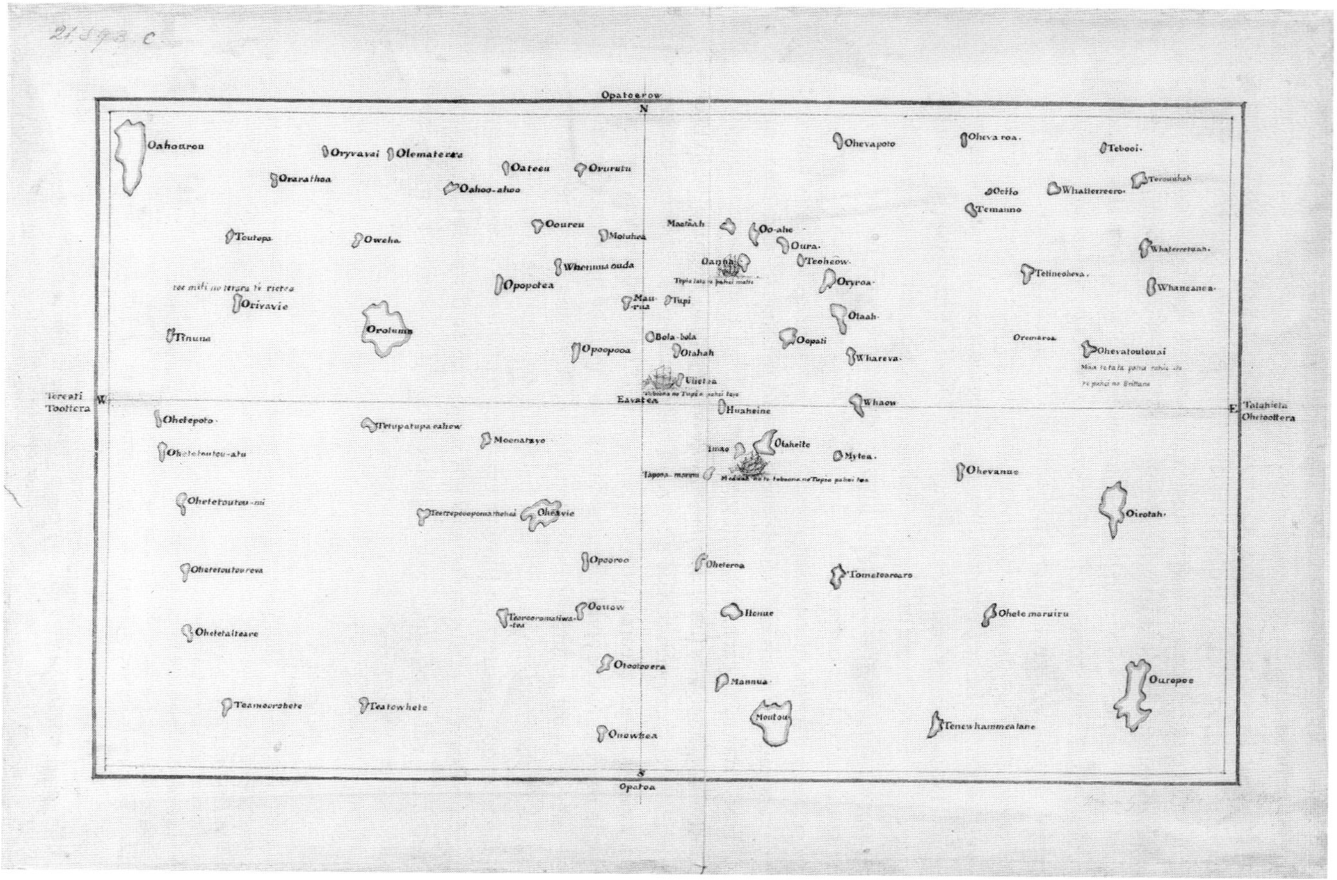

21.893 C

Opatoerow
N

Oahourou · Oryvavai · Olematere · Oateea · Orurutu · Ohevapoto · Oheva roa. · Tebooi.
Orarathoa · Oahoo-ahoo · Oetto · Whatterreero · Teraurah
Toutepa · Oweha · Ooureu · Motuhea · Maenah · Oo-ahe · Temanno · Whaterretuah.
Wherinna ouda · Oura · Teoheow · Tetineoheva.
Opopotea · Oangh · Oryroa · Whanzanea
tee mili no terara te rietra · Orivavie · Maa-roa · Tupi · Tipta lato no pahai malte · Olaah ·
Tinuna · Orotuna · Opoopooa · Bola-bola · Oopati · Oremaroa · Ohevatoulouai
Olahah · Whareva · Moa to tata patai rahie de te pahai no Brittane
Ulietea
Whehina ne Tupia ni pahai fea
Tereati Tootiera W · Ohetepoto- · Eavatea · Huaheine · Whaow · E Totahieta Ohetoottera
Oketetautou-alu · Terupatupa eahow · Moonatayo · Imao · Otaheite · Mytea. · Ohevanue
Tapona-mayou · Madont no te taboono ne Tupia pahai fea
Ohetetoutau-mi · Teettepooopoonathehei · Oheavie · Oieotah.
Ohetetoutaureva · Opooroo · Oheteroa · Tometeoroaro
Thereeramatiwatoo · Oottow · Henue · Ohete maruiru
Oketetaiteare · Otootooera · Ouropoo
Teamacrahete · Teatowhete · Mannua · Moutou · Tenea hammealane
Onewhea
S
Opatoa

Figure 34.2 Tupaia's map: chart of the Society Islands.

Borrowing from the 'spatial turn' in Pacific and other historiographies engaged with cultural geography, academic work on mobility analyses space not as 'an expanse travelled across' but as a dense site that creates and maintains social, political, and cultural relations.[54] Focusing on mobility opened up new areas of study and an extended historical scope. The Pacific region provides an ideal location through which to explore transnational and global approaches. The culture of space becomes 'an object of analysis and an interpretative grid for reinterpreting the colonial and imperial pasts'.[55] Spatializing empire has a variety of outcomes: it analyses how and where imperial ideologies and colonial practices emerged and interacted; it allows a focus on dynamic flows and counterflows (of ideas, goods, people, capital, technologies, and communication) that emphasizes transactions markedly different from the older imperial history model of centre and periphery; and it shifts attention to locations often distant from the Anglo-Euro-American focus of much scholarship, including the Pacific region. Such approaches shift from the nation-state model, encouraging comparison, and they enable new objects of analysis, such as the emergence of studies of the Pacific and Indian Oceans, whose waters lap many national shores but whose port towns sometimes find more in common with their adjacent oceanic 'Rim' cultures than with their inland national 'centres'.[56] Transport histories, trade routes, and oceanic movements come to the fore, and scholarly attention can move beyond 'first contact' encounters to histories of passage and exchange that pre-date European exploration voyages, and that follow through to the contemporary period.[57]

Importantly, Islanders and Europeans both come into view as active historical subjects, with traditions of knowledge, technologies of way finding, and modes of place-making and representation that reinstate forms of agency elided by images of Islanders waiting on the beach for the arrival of exceptional European travellers who then transformed (or destroyed) their

---

[54] T. Ballantyne and A. Burton, 'Introduction: the politics of intimacy in an age of empire', in T. Ballantyne and A. Burton (eds.), *Moving Subjects: Gender, Mobility, and Intimacy in an Age of Global Empire* (Chicago: University of Chicago Press, 2009), 1–28, at 3, citing Doreen Massey.
[55] Ballantyne and Burton, 'Introduction', 2.
[56] S. Sivasundaram, *Islanded: Britain, Sri Lanka, and the Bounds of an Indian Ocean Colony* (Chicago: University of Chicago Press, 2013); N. Worden, 'Writing the global Indian Ocean', *Journal of Global History* 12:1 (2017), 145–54; I. Hofmeyr, U. Dhupelia-Mesthrie, and P. Kaarsholm, 'Durban and Cape Town as port cities: reconsidering Southern African Studies from the Indian Ocean', *Journal of Southern African Studies* 42:3 (2016), 375–87.
[57] F. Steel, *Oceania under Steam: Sea Transport and the Cultures of Colonialism, c.1870–1914* (Manchester: Manchester University Press, 2011).

autochthonous world. Pacific peoples – like other Indigenous actors globally – engaged energetically and deliberately with the British (and broader) world that emerged as an uneven and opportunistic network throughout the eighteenth and nineteenth centuries.[58] As in other island cultures, productive tensions between Indigeneity (rootedness and place-based identity) and cosmopolitanism (the desire to engage with otherness) played out at the level of the individual and the community.[59] Individuals such as Mai and Tupaia joined European ships to further their own political and intellectual interests, to travel, and to gain new experiences to enrich them personally and to bring those experiences and knowledges back to their communities.[60] While disease and exploitation often dogged their experiences, the 'Fatal Impact' thesis of the Pacific failed to account for Pacific agency.[61] New approaches insist upon agency. Tracey Banivanua-Mar resituated the beginning of decolonization movements to the nineteenth century, arguing that Indigenous political movements

> had their roots in the early colonial period as a dialogue that Indigenous people maintained with colonial power, and in which they asserted their right to choose the best and reject the worst of colonisation. It began as localised responses, but quickly developed international and transnational linkages, shadowing the imperial networks of the nineteenth and twentieth centuries.[62]

A renewed focus on Indigenous mobilities has opened up colonial archives and sources for new readings of Pacific desires, agency, and politics in both pre- and post-colonial periods, and re-visioned decolonization as a process, not an event

---

[58] M. Stopp and G. Mitchell, '"Our amazing visitors": Catherine Cartwright's account of Labrador Inuit in England', *Arctic* 63:4 (2010), 399–413; M. Stopp, 'Eighteenth century Labrador Inuit in England', *Arctic* 62:1 (2009), 45–64; K. Fullagar and M.A. McDonnell (eds.), *Facing Empire: Indigenous Experiences in a Revolutionary Age* (Baltimore: Johns Hopkins University Press, 2018).

[59] Sivasundaram, *Islanded*.

[60] E. Elbourne, 'Indigenous peoples and imperial networks in the early nineteenth century: the politics of knowledge', in P. Buckner and R.D. Francis (eds), *Rediscovering the British World* (Calgary: University of Calgary Press, 2005), 59–85; J. Gascoigne, 'Cross-cultural knowledge exchange in the Age of the Enlightenment', in S. Konishi, M. Nugent, and T. Shellam (eds.), *Indigenous Intermediaries: New Perspectives on Exploration Archives* (Canberra: ANU Press, 2015), 131–46; Smith, 'Banks, Tupaia, and Mai'; V. Smith, 'Joseph Banks's intermediaries: rethinking global cultural exchange', in S. Moyn and A. Sartori (eds.), *Global Intellectual History* (New York: Columbia University Press, 2013), 66–86.

[61] A. Moorehead, *The Fatal Impact: An Account of the Invasion of the South Pacific, 1767–1840* (London: Hamish Hamilton, 1966).

[62] T. Banivanua Mar, *Decolonisation and the Pacific: Indigenous Globalisation and the Ends of Empire* (Cambridge: Cambridge University Press, 2016), 4.

(borrowing also from settler colonial studies, a particularly productive intellectual conjunction of new methodologies in the twenty-first century).[63]

An expanded Pacific is inaugurated in recent academic discourse, enabled by these spatial- and mobility-focused approaches. This is not only Hau'ofa's Oceania, but the 'Pacific Worlds' that are characterized by 'multiple seas, cultures, and peoples, and especially the overlapping transits between them'.[64] In such models, the Pacific is placed within long histories and interlocking movements within interlinked regions, so that Asia and the Pacific emerge through intermittent transits and transactions, performed at sites that might be variously characterized as 'transnational', 'translocal', or 'transcolonial'. Matt Matsuda argues that the Pacific 'is startlingly crowded with such episodes, where local actors were pulled into overlapping circuits of struggle and ambition'.[65] He connects pre-colonial spaces to contemporary policies of border protection and increasingly defensive nationalism, which appears determined to manage the accelerated mobility characterizing modern and contemporary worlds, including the Pacific. Yet even in such ambitious studies, the complex webs of states and nations must also make space for the rich biographies of individuals who personify the geopolitical tensions at play over extended historical periods.

Tupaia's Map, 1769–2019

This chapter concludes with an overview of how one Pacific Islander and his knowledge entered European intellectual history and academic discourse to illustrate the ongoing potency of Pacific encounters, ideas, and artefacts over 250 years. The Raiatean navigator and elite 'arioi priest Tupaia fascinated Europeans since his engagement with Cook's party at Tahiti in 1769.[66]

---

[63] R. Standfield (ed.), *Indigenous Mobilities: Across and Beyond the Antipodes* (Canberra: ANU Press, 2018); S. Konishi et al. (eds.), *Indigenous Intermediaries*; T. Shellam, M. Nugent, S. Konishi, and A. Cadzow, *Brokers and Boundaries: Colonial Exploration in Indigenous Territory* (Canberra: ANU Press, 2016); F. Driver and L. Jones, *Hidden Histories of Exploration: Researching the RGS-IBG Collections* (London: Royal Holloway, University of London, in association with the Royal Geographical Society (with IBG), 2009); J. Carey and J. Lydon (eds.), *Indigenous Networks: Mobility, Connections and Exchange* (New York: Routledge, 2014). On settler colonial studies, see P. Wolfe, *Settler Colonialism and the Transformation of Anthropology: The Politics and Poetics of an Ethnographic Event* (London: Cassell, 1999); L. Veracini, *Settler Colonialism: A Theoretical Overview* (Basingstoke: Palgrave Macmillan, 2010).
[64] Matsuda, *Pacific Worlds*, 2.   [65] Matsuda, *Pacific Worlds*, 6.
[66] Tupaia's life is most authoritatively told in A. Salmond, *The Trial of the Cannibal Dog: The Remarkable Story of Captain Cook's Encounters in the South Seas* (New Haven: Yale University Press, 2003); see also Salmond's *Aphrodite's Island: The European Discovery of Tahiti* (Auckland: Viking and Berkeley: University of California Press, 2009).

He had first observed Europeans during Wallis's visit on the *Dolphin*, and during the *Endeavour*'s visit he became a crucial translator, guide, and intermediary, aiding Banks in his acquisition of cultural artefacts, assisting Cook's and Banks's travels around Tahiti, and sharing time and techniques with the voyage's artists and draughtsmen. Tupaia's charisma, his *taio* friendship with Banks, his knowledge, and his spirited engagement with the Europeans ensured that he was welcomed on-board the expedition's next passage. These factors also ensured that many of the *Endeavour* journals mentioned Tupaia (named under a variety of orthographic forms), sketched his character and his knowledge, and speculated about his motivations. Tupaia entered academic discourse from this moment onwards, as a highly personalized representative of the exotic Pacific world that fascinated voyagers and their home audiences. In that discourse, Tupaia functioned both as an individually distinct, cosmopolitan eighteenth-century Islander, with his own complex (and still only partially understood) motivations, and a synecdoche of Pacific encounter.

Tupaia's presence in the archives lies not only in European representations, but also in material artefacts that he produced: eight watercolour drawings, including an iconic image of Banks trading a sheet of paper with Māori for a lobster, sketches of the Mahaiatea *marae*, botanical drawings, and *'arioi* rituals; and a map of most Polynesian island groups. These too entered European intellectual cultures and academic discourse, and across history they accrued a diverse set of meanings. Tupaia's archival traces are exemplary of the richness of the broader Pacific encounter archive: dense with European texts of various kinds, and filled with material artefacts that stretch from their Pacific origins to many global galleries, museums, universities, and libraries, which sought to place them within European intellectual culture. These diverse textual, material, and artistic representations of Pacific encounter were widely dispersed through circuits of the British Empire, science, and trade from the eighteenth century onwards by prolific collectors such as Banks, who used his Pacific collection both to establish a presence in national institutions such as the British Museum and Kew Gardens, and to further his scientific influence and patronage globally.[67] It is only recently that key aspects of that archive have been

---

[67] S. Werrett, 'Introduction: rethinking Joseph Banks', *Notes and Records: The Royal Society Journal of the History of Science* 73:4 (2019), 1–5; Gascoigne, *Science in the Service of Empire*.

meticulously researched and conserved.[68] In recent Pacific scholarship, better knowledge of the artefacts and their provenance, and academic collaboration with contemporary Pacific communities, have meant that individuals like Tupaia have come increasingly to the fore in their central role in major events in European voyaging, recasting these key moments in history not just as instances of imperial hegemony and Enlightenment science but also as densely imbricated, cross-cultural engagements that changed global history and brought about the modern world, jointly powered by Pacific and European knowledge.

Tupaia's map of the main Polynesian island groups is the most researched and resonant example of this, and it continues to influence academic discourse (Figure 34.2).[69] Emerging first in the voyage accounts of the *Endeavour* crew as material evidence of Tupaia's navigational expertise, the map was variously evaluated (and sometimes dismissed) by different sources as to its veracity and its usefulness.[70] Banks praised Tupaia's religious knowledge but noted that his most valuable skills lay in 'his experience in the navigation of these people and knowledge of the Islands in these seas; he has told us the names of above 70, the most of which he has been at'.[71] Cook declared Tupaia 'the likeliest person to answer our purpose' because of his superior knowledge of Island geography, Island produce, and religious laws and customs.[72] He empowered Tupaia to

---

[68] M. Jolly, 'Moving objects: reflections on Oceanic collections', in E. Gnecchi-Ruscone and A. Paini (eds.), *Tides of Innovation in Oceania: Value, Materiality and Place* (Canberra: ANU Press, 2017), 77–114; N. Thomas, J. Adams, B. Lythberg, M. Nuku, and A. Salmond (eds.), *Artefacts of Encounter: Cook's Voyages, Colonial Collecting, and Museum Histories* (Dunedin: Otago University Press, 2016); N. Chambers et al., *Endeavouring Banks: Exploring Collections from the Endeavour Voyage 1768–1771* (Sydney: Paul Holberton Publishing, University of Washington Press, 2016); H. Parsons, 'British and Tahitian collaborative drawing strategies on Cook's *Endeavour* voyage', in S. Konishi et al. (eds.), *Indigenous Intermediaries*, 147–68; S. Little and P. Ruthenberg (eds.), *Life in the Pacific of the 1700s: The Cook/Forster Collection of the Georg August University of Gottingen*, 3 vols. (Honolulu: Honolulu Academy of Arts, 2006); T. Weber and J. Watson (eds.), *Cook's Pacific Encounters: The Cook-Forster Collection of the Georg-August University of Göttingen* (Canberra: National Museum of Australia, 2006); B. Smith, 'Captain Cook's artists and the portrayal of Pacific peoples ' *Art History* 7:3 (1984), 295–312; A.L. Kaeppler, *'Artificial Curiosities': Being an Exposition of Native Manufactures Collected on the Three Pacific Voyages of Captain James Cook, R.N., at the Bernice Pauahi Bishop Museum, January 18, 1978–August 31, 1978* (Honolulu: Bishop Museum Press, 1978).

[69] See a full colour copy at www.bl.uk/collection-items/the-society-islands.

[70] For an overview of the various accounts, see Salmond, *Aphrodite's Island*, 203–5, 22. New work reconstructing the Tahitian cosmology that influenced Tupaia's mapping was begun by A. Di Piazza and E. Pearthree, 'A new reading of Tupaia's chart', *Journal of the Polynesian Society* 116:3 (2007), 321–40.

[71] J.C. Beaglehole (ed.), *The 'Endeavour' Journal of Joseph Banks 1768–1771*, 2nd edn (Sydney: Public Library of New South Wales with Angus and Robertson, 1963).

[72] J.C. Beaglehole (ed.), *The Journals of Captain James Cook on His Voyages of Discovery*, 4 vols. (Cambridge: Hakluyt Society, 1955–74), vol. I, 117.

pilot the ship through the Leeward Society Islands (and later around Aotorea New Zealand) so that Cook could learn more about Pacific navigation in order to inform his own navigational challenges, set by the Admiralty, and powered by Cook's practical ambition to fulfil his mission to enrich the British map of the Pacific and to locate the Great Southern Land. Various lists of island names dictated by Tupaia were transcribed by Cook and the ship's master Robert Molyneux, and various experiments in mapping were undertaken by Tupaia, beginning with charts of his home island Ra'iatea. Although Cook returned with a chart 'Drawn by Tupia's own hands', none of the original versions appears to have survived, although copies exist in various European archives.[73] Cook's comments about the chart were slight; several editors dismissed its contribution and significance; and it slipped into obscurity until the mid-twentieth century when Cook's definitive editor and biographer J.C. Beaglehole located a copy in Banks's papers in the British Library, and published it in 1955.[74] Tupaia's map steadily gained a place in academic literature about the Pacific: first, as 'part of a heated debate among historians and anthropologists' about ancient Polynesian navigation; then, as potent evidence of the vitality of ethnohistorical or post-colonial approaches to Pacific history; and lately, as part of 'Oceania's political and cultural renaissance'.[75] Ben Finney, among others, united archival research and experimental practical voyaging, consulting with Pacific communities and knowledge holders to produce new understandings of precolonial Pacific wayfinding.[76] More recently, scholars have drawn together European and Pacific traditions of voyaging and suggested that Tupaia's map provides evidence of island navigation and Oceanic knowledge, and others see it as a 'knowledge assemblage' that reveals collaborative map- and meaning-making between Tupaia and select members of the *Endeavour* crew.[77]

---

[73] Beaglehole (ed.), *The Journals of Captain James Cook*, vol. 1, 293.

[74] J. Cook, *Charts and Views: Drawn by Cook and His Officers and Reproduced from the Original Manuscripts*, ed. R.A. Skelton (Cambridge: Hakluyt Society at Cambridge University Press, 1955).

[75] L. Eckstein and A. Schwarz, 'The making of Tupaia's map: a story of the extent and mastery of Polynesian navigation, competing systems of wayfinding on James Cook's *Endeavour*, and the invention of an ingenious cartographic system', *Journal of Pacific History* 54:1 (2019), 1–95, at 2.

[76] B. Finney, 'Myth, experiment, and the reinvention of Polynesian voyaging', *American Anthropologist* 93:2 (1991), 383–404.

[77] Di Piazza and Pearthree, 'A new reading of Tupaia's chart'; D. Turnbull, '(En)-countering knowledge traditions: the story of Cook and Tupaia', in Ballantyne (ed.), *Science, Empire and the European Exploration of the Pacific*, 225–46; A. Salmond, 'Their body is different, our body is different: European and Tahitian navigators in the 18th century', *History and Anthropology* 16:2 (2005), 167–86; D. Turnbull, *Masons, Tricksters and Cartographers: Comparative Studies in the Sociology of Scientific and Indigenous Knowledge* (Amsterdam: Harwood Academic, 2000).

Most recently, an entire issue of one of the key journals for Pacific scholarship – the *Journal of Pacific History*, edited from the Australian National University – was dedicated to a book-length article comparing the three existing archival versions of Tupaia's map in order to reconstruct the map's method of construction and refining, and to attempt a 'conclusive interpretation of the chart as a whole'.[78] This fascinating archival exercise compares 1770, 1776, and 1778 copies to reconstruct a conjectured series of draft stages of Tupaia's map first undertaken on board the *Endeavour*, with Tupaia and European officers and select crew crammed around the great cabin's drawing table, seeking to communicate across different languages, navigational systems, and modes of representation. Eckstein and Schwarz paint a compelling picture of 'a collaborative, cross-cultural communication process that by default involved at least two, if not more partners', suggesting that Tupaia was lodged 'at the heart of knowledge production about the South Seas'.[79] Their complex and ambitious analysis imagines European draftsmen providing Tupaia with a rough sketch to fill in, then Tupaia inventing a new visual system to combine his navigational knowledge based on wayfaring chants, personal experience of the Ocean across various seasons, and astronomical bearings with the singular representational model of a European chart.[80] Like the Europeans around the drawing table, Eckstein and Schwarz bring in linguistic lists from the *Endeavour* archive and various journal accounts to build their case for Tupaia's *avatea* system (which situates positional north at the noon position of the sun as central to Polynesian wayfinding). They also take archival sources such as Tupaia's five Tahitian captions on the map – first written down by the *Endeavour* officers, then variously (and liberally) translated by subsequent sources – back to French Polynesia, where Hinano Teavai-Murphy worked with them to provide alternative translations.[81] Their reading of Tupaia positions him 'as a cultural intermediary whose ability to translate one highly complex system of wayfinding, of representational world-making and ultimately of cosmology into a very different order of knowledge far exceeded the abilities of any of his European interlocutors'.[82] Their vision is compelling. The series of responses published by leading scholars in the subsequent journal issue

---

[78] Eckstein and Schwarz, 'The making of Tupaia's map' contains a range of academic responses to Eckstein and Schwarz's new reading of Tupaia's map, and an additional authors' response.
[79] Eckstein and Schwarz, 'The making of Tupaia's map', 5.
[80] Eckstein and Schwarz, 'The making of Tupaia's map', 32.
[81] Eckstein and Schwarz, 'The making of Tupaia's map', 80–8.
[82] Eckstein and Schwarz, 'The making of Tupaia's map', 90–1.

indicate that the history, science, and mythology of Tupaia's map is not yet settled definitively, and it is both the natural world of the Pacific and the archival sources of European encounter that bring extra evidence to bear upon the broader arguments of the scholarly field.[83] Eckstein and Schwarz are perhaps most persuasive in their closing characterization of Tupaia's map as 'a living document of the enlarged world of Oceania', one which is both deeply historic and yet profoundly agentic in the present both for scholars and for Pacific communities.

Conclusion: An Infected Vision of the Pacific

This example demonstrates how pervasively the Pacific encounter entered European knowledge systems, archives, and intellectual thought and how it continues to provoke speculation and new attempts at knowledge production. From the outset, this encounter between cultures and knowledges was generative of new information, new interpersonal connections, and new visual, textual, and material forms that attempted to represent the novelty and opportunity of cross-cultural exchange. This archive of encounter has always been shot through with power, ideology, and racialized thought yet it cannot simply be reduced or dismissed for these European prejudices. Not least, it remains available for Pacific peoples – as well as scholars of diverse ethnicities and locations – to interpret, display, and contest.

Like Eckstein and Schwarz, Lisa Reihena engaged closely with the European archive of encounter to repeople Dufour's 1802 wallpaper with Pacific, Aboriginal, and Māori people and practices that she recognized, in response to the incomprehensible 'exotic' figures she saw depicted in the static museum display.[84] The 'infection' of her work's title is a subtle and multivalent signifier, referring to the venereal disease that Cook's ships brought to the Pacific, which troubled Cook's passage and management of his crew, and damaged Islander health. Yet it is also an infected point of view (she notes that the acronym POV is shared with Pursuit of Venus), a new and

---

[83] A. Anderson, 'Alternative perspectives upon Tupaia's mapmaking', *Journal of Pacific History* 54:4 (2019), 537–43; A. Di Piazza and E. Pearthree, 'Does the avatea system offer a new key for reading Tupaia's maps?', *Journal of Pacific History* 54:4 (2019), 543–9; B. Douglas, 'Tupaia's map', *Journal of Pacific History* 54:4 (2019), 529–30; L. Eckstein and A. Schwarz, 'Authors' response: the making of Tupaia's Map revisited', *Journal of Pacific History* 54:4 (2019), 549–56; A. Salmond, 'Hidden hazards: reconstructing Tupaia's chart', *Journal of Pacific History* 54:4 (2019), 534–37; D. Turnbull, 'Eckstein and Schwarz's translation of Tupaia's chart: the Rosetta Stone of Polynesian navigation?', *Journal of Pacific History* 54:4 (2019), 530–4.
[84] See Reihana's artist talks at www.inpursuitofvenus.com/artist-talks.

challenging perspective on the English explorers and their Enlightenment culture. Most importantly in her video work, Pacific performers put their own vision into the European vision of the Pacific, to make the familiar strange again. Tupaia, Banks, Parkinson, and Purea all feature in Reihana's re-visioning of Pacific encounters: their narrative traces are made to live anew and differently. Reihana's work challenges audiences to look again at the past, and to consider where they might choose to look, to identify, and to imagine themselves in the narratives of the past that continue, like Tupaia's map, to have a vibrant life in shaping aesthetic and cultural domains both in Oceania and in the global world with which the region is profoundly entangled.

35

The Phantom Empire

Japan in Oceania and Oceania in Japan from the 1890s Onward

GREG DVORAK

Na mo shiranu tōki shima yori,	From an island whose name I know not,
Nagare-yoru yashi no mi hitotsu ...	a coconut floated ashore ...*[1]

Drifting Coconuts, Forgotten Islands

At some point in 1898, famed Japanese folklorist Yanagita Kunio[2] was walking along the long, sandy beach of Iragonomisaki, Aichi Prefecture – not far from the site of the present-day Toyota car manufacturing factory – when he stumbled upon a dried coconut that had washed up in the surf. Fascinated by this and insistent that it proved Japanese connections to southern tropical islands via the Kuroshio (Pacific) Current,[3] he mentioned his discovery to his friend, the poet Shimazaki Tōson, who would later memorialize the moment in the first lines (above) of his wistful poem, 'Yashinomi' (Coconut), written in 1901 and set to music by Ōnaka Toraji in 1936.

I open with this episode to foreground the Japanese romance and engagement with Oceania that began around the turn of the twentieth century. Shimazaki's 'Coconut', a ballad of wanderlust and desire, is written in the voice of a restless spirit. These lyrics embody the dreams of the burgeoning Japanese modern nation-state as it looks yearningly towards the exotic world

---

[1] T. Shimazaki, *Shimazaki Tōson Zenshū II (Collected Works of Shimazaki Tōson, II)*. Tokyo: Shinchōsha, 1949 [1901]. Japanese names mentioned in the text in this chapter are written as per Japanese convention with family name first, except when a work published in English by an author with a Japanese name is cited, in which case I have written the family name last.
[2] Yanagita Kunio (1875–1962) was considered one of the founders of *minzokugaku* or Japanese folklore studies.
[3] Yanagita expounded upon this early discovery that Japanese origins were to be found in Okinawa and in the south in one of his final works published after the Pacific War, *Kaijō no Michi* (Passage on the Sea. 1961), but his 'drift' theories of migration were largely discredited by post-war researchers as being nostalgic for the Okinawan territories lost during the War and ungrounded in science, appropriating 'primitive' Okinawan culture for the sake of justifying Japanese imperialism.

that lies beyond its edges.[4] Today, it is mainly sung tearily by the bereaved elderly children of fallen Japanese soldiers from World War II, whose nostalgia and mourning for lost fathers and undelivered imperial promises are never soothed. Coconuts, as we shall see, are the stuff of both fantasies and nightmares.

Japan's historical involvement in Oceania goes largely unacknowledged today by most outside observers, let alone most contemporary Japanese. The visit of Japan's former emperor and empress to pay their respects to the war victims of Saipan in 2005 or Palau in 2015 ignited the curiosity of a new generation of younger Japanese who had no awareness of the extent of their nation's trans-oceanic trespasses, leading to journalism and books in Japanese about Japan's 'forgotten islands'.[5]

This chapter contemplates the traces of Japan's Pacific past – a phantom geography of buried histories, networks, and memories long forgotten. For many people in Japan this geography is an invisible and forgotten *nesia* – a veritable archipelago we might nickname 'Am-nesia' – that endures beneath the surface of its better-known nesian counterparts of Poly-, Mela-, and Micro-. For the countless war-bereaved families of Japanese war dead, many of these islands and waters are, in contrast, sites of memory, virtual cemeteries haunted by the phantoms of loved ones. But here I use the term 'phantom' more metaphoric-ally; like the uncanny phenomenon of the 'phantom limb' experienced by amputees, who feel their missing appendage hurt even though it has long been removed, many Pacific Islanders – especially in northern Oceania – viscerally sense the presence and sometimes the pain of Japan's enduring influence as if it were yesterday. By 1945, the superficial trappings of Japanese empire had largely been erased from most of Oceania – settlers, soldiers, towns, language, culture, and infrastructure abruptly excised after half a century of intense involvement and influence. Here I reference Merleau-Ponty's meditations on the phantom limb phenomenon, which he argues is not only the sense of a 'limb' that once was attached to the body but can also be an experience in some people who sense the presence of a limb that was never attached in the first place.[6] Many Islanders whose lives and lands were colonized and occupied by the

---

[4] M. Bourdaghs, *The Dawn that Never Comes: Shimazaki Tōson and Japanese Nationalism* (New York: Columbia University Press, 2003), 11.

[5] R. Hasegawa, *Chizu kara Kieta Shimajima: Maboroshi no Nihon-ryō to Nanyō Tankenka-tachi* (The Islands that Disappeared from the Map: Phantom Japanese Territories and Japanese Southern Explorers). Tokyo: Yoshikawa Kōbunkan, 2011; M. Inoue, *Wasurerareta Shimajima: 'Nanyō Guntō' no Gendai-shi* (Forgotten Islands: A Modern History of the South Sea Islands of Japan). Tokyo: Heibonsha Shinsho, 2015.

[6] M. Merleau-Ponty, *Phenomenology of Perception* (London: Routledge, 1986), 82–6.

Japanese empire not only contextualize their contemporary world in relation to the traumas and nostalgias of an empire that no longer exists, but also recuperate and perpetuate elements of imperial Japan in the present, as part of maintaining cultural integrity.

In English, very few histories of Japan's involvement in Oceania in the twentieth century exist, the most significant being Peattie's landmark volume *Nan'yō: The Rise and Fall of the Japanese in Micronesia, 1885–1945* (1988), which deals mainly with the political history of Japan's colonization of northern Oceania in the first half of the twentieth century. Aside from this, though primary sources and anthropological studies abound, recent histories that provide a critical and comprehensive overview in Japanese are also scarce. Kawamura, Yano, Kobayashi, Imaizumi, and others have provided nuanced considerations of Japanese empire in the Pacific Islands,[7] but further work is needed to compile and thread together these rich and complex narratives of interconnectivity, broadening the scope to embrace all of Oceania and contemporary considerations as well. This brief chapter does not promise to provide such a comprehensive narrative; it would be presumptuous to suggest that the entirety of Japan's engagement with Oceania could be covered in anything less than several volumes. It does, nonetheless, gesture towards some of the key themes that characterize Japanese historical linkages to the Pacific, especially Japan's colonization of Micronesia, an area it renamed the Nanyō Guntō (the South Seas Islands), to offer clues to the contours of this phantom empire today, and also how Japan projected, and to some extent continues to project, its power throughout the entire region.

Contrary to popular myths of an impenetrable, isolated, homogeneous, or consistent nation from ancient times, Japan itself is porous, diverse, and constantly changing – its manifestation as a unified nation-state being a relatively recent phenomenon.[8] Japan is itself an archipelago in the Pacific Ocean – over 6,850 islands, linked by water and undersea volcanic ranges to other archipelagoes, and its histories are deeply entwined with other islands

---

[7] M. Kawamura, *Nanyō-Karafuto no Nihon Bungaku* (Japanese Literature of the South Seas and Sakhalin) (Tokyo: Chikuma Shobō, 1994); Yano Tōru, *Nanshin no Keifu: Nihon no Nanyō Shikan* (The History of 'Southbound Expansion of Japan': Historical Patterns of Japanese Views on Southeast Asia) (Tokyo: Chikura Shobō, 2009); I. Kobayashi, 'Japan's diplomacy towards member countries of Pacific Islands Forum: significance of Pacific Islands Leaders Meeting (PALM)', *Asia-Pacific Review* 25:2 (2018), 89–103; Y. Imaizumi, *Nihon Teikoku Hōkaiki 'Hikiage' no Hikaku Kenkyū* (Comparative Studies of 'Returnees' during the Fall of the Japanese Empire) (Tokyo: Nihon Keizai Hyōronsha, 2016).

[8] Historian Oguma Eiji writes extensively about the myth of Japanese homogeneity and the production of Japan as a modern nation in the popular imagination in his groundbreaking work *A Genealogy of 'Japanese' Self Images* (Melbourne: Trans Pacific Press, 2002).

in its extended Pacific neighbourhood. Contemporary Japan reaches from the Arctic ice floes of Hokkaido in the north to the tropical reefs of Okinawa in the south, two poles of Indigenous lands that were violently annexed – the former being crafted out of the vast Ainu territories formally assimilated in 1869, the latter, out of the overthrown Ryukyu Kingdom in 1879.[9] But in the early half of the twentieth century, imperial conquest expanded Japan's boundaries much farther – from Sakhalin (Karafuto) in the north, to Manchuria in the west, across to Mili Atoll in the Marshall Islands to the east, and, during the war years, all the way down to the whole island of New Guinea (present day Papua New Guinea and West Papua). Though the empire was crushed by Japan's defeat in World War II, even today some of Japan's territories, like the island chains of Ogasawara (Bonin) and Iō (Iwojima) – administered as part of the Tokyo Metropolis – sit ambiguously in an area of the Pacific Ocean originally designated on European maps as 'Micronesia'.

Writer Shimao Toshio once declared the Japanese archipelagic complex to be its own insular Pacific island grouping he called 'Yaponesia', and in some ways, this is a useful (if problematic) concept to reflect on Japan's larger cultural articulations in the region.[10] Having once expanded in World War II to encompass much of Asia/Pacific, today the country only covers a relatively small geographic corner of Oceania; yet, legacies fraught with encounter, exchange, romance, violence, death, memory, and amnesia between Japan and the archipelagoes to its south and west constitute a phantom empire that still haunts the present. Its traces are hidden in plain sight in jungles, on beaches, and beneath the sea, with thousands of Pacific Islanders of Japanese or Okinawan heritage still seeking their families in Japan. The remains of countless Japanese soldiers lost during the war still sleep in the coral sediment of many Pacific places.

One of Japan's earliest historical records documenting linkages with 'strangers adrift from the South' is in the *Kokon Chomonjū*, a thirteenth-century document that describes these likely Pacific Islander visitors as *oni* (demons) who rode the Kuroshio (Pacific Current) north to the Izu region of

---

[9] The Indigenous names for these places are, Yaun-Mosir for Hokkaido itself and Ainu-mosir referring to all Ainu homelands (meaning, respectively, 'country land' and 'the quiet land of humans' – known before by Japanese as Ezo); and for the Ryukyu archipelago, Uruma (meaning 'the timespace between coral reefs'), according to anthropologist Imafuku Ryūta; see R. Imafuku, 'Noah's stories in shaky archipelagos: Martinique, Haiti, Fukushima', *Open Democracy*, 8 June, 2012.

[10] K. Hanazaki, 'Ainu Moshir and Yaponesia: Ainu and Okinawan identities in contemporary Japan', in D. Denoon, M. Hudson, and G. McCormack (eds.), *Multicultural Japan: Paleolithic to Postmodern* (Cambridge: Cambridge University Press, 2001), 117–31, at 129–30.

the country in 1171.[11] There were probably other maritime exchanges with a broader Oceanic community, and further research can illuminate deeper connections between Indigenous communities in Japan – particularly Okinawans – and Austronesian communities throughout Asia and Oceania. For the most part, however, despite their awareness of the coastal marine environment, Japanese perceptions of the oceanic world beyond the horizon belonged to the world of mythology.

Modern Japanese knowledge about Oceania only really began to proliferate in the late Edo period (seventeenth–nineteenth centuries), at a time when Japanese explorers began to venture out towards the Ogasawara Islands, and when European explorers' travel logs and maps were translated into Japanese. Ogasawara became a pivotal site of contact with Westerners, such as Commodore Matthew Perry's expeditions to Japan between 1853 and 1854, as well as an experimental staging ground from which Japanese pioneers and settlers would reach into the Mariana Islands.[12] Just before the Meiji Restoration that ended Japan's self-imposed isolation and 'opened' the country to the world, Japanese castaway Nakahama (John) Manjiro and his comrades were among the first to encounter Pacific Islanders in their own lands as they travelled all around Oceania.[13] Manjiro would also join the first Japanese diplomatic mission to the United States in 1860, which reported on its visit to Hawai'i.

Under an official state policy of emigration beginning in the late nineteenth century, Japanese and Okinawans – especially from rural and poorer families – began to seek economic opportunities outside Japan. Migrant sugar plantation labourers had already begun to settle in Hawai'i, for example, as early as 1868, and their experiences led to more nuanced and first-hand Japanese knowledge of Pacific places, at least from the perspective of life under Western colonialism. This knowledge slowly found its way back to Japan and would eventually lead to a Japanese interest and admiration for Hawaiian culture, particularly music and dance.[14] Japanese migration also would gradually give Hawaiians and other Pacific Islanders the awareness

---

[11] T. Akimichi, 'Japanese views on Oceania in modernist images of Paradise', in K. Yoshida and J. Mack (eds.), *Images of Other Cultures: Re-viewing Ethnographic Collections of the British Museum and the National Museum of Ethnology, Osaka* (Tokyo: NHK Service Center, 1997), 244.

[12] J. Rüegg, 'Mapping the forgotten colony: the Ogasawara Islands and the Tokugawa pivot to the Pacific', *Cross-Currents: East Asian History and Culture Review E-Journal* 23 (2017).

[13] J. Nagakuni and J. Kitadai, *Drifting toward the Southeast: The Story of Five Japanese Castaways Told in 1852 by John Manjiro* (New Bedford: Spinner Publications. 2003).

[14] Y. Yaguchi, *Akogare no Hawai: Nihonjin no Hawai-kan* (*Hawaiian Yearning: Japanese Perspectives on Hawai'i*) (Tokyo: Chūō Kōron Shinsha, 2011).

The Phantom Empire

that their islands were being inundated not only by European and American settlers but also by the 'Asian settler colonialism' that brought waves of Japanese, Chinese, Indian, and Filipino migrants throughout the region.[15] These were not one-way encounters: in 1881, as part of his world tour, Hawaiian King Kalākaua paid a visit to Japan and met the Meiji Emperor. He praised Japan's strength and, after encouraging his fellow monarch to lead Asian countries in fending off powerful Western regimes, he also proposed that Japanese Prince Komatsu marry Hawaiian Princess Kaiulani.[16] Japan would go on to dominate all of Asia and Oceania in the decades that followed, but this royal marriage proposal was rejected.

By the 1880s, Japanese had also built up a substantial population in Western Australia and Papua in the pearl diving industry. Communities of Japanese divers also lived in the commercial centre of Rabaul in German New Guinea, where the colonial government gave them the legal status of Europeans, unlike other Asian migrants.[17] In 1884, one party of Japanese pearlers heading back home from Broome got caught in a storm and shipwrecked in Lae, Marshall Islands, where they were reportedly murdered by order of *irooj* (chief) Larrelia. Investigating this incident became the pretext for an official government visit by explorers Suzuki Keikun (Tsunenori) and Gotō Taketarō, who used the mission as a chance to travel around the Marshall Islands and other parts of Oceania. They later chronicled their journeys in a fanciful account titled *Nanyō Tanken Jikki* (A Record of South Seas Exploration), a book by 'raconteur' Suzuki that embellished and conflated ethnography from various Pacific locales, including not only Micronesian islands but also Hawai'i, Sāmoa, and Indigenous Australia.[18] This journey, and Suzuki's subsequent voyages to Oceania – however spuriously documented – yielded colourful maps, illustrations, and descriptions that piqued the imaginations of elite readers back in Japan, encouraging

---

[15] C. Fujikane and J. Okamura, *Asian Settler Colonialism: From Local Governance to the Habits of Everyday Life in Hawai'i* (Honolulu: University of Hawai'i Press, 2008).

[16] Matsuda points out that, while more and more waves of Japanese were settling in the Hawaiian Islands, King Kalākaua impressed upon the Japanese emperor that it was Japan's destiny to lead Asia in confronting the formidable power of Western regimes, and that he would gladly serve as Japan's 'vassal'; see M.K. Matsuda, *Pacific Worlds: A History of Seas, Peoples and Cultures* (Cambridge: Cambridge University Press, 2012), 242.

[17] R. Crocombe, *Asia in the Pacific Islands: Replacing the West* (Suva: University of the South Pacific for the Institute of Pacific Studies, 2007), 45.

[18] J. Takayama, *Nankai no Daitankenka Suzuki Tsunenori (Suzuki Tsunenori, the Great Adventurer of the Southern Seas)* (Tokyo: Sanichi Shobō, 1995); R. Nishino, 'The awakening of a journalist's historical consciousness: Sasa Yukie's Pacific Island journeys of 2005–2006', *Japanese Studies* 37:1 (2017), 71–88.

the expansionism that was yet to come. Many of the original watercolour sketches that accompany the original manuscript in the Japan Diplomatic Records Office at the Ministry of Foreign Affairs in Tokyo, painted on thin paper, inscribe Japanese *ukiyo-e* style flourishes on Micronesian landscapes, early artistic colonizations that imagine Oceania as a Japanese frontier waiting to be settled.

Navigating Nanyō

Mark Peattie writes about how *nanshin*, or 'southern advance', was at first a vaguely defined and controversial expansionist dream of building up the southern frontier of 'Nanyō' (sometimes spelled Nan'yō in English).[19] Nanyō, written in Japanese with the characters for 'south' and 'seas', was a word that had already been in use in China[20] to refer to oceanic places but moreover to Chinese southern coastal areas, and later to refer to Southeast Asian sites beyond that. The anti-Western intellectual and expansionist Shiga Shigetaka was among the first Japanese writers to appropriate the concept of Nanyō as a term that corresponded more to regional/cultural spheres like 'the West' (Seiyō) or 'the East' (Tōyō).[21] For Japanese of the early twentieth century, Nanyō was thus an expansive third-space wilderness, a 'Southern Frontier' that loosely encompassed *all* of maritime Oceania and most of Southeast Asia as well. Any archival search in Japan today for the keyword 'Nanyō' is more likely to return results for Java, the Philippines, or even Australia rather than proper Pacific islands, as those resource-rich areas were more interesting to Japanese economic pioneers. This enlarged view of Greater Nanyō (Dai Nanyō), with Taipei as its main economic and administrative hub, and Micronesia as merely an insular nearby island buffer for the Japanese home islands, is an image that has not been articulated in many English-language works on this history, but viewing the region in this way can reveal Japan's bigger ambitions for expansion.[22]

---

[19] M. Peattie, *Nan'yō: The Rise and Fall of the Japanese in Micronesia, 1885–1945* (Honolulu: University of Hawai'i Press, 1988), 36–7.

[20] In Chinese, it is Nanyang.

[21] T. Yano, *Nanshin no Keifu: Nihon no Nanyō Shikan* (The History of 'Southbound Expansion of Japan': Historical Patterns of Japanese Views on Southeast Asia) (Tokyo: Chikura Shobō, 2009), 41–2.

[22] For more on Japan's expansive imagination of empire as portrayed through travel and tourism in Korea, Taiwan, and Manchuria in the twentieth century, see, for example, K. MacDonald, *Placing Empire: Travel and the Social Imagination in Imperial Japan* (Oakland: University of California Press, 2017).

Japanese engagement with Oceania did not intensify until the 1890s. At first, Japan's 'expansion' consisted simply of large numbers of Japanese migrants settling in places like the Philippines, Hawai'i, Thailand, and other sites around Asia and the Pacific. As a sort of backwater to which Japanese could emigrate, and where business opportunities might flourish, these southbound trajectories made sense. For many Japanese leaders, therefore, the pursuit of territory in Oceania seemed pointless. Yet, after Japan annexed Taiwan in 1895, and Korea in 1910, the prestige of controlling oceanic as well as continental territory, and of accessing more resources, began to generate appeal, and more and more influential figures began to write enthusiastically about the merits of Japanese southern expansion.

It was in this spirit of *nanshin* that Shiga, joined by other enterprising leaders like Hattori Toru and Taguchi Ukichi, began to imagine Nanyō as a vast space of potential for Japan. Building on initial business developments in

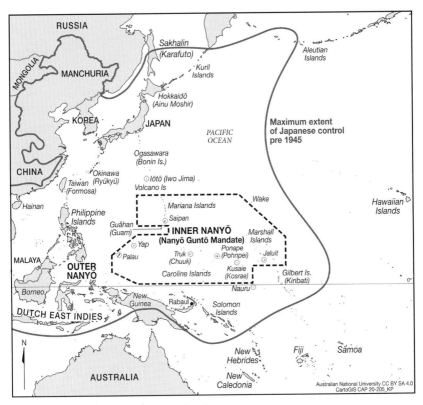

Figure 35.1 Map of Inner and Outer Nanyō.

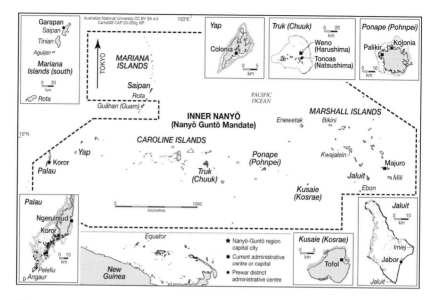

Figure 35.1 (cont.)

the Ogasawara Islands, which Japan had absorbed in 1875, Taguchi was one of several business leaders who struggled to build a successful trading business between Japan and Micronesia. Although this was ultimately unsuccessful, the fact that this was even attempted, and written about so extensively, led to other entrepreneurs taking risks, leading eventually to the formation of two trading companies, the Hiki and Murayama companies, which merged in 1908 to become the influential and ubiquitous Nanyō Bōeki Kaisha (NBK), the South Seas Trading Company, a corporation that still endures to the present day.[23]

As business interests ventured into the islands nearest to Japan, the idea of Nanyō grew from a vague geographic hinterland into concrete reality as more and more Japanese ventured out into Oceania. An early Japanese pioneer who became deeply involved in the Pacific Islands was Mori Koben, who hailed from a samurai family from Tosa (present-day Kōchi Prefecture), and had in his youth learned about Micronesia when he worked for the family of the explorer Gotō Taketarō.[24] This led to his joining a trading company that sent him to work as their representative, and in 1891 he

[23] Peattie, Nan'yō, 25.   [24] Peattie, Nan'yō, 27.

travelled to the Marianas and Pohnpei before finally settling in Chuuk, marrying a local chiefly woman and fathering many children.[25]

In the intervening years, the United States military fought with Spain in 1898, claiming Guam (Guåhan) and the Philippines, and also annexing the Hawaiian Kingdom. Financially ruined, Spain sold its territories in Micronesia to Germany in 1899. Mori somehow managed to weather this upheaval when German officials ousted other Japanese businessmen in the area, giving him status as a key representative who helped keep Japanese interests afloat in the early days of German rule.[26] But soon NBK and several other trading companies gained a foothold throughout the islands, expanding Japanese economic influence and presence.

Having entered into an alliance with the British Empire in 1902 to resist Russian expansion into Japanese territory, when Britain declared war on Germany in 1914 Japan offered to assist its ally in the Pacific region. Within months of declaring war on Germany, Japan swiftly occupied the Marshall Islands, Pohnpei, Kosrae, Chuuk, Yap, Palau, and Saipan with minimal resistance.[27] Japan then went on to attack German-held sites and ships in and around China, resulting in German surrender by November 1914. These islands soon began to appear on Japanese maps as the Nanyō Guntō (the 'South Seas Islands'), or alternatively 'Uchi Nanyō' ('Inner' Nanyō – as opposed to just Nanyō or 'Soto' Nanyō, the 'Outer', broader and vaguely defined expanse of non-Japanese territory to the south).[28] In 1922, under a League of Nations Class C Mandate, Japanese rule in these islands – which had been administered by the occupying Imperial Navy for eight years – was transferred to a civilian government called the Nanyō-chō, headquartered in Koror, Palau.

The Nanyō-chō

The new Nanyō Guntō did not encompass the entirety of what Europeans had referred to as 'Micronesia', let alone what Islanders themselves knew of their islands, their ancient seafaring routes, or genealogical connections.

---

[25] According to the Federated States of Micronesia Embassy in Tokyo, Mori's descendants now number in the thousands.
[26] I. Kobayashi Izumi, *Minami no Shima no Nihonjin (The Japanese of the Southern Islands)* (Tokyo: Sankei Shimbun Shuppan, 2010), 80–1.
[27] Peattie, *Nan'yō*, 43–4.
[28] Alternatively the distinction was made between Ura (Rear) Nanyō to refer to the Nanyō Guntō or Dai (Greater) Nanyō to refer to the broader region as a whole.

It did not include Kiribati, Nauru, or Guam, for example (the former two dominated by Britain, the latter by the United States). With the coming of Japanese administrators, business people, and ordinary settlers, the colonial histories of the Nanyō Guntō Islands drastically diverged from those of surrounding islands. Indigenous children in Guam studied American presidents and the English language, for example, while their relatives in Saipan studied about the Japanese emperor and Japanese grammar. In both cases, as with all colonial experiences throughout Oceania, Islanders were not encouraged by colonizers to value their own histories and cultures.

For the first years of Japanese rule in Micronesia, the Imperial Navy clumsily initiated an educational programme, taking over for the Western mission schools that had taught throughout the Nanyō Guntō. They also began to establish hospitals, a postal service, and various communication services. Japanese companies like NBK; Nanyō Kohatsu Kaisha (NKK), a development firm that built up sugar and other industries mainly in Saipan; or Nanyō Takushoku Kaisha (Nantaku), which focused especially on mining phosphate and other resources, began to set up business throughout the islands. Later, civilian administrators came, wearing their crisp white uniforms, operating within a bureaucratic structure that worked much like any Japanese provincial government, with a 'branch office' of the main Nanyō-cho Headquarters in Palau set up in the main town of each island group.

Japanese power and infrastructure were firmly established in each district in a way that no previous colonial entity had attempted in Micronesia. Traditional leaders were recruited into serving as largely symbolic *sonchō*, or village mayors, a way for Japanese to exploit the pre-existing power structure, while pulling chiefs away from their constituents, and realigning the true source of power in the islands with the imperial throne. In many places – like the extensive rural atolls throughout the region – at first there was virtually no Japanese presence or 'development' at all. For example, most of the Marshall Islands changed little in the first decade of Japanese rule and only a handful of atolls had Japanese residents. Jaluit Atoll (which Japanese pronounced Yarūto, imitating the German, not Marshallese, pronunciation of the name) became a small but bustling village of several hundred Japanese and Okinawan settlers, featuring a power plant, weather station, and other utilities, a public school for Islanders, a hospital – and several shops, selling kimono, noodles, *kakigōri* shaved ice, and other Japanese staples and delicacies. Later, schools and businesses would be erected on various distant islands throughout Micronesia, but away from district centres the most visible Japanese influence, if any, consisted only of pier facilities and a handful of shops. Still, land throughout the islands that had been collectively managed by Islanders was gradually privatized under Japanese rule, and then sold or leased, dramatically changing traditional land tenure and leaving a long-term mark on most places.

The first wave of migrants who came to these islands from the Japanese homeland under the Nanyō-chō administration were colonial elites – such as administrators, schoolteachers, doctors, and postal workers – and corporate businessmen sent by companies such as NBK. Fishermen, farmers, small businessmen, and other settlers from all throughout Japan would follow. With few exceptions, most of these first settlers were men. In some cases, Japanese businessmen followed in the tradition of Mori Koben, fathering children with local women, some choosing to remain long-term in the islands with their local girlfriends. Because so many of the islands of Micronesia have matrilineal societies (with the notable exception of patrilineal Yap), in some respects local women benefited from these liaisons, leveraging power to protect their land and bloodlines against Japanese conquest.[29] In more distant or rural areas, Japanese men, too, benefited from the protection afforded by marrying into local families, building up a meaningful sense of trust among Indigenous populations. Aside from Japanese authorities frowning on or forbidding such relationships, the bitter reality was that most of these businessmen were expected to enter into arranged marriages waiting for them back in Japan. Many never told their families back home about their wives or children in Micronesia. For Islanders, whose local customs often equated cohabitation with marriage, this came as a shock. Some men, to the displeasure of local communities, even formally married in Japan and then brought their new Japanese wives to the Nanyō Guntō to live alongside their Micronesian wives and children. Some younger Japanese men like Ishiwata Tatsunosuke (Figure 35.2) became deeply involved in local life, learning the language and buying land to pass down to their mixed-heritage children, earning them the respect of the communities where they resided.

Later, entire families would move to the region, lured by government incentives, advertisements that promised a comfortable lifestyle, job opportunities such as the NKK's booming sugar manufacturing plant in Saipan, good medical care and Japanese amenities, and warm weather. A steady flow

---

[29] Kobayashi, *Minami no Shima no Nihonjin*, 145–50.

Figure 35.2 Ishiwata Tatsunosuke was an employee of Nanyō Takushoku Kaisha (Nantaku) Phosphate Mining Division in Ebon Atoll, Marshall Islands, who married a Marshallese woman and had two daughters. Here he poses with local children on Ebon c. 1936.

of people, including thousands of Okinawans, began to emigrate to the Nanyō Guntō through the 1920s to 1930s, reaching over 70,000 people in 1938.

Race, Identity, and 'Development' in the Nanyō Guntō

In crafting the narrative of undeveloped primitive people in desperate need of civilization by a modern state, Japan used racialized ideologies to justify and perpetuate its colonial project. Showing the world that Japan could serve as an exemplary developing power was important to Japanese leaders, as politically it helped them to position Japan strategically on a par with Western nations as a contemporary, imperial nation-state. Under obligation by Mandate rules to notify the League of Nations about its progress towards developing Micronesia, Japan's reports were meticulously written in English and painted a portrait of Japan as a benevolent big brother who tended to the colonial burden of the 'backward' natives. This stood in contrast to Japan's treatment of other colonized subjects in its empire: unlike in the 'Outer Nanyō' colony of Taiwan – or in Korea, and later in Manchuria – where Japanese rule was far more militaristic and violent, colonialism in the mandated territories was a showcase for development. In 1933, Japan declared it would withdraw from the League of Nations, but it continued to submit its annual reports about the mandated territories of the Nanyō Guntō, even after its formal withdrawal in 1935, up until 1938, still emphasizing its responsibility to the colonized Islanders in its custody as a 'mandatory power'.[30]

What these reports did not indicate clearly to the world was that, as the Japanese population swelled throughout the Nanyō Guntō, a de facto racial hierarchy began to emerge, to be reinforced formally by official regulations, business practices, educational institutions, and ethnological discourses. To begin with, Japanese discursively erased all of the distinctions between the incredibly diverse societies and communities that stretched across nearly all of northern Oceania, from Palau in the far west to the edge of the Marshall Islands on the other side of the mandated territories. Instead of referring to people as 'Palauan', 'Yapese', or 'Pohnpeian', Japanese discourses flattened all Indigenous people into the categories *Kanaka* or *Chamoro*, two racialized groupings that were imagined to be present throughout the islands, determined by skin colour. *Kanaka* (a term appropriated from Polynesian languages and converted into derogatory slang by European colonists before it was adapted into Japanese) referred to 'Black' Islanders, who were the most numerous throughout the islands, and who Japanese determined were 'primitive, docile, and simple-minded' but 'hard-working'.[31] *Chamoro* is another stolen term: appropriated from the word Chamorro (CHamoru), usually used by Indigenous people of the Mariana Islands to describe their ethnic identity, Japanese officials reappropriated the word to refer any Islander in the entire Nanyō Guntō who had European mixed ancestry. Based on this anti-Black ideology, their whiteness was deemed to make them

---

[30] W. Higuchi, 'Japan and war reparations in Micronesia', *Journal of Pacific History* 30:1 (1995), 87–98, at 87.

[31] Here I am alluding to primary sources such as films, postcards, and photo books from the 1920s–1930s, which frequently used these tropes. One of the most explicit examples of the perpetuation of this narrative is Saeki Eisuke's 1932 film *Umi no Seimeisen: Waga Nanyō Shotō (Lifeline of the Sea: Our South Southern Islands)* (Yokohama: Yokohama Cinema Shōkai, 1932), 35 mm, 16 mm; 72 min. film, 'talkie' version (archived by Mainichi Films Company, Tokyo and Japan National Film Center, Tokyo).

Figure 35.3 Postcards of *Kanaka* (left) and *Chamoro* (right) produced during the 1930s (personal collection of the author). The postcard on the left, 'Customs of Kanaka at Saipan Islet', is captioned in Japanese by the words 'abundant male beauty' (*yutaka na dansei bi*), and an explanation that reads 'Kanaka Natives: The Kanaka race who live around the islands of Saipan decorate their bodies when they dance with aesthetic objects, such as necklaces and belts, objects more valuable than those of other Islanders and are therefore precious possessions'. The postcard on the right depicts a 'CHamoru' young woman from Jaluit, Marshall Islands (where no actual Indigenous CHamoru people would have lived).

more 'cultured' and intelligent than their Kanaka counterparts; so sophisticated that they all were said to keep pianos in their homes.[32] Even without having the slightest relationship to actual Chamorro people, Islanders who had European features – even if they lived on the opposite side of Micronesia from the Mariana Islands and would not identify as such – were referred to as *Chamoro*. Highly racialized studies were also conducted by Japanese scientists, such as the anthropometric research of Hasebe Kotondo, who compared and measured the skulls and facial features of Indigenous *Kanaka* versus *Chamoro* throughout the Nanyō Guntō in much the same spirit as

[32] This theme is also elaborated in the film *Umi no Seimeisen*.

the racist research on colonized 'Natives' undertaken by Western anthropologists in the same period (Figure 35.3).[33]

Racialized ethnological research was used as justification to promote Japanese narratives of supremacy, as well as the stratification of local society. Higuchi Wakako depicts the social pyramid in 1930s Garapan, Saipan, by describing a hierarchy in which Naichi ('mainland') Japanese were at the top, filling the most prestigious and powerful positions of administrators and corporate employees or private business owners. Below them were the *Chamoro* and Okinawans, who were roughly of equal standing, often running small businesses but usually working mainly as company employees, or as labourers like fishermen and farmers (such as Okinawans catching bonito and drying it to make *katsuo bushi*, an important industry in Japan). Koreans were on the next tier below, also working as labourers in different areas but joining Kanakas, who were considered to be inferior to them, in various service industries as low-wage earners.[34] However, this hierarchical racism was not endorsed by all Japanese experts or policymakers: colonial advisor and economist Yanaihara Tadao, for instance, was mindful of the racism Japanese themselves experienced from other countries and was an outspoken critic of this approach.[35]

Social infrastructure, nonetheless, treated Islanders as lower-class subjects. Public schools for Indigenous children, called *kōgakkō*, were situated throughout Micronesia and offered usually two to three years of education, while children with at least one Japanese or Okinawan parent (including Korean children) were sent to the eight-year primary schools, or *shōgakkō*, before going on to higher education in Japan. There were some exceptions to this, such as Micronesian children who managed to get a better education through the Japanese system, some being recommended to the *mokkō* carpentry school in Palau – even studying eventually in Japan and serving later in quasi-administrative roles. For the most part, however, the education offered to Islanders was rudimentary and simplistic, intended to make them dependent on Japanese and loyal to the empire. It was also quite disciplined and strict, but the teachers were often experienced and dedicated educators sent from Japan, some of whom continued lifelong correspondences with their students back in

---

[33] See K. Hasebe, 'Nanyō Guntō-jin no Kao Rinkaku-gata' (The facial shapes of South Sea Islanders), *Jinruigaku Zasshi (Anthropology Magazine)* 56:1, Bulletin Edition 639, January 1942.

[34] W. Higuchi, *Islanders' Japanese Assimilation and Their Sense of Discrimination* (Mangilao: University of Guam Micronesian Area Research Center, 1993).

[35] S. Townsend, *Yanaihara Tadao and Japanese Colonial Policy: Redeeming Empire* (Richmond, VA: Curzon Press, 2000), 197.

the islands even after they were transferred home. Micronesians who experienced this education system and spent their childhoods speaking Japanese often reflect on this highly unequal society with a mix of ambivalent bitterness and nostalgia – remembering the humiliation of being bullied and teased by peers or punished by a teacher, but also expressing a sense of respect for Japanese discipline that led to a productive society – in comparison to the chaos and disorder that erupted when the United States took over the administration of their islands after the war.[36] As Iitaka Shingo warns, however, it is dangerous to interpret literally Micronesians' appraisal of pre-war life under Japanese rule as being better than it is today, pointing out how these memories have been recontextualized in the post-war era under a different government and detached from the original experience.[37]

One element of Micronesian identity and community that Japanese officials interfered with relatively less was the church, even if Christianity itself effectively served as a form of segregating the community along racial lines. Japanese colonialism did not impose religious beliefs or practices like Shintōism and Buddhism on Pacific Islanders, at least not substantially. Islanders, most of whom were practising Christians who had already been influenced by Western missionaries in the nineteenth century, were allowed to continue to worship as they had before, and in fact Japan sent its own Japanese Protestant missionaries from the Congregationalist Nanyō Dendō-Dan.[38] Throughout the islands – but especially in devout Kosrae, where few Japanese were Christian – churches became places of refuge where self-governance could be nurtured among locals.[39] However, in practice, many Japanese rituals, including even the morning practice in public schools of facing Tokyo, reciting the Imperial Rescript on Education, and bowing to worship the emperor, could be interpreted as Shintō ceremonies. And as more shrines were built throughout the high islands in the approach to war, including the major national shrine (*kanpei-taisha*) Nanyō Jinja in Palau (completed in 1940), Islanders were forced to be involved in state Shintō rituals on a regular basis.[40]

[36] See, for example, M. Mita, *Palauan Children under Japanese Rule: Their Oral Histories* (Osaka: National Museum of Ethnology, 2009).

[37] S. Iitaka, 'Appropriating successive colonial experiences to represent national culture: a case analysis of the revival of war canoes in Palau, Micronesia', *People and Culture in Oceania* 24 (2009), 1–29, at 5.

[38] Peattie, *Nan'yō*, 84.

[39] A. Strathern et al., *Oceania: An Introduction to the Cultures and Identities of Pacific Islanders*, 2nd edn (Durham: Carolina Academic Press, 2017), 242.

[40] F.X. Hezel, *Strangers in Their Own Land: A Century of Colonial Rule in the Caroline and Marshall Islands* (Honolulu: University of Hawai'i Press, 1995), 212.

Despite these structural aspects, in this segregated society, the most marginalized groups often lived in similar areas and enjoyed social contact, and some degree of solidarity, with each other. For instance, an elderly Okinawan woman who was born in the Marshall Islands and grew up in Chuuk in the early 1930s described how she used to play with Chamorro and Korean children, and was still able to recite songs in both Korean and Chuukese at the age of 87. Another woman, the daughter of a Japanese administrator, lived on exactly the same island at the same time, but described a life in which she was kept away from local children, forced to wear shoes, and made to socialize only with other Japanese. But segregation was not always so rigid in Islanders' actual lived experience; many Palauans, for example, have fond memories of close Japanese playmates from their childhood, with whom they maintained relationships long after the war.[41]

Islanders in urban centres dealt with marginalization on their own land for the first time, in ways that had never been experienced in previous regimes of colonialism. In more distant island groups, Japanese or Okinawans were the minority, and often had to adapt by learning to speak the local language, especially if they had married into a local family. There were also notable tensions, even among Japanese in the islands, between those elites temporarily assigned to administer the island communities and enforce social rules, and the settlers who gradually adapted to their environments and broke those rules. As Tomiyama writes, Okinawans, too, were often discriminated against or marginalized by Indigenous Islanders, teased for being lower-class 'natives' of Japan, and, in places where Islanders were the majority, Okinawans' status was actually quite unstable.[42] Some Micronesians would also emulate Japanese anti-Korean bias as a way of positioning themselves on a better footing with the colonizer, a tendency that became more pronounced during the war years.

Complexities and nuances like these differentiated Japanese colonialism in Micronesia from other histories of European colonialism in Oceania, and even Japanese colonialism in Asia, generating different cultural memories and politics between even the closest of neighbouring islands. One example of this would be the case of the Mariana Islands where Guam suffered an abrupt military takeover and occupation by Japanese troops long after having been a US territory, yet Saipan was settled by Japanese civilians for several decades

---

[41] Mita, *Palauan Children under Japanese Rule.*
[42] I. Tomiyama, 'The "Japanese" of Micronesia: Okinawans in the Nan'yō Islands', in R.Y. Nakasone (ed.), *Okinawan Diaspora* (Honolulu: University of Hawai'i Press, 2002), 57–70, at 62.

before the war. Japan was more than merely an 'occupier'; its involvement was not fundamentally military in nature, nor was its outward objective to oppress the local people – on the contrary, its mandate was purportedly for their benefit. The majority of those who settled the Nanyō Guntō, aside from the elite business owners and officials, were the poorest of the poor from Japan, including colonized people from the overthrown Ryukyu Kingdom and the Korean peninsula. Japan's engagement was mainly a peacetime, civilian exercise in out-migration, development, and colonialism, but one justified in part by race – most importantly a rhetoric of protectionism from 'white', Western colonialism. The emerging ideology of the Greater East Asia Co-Prosperity Sphere in the late 1930s as an Asian-controlled, Japanese-led bloc that would resist Western colonialism – albeit by promoting the notion of Japanese racial superiority over all other Asians and Pacific Islanders – also made the Nanyō Guntō a peculiar space of resistance.

Nanyōism

Back in Japan, narratives of settlers' crossings to Oceania served as fodder for popular culture, merging with various fantasies of adventure and peril in the Pacific Islands that Japanese readers had inherited from translations of European literature and artistic depictions of a southern paradise. Books like Robert Louis Stevenson's *Treasure Island* or Paul Gauguin's *Noa Noa*, together with the emerging genre of Japanese accounts of the Pacific by Suzuki and others, were influential in the early twentieth century in creating an overarching narrative of conquest and civilization of the primitive 'Other'. This facilitated the positioning of Japanese as superior and more evolved compared with their Pacific counterparts, a trend that post-colonial critics Kawamura Minato and Sudō Naoto refer to as 'Tropicalism' or 'Nanyō Orientalism'.[43]

Nakajima Atsushi, a popular Japanese writer who emulated Robert Louis Stevenson's sojourns in Sāmoa by travelling to the Nanyō Guntō to restore his poor health, authored a travelogue and series of fictional works about Micronesia during his stay there in 1941–2.[44] Hijikata Hisakatsu, sometimes referred to as the 'Japanese Gauguin', was an ethnologist-artist whose iconic

---

[43] Kawamura, *Nanyō-Karafuto no Nihon Bungaku*; N. Sudō, *Nanyō Orientalism: Japanese Representations of the Pacific* (Amherst: Cambria Press, 2010).

[44] A. Nakajima, *Nanyō Tsūshin (Nanyō Communiqué)* (Tokyo: Chūō Kōron Shinsha, 2001 [1941–2]).

The Phantom Empire

woodblock carvings and prints became well-known representations of Nanyō Guntō culture back in Japan. Hijikata first travelled to Palau and then, disappointed with Japanese colonial influences there, moved on to reside in Satawal, just as Gauguin's disgust for French influence in Papeete and his search for an idyllic eden had led him to live in the Marquesas Islands.[45] Other artists, such as Japan-raised French woodblock printer Paul Jacoulet, also popularized images of Micronesia as a playground of desire and romance filled with beautiful Pacific Islander bodies.

One of the most famous examples of this tropicalist genre would be the serialized comic *Bōken Dankichi* (Adventurous Dankichi), by *manga* cartoonist Shimada Keizō, which appeared in the bestselling boys' magazine *Shōnen Kurabu* (Boys' Club) from 1933 to 1939.[46] The first episode begins with the brave young Japanese boy Dankichi and his trusty mouse companion Karikō (Mister Kari) shipwrecking after falling asleep on a fishing trip and getting washed up on the beach of an imaginary island somewhere in the 'South'. Not long after arriving on the island, Dankichi and Karikō discover that the island is inhabited by dangerous wild animals like lions and elephants (none of which actually exist in Oceania) and 'cannibalistic' dark-skinned people who pose a significant danger. These Islanders are drawn as happy ape-like men – largely featureless, big-lipped and wide-eyed, barefoot, clad in grass skirts with stacks of metal rings around their necks. Dankichi paints his skin black and infiltrates the tribe, but his disguise is foiled when a sudden rain shower washes away his skin colour. To avoid being killed and eaten, he sets a simple trap and ensnares the chief, easily convincing him to make him the new king of the island, a coronation which the Islanders gladly celebrate.

In subsequent manga episodes, Dankichi and Karikō's adventures mirror Japan's project of development and 'progress' in the Nanyō Guntō as they lead the Natives in establishing schools, hospitals, shops, and various other marks of 'civilization', based on the presumption that local people are 'primitive savages', and Japanese like Dankichi are their saviours. He even organizes the Islanders into an army to fight against Westerner invaders. Dankichi, who has little interest in local knowledge or culture, never attempts to pronounce the actual names of his Islander hosts, and arrogantly decides that he will just paint large white numerals on each of their chests, so that he can tell them apart – since to him (and the reader of the comic) they all look the same.

---

[45] Peattie, *Nan'yō*, 199.
[46] K. Shimada, *Bōken Dankichi Manga Zenshū (Compiled Collection of 'Dankichi the Adventurous')* (Tokyo: Kōdansha, 1976 [1939]).

Were the *Dankichi* comic not so popular throughout Japan, it could easily be dismissed as a passing fad, but it fuelled the dreams of young men in Japan to cultivate their own Pacific fantasies of life in Paradise, and most of the soldiers who would eventually be dispatched to the Pacific front would have read it as children. Bōken Dankichi is also often associated with pioneer Mori Koben, whose family grave back in Kōchi, Japan, is decorated with a plaque that commemorates the comic book character as if he were based on Mori himself (which apparently he wasn't). The boys of Kōchi Secondary School adapted the story of Mori marrying a local chief's daughter into a dance and song performance in which several boys covered their bodies with soot, waved around spears, and wore 'grass' skirts to mock Pacific Islanders based on the stereotypes they had gleaned from the comic.[47] Through the 1920s and 1930s, pictorial atlases and photographic postcards depicting so-called *dojin* (a derogatory word for 'natives' spelled with the characters 'dirt' and 'people') and their 'curious customs' were widely circulated throughout Japan, and this led to a racist fascination in Japan with 'primitive' people, especially Pacific Islanders. It was a popular pastime at drinking parties and local festivals, for example, to perform in ethnic drag and act the part of a 'savage'.

The Kōchi students' minstrel dance included a comical song about an island princess in the Marshall Islands who lazily dances all day, waiting for a Japanese man to seduce her. This dance and song was so popular that its lyrics would later be adapted in 1931 by Ishida Hitomatsu into the first-ever recording by Japan Polydor Records, a song called 'Shūcho no Musume' (The Chieftain's Daughter), which begins, 'My lover is the chieftain's daughter. She's black but in the South Seas she's a beauty.' Thus, the genre of 'Nanyō Odori' (South Seas dancing) was popularized, along with the image that Japan's new Pacific Island territories and the women who inhabited them were alluring, available, and eager for Japanese men to conquer. Though in fact a racist skit, Japanese colonists performed it commonly in the islands and regularly asked Islander women to play the role of the 'chieftain's daughter' as part of the routine. Much later, after the war and even up to the present day, variations of Nanyō Odori have been danced throughout Japan by the descendants of returnees from Micronesia, but less as parody than as a form of nostalgic cultural memory of another time.[48]

---

[47] T. Kisō, *Uta no Furusato to Kikō* (the birthplace and environment of songs) (Tokyo: Tokyo Hōsō Shuppan Kyōkai, 1986).
[48] G. Dvorak, *Coral and Concrete: Remembering Kwajalein Atoll between Japan, America, and the Marshall Islands* (Honolulu: University of Hawai'i Press, 2018), 61–91.

These narratives of 'tropicalism' primed some male settlers and soldiers sent to Micronesia to expect local women to fulfil their fantasies and to perceive local men as little more than able-bodied servants. Perhaps this is one of the reasons why the word kokan – which derives from the Japanese *kōkan*, meaning 'trade' or 'exchange' in Japanese – is still used today in Marshallese to refer to prostitution. But there were also many Japanese and Okinawan settlers who forged enduring and respectful relationships with their Pacific Islander contemporaries, building families and even taking some Islander family members back with them to Japan. Not only through a rigorous nationalistic and imperialistic education under Japanese rule, but also through deep and emotional ties to Japanese residents, many Islanders throughout the Nanyō Guntō expressed loyalty to the emperor. As the war approached, despite their ambivalences, Islander communities tended to share in Japanese defensive anticipation of the arrival of Allied forces on their shores. Poyer, Falgout, and Carucci mention, for example, that some Islanders would even go on to fight alongside the Japanese.[49]

Bombarded or Bypassed: Islands during the War

It is important to emphasize the massive shift that took place in the late 1930s in terms of Japan's relation to the Pacific Islands, as its posturing shifted away from economic expansion and settlement to militarism and defence. In the latter half of the 1930s, Japanese enterprises centred around Palau, Saipan, and Taiwan had begun to survey broader swaths of the South Pacific and Southeast Asia, including the Philippines, the Malay Peninsula, Indonesia, and significant parts of Melanesia, for further economic exploitation. Along with this expansion, more and more small settlements of Japanese began to live abroad, outside the aegis of Japanese governmental rule, but still within the broader scope of what Japanese maps referred to as 'Outer Nanyō', or simply 'Nanyō'.

The intertwined ideologies of *nanshin* and the 'co-prosperity sphere' crescendoed as tensions grew between Japan, the United States, and its allies on the international stage. Beginning with the second Sino-Japanese War in 1937, Japan initiated an unprecedentedly violent pursuit of raw materials, food supplies, and a bigger labour force, to feed its empire. In Oceania,

---

[49] L. Poyer, S. Falgout, and L.M. Carucci, *The Typhoon of War: Micronesian Experiences of the Pacific War* (Honolulu: University of Hawai'i Press, 2001), 121.

Japan's militarism began to manifest in the physical landscapes and seascapes of Micronesia as it started to fortify its territories in Nanyō Guntō, believing the islands to be an important launchpad for further expansion and a defensive cushion against Western retaliation. The propaganda film *Umi no Seimeisen* (Lifeline of the Sea), first released in 1933 as a documentary hewn from ethnographic footage, but re-edited and re-released by the Imperial Navy in 1938 with a heavily militaristic message, makes clear Japan's military use of the islands as a 'lifeline' to resources further afield, and as a barrier to protect the home islands.[50] Japan did not give many clues about when it actually began to fortify Micronesia, and various experts surmised that the building of airstrips or weather stations actually served the dual purpose of both civilian and military infrastructure. However, by the early 1940s, Japan had established significant naval bases at Chuuk and Kwajalein, with additional facilities on a number of atolls on the imperial eastern front in the Marshall Islands.[51] To build these bases, Japan enlisted the labour of hundreds of Japanese political prisoners, as well as over 10,000 Korean forced labourers drafted from their hometowns in Busan, Jeju, and elsewhere.[52] Meanwhile, Japanese civilians as well as Islanders were systematically moved away from key islands to make way for the first waves of personnel who worked on the bases, and then the tens of thousands of Japanese sailors and soldiers during the Pacific War, many of whom were being mobilized from the front in China and had never been to the tropics.

In December 1941, Japan bombarded US-military occupied Pu'uloa, on the island of O'ahu in the Hawaiian islands, a place known to most Americans as 'Pearl Harbor' – and the attack was launched from its bases in the Marshall Islands.[53] On the same day, Japanese forces would also launch attacks upon US-held Guam, Wake, and the Philippines, and the British-held territories Hong Kong, Singapore, and Malaya, as part of a coordinated effort to fend off interference with its planned *nanshin* invasion of 'Greater Nanyō' (Southeast Asia), itself partly a response to the total US oil embargo ordered

---

[50] Dvorak, *Coral and Concrete*, 44.   [51] Peattie, *Nan'yō*, 254.
[52] These Japanese political prisoners came from Abashiri and Yokohama prisons and numbered at least 400–500. US intelligence reports indicate that the largest numbers of male conscripted Korean labourers sent to Oceania, as of 1943, were roughly 10,000 in Chuuk, 1,600 in Nauru, 1,200 in Kwajalein, and 1,200 each in Mili and Wake; whereas a taskforce of the South Korean government more conservatively estimated that the number of confirmed conscripted labourers in the Nanyō Guntō was closer to 10,000 men. Dvorak, *Coral and Concrete*, 99. For further details on Korean forced labour, see D.C. Denfeld, 'Korean laborers in Micronesia during World War II', *Korea Observer* 15:1 (1984), 3–17.
[53] Peattie, *Nan'yō*, 257.

earlier that year. It was in this context that the USA and its allies declared war on Japan and the Pacific War began.

In the months that followed these initial confrontations in Greater Oceania, the Japanese military would occupy Wake, Kiribati, New Guinea, Guam (which it renamed Ōmiya Island), East Timor, and Nauru, in that order. In addition to its occupation of the Philippine Archipelago, Indonesia, and many parts of Southeast Asia, Japanese also made air attacks on Darwin, Broome, and Townsville, and a submarine attack on Sydney in Australia. In Guam, Rabaul, and several other sites, substantial Japanese civilian populations had already been living and were galvanized by these invasions. In 1942, the Japanese military landed in parts of the British-held Solomon Islands and in Bougainville, where they would fight with Australian, New Zealander, and American allied forces in this area to secure Japan's pivotal base in Rabaul. Many Islanders caught up in the fighting in Rabaul were captured and sent to the major naval base in Chuuk in the mandated Micronesian islands north of the equator, which was relatively close.[54]

In northern Oceania, the Battle of Midway of June of that year was a significant naval defeat for Japan, but in southern Oceania Allied Powers began to subdue Japanese power throughout the occupied territories in 1942–3 when they landed at Guadalcanal in the Solomon Islands and could surround Rabaul. Memories of this intense and bitter conflict remain in the consciousness of families throughout these parts of Melanesia today, including the traumatic recollections of forced prostitution by local women, or 'comfort women', under Japanese militarism.[55]

Back in the north, early Allied air raids between 1942 and 1943 had caused damage and casualties on many islands, but it was not until 1944 that US forces actually made invasions into the former mandated islands of the Nanyō Guntō, beginning with amphibious landings in the Marshall Islands and progressing across in a stepping-stone campaign towards Palau, Saipan, and Guam. On many islands, confrontations between Japanese and Americans had the effect of practically bulldozing the islands, leaving a wake of complete destruction and death followed by barely any effort by either party to clean up the mess. Islanders were recruited to bury the Japanese dead, an experience fraught with tension for a population that had been educated in Japanese language and customs and knew very little

---

[54] Crocombe, *Asia in the Pacific Islands*, 50.
[55] Y. Sekiguchi, *Senso Daughters* (Canberra: Ronin Films, 1990), 55 min. film; English version 1991.

about the American invaders. At the same time, most islands throughout Micronesia did not actually experience combat on land and were therefore bypassed or barricaded by US forces, leading to other bitter experiences, such as when starvation and cannibalism by Japanese captors provoked a coordinated revolt by Korean and Marshallese labourers in the Mili Atoll Rebellion of 1943, leading to the massacre of 170 Koreans and 84 Marshallese.[56]

Remembering and Forgetting

The scars of violence from Japanese aggression and the fighting between Japanese and Allied troops still run deep through the memories and genealogies of Pacific Islanders today. Japanese wartime violence varied from locale to locale: some Islanders, particularly English-speaking clergy, were targeted on suspicion of being spies for the USA and executed; other communities were forced to surrender their food to feed whole battalions and starved as a result. Many other Islanders throughout the Pacific Theater were killed in crossfire or air raids. In several other cases, Japanese military officials helped Japanese civilians and their Islander families escape from danger; however, by the end of the conflict, the Japanese presence throughout Oceania, and especially the former Nanyō Guntō, was all but snuffed out.

Over 500,000 enlisted Japanese were killed in Pacific Island places during the war, and if this number is combined with soldiers killed in the Philippines, island Southeast Asia, Ogasawara, and Okinawa, this number easily comprises most of the 2.1 million soldiers killed throughout the whole Pacific War.[57] The majority of these soldiers' remains are buried where they fell throughout the region. This number does not include Allied soldiers or millions of civilian deaths. More troublingly, there are no clear figures on how many Indigenous people – relegated to the sidelines on their own land – perished in the war throughout Oceania. What remained of the Japanese empire, aside from the war dead, were the burned-out concrete blockhouses, the remnants of infrastructure, knowledge of Japanese language and customs in many places, and of course the mixed-ancestry children of former Japanese or Okinawan settlers, who had to say goodbye to their fathers or uncles before they were either killed in the war or forcibly repatriated to Japan.

---

[56] For more details on this massacre, see Dvorak, Coral and Concrete, 107, and Poyer et al., The Typhoon of War, 226–9.
[57] Based on figures indicated on the map displayed at the Japan national secular memorial for war dead, the Chidorigafuchi National Cemetery, 'Number of Japanese Killed in Each of the Main Overseas War Zones during World War II'.

The Phantom Empire

Japanese government and colonial economic development had been a sustained feature of life in Micronesia for nearly thirty years, and a massive vacuum was left in its place. Thus it was with ambivalence that the American discourse of 'liberation' was celebrated in many places, amidst a profound sense of loss experienced by many Islanders.

After the war, as Japan finally began to gather the pieces of its national identity together, little by little Japanese began to engage with Oceania again. However, as Naoki Sakai has theorized, though American objectives were framed by different discourses in the post-war period, it could be said that the United States essentially inherited the Japanese empire and absorbed it into its own trans-regional project of military hegemony and economic development.[58] As Hara has elaborated, the establishment of the US Trust Territory of the Pacific Islands in 1947 is one Pacific example of how this transformation from a Japanese to an 'American Lake' took place, in an uninterrupted arc that now stretched from Hawai'i across to Guam and the Philippines.[59]

Its military transformed into a self-defence force under the post-war constitution, Japan's post-1945 connections to Oceania have primarily been through tourism, overseas development assistance, or obtaining resources such as fish, lumber, and oil.[60] Deep-freeze refrigeration technologies allowed the first long-distance tuna fishing operations to begin in the 1950s, sending boats on extended voyages throughout the Pacific Ocean, including the waters of the former Nanyō Guntō. It was in these early years, too, that unbeknownst to the Japanese public, the United States, in 1946, had begun testing its deadly atomic weapons on Bikini and Enewetak atolls in the Marshalls. Not even one year after dropping payloads of nuclear horror onto Hiroshima and Nagasaki, the USA went on to continue its attack on Japanese people in the *Daigo Fukuryūmaru* (Number 5 *Lucky Dragon*) fishing boat incident, in which a tuna fishing vessel carrying twenty-three Japanese crew was severely irradiated during the Castle Bravo hydrogen bomb test at Bikini on 1 March 1954.

---

[58] N. Sakai, 'On romantic love and military violence: transpacific imperialism and U.S.–Japan complicity', in K. Camacho and S. Shigematsu (eds.), *Militarized Currents: Toward a Decolonized Future in Asia and the Pacific* (Minneapolis: University of Minnesota Press, 2010), 206–16.

[59] K. Hara, *Cold War Frontiers in the Asia-Pacific: Divided Territories in the San Francisco System* (New York: Routledge, 2007).

[60] Although at the time of this publication, the Japanese Self-Defence Forces do not engage in Japan-led military campaigns, proposed changes to the Japanese constitution may result in Japan's ability to conduct its own military activities overseas. Additionally, Japanese Air Self-Defence aircraft already use American bases such as those at Kwajalein or Guam for refuelling, and Japanese forces collaborate with US and South Korean militaries for training in the Pacific from time to time.

This incident sparked massive protests throughout Japan against nuclear weapons and led to a sense of solidarity that lasts to the present day between Pacific nuclear testing victims, such as those from the Marshall Islands and French Polynesia, and Japanese *hibakusha* (radiation victims) from atomic bombings and now the failed Fukushima nuclear plant. The *Lucky Dragon* incident was also the inspiration behind the story of the nuclear mutant sea monster Godzilla, who was, effectively, born on Bikini Atoll. Historian Igarashi Yoshikuni theorizes how the *Godzilla* film franchise and its preoccupation with southern island locales revisits the theme of Yanagita and Shimazaki's 'drifting coconuts' theme in the post-war era, when the massive coconut-shaped egg of the frightening monster Mothra washes up on Japan's shores in the 1950s–1960s cinematic imagination, symbolically replacing Japan's pre-war dreams of southern expansion with post-war nightmares.[61]

Average Japanese people could not afford to travel abroad for many years after the war, but beginning around the time of the Tokyo Olympics in 1964, domestic resorts for honeymooners began to emulate a Pacific escape, and the study of hula became immensely popular throughout the country. For instance, the Jōban Hawaiians Center that opened in 1966 in Iwaki, Fukushima Prefecture, was the forerunner to Spa Resort Hawaiians, an artificial tropical-themed amusement park that still operates today and has served as a site for the PALM Japan-Pacific Islands Summit meetings. The post-war tourist gaze bypasses the defunct dreams of Nanyō Guntō/ Micronesia, setting its sights on Hawai'i, Tahiti, Aotearoa New Zealand, and other Polynesian places as sites for touristic pleasure and relief from the stresses of the everyday. Many in Japan today associate the Pacific with *sumo* wrestlers from Hawai'i or rugby players from Sāmoa, Tonga, and Fiji, but the most common Pacific image in Japan is propagated by hula and Tahitian dance studios, which are ubiquitous all over the country. Today, Japanese students of hula far outnumber Indigenous Hawaiian hula practitioners.[62] As Yaguchi has written, dancing hula as 'authentically' as possible has become for contemporary Japanese a way of embodying the imagined comfort of a Hawaiian paradise: another Orientalist fantasy of Japan's Pacific Other.[63]

---

[61] Y. Igarashi, 'Mothra's gigantic egg: consuming the South Pacific in 1960s Japan', in W. Tsutsui and M. Ito (eds.), *In Godzilla's Footsteps: Japanese Pop Culture Icons on the Global Stage* (New York: Palgrave Macmillan, 2006), 83–102, at 85–6.

[62] Lisette Flanary's film *Tokyo Hula* (2019) addresses the immense popularity of hula in Japan that has led to a steady proliferation of *halau* (schools) in Japan and increase in numbers of Japanese hula dancers that have surpassed their counterparts in Hawai'i.

[63] Y. Yaguchi, 'Longing for Paradise through "authentic" hula performance in contemporary Japan', *Japanese Studies* 35:3 (2015), 303–15.

Figure 35.4 'Yume no Hawai [Hawai'i Dreaming]: *Aloha Oe* Ukulele', by Kimura Ryōko, 2017, ink, mineral pigments, gold leaf on paper, folding screen, 186 × 166.7 cm.

Pre-war Japanese visions of Oceania that had revolved so heavily around Micronesia became tabu – too tied up in imperialistic narratives of conquest and wartime loss; moreover, travel to the US Trust Territory that replaced the Japanese mandate was off limits for the first decades after the war. Eventually, more Japanese tourists would begin to travel to Guam and to visit resorts in the former colonies of Palau and Saipan, but mostly for scuba diving and golf, and rarely with much awareness of the pre-war era or the immense Japanese influence in these islands.

Meanwhile, another type of post-war traveller was aware of little *but* the Japanese history in the Pacific Islands. The extensive membership of Nihon Izokukai, the Japan Bereaved Families Association, eligible for funding from the Japanese Ministry of Health and Welfare, began organizing pilgrimages to former Pacific War battlefields, in which family members of war dead throughout Oceania could retrace the steps of fallen soldiers as a way of mourning and conducting formal ceremonies to consecrate their graves far away from Japan. For these pilgrims, long unable to express their frustration and grief in Japan, such journeys are a way of reconnecting the severed memories and emotions of the past. Myriad organizations typically conduct several bereavement 'tours' every year, with many of the bereaved following prescribed Japanese government protocols for grave visitation, in lieu of any official policy to seek out and formally repatriate war remains to Japan. Some groups, but not all, exhume the presumed remains of Japanese, holding mass cremation ceremonies, and bringing the ashes home to the tomb of the unknown soldier at Chidorigafuchi Cemetery in Japan. This practice is plagued by a lack of DNA testing, and the alleged misidentification of Islander and Korean bodies as Japanese.[64]

'In the Pacific Islands', states Keith Camacho, who has written about comparative rituals of Indigenous, Japanese, and American commemoration, 'the making of history is a vibrant process of contestation and celebration'.[65] As the elderly generations who remember the war disappear, historical revisionism in Japan about wartime and colonial violence in Oceania has increased. Right-leaning memorialist groups travel to sites of former Japanese occupation, from Papua New Guinea to Pohnpei, building shrines and memorials to war heroes, despite having no family ties to the war dead. Some of these groups also practise 'bone-collecting' as an act of nationalistic service to redeem the glory of Japan's former empire, without the permission of bereaved families or the consent of local island landowners and governments. Taking advantage of Japanese public amnesia combined with the ambivalent recollections of Micronesians who sometimes remember Japanese colonialism as 'the good old days', historical revisionists have assertively embarked upon a project of memory laundering, hijacking Islanders' narratives of nostalgia in the service of Japanese right-wing nationalism. Journalists such as Sasa Yukie and *manga* cartoonists such as Kobayashi Yoshinori sanitize the past by attempting to portray Islanders as loyal pro-Japan (*shin-Nichi*) apologists, and history textbooks that detail Japanese violence in Oceania are effectively prevented from being published or approved

---

[64] See G. Dvorak, 'Who closed the sea? Postwar amnesia and the Pacific Islands', in L. Kurashige (ed.), *Pacific America* (Honolulu: University of Hawai'i Press, 2017), 229–46, at 237–8 and Dvorak, *Coral and Concrete*, 263.

[65] K. Camacho, *Cultures of Commemoration: The Politics of War, Memory, and History in the Mariana Islands* (Honolulu: University of Hawai'i Press, 2011), 177.

for use in classrooms.[66] Today, with such a pronounced lack of nuanced awareness about Pacific histories and the absence of Pacific voices in Japan, these discourses have a disproportionate influence on popular opinion.

Japan as an 'Island Nation'

The post-colonial image of Oceania is increasingly challenged, critiqued, and reimagined in some way by the substantial communities of Pacific Islanders who live in those countries. For example, Aotearoa New Zealand is home to many influential scholars, politicians, artists, and writers of Indigenous Māori or diasporic Pacific Islander descent – and their voices help to shape national contemporary and historical narratives of the Pacific Islands region. The 'Australian Pacific', 'French Pacific', or 'American Pacific' are discourses that are challenged from within, by local Islander diaspora. In contrast, few Pacific Islanders are able to participate in nuancing and confronting how the Pacific is understood within Japan or in the Japanese language. This is because the Pacific population of Japan is comparatively small, limited mainly to diplomats, students, rugby players and other athletes, and some individuals who have intermarried with Japanese citizens. The result is that Japan, despite significant emigration of its citizens, its pivotal role in the Pacific War, and its decades of colonial rule in Oceania, is somewhat disengaged from the cultural politics of the contemporary Pacific. This need not be the case.

Japanese often use the term *shimaguni*, 'island nation', when describing how isolated their country is from the rest of the world. From the perspective of Oceania and Pacific Islands history, this definition of 'island' could not be further from the lived experience of island interconnectedness, or further from the truth about Japan's deeply interconnected place in Oceania's contemporary reality. In March 2011, a tremendous earthquake triggered the not-so-Pacific Ocean to swallow up an enormous stretch of the north-eastern Japanese coastline, sweeping away 20,000 lives in a horrific tsunami. This event not only showed that all of Oceania was physically connected; it also revealed the sense of community shared throughout the region. The debris of millions of homes, buildings, and boats was swept around

---

[66] See also R. Nishino, 'The self-promotion of a maverick travel-writer: Suzuki Tsunenori and his southern Pacific Islands travelogue', *Nanyō Tanken Jikki. Studies in Travel Writing* 20:4 (2016), 1–14; Dvorak, 'Who closed the sea?'; T. Morris-Suzuki, *The Past within Us: Media, Memory, History* (New York: Verso, 2005). For more context on contemporary Japanese historical revisionism regarding the Pacific War, see M. Dezaki, *Shusenjo: The Main Battleground of the Comfort Women Issue* (USA: No Man Productions, 2018), 122 min. film.

the northern hemisphere, landing on beaches throughout, while the crippled Fukushima nuclear reactor released unprecedented quantities of radioactive waste into the ocean currents. Although Japan is often a major donor to Pacific Island countries, in the wake of this disaster Pacific nations, including many former colonies of Japan such as the Marshall Islands, aided Japanese victims by their generous outpouring of donations and offers of support.

This spirit of community and shared concern about both climate and nuclear issues across the ocean should not be overlooked in historicizing Japan's international relations with Pacific Island nations. Political scientist and Japanese government advisor Kobayashi Izumi identifies a moment in the 1980s when the newly autonomous former Japanese territories of the Republic of the Marshall Islands, the Federated States of Micronesia, and the Republic of Palau united in protest against Japanese government proposals to dump waste from nuclear power plants in the Marianas Trench. Their intervention compelled former Prime Minister Nakasone to promise to defend the wishes of these Pacific countries and subsequently led to the creation of further partnerships.[67]

Between Islanders, the shared memory of the Japanese colonial enterprise has contributed to a sense of connection to contemporary Japan, as well as serving as a tool of resistance for island communities in Micronesia when they faced the nuclear testing and neglect brought by the United States in the beginning of the Trust Territory years. Clever triangulation between Japanese, American, and Indigenous governance systems would eventually accelerate decolonization and effective leadership in independence movements, such as in the case of Federated States of Micronesia's first president Tosiwo Nakayama.[68] Previously colonized Pacific Islanders cleverly retooled and reappropriated structures left behind by the colonial and military eras. For example, Palauans revitalized canoe races that were once forced upon them by colonial authorities as a way of promoting national pride at the Festival of Pacific Arts.[69] Japanese words and concepts are still used extensively throughout communities across northern Oceania, such as in Palau, where they make up the majority of loanwords from any other language and serve as a mnemonic link for both locals and Japanese to shared pasts.[70]

---

[67] Kobayashi, 'Japan's diplomacy towards member countries of Pacific Islands Forum', 92.
[68] D. Hanlon, *Making Micronesia: A Political Biography of Tosiwo Nakayama* (Honolulu: University of Hawai'i Press, 2014).
[69] Iitaka, 'Appropriating successive colonial experiences'.
[70] D. Long and K. Imamura, *The Japanese Language in Palau* (Tokyo: National Institute for Language and Linguistics, 2013).

Arguably, this consciousness of the Japanese phantom empire in the islands keeps Micronesians politically aware of and engaged with Japan today, and the colonial legacy figures in development discourse as well.

Today, Japan is deeply engaged in development initiatives all across Oceania, including volunteer technical expertise through the Japan International Cooperation Agency (JICA) and educational/medical support through its Japan Overseas Cooperation Volunteers (JOCV) programmes, and its funding often aids in the construction of fishing bases, hospitals, and schools, throughout all independent Pacific Islands nations. These contributions are highly valued by Pacific communities, though some scholars have suggested that Japan's sole purpose in engaging in aid diplomacy is to garner better access to dwindling fisheries or other resources in various countries' territories.[71] Outside observers have also characterized Japanese aid as being a tool for leveraging itself against China in the region. Kobayashi argues, however, that long before China got involved in the Pacific, in the decades after the war, Japan had started providing Official Development Assistance to Sāmoa and Fiji by the 1970s, and that its reason for not extending aid elsewhere was simply that many other Pacific nations, including all of those once colonized by Japan, were not independent and able to engage in diplomatic relations until much later.[72] Additionally, as has been highlighted by widely publicized Korean litigation against Japanese corporations that profited from conscripted labour during World War II, some of the Japanese corporations who engage today in construction and infrastructure support throughout Oceania evolved out of the very companies that built up the pre-war Japanese empire or were enriched by wartime violence. Nonetheless, it is important to point out that these Japanese aid and cooperation programmes are instituted worldwide and are in fact not even as extensive as they are in other countries outside the Pacific Islands. Japanese volunteers also tend to be respected in island nations as being highly fluent in local languages and earnest in their missions of support.

Since 1997, the Japanese government has hosted summits between leaders of Pacific Islands countries and the Japanese prime minister every three years, known as the Pacific Islands Leaders Meetings, or PALM. These summits have been widely criticized for lumping all Pacific nations into one without consideration for local contexts, and they have tended to function less as

---

[71] For an example of this criticism, see S. Tarte, *Japan and the Pacific Islands: The Politics of Fisheries, Access, Aid and Regionalism* (Uppsala: Life and Peace Institute, 1995).

[72] Kobayashi, 'Japan's diplomacy towards member countries of Pacific Islands Forum', 91.

spaces of mutual dialogue than as opportunities for the Japanese government to promote its latest plans in the region. This underscores the fact that the Japanese Ministry of Foreign Affairs typically has not placed much emphasis on diplomacy with Pacific nations, and a handful of policy experts tend to dictate the terms of these relationships without opening up to insights from Islander leaders themselves. Tongan political scientist Kaitu'u Funaki explains that Pacific Island countries 'perceive themselves as being in a one-way relationship wherein Japan exists to assist [them] with their limitations', and that, rather than facilitate more mutual respect, trust and collaboration, PALM summits foster more dependency and lack of consultation, with Pacific Islanders as 'guardians of the ocean' on Japan's behalf.[73]

In the face of threats due to climate change, Japan is increasingly being called upon to consult and collaborate more effectively with its Oceanic counterparts. Bringing Pacific Islander and Asian youth to Japan to visit the areas affected by the tsunami and nuclear meltdown, the Japanese government began to present itself as a mentor in 'disaster preparedness'.[74] But in fact Pacific Islanders themselves have much more to teach the Japanese public about the Great Ocean and its stewardship, and people are beginning to listen. Marshallese artist and climate change activist Kathy Jetñil-Kijiner, herself possessing Japanese roots, has made several visits to Japan, where her poetry and performances, translated into Japanese, have begun to spread consciousness about the environmental colonialism of nuclear radiation and the global sea level rise caused by the careless emissions of industrialized nations.

In recent years, meaningful alliances have also been forged between Indigenous Ainu, Ryukyuans (Okinawans), and Pacific Islanders, and they have begun to redefine and subvert the Japanese government's pattern of paternalism in Oceania. Scholarly networks between post-colonial researchers based in Japan and their colleagues in Oceania have also created more forums for dialogue. Ainu, involved in United Nations Indigenous conventions but only formally recognized as Indigenous people under Japanese law in 2019, have been involved in networking for many decades in exchanges with their counterparts, including Māori, CHamoru, Hawaiian, and other Pacific communities. Trans-oceanic, Indigenous-led scholarly movements for demilitarization, centring around the nexus between Guam and Okinawa, have also

---

[73] K.P. Funaki and Y. Satō, 'Wanted: a strategic dialogue with Pacific Island countries', *The Japan Times* (28 January 2019).
[74] Here I am referring to initiatives like the JENESYS Program, spearheaded by the Japan International Cooperation Center (JICE).

begun to build new collectives of solidarity within the Asia Pacific region, involving a renewed interest in Okinawan-Micronesian experiences of colonialism, war, memory, and resistance. Indigenous artists from Japan have also begun to network with Pacific Islander artists via international exhibitions.

Legendary Tongan philosopher Epeli Hau'ofa once wrote that 'Oceania refers to a world of people connected to each other... For my part, anyone who has lived in our region and is committed to Oceania is an Oceanian.'[75] Despite this broad interpretation of what it means to connect and commit to Oceania, Hau'ofa wrote specifically in the same essay that Japan and other Asian countries 'do not have oceanic cultures, and are therefore not a part of Oceania'.[76] I would suggest that perhaps it is worth rethinking this divide between Asia and the Pacific, to consider in what ways the Japanese and Okinawan archipelagoes, with their intimate relationships to the sea and various Indigenous maritime histories, *do* indeed have Oceanic elements. Arguably, deeper and more nuanced engagements in Japan with truths about its pre-war and wartime imperial violence can create space to reimagine how to relate more meaningfully with the rest of the Pacific Ocean neighbourhood. How can Japan transcend its phantom empire to pursue an 'Oceanian' worldview – as a more conscious, equal partner in the perpetuation of a healthy, peaceful, and safe environment for the people and ecosystems of all who share these waters? It is one thing to imagine the serendipitous drifting of a coconut from faraway and forgotten isles of the past, but quite a different thing to envision what collaborative and creative navigations might be made possible towards a brighter and happier future.[77]

---

[75] E. Hau'ofa, 'The ocean in us', in A. Hooper (ed.), *Culture and Sustainable Development in the Pacific* (Canberra: Australian National University E Press and Asia Pacific Press, 2005), 32–43.
[76] Hau'ofa, 'The ocean in us', 38.
[77] I wish to thank Imayashiki Hiroshi, a former employee of the Toyota factory in Tahara, Japan, who invited me to give a talk to a local environmental preservation and surfing group in 2010 on Irago Beach, where I first learned about the very place where Yanagita's coconut washed ashore. I am also grateful to Nishino Ryōta for his generous feedback on earlier drafts of this chapter.

36

Blue Continent to Blue Pacific

JANE SAMSON

The unveiling of the new Pacific Hall at the Bernice Pauahi Bishop Museum in Honolulu, with its emphasis on an interconnected 'Blue Continent', was bold and invigorating. Opened in 2013, it presented the Pacific Ocean as the focus of historical attention in its own right; as an entity, not as a largely empty space whose histories were driven by neighbouring continents. Exhibits and events in the Pacific Hall were collected in, above, and around a central core rich in the histories and technologies of maritime travel. Over it all presided an extraordinary piece of art: *Anu'u Nu'u ka 'Ike* ('Learning step by step'). Created by over thirty students and master artists of Indigenous Pacific Island heritage, the mural expresses the ocean's physical, historical, and spiritual identities.[1]

I'd known intellectually that the Pacific's maritime environment connected people rather than isolating them, but the 'Blue Continent' approach enriched this perspective, stretching my own conceptions of the Pacific world, and prompting new questions about Pacific historiography. It's a tribute to the museum's success that the phrase 'Blue Continent' would become so ubiquitous, and this chapter will begin with an outline of the benefits of thinking in this way about the histories of a third of our planet. Then it will conduct a thought-experiment to explore two important questions: why a continent, and why a blue one? Like a kaleidoscope, this chapter will use different colours to create new patterns, not to question the usefulness of the 'Blue Continent', but to enhance the ways in which space, place, and vocabulary have invited the historical exploration of many different Pacific worlds. It will conclude with reflections on the newer concept of a 'Blue Pacific', returning to where it began with a celebration of Indigenous voices and agency in Pacific history.

---

[1] K. Meskin, 'Navigating *Moananuiākea*, the vast expanse of ocean', *Ka'Elele* (Fall 2013), 10.

These Pacific worlds have often featured the use of colours by colonizing outsiders to draw borders, and to divide Pacific bodies into 'races' in support of dispossession and exclusion. More recently, colour has underlined the unique role of Indigenous Pacific peoples, emphasizing their dignity and leadership in forming future Blue Pacific worlds. Since the Pacific Hall's opening in 2013, numerous visitors have acknowledged the power of 'raising the Blue Continent' to counter misconceptions about Pacific history.[2] Here I endorse Kerry Howe's insight that in traditional, Western academic life, each generation feels it has a uniquely insightful view of the past. The next generation, in turn, denounces the failings of its predecessors. But 'Different peoples may have different knowledge and perspectives. And Pacific history is certainly a much more diverse enterprise than it once was.' For example, 'such differences and diversities cannot readily be compressed into the binary categories of islander and non-islander'.[3] This chapter will use colour thought-experiments to glimpse something of the historical diversity of both 'islander' and 'non-islander' histories, not to come to a conclusion that puts all previous insights to shame, but to celebrate the fact that such closure is impossible. No kaleidoscope ever produces the same image twice: that is its gift.

Raising the Blue Continent

For Ramsey Taum, Hawaiian practitioner and instructor of Native Hawaiian culture and history, 'Raising the Blue Continent' was about taking a stand against the erosion of relationships by certain strands of Western political and economic philosophy. Historical voyaging should involve 'developing new eyes' as well as seeing new things: 'context changes content'.[4] New ways of seeing the Pacific world were in the air. In 2009 in Taiwan, the Kaohsiung Museum of Fine Arts had unveiled its exhibition 'The Great Journey: In Pursuit of the Ancestral Realm'. The entrance hall featured an enormous map of the Pacific marked up in both Mandarin and English, showing the Austronesian-speaking areas highlighted in green, including Taiwan.

Since the later eighteenth century, Euro-American theorists had proposed many models of prehistoric settlement in the Pacific. By the twenty-first century, although some questions remain, most academics agree that humans

---

[2] R. Taum, 'Ancient wisdom, future thinking: raising the Blue Continent', TEDx, Richardson Law School, University of Hawai'i, 29 September 2011, http://youtu.be/RJ1WKfofRMM.
[3] K.R. Howe, *Nature, Culture, and History: The 'Knowing' of Oceania* (Honolulu: University of Hawai'i Press, 2000), 83.
[4] Taum, 'Ancient wisdom, future thinking'.

arrived first through ancient migrations into what is now Australia, Tasmania, New Guinea, and some nearby islands in the southwest Pacific. At a later time, a movement of Austronesian language-speakers out of Taiwan generated the 'Polynesian' and Polynesian-outlier culture areas labelled by future European explorers and anthropologists. The point the Kaohsiung Museum wanted to make was that Taiwan, along with Madagascar, Aotearoa New Zealand, and Rapa Nui (Easter Island), could form the four corners of a Polynesian Continent: the 'Ancestral Realm'. As Alice Christophe notes, this emphasis on an 'inner Pacific' produces an occlusion of the 'Pacific Rim', notably mainland China and the Americas. It reintegrates Taiwan into the remarkable story of Indigenous Pacific navigation and migration, supporting the growing pride and profile of the remaining Indigenous Taiwanese.[5] It reaches into the Indian Ocean, following Austronesian language patterns. It's no coincidence that it also facilitates Taiwan's recent push for political recognition and economic contacts with Pacific nations.[6]

In some form or other, a 'Blue Continent' has now entered the social vocabularies of many Pacific-centred events. A 'Blue Continent Caucus' gathered at the annual Native Hawaiian Convention in 2015 to address a range of social and medical concerns in order to prepare briefing notes for members of Congress and lobby groups.[7] So many Pacifics – Pacific Rim, Asia-Pacific, Pacific Basin – have been articulated for the region by its largest rimworld neighbours, and not by the island nations at its heart. The Blue Continent's image of mutual dignity and collective responsibility has great appeal, inviting Pacific Islanders to shape the identity of their region, rather than having it shaped for them by others.

The historiographical contribution of an Indigenous Blue Continent has been just as substantial, long before the concept was named and popularized. Pacific scholars had long recognized the need to challenge Eurocentric notions of the primacy of Mediterranean and Atlantic histories. Well into the twentieth century, the significance of Pacific maps in textbooks and atlases was the lines of famous European explorers across its 'unknown' waters, and the extent of its colonized islands and territories. The triumphs of Western knowledge systems and colonial power were inscribed onto the oceans in lines of latitude and longitude. The stories told by the world's

---

[5] A. Christophe, 'What's in a map? Remapping Oceania in Taiwan museums through exhibitions', *Pacific Arts* 15:1–2 (2016), 8–20.
[6] See Chapter 59 by Stephanie Lawson in this volume.
[7] '14th Annual Native Hawaiian Convention, September 22–24, 2015', conference programme, 17, www.nhec.org/event/14th-annual-native-hawaiian-convention/.

oceans were, for these children of empire, stories of European adventure, superiority, and economic enrichment.

This was vital context for raising the Blue Continent. Decolonization in the Pacific in the 1970s had intensified the relevance of island-centred analysis, especially its emphasis on Indigenous agency and the importance of local historical circumstances. Pacific history did not begin and end with Europe. Scholars uncovered great riches in island archives and oral accounts, preserving them for academic analysis. The Blue Continent built upon this methodology, extending it outward. Aotearoa New Zealand, whose Indigenous population was Polynesian in origin, was not usually included with the tropical islands in Pacific Studies. Now it could be drawn back together with the rest of the Polynesian family in a new configuration. This was underlined by Māori: their response to the 1998 opening of *Te Papa*, the National Museum of Aotearoa New Zealand, had been mixed. The museum's mandate was to 'express the bicultural nature of the country', and its architectural features 'clearly encode the predominant value of biculturalism'.[8] This appealed to some Māori who prioritized a bicultural focus, but as one curator noted, 'That's fine but don't forget we are in the Pacific. I mean, the Pacific Ocean is absolutely paramount in this country. Māori came from the Pacific.'[9]

Various area studies programmes proliferated in the 1960s and 1970s, notably Australian Studies, New Zealand Studies, Southeast Asian Studies, Pacific Studies, Canadian Studies, and the like. The point was to emphasize the uniqueness of the local milieu. Out went those old, Eurocentric maritime maps with the voyages of Captain Cook carefully inscribed. In came maps, textbooks, and pedagogy, centred on particular regions. These areas were usually geographical ('Latin American Studies') or nation-state based ('Australian Studies'). What was once a topic in itself – the imperial history of the Pacific world – fragmented into at least a dozen separate programmes. At issue was what distinguished each area or country from others, not what drew them together. Pacific Studies included the tropical islands but usually not Aotearoa New Zealand or Australia; those had their own pedagogies, conferences, and publications. East and Southeast Asian Studies included the Pacific world only as an extension of continental priorities; the Pacific histories of the Philippines, for example, largely vanished in favour of

[8] M. Jolly, 'On the edge? Deserts, oceans, islands', *Contemporary Pacific* 13:2 (2001), 417–66, at 442.
[9] Cited in Jolly, 'On the edge', 461, n. 38.

attention towards its Asian connections.[10] Latin American Studies, like American or Canadian Studies, rarely ventured offshore. When they did, they seemed to pass Pacific Studies like ships in the night.[11]

In a revisionist challenge, Ron Crocombe noted that the extensive nineteenth-century contacts and exchanges between the new Latin American republics, Australia, Aotearoa New Zealand, and the Pacific Islands, were occluded by the diminished contact of the twentieth century. This meant 'little is generally known of either the past relationships or the future potentials'.[12] A re-engagement with the deep history of Oceanic–Latin American contacts is vital for the twenty-first century, if only to explain why, 'while everyone is aware of the growing importance of Pacific Basin inter-action', few people seem to be aware that the region is dominated numerically by its many island nations and the Pacific coast nations of Latin America.[13]

From seeds planted in the 1990s, transnational and transregional scholarship on the Pacific World began to blossom into the early years of the new century. Dennis Flynn's *Pacific Centuries* (1999), and the *Pacific World* series he co-edited with Arturo Giraldez, were important early interventions in favour of a new, maritime-centred approach. Pioneers of Russian Pacific history such as Glynn Barratt prompted American historians also to take their own nation's history back out to sea; until the end of the Cold War it was 'as though we refuse to recognize that Soviet vessels are not Johnny-come-latelies on the South Pacific scene'.[14] The same could be said of American historiography and its preoccupation with World War II as the beginning of serious engagement with the Pacific world. The post-Soviet era also invited Canadianists to move offshore to join Pacific Studies, New Zealand or Australian Studies specialists, and Asianists. Books about the transregional Pacific began to appear regularly.[15]

---

[10] P. D'Arcy, 'The Philippines as a Pacific nation: a brief history of interaction between Filipinos and Pacific Islanders', *Journal of Pacific History* 53 (2018), 1–23, at 2–4.

[11] J. Samson, 'Exploring the Pacific World', in D. Kennedy (ed.), *Reinterpreting Exploration: The West in the World* (Oxford: Oxford University Press, 2014), 154–71.

[12] R. Crocombe, 'Latin America and the Pacific Islands', *Contemporary Pacific* 3:1 (1991), 115–44, at 115.

[13] Crocombe, 'Latin America and the Pacific Islands', 115.

[14] G. Barratt, *Russia and the South Pacific 1696–1840*, vol. II, *Southern and Eastern Polynesia* (Vancouver: UBC Press, 1988), xii.

[15] Recent examples include J. Price, *Orienting Canada: Race, Empire, and the Transpacific* (Vancouver: UBC Press, 2011), and D. Igler, *The Great Ocean: Pacific Worlds from Captain Cook to the Gold Rush* (Oxford: Oxford University Press, 2013).

Why a Continent?

The idea of a 'Blue Continent' already had a rival towards the southern pole, where the oceanic Pacific world merges with the Antarctic continent in an unsettling embrace. The deep blue ice crevasses draw fault lines across both sea ice and glaciers, calving icebergs whose ancient blue fresh water dissolves in oceanic salt. Naming Antarctica 'the Blue Continent' goes back at least to the publication of *Antarctica: The Blue Continent* in 2002, and travel tours still use this phrase.[16] However, there seems to have been little thought given to the name apart from the blue colour of ancient ice.

I take the rhetorical point that by presenting the Pacific world as a 'Blue Continent', the Bishop Museum was countering the idea that the history of a maritime region is of less significance than that of a continental land mass. As Kerry Howe explains, 'Westerners, as fundamentally continental creatures, see islands as tiny dots of land and ignore the surrounding seas. Islands can thus seem small, and therefore insignificant and powerless.'[17] Thankfully, historiography has moved on from such landlocked condescension. Recent scholarship now regularly contrasts older historiographies with newer ones that recognize the historical and cultural richness of maritime environments.

A model was already available in the rise of 'Atlantic World' scholarship. In 1993 Paul Gilroy proposed that Atlantic World studies needed a radical shakeup, one that could be provided by taking the ocean itself 'as one single, complex unit of analysis' that would inevitably 'produce an explicitly transnational and intercultural perspective'.[18]

But some of the new transnational, maritime-centred studies of ocean worlds began with the Atlantic before proceeding on to the Indian Ocean and others, and only then tackling the Pacific world.[19] This hierarchy of value went largely unchallenged by Pacific regional specialists still focused on island groups, or individual islands, rather than the larger milieu, because

---

[16] D. McGonigal and L. Woodworth, *Antarctica: The Blue Continent* (Noble Park: The Five Mile Press, 2002).

[17] Howe, *Nature, Culture, and History*, 61.

[18] P. Gilroy, *The Black Atlantic: Modernity and Double Consciousness* (Cambridge, MA: Harvard University Press, 1993), 15.

[19] For example the 'Seas in History' series, edited by Geoffrey Scammel, which began with *The Atlantic* in 1999, concluding with D. Freeman, *The Pacific* (London: Routledge, 2010). By contrast, editors David Armitage, Alison Bashford, and Sujit Sivasundaram made a deliberate choice not to begin their book *Oceanic Histories* with the Mediterranean or Atlantic, but instead with three oceans, the Indian, Pacific, and Atlantic, arranged in that order in order to divert preeminence from the European world; *Oceanic Histories* (Cambridge: Cambridge University Press, 2018), 24–5.

'Pacific historians have not been inclined to consider the environment as a significant influence on cultural and historical patterns.'[20] An ironic situation indeed, given that the Pacific Ocean's maritime environment facilitated the growth and dispersion of those patterns.

This is the main reason why raising a 'Blue Continent' is fraught with contradiction. The concept's privileging of land masses as the normative location of history will perpetuate a significant problem in historiography. Pacific history, or any other maritime history, should be considered as important historically as that of the traditional continents: 'some maritime environments can be endowed with as much cultural value and detail as terrestrial environments. To truly understand the history of Oceania, we need to map its cultural seascapes as well as those on land.'[21] We also need to recognize how Western scholars have privileged the Atlantic over the Pacific. It has been doubly invisible to the Western academic gaze, because of the privileging of continents, and because of the perceived 'peripheral' status of the island nations within its vast embrace.

The critical importance of the Indigenous canoe as a miniature world, worthy of study in its own right, is a useful model for understanding the richness of the Pacific maritime environment. As Atlantic World historians have known for some time, the metaphor of the ship, and an emphasis on the maritime environment, can powerfully challenge traditionally land-locked historiographies. Paul Gilroy explains that the ship is 'a living, micro-cultural, micro-political system in motion' that focuses on the 'middle passage' and on the circulation of ideas and activists as well as the movement of key cultural and political artefacts: tracts, books, gramophone records, and choirs.[22] Why not in the Pacific as well? There is an old Hawaiian proverb: *He Wa'a He Moku, He Moku He Wa'a!* (A canoe is an island; an island is a canoe). There is a symbiotic relationship between space/place and history, meaning that Pacific histories are distinctively shaped by their maritime environment. A perpetuation of continental metaphors in Pacific history may not be the best way to encourage a maritime-centred approach, despite the Bishop Museum's best intentions. 'The Pacific is simply a "civilization without a center", and Oceanic space of movement, transit, and migration in a *longue durée* of local peoples and broad interactions.'[23] The image of an ersatz continent just doesn't capture the alterity and dynamism of Pacific worlds.

---

[20] Paul D'Arcy, *The People of the Sea: Environment, Identity and History in Oceania* (Honolulu: University of Hawai'i Press, 2006), 12.
[21] D'Arcy, *The People of the Sea*, 12.   [22] Gilroy, *The Black Atlantic*, 4.
[23] M.K. Matsuda, 'The Pacific', *American Historical Review* 111:3 (2006), 758–80, at 769.

Just as a kaleidoscope image might feature one dominant colour, while still including many others, this chapter will assume that all Pacific worlds are both hybrid and dynamic. But it's vital to remember that there are historical structures distinctive to Indigenous peoples and their experience of unequal power relations, especially under colonialism. Not only the resources of their islands and seascapes but the very blood and kinships of Islanders were co-opted for the scientific and consumer fashions of the day.[24] These structures have by no means disappeared with the end of formal colonial rule. This is another reason why I am reluctant to embrace a continental conception of the Pacific world. Islands, Islanders, and their maritime connections are simply too essential. There is an old saying that 'islands are for the schooling of continents'. I haven't been able to trace its origin, but this adage suggests that there is something unique about littoral, liminal, 'peripheral' space that opens up the human spirit. The Pacific's multitude of islands, and enormous coastlands, have much to teach the continents surrounding them. As the following colour experiments will show, the sheer extent of their reach can bring about some very unexpected connections.

'Black Pacific'?

Although African trade networks had extended to Southeast Asia for centuries, it was the imperial age that brought people of African ancestry together to an unprecedented extent in the Pacific. The recent appearance of books with 'Black Pacific' in their titles is therefore not surprising. Is the use of this colour helpful in discerning an important and distinctive set of historical connections?

A partially 'Black Pacific' has existed for centuries, if only in the European imagination. The naming of various regions of the vast Pacific world had stemmed from European curiosity about the ancestral origins of various Pacific peoples, but also from the European preoccupation with hierarchies of 'civilization' and, eventually, of 'race'.[25] Polynesia (many islands), Micronesia (small islands), and Melanesia (black islands) are Eurocentric labels of no Indigenous significance. In the southwest Pacific, unlike other areas, Europeans wished to highlight the people's darker skin colour, as

---

[24] See M. Arvin, *Possessing Polynesians: The Science of Settler Colonial Whiteness in Hawai'i and Oceania* (Durham, NC: Duke University Press, 2019).
[25] See Chapter 48 by Bronwen Douglas in this volume.

when they nicknamed Aboriginal Australians 'blackfellas'. To do this they had to overlook the vast diversity of physical appearance, languages, social organization, and cultural practices in what they named 'Melanesia'. They labelled the inhabitants 'savages', a powerful yet inconsistent term combining the superior imperial gaze with a grudging admiration of physical prowess: 'The armchair explorer James Greenwood assured his Victorian readership that the prototypical savage – "forest-haunting, clothes-eschewing, arrow-poisoning, [and] man-devouring" – remained "vigorous".'[26]

By the nineteenth century the colloquial name of a new labour trade – the 'blackbirding' of Melanesian Islanders – was drawing upon a repertoire of images, vocabulary, justifications, and protests relating to African slavery. As Clive Moore explains, 'Thinking resembling the racial justification for slavery was used to justify entrapment of Pacific Islanders, and even more liberal Europeans regarded the Islanders as "niggers" and "savages" who could be exploited brutally.'[27] What began with enslavement for the guano mines on islands west of Peru spread south and west to include new plantations in Fiji started during the cotton shortage of the American Civil War. In Queensland, sugar planters took advantage of Australia's tropical northeast. Often a mutually agreeable system of contract labour, 'blackbirding' also included kidnapping, especially in the earlier decades, and the work and living conditions of Melanesian labourers could be dire. Concerned humanitarians began calling for regulation, but an end to 'blackbirding' came only with the expulsion of Melanesians from the newly created nation of Australia in 1901.

Meanwhile the maritime environment offered alternatives to plantation labour for black people, whether African or Pacific in ancestry, and made its own creative contribution to race relations. Scholarship on the 'Black Atlantic' is helpful here. Paul Gilroy estimates that up to a quarter of the Royal Navy's sailors were Africans, some (maybe many) having escaped slavery by knowing their way around a ship and, in the famous words of Frederick Douglass, 'Talk sailor like an old salt.'[28] This kind of research can help us to get at what Robbie Shilliam named the 'deep relationship' binding multiracial groups together in the Pacific world.[29] One example is Julius

---

[26] Cited in G.K. Behlmer, *Risky Shores: Savagery and Colonialism in the Western Pacific* (Stanford: Stanford University Press, 2018), 8.

[27] C. Moore, *Making Mala: Malaita in Solomon Islands, 1870s–1930s* (Canberra: ANU Press, 2017), 111.

[28] Cited in Gilroy, *The Black Atlantic*, 13.

[29] R. Shilliam, *The Black Pacific: Anti-Colonial Struggles and Oceanic Connections* (London: Bloomsbury, 2015), 1–2.

S. Scott's *The Common Wind: Afro-American Currents in the Age of the Haitian Revolution* (2018). Scott's work includes the objects, ideas, documents, and movements which criss-crossed the Caribbean maritime world in the age of anti-slavery rebellions. Of particular interest is his notion of 'the mystique of the sea' as essential to this transnational resistance movement.[30] Did Pacific currents also blow 'masterless men', craftswomen with revolutionary pamphlets, whalers carrying anti-slavery medallions, and sailors with tricolor cockades, into the trans-Pacific world? Did this become a distinctive milieu, just as the Haitian-inspired movement had been: hybrid, subaltern, separate from the better-known French and American revolutions?[31]

African Americans in the Pacific made a distinctive contribution to Indigenous political and socio-economic awareness long before World War II. By the 1920s, a multiracial, transnational trading community had drawn together Indigenous peoples from throughout the islands, including New Guinea. This island's large size and internationally disputed territory had limited European activities there until the later nineteenth century; not until the scramble for the Pacific in the 1880s, under pressure from the nearby Australian colonies, did Britain claim the southeastern portion as a new colony, which it transferred to Australian rule in 1905. At the end of World War I, German New Guinea to the north was also transferred to Australian control. Australia presided over a strikingly brutal system of racial segregation, even by the standards of the time, and by the late 1920s a few members of the Papuan workforce had had enough. Some boats' crews had encountered African American sailors. Bohun, a 'boss boy', or cargo master, for the Melanesian Company, 'had been laughed at by American Negro sailors in Kavieng who told him that his wages (then 3/- a month) were too low and outlined how he might organize a strike'.[32]

As Bill Gammage observes, African American crew were not particularly well paid themselves, 'but the disparity was sufficient to rankle, and in 1929 Bohun [became] a strike leader'.[33] The Islanders were not the only ones drawing on attitudes imported from the interwar United States. One white resident of Rabaul, furious at the disappearance of so many of his servants during the strike, 'rang the police station to see whether [his] boys had been

---

[30] J.S. Scott, *The Common Wind: Afro-American Currents in the Age of the Haitian Revolution* (London: Verso, 2018).

[31] See Chapter 44 by Sujit Sivasundaram in this volume and S. Sivasundaram, *Waves across the South: A New History of Revolution and Empire* (Chicago: University of Chicago Press, 2020).

[32] B. Gammage, 'The Rabaul Strike, 1929', *Journal of Pacific History* 10:3 (1975), 3–29, at 6.

[33] Gammage, 'The Rabaul Strike', 6.

arrested, or shouted to their neighbours to find out what was going on. "My coon's not here", called one, "and the damned stove's not even lit".'[34] The strike was short-lived and its leaders were severely punished: Jim Crow in the South Seas.

On the other side of the Pacific, African American civil rights activists began to ponder whether Japanese expansionists could be useful allies. Perhaps because this seems such an unlikely connection, few historians have explored it. Recent Japanese scholarship offers tantalizing glimpses, particularly of the interwar period when circumstances fostered a fledgling black internationalism. The Harlem Renaissance prompted some African American activists to seek non-white allies in both political and economic terms. Marcus Garvey launched a trans-Pacific transportation venture with Japanese support called the 'Black Star Line Steamship Corporation'.[35] Booker Washington launched the *Colored American Magazine* as a vehicle for activism, including contributions with a trans-Pacific focus. Some articles strained to build a rationale for connections between Afrian Americans and Asians; one even attempted to construct the Japanese as an 'Oceanic Negro' capable of getting the upper hand over white Euro-Americans as 'part and parcel of the Negro race'.[36]

Notions of trans-Pacific blackness, or at least shared non-whiteness, became a significant security concern for American counter-intelligence during World War II. W.E.B. Dubois's visit to Japan in 1936 may or may not have originated in Japan's office of Wartime Negro Propaganda Operations, but at the very least it presented Japan with an ideal opportunity to influence a high-profile African American intellectual and activist in the wake of Japan's invasion of Manchuria. In return, Dubois developed a 'black Manchurian narrative' by regarding the newly named Manchukuo as a 'new colored state on the Pacific Rim'.[37] Malcolm X magnified the potential subversiveness of trans-Pacific blackness by 'posing the possibility of a transnational alliance among people of color', playing to white paranoia about Asia in general and Japan in particular.[38] Some African American soldiers in the Pacific theatre believed 'The japs wasn't like the white people

---

[34] Gammage, 'The Rabaul Strike', 19.

[35] E. Taketani, *The Black Pacific Narrative: Geographic Imaginings of Race and Empire between the World Wars* (Hanover, NH: Dartmouth College Press, 2014), 9. See also Akami Tomoko, *Internationalizing the Pacific: The United States, Japan, and the Institute of Pacific Relations in War and Peace, 1919–45* (London: Routledge, 2002).

[36] Cited in Taketani, *The Black Pacific Narrative*, 19.

[37] Cited in Taketani, *The Black Pacific Narrative*, 158.

[38] Taketani, *The Black Pacific Narrative*, 6.

said they was. They was colored just like us, and they didn't want to kill us, they just wanted to kill the white soldiers.'[39]

Probably the best-known impact on Pacific Islanders and Southeast Asians during World War II involves the status of African American servicemen: an acceleration of processes we saw earlier in the Rabaul Strike. Indigenous peoples observed dark-skinned men wearing the same uniforms as white men, handling the same impressive weaponry, and working towards the same goals. The roots of civil rights and independence movements such as Maasina Rule in Solomon Islands had developed before the war, possibly facilitated by the shared language training and multi-ethnic population of the mission schools.[40] But a shared, lived experience of the Pacific theatre was the catalyst for more militant expressions of Island nationalism. We can 'recast black internationalism geographically' by placing the Pacific world at the centre of analysis.[41] Perhaps Barack Obama was aware of this in 2009 when he told a Tokyo audience that he was 'America's first Pacific President' because he understood that 'Asia and the United States are not separated by this great ocean; we are bound by it.'[42]

'Yellow Pacific' to 'Asia-Pacific'?

The Asian peoples of the Pacific had their own harrowing relationship with Western colonialism and modernity in the region. As Judith Bennett notes in this volume, a fully transregional history of the Chinese Pacific diaspora has yet to be written, although its outlines are already clear.[43] I would like to broaden her call to include Korean, Japanese, and other Asians in the Pacific world, noting the use of colour by white Westerners to designate disparate Asian peoples as one 'race', and to create persistent structures of exclusion

---

[39] Cited in Taketani, *The Black Pacific Narrative*, 3.

[40] For an excellent recent analysis in the context of a particular Solomon Islands culture, see D. Akin, *Colonialism, Maasina Rule, and the Origins of Malaitan Kastom* (Honolulu: University of Hawai'i Press, 2013); for more on transnational and transregional connections see T. Banivanua-Mar, *Decolonisation and the Pacific: Indigenous Globalisation and the Ends of Empire* (Cambridge: Cambridge University Press, 2016).

[41] Taketani, *The Black Pacific Narrative*, 12.

[42] Cited in Taketani, *The Black Pacific Narrative*, 185.

[43] See Judith Bennett's Chapter 5 in Volume I. For a review of the recent literature see P. D'Arcy, 'The Chinese Pacifics: a brief historical review', *Journal of Pacific History* 49:4 (2014), 396–420. For a pioneering study of Asian foreign policy in the Pacific Islands, see R. Crocombe, *Asia in the Pacific Islands: Replacing the West* (Suva: University of the South Pacific for the Institute of Pacific Studies, 2007).

and persecution. Unlike 'black', the colour 'yellow' has not been embraced today as part of a proud identity.

It was Kaiser Wilhelm II who first labelled Asians *die gelbe Gefahr*, 'the yellow peril', amid falling white birthrates in Europe and North America in the later nineteenth century. Meanwhile, Chinese and other Asians had been trading with Pacific Islanders and Aboriginal Australians for millennia. In terms of Chinese migration, beyond these ancient trading patterns, *huashang* ('traders') were joined in the nineteenth century by the *huagong* ('overseas labourers') hired by colonial administrations and Euro-American businesses in the Pacific Islands as well as the rimlands. By the early twentieth century, *huaqiao* ('sojourners') had joined these earlier groups to form more settled Chinese communities and their distinctive Chinatowns. Another flow, since about 1980, are the transnational *huayi* ('ethnic Chinese') who have been settling, investing, and buying extensive property across the Pacific world and beyond.[44] In addition to these categories of migrants, Chinese also crewed and serviced vessels in Pacific port towns, suggesting that coastal China featured 'communities more orientated towards the sea than were the European cultures and communities that built, owned, and captained the vessels on which many Chinese shipped out'.[45]

Filipinos and Japanese were also shaping the development of new imperial borderlands from coastal British Columbia to the Priamur region of the Russian empire.[46] By the late nineteenth century, both Japan and the United States were expanding their Asian empires; after defeating Spain in 1898, American rule in the Philippines replaced the political context, but not the long history, of Filipino migration and community-building across the Pacific world. There is ample evidence of ancient Filipino exploration and trade into Micronesia, and from the earliest days of Spain's trans-Pacific empire, 'Manila-men' (and some women) crewed trade vessels, provided translation services, and worked at Spanish ports. By the late twentieth century, their expatriate numbers in the Pacific world were second only to China's, but their main migration routes had shifted. Where they had once established families in the Pacific Islands, the Blue Continent was increasingly

---

[44] D'Arcy, 'Chinese Pacifics', 398, outlines the terminology pioneered in Wang Gungwu, 'The study of Chinese identities in Southeast Asia', in J.W. Cushman and W. Gungwu (eds.), *Changing Identities of the Southeast Asian Chinese since World War II* (Hong Kong: Hong Kong University Press, 1988), 11–16.

[45] D'Arcy, 'Chinese Pacifics', 407.

[46] I. Saveliev, 'Migrants and borderland identity: a comparative study of Japanese communities in British Columbia and the Priamur region in the 1870s–1900s', *Forum of International Development Studies* 40 (2011), 79–94.

irrelevant after airlines enabled direct travel to the United States for work. 'This eastward orientation largely bypassed Oceania, which remained an area to fly over rather than a region to engage with in any substantial way', except for the US territories of Guam and Hawai'i.[47]

After yellow gold drew an unprecedented number of Asians across the Pacific, the Western colonial powers began to perceive their skills and endurance as threats. From California in 1849 to southeastern Australia in the 1850s, British Columbia in 1870, and on to the Klondike in the 1890s, Asians – mainly Chinese – flocked to the goldfields as part of a multiracial brotherhood of hopeful miners. A few women accompanied them, but at first this was a man's world where about 5,000 men flocked to the California rush from Australia and Aotearoa New Zealand alone, contributing 'a variety of the *genus* Pacific Man whose habitat is no particular country but the goldfields'.[48] At New Westminster, near present-day Vancouver, Chinese offering laundry and food services to the growing city were joined by those who had survived the gruelling task of building the Canadian Pacific railroad through two mountain ranges from the Canadian prairies to the Pacific coast.

In response to these growing communities, anti-Asian legislation proliferated in Australia, Aotearoa New Zealand, and North America from the 1880s onward, as governments and social discourses began to view Asia as an existential threat. From goldfields to Parliaments, so-called 'yellow hordes' became symbolic of white fears about the falling Caucasian birthrate, the supposed undermining of labour standards and wages, unfounded rumours about a 'white slave trade', and inaccurate understandings of disease outbreaks, among many other excuses. What became known as the 'White Australia' policy was a top priority for the new Commonwealth of Australia in 1901: 'Once viewed as a remote outpost of the British Empire, Australia could now be seen as central to the greatest geopolitical challenges of the twentieth century.'[49] Head taxes, housing restrictions, limited family migration, and outright immigration bans were usually focused on Chinese, but public prejudice in the United States and the British colonies against settlement tended to view all Asians as interchangeable threats. As Franck Billé explains, 'yellow peril' discourse was 'inherently fractured and multiple'.[50]

---

[47] D'Arcy, 'The Philippines as a Pacific nation', 17.
[48] G. Horne, *The White Pacific: U.S. Imperialism and Black Slavery in the South Seas after the Civil War* (Honolulu: University of Hawai'i Press, 2007), 153.
[49] F. Billé and S. Urbansky (eds.), *Yellow Perils: China Narratives in the Contemporary World* (Honolulu: University of Hawai'i Press, 2018), 23.
[50] Billé and Urbansky, *Yellow Perils*, 7.

By 1907 there were large Anti-Asian protests on the west coast of North America from San Francisco to Vancouver, generating desperate migration between Pacific ports by Chinese and others trying to flee draconian taxation and litigation from one jurisdiction to another.[51] Many reached a new potential home only to find that the panic had followed them. Swept up in the 'yellow peril' were migrants from British-ruled India. Despite coming from outside the Pacific region altogether, as so-called 'Asians' or 'coolies' they were usually unwelcome. The Japanese vessel *Komagata Maru* arrived in 1914 at Vancouver amid legal and political turmoil concerning immigration from other parts of the British empire, especially when the immigrants were non-whites. Confined to their ship in appalling conditions, the Punjabi passengers were eventually forced to return to India.[52]

But by no means were white people the only ones prejudiced against Asians. Anna Julia Cooper, a black feminist and activist in the late nineteenth-century United States, criticized the anti-black racism of her white feminist sisters, but reproduced 'yellow peril' tropes in her view of Chinese culture: 'The Chinese shoe of to-day does not more entirely dwarf, cramp, and destroy her physical powers, than have the customs . . . which from remotest ages have governed our Sister of the East, enervated and blighted her mental and moral life.'[53] Cooper's Orientalist descriptions of Asians, particularly Chinese women, demonstrate how powerfully 'yellow peril' discourse could spread beyond its Euro-American origins.[54]

Meanwhile, Japanese conceptions of the Pacific world are particularly important, not only because of their long history, but because they became a rationale for Japan's expanding Pacific empire in the early twentieth century. Like other Asians, Japanese crewed ships, set up businesses, and founded communities across the *Taiheiyō* (Pacific) Ocean for centuries. Numerous Japanese worked as indentured labourers in Hawai'i and in various countries in South America.

By 1936, the Japanese government had evolved a 'South Seas policy', including the creation of a South Seas Section in the Foreign Office, and a

---

[51] See E. Lee, 'Hemispheric Orientalism and the 1907 Pacific Coast race riots', *Amerasia Journal* 33:2 (2007), 19–47.

[52] Radicalized by their experiences, they were confronted by British police when trying to disembark in India, and this whole episode contributed to rising anti-British nationalism in India during and after World War I; see A.G. Roy, *Imperialism and Sikh Migration: The Komagata Maru Incident* (London: Routledge, 2017).

[53] Cited in H.H. Jun, *Race for Citizenship: Black Orientalism and Asian Uplift from Pre-Emancipation to Neoliberal America* (New York: New York University Press, 2011), 33.

[54] Jun, *Race for Citizenship*, 48.

South Seas Development Company to oversee Japanese migration and land acquisition in the Pacific world.[55] The issue of real estate was complicated by generalized anti-Asian discrimination around the region as articulated, for example, in the 1920 Alien Land Law in California. Japanese American homes, with their mantlepiece photographs of the emperor and Mount Fuji, were models of the aspirational American Dream. But after Pearl Harbor, such images returned Japanese Americans to the category of dangerous 'other', when recently they had been allies. On the American Pacific coast, and in British Columbia in Canada, Japanese citizens were forcibly removed from their homes and confined to detention camps. Japanese Americans in Hawai'i, however, were able to avoid a similar scale of detentions through the sheer strength of local interfaith and intercultural networks and leadership.[56]

The Japanese entanglement with Rapa Nui off the South American coast is a lesser-known case of transregional connections. The most geographically distant point with evidence of ancient Polynesian settlement, Rapa Nui is best known for its remarkable stone statues and for evidence of a widespread collapse in the local economy before the arrival of Europeans in the eighteenth century. Peruvian slave raiders and European diseases further shrank the population. After Chile annexed Rapa Nui in 1888, there was talk of ceding the island to Japan for badly needed income, but despite keen interest by the Japanese Navy, 'negotiations were informally discontinued due to the island's proximity to Australia and the detrimental effects that this might have had on the course of Anglo-Japanese and US–Japanese relations'.[57] Today, people of Japanese ancestry form large, thriving minority communities in Latin America and the islands: from 1990 until 2000 Alberto Fujimori was President of Peru, cultivating stronger economic ties with Japan, and eventually fleeing there amid charges of corruption and human rights abuses.

Meanwhile, the British colony of Fiji, annexed in 1874, was in need of non-Indigenous labour. Essentialized as primitive 'natives' in need of benevolent imperial protection, Indigenous Fijians were to stay in their villages; outside labour would need to be imported. As elsewhere in Southeast Asia and on Mauritius, the British turned to India, recruiting (often through corrupt

---

[55] Cited in G. McCall, 'Japan, Rapanui and Chile's uncertain sovereignty', *Rapa Nui Journal* 9:1 (1995), 1–7, at 3.
[56] T. Coffman (dir.), *The First Battle: The Battle for Equality in War-Time Hawaii* (San Francisco: Center for Asian American Media, 2006), DVD.
[57] McCall, 'Japan, Rapanui and Chile's uncertain sovereignty', 3. Also see C.H. Gardiner, *The Japanese and Peru, 1873–1973* (Albuquerque: University of New Mexico Press, 1975).

middlemen) tens of thousands of Indians to work on Fijian plantations owned mainly by Euro-American investors.[58] Unlike British Columbia or the Australian colonies, British officials deemed these 'Asians' to be useful, as long as they knew their place. However, after Fijian independence in 1970, their numbers grew to the point of threatening Indigenous control of the government. The result was military coups, the arrest and torture of Indo-Fijian leaders, and expulsion from the Commonwealth.[59] Today Fiji governs itself more peacefully and democratically, but the question remains: who is a Fijian?

Another focal point for nineteenth-century Asian connections in the Pacific is the prominent statue of Chinese nationalist Sun Yat-sen that stands in Honolulu's Chinatown. In the long history of Chinese in the transnational Pacific, 'the longest unbroken line of Chinese Pacific Islanders derives from the *huashang*, who arrived shortly after the middle of the 19th century'.[60] Many were drawn to Hawai'i as indentured labourers, family members, and prospective business owners. Sun, the future revolutionary and founding father of the Chinese Republic, was educated in the Hawaiian Kingdom, attending two denominational secondary schools in Honolulu in the late 1870s and early 1880s during King Kalākaua's reign. As Lorenz Gonschor explains, Sun's earliest ideas about modernizing China arose during this time, and he praised the Hawaiian Kingdom for providing a model of democratic, non-Western modernity.[61]

During the later twentieth century, political and economic confidence inspired Asians to create their own terminologies and identities within the Pacific region. In the 1980s we began to read of 'Asia-Pacific', especially in Asian business circles and educational materials: a direct English translation of the Japanese *Ajiataiheiyō chiiki*.

Launched in 1989, a new international organization for economic integration used this new terminology in its title: Asia Pacific Economic Cooperation (APEC). This Asian-inspired configuration was trans-Pacific, drawing economic ties across the ocean from Asia to Australia, Aotearoa New Zealand, Canada, and the United States. A remarkable transformation had taken place: at least at the official level, 'yellow peril' discourse had given

---

[58] For a general overview of Indian indenture during this period see C. Tumbe, *India Moving: A History of Migration* (Gurgaon: Penguin Random House, 2018).

[59] B.V. Lal, *Islands of Turmoil: Elections and Politics in Fiji* (Canberra: ANU Press, 2006).

[60] D'Arcy, 'Chinese Pacifics', 410.

[61] L. Gonschor, 'Revisiting the Hawaiian influence on the political thought of Sun Yat-sen', *Journal of Pacific History* 52:1 (2017), 52–67, at 58.

way to a more respectful (or at least pragmatic) understanding of the integration and importance of trans-Pacific economic ties. Officially, the age of Western imperial domination in many parts of Asia had given way to the era of decolonization and political independence.

However, Helen Jun warns us about the 'poverty of a focus on "racial prejudice"' by white people.[62] 'Contemporary black Orientalisms', especially in Pacific port cities like Los Angeles, need to be considered in their full scope, 'not merely as something white people do', because, in Jun's opinion, 'black disenfranchisement is structurally related to new Asian immigration and the rise of the so-called Pacific Rim economy'.[63] From the 1990s, real estate markets around the rimworld rapidly inflated under pressure from newly wealthy Asian elites, pricing local populations out of housing. Now anti-Asian prejudice and persecution is rising again in response to the COVID-19 pandemic, even as 'Black Lives Matter' and its allies are taking a broader consciousness of structural racism to the streets. Jun warns of America's 'worst yellow peril nightmare' not as an artefact of history, but as a significant danger yet to come.[64]

'Red Pacific'?

The flourishing 'Red Atlantic' historiography needs to be addressed here. Intended to highlight the role of Indigenous people as 'diplomats, soldiers and sailors, slaves, tourists, performers, and more',[65] studies of the 'Red Atlantic' depict the Indigenous peoples of the Americas as active agents in their own histories and as direct contributors to the creation of the modern Atlantic world. However, the word 'Red' was imposed upon Indigenous peoples by their imperial conquerors, and is not embraced as a form of self-identification. Given that, are there any advantages to thinking about a 'Red Pacific'?

Important as it has been in this chapter to highlight mobility and interconnection, trans-Pacific lines of communication were mainly constructed during an era of vastly unequal power relations. That era began in part when the first European explorers began calling Pacific Islanders, Aboriginal Australians, and some Southeast Asian peoples 'Indians'. From the day

---

[62] Jun, *Race for Citizenship*, 100.   [63] Jun, *Race for Citizenship*, 100.
[64] Jun, *Race for Citizenship*, 100.
[65] J. Weaver, *The Red Atlantic: American Indigenes and the Making of the Modern World, 1000–1927* (Chapel Hill: University of North Carolina Press, 2014), xi.

Christopher Columbus stepped ashore in what he thought was the 'Indies', successive generations of Europeans kept labelling Indigenous North Americans 'Indians', right across to the Pacific coast. In the nineteenth century, the description became 'Red Indians', to distinguish the Indigenous peoples of the Americas from subjects of the British Raj in India. Meanwhile, many British explorers continued to call newly encountered Indigenous peoples 'Indians',[66] right across the Pacific to the island of New Guinea, where newly named 'Indians' stared the original Southeast Asian 'Indies' in the face. Inscribed across more than half the planet, the imperial gaze erased local identities and circumstances, moving steadily and arrogantly westward from Europe.

Nevertheless, we can see some commonalities of experience. The pioneering work of David Chappell illustrates the value of a trans-Pacific approach to understanding Indigenous responses to the chaos and dislocation of colonialism. Successive diasporas of Indigenous peoples took ship with Europeans from the sixteenth century onward, crewing the voyages west from the South American silver mines and Californian ports to Guam, where recently rediscovered 'star caves' demonstrate the ancient history of navigation and exploration in Micronesia. From Manila to Asia, and on to Europe, they translated and negotiated for Spanish and Portuguese traders. More recently, they have emigrated to the rimworld in search of better opportunities for their families. 'With more familiarity and growing demand, Oceanian voyagers found niches ranging from proletarian kanaka to ennobled tourist'.[67]

For these reasons and more, a 'Red Pacific' would need a much longer timeline than the 'Red Atlantic' does. The vast geographical spread of the sweet potato tells us that at some point BCE, Pacific Islanders made first contact with today's Indigenous peoples of the coastal Americas. Prehistoric contacts, and possible genetic relationships, remain a matter of intense debate.[68] However, by the sixteenth century, Spanish activities in the Pacific were creating new and very different connections. The silver trade, identified by Dennis Flynn and Arturo Giraldez as the world's first fully globalized economic system, stretched from the Pacific coast of the

---

[66] For example, Captain Cook described meeting 'Indian Chiefs' at Tahiti and its neighbouring islands in 1768; J. Hawkesworth, *An Account of the Voyages Undertaken by the Order of His Present Majesty, for Making Discoveries in the Southern Hemisphere* (Dublin: James Williams, 1775), vol. II, I.

[67] D.A. Chappell, *Double Ghosts: Oceanian Voyagers on Euroamerican Ships* (Armonk, NY: M.E. Sharpe, 1997), 22.

[68] See chapters by David Christian, Lisa Matisoo-Smith, Stuart Bedford, Atholl Anderson, and José Miguel Ramírez Aliaga in Volume I.

Spanish-ruled Americas, to Guam and other Micronesian islands of the central Pacific, and on to Spain's colony in the Philippines on the doorstep of the Asian markets.[69] By the eighteenth century, French and British explorers and traders were challenging this 'Spanish Lake', creating a framework for Indigenous activities to enlarge their scope once again.

Captain James Cook visited the northwest coast of North America, and on the west coast of Vancouver Island he relied on Chief Maquinna's power to negotiate trade in valuable sea otter fur and timber in the region. Nineteenth-century Polynesian 'Kanakas' would later live and work on the same coast, while local First Nations traders and Native Americans would travel to Polynesia and beyond.[70] As late as 1930 a beaver weather vane watched over the site of the Hudson's Bay Company (HBC) post at the corner of Queen and Fort streets in Honolulu, and a carved beaver presided over the 'Beaver Coffee Saloon'.[71] Later, these connections between north and south Pacific worlds were occluded by the geographical boundaries of mid-twentieth-century 'Area Studies', as discussed earlier. Thankfully they are being redis-covered, not only in historical scholarship, but in current cultural exchanges. 'First Nations Art from British Columbia' brought Indigenous visual arts and crafts to Honolulu's East–West Centre in 2019–20, accompanied by gallery talks that included historical discussions of Hawaiian–Northwest Coast exchanges and new communities.[72]

Pacific Islanders also lived and traded from Asia to South America. Some carried sandalwood from their home islands to China at the behest of King Kamehameha of Hawai'i who, disgusted with the gouging harbour fees at Canton, retaliated by instituting fees of his own at Honolulu. Others worked on sealing, whaling, fur trade, and fishing vessels crisscrossing the Pacific. Ten Yapese caused a sensation in Hong Kong by wearing silk top hats purchased from an English merchant, and then discarding their loincloths during an impromptu performance for resident Europeans.[73] Today, numer-ous I Kiribati and other Pacific Islanders crew vessels throughout the Pacific world and beyond, joined by Filipinos and Bangladeshis.[74]

---

[69] D.O. Flynn and A. Giraldez, 'Born again: globalization's sixteenth century origins', *Pacific Economic Review* 13:3 (2008), 359–87.
[70] J. Barman, *Leaving Paradise: Indigenous Hawaiians in the Pacific Northwest, 1787–1898* (Honolulu: University of Hawai'i Press, 2006).
[71] R. Watson, 'HBC in the Hawaiian Islands', *The Beaver* (June 1930), 7–8.
[72] www.eastwestcenter.org/events/exhibition-first-nations-art-british-columbia.
[73] Chappell, *Double Ghosts*, 109.
[74] A. Couper, *Sailors and Traders: A Maritime History of the Pacific Peoples* (Honolulu: University of Hawai'i Press, 2009), 186–206.

Recent work on Indigenous mobility in the trans-Pacific world has echoed many of the themes of 'Red Atlantic' scholarship, but without using its colour-coded terminology.[75] Ideas, languages, economic patterns, and material culture were on the move along with Indigenous bodies. 'The world after the inauguration of the Red Atlantic', writes Jace Weaver, 'when Vikings kidnapped the Beothuk boys Vimar and Valthof, was forever and majorly different from what it was the moment before. That was true for both colonizer and colonized.'[76] Similar points could be made about Pacific culture contacts, from the famous encounters between European explorers and Islanders, to everyday intimacies and influences. On the *luau* table in Hawai'i is found the now-traditional *lomi lomi* salmon, the legacy of largely forgotten connections to the North American rimlands. Masters of preserving salmon, First Nations on the northwest coast taught their techniques to European and American visitors, and helped to crew the HBC supply ships to Honolulu, bringing barrels of salmon with them. Eaten on ships and in ports across the Pacific World since the nineteenth century, northwest coast salmon fed crews in the fo'csle, and enhanced the Japanese sushi chef's art.

Glynn Barratt, whose extensive work on Russia did so much to open up the study of its Pacific empire, has claimed a comparatively peaceful interaction with some Pacific peoples: 'Russia's maritime and hydrographic record in the Central Polynesia of the early nineteenth century is a particularly proud one, fully equal to the British or the French and almost free of violence and bloodshed.'[77] But he is speaking here mainly of Russian naval officers. Merchant captains were not usually as educated, or as morally scrupulous. Ryan Jones tells us of two Eveni girls from Siberia who appeared at the Russian Consul's office in Honolulu in 1860. They claimed to have been kidnapped and subsequently abandoned, adding their own distinctive experiences to a transregional story of Indigenous mobility and its costs.[78] Experiences like these embody, on an individual scale, the racist exploitation and dispossession that would engulf an entire continent – Australia – and would bring disease, war, and cultural dislocation to countless other peoples.

---

[75] For example N. Thomas, *Islanders: The Pacific in the Age of Empire* (New Haven: Yale University Press, 2010), and for a pioneering study of Indigenous Pacific travellers to London see C. Thrush, *Indigenous London: Native Travelers at the Heart of Empire* (New Haven: Yale University Press, 2016).

[76] Weaver, *Red Atlantic*, 268.

[77] G. Barratt, 'Russian activity among the Cook Islands, to 1820', *New Zealand Slavonic Journal* (1998), 34–98, at 35.

[78] R. Jones, 'Kelp highways, Siberian girls in Maui, and nuclear walruses: the North Pacific in a Sea of Islands', *Journal of Pacific History* 49:4 (2014), 373–95, at 384–5.

Entrepreneurs from the British settler colonies in Canada, and from the United States, entered the Pacific world with experience of lands cleared, by treaty or otherwise, of so-called 'Red Indians', and these connections are worth exploring more deeply than they have been to date. David Igler has noticed them:

> As much as any other set of factors, the US–Mexico War, the California gold rush, and US annexation of its initial Pacific Coast territories forever altered the oceanic connections and, in the process, reconfigured large portions of the coastal geography. For the expansionist United States, much of the *eastern* Pacific became the American *West*. [original emphasis][79]

The newly independent states of Central and South America were also expanding their Pacific frontiers. Peter Dillon, trading sandalwood and other products from the South Pacific Islands, noted people at Valparaiso from many islands, including Indigenous crew members who had jumped ship from various vessels and were working at the port for passage money to return home.[80] These longstanding connections between South America and the Pacific Islands motivated Peruvian labour traders to capture Islanders for work in the guano mines in the mid-nineteenth century. From Rapa Nui, the Marquesas Islands, and elsewhere, these forced labourers provided an unfortunate model for the 'blackbirding' of Melanesians. The labour ships, like most other vessels in the Pacific, featured Pacific Islander crew, such as the fifteen Māori aboard the whaler *Grecian* in 1863. They didn't necessarily realize that they were on a voyage to enslave fellow Indigenous peoples and, along with some of the Euro-American crew, abandoned ship at Sāmoa rather than continue on such a mission.[81] Even rare female Indigenous crew members could defy poor treatment: the steward on the American trader *Golden Cross* in 1862 'hove a jug at the captain's temple (lacerating it) and left without liberty'.[82] Indigenous women and men like her, along with their families, sustained the trans-Pacific sailortowns and their multiracial populations. 'Coastal entrepôts operated in a global geography of connection, not with nations or the capitals of other polities, but primarily, even exclusively, with other local port towns'.[83]

---

[79] Igler, *The Great Ocean*, 10.
[80] J.W. Davidson, *Peter Dillon of Vanikoro: Chevalier of the South Seas* (Oxford: Oxford University Press, 1975), 83–4.
[81] Couper, *Sailors and Traders*, 107–8.   [82] Couper, *Sailors and Traders*, 114.
[83] Armitage et al., *Oceanic Histories*, 5.

Some Pacific leaders drew the borders of an Indigenous Pacific even wider than Western conceptions of ethnic or racial boundaries. King David Kalākaua of Hawai'i was a proud scholar of his own people's culture, publishing *Legends and Myths of Hawaii* in 1888 and encouraging the academic study of Hawaiian history.[84] He was also an ambitious, outward-looking statesman. Before leaving on a world tour in 1881 – the first by any monarch in world history – he expressed a connection between Hawai'i's diversity and the need to protect its sovereignty:

> I desire the best welfare of all who gather under our flag in my dominions, and I believe that you who come from other lands, bringing with you the wealth, enterprise, and intelligence of those lands, sympathize with me in my desire to protect my native Hawaiian people, and strengthen my nation.[85]

From Kalākaua's perspective, Asians were an integral part of an Indigenous Pacific. In Japan during his world tour, he highlighted Hawai'i's democratic modernity, shared insights with the Meiji Emperor, and discussed an immigration agreement that could help Hawai'i to survive by ensuring a reliable labour supply. Kalākaua's kingdom was an independent nation, but Japan in the 1930s was an internationally recognized empire. In a shortlived attempt to cement an alliance between them against the rampaging Western colonial powers, Kalākaua proposed a marriage between his niece and a Japanese prince. An attempt to negotiate an equal treaty between the two countries was also shortlived, thwarted by British and American espionage, revealing a possible future for independent Indigenous sovereignty that was delayed but never forgotten.[86]

Pekka Korhonen notes that 'Pacific Age rhetoric seems to appear in cycles ... It has hibernated in the shelves of old libraries under a warm blanket of dust, until a new enthusiast has arrived with shining eyes and wiped the dust away.'[87] Sometimes those shining eyes belonged to Pacific Islanders: Kalākaua's initiatives, long before the phrase 'Asia-Pacific' entered

---

[84] B. Finney et al., 'Hawaiian historians and the First Pacific History Seminar', in N. Gunson (ed.), *The Changing Pacific: Essays in Honour of H.E. Maude* (Oxford: Oxford University Press, 1978), 308–16.

[85] S.L. Kamehiro, *The Arts of Kingship: Hawaiian Art and National Culture of the Kalākaua Era* (Honolulu: University of Hawai'i Press, 2009), 24.

[86] Gonschor, 'Revisiting the Hawaiian influence on the political thought of Sun Yat-sen', and his Chapter 49 in this volume.

[87] P. Korhonen, 'The Pacific Age in world history', *Journal of World History* 7:1 (1996), 41–70, at 69–70.

our common vocabulary, had attempted to bring Islanders and Asians together to stand up to Euro-American imperialism. Europeans may have created separate racial labels for 'yellow' and 'red' peoples at that time, but this was of no more importance to Kalākaua than it was to the countless mixed-race crews and families of the Pacific world. Today these trans-Pacific connections usually follow employment: female-dominated at resorts and factories, and male-dominated in fisheries and cargo shipping, reminding us that the Pacific world is also 'a regional capitalist formation'[88] in which economics, gender, and race continue to shape Indigenous communities. Any academic conception of a Red Pacific, like similar conceptions of a Red Atlantic, will always fall well short of the complex realities of life, trade, family, and geopolitics.

'White Pacific'?

The elephant in the room, the gaze that constructs all of these other kaleidescopic configurations as 'coloured', is of course the White Pacific. After early modern European explorers and cartographers created the first cartographic globes, the Pacific was increasingly pinned down, pulled away from the encircling Oceanus of European medieval imagination, and reconfigured as an inconveniently large space between continents. From the late fifteenth century the Portuguese explored and exploited Asia and Africa; the Spanish did the same with the Americas. In between was a Pacific filled with Europe's longing for gold, magical beasts, and tropical sex. Dangers abounded in its 'uncharted' vastness, including lingering death from scurvy and starvation. Britain's Captain James Cook contained it within its modern grid of latitude and longitude, lessening both the dangers and the fantasies: no more great southern continent, or magical beasts, and far less gold than anticipated. Tropical sex remains a fantasy pinned upon the Pacific map, although these days tourists of any sort in the Pacific Islands are as likely to be Asian as European or American. They are drawn to the colours of the Pacific world, including its vivid coral reefs and multicoloured fish. The impact of watervision, enabled by SCUBA technology and television from the 1950s, made Jacques Cousteau an international star, and brought the

---

[88] K.J. Leong, 'The many labors of the gendered trans-Pacific world', in C.C. Choy and J.T.-C. Wu, *Gendering the Trans-Pacific World: Diaspora, Gender and Race* (Leiden: Brill, 2017), 20–38, at 23.

spectacular beauty of the underwater Pacific to the sitting rooms of the Western world and beyond.[89]

Writing in 2001, historian of the Atlantic world David Armitage lamented that 'Until quite recently, Atlantic history seemed to be available in any color, so long as it was white.'[90] Here Pacific scholarship has a considerable advantage: since its inception in the 1960s, it has emphasized the central importance of Indigenous agency in detailed studies of culture contact in the islands. After the postcolonial revolution in the 1980s, Pacific Studies rarely succumbed to a totalizing, reductive view of colonial power. Unequal power relations could be held in creative tension with agency. Nevertheless, the Blue Continent needed to be raised because both geopolitics and academic analysis still tended to put white people and their empires at the focus of attention. Indigenous peoples responded in a wide variety of ways, but were not usually cast as setting the agenda, let alone determining the outcome. The Blue Continent was a powerful way of articulating something that was formative rather than responsive. After all, the connections, worldviews, explorations, and travels of Pacific Islanders had created Pacific worlds long before Europeans ever arrived.

However, by the nineteenth century the Pacific world had been mapped, reimagined, and promoted as a vehicle for white Euro-American interests. On his world tour in 1842, Sir George Simpson, governor-in-chief of the Hudson's Bay Company, called at Honolulu after inspecting company operations along the coasts of today's British Columbia, Washington, Oregon, and northern California. Simpson imagined a transregional Pacific trade network based on existing commodities such as sea otter fur from the northwest coast of North America and sandalwood from Hawai'i and other Pacific islands. British goods were exchanged for these items at Canton for tea and luxury goods. After becoming an official agent of the Hawaiian government along with Timoteo Ha'alilio and others, Simpson helped to promote Hawaiian independence among the Western colonial powers, eventually publishing his journal of the first known circumnavigation of the world by land. Reflecting on his trans-Pacific dreams of empire, Simpson envisioned the island of Oahu as 'the emporium of at least the Pacific ocean, for the products, natural and artificial, of every corner of the

---

[89] A. Elias, *Coral Empire: Underwater Oceans, Colonial Tropics, Visual Modernity* (Durham, NC: Duke University Press, 2019), 199–213.

[90] D. Armitage, 'The Red Atlantic', *Reviews in American History* 29:4 (2001), 479–86, at 479.

globe', and Honolulu, under benevolent British patronage, would become 'one of the marts of the world'.[91]

Here was the racialized superiority with which most of his white contemporaries viewed this profitable, inviting Pacific world. They poured into the British colonies of settlement from Vancouver Island and British Columbia to Aotearoa New Zealand and Australia. They pushed the boundaries of the United States westward. Talk of 'vanishing' Indigenous races, supposedly melting away before them, haunted catastrophic policies such as the residential school system in western Canada or 'White Australia' policies that included the Stolen Generation of mixed-race children forcibly adopted out to white families. As Stuart Banner observed, 'in some respects the peoples of the region had more in common in the nineteenth century than they do now'.[92] This old imperial network has recently been re-engaged by scholars interested in postcolonial and gender theory, among others, leading to a thriving comparative literature on settler colonialism.[93]

Is there still a 'White Pacific'? Demographically speaking, there never was. Caucasians have always been a minority racial group in this vast region, and settler colonialism did not always have a white face.[94] Economically speaking, the answer is equivocal. Many former colonial businesses remain, sometimes under new names. As recent mining scandals in Bougainville and elsewhere have demonstrated, transnational capitalism remains a powerful force. Asian financing, especially from China, has transformed any straightforward picture of white, Western economic colonialism. But is a focus on super-rich Asian elites just a distraction from the enormous ongoing influence of the United States and other traditional Western powers?

We must expose this question to the blinding white light of 'two suns': the era of nuclear testing in the Pacific world. From the Australian outback to

---

[91] G. Simpson, *An Overland Journey round the World during the Years 1841 and 1842*, vol. II (Philadelphia: Lea and Blanchard, 1847), 50–1.

[92] S. Banner, *Possessing the Pacific: Land, Settlers, and Indigenous People from Australia to Alaska* (Cambridge, MA: Harvard University Press, 2007), 1; also see J. Belich, *Replenishing the Earth: The Settler Revolution and the Rise of the Anglo-World, 1783–1939* (Oxford: Oxford University Press, 2011).

[93] Also see M. Lake, *Progressive New World: How Settler Colonialism and Transpacific Exchange Shaped American Reform* (Cambridge, MA: Harvard University Press, 2018); A.E. Coombes, *Rethinking Settler Colonialism: History and Memory in Australia, Canada, Aotearoa New Zealand and South Africa* (Manchester: Manchester University Press, 2006); J. Weaver, *The Great Land Rush and the Making of the Modern World, 1650–1900* (Montreal: McGill-Queen's University Press, 2003).

[94] S.X. Lu, *The Making of Japanese Settler Colonialism: Malthusianism and Trans-Pacific Migration, 1868–1961* (Cambridge: Cambridge University Press, 2019).

Bikini Atoll, Indigenous peoples were subjected to catastrophic environmental destruction and radiation damage. Entire islands were destroyed even more surely than they had been by phosphate mining. Communities were forced to relocate, sometimes very far from their home islands, only to find that the white light had permanently damaged their own bodies and those of their children. Public protest brought American testing to a halt in 1962 but France continued until 1996. Assisted by regional configurations such as the South Pacific Forum, the newly independent island nation of Belau created the first anti-nuclear constitution in world history in 1979. Aboriginal Australians and their allies, including British and American veterans of the Australian nuclear tests, began pressuring their governments for information and compensation. Although major powers on the other side of the Cold War also conducted nuclear testing, neither China nor the Soviet Union did so in the Pacific. The killing white light was unleashed only on the side of the Western allies.

The White Pacific is also a state of mind. Its importance has waxed and waned in twentieth-century American geopolitics, especially before World War II when 'the idea of the twentieth century as the Pacific Age died in 1929', to be replaced by an 'American Age' as proudly proclaimed by the publisher of *Life* magazine in 1941.[95] The growing environmental catastrophe in the region was not yet a priority, but nuclear non-proliferation was. At a conference in Canberra in 1970, representatives from Aotearoa New Zealand, Australia, and the United States met to consider the changing scene. Mary Boyd, providing a view from the southwest Pacific, used imagery that was both candid and shocking: the island groups of Micronesia, Polynesia, and Melanesia currently formed 'three great shields that guard the sea and air approaches from East and Southeast Asia to Australia, New Zealand, Hawaii, and the United States'.[96]

Here was rimbound thinking at its worst, with Pacific Islanders, their homelands, and their maritime environment reduced to nuclear 'shields'. Boyd also noted Indigenous protests against the outflow of capital from the islands, broken promises on capital development, and backlash against compulsory land appropriation for timber and mining industries. Of such stuff was postcolonial critique born, and the Blue Continent raised.

---

[95] Cited in Korhonen, 'The Pacific Age', 64.
[96] M. Boyd, 'The Southwest Pacific in the 1970s', in B. Brown (ed.), *Asia and the Pacific in the 1970s: The Roles of the United States, Australia, and New Zealand* (Canberra: ANU Press, 1971), 61–88, at 61.

'The population of the region was minuscule but the area's strategic value could be important', read Boyd's briefing, and to secure it 'either [the Islands] should be heavily subsidized or their people should be enabled to move out to the metropolitan powers' own territories, and so attain higher living standards'.[97] This breathtaking dismissal of the heart of the Pacific – its Islanders and their maritime environment – was merely one form of rim-world consciousness that would prevail for decades to come. As China and Taiwan fight for influence in various Pacific Island nations today, rimbound thinking is on the rise again. Even the new Trans-Pacific Partnership has no sovereign members inside the rim.

But how 'white' is all of this now that China's thinking matters just as much as the USA's? In an environmental and medical sense it is increasingly so: we cannot forget the white-hot devastation of nuclear testing as its genetic legacy continues to plague Indigenous peoples. We can see the growing number of gray-white, dead coral reefs that testify to reckless economic development and environmental irresponsibility going back to the age of Euro-American rule. White – an Asian colour of mourning – is on the rise in the Pacific world, in waters that used to nourish multicoloured reefs and their complex biomes. Whatever the fate of 'Asia-Pacific' may be under China's rising regional power, the White Pacific has already inscribed itself onto the body of the ocean itself.

Blue Pacific and Blue Planet

This chapter began with the wisdom of the canoe: the gift of Pacific Islanders whose recent policy gatherings have begun to promote a 'Blue Pacific' paradigm. Unlike a Blue Continent, a Blue Pacific underlines the importance of the maritime environment, and has recently been promoted by the Pacific Forum as a fresh articulation of regional identity and aspirations. Providing a touchstone for policies located firmly in local, island-centred priorities, the Blue Pacific provides

> The expression of a common sense of identity and purpose, leading progressively to the sharing of institutions, resources, and markets, with the purpose of complementing national efforts, overcoming common constraints, and enhancing sustainable and inclusive development within Pacific countries and territories and for the Pacific region as a whole.[98]

[97] Boyd, 'Southwest Pacific', 83.
[98] Pacific Islands Forum Secretariat, 'The framework for Pacific regionalism', www.forumsec.org/wp-content/uploads/2017/09/Framework-for-Pacific-Regionalism.pdf.

The Forum's 2014 'Framework for Pacific Regionalism' proclaimed that 'Pacific peoples are the custodians of the world's largest, most peaceful and abundant ocean, its many islands and its rich diversity of cultures.'[99] In his opening address to the Forum's 2017 meeting, Sāmoa's prime minister Tuilaepa Lupesoliai Sailele Malielegaoi observed that 'The Blue Pacific will strengthen the existing policy frameworks that harness the ocean as a driver of a transformative socio-cultural, political and economic development.'[100] Here the colour blue is a metaphor, source, goal, and motivation for change. It is also historically neutral, by which I mean that it was never used as a colonizing label for perceived racial or cultural groups during the colonial era, unlike red, yellow, or black. Meanwhile, the word 'Continent' is increasingly rare in official discourse. As discussed earlier, describing the Pacific world as a would-be land mass had disadvantages. The new 'Blue Pacific' regionalism is a gathering together of space, place, and purpose, but those spaces and places are proudly maritime ones. They need to be. The impact of climate change is already swallowing islands and threatening resources.

Because the Pacific world is *not* a continent, it is now 'at the centre of contemporary global geopolitics'.[101] After hosting climate change conferences, and making powerful interventions at conferences hosted elsewhere, Indigenous Pacific scholars and activists have raised their profile by challenging the idea that their region is similar to others. Their voices join the ancestral one of the late Tongan scholar Epeli Hau'ofa, who once wrote that a common Pacific identity would enable 'the protection of the ocean for the general good'. This was 'necessary for the quality of our survival in the so-called Pacific Century when, as we are told, important developments in the global economy will concentrate in huge [continental] regions that encircle us'.[102] The Blue Pacific is therefore of planetary significance, threatened by and contrasted with traditional continental geopolitics.

Here we must heed warnings about appropriation. So many scholars, activists, and politicians are now focused on rising sea levels and pollution in the Pacific that a 'Rush for Oceania' is underway. Critics both celebrate and lament the concept of a 'Blue Economy' that could invite fresh

---

[99] Pacific Islands Forum Secretariat, 'Opening address by Prime Minister Tuilaepa Sailele Mailelagaoi of Samoa to open the 48th Pacific Islands Forum 2017', 2, www.forumsec.org/opening-address-prime-minister-tuilaepa-sailele-mailelegaoi-samoa-open-48th-pacific-islands-forum-2017/.
[100] 'Opening address by Prime Minister Tuilaepa Sailele Mailelagaoi', 2.
[101] 'Opening address by Prime Minister Tuilaepa Sailele Mailelagaoi', 3.
[102] E. Hau'ofa, 'We are the ocean', in *We Are The Ocean: Selected Works* (Honolulu: University of Hawai'i Press, 2008), 41–59, at 42.

exploitation by the rimworld, even as it generates 'a space of resistance' for exploited Pacific peoples.[103] Academics have jumped onto the blue bandwagon, generating an 'oceanic turn in environmental history [that] indicates a larger cultural and political shift in which "blue" has, to some extent, succeeded "green"'.[104] Rob Wilson is sceptical, worrying that a Blue Pacific might provide a new refrain on a very old imperial tune for non-Indigenous academics and policymakers. Criticizing North American academics for simply adding a Hawaiian case study in order to make their book, art exhibit, or poetry collection about 'the Pacific', he speaks bluntly: 'Hawai'i is simply an easy place to write about, to laze and gaze around in for a week or two, to tour, and thereby to work up into a narrative, genre piece, or fantasy with global staying power and (alas) media clout.'[105]

The shifting colours and political geographies can get complicated. Samoan prime minister Tuilaepa introduced his 'Blue Pacific' concept at the United Nations Ocean Conference in June 2017 but, in the interim, as head of the Pacific Islands Forum Secretariat, Dame Meg Taylor opened a Fijian conference titled 'Promoting the Blue Green Economy'.[106] Presumably the 'green' reference in the conference title indicated possible areas of environment-related employment for Islanders; the conference subtitle was 'Enhancing Connectivity; Accessible Employment'. We are all familiar with 'green' movements, but 'blue' ones are new; a 'Blue Green' compromise was probably sensible.

In concluding an essay composed of colour thought-experiments, it's important to recognize that no single colour can facilitate a narrative sufficiently nuanced for the hybridities and complexities of the Pacific world. But colour can spark our imaginations. Recently the United Nations has been deploying oceanic imagery under the slogan 'One Planet, One Ocean' to encourage support for the Intergovernmental Oceanic Commission of UNESCO.[107] As Stefanie Hessler does, we could name this oceanic turn

---

[103] Reclaiming the Ocean Collective, 'The rush for Oceania: critical perspectives on contemporary oceans governance and stewardship', http://repository.usp.ac.fj/11405/1/SGDIA_WORKING_PAPER_SERIES_-_No._9_-_Rush_for_Oceania.pdf.

[104] Armitage et al., *Oceanic Histories*, 15.

[105] R. Wilson, *Reimagining the American Pacific: From South Pacific to Bamboo Ridge and Beyond* (Durham, NC: Duke University Press, 2000), ix.

[106] M. Taylor, 'Opening remarks to the 2017 Pacific Update', Pacific Islands Forum Secretariat, 20 June 2017 www.forumsec.org/secretary-general-dame-meg-taylors-opening-remarks-to-the-2017-pacific-update/.

[107] S. Sivasundaram, A. Bashford, and D. Armitage, 'Introduction: writing world oceanic histories', in Armitage et al., *Oceanic Histories*, 1–28, at 1.

'Tidalectics' and use it to reconfigure our politics, economics, and aesthetics, under the guidance of a Blue Pacific.[108] The Pacific Forum plans to launch a full 'Strategy for the Blue Pacific Continent' in 2050 (note the hybrid title that employs both the older continental conception as well as the newer Blue Pacific terminology). A recent call for statements of interest by stakeholders emphasized key issues such as climate change, the future of the Pacific Ocean and its resources, the competition for global power, economics, resilience, and the impact of COVID-19.[109]

A Blue Pacific may also underline the urgent necessities of our common fate on a Blue Planet. Humanity experienced a collective paradigm shift when we first viewed our world from the moon: a precious, blue island in the black ocean of space. Continents could be glimpsed beneath the encircling clouds, humbled by the vastness of Earth's oceans. There were no borders; no political or economic blocs; no 'natural' geopolitics. Instead there was a shared and vulnerable world; a planetary canoe voyaging around the sun. Long canoe voyages require the collection and careful conservation of drinking water, the preservation of canoe plants to provide food, shelter, and clothing, and the cherishing of ancestral knowledge and wisdom. What have we done with these treasures?

At the beginning of this chapter Ramsey Taum gave us an Indigenous Hawaiian perspective on raising the Blue Continent. Taum also believes that Earth is best understood as an island, not as a collection of continents, and this takes us back to the aphorism I mentioned at the beginning of this chapter: 'islands are for the schooling of continents'. The lessons that islands teach are about the dangerous consequences of discrimination and exploitation, and also about the possibility of a broad horizon. If anything is clear about their relationship with the Pacific world, it is that multiple histories have always been overlaid, recombined, and reborn in new forms. No two kaleidoscope images are alike, meaning that change and fresh possibilities are not only desirable, but inevitable.

This chapter's colour mapping has suggested a 4D Venn diagram of Pacific histories where sets of historical relationships interact and change over time.

---

[108] This term is itself a reconfiguration of Kamau Brathwaite's 'tidalectic' theory of Caribbean history as explained in *Rights of Passage* (Oxford: Oxford University Press, 1967); see S. Hessler (ed.), *Tidalectics: Imagining an Oceanic Worldview through Art and Science* (Cambridge, MA: MIT Press, 2018), esp. P. D'Arcy, 'Lessons for humanity from the ocean of ancestors', 117–26.

[109] Pacific Islands Forum, 'Building the Blue Pacific Continent', www.forumsec.org/pacific-regionalism/.

Cosmopolitanism and hybridity are important keynotes because the ocean has always been a web of interconnecting lines of communication. Other webs – of racism, colonialism, economic and environmental exploitation – also remain with us. Recent historical scholarship is rediscovering this complexity, and the histories of a Blue Pacific are still being imagined. The Indigenous island navigators taught well: the great ocean itself can speak, nurture, and continue to challenge us.

PART VIII

★

APPROACHES, SOURCES, AND SUBALTERN HISTORIES OF THE MODERN PACIFIC

37

Archives and Community Memory in the Pacific

OPETA ALEFAIO AND NICHOLAS HALTER

Dynamic and proactive archives are crucial for safeguarding and growing community memory and knowledge. Despite this, South Pacific Island archives are plagued by stark challenges which hinder their role. Principally, it is an issue of trust. The echoes and expectations of a not-too-distant colonial past have isolated archives from the communities they are supposed to serve. This is made worse by traditional archival practice, which has a narrow focus, and with characteristics and requirements that prevent Pacific archives from connecting with their communities. These dated archive practices concentrate on 'control' of archival holdings with less consideration for the 'accessibility' of these holdings to the general public. This is driven by assumptions that may be relevant in Europe and societies where the written record has a long history, but which do not fit the realities of the island nations of the South Pacific and other countries that are former colonies, where oral tradition has a more dominant role. Using the developments at the National Archives of Fiji from 2012 to 2019 as a case study, this chapter will examine the challenges to Pacific Island archives, reveal how acknowledging cultural norms is key for Pacific archives to build trust and establish relevance in the community, and demonstrate how connecting with community is critical to overcoming the obstacles which prevent archives from serving their communities as desired.

Traditional archival practice has a narrow focus, with characteristics and requirements which can hinder Pacific Island archives from connecting with their communities. Ideals of neutrality, passivity, and objectivity that were once championed by conventional archives are useful but they do not go far enough to suit Pacific Island contexts. Pacific Islands and cultures are marked by diversity, and cultural contexts are highly specific, subjective, and political. Archives not only reflect the circumstances of the past, they are also shaped by the context of the present. Today Pacific Island archives are increasingly reaching out to engage their communities and must find new ways to demonstrate that they are accessible, useful, and relevant. This presents many challenges for institutions which have inherited a colonial legacy yet operate in a post-colonial context. The preference for the written word over the Indigenous knowledge systems means that archives are regarded with suspicion, distrust, or apathy. This perception is reinforced by geography – archivists work on the colonial record in the urban metropole while memories are preserved in oral form in the villages. How do Pacific Island archives bridge this divide in the twenty-first century?

As one of the largest and most well-established archives in the Pacific Islands, the National Archives of Fiji (NAF) is an example of Indigenous-driven archival administration. This represents a newer paradigm in archival management, with Indigenous archivists experimenting with novel ways to merge cultural values and practices with archival principles and standards. The NAF's outreach and accessibility projects have brought the centrality of the Indigenous voice to the archives collection by rebalancing the colonial stories with community Indigenous memories. By making collections accessible through a variety of community outreach projects, the NAF has strengthened community knowledge and pride, empowered communities to tell new stories, revealed hidden and neglected histories, and sparked creative outputs, emotional responses, and local activism. This community-centred practice represents an exciting new phase in recordkeeping in a region where Pacific Island archivists are starting to be more actively involved in memory making and knowledge construction.

Traditional archival practices emphasized the importance of evidence over memory, and archival identity deemed collectors to be custodians of evidence. Principles of impartiality and authenticity were advocated by Sir Hilary Jenkinson of the Public Record Office in London in the early twentieth century. According to this Jenkinsonianism, 'His creed, the sanctity of Evidence; his Task, the Conservation of every scrap of Evidence attaching to the Documents committed to his charge; his Aim, to provide without prejudice or afterthought, for all who wish to know the Means of Knowledge ... the good Archivist is perhaps the most selfless devotee of Truth the modern world produces.'[1] As Pacific Island archives were established by colonial regimes in the region their success was judged by comparison to European ideals of the archive. Terry Cook argues that archival

---

[1] H. Jenkinson, 'The English archivist: a new profession', in R.H. Ellis and P. Walne (eds.), *Selected Writings of Hilary Jenkinson* (Chicago: Society of American Archivists, 2003), 236–59, at 258.

identity shifted in the 1930s from being custodians of evidence to active selectors and curators of cultural memory.[2] Evidence and memory 'evolved . . . in archival discourse in a kind of creative tension', as archives claimed to preserve the collective memory of nations and peoples yet ignored the selectiveness of memories. In the context of the Pacific Islands, subject to centuries of colonization by Europeans, Islander voices were often omitted in the collective memory of Pacific archives. Movements for self-determination and independence in the 1970s had far-reaching implications for the governance of many Pacific Islands, but the importance of the written record remained unchanged: 'Oral forms of recording memories have been undermined through social changes imposed by new economic patterns and educational practices, the growth of government and economic systems for which written recordkeeping is an integral support, and the expectation that memory is being kept elsewhere.'[3] One response by Pacific communities advocating for self-determination or Indigenous rights has been to reclaim and repatriate knowledge embedded in archives. This is highly sensitive and political, as archives are 'entangled in the reassertion of identities'.[4] Monica Wehner and Ewan Maidment argue that 'the struggle for repatriation of the past is a struggle for the right to control and possess the present'.[5] Thus Pacific Island archives are situated in a precarious position between communities and governments, while their relevance is determined by how often they are actively used. As Panitch noted, 'Far from standing as enduring monuments to the past, archives instead appear somewhat fragile, eternally subject to the judgement of the society in which they exist . . . the archives of the past are also the mutable creations of the present.'[6]

In this context, Pacific archives operate in difficult circumstances to reclaim and repatriate knowledge for their Indigenous communities. Cook argues that the advent of the digital age means that archiving is increasingly viewed as a participatory process in which the community is involved in 'collaborative evidence- and memory-making'. This involves 'a shift in core principles from exclusive custodianship and ownership of archives to shared stewardship and collaboration; from dominant-culture language, terminology, and definitions

---

[2] T. Cook, 'Evidence, memory, identity, and community: four shifting archival paradigms', *Archival Science* 13:2–3 (2013), 95–120, at 102.

[3] Cook, 'Evidence, memory, identity, and community', 197.

[4] Cook, 'Evidence, memory, identity, and community', 199.

[5] M. Wehner and E. Maidment, 'Ancestral voices: aspects of archives administration in Oceania', *Archives and Manuscripts* 27:1 (1999), 23–41, at 32.

[6] J.M. Panitch, 'Liberty, equality, posterity? Some archival lessons from the case of the French Revolution', *American Archivist* 59:1 (1996), 30–47, at 47.

to sensitivity to the "other" and as keen an awareness of the emotional, religious, symbolic, and cultural values that records have to their communities'.[7] The practical implications for Pacific archivists who wish to engage and empower their local communities is more uncertain. Evelyn Wareham's summary of archive development in the region considers it an act of evangelism in which archives must justify their system of knowledge to Indigenous communities that already maintain existing systems: 'to overcome distrust, archival practices must be adjusted so that they are transparent and understandable for local communities, and local people should be encouraged to use the records held'.[8] Until very recently, specific examples of this were not easily found in the South Pacific.

This chapter focuses on a series of innovative projects by Indigenous archivists at the NAF from 2012 to 2019 to develop a more community-focused practice. First, a brief history of the changing roles of Pacific Island archives, the establishment of the NAF, and the structural challenges they have faced is illustrative of the broader context of archive development in the Pacific. Next it considers the limitations of traditional archival practices, highlighting specific Indigenous Fijian protocols that enabled it to engage legitimately with communities. Finally, it considers a series of outreach projects run by the NAF and highlights specific cultural values that have a wider relevance for Pacific Island archivists who wish to build trust and establish relevance in the community.

The Establishment and Role of Archives in the South Pacific

Archival collections in the Pacific first emerged as a result of European exploration, as visiting collectors gathered a variety of objects, manuscripts, and maps related to their economic, political, military, or scientific interests. These rare collections were transported and stored outside the Pacific, where many remain today. With colonial rule in the Pacific Islands, government bureaucrats began to gather documentary records of colonial administration in the region, and the archives that were created were formalized as countries transitioned to independence in the 1970s. This corresponded with a global professionalization of the archives marked by the beginning of formal

---

[7] Cook, 'Evidence, memory, identity, and community', 113.
[8] E. Wareham, 'From explorers to evangelists: archivists, recordkeeping, and remembering in the Pacific Islands', *Archival Science* 2:3–4 (2002), 187–207, at 206.

training and the formation of professional organizations. In the South Pacific today, seventeen Pacific Island states and territories comprise the membership of the Pacific Regional Branch of the International Council on Archives (PARBICA). This organization was formed in 1981 for 'promoting the effective management and use of records and archives across the Pacific and preserving the region's archival heritage'.[9]

The National Archives of Fiji was initially established as the Central Archives of Fiji and the Western Pacific High Commission (WPHC) in 1954 after numerous efforts from bureaucrats who were interested in securing the colony of Fiji's documentary evidence for administrative effectiveness, as well as researchers concerned that vital research materials would be lost without a formal organization tasked with their care. Then in 1971, less than a year after Fiji attained independence, the records of the WPHC were relocated to other institutions and the Central Archives formally became the National Archives of Fiji (NAF) with an amendment of the Public Records Ordinance.[10]

NAF is responsible for two acts. These are the Public Records Act (PRA) Cap. 108 of the laws of Fiji and the Libraries Act Cap. 109 of the laws of Fiji. Together these laws give NAF its two main objectives.

The first objective is to attain, conserve, and make accessible important archival records and all publications printed and published in Fiji. Together the archival records and publications comprise a large portion of the nation's collective memory. The archival records act as the corporate memory of government. And for the general public they offer proof of decisions and activities, thus supporting their rights and entitlements. The publications complement the archival holdings as either synthesized interpretation of data found in those archives or externally, as commentary on the development of Fiji and the wider Pacific, and as creative works to educate, entertain, and inspire. In unison, these two broad categories of holdings form a vast reservoir of information for a wide array of users.[11]

The second objective is to enable evidence-based governance by supporting government recordkeeping. The PRA directs the Archives to support government agencies to care for their corporate records accurately.

---

[9] Pacific Regional Branch of the International Council on Archives, 2016, www.ica.org/en/parbica.

[10] A.I. Diamond, 'The Central Archives of Fiji and the Western Pacific High Commission', *Journal of Pacific History* 1:1 (1966), 204–11.

[11] O. Alefaio, 'Archives connecting with the community', paper presented at IFLA WLIC 2016, Columbus, OH: Connections, Collaboration, Community in Session 96, Asia and Oceania.

Authentic, accurate, accessible records provide the foundation for the smooth conduct of government business. NAF meets this obligation through records, surveys of agencies, and recordkeeping training for clients.

Combined, these responsibilities make NAF the National Archive, the National Library, and the government's recordkeeping authority and capacity-building body for managing information. This is a deep and encompassing set of responsibilities for the care and accessibility of the nation's information assets and documentary heritage. Unfortunately NAF is confronted with a significant group of obstacles that collectively and seriously undermine its function.[12] Namely, these are climate challenges, structural deficiencies, and lack of community trust.

Climate and Related Challenges

Firstly, the tropical climate of the South Pacific is a major threat to the safe care of aged and brittle records. The combination of high humidity and high temperature poses a direct threat to the long life of records in all formats. In addition, natural disasters such as cyclones and floods are a significant concern for Pacific heritage professionals. For example, in 2003, Category 5 tropical cyclone Heta with winds up to 296 kilometres per hour caused massive damage to the archives of Niue. It took a concerted effort over a number of years to get the archive back to basic functional working order.[13]

The next major difficulty for Pacific archives is extremely low societal awareness of both recordkeeping and archives as key enablers for administrative efficiency and accountable governance, as well as a crucial evidence base to guarantee the rights and entitlements of the public at large. This is played out broadly at two levels: firstly, in terms of government priorities, decision making, and resource allocation, and secondly, in terms of general acceptance and engagement by the community itself.[14]

Public heritage and information institutions receive very little support in the South Pacific. This is especially true for archives. In fact some South Pacific Island countries do not have a national archive: Nauru, Tokelau, and

---

[12] Alefaio, 'Archives connecting with the community'.

[13] T. McCormack, 'The Niue Archives Project', *Panorama* 2 (2008), 7–12; M. Enetama, 'Cyclone Heta: disaster preparedness and response. A brief report on actions taken by Pacific archives following recent disaster', *PARBICA 14: Evidence and Memory in the Digital Age*, conference paper, Sāmoa, 2011.

[14] S. Tale and O. Alefaio, 'We are our memories: community and records in Fiji', in J.A. Bastian and B. Alexander (eds.), *Community Archives: The Shaping of Memory* (London: Facet Publishing, 2009), 87–94.

Tonga are three examples. Those countries which do have archives are not likely to provide the resources needed. As the former deputy vice-chancellor of the University of the South Pacific Dr Esther Williams mentioned in her 1998 UNESCO study on the information needs of the Pacific Islands, 'Very few decision-makers and Pacific Island leaders will link good governance and accountability to the efficient management of public sector records . . . These institutions are given minimal recurrent funding and are barely surviving. There is a clear lack of political will to support development in these fields.'[15] This is also supported by Pacific archivists themselves who submit country reports on the status of their archives and developments impacting them during their biennial PARBICA conferences.

This lack of attention from decision-makers severely hampers archives from fulfilling their obligations. Document conservation, for example, is a core activity necessary to prolong the lifespan of records. Without this activity it is extremely difficult to ensure that records are accessible for today's use and into the future for generations to come. Sadly, most South Pacific archives are not able to perform this activity.[16] At the time of writing, only the French territory archives of New Caledonia and Tahiti, as well as the National Archives of Fiji, have working conservation laboratories.

It is not enough though to possess a conservation laboratory. It must receive the necessary level of resources to be effective. Air conditioners and dehumidifiers are necessary to counteract the tropical weather so detrimental to old paper records and newer electronic records. These are expensive and difficult to replace. The materials necessary for restoration works are also difficult to obtain. They are unavailable on the local market and must be flown in. They are also very expensive, and the limited funds provided mean that archives are forced to take a reactive approach rather than a proactive approach with their conservation programmes. Under such circumstances conservation and restoration efforts can only be applied to those records at the very highest risk. The archive is not able to provide remedial care to those documents needing attention though not yet at advanced or critical stages. These records, however, are likely to constitute a major portion, if not the majority, of the collection. Over time the lack of proactive conservation puts increasingly telling pressure on these records, cutting short their lifespan.

---

[15] E.B. Williams, *Information Needs in the Pacific Islands: Needs Assessment for Libraries, Archives, Audio Visual Collection and ICT Development in the Pacific Islands* (Sāmoa: UNESCO, 1998).
[16] Wareham, 'From explorers to evangelists'.

Advanced decay in records can cause concern in the user, and rightly so. A group of concerned Fiji citizens once wrote a letter to the Office of the Prime Minister to express their distress at the condition of some of the records they had seen at the National Archives of Fiji.[17] In his 1992 UNESCO report on the state of the National Archives of Fiji, Bower explained that inadequate funding and an inadequate staffing structure had had a negative impact on the ability of the archive to give its holdings the level of care required.[18]

Structural Deficiencies

Poor staffing levels provide a host of difficulties for archives. For one, the low numbers of staff mean 'back of shop' activities such as processing of consignments, applying of descriptive standards, and conservation efforts, all of which are the foundational work for an orderly archive, will be curtailed. This leads to worsening backlogs, making it difficult to exert meaningful control over the collection. In such a situation, misplacement and loss become a marked risk. Bower's survey in 1992 found that the National Archives of Fiji had been put in this very predicament.[19]

Staffing shortages were not just a matter of insufficient numbers caused by prolonged delays in recruitment. The organizational structure itself was distinctly inadequate. Bower also saw it as not only meagre and unbalanced, but stifling and demeaning. Frequent denials to repeated requests to address longstanding personnel, training, and infrastructure needs nudged Bower to make a key recommendation to elevate the Principal Archivist to departmental head status with the designation of National Archivist; to bring long-overdue clout in engaging with other government agencies and advocacy in general.[20]

The following decade did see some minor enhancement to the organizational structure in response to constant pressure and submissions to decision-makers, but those with the authority to act on recommendations largely resisted. By 2012, NAF's organizational chart continued to have three entire levels missing. For more than four decades, this predicament forced staff to

---

[17] T. Te'aiwa, personal discussion (Wellington, New Zealand, 2016).
[18] P. Bower, 'The state of the National Archives: Fiji', UNESCO Assignment Report RP/1990–1991/II.C(i) (1992).
[19] Bower, 'The state of the National Archives'.
[20] Bower, 'The state of the National Archives'.

leave the organization if they wanted to improve their lot. In short there was no real career path.[21] This meant that all on-the-job training and capacity building provided to a staff member was effectively lost to the NAF. Already stretched thin, NAF management were consistently having to request permission to recruit at entry level and somehow find time to train these newcomers, as a steady stream of experienced and valuable team members left for better prospects.[22]

Training and capacity building is another considerable constraint. There is not now, nor has there ever been, any formal education for archives, records management, or document conservation in Fiji. Only distance and online educational packages are available but these are too expensive for archives and records management professionals in the South Pacific. On-the-job training and the biennial PARBICA conference provide the only consistent capacity building opportunities. The need is great, especially in the light of technological advancements since the 1990s and the resultant growing public expectation that all relevant information should be accessible at the push of a button. While technology has great potential for improved efficiencies and services, in the Pacific it is often deployed on a project basis, leading to information silos and legacy systems whose usability over time is not planned for.[23] Poor deployment of technology and the terabytes of data it puts at risk poses a potential catalyst to detonate the multiple frailties listed above.

The obstacles dealt with so far cover the intense challenges caused by the tropical climate of the South Pacific region and structural deficiencies caused by the low regard of decision-makers towards recordkeeping and archives. We will now move to another set of problems caused by a lack of community trust in official archives which has resulted from echoing fears of the colonial experience and unfamiliarity with the role and uses of archives. This second set of obstacles was then amplified by traditional archiving concepts and practices which sought to maintain distance between the archivists and their clients in the name of neutrality and objectivity.

---

[21] O. Alefaio, 'Aim high: looking past our problems to get past our problems', 2018 Asia-Pacific Library and Information Conference (APLIC), keynote address (Gold Coast, Australia, 30 July–2 August 2018).

[22] Bower, 'The state of the National Archives'.

[23] O. Alefaio, 'Archival revival, heritage and social media: the example of the National Archives of Fiji', Oceanic Knowledges, conference paper (Canberra, Australian National University, 27–8 July 2017).

Lack of Community Trust

Archival institutions in post-colonial societies have a difficult time gaining traction. This occurs not only with the senior officials who have treated them as an indulgence at best and pointless Western 'white elephants' at worst; but also with the public for whom oral tradition is a cornerstone of existence. Under these conditions, archives are seen primarily as extraneous institutions whose primary focus is to preserve records created by former colonial masters (with their prejudices and limited understanding of the concerns of the colonized) for use by themselves and Western academics.[24] Against this backdrop it is easy for archives to be seen as a type of imposition, and trust in them is not abundantly overflowing. However broadly one might attempt to define archives, it is very difficult to allay the lingering notion that they exist to compete with and/or dominate native knowledge systems. Orality versus literacy is a daunting proposition for both archives and the public.

This was made even more challenging by shallow and outdated thinking which sought to minimize the role and value of oral tradition in general and Indigenous oral tradition in particular. In reality, Indigenous oral tradition contains scientific knowledge pertaining to architecture, seafaring, medicine, agriculture, fisheries, genealogies, and migration histories.[25] The knowledge is not static; rather, it is dynamic, put through numerous feedback loops, and evolving through phases of transmission between generations to encourage innovation and knowledge building.[26] It does, however, have shortcomings which make it sometimes inappropriate for modern administration and the business of government. And it is here that official archives as the repository for the permanent records of government have a crucial role for accountability and transparency of government by providing the evidence to help it meet its obligations, illuminate planning, enable effective programme implementation, and support the rights and entitlements of the public.[27]

---

[24] A. Cunningham, 'Archival institutions', in S. McKemmish, M. Piggott, B. Reed, and F. Upward (eds.), *Archives: Recordkeeping in Society* (Wagga Wagga: Charles Sturt University, 2005), 21–50.

[25] B. Biggs, 'What is oral tradition', in S. Vatu (ed.), *Na Veitalanoa me baleta na i tukutuku maroroi = Talking about Oral Traditions. Proceedings of a Workshop on Fijian Oral Traditions Held at the Fiji Museum, August 16th–August 21st, 1976* (Suva: Fiji Museum, 1977), 1–12.

[26] C. Peteru, 'Protection of indigenous knowledge', Preservation of Local and Indigenous Knowledge Workshop, conference paper (Suva, World Wide Fund for Nature and Department of Environment, 16–17 November, 1999).

[27] S. McKemmish, 'The smoking gun: recordkeeping and accountability', 22nd Annual Conference of the Archives and Records Association of New Zealand, 'Records and Archives Now – Who Cares?', keynote address (Dunedin, September 1998).

The value of the written record and recordkeeping systems notwithstanding, the 'foreignness' of archives is compounded by the memory of life under colonial masters. Many Fijians did not know the role of the archives and the ways in which it could benefit them, and more than a few viewed it with fear or a sense of futility.[28] As Eric Ketelaar argued, archives are a source of power and have been used by those in power as a means of dispossessing and dominating entire populations.[29] Decades after Fiji achieved independence in 1970, this sense of dispossession is still evident. There are those who are hesitant to use the archives out of fear that the information held there is secret and available only to senior administrators.[30] There is also concern that the information held in the archives is harmful. As shown by Fiona Ross, Sue McKemmish, and Shannon Faulkhead, colonial records created in a different time and under a different set of priorities often reflect the shortcomings of colonial administrators, revealing the unpleasant realities of the day. Interacting with such materials can be disturbing and even traumatic, particularly for the descendants of the 'subjects' described in those records.[31]

Those who are not dissuaded from visiting the archives are met by another set of obstacles. Firstly, the archives are located in the capital city of Suva in order to be in close proximity to the headquarters of government agencies, the source of records which feed the archives and also the first level of clients to recall such records to support operations and research. This can make visiting the archives an expensive exercise, particularly for those who have to travel long distances. Those who do travel to Suva from a long distance are not likely to 'waste' the short time they have in the capital with a visit to the archive.[32] Another impediment for users is that the vast majority of the records are in English. While Fiji has a high literacy rate, and English is one of Fiji's official languages, it is not the first language of a large portion of the population. Furthermore, the records are written in bureaucratic

---

[28] T. Balenaivalu, 'Designing how Pacific archives are perceived: using empathy and experimentation to make archives more "relevant" in a resource poor environment', Joint International Council on Archives (ICA), Australian Society of Archives (ASA), Archivists and Records Managers Association of New Zealand (ARANZ), Pacific Regional Branch of the International Council on Archives (PARBICA) conference, conference paper (Adelaide, 21–5 October 2019).
[29] E. Ketelaar, 'Access: the democratic imperative', *Archives and Manuscripts* 34:2 (2006), 62–81; E. Ketelaar, 'Archives as spaces of memory', *Journal of the Society of Archivists* 29:1 (2008), 9–27.
[30] Balenaivalu, 'Designing how Pacific archives are perceived'.
[31] F. Ross, S. McKemmish, and S. Faulkhead, 'Indigenous knowledge and the archives: designing trusted archival systems for Koorie communities', *Archives and Manuscripts* 34:2 (2006), 112–40.
[32] Balenaivalu, 'Designing how Pacific archives are perceived'.

language of the colonial era and bear very little resemblance to the type of English today's Fijians utilize. A working knowledge of the administrative history of government is also necessary to be able to navigate the records, interpret them, then match them with the real needs of the user, who may not necessarily know exactly what they are looking for. Usually only professional researchers are equipped with the skills and experience to conduct independent research in the archives, and the majority of the Fiji public are not professional researchers.[33]

In-house training for NAF staff prepares them to assist a variety of client requests, with a special focus on those who are first-time users possessing no familiarity with the collection or any idea of how to use them. But this approach assumes that the public will use the archives, as is the case in the Western world and in other nations with a deep and longstanding involvement with the written word. This assumption does not reflect reality, and poorly funded archives may not be in a strong position to change that reality. In the case of the NAF, under-resourcing resulting from the intermittent attention of government officials combined with traditional archival practice meant that the archives focused on their most pressing concerns; securing the collection, making safe the premises, and serving those entering the premises.

Traditional archival practice was valuable for laying the groundwork and establishing an archive in good working order. But in a post-colonial environment, access and usability have become more pressing concerns for heritage institutions seeking to demonstrate 'relevance' with both senior government administrators and the community. NAF has found that under these circumstances archives need to move in the opposite direction. Not only do they need to make their holdings and services more accessible by actively seeking out the community to develop a dialogue or relationship; they also have to deliver unique value to excite and inspire the community to collaborate and share knowledge. Ultimately, NAF must advocate on the behalf of archives by providing a positive feedback loop through government bureaucrats to decision-makers for increased resourcing. This would enable the archives to increase services and programmes to grow that connection to community.[34]

But this new thinking has its own challenges, as Wareham has stated, as advocating for what are largely colonial archives in a post-colonial Pacific is no simple matter.[35] Islander populations who have weathered evangelism,

---

[33] Balenaivalu, 'Designing how Pacific archives are perceived'.
[34] Alefaio, 'Aim high: looking past our problems to get past our problems'.
[35] Wareham, 'From explorers to evangelists'.

colonialism, and recently the driving forces of neoliberalism and development have little time for newer forms of proselytizing. Prospective engagement exercises to 'educate' or 'enlighten' the community can be seen as condescending and self-serving. Instead, as the remainder of this chapter demonstrates, the archives must approach the community using traditional protocols of introduction such as the presentation of *sevusevu*, a ceremonial presentation of *yaqona* by a visitor upon arrival, after gaining access to the community through long-standing governance channels of the Fijian Administration.

Negotiating Indigenous Spaces and Protocols

External parties are obliged to follow particular paths to connect to Fijian villages. These paths and their 'gatekeepers' are often colonial constructs, themselves introduced by the British colonial administration in the nineteenth century. This presents something of a paradox for archivists who must utilize colonial legacies and institutions in order to access the communities. When Fiji was ceded to Britain in 1874, successive policies introduced by governors Sir Arthur Gordon and John Bates Thurston created a Fijian Administration for the Indigenous population. This operated separately from the Indian administration which supervised the Indian indentured labourers who were brought to Fiji to work on sugar cane plantations as part of a British plan to develop the economy and protect the 'native' from dying out. Under the 1876 Native Affairs Ordinance, Gordon established councils in the districts and provinces, headed by a Great Council of Chiefs. Villages were headed by a *Turaga-ni-koro*, districts were led by a *Buli*, and each of the fourteen provinces was head by a *Roko*. The Native Lands Ordinance of 1880 also created *mataqali*, landowning groups, and, together with the Native Land Trust Board, divided Fiji into freehold land, state land, and *iTaukei* (Indigenous) land. Though Fiji secured its independence from Britain in 1970, some of these institutions and positions have remained and are necessary stepping stones for organizations to access Indigenous communities formally. For community outreach activities in the past, the NAF had to consult for permission first with the Provincial Councils before approaching the district and then village levels. Approvals attained through this chain provide a safe opportunity for archives to seek their audience, and through the presentation of *sevusevu* (if accepted) inform the community of their role and purpose.

The *sevusevu* is a ceremonial presentation of *yaqona* by a visitor upon arrival at the home, village, or meeting. *Isevusevu* are 'ceremonial offerings of *yaqona* [kava] by the host to the guest, or the guest to his host and done in respect of recognition and acceptance of one another'.[36] *Yaqona* are the dried roots of a plant (*Piper methysticum*) which are pounded into a powder and mixed with water. The drink, known as kava, serves a ceremonial purpose in many Pacific societies. The Fijian word *sevu* means 'taking the first fruits', either to the paramount chief or to God.

One key importance of the *sevusevu* is that it reinforces assumptions about rank, allowing members within a community to define their status relative to others. Brison states that 'the *sevusevu* expresses typically Polynesian notions of social ranking both through the ordering of drinking and through providing each "chief" or important person with a spokesman (Fijian: *mata ni vanua*)'.[37] In Fiji, *vanua* can be simply translated as 'land', but the term has multiple meanings. Ravuvu considers it as a sense of place, also as 'the people of the land, common descent, common bonds, parochialism, identity'.[38] Others have defined *vanua* as a landowning group in the legal sense or as a 'decision-making group' for traditional affairs.[39] Whilst studies of the *sevusevu* have emphasized the importance of the protocol for ascertaining social ranking within the village, they have failed to observe the reciprocal purpose – it allows the village to determine the ranking within visiting groups, a significance for the discussion of the Fiji Archives in the next section.

The *sevusevu* is also significant for reinforcing communal solidarity. This is reinforced through the actions and speeches of the people involved. Brison argues the 'theme of social embeddedness' is always present, which means 'framing everything an individual does as representing his or her group'.[40] This is important for conflict resolution and consensus decision-making, with the *sevusevu* being one part of a complex tradition system of reciprocation designed to minimize conflict. For important decisions to be made and communicated, the *sevusevu* provides one forum for this to occur, with the social presentation of the *yaqona* (or in other cases a *tabua*, whale's tooth), sealing the decision.[41] For new visitors, the ceremony is important for coming

---

[36] A. Ravuvu, *Vaka i Taukei: The Fijian Way of Life* (Suva: Institute of Pacific Studies, University of the South Pacific, 1983), 120.

[37] K.J. Brison, 'Constructing identity through ceremonial language in rural Fiji', *Ethnology* 40:4 (2001), 310.

[38] A. Ravuvu, *Vaka i Taukei*; A. Ravuvu, *The Fijian Ethos* (Suva: Institute of Pacific Studies, University of the South Pacific, 1987).

[39] See P. France, *The Charter of the Land. Custom and Colonization in Fiji* (Oxford: Oxford University Press, 1969); I.Q. Lasaqa, *The Fijian people before and after independence* (Canberra: ANU Press, 1984).

[40] Brison, 'Constructing identity through ceremonial language in rural Fiji', 309–26, at 314.

[41] S. Siwatibau, 'Traditional environment practices in the South Pacific: a case study in Fiji', *Ambio* 13:5–6 (1984), 365–8.

to an understanding about shared values. This is one of the most important functions for external groups visiting villages in the present day. And the act of remaining until the *tanoa* (kava bowl) is empty, symbolizes solidarity.

The *sevusevu* also has significant spiritual functions. Once a semi-religious rite, only high-ranking people were allowed to participate. Today they are more common, and every adult can participate in them regularly. The use of *matanivanuas* or spokesmen upholds the belief that high-ranking people are semi-divine and imbued with the power of ancestral spirits (*vu*). Thus it is still commonly believed that the ceremony ensures that visitors are protected from spirits whilst in the village. The formalized and ritualized pattern of speech and actions elevates the people and the discussions above worldly politics. Drinking kava is part of this process to infuse the sacred power of the spirits (*mana*) into society.[42]

The *sevusevu* plays an important role in Pacific research as well. Fijian scholar Unaisi Nabobo-Baba explained the importance of *sevusevu* as part of the 'Vanua Research Framework'.[43] In many cases it is a culturally appropriate protocol to obtain consent, because once the *sevusevu* is presented and accepted all the doors to the village have been opened. The social aspect of the ceremony also ensures that all members of the community are aware of the visitor's presence.

Community Outreach

Between 2012 and 2019 the NAF organized a series of outreach projects to engage with the local communities. This was part of a wider goal to promote public awareness of the archival collection and its relevance in order to encourage its use by a broader cross-section of society. Each activity represented a different approach to archival engagement that changed over time. Some of these projects were shaped by contextual factors at the time (whether support was provided by government or donor grants, or requested by specific communities), but they also represented a change in thinking within the archive staff as they reflected on the successes and challenges of each project. This was part of a process of establishing the

---

[42] J. Turner, '"The water of life": kava ritual and the logic of sacrifice', *Ethnology* 25:3 (1986), 203–14.
[43] U. Nabobo-Baba, 'Vanua Research Framework', *Sustainable Livelihood and Education in the Pacific Project (SLEP)* (Suva: Institute of Education, University of the South Pacific, 2007). See also U. Nabobo-Baba, *Knowing and Learning an Indigenous Fijian Approach* (Suva: Institute of Pacific Studies, University of the South Pacific, 2006).

avenues to enable community-centred practice. Three particular activities are outlined here – village visits to remote communities, community participation in the archival process, and a programme of digitizing and sharing historical images. Each activity highlights specific archival approaches that may have a wider relevance for Pacific archivists with similar community-centred goals.

Village Introductions

Fiji consists of many remote rural communities where accessibility is a major challenge. Some of these communities are scattered over 300 islands, while other villages are in remote mountainous areas of the two largest islands, Viti Levu and Vanua Levu. The NAF partnered with its sister department, the Library Services of Fiji, to commemorate World Book Day and carry out a literacy programme in the hinterlands of Viti Levu. To enable this, permission was attained through the stepping stones of the Fijian Administration to visit the proposed villages. Word was also sent out to neighbouring villages to draw as much participation as possible. Just as importantly, a partnership was struck with the divisional office of the Ministry of Education to facilitate the participation of schools in the area, which eagerly responded to the opportunity. *Sevusevu* presentations and other traditional practices were central to setting up and executing this programme, and the results were very encouraging. The active participation and positive feedback from the community proved to the NAF that carefully targeted outreach programmes facilitated through culturally relevant channels and practices was worthwhile. 'It is satisfying and heartening to see so many people, especially students, flocking and asking historical questions at the National Archives booth', remarked NAF team member Taito Raione in 2012.[44]

A short while later, after a number of similar outreach exercises with various partners, the NAF began visiting remote communities as part of newly launched 'Government Roadshow' programme, accompanying other government departments which would visit specific provinces or districts for a few days to share information and provide government services. The Rotuma Day Outreach in 2013 was typical of some of these early ventures. Rotuma is an isolated Polynesian island situated at the very north of the Fiji group which takes two days to reach by boat. The NAF provided copies of

---

[44] Alefaio, 'Archives connecting with the community'.

land records, genealogical records, historical photos, and audiovisual footage, much of which the Rotuman Islanders had never seen. Given that this was the first time that they were given access to their documentary heritage, many formed long queues to speak to the archival staff about the records and ask questions.[45] These face-to-face visits allow the archive staff to build personal relationships with the communities and to make the appropriate gestures necessary to share knowledge freely. This is also an important act of translation – not only are the archival staff translating the language from English to the local dialects, but they are also acting as a bridge between colonial records and Indigenous knowledge, and so they translate between two different cultural spaces. Many of the issues associated with family records and land records are highly sensitive and cannot be simply deposited in the communities. Some records may challenge or exacerbate pre-existing village debates. So it is important that these village visits take place over several days, allowing villagers time to consider the information, discuss it amongst themselves, and ask questions of the archivists. These often take place in informal settings, around the kava bowl, during meals or in the homes, as much as they do under a government tent in a village *rara* (open ground).

The success of these village visits rests upon the respect shown for customary protocols which ensure that visitors are properly introduced and accepted into traditional spaces. Traditional colonial archival practices assumed that archives were static institutions that would preserve records so that people could travel to access them. This static view was reinforced by the colonial records themselves which often presented the Pacific Islands and its people as passive. With time, Pacific archives like the NAF are beginning to realize that archivists must go out into the communities to engage them and take the records with them. Not only is the sharing of information important, but it is also the courtesy of introductions like the *sevusevu* which allows 'foreign' institutions like the archives to identify themselves and explain their goals to the communities.

Community Participation

Another step towards engaging the community began in 2014 with the sharing of Pacific indentured labourer records. In November 2014, the

---

[45] Alefaio, 'Archives connecting with the community'.

descendants of Pacific indentured labourers celebrated the 150th anniversary of their ancestors' arrival in Fiji. This community endured considerable hardship during their period of indenture and long afterward, and many had come to view their history negatively after an extended period of marginalization. They were a composite of various ethnicities, including many from the Melanesian region. The Melanesian labourers came from different islands and villages, but once in Fiji coalesced and formed new communities to survive. The NAF outreach team set up a stall at the anniversary celebrations to display records related to the labour trade, such as registers containing the names and islands of recruits. They were surprised by the response of many participants who were overcome with emotion upon sighting these records. According to the organizing committee chair Pateresio Nunu in 2015,

> Without the presence of National Archives most of the descendants will still rely on the verbal history relayed to them through stories. They are now confident that what they know is something that was recorded during that time then and there and are reliable information. Many of them were so moved they had tears in their eyes when they returned from your tent.[46]

The NAF responded to this encouraging feedback by turning its attention to the Melanesian and Indian indentured labourers to Fiji. Though digitization programmes are well advanced in archives around the globe, there is a relative lag in the Pacific due to financial and institutional constraints. The NAF collaborated with the University of the South Pacific to invite members of the public to assist with the data entry work. Over a period of three days, over a hundred volunteers worked in computer labs to transcribe copies of colonial registers into Excel spreadsheets, which could then be cross-checked later by archivists in order to create a catalogue of names that could be posted online and freely searchable. Many of the archive enquiries in Fiji are family history enquiries, with a substantial number from descendants of migrant labourers searching colonial registers.

This example of community participation in the archival process was relatively simple and small-scale, yet it had a significant impact on those involved. The indentured labour records are one of the most frequently requested records at the NAF because they contain traces of Indigenous lives and migrant voices. Contrary to traditional archival practices which ensure that documents are securely stored in controlled environments and viewed

---

[46] Alefaio, 'Archives connecting with the community'.

under strict conditions, this activity brought archives into the public domain and invited people to participate in the preservation of their documentary heritage and share their experiences. Such practices are powerful because they acknowledge the Indigenous owners of knowledge – in this case, the indentured labourers and their descendants. Acknowledging the traditional owners of land, of knowledge, and of history is an important aspect of Pacific Island cultural values.

Co-creating Archives

Photographic and audiovisual collections are some of the most engaging records held by the NAF, but until recently have been difficult for the general public to access. The growing impact of this archival community outreach was earning increased credibility with senior government administrators, enabling the NAF to take on new activities to demonstrate the unique value of documentary heritage and strengthen the connection with the community.

The digitization programme by the NAF and its use in public fora such as social media and television has allowed for greater community participation in the archive, including, to a limited extent, content co-creation. In 2006, Fiji's official historical audiovisual and photographic collection, consisting of 2,000 hours of audiovisual footage and 200,000 historical photographs, was brought to NAF for temporary storage. In 2012, the NAF assumed full ownership of these materials. A new team was established to start working on the photographs and 1 million Fiji dollars was acquired to restore and digitize almost all the footage (97 per cent of the footage was salvaged). Following the successful conclusion of the project in December 2013, NAF formed a partnership with the agency which created the footage to enable its curation and repackaging into a digestible educational programme called 'Back in Time' for free-to-air television. This provided the access for the public to its heritage at no extra cost. This television programme proved very popular as it put forgotten histories and practices back into current-day discourse. The footage contains many cultural practices which have since passed from everyday life, or which have become totally dormant.[47]

According to one journalist from the *Fiji Sun* in 2015:

---

[47] Alefaio, 'Archives connecting with the community'.

we need to know how our culture has evolved over the years, and the developments that have taken place, and why they did that in those days and why they are not being done now ... but unless you know what happened then, which is recorded by the video, we wouldn't know, because people have died, people who knew, who had the knowledge and probably the skills have gone, but the film has got it all recorded, so we can watch it and learn and probably try and revive.[48]

The footage has since been used by the Ministry of iTaukei Affairs to revitalize such practices in the communities which hold ownership. This television programme has run over four seasons and has over 150 episodes.

The NAF also experimented with using social media as a platform to share historical images. Though village visits encouraged deep impact with specific communities, a strategy was developed in 2015 to use social media to increase the breadth of that impact. One unintended consequence of this action was the immediate feedback generated by the community, which helped to identify unlabelled photos and provide additional historical information with which to corroborate details in the images. For example, to commemorate International Biodiversity Day the NAF posted on Facebook an image of a traditional fish drive on the island of Beqa (see Figure 37.1). This brought animated discussion, with Indigenous Fijians from all parts of Fiji discussing their histories around this practice. Then one user, a member of a high-ranking family of the villagers in the photograph, gave a full description of the cultural significance of such a fish drive. He described the various clans involved, and the conservation protocols put into place two to three years before the fish drive to ensure the success of the drive and the sustainability of marine resources. He named the special occasions the catch was used for, and so on. Through this public Facebook discussion, the user was able to demonstrate and assert his community's customary knowledge and ownership. This social media strategy to connect with community not only enabled him to access his documentary heritage, it also enabled him to write his history in a public forum for all to become engaged.

According to Facebook this post received over 7,700 likes and reached over 100,000 Facebook accounts. That amounts to an engaged audience (likes comments and shares) approaching 1 per cent (0.85 per cent) of Fiji's population and a total audience (total number of accounts exposed to the post) of about 11 per cent (11.11 per cent) of Fiji's population. This post is not among the NAF's four most popular posts. According to Facebook the most

---

[48] Alefaio, 'Archives connecting with the community'.

Figure 37.1 Beqa villagers' traditional fish drive, 1947.

popular post reached 162,000 accounts and was liked 138,000 times. That is an overall audience of about 18 per cent of Fiji's population and an engaged audience of 1.5 per cent.

Technology that allows archives to digitize and share images has allowed the communities to take full ownership of the historical images and start adding precious additional information to them. In the archives, these photos were disorganized and uncatalogued, unceremoniously dumped and in an advanced state of decay. But through the Facebook posts the public are commenting on who is in the photographs, where or when these may have been taken, and how they themselves are personally connected to the images. In short, the public are 'making history'. This is a form of content creation that allows archivists and villagers from two different spaces to share knowledge that benefits one another. It also creates a space for oral histories to inform written colonial records and deepen our knowledge of historical events.

The increased visibility and acceptance of the NAF has also enabled it to work with other parties to make accessible Fijian heritage held abroad.

The NAF has established a relationship with the Fijian Art Research Project jointly hosted by the Sainsbury Research Unit at the University of East Anglia (UEA) and the Museum of Archaeology and Anthropology at the University of Cambridge (MAA), to post on the NAF Facebook page images of Fijian heritage in their collection. This has given Fijians access to cultural material not held in Fiji. These items and designs are sometimes controversial, because they are no longer found in Fiji today. Certain *masi* or *tapa* (bark cloth) designs have caused animated debate because the designs are no longer used in contemporary pieces, and consequently showing this to the Fijian public has broadened previously narrow ideas of what 'Fijian' art is. More than just (re)discovering lost heritage, practices, and ideas, this has also underlined the ongoing relevance of archives as public institutions that have much to contribute to contemporary debate about memory, identity, and knowledge. Using documentary heritage held in trust within archives is not simply about living in the past, but is as much about making the present and building for the future. This collaboration took another big step with the 2018 sharing (or 'repatriation') of 3,000 historical photographs of Fiji by the MAA with NAF to support public outreach and education. NAF has full permission to reproduce the images, with the condition that the MAA be properly acknowledged and that any contextual information (metadata) contributed by the public be passed along to MAA.

With the rapid pace of technological advancements, archival institutions are well placed to experiment with new technologies because they have the expertise, funding, and equipment that local communities may lack. For Indigenous communities concerned with the loss of knowledge and tradition by natural attrition, archival institutions are well placed to connect sources and people to remote communities using technology. This presents a contradiction for those interested in preserving historical memories at the local level who rightly question whether archival institutions can or should be trusted. This is the challenge facing Pacific archives which must simultaneously accept their colonial inception and convince local communities that they can open new possibilities for sharing and protecting Indigenous knowledge. This is further underlined by the NAF's participation in the Pacific Virtual Museum (PVM) project led by the National Library of New Zealand and the National Library of Australia, with funding and support from the Australian Department of Foreign Affairs and Trade (DFAT) and the New Zealand Ministry of Foreign Affairs and Trade (MFAT). The aim of the PVM is to connect Pacific Islanders with their documentary heritage by providing an 'online portal that provides an easy single access point to digitised Pacific cultural heritage items held in different museum, gallery and library collections around the world'.[49]

Demonstrated relevance and impact in the community also brought increased trust with senior government administrators. For example, public outreach and engagement was not a funded activity in 2011. After the initial pilot carried out in 2012, the NAF was given an allocation of 20,000 Fijian dollars in 2013, resulting in eleven outreach programmes. By 2018, this had increased to 100,000 Fijian dollars, enabling thirty-six outreach programmes. At this point NAF's expertise and the unique value it provided had become highly acknowledged and sought after by all ethnicities and provinces, for national events as well as regional and international events hosted locally in Fiji.[50]

Positive community feedback also helped secure project funding of 1,000,000 Fijian dollars for the salvaging and digitization of the national audiovisual collection of over 2,000 hours of footage. The benefits that came from connecting with the community helped the NAF to address longstanding internal issues. Funding on the whole saw a steady increase for the NAF, rising from 405,000 Fijian dollars in 2011 to 1,889,000 Fijian dollars by 2018. This finally facilitated a solution to the deeply set and ongoing personnel woes described by Bower, rising from a staff establishment of nineteen in 2011 to thirty-six in 2018.[51] The NAF now has a balanced organizational structure, providing a career path for all who enter its service.[52]

Conclusion

The archives, as both repository and catalyst for sparking community conversations and thinking, can have a key role to play in nurturing the memory and knowledge of society. In the South Pacific the ability of archives to meet this potential has been severely curtailed, as discussed early in this chapter. This is due principally to the low priority with which they have been seen by senior administrators, as well as the lack of interest and the suspicion they have received from the wider community. The underlying tension at the root of this hesitancy and distrust is a legacy of the outdated colonial practice of elevating Western knowledge systems at the expense of Indigenous

---

[49] National Library of New Zealand, Pacific Virtual Museum, https://natlib.govt.nz/about-us/collaborative-projects/pacific-virtual-museum, accessed 25 April 2020.
[50] Alefaio, 'Aim high: looking past our problems to get past our problems'.
[51] Bower, 'The state of the National Archives'.
[52] Alefaio, 'Aim high: looking past our problems to get past our problems'.

knowledge systems. Today's reality undermines this historical assumption. South Pacific Island nations need to take ownership of and elevate both systems. We stand to lose out if either or both of these is not functioning at the levels needed. The primacy of literacy over orality is a proposition pushed by those seeking to achieve an advantage. Archives, because of their colonial origin and early function, are easily seen as representing that legacy of domination and subjugation.

Without the resources needed to face a daunting array of challenges, archival practitioners turn to their training to address what they feel is 'in their control'. This generates positive increments in their work. They pull inwards, focusing on the 'control' aspect of their jobs by dispassionately applying archival techniques to the collection, ostensibly to make it more 'usable', but without making a concerted effort to go out proactively to the community to make sure it is used. This was not without its advantages; in the case of Fiji it meant that a very good archival foundation was put in place, though poor resourcing over a period seriously undermined this.[53]

To make the most of the good work of earlier archivists, the NAF in 2012 took the archives to the community, but only after the proper approvals were attained through established channels trusted by the community in order for the NAF to make a formal introduction and then provide unique value to a welcoming audience. The success of this exercise and the support it won from officials responsible for prioritizing and apportioning resources enabled the NAF to develop more services and initiatives targeted at demonstrating value through community engagement. This opened the eyes of the public to their heritage and the possibilities that brought with it.

When Pacific Island archives engage with their communities on multiple levels for extended periods, they can become a trusted agent for the dynamic collection and recollection, imagining and reimagining, of their society. Without sustained community engagement, and without dynamic archives, Pacific Island communities over time will be left wondering what they know and what they don't know. They will be bogged down and hampered by the illusory question of literacy versus orality. The truth is, there is more than enough space for both. The truth is we need them both. And Pacific Island archives can be a key point of confluence to acknowledge this, and grow this understanding, in order to benefit their peoples.

---

[53] Bower, 'The state of the National Archives'.

38

Missing in Action

Women's Under-representation and Decolonizing the Archival Experience

SAFUA AKELI AMAAMA

Introduction

The archival record, in all its forms, plays a significant role in the documentation of histories, peoples, and events. In the Pacific region, archival collections typically reflect their respective colonizers' interests, are written in colonial languages, and are confined in different and far-flung collections. Furthermore, underlying these archives lies a complex variety of gender issues. Hence, this chapter considers the broad archival record in Oceania as a body of privileged knowledge embedded within the deep material cultures of the Islands and oftentimes strongly evoking emotions and memory. It seeks to privilege women's experience and voices to generate meaningful discussions. As Natalie Harkin eloquently expresses of Australian Aboriginal archives,

> Our family archives are like maps that haunt and guide us toward paths past-travelled and directions unknown. We travel through these archives that offer up new stories and collections of data, and a brutal surveillance is exposed at the hands of the State. We gain insight into intimate conversations, letters, behaviours and movements, juxtaposed with categorisations of people, places, landscapes and objects. These records are our memories and lives; material, visceral, flesh and blood.[1]

As I myself recall some early archive memories, I fondly remember my paternal grandmother, Palepa Ioane Akeli (1923–2008), and her well-worn exercise book, a volume that she kept with her bible in which she documented her life story and genealogy. Grandmother was born in Ti'avea

---

[1] N. Harkin, 'The poetics of (re)mapping archives: memory in the blood', *Journal of the Association for the Study of Australian Literature* 14:3 (2014), 1–14.

village on the southeast coast of Upolu, where she had met and married my grandfather, Ioane Akeli (1922–94), a son of a Catechist minister of the Catholic Church who was stationed at Ti'avea. Soon after, they enrolled in the Catholic seminary at Moamoa which had been established by the French mission as an educational institution to train Samoan Catechists. In this role, Catechists and their wives oversaw parish activities and church rites on behalf of the priests.[2] After graduating from the seminary, my grandparents took up their first village post in Samata (1949–54), located in Savai'i. At the time, grandmother was pregnant with their third child and, on arriving at the village, had to live with the high chief for a few months as no residence was available. Grandmother described a difficult settlement period in a new village, far away from their families in Upolu. Moreover, my grandfather had to work the plantations to earn a small income to supplement their subsistence living. Over their forty-five years of missionary service, my grandparents worked in several villages: Safa'i (1955–60), Fa'ala (1961–6), Satitoa (1967–76), Samatau (1977–87), and Si'umu (1987–94), and went on to have ten children, one of whom died at aged two. Many of grandmother's stories have been richly documented in her exercise book, including the loss of her child, her childhood memories, stories of her father as part of the Mau movement (1926–36), her birthing experiences outside of the hospital, and the 1970 visit of Pope Francis VI to Sāmoa.

During a visit to New Zealand in 1994, my grandfather passed away unexpectedly, and, at the request of their parish in Si'umu, he was laid to rest in front of the village Catholic church. Grandfather too was an avid writer and kept a tattered brown ledger which held oratory speeches, genealogies, and birth records. After their passing, these records were sought after by family members, as many by this time lived outside of Sāmoa. I hold these memories with deep affection since these private records lie outside institutional repositories. However, their stories, as with many others, are buried under or absent from the state and church archives which tend to focus on the accounts provided by European missionaries.

In this chapter, I reconsider the archival experience both as a personal journey and as part of my work as an academic historian. By sharing these insights, I hope to contribute towards reframing the archival record as an embedded part of material culture by focusing on women's under-representation and the associated affective histories and memories. Hence,

---

[2] A. Hamilton, 'The French Catholic Mission to Samoa 1845–1914', PhD thesis, Australian National University, Canberra, 1997.

this chapter considers the broad archival record as a body of privileged knowledge embedded within deep material culture and strongly evoking emotions and memory.

Pushing the Archival Lens

Internationally, the overarching body of frameworks overseeing the archives is situated under the United Nations Educational Scientific and Cultural Organization (UNESCO) such as the International Council on Archives (ICA) which was established in 1948. As defined by ICA, archives are 'the documentary by-product of human activity retained for their long-term value'. Moreover:

> They are contemporary records created by individuals and organisations as they go about their business and therefore provide a direct window on past events. They can come in a wide range of formats including written, photographic, moving image, sound, digital and analogue. Archives are held by public and private institutions and individuals around the world.[3]

According to this definition, archives encompass a broad range of characteristics as they are situated within various spaces and are created by people and institutions. Hence the practice of archiving, as Christen argues, requires flexibility to accommodate multiple knowledge systems: 'incorporating Indigenous knowledge systems into library and archive practices will not just enhance relationships and create access to records, but more importantly, it has the potential to decolonize archival practices and modes of access'.[4] Regionally, the establishment of the Pacific Regional Branch of the International Council on Archives (PARBICA) in 1981 has contributed towards this pursuit. Over the last few decades, PARBICA has documented the challenges of the archival landscape across the region in the areas of training, disaster preparedness, digitization, and conservation.[5] Similarly, the Pacific Islands Association of Libraries, Archives, and Museums (PIALA),

---

[3] See International Council on Archives website, www.ica.org/en.
[4] K. Christen, 'Tribal archives, traditional knowledge, and local contexts: why the "s" matters', *Journal of Western Archives* 6:1 (2015), 1–19.
[5] M. Crookston, 'Record keeping for good governance in the Pacific: the work of the Pacific regional branch of the International Council on Archives', *Archifacts* (2011), 73–83; M. Hoyle and L. Millar, 'The challenge of records and archives education and training in the Pacific', *Archives and Manuscripts* 32:2 (2011), 114–41; D. Wickman, 'Recordkeeping legislation and its impacts: the PARBICA recordkeeping for good governance toolkit', *Comma, International Journal on Archives* (2012), 51–9.

established in 1981, has provided avenues to collaborate across institutions, although it focuses mainly on Micronesia.[6]

Geographically, the Pacific region covers twenty-two countries, spanning from Hawai'i in the north and Rapa Nui in the east, to Australia and New Zealand in the south. Overall, the Pacific Ocean is home to 9 million people (excluding Australia and New Zealand), living on '200 high islands and 2,500 low islands or atolls', with a combined land mass of 91,099 square kilometres and an Exclusive Economic Zone of 27,449,000 square kilometres. Evelyn Wareham's 2002 survey on the state of Pacific archives notes the challenges posed by the region's vastness and highly diverse traditional systems of archiving, stating that 'Pacific island archives vary in resources from the relatively well-established National Archives of Fiji and Papua New Guinea to understaffed archival services with little storage space or authority over the disposal of government records.'[7] Moreover:

> a number of countries, including Nauru, Tonga, and Sāmoa, continue to have no legislative mandate over government records, no repositories, and no knowledge of archival systems, leaving government records either in a state of complete neglect or in the overcrowded registries of government departments.[8]

Decades earlier, the archives had undergone several transformational turns. For example, in its first volume of the *Journal of Pacific History* (1966), a section titled 'From the Archives' was created to highlight the discovery of lesser-known archives such as missionary accounts, anthropological writings, naval records, ships logs, journals, company papers, and unaccessioned manuscripts.[9] Since the opening of the Research School of Pacific Studies (RSPacS) at the Australian National University (ANU) in 1946, founding editors James Davidson and H.E. Maude, both from the Department of Pacific History, had developed the idea of a journal publication.[10] Having expanded since its inception in 1966, the *Journal of Pacific History* (2019) now produces four annual issues and is accessed online via the publisher Taylor & Francis. The editorial board includes a number of non-ANU scholars and continues to include a section on 'Narratives and Documents' which accommodates articles featuring archival discoveries and innovations.

---

[6] See Pacific Islands Association of Libraries, Archives, and Museums website: https://piala-pacific.wixsite.com/piala-pacific.
[7] E. Wareham, 'From explorers to evangelists: archivists, recordkeeping, and remembering in the Pacific Islands', *Archival Science* 2 (2002), 187–207.
[8] Wareham, 'From explorers to evangelists'.   [9] *Journal of Pacific History* 1:1 (1966), 183–203.
[10] D. Munro and G. Gray, '"We haven't abandoned the project": the founding of the *Journal of Pacific History*', *Journal of Pacific History* 48:1 (2013), 63–77.

Progress since the 1960s in the documentation of work associated with the Pacific Islands parallels the emerging post-colonial period when nations were transitioning into a new era of independence. In this period, the academic community was keen to preserve archival sources in order to support the writing of new histories that highlighted oral history accounts as valid sources.[11] The 'island-centred' perspective encouraged in the 1960s and 1970s provided a new turn in the writing and conceptualization of Pacific histories.[12] Thus, a new wave of Pacific Island scholars such as Sione Lātūkefu (1927–95), Epeli Hauʻofa (1939–2009), Albert Wendt (b.1939), and Malama Meleisea (b.1948) emerged from this school of thought, making significant inroads in the documentation of new histories and the archival record.[13] Archiving the work of these Pacific scholars is important for communities, within academia and beyond, since their body of work maintains a pivotal reference point for emerging scholars.

Parallel to these events, since 1968, the ANU Pacific Manuscripts Bureau has provided a wealth of information on the Pacific region for preservation purposes. However, accessibility for users in the Pacific Islands continues to be a challenge, despite online links to microfilm, audio recording, and photographic and printed publications collections. As Wareham states:

> Documentary records were often not created by local communities and are not held in island countries. Many strands of the Pacific documentary record have been absent from the region almost since their creation. Evidence of the past of the Pacific in the records of explorers, travellers, missionary organizations, trading companies, imperial policy-makers, and scientific researchers are held in the homelands of the record-makers.[14]

On the issue of preservation and related responsibilities, as late as the nineteenth century, in a letter to the editor of the Dunedin-based *Evening Star* (1898) newspaper which was launched in the 1860s, a member of the public, Ka Lofa contended that 'Before too late (all the old customs and ceremonies will soon be things of the past) some wealthy colonists should fit out a vessel

---

[11] B. Douglas, 'Pasts, presents and possibilities of Pacific history and Pacific studies: as seen by a historian from Canberra', *Journal of Pacific History* 50:2 (2015), 224–8.

[12] Douglas, 'Pasts, presents and possibilities'.

[13] M. Meleisea and P. Schoeffel, 'Forty-five years of Pacific Island Studies: some reflections', *Oceania* 87:3 (2017), 337–43; E. Hauʻofa and N. Thomas, '"We were still Papuans": a 2006 interview with Epeli Hauʻofa', *Contemporary Pacific* 24:1 (2012), 120–32; S. Lātūkefu, 'Oral traditions: an appraisal of their value in historical research in Tonga', *Journal of Pacific History* 3 (1968), 135–43.

[14] Wareham, 'From explorers to evangelists', 199.

with scientists and visit a few groups in order to preserve in our archives concrete facts of bygone traditions and ceremonies.'[15]

It appears that the concern for the preservation of the archives was seen to be the responsibility of 'wealthy colonists' and 'scientists'. Moreover, the role of the state in facilitating the transfer of historical records was essential in the practice of archival information. For example, in 1929, archives held in the old British Consulate in Sāmoa were transferred to the Alexander Turnbull Library as a result of a move by the Internal Affairs Department 'to collect and classify official records of the Dominion which may have an historical value'.[16] However, increasingly, since the 1990s, the role of the state in countries like New Zealand shifted towards 'democratizing' collections and focused on engaging with the community and providing access to multiple collection stories.[17] Thus, the emerging cultural centres and communities requesting dialogue with institutions is an important conversation to be had in terms of the transformational shift in legislative frameworks and legal recognition.

One way in which communities are actively engaging in this area of public history involves online platforms. Recently, I was directed to a new website platform organized by the Australian South Sea Islanders (Port Jackson) (ASSIPJ) which details the history, vision, and mission of ASSIPJ including representation, healing, and family connection.[18] Containing a rich offering of video recordings, images, chronologies, and reports on the ASSI communities, the website presence reveals a strong governance body of experts and advisors.[19] This example demonstrates an avenue of flexibility that includes the combination of the state, communities, and academic scholars and thus encompasses multiple spaces, created by people and institutions.

Searching for Women's Narratives

Whose interpretation takes precedence is continually challenged and under siege; the predominant stories and master narratives compete with the less acknowledged minor narratives for recognition.[20]

---

[15] *Evening Star*, 14 May 1898.   [16] *Auckland Star*, 22 August 1929.

[17] UNESCO, *Museums, Libraries and Cultural Heritage: Democratising Culture, Creating Knowledge and Building Bridges* (Hamburg: Druckerei Semann, 1999), 9–11.

[18] See Australian South Sea Islanders Port Jackson, www.assipj.com.au/ (accessed 12 October 2019).

[19] Australian South Sea Islanders Port Jackson.

[20] J. Bastian, 'Records, memory and space: locating archives in the landscape', *Public History Review* 21 (2014), 45–69.

In reference to the quotation above, my grandmother's personal story exemplifies the narratives absent from the state and church archival record, even though the work of Catechists was crucial in the Catholic mission apparatus since they lived in the village and participated in church and village events. These absences are further revealed in the work of annotated bibliographies such as one example focusing on Māori *Wahine* (Women) in which Honiana Love states, 'Making this information more accessible to all people will help provide an insight into the lives of some of the least accessible and therefore least visible members of New Zealand society.'[21] The visibility of women has been highlighted by scholars who cite areas needing improvement, including collaborations between archivists, scholars, and museum professionals.[22] For the Pacific region, scholarship on women's histories is sporadic at best, with very few histories exploring this area. In recent times, histories on women, war, and conflict have enabled women's voices to come to the fore of this experience.[23] Within the writing of these recent histories, scholars are highlighting archives and repositories as key components in the evaluation of histories and family connections. For Sāmoa, there has been a record of documenting strong ancestral female figures through various publications which focus on genealogy associated with hierarchy.[24] This historic focus on rank and status, however, also neglects the general lives of ordinary women. In Guam, Anne Hattori's review of national curriculum textbooks provides tangible evidence of women's invisibility, even by Indigenous authors. However, women themselves in the legislative space actively challenged the political discourse and asserted their own voices.[25] For the Australian context in relation to the national inquiry on the Stolen Generation of Aboriginal and Torres Strait Islander children, Trish Luker contends the 'affective politics of reconciliation

---

[21] H. Love, 'Nga Korero E Pa Ana Ki Nga Wahine Māori: a guide to manuscripts and archives on Māori women held at the Alexander Turnbull Library', Master of Library and Information Studies, School of Communications and Information Management, Victoria University of Wellington, 2000, vi.
[22] T. Clery and R. Metcalfe, 'Activist archives and feminist fragments: claiming space in the archive for the voices of Pacific women and girls', *Education as Change* 22:2 (2018), 1–29.
[23] J. Bennett and A. Wanhalla (eds.), *Mothers' Darlings of the South Pacific: The Children of Indigenous Women and US Servicemen, World War II* (Honolulu: University of Hawai'i Press, 2016).
[24] C. Ralston and N. Thomas (eds.), *Sanctity and Power: Gender in Polynesian History*, special issue, *Journal of Pacific History* 22:4 (1987); A. Kramer, *Salamasina: Scenes from Ancient Samoan Culture and History*, trans. Brother Herman (Pago Pago, American Sāmoa: Association of the Marist Brothers' Old Boys, 1949).
[25] A.P. Hattori, 'Textbook tells: gender, race, and decolonizing Guam history textbooks in the 21st century', *AlterNative* 14:2 (2018), 173–84.

have been challenged by claims to sovereignty in relation to records management'.[26] These are only some of the complex issues which surface from the problematic archival praxis. There is a need to reconfigure the cataloguing process within collections to include women's archival documents in the metadata produced. However, this requires commitment towards analysing archives, as Christen contends:

> Collecting institutions, be they archives, libraries, or museums, are in a unique position to tackle the educational and social aspects of our current intellectual property landscape as it pertains to Indigenous cultural heritage materials. Shifts in how and why these institutions choose to collect, manage, and define their materials can set a new tone for the circulation and use of cultural materials.[27]

For example, in my search for women's archival stories associated with leprosy from the 1890s to the 1920s, aside from the European missionary sisters who managed the care of leprosy sufferers, very few records documented the experience of women who supported family members or were themselves leprosy sufferers.[28] Thus, the majority of the archives – which were written in English, French, German, and Samoan – were created by men, most of whom were either working in government, were chiefs of a village, or were affiliated with the church.

Hence, activism has played a central role in the archival process, particularly in considering the fact that 'the public domain has been a space that has been historically hostile for Indigenous peoples because much of their cultural patrimony was treated as a source of knowledge for all humankind despite its location within local cultural systems'.[29] Scholars such as Clery and Metcalfe argue that archives do not focus on 'local responses or experiences' but rather 'often prioritise stories about conflict and war, about national and political manoeuvrings'.[30] Historian Patricia O'Brien's biography of Ta'isi Olaf Nelson attempts to present women in the story, such as Olive Virginia Malienafau Nelson (1917–70), the first Samoan woman in New Zealand to graduate with a law degree in 1936 and admitted into the

---

[26] T. Luker, 'Decolonising archives: indigenous challenges to record keeping in "reconciling" settler colonial states', *Australian Feminist Studies* 32:91–2 (2017), 108–25.

[27] Christen, 'Tribal archives, traditional knowledge, and local contexts', 14.

[28] S. Akeli Amaama, 'Cleansing Western Samoa: leprosy control during New Zealand Administration, 1914–1922', *Journal of Pacific History* 52:3 (2017), 360–73.

[29] Christen, 'Tribal archives, traditional knowledge, and local contexts', 13.

[30] Clery and Metcalfe, 'Activist archives and feminist fragments', 2.

Supreme Court.[31] However, archives pertaining to the women's Mau movement are located not in Sāmoa but in the Geneva Archives in Switzerland, not only distant but also restrictive by requiring permission to access. This is problematic for students and staff who lack funding support to enable the exploration of these important histories.[32]

The search for women's narratives in the archival records takes commitment by professionals to evaluate the archives and annotate specific collections. The post-colonial period has provided space for countries to reinterpret and reorganize their archives to assist community engagement. Thus, the issue of reconstructing the archives requires historical background to the collections better to understand how documents were stored and retrieved. The post-colonial period ignited views on how new and emerging states needed to capture their histories and transition towards independence and the need for communities to engage with archives pertaining to their histories. Therefore, as Harkin argues, 'The archive is at odds with itself, functioning through a paradoxical logic. It is both sacred space *and* colonial object; it drives us to both recover *and* preserve the past; it protects *and* patrols, regulates *and* represses.'[33]

In October 2018, I was invited to attend a workshop facilitated by the German Museums Association (GMA) which included representatives from various institutions and countries such as Bolivia, Turkey, New Zealand, Australia, Sāmoa, United States, France, and Nigeria. Some of the heated discussions focused on the affective ties associated with objects and archives, in that most German institutional inventories are inaccessible due to various reasons, including language. Although work in this area requires commitment, access to women's stories is potentially provoking. Through museum institutions in Germany, discussions with colleagues include the archival record, its accessibility, decolonizing the frame of reference, and the need to translate museum inventories into English.

Documentation plays a significant role in the narratives that can be drawn from lived experiences. As a result of these discussions, the GMA guidelines were revised into a second draft and published online for public circulation.[34] Archives, as scholars rightly contend, are viewed no longer as 'neutral', but

---

[31] P. O'Brien, *Tautai: World History and the Life of Taʻisi Olaf Nelson* (Wellington: Huia Publishers and University of Hawaiʻi Press, 2017).
[32] Currently, O'Brien and colleagues at NUS are looking to develop a history workshop to generate interest in the writing of histories which will place these difficulties within the context of resource-constrained Pacific institutions.
[33] Harkin, 'The poetics of (re)mapping archives', 10.
[34] See www.museumsbund.de/publikationen/guidelines-on-dealing-with-collections-from-colonial-contexts-2/.

as constructed by creators (directly and indirectly) for multiple reasons. Having worked in both a national museum and a university environment, I came to understand that the politics of representation is at the heart of consultations and community engagement. Hence, accountability for institutions to democratize their collections is fundamental to their existence and to the communities they aim to serve. Therefore, what commitments are institutions tied to in respect to archives? This next section reviews how relationships can be better managed to provide opportunities to engage with partners in a beneficial way.

Archival Memories and Affective Articulations

In 2015, during my history PhD studies, I visited the National Library of New Zealand (NLNZ) in Wellington as I was critiquing a photographic exhibition on Sāmoa which had been displayed in 1998. After discussions with the archivist, the NLNZ was keen to donate images to an institution. Therefore, in 2017, through discussions with the then Director of the Centre for Samoan Studies, the National University of Sāmoa accepted the donation of photographic images from the NLNZ with the support of the New Zealand High Commission in Sāmoa. These originally were part of the *Va'aomanu Togimamanu e ata, tala ma fa'atufugaga o le fa'aaliga o au measina – An Exhibition Celebrating the History and Culture of Sāmoa* (1998), curated by Samoan lecturer Tupuola Malifa who was at the time based at Victoria University of Wellington. I recall meeting a visitor at the exhibition launch who was drawn to the images and Samoan text of a history previously unknown to him. This bilingual exhibition now hangs on the wall at the Centre for Samoan Studies as a reminder of Sāmoa's complex history and the need for institutions to continue the dialogue. The collective celebratory exhibition cited above drew on several different elements such as language, images, and context. However, as Bastian contends, archives are 'dynamic, part of an ever-evolving continuum, always in a state of creation, open to new interpretations and offering new dimensions of meaning depending on who is reading them, under what conditions and where'.[35]

In this exhibit, the photographs captured in the colonial period were produced and manufactured for multiple purposes by those in privileged positions. Consequently, they hold powerful messages about a past that continues to require critique. Likewise, the entire archival record is

---

[35] Bastian, 'Records, memory and space', 50.

considered a rich body of material culture, including private letters, government reports, missionary dossiers, photographs, and medical reports. For a historian, such material enables the reconstruction of a time in history (or present), shedding light on relationships and network connections. However, the paper record provides information that reveals the lives and memories of those who have gone before. A few years ago, I came across archival records pertaining to New Zealand's Goodwill Mission to Sāmoa in 1936 which changed the course of the Mau resistance movement. The records had been filed under 'Education' in the Archives New Zealand repository and were discovered accidentally.[36]

When considering the affective nature of archives, there is a requirement for an understanding of how documents and sources are created and positioned to tell particular stories. The emerging discourse of 'archives of feeling' foregrounds how sources can express emotions, values, and ephemeral elements associated with archives that require consideration. I have drawn largely from the work of Ann Cvetkovich, who argues that the feelings of ordinary people in the archival record, especially the stories and experiences of women and queers, have been neglected in the field of historical trauma studies.[37] This deeply resonates with the challenges I faced in attempting to highlight the trauma of stigma, violence, and isolation associated with leprosy in colonial Sāmoa. Some of the questions raised include: How do we ensure women's voices are represented and decolonized in the archival record? How can we ensure their lived experiences find a place in scholarly debate and discussion? Where are women's voices to be found? How do we work with oral stories where archives do not exist? These questions are by no means new and have continued to challenge my practice as a historian. Institutional processes have privileged the colonial archive, and, for scholars, unpacking the box requires skill and tact in understanding the broader architecture of the colonial project.

Moving into the Digital Future

According to Tough, technological changes have transformed the processing of information: 'The two most significant changes of the last century came

---

[36] S. Akeli Amaama, 'A goodwill mission? Revisiting Samoa–New Zealand relations in 1936', *New Zealand Journal of History* 53:2 (2019), 65–82.
[37] A. Cvetkovich, *An Archive of Feelings: Trauma, Sexuality, and Lesbian Public Cultures* (Durham, NC: Duke University Press, 2003).

with the development of programs that could process text and the development of Windows operating systems.'[38] This bodes well for the future digitization of archives and raises issues about access, storage, security, and maintenance. In some instances, archives 'were imposed on the indigenous cultures of Oceania by colonizing powers, as an introduced technology, which altered or displaced established practices'.[39] Furthermore, 'written recordkeeping is a necessity for modern governance, economic systems, and cultural needs in the Pacific islands, and archives have a vital role to play in documenting rights and entitlements and enabling interpretation of the events of the past'.[40] The move to digital includes judicial records pertaining to archival sources. Kathleen Birrell argues that within the Australian legal archive, 'While the Indigene is perpetually determined by the law in continuous acts of violent (mis)recognition, the alterity of indigeneity is constitutive of the law itself, as a persistent and spectral ambivalence within it.'[41] Archival records hold powerful assumptions which can change worldviews and physical boundaries. In the Pacific region, court records pertaining to land and titles have implications for communities, as do the historical records and scholarly publications. Thus, recordkeeping has been utilized as a controlling mechanism: 'In judicial systems from New Zealand to Sāmoa, the cultural knowledge of land rights, related in orally remembered genealogies and recorded in written land records, continues to have vital economic significance in proving descendants' rights.'[42]

A few years ago, a close friend enquired about records pertaining to her great-grandfather who had been a key leader in the Mau resistance movement. In reviewing my files, I was able to share records from newspapers and files of unpublished manuscripts. Subsequently, she shared these documents with family elders at a family reunion, who were grateful to have records of a loved one who played a significant role in Sāmoa's journey towards independence. However, some of these records were accessed via digital platforms provided by different institutions. This accessibility and archival experience placed me in a privileged space, and while I was keen to share information, I was also aware of the tension of the archival record.

---

[38] A. Tough, 'Good government and good governance: record keeping in a contested arena', *Journal of the Eastern and Southern Africa Regional Branch of the International Council on Archives* 36 (2017), 108–15.
[39] Wareham, 'From explorers to evangelists', 187.   [40] 'From explorers to evangelists', 187.
[41] K. Birrell, '"An essential ghost": indigeneity within the legal archive', *Australian Feminist Law Journal* 22 (2010), 81–99.
[42] Wareham, 'From explorers to evangelists', 202–3.

Records can be used to validate, define, and redefine social relationships and resources. Here the role of the archivist is fundamental to provide a structure that accommodates the political discourse associated with these records.[43] The National University of Sāmoa is leading the development of the National Digital Library, which is funded by the United Nations Development Programme. The process of preserving records on a national scale requires international support for hardware and software, as well as capacity building. However, this requires a solid infrastructural framework and information-sharing across ministries, which is an ongoing challenge.

An area of concern is historical business records from the Pacific; entrepreneurial ventures had far-reaching opportunities and at times failed in their course. In 2018, while working at the Centre for Samoan Studies, a German museum collaboration emerged to develop an exhibition relating to the Goddefroy und Sohn Company which had established itself in Sāmoa (and other places) in 1857. The German plantation monopoly and labour exploitation has been documented by scholars such as John Moses, Doug Munro, and Ben Featuna'i Liua'ana. However, I was keen to explore the contribution women made to the plantation economy. Moreover, the Chan Mow Supermarket Chain established in 1950 by Lotte Chan Mow and Chan Yat Mow also deserves exploration within the written archives. In just these two examples, developing these worthy archives will require relationship-building and scoping of the archival record, both literary and oral.

As has been highlighted by researchers, resources and storage for archives is a pressing issue, particularly for the tropical region where climate conditions are unstable. While I was a curator at Te Papa, I recall a visit by Cook Island members of parliament to the museum and their request to leave records and objects at the museum until the Cook Islands had a proper facility with the right conditions. These concerns are very real in the region and require continued support. Despite the focus on government records in Pacific archival collections, civil society organizations with a strong advocacy position should have support in the archival recordkeeping process.[44] This recognizes the parallel existence of oral and literature sources within communities, as Tough notes:

---

[43] J.R. O'Neal, '"The right to know": decolonizing Native American archives', *Journal of Western Archives* 6:1 (2015), article 2, 6.

[44] M. Olhausen, 'The archival challenges and choices of a small non-profit organization attempting to preserve its unique past', *Journal of Western Archives* 10:2 (2019), 1–14.

Instead orality and literacy continue to co-exist in differing mixes throughout the region, and many indigenous peoples maintain both oral and written means of creation, transmission, and preservation of records despite long knowledge of literacy. In this context, written records may tell partial stories, and yet still lack an easy relationship with the communities to whom they related.[45]

These groups and associations play a vital role in providing civil support to multiple communities, and their stories are just as important in providing a broader view of the political and social landscape in the Pacific. For example, women's crisis centres in Fiji and Vanuatu are transforming lives and assisting in empowering women, as are the Lesbian, Gay, Bisexual, Queer, and Intersex community organizations. Archives must work to access documents from such important social groups, in addition to the traditional government archives.

With digital tools and applications providing new opportunities to communicate information, methods of archiving the digital interface such as Facebook have enabled powerful sharing platforms. Where communication was once a private affair, the new age of digital futures has extended this network rapidly and widely in a matter of seconds. Moreover, recent events on Wikileaks and the Cambridge Analytics point to complicated issues regarding archival security and the ability, or inability, of security-conscious governments to control the news feed: 'The organisations that have made the greatest progress in electronic Records Management tend to be those that hold the most sensitive and the most important records.'[46] Despite the sensitive nature of 'big data', Archives New Zealand are digitizing more of their records, making them available to Pacific-based scholars, although these associations depend on colonial historical ties to various groups, and research topics of interest.

Conclusion

The archive genealogy in respect to Pacific histories continues to be located in far-flung places, and its existence poses many spaces of tension. As a collector and interpreter of information, I acknowledge my activism and the challenges faced in my work. This chapter provides insights into some of the progress, as well as some of the dilemmas faced by the caretakers of the

---

[45] Wareham, 'From explorers to evangelists', 197–8.
[46] Tough, 'Good government and good governance', 110.

archival record, and offers some suggestions towards improvement. The locations of repositories should no longer be an issue in light of the utilization of the digital platform to provide researchers and scholars the opportunity to access records. However, problems of sustainability and infrastructure continue to pose challenges and questions. For example, since the National Archives Records Authority (NARA) was established in 2013 under the *Public Records Act* (2011), Sāmoa has engaged in digitizing records, particularly the German archives, via a project with Archives New Zealand and Germany. However, much of this work is inaccessible to researchers. In 1999, Sam Kaima noted: 'Archives and records are both an information source and an important cultural heritage and better management patterns and preservation methods must be put in place now to ensure that the benefits of records and archives are realized in the island nations.'[47]

This chapter has demonstrated the progress in some areas in terms of information-sharing, particularly via the digital platform. However, there continues to be a need to develop community protocols of ethics and use to enable further dialogue with institutions, private collections, and multiple communities. The departure point for this chapter was my grandmother, since her act of recordkeeping and transmitting stories orally and literally has deeply affected my academic practice as a historian. However, the means to assert women's voices continues to be a reflective process to ensure underrepresented narratives are given spaces to speak and thrive.

---

[47] S. Kaima, 'Education and training for archivists and record keepers in the Pacific', *Information Development* 15:1 (1999), 51–5.

39

Rethinking Gender and Identity in Asia and the Pacific

ANGELA WANHALLA

Since the 1980s, a focus on gender relations has opened up new questions about the Pacific past across a diverse set of issues.[1] Health, sexuality, war, the family, reproduction, and many other areas have benefited from the analytical insights made possible by gender as a 'category of analysis'.[2] Gender, as Patricia O'Brien has argued, has been 'vital to understanding the cultural kaleidoscope of the Pacific'.[3] For instance, recognition that gender is a socially constructed category and system of meaning has produced an influential body of scholarship on Western representations of Pacific bodies since the eighteenth century across a range of cultural texts.[4] Because gender is woven into the structure of institutions, the allocation of resources, and the sexual division of labour, it has been a particularly fruitful area for the examinations of power and rank in Indigenous societies, while studies of cross-cultural encounters have highlighted the centrality of gender and sexuality to imperial and colonial projects.[5]

---

[1] The research for this chapter was supported by a Royal Society Te Apārangi Rutherford Discovery Fellowship, generously provided through Government funds.

[2] J.W. Scott, *Gender and the Politics of History* (New York: Columbia University Press, 1988).

[3] P. O'Brien, 'Gender', in D. Armitage and A. Bashford (eds.), *Pacific Histories: Ocean, Land, People* (Basingstoke: Palgrave Macmillan, 2014), 238–304, at 282.

[4] Some examples include: B. Creed and J. Hoorn (eds.), *Body Trade: Captivity, Cannibalism and Colonialism in the Pacific* (New York: Routledge, 2001); P. O'Brien, *The Pacific Muse: Exotic Femininity and the Colonial Pacific* (Seattle: University of Washington Press, 2006); K. Rountree, 'Re-making the Māori female body: Marianne Williams's Mission in the Bay of Islands', *Journal of Pacific History* 35:1 (2000), 49–66; A. Jones and P. Herda (eds.), *Bitter Sweet: Indigenous Women in the Pacific* (Dunedin: Otago University Press, 2000).

[5] P. Herda, 'Introduction: writing the lives of some extraordinary Polynesian women', *Journal of the Polynesian Society* 123:2 (2014), 113–28, at 109. M. Jolly, *Women of the Place: Kastom, Colonialism and Gender in Vanuatu* (Philadelphia: Harwood, 1994); M.C. Rodman, *Far from Home: British Colonial Space in the New Hebrides* (Honolulu: University of Hawai'i Press, 2001); K. Ram and M. Jolly (eds.), *Maternities and Modernities: Colonial and Postcolonial Experiences in Asia and the Pacific* (Cambridge: Cambridge University Press, 1997); C. Ralston and N. Thomas (eds.), *Sanctity and Power: Gender in Polynesian History*, special issue *Journal of Pacific History* 22 (1987).

In the context of gender and colonialism – a particularly productive area of inquiry in Pacific history – historians have sought to assess how far Indigenous women retained agency and power, or were constrained by male-dominated colonial institutions.[6] By the 1990s, scholars of gender and empire recognized that European women were agents of the imperial effort, had helped advance projects of colonial settlement, and had gained material advantages from colonization. In Anne McClintock's words, 'white women were not the hapless onlookers of empire but were ambiguously complicit both as colonizers and colonized, privileged and restricted, acted upon and acting'.[7] In the Pacific, historians have examined, for instance, European women as missionary wives and workers, women's role in the settlement of the Pacific, and their impact upon race relations and the evolution of colonial policies.[8] Since then, investigations into gender and sexuality within colonial contexts have demonstrated the various ways in which imperial projects of territorial, military, and political expansion were intimate in character and nature. Of particular importance is Ann Laura Stoler's analysis of race, gender, and colonialism in the Dutch East Indies, which has been influential in rethinking the scale and character of imperial endeavour and colonial governance.[9]

Interracial relationships, cross-cultural families, and mixed-race children are key areas where scholars have assessed the ties between intimacy, race, and colonial governance. These are of particular significance for Asia and the Pacific: two regions shaped and connected by the imperial trade, migration, and labour relations that inaugurated cross-cultural relationships and saw the emergence of mixed-race families who were the focus of official concern.

---

[6] For instance, J. Linnekin, *Sacred Queens and Women of Consequence: Rank, Gender, and Colonialism in the Hawaiian Islands* (Ann Arbor: University of Michigan Press, 1990); N. Te Awekotuku, *Mana Wahine Maori: Selected Writings on Maori Women's Art, Culture and Politics* (Auckland: New Woman's Press, 1991); A. Mikaere, *Colonising Myths: Māori Realities* (Wellington: Huia, 2011).

[7] A. McClintock, *Imperial Leather: Race, Gender and Sexuality in the Colonial Conquest* (London: Routledge, 1995), 6.

[8] C. Ralston, 'The study of women in the Pacific', *Contemporary Pacific* 4:1 (1992), 162–75, at 166. For instance, A. Inglis, *'Not a White Woman Safe': Sexual Anxiety and Politics in Port Moresby, 1920–1934* (Canberra: ANU Press, 1974); C. Knapman, *White Women in Fiji, 1835–1930: The Ruin of Empire?* (Sydney: Allen & Unwin, 1986); C. Bulbeck, *Australian Women in Papua New Guinea: Colonial Passages 1920–1960* (Cambridge: Cambridge University Press, 1992); P. Grimshaw, *Paths of Duty: American Missionary Wives in Nineteenth-Century Hawaii* (Honolulu: University of Hawai'i Press, 1989).

[9] A.L. Stoler, *Carnal Knowledge and Imperial Power: Race and the Intimate in Colonial Rule* (Berkeley: University of California Press, 2002); A.L. Stoler (ed.), *Haunted by Empire: Geographies of Intimacy in North America History* (Durham, NC: Duke University Press, 2006).

Interracial relationships and mixed-race children were an almost universal outcome of cross-cultural encounters and meetings between newcomers and local peoples across the Pacific, inclusive of Australasia, Southeast Asia, and the Pacific Northwest from the nineteenth century. Yet, as Patricia O'Brien has argued, 'traditional historical narratives, which have been preoccupied with public deeds of white men' often overlook or downplay the significance and legacies of these couples and their families.[10] In recent decades, though, mixed-race families and communities have been important vehicles for sociologists and anthropologists to elaborate on the nuances of race and identity in contemporary contexts, while an important body of work by feminist historians has foregrounded the centrality of Indigenous women to founding cross-cultural communities in the Pacific.

Gender and identity have been interrogated from a variety of locations and spaces, notably the beaches, towns, cities, and treaty ports where cross-cultural encounters took place and new communities were forged. At certain points across these various sites, interracial marriage was accepted, encouraged, or prohibited, while mixed-race children were perceived either as a source of racial degeneration or as symbolic of racial harmony, progress, and the promise of a cosmopolitan future. As the embodiment of racial transgression between newcomer and host communities, interracial couples and their children were the subject of imperial and colonial strategies of control and regulation. As Ann Laura Stoler has argued for the Dutch East Indies, children of mixed ancestry 'straddled the divisions of ruler and ruled [and] threatened to blur the colonial divide'.[11] They were often perceived by administrations as embodying a 'tension of empire' between inclusionary discourses and exclusionary practices.[12]

This chapter surveys interracial relationships and colonial debates about race-mixing as they played out in particular locations across Asia and the Pacific. It touches on the earliest beach and port communities forged out of trade and extractive resource industries, including the value of cross-cultural relationships to these economies and the ways in which local communities responded. It also traces the emergence of ideas about the effects of race-mixing

---

[10] O'Brien, 'Gender', 292–3.
[11] A.L. Stoler, 'Making empire respectable: the politics of race and sexual morality in twentieth-century colonial cultures', in A. McClintock, A. Mufti, and E. Shoat (eds.), *Dangerous Liaisons: Gender, Nation, and Postcolonial Perspectives* (Minneapolis: University of Minneapolis Press, 1997), 344–73, at 349.
[12] A.L. Stoler, 'Sexual affronts and racial frontiers: European identities and the cultural politics of exclusion in colonial Southeast Asia', in F. Cooper and A.L. Stoler (eds.), *Tensions of Empire: Colonial Cultures in a Bourgeois World* (Berkeley: University of California Press, 1997), 198–237, at 198.

that circulated globally, but were shaped, too, by local circumstances, and informed colonial policies and census categories. Individuals and families, though, navigated personal and collective identities in ways that rarely ever matched the racial categorizations imposed by juridical regimes, and did so in ways that often confounded colonial policies and strategies of control.

Race, Sex, and Empire

Historians of the Pacific called for investigations into cross-cultural families and communities in the 1960s, although gender would not be explicitly addressed as a site of analysis for several more decades. In an agenda-setting 1966 article, J.W. Davidson argued studies 'of the immigrants themselves and of the [beach and port] communities they founded' were needed.[13] Recognizing the importance of legal regimes to imperial rule, Davidson identified a 'lack of studies of mixed-blood communities which come into being as a consequence of migration to the islands' and the legal distinctions associated with these peoples.[14] An early focus were the 'beachcomber' communities established by a polyglot group of sailors, deserters, whalers, and traders from the late eighteenth century. Since then, the beach has become an important location for Pacific history, characterized as a liminal space, both separating and connecting different communities.[15] In 1964 Harry Maude made, in his words, 'an attempt to study the first of these European immigrant groups, the beachcombers, who appear to have been largely neglected by anthropologists and historians interested in the study of acculturation'.[16] Caroline Ralston's extended study, published in 1977, focused on the beach towns and ports of Russell, Levuka, Apia, Honolulu, and Papeete forged out of the global trade in whales, sandalwood, fur skins, and coconut oil that relied on the exploitation of local resources controlled by Indigenous communities.[17] In 1982, Harry Morton addressed the whaling economy, including aspects of its social dimensions, that flourished in New Zealand during the first half of the nineteenth century.[18]

---

[13] J.W. Davidson, 'Problems of Pacific history', *Journal of Pacific History* 1:1 (1966), 18–19.
[14] Davidson, 'Problems of Pacific history', 19.
[15] G. Dening, *Beach Crossings: Voyaging across Times, Cultures and Self* (Carlton: Miegunyah Press, 2004).
[16] H.E. Maude, 'Beachcombers and castaways', *Journal of the Polynesian Society* 73: 3 (1964), 254–93, at 254.
[17] C. Ralston, *Grass Huts and Warehouses: Pacific Beach Communities of the Nineteenth Century* (Canberra: ANU Press, 1977).
[18] H. Morton, *The Whale's Wake* (Dunedin: Otago University Press, 1982).

These masculine worlds of maritime and resource extraction have attracted continued attention. Lines of enquiry have focused on the extent to which these men crossed cultures and integrated into Indigenous communities, examining the characterization of beach communities as immoral and lawless frontiers where violence and prostitution were rife.[19] As David Haines and Jonathan West point out in their discussion of the 'crew cultures' that underpinned the Tasman World in early nineteenth-century Australasia, the descriptions and behaviours associated with ships and the social dynamics of shore-based maritime industries are highly gendered. It is not uncommon, for instance, for popular and scholarly accounts of maritime industries to be populated by men characterized as risk-takers, adventurers, and entrepreneurs, who were rebellious, lawless, hot-headed, and violent, and endured brutal conditions and dangerous work.[20]

Early scholarship strove to detail the impact of sailors, traders, and castaways upon local communities, but the contribution of Indigenous women to the success of the various extractive industries was often overlooked. When women appeared, it was as wives, companions, and providers of domestic labour. Since the 1980s, feminist historians have produced an important body of work that has identified the significance and value of cross-cultural relationships to the establishment of early extractive industries. Led by scholars of the Canadian fur trade, this work has demonstrated the crucial importance of intimacy and Indigenous women's labour to the establishment of economies of trade and exchange, and to the settlement of newcomers within tribal territory.[21] They have highlighted a diverse set of arrangements ranging from brief encounters and commercial sex to meaningful marriages and, in addressing the nature and character of intimate relationships, feminist scholars have been particularly concerned with illuminating the extent to which Indigenous women exercised agency and power within extractive economies.

Work focused on tracking the evolution of cross-cultural relationships over a longer temporal scale, and, after the decline of industry, has brought

[19] T. Bentley, *Pakeha-Maori: The Extraordinary Story of the Europeans Who Lived as Maori in Early New Zealand* (Auckland: Penguin, 1999); S.W. Milcairns, *Native Strangers: Beachcombers, Renegades and Castaways in the South Seas* (Auckland: Penguin, 2006).

[20] D. Haines and J. West, 'Crew cultures in the Tasman World', in F. Steel (ed.), *New Zealand and the Sea: Historical Perspectives* (Wellington: Bridget Williams Books, 2018), 181–200.

[21] S. Van Kirk, *Many Tender Ties: Women in Fur-Trade Society, 1670–1870* (Norman: University of Oklahoma Press, 1980); J.S.H. Brown, *Strangers in Blood: Fur Trade Company Families in Indian Country* (Vancouver: UBC Press, 1980); A. Perry, *On the Edge of Empire: Gender, Race and the Making of British Columbia* (Toronto: University of Toronto Press, 2001).

the emotional dimensions of intimacies to the centre of analysis, demonstrating that sexual commerce, trade, or political alliances are not the only interpretations available for understanding patterns of intimacy in early cross-cultural histories.[22] In New Zealand and Sāmoa, early patterns of interracial marriage often followed Indigenous custom, whereby newcomer men (traders, whalers, and merchants) were folded into local communities through marriage for reasons of political alliance and also to access potential wealth that may derive from trade relationships. Marriage to an Indigenous woman of high rank cemented an alliance and provided newcomer men with patronage, although they were subject to the dictates and protocols of the Indigenous communities in which they resided.[23] Similarly, in the eighteenth and nineteenth centuries Marshall Islanders used a range of strategies to manage foreign sailors and traders, including providing them with land and bringing them into familial relationships 'to secure loyalty and share resources and knowledge across genealogies'.[24] Prioritizing how gender relations operated within Indigenous political and cultural contexts demonstrates that marriage accorded newcomer men the status of kin, and, as such, they were obligated to support their family financially and emotionally, and to contribute to wider collective needs.[25]

Depending on location, the nature and pattern of interracial marriage often echoed forms of gendered authority and leadership in Indigenous communities. In cultures where women of rank exercised power and authority, such as the Chinookan peoples of the lower Columbia River in modern-day Oregon, they had the freedom to choose to engage in intermarriage with traders and gained advantage from the economic and social opportunities marriage provided, both personally and collectively.[26] Likewise, in southern New Zealand, where shore whaling was the prominent industry in the 1830s

---

[22] A. Wanhalla, *In/visible Sight: The Mixed-Descent Families of Southern New Zealand* (Wellington: Bridget Williams Books, 2009).

[23] P. Shankman, 'Interethnic unions and the regulation of sex in colonial Samoa, 1839–1945', *Journal of the Polynesian Society* 110:2 (2001), 119–48, at 121; D. Salesa, *Racial Crossings: Race, Intermarriage, and the Victorian British Empire* (Oxford: Oxford University Press, 2011); A. Wanhalla, *Matters of the Heart: A History of Interracial Marriage in New Zealand* (Auckland: Auckland University Press, 2013). For China, see E.J. Teng, *Eurasian: Mixed Identities in the United States, China and Hong Kong, 1842–1943* (Berkeley: University of California Press, 2013).

[24] M.C. LaBriola, 'Planting islands: Marshall Islanders shaping land, power, and history', *Journal of Pacific History* 54:2 (2019), 182–98, at 183.

[25] K. Stevens and A. Wanhalla, 'Intimate relations: kinship and the economics of shore whaling in southern New Zealand', *Journal of Pacific History* 52: 2 (2017), 135–55.

[26] D. Peterson-del Mar, 'Intermarriage and agency: a Chinookan case study', *Ethnohistory* 42:1 (1995), 1–30.

and 1840s, marriage patterns reflected hierarchies of rank and power in Indigenous society, and these mapped onto the political and social structure of the shore-based whaling station. As Atholl Anderson's close analysis of the 140 cross-cultural couples and their families in southern New Zealand has demonstrated, women of high rank often married the owner or manager of a station.[27] Women gained advantages from entering marriage alliances with German and American traders who settled on the Marshall Islands. Marriage gave them access to goods and resources, from which they derived personal wealth and status, while women of commoner background gained land rights through an alliance with a man 'planted' in a location through the gift of land. These rights were transferred to future generations.[28]

At the other end of the spectrum, cross-cultural relationships brought into being by maritime economies could be exploitative in nature, and, for some women, abandonment and mistreatment were a central part of their experience.[29] Maritime industries were characterized by violence, and the link between involuntary mobility and Indigenous women's labour is particularly prevalent in the sealing industry around Australia's Bass Strait, where it was not uncommon for Aboriginal women to be abducted as workers and sexually abused.[30] Research on the North Pacific suggests taking captives was a characteristic of Russian imperial strategy and economic expansion, although men who worked in the sea otter industry did marry into local communities too.[31]

Early maritime economies continue to attract attention, but recently there has been a call for a renewed focus on the place of the extractive industries in 'the larger histories of capitalist expansion and empire-building'.[32] Economically focused histories helpfully highlight the global dimensions of maritime cultures, in terms of both a polyglot employee base and the economic significance of the industry. However, there is a danger that such

---

[27] A. Anderson, *Race against Time: The Early Maori-Pakeha Families and the Development of the Mixed-Race Population in Southern New Zealand* (Dunedin: Hocken Library, 1990).

[28] LaBriola, 'Planting islands', 196.

[29] D. Haines, 'In search of the "whaheen": Ngai Tahu women, shore whalers, and the meaning of sex in early New Zealand', in T. Ballantyne and A. Burton (eds.), *Moving Subjects: Gender, Mobility, and Intimacy in an Age of Global Empire* (Urbana: University of Illinois Press, 2009), 49–66.

[30] L. Russell, *Roving Mariners: Australian Aboriginal Whalers and Sealers in the Southern Oceans, 1790–1870* (New York: SUNY, 2012).

[31] R.T. Jones, 'Kelp highways, Siberian girls in Maui, and nuclear walruses: the North Pacific in a Sea of Islands', *Journal of Pacific History* 49: 4 (2014), 373–95, at 383–4.

[32] T. Ballantyne, *Webs of Empire: Rethinking New Zealand's Colonial Past* (Wellington: Bridget Williams Books, 2012), 126.

approaches could occlude the specific forms of gendered labour that enabled this thriving pattern of exchange and inadvertently reassert a narrative of the ocean as a masculine space and maritime industries as men's work. Pacific scholars have amply demonstrated that the labour of Indigenous men and women in early maritime industries[33] – a key location for cross-cultural marriage and the formation of mixed descent communities – was sustained by local kinship networks. It was often family networks that encouraged men's and women's engagement in shore whaling, for instance where they worked as crew, station employees, and producers of key trade goods.[34] For these reasons, the intimate ties forged between Indigenous peoples and foreign men have to be integrated into economic analysis, for this will deepen understandings of how gender, power, and rank shaped labour relations within the colonial maritime world. Indigenous women, for instance, managed homes and domestic economies, worked on gardens, wove baskets, and gathered food. Just how far class and rank shaped Indigenous people's participation in maritime economies, and the kind of labour women and men performed, requires deeper investigation.

Questions of Indigenous agency and power remain central to scholarship on early cross-cultural communities where kinship and marriage have been identified as key management strategies. In foregrounding agency and women's experiences, scholars have provided greater nuance to historical interpretations of the nature and pattern of early cross-cultural intimacies that in the past often relied heavily upon the accounts of resident missionaries, who tended to construct the relationships between Indigenous women and foreign men as a form of slavery or as prostitution. Drawing from Christian understandings of gender and morality, missionaries identified Indigenous men as instigators of a trade in women's bodies and drew connections between the treatment of women in non-European societies and the 'civilized' status of Indigenous cultures more broadly.

New Zealand's missionaries, who arrived in the north of the country in 1814 and had spread to the southern reaches of the country by 1840, regularly condemned European men for their treatment of local women, often characterizing it as sexual commerce, and regarding women's labour as a form of exploitation and further evidence of male brutality. In the Bass Strait, visiting humanitarians, such as the Quakers James Backhouse and George

---

[33] P. D'Arcy, 'Forum introduction: women and the sea in the Pacific: a neglected dimension', *International Journal of Maritime History* 20:2 (2008), 259–64, at 259.
[34] Stevens and Wanhalla, 'Intimate relations'.

Washington Walker examined by Penelope Edmonds, collected testimonies from Aboriginal women involved in the sealing industry in the early 1830s in order to mobilize humanitarian sentiment and action.[35] At Levuka, Fiji, a local missionary's claim that an exchange of goods, probably a form of gift exchange to confirm a marriage that followed local custom, or a payment for domestic labour, was a trade in women akin to slavery prompted the New South Wales government to issue an anti-slavery proclamation in 1852, in an 'unprecedented attempt' at 'jurisdictional imperialism'.[36] In advancing arguments about the respectability of their marriages, which were centred on the cultural protocols and practices of the local community, Levuka's European residents challenged claims about the existence of a lawless and immoral frontier.[37] At the same time, instances of missionaries who 'back-slided', including some who fathered children with local women, such as William Colenso of the Church Missionary Society in New Zealand, exposed the hypocrisy of missionary moralizing.[38]

Cross-cultural relationships came in many forms and could encompass affection, but also be exploitative and coercive in nature. Newcomers were also diverse. Traders, whalers, sailors, and castaways have attracted the bulk of scholarly attention to date, especially in Australia and New Zealand, but those who married into local communities came from a range of backgrounds. The shipboard world was comprised of a polyglot workforce, and the onshore stations reflected the cultural and linguistic diversity of the maritime world of work. Writing of Ruapuke, an island located in southern New Zealand, the resident missionary Johannes Wohlers characterized it as a 'gathering place' for newcomers from around the world. To 'describe them as European does not seem to me to be correctly applicable', wrote Wohlers in 1846, because the men who lived and worked there came from the United States, Australia, Tahiti, and other parts of the globe.[39]

Whaling attracted a diverse workforce, as did the fur trade in the Pacific Northwest. Along with British traders, French Canadians worked in the fur

---

[35] P. Edmonds, 'Collecting Looerryminer's "testimony": Aboriginal women, sealers, and Quaker humanitarian anti-slavery thought and action in the Bass Strait Islands', *Australian Historical Studies* 45:1 (2014), 13–33.

[36] J. Samson, 'Rescuing Fijian women? The British Anti-Slavery Proclamation of 1852', *Journal of Pacific History* 30: 1 (1995), 22–38, at 23.

[37] Samson, 'Rescuing Fijian women?', 37–8.

[38] A. Wanhalla, '"The natives uncivilize me": missionaries and interracial intimacy in early New Zealand', in P. Grimshaw and A. May (eds.), *Missions, Indigenous Peoples and Cultural Exchange* (Brighton: Sussex Academic Press, 2010), 24–36.

[39] Wohlers cited in Wanhalla, *Matters of the Heart*, 9.

trade, and Indigenous Hawaiians were a presence from the early nineteenth century.[40] At Fort Vancouver, the principal post in the Pacific Northwest (located in modern-day Washington State), 122 of the 535 men employed there between 1827 and 1860 were from Hawaii.[41] Many married into local families, and remained in the region after the fur trade came to an end.[42] Similarly, by the 1880s, as a result of their engagement in whaling and other forms of maritime industry, around 800 Chamorro men from the Mariana Islands were living in Honolulu where they too intermarried, some with Hawaiian women, and lived the rest of their lives there.[43]

Research on migrant and labour histories has brought to light the immense diversity of cross-cultural couples in colonial societies. In Sāmoa, indentured labourers from Melanesia and China, introduced under the German administration (1900–14), formed relationships with local women, as did migrant labourers from Japan, China, Java, Indochina, India, and Vanuatu imported by the French administration to work in New Caledonia's nickel mines and plantations in the late nineteenth century.[44] Chinese indentured labourers were brought to French Polynesia from 1865, to German New Guinea from 1891, and to German-controlled Nauru and Banaba from 1906.[45] In Australia, the histories of Aboriginal–Asian relationships have been explored, notably in the pearl shell industry prominent in the north from the late nineteenth century. Dominated by migrant workers from Japan and Indonesia, pearl-shelling brought these men into contact with local Aboriginal women whose skills and local knowledge were critical to that industry's establishment.[46] Likewise, Filipino men were recruited to work on ships engaged in resource extraction and trade for the China and European markets in the nineteenth century, and into the pearl-shell industry in the Torres Strait where they settled and often married into Aboriginal

---

[40] J. Barman, 'New land, new lives: Hawaiian settlement in British Columbia', *Hawaiian Journal of History* 29 (1995), 1–32, at 2; J. Barman, *French Canadians, Furs, and Indigenous Women in the Making of the Pacific Northwest* (Vancouver: UBC Press, 2014).

[41] Barman, 'New land, new lives', 2.

[42] J. Barman and B.M. Watson, *Leaving Paradise: Indigenous Hawaiians in the Pacific Northwest, 1787–1898* (Honolulu: University of Hawai'i Press, 2006).

[43] R.F. Rogers, *Destiny's Landfall: A History of Guam*, rev. edn (Honolulu: University of Hawai'i Press, 2011), 99.

[44] A. Muckle and B. Trépied, 'The transformation of the "métis question" in New Caledonia, 1853–2009', in F. Fozdar and K. McGavin (eds.), *Mixed Race Identities in Australia, New Zealand and the Pacific* (London: Routledge, 2017), 116–32, at 116.

[45] P. D'Arcy, 'The Chinese Pacifics: a brief historical review', *Journal of Pacific History* 49:4 (2014), 396–420, at 410.

[46] R. Balint, 'Aboriginal women and Asian men: a maritime history of color in white Australia', *Signs: Journal of Women in Culture and Society* 37:3 (2012), 544–54, at 545, 546.

communities.[47] In recent decades, sociologists, anthropologists, and demographers have illuminated the little-known histories of Māori-Chinese families and the relationships forged between Māori and Croatians who worked alongside each other on the northern gumfields in early twentieth-century New Zealand.[48]

Interracial relationships also flourished in the treaty ports of colonial Asia, especially Hong Kong, Shanghai, and China from the 1840s. After its defeat in the First Opium War (1839–42), and the signing of the Treaty of Nanjing, China was forced to cede Hong Kong to Britain and open five treaty ports.[49] Further treaties with other imperial and trade powers followed, and goods and people flowed in and out of these locations, connecting China to the island Pacific, North America, and Europe. American, French, British, and other foreigners established themselves as merchants, traders, missionaries, and administrators at China's treaty ports, while Chinese men looked outwards from the ports. They sought economic opportunity during the gold rushes in Australasia and North America, while labour contracts fostered the movement of men to other parts of Asia and the Pacific. Similar patterns operated in Japan, after it opened a series of treaty ports in the 1850s, which fostered trade as well as interracial relationships between Japanese women and foreign men.[50]

Particular patterns of cross-cultural relationships arose out of these mobilities. In Japan, relationships ranged from temporary alliances through to legal marriages, but also included commercial sex.[51] In China, foreign men forged either temporary arrangements or marriages with Chinese women; children were born to missionaries who married Chinese converts; the overseas Chinese, who migrated for education, or economic opportunity, formed relationships with European women in the United States, New Zealand, and Australia, while migrant labourers created families in the island Pacific.[52]

---

[47] P. D'Arcy, 'The Philippines as a Pacific nation: a brief history of interaction between Filipinos and Pacific Islanders', *Journal of Pacific History* (online first) (2018), 53 (2018), 1–23, at 15.

[48] M. Ip, 'Maori–Chinese encounters: indigine–immigrant interaction in New Zealand', *Asian Studies Review* 2:2 (2003), 227–52; M. Ip, *Being Maori Chinese: Mixed Identities* (Auckland: Auckland University Press, 2008); M. Ip (ed.), *The Dragon and the Taniwha: Maori and Chinese in New Zealand* (Auckland: Auckland University Press, 2009); S. Bozic-Vrbancic, *Tarara: Croats and Maori in New Zealand, Memory, Belonging, Identity* (Dunedin: University of Otago Press, 2008).

[49] Teng, *Eurasian*, 3.

[50] G.L. Leupp, *Interracial Intimacy in Japan: Western Men and Japanese Women, 1543–1900* (London: Continuum, 2003).

[51] Leupp, *Interracial Intimacy in Japan.*   [52] Teng, *Eurasian*, 6.

Settler populations varied too. German planters, merchants, and traders formed families with local women in nineteenth-century Sāmoa, Tonga, and Fiji. German residents forged cross-cultural families in New Guinea, as did the British traders based at Port Moresby in the 1880s and 1890s, along with a range of non-European migrant workers.[53] In the early stages of colonial administration, it was not uncommon for employees in the colonial service to marry into local communities. Damon Salesa, writing about Sāmoa, refers to these as 'strategic intimacies': a set of relationships and personal associations that emerged in moments of uncertain jurisdictions and there created a 'domain that was at once tactical and strategic, imperial and intimately local'.[54] Whether entered into for affective or strategic reasons, such relationships directly connect interracial intimacies with colonial power and help illuminate how personal associations were entangled in settler colonial practices of dispossession.[55] As this pattern highlights, interracial relationships continued to flourish after territories were formally annexed, despite regulation or prohibition.

Regulating Intimacy

Annexation of territories by imperial regimes brought about a change in circumstances for couples. Depending on the location, the time period, the administrative or governing force, and the 'racial crossings' involved, couples were subjected to juridical regimes that sought to regulate interracial contact and limit the possibility of interracial marriage. In some territories, political leaders encouraged interracial relationships to help advance the colonial project.[56] Restrictive policies, surveillance, and regulation of marriage have been identified as important strategies of governance and 'significant indicators of colonizing white societies' management strategies of subject groups'.[57] This shift from freedom to control, accompanied by a hardening

---

[53] M. Goddard, 'A categorical failure: "mixed race" in colonial Papua New Guinea', in F. Fozdar and K. McGavin (eds.), *Mixed Race Identities in Australia, New Zealand and the Pacific* (London: Routledge, 2017), 133–46, at 135.
[54] D. Salesa, 'Samoa's half-castes and some frontiers of comparison', in A.L. Stoler (ed.), *Haunted by Empire: Geographies of Intimacy in North American History* (Durham, NC: Duke University Press, 2006), 71–93, at 72.
[55] A. Wanhalla and L. Paterson, '"Tangled up": intimacy, emotion, and dispossession in colonial New Zealand', in P. Edmonds and A. Nettelbeck (eds.), *Intimacies of Violence in the Settler Colony: Economies of Dispossession around the Pacific Rim* (Basingstoke: Palgrave Macmillan, 2018), 179–200.
[56] See Salesa, *Racial Crossings*.
[57] P. Grimshaw, 'Interracial marriages and colonial regimes in Victoria and Aotearoa/New Zealand', *Frontiers* 23: 3 (2002), 12–28, at 12.

of racial attitudes signified by the implementation of restrictions on marriage across racial lines, characterizes the scholarship on mixed-race families and interracial marriage, including in Asia and the Pacific.[58]

For the Pacific the most extensive studies of interracial marriage and colonial regulation come from New Zealand, Australia, and Sāmoa, along with the Pacific Northwest. New Zealand did not prohibit interracial marriage after British annexation in 1840. As Damon Salesa has argued in his examination of Victorian racial ideologies and interracial marriage, Britain annexed New Zealand during a period when racial amalgamation philosophy was prominent in metropolitan intellectual and official circles. Promoted as a key feature of the New Zealand Company, Edward Gibbon Wakefield's private colonization venture, and taken up by the colony's early governors, racial amalgamation promised the political, economic, and social incorporation of Indigenous peoples into British institutions, but it also encompassed biological absorption through marriage. In a colony where interracial relationships were customary, New Zealand's political leaders promoted racial amalgamation in order to shore up European access to land. In light of the direct relationship between marriage and colonization, Salesa argues, 'properly managed and administered racial crossings could be beneficial and helpful to race relations and colonial rule'.[59] For 'racial crossings' to be beneficial to advancing land settlement, interracial marriages had to be legally recognized. New Zealand's nineteenth-century racial policy emphasized Māori assimilation to British modes of life, and interracial marriage, as long as it conformed to the Western Christian model, was encouraged as one strategy for bringing about racial amalgamation and successful colonization.

New Zealand's colonial political leaders were not alone in regarding interracial marriage as a strategy for protecting the property and inheritance rights of European men. Some jurisdictions in the American West with longstanding histories of cross-cultural relationships forged out of the fur trade initially hesitated to prohibit marriages between settlers and Indigenous women because, argues Peggy Pascoe, these marriages advanced land settlement in regions sparsely populated by Europeans.[60] Prior to the passage of an 1866 anti-miscegenation law in Oregon, the courts in that territory recognized interracial marriages contracted in accordance with Indigenous

---

[58] Shankman, 'Interethnic unions', 120.   [59] Salesa, *Racial Crossings*, 26.
[60] P. Pascoe, *What Comes Naturally: Miscegenation Law and the Making of Race in America* (Oxford: Oxford University Press, 2009), 95.

custom in order to secure the property rights of the European husband and effect the transfer of land out of Indigenous control.[61]

As colonial regimes matured, interracial relationships that were once acceptable to officials in some jurisdictions, primarily because they advanced the project of settler colonialism, were increasingly stigmatized or outlawed. From the 1860s, for instance, state lawmakers instituted a patchwork of anti-miscegenation laws in Washington and Oregon, following the lead of California. Such laws were designed to reinforce racial hierarchies, but as Pascoe has argued these 'bans on interracial marriage conflicted with long-standing conceptions of white men's sexual freedoms and civil rights, including the right to choose their own wives and control their own property'.[62]

An absence of legal prohibition should not be equated with tolerance for interracial relationships. In emerging colonial societies, such as New Zealand and British Columbia, where no legal prohibitions existed, social and moral pressure was applied to prevent interracial relationships. In these territories, cross-cultural relationships were often stigmatized as immoral; associated with forms of marriage common to an earlier era characterized as an 'uncivilized' and lawless masculine frontier. By the mid-nineteenth century, connections were drawn in New Zealand between the perceived promiscuity of Māori women, the nature of interracial relationships, and social degradation during a time of heightened racial tension.[63] Managing interracial relationships through social marginalization and exercising moral and social control over the Indigenous population were essential strategies for generating colonial respectability. For instance, in colonial British Columbia, local officials and settlers sexualized Indigenous women as prostitutes, arguing they were a threat to the moral order.[64]

Some marriages attracted more attention from the state than others. Across the American West, with its multicultural populations formed out of the fur trade and the 1849 California gold rush, legal prohibitions on interracial marriage were passed between the 1860s and the 1930s that targeted and racialized Asian settlers. Depending on the state, 'marriages between Whites and American Indians, native Hawaiians, Chinese, Japanese, Filipinos, Koreans, and Hindus' were progressively outlawed.[65] In 1866, Oregon passed a law outlawing marriage with Chinese and Indigenous

---

[61] Pascoe, *What Comes Naturally*, 96.   [62] Pascoe, *What Comes Naturally*, 11.
[63] Wanhalla, *Matters of the Heart*, 95.
[64] J. Barman, 'Taming aboriginal sexuality: gender, power and race in British Columbia, 1850–1900', *BC Studies* 115/16 (1997/8), 237–66; Perry, *On the Edge of Empire*.
[65] Pascoe, *What Comes Naturally*, 2.

Hawaiians.[66] It was the only state in the American West to target this group (a number of whom moved north to British Columbia), but one of many to impose prohibitions on the marital freedom of Chinese men who were targeted at a time of growing anti-Chinese sentiment.[67] California introduced an anti-miscegenation law in 1850 to prohibit marriage between whites and African Americans, including 'mulattoes', and in 1880 extended that law to encompass marriages between whites and 'Mongolians'.[68] Oregon extended its prohibitions on interracial marriages in 1893, adding 'Mongolian' to a prohibited list that already included African Americans, Chinese, Hawaiians, and Indigenous peoples, but also imposed a blood quantum rule.[69] In the early twentieth century, Japanese and 'Malays' became targets of anti-miscegenation laws in the American West.

Restrictive immigration laws passed in the 1880s were gradually tightened in the 1890s and into the first decades of the twentieth century around the Pacific, and in some jurisdictions these restrictions were accompanied by prohibitions on marriage. Scholars have tracked these restrictions in the United States, but also in a range of other locations. For instance, the recruitment of Chinese labourers to Sāmoa was inaugurated under the German administration from 1903. Over 3,000 Chinese men were brought into the territory, but by 1910 interracial marriages had been prohibited, while laws that restricted interracial socializing were also in place.[70] Influenced by a eugenic ideology prominent in the 1920s, New Zealand continued the German administration's restrictions on marriages, claiming such prohibitions would halt racial degeneration and prevent racial pollution.[71] In Australia, Asian–Aboriginal relationships were restricted at a time when their existence undermined the project of White Australia.[72]

Although the numbers are unknown, European women did marry Indigenous men. These relationships tended to attract condemnation from officials and commentators, especially in the settler colonies, for they

---

[66] Pascoe, *What Comes Naturally*, 80.   [67] Pascoe, *What Comes Naturally*, 83.

[68] Pascoe, *What Comes Naturally*, 85.   [69] Pascoe, *What Comes Naturally*, 85.

[70] Shankman, 'Interethnic unions', 129; B. F. Liua'ana, 'Dragons in little paradise: Chinese (mis-)fortune in Samoa, 1900–1950', *Journal of Pacific History* 32:1 (1997), 29–48.

[71] Shankman, 'Interethnic unions', 133.

[72] Balint, 'Aboriginal women and Asian men', 548; J. Martínez, 'Indigenous Australian–Indonesian intermarriage: negotiating citizenship rights in twentieth-century Australia', *Aboriginal History* 35 (2011), 177–95, at 181.

challenged racial hierarchies and assumptions of white masculine superiority. When these relationships were publicly debated in New Zealand, commentators interpreted their existence in two ways. First, they assumed women were coerced into marriage, reflecting a widely held belief in Māori men as sexually aggressive, but in instances where it appeared the marriage was the result of personal choice, it was assumed the bride was of a low class, and the marriage was therefore symbolic of her moral degradation.[73]

Depictions of non-European men as violent and lacking sexual restraint were widespread. Public and political rhetoric identified Asian men, especially, as a sexual danger to white women, which was reflected in widely circulated sensationalist newspaper accounts of European women married to Chinese men. In December 1899, for instance, New Zealand's *Otago Daily Times* published an article, which originally appeared in an English newspaper, called 'Ladies of title who have married black men'.[74] It told of a 'pretty and well-born Scots girl, possessed of a fortune of her own' who married 'a full-blooded Chinaman'; the 'Indian Prince Dhuleep Singh and his full-blooded white wife, Lady Ann Coventry'; German, Italian, and French women who had married Japanese men; and an English woman 'of excellent birth' who married a Moroccan. Published for entertainment, and chosen because of the hint of scandal attached to the subject, it also drew upon popular narratives about white women's virtue lost at the hands of scheming 'black' men who styled themselves 'princes' in foreign countries in order to seduce European women for their money. A rhetoric connecting white women's morality with social and racial degradation underpinned anti-Asian sentiment in the United States.[75] Such views informed legal prohibitions on interracial marriage, which were often justified as a protective measure to secure white women's virtue. At the same time, ideas that interracial mixing with 'Asiatics' threatened the virility and the quality of the white race permeated public discussion about national strength across the colonial Pacific.[76]

---

[73] See Wanhalla, *Matters of the Heart*, 111.
[74] *Otago Daily Times* (Dunedin, New Zealand), 7 December 1899, 7.
[75] H. Yu, 'Mixing bodies and cultures: the meaning of America's fascination with sex between "Orientals" and "Whites"', in E. Reis (ed.), *American Sexual Histories* (Oxford: Blackwell, 2000), 446–58.
[76] Pascoe, *What Comes Naturally*, 78.

The 'Problem' of Race-Mixing

In every location where interracial marriage was prominent, mixed-race children attracted official attention because they destabilized notions of fixed racial hierarchies and embodied racial transgressions that undermined the social and moral respectability of colonial societies. Writing of the 'métis question' that was prominent across the French colonial empire, Emmanuelle Saada characterizes the debate as 'a meeting place for a wide range of anxieties about colonial society, touching on racial mixing, illegitimacy, and the definition of citizenship'.[77] Similar concerns were expressed about 'half-castes' and 'Eurasians' across the British Empire. Political and religious leaders in the colonies developed a set of strategies in order to manage the 'problem' of mixed-race children who were delineated into two groups: those formally acknowledged by their European parent, or those who had been 'abandoned', a designation used even though the children were in the care of their mother and wider kin.

If 'properly managed', the potential contribution of mixed-race children to colonial development could be realized, as exemplified by an 1856 Board of Inquiry into Native Affairs New Zealand when it reported that 'occupying as they do an intermediate station between the Europeans and natives, [those of mixed ancestry] have neither the advantages of the one, or, the other, and whose future destiny, may, by proper management, be directed in the well-being of the Colony, or by neglect, be turned in a contrary course'.[78] Of particular concern were those children deemed to have been left destitute or 'abandoned' by the European father.[79] An absent European parent was particularly problematic because the cultural assimilation and socialization of mixed-race children to colonial norms required a European parent to be present in the home.

'Abandonment' was a colonial keyword that both critiqued male behaviour in the colonies and authorized interventions for assimilatory purposes. Religious and charitable organizations, sometimes with state support, stepped into the paternal role, establishing schools or orphanages specifically for mixed-race children so they could 'fit' them for participation in colonial society.[80] In Hong Kong, rising anxiety about the 'Eurasian problem' during the 1860s resulted in the establishment of a school specifically for these

---

[77] E. Saada, *Empire's Children: Race, Filiation and Citizenship in the French Colonies*, trans. A. Goldhammer (Chicago: University of Chicago Press, 2012), 3.
[78] 'Land for half-caste children', LE1/1890 1856/66, Archives New Zealand, Wellington.
[79] Saada, *Empire's Children*, 4.
[80] For a comparative analysis of colonial debates about mixed-race children and strategies of intervention from the late nineteenth to the mid-twentieth century see C. Firpo and M. Jacobs, 'Taking children, ruling colonies: child removal and colonial subjugation in Australia, Canada,

'abandoned' children, and similar concerns led the Anglo-American community in Shanghai to establish a Eurasian School in 1870.[81]

Fears about the political threat posed by a disinherited and disaffected population to the security of colonial society led some jurisdictions to recognize paternity legally in order to secure the economic future of mixed-race children which, it was hoped, might cultivate loyalty to the state. In 1933, several years after a decree defined the status of métis children in French Indochina, New Caledonia's administration formally recognized the French paternity of 'métis born to unknown parents', giving them citizenship rights.[82] In contrast, under German law, paternal ancestry defined one's rights, which meant that in the colonies mixed-race children inherited the economic and political status of their European father. Wary of granting the population too much political and economic power, the German administration codified the inheritance rights of mixed-race children in Sāmoa, distinguishing between those born within legal marriage and those who were not.[83] Children born within legal marriage were granted their father's status and registered as 'European half-castes', and those born illegitimately were classified as 'Native half-castes'.[84] New Zealand's administration of Sāmoa (1920–62) continued the German restrictions on interracial marriage and refined the system of racial categorization. Europeans were defined as including those of Samoan ancestry, but only if they were of legitimate birth and of no more than 50 per cent 'blood'.[85] Even though these categories did not accord with personal identity, one's racial status mattered for it defined access to education, voting rights, employment opportunities, and social standing, and it shaped family aspiration.

To 'properly manage' those of mixed ancestry, colonial administrations created legal categories of identity based on 'blood'.[86] 'Race', as Warwick Anderson has argued, 'was a major criterion of citizenship and could even

---

French Indochina, and the United States, 1870–1950s', *Journal of World History* 29:4 (2018), 529–62.

[81] Teng, *Eurasian*, 7.

[82] Muckle and Trépied, 'The transformation of the "métis question" in New Caledonia', 120; Saada, *Empire's Children*, 1 and 3.

[83] D.J. Walther, 'Sex, race and empire: white male sexuality and the "other" in Germany's colonies, 1894–1914', *German Studies Review* 33:1 (2010), 45–71, at 57.

[84] Shankman, 'Interethnic unions', 126; S. Tcherkézoff, 'Multiculturalism and construction of a national identity: the historical case of Samoan/European relations', *New Pacific Review* 1:1 (2000), 168–86, at 171.

[85] Shankman, 'Interethnic unions', 132.

[86] Z.L. Rocha, 'Re-viewing race and mixedness: mixed race in Asia and the Pacific', *Journal of Intercultural Studies* 39:4 (2018), 510–26.

decide whether one counted as an inhabitant in the national census ... Mixed-race peoples might be disparaged as degenerate, validated as forming stable communities, absorbed into white populations, or counted as indigenous.'[87] Demographic change was mapped through census categories, which themselves were informed by Victorian racial science, reflected in the use of terms like 'half-caste' and 'quarter-caste'. Census data on ethnic composition was variously used to monitor racial fitness and national health, to explain Indigenous depopulation, and to make claims about the positive and negative impacts of interracial marriage. Census data informed scientific theories about racial progress, decline or strength, and influenced the colonies policies.

Colonial interventions directed at mixed-race children were informed by scientific theories about the role of 'race mixing' in promoting racial degeneration or conversely its role in racial improvement.[88] There were two competing views: that 'half-castes' were physically robust, healthier, and more fertile than Indigenous peoples (who were popularly believed to be dying out); or that races were biologically distinct and racial differences were fixed. It was feared that the mixing of distinct races or 'species' would produce unfertile 'half-castes' who would bring about racial degeneration. Such views were reflected in the 'characterization of half-castes as infertile, prone to illness, lacking vitality, and combining the worst elements of both parental lines'; however, these negative views, which were commonplace in racial thought from the late nineteenth century, 'co-existed with enthusiastic appraisals'.[89]

Theories that 'racial crossings' either would produce degenerate 'hybrids' or could be a force for racial strength prompted investigations into the health and fertility of mixed-race populations that aimed to measure racial difference and interpret the biological consequences of miscegenation.[90] In 1888, for instance, Hong Hong based Scottish doctor James Cantile distributed between 400–500 questionnaires to physicians in Japan, China, and the Straits Settlements for the purpose of an investigation into the 'life history of Eurasians'. Cantile defined 'Eurasian' broadly as any child where the 'parent

---

[87] W. Anderson, 'Racial conceptions in the Global South', *Isis* 105 (2014), 782–92, at 783.

[88] D. Salesa, '"Troublesome half-castes": tales of a Samoan borderland', MA thesis, University of Auckland, 1997, 2. Also see Shankman, 'Interethnic unions'.

[89] V. Luker, 'The half-caste in Australia, New Zealand, and Western Samoa between the wars: different problem, different places?', in B. Douglas and C. Ballard (eds.), *Foreign Bodies: Oceania and the Science of Race, 1750–1840* (Canberra: ANU Press, 2008), 307–35, at 312.

[90] N. Stepan, *Picturing Tropical Nature* (Ithaca, NY: Cornell University Press, 2001).

on the one side is usually of European stock' in order to justify the inclusion of Australia, New Zealand, and Pacific Islands 'in the scope of the enquiry', despite the very different histories of cross-cultural mixing and racial dynamics in these places.[91] Of the 400 to 500 questionnaires distributed, Cantile received just nineteen responses.

Reflecting popular racial thinking about the relationship between 'race mixing' and racial degeneration or improvement, the questionnaire asked respondents to comment on the health, fertility, and intellectual capacity of the 'Eurasian' population. Many of the New Zealand respondents drew connections between biology and moral character. One claimed the longevity of the mixed population was 'a little below the European average on account of the sins of the fathers in the case of illegitimates – quite up to the average in the case of married parents'.[92] Many praised the physical attractiveness of children born to European fathers and Māori mothers, but claimed that they were intellectually and physically inferior to the European parent. Fertility and longevity increased, claimed an official in New Zealand's Native Department, only when those of mixed ancestry married Europeans, thereby producing 'a finer race in every way than the first cross – more approaching the European in physique, mental calibre, constitution and character'.[93]

During the interwar years, American sociological and anthropological investigations turned to Asia and the Pacific as key locations from which to theorize how 'race mixing' might shape racial futures. According to Emma Teng this research 'focused quite centrally on race mixing in Asia' as it was 'an area of the world that has exhibited immense diversity in its histories of cross-cultural contact, trade, migration, conquest, colonialism and nation-building'.[94] Alongside American-led research in Asia, between the 1910s and 1940s around twenty major studies of 'the physical features and social life of mixed peoples' took place in the Pacific, with a particular focus on Hawai'i.[95] There, argues Warwick Anderson, the story of intellectual investigations into 'race-mixing' in the twentieth century has a distinctive character defined by

---

[91] D. Pomfret, 'Raising Eurasia: race, class and age in French and British colonies', *Comparative Studies in Societies and History* 51:2 (2009), 314–43, at 321.
[92] Questionnaire Response, Table 1: Evidence as to the children of European males and Maori females, undated, Enquiry into the life-history of Eurasians (1888), James Cantile Papers, MS.1499, Wellcome Collection, London.
[93] Questionnaire Response, Table 1: Evidence as to the children of European males and Maori females, 9 April 1888, MS.1499.
[94] E.J. Teng, 'The Asian turn in mixed race studies: retrospects and prospects', *Asia Pacific Perspectives* 14:2 (2017), 80–5, at 82.
[95] W. Anderson, 'Ambiguities of race: science on the reproductive frontier of Australia and the Pacific between the wars', *Australian Historical Studies* 40:2 (2009), 143–60, at 146.

an openness to its possibilities.[96] Sociological investigations, however, were used to justify further harsh state interventions, such as in Australia where in the 1930s 'half-caste' children, collectively known as the Stolen Generations, were forcibly removed from their families and placed in institutions under a policy of absorption.[97]

A great deal of the scholarship on 'race-mixing' has focused on the intellectual traditions of Western thinkers and colonial scientists, but recent research has explored other locations and intellectual cultures. Increasingly, Indigenous perspectives on interracial marriage and 'race mixing' are being explored. While scholarship on the relationships forged in the early maritime beach communities has begun to address the place of interracial marriage within Indigenous cultural worlds, there has been much less attention paid to intellectual and political debate within Indigenous societies. In an important intervention into the historiography Lachy Paterson explored the 'half-caste' debate in Māori-language newspapers. He found that the 'half-caste question' was important to Māori in the late nineteenth century, but it was not framed as an issue about 'race' or racial exclusion.[98] Rather, Māori leaders were concerned about the role of interracial marriage in effecting land loss and its potential for eroding Māori culture.[99]

In Japan and China, intellectuals debated the merits of 'race mixing' during the first half of the twentieth century. At this time eugenic thinking was particularly prominent and encouraged a body of research on the nature and effects of 'racial hygiene', which encompassed debates over the consequences of 'race-mixing'.[100] Japanese sociologist Takahashi Yoshio argued interracial marriage had eugenic outcomes, as did Chinese philosopher Kang Youwei, who supported interracial marriage in aid of 'racial improvement'.[101] Whether 'race mixing' was conceived as a positive force or not, these debates, and the associated social-scientific investigations, were more than abstract: they shaped racial policies, gave rise to invasive interventions into family life, justified legal prohibitions based on race, and cultivated social marginalization that enforced generational silences about ancestry, culture, belonging, and identity.

---

[96] Anderson, 'Racial conceptions', 783.

[97] Anderson, 'Ambiguities of race', 146; H. Reynolds, *Nowhere People* (Camberwell: Penguin, 2005).

[98] L. Paterson, 'Hāwhekaihe: Māori voices on the position of "half-castes" within Māori society', *Journal of New Zealand Studies* 9 (2010), 135–56.

[99] Paterson, 'Hāwhekaihe', 146–7.

[100] T. Morris-Suzuki, 'Debating racial science in wartime Japan', *Osiris* 13 (1998), 354–75, at 361.

[101] Teng, 'The Asian turn', 81. On Japan see N. Hoshino, 'Racial contacts across the Pacific and the creation of *minzoku* in the Japanese empire', *Inter-Asia Cultural Studies* 17:2 (2016), 186–205.

Families and Households

Patterns of interracial relationships, colonial regimes of regulation, and the imposition of colonial racial categories have been key areas of scholarly investigation. More recently, scholars have paid attention to cross-cultural families themselves in order to foreground the voices and experiences of interracial couples and their children.[102] Biography and life histories have been particularly important methodologies for exploring lives lived 'in-between' worlds,[103] while an increasing number of personal narratives have exposed the deliberate generational silence and shame associated with being of mixed ancestry.[104] With terms like 'half-caste' and 'Eurasian' widely used in metropolitan and colonial print media, families sought to erase a past where moral character was often linked to biology. As Emma Teng has argued, mixed-race individuals had to 'negotiate identity' in order to navigate racial categories and social stigma.[105]

Historians have yet to address fully the shape of interracial households, their social and cultural dynamics, or the emotional worlds of cross-cultural families in the colonial era in depth. This is primarily due to the nature of the available textual record: it is through policy interventions, racial science, and racial categories that those of mixed ancestry have entered the archives, and these colonial sources dominate scholarly frameworks of inquiry.[106] Even though the 'intimate relations of household and families [are] where racial crossings were lived and experienced' it is far easier to trace the histories of interracial marriage and mixed-race children through the abundant official archive and public discourse than from the perspectives of the couples or their children.[107]

---

[102] J. Binney, '"In-between" lives: studies from within a colonial society', in T. Ballantyne and B. Moloughney (eds.), *Disputed Histories: Imagining New Zealand's Pasts* (Dunedin: Otago University Press, 2006), 93–118; Wanhalla, *In/visible Sight*; Teng, *Eurasian*; J. McCabe, *Race, Tea and Colonial Resettlement: Imperial Families, Interrupted* (London: Bloomsbury, 2017); A. Perry, *Colonial Relations: The Douglas-Connolly Family and the Nineteenth-Century Imperial World* (Cambridge: Cambridge University Press, 2015).

[103] For instance, D. Salesa, 'Emma and Phebe: "weavers of the border"', *Journal of the Polynesian Society* 123:2 (2014), 145–67; L. de Bruce, 'Histories of diversity: Kailoma testimonies and "part-European" tales from colonial Fiji (1920–1970)', *Journal of Intercultural Studies* 28:1 (2007), 113–27.

[104] L. Russell, *A Little Bird Told Me: Family Secrets, Necessary Lies* (Crows Nest, NSW: Allen & Unwin, 2012).

[105] Teng, *Eurasian*.   [106] Salesa, *Racial Crossings*.

[107] Salesa, *Racial Crossings*, 8; Muckle and Trépied, 'The transformation of the "métis question" in New Caledonia', 120.

Close studies of couples and households can help identify the extent to which state policies shaped the pathways of families, in addition to how identity was formed and expressed. While it is true that interracial marriage was utilized as a force for assimilation into settler society, some families did try to resist this injunction. Recent work centred in Indigenous models of kinship, for instance, has shown that cross-cultural couples and households on the Marshall Islands and in southern New Zealand operated mainly with Indigenous aspirations in mind.[108] For instance, Marshallese women absorbed traders into genealogies, thereby gaining access to land, and in doing so ensured political and economic futures for their children.[109] In southern New Zealand homes, Māori was the lingua franca, and particular customs and cultural practices were maintained, including vitally important traditions related to food production. As Michael Stevens has pointed out, sometimes European family members participated in these practices, helping cultural knowledge to be maintained and passed down the generations.[110] Likewise, in the Pacific Northwest interracial marriage was a force for connection, rather than the disintegration of culture, for 'kinship was at the core of the Indigenous economy and intermarriage was the glue that held the Pacific Northwest region together'.[111] Kinship connections underwrote economic engagement in certain industries, such as the hop fields, for participation in these endeavours enabled families to gather as a community and engage in and maintain important cultural practices.

Historians have shown that the outcomes for mixed-race families after the treaty ports closed and the resource-based economies came to an end depended upon class and social standing. In southern New Zealand, whalers transitioned into fishing and small-scale farming, maintaining their families on small parcels of land made available to them by their Māori kin. Very few became large landholders, but a small number, like the former whaler John Howell, gained wealth, status, respectability, and power. His standing, and that of his family, was enabled by property ownership, itself made possible

---

[108] Stevens and Wanhalla, 'Intimate relations'; K. Stevens, '"Gathering places": the mixed descent families of Foveaux Strait and Rakiura/Stewart Island, 1824–1864', (BA research essay, University of Otago, 2008.
[109] LaBriola, 'Planting islands', 197.
[110] M.J. Stevens, 'An intimate knowledge of "Maori and mutton-bird": Big Nana's Story', *Journal of New Zealand Studies* 14 (2014), 106–21.
[111] V. Parham, '"All go to the hop fields": the role of migratory and wage labor in the preservation of indigenous Pacific Northwest Culture', in G.D. Smithers and B.N. Newman (eds.), *Native Diasporas: Indigenous Identities and Settler Colonialism in the Americas* (Lincoln: University of Nebraska Press, 2014), 317–46, at 324.

by the economic and political advantages that came from marriage to a woman of high rank.[112] In her examination of how five mixed-race families forged out of the fur trade made the transition to settlers in Victoria, British Columbia, Sylvia Van Kirk found wealth and property shaped family aspiration and colonial respectability.[113] In Hong Kong, some mixed-race families rose to prominence as a result of their business and social connections.[114] Men found employment as intermediaries at the treaty ports and in the Chinese Customs Service as interpreters or as public servants, while women's social advancement depended upon access to education and a good marriage.[115] Likewise, in colonial New Zealand, some fathers sought to gain respectability and economic mobility through education, while those with good connections made use of their networks and personal associations to obtain employment for their sons in the public service or good marriages for their daughters.[116]

Interpretations of family aspiration have been largely defined by the availability of personal writings, often dominated by the literate elite, while the more common experience for most people of mixed ancestry was economic and social marginalization. It is much harder to elaborate on the experiences of working-class families of mixed heritage, as they rarely left memoirs or personal writings. In my work on the mixed-descent families who lived at the Taieri Native Reserve in New Zealand from the 1830s to the 1940s I have argued for the importance of marriage patterns and kinship in tracing the fortunes of working-class families and their sense of cultural identity. Few of these families left behind personal archives, but their kinship connections demonstrated they were deeply entwined with the political and cultural world of Ngāi Tahu, the tribe to which they were affiliated through their maternal whakapapa (genealogy). Under the national census many of the Taieri residents were categorized as 'half-caste' or 'quarter-caste', but their way of life, engagement in tribal politics, cultural practices, and lingua franca identified them as Māori, and that is how many of them saw themselves.[117] Few such detailed community investigations have been attempted, but our understanding of identity formation within the context of colonialism

---

[112] K. Stevens, '"Every comfort of a civilized life": interracial marriage and mixed race respectability in southern New Zealand', *Journal of New Zealand Studies* 14 (2014), 87–105.
[113] S. Van Kirk, 'Tracing the fortunes of five founding families of Victoria', *BC Studies*, 115/16 (1997/8), 149–79.
[114] C. Ladds, 'Eurasians in treaty-port China: journeys across racial and imperial frontiers', in J. Leckie, A. McCarthy, and A. Wanhalla (eds.), *Migrant Cross-Cultural Encounters in Asia and the Pacific* (New York: Routledge, 2016), 19–35, at 19.
[115] Teng, *Eurasian*, 10.   [116] Wanhalla, *Matters of the Heart*.   [117] Wanhalla, *In/visible Sight*.

would be greatly enhanced by a close analysis of land, language, and cultural practice to identity formation within families and communities, set alongside the impacts of race-based colonial policies and legal categories.

The fate of non-European men is often discussed within the context of studies of labour migration, or of the anti-Asian sentiment prominent from the late nineteenth century. This emphasis on the discrimination and legal restrictions they faced, which were undeniably powerful forces for population control, has tended to produce an often-repeated line of argument that non-European migrant workers, who were predominantly male, were unable to form families. Kate Bagnall's nuanced and sensitive studies of Chinese-European couples in colonial Australia challenge standard historical interpretations. In reconstructing the lives of couples and their children Bagnall enlarges our understanding of the role these families played in colonial life and illustrates how family formation was a vital part of the Chinese experience in colonial Australia. Countering established claims about the transitory and male-dominated Chinese population, Bagnall argues that 'twentieth-century histories of the nineteenth-century Chinese Australian community, based primarily on official reports, newspapers and other published writings by white (almost exclusively male) commentators, often took on the biases of their sources, describing an absence of Chinese family life in the colonies and the consequent "vice" and "immorality" that occurred'.[118] Australia's twentieth-century histories of Chinese in the nineteenth century 'were predominantly written as histories of men without families. Family formation was seen as possible only by a return to China or, in rarer instances, by the migration of a Chinese wife.'[119]

A similar pattern can be seen in the New Zealand scholarship, where the emphasis is on anti-Chinese discourses and immigration restrictions. Chinese men did face numerous difficulties in establishing families within a context of racial intolerance and restrictive immigration, but there is evidence that many formed enduring relationships.[120] Focusing on intellectual discourses and high-level official debates about race-mixing, largely dominated by white male intellectuals, tends to frame mixed-race families as a racial and social problem and often sidelines the experiences of individuals whose very existence

---

[118] K. Bagnall, 'Rewriting the history of Chinese families in nineteenth-century Australia', *Australian Historical Studies* 42:1 (2011), 62–77, at 63–4.
[119] Bagnall, 'Rewriting the history of Chinese families', 71.
[120] M. Ip, 'Redefining Chinese female migration: from exclusion to transnationalism', in L. Fraser and K. Pickles (eds.), *Shifting Centres: Women and Migration in New Zealand History* (Dunedin: University of Otago Press, 2002), 149–66.

challenges a history largely framed by sojourning and transit. Turning our focus to lived experience within families and cross-cultural households is vital to opening up new sites of inquiry, and this can be achieved without denying the force and impact of anti-Chinese sentiment and policies. As Bagnall argues for Australia, and as is applicable to other locations with similar histories, bringing interracial relationships and family into the centre of scholarly work 'changes long-held assumptions about the lives of Chinese men in the colonies, of their domestic arrangements and social lives'.[121] As Paul D'Arcy has argued, undertaking studies of Chinese marriage in the Pacific locations they settled will enable deeper insight into how households were formed and the extent to which cultural traditions and values shaped personal identity.[122]

An important body of scholarship that draws upon personal narratives, often written by descendants of early cross-cultural unions, has demonstrated lived experience and personal identities rarely ever aligned with colonial classifications.[123] Personal narratives have exposed the histories of shame, silence, and deliberate forgetting as being authorized, legitimated, and validated by social-scientific investigations and discourses.[124] Lucy de Bruce, for instance, has used personal narratives and oral histories to foreground *kailoma* (European-Fijian) perspectives. Covering the period from 1920 to independence in 1970, de Bruce's aim was to centre 'previously voiceless communities' in Fiji's history and to privilege Indigenous knowledge systems rather than Western ideas about race and identity that perceived 'mixed bloods as debased, contaminated or immoral'.[125]

Since the 1990s, an important body of scholarship has traced patterns of interracial marriage, addressed the direct impacts of colonial policies on people's lives, unravelled the impacts of legacies of racial science, and illuminated how generational silence and erasure were practices underwritten by state intrusion and racial discourses. Although this is now a mature and sophisticated scholarship, there is scope for further research. There is a need for more studies of cross-cultural families and communities to add nuance and depth to identity formation. We need to continue to expand the scope of these studies to encompass a variety of relationships, notably migrant–Indigenous encounters

---

[121] Bagnall, 'Rewriting the history of Chinese families', 77.
[122] D'Arcy, 'Chinese Pacifics', 412.
[123] Z.L. Rocha and M. Webber (eds.), *Mana Tangatarua: Mixed Heritages, Ehnic Identity and Biculturalism in Aotearoa/New Zealand* (London: Routledge, 2018); F. Fozdar and K. McGavin (eds.), *Mixed Race Identities in Australia, New Zealand and the Pacific* (London: Routledge, 2017); L. de Bruce, 'A tartan clan in Fiji: narrating the coloniser "within" the colonized', in B.V. Lal and V. Luker (eds.), *Telling Pacific Lives: Prisms of Process* (Canberra: ANU Press, 2008), 93–105.
[124] Teng, 'The Asian turn', 80.   [125] de Bruce, 'Histories of diversity', 113.

Most importantly, research is required that centres Indigenous and Asian cultural contexts and perceptions of interracial marriage and mixed-race children. Close studies of family aspiration set within Indigenous frameworks of knowledge help to identify both the impacts of colonial legal regimes and how individuals and families responded to colonial racial categories. When thirteen people from the Taieri community, in New Zealand, signed their names to a petition in December 1892, some of the signatories added the phrase 'half-caste' alongside their name. This was not a claim to a personal identity, but a pragmatic response to legislative mechanisms passed between 1877 and 1885 in fulfilment of promises to provide land, separate from native reserves, for those of mixed ancestry in Ngāi Tahu territory.[126] Originally written in te reo Māori, the petitioners identified their primary identity as Māori, arguing for restitution 'because our ancestors had a right to land and from them it passed to our parents by whom we were begotten as members of the Ngaitahu and Ngatimamoe'.[127] Their use of colonial terminology points to the pervasiveness of race, but also their ability to navigate colonial categories for the benefit of their family and community.

Foregrounding the testimonies of families decentres colonial notions of identity and belonging based around 'race' and 'blood'. Nonetheless, the juridical regimes and categories of race and status imposed by colonial administrations have left deep legacies, particularly with respect to rights and identity. As Margaret Jolly has argued, 'the spectre of racial and cultural mixing' in the colonial past 'haunts' the present in relation to matters of landownership and citizenship.[128] In Hawai'i, for instance, the notion of 'blood' as central to identity 'generates processes of identification which fracture contemporary Hawaiian claims for sovereignty and self-determination'.[129] Tracing the histories of interracial marriage and 'race-mixing' in colonial Asia and the Pacific has immense value for interpreting and understanding contemporary political discourses, but attending to these histories also helps to foreground the particular circumstances in which families and communities were formed and the gendered dimensions of colonialism.

---

[126] A. Wanhalla and K. Stevens, '"A class of no political weight": interracial marriage, mixed-race children, and land rights in southern New Zealand, 1840s–1880s', *History of the Family*, published online, 23 May 2019.

[127] Robert Brown and 12 others, Petition to Alfred Cadman, Native Minister (trans.) 13 December 1892, MA1 1892/2250, Archives New Zealand, Wellington.

[128] M. Jolly, 'Oceanic hauntings? Race–culture–place between Vanuatu and Hawai'i', *Journal of Intercultural Studies* 28:1 (2007), 99–112, at 99, 100. See J.K. Kauanui, *Hawaiian Blood: Colonialism and the Politics of Sovereignty and Indigeneity* (Durham, NC: Duke University Press, 2008).

[129] Jolly, 'Oceanic hauntings?', 108.

40

Fifty Years of The Hawaiian Nation

Integrations of Resistance, Language, and the Love of Our Land

JONATHAN KAY KAMAKAWIWOʻOLE OSORIO

Pacific Islands History and its children, Pacific Islands Studies, Hawaiian Studies, Māori Studies and the like, grew up not in the shadow of a global Indigenous education movement, but as leaders and innovators in that movement. In this chapter I will explore the development of a Hawaiian-based literature beginning in the 1980s and the emergence of diverse new curricula and departments at the University of Hawaiʻi.

As undergraduates, and then graduate students, of young professors David Hanlon and Brij Lal, we learned that perspective changed one's whole understanding of history. The mere publication of a study did not ensure a necessarily accurate portrayal of a person, people, or community, and certainly did not provide a whole picture. This may seem obvious today. But for post-World War II generation American-schooled Native Hawaiians, these lessons on perspective were an intellectual liberation.

In the 1970s, the Pacific Islands academy wrestled with the legitimacy of oral testimonies, and how they were to be regarded in comparison to written documents produced by drifters, explorers, traders, missionaries, and colonial administrators, in Aotearoa and in Hawaiʻi. A new social and academic movement was born, focusing on reviving our native languages. While some scholars in Aotearoa such as Ranginui Walker clearly perceived the post-colonial possibilities connected to the revival of te reo Māori, in Hawaiʻi, where language loss was far more severe than in Aotearoa, the immediate focus was simply on rescuing ʻōlelo Hawaiʻi from what was generally believed to be an inevitable extinction.[1]

The creation of Pūnana Leo in Hawaiʻi, modelled after Kohanga Reo in New Zealand, was a significant development that drew public attention and commitment in Hawaiʻi to the task of rescuing the language, creating a teaching curriculum, and recruiting hundreds of teachers and thousands of children

---

[1] R. Walker, *Ka Whafai Tonu Matou: Struggle without End* (Auckland: Penguin Books, 2004).

233

and their families into a Hawaiian immersion education. But language reclamation was also connected to the cultural revivals of hula, voyaging, traditional agriculture, and the rise of a new professional class of Native Hawaiian academics and professionals in law, medicine, social work, public health, and politics.

'Ōlelo Hawai'i was also intimately connected to the political activism and protest of the 1970s, and ultimately to the construction of a new state constitution in 1978 in which the Hawaiian language and Hawaiian Studies became requirements in the state's public school system. A significant part of the Hawaiian political movements of the forty years since has been focused on holding the state and agencies like the Department of Education responsible to the law. This would lead to a dramatic growth in Hawaiian Studies and Hawaiian language at the University of Hawai'i, and a concomitant increase in Hawaiian political activity, not as collaborative agents in the state political system, but as a vocal and often effective opposition and resistance to militarization, untrammelled urbanization, and tourism.

The genealogy of this intellectual growth can be traced through at least three lineages that are distinct and at the same time significantly connected: resistance and political sovereignty (Kū'ē and Kū'oko'a); cultural revitalization ('Ōlelo Hawai'i); and environmental care (Aloha 'Āina). In this second decade of the twenty-first century no serious study of modern Hawai'i can take place without some understanding of all of these intellectual lines.

Kū'ē and Kū'oko'a (Resistance and Sovereignty)

The early 1980s saw a rise in the critical analysis of American and European colonialism in Hawai'i through the works of Indigenous scholars such as Haunani-Kay and Mililani Trask, Lilikalā Kame'eleihiwa, Pōkā Laenui, and Kekuni Blaisdell. Following the theoretical footsteps of Albert Memmi, Frantz Fanon, Ngūgī wa Thiong'o, and Michel Foucault, Trask and others laid a foundation for later writers like Kanalu Young, Jon Osorio, and Noenoe Silva to develop a deepening critique of Euro-American racism and exploitation in Hawai'i and in Oceania.

Trask's primary work, *From a Native Daughter* (1993), has had the greatest influence on political and historical scholarship in Hawai'i to the present day.[2] But close at hand is Lilikalā Kame'eleihiwa's historical account of the 1847 Māhele, *Native Land and Foreign Desires*, a transformation of traditional

---

[2] H.-K. Trask, *From a Native Daughter: Colonialism and Sovereignty in Hawai'i*, rev. edn (Munroe: Common Courage Press, 1999 [1993]).

land tenure that created a system of property to assist the new-born sugar industry and its American missionary creators.[3] Together, these works provided a sophisticated critique of capitalism and imperialism and a solid intellectual foundation for understanding and valuing traditional Hawaiian ideas through our own language and our own cultural metaphors.

Haunani-Kay Trask did not feel herself limited by her lack of fluency in the Hawaiian language and argued repeatedly for continual pressure on the US government and the State of Hawai'i to return lands and political authority to the Native people in Hawai'i. She and her sister Mililani established solid diplomatic relationships with other Indigenous peoples on the American continent and in Oceania. In 1987 they formed the first Native Hawaiian governing initiative, Ka Lāhui Hawai'i, and within three years had registered more than 20,000 native citizens.

Ka Lāhui and the later advocacy for the restoration of the Hawaiian Kingdom were closely related to the research and writing that came initially out of the Kamakūokalani Center for Hawaiian Studies and later from the Indigenous Politics section of the Department of Political Science – both departments at the University of Hawai'i at Mānoa. With a major focus on the nineteenth-century Hawaiian Kingdom, it is not surprising that over time more and more of the Native scholarship has been focused on Hawaiian language sources from nineteenth- and twentieth-century authors.

In 1998 George Terry Kanalu Young published *Rethinking the Native Hawaiian Past* that focused on the hana lawelawe,[4] the serving chiefs to the higher ranked Ali'i Nui in Hawaiian society.[5] Young was harkening to the lessons learned under the tutelage of David Hanlon and Brij Lal to focus on the non-elite, or in this case the lesser elite, as a way of understanding the ancient Hawaiian political society. But he brought a much more powerful narrative to the study of contemporary Hawaiians like Kalepa Johnson and his nineteenth-century ancestor, Noble Charles Kana'ina. He brought an ability to convey their lives meaningfully to Hawaiians, allowing a whole generation of Native Hawaiian undergraduate and graduate students to identify with historical figures and to feel more connected to the culture through them.

Jonathan Osorio's 2002 history of the Hawaiian Kingdom, *Dismembering Lāhui*, studied the Kingdom legislatures and the construction of four constitutions between 1840 and 1887 to describe the Kānaka Maoli reaction and strategies to

---

[3] L. Kame'eleihiwa, *Native Land and Foreign Desires: Ko Hawai'i Āina a me Nā Koi Pu'umake a ka Po'e Haole* (Honolulu: Bishop Museum Press, 1992).
[4] The author prefers the language not be exoticized through the use of italicization.
[5] K.G.T. Young, *Rethinking the Native Hawaiian Past* (New York: Garland, 1998).

the slow and insinuative process of colonization and the dispossession that came with it.[6] But Noenoe Silva's *Aloha Betrayed* (2004) went farther than any other work in this period to recognize the strategies that Kānaka adopted to record their way of life and to register their political values and criticism of the growing American presence in Hawai'i by focusing on the Hawaiian-language nupepa (newspapers) of the 1860s and 1870s.[7] Silva would inspire the next generation of Hawaiian scholars to document and understand our history through the powerful writings of the nineteenth-century authors and editors in their own language and in the medium of the newspapers that published them.

Some authors like Keanu Sai and political science professor Noelani Goodyear-Ka'ōpua found more than enough material in English-language documents and brought a reassertion of the Trask-style political analysis in the following decade with Ka'ōpua's *The Seeds We Planted* (2013) and *A Nation Rising* (2014).[8] These works looked at the Hawaiian charter school movement and the various protest movements that deeply affected the political society of Hawai'i from the 1970s to the present. But it was Keanu Sai's research and advocacy in the late 1990s, leading to the 2011 publication of *Ua Mau ke Ea: Sovereignty Endures,* that may have had the largest effect on Hawaiian political movements.[9] His portrayal of the takeover of the Hawaiian government as a prolonged occupation by the United States has influenced the current generation of young scholars who have written half a dozen theses and dissertations based on his theories. Furthermore, his ideas have contributed to the rise of several Hawaiian Kingdom entities and perhaps thousands of people who insist that the reinstatement of the nineteenth-century kingdom government is the only proper remedy for the illegal taking of our government and lands in 1893.

Kamana Beamer's *No Mākou ka Mana: Liberating the Nation* (2014) affirmed Sai's insistence that the creation and operation of the constitutional monarchy in Hawai'i was a proactive and successful attempt to protect the Islands' political sovereignty during the critical 1840s when Europeans were seizing strategic places in the Pacific.[10] Perhaps the larger issue, that colonization in

---

[6] J.K. Osorio, *Dismembering Lāhui: A History of the Hawaiian Nation to 1887* (Honolulu: University of Hawai'i Press, 2002).

[7] N.K. Silva, *Aloha Betrayed: Native Hawaiian Resistance to American Colonialism* (Durham, NC: Duke University Press, 2004).

[8] N. Goodyear-Ka'ōpua, *The Seeds We Planted: Portraits of a Native Hawaiian Charter School* (Minneapolis: University of Minnesota Press, 2013).

[9] D.K. Sai, *Ua Mau ke Ea, Sovereignty Endures: An Overview of the Legal and Political History of the Hawaiian Islands* (Honolulu: Pū'ā Foundation, 2011).

[10] B.K. Beamer, *No Mākou ka Mana: Liberating the Nation* (Honolulu: Kamehameha Schools Press, 2014).

Hawai'i is no simple matter of white domination and native surrender, is what characterizes Kānaka Maoli scholarship over the past two decades.

For all of these teacher/author/activists since Trask, the recovery of political power for Hawaiians was the most important goal, and for all of us it was a power independent of the American state that we have pursued. Unlike Asian Americans in Hawai'i who leveraged many decades of political powerlessness in the pre-World War II plantation economy to rise to political supremacy by 1960, Native political aspirations are not about taking over the legislature, the courts, and the governor's office. Genuine political leaders in the Hawaiian community may favour full independence from the USA, or a nation-within-a-nation relationship with the Americans, but what they seem to be in agreement about is that a Hawaiian government would be separated, if not wholly from the USA, at least from the State of Hawai'i.

'Ōlelo Hawai'i (Hawaiian Language)

The notion that we are a distinct people with distinct rights in our homeland is almost certainly linked to a sense that our culture lives on in, rather than merely through, some sense of racial or historical entitlement. Hula and traditional voyaging are well-publicized resurgences and they come with the usual problems of commercial exploitation. Less publicized are other revivals: medicinal healing arts (lā'au lapa'au); religious ceremony (ho'omana); traditional agriculture and aquaculture. Kānaka Maoli in the twenty-first century are relearning practices and rituals that were either gone or disappearing in their parents' and grandparents' generations. Nowhere is this more evident than in the speaking of the language itself.

Following the Māori Kohanga Reo model, Hawaiian language preschools, called Pūnana Leo, were formed in 1984, opposing an 1896 law that required education in the English language in Hawai'i. Three years later the founders of Pūnana Leo, Kauanoe Kimura, Pila Wilson, and Kauanoe Kamanā, were able to secure legislation creating and funding Kula Kaiapuni, Hawaiian language immersion schools located within already existing public elementary schools in Keaukaha and Waiau. These efforts were forged in protest and, in ways similar to the sovereignty protests, challenged the legitimacy and morality of the American takeover.

But the Hawaiian language movement, like the cultural and political movements of the 1980s onwards, was also affected by the 1978 constitutional reform in Hawai'i that created the Office of Hawaiian Affairs, opening the way to recognizing Native Hawaiian land claims and requiring the teaching of Hawaiian language and Hawaiian culture in Hawai'i's public schools. Kānaka Maoli delegates to the Constitutional Convention, including a future governor, were largely responsible for these reforms, but it is noteworthy that Kānaka political activity has largely remained outside of the electoral system and has continually focused on social and cultural goals such as improving Native health and education and reviving 'ōlelo Hawai'i.

Hawaiian political aspirations are almost entirely cultural aspirations, a deep desire to bring about acknowledgement and application of our values and traditions, of our arts and sciences. Ka Haka 'Ula o Ke'elikōlani College of Hawaiian Language at the University of Hawai'i at Hilo is the centre of language reclamation and where the founders of Pūnana Leo have created a language immersion and instructional model that reaches from the preschool child to the PhD. At Kawaihuelani Center for Hawaiian Language at University of Hawai'i at Mānoa, an increasing scholarship plumbing the huge literary archive of the Kingdom's Hawaiian-language newspapers seeks a better understanding of the ancient Hawaiian culture and history through the lens of the nineteenth-century Hawaiian observers, composers, writers, and political leaders. In different ways both programmes emphasize a Kānaka Maoli perspective, one that can only be discernible through 'ōlelo Hawai'i.

At Mānoa, Puakea Nogelmeier's *Mai Pa'a I Ka Leo: Historical Voices in Hawaiian Primary Materials* (2010) sets a foundation for a good many of the publications based on Hawaiian language sources since then.[11] Nogelmeier, not native himself, taught advanced Hawaiian language to scores of Kānaka Maoli students like myself at the University of Hawai'i from the 1980s on and introduced research into nupepa, an archive of quarter of a million newspaper pages recorded on microfilm and microfiche.

Many of his haumāna (students) have in turn become extremely productive and influential researchers and historical writers, including Kapā Oliveira, ku'ualoha ho'omanawanui, Bryan Kuwada, Tiffany Ing, and Alohalani Brown.[12] Noenoe Silva's 2017 masterpiece, *The Power of the Steel Tipped Pen*, examines the life and writing of late nineteenth-century writers Joseph Kanepu'u and Joseph Poepoe, an intellectual history of Hawaiian literature.[13] Bryan Kuwada's work on translation, focusing on the Hawaiian authors who

---

[11] M.P. Nogelmeier, *Mai Pa'a I Ka Leo: Historical Voices in Hawaiian Primary Materials, Looking Forward and Listening Back* (Honolulu: Bishop Museum Press, 2010).

[12] T. Ing, *Reclaiming Kalākaua: Nineteenth Century Perspectives on a Hawaiian Sovereign* (Honolulu: University of Hawai'i Press, 2019).

[13] N. Silva, *The Power of the Steel Tipped Pen: Reconstructing Native Hawaiian Intellectual History* (Durham, NC: Duke University Press, 2017).

translated European classics like *Ivanhoe, Tarzan, Bluebeard*, and *Twenty Thousand Leagues under the Sea*, discusses the implications of those translations as kingdom-era popular culture among Kānaka Maoli and what that suggests about assimilation, hybridity, and simply cultural change.[14]

Increasingly, academic studies of Hawaiian history and culture by researchers who have no knowledge of our language simply do not enjoy a great deal of credibility or relevance for Native scholars. The political origins of this academic view are certainly clear. The vast majority of European and American publications about Hawai'i and Hawaiians in the twentieth century have followed narrative patterns that impose a certain view of Hawai'i and its people that merely reinforces Euro-American superiority. Trask, no speaker of the language herself, is one of the first Native scholars to point this out. However, the contemporary focus of Hawaiian writing aims to understand the particularities of Indigenous ideas, practices, and values through the lives of the nineteenth-century Kānaka who described themselves, others, and the Hawaiian world that was changing in front of them.

Aloha 'Āina (Loved by the Land)

Kānaka Maoli are distinguishing themselves not only through ancestry and language but through cultural values and practices directed at knowing and managing land and other natural resources. From the early struggles to prevent urbanization of agricultural communities on O'ahu and the successful protest of the US military's operations on Kaho'olawe in the 1970s, care for the land (Aloha 'Āina) is the clearest and most consistent political advocacy that unites Hawaiians across the political spectrum.

This is reflected in an increasing presence and weight of Kānaka Maoli in environmental sciences and in social sciences like geography and urban and regional planning. An increasing number of Generation X and millennial scholars bring a fluency in Hawaiian earned either as immersion school students or as graduates of Hawaiian Studies and Hawaiian Language in Hilo and Mānoa. Fluency allows them to examine the nineteenth-century records and establish a clearer picture of the physical transformation of Hawai'i through the sugar plantation economy and the American militarization of O'ahu.

This research is also producing a very clear conceptual continuity of Aloha 'Āina from the eighteenth- and nineteenth-century mele (songs) that were

---

[14] B.K. Kuwada, 'How blue is his beard? An examination of the 1862 Hawaiian language translation of "Bluebeard"', *Marvels & Tales* 23:1, (2009), 17–39.

composed celebrating hundreds of places in Hawai'i, and the people for whom those places were known, to the cherishing of traditional practices that sustained the subsistence economy even through the rapid modernization and alienation of land over the past two centuries. Kānaka Maoli scholarship is becoming more and more particularized, focusing on specific places, such as No'eau Peralto's dissertation on the Ahupua'a of Koholālele and Kuka'iau on Hawai'i island's Hāmākua coast, using older mele and stories gleaned from Hawaiian-language newspapers to describe the community that lived in those ahupua'a before sugar levelled that history in the twentieth century.[15] More recently, Jamaica Osorio orientates her retelling of the Hi'iaka saga around Aloha 'Āina values in order to investigate the particularities and diversities of relationships among Kānaka before Christianty and colonization levelled them.[16] Finally, Kahikina DeSilva's 2018 dissertation, 'Iwikuamo'o o ka Lāhui: Nā Mana'o Aloha 'Āina i nā Mele Nahenahe', discovers the constant and continuous affirmation of Aloha 'Āina in virtually all mele composed in our language.[17]

Ethnic Studies professor Davianna McGregor's 2007 work *Na Kua 'āina: Living Hawaiian Culture* tells the story of the 'back country' people who continued subsistence practices into the twenty-first century despite enormous pressures from urbanization and tourism.[18] As a Protect Kaho'olawe 'Ohana activist herself, McGregor epitomizes something essential about the contemporary Kānaka Maoli scholar: that research and publication are almost always intimately connected with the author's personal commitment to protecting Hawaiian communities and sacred places.

University of Hawai'i Law School professor Kapua Sproat, and Malia Akutagawa (Law/Hawaiian Studies), work on enabling Hawaiians' access to land and re-establishing subsistence and ceremonial activities. Sproat writes about Hawai'i Supreme Court decisions that have clarified Native Hawaiian land rights connected to Kingdom laws and traditional and customary practices.[19] Akutagawa, who has worked in fishpond reclamation

[15] N. Peralto, 'Kokolo Mai Ka Mole Uaua O 'Ī: the resilience and resurgence of Aloha 'Āina in Hāmākua Hikina, Hawai'i', PhD thesis, University of Hawai'i, Mānoa, 2018.

[16] Jamaica Osorio, '(Re)membering 'Upena of Intimacies: a Kanaka Maoli Mo'olelo beyond queer theory', PhD thesis, University of Hawai'i, Mānoa, 2018.

[17] K. DeSilva, 'Iwikuamo'o o ka Lāhui: Nā Mana'o Aloha 'Āina i nā Mele Nahenahe', PhD thesis, University of Hawai'i, Mānoa, 2018.

[18] D.P. McGregor, *Nā Kua 'Āina: Living Hawaiian Culture* (Honolulu: University of Hawai'i Press, 2006).

[19] M.K. MacKenzie, S.K. Serrano, D.K. Sproat, A.K. Obrey, and A.K. Poai, *Native Hawaiian Law: A Treatise* (Honolulu: Kamehameha Publishing, 2015).

and management on Moloka'i since childhood, writes handbooks on community management of resources and is an important resource for the rural communities on that island.[20]

More and more Kānaka Maoli like Kiana Frank, Rosie Alegado, Mehana Blaich Vaughan, and Noelani Puniwai are matriculating into science and engineering fields and developing new insights into understanding the land- and seascapes that have housed Native communities for millennia. As of this writing, Hawaiian Studies professor Kamana Beamer is preparing his second book, this one on water use and regulation. Fluent in 'ōlelo Hawai'i, they all bring a deeper understanding of how traditional communities lived on the land and the extent to which the 'āina has shaped the Hawaiian values and character. Indeed their research is beginning to change the curriculum of 'hard sciences' on the University of Hawai'i at Mānoa campus. Colleges that house tropical agriculture, natural resource management, oceanography, and environmental sciences are competing for PhD students fluent in Hawaiian, and with a track record of community involvement and organization.

The story of Hawaiian political organizing and protest is more than inspiration to Kānaka Maoli because it is framing and instructing a cultural ethos that reasserts itself again and again. The rescue of Kaho'olawe (1976–2003), opposition to geothermal development (1989–92), and protest against an astronomy zone at the summit of Mauna Kea (1998–2019) are a continuous unfolding of one narrative: Kānaka Maoli are pilina (connected) to the 'āina and every story of our people is, in one way or another, the story of that relationship.

Philosophically, Hawaiian scholarship has also been deeply affected by new ways of looking at natural phenomena and how to understand the ways that our social and physical universe behaves. Hawai'i Community College professor Pua Kanahele has taught a method of analysing and categorizing knowledge called Papakū Makawalu (eight eyes) which entails broad inquiries into how our ancestors named phenomena through their understanding of the relationship between the physical world and human existence.[21] Kanahele's influence on Hawaiian scholars is at least as significant as Keanu Sai's influence on political advocacy, and it is safe to say that few contemporary Hawaiian authors write without at least an awareness of her methodology.

---

[20] M. Akutagawa, L. Han, E. Noordhoek, and H. Williams, 'Molokai Agriculture Needs Assessment, a Molokai-Pedia project of Sust 'āina Ble Molokai', unpublished, 2011.
[21] P.K. Kanahele, *Ka Honua Ola: 'eli 'eli Kau Mai (The Living Earth: Descend, Deepen the Revelation)* (Honolulu: Kamehameha Publishing, 2011).

Kanahele's lifelong study of hula and mele is a part of the narrative of Hawaiian music and its connection to Aloha 'Āina. Hundreds of popular songs composed in the past and present centuries celebrate the meaningfulness of myriad places in Hawai'i that are cherished for their beauty and their connection to remembered individuals. Cultural icons like Israel Kamakawiwo'ole and Liko Martin, Keola Beamer, Dennis Kamakahi, Kihei Nahale'ā, Keali'i Reichel, Jerry Santos, the late Edith Kanaka'ole and her descendents, Pua Kanahela, and Kekuhi Kanahele have strengthened Hawaiian poetic traditions and brought new vitality to a Hawaiian recording industry that rivals Nashville for its sustaining presence and contemporary relevance.

Moreover, Hawaiian performers and political protest have been inseparable from the beginning of the modern Hawaiian political movements. Liko Martin co-wrote 'Nānakuli Blues' in 1969, presaging Kokua Hawai'i's attempt to prevent the eviction of pig farmers from Kalama Valley to make way for a new subdivision. I remember hearing (and singing) this song over the past fifty years at public hearings and sovereignty gatherings. Israel Kamakawiwo'ole's rendition of 'Hawai'i '78' continues to be a haunting reminder of how the beauty of the land has been compromised by urbanization.

The Hawaiian music community has also been directly involved in political advocacy, most notably in 1998 when the Hawai'i State Senate attempted to pass a bill that would compromise access gathering rights enjoyed by Native Hawaiians since Hawai'i Supreme Court decisions between 1978 and 1994. Senate Bill 8 would have required Native Hawaiians to register to practise traditional religious, cultural, and subsistence practices on undeveloped land. Pua Kanahele, Reichel, the late Leinā'ala Heine, and Victoria Holt-Takamine brought their halau (school of hula) together and under the name 'Īlio'ulaokalani (Red Dog of the Heavens) held a vigil at the State Capitol, drumming in unison every hour on the hour while holding press conferences and pressuring legislative members.

Not all attempts to protect a community or a sacred space have been as successful as 'Īlio'ulaokalani or the Protect Kaho'olawe 'Ohana, but they tend to be at least as persistent. The creation of a 'Science District' at the summit of Mauna Kea has received a slowly mounting resistance that came to a head in 2015 when the Thirty Meter Telescope project was approved by the State Board of Land and Natural Resources after months of mostly opposing testimony. Coordinated by social media, hundreds of people from many places in the world, including Standing Rock, blocked the road and a dozen people were arrested. The governor of Hawai'i called for a halt in the construction in April 2015, though as of this writing it is expected to resume.

Hopena (Conclusion)

These three lineages have provided meaningful political and social progress and leadership for Kānaka Maoli in Hawai'i and have formed and guided Native Hawaiian academic research and publications for some forty years. I believe that the academic scholarship has been profoundly unifying in a Native community that has seemed to reject political unification over diverse and multifaceted expressions of sovereignty. There is almost no public disagreement among Native writers over content and method. Perhaps this is because we have been so critical of the American and European literature devoted to Hawai'i from when my generation first began entering higher education in the 1960s.

While criticism of haole (Caucasian) writers and lecturers goes back further through the novels and memoirs of John Dominis Holt and the translation work of Rubellite Kawena Johnson, the simple truth is that outside of Ralph Kuykendall's three-volume history of the Kingdom and Gavan Dawes's *Shoal of Time* (1968) there were very few works in English that gave a clear chronology of Hawai'i's history from 1777, and neither of them understood the Hawaiian language or considered that vast nineteenth-century archive of *nupepa* relevant to the story.

American authors continue to produce books about Hawai'i history, notably Sarah Vowell's 2011 *Unfamiliar Fishes* and James Haley's *Captive Paradise* (2014). But to say that they have little influence within the burgeoning Native canon is to give them too much credit. These works do not rise on anyone's horizons, and with very few exceptions Native writers simply aren't taking the time to contest the assumptions and methods of foreign writers. In fact, I don't believe we are reading their work.

In some ways Hawai'i is a world apart and distinct from everywhere else. Whether our preoccupation with Hawai'i as the centre and raison d'être of our academic lives is the result of America's purposeful and shabby assimilation effort of the twentieth century, an assimilation that left my parents' generation and mine almost completely ignorant of our past, is not really the point. We may have been making up for lost time and reconnecting with our great-grandparents who tried to leave a written record to guide our search for identity. But the point is, we are not really much interested in anything else, or in anyone else's opinion of Hawai'i for that matter. Indeed, we know that there is a tidal wave of copy about the islands in tourist magazines, in popular novels, in film, television, and social media, that capitalizes on our efforts to reclaim and dignify our language and culture. In the end, I am not sure that we distinguish between the claims made at Mauiwowee.com and the historical analysis of Sarah Vowell.

We should consider what this all portends. That there is a cleavage of direction and focus between Indigenous and Western scholars cannot be doubted. But ignoring the influence that haole have on the larger academy and in the global culture seems naively dangerous. Even the two critical reviews that I have conducted since 2010 – Nicholas Thomas's *Islanders: The Pacific in the Age of Empire* and Carol McClennan's *Sovereign Sugar* – made the point that these very excellent works were only tangentially important to Kānaka Maoli scholarship. And there are Kānaka Maoli authors like Noelani Arista, who, in *The Kingdom and the Republic*, specifically contend with historians who do not work with Hawaiian language texts and whose perspectives on Hawai'i demonstrate not just a lack of understanding of the Hawaiian people but a dismissal of the contemporary Hawaiian as anything but a dark-skinned American.[22] A very recent *University of Hawai'i Law Review* publication by a respected juror, the late James Burns, made an astonishingly archaic argument about the history of the American takeover of Hawai'i, relying on the testimonies of the nineteenth-century haole conspirators as evidence that the Hawaiian Kingdom was never more than an incompetent copy of modern democracies. The not-so-subtle racism in his article was not just in the argument, but also in the fact that he ignored the accumulation of data in nearly three decades of publications by Native authors that have produced deep and highly acclaimed studies of the Hawaiian Kingdom.

It is not as though our scholarship is unnoticed, however, and the extent to which Kū'ē, 'Ōlelo, and Aloha 'Āina are showing up in the literature of Hawai'i, and carried onward by newer and older scholars on the North American continent, is a testament to the integrity of our three themes whenever they are woven together. Thus, the emerging Kānaka Maoli scholarship is sharp and particular to place, grounded in observations of our natural world that are hundreds of years old, and married to a developing need to understand the philosophical underpinnings of those observations.

At a recent undergraduate research conference, five UH professors presented a panel entitled 'Kane and Kanaloa Are Coming: Are We Ready to Receive Them?' This panel was a conversation about the need to deal with climate change through a better understanding of the ways in which our Islands' natural forces interact and how our ancestors knew those relationships through the relationships of our deities. This panel was composed of wahine who earned their PhDs in the natural sciences – Oceanography,

---

[22] N. Arista, *The Kingdom and the Republic: Sovereign Hawai'i and the Early United States* (Philadelphia: University of Pennsylvania Press, 2019).

Microbiology, Molecular Cell Biology, Engineering, and Natural Resource and Environmental Management – and they offered not just a hybridization of traditional and European understanding of how the universe behaves, but also a new paradigm for perceiving the relationships between natural phenomena, employing a logic that relies on a knowledge of ancient religious practices and philosophies and presenting a new way for projecting that understanding in curriculum and pedagogy.

Time will tell whether we are looking at a paradigmatic change in how we create and organize knowledge, and whether these changes have currency in the wider world, but we are certainly in need of rebuilding trust globally in the 'academy'. Up on Mauna Kea thousands gathered in midsummer 2019 to protect the sacred mountain from the construction of the Thirty Meter Telescope. An important discourse is unfolding that at first pits science and technology against a Native sense of sacredness, but is quickly maturing into a critique of knowledge itself. As even scientists begin to use terms like 'colonial science', and to question the propriety and ethics of a research project that harms the environment, marginalizes a people, and relies on brute force to counter protest and resistance, we may be seeing the opening of conceptual doors that could have profound implications for the future of education and the welfare of our planet.

Perhaps we are seeing the beginning of a real revolution in thinking and education that more directly challenges philosophies grounded in white supremacy and the naked accumulation of wealth and resources as the keys to progress and power. Over a month-long period, we watched with awe as the young Kia'i (guardians) of the mountain have kept the State off-balance, unsure of itself, and unable to begin the construction of the telescope, with the principle of Kapu Aloha, a loving devotion to the sacred, and also a discipline of love and caring. At this point, half a millennium since Magellan landed on Guam and began, with murder, the rapacious conquest of the Pacific, may we not hope that we are turning that story back on itself?

41

Pacific Literature and History

ALICE TE PUNGA SOMERVILLE

Ours is a sea of writing. Historians, anthropologists, and linguists pore over documents, putting together paper puzzle pieces and figuring out how they fit. Social scientists, educators, development specialists, NGO administrators, activists, scientists, cultural specialists, politicians, journalists, preachers, entrepreneurs, and social media junkies spend hour after hour stringing words into sentences, and sentences into paragraphs (or hashtags). Thanks to the deeply stalkerish tendencies of the colonial project, archives are groaning with paper on which our lives, perspectives, experiences, and knowledges have been transcribed. In the Pacific we like to hold paper writing alongside other kinds of texts and sources: oral, musical, woven, carved, danced, and so on. Tatau, moko, veiqia, kakau kirituhi, record, communicate, and adorn our bodies. Small slabs of very old carved wood bear the evidence of Rongorongo, the currently indecipherable script produced in Rapa Nui. But none of these other texts lessen the value of alphabetic writing – they just place it in a broader context of articulation and representation.

The relationship between history and literature is a longstanding question, and the Pacific a place in which the line between the two sometimes feels incredibly fuzzy and at other times feels thickly stark. In this region, we cannot even begin the conversation without first engaging 'Towards a new Oceania', the ferociously clear essay Maualaivao Albert Wendt first published in 1976.[1] Written soon after completing an MA in history, and after his first novel and collection of short fiction had been published, the essay is a 'break

---

[1] A. Wendt, 'Towards a new Oceania', *Mana Review: A South Pacific Journal of Language and Literature* 1:1 (1976), 49–60. For a fascinating discussion of the context of this essay's publication and republications, see also G. Whimp, 'A search for the New Oceania', *Contemporary Pacific.* 22:2 (2010), 382–8.

up' letter with history. The (creative) writer is clear about his position from the now-famous first paragraph of the essay: 'only the imagination in free-flight can grasp its plumage, shape and pain'. Wendt's essay is eerily relevant over forty years later. Importantly, though, his essay does not simply repudiate or mock history as a project. Instead, it charts a much broader scope of what *counts* as history, and the role of creative writers in seeking to produce history in the region.

Wendt is not the only Pacific person who has been thinking about the relationship between history and literature in the context of the region. The three sections of this chapter respond to specific comments about this relationship, from Tahitian novelist and poet Chantal Spitz, Papa'ā/Cook Islands Māori scholarly couple Ron and Marjorie Crocombe, and Hawai'i-based New Zealand Māori poet, artist, and scholar Vernice Wineera respectively.[2] This chapter cannot attempt, and does not seek, to represent the wide range of writers, texts, or literary histories in the Pacific Ocean. There are ample bibliographies and surveys of the field that do not need reproduction or paraphrase here; this is not a Pacific literary history.[3] Instead, the three sections of the chapter pose three ways in which Pacific writers and literary scholars have engaged (and might engage) with Pacific histories. The first section looks at the ways in which Pacific creative texts tell/recite/produce histories of the region. The second takes the reciprocal view: what a literary studies approach to archives not primarily understood as 'Pacific literature' might contribute to our thinking about Pacific literary history. Finally, the chapter takes the focus of this whole volume at its word by focusing on the region *as a region*: it thinks about the ways in which particular texts by Indigenous Pacific people respond to, reflect on, and produce the vast Pacific we call home.[4]

---

[2] Please note that in this chapter, New Zealand Māori is used to distinguish Indigenous people from New Zealand from those Indigenous to the Cook Islands who also describe themselves as Māori.

[3] The three main texts that survey Pacific literary history at the regional level are Subramani, *South Pacific Literature: From Myth to Fabulation* (Suva: University of the South Pacific, 1985), M. Keown, *Pacific Islands Writing: The Postcolonial Literatures of Aotearoa/New Zealand and the Pacific* (Oxford: Oxford University Press, 2007), and S. Najita, *Decolonising Cultures in the Pacific: Reading History and Trauma in Contemporary Fiction* (New York: Routledge, 2006).

[4] With due recognition to Vernice Wineera, whose poem 'Heritage' ends 'I am taking my place / on this vast marae / that is the Pacific / we call home.' V. Wineera, *Into the Luminous Tide: Pacific Poems* (Provo: Centre for the Study of Christian Values in Literature/BYU, 2009).

ALICE TE PUNGA SOMERVILLE

'She Washes away This Dirt by Writing': Pacific Texts Telling Pacific Histories

In the final pages of Tahitian writer Chantal Spitz's extraordinary 1991 novel *L'île des rêves écrasés* that entered the Anglophone Pacific via Jean Anderson's 2007 translation *Island of Shattered Dreams*,[5] the main character Tetiare embarks on a process of writing. Her travels around the Pacific have been fuelled by her desire to reconnect with Indigenous people around the region whose longstanding relationships have been cut short by colonialism: 'She has discovered them. Peoples of the first people, attempting through little disorganized movements to shake off the Foreigner and immerse themselves again in their origins, to be themselves, the lost children of this huge family in search of one another.'[6] Upon her return, in the final pages of the novel, she reflects on the ways colonialism in her home islands has shaped her life and thinking – not only about the world and the broader region, but about herself. Specifically, she recalls being told as a child that Mā'ohi people cannot write, and responds: 'She washes away this dirt by writing.'[7]

The image of washing away colonialism is, of course, a provocative inversion of the colonial trope (famously conveyed in soap advertisements) of removing nativeness in order to become clean. If cleanliness is next to Godliness and whiteness also has a special proximity to perfection, then it follows that whiteness and cleanliness become merged. Nativeness, on the other hand, is framed as a kind of contamination: dirt, rot, disease. Spitz challenges this by thinking about colonialism itself as a kind of 'dirt' – not the nurturing 'dirt' of soil and land, but 'dirt' in the sense of filth. In the context of a novel that thinks about the consequences of French weapons testing in the French Occupied Pacific, including the ultimate environmental and human contamination of radioactive fallout as well as other kinds of pollution produced by the infrastructure of testing, this image of Tetiare 'wash [ing] away this dirt' reinforces the embodied grime of the colonial project in this part of the region.

The image of 'wash[ing] away this dirt' also gently echoes a Christian baptism, in which an inheritance of sin is washed away through the use of water. In this reading of the phrase, the original sin Tetiare has inherited is colonialism; something that is both unavoidable and fundamentally unjust. The inescapability of original sin also resonates with the novel's focus on the

---

[5] C. Spitz, *Island of Shattered Dreams* (Wellington: Huia Publishers, 2007).
[6] Spitz, *Island*, 121.   [7] Spitz, *Island*, 210.

248

experiences of colonialism in a series of generations in one family, and the unwanted but ongoing legacies of French 'dirt' inherited by different family members. Reversing the symbolism of the church, however, that (regardless of the brownness of actual Jesus) in colonial contexts models a dynamic of white missionaries (usually men) coming to wash abject Indigenous people of their sins, this 'wash[ing]' is undertaken by a brown woman. A final echo with Christian baptism is found in the combination of water and words: the 'wash[ing]' of sins takes place not merely by the presence of liquid but also by particular words intoned by the person performing the rite. Likewise, words are central to Tetiare's response to deeply ingrained colonialism: the washing itself is performed 'by writing'; by the production of language on her own terms.

Another reading of this image would focus on the idea of writing as a process of washing that gestures towards, but logically cannot be restricted to, physical dirt. The 'dirt' she is washing is psychological and spiritual, emphasizing the ways in which colonialism cannot be understood only as a network of physical violence, economic/material exploitation, or human mobility (forced or otherwise). The most obvious connection to this idea is the famously titled book by Ngũgĩ wa Thiong'o, *Decolonising the Mind*,[8] in which the Kenyan writer and scholar articulates the kinds of mental and emotional work that decolonization demands: it is not enough to speak of political independence, new flags, or even pieces of paper confirming that lands or waters are passing backwards and forwards between human hands. Likewise, it is not enough to trace battles, individuals, or treaties: histories that seek to understand the myriad consequences – but also *tools* – of colonialism need to reckon with the world of thoughts and feelings. Fijian historian Tracey Banivanua-Mar traced these broader affective, social, and cultural contexts of colonialism and independence across the Pacific region in *Decolonisation and the Pacific: Indigenous Globalization and the Ends of Empire*.[9] Because the damage she recalls from her childhood is discursive – she specifically recalls a teacher belittling her as a child – Tetiare 'washes away this dirt by writing'.

Thinking about Spitz's novel in relation to Thiong'o's book highlights the connections between Pacific and other anti-colonial worlds, but there's another

---

[8] Ngũgĩ wa Thiong'o, *Decolonising the Mind: The Politics of Language in African Literature* (Portsmouth: Heinemann, 1986).
[9] T. Banivanua-Mar, *Decolonisation and the Pacific: Indigenous Globalization and the Ends of Empire* (Cambridge: Cambridge University Press, 2016).

book called *Decolonising the Mind*, published much more recently by Ulli Beier about the history and role of the arts in Papua New Guinea, which affirms this connection.[10] Origin stories about the development of contemporary Pacific literature often focus on a small number of sites where key writers and texts appeared to emerge in the 1960s and 1970s. Beier's text recalls writers and other artists connected to one of these sites, Papua New Guinea, in which the vibrant and diverse Indigenous communities of that place were both energized and catalysed by the pathway to political independence from Australia in 1975. Another set of origin stories for contemporary Pacific literature coheres around the University of the South Pacific campus in Laucala (Suva); several key people attached to that campus as staff and students produced a critical mass for creative energy and output. Finally we can look to the origin stories of writing by local Indigenous, and migrant Pacific, people in Hawai'i and New Zealand; these stories of origins often but not always trace the links between the literary communities in those places and the networks of writers around the region. Of course histories are produced by historians who are often in turn produced by institutions; this is as true for literary histories as for any other kind. And so it is not surprising that these stories of literary origins also map onto key educational institutions in the region (UPNG, USP, New Zealand universities and teacher training colleges, and University of Hawai'i), both because those are the sites where writing communities have formed and had resources to publish, but also because those are the sites from which these origin stories are produced. In PNG, Pacific literature started at UPNG. In Fiji, Pacific literature started at USP. And so on. What this means for the many histories we might trace from literary tributaries in islands without major regional institutions is an open question.

Some producers of Pacific literary texts tell histories that other kinds of historians have not (yet) engaged, perhaps because they haven't asked those questions, and perhaps because the questions themselves are off the radar to some people and approaches. Certainly it is always helpful to caution against reading literary texts as if they were mere interviews from the field in a social science research project, or as if they are magically distilled 'Truth' from inside the heads of ethnographic others. And yet, we find experiences and perspectives documented and explored in Pacific literary texts that we do not find on other pages. We might look, for example, at Albert Wendt's *The Mango's Kiss* in which he conveys a turn-of-the-century Sāmoa that is

---

[10] U. Beier, *Decolonising the Mind: The Impact of the University on Culture and Identity in Papua New Guinea, 1971–74* (Canberra: Pandanus Books, 2005).

cosmopolitan, complex, and thoughtfully engaged with the cultural, intellectual, economic, and educational opportunities that connect their place with the world. The main character ends up living in New Zealand at a boarding school where she connects with Māori students and the broader contexts for understanding colonialism in Sāmoa. Or, for another treatment of Indigenous people interacting in global racialized networks, we might consider Patricia Grace's *Chappy* in which a European-born grandson returns to his Māori grandmother to hear about the many strands that are woven through their tribal home place, including the arrival of a Japanese soldier during World War II and a marriage that connects Aotearoa and Hawai'i. In the context of historical (and cultural) worlds in which the voices of non-Indigenous scholars (historians, but also – maybe especially – anthropologists) are by far the loudest, Vincent Eri's *The Crocodile* imagines its way into the perspective of an Indigenous man from early twentieth-century Papua and New Guinea, tracing his experiences of schooling, village life, World War II military engagements, and so on. We might also look at Grace Mera Molisa's supple poetry that articulates the many intersecting politics negotiated by ni-Vanuatu women in the 1980s, or Kathy Jetñil-Kijiner's insistent poetry that draws connections between family stories, weapons testing, and anti-Micronesian prejudice in Hawai'i.[11]

One of the particular contributions of literary work relates to what Wendt described as 'the imagination in free flight': the ability to tell histories without being constrained by secularism or materiality. Pacific writers tell histories in a way that 'history' either cannot or does not tell them. In literary texts, it is possible to link practical, observable, tangible things to spiritual, sacred, cultural influences. Ghosts, ancestors, land, whales: they're all there, active, agentic, and conscious parts of the story. Literary conventions of allegory and satire provide opportunities for Pacific writers resoundingly to critique power structures and colonial histories: Hau'ofa's novel *Kisses in the Nederends* and short story collection *Tales of the Tikongs* are iconic examples,[12] but we also might consider texts like Lemanatele M. Kneubuhl's 2006 novel *The Smell of the Moon*.[13] Literary texts can also directly address, or challenge,

---

[11] A. Wendt, *The Mango's Kiss* (Auckland: Vintage, 2003); P. Grace, *Chappy* (Auckland: Penguin, 2015); V. Eri, *The Crocodile* (Milton, Queensland: Jacaranda Press, 1970); G.M. Molisa, *Black Stone: Poems* (Suva: Mana Publications, 1983); K. Jetñil-Kijiner, *Iep jāltok* (Tucson: University of Arizona Press, 2017).

[12] E. Hau'ofa, *Kisses in the Nederends* (Auckland: Penguin, 1987); E. Hau'ofa, *Tales of the Tikongs* (Auckland: Penguin, 1983).

[13] L.M. Kneubuhl, *The Smell of the Moon* (Wellington: Huia, 2006).

colonialism in ways that conventions of non-fiction tend to treat with timidity through gesture. Samoan poet Tusiata Avia's 'Ifoga', for example, is a marvellously direct, angry, teasing poem that directly addresses the then prime minister of New Zealand whose apology for New Zealand's colonial wrongs are suggestively and playfully reframed in the context of the traditional Samoan convention of seeking to restore a relationship.[14] Loa Niumeitolu's poem 'when we tell' acknowledges the arrival of English as a language to Tonga, but pushes back on the idea that linguistic and cultural imperialism is a completed project in the islands: when we speak English – but also when we write it – 'we've got to have a Tongan way / of doing it'.[15]

'Largely Untapped Wealth': Literary Engagements with Historical Texts

Our sea is a sea of writing but it's also a sea of writers. Pacific people have been producing written texts for as long as writing has been in the region. Some days, this feels incredibly obvious. We consider the vast range of newspapers, letters, petitions, biographies, novels, poetry, plays, and so on produced by people Indigenous to the Pacific region, and we are overwhelmed by the sheer bulk of pages. Hawaiian historian Noelani Arista writes about the formidable size of the Hawaiian language archive, and the opportunities but also obligations it demands of historians of Hawai'i.[16] But other days, like the days when we talk about Pacific literature emerging in the 1960s and 1970s, or when literary scholars (or historians) from elsewhere treat the Pacific as so peripheral and unimportant that it couldn't *possibly* be anything but new or emergent, it can feel quite small. Partly, of course, this sense of the size of the field depends on whether you have a separate shelf for certain kinds of texts called 'Pacific literature', or whether you think about Pacific literary studies as an approach to all kinds of written (and perhaps other) texts that will of course engage those conventional literary genres but will happily critically engage (and deliberately seek – this is key as discussed below) any written texts produced by Pacific people.

[14] T. Avia, *Wild Dogs under My Skirt* (Wellington: Victoria University Press, 2004).
[15] L. Niumeitolu, 'when we tell', in *Whetū Moana: Contemporary Polynesian Poems in English* (Auckland: Auckland University Press, 2003), 167.
[16] N. Arista, 'Ka Waihoma Palapala Manaleo: research in a time of plenty: colonialism and ignoring the Hawaiian language archive', in T. Ballantyne, L. Paterson, and A. Wanhalla (eds.), *Indigenous Textual Cultures: Reading and Writing in the Age of Global Empire* (Durham, NC: Duke University Press, 2019), 31–59.

Pacific Literature and History

In their 1961 essay 'Early Polynesian authors – the example of Ta'unga', Ron and Marjorie Crocombe focus on nineteenth-century Cook Islander Ta'unga but warn against making what Epeli Hau'ofa would call 'belittling' assumptions about Pacific writing: 'One's first reaction may well be that Ta'unga is unique, but this would be quite incorrect even if we were to confine our documentary research to the single island of Rarotonga with a population, in Ta'unga's time, of under 3000.'[17] Shortly after, in 1965, Marjorie Crocombe published a book for use in Cook Islands schools that appeared in an English version called *Two Hundred Changing Years* and in Cook Islands Māori called *Ko e ua e teau tau Hikihikifano*. This history of the Cook Islands, produced by the Islands Education Division of the New Zealand Department of Education in connection with the Department of Island Territories, includes a chapter titled 'Maretu – who wrote some islands history', that introduces readers to the first Rarotongan writer whose unpublished manuscript sits in the library of the Polynesian Society in Wellington. As with Ta'unga, Crocombe does not suggest this one writer is a lone figure, however: 'Maretu is not the only one of the old people who wrote history, though he was the first',[18] and after naming two other specific authors (Tamuera Terei and Teariki Taraare) and encouraging children to talk to their parents about the genealogy books they may have in their own family homes, she ends the chapter with a hope that future Pacific historians may be among those reading the book. A few years later, in 1968, in an introduction to their painstakingly compiled and translated book of Ta'unga's writing, Ron and Marjorie Crocombe again urged their readers to consider what they called the 'at present *largely untapped wealth* of historical source material written by the Pacific Islanders'.[19]

In 1979, just over a decade after the Crocombes' *The Works of Ta'unga* appeared, Margaret Orbell published a review of the book *Directions in Pacific Traditional Literature: Essays in Honor of Katharine Luomala* in the *Journal of the Polynesian Society*. Her review of the Festschrift is robust and interesting, and

---

[17] R. Crocombe and M. Crocombe, 'Early Polynesian authors – the example of Ta'unga', *Historical Studies: Australia and New Zealand* 10:37 (1961), 92–3.

[18] M. Crocombe, *Two Hundred Changing Years: A Story of New Zealand's little Sisters in the Pacific – the Cook Islands, the Tokelau Islands, and Niue Island* (Wellington: Islands Education Division of the New Zealand Department of Education for the Department of Island Territories, 1962). Marjorie Crocombe later edited and published Maretu's works in 1983 as Maretu and M.T. Crocombe, *Cannibals and Converts: Radical Change in the Cook Islands* (Suva: Institute of Pacific Studies, University of the South Pacific, 1983).

[19] R. Crocombe and M.T. Crocombe, *The Works of Ta'unga: Records of a Polynesian Traveller in the South Seas, 1833–1896* (Canberra: ANU Press, 1968), emphasis added.

she spends some time commenting on various disciplinary approaches to Pacific literatures. In this case, she means Pacific literatures broadly – and particularly referring to what we might also think of as oral traditions and folklore. Having identified the central place of texts to the kind of work the literary scholar carries out, Orbell notes: 'One problem has been that texts recorded on anthropological expeditions have very frequently not been edited and published, both because of the difficulties which this can present and, often, because literary studies have been peripheral to the main interests of the persons concerned.'[20] This idea that literary studies has been peripheral to the study of the Pacific echoes the casting of the entire region as a peripheral space by visitors, scholars, politics, and discourse for centuries. It also leapt out at me, I confess, partly for personal reasons because a prominent Māori Studies scholar has used precisely that word to describe my own literary studies work in relation to that field. But it also leapt out because it nudged me to think more about the various possibilities of interdisciplinary work as a way to respond to the ways in which, for example, anthropological and historical work (or, perhaps, their methods and emphases) have had precedence in scholarly engagements with the Pacific.

Certainly this small book review published in 1979 packs a punch. It speaks from its own time – when there were not yet many scholars of the contemporary written literature of the Pacific region, and when many of the people we now think of as key 'foundational' contemporary Pacific creative writers had not yet published or had only published a few works. To conclude her review, Orbell writes about how the sheer wealth of Pacific literary texts leads her to think about the kinds of questions – and thus the kinds of askers – they demand. For the purposes of this discussion, it seems worth quoting at length:

> But what of the future? No very clear 'directions' for the study of the traditional literatures of the Pacific are apparent in this collection. Anthropologists, certainly, will continue to examine the social functions of these literatures. This is a very necessary task, and one trusts that literary scholars will learn from them. But one begins to wonder whether there will, in fact, be such scholars. In the field of Pacific studies there are many anthropologists and a considerable number of linguists, but very few students of the literature. (Whether we call such people folklorists or literary scholars makes, or should make, little difference.) Perhaps one can take

[20] M. Orbell, 'Directions in Pacific Traditional Literature: Essays in Honor of Katharine Luomala [review]', Journal of the Polynesian Society 88:1 (1979), 106–9.

some encouragement from the fact that, as the editors of this collection note, Pacific Islanders are now voicing the criticism that folklorists in the past have not published enough texts and translations. This new concern for the literary heritage of the Pacific may help to produce more interest in it among scholars, also.[21]

For Orbell, the 'literary heritage' is the 'traditional literatures of the Pacific', whereas it is possible also to expand this to include more recently composed written texts ('contemporary' – although that becomes a hollow term after five decades of energetic literary production). And yet Orbell's claims are as relevant now as they were forty years ago. How many classes focused on Pacific literature are taught anywhere in the world? How many people writing about Pacific writing have undertaken any training in the field? We still don't have discipline journals or a scholarly association. It is still possible to discover the Pacific and five minutes later declare yourself an expert in the field; it is still possible to publish critical work that assumes things started in the later twentieth century. Orbell and the Crocombes, writing out of very different disciplinary spaces, convey their sense of a Pacific which is full to the brim of writers and writing, full to the brim of written texts. In many ways, of course, Orbell's review speaks to, or echoes, the idea that the Crocombes had expressed almost two decades earlier in 1961: the problem is not a lack of texts but a lack of scholars and critical consideration of those texts. The writings identified by the Crocombes and by Orbell are texts with which literary scholars can do all kinds of work. Yes, these texts are 'historical source material'. Yes, they're even ethnographic sources. But they are also our literature. They are our people doing amazing things with new words and new expressive forms. They are our people speaking to us across time.

It is worth mentioning here that the field of Pacific literary studies, like all scholarly fields, has changed over the years, and in particular the scope of the objects of study has expanded from poetry / short fiction / novels to include not only film and new media texts but also a much wider range of written texts. One of the influences on these recent conversations in Pacific literary scholarship is perhaps traceable to the intersections some scholars have noted between engagements with Pacific texts and Indigenous literary studies. In Indigenous literary studies, particularly but not only in North America,[22] key scholars like Robert Warrior, Craig Womack, Daniel Heath Justice, Chadwick

---

[21] M. Orbell, 'Directions in Pacific Traditional Literature'.
[22] An important exception is P. van Toorn's *Writing Never Arrives Naked: Early Aboriginal Cultures of Writing in Australia* (Canberra: Aboriginal Studies Press, 2006).

Allen, and Lisa Brooks have sought to enlarge the range of texts engaged by literary scholars. Pacific scholars have responded by thinking about Pacific literary approaches to all kinds of texts, and the conscious assemblage of archives *as literary archives* connected to specific sites, islands, communities, or nations. To provide a sense of the kinds of historical texts (and archives) that are productively engaged by literary studies, it is worth considering some examples. One critical space where historical and literary studies most closely overlap is the study of life writing: biographies and autobiographies. Whereas the Pacific historian might have an interest in these texts as documents produced in particular moments that can be drawn into broader analysis of historical sources, a Pacific literary scholar might focus on those texts authored by Pacific people and read them alongside texts in other genres – poetry, fiction, plays, non-fiction. Indeed, many Pacific-authored autobiographies are produced by people who have also published writing in other genres. (Certainly there is a small number of biographies of Pacific writers, which are also naturally of interest to the literary scholar,[23] but these are very few relative to the number of writers whose lives and works deserve such treatment, and like Crocombe in 1965 I find myself rather hoping that people might read these words and feel inspired to add to this oeuvre. We need more biographies of Pacific writers!)

To consider the kinds of texts that might be engaged by historians but could just as productively be read as Pacific literature, and contribute to our understanding of Indigenous literary production in the region, we can turn to the example of four specific Indigenous Pacific people who wrote during the nineteenth or early twentieth centuries. Let's be clear from the start: all four of them are men, all wrote from a fairly young age, and all four were deeply connected to Christian missionary enterprises of various kinds. All four also travelled, albeit on different scales, and their mobility is as interesting as the places they were from or ventured to. And yet these examples were all very different. Most obviously, they come from four different places: according to contemporary nation-state boundaries (not that any of these existed at the time they wrote), one from the Cook Islands, one from Fiji, one from PNG, one from New Zealand. Or, as they might have described their different home places: one from Rarotonga, one from Tailevu, one from Kono/New Ireland, and one from Kororareka. While one wrote in a number of sites in

---

[23] For example, P. Sharrad, *Albert Wendt and Pacific Literature: Circling the Void* (Auckland: Auckland University Press, 2003); U. Ojinmah, *Witi Ihimaera: A Changing Vision* (Dunedin: Otago University Press, 1993); see also B. Nālani McDougall's work on Haunani-Kay Trask.

Polynesia and Melanesia, one wrote in Fiji, one wrote in New Ireland/New Britain, and one wrote in Norfolk Island, Australia, and London. Although they were all, at least according to their writing, devout in their Christian faith, their connections to mission work were very different and they were variously knowledgeable about the traditional knowledges of their people. With the exception of Mowhee, whom we have no reason to suspect was literate in his first language, the other texts have come into the world as English-language publications, and so bear the marks as well as the labour of translation. Their texts have had very different archival journeys, and as far as I am aware this is the first time they have been considered side by side.

Mowhee (whose name was written before orthographic conventions of the New Zealand Māori language were standardized; his name would now be spelled 'Māui') was from the Bay of Islands in the north of New Zealand. He travelled to Norfolk Island as a nine or ten year old in the first decade of the nineteenth century, where he lived with a white family, the Drummonds, and starting using the name Tommy Drummond. He attended school there, and when the family moved to New South Wales in Australia he got bored with farm work and ended up moving to live with (and continue his education in) the household of Samuel Marsden, who was chaplain of the NSW colony and oversaw missionary work in New Zealand as well. Mowhee returned to his original home in 1814, having spent almost half his life away, and although it was anticipated he would stay there he had heard so much about England that he boarded a ship bound for London in 1815. In May 1816, the boat docked in the Thames and the captain of the vessel on which he had been travelling brought Mowhee to the Church Missionary Society whose offices were nearby. Arrangements were made for Mowhee to stay under the care of the CMS and specifically the Rev. Basil Woodd from then until his untimely passing shortly after Christmas later that year. At some point, Woodd asked Mowhee to write a memoir so he could remember him once Mowhee returned home to New Zealand. Mowhee was apparently some way into this task when he became unwell and passed away. The original manuscript written by Mowhee has not (yet) been found, but Woodd sought posthumous publication of the memoir in a range of missionary publications in the years following his death. Each of these published versions is slightly different, and all bear the mark of Woodd, who enthusiastically edited and finished off Mowhee's autobiography from his own recollections.

In his introduction to an 1817 publication of Mowhee's memoir, with considerably more detail than the more widely known 1818 version titled

'Memoir of Mowhee' that appeared with an ink drawing of the author in the *Missionary Papers* the following year,[24] Basil Woodd writes about his grief immediately after Mowhee's passing, and especially his deep regret and despair that Mowhee didn't return to New Zealand to carry out the mission work he'd been prepared for and was so enthusiastic about: 'These pleasing prospects [of Mowhee going home] are now, alas! but as a dream when one awaketh. Mowhee is no more!'[25] But Woodd goes on to note in the *Missionary Register* that he was comforted when he realized the significance of Mowhee's writing: 'This thought then occurred to me – Mowhee is dead, but his work is not yet done. Let his Grave address his countrymen!'[26] Interestingly, although the *Missionary Papers* was explicitly aimed at a British Sunday School readership, Woodd's main interest in seeking publication of the heavily annotated manuscript was not primarily the edification or even interest of European readers but Mowhee's own people:

> Let Mowhee's family be especially considered. Perhaps they may read, or at least hear it, with some interest: and thus we may say of Mowhee 'By it, he, being dead, yet speaketh.'[27]

He then directly addresses the future Māori reader of this text:

> And, O Native of New Zealand! Whoever thou art that mayest hear or read this little Tract, remember that Mowhee, on his death-bed, remembered and prayed for thee.

I remember feeling surprised, and quite moved, and maybe even interpellated, when I (a 'Native of New Zealand') sat in an air-conditioned archive in Birmingham reading these words. Were they really for me?

Ta'unga, of course, is the writer on whom the Crocombes have already undertaken such rich and compelling work. He was born in Rarotonga but travelled through the Pacific region as a missionary and produced unparalleled ethnographic and descriptive accounts of communities he lived with, especially in what we now call New Caledonia. Ta'unga wrote prolifically from a young age and, it seems, at various times throughout his long life. Ron and Marjorie Crocombe describe the process of coming into contact

---

[24] Mowhee and B. Woodd, 'Memoir of Mowhee, a New Zealander who died at Paddington, December 28, 1816', *Missionary Papers* 10 (1818), n.p.

[25] B. Woodd, 'Memoir and obituary of Mowhee, a young New Zealander, who died at Paddington, December 28, 1816', *CMS (Church Missionary Society) Missionary Register* (February 1817), 71–9.

[26] Mowhee and Woodd, 'Memoir of Mowhee'.

[27] Woodd, 'Memoir and obituary of Mowhee', 79.

with his writing through a serendipitous mistake (literally it was on the other side of the page of something else they had asked to see), and painstakingly sought fragments of his writing in various institutions around the world. After locating, translating, and editing his writing, they published *The Works of Ta'unga: Records of a Polynesian Traveler in the South Seas 1833–1896*. In his foreword to the book, H.E. Maude gestures to not only the ethnographic and historical but the literary significance of Ta'unga's writing. He finishes his remarks with:

> Fortunately for us Ta'unga was writing in the earliest, and I submit the finest, age of Polynesian literature ... he writes naturally and entirely without self-consciousness, with all the freshness of early English prose. To conclude, *The Works of Ta'unga* is not only an important primary source for the student of Pacific history or anthropology; it possesses the additional merit of being an absorbing literary treat.[28]

Indeed, Ta'unga's collection of works has been described as an 'instant classic'.

Epeli Rokowaqa, also known as Mokunitulevu na Rai, came from Maumi in the district of Bau in the province of Tailevu. Rokowaqa was undertaking religious training at Navuloa Methodist Mission Institution at Tailevu in the late nineteenth century when he produced a manuscript that was later published under the Fijian title *Ai Tukutuku Kei Viti*.[29] In 2013, Kolinio Rainima Meo, an educator and public servant who has since passed away, published an edited transcription and retranslation of writing which Rokowaqa had produced in the late 1800s. Meo produced two translations: one in English, and one in Bauan, the widely used 'standard' Fijian dialect. Meo had come into contact with them through his professional work when he was involved in the Fijian Ministry of Education, and grew increasingly interested in them. The two books, not easily available outside Fiji, could be purchased for a period of time from the bookstore at University of the South Pacific's Laucala campus in Suva. Rokowaqa's writings are presented, like Ta'unga's, as historical and ethnographic work. He covers a wide range of topics, from various traditions about Fijian origins and traditional culture, social organization and links between people and land, and customs.

---

[28] Crocombe and Crocombe, *The Works of Ta'unga*, 4.

[29] E. Rokowaqa, *Ai Tukutuku Kei Viti: sa vola ko Rev. Epeli Rokowaqa* (Suva: [Methodist Missionary Magazine], 1926). The only version of this I have seen is in the personal collection of Professor Paul Geraghty at University of the South Pacific; it does not list a publisher.

Another Indigenous Pacific person whose manuscript describes his own life and religious faith but also the broader knowledges through which he and his people know the world is Ligeremaluoga, whose work was translated by missionary Ella Collins and published in Adelaide as *The Erstwhile Savage: An Account of the Life of Ligeremaluoga (Osea)* in 1932.[30] The text may have gone quite quickly out of print but it was not off the radar: an excerpt was included four decades later in Ulli Beier's 1974 anthology of mostly contemporary ('new') writing called *Niugini Lives*, although Beier (the German writer, teacher, and curator who had recently moved with his family to Niugini from Nigeria and who later wrote the book titled *Decolonising the Mind*) explained that 'he sees his own culture through the missionary's eyes' and the text was 'included here for historical rather than literary reasons'.[31] What Beier – who preferred his Indigenous writers to be anti-colonial and artistic in certain terms – meant by this comment is clear: he did not believe the text had any literary merit (let alone being, as Maude described Ta'unga's text, 'a literary treat'!) but considered it should be acknowledged for its place in PNG's literary history. Another four decades later, our thinking about the kinds of things Pacific literary studies can do with a text have shifted again, and scholarship in a range of fields has been pushed to reconsider Indigenous figures who stand out in the historical record. These critical shifts have primarily been pushed forward by members of the communities from which certain individuals come, who are dissatisfied with the limited range of character types allocated for Indigenous people: freedom fighters / savages, mockable sellouts, or 'caught between two worlds'. But a recent republication by UPNG Press in 2016 of Ligeremaluoga's book in its entirety draws our attention to a shift in PNG's sense of its own intellectual history, and to the kinds of literary and historical scholarship that find other ways to engage with this kind of work. In the front of the text is a letter with a letterhead from UPNG's School of Medicine and Health Sciences – the writer is an academic, David Linge, who thanks the press for being keen to republish his father's work.[32]

For Basil Woodd in 1817 London, having spent seven months with Mowhee and being passionately committed to a just-ramping-up global missionary enterprise, the idea that Māori people would read his and

---

[30] Ligeremaluoga, *The Erstwhile Savage: An Account of the Life of Ligeremaluoga (Osea) – An Autobiography* (Melbourne: Cheshire, 1932).
[31] U. Beier, *Niugini Lives* (Milton, QLD: Jacaranda Press, 1974).
[32] Ligeremaluoga, *The Erstwhile Savage: An Account of the Life of Ligeremaluoga (Osea), An Autobiography* (Port Morseby: UPNG Press, 2016).

Mowhee's words that he was writing was obvious to the point he could directly address them/us – 'O Native of New Zealand!' But, because of how things turned out in the following two centuries, until recently few people have engaged with Mowhee's work at all. I followed a little pathway of paper breadcrumbs back to his writing when I found myself dissatisfied by the story I was telling my students (in literary studies, Indigenous studies, and Pacific studies classrooms) that 'our' literatures emerged in the 1960s. Two other scholars have engaged Mowhee's writing: Alison Jones and Kuni Jenkins, New Zealand education scholars whose interests in literacy and its specific history in Māori contexts led them to research and write a book about early writing between Māori and Pākehā.[33] After two centuries of being told that Indigenous writing is only ever recent, I find myself being more surprised than Woodd to read Mowhee's memoir. How can we produce and nurture a collective memory of the region in which the existence of a historical text written by Mowhee (and Ta'unga and Ligeremaluoga and Rokowaqa) seems as obvious to us as the existence of a future Māori readership was to Woodd in 1817? What are the stakes of being able not only to imagine future readers but to imagine past writers? Each of these men wrote texts that can be equally engaged by the historian, the literary scholar, the anthropologist, the Pacific studies specialist, and so on – including, of course, and hopefully first and foremost, their own families and communities.[34] However, it it worth noticing the pathways of these texts through production and first publication (including translation), then through archives, to later publication, and finally to critical engagement. For all kinds of reasons, few historians have dealt with these texts. How many Pacific historians have the capacity to work in the many Indigenous languages in which whole manuscripts are written and are then sitting, neatly waiting, on archive shelves? How many historians read literary anthologies on the off-chance there might be a 1932 Niugini text wedged in there? How many historians of Cook Islands Māori or New Zealand Māori experiences focus on lives lived, and words written, beyond the political borders of their contemporary nation-states? We are talking here about the questions that we ask, and the bookshelves and archives those questions make visible. And particularly, when the desire to seek and engage writing by ancestors (however broadly conceived) is undertaken by Indigenous students and scholars – for whom the stakes and possibilities of

---

[33] A. Jones and K. Jenkins, *He Kōrero, Words between Us: First Maori–Pakeha Conversations on Paper* (Wellington: Huia, 2011).
[34] Of course, this is not to suggest that family members or communities are not also discipline specialists.

this kind of work have a different and particular charge – we are talking about who is asking the questions in the first place.

To provide another kind of example of the overlapping, interwoven work of literary and historical studies, we can spend a bit longer thinking about the problem of literary achievements of the 1960s and 1970s being celebrated as 'firsts' despite all of these texts that pre-date them. The idea of 'Niugini' into which Beier stitches Ligeremaluoga is an anachronism: from the stance of the soon-to-be-independent state of Papua and New Guinea in 1974, and certainly from the decades-of-independence state of Papua New Guinea now, one can look back and incorporate any writer who is an ancestor of communities living within the boundaries of those nations at that time. To clarify with another example, it is a truth that Mowhee is the first published Māori writer, but it is just as true that in 1816 Mowhee would not have thought of himself as Māori at all. So, Osea Ligeremaluoga lived in which nation-state as he wrote? The site of the 1932 book publication – Adelaide – gives us a clue: at the time, Australia was the colonizing power over his home place. So, when we seek to trace PNG's literary history it makes sense to look at literary publications in PNG as well as sole-authored texts like *The Erstwhile Savage*. But when we understand the role of periodicals in the publication histories of many Indigenous writers around the Pacific region, we find ourselves standing in front of other bookshelves.

The University of Melbourne library holds a mid-twentieth-century publication called *Pacific Reading* – this sounds like the kind of thing with which all Pacific literary scholars worth their oceanic salt would be familiar.[35] It was a magazine produced by the South Pacific Literature Bureau (SPLB), another thing that sounds like it should be known by scholars of this field. The South Pacific Commission, an entity made up of the colonial powers in the Pacific region established in 1947, was still in its early days when H.E. Maude, a former colonial manager who had moved into academia, proposed the establishment of the SPLB. Rather than being a publishing house or distribution network itself, the Bureau sought to act as a go-between; the purpose of the Bureau was to advise, support, and facilitate the production and distribution of literature around the region. The magazine was published in Sydney from 1952, and featured essays on relevant topics, information about how to acquire reading materials, and a section in which the editor reviewed (quite frankly) a wide range of texts for consideration. The magazine is fascinating,

---

[35] After first reading this magazine in Melbourne, I later found it was also held in the Pacific Collection at the University of the South Pacific – Laucala campus.

as is the institution that produced it. And yet, neither is mentioned in any account of Pacific literary history; neither features in any history of writing or literacy in the region; and only brief gestures are made towards them in histories of the South Pacific Commission (later known as the South Pacific Community).

What are the questions we do not ask that lead us to not know about the SPLB or *Pacific Reading*? How might our well-worn dominant accounts of Pacific literary history leave room for us to continue to imagine that such institutions, publications, and writers are out there on a small number of library bookshelves? How might we trace the influence of something that made its own vibrant contribution in particular times and places but has been expunged from our recollection of how literary history unfolded in this region? It is valuable to consider the SPLB on its own terms and in the context of the Pacific, but Banivanua-Mar has argued that in the twenty-first century it can be difficult to imagine the ways in which the mid-twentieth-century Pacific region was deeply, if not reciprocally, networked with other parts of the colonized world. Taking a step back, we see that literary (and, later, filmstrip and film) texts also connect this region to broader networks, especially during the mid-century moves towards anti-colonialism and independence. Indeed, the SPLB is one of many similar institutions, including several in Africa ('by the mid 1950s, there were seven Commonwealth Literature Bureaus in East and West Africa, as well as several others in the Congo, Sudan, South Africa, Liberia and elsewhere'[36]), others elsewhere in the Anglophone colonial world and, later, a PNG Literature Bureau (est. 1968).

'Walking on Water': The Ocean and the Page

The failing, of course, of much Pacific history is that it has been so deeply captured by the nation-state system, by particular colonial networks, and by a commitment to – if not Truth – a certain kind of reality. And, this is reflected in the content but also the form of a lot of historical scholarship from and about the region. Students and scholars of Pacific history read and cite Wendt's and Hau'ofa's now-canonical calls to dynamic decolonized regionalism, but seldom engage their authors' deep commitments to, and strong arguments about, the creative arts as a key site for this Oceania to be imagined and brought into being.

[36] E. Ellerman, 'The Literature Bureau: African influence in Papua New Guinea', *Research in African Literatures* 26:4 (Winter 1995), 206–15, at 206.

New Zealand Māori poet, artist and scholar Vernice Wineera has been living in Hawai'i for most of her adult life; a longstanding member of the multi-generational Pacific Mormon community in Lā'ie, when her collection of poetry *Mahanga* was published by BYU-Hawai'i in 1979 it was the first collection of poetry by a Māori woman. As a Māori woman on Hawaiian land, Wineera's residence in Hawai'i draws our attention to the many kinds of intra-island mobility in which Pacific people engage. Across her body of work, including in her most famous poem 'Heritage', whose final lines 'I am taking my place / on this vast marae / that is the Pacific / we call home' are echoed in the first section of this chapter, Wineera reflects on the ancestral, historic, and relational dimensions of the ocean. Wineera published a poem titled 'Walking on water' in a 1979 issue of *Mana*, a Fiji-produced journal of literary studies that was originally published as the *Mana Annual*, which in turn emerged from a section titled 'Mana' compiled and edited by Marjorie Crocombe as a regular feature in the Australia-based magazine *Pacific Islands Monthly* between 1973 and 1976.[37] The poem reflects on the role of the poet, the writer, in the Pacific, and suggests that poetry – and I would add writing – is inextricable from the concerns of history. 'Walking on water' opens: 'The poet walks on water, knowing full well / the transparency of the membrane / that keeps him afloat / on an ocean of ideas.' The poem ends with an echo of this opening and confirms that the argument of the poem has particular resonance for Pacific writers: 'Poetry is walking on water. / Pacific poets know this / more poignantly than all the world.' The ocean in the poem is both literal and metaphoric: the Pacific poet engages the vast geographic as well as intellectual span of the region. The 'membrane' on which Pacific writers stand is 'transparen[t]' – visible from its effects (a standing poet who appears to be 'afloat') – but the depth and structure that makes this possible can be seen simultaneously.

There is not scope in this chapter to engage the poem in its depths, but it is worth focusing on one section of it in particular: 'for some of us, / life is not all anguish not remorse, / but a series of progressive steps towards a cosmic whole, / and the worst we can suffer is to forget / the past events that shape us yet / and touch the soul.' Wineera casts struggle, including 'anguish and remorse', as the outcome of disconnection; their remedy is found in its opposite – 'steps towards a cosmic whole'. Despite the many kinds of suffering in the Pacific, 'the worst' is 'to forget'. This is an argument about history made

---

[37] V. Wineera, 'Walking on water', *Mana* (1979), 30–1.

in the negative: rather than saying that remembering is important, the poem speaks about the stakes of forgetting. Wineera calls us to recall and understand the histories that continue to be felt. The question is not whether 'past events ... shape us / and touch the soul'; the question is only whether we know those 'past events' to the extent that we can understand the ways in which we have been shaped and, indeed, our own 'soul[s]'. Wineera's poem is tied to history in another way, of course: we can only read it when we turn back to pages published in 1979 and find it there. The tracing of literary histories brings us into relationship with literary expressions of history and historical thought. Writing is a pathway to history, and to historical thought, but seeking and identifying Indigenous-authored texts can also be a nourishing end point of (literary) historical scholarship. It could be that Tetiare is 'walking on water' as she washes away dirt by writing; making another loop back to a Christian reference, we find Pacific people engaging in writing as an act of faith that enables them to overcome what appears to be impossible; to move; to connect. Perhaps the SPLB 'shape[s] us yet'. Maybe the writing of Rokowaqa, Mowhee, Ta'unga, Ligeremaluoga and all the rest has the capacity to 'touch our soul' and propel us 'towards a cosmic whole'.

42

Film and Pacific History

ALEXANDER MAWYER

This chapter approaches the history of the cinema of Oceania as a window on the shifting beliefs, values, and relational understandings of filmmakers and their communities about the region. Embroiled in the dynamics of encounters between outsiders and insiders crossing imagined or actual beaches of Pacific worlds, the region's film history has seen a dramatic turn from a cinema of Oceania to what might be called an Oceanian cinema as decolonizing and empowering works by Indigenous and local filmmakers emerged in the last decades of the twentieth century.

From the Cinema of Oceania to Oceanian Cinema: Twentieth-Century Film and Pacific History

The Pacific Islands have been inextricably entangled in European, American, and global imaginations since the earliest encounters between Oceanian peoples and Spanish, French, or British navigators, their diverse crews, and the even more diverse popularizers of encounter narratives. While a sea of scholarly work has been devoted to the representation of Oceania across media from the eighteenth century to the present, film has received relatively meagre attention despite being the superseding medium for the region's representation since the twentieth century's dawning. Pacific Islands on film, real and imaginary, have been the setting for every kind of fiction from stark morality plays to escapist idylls and fantastical adventures, war films, horror flicks and monster movies, romances and romantic comedies, musicals, animated shorts and features, and often included odious dimensions that ignored or worked to justify the depredations of colonial powers. At the same time, a striking amount of film grasping at the actualities of Pacific worlds was shot as travelogues, documentaries, newsreels, propaganda shorts, and visual ethnographies. In Oceania's cinema history, fiction has frequently pretended to be non-fiction, and many putatively non-fictional films set in Oceania over the twentieth century relied on narrative conventions associated with fiction to frame Pacific worlds, sometimes consciously and explicitly, but at times inexplicitly and outside filmmakers' awareness.

For those not living within Oceania or those not rooted in home island communities, cinema may have played the leading role in how the region was perceived, often below the threshold of audience awareness, with profound implications for day-to-day encounters, tourism and island development projects, colonial administration, and economic, political, and social dynamics from local to global scales. The mechanisms or causal chains of such impacts may be hard to trace. However, in their simplest operations they might be identified as the way films, regardless of genre, provide audiences with an assemblage of visualized expectations about the character of Pacific worlds and their societies, persons, and natures. Seeing is, as the proverb goes, believing. The history of the cinema of Oceania thus opens a window on the shifting beliefs, values, and relational understandings of filmmakers and their communities of origin about Oceania over time; on the historically embedded conditions of production for individual films; on the persistence and transmission of particular aesthetic or conceptual regimes; on contemporary relationships to the various pasts constituted in and by cinema history; and finally on Indigenous and local responses to the representational practices of others, including the ultimate response of seizing control of the camera oneself.

Today, the interplay between the non-fictional and fictional continues to be a significant dynamic. An era of enduring colonial legacies and continuing decolonization is mirrored in film in the frequent disparity between reductionist, othering, and fantastical non-Indigenous visions of the Pacific and alternative visions of island homelands with multihued and variegated histories evident in potent Indigenous filmmaking since the 1990s. This chapter offers a brief account of the emergence of filmmaking in and of the Pacific Islands and illuminates the development, diversity, and size of this cinema over the twentieth century. It observes that a relatively small number of classic films, 'the usual suspects', have been the focus of discussion and many other films and even whole genres still wait to be interrogated by scholars and students alike. This chapter also characterizes and offers cross-genre examples of emerging, persistent, and changing visual and conceptual regimes evident over the course of twentieth-century film. Finally, in contrast with the cinema of Oceania that is the focus of most of this chapter, it concludes by encouraging energetic attention to the potent, transformative birth of an Oceanian Cinema in the work of Indigenous and local filmmakers in the last decades of the twentieth and early years of the twenty-first century.

Setting Light Sails

The history of filmmaking, an art of light and shadow, has deep roots. Since the invention of magic lanterns during the Renaissance, various technologies have taken advantage of a human cognitive and optical phenomena loosely referred to as the persistence of vision, in which the cognition of perception is tricked into accepting the succession of a certain number of still images per second as a continuous flow. As with popular children's flip books, the result is the mental impression of a series of images as being in motion. Shortly after the early nineteenth-century invention of photography using photo-sensitive chemicals, notably metallic salts on a polished metal or glass backing, the possibility of producing 'moving images' was in the air.

By the later decades of the nineteenth century, a number of technical developments including series photography by Edward Muybridge and celluloid film by Hannibal Goodwin and George Eastman, and innovations in camera and projection equipment to record and play back images on celluloid, established the conditions of possibility for filmmaking as a creative practice. For those interested in the technical history of this transformative art form, the early years of film history are full of extraordinary stories and developments. In this period of fast-moving invention, Thomas A. Edison and his assistant W.K.L. Dickson developed the kinetoscope and the Lumière brothers developed the cinématographe more or less simultaneously. In the wake of these technical breakthroughs, narrative filmmaking took off and all but instantaneously reached Oceania.

Only a few years after the inventors of film and film equipment emerged from garages and studios in New Jersey, Paris, and Berlin, camera-wielding filmmakers began descending upon global populations, including the Pacific Islands. Local newspapers recorded the excitement of early film screenings in Auckland in 1896 and Honolulu in 1897.[1] The same period saw moving picture cameras brought to bear on Pacific lives, though very little of this early footage survives.

---

[1] See M. Blythe, *Naming the Other: Images of the Māori in New Zealand Film and Television* (London: Metuchen, 1994); R.C. Schmitt, *Hawaii in the Movies 1998–1959* (Honolulu: Hawaiian Historical Society, 1988).

Filmmaking has never occurred in a historical vacuum. For more than a century, filmmakers and audiences have been entangled in the visualization of subjective human experiences in Pacific worlds, linked in dense webs of historical, political, commercial, and cultural forces. Contemporary filmmaking, increasingly propelled by the restorative visions of local and Indigenous artists and scholars, inherits an immense visual and conceptual baggage. Recent revisionist or transformative films can be seen as focal points for much of what has passed before. For Indigenous filmmakers the juxtaposition of past and present is particularly fraught, because the content of so much prior film is deeply entangled with histories of displacement, and because film has been used to support or justify colonial settlerism, the erasure of Indigenous voices and experiences, struggles over civil and political rights in the corrosive maelstrom of globalizing capitalism, the actions of colonial states, and the persistence of pre-emptory disregard by Euro-American or Asian transient visitors and tourists of the rights and persons of Indigenous and local communities across the region. Both Euro-American and Indigenous film traditions have been shaped by the entangled interests and intimacies of various colonial and local actors and institutions. The cinema of Oceania reflects, embodies, and perhaps amplifies the resulting tensions.

Individuals and collectives living in continental contexts far from Oceania's shores, and almost entirely unknowledgeable about the lived histories and experiences of the region's peoples, have almost certainly been shaped over time by their repetitive experiences of often seductive, seemingly available Pacific worlds. Films like *Blue Lagoon*, either the 1948 version or the 1980 remake – young Euro-American castaways come of age on a remote Fijian island where, aside from fears of supposedly dangerous natives intruding into the site of paradise, the characters' primary anxieties seem to be the potential for sexual encounter – were perhaps never merely entertainment. Non-Oceanian viewers may have been inclined, trajected, implanted with a seed of possibility for one day travelling as tourists to Fiji or elsewhere in an idealized, liberating, sexualized, and receptive Oceania. Such films may have shaped not just the motivation but the enactment and performance of the tourist experience in Oceania by providing ready-made ideas for how to see, feel, or act within Pacific landscapes and communities. To appreciate the potential force of such a prospective crafting of experience, one must consider all the screenings, not just of *Blue Lagoon*, but of many thousands of other films similarly set in Oceania and shown on the big screen or, later, television. Over the entire twentieth century, films often reinforcing or quoting one another in a dense intertextual web over countless viewings globally shaped the ways Oceania and Pacific worlds have been imagined within and outside the region, including sometimes shockingly persistent and durable representational tropes.

Tempest of Images: Navigating Film in the Entangled Histories of Pacific Worlds

From the late 1890s to the early twentieth century, the first films shot in Oceania were largely produced by itinerant film artists and scientific expeditions circumnavigating the globe. They frequently possessed a framework of actuality intended to bring distant places and peoples into the sensory experience of the filmmaker's home audience, for instance as travelogues focusing on scenes of the particularity of everyday experience. Even early narrative films drew on the conventions of 'being there' to frame their stories. And yet the earliest films from the region also cultivated an intense atmosphere of romantic otherness, introducing from the first an aura of unreality. This tension between actuality and unreality is among the most poignant conventions of early Pacific filmmaking and perhaps the most significant characteristic of the cinema of Oceania.

The intrusion of film in the region is evident by 1898 when one of Thomas Edison's film crews took a striking sequence of native Hawaiian youths diving. Now in the US Library of Congress *Kanaka Diving for Money, No. 2* and *Boys Diving HI6361* are among the absolute oldest surviving film footage from anywhere in Oceania. Subsequent footage by the Edison Company, taken by Robert Bonnie in Hawai'i in 1906, shows scenes of island infrastructure and social activities, including a long camera pan probably from a boat or canoe, from the wharf area of Aloha Towers to Waikiki, cross-cut with sequences of haole (non-Hawaiian) vacationers and Indigenous Hawaiians at the beach adorned in the bathing costumes of the day, including a short shot of an outrigger catching a wave into shore. Filmed in the immediate wake of the American occupation of Hawai'i, it is difficult to imagine a more prescient archetype for Oceania. Accompanying footage includes extraordinary shots of American military officers parading alongside settler families visualized as local, profoundly framing and naturalizing a colonial vision of the American presence in these islands focused on power rather than pleasure. Such images of Victorian release and Indigenous or local pleasure certainly communicated something to American theatre-goers and foreshadow the extent to which American-occupied Hawai'i would be entangled in tourism, militarism, and their linkages. Also notable in 1898, the Cambridge Anthropological Expedition to the Torres Strait led by Alfred

Court Haddon produced short films of Torres Strait persons' cultural practices, including traditional songs and dances.

Films made in the early years of the new century were also produced in Micronesia, New Guinea, and New Zealand. The film *Neu-Guinea* (1904–6) offers a view of life among the people of German-occupied New Guinea in the first years of the century. *Voelkenkunliche Filmdokumente aus der Sudsee* (1910) documents aspects of Pacific cultures under German control, including ceremonial dances in the Caroline Islands, Chuuk, and the Bismarck Archipelago. The latter part of this short film focuses on pottery, weaving, and fire making. In Aotearoa New Zealand, Alfred Whitehouse is thought to have filmed around ten shorts between 1898 and 1900. Of the Whitehouse footage, the oldest survivor is *The Departure of the Second Contingent for the Boer War* (1900) which, like Edison's 1906 footage, draws pointed attention to European colonial militarization in Pacific worlds. Other early films in Aotearoa New Zealand focused on documenting cultural dimensions of Māori practices; for instance *Poi Dances at Whakarewarewa* (1910) is a two-minute fragment showing *haka poi* (a dance performed with poi balls, small globes swung at the ends of cords of varying lengths). World War I interrupted film production in the Pacific, especially evident in the film history of New Zealand. Footage in the wake of the war including *Te Hui Aroha ki Turanga/Gisborn Hui Aroha* (1919), a record of the week-long Hui Aroha celebration in honour of the returning Māori Pioneer Battalion, again suggests the intersection of local worlds entangled with global military and colonial projects. Across the earliest films made in Oceania, a significant multi-polar project documenting otherness in cultural practice and personhood is perceptible, reanimating ongoing Euro-American fascination with cultural encounters, encouraging global travel, and supporting an ethos of colonial military presence.

Early film in Oceania also included narrative fiction. A nascent Hollywood literally inventing the American feature film quickly introduced storytelling in Pacific settings. *The Shark God* (1913) depicts a love affair between a chiefly woman and 'shark god' in Hawai'i. *Hearts Adrift* (1914), starring Mary Pickford, appears to have been the first film to use the female volcano sacrifice trope introduced in 1908 by Richard Tully's popular play *Birds of Paradise. Aloha Oe* (1915) and *Beachcomber* (1915) both wove narrative conventions around romantic sub-plots to suggest that Hawai'i was a receptive natural home for American persons. Daniel Defoe's *Robinson Crusoe*, based on the Pacific experiences of Alexander Selkirk, promptly appeared on the screen twice, in 1916 and 1917, suggesting that Hollywood's practice of remaking exceedingly similar films was a foundational development of filmmaking. For instance, D.W. Griffith's notorious *The Idol Dancer* (1920), in which a drunken beachcomber is resuscitated and sustained by a young woman in a 'South Sea' village, directly echoes scenes and themes audiences had just recently encountered in Harry Carey's *Brute Island*, also known as *McVeagh of the South Seas* (1914). Harry Carey starred in another Oceania-set film, a very early work by John Ford called *Wild Women* (1918), an extraordinary early genre mash-up in which a rodeo-winning cowboy on a bender in San Francisco sees a hula dance in a bar. Asleep that evening, he dreams of being cast away with his cowboy friends on a South Pacific island, kidnapped by the island's queen, and forced to marry her daughter, a hula-dancing princess. Clearly, early fictional features did not always play to now-familiar and expected tropes. Similarly curious, Fox studio's *Fallen Idol* (1919) is interesting for its plotline of a Hawaiian princess invited to visit California. The racial or ethnic prejudices of her elite hosts are revealed when one of their nephews begins to court her. The plot is interestingly echoed in Richard Oswald's 1933 German film, *Die Blume von Hawaii/Flower of Hawaii* imaging another Hawaiian ali'i woman working as a waitress in Paris before being forced home to marry the king despite her established love for an American officer.

Giants of early European cinema also brought their production teams to the region. In 1912, the famous French filmmaker George Méliès's brother Gaston and his wife Hortense-Louise de Mirmont produced *A Ballad of the South Seas* in Papara, Tahiti. Gaston Méliès also shot three films in Aotearoa New Zealand including *Hinemoa* (1913), *Loved by a Māori Chieftess* (1913), and *The River Whanganui* (1913). Unfortunately, little is known about these Méliès films. The negatives were shipped to the USA and processed there, and subsequently lost, reflecting the fragility and impermanence of early film negatives and positives. It is unlikely that any of these films was ever screened in the region. The same is not true for George Tarr's film, also titled *Hinemoa*, which premiered at Auckland's Lyric Theater in 1914 and is generally heralded as New Zealand's first feature film. Australian films in this period are notable for footage of Papua New Guinea and the Torres Strait, often now surviving only in fragments, but also include Raymond Longford and Lottie Lyell's pioneering *Mutiny on the Bounty* (1916), from which only stills survive, and their *A Māori Maid's Love* (1916) filmed 'on location', again lost. What we know of these films exemplifies the period's remarkable ambivalence towards the perceived danger of crossing cultural, social, and sexual boundaries. In the plot by Longford and Lyell, an unhappily married surveyor named Graham is sent to work in New Zealand, where he falls in love with a young Māori woman. They have a child together but the mother dies in childbirth. Caught between worlds, the father gives the baby to a Māori man named Jack who later kills Graham. Like most of the 'lost silents' of this early cinema period, what we know of these films is extrapolated from period newspapers, surviving still shots, and occasional interviews or film-makers' autobiographies. Anywhere from 75 to 90 per cent of all film produced before 1929 is thought to be no longer in existence.

Whether framed as actuality or fiction, early narrative films of Oceania show competing visions of the relationships between Pacific worlds, colonial and global audiences, and historical perspectives in an era of profound social, technological, and cultural change at the onset of the twentieth century. The fragmentary nature of surviving early cinema is a potent reminder that scholarship is sometimes faced with the necessity of extrapolation or recon-struction. Nevertheless, quite a bit of very early film about Oceania has not yet received scholarly attention. Few early feature films have been unpacked for their contributions to representational tropes, narrative conventions, or insight into Euro-American or Australian/Pākehā-New Zealander under-standings of Pacific worlds and their histories, cultures, and politics at the end of the nineteenth and the beginning of the twentieth centuries.

Filmmaking in the 1920s increasingly reflected the interests of escapist romance and adventure-seeking American and global audiences after the trauma of World War I, and often drew on popular novels reflecting a developing close relationship between Hollywood and American writers. American audiences flocked to *Adventure* (1925), a Jack London-inspired story of yet another Indigenous woman who saves a European colonist in the Solomon Islands from disease and failure. Other well-known literary works that found their way to film included Somerset Maugham's story 'Rain' which first appeared on the screen as *Sadie Thompson* (1928). Robinson Crusoe was re-filmed at least four times during this decade, in 1921, 1924, 1925, and 1927. While a literal viewing of Robinson Crusoe films would reveal an Africa-entangled story, the actual historical relationship of Defoe's work to Oceania shows how certain imaginaries of the primitive or the exotic are geographically collapsed, and how Oceania's histories are often used as source materials by Euro-American artists without contextual regard. Certain stories and representational tropes return again and again. *The Altar Stairs* (1922), *As a Man Desires* (1925), *Aloma of the South Seas* (1926), and Victor Fleming's notable *Hula* (1927) starring Clara Bow playing the audacious daughter of a wealthy American planter family in Hawai'i, well exemplify how some representational tropes had become established conventions by the mid-1920s. Interest in Pacific themes also motivated technical innovations in film production itself, including underwater and undersea cinematography. The American studio tale of the rapacious, dangerous, and morally ambiguous South Pacific pearl industry, *Vengeance of the Deep* (1923), attracted audiences with what is sometimes identified as the first-ever underwater action footage shot on a back lot. The title and much of the plot was interestingly reused in Australia in 1937, in a film that was eventually released as *Lovers and Luggers*.

For scholars, many of the most cited and discussed films entangled in Pacific worlds were realized in this decade. *Moana: A Romance of the Golden Age* (1926), *White Shadows in the South Seas* (1929), and *The Pagan* (1929) all made claims to actuality and to depictions of the lifeways of Pacific worlds for American and European audiences. This struck reviewers and film audiences of the day as wholly new. *Moana*, the follow-up and putative sequel to Robert Flaherty's *Nanook of the North* (1922), is generally credited as among the first documentaries. However, all three of these films utilized narrative conventions borrowed from novels and other media to introduce ideas of romance, colonial authority, religion and conversion, social norms and morality, and the question of human freedom. Films from New Guinea and Tahiti highlighted a relationship between romance, traditional authority, and the intervention of Western economies such as the pearling industry. Australian photographer Frank Hurley's actuality film *Pearls and Savages* (1921, revised for 1924) and his feature *Pearl of the South Seas* (1926) grapple with this industry by combining intimations of verisimilitude with seductive and beguiling doses of fiction. The fake documentary on the cultural practices around cannibalism staged by André-Paul Antoine and Robert Lugeon in the New Hebrides, *Chez les mangeurs d'hommes* (1928), is a good candidate for the most extreme pretence to the conventions of actuality while actually presenting an exploitative fiction. The colonial project of exploring putative frontiers in support of resource extraction is a major plot point in many of these early films and was certainly not confined to pearling. For instance *Sugar Cane Hunting* (1929), about the US Agricultural Department's 1928 botanical expedition to PNG, was suggested by Josh Bell as exemplary of cinematic narratives of 'scientific triumph and discovery'.[2] Also shot in Papua New Guinea, *Jungle Woman* (1926) – the story of the narrative hero's search for gold including romance with an Indigenous woman – is another

---

[2] J.A. Bell, 'Sugar plant hunting by airplane in New Guinea: a cinematic narrative of scientific triumph and discovery in the "remote jungles"', *Journal of Pacific History* 45:1 (2010), 37–56.

obvious example of an expedition and resource exploitation film pretending not to be a fictional feature.

New Zealand films of this period including *He Pito Whakaatu i te Hui i Rotorua* (1920), *He Pito Whakaatu i te Noho a te Māori i te Awa a Whanganui* (1921), and *The Māori as He Was* (1928) illustrate continuing Pākehā attempts to frame Māori communities within particularly historicized visions of past lifeways and prior golden ages and at times seem to co-present Māori communities and New Zealand's natural wonders as suitable for economic exploitation, including a growing tourist industry. *The Romance of Hine-Moa* (1927), a romantic feature by Gustav Pauli, offered another version of the Hinemoa legend in collaboration with the local community on location around Lake Rotorua. This film too is lost. Some films of this decade offered decidedly different perspectives. *He Murimuri Aroha ki nga Morehu o Maungapohatu* (1928) is about the Māori prophetic leader Rua Kenana (1896–1937), whose vision included economic independence from Pākehā, the return of Māori land, the departure of the Pākehā, and the coming of a Māori millennium.

Films made about the Pacific Islands in the 1930s show a continued expansion of technical and narrative sophistication. *Tabu: A Story of the South Seas* (1931) was the first Pacific film to win an Academy Award (for cinematography). The fiery death of the heroine in *Aloha* (1931) and, one year later, Dolores del Rio's death in King Vidor's *Bird of Paradise* (1932) profoundly entrenched the mythos of the volcano sacrifice for American and global audiences. *In the Wake of the Bounty* (1933) and *Mutiny on the Bounty* (1935), the third Bounty film and the first to use the text of the wildly popular historical fiction of Charles Nordoff and James Hall, demonstrated the growing fascination with the Bounty story. Interest in the Robinson Crusoe story remained strong, Douglas Fairbanks Sr starred in the comedy *Mr. Robinson Crusoe* (1932). A colourful 'talkie' version of Maugham's *Rain* (1932) appeared. *The Hurricane* (1937) for which Director John Ford won an Academy Award and *Typhoon Treasure* (1938), which had much the same plot, established a connection between themes of human corruption, in Tahiti and Papua New Guinea respectively, and redemption through the destructive and cleansing forces of nature. Films like *Typhoon Treasure* also mark the beginning of Hollywood's near monopoly of Pacific films. One of the most interesting facets of the first twenty-five years of filmmaking is that Pacific films were regularly filmed in the islands on which they were set. But by the end of the thirties and until the late twentieth century when relocalization, democratization, and Indigenization of Pacific filmmaking can be said to have begun, relatively fewer commercial films were actually produced on islands other than Kauai and Oahu. Why this came to pass is an interesting question. The answer is probably to be found in the production needs of the 'talkie'. While cameras are fairly portable, sound equipment made studio production a necessity for all but the best-budgeted films.

Films about Māori in the 1930s again often centred on representations of a putatively passing-away lifestyle of particular interest to European travellers, frequently recorded around Rotorua, including *The Māori: Everyone Bathes on Washing Day at Rotorua* (1930) and *Rotorua N.Z.* (1930). Australian expansion into Papua New Guinea was also recorded on film. *Guinea Gold – A Romance of Australian Enterprise* (1932), an account of gold mining in Papua which focuses on the mechanics of exploitation through discovery and transportation of machinery, and *Death Drums of New Guinea* (1932), which offers a record of the Kolle expedition up the Fly River in Papua and featuring the circumstances and details of a cultural practice identified in the film as a 'devil dance', illuminate the Australian penetration into Papua New Guinea as a search for riches and political dominion. Another film of this decade worth noting is *Île de Pâques* (1935), a record of the arrival of the Belgian naval ship *Mercato* at Rapa Nui to collect two well-known scientists including Alfred Métraux, which has additional interest for scholars outside Pacific studies as a somewhat prescient allegory for Europe's descent into the maelstrom of world war. The wildly influential *Island of Lost Souls* (1932), based on H.G. Wells' 1896 novel about a mad scientist's social and genetic experiments on a South Pacific island near Sāmoa (destined to be re-filmed many times including 1977, 1996, 2004, and 2018), and the utterly seminal *King Kong* (1933), whose home island was somewhere in the far South Pacific, are key early horror and monster films set in Oceania. As well as witnessing the continuing expansion of film genres including musicals and animations such as *Betty Boop: Bamboo Isle* (1932) or Disney's *Hawaiian Holiday* (1937), films of Oceania in the 1930s demonstrate the achieved solidity and persistence of themes of moral ambiguity, colonial exploitation, and narrative exploration of existential questions of human freedom and social bondage.

Features depicting the Pacific war in both fictional and documentary form began to appear on the silver screen as early as 1940 and continued to be a major Hollywood genre into the 1960s. Generally, these films are emotional thrillers like *Wake Island* (1942), whose function as propaganda was to rouse public opinion. These films tended towards abstraction and an absence of details. Islands took on new meanings, as did the vast distances between them in races for refuelling or repair stations, and submarine chases. *Wings over New Guinea* (1942) envisioned a typical day in the RAAF in Papua, during the war. *East Coast District Nurse* (1946) presented a day in the life of a rural nurse in remote coastal areas of New Guinea towards the war's end. *Jungle Patrol* (1944) illustrated the obstacles faced by an eight-man Australian patrol seeking to take a Japanese-held ridge. Such films documented war in the Pacific at ground level and sometimes featured Pacific Islanders not as 'others' in possession of exploitable resources, or focal points of sexual desire in Euro-American fantasies, but as invisible pawns in a vast conflict between Axis aggression and Allied liberation, particularly in American films of the period.

This is not the only way Islanders were refigured during the forties. During this decade, visual anthropology came into its own as an increasingly standard ethnographic tool for documenting the traditional lifeways of Pacific peoples. In the immediate wake of the war, American researchers formulated ethnographic films such as *The Polynesians of Kapingamarangi* (begun in 1947 and completed in 1950) and *Mokil* (1948) which depicted the fixed or unchanging cultural practices of two atoll peoples and promoted the idea of cultural preservation through documentation. Oceanic cinema to this point, with the exception of *Moana: A Romance of the Golden Age*, tended to focus on plot elements of change, cultural fluidity, and hybridity. Also, like *Moana*, these films depicted communities as highly socially ordered and idyllic rather than as tempestuous and full of the complexities of everyday human affairs and as essentially unchanging in time. In the forties, there was also a continuation of the Pākehā film thematic depicting Māori daily life with films such as *Māori Village* (1945) and *Māori School* (1947). Hollywood's mythical or historically fictitious Pacific presentation was also still apparent, for instance in another Maugham feature based on his story *The Moon and Sixpence* (1942). However, Maugham's themes of colonial ennui and moral backsliding were largely overshadowed by the events of the typhoon of war that utterly transformed many of Oceania's communities, societies, and politics. Among the most evident features of Oceania's cinema in this decade is the fundamental tension between the transformative war machine deployed on Pacific islands and post-war attempts to recapture a timeless cultural and social world despite all contrary evidence and lived experience.

In 1950, Samoan-German artist John Kneubuhl wrote and directed perhaps the first Indigenous feature film, *Damien*, about Father Damian's fatal mission on Molokai. The 1950s are also notable for the role of American nuclear testing in the Marshall Islands and for another pinnacle of classic island misrepresentation, *South Pacific* (1957). Indeed, at the time of the Bravo tests

(1954) most of the world's existing colour film stock was brought to the Marshall Islands. Much of this footage, at least 6,000 hours, was only declassified in 1997. Meanwhile, war films continued to proliferate during this decade. *Between Heaven and Hell* (1956) and *Mr. Roberts* (1955) exemplify this trend. *Between Heaven and Hell* featured staged assaults, amphibious landings, and epic combat with the entire Oahu-based Marine Corps as extras. *Mr. Roberts*, about a ship and a world gone mad, is notable for popularizing the concept of cargo cults. The war films of this decade suggest that filmmakers and audiences were unsated by the war and its propaganda and wanted to continue the exploration of World War II themes. In *From Here to Eternity* (1953), the old theme of Western corruption purified by the region's natural forces (as in *The Hurricane* or *Typhoon Treasure*) was reimagined, with the Japanese standing in as the 'force of nature' prefigured by the cleansing tide that sweeps over Burt Lancaster and Deborah Kerr on the glistening Oahu beach as they consummate their adultery. Hollywood was not the only film industry to explore a new ambivalence about Oceania and Pacific islands. Little noticed elsewhere, the American 1953 film *The Beast from 20,000 Fathoms* was translated into Japanese as *Genshi Kaijū ga Arawareru* (原子怪獣現れる), or *An Atomic Kaiju Appears*, and featured polar atomic experimentation awakening a titanic monster which makes its way to New York City in some pique at having its eldritch slumber disturbed. Japanese Atomic Kaiju promptly proliferated, with substantial connections to the former Japanese colonies in Micronesia which were home to *Gojira* (1954), *Rodan* (1956), and others. By the release of *Mosura* (1961), sub-plots included substantial representations of Pacific Islanders which both differed from yet echoed Euro-American representational tropes of primitivism, benign colonialism, and a desire for restoration of colonial ties between Japan and the islands severed by the Americans as an outcome of World War II.[3] Despite a vast output of Pacific fantasies and WWII plots, perhaps the freshest theme of the 1950s was a rising ambivalence about the moral and economic right of colonial or Western capital powers to seize Pacific resources. Potent discourses around decolonization, for instance, were seen in films such as *Colonialism: Ogre or Angel?* (1957), which examined British colonies on the eve of self-determination in the Pacific and elsewhere.

The political and cultural revolutions that jolted the 1960s around the globe and in Oceania transformed the practice of filmmaking and the study of film.

---

[3] A. Mawyer, 'Video irradient: Micronesia and monsters in post-war Japanese film', MA thesis, University of Chicago, 1999.

As a medium, film was itself radicalized and the decade was characterized by a renewed interest in redefining film conventions. At the same time, film audiences in the USA, France, and elsewhere, polarized by civil rights movements and the Vietnam and Algerian wars, became more sensitive to film messages. The study of film also underwent a profound change. Even as film critics and scholars took a new seriousness to their work, they found themselves called out by more traditional disciplines for lacking a rigorous method or theoretical grounding. In response, film scholars embraced literary theorists and began to articulate films as texts to be deciphered, decoded, deconstructed, or otherwise read. No doubt this was also spurred on by the growing presence of television. The 1960s also saw a resurgence of ethnographic film as smaller cameras and relatively portable sound recording equipment made filmmaking an affordable possibility for more researchers. War films like *PT-109* (1963) which depicted John Kennedy's war experiences in the Solomon Islands and spoofs like *Ensign Pulver* (1964), the sequel to *Mr. Roberts*, continued to be produced. The fascination with more intricate symbolic levels in World War II films also led to *In Harm's Way* (1965), a descendant of *From Here to Eternity* which further explored the concept of war as a purifying storm that redeems the Western obsession with political power and sexual guilt. The most popular Pacific feature of the decade was easily *Mutiny on the Bounty* (1962), which combines pre-war plot interests with post-war sensibilities. A new genre appeared on the scene in the mid-sixties when enthusiastic Californian audiences propelled the production of surf movies into Pacific locales in such films as *Endless Summer* (1965). While most films of the 1960s echo and reproduce narrative conventions and representational tropes about Oceania familiar across the first half of the twentieth century, each of the films above might be seen as radical in different ways, offering audiences in their moment of cinematic release a subtle subversion of American, or broadly Western, normative expectations about class, race, education, sexuality, human liberty, or the value of labour.

Western and Asian filmmakers and audiences in the 1970s continued to be fascinated by long-established narrative tropes of Pacific worlds. The most important development in this decade was the birth of an Indigenous film aesthetic and the emergence of an early cohort of Pacific Islander filmmakers in Aotearoa, Hawai'i, and beyond. A number of the Micronesian Transition Series films, which began in 1969 and focused on the changing lifeways of Micronesian peoples, emphasizing the persistence of tradition, were produced by Micronesian writers and directors. Although none of these filmmakers appears to have produced films for a commercial audience, Māori director Barry Barclay came onto the global scene in 1974 with his television series about Māori traditions, *Tangata Whenua*. In New Zealand feature films, a more openly political film agenda was not limited to young Māori directors as in Pākehā director Roger Donaldson's *Sleeping Dogs* (1977) which brought Māori issues to mainstream film. In the USA, John Kneubuhl came into prominence with the success of *Hawaii 5-O*, among his other work writing and directing for Hollywood. Films from newly independent nations were also an important dynamic. Dennis O'Rourke's first film, *Ileksen: Politics in Papua New Guinea* (1978), recorded the exuberance of independence and inaugurated a new age of contemporary film ethnographies. Similarly, *Iu Mi Nao: Solomon Islands Regain Independence* (1979) examined a critical juncture in political history through Islander comments, song, dance, and cultural performance.

In the 1980s, O'Rourke developed a new, reflexive ethnography in documentary film. *Yap: How Did You Know We'd Like TV?* (1982), *Half Life: A Parable of the Nuclear Age* (1986), and *Cannibal Tours* (1987) reframed Oceania's representation in documentary film. This decade also marked further explorations by Indigenous filmmakers, especially in New Zealand where film equipment was relatively easily accessed. Merata Mita's *Bastion Point* (1981) and *Patu!* (1983) both appropriated news images to create alternative readings of transformative national events, as when the Bastion Point protesters sought to regain valuable land in Auckland and occupied the site for many months before being removed by police. *Patu!* recorded how local and global sociopolitical contradictions and tensions were made visible in the visit to Aotearoa of the South African rugby team in the years prior to the end of apartheid. With her film *Mauri* (1988), Mita and other Māori directors like Lee Tamahori, after a series of critically acclaimed commercials, and Barry Barclay with *Ngati* (1987), emerged as feature directors. Feature films recentring culturally grounded visions of Melanesia also date to this decade. Australian Chris Owen's *Jakupa* (1981) is the story of a village man from Papua whose art takes him abroad to Australia. Writer and director Albert Toro's *Tukuna* (1984) depicted the tension between tradition and personal ambition and how the resulting pressures can turn a young man to grog. Both films are in Tok Pisin and reached global audiences. *Tukuna* offers a Papuan play on the universal theme of alienation from one's elders and their expectations. The eighties were also notable for the increased quality, availability, and affordability of video equipment. This boom was particularly notable in Hawai'i, where a large group of videographers emerged as a potent force of local political expression – a bellwether for events occurring throughout the Pacific. Looking back on this period, Rotuman filmmaker Vilsoni Hereniko noted that in Hawai'i the documentary had become 'a weapon for change among political activists and cultural stewards'.[4]

In a famous passage at the end of the preface to the *Philosophy of Right*, Hegel noted that the owl of Minerva only takes flight at dusk.[5] John Patrick Shanley's holographic and virtuosic deployment of over a century of Hollywood conventions and cinematic tropes in *Joe vs. the Volcano* (1990) suggested at the very outset of the decade that – like a body of scholarly activity whose synthetic analytical coherency suggests that dusk has arrived – the American and non-local or non-Indigenous cinema of the Pacific region was a finished project. A number of films over the 1990s suggest an era of fashionable retro, resurrecting films from Oceania's cinematic past. These include the war movie genre in *McHale's Navy* (1996) and *Up Periscope* (1996); mythical Oceania and classic concerns with governance, power, order, and colony in *The Island of Dr. Moreau* (1996) in its fourth major filming; Kevin Costner's post-apocalyptic and post-Indigenous Oceania in *Waterworld* (1995), or his problematically historicalish fiction *Rapa Nui* (1994). The decade culminated in the perhaps never-far-from-mind settler colonial fantasy of Oceania's islands as terra nullius, empty lands that can be blank slates for the establishment of Euro-American cultural practices and an ethos of individual, personal development and self-fulfilment in Tom Hanks's massively successful *Castaway* (2000) as the first moment of the new millennium.

Meanwhile, in the period bracketed by Tom Hanks's *Joe vs. the Volcano* and *Castaway*, the assertive, visionary, restorative, indigenizing, and localizing work of Pacific Islander filmmakers, notably Barry Barclay, *Te Rua* (1991), Lee Tamahori, *Once Were Warriors* (1994), and Sima Urale, *O Tamaiti* (1997) furthered their intersecting project of challenging, recasting, and inverting customary conventions of the cinema of Oceania, and, by creating new globally circulating representations to stand in their place, began decolonizing minds. In Barclay's thinking, this process was one where filmmakers were responsible for taking control of one's own images in a potently place-based, place-addressing, yet community-transcending manner.[6] By the end of the 1990s, and in the films of the 2000s, it appears that the fundamental

---

[4] See V. Hereniko, 'Representations of cultural identities', in K.R. Howe, R.C. Kiste, and B.V. Lal (eds.), *Tides of History* (Honolulu: University of Hawai'i Press, 1994), 406–34; V. Hereniko 'Representations of Pacific Islanders in film and video', *Documentary Box* 14 (1999), 18–20.
[5] G.W.F. Hegel, *The Philosophy of Right*, trans. A. White (Indianapolis: Hackett, 2015).
[6] B. Barclay, *Our Own Image* (Auckland: Longman Paul, 1990).

tension in the cinema of Oceania had become a dynamic struggle between colonial, decolonial, and anti-colonial sensibilities, imaginaries, and stances, and that producing a film must be considered as much a political as an artistic act.

The twenty-first century is beyond the historical scope of this chapter. Nevertheless something extraordinary is emerging in the wake of the local and Indigenous artists, activists, and filmmakers whose work is a notable feature of Oceania's cinema since the 1990s. The global success and reception of *Whale Rider* (2002) made it clear that the next generation of non-Indigenous but often local filmmakers like Pākehā director Niki Caro, working with a novel by Māori author Witi Ihimaera, would fundamentally realign the camera's eye from the island out, rather than into the region via the Euro-American continental gaze. This alignment of narrative convention, ethical positionality on the question of who should control and have agency over the stories being told, and representational orientation towards Oceanian people's own views of themselves was evident again in the romantic comedy *Sione's Wedding* (2006) by another Pākehā director, Chris Graham. A rapidly growing number of new voices hailing from diverse Oceanian communities also arrived in the early 2000s as visible in films including Hereniko's *The Land Has Eyes* (2004) and Taika Waititi's *Boy* (2010) or *Hunt for the Wilderpeople* (2016) as a growing number of Indigenous directors cut their teeth in TV, films shorts, art school, and professional practice. In retrospect 2014 appears to have been a watershed year with Tusi Tamasese's *The Orator: O Le Tulafale* (2014), Toa Fraser's *Dead Lands* (2014), and Himiona Grace's *The Pa Boys* (2014). The continuing career and influence of Taika Waititi and the possibility of extending Māori and Pākehā sensibilities into ever greater generic breadth was also evident with *What We Do in the Shadows* (2014). While Waititi is not the first Pacific Islander filmmaker to make it big in Hollywood, there is something strikingly different about his relationship to Oceania and its historical and contemporary traumas and concerns, even in a science fictional alternative universe, like *Thor: Ragnarok* (2017) where allusions to the great Pacific garbage patch and the dispossession of Indigenous inhabitants of far-flung worlds speak to Oceania's histories. Given the breadth, range, embeddedness, emergent conventions, orientations, and alignments of this new period, it seems time to note that something like an Oceanian Cinema has emerged with a restorative re-mediation of representational futures for Pacific worlds. Beyond the scope of this chapter, the aesthetics, ethics, techniques, protocols, and filmic sensibilities that constitute an Oceanian Cinema will continue to be an immensely productive engagement.

An Ocean of Cinema Histories

Most of us have deep, nuanced, and intimate relationships with moving images rooted in our earliest youth. These relationships are both affective and perspectival, conceptual and experiential, motivated and motivating. They are ways of seeing, thinking, feeling, and acting in the world. They are not easily identified simply by accounting for patterns in the kinds of stories, ways of storytelling, and embedded beliefs and values constituted by a cinema, in this case the cinema of Oceania. The theatres which reshaped and mediated downtown areas in islands and communities across the region; the social histories and cultural practices of viewing films in particular Oceanian communities and contexts; the lived experiences of communities in which films were made; the complexities of participation for the often little-credited Pacific Islander actors whose presence in time-and-place was captured in films, both those produced 'on location' or in studios over the century; the accidental or contingent documentation of architecture or civic institutions or the ebbs and flows of actual social life, or even the natural land- and seascapes captured in films shot on location; the construction and actualization of more or less realistic or fantastic visions of Pacific worlds by producers and their hundreds or thousands of collaborators in the realization of any given film; the social and cultural conditions, broadly conceived, which underlie and made possible the drafting of particular scripts with particular themes, visualized in particular ways in particular decades by particular filmmakers, towards particular ends; all of these, among others, could profitably be pursued in an ever-expanding historical engagement with films in and of Oceania, including reflection on the role of cinema in the constitution of the contemporary.

This chapter offers only one path or navigation across the fluid history of twentieth-century film, with the goal of providing a broader sense of the range of genres, the number and kind of films that deserve critical attention, and the conceptual and visual context in which a twenty-first-century Oceanian Cinema has emerged in response to the twentieth-century cinema of Oceania. At the same time, for students of twentieth-century Pacific histories, there is an extraordinary potential in old film to make sense of the power of representational regimes and the effects of such power in and upon Pacific worlds.

This chapter is organized temporally by decade for convenience only. Alternative ways of organizing particular constellations of films undoubtedly exist. The characteristics and conventions of the cinema of Oceania are as varied as currents in the sea. However, it seems clear that a set of thematic plot elements, character types, constructed social spaces, aesthetic regimes, moral and ethical conventions, enduring motivations, and social politics has remained consistent over more than a century – a particular combination of tropes wholly distinct from the cinemas of other regions and with which many of us may already be consciously or unconsciously familiar.

Romanticism and pastoral themes are evident from the earliest silent films of the twentieth century to the present, including a dark romanticism that might be seen as something like the Oceanic Gothic as in *Rain*, or *Sadie Grey*. Somewhat more difficult to tease out but still relatively common is a filmic summoning of classicism, a framing of Pacific worlds as something like a Golden Age comparable to classical Greece or Rome. The various *Bounty* mutiny films, saturated with fantasies of Tahiti as seen through the imagined eyes of eighteenth-century British sailors, remain perhaps the best examples. Similarly the representing of Pacific worlds as natural laboratories, or sites of scientific knowledge production, also cuts through many different genres and is found not only in documentaries and ethnographies but even in the horror genre, such as *The Island of Dr. Moreau*, or even Reginald le Borg's comprehensive horror mashup *Voodoo Island* (1957, re-released as *Silent Death* in 1963). Beyond the kinds of representational frameworks identified by Smith or already frequently discussed in the existing literature, there is a wide variety of other representational frames that have become tropes or conventions, such as Pacific naturalism (in which Pacific worlds, their human communities notwithstanding, are nature spaces, spaces where the human is not, or where humans are close to being natural objects); ecologicalism (wherein Pacific worlds have been fostered in an ecological balance, frequently maintained by human agency, which is easily disturbed leading to catastrophes like typhoons, volcanic eruptions, or sinking islands); instrumental naturalism (representations of nature as ready-made or ready-to-hand); insular marginalism (representations of islands as disjointed, distant, lost in a far sea, fragile, hyper-bounded); insular determinism (representations of the limits of human agency in the face of island nature, sometimes including human nature on islands). These and others join moralism, sacralism, sexuality and sensualism, primitivism, exoticism, escapism, the teratological, and militarism as common representational frameworks in the history of Oceania's cinema.

While the narrative framework of any given film may be centred around one or only a couple of key representational tropes, as the frame and engine so to speak of the narrative, many films in the cinema of Oceania frequently draw upon a number of these patterns in often familiar intersections. Constituted as particular ways of perceiving, conceiving, experiencing, and responding to Pacific worlds, these frames have been anchors for representations of Oceania in film, institutionalized over time as conventions, and influenced audiences globally and locally. From Edison's cinematographers' footage in 1898 or 1906 to Tom Hanks's perfect fantasy of settler colonial freedom (a receptive island, no Islanders, and only one's own baggage and volleyball for company), one might argue that Euro-American filmmakers have more or less explicitly sought to surveille, understand, and thereby control Pacific peoples and places by presenting, representing, and promoting the entailments of those representations. Critical questions might include how film representations of Pacific Islanders and locales upheld the self-legitimating logics of the region's colonial regimes, how much Oceanian people's experiences of themselves has been affected by the same processes that fuel tourist imaginations, or how film-mediated portrayals have influenced economic realities. For scholars, much work remains to be done on the ways in which cinema has inherited, reproduced, resisted, contested, innovated, transformed, rejected, and renewed representations of Pacific worlds. Today, however, Indigenous and local filmmakers in Oceania are reforming, revising, responding to, or remediating these representations as they craft an Oceanian Cinema in the twenty-first century.

43

The Visual and Performing Arts
of the Pacific

A Historical Overview

ADRIENNE L. KAEPPLER

The many layers of traditional knowledge and recorded history of Pacific arts interact with politics and change that bring us into the twenty-first century. An author today faces questions of balance among Indigenous art content and its origins; Western history as recorded by Europeans, Americans, and others; Western artists and modernism; and Indigenous contemporary artists and intangible knowledge.[1]

Two of the first problems are how the term *art* can be used for cultures that do not have a similar concept, and what art consists of. I shall address architecture, sculpture, textiles and clothing, body art and ornaments, and other visual arts, as well as music, dance, and poetry, using my earlier concepts about art and aesthetics. In Pacific Island cultures, traditional arts are not separated from each other or from daily or ceremonial life, and most Pacific languages do not have Indigenous words or concepts for art as a separate category. A perspective that makes the term *Pacific art* meaningful is the following: Pacific arts encompass cultural forms that result from creative processes that use or handle with skill words, sounds, movements, materials, scents, or spaces in such a way that they formalize the non-formal. Aesthetics can then be characterized as culturally specific, evaluative ways of thinking about such cultural forms. Some basic concepts, skill, and indirectness help us understand these cultural forms. Indirectness is highly developed and culturally valued; skill or ability is necessary to carry it out. Hidden or veiled

---

Parts of this chapter are based on and excerpted from my earlier writings on the subject, where they are fully illustrated. See Kaeppler et al., *L'art océanien*; Kaeppler, *The Pacific Arts of Polynesia and Micronesia*.

[1] For general surveys of Paciific Island art forms, see A.L. Kaeppler, C. Kaufman, and D. Newton, *L'art océanien* (Paris: Citadelles & Mazenod, 1993); and A.L. Kaeppler, *The Pacific Arts of Polynesia and Micronesia* (Oxford: Oxford University Press, 2008).

meanings are unravelled layer by layer until the metaphors on which they are based can be understood. An object, ceremonial complex, or perform-ance cannot be fully apprehended or understood in isolation, but must be related to underlying social and cultural ideas and evaluated according to Indigenous aesthetic principles. In this chapter, I address these concerns, give an overview of Pacific art as it changed over time, elaborate on some exemplary works of art as found today in museums of the world, and give examples of contemporary use of traditional arts.

Europeanized written and depicted history begins with journals and illustrations of ship captains and artists who recorded what they saw as well as they could. Among the first were Spanish, Dutch, and British explorers. The Dutch voyagers Jacob Le Maire and Willem Schouten visited Tonga in 1616 and published an illustration with a double-hulled canoe; Dutch explorer Abel Janszoon Tasman from 1642 to 1644, as part of the Dutch East India Company, was apparently the first European to sight Tasmania and Aotearoa New Zealand; and Dutch West India Company explorer Jacob Roggeveen, on an exploring trip to find Terra Australis, located some of the Society Islands and landed on Easter Island in 1722. The illustrations in his book show the level of fantasy that pervaded this part of the world! Even earlier was the lesser-known Spaniard Álvaro de Mendaña, who landed on and mapped some of the Marquesas Islands and the Solomon Islands in 1595. These early contacts recorded objects such as ceremonial sites, houses, canoes, clothing, and even tattoos, but no objects or works of art can be traced to them.

The earliest corpus of Pacific objects that can be identified today consists of some 2,000 pieces collected during the three Pacific voyages of Captain James Cook from 1768 to 1780 and the illustrations that derive from these voyages. Many of these objects are today considered important art objects to European owners and museums because they were among the first such objects brought to Europe and are 'pristine' (in that European influence in their production or use is minor or absent).[2] They were received into eighteenth-century enlightened Europe as 'artificial curiosities' (objects made by people) as distinguished from 'natural curiosities' (things made by God) and described in glowing terms. The carving was 'singular', the cloth made of bark 'curious', the incising 'ingenious'.

---

[2] A.L. Kaeppler, 'Artificial Curiosities': Being an Exposition of Native Manufactures Collected on the Three Pacific Voyages of Captain James Cook, R.N., at the Bernice Pauahi Bishop Museum, January 18, 1978–August 31, 1978, ed. Museum Bernice P. Bishop (Honolulu: Bernice P. Bishop Museum, 1978); R. Joppien and B. Smith, The Art of Captain Smith's Voyages, 4 vols. (Oxford: Oxford University Press, 1985–7).

Other collections from the eighteenth and the first half of the nineteenth century from which at least some objects can be identified include those from Henry Wilson and George Keate of the British East India Company, whose ship *Antelope* was wrecked in Palau in 1781; Wilson and Keate, accompanied by Prince Lee Boo, took numerous artefacts back to England, now in the British Museum. George Vancouver followed Cook's path (1791–5). The Spaniard Alessandro Malaspina, a Tuscan in the service of the Spanish Navy, visited Guam, Aotearoa New Zealand, Australia, and Tonga (1789–94), and some of his objects are in the Museo de América, Madrid. Louis Antoine de Bougainville, the first Frenchman to make significant discoveries in the Pacific (1766–9), took possession of Tahiti for France, even though it had been visited by British explorer Samuel Wallis on HMS *Dolphin* the previous year. Objects collected by von Krusenstern and Langsdorff (1803–6), Lisiansky (1803–6), Kotzebue (1815–18), and Bellingshausen (1819–21) are in St Petersburg; and pieces from Dillon (1827–8), Freycinet (1817–20), Duperrey and Collet (1822–5), and Dumont d'Urville (1826–9, 1837–40) can also be traced. George Byron and others on HMS *Blonde* (1824–6) collected many important objects that are now in numerous collections, including the Pitt Rivers Museum, Oxford. Whaling voyages starting in 1801 brought important objects to the United States of America, which can be found in the Peabody Museum, Salem, and other maritime museums in the northeast United States; and the large collection from the US Exploring Expedition under Charles Wilkes (1838–42) is in the Smithsonian Institution, Washington, DC, and in other collections to which items were dispersed. Unexpected early pieces can be found in surprising places, such as the collection of the private traveller Gordon Augustus Thompson from the 1830s, now in Belfast and the Solomon Islands collection made by Julius L. Brenchley in Maidstone, Kent. Important collections were made by early Christian missionaries: many, assembled by the London Missionary Society, are now in the British Museum, and those made by the American Board of Commissioners for Foreign Missions are now in the Bishop Museum, Honolulu, and scattered in the eastern United States.

Collections from the second half of the nineteenth and the twentieth century saw a whole new series of collectors – interested travellers, more missionaries, collectors for museums, and anthropological fieldworkers, as well as German expeditions and trading firms such as Godeffroy and other independent traders. The Hamburg Scientific Foundation (Hamburgische Wissenschaftliche Stiftung, 1908–10), coordinated by Georg Christian Thilenius, chartered the ship *Peiho* and travelled widely in the Pacific.

The results included at least thirty-one published volumes and 15,000 objects. Anthropologists stayed for significant periods of time and carried out detailed research, which included important Indigenous knowledge about Micronesia and Melanesia/New Guinea. The Hamburg-based Godeffroy Museum obtained large collections from Fiji and Sāmoa, most of which are now in Leipzig, while the collections made by Krämer in Sāmoa, Arning in Hawai'i, and others are in the Berlin Museum and scattered in Germany. The German colonization of parts of the Pacific resulted in large collections, especially from Micronesia.

The Reishek collection of Māori artefacts is in Vienna. Collections from this period in France include the Hawaiian collection of Ballieu, French consul in Honolulu. Collections in Britain include those of Anatole von Hugel, Sir Arthur Gordon, and Alfred Maudsley (from Fiji and elsewhere), now in the University Museum of Archaeology and Anthropology, Cambridge (Figure 43.1). Sir George Grey's New Zealand Māori collection is in the British Museum, as are collections made in Easter Island on HMS *Topaze* in 1868 and by Katherine Routledge in 1914. Collections made by W.J. Thomson on the USS *Mohican* in Easter Island in 1886 are in the Smithsonian Institution, Washington, DC, as are collections made by Albert Steinberger in Sāmoa in the 1870s.

Although New Guinea was sighted by early Dutch and Spanish ship captains, exploration did not really take place until the 1870s, and the first European to carry out sustained research was the Russian explorer and anthropologist Nicholai Mikloukho-Maclay, also from the 1870s.

In their new European and American contexts, these eighteenth- and nineteenth-century objects floundered without theoretical frames, finding their ways to cabinets of curiosities, natural history collections, and curio shops, waiting to be 'discovered' another time by those who might regard them with more dignity and honour – indeed, waiting to be recontextualized into alien visions and aesthetic systems, as their own Indigenous contexts were puzzling unknowns.

During the twentieth century, important collections were made by museums and anthropologists, who began to consider the objects, contexts, and Indigenous knowledge as art. Bishop Museum expeditions, notably the Bayard Dominick Expeditions to the Society Islands, Marquesas, Tonga, and the Austral Islands, as well as the Mangareva Expedition, yielded important collections and monographs. The expedition to Easter Island by Lavachery and Métraux from the Brussels Museum and the Musée de l'Homme resulted in collections and monographs. John L. Young of Tahiti and New

Figure 43.1 Exhibit case of Fijian ivory ornaments acquired by Anatole von Hugel, Sir Arthur Gordon, and Alfred Maudslay.

Zealand, Eric Craig of New Zealand, and J.S. Emerson of Hawai'i sold their collections to museums in Hawai'i, New Zealand, and elsewhere. Other collectors who never travelled to the Pacific, such as Ratton, Oldman, Fuller, Beasley, and Hooper, collected Pacific objects in Europe, and traded and sold them, and they can now be found in museums in Britain, Europe, Australia, Aotearoa New Zealand, the United States, and Japan.

Some of these objects, resold over and over, are also in various private collections in Paris, London, Geneva, New York, and elsewhere. Polynesian objects are today considered the Rolls Royce of collections, sought after and expensive, and even 'required' to add diversity to art collections, while New Guinea pieces are admired and often collected because of their 'savage strangeness', particularly by twentieth-century modernists. Some collectors are interested in Pacific objects for their own sake, admiring them for their form and rarity, rather than for their original use or meaning. These collections have been studied and interpreted by academic fieldworkers and armchair anthropologists, as well as artists and art historians, primarily in Britain, France, Germany, and the United States. More recently, they have become objects of cultural patrimony and ethnic identity, increasingly important to Pacific Islanders themselves. Efforts to repatriate them to local museums and cultural centres have been successful in Hawai'i, Aotearoa New Zealand, and French Polynesia, where they are treated as historical valuables to be admired by visitors and venerated by their makers' descendants.

Exhibitions of Pacific Art

Early public displays of Pacific art took place in the Trocadero, Paris; Ethnographic Museum, Berlin; British Museum, London; Smithsonian Institution, Washington, DC; there were also presentations in private galleries in New York and Paris. The earliest international exhibition of Pacific art with which I am familiar was 'Arts of the South Seas' at the Museum of Modern Art, New York, in 1946. This resulted in the widely used book of the same title and was followed by a similar exhibit by Wingert, 'Art of the South Pacific Islands', at the De Young Museum, San Francisco, in 1953. Large-scale, comprehensive exhibits include 'The Art of the Pacific Islands' at the National Gallery of Art, Washington, DC, in 1979, and the 2018–19 exhibit 'Oceania' at the Royal Academy, London, and Quai Branly, Paris. The only truly international one was the 1979 National Gallery of Art exhibit, as objects from the 1946 exhibit were primarily from North America, and those in the 2018 exhibit included objects primarily from Europe. Along the way were large- and small-scale exhibits on specific subjects, such as objects from Cook's voyages, New Zealand Māori, New Ireland, Hawai'i (featherwork), and Fiji. These exhibitions have now become so expensive that it is unlikely that many more will occur.

The Arts of the Pacific

Some of the earliest Pacific art is the archaeologically defined cultural tradition known as the Lapita cultural complex, having spread from the Bismarck Archipelago (New Ireland, New Britain) along the coast of New Guinea, through much of Melanesia, and into Polynesia. Lapita, named after the site in New Caledonia where it was first identified, is distinguished by earthenware ceramics with a characteristic decorative system. It is the most important prehistoric cultural tradition for understanding the prehistory of art in much of the Pacific. Over time and space, the ancestral cultures diversified and eventually formed the historic cultural complexes now grouped together under the terms Melanesia ('black islands', which includes closely related New Guinea), Micronesia ('small islands'), and Polynesia ('many islands'). These areas are the focus of this chapter.

Pacific art encompasses art forms resembling those elsewhere in the world, and for convenience I divide them into five overlapping categories: the organization of space and architecture; sculpture and carving traditions; fibre and textile arts; body ornamentation and scent; and the oral, musical, and movement arts. Along the way, vignettes of specific artistic forms in various cultures will be presented. For a comprehensive overview of art in numerous Pacific cultures, see the book by Kaeppler, Kaufmann, and Newton (1993, 1994, 1997, in French, German, and English), and also the series of books published by the Pacific Arts Association, beginning in 1983. A similar encyclopaedia of music and dance has been produced by Kaeppler and Love.[3]

Many Pacific creations were meant to endure, while others were made to be used once and discarded. Time and energy were freely lavished on objects such as sculptures and fine mats in Polynesia that were to be passed as heirlooms from generation to generation. In contrast, in New Guinea the time-consuming construction of men's houses and the fabrication of ritual objects made within included huge masks that made a spectacular appearance and were shortly after discarded. To understand these uses, an exploration of the inter-relationships of the arts is useful. In examining the layout of space, for example, we need to explore how one moves in space, what one wears, carries, or says while moving, and how these elements change according to contexts and activities.

Ceremonial Sites, Monuments, Architecture

In 1722, when Roggeveen chanced upon Rapa Nui (Easter Island), large stone statues lined parts of the shoreline. In 1768–79, Cook's artists depicted houses in the Society Islands, Aotearoa New Zealand, Tonga, New Caledonia, Vanuatu, and Hawai'i. In 1781, Keate recorded Palauan houses and village layouts. So-called first-contact visitors to New Guinea marvelled over the

---

[3] A.L. Kaeppler and J.W. Love, *Australia and the Pacific Islands* (New York: Garland, 1998); Kaeppler et al., *L'art océanien.*

The Visual and Performing Arts

elaborate A-frame houses, and even the Indigenous Society Islands artist Tupaia drew a community/ceremonial house in 1769–70. These early illustrations, along with later photographs and more than a century of archaeological and ethnographic research, have been important for our knowledge and understanding of how Pacific Islanders conceptually organized their worlds and how they physically manipulated their environment. Architectural forms and ritual areas can be considered the aesthetic organization of space as well as major works of art.

Micronesia has variety and richness in architecture and spatial layout. In the Mariana Islands, architectural sites (some dating from 1000 CE) consisting of double rows of megalithic columns called *latte* with upturned hemispherical capstones were the bases for large wooden structures.

The most dramatic site in Micronesia and possibly the whole Pacific is on the southeast side of Pohnpei. This is the ceremonial complex of Nan Madol, situated in a shallow lagoon and made up of ninety-two natural and artificial islets related to specialized activities. The islets are separated by waterways navigable by canoe. Most of the walls are made of huge basalt boulders and prismatic basalt columns that were quarried miles inland and ferried by sea to the site. At its zenith, 1000–1500 CE, Nan Madol housed as many as 1,000 people. The basalt columns were laid horizontally in stacks to form the outside retaining walls; shorter columns were laid perpendicularly between them – a type of construction known as headers and stretchers. Inside the walls are stone pavings, platforms, and house foundations. Associated with the ruins are large rocks for pounding *sakau* (kava) for ceremonial drinking. Nan Madol was the seat of the Sau Deleur dynasty, then the ruling line of Pohnpei, and formed an 81-hectare political and religious centre. It was composed of two main areas intersected by a waterway: a religious centre, where religious leaders lived and major tombs were located, and an administrative centre, where royal dwellings and ceremonial areas were located. A large seawall protected the entire area from the sea. The most impressive islet is Nan Dauwas, the site of a royal tomb with a large crypt and platforms, with retaining walls 7.5 metres high upswept at the corners and entryways. Protected by a seawall 4.5 metres high and 10.5 metres thick, Nan Dauwas was orientated on an east–west axis, used by navigators to indicate points of the rising and setting sun.

The islet of Pahn Kadira was the residence of the Sau Deleur and his immediate family, with houses for his visitors. It was outlined with stacked prismatic basalt walls some 4.5 metres high with an entryway 4 metres wide. The Sau Deleur's own house had a courtyard of interior walls 2.4 metres thick. Idehd islet was the main religious centre, where agricultural rituals were held.

A great salt water eel, the medium between the people and the Sau Deleur's god, lived on this islet. At the end of certain rituals, a sacrificial turtle was given to it – which, if accepted, indicated that all was well on Pohnpei. Peinering islet was the centre for making and storing coconut oil used for ceremonial anointing of living and dead and for lighting. A priest responsible for the production of this oil lived on the islet. Archaeological investigations have found Pohnpei-made pottery, shell adzes, other tools, and shell ornaments.

The importance of Nan Madol has been internationally recognized, and it is now a UNESCO heritage site. A similar prehistoric ceremonial complex, Lelu, dated c. 1200 to 1400 CE, is found 550 kilometres to the east, on Kosrae.

In New Guinea, the conceptual organization of space is quite different and incorporates the geography of mountains and river systems. Large ceremonial men's houses that dominated the landscape were characteristic. The houses, masks, and ceremonies of the Papuan Gulf area were documented by F.E. Williams in the early twentieth century, and many in-depth anthropological studies have been carried out since then. Examples of the masks and ritual objects have been collected, as well as entire houses, and reside in museums. A large collection of masks and other ceremonial materials, and thousands of photographs, amassed by A.B. Lewis, is now in the Field Museum, Chicago (Figures 43.2 and 43.3). From 1909 to 1913 he collected thousands of objects, which, along with other collections purchased at the same time, now amount to some 30,000 objects, comprising one of the largest Melanesian collections in the world. Other collections from New Guinea and the nearby areas of New Ireland and New Britain are in Berlin, Hamburg (Figure 43.4), and other German museums. The large A-frame architecture has been retained in community buildings, such as the Parliament building.

The Polynesian organization of space is different again and includes vertical ordering of the sea, land, and skies. Settlement patterns, spatial orientation, shape of ceremonial sites, height, and the alignment of houses and their internal divisions reveal relationships between gods and people, between chiefs and commoners, and between men and women. Fijian villages are divided between seaward areas (considered chiefly) and landward areas (considered common), and houses repeat this spatial orientation. In the analysis of houses in Moala, Fiji, Marshall Sahlins notes that the village was 'divided down the long axis into a "chiefly side", traditionally set parallel to the sea, and a "common side" towards the inland'.[4] Each end was associated

---

[4] M. Sahlins, *Moala: Culture and Nature on a Fijian Island* (Ann Arbor: University of Michigan Press, 1962), 32.

Figure 43.2 Four men wearing Semese masks, Kerema, Papua New Guinea, 1 March 1911.

with a side, so that the chief of the house was associated with one end and one side, which Sahlins argues is a modelling system for dual organization, tripartite organization, and the four-class system of the Moalan social order. Godhouses (*bure kalou*) had striking pointed roofs. Images of the gods and pieces of barkcloth, through which the gods descended, were placed inside.

In Tonga, huge elevated rectangular stone tombs mark the historic gravesites of the Tuʻi Tonga, the highest-ranking lineage. The great oval houses of the chiefs were distinguished by complex rafter formations and rafter lashings, which incorporated designs formed from coconut-fibre sennit of two colours (Figure 43.5). The highest chiefs of the Kauhalauta lineage groups lived inland, while the lesser chiefs of the Kauhalalalo lineage groups lived close to the sea. Special mounds used by chiefs for resting (*esi*) and snaring pigeons (*sia heu lupe*) were elevated in height.

In Sāmoa, houses were, and still are, laid out with a specific order in relation to the village pathways, the concepts of centre and periphery, and the orientation of the *malae* (village green), with the chief's house and guest houses, round or oval in shape, in the most important positions, raised on earth and stone platforms. Formal kava drinking ceremonies take place on

Figure 43.3 Back of sacred or tamburan house (built 1551), Wakde, Papua New Guinea, 1 May 1911.

Figure 43.4 Masks from Melanesia, with a focus on New Britain and New Ireland.

Figure 43.5 Engraving of a kava ceremony inside a ceremonial house in Tonga, after a drawing by John Webber from the Atlas to Cook's Third Voyage, Smithsonian Institution Libraries.

the *malae*, with each person accorded a specific place, depending on his personal prestige and the rank of his title. Mounds believed to have been for snaring pigeons in the interior of the islands were elaborated into star shapes or ray shapes, related to concepts about the shapes of animals and natural phenomena personified by the gods. In addition, snaring pigeons was metaphorically associated with acquiring wives. A common form of these mounds had eight rays, possibly relating to the god Tagaloa, who had eight livers outside of his body, as well as Fe'e, the octopus god. The shapes of mounds with different numbers of rays are associated with gods and traditional lore dealing with the sun, turtles, and eels.[5]

In East Polynesia, ceremonial sites with stone or wooden images and chief's living sites marked the religious and societal centres of social action. In large islands, such as Hawai'i and the Society Islands, chiefs lived with their people in settlements laid out according to mythological or social rules,

[5] D.J. Hedrich, 'Towards an understanding of Samoan star mounds', *Journal of the Polynesian Society* 100:4 (1991), 381–435, at 381, 415.

which divided the island into wedge-shaped sections from mountain to sea, thereby giving access to fishing areas, agricultural areas, and mountains that were the home of wild plants and birds. Religious sites in Hawai'i varied from simple fishing shrines to elaborate high-walled enclosures (*heiau*) used for rituals of state importance. Rectangular in shape, *heiau* were often built at the top of a hill or slope of a mountain range, parallel or at right-angles to the shoreline, as part of the cultural landscape. A pavement of pebbles lay at the end where the images would be placed, and it was here the rituals were carried out. In the eighteenth century, a series of large images were arranged in a crescent, with the most important image, usually a smaller one, placed at the centre. Important structures included the *lele*, on which offerings were placed; the *anu'u*, 'oracle tower', in which religious specialists enacted ceremonies; a *hale pahu*, where drums were played facing the *lele*; a *mana* house, in which the most important image and other ritual objects were kept; and a *mua* house, a shedlike structure used for baking pigs and preparing offerings. *Heiau* plans varied according to use, landform, and importance.

Household furnishings included plaited floor and sleeping mats, and neckrests carved of wood or bamboo. Human figures were sometimes incorporated into the houses, such as in Māori houseposts. In Fiji and Tonga, sculptured hooks were hung from rafters to protect the important objects hung from them. Beautifully finished wooden bowls were carved with human figures in Hawai'i; humans, turtles, and birds in Fiji; multiple legs in Sāmoa; and incised designs in the Marquesas, the Austral Islands, and the Admiralities. Shaped and decorated gourd containers were used in Hawai'i and New Zealand. Neckrests and stools had a sleek, modern look. In early West Polynesian archaeological contexts, pottery was decorated with Lapita designs. Tools used in food preparation, such as stone pounders, might be decorated with human images or take aesthetically abstract forms. Even tools and fishhooks were varied and beautiful in materials, shapes, and lashings.

Sculptured Houses in Aotearoa New Zealand

The conceptual organization of space among the Māori of Aotearoa New Zealand includes large ceremonial areas called *marae* and the buildings within them, which reveal visual stories about the origin of the universe and the origin of carving, as well as social and religious metaphors about ancestors and gods. Indeed, Māori woodcarving is a consummate example of continuity, change, innovation, and variety within a tradition of Pacific art.

The Visual and Performing Arts

From the primary void or chaos, the Sky Father, Rangi, and the Earth Mother, Papa-tuanuku, lay together in a warm embrace. Their offspring were the four great gods, Tane (god of the forests), Tangaroa (god of fish and reptiles), Tu (god of destruction), and Rongo (god of cultivated foods), and two specialized gods, Haumia (god of uncultivated foods) and Tawhiri (god of the winds). Cramped in dark quarters, the children debated how they could separate their father and mother and bring light to the world. Tawhiri disagreed, but the others attempted to separate their parents. Tane succeeded but, finding his arms too short, he placed his head against mother earth and pushed his father up with his feet. Tawhiri rose with his father and sent his offspring – the four great winds, small violent winds, clouds of various kinds, and hurricanes – against Tane. Tawhiri's brothers and their offspring were terrified. Tangaroa's fish offspring plunged deep into the sea, but the reptiles sought safety in Tane's forests. Rongo and Haumia hid themselves in mother earth. Tu withstood Tawhiri's wrath and finally defeated him, but Rangi and Papa have never been reconciled to their separation, and even now Papa's sighs rise to Rangi as mist, and Rangi's tears fall to Papa as dewdrops.

This Māori creation story is often depicted as part of *pataka* (raised storehouses) and meeting houses. Rangi and Papa may be depicted in their pre-separation embrace. Tane may be depicted as the personification of the sun and fertilizer of the land and its creatures, and Tangaroa may be depicted as an embodiment of the sea and its creatures.

Traditionally the *pataka* (storage house) was the more important building on or near a *marae* and was raised on stilts to be seen from some distance. Used to store important objects and prestigious preserved foods, *pataka* signified the importance of the chief and his people. Often carved with symbols of fertility and abundance, the carved thresholds, bargeboards with a figure at the apex, doorways, and side panels incorporate visual associations with the Māori cosmos and *tapu* rituals. One of the few existing *pataka* is in the American Museum of Natural History, New York. It was carved by a few traditional craftsmen at the beginning of the twentieth century and was probably never used on a *marae* (Figure 43.6).

Today, with the demise of the *pataka*, a meeting house is the large important structure on the *marae* and incorporates important messages about the gods and ancestors of the tribe. The carved A-shaped bargeboards with a carved human figure or human head placed at the apex (*tekoteko*) beckons its users into a recessed entryway and through a door situated off-centre to the left surmounted by a carved lintel. Upon crossing this sacred boundary into

Figure 43.6 Māori storehouse (*pataka*), late nineteenth/early twentieth century, as mounted in 1984 for the Hall of Peoples of the Pacific, American Museum of Natural History, New York.

the house, marked by the doorway lintel, one enters into a horizontally and vertically ordered space conceptualized as a model of the cosmos and a metaphor of the history and embodiment of the ancestors of the group. The sky father encloses his progeny as he embraces the Earth, and like the primary void, it is dark inside. Tane, god of the forests, also personifies the house, as the building materials are taken from his domain. Inside, the carved ancestors express the corporate status of the group and the wider symbolic and genealogical relationships among its members.

In addition to Rangi, Papa, and their offspring, the house is a metaphor for the prostrate body of an ancestor, who may be the captain of a founding tribal canoe or the founder of the group. This ancestor is carved as a *tekoteko* at the apex of the bargeboards (*maihi*), which represent his arms and fingers. A ridgepole (*kaho*) runs the length of the ceiling at the centre of the house; this represents the ancestor's spine, replacing the earlier carved metaphorical hull of the war canoe. Painted rafters (*heke*) run from the ridgepole to the sides, representing the ancestor's ribs. Ridgepole supports, often with a human ancestral figure carved in the round at the base, reach floor to ceiling. The carved slabs along the sides of the house (*poupou*) represent the more recent ancestors of the group that owns the house and allude to its genealogy. These *poupou* alternate along the sides of the house with plaited wall panels (*tukutuku*). Plaited floor mats cover the floor. The right side (as viewed from outside the doorway) is considered tabu, the important side, and, depending on context, is reserved for visitors and men; the left side, considered less important, is used by local people and women. The right side can be associated with death and is where coffins are placed; the left side is *noa*, and associated with life.

Most of the tribes and *iwi* will no longer permit illustrations of their meeting houses, so I direct you to the many illustrations that have been published over the years, especially by Roger Neich for both traditional and contemporary forms of the meeting house.[6]

Sculpture and Carving Traditions

Sculpture was executed in the round, in high or low relief, by incising, and as part of houses. In addition to wood, sculpture was fabricated from wicker and feathers in Hawai'i, barkcloth-covered sedge in Rapa Nui, ivory in Tonga and Fiji, and greenstone in Aotearoa New Zealand. Relief carving was particularly characteristic of Aotearoa New Zealand, especially the carved wooden house panels and treasure boxes, while elaborate incising, sometimes with ivory inlay, was highly developed in Tongan and Fijian weapons. Carved staves, clubs, and other ceremonial objects were symbols of sacred power, rank, and prestige, as were such unusual objects as carved stilt steps in the Marquesas.

In some areas, canoes and their accoutrements were considered the epitome of artfulness. Māori war canoes had intricately carved prow and stern pieces, with relief-carved washstrakes, paddles, and bailers. Society Island canoes had carved, elevated endpieces with human sculptures

---

[6] R. Neich, 1994. *Painted Histories: Early Figurative Painting* (Auckland: Auckland University Press, 1994), and *Carved Histories: Rotorua Ngati Tarawhai* (Auckland: Auckland University Press, 2001).

Figure 43.7 Fijian wooden sculptures from the US Exploring Expedition, 1840. Magnificent Voyagers exhibit, National Museum of Natural History, Washington, DC, 1985.

mounted at the termini. Large oceangoing vessels, sometimes consisting of two hulls connected by a platform, with shelter and fire-building capability, were used for long-distance voyaging, exploration, and settlement. Human sculpture had an uneven distribution, being most important in Central and East Polynesia, and absent in many other areas. Stone sculptures have become signature objects, such as huge Easter Island figures and medium-sized temple figures from the Marquesas. A similar range in size was found in wood sculpture: large temple images from the Marquesas and Hawai'i; medium-sized images from Tonga, Fiji (Figure 43.7), Aotearoa New Zealand, Mangareva, Cook Islands, Society Islands, and Austral Islands; and small figures from Easter Island, Hawai'i, Aotearoa New Zealand, and New Guinea.

Sculptures, especially wooden ones, incorporated dynamic energy and symbolic form. The knees were often bent, as if ready to spring into action, and the body was sometimes individualized with painted or incised designs, thought to represent tattoo or body paint. Sculptures were sometimes activated by attaching feathers and by calling the gods and ancestors to them with sung prayers and offerings; others could be deactivated by removing their eyes.

Figure 43.8 Rapa Nui barkcloth sculptures.

Besides the well-known wood sculptures of Rapa Nui, sculptures were also made of a rigid plant structure covered with barkcloth (*mahute*), which was rare and valuable, as plants for its fabrication did not grow well. Only five such constructions are known, two of which are in the Peabody Museum at Harvard University. One of the Harvard figures is essentially naturalistic in form; though the face is reminiscent of a bird face in profile, the body is rounded, and the hands are distinctly human. The back has a well-formed vertebral column with distinct vertebrae, which continue up over the top of the head (Figure 43.8, left). The second body form is known from two examples – in the Peabody Museum, Harvard, and in the Ulster Museum, Belfast. In this form, the head is quite naturalistic in its proportions, but the body is flat (Figure 43.8, right). These figures appear to be receptacles for the ancestral gods, high-status versions of the lesser-ranked wooden figures, and were worn by chiefs in the same way that lesser-status individuals wore wooden figures around their necks during feasts and on ceremonial occasions.

Fibre and Textile Arts

In some areas of the Pacific, fibre and textile arts ranked equally with, or even more importantly than, carving traditions. The making of textiles was usually,

Figure 43.9 Dress worn by the chief mourner at a funeral ceremony in Tahiti.

but not exclusively, women's work and illustrates the important contribution of women to Pacific art. Particularly important was coconut-fibre sennit, made by men, and the aesthetic ramifications of the sennit made from it, by braiding, twisting, and knotting by religious specialists. In the Society Islands, images of lesser importance (*ti'i*) were carved of wood, while images made of coconut fibre (*to'o*) were more important and were activated by the addition of red feathers. In Hawai'i, human sculptures made of a basketry base and covered with red feathers were the most important images.

Clothing and personal adornment were carried to elaborate heights. Barkcloth wraparound skirts and *malo* (loin coverings) were decorated with complex designs in Hawai'i. An extraordinary ceremonial costume from the Society Islands was the mourning dress, worn by a chief mourner at funeral ceremonies of high-ranking individuals (Figure 43.9).

Aotearoa New Zealand Māori used fibres of a native flax which were weft-twined (the loom was not used in Polynesia) into cloaks that combined warmth

The Visual and Performing Arts

Figure 43.10 Presentation of fine mats (*'ie tōga*) at the death of distinguished elder Fa'animo. Falealupo village, Sāmoa.

with prestige. Flax cloaks with special borders (*taniko*) incorporated designs by intertwining elements of different colours.

Mats with plaited designs were made from pandanus, flax, and other leaves in Aotearoa New Zealand, and sedge in Ni'ihau Island in Hawai'i. The most important valuables, especially in West Polynesia, were fine mats, usually plaited from specially prepared pandanus strips, sometimes as many as thirty to the inch, which were named and imbued with their owner's *mana*. These were displayed during important rituals, such as funerals and weddings, and were inherited from generation to generation. The aesthetic criteria by which they were evaluated included fineness, colour, type of leaf from which they were made, how old they were, and most importantly on what occasions they had been used in the past and by whom. In Sāmoa, the tradition continues into the twenty-first century and the first presentation of new fine mats (*'ie tōga*) is a major event. They are used for presentations, such as at the death of family member or an important village elder (Figure 43.10). The addition of red feathers was an important element and the presentation itself was an aesthetic act.

Micronesians are well known for loom weaving (Figure 43.11). Backstrap looms were used in Kosrae and Pohnpei. They were strung with a continuous spiral warp, which encircled a warp-beam attached to a frame and a second unattached warp-beam (or breast-beam); these were separated from each other by half the desired finished length of the fabric. The breast-beam was tied to a strap that encircled the waist of the weaver, whose body tension held

Figure 43.11 Micronesian exhibit of weaving and important objects, 1970s. National Museum of Natural History, Washington, DC.

the warp taut. In other areas, such as the Marshall Islands, a continuous spiral warp was wrapped around a series of wooden pegs set into a benchlike loom.

The resulting cloth was varied in design, colour, and decoration. Fibres used were primarily from banana stalks and the inner bark of the hibiscus tree. Traditional colours were black, red, and yellow, but European dyes in blue, purple, green, and a brighter red were introduced early. Decoration consisted of shell and glass beads, and European yarn or thread unravelled from European cloth.

Pohnpei and Kosrae were the homes of fine loom-woven textiles, especially narrow belts with woven patterns and shell and glass bead decoration. These banana-fibre belts were about 15 centimetres wide, with warp so fine that they sometimes numbered thirty warps per centimetre. In Kosrae, the design was strung into the warp by tying in differently coloured threads, while the weft primarily bound the warps together into a fabric. In the Marshall Islands, famous for canoes and navigation stick charts, the women excelled in two-dimensional designs of plaited dress mats. About a metre square, designs were worked in with darker-coloured hibiscus fibre forming bands around a central, undecorated section. These pandanus-leaf dress mats were worn in pairs by

The Visual and Performing Arts

women; one mat hung like an apron in front, and the second mat overlapped it, back to front; both were held in place by a cord. In Kiribati, armour was made of intricately intertwined coconut fibre and pufferfish helmets.

Basketry traditions, technologically related to mat-making, reached high points in Fiji, Aotearoa New Zealand, and Tonga, where a variety of forms were made from creepers, coconut fibre, coconut leaves, flax, or pandanus-leaf strips twined around bundles of coconut-leaf midribs.

Textiles made from the inner bark (or bast) of certain trees are widespread and are well known around the world, particularly in Asia, Indonesia, South America, and Africa. Some of the finest barkcloth was made by beating the inner bark of the paper mulberry (*Broussonetia papyrifera*), cultivated specifically for the purpose, and carried with Pacific Islanders as they migrated from island to island. Other useful plants include breadfruit (*Artocarpus*), banyan (*Ficus*), and in Hawai'i an endemic nettle *Pipturus* (*māmaki* in Hawaiian). In the Pacific, the uses of barkcloth reached high points in Melanesia and Polynesia. In New Britain, huge masks and sculptures were featured in spectacular ritual performances that took place in outdoor sacred spaces at night with huge bonfires, or as ritual headdresses used for daytime performances. In Polynesia, barkcloth was considered a 'valuable' and categorized with distinctive terms (such as *iyau*, *koloa*, and *tōga* in Fiji, Tonga, and Sāmoa, respectively) to separate them from food and other products usually associated with men. The fabrication of barkcloth was usually women's work, but the resulting product was often sacred to men, women, and the gods. In the Cook Islands, images of gods and ancestors were wrapped with cloth and fibre attachments, the most remarkable of which is the staff god from Rarotonga now in the British Museum. About 3.5 metres long, the wooden figure is wrapped with a huge bale of barkcloth, embellished with red feathers and pearlshell pieces. The carved wooden section of the image includes an upright head, a phallus at the opposite end, and horizontal secondary figures near the ends of the staff. In the British Museum example, the barkcloth remains intact, but in similar figures in other collections the barkcloth was removed when given to missionaries and other Westerners, apparently because it was the barkcloth wrapping that made them sacred.

Rapa Nui chiefs showed their status by wearing barkcloth cloaks and belts formed of oval turtleshell plates enclosed in lengths of barkcloth. Rapa Nui people were especially anxious to obtain barkcloth when Cook's second Pacific voyage called there; Tahitian barkcloth was exchanged for feathered headdresses and other objects.

Barkcloth is intimately associated with the aesthetics of presentation, which can transform a two-dimensional cloth into a three-dimensional object.

Barkcloth was often presented attached to a person of rank and then presented in a dramatic flourish. In Fiji, a chief presented himself to a higher chief clothed in hundreds of feet of narrow barkcloth and disrobed, either by spinning to unravel wrapped barkcloth or by dropping a huge looped barkcloth dress as an aesthetic gesture in honour of the receiving chief. In Tahiti, not only was barkcloth presented wrapped around a high-ranking individual, but it was accepted in the same manner, unwound from the giver and rewound onto the receiver, making people into three-dimensional objects. No Tahitian gift presentation was complete without a large piece of barkcloth.

Tongan barkcloth is distinguished by its magnitude and metaphorical designs. Finished pieces, sometimes as large as 5 by 50 metres, are categorized by colour and design organization as *ngatu*, *ngatu uli* (black *ngatu*), and *fuatanga*. These huge pieces were, and are, used as pathways, carried as presentation pieces (Figure 43.12), and held to form three-dimensional sites, such as surrounding a royal tomb.

Figure 43.12 Presentation of a large Tongan barkcloth to Sinaitakala Fakafonua for a ceremony in honour of her marriage the following day to the Tongan Crown Prince. It was accompanied by further gifts, traditional dancing, a brass band, and extended family members. Maʻufanga, Tonga, 10 July 2012.

In islands and groups where making barkcloth has lain dormant for some time, some of these ritual and ceremonial uses exist primarily in memory. Today, the magic of turning bark into cloth is being widely revived and used in many places in the Pacific.

Feathered Textiles

Among the most distinctive and visually spectacular Hawaiian works of art were feathered cloaks, capes, and helmets, feathered god figures, a feathered sash that carried with it the right to rule, a unique feathered 'temple', and feathered standards called *kahili*, which heralded the presence of individuals of rank. Feathered cloaks, capes, and helmets were visual objectifications of social inequality. They were worn by male chiefs in dangerous or sacred situations and carried the social metaphor that one's genealogy is one's sacred protection (Figure 43.13). The feathers were primarily red from a honeycreeper (*'i'iwi*). Designs were incorporated as the feathers were tied to the backing of knotted fibre by adding yellow feathers, or occasionally black or green feathers from other honeycreepers or honeyeaters. Yellow feathers were plucked from birds that were primarily black – the yellow tufts

Figure 43.13 Hawaiian feathered cape and helmet as mounted in 1971 for the Hall of Peoples of the Pacific, American Museum of Natural History, New York.

removed, and the bird released – making yellow feathers rare and valuable. Made of a basketry foundation, feathered helmets, *mahiole*, were sometimes worn with the cloaks.

Body Ornamentation and Personal Objects

Tattooing and body painting were important in many parts of the Pacific, but especially in the Marquesas, Aotearoa New Zealand, Rapa Nui, Sāmoa, and Hawai'i, and cicatrization was found in the Solomons. These forms of permanent decoration were most extensive on men, but also used by women, and were associated with rank, status, and genealogy.

Ornaments, made of carved whale ivory, turtleshell, greenstone, carved or unaltered dog teeth, boar tusks, landshells, seashells, and porpoise teeth, were worn on necks, arms, legs, and ears.

Feathered headdresses were worn by chiefs in Hawai'i, the Society Islands, the Austral Islands, Sāmoa, Tonga, and the Marquesas, while necklaces, belts, and girdles made of feathers were widespread. Flower ornaments ranged from simply strung whole-flower necklaces to complex constructions of flower petals and ribbons of inner bark of hibiscus. Human hair was used for wigs in Fiji, adorned headdresses in Sāmoa, was worn on shoulders, arms, and legs in the Marquesas, and was made into finely braided neck, hair, or waist ornaments in the Society Islands, Hawai'i, Tuamotus, Tongareva, and the Austral Islands.

Oral, Musical and Movement Arts

A most important universal art in the Pacific was oral: poetry, oratory, and speechmaking. Besides proverbs, prayers, genealogical recitations, and historical and legendary accounts rendered in poetry or prose, oral literature was often the basis of music and dance. Traditionally, poetic texts were intoned with a small number of pitches and in a narrow melodic range. Polyphony also occurred, often in two parts (the lower part a drone), but occasionally with as many as six parts.

Musical instruments – log idiophones, drums (Figure 43.14), and rattles of various kinds – were works of art in themselves. The rapid spread of introduced *'ukulele* and guitar changed the way music was conceptualized and began the tradition of what has been called pan-Pacific pop. In the last decades of the twentieth century, reggae from Jamaica and other popular genres added further dimensions to this composite art.

The Visual and Performing Arts

Figure 43.14 Hawaiian drum, *pahu*.

In Polynesia, dance is a stylized visual accompaniment to poetry: performers usually face an audience and tell a story by alluding to selected words of the text with movements of the hands and arms, while the legs and body serve mainly for rhythm and keeping time, or are not used at all, as in sitting dances. In Melanesia/New Guinea, performances are more ritually based, often associated with male initiation, and performers often move as a group across ritual spaces or in inward-facing circles.

In many parts of the Pacific, dance has become more pantomimic, attempting to convey a story to audiences that do not speak the language (such as tourists) or no longer know the specialized language of metaphor and hidden meaning. But some performing arts have had a continuous oral transmission from the temple to today. For example, Hawaiian Mary Kawena Pukui, totally immersed in hula traditions evolved from the eighteenth century, composed a hula in the 1950s in honour of the snow goddess, Poliʻahu, which has passed to her descendants (Figure 43.15, right). A Hawaiian carver makes perfect replicas of drums in museums for performances at Hawaiian festivals (Figure 43.15, left).

Figure 43.15 Hawaiian hula performances, left with replica of the *pahu* in Canterbury Museum (above) made by Kanaʻe Keawe, 2018, played by Laʻakea Perry with dancers from his Hula Halau, Ke Kai o Kahiki. Merrie Monarch Festival, 2019, Hilo, Hawaiʻi; right hula *pahu*, performed by Kuhilani Suganuma dancer and Kalena Silva musician on a *pahu* made in 1985 by Kanaʻe Keawe.

Contemporary artists have continued and recycled many artistic traditions and have added new ones. Although modern Pacific art often involves borrowing from the West and the East, the incorporating traditional system shapes products into their final forms. Thus, while the traditional incised and painted housefronts of Belau meeting houses retain their traditional uses, the aesthetic aspects find modern expression in contemporary houses and in small tourist carvings. Contemporary abstract sculptures of traditional Hawaiian gods combine Hawaiian religious concepts with Western aesthetic concepts, while contemporary modern Māori carvings transform traditional themes into new ones. These new works depend on knowledge of the traditional aesthetic systems in which the artists have immersed themselves to create new forms based on their own backgrounds and experiences, producing fine art that makes Pacific themes understandable in today's world.

PART IX

*

CULTURE CONTACT AND THE
IMPACT OF PRE-COLONIAL
EUROPEAN INFLUENCES

44

The Pacific in the Age of Revolutions

SUJIT SIVASUNDARAM

In the age of revolutions, the Pacific was dramatically moulded from a 'Sea of Islands' into 'islands in a far sea'.[1] This ocean of dense Indigenous habitation, memory, and connection experienced a violent transition as it was hemmed in by modern formations of empire, knowledge, and culture.

In this chapter, I recontextualize the 'age of revolutions', so often cast as a European phase of transition to modernity, as a Pacific concept of conflict and contestation. This is because it is necessary to approach the decades that straddled the late eighteenth and early nineteenth centuries from the perspective of Pacific Islanders as well as Outlanders. It is also necessary to have a wide sense of the period's remit, encompassing politics, culture, and knowledge, rather than assuming that the age of revolutions should be defined by the French Revolution or the American Revolution and that it is a period that should begin with the benchmark of these grand revolutions. At the same time, given the slippery conceptual moorings of what revolution means in this period, akin to its slipperiness now, it is necessary to avoid a romanticization of this age as one entirely of liberty and resistance. For the imposition of liberty or humanitarianism could become part of the arsenal of imperial benevolence and protectionism.

The chapter begins with a lesser-known voyage, that of Peter Dillon, which it tracks across the Pacific and Indian Oceans in order to show how different strands of the age of revolutions could cohere around oceanic voyaging and across the global South. This is a microhistory of the revolutionary age. It then moves into more elite Anglo-French encounters in the Pacific and illustrates what these imperial tussles looked like in the Pacific setting. It grounds the story in Tasmania, in order to illustrate the local

---

[1] This follows, Epeli Hau'ofa, 'Our Sea of Islands', in *Contemporary Pacific* 6 (1994), 147–61.

workings of the age of revolutions. In tracking how the Pacific could remould the meanings of the age of revolutions, the intent is to place this 'Sea of Islands' at the centre of world history, as it should be.

The argument points to the opening up of many possibilities in this age: for the definition of human beings as much as imperial violence; for agency as well as war; and for commercial and environmental exploitation. The chapter ends with this suggestion: the 'age of revolutions' in the Pacific may also be approached as a making of place on the globe across these many scales, individual, territorial, political, and cultural included. Once again, this is in keeping with how a 'Sea of Islands' was becoming 'islands in a far sea' as the nineteenth century proceeded.

A Microhistory

'I will stick you on the Forecastle and set the Otaheiti men to shoot you.'[2] This was one of Peter Dillon's favourite expressions, as he captained the 400-ton *St Patrick*, which sailed from Valparaiso in Chile, in October 1825, to Calcutta, the bustling British imperial hub. Dillon was an erratic maritime adventurer and private trader with aspirations to greatness; an Irishman born in French Martinique in 1788.[3] He had a penchant for storytelling. He venerated Napoleon and named one of his sons after the general.[4] Seen from this perspective, perhaps the threat to arrange the shooting of his white sailors was Napoleonic in its violence. He pitted his European crew against the Tahitians on board and stirred the possibility of mutiny among his white men. Dillon was known for fostering very close relationships with South Pacific Islanders, an attachment which originated from his residency in Fiji in 1808–9, when he made 'considerable progress in learning their language'.[5] He claimed to have been adopted as the son of a chief after living on Borabora on the Society Islands from 1810–12.[6] George Bayly, third mate on the *St Patrick* who kept a journal of his time with Dillon, wrote of his release from

---

[2] G. Bayly, 'Journal on the *St. Patrick*, 8 October 1825 to 31 August 1831', reproduced in G. Bayly, P. Statham-Drew, and R. Erickson (eds.), *A Life on the Ocean Wave: The Journals of Captain George Bayly* (Melbourne: Miegunyah Press, 1998), 79.
[3] J.W. Davidson, *Peter Dillon of Vanikoro: Chevalier of the South Seas*, ed. O.H.K. Spate (Oxford: Oxford University Press, 1975), 13.
[4] Davidson, *Peter Dillon*, 71.   [5] Davidson, *Peter Dillon*, 16–17.
[6] E. Baigent, 'Dillon, Peter (1788–1847)', *Oxford Dictionary of National Biography* (Oxford: Oxford University Press, 2004); online edn, October 2008.

Dillon's aggressive captaincy in reaching Calcutta: 'never was a captive bird more pleased to get its liberty than I was'.[7]

The muster of the *St Patrick* is revealing; it had a crew forged by the age of revolutions. These ships made these astounding journeys through the labour and skill of multicultural crews. The *St Patrick* sailed under Chilean colours to Calcutta and the Europeans were recorded in the port register on leaving Valparaiso as 'naturalized Chileans'. Dillon himself was entered as 'Don Pedro Dillon'. The ship also had an 'enormous green flag with [a] yellow Irish harp in it'. In Ireland, under the influence of the French Revolution, a radical movement, the United Irishmen, mounted a campaign for an Irish republic leading to a rebellion in 1798. They used a green flag with a harp. Twenty British sailors who joined the crew had served in Chile's war of independence against Spain, under the command of Thomas Cochrane, a British naval officer who played a pivotal role in the rebel navies of Chile, Peru, and Brazil in the 1820s.[8] These men combined with a crew of Polynesians who had laboured under Dillon's command in a previous voyage in the *Calder*, from Sydney to Valparaiso. The *Calder*'s crew included an equal number of Europeans and Polynesians, and the Polynesians were mostly Tahitians, named by Dillon perhaps in an act of mockery, 'Governor Macquarie', after the Governor of Sydney; 'Major Goulborn', after the colonial secretary of New South Wales, and so on. Given the fighters from Chile, it is ironic and rather fitting of this age of revolutions, which could include counter-revolutionary empires, that Dillon was obsessed with aristocratic status and pedigree.[9]

It was not only the social makeup of this voyage that should point to the age of revolutions; the manner in which social classifications and hierarchies could be upheld as much as inverted is also worthy of note. The *Calder* also had on board a Chinese cook and a Bengali steward.[10] In another contradiction, indicative of the slippery quality of racial relations, Dillon's fondness for Polynesians did not extend to the Bengali. The captain kept a sheet headed 'Crimes' on which he listed the Bengali's wrongs, including the breaking of crockery or the loss of spoons overboard.[11] As the diverse crew of Dillon's vessels demonstrates, Dillon's travels came out of the work of men from

---

[7] Bayly, 'Journal on the *St. Patrick*', 79. [8] Davidson, *Peter Dillon*, 98–9.
[9] For Dillon's obsession with pedigree and status, see G. Obeyesekere, *Cannibal Talk: The Man-Eating Myth and Human Sacrifice in the South Seas* (Berkeley: University of California Press, 2005), 206
[10] Davidson, *Peter Dillon*, 95 [11] Davidson, *Peter Dillon*, 96.

Bengal and China who travelled to Latin America, Polynesians who arrived in India, and European freedom-fighters from Chile in the Indian Ocean.

If characteristically mixed in its composition as well as its cultural politics, the *St Patrick*'s journey became unusually important. Before docking at Calcutta, Dillon and Bayly solved one of the greatest mysteries of their time, the fate of the disappeared French navigator Jean François de Galaup Comte de La Pérouse. When Dillon came to the island of Tikopia, the remains of an extinct volcano remotely positioned in the southwest Pacific, he looked for some old friends who he had left there when an officer on the *Hunter* in 1813. These friends had disembarked after a dramatic and now controversial episode involving the *Hunter*'s call in Fiji to collect sandalwood and bêche de mer. It resorted to force on that occasion in order to procure the goods, and Dillon wrote that a 'cannibal feast' was being prepared by the Fijians for the bodies of those slain. In one recent interpretation, Dillon's tale of the Fijian cannibals is a narrative of self-delusion.[12] Now, fifteen years after the *Hunter*'s visit, when several canoes approached the *St Patrick*, there appeared a man called Joe, a 'lascar' or Asian seaman, who kissed Dillon's hands and feet. The *Hunter* had dropped Joe off at Tikopia on Dillon's previous visit. He was the informant who would help to solve the puzzle.[13]

Originating from the Persian via Portuguese, 'lascar', the term used to describe Joe, became a racialized term for non-white seamen and was used by the British for Asian and mostly Indian sailors in this period.[14] Joe's South Asian extraction is clear in Bayly's telling of the story: 'He appeared to have almost forgotten his native language and spoke at random, Bengallee, English, the Fijee and Tucopean.'[15] Elsewhere he was described as 'married on the island and comfortably settled'.[16] Bayly noted that his own country-men – presumably Indians on board the *St Patrick* – could not understand Joe. Dillon was also pleased to hear that a Prussian, Martin Buchert of the *Hunter*, was still alive. In what may have well been an exaggerated account, Buchert was said to have killed twenty-seven Fijians with twenty-eight shots in Fiji.[17] 'His only garment now was a mat round his middle. He was tattooed

---

[12] For this claim see, Obeyesekere, *Cannibal Talk*, 192–222.

[13] Bayly, 'Journal of the *St. Patrick*', 65.

[14] For more information on 'lascars' and rebellion see A. Jaffer, *Lascars and Indian Ocean Seafaring, 1780–1860* (Rochester: Boydell and Brewer, 2015).

[15] Bayly, 'Journal of the *St. Patrick*', 65. See also P. Dillon, *Narrative and Successful Result of a Voyage in the South Seas: Performed by the Order of the Government of British India, to Ascertain the Actual Fate of La Pérouse's expedition*, 2 vols. (London: Hurst, Chance & Co. 1829), vol. I, 32.

[16] *Bengal Hurkaru*, 26 September 1826.

[17] 'Editorial note', in Statham and Erickson (eds.), *A Life on the Ocean Wave*, 64.

all over his body and had several marks on his face.'[18] The artefact which solved the mystery of the lost navigator was around Joe's neck. It was a curious old silver guard which, in the end, Bayly managed to buy for a bottle of rum. Upon examining it, he wrote, 'we thought we discovered the initials of the "Comte de la Perouse"'.[19] This assertion was in fact erroneous.[20] The sword guard was taken back as a relic to Calcutta. There it was minutely examined by members of the Royal Asiatic Society of the city, the intellectual association which presided over Orientalist inquiries in the subcontinent.[21] This story shows how the Pacific was being located within global circuits of migration, exchange, and knowledge in this era. Not only was Calcutta becoming connected with the Pacific, but it was now possible to meet a South Asian in Tikopia.

It was not only this relic which created a stir in Calcutta when the *St Patrick* moored. Two Māori men who were sons of chiefs had taken passage with Dillon after the *St Patrick* stopped in New Zealand for timber, adding even further to the incredible itineraries which lace this story. The Calcutta newspaper, the *Bengal Hurkaru,* noted that the ship had on board Brian Boroimbe, a 'New Zealand Prince, who considers and by his *genealogical tree* can prove himself to be a lineal descendant from his namesake, the celebrated King of Ireland [Brian Boru], who died gallantly fighting for his country against the Danes at Clon'. Brian's appearance was said to be 'prepossessing' and his 'demeanor in every respect indicative of the ancient and noble blood that flows through his veins'.[22] Also among the arrivals was 'His Excellency Morgan McMurroch, aide-de-camp'. The so-styled Prince was fêted in Calcutta – taken to breakfast, dinner with the merchants in the settlement, a performance of Shakespeare's *Henry IV* – and received by the Acting British Governor-General in the official country residence in Barrackpore, where the Polynesians with Dillon performed dances and chants and were given gifts. Brian was given a captain's uniform, a sword, and a medal carrying the likeness of George IV, which he proceeded to wear around his neck.[23] Even as the Indian and Pacific oceans were being knitted together by the likes of Dillon or Joe, on the same ships, Pacific Islanders

---

[18] Bayly, 'Journal of the *St. Patrick*', 65.
[19] Bayly, 'Journal of the *St. Patrick*', 66. See also Dillon, *Narrative*, vol. 1, 39–40.
[20] Davidson, *Peter Dillon*, 108.
[21] Bayly, 'Journal of the *St. Patrick*', 78. See also *Bengal Hurkaru*, 7 September 1826.
[22] *Bengal Hurkaru*, 5 September 1826.
[23] *The India Gazette*, 14 September 1826, for how Brian wore the medal of George IV around his neck.

were making long-distance travels such as these in novel directions and finding themselves wrapped within discourses of monarchy which were themselves in contest and flux in this period.

In 1826, Calcutta was gripped by its post-Napoleonic war in Burma with the kingdom of Ava. Those with apprehensions linked to this war attacked Morgan as he landed off the *St Patrick* in his 'feathered War-Cloak'. According to a newspaper report, onlookers were 'struck with the form of the man, which combined Herculean strength with perfect ease, grace and symmetry'.[24] When he landed, the *chowkidars* or gatekeepers drew their scimitars, thinking that Morgan was a Burmese general coming to Calcutta as a spy. The gatekeepers thought it 'not improbable that his army would follow in the night, and storm Fort William'. Morgan's response was a Māori war cry. Some Europeans, or in another account Peter Dillon's clerk, 'promptly interfered and [Morgan's] hand was arrested in the act of dealing a death-blow'.[25] Morgan was marched to the police, followed by what the newspaper recorded to be 3,000 Indians. This story may have been embellished by the *Bengal Hurkaru*, in keeping with the tenor of the newspaper's other comments on Morgan. It reported that Morgan had a 'very just idea of the initiatory principles of Political Economy' and that he was 'determined to perfect himself in the science before he leaves the Presidency [of Bengal]'. He had asked, it was alleged, for instruction in the making of railroads, steam coaches, wheels, and the principles of phrenology, the science of the head. This may indicate Māori curiosity, but the tone of commentary was derogatory. The reportage may also indicate that Morgan's head was examined for character by a phrenologist. *The India Gazette*, meanwhile, poked fun at the prince, noting the rumour around town of the cannibal propensities of New Zealanders. '[A]t least during the time that he has been on shore here, [he] has fed very much like a good Christian.'[26]

These reports are in keeping with the reception of Pacific Islanders on the other side of the world, in London, in the aftermath of Captain Cook's voyages. There they were taken first as ennobled representatives of a culture uncorrupted by civilization and second as men who had fallen from divine grace who resorted to all manner of sins, including cannibalism. Calcutta could now act as London for these southern oceans. Dillon's attempt at the display of Māori also indicates the reach of Māori travellers, including Māori

---

[24] *Bengal Hurkaru*, 11 September 1826, for all information in this paragraph.
[25] For the other account, see *The India Gazette*, 14 September 1826.
[26] *The India Gazette*, 4 September 1826.

The Pacific in the Age of Revolutions

serving on board sealers and whalers, into the heart of the Indian Ocean.[27] Brian and Morgan's journey was parallel and yet opposite in direction to that of Joe who took on the ways of Tikopia.

These astounding itineraries of the age of revolutions, from New Zealand to India and from India to Tikopia with sideways glances to Burma, in addition to Dillon's own trajectory, serve as a template for empire; however, the intent of individual Māori and the British who received them is also worth probing. These visitors wished to increase their authority in New Zealand and came to Calcutta, like Hongi Hika, the so-called 'Māori Napoleon' who travelled to London in 1820, was presented to the king, and finally returned home with muskets, powder, and shot. Bayly wrote of how Māori spoke of Hongi when the St Patrick arrived in New Zealand: 'After [Hongi] returned to his native country he gave out that he would never desist from killing and eating his countrymen till they made him King the same as King George in England.'[28] Bayly noted that Brian and Morgan too were to 'try their fortunes in obtaining Muskets and Gunpowder from the Merchants of Calcutta'.[29] The spread of the European musket across the far reaches of the Pacific was itself a token of how European wars and Pacific Island contests were interrelated; the techniques and scale of war were shifting in the early nineteenth century. Those who went to war with Europeans, as well as those fighting neighbouring regimes or political elites, had to arm themselves as Europeans did.[30] The British imperial war machine was tied together with an extractive fiscal state and new modes of information gathering. War is not a theme which springs out of Dillon's or Bayly's narrative, yet this is a romanticism worth guarding against in interpreting these travellers and their relations with the peoples of Asia, Africa, and Oceania and the consequences which followed in their wake.

Note, for instance, the conversation between Brian and Dillon at Budge Inn. Why, Brian pondered, did the staff treat Dillon with such attention? When it was explained to him that this was because Britain had taken the country, Brian observed: 'you will come and take my country too, I have no

---

[27] For the resettlement of New South Wales convicts in Calcutta see C. Anderson, 'Multiple border crossings: convicts and other persons escaped from Botany Bay and residing in Calcutta', *Journal of Australian Colonial History* 3:2 (2001), 1–22. Brian and Morgan's journey is in keeping with the spike in the global dispersal of Māori in the first three decades of the nineteenth century. See V. O'Malley, *Haerenga: Early Māori Journeys across the Globe* (Wellington: Bridget Williams Books, 2015).

[28] Bayly, 'Journal on the St. Patrick', 56.   [29] Bayly, 'Journal on the St. Patrick', 62.

[30] This point about warfare and the spread of weapons across the Pacific is further explored in my *Waves across the South: A History of Revolution and Empire* (Chicago: University of Chicago Press, 2020).

doubt, as you have taken this'.[31] Brian was absolutely correct: these wavy paths encompassing the ship he arrived on, which traversed the Indian and Pacific oceans, connected maritime power to imperialism. The *Bengal Hurkaru*, reporting Brian's visit to Barrackpore, imagined him returning home to New Zealand and providing a safe haven for British ships which would touch in any territory under his control. It added this line in support of Brian's credentials as a friend of Britain: 'The dominions over which Brian's father presides extend from Cape Palliser to the River Thames, and the largest, straightest and most durable spars in the world are easily procurable there.'[32] Spars of such height growing close to the water could be invaluable for the Royal Navy. The reception accorded Māori on Dillon's voyage pointed to the prospect of an empire of trade riding the waves. Elsewhere the fate of Māori lands was in prospect. The *India Gazette* hoped that Brian would be sent back not with weapons but with 'the instruments of agriculture and husbandry, and duly instructed in their use, and be provided with the means of raising in his own country, grains, vegetables, and fruits, that are not now indigenous to it'.

The journeys of these men, known only by crude nicknames such as Joe, or 'Choulia' as he was called by one Indian newspaper, and Brian and Morgan, were part of a whole host of other journeys across the waters of the South.[33] It would be wrong to see the *Calder* and *St Patrick* as passing without company across these great oceans – the seas were becoming populated in new ways as Europeans were arriving in greater numbers and encountering the Pacific Islanders, Asians, and Africans who travelled across these waters. While the number of official British vessels in these seas was still small, nevertheless ships of all kinds, private and official, British and non-British, came upon each other.[34] Valparaiso had a series of American and British vessels in harbour, and during Bayly's time there a Spanish brig was brought to harbour by a crew that had mutinied, murdered their officers, and wished to deliver the vessel to the patriots of Chile.[35] At Tahiti, the *St Patrick*

---

[31] *The India Gazette*, 14 September 1826.   [32] *Bengal Hurkaru*, 12 September 1826.

[33] For the name 'Choulia' see *The India Gazette*, 28 September 1826. I thank Jane Samson for her suggestion that these Māori may in fact have attempted to appropriate the *mana* of the Irish warriors. This is an intriguing suggestion.

[34] H.V. Bowen, 'Britain in the Indian Ocean region and beyond: contours, connections, and the creation of a global maritime empire', in H.V. Bowen, E. Mancke, and J.G. Reid (eds.), *Britain's Oceanic Empire: Atlantic and Indian Ocean Worlds, c.1550–1850* (Cambridge: Cambridge University Press, 2012), 45–65, at 52.

[35] Bayly, 'Journal on the *Calder*, 23 March 1825 to 12 June 1825', in Bayly et al. (eds.), *A Life on the Ocean Wave*, 42, 46.

came across a British whaler, the *Fawn*, in addition to some American whalers and a merchant ship. At Huahine it met a 300-ton American whaler, and in New Zealand the *Emily*, another whaler, as well as the *Larne*, a British ship of war, and the *Sir George Osborne* on the way to pearl in the Marquesas.[36] In the East Indies, between Papua New Guinea and Christmas Island, it came across an American ship trading between Philadelphia and Canton.[37] The American Revolution released American traders from the East India Company's monopoly, making them flock to the Pacific in the age of revolutions.

Having set out the Dillon voyage as a microhistory of the age of revolutions, it is worth once again summarizing the features that arise from it as a means of bringing this story together. In demographic terms, its crew was forged by the age of revolutions; but the dramatic journeys that are evident here, including how Calcutta could serve as a hub and draw the Pacific to itself, indicate the political changes of this age. They point to the rise of the British in India, an event which itself was tied to the changing politics of another ocean, the Atlantic. This imperial expansion reverberated across to Aotearoa New Zealand. These political changes did not simply give rise to the revolt of a 'many headed hydra', to use a phrase utilized by Atlantic historians. For empires were moving in these pathways across the Indian and Pacific oceans too. But in addition to demography, migration, and politics, the nature of the age of revolutions is also evident in the languages of race, class, and gender, as well as those of royalty and aristocracy. These languages were being defined and this was a newly classificatory age; but these classifications were slippery and open to reinvention. The expansion of commercial engagements of all kinds, together with a regime of surveillance, is also a feature of what the Pacific came to stand for in this age.

Anglo-French Tussles in the Pacific's Age of Revolutions

Yet to return to the puzzle that Dillon helped solve, the politics of the age of revolutions might also be approached from the elite explorations of the era, such as that of La Pérouse, and what they meant within the region itself. To summarize, Peter Dillon sailed across the Indian Ocean to Calcutta, with the sword guard and his Māori sojourners, and strategically generated interest by

---

[36] Bayly, 'Journal on the *St. Patrick*', 51, 54, 56 and 62.
[37] Bayly, 'Journal on the *St Patrick*', 73.

circulating his reports through Indian newspapers, the *Bengal Hurkaru* being the first to report on this discovery. Dillon's aim was to further his bid to command an expedition to investigate the missing La Pérouse.[38] In a book published to cement his fame as the problem solver, and to add to his pocket, Dillon provided this account of an interview on Vanikoro, in the Santa Cruz group:

Q. 'How were the ships lost?' – A. 'The island is surrounded by reefs at a distance off shore. They got on the rocks at night, and one ship grounded at Wannow, and immediately went to the bottom.'

Q. 'Were none of the people from the ship saved?' – A. 'Those that escaped from the wreck were landed at Wannow, where they were killed by the natives. Several also were devoured by the sharks, while swimming from the ship.'

Q. 'How many people were killed at Wannow?' – A. 'Two at Wannow, two at Amma and two more near to Paiow. These were all the white men who were killed.'

Q. 'If there were only six white men killed on shore, how, or from whence, came the sixty sculls [*sic.*] that were in the spirit house at Wannow, as described by Ta Fow, the hump-backed Tucopian, and others?' – A. 'These were the heads of people killed by the sharks.'

Q. 'How was the ship lost near Paiow?' – A. 'She got on the reef at night, and afterwards drifted over it into a good place. She did not immediately break, for the people had time to remove things from her, with which they built a two-masted ship' . . .

Q. 'Had these people no friends among the natives?' – A. 'No. They were ship spirits; their noses were two hands long before their faces. Their chief used always to be looking at the sun and stars, and beckoning to them. There was one of them who stood as a watch at their fence, with a bar of iron in his hand, which he used to turn round his head. This man stood only upon one leg.'[39]

So what is the headline? La Pérouse's ships had come to their end in the midst of a hurricane. Though some of the crew remained, most of them sailed away in a small vessel, which they built as noted in this interview, never to be seen again. Evidently, before they left, their astronomical interests and their manners had bewildered the inhabitants of Vanikoro. Yet around the disappearance of this expedition is arrayed a series of political stand-offs which drew in the high politics of the age of revolutions.

---

[38] See Davidson, *Peter Dillon*, 124ff.   [39] Dillon, *Narrative*, vol. II, 159–69.

These years saw three French exploratory voyages to the Pacific, each under dramatically different circumstances indicating different phases in the history of France: first, under the command of Comte de La Pérouse (1785–8) and with the authority of an absolute monarch, Louis XVI; second, under de Bruni d'Entrecasteaux (1791–4), to search for the lost La Pérouse with the sanction of the National Assembly; and third, by Nicolas Baudin (1800–3), under instruction by Napoleon.[40] It was an impatient national interest that prompted the expedition to search for La Pérouse. A petition drawn up early in 1791 from the Société d'Histoire Naturelle bemoaned that France had waited for two years for the return of its famous explorer:

> Perhaps he has run aground on some island in the South Seas from whence he holds out his arms toward his country, waiting in vain for his liberator . . . And the decent nation that expected to reap the benefits of his labors also owes him its concern and its assistance.[41]

La Pérouse was to be France's response to Cook, and that these explorations were shaped by rivalry is evident in how his ships were as solid and heavy as those chosen by Cook. A French spy, taking the guise of a Spanish trader named Don Inigo Alvarez, sought out information about Cook's expedition for La Pérouse's mission and found John Webber, Cook's artist, to be a particularly useful source of information. Alvarez sat for a portrait by Webber. The expedition's origin prior to the revolutionary years, and its connection to the politics of the time, is also nicely illustrated by one contemporary diarist who held that Napoleon Bonaparte expressed an interest in joining the voyage, along with one of his compatriots at the École Militaire.[42]

While the voyage was underway, the multiple eyes that watched it clearly bore down heavily on La Pérouse. La Pérouse was anxious about whether his discoveries would be overtaken by the British successors of Cook. Distinguishing French exploration from British exploration, he commented on the news of 'evidence more of the large means the English dispose of than

---

[40] For analysis of the relationship between these three voyages see N. Starbuck, *Baudin, Napoleon and the Exploration of Australia* (London: Pickering and Chatto, 2013), Introduction. See also J. Dunmore, *French Explorers in the Pacific* (Oxford: Clarendon Press, 1965), vol. I.
[41] Cited in R. Williams, *French Botany in the Enlightenment: The Ill-Fated Voyages of La Pérouse and His Rescuers* (Dordrecht: Kluwer Academic, 2003), 107. For discussion of La Pérouse's agenda see Dunmore, *French Explorers*, 261–2. For the explorer's biography and further details of the mission see also J. Dunmore, *Pacific Explorer: The Life of Jean-François de La Pérouse, 1741–1788* (Palmerston North: Dunmore Press, 1985), esp. chapter 13.
[42] Dunmore, *Pacific Explorer*, p. 203

of their judgement'.[43] Given the range of expectations heaped on it, the displeasure that arose when La Pérouse lost the whole of his crew is indeed understandable. As the compiler of his journal, published from records sent home, wrote: 'our new Argonauts have all perished'.[44] An English compiler who had sailed with Cook noted that La Pérouse had operated in a state of continual anxiety because of the enormity of the task, combined with over-ambitious timetabling which created 'perpetual hurry'.[45]

D'Entrecasteaux came agonizingly close to success in his search for La Pérouse. Rumours had spread by this time that the navigator's end had come at British anti-republican hands.[46] It was just at this time, in 1788, that the British First Fleet had first founded an outpost for convicts in Australia. La Pérouse himself had touched at Botany Bay, now near Sydney, just five days after the First Fleet, and met British captain John Hunter. Could contrasting modes of engaging with the Pacific world, tied to French philosophy and British colonization, indicate antipathy to French voyagers on the part of the British and so explain the disappearance? From Botany Bay came La Pérouse's fateful last official letter, dated February 1788, promising to do 'exactly what my instructions require me to do ... But in such a way as to enable me to go back north in good time to reach the Isle de France [Mauritius] in December.'[47] The first news of La Pérouse reached D'Entrecasteaux while he was in Cape Town. In his journal he recorded a testimony received in Cape Town via Mauritius of what had been seen by Hunter in the Admiralty Islands, north of present-day New Guinea. Hunter later gave this account of what he had seen:

> Being near the Admiralty Islands on May the 31st 1791, five large canoes came off from the nearest Island, in each of which were eleven men ... They held up various articles which they seemed desirous of exchanging, such as lines, shells, bundles of darts or arrows ... One of them made various motions of shaving, by holding up something in his hand, with which he frequently

---

[43] La Pérouse to the Minister, dated Awatska, 29 September 1787, in J. Dunmore (ed.), *The Journal of Jean-François de Galaup de la Pérouse, 1785–1788* (London: Hakluyt Society, 1994), 533–4, at 533.

[44] Jean-François de Galaup, Comte de La Pérouse, *The Voyage of La Pérouse Round the World, in the Years 1785, 1786, 1787 and 1788 translated from the French*, ed. M.L.A. Milet Mureau (London: John Stockdale, 1798), ii.

[45] J. Burney, *A Memoir on the Voyage of d'Entrecasteaux in Search of La Pérouse* (London: Luke Hansard, 1820), 4–8, at 8.

[46] L.R. Marchant, 'La Pérouse, Jean-François de Galaup (1741–1788)', in *Australian Dictionary of Biography*, National Centre of Biography, Australian National University, http://adb.anu.edu.au/biography/la-perouse-jean-francois-de-galaup-2329/text3029.

[47] La Pérouse to the Minister, dated 7 February 1788, in Dunmore (ed.), *The Journal*, 541–2.

The Pacific in the Age of Revolutions

scraped his cheek and chin. This led me to conjecture that some European ship had been lately among them, and I thought it not improbable that it might have been M. de la Pérouse.[48]

D'Entrecasteaux believed that his compatriots in Mauritius, where he had served as Governor General, had misunderstood or exaggerated the news. Surely Hunter would have persevered in a rescue if he sincerely believed that he had discovered shipwrecked Frenchmen or at least the signs of their influence. The 'sacred duties of mankind' would have over-ruled other considerations of weather or even national difference.[49] Regardless of his doubts, d'Entrecasteaux made up his mind; he would sail to the Admiralty Islands. When he finally got there, he decided that the reports of La Pérouse were uncorroborated.

If the politics of the age of revolutions was evident at the beginning of this expedition, it was also evident in its ending. *La Recherche* and *L'Espérance*, two of D'Entrecasteaux's ships, were sold by auction in Batavia at the end of 1794.[50] D'Entrecasteaux had died of illness by this time, and his expedition had been stalled not only by news from Europe, but by the internal politics of the crew itself. Royalist and republican commitments divided the crew. The expedition's papers were seized at St Helena by the British and kept in London under the protection of the royalist who was the final commander of the expedition.[51] Natural historical cases found their way to Paris as a result of the ingenuity of a republican naturalist.[52] The remains of the voyage were thus affected by revolutionary politics. Yet, it is important to deepen the story by localizing it. One might turn to any number of places in the Pacific 'Sea of Islands' to do this, but in this chapter I turn to Tasmania.

Thinking with Tasmania

The rivalry between European explorers is easily traced in the origins of the settlement of what was initially called Van Diemen's Land,

---

[48] Burney, *A Memoir*, 10–11. Burney reports that this is from the *Historical Journal of Transactions in New South Wales*.
[49] Bruny D'Entrecasteaux, *Voyage to Australia and the Pacific 1791*, trans. E. Duyker and M. Duyker (Carlton: Melbourne University Press, 2001), 16.
[50] D. Johnson, *Bruny D'Entrecasteaux and His Encounter with Tasmanian Aborigines: From Provence to Recherche Bay* (Lawson, NSW: Blue Mountain, 2012), 72.
[51] D'Entrecasteaux, *Voyage to Australia*, xxxvi.
[52] See M. Labillardière, *An Account of a Voyage in Search of La Perouse, Undertaken by Order of the Constituent Assembly of France and Performed in the Years 1791, 1792 and 1793 Translated from the French*, 2 vols. (London: J. Debrett, 1800), xix.

later Tasmania and now Lutruwita. One way of doing this is to work with the writings of a naturalist, François Péron, who was on another French expedition, that of Nicolas Baudin, and who spent time on Van Diemen's Land. Péron compiled a memoir to the French government on why it was necessary to annex New South Wales, accusing the English of an 'invasion'.[53] The link to the revolutionary age can be seen in the raising of the British flag on Tasmania directly in the aftermath of rumours that the French were going to take it. Leaving the politics aside, Péron's natural history is a bridge to a deeper sense of the age of revolutions in Tasmania.[54] Within his natural historical writings, Péron's account of seals is especially detailed, arising from his observations while stranded in King Island in the Bass Strait, between Tasmania and mainland Australia, for twelve days in 1802.[55] It links these explorations to the history of seals and sealing, an important trade in the early history of Tasmania. Here we see vital debates, characteristic of the period, about slavery, piracy, liberty, and reform.

Natural exploitation – and in particular the period's ideology of 'improvement' – drove Tasmania's colonization.[56] Escaped convicts, sealers, and whalers responded to the natural resources of Tasmania. Sealers were cast as 'seawolves' in the period, a term which places them next to pirates, and the southern seal fishery is estimated to have taken 7 million seals in fifty years, an extreme case of natural historical depredation.[57] From 1810, populations of sealers lived with Indigenous women in the Bass Strait. The community was polyglot, including English, Irish, American, Portuguese, 'lascar', New Zealand, Tahitian, and Australian Aboriginal members.[58] By the second decade of the nineteenth century, reports of these communities were circulating in

---

[53] On the proposal of an invasion see J. Fornasiero and J. West-Sooty (eds.), *French Designs on Colonial New South Wales* (Adelaide: State Library of South Australia, 2014), 'Introduction', 102.
[54] On the rise of a new kind of science in the age of revolutions see P. Manning and D. Rood, *Global Scientific Practice in the Age of Revolutions* (Pittsburgh: University of Pittsburgh Press, 2016). For Péron's anthropology see S. Konishi, 'François Péron's meditation on death, humanity and savage society', in A. Cook, N. Curthoys, and S. Konishi (eds.), *Representing Humanity in the Age of Enlightenment* (London: Pickering and Chatto, 2013), 109–22.
[55] H.M. Micco (ed.), *King Island and the Sealing Trade, 1802* (Canberra: Roebuck Society, 1971), 38.
[56] For more on the ideology of natural improvement as part and parcel of this period, see R. Drayton, *Nature's Government: Science, Imperial Britain and the 'Improvement' of the World* (New Haven: Yale University Press, 2000).
[57] For the first colonial sealers' arrival, see P. Cameron, *Grease and Ochre: The Blending of Two Cultures at the Colonial Sea Frontier* (Launceston: Fuller's Bookshop, 2011), 51, 61–2; and 70 for 'seawolves'; for estimate of depopulation see Russell, *Roving Mariners*, 102. For 'piracy' in the age of revolutions see S. Layton, 'Discourses of piracy in an age of revolutions', *Itinerario* 35 (2011), 81–97.
[58] B. Plomley and K.A. Henley, *The Sealers of Bass Strait and the Cape Barren Island Community* (Hobart: Blubber Head Press, 1990).

Sydney, allowing Rev. John McGarvie to write of them as 'runaways' who had come ashore in the Strait and who had become acquainted with 'old Munro', who with his 'black wife' led them into 'all the secrets of the mysterious traffic & routes in these dangerous straits'. Munro, one of the earliest resident sealers, was described as the 'owner & king' of Preservation Island.[59] This mention of 'runaways' indicates that this history of sealing intersects with convicthood.

The events which occurred in the midst of these sealing communities may be seen as an outworking of the revolutionary moment. Before turning to that history it is important to stress at first that the trade is one aspect of the extraordinary violence which unfolded in Tasmania as Aboriginal resistance spiked from the late 1820s. One of the driving factors of the brutal Tasmanian wars which saw the hunting down of Aboriginal Tasmanians and retaliatory violence towards settlers was the arrival of retired naval and army officers of the Napoleonic wars and other refugees of the period to settle Van Diemen's Land, including the children of colonial officials and offspring of the landed gentry of Britain. As the colonial population increased sixfold from 1817 to 1824, the island was changed from 'a creole society based on small-scale agriculture, whaling and sealing to a largely pastoral economy based on the production of fine wool'.[60] The policy taken to contain the violence between the settlers and the Aboriginal Tasmanians was driven by the contradictory commitments to militarism and humanitarianism, a characteristic blend for the period. These are some of the signs of the age of revolutions in Tasmania: the establishment of military posts, a field police, and the scouring of the land by armed parties, making this one of the most heavily policed territories at this time;[61] the use of martial law over more than three years from 1828, justified as opening up the prospect of conciliation through terror but used to kill Aboriginal Tasmanians; a 'Black Line' in 1830, devised perhaps with strategies utilized against the French and using expertise of warfare in India and in the Peninsular War and the model of imperial hunts, as a human chain comprising troops, convicts, and settlers, which sought to drive the Aboriginal Tasmanians into a confined ground; and, the application of commitments to 'civilization', honed after the abolition of slavery and as a

---

[59] Rev. J. McGarvie, 'Manuscript on convict escapees', MS 400482, National Library of Australia, Canberra, 0608; for Munro's assistance to escaped convicts see Plomley and Henley, *The Sealers of Bass Strait*, 6.
[60] L. Ryan, *Tasmanian Aborigines: A History since 1803* (Sydney: Allen & Unwin, 2012), 74; and the paragraph also draws from 132–3.
[61] On Van Diemen's Land as one of the most policed countries in the world at this point, see discussion in J. Boyce, *Van Diemen's Land: A History* (Melbourne: Black, 2008), 174.

result of evangelical religion, to the transportation and confinement of Aboriginal Tasmanians in the Bass Strait, leading to their death.

There was a rhetorical and cultural imbrication of the sealing and whaling communities in the Bass Strait with the language of the age of revolutions, as revealed in the important writings of the evangelical humanitarian and later 'protector' of Aboriginals, George Augustus Robinson, who oversaw the removal of Aboriginal Tasmanians to the Bass Strait.[62] For Robinson, the sealers were 'wretched men': for 'to abolish the Slave Trade the Govt. at home has expended millions – and that it should exist in this her colony is certainly improper and Disgraceful. These men put the Govt. at defiance.'[63] Already by this point there were calls for the management of these sealing communities, and these calls resonated with the reformation of imperial government in a liberal imperial age. One 1826 report addressed to Governor Arthur of Van Diemen's Land, by a naval officer, described the Strait as 'one continual scene of Violence, Plunder, and the commission of every species of Crime'. It called for tighter checks on the passengers of sealing vessels in order to stem the arrival of escaping prisoners from Sydney to the Strait and their transformation to sealers; a restriction of the period and season during which sealing is allowed to five or six weeks in order to prevent seal pups being killed too young; and the making of a 'Government settlement' on one of the islands with civil and military force.[64] This call for a military settlement presaged the eventual formation of Robinson's reserve for Aboriginal Tasmanians.[65] An act regulating the shipping of Van Diemen's Land, including measures to prevent the stowaway of escaped convicts in vessels, was passed in 1833 in the midst of the Tasmanian War.[66] For Robinson himself, the exercise of liberal reform was exemplified by the rescue of Indigenous women who lived with sealers.

---

[62] For recent transnational readings of Robinson, see A. Johnston and M. Rolls (eds.), *Reading Robinson: Companion Essays to Friendly Mission* (Clayton: Monash University Press, 2012 [2008]).
[63] Papers of George Augustus Robinson, vol. 8, part 3, Van Diemen's Land, 31 Oct. 1830–28 Feb. 1831, p. 68, A 7029, Mitchell Library (hereafter ML), Sydney. For more on the status of abolitionist discourse in the Bass Strait see P. Edmonds, 'Collecting Looerryminer's "testimony": Aboriginal women, sealers, and Quaker humanitarian anti-slavery thought and action in the Bass Strait Islands', *Australian Historical Studies* 45 (2014), 13–33.
[64] Letter from W. Balfour, Naval Officer, to Lieutenant Governor Arthur, dated 30 May 1826, cso1/36, Tasmanian Archives and Heritage Office (hereafter TAHO), Hobart.
[65] See for instance the tissue map of James Allen, the Medical Officer on Flinders Island from 1834 to 1837 and son-in law to Robinson, NG 1419, TAHO, Hobart.
[66] 'An Act for the better preservation of the Ports, Harbours, Havens, Roadsteads, Channels, navigable Creeks and Rivers in Van Diemen's Land, and the better regulation of the Shipping in the same', cro29/1/14, TAHO, Hobart.

The Pacific in the Age of Revolutions

As a humanitarian, he wrote that they had been 'taken from their country' and that the kidnaps had involved white men tying the women's hands and forcibly conducting them to their boats, transporting them to the islands of the Bass Strait. When a 'plurality' were 'possessed', a 'favourite [was] selected, who is exonerated from labour and to whom the others are compelled to submit'.[67] One sealer – Thomas Tucker – was alleged to have shot male Aboriginal Tasmanians while being 'most active' in the pursuit of native women. The 'unmerited cruelty' was evident in the scars on the women. Robinson presented a catalogue of these women's names and stories and he made certain to indicate which had been rescued and placed in his establishment. Among the lists is a woman who was taken by a 'man of colour', another who still had a 'husband among the Blacks' and others who were passed, bartered, and sold between the sealers. There are accounts of women beaten with sticks; for instance one woman reportedly told Robinson how a sealer had wounded her on the head when she lost one of his dogs. In one horrific story, Worethmaleyerpodyer was described thus by Robinson:

> About 20 years of age fine . . . Woman native of the District of Pipers river was forcibly taken from her country by a Sealer name James Everitt [who came to the Strait after the wreck of a whaler in 1820], by whom she was afterward murdered on Woody Island by malicious shooting her through her Body with a Musket Ball because she did not clear the Mutton Birds to please him . . .[68]

Worethmaleyerpodyer's grave was pointed out to him.[69] Yet despite the commitment to the extension of liberty and freedom evident here, and its lineage in the history of abolition, the extent of agency that Robinson attributed to these women is certainly minimal. Robinson's activities as a humanitarian were premised on the interventionism of the age. The women were presented as relying on his rescue.

In addition to such a perspective, it is still important to see the signs of mutuality and the agency of these Aboriginal women at this time of profound change. Robinson reported on women who escaped the sealers and rejoined their communities. This means that his writings cannot be taken, even in their own terms, as indicators of a lack of female agency.

---

[67] 'Register of Names and Descriptions of Native Women forcibly taken away by the sealers and retained by them on the Straits', in DLADD219, Item 9, ML, State Library of New South Wales, Sydney.
[68] From 'Register of Names and Descriptions of Native Women'; note that this murder is not the only one recorded in these papers.
[69] C. Bateson, *Dire Strait: A History of Bass Strait* (Sydney: Angus Reed, 1973), 63.

For instance, a woman who Robinson named Tarerenorer was said to have committed 'dire outrages on the Settled Districts' after escaping from the sealers, and to have then returned to the sealing community. It was then that she was placed in Robinson's custody.[70] Yet that the agency he attributed to Aboriginal Tasmanians is minimal becomes clear when one reflects on how these women were the prime providers for their families, responsible for gathering food from both coast and sea, and known for their swimming, diving, and sea-voyaging.[71] In contrast, James Kelly of Hobart, provides a fuller account of their role along these lines, and prevents them being cast simply as abducted females.

Kelly's crew gave six women a club each and watched the unfolding events. The women crept up close to the seals and lay down with their clubs alongside them; 'some of the seals arose their heads up to look at their new visitors and smell them'. The women then imitated the seals, following the same motions, lifting elbows and hands and scratching themselves as the seals did. It was only an hour later that they suddenly rose and struck the seals on the nose, thus killing them. '[I]n an instant they all jumped up as if by Magic and killed one more each ... they commenced loud laughing and dancing as if they had gained a great Victory over the seals.' They then swam with the dead seals, which presumably required great strength, and brought them to the watching men. On the following day, the women took the lead in killing seals. They also proceeded to roast seal flippers and shoulders. Kelly's vivid portrayal of the women workers could not have been penned without George Briggs as his aide. Briggs was recognized by these communities, having resided in the Strait as a sealer, and having 'two wives and five children' in the Strait. Kelly wrote that Briggs had 'acquired the Native Language'.[72] Kelly reported that the women cried when they were about to leave, and they asked Briggs to wait for a dance, the marker of the end of an agreement or exchange.[73] Three hundred people, including men and children, proceeded to dance at Eddystone Point. The women began 'forming a circle and dancing round the heap of dead seals ... putting themselves into the most singular attitudes'. 'The men then commenced a

---

[70] 'Register of Names and Descriptions of Native Women'.
[71] Cameron, *Grease and Ochre*, 18–19, 42–3.
[72] James Kelly, 'Discovery of Port Davey and Macquarie Harbour, 12 December 1815 – 30 January 1816', TAHO: MM134, p. 49. See also the description of the Kelly voyage in Bateson, *Dire Strait*, 41; for some other discussion of Briggs see Plomley and Henley, *The Sealers of Bass Strait*, 18, and Cameron, *Grease and Ochre*, 74–5.
[73] For dancing as marking the culmination of 'reciprocal exchange' see Cameron, *Grease and Ochre*, 96.

sort of sham fight with spears and waddies then – dancing round the heap of dead seals and striking their spears into them as if they were killing them.'[74]

The age of revolutions as seen from Tasmania should thus encompass the politics of annexation and war, exploration, settlement and surveillance, knowledge-making, and imperial humanitarianism and reformed government. It should also include the continuing possibilities open to Aboriginal people – like those who Kelly watched – to find their own paths.

Conclusions

This is a preliminary sampling of the rich and deeply troubling material that awaits study if we are to consider the Pacific in the late eighteenth and early nineteenth centuries as being at the heart of the age of revolutions, a global moment of conflict and contestation. Bringing it to the centre of this period is to argue that places far from Europe could inflect and change the politics of this moment. It also challenges one of the most Eurocentric terms of periodization in historiography.

Accordingly, it is possible to see the horrific wars of Tasmania as akin to but different from those in Europe in this period, or the modes of reform tied to anti-slavery and anti-piracy around sealing, for instance, as particular and yet linked with similar reforms in the Atlantic world. If we work with the notion of the 'Sea of Islands', the Pacific as a space of dense Indigenous connection, the tragedy here is that Tasmania was being woven into global maps; warfare on Tasmania was being interpreted in relation to that far away, just as Māori were being received in Calcutta like Burmese. This globalization was violent and the place-making which was afoot was rendering the 'Sea of Islands' into 'islands in a far sea'; in the latter conception these sites were ripe for colonization and extraction in an expanding system of migration, commerce, and shipping. Meanwhile, a politics of race, gender, and social reform was unfolding which was interventionist and imperial, denying a voice to local peoples. However, as in the Māori case and elsewhere in the Pacific, new vocabularies of monarchy were giving rise to new possibilities for Indigenous elites. In these ways, though globalization and empire were generating great transformation in these decades, there was still a possibility for Pacific peoples, including Tasmanian Aboriginals, to assert their agency.

[74] Kelly, 'Discovery', 72.

This chapter includes microhistories of elite and less elite voyages as well as social and cultural changes in Tasmania. Methodologically, it is important to bridge these various vectors and scales if we are to make sense of this period of transformation and its effects. Long-distance relations across the Indian and Pacific Oceans, towards the north and India, and across the south with sealers and whalers to southern Africa, has revealed itself in the events studied here. Yet, the intent was also to study the making of Tasmania on the globe as a way of avoiding a prioritization of long-distance relations for the definition of the Pacific's age of revolutions. To argue in this way is not to provincialize, localize, or globalize the Pacific in historiographical terms, but rather to show how it could remake, resist, and contribute to the making of the global.

45

Disease in Pacific History

'The Fatal Impact'?

VICKI LUKER

We have fallen on a new Age, io e.
Infectious disease is spreading amongst us, io e.[1]

After the arrival of European ships, a new age of infectious disease arrived in Fiji. According to the *meke* (dance poem) above,[2] the first epidemic was introduced to Fiji in the late 1700s. This important Indigenous source was recorded by the Fijian public servant Ilai Motonicocoka in the late 1800s; however, his scholarship was later contested.[3] This is a fitting way to introduce a set of debates about a European 'Fatal Impact' on Pacific peoples because of two central questions. Did the coming of European ships really bring a new age of infectious disease to the island Pacific? Was this new age responsible for steep demographic decline before formal colonial rule was implemented?

Personally, I answer 'yes' to the first question: the coming of European ships did bring a new age of infectious disease to the island Pacific. But I doubt that any answer to the second question would be valid in all contexts because the demographic effect of this varied widely: some populations crashed catastrophically; others simply carried on. Besides, do answers to these questions matter 200 or more years later? I will review the 'Fatal Impact' debate with some pain, because early critics of the 'Fatal Impact', whom I call the 'anti-Fatal-Impactists', have left a regrettable legacy, as I will

---

[1] I. Motonicocoka, 'The story of the "lila balavu" (wasting sickness) and of the cokadra (dysentery); and the *meke* (ballads) relating to those events', in *Report of the Commission Appointed to Inquire into the Decrease of the Native Population* (Suva: Edward John Marsh, Government Printer, 1896), appendix 1, [np] (hereafter DR). According to Motonicocoka, the meke was composed by two female prisoners of war brought from Buretu to Bau much earlier in the nineteenth century.
[2] DR.Mot.
[3] For Motonicocoka, see P. France, 'The Kaunitoni migration: notes in the genesis of a Fijian tradition', *Journal of Pacific History* 1 (1966), 107–13, esp. 110 and 112 plus 112 n. 28.

explain. Disease in Pacific history warrants re-evaluation, not least because few students recall either the original debate or its consequences.

Introduction

The period reviewed in this chapter will be the 'classic era of European scientific voyaging',[4] from the late 1700s till the mid-nineteenth century, well before the implementation of colonial rule in most of Polynesia, Melanesia, and Micronesia,[5] and including the voyages of whalers, traders, and mission ships. Aubrey Parke, speaking of Fiji, terms these years 'proto-colonial'.[6] This era also preceded modern census-taking[7] and modern understandings of disease transmission, diagnosis, and prevention. Today, introduced infectious diseases in the island Pacific are usually understood as the sexually transmitted syphilis and gonorrhoea, or other infections which in the West came to be known as 'acute' such as measles, mumps, influenza, whooping cough, and dysentery. 'Coughs came with white men, so did dysentery', as Motonicocoka's fellow countrymen declared.[8] To use the explanation employed by many scholars since William McNeill, such acute infections have been described as 'crowd diseases' that evolved in the cities of the continents; there they became diseases of childhood.[9] But after their introduction to the Pacific Islands, these 'crowd' or childhood diseases affected older people. While Islander communities had some infectious diseases

[4] B. Douglas, 'In the event: indigenous countersigns and the ethnohistory of voyaging', in M. Jolly, S. Tcherkezoff, and D. Tryon (eds.), *Oceanic Encounters: Exchange, Desire, Violence* (Canberra: ANU Press, 2009), 175–98, at 175.
[5] This nomenclature is based on J. Dumont D'Urville, 'Sur les îles du *Grand Océan*', *Bulletin de la Société de Géographie* 17 (1832), 1–21; trans. I. Ollivier, A. de Biran, and G. Clarke as 'On the Islands of the Great Ocean', *Journal of Pacific History* 38:2 (2003), 163–74, and it remains controversial. I use the terms geographically only. For an outline of its effects on the writing of history and on European ways of viewing the Pacific, see P. D'Arcy, 'Cultural divisions and island environments since the time of Dumont d'Urville', *Journal of Pacific History* 38:2 (2003), 217–35. John Miles lists voyages of exploration from 1511 till 1842, but I will concentrate on the period after 1767; J. Miles, *Infectious Diseases: Colonising the Pacific?* (Dunedin: University of Otago Press 1997), 115–16.
[6] A. Parke, *Degei's Descendants: Spirits, Place and People in Pre-Cession Fiji*, ed. M. Spriggs and D. Scarr (Canberra: ANU Press, 2014), xix.
[7] While the missionaries often attempted censuses, and their figures may be more reliable than previous European counts, they were subject to many limitations. Also, contemporaneous Indigenous estimations, based on such things as tribute or men available for battle, indicate that Indigenous leaders had compelling interests in population. But today demographers lament the quality of data from many Pacific Island countries. G. Haberkorn, 'Pacific Islands' population and development: facts, fictions and follies', *New Zealand Population Review* 33/4 (2008), 95–127.
[8] DR 31.
[9] W.H. McNeill, *Plagues and Peoples* (Garden City, NY: Anchor Press, 1976), 50–1 (repr. Harmondsworth: Penguin, 1979).

Disease In Pacific History

before the European ships came, such as yaws, generally they had been insulated, to varying degrees, from continental epidemiologies.

Not all introduced infections were 'European'. Syphilis, which early European navigators did not distinguish from gonorrhoea, perhaps originated in the Americas.[10] Malaria had long been endemic in parts of New Guinea, the Solomon Islands, and Vanuatu, but spread during the colonial era.[11] A fungal skin infection, known as Tokelau ringworm, spread from indentured Tokelauans to Fijians in the nineteenth century.[12] Tuberculosis and leprosy had been present in some Pacific Island populations for millennia, and here again European transportation systems acted as a powerful vector.[13]

Many on board 'European' ships, especially in the nineteenth century, had little or no European ancestry; Islanders themselves were prized as crew and missionaries.[14] Nor should we discount Indigenous shipping. The late eighteenth to the mid-nineteenth century was a particularly active period of Indigenous seafaring;[15] Tongans, for example, sailed to and from Sāmoa and Fiji. Finally, many Islanders lived well inland, especially those not 'contacted' for the first time by Europeans until the mid-nineteenth century in the southwest Pacific.[16] For them, introduced diseases travelled overland.[17]

[10] McNeill, *Plagues and People* (1979 edn), 185, 186, 202–3, 304 n.2, 308 n.35.
[11] J.A. Cattani, 'The epidemiology of malaria in Papua New Guinea', in R.D. Attenborough and M.P. Alpers (eds.), *Human Biology in Papua New Guinea: The Small Cosmos* (Oxford: Oxford University Press, 1992), 302–12. See also J.A. Bennett, 'Malaria, medicine, and Melanesians: contested hybrid spaces in World War II', *Health and History* 8:9 (2006), 27–55. Black noted that European influence was 'the cause of [malaria's] increase and spread'; R.H. Black, 'The epidemiology of malaria in the Southwest Pacific: changes associated with increasing European contact', *Oceania* 27:2 (1956), 136–42, at 142.
[12] DR 32.
[13] On leprosy, see V. Luker, 'The lessons of leprosy? Reflections on Hansen's Disease in the response to HIV and Aids', *Journal of Pacific History* 52:3 (2017), 388–90; on tuberculosis, see K. Viney, 'Problems and prospects for tuberculosis prevention and care in the Pacific Islands', PhD thesis, Australian National University, Canberra, 2015.
[14] D.A. Chappell, *Double Ghosts: Oceanian Voyagers on Euroamerican Ships* (Armonk, NY: M.E. Sharpe, 1997). For Islander missionaries being blamed for the introduction of epidemic infections into New Caledonia, see e.g. R.G. Crocombe and M.T. Crocombe, *The Works of Ta'unga: Records of a Polynesian Traveller* (Canberra: ANU Press 1968), 59.
[15] D'Arcy, 'Cultural divisions and island environments', 232.
[16] Epeli Hau'ofa suggests caution when using the term 'contact'; E. Hau'ofa, 'Epilogue, pasts to remember', in R. Borofsky (ed.), *Remembrance of Pacific Pasts: An Invitation to Remake History* (Honolulu: University of Hawai'i Press, 2000), 453–71, at 455. In this chapter, 'contact' refers to early interactions between a local Indigenous people and European or other carriers of infection.
[17] But their experience falls largely outside the chronological span of this discussion, as does the SS *Talune*, which brought the influenza pandemic to the colonies of Fiji, Western Sāmoa and Nauru, and the protectorate of Tonga in 1918.

The variations in introduced disease must also be noted. 'Know one [outbreak], and you know ... one [outbreak].'[18] The overall Pacific picture is dynamic, variegated, and changing. If one elides differences in pathogens, different 'European' and Indigenous conditions abound. At some ports of the Pacific – such as Honolulu in Hawai'i, Matavai Bay in Tahiti, the Bay of Islands in New Zealand, or Port Jackson in Australia, many 'European' ships docked during the early nineteenth century. Over time some ports grew, and became greater sources of disease transmission, due in part to Indigenous migration accompanied by pauperization and overcrowding. Some Indigenous communities were already large without the formation of such a port, such as in Fiji's Rewa Delta, which may have supported a population of 35,000 to 40,000.[19] In cases like this, a difference in disease resistance involves the pre-existing local disease profile. At the time, some European observers assumed that yaws granted immunity to syphilis, making only Indigenous people unprotected by yaws vulnerable to introduced syphilis.[20] Meanwhile, endemic malaria in New Guinea, the Solomon Islands, and Vanuatu was among the factors that delayed formal colonialism. Thus malaria had a 'Fatal Impact' on Europeans![21]

The Opposition to 'Fatal Impact'

The Fatal Impact, by Alan Moorehead, was first published in 1966 and much republished.[22] This popular history narrated a tale of European destruction of the peoples and environments of Tahiti, Australia, and the Antarctic, focusing

---

[18] The above quote paraphrases A. Kurchanski, *The Rules of Contagion* (London: Profile Books, 2020), 3.

[19] J.T. Parry, *Ring Ditch Fortifications in the Rewa Delta, Fiji, Air Photo Interpretation and Analysis*, Bulletin of the Fiji Museum 3 (1977), 73.

[20] Pirie thinks it unlikely that the yaws syndrome existed throughout the eastern extremities of human settlement of the Island Pacific; P. Pirie, 'The effects of treponematosis and gonorrhoea on the populations of the Pacific', *Human Biology in Oceania* 1:3 (1972), 187–206. The theory he propounds may explain the predominant occurrence of Generalized Paralysis of the Insane among the Indigenous inmates of St Giles, who were thought not to have suffered the necessary infection of syphilis; J. Leckie, *Colonizing Madness: Asylum and Community in Fiji* (Honolulu: University of Hawai'i Press, 2020), 44, 129, 135–40.

[21] D. Denoon, S. Firth, J. Linnekin, M. Meleisea, and K. Nero (eds.), *The Cambridge History of the Pacific Islanders* (Cambridge: Cambridge University Press, 1997), 115. The first Germans who attempted settlement of New Guinea died from malaria, and mortality from malaria among Polynesian missionaries to Papua and the Solomon Islands was breathtaking; P. Curtin, *Disease and Empire: The Health of European Troops in the Conquest of Africa* (Cambridge: Cambridge University Press 1998).

[22] A. Moorehead, *The Fatal Impact: An Account of the Invasion of the South Pacific* (London: Hamish Hamilton, 1966).

especially on diseases introduced by the first two voyages under Captain Cook. Moorehead also lamented the introduction of Christianity, muskets, alcohol, capitalist exploitation, and foreign laws, and noted the ecological damage of European whaling and sealing.

The first anti-Fatal-Impactists were academic Pacific historians, specifically the contemporaries and followers of James Wightman Davidson, who became the world's first professor of Pacific History at the Australian National University in Canberra. In 1966, the inaugural issue of the *Journal of Pacific History* published Davidson's agenda for Pacific history, especially the importance of Indigenous voices and agency.[23] Moorehead's book summed up all that Davidson and his circle opposed, especially the belief that Europeans always had an outsized influence upon Indigenous peoples. Perhaps the greatest anti-Fatal-Impactist was Kerry Howe, simultaneously influential in Pacific history and in the history of his native Aotearoa New Zealand. He studied at the ANU, was in Davidson's department,[24] and summarized the objections to Moorehead's Fatal Impact analysis: 'The Pacific Islanders seldom featured ... and when they did they were usually portrayed as helpless, passive, inferior, and the objects of European initiatives, not subjects in themselves.'[25]

Howe praised the 'new Pacific historians'[26] like Norma McArthur, who had 'shown that for the most part the alleged depopulation of Pacific islands in the nineteenth century – the topic that so obsessed generations of commentators – is a myth, and one usually created by Europeans who looked for what they wanted to see'.[27] Howe regarded her as the new authority on the demography of Islanders,[28] and as a result her 1967 *Island Populations of the Pacific* stifled debate about Pacific Island population decline before it could

---

[23] J.W. Davidson, 'Problems of Pacific history', *Journal of Pacific History* 1:1 (1966), 5–22. This agenda had been delivered more than a decade earlier, so was not new. For a biography, see D. Denoon, 'Davidson, James Wightman (Jim) (1915–1973)', in *Australian Dictionary of Biography*, vol. XIII (Melbourne: Melbourne University Press, 1993).

[24] For Kerry Howe's time at the Australian National University, see K.R. Howe, 'Recalling the Coombs – Pacific History 1970–73', in B.V. Lal and A. Ley (eds.), *The Coombs, House of Memories?* (Canberra: Pandanus Press, 2006), 265–8.

[25] K.R. Howe, *Where the Waves Fall: A New South Sea Islands History from First Settlement to Colonial Rule* (Honolulu: University of Hawai'i Press, 1984). Howe's perhaps best-known statement against the 'Fatal Impact', as defined by this chapter, was K.R. Howe, 'The fate of the "savage" in Pacific historiography', *New Zealand Journal of History* 11:2 (1977), 137–54.

[26] Howe, *Where the Waves Fall*; for 'new', see the book's subtitle, preface, chapter title on 347 and elsewhere in the book.

[27] Howe, *Where the Waves Fall*, 351.

[28] As late as the turn of the century, Howe described her as having written 'the best foundational survey of [Pacific] island populations'; K.R. Howe, *Nature, Culture, and History: The 'Knowing' of Oceania* (Honolulu: University of Hawai'i Press, 2000), 98 n.14.

properly begin.[29] While she was originally a mathematician, McArthur's history doctorate had studied the impact of epidemic disease on the population of Aneityum in what is now Vanuatu, finding evidence of steep, disease-induced depopulation.[30] Her dismissal of most European scholarship in her field resonated with her Australian and New Zealand colleagues and exposed important miscalculations.[31] She ridiculed the idea that the despair of Islanders had any role in population decrease, laughing at still current theories about the importance of psychology.[32] McArthur and the anti-Fatal-Impactists in Canberra seemed unaffected by contemporaneous trends in North American scholarship and beyond.

A North American Challenge

In 1966 Henry Dobyns published an influential article on the upward revision of Indigenous American populations before conquest.[33] Dobyns included a number of sources such as archaeology and oral traditions in addition to the colonial population estimates which had been McArthur's sole source. Simultaneously, North American scholars were working on the impact of new diseases in world history. The big names in this endeavour were William H. McNiell and Alfred Crosby.[34] McNeill wrote of 'disease pools',

[29] I.C. Campbell, 'More celebrated than read: the work of Norma McArthur', in D. Munro and B.V. Lal (eds.), *Texts and Contexts: Reflections in Pacific Islands Historiography* (Honolulu: University of Hawai'i Press 2006), 98–110, at 98.
[30] N. McArthur, 'Population and prehistory: the late phase on Aneityum', PhD thesis, Australian National University, Canberra, 1974.
[31] Some difficulties with population data of the Island Pacific, especially death registration, are still being addressed.
[32] W.H.R. Rivers, 'The psychological factor', in W.H.R. Rivers (ed.), *Essays on the Depopulation of Melanesia* (Cambridge: Cambridge University Press, 1922), 84–113. Rivers was medically trained and particularly interested in psychiatry. His psychological factor was only one of his suggested explanations for population decline; and while he failed to recognize the importance of suppressed fertility due to disease as a factor, distress might not be so inapplicable after all. See T. Bayliss-Smith, 'Colonialism as shell-shock: W.H.R. Rivers's explanations for depopulation in Melanesia', in E. Hviding and C. Berg (eds.), *The Ethnographic Experiment: A.M. Hocart and W.H.R. Rivers in Island Melanesia, 1908* (New York: Berghahn Books, 2014), 179–213; J.A. Bennett, 'A vanishing race or a vanishing discourse? W.H.R. Rivers's "psychological factor" and the depopulation in the Solomon Islands and the New Hebrides', in Hviding and Berg (eds.), *The Ethnographic Experiment*, 214–51.
[33] H. Dobyns, 'Estimating aboriginal American population: an appraisal of techniques with a new hemispheric population estimate', *Current Anthropology* 7 (1966), 395–416. Dobyns refers to the work of Cook and Borah. See also H.F. Dobyns, *Their Number Become Thinned: Native American Population Dynamics in Eastern North America* (Knoxville: University of Tennessee Press, 1983).
[34] McNeill, *Plagues and People*; A.W. Crosby, *Ecological Imperialism: The Biological Expansion of Europe, 900–1900* (Cambridge: Cambridge University Press, 1986).

with Oceania the last region of the world to be incorporated. In 1986 Alfred Crosby published *Ecological Imperialism*, which featured the European take-over of New Zealand. As the title of the book suggests, Crosby argued that colonialism was aided by the germs and animals enjoyed, at first unwittingly, by Europeans in their portmanteau biota. Later Crosby was to quip that Cortez did not conquer America – smallpox did.[35]

While the upward revision of the North American population remains contested,[36] there can be no doubt that Indigenous experiences in the Pacific Islands and the Americas had challenged academic assumptions.

Drawing on American revisionism, David E. Stannard, a historian of American Studies in Honolulu, published *Before the Horror: Hawaiian Population on the Eve of European Contact* in 1989. In effect, he brought back, transformed, and renamed 'The Fatal Impact' as 'The Horror'.[37] Stannard's slim volume argued that accepted estimates of the Hawaiian population at 'contact' were too low. The volume included responses from two of the authorities with whom Stannard disagreed, Eleanor Nordyke and Robert Schmitt. According to Stannard, Hawaiians, who were generally estimated to be around 250,000, should have been numbered at 800,000 at least. His upward revision was welcomed by Hawaiian nationalists such as Haunani-Kay Trask.[38] Stannard depicted anti-Fatal-Impactists as hopelessly old-fashioned and/or illogical, giving them no credit for trying something new.[39]

A major achievement by Stannard was to show how new infections can repress fertility. The effects of introduced syphilis and gonorrhoea were already recognized, but Stannard highlighted the longer term effects of other introduced diseases on the ability of Indigenous women to conceive and bear healthy children.[40] For this reason among others, he argued against

---

[35] A. Crosby, 'Interview', *Environmental History* 14:3 (2009), 562.
[36] D. Henige, *Numbers from Nowhere: The American Indian Contact Population Debate* (Norman: University of Oklahoma Press, 1998) and P. Kelon, *Epidemics and Enslavement: Biological Catastrophe in the Native Southeast* (Lincoln: University of Nebraska Press, 2007).
[37] D.E. Stannard, *Before the Horror: The Population of Hawaii on the Eve of Western Contact* (Honolulu: University of Hawai'i Press, 1989).
[38] H.-K. Trask, 'Hawaii, colonization and decolonization', in A. Hooper, S. Britton, R. Crocombe, J. Huntsman, and C. Macpherson (eds.), *Class and Culture in the South Pacific* (Suva: Institute of Pacific Studies, 1987), 157–75, at 172–3 n.2.
[39] To be fair, he cites McArthur favourably as a co-author of a piece that serves one angle of his argument; Stannard, *Before the Horror*, 33, 34–6, 88 n.3, 89 n.5.
[40] D.E. Stannard, 'Disease and infertility: a new look at the demographic collapse of native populations in the wake of Western contact', *Journal of American Studies* 24:23 (1990), 325–50.

infanticide as a cause of Hawaiian depopulation.[41] Dismissing this idea as a colonialist myth, he pointed out that European scholarship had been inclined to 'blame the victim', attributing Indigenous decline to Indigenous practices (such as infanticide, other forms of killing, lack of nursing).[42] In the small world of Hawaiian Studies and historians of disease, Stannard's challenge led to a flurry of literature both for and against him.[43]

An issue which Stannard's work implicitly highlighted was survival.

The Post-colonial Turn

David A. Chappell published an article in 1995 that went to the heart of a central problem with both the 'Fatal-Impactists' and the 'anti-Fatal-Impactists': both could be seen as 'colonial'.[44] Fatal-Impactists glorified the effect of Europeans; anti-Fatal-Impactists said that Europeans had no effect. While the Fatal Impact denied native agency, the anti-Fatal-Impactists bestowed it to deny the colonialists' agency in depopulation. Because their work could be seen as apologizing for colonialism, low-counters such as McArthur could now be called 'colonialist', when that was far from her own intention, or that of the other anti-Fatal-Impactists who revered her demographic authority. Chappell tried to get beyond the dichotomy of agent–victim which he saw as dominating Pacific historiography to the time of his writing. In so doing, without explicitly invoking Stannard, he argued that victims of depopulation could be agents. '[F]atal impact' warranted another look, according to Chappell, 'because polemics have prevented Pacific historians from adequately dealing with disease'.[45] He believed that 'agency'

[41] D.E. Stannard, 'Recounting fables of savagery: native infanticide and the functions of political myths', *Journal of American Studies* 25:3 (1991), 381–418.
[42] Brantlinger referred to proleptic elegy, that is, the lament on the passing of Native populations before they had passed; P. Brantlinger, *Dark Vanishings: Discourse on the Extinction of Primitive Races, 1800–1930* (Ithaca, NY: Cornell University Press, 2003), 3.
[43] This includes T.L. Hunt et al., Book review forum, *Pacific Studies* 13:3 (1990), 255–301; P.V. Kirch's review of *The Horror* in *Contemporary Pacific* 2:2 (1990), 394–6; A.W. Crosby, 'Hawaiian depopulation as a model for the Amerindian experience', in T. Ranger and P. Slack (eds.), *Epidemics and Idea: Essays on the Historical Perception of Pestilence* (Cambridge: Cambridge University Press, 1992), 175–201; A.F. Bushnell, '"The Horror" reconsidered: an evaluation of the historical evidence for population decline in Hawai'i, 1778–1803', *Pacific Studies* 16:3 (1993), 115–62; O.A. Bushnell, *The Gifts of Civilization: Germs and Genocide in Hawaii* (Honolulu: University of Hawai'i Press, 1993).
[44] D.A. Chappell, 'Active Agents versus passive victims: decolonized historiography or problematic paradism?', *The Contemporary Pacific* 7:2 (1995), 303–26.
[45] Chappell, 'Active agents', 316. An early attempt to construe Indigenous agency in health provision, and to subvert the binary related to agency versus victim was Anne Perez Hattori's chapter on midwives in A.P. Hattori, *Colonial Dis-ease? US Navy Health Policies and the Chamorro of Guam* (Honolulu: University of Hawai'i Press, 2004, 91–123). Attempts have since been made

and 'victimhood' could coexist at any one time. Victimhood need not be partnered with passivity, and all agents were in a sense the victims of circumstance, or, as he wrote in his abstract: 'actors tend to be embedded in structures'.[46] Victimhood could also be empowering; it could connote injustice and be a tool for redress.[47]

Patrick V. Kirch (an archaeologist) and Jean-Louis Rallu (a historical demographer) edited a volume published in 2007[48] that asked the question of proto-colonial population decline in the long-term context of changes to Pacific Island populations, especially in islands that founding settlers had to sail beyond the horizon from their homeland to reach. They also took issue with the Norma McArthur tradition. They saw the question of population decline after 'contact' as one that should be left for archaeologists to decide. Although they supported the idea of steep proto-colonial demographic decline due to introduced diseases, fieldwork had not yet provided any firm answers. Nevertheless Kirch believed that the decline and, in some cases, collapse of Pacific Island populations was an 'essential' story, and the editors hoped their book would inspire others 'to join us on that road'.[49]

Regarding Hawai'i, Kirch agreed that the introduction of diseases from the earliest interaction with Cook would have had a negative effect on Indigenous mortality and fertility and that the actual archipelagic population on the eve of 'contact' was 'perhaps unknowable'.[50] But he did not follow Stannard in advocating a population of 800,000–1,000,000 and subsequent commentators took their lead from him in advocating a population of 500,000.[51] Several chapters in the collection focused on Hawai'i, but Roger Green shared findings from decades earlier on Sāmoa, generating vociferous objections from Derek Freeman and, later, by inference, from Norma McArthur herself.[52]

---

to reconsider disease. For example, for the consideration of the lived experience of disease see S. Archer, *Sharks upon the Land: Colonialism, Indigenous Health, and Culture in Hawai'i, 1778–1855* (Cambridge: Cambridge University Press, 2018) and the revisionist treatment by J. Samson, 'The sleepiness of George Sarawia: the impact of disease on the Melanesian Mission at Mota, c. 1870–1900', *Journal of Pacific History* 52:2 (2017), 156–71.

[46] Chappell, 'Active agents', 326.

[47] See e.g. Hattori, *Colonial Dis-ease*, 15, which notes the shift from 'done to' historiography.

[48] P.V. Kirch and J.-L. Rallu (eds.), *The Growth and Collapse of Pacific Island Societies: Archaeological and Demographic Perspectives* (Honolulu: University of Hawai'i Press, 2007).

[49] P.V. Kirch, 'Concluding remarks', in Kirch and Rallu (eds.), *The Growth and Collapse of Pacific Island Societies*, 326–37, at 337.

[50] P.V. Kirch, '"Like shoals of fish": archaeology and population in pre-contact Hawai'i', in Kirch and Rallu (eds.), *The Growth and Collapse of Pacific Island Societies*, 52–69, at 53.

[51] E.g. Archer, *Sharks upon the Land*, 28.

[52] R.C. Green, 'Protohistoric Samoan population', in Kirch and Rallu (eds.), *The Growth and Collapse of Pacific Island Societies*, 203–31, at 217.

Christophe Sand and co-authors finished their contribution concerning New Caledonia with the testimony of Poindi-Poweu that he 'was the last pagan of the region, and his life had been completely molded by a tragedy that came from abroad: epidemics'.[53]

Kirch and Rallu's volume marked a milestone in the stand-off between the low- and high-counters: between Norma McArthur and Stannard. It came down on the side of the high-counters, although its message was: high, but not too high. Though Rallu had felt personally attacked by the McArthur tradition,[54] she did not endorse Stannard. But their collection was lopsided in three respects. First, the category 'Pacific Islands' was, understandably, geared towards Polynesia, and particularly Hawai'i and French Polynesia. What about the Solomon Islands or Papua New Guinea? Second, it focused on a rather old-fashioned approach to archaeology, disregarding Indigenous testimony[55] and endeavouring to be as scientifically rigorous as McArthur.[56] But more importantly, the volume was methodologically uneven: one of the editors was a historical demographer, but only one chapter was written from this perspective.[57] Thirdly, discussion focused narrowly on the population of Pacific Island societies, neglecting discussion of the introduction of disease. If, like me, you accept the possibility that decline might have been steep post-'contact', then you must look elsewhere for the latest thinking on disease transmission and prevalence.

Contemporary Concerns

Ironically, while the Horror is now generally accepted among historians, and interest in infectious diseases has ultimately been replaced by chronic,

---

[53] C. Sand, J. Bolé, and A. Ouétcho, 'What were the real numbers? The question of pre-contact population densities in New Caledonia', in Kirch and Rallu (eds.), *The Growth and Collapse of Pacific Island Societies*, 306–25, at 315.

[54] For Jean-Louis Rallu's experience, see J.-L. Rallu, 'Pre- and post-contact population in island Melanesia: can projections meet retrodictions?' in Kirch and Rallu (eds.), *The Growth and Collapse of Pacific Island Societies*, 15–34, at 16–17.

[55] Kirch and Rallu were unlike Stannard, who gestured towards Indigenous memory, but did not show what this evidence was or how his case was shaped by it; and unlike someone such as Aubrey Parke, who tried to combine Indigenous evidence with archaeological findings. See e.g. M. Spriggs, 'Aubrey Parke; an enthusiastic amateur in Fiji?' in A. Parke, *Degei's Descendants, Spirits, Place and People in Pre-cession Fiji*, ed. M. Spriggs and D. Scarr (Canberra: ANU Press, 2014), xii–xiii.

[56] I am reminded of Christina Thompson's comment on the mid-twentieth-century desire for mathematical accuracy; C. Thompson, *Sea People: The Puzzle of Polynesia* (New York: HarperCollins, 2019), 257.

[57] Rallu was of course cited as co-author of the introduction that was evidently largely written by Kirch. P.V. Kirch and J.-L. Rallu, 'Long-term demographic evolution in the Pacific Islands', in Kirch and Rallu (eds.), *The Growth and Collapse of Pacific Island Societies*, 1–14.

non-communicable diseases such as diabetes, more attention than ever has been given to the variation within the island Pacific. The 'Fatal Impact' and its critics seem outmoded now, and there is no single position that encompasses all Pacific history as the anti-Fatal-Impactists seemed to promise. The question of the initial decrease of the Indigenous popuations after 'contact' is extremely important for living island communities, but has fallen out of academic view to become a narrow specialist concern, particularly of archaeologists. Yet the archaeologists have no firm answers on the size of populations prior to 'contact'. There is little attention paid to the nature of the diseases introduced, and there is an uncritical acceptance of steep Indigenous population decline due to introduced diseases.

If funding and interest can be found, I would advocate two kinds of research. First, I would exhort historians of particular Indigenous communities to focus on the questions of when colonialism came to their community, whether their community experienced a proto-colonial decline, and whether there is evidence of introduced diseases. More generally, I would suggest that someone examine records of people-moving, such as shipping. For example, Tahiti was a favoured port of call for ships, and presumably this single factor resulted in repeated primary introductions of diseases by crewmen from other environments. However, other island populations were not exposed to those primary introductions. Were they exposed to secondary introductions? And what factors (such as shipping speeds, conditions on board, conditions in place of origin) influenced primary introductions? In the absence of firm data, one is left to speculation, circumstance, and the serendipity of sources. But perhaps a researcher can weave together the views of individual researchers on their communities of special interests.

I accept that, in the long nineteenth century, European estimates of Indigenous populations were unreliable. I also accept that the Indigenous population may have already declined when the European demographic data (such as mission censuses) became more reliable. But the Fiji example is one where the records that remain suggest that the proto-colonial toll of introduced disease was heavier than perhaps the anti-Fatal-Impactists thought. I am therefore open on these grounds to the possibility of steep, proto-colonial declines. On the other hand, it is likely that the Highlands of PNG were home to communities that did not decline in the period leading to formal colonization, although they felt the effects of influenza. There were no doubt communities which boomed demographically in the proto-colonial period.

Secondly, the emphasis on epidemics as a cause of depopulation distracts from the other effects of new diseases. Epidemics are dramatic and obvious. But what about epidemics that became regular events, or the way that newly introduced diseases became endemic in local populations, either because the local population was large enough, or because the disease (or strain of the disease, such as tuberculosis) was not acute, but chronic? Norma McArthur had noted how epidemics could reduce the number of women coming to reproductive age, and there were other ways in which the reproductive ability of women could be reduced. One was the introduction of syphilis and gonorrhoea. The introduction of syphilis appears to have been particularly marked among those populations in Polynesian areas that did not feature yaws, since yaws seems to have granted some immunity to syphilis. Venereal diseases certainly limited the number of Indigenous children brought into some parts of the Pacific world. But on the other hand, in Fiji at least, population decline in the early 1890s was due not to fewer children being born but to more children combined with higher infant mortality. Children were being born sooner because the previous child had died of introduced diseases, making the mother sexually and reproductively available. I have explained this dynamic elsewhere. But it is possible for the fertility rate of each woman to be high, but infant mortality due to introduced diseases to be too high too.

Given the variability of the communities of the island Pacific during the long nineteenth century, and beyond both the beginning and the end zones, I would wish that prior commitments to support 'The Fatal Impact' or 'The Horror' or the criticism of 'The Fatal Impact' would be suspended in individual cases, so that a priori one does not rule out the opposite of one's commitment having occurred. As indicated earlier, support of 'The Fatal Impact' or 'The Horror' tends to favour the great diminution of Indigenous populations due to introduced diseases. On the other hand, the anti-Fatal-Impactists tend to favour low or no decline of the Indigenous population due to imported disease.[58] So I hope that every researcher looks into the possibility that their community diminished or otherwise on 'contact'. How you, as a researcher, go about this question is up to you.

---

[58] For literature against the idea of virgin soil epidemics, see D.S. Jones, 'Virgin soils revisited', *William and Mary Quarterly* 60:4 (2003), 703–42; for the earlier viewpoint, see A. Crosby, 'Virgin soil epidemics as a factor in the aboriginal depopulation in America', *William and Mary Quarterly* 33:2 (1976), 289–99.

Conclusions

Let me return to the main questions of this chapter. I defined 'The Fatal Impact' as the steep decline of Indigenous Pacific populations due to the introduction, by Europeans, of new, infectious diseases. Many readers probably accept this idea, but at the outset of Pacific History as a discipline, such a decline was strenuously rejected on what seemed to be good grounds. Thus 'The Fatal Impact' involves a historiographical argument, including a debate about disciplinary methodology and the motivations of students.

Regarding initial population size, the anti-Fatal-Impactists were, following Norma McArthur, low-counters. But the Horrorists were 'high-counters', after Stannard, who applied to Hawai'i the upward revision of an American school of Indigenous population studies. While each side agreed that introduced disease had been the main reason for the decline of island populations where decline occurred, the low-counting anti-Fatal-Impactists took a narrow view of 'disease as epidemic' while the Horrorists took a wider view. Stannard did well to focus on the limiting effects on reproduction caused by many introduced diseases as well as the mortality caused by introduced diseases.

As a result, anti-Fatal-Impactists and their successors the Horrorists took opposite views on the crash of Islander populations following European interaction. The anti-Fatal-Impactists not only had a lower population level from which to drop, but a narrower concept of the effects of introduced disease. The Horrorists tended to favour larger numbers at 'contact', thus proposing a higher level from which the population could drop, and they had a wider concept of the effects of introduced disease. While each side was 'anti-colonial' in its own way, and other similarities have been noted, the radical difference between the two was their vision of Indigenous agency. According to the anti-Fatal-Impactist, the infected Islander was not a victim, but instead an agent; according to the Horrorists, the Native was both a victim and an agent.

To go back to the second question: it is likely that, in some Pacific Island populations, the introduction of new diseases may have been the main factor in local population decline. Even if too much attention has focused on epidemics in the longer term, often a disease known to Europeans as a childhood illness, or a chronic complaint, manifested among Islanders as a virulent epidemic. This process might have been invisible to Europeans on ships because they left before the epidemic took hold. Finally, epidemics may have been more lethal on first introduction than later on. Matthew Spriggs argued that depopulation on Aneityum may have been steeper in the early decades of 'contact'.[59]

So I conclude that 'one size does not fit all'. Kerry Howe has more recently taken the position that, while some populations decreased, others did not, even though he remains a low-counter. Epeli Hau'ofa, who gave the classic and inspiring statement of Indigenous agency, also represents the tendency to dismiss the agency language of the Fatal Impact and everything it entailed, while embracing the Horror.

The Horrorists, who succeeded the anti-Fatal-Impactists, have also tended too readily to generalize. While in the long nineteenth century some populations did suffer terrible disease and left descendants, this was not the whole story. One could assume that some communities did not indeed survive. One might also assume that some communities in this era survived and flourished, little touched by Europeans, their representatives, and their 'European' diseases

So can we bid farewell to the term 'Fatal Impact'? It is an old term, with connotations of a lack of Indigenous agency. Anti-Fatal-Impactists may belong to a bygone era too, but they were trying something new. Their dismissal of steep, initial population decline was, in the case of Norma McArthur, tied to efforts to apply rigorous mathematical methodology to woolly numbers and to remove from the foreground European vainglory. In so doing, The anti-Fatal-Impactists could be accused of 'excusing' colonialism and minimizing colonialism's ill-effects, for instance with regard to the consequences of new diseases. In so doing, the Anti-Fatal-Impactists, in an old-fashioned way, may have downplayed both the biological aspects of colonialism and the ability of Islanders to survive such onslaughts. These could be seen as fundamental weaknesses of their position.

---

[59] M. Spriggs, 'Vegetable kingdoms: taro irrigation and Pacific prehistory', PhD thesis, Australian National University, Canberra, 1981, esp. chapters 2–4.

46

The Culture Concept and Christian Missions in the Pacific

HELEN GARDNER

From the Spanish Jesuits, who arrived first on the island of Guam in 1688 then spread the gospel through the Marianas,[1] to the stream of missions, both Protestant and Catholic, which swept through Oceania in the following centuries, European missionaries struggled to understand and describe the lives of the people they encountered. From high islands and coral atolls priests and reverends reported back to Europe on the polity, the religion, or the kinship of the peoples with whom they worked, using terms such as 'tradition', 'custom', or 'practice' or their Spanish, French, or German equivalent, often prefaced with 'primitive' or 'savage'.[2] Except for German missionaries, the word they did not use – up until the twentieth century – was 'culture'. For English-speaking missionaries, at least, 'culture' referred to refinement and the attainment of civilization. It was reserved for the higher classes and almost exclusively to Europeans. Yet, in a remarkable shift for a single word, 'culture' – led by the new discipline of anthropology – largely lost its older meaning, to emerge in the twentieth century as a new conceptual tool for the understanding and describing of human difference. As professional anthropologists arrived in Oceania they honed the culture concept to insist on the plurality of cultures and to defend Islander traditions and customs. Many did their research with the assistance of in situ missionaries, who were eager to engage in the new disciplines. Most anthropologists, however, viewed mission as the enemy of 'culture', yet from the 1930s many missionaries trained in anthropology and the culture concept was picked up by theology.

The term 'culture' is now so paradigmatic in global thought and deployed so frequently in historical and contemporary analyses that it is easy to forget that it

---

[1] F. Hezel, 'From conversion to conquest: the early Spanish mission in the Marianas', *Journal of Pacific History* 17:3 (1982), 115–37.

[2] B. Douglas, '"Novus Orbis Australis": Oceania in the science of race, 1750–1850', in B. Douglas and C. Ballard (eds.), *Foreign Bodies: Oceania and the Science of Race 1750–1850* (Canberra: ANU Press 2008), 99–155, at 99.

has a history. This chapter will explore first how Christian missionaries in the Pacific represented the customs and societies of those with whom they worked in the period prior to the introduction of the culture concept. From the middle of the twentieth century an anthropologically inspired understanding of human difference became central to theology and missiology and radically changed the relationship between mission societies and their converts. As the missions and the colonies of the Pacific decolonized, the new independent churches of the Pacific deployed the theologies of culture – known as contextualization or enculturation – as the heart of their churches and their nations.

The culture concept is notoriously difficult to define and much debated by anthropologists; indeed the history of the term within the discipline is opaque. This chapter is concerned with 'culture' beyond the discipline where missionaries and theologians picked up the idea as a set of established principles, ignoring the debates at the core. The concept has also shifted in ways difficult for historians to track but these key points are generally accepted, at least for the twentieth century. 'Culture' is a means of under-standing human behaviour according to three key precepts. First that cul-tures are relative: people are born into, shaped by, and understand the world according to their culture. Therefore, no culture holds the absolute truth – indeed for extreme cultural determinists, truth itself is culturally determined, as is morality. Second, that cultures are plural: all cultures are equally valid and should coexist. Finally, cultures are holistic and bounded: people identify themselves and others as members of a single defined culture.[3]

As we now live under the paradigm of culture, reading missionary texts written before the adoption of the concept can be disconcerting. The lack of pluralism or relativism in old missionary accounts appears insensitive at best and racist at worst. Many missionaries arrived on the beaches of Pacific islands believing that conversion proved that God's favoured species was one and that the converted Islander would quickly assume the mantle of the civilized European. They saw no problem in emphasizing the life practices of pre-Christian Islanders as 'savage' or 'primitive' in letters and reports home. Historian Jane Samson describes this as the simultaneous 'brothering' and 'othering' of missionary work.[4] Brothering claimed the essential unity of the human species and provided the theological argument for the value of

---

[3] G.W. Stocking Jr, 'Introduction: the basic assumptions of Boasian anthropology', in G. Stocking (ed.), *A Franz Boas Reader: The Shaping of American Anthropology 1883–1911* (Chicago: University of Chicago Press, 1982), 19.

[4] J. Samson, *Race and Redemption: British Missionaries Encounter Pacific Peoples, 1797–1920* (Grand Rapids, MI: Eerdmans, 2017), 1–11.

The Culture Concept and Christian Missions

missionary work. Brothering also showed that mission was a gendered activity. Indigenous and European women were equally as important in the day-to-day negotiation of conversion but men largely chronicled the events and saw themselves as the key agents of change. As for 'othering', missionaries recoiled from many of the life practices of Islanders. These differences became an argument for conversion and a source of lurid tales for home congregations.[5] Yet missionaries knew that while these customs appeared strange, they were none-the-less systematic. Moreover, they quickly realized that conversion did not lead to the adoption of European ways. Many were deeply disappointed, often crushed, by the repeated evidence that those who learned to read Bible passages in Islander languages printed on wooden presses, who 'took the sulu' or cut their hair or *louted* (worshipped) to the Christian God, in Tahiti, Fiji, Sāmoa, and Tonga, remained steadfastly Tahitian, Fijian, Samoan, or Tongan in their social practices.

Some missionaries puzzled over the best means of representing the lives of others. In the early part of the nineteenth century, Lancelot Threlkeld, who worked in Raiatea but spent much of his working life among the Awabakal people of the Newcastle region of New South Wales, described in great detail his Aboriginal neighbours through his close friend Bierban.[6] Threlkeld sought to challenge audience expectations of Aboriginal primitivism by relativizing their practices and hinted at a shared psyche. Yet he maintained a clear hierarchy of belief systems: 'We pity the deep ignorance of the aborigines in their to us silly practices' but, he noted, they were no more foolish than the 'childish practices of Europeans who engaged in the spirit rapping and table turning of spiritualism'.[7]

While missionaries might belittle the gods and spirits of Pacific communities, their translation work demanded close engagement with local cosmologies and deities.[8] John Inglis on Aneityum in Vanuatu (then the New Hebrides) was grateful that the Aneityumse language proved a worthy vehicle for Christian scripture.[9] Yet, even as they sought equivalent terms

[5] For an excellent overview of the pre-Christian practices of Pacific Island people and their responses to Christian mission, see J. Barker, 'Religion', in M. Rapaport (ed.), *The Pacific Islands: Environment and Society* (Honolulu: University of Hawai'i Press, 2013), 214–24.
[6] N. Gunson (ed.), *Australian Reminiscences & Papers of L.E. Threlkeld: Missionary to the Aborigines 1824–1859*, vol. I, Australian Aboriginal Studies 40 (Canberra: Australian Institute of Aboriginal Studies, 1974), 44.
[7] L. Threlkeld, in Gunson (ed.), *Australian Reminiscences & Papers of L.E.Threlkeld*, vol. I, 52.
[8] S. Fenton (ed.), *For Better or for Worse: Translation as a Tool for Change in the South Pacific* (Manchester: St Jerome, 2004).
[9] H. Gardner, 'New heaven and new earth: translation and conversion on Aneityum', *Journal of Pacific History* 41:3 (2006), 293–311, at 298.

for concepts such as faith, sacrifice, heaven, and hell, most believed they must go head to head against the 'false' gods of Islanders. Joseph Waterhouse of Fiji recalled with relish his response to a rock identified by locals as transcendent and imbued with special significance. He 'filled the Natives with alarm and dismay by raising my foot and giving the god a hearty kick'.[10]

To the initial delight of missionaries, Pacific communities showed great enthusiasm for the new faith, which drew familiar and beloved practices into Christian forms and forged new forms of worship.[11] However, once released, Christianity was not easily contained. Māori prophets, for example, reframed the scripture they read in te reo Māori after the great baptisms of the 1830s.[12] They claimed a closer allegiance to the real message of the Bible and insisted that white missionaries who rejected their readings were opposed to the will of God.[13]

From the origin of Christian mission to the Pacific, missionary texts were mined for linguistic, religious, or technological evidence by social theorists. In the latter part of the nineteenth century, missionaries were directly approached to answer questionnaires set by those beguiled by the idea of social evolution and determined to identify the arc of human development from 'primitive' to 'civilized'. While missionaries were often willing to contribute, many were unconvinced by European theories. Their constant contact with those described as ignorant and barely social destabilized their expectations, while Indigenous lives and practices revealed the paucity of the evolutionist paradigm. As anthropology moved to the academy, missionaries such as Methodist Lorimer Fison from Fiji and Anglican Robert Codrington from the Melanesian Mission debated the failings of Northern ideas. They were drawn especially to the Oxford anthropologist E.B. Tylor, who accepted social evolutionism yet sought a deeper understanding of Indigenous lives and recognized the need for new conceptual tools to represent the lives of those deemed 'primitive'. He began his two-volume work *Primitive Culture* (1871) with his famous definition of his rebranded word 'culture'.

---

[10] N. Gunson, *Messengers of Grace: Evangelical Missionaries in the South Pacific 1796–1860* (Oxford: Oxford University Press, 1978), 209.

[11] B. Hindmarsh, 'Patterns of conversion in early Evangelical history', in B. Stanley (ed.), *Christian Missions and the Enlightenment* (Grand Rapids, MI: Eerdmans 2001), 71–98, at 91.

[12] B. Elsmore, *Mana from Heaven: A Century of Maori Prophets in New Zealand* (Tauranga: Moana Press, 1989), 27–31.

[13] Elsmore, *Mana from Heaven*, 391–8.

> Culture, or civilization, taken in its broad, ethnographic sense, is that complex whole which includes knowledge, belief, art, morals, law, custom, and any other capabilities and habits acquired by man as a member of society.[14]

Tylor's 'culture' folded what had previously been termed customs and social practices into a single catchall term. However, as historian Stocking points out, Tylor's new definition of culture still lacked relativism or pluralism and was synonymous with civilization.[15] It was another forty years before the word began to take on its twentieth-century meaning.

Missionaries were both contributors to and critics of European theories. Following years of investigation into the kinship systems of Oceania, Fison, influenced by Codrington, became increasingly suspicious of what we would now call Eurocentrism. The problem was in method and approach, and the answer, he believed, was for the observer to acknowledge they were trapped in their own world. In an early expression of the culture concept, Fison described the difficulty of crossing the gulf between the 'mind-world' of the observer and the observed: 'To get at the real meaning of the facts we must learn to see in them what the savage sees, and in order to do this we must get out of our own mind-world and into his. We must unlearn before we can begin.'[16] His, however, was a rare voice as missionaries were increasingly drawn to evolutionary theories of human development, which seemed to be proved by the spread of imperial rule in Oceania.

The Challenge to Mission

By the end of the nineteenth century, Protestant and Catholic missions had made their way across the Pacific, leaving only some of the heavily populated islands of Melanesia and the Highlands of New Guinea uncontacted. The empires followed from the mid-nineteenth century, often through the machinations of their missionaries. By the turn of the twentieth century, most of the island groups of the Pacific were under imperial rule. Now the twin and often-entangled demands of mission and colonial administration fell on those deemed both spiritually and politically backward. Yet Christian mission was about to be challenged from within, and particularly from the

---

[14] E.B. Tylor, *Primitive Culture: Researches into the Development of Mythology, Philosophy, Religion, Art, and Custom* (London: John Murray 1871), 1.

[15] G.W. Stocking Jr, 'Matthew Arnold, E.B. Tylor and the uses of invention', *American Anthropologist* 32 (1963), 784–5.

[16] L. Fison, 'Address of the president to Section G Anthropology', in A. Morton (ed.), *Report of the Australasian Association for the Advancement of Science* (1892), 144–53, at 151.

Pacific Rim. At the World Missionary Conference in Edinburgh 1910, missions were quizzed on how far they had advanced towards Anglican Henry Venn's mid-nineteenth-century goal of self-supporting, self-governing, self-extending native churches. Chinese theologian Cheng Jingyi was one of only eighteen non-European Christians among the 1,215 delegates, but he inspired the assembly with a call for ecumenism in China.[17] Cheng reminded the delegates that 'The Church of Christ is universal, not only irrespective of denominations, but also irrespective of nationalities.'[18] Japanese Christians joined the demand for greater church autonomy and a 'national' church reflecting the character of the people. The Asian delegates, however, were no match for the racial theories then dominant in European churches. European missionaries ruled, according to the final report from the conference, because they came from the 'vigorous' and 'progressive' European races, full of 'bustling activity', while oriental Christians were more contemplative and mystical. As historian Brian Stanley noted, 'European dominance was paradoxically both the root of the problem and yet also indispensable to the solution.'[19]

Yet Chinese converts influenced their European missionaries. Anglican Roland Allen was forced from his first mission to northern China by the Boxer Rebellion and in 1904 returned to England, where he addressed the doubts raised by his experiences. *Missionary Methods: St Paul's or Ours* (1912) compared the early years of the Christian faith, where conversion was rapid and churches spread quickly, with the modern missionary practice of maintaining control from the imperial centre, instituting an extensive period of testing before ordination or the leaving of churches to local converts. The problem, Allen claimed, was the arrogance of the imperial European convinced their race and their methods were essential to success, and that mission churches must be a faithful reflection of the sending church.[20] He was particularly critical of the well-built and well-equipped mission house as both material and metaphor for contemporary mission methods. It provided a bunker for the mission family while maintaining a distance from local communities and signalled mission intentions of a long residence.

---

[17] On the three selves principle in Edinburgh see B. Stanley, *The World Mission Conference Edinburgh 1910* (Grand Rapids, MI: Eerdmans, 2009), 132–66.
[18] Stanley, *The World Mission Conference*, 111–12.
[19] B. Stanley, 'The church of the three selves: a perspective from the World Missionary Conference, Edinburgh, 1910', *Journal of Imperial and Commonwealth History* 36 (2008), 435–51, at 447–8.
[20] R. Allen, *Missionary Methods: St Paul's or Ours* (London: Robert Scott 1912), 8.

The Culture Concept and Christian Missions

Allen's critique could be readily applied to the Pacific, where large well-appointed mission houses signalled the power of the white missionary family and were often a proxy for a distant colonial administration.[21] Believing in the long process of Christian conversion and seduced by racial theories, missionaries considered themselves essential to the wellbeing of their 'child-like' congregations. Failing missionary faith in their congregations could be measured in ordination. Few churches in the Pacific, either Protestant or Catholic, fully ordained more than a handful of converts in the period from the 1880s to the 1930s though many received training to the level of pastor or teacher who provided the second generation of converts.[22]

A few Pacific Christians forged independent churches. Labourers returned from the sugar cane fields of Queensland to the Solomon Islands with the faith taught to them by Evangelical Florence Young. Peter Abu'ofa established a mission school on the island of Malaita with the intermittent assistance of Young and her family. Following early failures, Abu'ofa's school became the base for the South Seas Evangelical Mission. The church bridged ethnic and clan differences, allowed interaction with sympathetic Europeans, and became the largest and most politically active organization in the island in the century to come.[23]

Most Pacific Christians, however, remained under the thumb of their European missionaries, though many chafed under church and colonial restrictions. Fijian Apolosi Nawai became a thorn in the side of both the Methodist mission and the British administration when he formed his own company, aiming to break the stranglehold of European and Indian commerce in the Islands. Apolosi's company offered an alternative to both the British administration – using Fijian versions of British titles – and the Methodist mission with a new faith that harnessed Christianity to a nationalist call to remake Fiji.[24] The British were alarmed by wide support for

---

[21] See, for example, Malinowski's description of the mission home of William and Francis Saville on the island of Mailu with its sweeping views, spacious verandas, and hardwood fittings. M.J. Young, *Malinowski: Odyssey of an Anthropologist 1884–1920* (New Haven: Yale University Press, 2004), 328.
[22] In relation to Micronesia clergy training see, for example, F.X. Hezel, 'Christianity in Micronesia', in C.E. Farhadian (ed.), *Introducing World Christianity* (Malden: Wiley-Blackwell, 2012), 230–43, at 236–7.
[23] C. Moore, 'Peter Abu'ofa', in *Solomon Islands Historical Encyclopaedia 1893–1978*, www.solomonencyclopaedia.net/biogs/Eooohttp://www.solomonencyclopaedia.net/biogs/Eooo356b.htm356b.htm; D.W. Akin, *Colonialism, Maasina Rule and the Origins of Malaitan Kastom* (Honolulu: University of Hawai'i Press, 2013), 27–8.
[24] M. Kaplan and J.D. Kelly, 'Rethinking resistance: dialogics of "disaffection" in colonial Fiji', *American Ethnologist* 21 (1994), 123–51, at 135–6.

Apolosi's company, and he was deported from Fiji in 1917 under the Disaffected or Dangerous Natives Ordinance.[25]

Early twentieth-century arguments against the colonial missionary began to influence mission thought and resonated with those who formed close friendships in local communities. Methodist missionary to indentured Indians in Fiji, John Burton spent many hours in conversation with his Hindu friend Pandit Totaram Sanadhya discussing theology and philosophy; both 'determined not to be converted by the other'. In 1914 Burton began writing on the Hindu revival and urged his readers to recognize the value of Eastern faiths.[26] Yet it was one thing to acknowledge the aspirations of Asian Christians, believed to be high up the evolutionary ladder, and another to accept the capabilities of those deemed too 'primitive' to manage. In the same year that Burton publicly suggested a more sympathetic approach to Islam and Hinduism, his colleague Joseph Bowes, president of the Queensland Methodist Conference, made a damning assessment of Aboriginal abilities in settler colonial Australia using contemporary theories of race. The scientific view of Aboriginal people, he claimed, explained the advance of the civilized 'human' in contrast to the pre-glacial Aboriginal 'creature'.[27]

As missions began a slow turn to self-criticism from the height of imperial hubris, pushed especially by their Asian converts, social anthropology was deploying the developing disciplines of psychology, statistics, and physical anthropology to test distinctions between human societies. In the late 1880s German American anthropologist Franz Boas provided an important crack in the idea that all people were on a ladder of human development. A year spent among the Inuit of Baffin Island, including an Arctic winter, revealed to him the conceit of European superiority. Based on his previous study of perceptions of light, Boas developed a certain relativism in his analysis. In 1888 he published his critique of the evolutionism of contemporary anthropology and challenged the obsession with comparing one society to another.[28] Boas continued to dispute the single line of social evolution through the 1890s, preferring instead a branching tree in which human

---

[25] Kaplan and Kelly, 'Rethinking resistance', 137.

[26] C. Weir, 'An accidental biographer? On encountering, yet again, the ideas and actions of J.W. Burton', in B.V. Lal and V. Luker (eds.), Telling Pacific Lives (Canberra: ANU Press 2008), 215–66, at 221.

[27] J. Bowes, 'The Australian Aborigine', in J. Colwell (ed.), A Century in the Pacific (Sydney: William H. Beale 1914), 153–4.

[28] G.W. Stocking Jr, 'Boas and the culture concept in historical perspective', American Anthropologist 68 (1966): 871.

The Culture Concept and Christian Missions

societies took many paths. At this stage, however, his use of the term 'culture' was in its humanist sense: i.e. synonymous with civilization.[29]

Boas spent the first two decades of the twentieth century caught between the measurements of the human body and mind, and cultural anthropology, which was continuing a cautious push for relativism. While he developed arguments for the acknowledgement of local customs as a single unified culture, the idea was popularized by his student Margaret Mead, who conducted fieldwork in American Sāmoa, then largely a London Missionary Society field. The first popular deployment of the culture concept in an influential text, however, came from Bronislaw Malinowski's study on the island of Kiriwina in the Trobriand group in Australian-administered Papua, home also to a resident Methodist missionary from the Australasian Methodist Church.

Malinowski's *Argonauts of the Western Pacific* (1922), drawn from fieldwork conducted during World War I, became a standard in anthropology. Trained in Britain but deeply immersed in the global literature of all the social sciences, especially psychology, Malinowski's 'culture' was largely relativist, pluralist, and holistic, though it was certainly not reflexive. The culture concept did not apply to the cosmopolitan Pole. His mentor, James Frazer, maintained an evolutionist perspective and in the Preface positioned Trobriand Island 'culture' on the 'scale of savagery'.[30] Malinowski believed in the 'anatomy of culture'; Trobriand culture was analogous to the working human body, each part dependent on the other, an idea known as functionalism. According to Malinowski, and other anthropologists at the time bent on 'salvaging' the details of 'primitive' life, 'savage' cultures were 'dying away under our very eyes'.[31] As Trobriand culture was held to be fragile, any demands for change, such as missionary strictures on dancing or colonial restrictions on canoe travel, were a threat to the whole. According to functionalism, missionaries were, by default, a danger to their converts, for change invariably led to decay and/or death. In his footnotes, Malinowski was especially critical of LMS missionary Charles Abel, though he acknowledged his friendship with the Methodist missionary to Kiriwina, Matthew Gilmore, on whom he was dependent for his knowledge of language and

---

[29] Stocking, 'Boas and the culture concept', 871.

[30] J. Frazer, 'Preface', in B. Malinowski, *Argonauts of the Western Pacific: An Account of Native Enterprise and Adventure in the Archipelagoes of Melanesian New Guinea* (London: Routledge & Kegan Paul, 1922), i–xxi, at xiv.

[31] Frazer in Malinowski, *Argonauts of the Western Pacific*, xv.

customs.[32] Yet he detested missionaries as a category and wrote a sustained attack in his diary:

> Mentally I collect arguments against missions and ponder a really effective anti-mission campaign. The arguments: these people destroy the natives' joy in life; they destroy their psychological raison d'être. And what they give in return is completely beyond the savages. They struggle consistently and ruthlessly against everything old and create new needs, both material and moral. No question but that they do harm.[33]

Malinowski's hatred of mission was not just the knee-jerk reaction of the atheist, but a profound rejection of the mission project of human change. As a result, however, he and many others who followed were in danger of fetishizing the purity, fragility, and value of 'pure' Indigenous cultures.[34]

Six years later Margaret Mead published *Coming of Age in Samoa* (1928). Her readable tale of Samoan culture with its explicit critique of American adolescence, in comparison to the casual easy-going sex life of Samoan girls, proved enormously successful and spread the culture concept into a large general readership. Over the next fifty years, more than a million copies were sold in sixteen languages, though Samoan was not one of them.[35] Mead's analysis offered a new reading of primitivism. Under her pen, 'primitive' people had an important lesson for 'civilized', indeed corrupted, modern man and woman. Her crusade was in her subtitle, *A Psychological Study of Primitive Youth for Western Civilization*. Mead laid down the gauntlet in the introduction and identified conservative Christian America as the enemy of enlightened anthropology and happy American teenagers. The book was a challenge to those who fulminated from the pulpit and who responded to 'missionary crusades' on the threat of aimless youth. Her study of the sex lives of Samoan girls promised a release valve for 'juvenile delinquency', the new scourge in American life.[36]

Mead knew she was making her argument from Christian Sāmoa. Most Samoans had converted through the 1850s and 1860s. The faith first appeared on the iron-bound coast of the islands in the 1830s when Tongan Christians, plying

---

[32] J. Burton and O.A. Burton, 'Some reflections on anthropology's missionary positions', *Journal of the Royal Anthropological Institute* 13 (2007), 209–17, at 212.

[33] B. Malinowski, *A Diary in the Strict Sense of the Term* (London: Athlone Press, 1967), 41.

[34] Young, *Malinowski*, 213

[35] P. Shankman, *The Trashing of Margaret Mead: Anatomy of an Anthropological Controversy* (Madison: University of Wisconsin Press, 2009), 101.

[36] M. Mead, *Coming of Age in Samoa: A Psychological Study of Primitive Youth for Western Civilization* (New York: William Morrow 1928), 1–14.

The sea routes between Fiji, Sāmoa, and Tonga, landed with tales of a new god told to them by Methodist missionaries. Within ten years European missionaries appeared in Sāmoa and were guided to the most auspicious sites for Christian success by Tongan converts who knew the allegiances and political landscape of the islands. By the 1920s Samoans had long been Christian, literate in Samoan but with almost exclusively Christian texts. Many had taken the faith to Melanesia and hundreds had died for their efforts. Mead's view of culture as a hermetically sealed world, in which outside influences mattered little, implied that Christianity had been swallowed whole by *faa' Samoa* (the Samoan way).[37] Culture was sovereign. While colonization had 'drawn the teeth' of Samoan culture the people lived the life of lotus eaters, content, compliant, and lacking in the passions that led to unhappiness.

As Mead was publishing her argument for Samoan culture against conservative Christian America, European missionaries came under fire from their converts. The International Board of Missionaries met in Jerusalem in 1928 for the first time since Edinburgh, under the theme 'Indigenous churches'. In sectional meetings, delegates considered withdrawing from the field and the practical issues of handing power to local people. Chinese Christians demanded a church to reflect Chinese culture. Chang Ching Yi claimed: 'We are moved by the positive power of a great ideal. Every nation has its special characteristics. Is it not a great duty we owe to God and to mankind to develop the religious talent of our people, and to contribute our share to the religious ideas of the world?'[38]

The European delegate from the Pacific, Frank Lenwood of the London Missionary Society, was not persuaded by the call for the end of mission. He warned the assembly that, 'Among primitive peoples the policy of withdrawing the white missionary is based on failure to think out the problems and is almost certain to issue in disaster.' Lenwood reported that efforts to remove European missionaries had failed in Hawai'i, South Africa, and British Guiana. The problem, he insisted, alert to new sensibilities, was not the 'primitiveness' of the Indigenous people but the venal nature of European commerce: 'primitive' people required protection from the impact of 'white and Asiatic races' if they and their churches were to flourish.[39] Lenwood

---

[37] E. Leacock, 'Anthropologists in search of a culture: Margaret Mead, Derek Freeman, and all the rest of us', in L. Forestel and A. Gilliam (eds.), *Confronting Margaret Mead: Scholarship, Empire and the South Pacific* (Philadelphia: Temple University Press, 1992), 3–30.
[38] Box 261003 IMC Committees Jerusalem March 24–April 8 1928. Folder 'Church and Mission', World Council of Churches, Geneva archive.
[39] Box 261003 IMC Committees.

acknowledged that the South Pacific missions had clearly met one of the three requirements of the Indigenous church; they were supported financially by their Pacific Islander congregations. They were also extending churches, given the huge movement of Islanders as pastors throughout the Pacific, but these successes were not considered sufficient for the end of European mission.

While these paternal ideas may have sounded convincing in the olive groves of Jerusalem where no Pacific Island Christians were present, they did not acknowledge growing Islander discontent towards European missionaries and colonial administrations, particularly in Sāmoa where the Mau movement was challenging both the American and the New Zealand administrations and the missions. While Mead insisted the Samoan hierarchy in American Sāmoa found a happy fit with the US Navy and all were grateful for the benefits of civilization, this was not the case.[40] From the time the deed of cession in 1899 handed the eastern islands of Sāmoa to America, Samoans had been protesting intermittently against American naval rule. As Mead was writing her dissertation, twenty-nine American Samoan chiefs sent a letter to President Coolidge asking for representative government and equal rights with US citizens. The year before *Coming of Age* was published, chiefs supportive of Mau formed the Committee of the Samoan League and organized a copra boycott as a form of tax resistance.[41] By the late 1920s Western Sāmoa was in a state of open rebellion against military rule from New Zealand. The Jerusalem Meeting was held as Mau chiefs were becoming increasingly suspicious that their missionaries supported the New Zealand administration, especially when a former missionary, Reverend F.G. Lawes, was appointed New Zealand Secretary of Native Affairs at the height of the tensions.[42] Offerings to the churches suffered when missionaries spoke against the Mau and anger towards mission reached its height when the Great Council meeting for Christians throughout Sāmoa was dismissed by the LMS mission in 1928.[43] The year after the conference in Jerusalem, New Zealand troops opened fire on a peaceful Samoan protest, killing at least eight.

[40] Mead, *Coming of Age in Samoa*, 272–6.
[41] D.A. Chappell, 'The forgotten Mau: anti-navy protests in American Samoa, 1920–1935', *Pacific Historical Review* 69 (2000), 217–60, at 248–9.
[42] P. O'Brien, 'Bridging the Pacific: Ta'isi O.F. Nelson, Australia and the Sāmoan Mau', *History Australia* 14 (2017), 1–19, at 3.
[43] I. Breward, 'Christianity in Polynesia', in C.E. Farhadian (ed.), *Introducing World Christianity* (Malden, MA: Wiley-Blackwell, 2012), 218–29, at 224.

The troubles were not confined to Sāmoa. In January 1929, Methodist and Catholic plantation workers in the Australian New Guinea mandate went on strike for higher wages and congregated at their respective mission stations expecting support. None was forthcoming though the Methodist mission was later accused, incorrectly, of leading the unrest. The ringleaders were flogged and jailed with hard labour and the rest were sent back to work with the same conditions.[44] LMS Samoan pastors in Papua were unsuccessful in their claim for their own district as overseas missionaries. They were angry at their inadequate pay and the failure of many European missionaries to treat them as colleagues.[45] Indian Christians in Fiji were also aggrieved over lower rates of pay and their poor conditions when compared to their European counterparts who lived more comfortable lives in the mission stations.[46] Both anthropology and mission struggled to incorporate the political realities of the lives of the people they were working with; anthropologists were focused on the salvage of pre-colonial cultures while missions were too closely aligned with colonial administrations to respond to the demands of their congregations.

By the late 1920s, anthropology and the culture concept were coming into mission through new forms of training. In the same year as the Jerusalem conference, professor of anthropology Radcliffe-Brown at Sydney University admitted fifteen missionaries to a special short course of anthropology devised for the training of colonial officers for the Australian territory of Papua and the new mandate of New Guinea.[47] The short course was maintained under the leadership of Radcliffe-Brown's successor, former Anglican priest A.P. Elkin.

In France, Protestant missionary Maurice Leenhardt returned from his mission to New Caledonia and began to produce both anthropological articles and books beginning in 1922. He held key posts in French anthropology, as the president of the Société des Océanistes and head of the Pacific section at the Musée de l'Homme. Following Marcel Mauss and preceding Claude Lévi-Strauss, he was professor at the École Pratique des Hautes

---

[44] B. Gammage, 'The Rabaul Strike 1929', *Journal of Pacific History* 10 (1975), 3–29.
[45] S. Mullins and D. Wetherell, 'LMS teachers and colonialism in Torres Strait and New Guinea, 1871–1915', in D. Munro and A. Thornley (eds.), *The Covenant Makers: Islander Missionaries in the Pacific* (Suva: Pacific Theological College and Institute of Pacific Studies, University of the South Pacific, 1996), 196–209, at 201–4.
[46] K. Close Barry, *A Mission Divided: Race, Culture and Colonialism in Fiji's Methodist Mission* (Canberra: ANU Press, 2015), 113–14.
[47] T. Wise, *The Self-Made Anthropologist: A Life of A.P. Elkin* (Sydney: George Allen & Unwin 1985), 74.

Études.[48] While deeply entrenched in French anthropology, Leenhardt continued his support for this first vocation. He assumed responsibility for foreign missions, assisted in the training of missionaries, and advanced mission studies.[49]

In the decades following the Jerusalem Conference there were grass-roots rebellions against missions and/or colonial administrations throughout the Pacific. At the same time, the anthropological culture concept was spreading into theology and the number of missionaries trained in some form of anthropology was increasing. The term culture entered mainstream theology in the 1940s as missiology courses were established, particularly in North America.

Catholic theologian Christopher Dawson delivered the Gifford Lectures in 1947 on the theme of Religion and Culture. He saw 'culture' as a neutral term, which allowed the separation of religious belief from theological and philosophical judgement.[50] Dawson's analysis was particularly dependent on Ruth Benedict's *Patterns of Culture* (1934).[51] Another of Boas's students, Benedict was instrumental in spreading the developing concept beyond the discipline. She essentially untethered culture from history allowing for a much broader application of the term. Cultures, she claimed, were of such infinite variety that their origins and trajectory could not be explained. Anthropologist Kroeber described the book approvingly as largely 'propaganda for the anthropological attitude'.[52]

Yet in the Pacific, from where the culture concept was first popularized, the core precepts meant little to Pacific Islanders. As Dawson was preparing his lecture, the British administration and the Anglican Melanesian Mission were facing a revolt on the island of Malaita in the Solomon Islands. Many Malaitans had engaged in the labour trade to Queensland in the late nineteenth and early twentieth centuries where they became adept at managing their own religious and tabu demands and found ways of dealing with ethnic rivalries when brought into close contact on plantations.[53] These experiences

---

[48] J. Clifford, 'Reciprocity and the making of ethnographic texts. The example of Maurice Leenhardt', *Man* 15 (1980), 518–32, at 518.

[49] M.R. Splinder, 'The legacy of Maurice Leenhardt', *International Bulletin of Missionary Research* 13:4 (1989), 170–4, at 170.

[50] Recent theology has questioned the neutrality of the term. See, for example, A. Thompson, *Culture in a Post-Secular Context: Theological Possibilities in Milbank, Barth and Bediako* (Eugene: Pickwick Publications, 2014), 12.

[51] C. Dawson, *Religion and Culture: Gifford Lectures* (Washington, DC: Catholic University of America Press 1948), 37, 79.

[52] A.L. Kroeber, 'Review *Patterns of Culture*, Ruth Benedict', *American Anthropologist* 37 (1934), 689.

[53] D. Akin, *Colonialism, Maasina Rule and the Origins of Malaitan Kastom* (Honolulu: University of Hawai'i Press, 2013), 20–8.

The Culture Concept and Christian Missions

assisted in the development of a powerful movement known as Maasina Rule. Of the nine leaders chosen to represent the regions of Malaita, five were from the South Seas Evangelical Mission.[54] Their aims were to develop centralized villages with large communal gardens, to codify customs – keeping those deemed worthy and rejecting those that were not – and to form an Indigenous government structure outside of British colonial control. As anthropologist David Akin notes, this was far from the classical anthropological concept of culture – a rigid structure of unchanging laws and practices based on historical precedent. Instead, Maasina Rule members shaped their customs according to their political, spiritual, and economic needs. Christians were at the forefront of the movement.

Across the Pacific in the post-war period, the question of custom was becoming more important as Pacific Island Christians gained greater power within their missions. Alan Tippett, Methodist missionary to Fiji from 1942, who was to be a key figure in mid-century missiology, described with approval a new mood for self-expression in post-war Fiji and worked to revise the Methodist constitution to enhance Fijian power within the mission. Yet he struggled, as did many missionaries, with the unexpected forms of Islander demands and the anti-imperial, anti-mission implications of Indigenous claims for autonomy. This was much more challenging than the orderly devolving of power to the highest Fijian leaders of the church based on chiefly customs. Tippett's own experiences were instructive. He was called to minister to the chiefly island of Bau after their previous missionary had been forced to leave following his declaration that he was 'against custom' at a chiefly gathering that 'went cold' at his speech.[55] At first, Tippett despaired over the lack of religious enthusiasm in the district, yet, when it came, he was uneasy over its anti-colonial implications. In 1955 Ratu Emosi from the Bau/Ra division of the Methodist circuit attracted a large number of followers by calling for the separation of the Fijian synod from the Australian Methodist church, using a drama on the coming of the gospel to Fiji. The play ended with the tearing down of the British flag and the raising of one designed by Emosi.[56]

Following training in social anthropology at the American University in history, social anthropology, and archives, Tippett returned to Fiji

---

[54] Akin, *Colonialism*, 166, 171.
[55] G. Dundon, '"Walking the road" from colonial to post-colonial mission: the life, work and thought of the Reverend Dr Alan Richard Tippett, Methodist missionary in Fiji, anthropologist and missiologist, 1911–1988', PhD thesis, University of New South Wales, 2000.
[56] Dundon, '"Walking the road"', 97–8.

determined to teach anthropology to Fijian students and began to explore how the 'Fijian cultural pattern' played out in Fijian Christianity based on the linguistic work of anthropologist Edward Sapir.[57] This was the European culture concept, which understood Fijian life paths as distinct unified systems, not the Pacific idea of custom as a more fragmented and dynamic set of practices deployed and developed in response to the challenges of colonialism and everyday life.

In the 1950s, the culture concept was adopted into broader liberal theology with American theologian H. Richard Niebuhr's best-selling *Christ and Culture* (1951), currently in its 11th edition. Niebuhr acknowledged that culture was an anthropological term and that he was using it in a layman's sense; his definition came from Malinowski's entry on 'culture' in the *Encyclopaedia of Social Sciences*, vol. IV, and Dawson's *Religion and Culture*, as well as Benedict's *Patterns of Culture*.[58] Niebuhr reviewed the theological relationships between Christ and society and laid out five theological perspectives; two suggested that Christ was opposed to culture and two had a positive view that Christ ordered and fulfilled culture. Those theologies in opposition to culture, that Christ demanded authority over culture, were rejected by many liberal churches in the decades that followed. Missionaries and Pacific Islanders were inspired by Niebhur's second analysis of culture in theology, that Christ was in culture, the 'Messiah of their society, the perfecter of its true faith, the source of its holiest spirit'.[59] Or the final reading, that Christ fulfilled culture, leading to a 'transformed human life in and to the glory of God . . . through the grace of God'.[60]

Through the 1960s the culture concept spread into the Pacific via the ecumenical church meetings held throughout the region and the spread of theological theories of culture to the theological colleges. From now, the concept mingled with the Pacific idea of custom or kastom. The first meeting of Pacific Island churches and missions held at the London Missionary Society theological college at Malua in Sāmoa insisted, 'The Coconut curtain has lifted': an acknowledgement of the previous isolation of the sectarian riven churches of the Pacific and an implicit call for the decolonization of the churches of the Pacific.

The conference was the brainchild of two Pacific Island clergy, Fijian Setereki Tuilovoni and Tongan Sione Havea. Both undertook theological

---

[57] Dundon, '"Walking the road"', 128, 139.

[58] H.R. Niebuhr, *Christ and Culture* (New York: Harper and Row, 1951), 32–3.

[59] Niebuhr, *Christ and Culture*, 83.   [60] Niebuhr, *Christ and Culture*, 196.

The Culture Concept and Christian Missions

training in the USA where they joined an informal international network of young politically active third world Christians keen to challenge the colonialism of the missions and the empires.[61] The Samoan Conference was organized by the World Council of Churches, which funded Pacific Island clergy to meet away from their European mission boards. One of the speakers was Solomon Islander the Reverend later Bishop Leonard Alafurai, who was well versed in the Niebuhr culture concept: 'Christ came and fulfilled all cultures and all people', he claimed, a common refrain from those trained in anthropologically inspired theology.[62] Christianity, therefore, was not opposed to culture; instead cultures were made by God and were fulfilled by the revelation of Christ.

From this conference came the Pan Pacific ecumenical Theological College in Suva, Fiji. The new college would be staffed by six full-time tutors covering the standard theological college topics but also sociology and anthropology augmented with visiting lecturers in these disciplines.[63] A *Pacific Journal of Theological Studies* was launched with a focus on issues such as land tenure, marriage customs, and other Pacific practices as well as the acknowledgement of the 'sacraments in our differing traditions'.[64] The other institution foreshadowed at this conference was the Pacific Conference of Churches, a staunchly political organization which supported decolonizing churches and nations and responded to environmental threats to the Pacific.[65]

The second conference was held on the island of Lifou in 1966. Here, sectional meetings with clergy and lay delegates discussed particular issues and reported back to the assembly.[66] One session, 'The place and function of custom', led to lively discussions on the source of cultural practices: 'some members believe that custom is a way of life given by God to man while others feel that it is a man-made institution containing both good and evil'. Participants overwhelmingly described custom as a positive force, which could 'integrate society in a harmonious and familiar pattern', and provide stability and stimulus for development. Indeed custom regulated society and

---

[61] K. Close Barry, 'The Reverend Setereki Tuilovoni: mobile Pacific leader in the decolonisation era', *Journal of Pacific History* 50 (2015), 149–67, at 154.
[62] L. Alafurai, *Beyond the Reef: The Records of the Conference of Churches and Missions in the Pacific* (Apia: Malua Theological College, Western Sāmoa, 1961), 31.
[63] *Theological Education in the Pacific* (London: Theological Education Fund Committee of the International Missionary Council, 1961), 17.
[64] *Theological Education in the Pacific*, 33.
[65] J. Garrett, *Where Nets Were Cast: Christianity in Oceania since World War II* (Suva: Institute of Pacific Studies, 1997), 231.
[66] Garrett, *Where Nets Were Cast*, 9.

prepared it for the gospel. Pacific Christians were especially plural: 'All people have customs. It is the purpose of God, by the Gospel, continuously to transform and recreate customs'; and they insisted on the dynamism of customs which 'are not static but constantly changing'. Discussion groups recommended that 'expatriate missionaries should study the customs and culture of the place where they serve' and that 'church schools should include a course on custom, instructing students in the custom of their people' as well as the relationship between custom and the Gospel. Clearly the Europeans who devised the questionnaire were uncertain. They included leading questions on the dangers of bride price and the commodification of women. Yet the delegates maintained their positive perspective. Customary marriages and initiations were acknowledged as a 'wholesome social custom' and a study of dancing in the New Hebrides revealed that, of the four classes of dance, only one was evil so the others were permitted and encouraged.[67]

The Pacific Theological College opened in 1966 and was immediately engaged in the theological movements of the 1960s, led by the incorporation of the culture concept into theology and missiology. The theology of contextualization for Protestants, or inculturation for Catholics, became the principal method of the new college. This is amply illustrated from a sample of the titles of the divinity theses from 1968–73.

Tanielu, L.I., 'A study of the Ministry of the Congregational Christian Church in Samoa and the influence of social organisation, traditions and customs', Bachelor of Divinity thesis, 1968.

Aseta, Galuefa, 'Gospel in Samoan setting', Bachelor of Divinity thesis, 1969.

Nabetari, Baiteke, 'Indigenisation of worship in the Gilbert Islands', Bachelor of Divinity thesis, 1970

Hagesi, Robert, 'Towards localization of Anglican worship in the Solomon Islands', Bachelor of Divinity thesis, 1972.

Itaia, Maunaa R., 'The transmission of the Christian concept of God from one culture to another', Bachelor of Divinity thesis, 1973.

As Pacific clergy spread the new theologies, they began to embrace local practices. Catholics on Pohnpei, for example, now raffle off kava roots to raise funds where the first missionaries demanded abstinence from kava as

---

[67] 'Report of Commission on Custom for Further Discussion', First Assembly of the Pacific Conference of Churches, Lifou, Box 42.3.119 WCC General Secretariat Country Files and Correspondence 1938 1946–1995: Pacific, World Council of Churches Archive, Geneva.

proof of Christian sincerity.[68] Black Christs began appearing in churches around the Pacific.[69]

In the years to come, many Pacific clergy and prominent lay Christians became involved in the decolonization of their nations backed by the Pacific Conference of Churches. Culture and kastom became the nucleus of new nations. Vanuatu, which faced the dual issues of the French–British Condominium, became independent under prime minister and Anglican priest Walter Lini, with five ordained Presbyterian pastors in the cabinet, most trained at the Pacific Theological College in Suva.[70] At the heart of the nation was the Vanuatu Cultural Centre (Vanuatu Kaljoral Senta); originally a small museum, it became the umbrella organization over institutions such as the National Archives, the National Museum, and the Fieldworkers Unit for the collection and protection of culture and heritage. In contrast to the decolonization of Asia and Africa, the constitutions for the Pacific Islands almost invariably begin with a preamble that acknowledges both the Christian faith of the citizens and their traditions and cultures.

Networks of Pacific Christians moved between pulpit and parliament, bringing the theologies of inculturation or contextualization with them. Bougainville Catholic priest John Momis was steeped in inculturation theologies and was a key figure in the formation of the Papua New Guinea constitution as well as being the Member for Bougainville.[71] Devout Catholic layman Bernard Narokobi, and first attorney general of Papua New Guinea, wrote *The Melanesian Way* to show how Melanesian Christianity was deeply embedded in Melanesian spiritual practices.[72] Lay preacher in the South Seas Evangelical church Peter Kenilorea became the first prime minister of the Solomon Islands in 1978.[73]

Women, however, struggled, for missions and colonies included women only on the peripheries. Colonial forms of indirect rule almost invariably ignored the traditional place of women in the power structures of the Pacific

---

[68] Hezel, 'Christianity in Micronesia', 232, 237.

[69] See, for example, the description of the iconography of the church of the Merukun of the Sepik region, in P. Peltier, 'Men's houses and other people's houses', in S. Tcherkézoff and F. Douaire-Marsaudon (eds.), *The Changing South Pacific: Identities and Transformations* (Canberra: ANU Press, 2008), 63–84, at 78.

[70] H. Gardner, 'Praying for independence: the Presbyterian Church in the decolonisation of Vanuatu', *Journal of Pacific History* 48:2 (2013), 122–43, at 142.

[71] D. Denoon, *A Trial Separation: Australia and the Decolonisation of Papua New Guinea* (Canberra: ANU Press, 2012), 113.

[72] B. Narokobi, *The Melanesian Way* (Port Moresby: Institute of Papua New Guinea Studies, 1980).

[73] P. Kenilorea, www.solomonencyclopaedia.net/biogs/E000525b.htm.

and the missions and churches were unreflexively paternalistic, very few allowing the full ordination of women.[74] While Pacific churches and nations decolonized at the height of second-wave feminism and women reached for a place in the new institutions, few succeeded. Indeed, historian Anne Dickson-Waiko argued that women held such minor roles in colonialism and mission in Papua New Guinea that they were only truly colonized following independence. Indigenous men were determined to honour a reified version of pre-colonial culture, which included the return of women to the village.[75] Pacific women's voices were heard in the radical theologies of third world Christianity in the post-independence period but they made little headway in the formal structures of Pacific churches. Yet women retain a powerful voice in Melanesian villages, where they organize in Christian fellowship groups and hold male politicians to the standards of both Christian and cultural ethics of equality and reciprocity. Their collective 'everyday modernity', Douglas claims, is a 'counterpoint to the heavy formal male domination of all Melanesian politics'.[76]

Conclusion

Culture has a history and can be tracked in its most popular form to key texts originating from engagement with Pacific Islanders in the 1920s. The West's 'turn' to culture in the post-war period was paralleled by the theological engagement with culture, first as a 'neutral' term, then as a reified source of social wellbeing and authenticity, which provided the bedrock for decolonizing churches and nations. The spread of the culture concept into theology and the return of the idea to the Pacific from where it was first developed granted European missionaries the space to accept the practices of their converts and encouraged the decolonization of missions to churches. Pacific Islanders, who had maintained cultural forms from the origin of Christian mission and through the spread of colonization, now repositioned these practices as part of a new claim for cultural, religious, and national identity. They were led by Pacific clergy and devout Christian politicians, who were deeply immersed in theologies of enculturation or contextualization.

---

[74] M. Ropeti, 'One Gospel: Pacific Island women's perspective and response to Rev. Marie Ropeti', *Pacific Journal of Theology* 17 (1997), 31–53.
[75] A. Dickson-Waiko, 'Women, nation and decolonisation in Papua New Guinea', *Journal of Pacific History* 48:2 (2013) 177–93.
[76] B. Douglas, 'Christianity, tradition and everyday modernity: towards an anatomy of women's groupings in Melanesia', *Oceania* 74:1/2 (2003), 6–23, at 7.

47

Trading Nature in the Pacific

Ecological Exchange prior to 1900

DAVID IGLER

The title of this chapter echoes Jennifer Newell's superb monograph, *Trading Nature: Tahitians, Europeans, and Ecological Exchange*, which examines a set of environmental relationships unique to Tahiti but also global in nature.[1] Tahiti, in this way, reveals the ecological shifts, species invasions, and biological effects of many places around the world during the era of European imperialism in the late eighteenth and early nineteenth centuries. Newell's work explores unique features for the study of Tahiti, and, more broadly, for Pacific scholars interested in the 'wide ranging impacts' of ecological exchange.[2] Those features include the circumstance of Cook, Wallis, and Bougainville each 'discovering' Tahiti within a three-year period (1767–9), as well as the unparalleled archive of documents they generated about the islands and the Islanders themselves. A second feature transpired two decades later, when Captain Bligh led the archetypal expedition in ecological transplantation by successfully bringing Tahiti's breadfruit trees around the world to Britain's slave colonies in the West Indies. Paradise found, paradise transplanted. And yet the most compelling feature in *Trading Nature* may not be those items transported from Tahiti but instead those things introduced to the islands: plants, animals, birds, and bacteria from all points of the globe. In short, an assortment of the world's biomatter arrived at the Society Islands, initially in the canoes of Indigenous voyagers and later under the aegis of European ventures.

Tahiti received new species at a fairly astonishing pace, all for the 'improvement' of the islands and certainly intended for the benefit of future provision-starved voyagers. Introduced animals – including cattle, donkeys, goats, guinea pigs, horses, rabbits, sheep, new varieties of dogs and pigs, and

---

[1] J. Newell, *Trading Nature: Tahitians, Europeans, and Ecological Exchange* (Honolulu: University of Hawai'i Press, 2010).
[2] Newell, *Trading Nature*, 8.

a pregnant cat gifted to 'Queen' Purea by Samuel Wallis in 1767 – found their way to Tahiti prior to 1800. A similar variety of birds also arrived during this period, ranging from Australian parrots to English turkeys and Spanish hens. Plants constituted the largest number of introduced species; by Newell's account, dozens of varieties of fruits, vegetables, legumes, trees, and seeds were transported to Tahiti, the vast majority as intentional imports for the benefit of Tahitians and European visitors alike.[3] Some species invaded and multiplied with evident impact, while others existed as relatively harmless additions to Tahiti's natural diversity. Tahitians, for their part, welcomed many of these introduced species, and, according to Newell, the Islanders maintained 'much more of a controlling hand [over the natural production] than the voyagers found comfortable'.[4] However, the Islanders could not exert control over the viral and bacterial agents introduced by voyagers. Disease devastated the Indigenous people of Tahiti and their population plummeted within two generations of the first arrivals.[5]

Taking a wider perspective beyond Tahiti, this chapter examines the transportation and introduction of biota that accompanied the human settlement, migration, and colonization of the island Pacific and continental coastlines. The 'trading' of nature transpired over the *longue durée* of human habitation, making possible the migration of Indigenous groups since ancient times and sharply escalating with the appearance of Europeans prior to 1800. While some biota arrived intentionally, as suggested by many of the Tahitian examples, other species came unintentionally in the shadows of exploration and commercial exchange. Scholars have utilized many terms to describe these transformative processes: 'ecological revolutions', 'the Columbian/Magellan Exchange', 'green imperialism', and 'tending the wild', among others.[6] Such concepts are undoubtedly useful for understanding large-scale changes to

---

[3] Newell, *Trading Nature*; for an excellent accounting of these introductions, see appendix B, 213–24, at 224.
[4] Newell, *Trading Nature*, 195.
[5] On the biological impact faced by Tahitians and other Pacific Islanders, see P.V. Kirch and J.-L. Rallu (eds.), *The Growth and Collapse of Pacific Island Societies: Archaelogical and Demographic Perspectives* (Honolulu: University of Hawai'i Press, 2007); Newell, *Trading Nature*, 113.
[6] C. Merchant, *Ecological Revolutions: Nature, Gender, and Science in New England* (Chapel Hill: University of North Carolina Press, 1989); A. Crosby, *The Columbian Exchange: Biological and Cultural Consequences of 1492* (Westport, CT: Greenwood, 1972); R.H. Grove, *Green Imperialism: Colonial Expansion, Tropical Island Edens, and the Origins of Environmentalism, 1600–1860* (Cambridge: Cambridge University Press, 1995); M.K. Anderson, *Tending the Wild: Native American Knowledge and the Management of California's Natural Resources* (Berkeley: University of California Press, 2005); S. Hackel, *Children of Coyote, Missionaries of Saint Francis: Indian–Spanish Relations in Colonial California* (Chapel Hill: University of North Carolina Press, 2005).

human societies and natural environments, and this chapter examines specific instances in the Pacific denoted by these terms. Equally important is the way scholars have narrated the formative 'changes to the land' (and sea) in ways that move beyond simple lists of introductions, transplantations, and extinctions. Given the nature of the Pacific – a collection of seas covering one-third of the Earth – narrative strategies that emphasize the motivations for and consequences of the oceanic transit of species offer some of the most compelling routes into the histories of ecological change. Stories that speak to environmental change illuminate human intention, ambitions, and sometimes folly. They reflect the significance of human culture as a primary component of ecological transformation.

Trading Nature in the 'Outrigger' Age

The vast distances of the Pacific Ocean challenge the imagination in the same way those distances challenged actual voyagers centuries ago. For instance, the Society Islands are located some 4,000 nautical miles from California's Channel Islands – an unimaginable journey during the millennia of Polynesian eastward migration, and only slightly more imaginable during the period when Cook, Wallis, and Bougainville arrived at Tahiti and found, according to one naturalist, 'the truest picture of an arcadia'.[7] But extensive spatial distances often mask parallel historical circumstances. In the same year (1769) that Cook's entourage crossed the beach at Matavai Bay, Tahiti, Spanish soldiers and Franciscan missionaries established their beachheads of colonization on the coast of Alta (or Upper) California. And, in the same way that Europeans introduced a host of new biota to Tahiti, the Spanish newcomers brought plants, animals, and germs to coastal California – a place long depicted by cartographers as a massive Pacific island directly off the North America coast.[8] The geographic distances between the simultaneous landings in Tahiti and California are certainly counterbalanced by the similar historical and cultural processes, which include expansionistic European empires, missionary zeal, and exploratory ambitions. Meanwhile, the ecological factors of empire in each place played a powerful role in refashioning the land to the settlers' desire and profit.

[7] J.C. Beaglehole (ed.), *The Endeavor Journal of Joseph Banks, 1768–1771* (Sydney: Public Library of New South Wales with Angus and Robertson, 1963), 252.
[8] R. Solnit, 'Notes on California as an island: there's truth in old maps', *Boom: A Journal of California* 4 (2014), 36–45.

But Europeans were hardly the first instigators of biotic transfers or ecological management in either location. Among the longest-inhabited group of islands in the eastern Pacific was those populated by the *Michumash*, known in more recent times as the Chumash residents of the Channel Islands off the coast of Santa Barbara. Probably first visited by ancient migrants on the coastal 'kelp highway', this island chain shows continuous settlements by Chumash and Tongva people for the past 10,000 years.[9] These first settlers fashioned an export economy of microlith points (chert) and shell beads for currency – hence the name 'Michumash' bestowed on them by mainland Chumash, which roughly translates to 'makers of shell bead money'.[10] The people crossed to the mainland trade centre called *Qasil* on plank canoes (*tomol*) and returned to the islands with a variety of biota, including seeds, small animals, and 'canoe plants' – a term denoting the widespread transfer of biota by Islanders in the Pacific. The Island fox (*Urocyon littoralis*), the Island oak (*Quercus tomentella*), and numerous other species descend from mainland ecologies, demonstrating an extensive history of exchanges between the islands and California's coastal mainland.[11]

The trading of nature by California's Indigenous groups flourished due to what M. Kat Anderson describes as the 'tending of the wild'. The Native peoples transformed the products of nature into foods and tools, and exchanged those items through trade networks while introducing new species to different locales. Rather than reaping the bounty from a static nature, California Native groups 'tended' the landscape through various interventions, including the widespread use of fire. Controlled and communal burns, usually lit in the autumn months, 'was the most significant, effective, efficient, and widely employed vegetation management tool of California Indians tribes'.[12] Whether lit intentionally or by lightning, somewhere between 2.4 million and 5.25 million hectares of California burned on an annual basis. The resulting landscape exhibited bounteous vegetation and well-managed habitats, allowing for a healthy trade in nature's productions along California's coast and the interior.[13] Anderson's concept of 'tending the

---

[9] J.M. Erlandson et al., 'The Kelp Highway Hypothesis: marine ecology, the coastal migration theory, and the peopling of the Americas', *Journal of Island and Coastal Archaeology* 2 (2007), 161–74.
[10] J. Arnold (ed.), *The Origins of a Pacific Coast Chiefdom: The Chumash of the Channel Islands* (Salt Lake City: University of Utah Press, 2001); L. Gamble, *The Chumash World at European Contact: Power, Trade, and Feasting among Complex Hunter-Gatherers* (Berkeley: University of California Press, 2008).
[11] K. Lightfoot and O. Parrish, *California Indians and Their Environment* (Berkeley: University of California Press, 2009).
[12] Anderson, *Tending the Wild*, 136.   [13] Hackel, *Children of Coyote*, 25.

wild' – which explicitly rejects the idea of Indigenous people lacking the ability to manage or impact their environment – applies equally well to many Native groups throughout the Pacific.

For some scholars, the phrase 'tending the wild' may seem like a polite way of characterizing the actions of nature's most troublesome species, human beings. Throughout Polynesia human settlers introduced their 'portmanteau biota' of plants and animals, burned pre-existing forests, cleared hillsides, and set about the urgent business of creating a highly managed landscape, a landscape later *discoverers* would idealize as an original paradise.[14] 'Sustaining human life in Remote Oceania', Matthew Spriggs writes of the earliest settlers, 'may well have been impossible' without the radical disturbance caused by introduced species, extensive clearing of forests, and intensive agricultural systems. Rather than 'landscape degradation', Spriggs argues, such disruption might best be viewed as 'landscape enhancement' from an anthropocentric perspective – 'an island's capability for feeding its human population'.[15] Trading nature, in this context of Polynesian settler populations, involved some serious trade-offs in terms of what *belonged* on an island during the Anthropocene.

'Belonging' in an ecosystem represents a contentious issue for all species, given the fact that species compete over time for space, resources, and dominance. At the same time, belonging suggests a sense of one's rightful place, one's claim to being a native plant, animal, or human. Can any species – birds, trees, mammals, and so on – assert native status given the fact that 'on islands, everything has come from somewhere else[?]'[16] Historian Daniel Lewis ponders this question in his study *Belonging on an Island: Birds, Extinction, and Evolution in Hawai'i*. His story involves not only introductions and extinctions but also the very origins of this island chain. The Hawaiian islands burst through the ocean's surface from volcanic action, with island after island expiring and disappearing back under the Pacific swell during Deep Time. Species arrived and evolved, and many if not most of them disappeared over geological periods with humans playing no part.[17]

---

[14] A. Crosby, *Ecological Imperialism: The Biological Expansion of Europe, 900–1900* (Cambridge: Cambridge University Press, 1986), 89.

[15] M. Spriggs, 'Landscape catastrophe and landscape enhancement: are either or both true in the Pacific?' in P.V. Kirch and T. Hunt, *Historical Ecology in the Pacific Islands: Prehistoric and Environmental Landscape Change* (New Haven: Yale University Press, 1997), 81, 99.

[16] D. Lewis, *Belonging on an Island: Birds, Extinction, and Evolution in Hawai'i* (New Haven: Yale University Press, 2018), 12.

[17] On plants in Hawai'i, see K. Nagata, 'Early plant introductions in Hawai'i', *Hawaiian Journal of History* 19 (1985), 35–61.

But when the first human settlers from the Marquesas arrived in the Hawaiian islands 1,000 years ago, they accelerated a pattern of disruption (and enhancement) found throughout the island Pacific: the extinction of certain species that formerly lived there. As Lewis notes specifically of avian disappearances, 'human colonization across forty-one Pacific islands caused the global extinction of nearly 1,000 species of birds'.[18]

In exchange for the extinction of bird species and other life forms, the settlers of Hawai'i introduced a familiar menagerie of fellow travellers, including rats, chickens, pigs, fowl, lizards, snails, and dozens of plant varieties – all stuff packed on the ancestors' double-hulled canoes for future sustenance. Either by intention or not, the ancestors also carried with them the Polynesian rat (*Rattus exulans*), which over time played a significant role in island deforestation and the extinction of lowland birds.[19] Some introduced species thrived alongside the human settlers, while endemic birds such as the Stumbling Moa-nalo (*Ptaiochen pau*) was swept into the dustbin of history. The Stumbling Moa-nalo had little chance of survival; it was a large, flightless, and probably tasty bird – certainly an attractive meal for the masses of new Islanders, whose population rapidly grew and spread out across the Hawaiian island chain. In the end, the human settlers prospered due to what they brought, what they found, and how they engineered the island landscape for human habitation.

Along with Rapa Nui (Easter Island) and Aotearoa (New Zealand), the human colonization of the Hawaiian islands transpired near the end of the most successful maritime migration in human history. Oceania came into being (as a populated portion of the globe) through human ingenuity and discovery, continual eastward voyages and westward returns, and a multitude of transits embedded in the ancestors' memories. Ancient Lapita cultures spread to the east into Tonga and Samao more than 2,000 years ago, at which point 'an Oceanian world began to launch toward unexplored islands' through 'successive chains of migration', according to Matt Matsuda.[20] To each new island home the settlers brought fauna (primarily dogs, chickens, pigs, and rats) as well as familiar flora (breadfruit, bananas, taro, yams, and pandanus); everywhere they introduced human-controlled fire to clear the land as well as to control or eradicate species of lesser value. They practised an inter-island trade of useful and ceremonial goods in a fashion that

---

[18] Lewis, *Belonging on an Island*, 10.   [19] Lewis, *Belonging on an Island*, 37–9.
[20] M.K. Matsuda, *Pacific Worlds: A History of Seas, Peoples, and Cultures* (Cambridge: Cambridge University Press, 2012), 19.

harkened back to the *kula* voyages of eastern New Guinea, and those voyages also included the intentional transportation of canoe plants for diversifying the biota at home.[21] The Pacific, in 'Indigenous time', was a culturally diverse creation layered on top of intersecting 'native seas' and altered island ecosystems.[22]

The Transportation of Nature in an Era of Empires

Extinctions continued at a rapid pace as European empires explored and exploited the Pacific in the eighteenth and nineteenth centuries. For instance, Ryan Tucker Jones opens his book *Empire of Extinction* with the mordant line: 'On an unrecorded day in the 1760s, the last Steller's sea cow (*Rhytina borealis*) died.'[23] A hunter may have killed it or possibly it died of loneliness, but regardless, the Russian empire's assault on marine life in the North Pacific had a devastating impact on the 'strange beasts of the sea' *and* the Indigenous communities forced to hunt them. Steller's sea cow paid the ultimate price. And yet somewhere in that empire of slaughter, profit, and power lay the seeds of mounting interest about the natural world and concern for the costs of environmental exploitation. As Jones shows, natural scientists like Martin Sauer and Georg Heinrich von Langdorff raised valuable questions about species in particular locales and the need for conservation efforts. The Russians introduced Eurasian species (rats, pigs, cattle, and wheat) in a fashion similar to other colonizing groups, but these and other naturalists also developed ideas that anticipated later conservation actions and, tangentially, the field of environmental history.

Chronicling the environmental history of the entire island Pacific represents a gargantuan task due to spatial, temporal, cultural, and technological factors. Writing that history in a single journal article – an article with deep insight and a compelling conceptual framework – is a singular achievement and one that is certain to attract many young scholars to the field.

---

[21] On the early migrations and settlement of Oceania, see K.R. Howe, *Vaka Moana: Voyages of the Ancestors: The Discovery and Settlement of the Pacific* (Auckland: David Bateman, 2006); P.V. Kirch, *A Shark Going Inland Is My Chief: The Island Civilization of Ancient Hawai'i* (Berkeley: University of California Press, 2012); D. Armitage and A. Bashford (eds.), *Pacific Histories: Ocean, Land, People* (Basingstoke: Palgrave Macmillan, 2014), 1–74; B. Malinowski, *Argonauts of the Western Pacific: An Account of Native Enterprise and Adventure in the Archipelagoes of Melanesian New Guinea* (London: Routledge & Kegan Paul, 1922).

[22] D. Salesa, 'The Pacific in indigenous time', in Armitage and Bashford (eds.), *Pacific Histories*, 31–52.

[23] R.T. Jones, *Empire of Extinction: Russians and the North Pacific's Strange Beasts of the Sea, 1741–1867* (Oxford: Oxford University Press, 2014), 1.

J.R. McNeill's 'Of rats and men: a synoptic environmental history of the island Pacific', published in the *Journal of World History* in 1994, more than accomplished these ends.[24] It not only offered an exhaustive selection of potential topics for future researchers, but also provided a narrative that moved fluidly from 'pre-human' times to the present. McNeill temporally divided his study through changes in transport and technology – the 'ages' of the outrigger, the sailing ship, and the steamship – observing at the outset that the island Pacific 'exhibits eras of calm interrupted by spurts of torrential change' closely aligned to the new forms of transport. He ends the essay with a caution about the 'costs' of 'the end of isolation' in the island Pacific, which refers to the host of externally driven destructive forces ranging from introduced European pathogens to extractive industries and atomic testing. 'Little of the actual environmental change was desired or intended', he concludes. 'The law of unforeseen consequences is a potent one, in history as in ecology.'[25]

McNeill's essay encompasses far more than is implied with the subtitle 'a synoptic environmental history of the island Pacific'. Instead, 'Of rats and men' is a richly comprehensive examination of human and environmental change across a large swath of the world's biggest ocean, filled with analytical insight and unexpected turns. Invasive and introduced species run amok across the island Pacific, as successive waves of rats, humans, and other creatures find their niches by displacing previous inhabitants. But if the environmental changes were not 'desired or intended', as McNeill correctly posits, many of the causes of change were nonetheless observed, documented, and even feared at the time. This gets at the issue of what contemporaries *knew*, and to what extent they recorded that knowledge. For instance, did Captain James Cook recognize the dangerous impact that sexually transmitted diseases would have on Hawaiians when he came across that island chain in 1777? He certainly did, given his knowledge of 'venereal complaints' from so many of his crew, and, as Cook wrote in his journal, he 'ordered that none who had the venereal upon them should go out of the ships'.[26] Regardless of his efforts, 'connections' between sailors and island women took place almost immediately, forcing Cook subsequently to document the failure of his preventive measures: 'the very thing happened that

---

[24] J.R. McNeill, 'Of rats and men: a synoptic environmental history of the island Pacific', *Journal of World History* 5:3 (1994), 299–349.

[25] McNeill, 'Of rats and men', 300, 340, 341.

[26] J.C. Beaglehole (ed.), *The Journals of Captain James Cook on His Voyages of Discovery*, 4 vols. (Cambridge: Hakluyt Society, 1955–74), vol. III, part 1, 265.

I had above all others wished to prevent'.[27] Upon his return to Hawai'i less than a year later, the Islanders confronted Cook with corporeal evidence of the new disease among them. In the history of trading natures, few introductions (and the resulting consequences) were more closely and immediately observed than this tragic incident.

Pacific voyagers documented a range of similar phenomena as European empires entered the Pacific in the late eighteenth and early nineteenth centuries. Logbooks, journals, and artistic work include many accounts of introduced species in order to demonstrate both the successes and failures of trading nature. When the artist Ludwig Choris arrived on Oahu in 1816, he quickly began filling his notebooks with sketches of the tropical landscape, the built environment, the Hawaiian people, and their spiritual icons. His drawings and subsequent lithographs show island palm trees bending in the wind while symbols of European technology (such as the masts of sailing ships and European style buildings) denote the colonial presence of foreigners. A few of his images intentionally juxtapose elements of what pre-existed on the islands with what outsiders introduced. For example, Choris's depiction of the main commercial port in 'Port of Honolulu' (titled 'Port d'hanarourou' in his book of lithographs, published in Paris in 1822) looks outward from the coast towards the bay, showing the hybrid influences that had made this place 'un grand Caravanserai' (the great caravansary) of the Pacific, as named by an earlier French visitor.[28] In the foreground of Choris's image, adjacent to the many Hawaiians who gather in conversation, stand two pigs and a number of cattle being driven forward by a *paniolo* on horseback. The image of livestock and swine seems almost natural, except for the fact that cattle and horses had only arrived on the island twenty years earlier. By the time of Choris's visit, domesticated livestock were fairly well ensconced in some parts of the islands' agricultural landscape.

Throughout the conquest of the Americas, Europeans lowered cattle and horses from the first ships to the beachheads of colonization. Along with soldiers and missionaries, livestock were deployed in the vanguard of empire. These large domesticated – and sometimes barely domesticated – ungulates arrived in Hawai'i on George Vancouver's ship *Discovery* in 1793. He brought

---

[27] Beaglehole (ed.), *The Journals of Captain James Cook*, vol. III, part 1, 276. On this episode see D. Igler, *The Great Ocean: Pacific Worlds from Captain Cook to the Gold Rush* (Oxford: Oxford University Press, 2013), 54–8.

[28] L. Choris, *Voyage pittoresque autour du Monde: avec des portraits de sauvages d'Américque, d'Asie, d'Afrique* (Paris: Fermin Didot, 1822); C.P.C. Fleurieu, *Voyage autour du Monde: pendant les années 1790, 1791 et 1792* (Paris: De l'Imprimerie de la République, 1798–1800), vol. I, 410.

one bull and one cow, both ill from a voyage that was not only long but also unanticipated (for the cattle). Neither animal was 'able to stand on their legs', wrote Vancouver, who feared his mission of colonizing Hawai'i with edible beef-on-the-hoof could perish at any moment.[29] And yet they survived, and successive imports of cattle from California and elsewhere increased the stock. By Choris's time, a modest number of feral cattle (probably belonging to Hawaiian royalty) roamed the hillside and valleys; 'bullock-hunting' parties would track down the wild cattle at the request of the ruling *ali'i*. Foreigners likely owned more cattle than the Hawaiian royals: the Spaniard Francisco de Paula Marin had a sizeable herd, as did an African American settler named Anthony Allen (a former sailor on the *Lelia Byrd*, and born into slavery in 1774), who owned fenced acreage on Oahu and traded milk to locals and ship captains alike. Hannah Holmes Davis, who was half Hawaiian by virtue of her *ali'i* mother, owned a sizeable herd near Honolulu and carried on an active beef trade with 'whalers and other vessels visiting the Islands', according to her son, the well-known merchant William Heath Davis Jr. These individuals comprise only a few of the people engaged in 'cattle colonialism', which historian John Ryan Fischer describes as 'central to the interconnections and transformations of the late eighteenth-century and early nineteenth-century Pacific'.[30]

In contrast to McNeill's narrative, which offers a panoramic view of the ocean and its multitude of ecological shifts, Fischer focuses specifically on cattle introductions and pastoral culture in the context of Hawai'i and California. *Cattle Colonialism* echoes the 'ecological imperialism' arguments of Alfred Crosby's work on the Columbian Exchange, but his work also spotlights 'the legal, economic, and social frameworks that each European power brought with the animals that determined their value as implements of colonization'.[31] Cattle severely disrupted the subsistence patterns of Indigenous populations in both Hawai'i and California, and pastoral culture contributed to new systems of land tenure introduced in the 1850s. Although cattle represented only one of countless introduced species, they played a powerful role in the economic and legal frameworks that gave power to colonial systems in the mid-nineteenth century. Fischer's argument, it should be noted, is also specific to cattle as opposed to a fully encompassing

---

[29] G. Vancouver, *A Voyage of Discovery to the North Pacific Ocean and Round the World, 1791–1795*, ed. W.K. Lamb (London: Hakluyt Society, 1984), vol. III, 806.
[30] J.R. Fischer, *Cattle Colonialism: An Environmental History of the Conquest of California and Hawai'i* (Chapel Hill: University of North Carolina Press, 2015), 118–19; 8.
[31] Fischer, *Cattle Colonialism*, 6.

Columbian Exchange. Following Crosby's pioneering work, Atlantic scholars successfully outlined the circulation of biota and germs between Europe, Africa, and the Americas constituting a set of 'exchanges'. Few Pacific scholars believe such a coherent system (such as a 'Magellan Exchange') of trade-offs and exchanges existed in the Great Ocean, given its size and multiple regions interconnected with the surrounding continents and European shipping.

What motives inspired the individuals who introduced specific species to particular places around the Pacific? In many instances, the trading of nature reflected one element of larger imperial goals to civilize, colonize, and transform an unfamiliar landscape into a more familiar setting. As the naturalist George Forster mused in 1777, 'I cannot help thinking that our late voyage would reflect immortal honour to our employers, if it had no other merit than stocking Taheitee with goats, the Friendly isles and New Hebrides with dogs, and New Zealand and New Caledonia with hogs.'[32] The 'employers', in this instance, most directly refer to the British Admiralty that funded the expedition to the Pacific, but in a more meaningful way Forster's statement reflected the empire's goal of 'stocking' potential island colonies with consumable trade items. Forster's employer was the British Empire, writ large. The Islanders themselves may in some way benefit from animal husbandry, but this hardly seems to be Forster's primary message. Nor does Forster's comment suggest that Indigenous Islanders had any desire for the 'stocking' of their homes with alien species – species that were often quite destructive to native flora and fauna.

Some voyagers could not imagine that a local population would fail to benefit from the intentional implantation of a cherished species brought from afar. Kadu, a Caroline Islander who joined Otto von Kotzebue's expedition to the North Pacific on board the *Rurik*, was struck by the 'misery of the inhabitants' when he went ashore at Unalaska Island in 1817. According to the naturalist Adelbert von Chamisso, Kadu 'surveyed this desolate earth, devoid of all trees', and quickly concluded that the island suffered from a lack of useful plants, tropical trees, and, more specifically, coconut palms. Fortunately, the *Rurik* carried a load of coconuts from the Marshall Islands and Kadu went about the business of planting them in the rocky soil despite Chamisso's admonishment 'that [Kadu's efforts] would be completely superfluous'.[33] Chamisso presented this episode as an example of Kadu's deep

---

[32] Newell, *Trading Nature*, ix.
[33] A. Chamisso, *A Voyage around the World with the Romanzov Expedition in the Years 1815–1818 in the Brig Rurik, Captain Otto von Kotzebue*, ed. and trans. H. Kratz (Honolulu: University of Hawai'i Press, 1986 [1836]), 266–7.

empathy for the inhabitants of Unalaska – how could they possibly exist without palm trees? – but the naturalist also used the incident to indicate the Islander's naivety. And yet how naive was Kadu for believing palm trees could grow on this island? In fact, he had good reason to imagine coconuts might successfully propagate on an island 6,500 kilometres from his homeland. He had already learned of the *Rurik*'s officers introducing various biota on Pacific islands, and upon arriving at Unalaska he immediately noticed the cattle brought there previously by Europeans. Kadu had seen cattle for the first time on an island earlier in the voyage and he was fascinated by the way these large and ungainly creatures could accustom themselves to an island environment where they did not appear to belong naturally. If cattle could survive on Unalaska, surely his island staple of coconuts could thrive on the island to the great benefit of the local inhabitants.

Coconut palms, cattle, pigs, birds, and pathogens – these and many other products of nature feature prominently in the accounts penned by voyagers, who generally viewed their intentional introduction of new biota as beneficial to Indigenous communities. Those communities frequently took a different view, and their resistance to foreign intrusion was partially motivated by the threat posed by introduced agents. The arrival of a foreign vessel could inspire well-warranted alarm from a local group, who sometimes 'warned off' vessels from approaching shore. Indeed, such resistance occurred repeatedly from the time of Cook's voyages in the 1770s to the early 1840s, when the United States Exploring Expedition sailed through Oceania and was periodically warned off by Islanders. In such instances, the Islanders' defiance represented an assertion of rights to their own sovereign land, but they also opposed the introduction of some things foreigners carried with them, such as the harmful maladies brought by foreign vessels.[34] Also, explorers like Cook generally did not ask permission when they introduced crops or strange animals; at Huahine, in the Society Islands, Cook ordered sailors to plant a garden with vines, melons, pineapples, and various trees, in addition to landing goats, chickens, a pair of rabbits, a horse and a mare, and sheep.[35] Cook believed in the benefits of such implants, while the people of Huahine watched the proceedings and weighed their options under the gaze of armed marines. They could decide what to do with these new plants and animals once the strangers sailed away.

[34] Igler, *The Great Ocean*, 62–3.
[35] A. Salmond, *Bligh: William Bligh in the South Seas* (Berkeley: University of California Press, 2011), 88.

The most notorious episode in the annals of trading nature in the Pacific involves not the introduction of a new species but instead the transplantation of a specific plant: *Artocarpus altilis*, better known as breadfruit. The global dimensions of this event – an attempt to transport breadfruit cuttings from Tahiti to numerous British Caribbean slave islands and also to the Royal Botanical Gardens at Kew – is frequently elided by the high-seas drama of its first voyage.[36] In 1789, Captain William Bligh acquired the desired breadfruit cuttings in Tahiti only to face the wrath and mutiny of his crew on the *Bounty*, led by first mate Fletcher Christian. Bligh and eighteen others were set adrift in a boat, while the mutineers sailed off on the *Bounty* to face their various fates. For obvious reasons, the resulting *human* drama of mutiny, capture, shipwreck (of the *Pandora*), rescue, court-martial, acquittal, and public hangings became well-trod historical narrative, while the less sensational environmental story of transplanting breadfruit received less public recognition.

Fortunately, historian Anne Salmond's study of the famous captain (*Bligh: William Bligh in the South Seas*) weds the *Bounty* drama to a global context of empire and the environmental story of species transplantation. The empire had many objectives with the breadfruit transportation, including the need to find a new source of calories for its enslaved African plantation workers in the Caribbean, the conjoining of South Pacific naval expeditions with West Indies wealth-producing colonies, and the aggressive collecting of the world's flora and fauna for the profit of science and commerce.[37] Coordinating this latter goal for the Crown and the Royal Society was Joseph Banks, who served as Cook's naturalist on his first Pacific voyage and would largely direct England's government-sponsored science for the next thirty years. Banks, Salmond argues, busily sent plant collectors 'around the world to bring back a stream of new species' to London 'where they were transplanted, grown and studied'. He had a particular fixation with breadfruit due to his many months in Tahiti with Cook. Breadfruit, he wrote at the time, 'is procured [in Tahiti] with no more trouble than that of climbing a tree and bringing it down'.[38] Surely, he believed, the British should transport this Tahitian staple

---

[36] For two examples of histories that address the global dimensions of the breadfruit transplantation, see Salmond, *Bligh*, and E. DeLoughrey, 'Globalizing the routes of breadfruit and other bounties', *Journal of Colonialism and Colonial History* 8 (2007), https://muse.jhu.edu/.
[37] On these themes of science, empire, and commerce, see P. Fara, *Sex, Botany and Empire: The Story of Carl Linnaeus and Joseph Banks* (New York: Columbia University Press, 2003); and J. Gascoigne, *Science in the Service of Empire: Joseph Banks, the British State, and the Uses of Science in the Age of Revolution* (Cambridge: Cambridge University Press, 1998).
[38] Salmond, *Bligh*, 108.

food to the enslaved workers in other British tropical colonies. Imperial science, in this sense, would function as an organizing tool of nature's productions by shuttling what bountifully grew in one place to a different place in need of the crop. The act embodied pure 'benevolence', according to Banks's colleague Bryan Edwards: 'it is that of spreading abroad the bounties of creation by transplanting from one part of the globe to another such natural productions as are likely to prove beneficial to the interests of humanity'.[39]

The actual transplantation of breadfruit proceeded with little trouble once the *Bounty* debacle had passed. While Pacific Islanders greatly valued the breadfruit (*uru* in the Society Islands) for both its generous harvest and its shade-producing trees, Europeans generally viewed the fruit for its more basic features – it was easily stored and rich in calories. The ancient ancestors of Islanders had brought the breadfruit cuttings on their earliest canoe voyages, easily planting the specimens where they settled. The British realized they could do the same in the Caribbean, while erroneous rumours of the French transporting breadfruit to its West Indies colonies forced a competitive urgency to the matter.[40] When Bligh's ship *Providence* arrived in Matavai Bay in April 1792, his gardeners immediately set to the task of cutting and potting breadfruit specimens, eventually making a full cargo comprised of '780 large, & 3012 small Pots: 35 Tubs and 28 boxes of Bread Fruit'. Bligh delighted in the ease of this operation as well as the 'good will' of the people of Tahiti, a place he considered the 'Paradise of the World'.[41]

Bligh's 'paradise' metaphor echoed Joseph Banks's initial description of Tahiti as 'the truest picture of an arcadia' he could envision.[42] In their eyes, Tahiti's tropical climate produced not only welcoming inhabitants but also a harvest of breadfruit that simply awaited transfer to any number of places in the empire. The tree itself, writes Greg Dening, was 'the very symbol of a free and unencumbered life, from the island of freedom, Tahiti'.[43] The empire valued these places of apparent freedom and generosity in part because they validated the righteousness of the empire, but also because they stood in stark contrast to those imperial spaces that embodied the denial of human freedom, such as the slave islands of the West Indies. The transfer

---

[39] Brian Edwards, cited in DeLoughrey, 'Globalizing the routes of breadfruit and other bounties', 11.
[40] Newell, *Trading Nature*, 152.   [41] Salmond, *Bligh*, 393; 395.
[42] Banks, *Journals*, vol. 1, 252.
[43] G. Dening, *Mr Bligh's Bad Language: Passion, Power and Theatre on the Bounty* (Cambridge: Cambridge University Press, 1992), 11.

of this one natural product would not alter the system of slavery, but it just might increase the productive capabilities of those who laboured in bondage for the empire's commercial advantage.

The *Providence* arrived in the West Indies in January 1793 with its cargo of breadfruit cuttings for dispersal among the British colonies. At St Vincent the crew offloaded more than 500 potted breadfruit plants to the dock, where a long line of enslaved Africans gathered the plants for transfer to the island's botanical garden. The same process ensued the following week at Point Royal Harbor, Jamaica, and Bligh put a gardener in charge of overseeing the plants' proper dispersal among the island's counties and their transfer to other nearby British slave islands. The breadfruit trees matured rapidly in the tropical Caribbean climate, but according to Anne Salmond the intended beneficiaries cared little for the new addition to their diet.[44] Bligh and Banks considered the operation a huge success, and the *Providence* returned to England with hundreds of botanical cuttings from Tahiti and the West Indies. When Bligh died two decades later, his tombstone memorialized 'the celebrated navigator who first transplanted the Bread fruit tree from Otaheite to the West Indies'.[45] The tombstone offered no information about the *Bounty* mutiny.

Few introduced species received similar graveyard recognition, especially in Australia where a very long list of imported plants and animals refashioned the continent's landscape beginning in the late eighteenth century. Australia gathered a slew of plants, animals, birds, insects, and diseases due to the efforts of explorers, traders, and the steady influx of convict settlers in the early nineteenth century.[46] In the two decades surrounding the 1850s gold strikes in Western Australia, at least a dozen new animal species arrived, including the red fox, feral cat, feral pig and donkey, water buffalo, camel, and of course, the European rabbit that multiplied by the tens of millions and soon over-ran most coastal and interior regions.

Alongside the animals came a host of plant species, ranging from almost one hundred different weeds to more prominent flora such as varieties of prickly pear from South America.[47] Intended for the purpose of fencing fields and also to produce red dye from the cochineal insect that feeds on the plant,

---

[44] Salmond, *Bligh*, 431.   [45] Salmond, *Bligh*, 472.
[46] L. Robin, 'Australia in global environmental history', in J.R. McNeill and E.S. Mauldin (eds.), *A Companion to Global Environmental History* (Chichester: Wiley-Blackwell, 2012), 182–95.
[47] 'The prickly pear story', The State of Queensland, Department of Agriculture and Fisheries (2016), 1–3, www.daf.qld.gov.au/__data/assets/pdf_file/0014/55301/IPA-Prickly-Pear-Story-PP62.pdf.

the large cacti rapidly advanced across Western Australia and covered some 23 million hectares by 1920, at which point officials in the aptly named Commonwealth Prickly Pear Board viewed the plant's colonizing success as a dangerous infestation on par with the hordes of rabbit. Chemical control efforts failed, except for the use of arsenic pentoxide that had the adverse effect of killing farmers and livestock when not properly handled. During the 1920s officials experimented with various 'natural' control agents, and they found success with the importation of the American moth *Cactorblastis cactorum*. Billions of *Cactorblastis* eggs were released across the cacti-ridden landscape and the plant gradually died out, making way for settlers and the 'revitalization' of 'townships that had been stagnant in the 1920s'.[48] In celebration of the successful prickly pear eradication, the townspeople of Boonarga constructed a 'Cactoblastis Memorial Hall' while the Commonwealth Prickly Pear Board produced a film titled *The Conquest of the Prickly Pear* (1935).[49] In sum, trading nature via introduced species (such as the prickly pear) involves both unintended consequences and occasionally the celebration of hard-fought conquests.

About the same time that feral cats (*Felis catus*) arrived in Australia, thousands of young men departed from the country and crossed the Pacific in search of California gold. One of them brought *Eucalyptus* seeds, and by the end of the 1850s the largest nursery in San Francisco offered the saplings for sale. California had a tree deficit, at least according to some migrants. 'Post Gold Rush settlers did not feel content with the existing landscape', writes Jared Farmer in *Trees in Paradise*. 'It looked deforested. It looked unfinished. A land blessed with so much sunshine, warmth, and fertility demanded more greenery, flowers, and shade.'[50] Why not import some additional shade? Californians planted *Eucalyptus* (primarily the blue gum variety) by the tens of thousands in the cooler coastal valleys. They grew tremendously fast, provided abundant shade (but not useful building material), and, according to some early boosters, *Eucalyptus* could counter miasmic 'fevers' due to the 'camphorous' odour the tree emitted.[51] However, did they *belong* in the state, as Dan Lewis queried regarding certain bird species in Hawai'i? Not until the post-war decades did 'native' plant enthusiasts

---

[48] 'The prickly pear story', 3.
[49] *The Conquest of the Prickly Pear* can be viewed at https://faclibrary.com/Title-Details.aspx?tid=2&titlename=The+Conquest+of+Prickly+Pear.
[50] J. Farmer, *Trees in Paradise: The Botanical Conquest of California* (Berkeley, CA: Heyday, 2017), 117.
[51] Farmer, *Trees in Paradise*, 126.

question if *Eucalyptus* belonged in California. Some environmentalists readily accepted the idea that species brought to the state in the 1850s belonged, while critics associated *Eucalyptus* with a variety of other unwelcome immigrants – a sort of 'botanical xenophobia', Farmer observes.[52]

Farmer's narrative of native and non-native trees in California offers a healthy reminder that the intentional introduction of species can later manifest in unique cultural politics, resistance, and questioning of what's considered 'natural'. Did Islanders accept or tear up the gardens planted by explorers and naturalists? Could Māori ever come to view sheep as anything but a four-footed accessory to the British colonizers, only far more numerous? As early as 1877, one *Eucalyptus* critic charged: 'This absurd vegetable is now growing all over this State … It asserts itself in long twin ranks, between which the traveler must run a sort of moral gauntlet.' Another detractor cited natural rather than moral concerns, observing that the tree had an 'insatiable thirst' for groundwater; it was little more than a 'venomous feeder upon moisture and soil nutriment'.[53] *Eucalyptus* simply did not belong in California's natural environment, charged these individuals, and, more to the point, it exploited the state's most fickle and contentious resource: water. However, if *Eucalyptus* represented a water-wasting invader, then what of the nineteenth-century crops like corn, barley, and wheat imported by Spaniards, to say nothing of the introduced cattle, horses, and sheep that relied on water-intensive European grasses and alfalfa that covered the state? Obviously, food production trumped shade and beauty. But carrying the argument forward to today's agricultural economy, where would the state be without its most valuable crop – *Cannabis* – first brought to California as hemp by Spaniards in the 1790s?[54] Much of California's seemingly distinctive and highly managed landscape actually arrived from somewhere else, as did its human populations going back for more than 10,000 years.

For those earliest human migrants, California's landscape offered a fairly diverse biota and a pleasant climate upon which their small populations could grow. Some places in and around the Pacific were not so accommodating, which raised the stakes in terms of the impact caused by introduced species. The Polynesian migrants who arrived at the most distant eastern island of Rapa Nui around 1200 CE may have decided it resembled a viable place to call 'home', or alternatively they may have been exhausted, adrift, and no longer concerned about which land offered refuge from the sea.

---

[52] Farmer, *Trees in Paradise*, 207. [53] Farmer, *Trees in Paradise*, 128, 129.
[54] Hackel, *Children of Coyote*, 279.

The soil was not rich but towering palm trees (*Paschalococos disperta*) grew aplenty, sea turtles populated the beach, and many land birds looked edible. 'Rapa Nui was not a Polynesian Paradise', write Terry Hunt and Carl Lipo, in regards to the irregular rainfall, poor soil, and persistent winds.[55] But the Islanders made the place sustainable. Jared Diamond reads it differently: the Rapa Nui Islanders carelessly exhausted the resources, knowingly deforested the land until some Islander 'cut down the last palm tree', and society 'spiral[led] into chaos and cannibalism'.[56]

Diamond's story is one of human folly leading to ecological and societal 'collapse', whereas other scholars demonstrate the dangerous consequences of introduced biota to an isolated island with a small human population – a population hit hard by introduced species but one that fully survived to today. In this context, trading nature certainly held some dire effects. The ancient voyagers arrived with rats (*Rattus exulans*) in their canoes, either intentionally or unintentionally. Similar to other Pacific islands (such as parts of Hawai'i), the rat population expanded rapidly and consumed the palm forests much faster than the human felling of individual trees. Agricultural production in the coastal swamp forests increased the food supply while also adding to the decline of native palms, according to archaeologist Atholl Anderson.[57] By the late eighteenth century, the rat-induced 'deforestation of Rapa Nui was complete, or nearly complete', while the human population may have entered a period of decline but had certainly not collapsed.[58] It required the introduction of European diseases to initiate the island's steep population decline of the late 1700s and early 1800s, as exploratory and trade vessels stopped at Rapa Nui and engaged with the Islanders. Decades earlier a Dutch expedition led by Jacob Roggeveen reported no sign of an ecological-social disaster on the island, but circumstances changed following the visits of French, British, and other European voyagers in the late eighteenth century. At this time, the trading of nature included the 'diseased goods' that arrived on many European vessels, resulting in a steep decline of the island population.[59]

---

[55] T. Hunt and C. Lipo, 'Ecological catastrophe, collapse, and the myth of "ecocide" on Rapa Nui (Easter Island)', in P. McAnany and N. Yoffee (eds.), *Questioning Collapse: Human Resilience, Ecological Vulnerability, and the Aftermath of Empire* (Cambridge: Cambridge University Press, 2010), 21–44, at 24.

[56] J. Diamond, *Collapse: How Societies Choose to Fail or Succeed* (New York: Viking, 2005), 63, 68.

[57] M. Prebble, A. Anderson, and D.J. Kennett, 'Forest clearance and agricultural expansion on Rapa, Austral Archipelago, French Polynesia', *Holocene* 23 (2013), 179–96, at 195.

[58] Hunt and Lipo, 'Ecological catastrophe', 36, 38–9.

[59] D. Igler, 'Diseased goods: global exchanges in the eastern Pacific Basin, 1770–1850', *American Historical Review* 109:3 (2004), 693–719. For a brief mention of the Roggeveen voyage, see Hunt and Lipo, 'Ecological catastrophe', 26.

Conclusion

The species comprising the world's biomatter constantly evolve, migrate without human activity, take passage with human movement, and enter periods of diversification and intense competition. Extinctions also factor into the Earth's shifting biomatter. The rising rate of species extinction during the Anthropocene – which ecologists estimate is one thousand times the background rate – calls attention to the severe impacts caused by human action, leading renowned biologist E.O. Wilson to propose a 'half-earth' set aside for the preservation of species and natural systems.[60] The Pacific Ocean and its thousands of inhabited islands would figure prominently in any global plan for species preservation, just as it figures prominently in all climate change scenarios due its size and potential for disruption or stability.

The high rate of species extinction in the Pacific represents a logical, if unforeseen, culmination of trading nature over the past millennia. Before human habitation, species moved about the Pacific at a slower pace but still managed to compete for resources in new niches, sometimes muscling aside previous occupants. Subsequent human travels around the Pacific added the element of social intention and culture to the transfer of species: even the earliest migrants chose specific biota as travelling companions, while trade and population growth increased the pace of chosen species moving from place to place. The transfer of biota only multiplied in recent centuries. New crops and unsuspected weeds, bird species and quadrupeds, plants of the ornamental or utilitarian sort, people by the millions, selected microbes carried by humans or animals, stowaway vermin and celebrated transplantation enterprises – different species shifted by the thousands in the ages of sailing vessels, steamships, and air travel. Biologists and biogeographers quantify and assess this massive trading of nature in and around the Pacific, while historians, anthropologists, and storytellers attempt to explain these changes as part and parcel of human narratives.

This chapter has attempted to demonstrate how historical narratives articulate different meanings of trading nature and, more broadly, humanity's interactions with non-human nature. Rather than living apart from nature or intuitively seeking an ethereal harmony with the environment, Indigenous peoples' 'tending of the wild' assumed a variety of forms. Most groups utilized fire extensively to manage the landscape, while communities

---

[60] E.O. Wilson, *Half-Earth: Our Planet's Fight for Life* (New York: Norton, 2016). For a discussion of extinction rates, see Lewis, *Belonging on an Island*, 11–41.

everywhere intentionally introduced species to further food production and social 'reproduction'. Settler populations transported their own flora and fauna ('portmanteau biota') as a means to survive, but they were also motivated by the human need to create a sense of 'belonging' in a new place. What belonged in any particular location often came at the cost of people deciding what did not belong; such trade-offs remade the landscape and resulted in the disappearance or extinction of numerous species.

The transportation of some biota (such as breadfruit) received widespread attention and even celebration in the age of European scientific exploration, but is there any reason to believe ancient settlers did not celebrate their own successful species transportations? Most likely they did. The motivations for species transfers frequently appear obvious, but as John McNeill observes, the 'unintended consequences' could be tragic to the existing environment and human populations alike. The motivations, especially in the latter age of scientific environmental management, might include the control of one introduced species (such as prickly pear in Australia) via the introduction of a different species (an American moth). Now, in the era of environmentalism, debates over the value of 'native' species leads to the troubling issue of what *native* actually means, given the fact that most things come from somewhere else. Trading nature through introductions and land management has a very long history, and the most compelling narratives created by scholars utilize a broad lens and a lengthy timeframe in order to make sense of natural and human complexity.[61]

---

[61] This summary draws from the following works: Anderson, *Tending the Wild*; Merchant, *Ecological Revolutions*; Lewis, *Belonging on an Island*; Salmond, *Bligh*; Newell, *Trading Nature*; McNeill, 'Of rats and men;' Farmer, *Trees in Paradise*.

48

Seaborne Ethnography to the Science of Race, 1521–1850

BRONWEN DOUGLAS

This chapter investigates the production of varied European knowledges about the Indigenous inhabitants of the insular Pacific from the early sixteenth to the mid-nineteenth centuries. I address liaisons of two entwined cognitive modes glossed as 'facts' and 'systems' – terms borrowed from the French comparative anatomist Cuvier, who condemned 'systems' conceived 'in the study' while vaunting 'the more solid edifice of facts and induction'.[1] 'Facts' denotes 'seaborne ethnography':[2] written, drawn, or toponymic outcomes of fleeting encounters with Pacific Islanders by European voyagers unfamiliar with their languages, practices, or ideas. 'Systems' refers to both the deductive appropriations of such information by savants in Europe from the 1740s and the inductive reflections of travelling naturalists after 1770. My scientific focus is partly 'geographic', identifying cartographic residues of encounters in place. However, it is mainly 'anthropological', surveying the deployment of seaborne ethnography in diverse, shifting explanations for human difference proposed in the 'science of man'.

As representations of people, their actions, and lifestyle, seaborne ethnography resulted from situated human encounters during maritime voyages. Such knowing is dialogic rather than linear, shaped by contexts and by traces of the actions and agency of local people.[3] I consider inductive and deductive uses of Pacific facts by mapmakers, travelling naturalists, and savants, especially in theories about human diversity proposed in the 'science of man' – an umbrella term for the eighteenth-century natural history of man and the

---

[1] G. Cuvier (ed.), 'Rapport sur un ouvrage manuscrit de M. André . . .', *Mémoires de la classe des sciences mathématiques et physiques de l'Institut national de France*, premier semestre (1807), 128–45, at 136–7. Unless otherwise indicated, all translations are my own.
[2] B. Douglas, 'Seaborne ethnography and the natural history of man', *Journal of Pacific History* 38 (2003), 3–27.
[3] B. Douglas, *Science, Voyages, and Encounters in Oceania, 1511–1850* (New York: Palgrave Macmillan, 2014), 18–22.

nineteenth-century science of race (or raciology), synonymous with anthropology from the 1820s.

My spatial focus – the insular Pacific, New Guinea, and nearby islands – is thematically dictated. For nearly three centuries before 1800, seaborne ethnography was almost the sole conduit for very limited European knowing of people and places in that maritime zone. The North Pacific islands of Guam, Rota, Tinian, and Saipan were a single exception.[4] With colonization by Spain in 1668, the rapidly diminishing Chamorro population was thereafter described in some detail by foreign residents and missionaries familiar with people and language. Across the Pacific, seaborne ethnography remained a significant anthropological resource for a half-century after 1800, complemented and then supplanted by information from resident missionaries, traders, consular or colonial officials, and eventually field anthropologists.

Europe's limited or non-existent Pacific presence until the later nineteenth century contrasts strikingly with the immense span of waterborne human occupation revealed by Indigenous knowledge, archaeology, linguistics, and related sciences. At least 30,000–60,000 years ago, modern human beings settled the expanded Pleistocene land mass of Sahul (New Guinea, Australia, and Tasmania) and the islands of Near Oceania (Bismarck Archipelago and the main Solomons chain). From about 4,000 years ago, Austronesian-speaking seafarers colonized the far-flung archipelagoes, islands, and atolls of Remote Oceania, mostly well before Europeans developed equivalent wayfinding capabilities.[5] The larger islands and archipelagoes, and the ocean as a whole, were unnamed until encompassed by European toponyms. But everywhere constellations of named Indigenous places and communities were interlinked in overlapping patterns of movement, ritual, trade, and exchanges. Those remarkable histories are palimpsest and counterpoint to my prosaic story.

Seaborne Ethnography before the Science of Man

This section sketches two instances of the meagre but influential information recorded by sixteenth- and seventeenth-century European South Sea navigators. For 250 years after Magellan's pioneer passage in 1520–1, most of the

[4] US Territory of Guam and US Commonwealth of the Northern Marianas.
[5] P.V. Kirch, 'Peopling of the Pacific: a holistic anthropological perspective', *Annual Review of Anthropology* 39 (2010), 131–48.

great ocean remained a cartographic void, crossed by Spain's northern galleon routes and sporadic European voyages which 'discovered' only parts of the New Guinea coastline and scattered islands – that were often lost due to technical incapacity to determine accurate longitude. Before the 1770s, few voyagers' accounts were published as integral narratives. Important exceptions include a French abridgement of the narrative of the Italian scholar Pigafetta who sailed with Magellan.[6] The so-called 'eighth' memorial of Quirós to the king of Spain, describing a range of Pacific Islanders encountered, evaded state censorship to be published in 1610 and was quickly translated into major European languages.[7] Narratives of the South Sea travels of the Englishman Dampier were much translated and widely read.[8] Generally, however, information about people encountered by voyagers was accessible only as summaries in chronicles or histories or condensed in collections of 'voyages'.

From first European contacts until the post-colonial era, foreign interest in Pacific Islanders was embodied – as potential Christian converts, opponents or subjects of colonialism, labour force, or customers. From the mid-eighteenth century, the science of man objectified Indigenous 'varieties' or 'races' as facts in anthropological inquiry. Before then, lack of interest in conceptualizing such human groupings and the pragmatic needs of navigation meant that the most significant scientific impact of early voyages was cartographic. However, I am more concerned with the ethnographic subtexts of early maps than with cartography per se.[9]

The words applied to Indigenous people in European texts are often highly pejorative. While acknowledging that they may be hurtful to living descendants, I cite them in context for two reasons: to emphasize that they are historical rather than natural constructs; and to expose their absurdity to critical scrutiny. Such a strategy discredits both the words and their governing mentalities in ways that burying or ignoring them cannot do.

---

[6] [A. Pigafetta], *Le voyage et navigation, faict par les Espaignolz* ... (Paris: Simon de Colines, [1525]).

[7] C. Sanz, *Australia su descubrimiento y denominación: con la reproducción facsímil del memorial número 8 de Quirós en español original, y en las diversas traducciones contemporáneas* (Madrid: Ministerio de Asuntos Exteriores, 1973).

[8] W. Dampier, *A New Voyage Round the World* ... (London: James Knapton, 1697), and *A Continuation of a Voyage to New-Holland, &c. in the Year 1699* (London: James Knapton, 1709).

[9] B. Douglas, 'Naming places: voyagers, toponyms, and local presence in the fifth part of the world, 1500–1700', *Journal of Historical Geography* 45 (2014), 12–24.

Magellan: 'Island of Thieves' 1521

The first encounter between Pacific Islanders and European voyagers occurred near the end of Magellan's tortuous Pacific crossing of nearly four months across an almost empty ocean. On 6 March 1521, the Spanish saw several islands. Pigafetta's *Voyage* blends classic modes of historical and ethnographic enunciation, beginning with a vivid passage in the preterite or past historic tense:

> And the captain general wanted to anchor at the large [island] to take some rest, but can not due to the people of this island, who entered the ships and plundered all sorts of things, so that ours could not protect themselves from them. And [the men] wanted to strike the sails in order to go ashore. And the furious captain landed with forty armed men, & burned forty or fifty houses, with many of their boats, and killed seven of them, and recovered a skiff that they had stolen. And immediately left.[10]

Out of all proportion to the insult suffered, the Spanish reaction signified not only the brutal arrogance of conquistadors towards people they considered 'heathen' and 'barbarous', but their own plight and vulnerability to the unfettered agency of a large resident seafaring population.[11]

Pigafetta then switched tense to the 'ethnographic present' to sketch an empirical description of the Islanders. The men 'go naked', have long black hair, are as tall as the Spanish, well built, and 'olive' in skin colour. The women also 'go naked' and 'are beautiful & delicate & whiter than the men'. With no possible expertise, Pigafetta asserted that they have 'no lord' and 'worship nothing'. A marginal heading 'Thievish people' condenses his concluding barb: 'This people is poor, extremely ingenious, & very thievish. And for this our people called it the island of thieves', *los Ladrones* in Spanish.[12] Yet Magellan had evidently first labelled these islands *de las Velas Latinas* (of the lateen sails).[13] The toponym *de las Velas* appears in a few sixteenth-century Portuguese manuscript maps and a handful of published Dutch maps based on them, but vanishes after 1700.[14] While registering

---

[10] [Pigafetta], *Voyage*, fol. 15r–15v.   [11] Douglas, *Science*, 41–68.

[12] [Pigafetta], *Voyage*, fol. 16r–16v.

[13] A. de Herrera y Tordesillas, *Historia general de los hechos de los Castellanos en las Islas i Tierra firme del mar Oceano* . . ., 4 vols. (Madrid: Iuan Flamenco and Iuan de la Cuesta, 1601–15), vol. II, 6.

[14] A. Cortesão, 'António Pereira and his map of circa 1545: an unknown Portuguese cartographer and the early representation of Newfoundland, Lower California, the Amazon, and the Ladrones', *Geographical Review* 29 (1939), 205–55, at 220–4; A. Cortesão and A. Teixeira da Mota (eds.), *Portugaliae Monumenta Cartographica*, 6 vols. (Lisbon: Comemorações do V Centenário da

Figure 48.1 Anon., 'Ladrones', Chinese ink and paint on rice paper, in [Sino-Spanish (Boxer) Codex], [c. 1590].

appreciation rather than disgust, this discarded term also attests to local agency, in this case superlative seamanship.

The Indigenous protagonists in the encounter were Chamorro, almost certainly inhabitants of Guam. Drawings of two armed men labelled 'Ladrones' feature in the 'Boxer Codex', a richly illustrated late sixteenth-century ethnographic manuscript prepared for a Spanish governor in Manila (Figure 48.1).[15] Possibly drawn by a Chinese artist, these unflattering, distorted figures are probably the earliest surviving visual representations of Pacific Islanders. Annexed by Spain in 1565, Guam was henceforth a stopover on the Manila Galleon Route until formally colonized in 1668, when the group was renamed Marianas after the Spanish Queen. However, the derogatory appellation Ladrones was scarcely challenged in global mapmaking until the nineteenth century and persisted until at least the 1930s.

Morte do Infante D. Henrique, 1960–2), vol. III, 97–100; P. Plancius, *Insulae Moluccae* ... ([Amsterdam, Cornelis Claesz], 1592–4).
[15] Anon., [Sino-Spanish (Boxer) Codex], [c. 1590], LMC 2444, Lilly Library, Indiana University, Bloomington, IN; C.R. Boxer, 'A late sixteenth century Manila MS', *Journal of the Royal Asiatic Society of Great Britain and Ireland* 1/2 (1950), 37–49, at 37–8, 45–8.

Magellan was killed about a month after leaving Guam in a reckless assault on an island in the archipelago later named the Philippines. Pigafetta was among twenty-two survivors of the expedition, including four 'Indians', who completed the circumnavigation of the globe in September 1522. They were interviewed in depth, including by the chronicler Pietro Martire, who mentioned the toponym Ladrones,[16] and the Portuguese chartmaker Diogo Ribeiro. A contributor to preparations for Magellan's voyage and later an official Spanish cosmographer, Ribeiro inscribed the Pacific islands seen by Magellan on a manuscript planisphere of 1525.[17] They include *los Ladrones*, subsequently deformed into *Ins. p̄donum* in Münster's widely circulated 1540 re-edition of Ptolemy's *Geographia*.[18] Renaissance mapmakers thereby disseminated a cartographic calumny which long endured as a signified (meaning) unmoored from its referents, the local actions that had provoked it.

Dampier: Guam 1686; New Guinea 1700

In May 1686, the erstwhile buccaneer Dampier spent nearly two weeks anchored off Guam as a crew member of the English merchantman-privateer *Cygnet*. In *A New Voyage Round the World*, the first of his wildly popular travel narratives, Dampier reported that the 'Native *Indians*' of the island – a Spanish colony for two decades – were drastically reduced to 'not above 100' by voluntary exile to islands further north, following an unsuccessful attempt to expel the Spaniards. Dampier noted a garbled version of the new Spanish eponym for the archipelago – 'The *Spaniards* of late have named *Guam*, the Island *Maria*' – but retained the appelation '*Ladrone* Islands'.[19]

As a maritime trader and avid naturalist, Dampier described the island's 'Fruits' and the Islanders' canoes in considerable detail, while consigning people to a brief ethnographic passage: 'strong bodied, large limb'd and well shap'd'; 'black and long' hair; 'meanly proportioned' eyes; 'pretty high' noses; 'pretty full' lips; 'long-visaged, and stern of countenance'. A moral addendum commended approved conduct: 'we found them to be affable and

---

[16] P. Martire d'Anghiera, *De Orbe Novo* (Compluti: Michaelé de Eguia, 1530), fol. lxxviii.

[17] [D. Ribeiro], [Carta Castiglioni], 1525, Biblioteca estense universitaria, Modena, http://bibliotecaestense.beniculturali.it/info/img/geo/i-mo-beu-c.g.a.12.html.

[18] C. Ptolemy, *Geographia universalis . . .*, ed. S. Münster (Basel: Henricum Petrum, 1540); T. Suárez, *Early Mapping of the Pacific* (Singapore: Periplus, 2004), 50–1.

[19] Dampier, *New Voyage*, 290–1, 300–1; all emphases in citations from Dampier are original.

courteous'. Brief ethnological (comparative) remarks punctuate the ethnography, invoking Dampier's wide experience in the East and West Indies and the Americas: the 'Native *Indians*' of Guam 'are Copper-coloured, like other *Indians*'; they are 'very ingenious beyond any people, in making Boats, or Proes, as they are called in the *East Indies*'; and they are 'not less dexterous in managing than in building these Boats', which 'sail the best of any Boats in the world'.[20]

In early 1699, the Admiralty despatched Dampier, now a renowned author, on an official voyage 'for making Discoveries in foreign Parts', specifically New Holland (Australia), New Guinea, and *Terra Australis* (the south land).[21] After five weeks on the west coast of New Holland and in Timor, he sighted New Guinea on New Year's Day 1700. For nearly four months, Dampier coasted the great island's northern margins and outliers.[22] Successive ethnographic commentaries in *A Continuation of a Voyage to New-Holland* reference encounters with particular people whose appearance and behaviour coloured his descriptions and judgements. At a small island off New Guinea's northwest coast, called Pulau Sabuda by 'the Natives', he recorded striking physical variation: between 'a sort of very tawny *Indians*, with long black Hair', whose 'manners' reminded him of people in the East Indies and who seemed 'to be the chief'; and 'shock Curl-pated *New-Guinea Negroes*', many 'Slaves to the others', but 'not all'.[23] Several weeks later, Dampier described large communities of 'strong well-limb'd *Negroes*' encountered in 'New Britain' (Bismarck Archipelago, Papua New Guinea). Physically, they were 'very black', with 'Hair naturally curl'd and short'. Materially, they were 'very dextrous active Fellows' whose double outrigger canoes were 'very ingeniously built'. Morally, he was offended by their 'treacherous', 'shy and roguish', 'very daring and bold' demeanour. These moral terms encode instances of Indigenous agency: determination to interact on their own terms and resolute refusal to engage in 'a friendly Commerce' for anything other than coconuts. Thwarted and alarmed, Dampier resorted to pre-emptive use of gunfire 'to strike some terrour into the Inhabitants' in order to obtain vitally 'necessary' wood and water; and he condoned the crew's armed raids on local hog supplies.[24]

---

[20] Dampier, *New Voyage*, 291–301.
[21] Admiralty to Dampier, 'Instructions', 30 November 1698, in Great Britain Parliament, *Journals of the House of Commons from November the 16th 1699 . . . to May the 25th 1702 . . .* (s.l., s. n., 1803), 87–8.
[22] Dampier, *Continuation*, 92–158.   [23] Dampier, *Continuation*, 100.
[24] Dampier, *Continuation*, 117–48.

Dampier's influence on mapping the South Sea was markedly less than that of earlier Spanish and Dutch voyagers.[25] However, the ethnological implications of his sporadic comparison of physically stereotyped 'Indians' and 'Negroes' are profound. By the seventeenth century, Spanish condensation of the entire hemisphere comprising the West Indies, the Americas, the Pacific Islands, and the East Indies into *las Indias* (the Indies) had made 'Indian' an ambiguous concept. Sometimes denoting an inhabitant of India or either Indies, it could also be a general synonym for 'native'.[26] Dampier explicitly differentiated 'the common *Indians*', in the restricted sense, from 'the *Negroes* of Guinea'[27] – a phrase imbued with ever-deepening negative connotations from the mid-fifteenth century by association with the expanding West African slave trade. Yet Dampier's usage is a descriptive contrast rather than a racial dichotomy. He hardly used the word race and his primary criterion of human difference was a deeply ethnocentric conception of relative civility. As a buccaneer, he learned compassion for 'the inland people' in the East Indies, whom 'the civilized *Indians* of the maritime places, who trade with Foreigners', caught and sold 'for Slaves; accounting them to be but as Savages, just as the *Spaniards* do the poor *Americans*'. His narrative brackets 'wild *Indians*' in central America, 'who have not the use of Iron', with '*Savage Indians*' and African '*Negroes*'.[28] But unlike apologists for the slave trade or nineteenth-century raciologists, his confidence that 'Negroes' were capable of civilization through trade is evident in his contention that the 'very black, strong, and well-limb'd People' of New Britain might 'be easily brought to Commerce', despite his own failure to do so in 'present Circumstances'.[29]

Colonial Imaginings

Dampier's narratives put *Terra Australis* at the forefront of competing British and French colonial fantasies. His favourable assessment of the inhabitants of New Britain and conclusion that 'this Island may afford as many rich Commodities as any in the World' were portentous. An updated edition of Harris's 'collection of voyages and travels' contains a map of Dampier's 'Discoveries' in New Guinea (Figure 48.2), with a commentary recommending New Britain's 'great Advantages' for 'settling a Colony'.[30] In 1752, the

---

[25] Suárez, *Early Mapping*, 39–112.   [26] Douglas, *Science*, 47, 58–73, 80–99.
[27] Dampier, *Continuation*, 537.   [28] Dampier, *New Voyage*, 85, 456–7, 486, 536.
[29] Dampier, *Continuation*, 148.
[30] E. Bowen, 'A map of the discoveries made by Captn. Willm. Dampier in the Roebuck in 1699', in J. Harris, *Navigantium atque Itinerantium Bibliotheca* . . ., [ed. J. Campbell], 2nd edn, 2 vols. (London: T. Woodward et al., 1744–8), vol. I, 125.

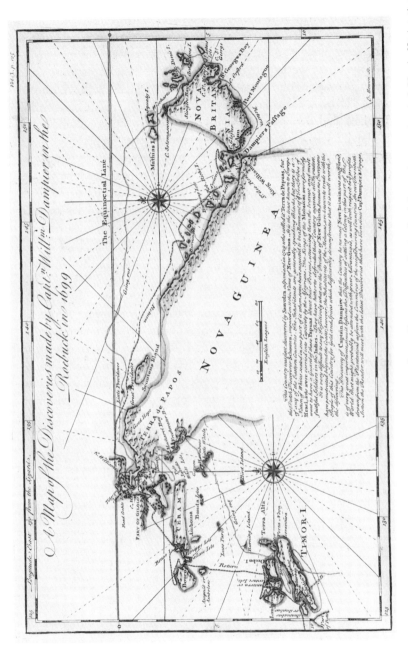

Figure 48.2 E. Bowen, 'A map of the discoveries made by Captⁿ. Willm. Dampier in the Roebuck in 1699', engraving, in J. Harris, *Navigantium atque Itinerantium Bibliotheca* ... (1744), vol. 1, facing 125.

French polymath Maupertuis listed the 'discovery' of the *Terres australes* as the most urgent and worthy project whereby an enlightened prince might advance 'Commerce' and 'Physics' (natural science).[31] Grounded in a digest of voyage texts, Brosses differentiated the earliest regional cartography of 'this fifth part of the world'. He proposed two novel toponyms: Australasia (from Latin *australis*, south), a largely speculative land mass in the southwest Pacific; and Polynesia (from Greek *poly-*, many, and *nēsos*, island), comprising 'everything contained in the vast Pacific Ocean'.[32] Both terms endured to the present, though with labile geographic content and racial implications.

Brosses, too, identified New Britain as the most favourable site for a future colony, due mainly to Dampier's positive assessment of the country and its inhabitants' potential for commerce.[33] Within a decade, John Callander plagiarized Brosses's work in English translation and pirated his colonial prospectus 'to the Advantage of Great Britain'.[34]

Seaborne Ethnography in the Natural History of Man

This section samples the initially limited but steadily growing impact of seaborne ethnography in the Pacific in the natural history of human varieties, pioneered by the French naturalist Buffon. Regionalized with respect to the Pacific Islands by Johann Reinfold Forster, naturalist on Cook's second Pacific voyage of 1772–5 with his son Georg, this inquiry was transmogrified into the nascent science of race by the German comparative anatomist-anthropologist Blumenbach.

Buffon and Dampier

In 1749, when natural history normally considered man only as individual, Buffon published a groundbreaking catalogue of the 'varieties in the human species', drawn largely from travellers' accounts.[35] The Pacific Islands figure negligibly in this volume, since the essay predated the flood of information produced by the great scientific voyages after 1766. Dampier was Buffon's

---

[31] P.L. Moreau de Maupertuis, *Lettre sur le progrès des sciences* (s.l., s.n., 1752), 1–29.

[32] C. de Brosses, *Histoire des navigations aux terres australes* . . ., 2 vols. (Paris: Durand, 1756), vol. I, 77–80.

[33] Brosses, *Histoire*, vol. I, i, 2–4; vol. II, 128, 169, 380–99.

[34] [C. de Brosses], *Terra Australis Cognita: or Voyages to the Terra Australis* . . ., trans. and ed. J. Callander, 3 vols. (Edinburgh: A. Donaldson, 1766–8).

[35] G.-L. Leclerc, comte de Buffon, 'Variétés dans l'espèce humaine', in *Histoire naturelle, générale et particulière* . . ., 15 vols. (Paris: Imprimerie Royale, 1749–67), vol. III, 371–530.

primary ethnographic authority on the 'very diverse' inhabitants of the vast zone extending from the coasts of India, to island and mainland Southeast Asia, New Holland, New Guinea, and the western Pacific Islands.[36] Beyond empirical detail, Dampier provided key evidence for Buffon's pioneer thesis on the 'causes' of human 'varieties'. He juxtaposed Dampier's descriptions of the 'Papuans or Negroes' of New Guinea and New Britain ('true Negroes', '*because*' their homeland was crossed by 'burning' winds) and the 'less black' inhabitants of New Holland ('where the heat of the climate is not as great, *because* this land . . . [is] further from the equator'). Such imagined physical contrasts underwrote Buffon's argument that 'the climate' was 'the first and almost unique cause of men's colour'. Dampier thus helped 'prove' Buffon's conviction that, as the original 'single species of men' spread across the globe, they changed under the influence of 'external and accidental causes', resulting in the production of stable, but not irreversible, 'varieties of the species'.[37] Buffon's reasoning was confirmed by subsequent South Sea voyage narratives, particularly those of Bougainville and Cook.[38]

Buffon's writings have been condemned in modern hindsight as the wellspring of 'the entire racialist theory', but this teleological reading misconstrues his erratic concept of race and aversion to taxonomy.[39] My point is made in this western Pacific example: having rehearsed Dampier's ethnographic description of the inhabitants of Guam, Buffon declared that the people of Formosa (Taiwan) and the Marianas Islands '*resemble*' each other physically and seemed 'to form a separate race different from all the others nearby' – specifically, 'the Papuans & the other inhabitants of the lands near New Guinea, [who] are true blacks & *resemble* those of Africa'.[40] These adjacent assertions, mirroring Dampier's stereotyped '*Indians*' and '*Negroes*', might be seen to prefigure later racial differentiation of Micronesians and Melanesians (see below). But, as with Dampier, it is inappropriate to attribute a modern racial system to Buffon. His ambiguous usages of the collective noun 'race' range from a 'narrow' genealogical sense, synonymous with 'kind', 'variety', or 'nation', to an 'extended' sense connoting

---

[36] Buffon, 'Variétés', 385–6, 392, 396, 400–2, 407–10.

[37] Buffon, 'Variétés', 407–10, 520–2 my emphasis, 528–30.

[38] G.-L. Leclerc, comte de Buffon, *Servant de suite à l'histoire naturelle de l'homme*, in *Histoire naturelle, générale et particulière . . .: Supplément*, 7 vols. (Paris: Imprimerie Royale, 1777–89), vol. IV, 539–55.

[39] T. Todorov, *Nous et les autres: la réflexion française sur la diversité humaine* (Paris: Seuil, 1989), 119–28; cf. Douglas, *Science*, 106–7.

[40] Buffon, 'Variétés', 406, 410–11, my emphasis.

climatically induced 'singular resemblance' in widely dispersed, unrelated 'peoples' occupying a similar latitude.[41]

Dampier and Buffon shared the distaste for dark skin colour long ingrained in 'white' Euro-American sensibilities. Before the 1770s, however, natural history generally took human physical variations to be transient products of the effects of climate, lifestyle, and station on members of the single human race. Human diversity was primarily attributed to religion and alleged degree of 'civility' or its lack, which correlated unevenly with skin pigmentation. But from the fifteenth century, these criteria converged in the growing nexus between 'heathen', 'barbarous', 'black' African 'Negroes', and chattel slavery.[42]

J.R. Forster: Observations of a Travelling Naturalist

Most scientific voyagers of the late eighteenth century had no more interest in classifying human beings than did Dampier. A notable exception was J.R. Forster, who devoted nearly two-thirds of his *Observations* on 'physical geography, natural history, and ethic philosophy' to the 'human species'.[43] Brosses did not systematically class the inhabitants of Australasia and Polynesia but coalesced them, following Quirós, into 'so many races of men of diverse kinds, & different colours, placed in the same climates at such short distances from each other'.[44] Forster, in contrast, split them into 'two great varieties of people': 'the one more fair, well limbed, athletic, of a fine size, and a kind benevolent temper; the other, blacker, the hair just beginning to become woolly and crisp, the body more slender and low, and their temper, if possible more brisk, though somewhat mistrustful'. Claiming to privilege 'facts' over 'systems formed in the closet', Forster inferred this binomial classification from personal observation in places visited during the voyage, assigning their populations to one or other category: the 'first race' in Tahiti, the Society Islands, Marquesas, Friendly Islands (Tonga), Easter Island, and New Zealand; the 'second race' in New Caledonia and the New Hebrides (Vanuatu).[45]

As a Lutheran pastor, Forster did not doubt that '*all mankind*' were '*of one species*' and all varieties 'only accidental', while insisting on a universal human potential to 'progress' towards 'civilization'.[46] Yet as a naturalist, he

---

[41] Buffon, 'Variétés', 372, 433, 447–8; Buffon, *Servant de suite*, 462–3, 478.
[42] Douglas, *Science*, 10–12, 39–46, 74–8.
[43] J.R. Forster, *Observations Made during a Voyage Round the World* ... (London: G. Robinson, 1778), 212–609.
[44] Brosses, *Histoire*, vol. I, 334; vol. II, 348.   [45] Forster, *Observations*, ii, 228, 258.
[46] Forster, *Observations*, 252, 257, original emphasis, 285–307.

explained the 'evident difference' between the 'two different tribes' he had seen living in virtually 'the same climate' by supposing that they were 'descended from two different races of men'. Brosses and Forster used 'races' in the eighteenth-century collective sense, loosely synonymous with 'varieties', 'kinds', or 'tribes'. Both reinscribed an old conjectural history to hypothesize, in Brosses's case, that island Southeast Asia and New Holland were originally settled by an 'old race' of 'brutish', 'frizzy-haired blacks'; in Forster's, that 'the first and aboriginal inhabitants' of the Pacific Islands were a 'black race' of 'Papuas', 'all cannibals', who still occupied New Guinea, the New Hebrides, and remote areas of the Philippines and Maluku (eastern Indonesia). Both imagined that 'foreign colonies' of 'fairer', 'more civilized Malay' immigrants must have destroyed or dispersed these supposedly autochthonous blacks.[47] This equation of darker skin colour with primordiality, cannibalism, and absence of civility ominously foreshadowed aspects of nineteenth-century racialist discourses.

Blumenbach: 'Natural Varieties of Mankind' to 'Principal Races'

From the late eighteenth century, the venerable dogma of human similitude – labelled monogenism in the 1850s in opposition to polygenism – was severely compromised by swelling belief in the essential inequality of races, newly reified as permanent, innately physical, hereditary entities and conceived by polygenists as originally separate species.[48] A key precursor of the biologization of human difference and emergence of racial taxonomy, Blumenbach drew liberally on Pacific materials to illustrate his long-emergent monogenist thesis of diversity within the single human species.

In the second edition of his landmark Latin study 'on the natural varieties of mankind', Blumenbach made the 'new southern world' a fifth human variety, divided by J.R. Forster into 'two Tribes'.[49] In the third edition, Blumenbach renamed his 'five principal varieties' as 'Caucasian', 'Mongolian', 'Ethiopian', 'American', and 'Malay'.[50] Citing comparative language tables, including those

---

[47] Brosses, *Histoire*, vol. II, 348, 378–80; Forster, *Observations*, 228, 276, 281–4; Douglas, *Science*, 89–91.

[48] Douglas, *Science*, 13–16, 106–11, 162–5, 201–5, 252–7; B. Douglas, 'Climate to crania: science and the racialization of human difference', in B. Douglas and C. Ballard (eds.), *Foreign Bodies: Oceania and the Science of Race 1750–1940* (Canberra: ANU Press, 2008), 33–96.

[49] J.F. Blumenbach, *De Generis Humani Varietate Nativa*, 2nd edn (Goettingen: A. Vandenhoek, 1781), 52, original emphasis.

[50] J.F. Blumenbach, *De Generis Humani Varietate Nativa*, 3rd edn (Gottingen: Vandenhoek & Ruprecht, 1795), 284–7.

published in the narratives of Cook's first and third voyages, he justified the final category on the grounds that 'by far the most men' of this widely dispersed variety spoke the 'Malay idiom'.[51] But Blumenbach also stressed the enigma of their great physical diversity in supposed 'beauty' and 'other bodily characters', personified in 'the Otaheitians [Tahitians]' amongst whom Bougainville had reported 'two very different races of men': one very tall, 'as white as us', with European facial features; the other of 'average' size and like 'Mulattos' in 'colour & features'.[52]

Blumenbach further deduced an east–west cline across the Pacific in skin colour, stature, and features: from Bougainville's 'paler' Tahitians, to his Tahitian 'Mulattos', who resembled the inhabitants of 'more westerly islands', amongst whom 'the New Hebridean islanders gradually approach to the Papuans and New-Hollanders'. They in turn converged imperceptibly with 'the Ethiopian' (African) variety, to which they might fittingly be assigned.[53] Blumenbach's primary authority for this presumed somatic continuum was Quirós, whose 'eighth' memorial he read in Dalrymple's English translation. Blumenbach applauded Quirós for having 'carefully divided the variety of men who inhabit the Pacific Ocean' by calling some 'whitish' and comparing others to 'the Mulattos' and 'the Ethiopians'.[54]

Blumenbach, however, anachronistically ascribed his own taxonomic agenda to Quirós, who had twice crossed the Mar del Sur from Peru on expeditions of colonization (in 1595) and exploration (in 1605), latterly as commander. The eighth memorial is one of more than fifty he despatched seeking support for further voyages.[55] It catalogues a locally varied kaleidoscope of skin and hair colour *within* both eastern and western Pacific populations: 'their colours are white, brown [*loros*], mulattos, and Indian, and mixtures of one and the others: the hair of some is black [*negros*], thick and loose, of others is twisted and frizzy, and of others very fair and thin'.[56] Blumenbach's categorical misreading of this passage might have stemmed from Dalrymple's mistranslation of Quirós's Spanish adjective *loro* (meaning 'between white and black') as the English noun 'Negroes' ('Ethiopians').[57] At a time when systematic human classification was scarcely conceivable,

---

[51] Blumenbach, *Generis Humani*, 3rd edn, 320, note x.
[52] Blumenbach, *Generis Humani*, 3rd edn, 320, note y.
[53] Blumenbach, *Generis Humani*, 3rd edn, 320–1.
[54] Blumenbach, *Generis Humani*, 3rd edn, 321, note z; A. Dalrymple, *An Historical Collection of the Several Voyages and Discoveries in the South Pacific Ocean*, 2 vols. (London: The Author, 1770–1), vol. 1, 162–74.
[55] P.F. de Quirós, *Memoriales de las Indias Australes*, ed. O. Pinochet (Madrid: Historia 16, 1990).
[56] Sanz, *Australia*, 23.   [57] Dalrymple, *Historical Collection*, vol. 1, 164.

Quirós pragmatically invoked the variegated appearance of South Sea Islanders as evidence for the occurrence of 'much commerce and intercourse' and 'the vicinity of more civil people', in his tenacious campaign to prove the reality of an unknown southern land, ripe for conversion, exploitation, and colonization.

Prime illustration of 'insensible transition' within and between varieties, the Malay variety confirmed Blumenbach's principled commitment to the concept of the singularity of the human species.[58] Yet two years later, writing in German, Blumenbach relabelled Latin *varietates*, 'varieties', as *Hauptrassen*, 'principal races', and endorsed the German philosopher Kant's portentous redefinition of a race as a stable, 'classificatory distinction of the animals of one and the same stem stock [*Stammes*], insofar as it is inevitably hereditary'.[59] In 1806, Blumenbach diluted his concept of insensible transition between varieties by reconstituting 'the black Papuans at New Holland, etc.' as a 'people' whose 'more or less striking conformation' so distinguished them from the 'brown' Pacific Islanders that they might be considered a 'separate subspecies' of the Malay 'race'.[60]

Seaborne Ethnography and the Science of Race

Scientific voyages in the Pacific supplied much factual grist for comparative anatomy, biology, and anthropology. New materials from beyond Europe were exploited by the science of race to discredit traditional climatic explanations for human differences and normalize hereditarian theories. With particular reference to the polysemic category 'the Papuans', this section considers the inductive entanglement of experience and discourse in works by voyaging naturalists: Georg Forster who accompanied Cook; the French naval medical officers Quoy, Lesson, and Hombron, co-opted as naturalists on four successive expeditions to the Pacific between 1817 and 1840; and the navigator-naturalist Dumont d'Urville who commanded the final two voyages and sailed on three. These men mobilized the experiential authority of encounters with particular Pacific people to apply or repudiate abstract racial theories or infer their own racial generalizations. Reception of voyagers'

---

[58] Blumenbach, *Generis Humani*, 3rd edn, 322.
[59] J.F. Blumenbach, *Handbuch der Naturgeschichte*, 5th edn (Göttingen: J.C. Dieterich, 1797), 23–4, 60–3; I. Kant, 'Bestimmung des Begriffs einer Menschenrace', *Berlinische Monatsschrift* 6 (1785), 390–417, at 407.
[60] J.F. Blumenbach, *Beyträge zur Naturgeschichte*, 2nd edn, 2 vols. (Göttingen: H. Dieterich, 1806–11), vol. I, 72.

impressions by savants in Europe is exemplified in texts by Kant, Cuvier, the French zoologist Blanchard, and the English ethnologist Prichard.

Georg Forster and Kant

In his precocious narrative of Cook's second voyage, the younger Forster anticipated empirically his father's formal binary division of Pacific humanity. At the island of Malakula (Vanuatu), the expedition encountered a population whom Cook disparaged as 'the most ugly, ill-proportioned people' he had seen.[61] In earlier work, I argued that Malakulan agency – indifference to European goods and refusal to trade provisions – goaded Cook the anxious commander into what Forster called 'an ill-natured comparison between them and monkies'. In contrast, Forster the eager savant admired the 'great sprightliness' of their features and their 'quick comprehension' of the visitors' gestures and sounds. He also differentiated them as 'a race totally distinct' in 'form', 'language', and 'manners' from the 'lighter-coloured nation' seen earlier and hypothesized their identity with the 'black race' earlier reported in 'New Guinea and Papua'.[62]

A decade later, in a paper on 'human races', Forster dichotomized the South Sea Islanders more harshly: 'these two so markedly different peoples', one 'light-brown' with 'pleasing' facial features, the other 'black' and 'uglier'. This paper initiated a polemical interchange with Kant in which Forster posed as the 'clear-sighted and reliable empiricist' against the 'biased systematist'.[63] Rejecting as empirically unsustainable Kant's belief in the reality of discrete, 'inevitably hereditary' races within a single human species of common ancestry, Forster argued that everything in holistic nature 'is connected by nuances' and 'does not follow our classifications'.[64] He reinscribed the conventional definition of 'race' as an equally 'changeable, accidental' synonym of 'variety' and asserted authoritatively that voyagers only applied race to South Sea Islanders to imply 'a crowd of people' of 'idiosyncratic' form and 'unknown origin' – Buffon's 'extended' sense. So 'the Papuans and the black Islanders of the South Sea incidentally related to them' were called a race to differentiate them from nearby 'light-brown people of

[61] J. Cook, *A Voyage Towards the South Pole and Round the World* ..., 2 vols. (London: W. Strahan and T. Cadell, 1777), vol. II, 31–6.
[62] G. Forster, *A Voyage Round the World in His Britannic Majesty's Sloop, Resolution* ..., 2 vols. (London: B. White, J. Robson, P. Elmsly, and G. Robinson, 1777), vol. II, 205–31; Douglas, *Science*, 98–100.
[63] G. Forster, 'Noch etwas über die Menschenrassen', *Teutsche Merkur* (October 1786), 62, 64–5.
[64] Forster, 'Noch etwas über die Menschenrassen', 77, 85–6, 155, 160.

Malay origin'.[65] Yet Forster's uncompromising empiricism also drove him to deride as 'indemonstrable dogma' the orthodox premise of a single common human origin – championed by Buffon, J.R. Forster, Blumenbach, and Kant – since 'indisputable historical evidence' for descent from 'a common parental couple' was entirely lacking. In a portent of the racialist polygenism of the nineteenth century, Forster was prepared to imagine the 'heresy' that 'there are several original human stem stocks [*Menschenstamme*]' and query whether 'the Negro' might constitute 'a second human species'.[66]

That Forster's flirtation with proto-polygenist heterodoxy was a rhetorical device to unsettle Kant's teleology and deductive logic is suggested by his subsequent 'findings' in a long panegyric of Cook and his voyages: that they had shown 'human nature' to be 'everywhere climatically distinct', but also '*specifically* the same' in 'organization', 'instincts', and 'development'.[67] Forster's hostile critique provoked Kant to respond in the same magazine. Distorting Forster's empirical objections, Kant reinforced his earlier thesis that natural history needed a teleological concept of race as an inevitably hereditary character.[68]

Forster and Kant personify the opposition of voyaging naturalist and sedentary philosopher and their distinct epistemological modes. In contrast to Forster's professed inductivism, Kant made his deductive stance explicit: 'you find in experience what you need only if you know beforehand what to look for'.[69] Kant's insouciance about facts is evident in casual asides on the physical appearance and skin colour of Pacific Islanders, inserted to buttress an a priori argument and infuriating to Forster.[70] With respect to 'the Papuans', Kant salvaged theory in the face of a seeming empirical anomaly by reconfiguring them and adjacent discrepant 'races' as 'not aborigines' but 'foreigners', displaced from west to east by an unknown cause.[71]

Quoy and 'the Papuans'

Quoy was chief surgeon-naturalist on Freycinet's circumnavigation of 1817–20 and professor and naturalist on Dumont d'Urville's voyage of

---

[65] Forster, 'Noch etwas über die Menschenrassen', 79–80, 159–60, 164.
[66] Forster, 'Noch etwas über die Menschenrassen', 79–81, 86, 154–66. On polygenism, see Douglas, 'Climate to crania'.
[67] G. Forster, 'Cook, der Entdecker', in *Geschichte der See-Reisen und Entdeckungen im Süd-Meer* . . ., 7 vols. (Berlin: Haude und Spener, 1787), vol. VI, 86, my emphasis.
[68] I. Kant, 'Ueber den Gebrauch teleologischer Principien in der Philosophie', *Teutsche Merkur* (January 1788), 36–52; (February 1788), 107–36.
[69] Kant, 'Bestimmung', p. 390.   [70] Forster, 'Noch etwas über die Menschenrassen', 64–8.
[71] Kant, 'Ueber den Gebrauch teleologischer Principien', 124.

1826–9. His protégé Lesson was pharmacist-naturalist and ultimately surgeon on the intermediate circumnavigation of Duperrey in 1822–5. Hombron was chief surgeon-naturalist on Dumont d'Urville's final voyage of 1837–40. All four expeditions traversed vast Pacific spaces and encountered very varied populations, putting in sharp experiential relief the monogenist conundrum of extreme physical and social diversity in a single human species of common origin.[72] These naturalists' main remit was natural history generally, within which 'man' as zoological object was 'first link in the animal chain'.[73] They contributed variously to the ethnography, physical anthropology, and taxonomy of Pacific Islanders and their work instantiates the metamorphosis of the natural history of man in Oceania to the science of race.

Like all naturalists on French Pacific voyages from 1800 to 1830, Quoy and Lesson followed Cuvier's taxonomic principles and insistence on the primacy of physical organization.[74] Cuvier's opinion mattered because, ensconced in the most powerful institutions of French science, he oversaw the naturalists' professional instruction and assessment. Cuvier's expressed commitment to inductive reasoning clearly did not extend to anthropology, given his a priori conviction that racial inequality was a real, immutable product of human physical organization, especially cranial structure and the size of the brain.[75] In a brief zoological overview of 'Bimana or man', he divided the seemingly 'unique' human species into three 'eminently distinct' 'races' – 'white', 'yellow', and 'black' – constituted by 'certain hereditary conformations'. He extolled the white race ('to which we belong') and damned the others, particularly the black race, whose 'projecting snout and thick lips, put it patently close to the apes'. He was indecisive about the racial location of the 'handsome' Malays, including the South Sea Islanders, or of 'other men' generalized as 'Papuans' – 'frizzy-haired', 'black', 'negroid', and 'all extremely barbarous'.[76]

Quoy began his first voyage professing the humanist conviction that the 'natives' he expected to meet were 'barbarous only by lack of judgement and civilization' – a more Buffonian than Cuvierian position.[77] Yet he never

---

[72] Douglas, *Science*, 161–286.

[73] J.-R.C. Quoy and J.-P. Gaimard, *Zoologie, Voyage autour du monde . . . pendant les années 1817, 1818, 1819 et 1820 . . .* (Paris: Pillet aîné, 1824), 1.

[74] G. Cuvier, *Leçons d'anatomie comparée*, 5 vols. (Paris: Crochard, Fantin, 1800–5); G. Cuvier, *Le règne animal distribué d'après son organisation . . .*, 4 vols. (Paris: Deterville, 1817), vol. I, 1–61; R.-P. Lesson, *Manuel de mammalogie . . .* (Paris: Roret, 1827); Quoy and Gaimard, *Zoologie*, [ii].

[75] Cuvier, *Leçons*, vol. II, 2–10.   [76] Cuvier, *Le règne animal*, vol. I, 94–9.

[77] J.-R.C. Quoy, 'Voyage autour du monde, pendant les années 1817, 1818, 1819, & 1820: Journal', 1817–20, [i]–[iii], R-2520-11702, Archives centrales de la Marine, Service historique de la Défense, Rochefort, France.

doubted the physical reality or inequality of human races and decades later invoked personal observation of the alleged 'degradation' of Aboriginal Australians to deny human 'unity' and endorse the polygenist position that 'the creator made several species of men'.[78]

Quoy's published anthropology comprises two short chapters 'On man' prefacing thick *Zoologie* volumes co-authored with his surgeon-naturalist colleague Gaimard. The first is not a racial taxonomy but an inductive distillation of the 'physical constitution of the Papuans'.[79] The term Papuan was of uncertain derivation and ambiguous usage.[80] The sixteenth-century Portuguese chronicler Galvão reported that islands east of Maluku were populated by 'black' people with 'frizzy hair' whom Malukans called Papuans. They extended the name to the inhabitants of a long coastline southeast of these islands, because of their similar appearance, and 'therefore' the Portuguese did likewise. In 1545, this 'coast of the Papuans' was named New Guinea by a Spanish traveller, by analogy with African Guinea.[81] The erratic signifieds of 'Papuans' within natural history are sampled above: Buffon's indecisive 'Papuans or Negroes of New Guinea'; Blumenbach's and Cuvier's 'black' Oceanians collectively, associated with Africans; Forster's loose identification with unrelated 'black Islanders', to discredit Kant's teleology of race; and Kant's displaced 'foreigners', in defence of his theory. The toponym Papua was long an alternative name for all or part of New Guinea and the Papuan islands to its west. In modern usage, it designates the Indonesian provinces of Papua and West Papua (including Raja Ampat, formerly the Papuan islands) and the southern part of the nation of Papua New Guinea.

Quoy's writings highlight the uneasy fit between recalcitrant facts and rigid racial systems. He inferred his category Papuan empirically, from 'direct' observation of 'several hundred natives who came to trade' while the ship was anchored for three weeks in the Papuan islands near Waigeo. Limiting the term to the inhabitants of Waigeo and neighbouring islands, he

---

[78] J.-R.C. Quoy, [Autobiographie], 1864–8,175, Papiers Quoy, MS 2507, Médiathèque Michel-Crépeau, La Rochelle, France.
[79] Quoy and Gaimard, *Zoologie*, 1–11.
[80] J.H.F. Sollewijn Gelpke, 'On the origin of the name Papua', *Bijdragen tot de Taal-, Land- en Volkenkunde* 149 (1993), 318–32.
[81] A. Galvão, *Tratado . . . dos diuersos & desuayrados caminhos, por onde nos tempos passados a pimenta & especearia veyo da India ás nossas partes, & assi de todos os descobrimentos antigos & modernos, que são feitos ate a era de mil & quinhentos & cincoenta . . .* (Lisbon: Ioam de Barreira, 1563), fols. 57r–57v, 67r, 76r.

Figure 48.3 S. Leroy, [Îles des Papous: Divers portraits de naturels vus sur l'île Rawak], watercolour (n.d).

sharply differentiated them from the 'black' but otherwise dissimilar race reported in New Guinea itself, said to be 'true Negroes'.[82]

The Papuans defied Quoy's presumption of the physical and mental reality of discrete races. Unable to discern their 'distinctive characters', he concluded that 'mixing of individuals' in a dense island cluster had produced a 'multitude of nuances' that made it hard to determine the component races, 'denatured' by 'fortuitous crossings'. He saw combinations of particular physical traits he associated with 'Malays', 'Negroes', 'Chinese', or 'Europeans', all living 'freely' together 'as if forming a single people'.[83] Visual diversity is manifest in portraits of Papuans by the midshipman Pellion, as redrawn for engraving by Leroy (Figure 48.3). Quoy's primary focus was zoological – a study of the skull as 'bony envelope' for the brain, based on six skulls stolen from a tomb. However, he sent the plundered

---

[82] Quoy and Gaimard, *Zoologie*, 2–6.
[83] Quoy, 'Voyage', 141; Quoy and Gaimard, *Zoologie*, 4–6.

Seaborne Ethnography to the Science of Race

skulls to Cuvier's bitter enemy, the German physiologist Gall who founded phrenology, the controversial science of the cerebral localization of 'moral and intellectual faculties'. Quoy marvelled that his own ethnographic 'observations' confirmed (and racialized) the 'faculties' Gall identified in the six skulls, notably 'mistrust' ('an instinct in half savage men, like most animals') and a 'dreadful penchant' for murder ('probably' source of the skulls themselves).[84]

Quoy was backhandedly complimentary about the Papuans, their 'in no way unpleasant' features and 'not coarse' laughter. He concluded optimistically that they were 'capable of education' and only needed 'to exercise and develop their intellectual faculties' to become a distinguished variety of the human species.[85] The idea of racial crossing was his conceptual circuit-breaker to rationalize chaotic perceptions and distance relatively admired people from the reviled stereotype of 'the Negro'. At this point, his argument is more 'environmentalist' than innatist. I also read traces of the textual impact of Indigenous agency in that sustained humanist logic, testament to the prudent tactics the inhabitants adopted to control the ship's presence without overt menace or violence. Thus managed, Quoy experienced and recorded these Pacific encounters in largely positive terms.

Travelling Taxonomies

In 1822, the new Société de Géographie in Paris offered a gold medal as prize for a memoir on the 'origin', 'differences', and 'similarities' of the 'various peoples' of Oceania, beginning with their 'shape' and 'physical constitution'.[86] Lesson, Quoy, and Dumont d'Urville all tackled the topic on return to France, self-consciously trying to convert their empirical authority as voyagers into wider scientific credibility. However, the prize lapsed without award in 1830.

The first of numerous iterations of Lesson's formal taxonomy of 'the varieties of the human species' in the Pacific appears in the opening chapter of the *Zoologie* volumes of Duperrey's voyage.[87] Beginning with a global tripartite division – effectively Cuvier's – into 'Hindu-Caucasic', 'Mongolic', and 'Black' races, Lesson vaunted his own originality and the 'remarkable

---

[84] Quoy and Gaimard, *Zoologie*, 1–3, 7–10.   [85] Quoy and Gaimard, *Zoologie*, 11.
[86] Anon., 'Programme des prix mis au concours dans la première assemblée générale annuelle de l'an 1822', *Bulletin de la Société de Géographie* 1 (1822), 65–6.
[87] R.-P. Lesson, 'Considérations générales sur les îles du Grand-Océan, et sur les variétés de l'espèce humaine qui les habitent', in R.-P. Lesson and P. Garnot, *Zoologie*, 2 vols., *Voyage autour du monde . . . pendant les années 1822, 1823, 1824 et 1825 . . .* (Paris: Arthus Bertrand, 1826–30), vol. I, 36–113.

409

modifications' in his classification.[88] But the result is a convoluted regional racial hierarchy subdivided into five branches with an idiosyncratic nomenclature at odds with current usages: thus, though the toponym Oceania normally spanned the entire fifth part of the world,[89] Lesson limited it to the eastern Pacific Islands. He lauded the Hindu-Caucasic 'Oceanian race' as 'superior' to all other South Sea Islanders in 'beauty' and bodily conformation. He assigned the 'good-looking' 'Carolinians' of the North Pacific to the Mongolic race. He split the 'black race' into two branches distributed between four varieties. A 'Caffro-Madagascan' branch comprised the Papuans and the Tasmanians. An *Alfourou*' branch combined a 'repulsive' Negro variety, inhabiting the interiors of New Guinea and some large Malay islands, with the 'miserable', 'blackish' 'Australians' relegated to the base of the racial hierarchy.

Lesson consistently espoused the 'fundamental idea, that man comprises only one *unique species*', while insisting on its permanent diversification by the 'real and profound characters' of race.[90] Yet personal experience in the Pacific regularly confounded his racial presumptions, prompting marked inconsistency in his empirical writings on the Papuans and their neighbours. Following a fleeting seaborne encounter with six men from Buka (Bougainville, Papua New Guinea), his journal confidently assigns them to the 'race of the Papuans' on the basis of 'characteristic' physiognomy and bouffant hairstyles. After a longer stay in nearby New Ireland, he described the inhabitants as a 'Negro race' with 'woolly' hair worn in braids who differed 'much' from their Papuan 'neighbours' in Buka.[91] However, he evidently thought better of his initial impression since 'differ *much*' is corrected to 'differ *little*'.[92] Empirical confusion is compounded in Lesson's formal taxonomy by shifts between narrow and more generalized meanings of the term Papuan.[93] He noted Quoy's specialized sense defining a 'hybrid species' of 'Negro-Malays' occupying the Papuan islands and the northwest coast of New Guinea. A broader signified designates 'Negroes' who inhabited the New Guinea littoral and the island groups as far east as Fiji, plus the Tasmanians, but not the 'Australian Negroes' supposedly 'aboriginal' to

[88] Lesson, 'Considérations', 2, 36.
[89] A.-H. Brué, 'Océanie ou cinquième partie du monde . . .', in *Grand atlas universel . . .*, plate 36 (Paris: Desray, 1815).
[90] Lesson, 'Considérations', 34, original emphasis; R.-P. Lesson, *Description de mammifères et d'oiseaux récemment découverts . . .* (Paris: Lévêque, 1847), 14.
[91] R.-P. Lesson, [Manuscrit d'une partie du voyage de la Coquille], 2 vols., vol. II, 274–5, 310, 313, original emphasis, MS 1793, Muséum National d'Histoire Naturelle, Paris.
[92] My emphasis. [93] Lesson, 'Considérations', 84–101.

inland New Guinea and New Holland. Eventually, Lesson conflated the once 'opposite' Bukans and New Irelanders as Papuans, Negroes, or Papuan Negroes.[94] Still later, he fantasized that the 'Papuans of New Guinea' were 'evidently' descendants of ancient Egyptians, because their armbands and decorations on their wooden headrests were similar to those found in Egyptian tombs.[95]

Quoy's later chapter 'On man', written after his return from Dumont d'Urville's voyage, constitutes forty-four pages of the four-volume *Zoologie*.[96] Claiming pure inductivism – limited to 'our own observations' – this work epitomizes hardening European presumptions about human differences during the 1820s. Quoy froze J.R. Forster's fluid 'two great varieties' of South Sea Islanders into 'two very distinct races', 'yellow' and 'black', whose differences were real 'zoological characters' embodied in the 'fundamental base' of physical organization. He had 'observed' the yellow race in New Zealand, Tonga, Hawai'i, Tikopia, and the Caroline Islands; the black race in Waigeo, New Guinea, New Ireland, Vanikoro, Fiji, and New Holland. Deeply racialist in language and tone, this chapter subordinates climatic determinism to zoological. Quoy's belief in the physical reality of a fixed racial hierarchy is clear in the bleak prognosis that, 'under European influence', the yellow race would 'stride rapidly towards civilization' while the black remained 'stationary in its ignorance and barbarity'.[97]

Repeated references to the 'black *species*' insinuate the disbelief in human specific unity Quoy expressed openly in old age.[98] This lexical obfuscation signals his struggle to negotiate the tension between monogenist orthodoxy, still expected in the official genre of voyage publications, and the confident, increasingly polygenist materialism of the science of race, with which he sympathized. I argue, however, that the tonal shift between Quoy's two chapters is not purely a reflex of European discourses or stereotypes. Rather, it is also an empirical register of his disconcerting exposure to the unpredictable, 'mistrustful' behaviour and alleged sexual jealousy of 'the black race', particularly in Vanikoro, in stark contrast to the 'joyous', sexually

---

[94] R.-P. Lesson, *Voyage autour du monde . . . sur la corvette la Coquille*, 2 vols: (Paris: R. Pourrat frères, 1839), vol. II, 13, 35, 56.
[95] Lesson, *Description*, 76.
[96] J.-R.C. Quoy, 'De l'homme', in J.-R.C. Quoy and J.-P. Gaimard, *Zoologie*, 4 vols., *Voyage de découvertes de l'Astrolabe exécuté . . . pendant les années 1826–1827–1828–1829* (Paris : J. Tastu, 1830–5), vol. I, 15–59.
[97] Quoy, 'De l'homme', 16–17, 46–53.   [98] Quoy, 'De l'homme', 29, 35, 47, my emphasis.

Figure 48.4 L.-A. de Sainson, 'Vanikoro: vue du village de Nama', lithograph, detail, in J. Dumont d'Urville, *Atlas, Voyage de la corvette l'Astrolabe* ... (1833), plate 183.

complaisant welcome given by the 'yellow race', particularly at the neighbouring island of Tikopia (both eastern Solomon Islands).[99]

As in Malakula during Cook's visit, Vanikoran appearance, self-possession, and refusal to trade provisions infuriated Quoy's commander Dumont d'Urville. The ensuing racial vitriol in his *Histoire* of the voyage is at odds with his pragmatic descriptions of several friendly encounters and his publication of the artist Louis-Auguste de Sainson's lyrical depiction of the affable reception of French sailors by Vanikoro villagers (Figure 48.4).[100] Having lauded the Tikopians as 'naturally mild, joyful and friendly', Dumont d'Urville characterized the Vanikorans in a string of disagreeable epithets: disgusting, lazy, stupid, fierce, greedy, timid, suspicious, and 'naturally' hostile to Europeans. He extrapolated these traits to 'the black Oceanian race' in general and deplored the 'natural antipathy of the black races to the white'.[101] Conversely, I read both suspicion and hospitality not as 'natural' racial characters but as contextually specific Indigenous tactics to control or profit from the presence of foreigners.

Dumont d'Urville addressed the essay prize questions on return from his circumnavigation as Duperrey's first lieutenant, but the resulting manuscript remains unpublished. Following his first voyage as commander, with the prize now withdrawn, he published a seminal scientific paper on the islands

---

[99] Quoy, 'De l'homme', 48; Douglas, *Science*, 226–51.
[100] J. Dumont d'Urville, *Histoire du voyage*, 5 vols., *Voyage de la corvette l'Astrolabe exécuté ... pendant les années 1826–1827–1828–1829* ... (Paris: J. Tastu, 1830–3), vol. v, 145, 166–7, cf. 160, 175–83.
[101] Dumont d'Urville, *Histoire du voyage*, vol. v, 112, 145–6, 166, 214.

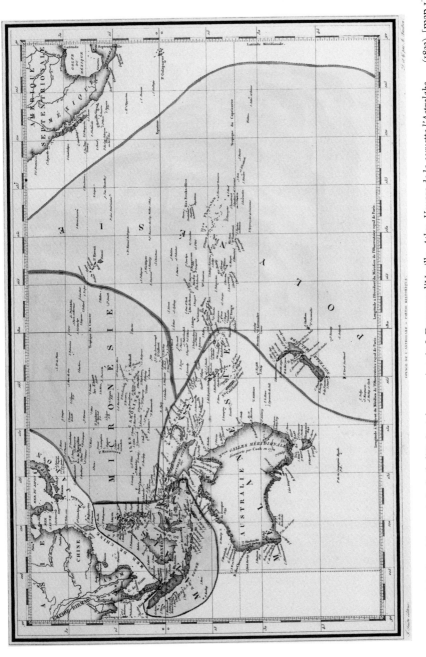

Figure 48.5 A. Tardieu, 'Carte générale de l'Océanie', engraving, in J. Dumont d'Urville, Atlas, *Voyage de la corvette l'Astrolabe* ... (1833), [map 1].

and people of Oceania – 'fruit' of a dozen years of study, observations, and worldwide travel. An illustrative map (Figure 48.5) partitions the Pacific Islands into Polynesia, Micronesia, and the overtly racialist neologism Melanesia (from Greek *melas*, black) for 'the homeland of the black Oceanian race'. Like Quoy, Dumont d'Urville congealed Forster's labile varieties into 'two truly distinct races', one 'black', the other 'copper-coloured'. He streamlined Lesson's tortuous racial taxonomy into a now classic regional nomenclature: the 'black race' – 'the Melanesians' – were the 'true natives' of Oceania or at least 'first occupants'; the 'copper-coloured' race – 'the Polynesians' and 'the Micronesians' – were progeny of 'conquerors' from the west who supplanted or intermixed with the 'primitive race of Melanesians'. The 'Papuans' were perhaps 'a handsome variety of the Melanesian race' or more recent immigrants from the Indian Ocean.[102]

Dumont d'Urville's article generalizes selective observation – particularly in Tikopia and Vanikoro – by correlating skin colour, behaviour, and physical appearance with language, institutions, religion, intellect, and morality to formulate an abstract racial hierarchy. Damning Melanesians as 'hideous', linguistically 'very limited', lacking regular government, laws, or religion, and 'natural enemies of the whites', he ranked them 'generally very inferior' to Polynesians and Micronesians. Like Lesson (who accused him of plagiarism),[103] he posited a tripartite global hierarchy of 'white', 'yellow', and 'black' races into which his Oceanian races slotted as 'branches' of the 'black race of Africa' and the 'yellow race' of Asia, respectively. He transmuted Brosses's and Forster's conjectural histories of ancient migrations and displacements into chilling biological reality and colonial fact; a 'law of nature', resulting from 'organic differences' in the 'intellectual faculties' of the diverse races, ordained that the black 'must obey' the others 'or disappear' and that the white 'must dominate'.[104]

Polygeny in the Pacific

By 1830, polygenism was the most strident voice in anthropology in France, if not yet the dominant Euro-American discourse it would be after 1850. Concurrently, many professed monogenists were increasingly complicit in racialist agendas. Implied in Quoy's aforementioned equivocation, the

---

[102] J. Dumont d'Urville, 'Sur les îles du grand océan', *Bulletin de la Société de Géographie* 17 (1932), 1–21; trans. I. Ollivier, A. de Biran, and G. Clarke as 'On the islands of the Great Ocean', *Journal of Pacific History* 38:2 (2003), 163–74.
[103] Lesson, *Description*, p. 21.   [104] Dumont d'Urville, 'Sur les îles', 3, 11–21.

Seaborne Ethnography to the Science of Race

transition is patent in the published anthropological record of Dumont d'Urville's final voyage of 1837–40. The expedition's striking material legacy is a collection of fifty-one plaster busts cast in situ by the phrenologist Dumoutier, an egalitarian humanist and staunch monogenist. Moulding heads in the field demanded patient negotiation, tact, and prolonged intimacy with Indigenous subjects, whose behaviour at times provoked Dumoutier to harsh or racialized language. The busts preserve a powerful, intensely moving individual presence which disrupts the project of racial typification in the anthropological *Atlas* produced under Dumoutier's direction. Systematically measured, photographed, lithographed, and labelled, the busts are simultaneously personalized with names and racialized as examplars of Dumont d'Urville's regional toponyms (Figure 48.6).[105]

Since Dumoutier published little about the voyage, its primary anthropological outcomes are three polygenist works. A volume *De l'homme* (On man) by Hombron inaugurates a five-volume *Zoologie* co-authored with the junior surgeon Jacquinot, who devoted the second volume to 'human races'. Blanchard, a zoologist at the Muséum national d'Histoire naturelle in Paris with no Pacific experience or anthropological credentials, mined Dumoutier's *Atlas* and his collection of busts and fifty-one skulls to produce a volume on *Anthropologie*. The hallmarks of Hombron's and Blanchard's treatises are harsh racialism and fervent race pride.

Hombron's book is a prolix amalgam of polygenism and Christian piety. Claiming wide observation in South America and Oceania, he split the 'human series' into several distinct species, formed sequentially to occupy particular 'centres of creation' and clustered into three 'natural families' distinguished by 'degree of intelligence'. The 'family of blacks' ranks lowest as 'inferior species' of the 'primitive human creations'. The 'copper-coloured' family, including the eastern Oceanians or Polynesians, was created next and ranks more highly. The 'Aryan race' of the 'great white human family' was created last and ranks first as 'logical consequence of the union of matter and intelligence'.[106]

The theme of 'hybrids' was Hombron's theoretical keystone, as for many polygenists who rejected Buffon's monogenist breeding criterion for

---

[105] [P.-M.A. Dumoutier], *Atlas anthropologique, Voyage au pôle sud et dans l'Océanie . . . pendant les années 1837–1838–1839–1840 . . .* (Paris: Gide, 1846); Douglas, *Science*, 259–77.

[106] J.-B. Hombron, *De l'homme dans ses rapports avec la création*, vol. I in J.-B. Hombron and H. Jacquinot, *Zoologie*, 5 vols., *Voyage au pôle sud et dans l'Océanie sur les corvettes l'Astrolabe et la Zélée . . . pendant les années 1837–1838–1839–1840*, (Paris: Gide, 1846), 98–105, 130–3, 248–328, 395–401.

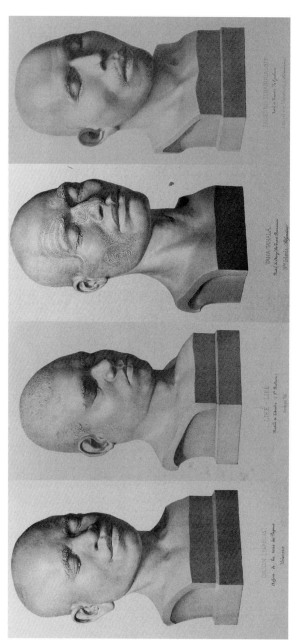

Figure 48.6 L.A. Bisson, 'Orion (Papouas) ... Mélanésie' [teenaged Papuan 'slave', Maluku]; 'Liké-liké ... Archipel Viti' [woman, Fiji]; 'Taha-Tahala ... (Polynésie)' [man, New Zealand]; 'Faustino-Tchargualoff ... (Micronésie)' [man, Guam], lithographed photographs, in [P.-M.A. Dumoutier], *Atlas anthropologique, Voyage au pôle sud et dans l'Océanie* ... (1846), plates 11, 5, 13, 10.

Seaborne Ethnography to the Science of Race

including all human varieties within a single species.[107] Postulating western Oceania as epicentre of the 'mixing of species', Hombron contended that only parents of proximate species could produce fertile offspring and that unions between species low in the human series generated 'a kind of monstrosity'.[108] He envisaged a future whitewashed by sustained crossbreeding in which man comprised a 'single' race, 'civilization' was general, and 'inferior races and species' were dispatched to the 'archives of history'.[109]

A case study provides an extreme example of the tension between empirical authority and raciological deduction evident in the work of all the naval naturalists discussed. In April 1839, the expedition anchored for a week in Triton Bay at New Guinea's southwestern end. In a journal extract and an ethnographic 'description', Hombron admitted seeing only a 'small number of inhabitants' but reified them into a taxonomic category – 'a métis race' of Malays and Papuans. He described a lighter-coloured 'few', presumed to be 'the chiefs', as better built, better looking, and more 'vigorous' than either parent race. He differentiated them from Quoy's 'Métis of Waigeo' on the grounds of their greater 'beauty' and sought its 'cause' in 'different origins'. He reconfigured the Waigeo Papuans as offspring of the crossing of Papuans with Malays of Maluku, whose 'brown skin' and 'very coarse' features betrayed their 'frequent mixings' with the 'ancient aborigines' of the larger East Indian islands and New Guinea. In contrast, the inhabitants of Triton Bay bore the physical imprint of relations with the 'infinitely more handsome Malays' of Celebes (Sulawesi) and the Sunda Islands (both Indonesia).[110]

Hombron boasted that being 'on the spot' in Triton Bay showed him the 'simple relationship' between physical appearance, geographical location, and hybrid origins as his key to unravelling the 'confusion of species and races' in Oceania.[111] His volume 'On Man' reconstitutes the Papuans as a distinctive, 'agreeable' species inhabiting the New Guinea littoral, quite different from the 'very ugly' race of black-Malay hybrids widespread in Maluku.[112]

---

[107] C. Blanckaert, 'Of monstrous métis? Hybridity, fear of miscegenation, and patriotism from Buffon to Paul Broca', in S. Peabody and T. Stovall (eds.), *The Color of Liberty: Histories of Race in France* (Durham, NC: Duke University Press, 2003), 42–70.
[108] Hombron, *De l'homme*, 85, 275–84. [109] Hombron, *De l'homme*, 104–5.
[110] J.-B. Hombron in J. Dumont d'Urville, *Histoire du voyage*, 10 vols., *Voyage au pôle sud et dans l'Océanie ... pendant les années 1837–1838–1839–1840 ...* (Paris: Gide, 1841–6), vol. VI, 311–13; J.-B. Hombron, 'Aperçu sur la côte nord de l'Australie et sur la côte sud de la Nouvelle-Guinée; description de leurs habitants', *Comptes rendus hebdomadaires des séances de l'Académie des Sciences* 20 (1845), 1568–73, at 1572.
[111] Hombron in Dumont d'Urville, *Histoire du voyage*, vol. VI, 313; Hombron, 'Aperçu', 1572; Hombron, *De l'homme*, 302.
[112] Hombron, *De l'homme*, 291, 296–8, 302–3.

He rebuked Malukan application of the term Papuan to everyone from New Guinea or neighbouring islands – thereby ironically correcting longstanding Indigenous usage of a local term which his science had indirectly appropriated from that usage.[113]

Blanchard wrote his *Anthropologie* as Dumoutier's surrogate but his unbending adherence to zoological system lacked the travelling naturalists' fugitive empirical sensibility. He subverted Dumoutier's monogenism by reading his *Atlas* and skull collection as proof of the 'specific plurality' of the human genus and the simultaneous creation of many 'original stocks' in the countries they still occupied. Blanchard allowed no human 'equality', pronouncing those whose heads were 'contracted on top and in front and elongated behind' and whose jaw bones 'projected' to be bereft of 'genius or even talent'. Such permanent 'anthropological' characters coincided with predetermined 'moral' and 'intellectual' traits, 'state of civilization', and 'degree of intelligence', with little capacity for modification. So Papuan crania proved them to be 'inferior' to Polynesians and Micronesians and that 'inferiority' was manifest in their 'every action', as recorded by voyagers.[114]

Mainly on cranial evidence, Blanchard distinguished three 'very distinct types' in the Pacific: Micronesian, Polynesian, and Papuan, the last two allegedly 'true natives' of lands they inhabited. He fitted them into an a priori hierarchy of relative physical and moral 'superiority' or 'inferiority', starting from the 'European type', whose 'physical characters' coincided with the greatest 'mass of intelligence'. Adjacent to the Pacific, the 'half-civilized' Malays had migrated from the Asian mainland and supplanted the original inhabitants of the islands they colonized. Though 'inferior' to Europeans, the 'Malay type' was 'greatly superior' to the Micronesian, which in turn ranked above the Polynesian. The Papuans or 'Oceanic blacks' were in general an 'inferior anthropological type', condemned physically to permanent occupation of 'one of the last degrees of human civilization'.[115]

Though Blanchard's *Anthropologie* is part of the 23-volume official publication of Dumont d'Urville's final voyage, it epitomizes the appropriation and exploitation of travellers' work by a rigidly deductive science. In the process,

---

[113] Hombron, *De l'homme*, 283.
[114] E. Blanchard, *Anthropologie, Voyage au pôle sud et dans l'Océanie ... pendant les années 1837–1838–1839–1840 ...* (Paris: Gide et J. Baudry, 1854), 7–13, 19, 35–6, 45, 49, 120, 256–7.
[115] Blanchard, *Anthropologie*, 133, 199–216.

he restored the blanket application of the term Papuan to 'Oceanic blacks' or 'Melanesians', thus jettisoning four decades of existential struggle by naval naturalists to reconcile ambiguous personal observation of actual living persons with raciology's neat categorical pigeonholes.

Conclusion

Throughout these three centuries, most navigators took for granted both human specific unity and human differences. The main mode of enunciation in their narratives is seaborne ethnography – reports of situated encounters and events using the preterite tense, often complemented by generalized impressions of particular populations using the ethnographic present. Before the mid-eighteenth century, the primary scientific interest in such materials was toponymic and cartographic. From the outset, some European navigators speculated on the enigma of human origins in the Pacific but few engaged directly with the science of man after its Buffonian efflorescence within natural history. Even Dumont d'Urville's rare excursion into inductive racial theorizing marvels that his empirically grounded 'system' unwittingly mirrored the 'opinion' of the 'celebrated physiologist' Cuvier.[116]

From 1770, the liaison of seaborne ethnography with the science of man was embodied in naturalists with responsiblity for zoology on Pacific-wide voyages. They include the Forsters and nineteenth-century French naval naturalists whose regional treatises on man as an animal species mostly use the present tense. However, the mismatch of theory and practical experience means that traces of Indigenous presence and agency infiltrate these works, especially in slippages between zoological precept and anecdotes of personal encounters phrased in the preterite. Cook's other naturalists did not systematically address the science of man, though their journals are cannibalized in narratives of his voyages. Other notable voyage naturalists who published on man, but with narrower regional expertise, include Chamisso, Darwin, Hale, and Pickering. Appropriated in detail by Buffon, Blumenbach, and Prichard, the works of navigators and travelling naturalists were cherry-picked by raciologists whose deductive systems were largely immune to the imprint of encounters with actual people.

---

[116] Dumont d'Urville, 'Sur les îles', 2, 21, note.

The Pacific's changing salience in anthropology is exemplified in Prichard's successively more voluminous treatises on the 'physical history of man(kind)'.[117] The first draws heavily on seaborne ethnography in Cook voyage narratives and makes South Sea populations analytically central.[118] The region's relative empirical significance declines in later editions, but is acknowledged in the second as Prichard's most prolific source of 'facts', while 'Oceanic races' retain considerable interpretative value in the third.[119] This final edition cites Dumont d'Urville, Quoy, and Lesson verbatim and at length, despite implying that they believed in 'an original diversity of races'.[120] The unyielding monogenist commitment of humanist Prichardian ethnology stemmed the polygenist tide in Britain before 1850. But in naturalizing racialized terminology and logic, Prichard's later work is symptomatic of the steady hardening of the language of human difference after 1800 and its contribution to the transformation of anthropology into raciology outlined in this chapter.

---

[117] Douglas, '"Novus Orbis Australis"'.

[118] J.C. Prichard, *Researches into the Physical History of Man* (London: J. and A. Arch, 1813).

[119] J.C. Prichard, *Researches into the Physical History of Mankind*, 2nd edn, 2 vols. (London: J. and A. Arch, 1826), vol. I, 365; J.C. Prichard, *Researches into the Physical History of Mankind*, 3rd edn, 5 vols. (London: Sherwood, Gilbert, and Piper, 1836–47), vol. v, 1–285.

[120] Prichard, *Researches*, 3rd edn, vol. I, vii–viii, 249–57, 298–302; vol. v, 212–57.

PART X

★

THE COLONIAL ERA IN THE PACIFIC

49

Political Developments in the Pacific Islands in the Nineteenth Century CE

LORENZ GONSCHOR

Introduction

For the political evolution of the archipelagoes of Oceania as we know them today, the nineteenth century was of crucial importance. In conventional historiography, the most striking feature of historical development during that century has been the establishment of colonial rule over virtually every archipelago. While the century started with barely any European colonial presence (except for the Marianas, considered an outpost of the Spanish Philippines, and Norfolk Island, considered an outpost of the British penal settlement in Australia), at the turn of the twentieth century every island was being claimed directly or indirectly as falling under the dominion of one of the Western powers.

Yet it would be misleading to regard the nineteenth century as simply a period of transition towards colonial rule. Instead, the century was first and foremost one of transformation, modernization, and hybridization of Indigenous systems of governance. This led to the emergence of one major nation-state in Oceania that played a significant role in world politics – the Hawaiian Kingdom – and the emulation of that model by several others. Before the very end of the century it was by no means a foregone conclusion that those emerging island states would be forced under Western imperial rule, and it would be ill-advised to delve into a teleological view of history based on the subsequent colonial period. As Andrew Robson phrased it, for most of the century 'everything was in a state of flux [and n]o one knew what the ultimate political fate of the islands would be'.[1]

---

[1] A. Robson, *Prelude to Empire: Consuls, Missionary Kingdoms and the Pre-colonial South Seas Seen through the Life of William Thomas Pritchard* (Vienna: Lit Verlag, 2004), 173.

From Ancient States to Modern States

Instead of telling the story backwards from the vantage point of later colonial or pseudo-colonial rule, it is thus a more suitable approach to start our analysis with the political dynamics of Indigenous political systems and their previous evolution in the classical period, before the Western encounter. Most interesting from this point of view is the fact that in three islands or archipelagoes – the Hawaiian islands and Tonga in Polynesia, and Kosrae in Micronesia – the Indigenous political systems had developed from kinship-based societies into primary states, comparable to developments in ancient Egypt and Mesopotamia, the Indus valley, China, Mesoamerica, and the Andean Highlands.[2] Archaeologist Robert Hommon thus refers to the political system in operation in the Hawaiian Islands in the mid-eighteenth century as the 'Ancient Hawaiian State' and argues that the centralized political system in Tonga should similarly be seen as an ancient Oceanian state.[3] When Western contact in the late eighteenth and early nineteenth centuries brought the idea of the modern state into the region, the more stratified societies held an advantage over their more politically fragmented neighbours in making the transition.

It was in Hawai'i that such a process was most successful. Over the many centuries since its settlement by eastern Polynesians, centralized chiefdoms had developed on each of the archipelago's larger islands and in time evolved into 'kingdoms' or 'early states'.[4] As early as twenty generations before Western contact (about the thirteenth century CE), Hawai'i Island king Kalaunuiohua had temporarily conquered about three-quarters of the archipelago and attempted to create a unified kingdom.[5] In the decades after Captain Cook's fateful visit in 1778 this vision resurfaced, and several rival island kings fought a series of wars for supremacy. It was the young *ali'i* (nobleman) Kamehameha from Hawai'i Island (c. 1858–19) who eventually succeeded in unifying the archipelago and in consolidating the different

---

[2] P.V. Kirch, *How Chiefs Became Kings: Divine Kingship and the Rise of Archaic States in Ancient Hawai'i* (Berkeley: University of California Press, 2010); R. Cordy and T. Ueki, 'The development of complex societies on Kosrae', Unpublished paper presented at the 48th Annual Meeting of the Society for American Archaeology, 1983.
[3] R. Hommon, *The Ancient Hawaiian State: Origins of a Political Society* (Oxford: Oxford University Press, 2013).
[4] Hommon, *The Ancient Hawaiian State*; R. Cordy, *Exalted Sits the Chief: The Ancient History of Hawai'i Island* (Honolulu: Mutual Publishing, 2000).
[5] C.K. Cachola-Abad, 'The evolution of Hawaiian socio-political complexity: an analysis of Hawaiian oral traditions', PhD thesis, University of Hawai'i, 2000, 305–8.

kingdoms into one, while streamlining its administration by incorporating British concepts of governance.[6]

Under Kamehameha's successors (his sons Kamehameha II and III, 1797–1824 and 1814–54), the transition from ancient to modern state continued. After converting to Christianity brought to the islands by American Congregationalist missionaries in the mid-1820s, the Hawaiian court put in place a long series of legal and political modernization projects.[7] These included a written constitution in 1840 – one of the earlier ones in the world, when many European nations were still absolute monarchies – a compulsory education system which led to one of the world's highest literacy rates, and a large-scale land reform process that created private landownership but also protected the traditional land rights of native tenants.[8] In 1843, Hawai'i was recognized as an independent state in a joint declaration by Great Britain and France, the first, and for almost the entire century the only, non-Western nation to achieve such a status.[9] Under the third generation of the dynasty (Kamehameha IV and V, 1834–64 and 1830–73), the political system was further modernized, including a move away from missionary influence towards secularism.[10] This tendency intensified under their successor King Kalākaua (1836–91) in the 1870s and 1880s, who promoted the development of a national culture based on classical Hawaiian values, and at the same time positioned himself in the global modernity of the Victorian age, epitomized by various monuments and performances created during his reign.[11]

The developments of the Hawaiian Kingdom thus presented are best understood through three theoretical concepts of parity, similitude, and hybridity. Parity, according to Niklaus Schweizer, 'signifies an effort to be taken seriously by the Western powers, to be accepted as an equal and

---

[6] D.K. Sai, *Ua Mau ke Ea, Sovereignty Endures: An Overview of the Political and Legal History of the Hawaiian Islands* (Honolulu: Pū'ā Foundation, 2011); P. D'Arcy, *Transforming Hawai'i: Balancing Coercion and Consent in Eighteenth-Century Kānaka Maoli Statecraft* (Canberra: Australia National University Press, 2018).

[7] C. Klieger, *Kamehameha III: He Mo'olelo no ka Mo'i Lokomaika'i: King of the Hawaiian Islands, 1824–1854* (San Francisco: Green Arrow Press, 2015); N. Arista, *The Kingdom and the Republic: Sovereign Hawai'i and the Early United States* (Philadelphia: University of Pennsylvania Press, 2019).

[8] K. Beamer, *No Mākou ka Mana: Liberating the Nation* (Honolulu: Kamehameha Schools Press, 2014), 142–52.

[9] Sai, *Ua Mau ke Ea*, 10; Beamer, *No Mākou ka Mana*, 16, 138.

[10] R. Kuykendall, *The Hawaiian Kingdom*, vol. II, *1854–1874: Twenty Critical Years* (Honolulu: University of Hawai'i Press, 1953); Beamer, *No Mākou ka Mana*, 170–4.

[11] S.L. Kamehiro, *The Arts of Kingship: Hawaiian Art and National Culture of the Kalākaua Era* (Honolulu: University of Hawai'i Press, 2009); H. Johnston, *Ho'oulu Hawai'i: The King Kalākaua Era* (Honolulu: Honolulu Museum of Art, 2018).

to be accorded the civilities and privileges established by international law'.[12] In order to achieve such parity with the West, a non-Western state would use a certain degree of similitude, which Jeremy Prestholdt describes as 'a conscious self-presentation in interpersonal and political relationships that stresses likeliness'.[13] Yet, rather than fully assimilate to Western models, these innovations would be selectively appropriated and combined with Indigenous concepts to create something unique, which Kamanamaikalani Beamer refers to as a system of hybridity, arguing that Hawaiian rulers 'used traditional structures and systems of knowledge in an attempt to construct a modern nation-state' while 'modifying existing structures and negotiating European legal forms which created something new, neither completely Anglo American nor traditionally Hawaiian, but a combination of both'.[14] Similar strategies, employing some degree of similitude to achieve parity while creating a hybrid political system, were typical of non-Western states in other parts of the world that successfully modernized themselves and thereby escaped formal Western colonization, such as Japan and Thailand.[15]

Among the other islands of Oceania, the one most similar to Hawai'i in its employment of such strategies was the Kingdom of Tonga. Unlike Hawai'i, the smaller Tongan archipelago had already been a unified polity in classical times, with a diarchy of a sacred and a secular king ruling the archipelago from an urbanized settlement on Tongatapu. Following the Western encounter, and possibly in response to it, the classical system collapsed around the turn of the nineteenth century, and Tonga became fragmented into numerous warring chiefdoms.[16] The establishment of a Wesleyan Methodist mission in 1822 coincided with the rise of the warlord Tāufaʻāhau (1797–1893), who converted to their religion, took the name of George Tupou, after King George of Britain, and through a series of wars and alliances succeeded through the middle of the nineteenth century in reunifying the Tongan islands as a Christian Kingdom under his rule, later copying the Hawaiian model and creating a constitutional monarchy

---

[12] N. Schweizer, *Turning Tide: The Ebb and Flow of Hawaiian Nationality*, 3rd edn (Berne: Lang, 2005),177.

[13] J. Prestholdt, 'Similitude and empire: on Comorian strategies of Englishness', *Journal of World History* 18:2 (2007), 113–38, at 120.

[14] K. Beamer, 'Na wai ka Mana? ʻŌiwi agency and European imperialism in the Hawaiian Kingdom', PhD thesis, University of Hawaiʻi. 2008, 30, 177.

[15] For a detailed discussion, see L. Gonschor, 'A power in the world: the Hawaiian Kingdom as a model of hybrid statecraft in Oceania and a progenitor of pan-Oceanianism', PhD thesis, University of Hawaiʻi, 2016, 35–41.

[16] I.C. Campbell, 'The demise of the Tuʻi Kanokupolu: Tonga 1799–1827', *Journal of Pacific History* 24:2 (1989), 150–63.

Political Developments in the Nineteenth Century

Table 49.1 *Chronology of Oceanian constitutions.*

1825	Kingdom of Tahiti (amended 1842)
1840	Hawaiian Kingdom (amended 1852 and 1864)
1867	Kingdom of Bau [Fiji] (amended 1869)
1869	Chiefdom of Lau and Tovata Confederacy [Fiji]
1869	Kingdom of Mangareva
1871	Kingdom of Fiji (amended 1873)
1873	Kingdom of Sāmoa (amended 1875)
1875	Kingdom of Tonga
1877	Kingdom of Raiatea
1894	Kingdom of Aotearoa [in rebellion against British rule]

in 1875.[17] (For a list of Oeanian constitutions, see Table 49.1.) Like the Kamehameha dynasty, George Tupou built a hybrid political system, based on Indigenous Tongan concepts of governance, into which elements of British and other Western systems were incorporated. The long life of George Tupou, who was in control of these developments for most of the century, provided a factor of stability that was absent in Hawai'i. On the other hand, however, the sociopolitical unification of Tonga was less thoroughly accomplished on the ground. Regional challenges to Tupou I's rule by powerful local chiefs on the main island of Tongatapu endured until the 1850s.[18]

The Impact of Christian Conversion and Literacy

In both Hawai'i and Tonga, the impulse to create a unified modern state arose out of Indigenous political dynamics, but in Tahiti and the other Society Islands, conversion to Christianity formed a crucial element in the development towards state formation. Conversion and collaboration with missionaries had also been an important element in Tāufa'āhau's campaigns to reunify Tonga, and of Kamehameha III's constitutional reforms, but in Tahiti's case Christianity was perhaps the most defining element of the new political system that developed in the early nineteenth century. While certainly more stratified than some other Polynesian societies, classical Tahiti lacked centralized political structures like Hawai'i and Tonga and

---

[17] S. Lātūkefu, *The Tongan Constitution: A Brief History to Celebrate its Centenary* (Nuku'alofa: Tonga Traditions Committee, 1975), 28–63.
[18] I.C. Campbell, *Island Kingdom: Tonga Ancient and Modern*, 2nd edn (Christchurch: Canterbury University Press, 2001), 87.

was instead fragmented into a number of medium-sized chiefdoms. After high chief Pomare II (1782–1821) of the northwestern districts of Tahiti had converted to the Protestantism brought to the country by the London Missionary Society (LMS), he defeated his traditionalist enemies in 1815 and created a centralized Christian monarchy in which he held the title of king while the other high chiefs were appointed as district governors.[19] In his war of unification, Pomare was allied with several convert chiefs from the Leeward Islands of Huahine, Raiatea, and Bora Bora, each of which established similar Christian kingdoms. With the help of Society Islands converts, similar processes of transition from traditionalist chiefdoms to Christian states also happened on the neighbouring Austral and Cook Islands.[20] Importantly, however, there was no archipelago-wide unification in any of them and the newly founded Christian states remained relatively small in scale, compared to Hawai'i and Tonga.

Because of the importance of Christian conversion in their formation, the Society Islands polities, George Tupou's Kingdom in Tonga, and Hawai'i under Kamehameha III have at times been labelled 'missionary kingdoms' or 'Christian theocracies'.[21] While missionaries certainly played an important role in each of these archipelagoes, the main agents in each of the mentioned political developments were the Indigenous leaders who made the ultimate decisions, which in Tahiti's case included Pomare II, other chiefs, and eventually his daughter Pomare IV (1813–77).[22] In Hawai'i, it was Kamehameha's widow Ka'ahumanu (c. 1768–1832), and then Kamehameha III and other Hawaiian ali'i, not the American missionaries, who decided matters of law and order. Later, Kamehameha IV and V removed all remaining missionaries from government offices.[23] Claire Laux's identification of Tonga as a 'long-lasting Protestant "theocracy"'[24] is equally problematic, given the deep-seated conflict between King Tupou I and the mission

---

[19] C. Robineau, 'La construction du premier État tahitien moderne', in P. de Dekker and P. Lagayette (eds.), *Etats et pouvoirs dans les territoires français du Pacifique* (Paris: L'Harmattan, 187), 28–43.

[20] J. Sissons, *The Polynesian Iconoclasm: Religious Revolution and the Seasonality of Power* (New York: Berghahn Books, 2014); R.P. Gilson, *The Cook Islands 1820–1950* (Wellington: Victoria University Press, 1980).

[21] C. Laux, *Les théocraties missionnaires en Polynésie au XIXe siècle: des cités de Dieu dans les Mers du Sud?* (Paris: L'Harmattan, 2000); I.C. Campbell, *Worlds Apart: A History of the Pacific Islands* (Christchurch: Canterbury University Press, 2003), 88.

[22] C.A. Sampson, 'Tahiti, George Pritchard et le "mythe" du "royaume missionnaire"', *Journal de la Société des Océanistes* 29:38 (1973), 57–68.

[23] Arista, *The Kingdom and the Republic*; Beamer, *No Mākou ka Mana*.

[24] Laux, *Les théocraties missionnaires*, 31.

Political Developments in the Nineteenth Century

towards the end of the century – a conflict won by the king, not the missionaries.[25] Even in the three small island kingdoms under French Catholic influence – Mangareva, 'Uvea, and Futuna – where the word 'theocracy' was used most widely by contemporary observers,[26] the term is questionable. Despite the strong influence exercised by priests on these islands such as Honoré Laval (1808–80) on Mangareva and Pierre Bataillon (1810–77) on 'Uvea, the islands were still ruled by their Indigenous kings (Maputeoa, c. 1814–57, and Vaimua Lavelua, d. 1858, respectively).

But arguably the most enduring influence of the missionaries was the creation of literary languages.[27] Choosing the dialects of the main islands of each major archipelago as the basis for Bible translations and other written materials for religious instruction, the missionaries and their native collaborators thereby contributed to the forging of national identities in Polynesia.[28] This is a good example of Benedict Anderson's argument that the development of printed matter in a standardized language was one of the key factors in nation-building, since it promotes the idea of an 'imagined community' of readers and writers of this language. This means that the ability to read printed material in a common language is a major element in socially constructing 'nations', i.e. communities that include large numbers of people who do not know each other individually yet strongly identify with such communities in similar ways that people identify with smaller, actual communities such as families and descent groups.[29]

Once again, Hawai'i took the lead. Among the millions of pages written and printed in Hawaiian during the nineteenth century was Oceania's first newspaper, the missionary-edited *Ka Lama Hawaii*, which appeared in 1834. From the 1860s onwards, a diverse print media landscape emerged in the Hawaiian islands, with up to five Hawaiian-language newspapers being published concurrently, in addition to several in English, and later in Chinese, Portuguese, and Japanese to cater to diverse immigrant

---

[25] N. Rutherford, *Shirley Baker and the King of Tonga*, 2nd edn (Honolulu: University of Hawai'i Press, 1996).
[26] Laux, *Les théocraties missionnaires*, 204.
[27] G.S. Parsonson, 'The literate revolution in Polynesia', *Journal of Pacific History* 2 (1967), 39–57; R.E. Lingenfelter, *Presses of the Pacific Islands 1817–1867: A History of the First Half Century of Printing in the Pacific Islands* (Los Angeles: The Plantin Press, 1967).
[28] Because of a stronger focus on the importance of individually reading the scriptures in Protestantism, archipelagoes primarily missionized by Protestants tended to have a larger corpus of written native-language materials than those under the influence of Catholicism.
[29] B. Anderson, *Imagined Communities: Reflections on the Origin and the Spread of Nationalism* (London: Verso, 1991), 33–46.

communities.[30] Large amounts of Indigenous-language print matter were also produced in Aotearoa New Zealand, where they contributed to the formation of a Māori national identity.[31] An impressive corpus of writing, including religious and secular books and periodicals, was also created in Tahitian, Cook Islands Māori, Tongan, Samoan, and Fijian, as well as various other island languages.[32]

Creating these 'imagined communities' of language readers and writers also led to the development of national historiographies. Various Hawaiian scholars authored and published extensive essays on the political and social history of their archipelago, the most prominent of whom was Samuela Mānaiakalani Kamakau (1815–76), whose monumental history of the early Kamehameha dynasty, originally published in newspapers during the 1860s and 1870s, was recently republished in book form.[33] In the other archipelagoes, some shorter texts were published, for example Matia Puputauki's 1852 history of the classical kings of Mangareva,[34] but most comparable works remained in manuscript form – referred to as *puta tupuna* (ancestral books) in Tahitian – to be published only posthumously towards the end of the twentieth or at the beginning of the twenty-first century.[35]

Interconnected State-Building

These processes of state-building and modernization did not happen in isolation and should be seen as interconnected parts of large networks of

---

[30] H.G. Chapin, 'Newspapers of Hawai'i 1834 to 1903: from "He Liona" to the *Pacific Cable'*, *Hawaiian Journal of History* 18 (1984), 47–86; N. Silva and I. Badlis, 'Early Hawaiian newspapers and Kanaka Maoli intellectual history, 1834–1855', *Hawaiian Journal of History* 42 (2008), 105–34; M.P. Nogelmeier, *Mai Pa'a I Ka Leo: Historical Voice in Hawaiian Primary Materials, Looking Forward and Listening Back* (Honolulu: Bishop Museum Press, 2010).

[31] J. Curnow, N. Hopa, and J. McRae (eds.), *Rere atu, taku manu! Discovering History, Language and Politics in the Maori-Language Newspapers* (Auckland: Auckland University Press, 2002); L. Paterson, 'Print culture and the collective Māori consciousness', *Journal of New Zealand Literature* 18:2 (2010), 105–29.

[32] For a tentative list of periodicals in each of these languages, see Gonschor, 'A power in the world', appendix 3.

[33] S.M. Kamakau, *Ke Kumu Aupuni: Ka Mo'olelo Hawai'i no Kamehameha Ka Na'i Aupuni a me kāna Aupuni i Ho'okumu ai* (Honolulu: 'Ahahui 'Ōlelo Hawai'i, 1996); S.M. Kamakau, *Ke Aupuni Mō'ī: Ka Mo'olelo Hawai'i no Kauikeaouli Keiki Ho'oilina a Kamehameha a me ke Aupuni āna i Noho Mō'ī ai* (Honolulu: Kamehameha Schools Press, 2001).

[34] M. Puputauki, *E mau Atoga Magareva Akataito* (Honolulu: Imprimerie Catholique, 1852).

[35] E.g. Maretu, *Cannibals and Converts: Radical Change in the Cook Islands*, trans. and ed. M.T. Crocombe (Suva: Institute of Pacific Studies, University of the South Pacific, 1983); B. Saura (ed.), *La lignée royale des Tama-toa de Ra'iātea (Îles-sous-le Vent): Puta 'ā'amu nō te 'ōpū hui ari'i Tama-toa nō Ra'iātea* (Papeete: Service de la Culture et du Patrimoine de Polynésie Française, 2003).

state formation, modernization, and institutional transfer. The latter is a concept first developed by Eleanor Westney to describe the selective appropriation of Western features in nineteenth-century Japan, and subsequently picked up by Peter Larmour in relation to Pacific Islands states.[36] In nineteenth-century Oceania, such hybridized political systems and institutions were then, in turn, transferred to other archipelagoes.

There were three centres of political development from which such institutional transfer took place (see Figure 49.1). Chronologically first was Tahiti, where Pomare II's conversion and the creation of a unified Christian kingdom quickly influenced neighbouring societies in the Society, Austral, and Cook Islands, and eventually Hawai'i, where the traditional state religion was abolished in 1819 before any missionary presence.[37] Pomare's kingdom enacted Oceania's first written legal code in 1819, containing mainly Old Testament-inspired prohibitions, but also some classical Tahitian regulations. After Pomare's death, the code was amended in 1825 to include provisions for a partly elected legislative assembly. Hence the Tahitian kingdom actually preceded Hawai'i in having a constitutional monarchy.[38]

Similar to the spread of Christian conversion itself, the 1819 and 1825 law codes – including translated new key terms such as *ture* (from Hebrew *torah*) for law and *tāvana* (from English governor) for district chief – spread around central eastern Polynesia as templates for similar foundational documents in Christian kingdoms of the Society, Austral, and Cook Islands during the 1820s and 1830s. Some elements of this new legal system, including the term *ture* for law, spread beyond the sphere of influence of the LMS, for instance to Roman Catholic Mangareva and later Rapa Nui, and to mainly Anglican-influenced Aotearoa New Zealand, where an embryonic state project was launched in 1835 as a confederation among the Ngāpuhi in the far North Island.[39] LMS and Wesleyan missionaries (both Europeans and native converts) brought the law templates further west, to Sāmoa and Tonga, where the first local law codes were equally modelled on those from the Society Islands.[40]

---

[36] D.E. Westney, *Imitation and Innovation: The Transfer of Western Organizational Patterns to Meiji Japan* (Cambridge, MA: Harvard University Press, 1987); P. Larmour, *Foreign Flowers: Institutional Transfer and Good Governance in the Pacific Islands* (Honolulu: University of Hawai'i Press, 2005).
[37] Sissons, *Polynesian Iconoclasm*, 62–4.
[38] B. Gille, *Histoire des institutions politiques à Tahiti du XVIIe siècle à nos jours* (Papeete: Ministère de l'Éducation de la Polynésie Française, 2006), 19.
[39] Gonschor, 'A power in the world', 378–81; P. Moon, *Fatal Frontiers: A New History of New Zealand in the Decade before the Treaty* (Auckland: Penguin Books, 2006), 102–4, 111–14.
[40] J.W. Davidson, *Samoa mo Samoa: The Emergence of the Independent State of Western Samoa* (Oxford: Oxford University Press, 1967), 41; Lātūkefu, *The Tongan Constitution*, 20–4.

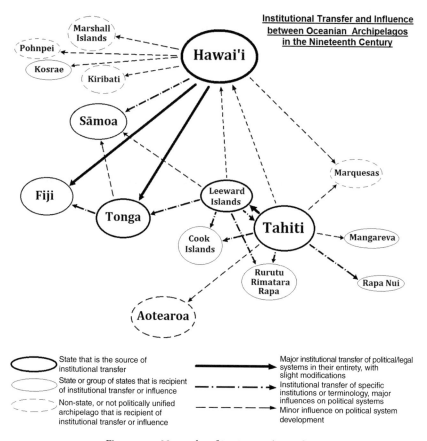

Figure 49.1 Networks of institutional transfer.

As a comparatively stable centralized state that was not merely a newly invented Christian nation like Tahiti, but additionally rooted in a classical 'ancient state' society, the Kingdom of Tonga also became a model for state-building in surrounding archipelagoes. In Fiji, Tongan nobleman Ma'afu (c. 1825–81) had established himself as a local warlord and was creating a polity modelled on that of his cousin King George Tupou I.[41] The Tongan king visited Sāmoa several times in the 1840s, and Samoan leaders in turn sent a delegation to Tonga in 1875 to learn about the Tongan system of governance (Figure 49.1).[42]

---

[41] R.A. Derrick, *A History of Fiji* (Suva: Government Press, 1950), 188 n.8; J. Spurway, *Ma'afu, Prince of Tonga, Chief of Fiji: The Life and Times of Fiji's First Tui Lau* (Canberra: ANU Press, 2015).
[42] Untitled and unsigned article in Tongan newspaper *Koe Boobooi* (July/August 1875), 37.

Political Developments in the Nineteenth Century

Arguably the most influential political model in the region, however, was the Hawaiian Kingdom. During the second half of the century, the Hawaiian constitution, revised in 1852 and 1864 to secularize and democratize it, was substantially copied to produce constitutions for Fiji and Tonga, and served as one of the main models for the constitution of Sāmoa. It all started with Hawai'i's diplomatic representative in Sydney, Charles St. Julian (1819–74), taking an active interest in the western Polynesian islands in the 1850s.[43] In an exchange of letters with King George Tupou I of Tonga, St. Julian recommended reforming the Tongan constitutional and legal system along Hawaiian lines. In 1873, Shirley Baker (1863–1903), a former Wesleyan missionary who served as Tupou I's chief advisor, obtained a copy of Hawai'i's 1864 constitution from St. Julian's successor Edward Reeve (1822–89). In 1875 the Tongan king enacted a slightly modified version as Tonga's constitution, a document that in amended form is still the basic legal document of Tonga today.[44]

Meanwhile, in Fiji, the most powerful Indigenous chief, Cakobau of Bau (c. 1815–83), had created a constitutional kingdom based on the Hawaiian constitution in 1867. By 1871, his embryonic state had united itself with other chiefdoms, including the one established by Ma'afu, to create a unified Kingdom of Fiji on the Hawaiian model, and St. Julian had moved there to become Fiji's Chief Justice for the remainder of the existence of Cakobau's kingdom.[45] The Ta'imua (principal chiefs) of Sāmoa created their own constitutional state in 1873, partly influenced by St. Julian's earlier advice,[46] and in 1875 the Samoan constitution was amended under the advice of American diplomat Albert Steinberger (1840–94), who had previously visited Hawai'i to learn more about Hawai'i's constitutional template from King Kalākaua.[47] In each of the archipelagoes participating in institutional transfer

[43] M. Diamond, *Creative Meddler: The Life and Fantasies of Charles St. Julian* (Melbourne: Melbourne University Press, 1990).

[44] S. Lātūkefu, *Church and State in Tonga: The Wesleyan Methodist Missionaries and Political Development, 1822–1875* (Honolulu: University of Hawai'i Press, 1974), 201–2.

[45] E. Crane, 'King Cakobau's government or, an experiment in government in Fiji: 1871–1874', MA thesis, University of Auckland, 1938; D. Routledge, *Matanitū: The Struggle for Power in Early Fiji* (Suva: University of the South Pacific, 1985).

[46] C.G. Powles, 'The persistence of chiefly power and its implications for law and political organisation in Western Polynesia', PhD thesis, Australian National University, 1979, 91; M. Meleisea, *The Making of Modern Samoa: Traditional Authority and Colonial Authority in the Modern History of Western Samoa* (Suva: Institute of Pacific Studies, University of the South Pacific), 36.

[47] 'Le Talaiga o le Saolotoga'/'Declaration of Rights', 'Le Faavae'/'Constitution', 18 May 1875, Steinberger collection, Elloy papers B.6.4, Archives of the Catholic Archdiocese of Apia, Sāmoa; M. Torodash, 'Steinberger of Samoa: some biographical notes', *Pacific Northwest Quarterly* 68:2 (1977), 49–59, at 54–5.

from Hawai'i, the kings or chiefs were advised by exceptional Western advisors who went against common settler interests and therefore antagonized the imperialist powers. Both Steinberger and Baker ended up being removed from office and deported by invading British navy ships, in 1876 and 1890 respectively.[48]

Oceanian Regionalism and International Politics

The political ideas emanating from Hawai'i were not limited to providing models for state formation elsewhere. In fact, Hawaiian leaders and diplomats envisioned a unification of all the burgeoning state-building projects into a large Oceanian confederation. Again, it was the visionary diplomat St. Julian, himself not Hawaiian but deeply committed to the government he served, who first formulated this idea in the 1850s, initially in letters to Hawai'i's minister of foreign affairs, and then in an official report published in 1857. Such a pan-Oceanian polity, he argued would be able to withstand foreign colonialism and be, in his own words, 'a power in the world'.[49]

However, St. Julian's ideas remained largely theoretical and were not always met with enthusiasm from Honolulu, to the point where he moved to Fiji and contented himself with serving Cakobau's government as related above. During the short reign of the inexperienced King Lunalilo (1835–74) in Hawai'i in 1873 (between the Kamehameha and Kalākaua dynasties), a Hawaiian government friendly to US expansionist interests completely disavowed the hesitant pan-Oceanian policy of Lunalilo's predecessors and closed down Hawaiian diplomatic posts in the Pacific Islands. St. Julian's equally idealistic successor Edward Reeve therefore attempted to transfer the championship of the pan-Oceanian movement to Tonga and discussed with Shirley Baker how to build the 'power in the world' from a Tongan base instead. But George Tupou I apparently did not pursue the idea further.[50]

However, it was Hawai'i's last king, Kalākaua, who not only resurrected pan-Oceanianism but made it a core tenet of Hawai'i's foreign policy. Merely days after taking the throne, Kalākaua resumed correspondence with Cakobau of Fiji, and in 1875 he provided the primary outside support for the new

[48] R.P. Gilson, *Samoa 1830–1900: The Politics of a Multi-Cultural Community* (Oxford: Oxford University Press, 1970), 321–31; Rutherford, *Shirley Baker and the King of Tonga*, 201–19.
[49] C. St. Julian, *Official Report on Central Polynesia: With a Gazetteer of Central Polynesia by Edward Reeve* (Sydney: John Fairfax and Sons, 1857).
[50] J. Horn, 'Primacy of the Pacific under the Hawaiian Kingdom', MA thesis, University of Hawai'i, 1951, 42 n. 39.

Samoan state that was being built by the Taʻimua and Steinberger. Having been the first head of state in history to circumnavigate the world in 1881, where he witnessed both the expansion of European colonial empires and the non-Western societies' resistance to it,[51] Kalākaua intensified his pan-Oceanian policy. Together with his head advisor and premier Walter Gibson (1822–88), Kalākaua issued a proclamation in 1883, appealing to the Western powers to 'recognize the inalienable right of the several native communities of Polynesia to enjoy opportunities for progress and self-government', and stating that it was Hawaiʻi's duty 'to lift up a voice among the nations in behalf of sister islands and groups of Polynesia'.[52] Subsequently, a Hawaiian diplomatic envoy was sent to Kiribati in 1883 to follow up on several petitions for advice, protection, or in some cases the outright Hawaiian annexation of their islands.

In late 1886, as a symbol of his commitment to Oceanian unity, Kalākaua created the Royal Order of the Star of Oceania and commissioned a Hawaiian diplomatic delegation to go to Sāmoa to assist the Samoan government led by Malietoa Laupepa (1841–98), currently under siege by a rival chief whose claims Germany supported. In February 1887, the delegation led by Hawaiian politician and journalist John E. Bush (1842–1906) convinced Malietoa to sign a treaty of political confederation between Hawaiʻi and Sāmoa. Bush's mission was to move on to Tonga and the Cook Islands and invite them to join in the confederation as well, and then to follow up on the I-Kiribati petitions.[53] The Hawaiian legation was supported by Hawaiʻi's only navy ship, HHMS *Kaimiloa* ['the far seeker'], a powerful symbol that combined the classical Hawaiian search for knowledge and the maritime orientation of Oceanian civilization with selectively appropriated Western technology. The ship epitomized pan-Pacific hybrid modernity as an alternative, non-colonial vision for Oceania's future.[54] The project was brought to an abrupt end, however, by the coup d'état by American missionary descendants against the Hawaiian government and, almost simultaneously, a German naval invasion of Sāmoa accompanied by a threat of war against Hawaiʻi.[55]

---

[51] W.M. Gibson (ed.), *King Kalakaua's Tour round the World. A Sketch of Incidents of Travel, with a Map of the Hawaiian Islands* (Honolulu: P.C. Advertiser Co., 1881).
[52] 'Protest', appendix to *Report of the Minister of Foreign Affairs to the Legislative Assembly of 1884* (Honolulu: P.C. Advertiser Steam Print, 1884).
[53] Horn, 'Primacy of the Pacific', 107.
[54] K. Cook, *Return to Kahiki: Native Hawaiians in Oceania* (Cambridge: Cambridge University Press, 2017), 151–2; L. Gonschor, *A Power in the World: The Hawaiian Kingdom in Oceania* (Honolulu: University of Hawaiʻi Press, 2019), 97–100.
[55] Meleisea, *The Making of Modern Samoa*, 39; Horn, 'Primacy of the Pacific', 181; Gonschor, *A Power in the World*, 100–1.

Short-lived as it may have been, King Kalākaua's far-sighted international-ism was aiming not merely at the building of a pan-Oceanian polity, but to extend its influence beyond the islands to the Pacific Rim. While visiting the rulers of Japan, China, Thailand, and Johor (in today's Malaysia) during his 1881 circumnavigation, Kalākaua developed pan-Asian ideas and promoted a collaboration of all remaining independent non-Western states to halt the expansion of European imperialism, a concept pioneering similar ideas spreading in Asia in the early twentieth century.[56] Hawai'i played a decisive role in revising Japan's unequal treaties in the 1890s: up to that time Hawai'i was the only non-Western nation with a full level of recognition and its own unequal treaty privileges in Japan, but, unlike Western states, Hawai'i was willing to give this up as a gesture of solidarity.[57] Furthermore, Hawaiian influence had a part in the modernization of China in the early twentieth century. The Chinese revolutionary leader Sun Yat-sen was educated in Hawai'i during Kalākaua's reign and repeatedly referred to Hawai'i as one of the conceptual models for his own political reforms in China.[58]

Indeed, the Hawaiian Kingdom was more globally connected than any other country of a comparable size at the time. At the peak of its inter-national involvement in 1887, there were 103 Hawaiian embassies and con-sulates worldwide.[59] And this figure does not include the various special diplomatic delegations sent to attend events of global importance such as Queen Victoria's Golden Jubilee in 1887, various world exhibits,[60] and the 1884 International Meridian conference that set Greenwich as the universal zero median.[61] Hawai'i also concluded over twenty international treaties and joined the International Postal Union, a predecessor to the League of Nations and the UN, in 1882 (Table 49.2).[62]

---

[56] C. Aydın, *The Politics of Anti-Westernism in Asia: Visions of World Order in Pan-Islamic and Pan-Asian Thought* (New York: Columbia University Press, 2007).

[57] 'Exchange of notes between Hawaii and Japan respecting Consular Jurisdiction, 18 January 1893/10 April 1894', in *The Consolidated Treaty Series, 1648–1919*, vol. CLXXX (Oxford: Oxford University Press, 1969), 125.

[58] L. Gonschor, 'Revisiting the Hawaiian influence on the political thought of Sun Yat-sen', *Journal of Pacific History* 52:1 (2017), 52–67.

[59] 'Diplomatic and Consular Representatives of Hawaii Abroad', printed broadsheet dated 1 June 1887, copy in Miscellaneous Foreign 1890, FO&Ex, Hawai'i State Archives.

[60] P.H. Hoffenberg, 'Displaying an Oceanic nation and society: the Kingdom of Hawai'i at nineteenth-century international exhibitions', in R. Fulton and P.H. Hoffenberg (eds.), *Oceania and the Victorian Imagination: Where All Things Are Possible* (Aldershot: Ashgate, 2013), 59–76.

[61] G.L. Fitzpatrick and R.M. Moffat, *Mapping the Lands and Waters of Hawai'i: The Hawaiian Government Survey* (Honolulu: Editions Limited, 2004), 30.

[62] Hawaiian Kingdom Government, *Treaties and Conventions Concluded between the Hawaiian Kingdom and other Powers since 1825* (Honolulu: Elele Book, Card and Job Print, 1887).

Political Developments in the Nineteenth Century

Table 49.2 *Treaties of Pacific states, 1800–1900.*

Hawai'i

1826	Draft commercial agreement with the USA (not ratified)
1836	Equal treaty with Great Britain
1837	Equal treaty with France
1839	Disadvantaging unequal treaty with Great Britain
1846	Disadvantaging unequal treaties with France and Great Britain
1846	Equal treaty with Denmark
1848	Equal treaty with Hamburg
1850	Equal treaty with the USA
1852	Equal treaty with Great Britain
1852	Equal treaty with Sweden-Norway
1854	Equal treaty with Bremen
1858	Equal treaty with France
1863	Equal treaty with Belgium
1863	Equal treaty with Spain
1864	Equal treaty with the Netherlands-Luxemburg
1864	Equal treaty with Italy
1864	Equal treaty with Switzerland
1869	Equal treaty with Russia
1871	Advantaging unequal treaty with Japan
1875	Equal treaty with Austria-Hungary
1879	Equal treaty with Germany
1882	Equal treaty with Portugal
1882	Party to Universal Postal Union treaty
1887	Confederation treaty with Sāmoa
1893–4	Agreement with Japan to end extraterritoriality

Tahiti

1826	Draft commercial agreement with the USA (not ratified)
1838	Equal treaty with France
1839	Disadvantaging unequal treaty with France

Leeward Islands

1826	Raiatea draft commercial agreement with the USA (not ratified)
1868	Huahine convention with the 'French protectorate government in Tahiti'
1879	Huahine draft equal treaty with Germany (not ratified)

Tonga

1855	Convention with France (not filed as a treaty in France)
1865	Equal treaty with Bua [Fiji]
1865	Advantaging unequal treaty with Lakeba [Fiji]
1876	Equal treaty with Germany, from 1870 de facto unequal
1879	Disadvantaging unequal treaty with Great Britain (amended in 1891)
1888	De facto disadvantaging unequal treaty with the USA
1900	Disadvantaging unequal treaty with Great Britain (de facto protectorate)

Table 49.2 (cont.)

Sāmoa

1839	Draft commercial agreement with the USA and Great Britain (not ratified)
1875	Draft equal treaty with Hawai'i (not ratified)
1878	Disadvantaging unequal treaty with the USA
1879	Disadvantaging unequal treaty with Germany
1879	Disadvantaging unequal treaty with Great Britain
1887	Confederation treaty with Hawai'i

Fiji

1840	Bau draft commercial agreement with the USA (not ratified)
1855	Bau draft agreement with the USA (not ratified)
1858	Bau convention with France (not filed as a treaty in France)
1865	Bua equal treaty with Tonga
1865	Lakeba disadvantaging unequal treaty with Tonga

Various small islands

1844	'Uvea disadvantaging unequal treaty with France (unratified until protectorate in 1887)
1878	Funafuti draft disadvantaging unequal treaty with Germany (not ratified)
1878	Jaluit draft disadvantaging unequal treaty with Germany (not ratified)

In the other emerging states of Oceania, international relations and diplomacy were less developed. Several of them had international treaties, but they were usually unequal, like those of Asian nations. There was one other example of international diplomacy: the Ta'imua of Sāmoa commissioned high chief M.K. Le Mamea (c. 1830–c. 1910) as a Samoan diplomat to travel to the United States to negotiate a treaty in 1879,[63] although the earlier voyage by King George Tupou I to Sydney in 1853 may be seen as a similar venture.[64] Also throughout the century, various Māori delegations travelled to the United Kingdom, including some that should be seen as quasi-diplomatic, i.e. representing attempts of Māori political entities to obtain recognition as equals to the British Crown, including Ngāpuhi paramount chief Hongi Hika (c. 1772–1828) in 1820 and Māori King Tāwhiao (c. 1822–94) in 1884.[65]

---

[63] Davidson, *Samoa mo Samoa*, 69–71; Gilson, *Samoa 1830–1900*, 349.
[64] Lātūkefu, *Church and State in Tonga*, 161–2.
[65] V. O'Malley, *Haerenga: Early Māori Journeys across the Globe* (Auckland: Bridget Williams Books, 2015).

Political Developments in the Nineteenth Century

Developments in Micronesia and Melanesia

While this chapter focuses mainly on developments in Polynesia (and Fiji), some of them were mirrored in the neighbouring region of Micronesia as well, although on a smaller scale.[66] Although there were relatively few changes from traditional politics in western Micronesia during the early to mid-1800s (except of course the Marianas that had been under Spanish colonial rule for two centuries), American and Hawaiian Congregationalist missionaries were active in Kiribati, the Marshalls, Kosrae, and Pohnpei.[67] In each of these islands and archipelagoes, literary languages created in the missionizing process contributed to the formation of national, or sub-national, identities as they still exist today. Interestingly, on Kosrae, the only other primary state society in Oceania besides Hawai'i and Tonga, the traditional monarchy of the *tokosra* (kings) appears to have been slowly eroded under the influence of Congregationalist Christianity and the impact of devastating disease and disorder created by visiting whaling ships, rather than being transformed into a modern constitutional state. However, Kosraeans did quickly assume control of the mission church, with various political leading figures taking positions as church ministers.[68] On Pohnpei, traditional chiefs resisted political change as much as they could, while Henry Nanpei (1862–1928), a chiefly convert with business interests, attempted to form a more modern system of government partly based on ideas from Hawai'i.[69]

Hawaiian connections and state formation projects influenced by Honolulu were most evident in Kiribati, where several chiefdoms attempted to constitute small-scale copies of the Hawaiian Kingdom. On the atoll of Abemama, its independently minded ruler Binoka (c. 1844–91) prohibited the presence of missionaries while at the same time entertaining the idea of becoming the Gilbertese Kamehameha and conquering the entire archipelago, for which he attempted to solicit Kalākaua's help.[70]

---

[66] F.X. Hezel, *The First Taint of Civilization: A History of the Caroline and Marshall Islands in Pre-Colonial Days, 1521–1885* (Honolulu: University of Hawai'i Press, 1983); as an exemplary case study, see D. Hanlon, *Upon a Stone Altar: A History of the Island of Pohnpei to 1890* (Honolulu: University of Hawai'i Press, 1988).

[67] N.J. Morris, 'Hawaiian missionaries abroad, 1852–1909', PhD thesis, University of Hawai'i, 1987; Cook, *Return to Kahiki*, 32–94.

[68] Hezel, *The First Taint*, 161, 169; E.M. Buck, *Island of Angels: The Growth of the Church on Kosrae, Kapkapak lun Church fin acn Kosrae, 1858–2002* (Honolulu: Watermark, 2005).

[69] D. Hanlon, 'Another side of Henry Nanpei', *Journal of Pacific History* 23:1 (1988), 36–51, at 40.

[70] H.E. Maude, 'Baiteke and Binoka of Abemama: arbiters of change in the Gilbert Islands', in J.W. Davidson and D. Scarr (eds.), *Pacific Islands Portraits* (Canberra: ANU Press, 1976), 201–24; letter, Tem Binoka to Kalākaua, 23 September 1883, Hawaiian Officials Abroad, Special Commission to Western and Central Polynesia 1883–4, FO&Ex, Hawai'i State Archives.

In Melanesia beyond Fiji, political transformations were more local in scale, as the islands were linguistically and culturally highly diverse and politically fragmented. Unlike Polynesia and Micronesia, it was only later European colonial conquests that forcefully unified Melanesian archipelagoes such as the Solomons or the New Hebrides (Vanuatu) into larger political entities. For pre-colonial movements of nation-building the islands were too fragmented linguistically (dozens of mutually unintelligible languages) and politically (chiefdoms or other traditional polities rarely encompassed more than a few villages or a single island).[71] However, traditional leaders in areas near missionary stations used that influence to enhance their position, and to create embryonic 'Christian chiefdoms', e.g. on the Loyalty Islands near New Caledonia, and in some parts of the New Hebrides.[72]

Another factor influencing political developments in Melanesia was trader and settler adventurism in areas not yet claimed as colonial possessions. For instance, European settlers founded an independent community named Franceville in the New Hebrides (the predecessor of Vanuatu's capital Port Vila)[73] and Samoan-American businesswoman Emma Coe created a state-like business empire in the Bismarck Archipelago.[74] Other economic interests with political consequences included sandalwood extraction and the labour trade, often but not always taking slavery-like forms (referred to as 'blackbirding'). Some of these activities were strangely intertwined with Hawaiian pan-Oceanianism, as one of the early sandalwood harvesting expeditions to the New Hebrides was organized by Hawaiian *ali'i* Boki Kamā'ule'ule (c. 1785–c. 1829) in the 1820s,[75] similar to another one by Fiji-based Tongan prince Ma'afu in 1842.[76] Later in the 1850s, some of St. Julian's associates in Sydney attempted to create a settler-adventurer state in the Solomon Islands while claiming affiliation with

---

[71] K.R. Howe, *Where the Waves Fall: A New South Sea Islands History from First Settlement to Colonial Rule* (Honolulu: University of Hawai'i Press, 1984), 279ff.; J.A. Bennett, *Wealth of the Solomons: A History of a Pacific Archipelago, 1800–1978* (Honolulu: University of Hawai'i Press, 1987).

[72] E.g. K.R. Howe, 'The fortunes of the Naisilines: portrait of a chieftainship', in D. Scarr (ed.), *More Pacific Islands Portraits* (Canberra: ANU Press, 1978), 1–18.

[73] K.S.K. Cawsey, *The Making of a Rebel: Captain Donald Macleod of the New Hebrides* (Suva: Institute of Pacific Studies, University of the South Pacific, 1988), 391–403.

[74] D. Salesa, 'Emma and Phoebe: "weavers of the border"', *Journal of the Polynesian Society* 132:2 (2014), 145–68.

[75] Kamakau, *Ke Aupuni Mō'ī*, 60–1.   [76] Spurway, *Ma'afu*, 38–41.

Hawai'i, and Kalākaua's diplomatic emissary to Kiribati in 1883, Captain Alfred Tripp (1840–1913), was also a labour recruiter in the New Hebrides.[77]

Imperialist Encroachment

Even though the modernization and hybridization of Indigenous political systems was the most important political development during the 1800s, the nineteenth century, especially its last quarter, saw increasing colonial encroachment. Generally, colonial rule was undesired and often resisted by Islanders. In some cases, however, native rulers consented to colonial take-over, sometimes as a last resort, either to hold on to tenuous positions of power within their societies, or to prevent takeover by another Western power that was perceived as more hostile. The relation of missionaries to colonialism was similarly ambiguous. At times, missionary activity directly precipitated imperial intervention; in other cases missionaries supported the resistance of native governments against such takeovers. Merchants and traders, who were often antagonistic to both missionaries and native governments, frequently supported the establishment of colonial rule, as it would provide security for their business interests while giving them special privileges over natives in a system of racial hierarchy (Table 49.3).

The first major colonization event in the nineteenth century was the claiming of Aotearoa New Zealand by the United Kingdom in 1840 by way of the treaty of Waitangi. Probably the most well-researched and debated treaty between Indigenous communities and an imperial power, the relationship it established between Māori and the British Crown was contested from the beginning. Complicating the situation was the earlier 1835 declaration of independence of an embryonic Māori nation-state in the far north of the country, in which the key Māori term 'rangatiratanga' was translated as 'independence', whereas the same word was rendered as mere 'governance' in the English version of the Waitangi treaty.[78]

As the only instance of classical settler colonialism in Polynesia akin to developments in North America and Australia, Britain's violation of the Waitangi treaty in order to take possession of lands for settlers led to various

---

[77] Horn, 'Primacy of the Pacific', 26–30; Diamond, *Creative Meddler*; A. Tripp, 'Report by Special Commissioner Alfred Tripp, 17 June 1884', Hawaiian Officials Abroad, Special Commission to Western and Central Polynesia 1883–4, FO&Ex, Hawai'i State Archives.
[78] C. Orange, *An Illustrated History of the Treaty of Waitangi* (Auckland: Bridget Williams Books, 2004); T. Bennion, 'Treaty-making in the Pacific in the nineteenth century and the Treaty of Waitangi', *Victoria University of Wellington Law Review* 35:1 (2004), 165–205.

Table 49.3 *Timeline of colonial claims up to 1901.*

1668	Mariana Islands (Spain)
1788	Norfolk Island (Great Britain)
1838	Pitcairn (Great Britain)
1840	Aotearoa New Zealand (Great Britain)
1842	Marquesas Islands (France)
1847	Tahiti (French protectorate)
1853	New Caledonia (France)
1871	Mangareva (French protectorate)
1874	Fiji (Great Britain)
1875	Bonin Islands (Japan)
1880	Tahiti (France), Raiatea (French protectorate)
1881	Mangareva and Rapa (France)
1885	Eastern New Guinea (divided between Great Britain and Germany); Marshall Islands (Germany); Caroline Islands (Spain)
1887	'Uvea [Wallis] (French protectorate); New Hebrides (joint British-French protectorate)
1888	Rapa Nui (Chile); Nauru (Germany); Cook Islands (British protectorate); Futuna (French protectorate)
1889	Rurutu and Rimatara (French protectorates); Tokelau (British protectorate); Sāmoa (tripartite German-British-US protectorate)
1892	Gilbert and Ellice Islands (British protectorates)
1893	Solomon Islands (British protectorate)
1895	Bora Bora and Huahine (France)
1897	Raiatea (France)
1898	Hawai'i (US occupation); Guam (USA)
1899	Caroline and Northern Mariana Islands (Germany)
1900	Sāmoa (divided between Germany and USA); Tonga (British protectorate); Cook Islands Niue (Great Britain); Rurutu (France)
1901	Rimatara (France); Niue (Great Britain)

Māori resistance movements throughout the rest of the nineteenth century, which were so fierce as to necessitate deployment of the British Royal Troops. This included a belated movement to construct a monarchical nation-state in the central North Island – comparable to earlier developments in tropical Polynesia – with paramount chief of the Tainui confederation Pōtatau Te Wherowhero (c. 1770–1860) being elected and crowned Māori king in 1858, founding a movement still in existence today. In the end, due to this and other more locally based resistance movements, the 1840 British sovereignty claim over Aotearoa took until the early 1900s to be implemented fully.[79]

---

[79] P. Cleave, 'Tribal and state-like political formations in New Zealand Maori society 1750–1900', *Journal of the Polynesian Society* 92:1 (1983), 51–92; J. Belich, *Making Peoples:*

Political Developments in the Nineteenth Century

The British foothold in Aotearoa, where there had also been a small French settlement in Akaroa Bay on the South Island, prompted France to pursue its own colonial sphere in the Pacific more aggressively. In 1842, France declared the Marquesas Islands to be a French colony even though a colonial presence was subsequently only established on Tahuata in the south and Nuku Hiva in the north.[80] A few months later, French intervention in favour of persecuted Catholic missionaries in Tahiti led to the proclamation of a protectorate over Pomare IV's kingdom, leading to a protracted war against fierce Tahitian resistance, which was only concluded in 1847 with the queen's signing of a definitive protectorate agreement. The three Leeward Islands kingdoms, on the other hand, had their independence guaranteed by an Anglo-French declaration.[81]

The situation was quite different on 'Uvea, Futuna, and Mangareva, where French Catholic missionaries had been influential and local political systems had subsequently redefined themselves as 'Catholic kingdoms'. Consequently, France was seen not as an enemy but as a fellow Catholic power. Informal protectorates were thus agreed upon in 1844, as far as can be gathered, in a consensual way. But after France secularized and moved away from Catholic influence in the latter parts of the century, there were instances of resistance as well. The Kingdom of Mangareva formally revoked the French protectorate in 1870, and only after repeated shows of French naval force was the protectorate reinstated in 1871 and annexation accomplished in 1881.[82]

In 1853, France claimed possession of New Caledonia, where it mirrored previous British colonial models in Australia by establishing a penal colony and later large ranches on land confiscated from the large island's Indigenous Kanak people, who were confined to 'reserves'. The large Melanesian island subsequently became the only other typical settler colony in Oceania besides Aotearoa New Zealand. On the smaller offshore islands Kanak remained in the majority, and kept the bulk of their land; however, massive dispossession of the Kanak tribes on the mainland led to a fierce pan-tribal resistance

---

A History of the New Zealanders, from Polynesian Settlement to the End of the Nineteenth Century (Honolulu: University of Hawai'i Press, 1996), 261–4.

[80] G. Dening, *Islands and Beaches: Discourse on a Silent land, Marquesas, 1774–1880* (Chicago: The Dorsey Press, 1980); M. Bailleul, *Les Îles Marquises: histoire de la Terre des Hommes du XVIIIème siècle à nos jours* (Papeete: Ministère de la Culture de Polynésie Française, 2001), 90–4.

[81] Newbury, *Tahiti Nui: Change and Survival in French Polynesia 1767–1945* (Honolulu: University of Hawai'i Press, 1980); Gille, *Histoire des institutions politiques*, 33.

[82] H. Laval, *Mémoires pour servir à l'histoire de Mangareva, ère chrétienne 1834–1871*, ed. C.W. Newbury and P. O'Reilly (Paris: Musée de l'Homme, 1968), xcix–cviii.

movement in 1878, led by chief Atai (d. 1878), that needed massive French military force to be suppressed.[83]

The next major archipelago to fall under colonial rule was Fiji in 1874. Cakobau and some other Fijian chiefs had for a long time been ambivalent about a possible cession of their islands to the Britain, but in the 1870s had decided to follow the Hawaiian model of an independent constitutional state instead. But Britain refused to recognize the Fijian government while the British consul and other British officials actively sabotaged it and encouraged British subjects to disavow its authority,[84] while support from Hawai'i temporarily lapsed during King Lunalilo's short rule in 1873. All of this hastened the demise of the Fijian Kingdom and gave Cakobau and his collaborators in the Fijian government virtually no other choice but to agree to the humiliating procedure of a 'deed of cession' to Great Britain in October of 1874 as mere 'native chiefs', as if the constitutional kingdom of Fiji had never existed. Subsequently, Fiji became the centre of British colonial activity in Oceania, its governor taking the additional title of High Commissioner for the western Pacific in 1877. In stark contrast to Baker and Steinberger mentioned above, Cakobau's main foreign advisor, John B. Thurston (1836–97), reconciled himself with the colonial administration and made a career therein, ending up as Governor and High Commissioner 1885–7, and 1888–9.[85]

The 1880s saw a scramble to colonize the remaining archipelagoes: in 1880, France annexed its Tahitian protectorate by agreement with King Pomare V (1839–91) and in the following years widely extended its East Polynesian colonial possessions by forcing protectorates or annexations onto the Leeward Society Islands of Raiatea, Huahine, and Bora Bora, as well as on the Austral Islands. It then led massive military expeditions to the Marquesas to implement the 1842 claims on the ground. Resistance in the Leeward Islands endured until the mid-1890s, especially on Raiatea, where it took a protracted war to suppress insurgents led by Teraupoo (c. 1855–1918).[86]

---

[83] M. Millet, *1878, carnets de campagne en Nouvelle-Calédonie: précédé de La guerre d'Ataï, récit kanak*, ed. A. Bensa (Toulouse: Anacharsis, 2013).
[84] Crane, 'King Cakobau's government', 134–5; Routledge, *Matanitū*, 166–7.
[85] D. Scarr, *The Majesty of Colour: A Life of Sir John Bates Thurston*, 2 vols. (Canberra: ANU Press, 1973).
[86] Newbury, *Tahiti Nui*, 220; B. Saura, *Histoire et mémoire des temps coloniaux en Polynésie française* (Papeete: Éditions au Vent des Îles, 2015), 194–213.

Political Developments in the Nineteenth Century

At the same time, recently unified Germany became a new player in the field. Already involved in the Pacific copra trade, Bismarck's empire began aggressively pushing for colonial expansion in the 1880s. After claiming northeastern New Guinea, Germany made an agreement with Britain in 1885 to divide most of Melanesia and Micronesia into spheres of influence, declaring the Bismarck Archipelago and the northern Solomons, as well as the Marshall Islands, to be under German sovereignty, adding Nauru in 1888.[87] Further German claims in Micronesia clashed with those of Spain, which had seen most of Micronesia as a vaguely defined hinterland of its colonial possessions in the Marianas. German activity thus precipitated a formal Spanish annexation of the Caroline archipelago in 1885, meeting especially fierce resistance on Pohnpei, whose population was either traditionalist, or Hawaiian- and US-affiliated Protestant.[88] In 1887 the German navy invaded Sāmoa, installing a German puppet government and in the process destroying Kalākaua's burgeoning Polynesian confederation. Pressure from the other powers with interests in Sāmoa (Britain and the USA) prevented Germany from permanently taking over the Samoan archipelago at the time, but after an unsuccessful attempt to install a tripartite protectorate, Sāmoa ended up being divided between the USA and Germany in 1900, with the latter obtaining the bulk of the archipelago.[89]

Britain was more reluctant to join in the latest imperial race since it was already saturated with colonial possessions in the region. Nonetheless, in the face of French and German competition, Britain felt compelled to act, and proclaimed protectorates over some remaining archipelagoes, including the Cook Islands in 1888, Tokelau in 1889, the Gilberts in 1892, and the Solomons in 1893, later annexing them as colonies.[90] Even Tonga, hitherto a stronghold of native rule, was invaded by the British navy in 1890 to force the installation of a pro-British administration. This was followed by a new act of gunboat diplomacy in 1900 to force King George Tupou II (1874–1918) to sign a de facto protectorate treaty which remained in force until the late

---

[87] S. Firth, *New Guinea under the Germans* (Melbourne: Melbourne University Press, 1984); H.J. Hiery (ed.), *Die Deutsche Südsee 1884–1914: Ein Handbuch* (Paderborn: Ferdinand Schöningh, 2001).
[88] Hanlon, *Upon a Stone Altar*, 147–97.
[89] Davidson, *Samoa mo Samoa*; Meleisea, *The Making of Modern Samoa*.
[90] D. Scarr, *Fragments of Empire: A History of the Western Pacific High Commission, 1877–1914* (Canberra: ANU Press, 1967), 252–90. Annexation as colonies took place for the Cook Islands in 1900, for Niue in 1901, and for the Gilberts in 1917. The Solomons became a de facto colony despite continuing to be officially named 'protectorate'.

twentieth century, but was not followed by annexation.[91] However, tired of ruling too many small colonies, the Colonial Office in London quickly turned two of its new possessions (Cook Islands and Niue) over to its already largely self-governing settler colony of New Zealand where premier Richard Seddon was developing regional imperialist ambitions of his own.[92] Similarly, Norfolk Island was turned over to Australia, and after World War I, Germany's possessions falling under British mandate would be divided between Australia and New Zealand rather than run directly by London.

In Hawai'i, on the other hand, direct moves of colonization by a foreign power were prevented by the kingdom's unique standing as a recognized nation-state. Instead, its imperialist subjugation was achieved by an unholy alliance of local descendants of American missionaries and burgeoning imperialist circles in the United States.[93] First, the missionary families and their armed militia staged a domestic coup against King Kalākaua in 1887. Five years later, they conspired with the US diplomatic representative in Honolulu against the king's successor, Queen Lili'uokalani (1838–1917), in order to destroy Oceania's most advanced state and have its land taken over by the United States, precipitating a US military invasion and the installation of a puppet government in 1893. Later that year, the US government disavowed the invasion and negotiated an executive agreement with the queen to have her constitutional government restored. That promise was never kept. Meanwhile, the missionary sons who had risen to power during the invasion established an apartheid-like dictatorship, calling itself the 'Republic of Hawai'i', and hired foreign mercenaries to run the islands as a police state.[94] When the imperialist faction took power in Washington in 1897, an attempt was made to annex the islands formally, but this was thwarted by massive petitions submitted by Hawaiian patriots to the US Congress.[95] During the Spanish-American War in 1898, however, the US Congress passed a resolution to annex Hawai'i without a treaty, defying both the US constitution and international law. This created a US occupation that Beamer refers to as 'faux-colonial', since it resembled colonial rule over other

---

[91] Campbell, *Island Kingdom*, 111–12, 132–7.
[92] D. Salesa, 'A Pacific destiny: New Zealand's overseas empire, 1840–1945', in S. Mallon, K. Mahina-Tuai, and D. Salesa (eds.), *Tangata o le Moana: New Zealand and the People of the Pacific* (Wellington: Te Papa Press, 2012), 97–122.
[93] T. Coffman, *Nation Within: The History of the American Occupation of Hawai'i*, 3rd edn (Durham, NC: Duke University Press, 2016).
[94] Beamer, *No Mākou ka Mana*, 198–223.
[95] N. Silva, *Aloha Betrayed: Native Hawaiian Resistance to American Colonialism* (Durham, NC: Duke University Press, 2004).

Political Developments in the Nineteenth Century

archipelagoes, yet left the Hawaiian Kingdom in a state of constitutional limbo, an unresolved situation that would resurface in the late twentieth and early twenty-first century.[96]

Through its victory in the Spanish-American War, the United States also supplanted Spain as an imperial power in the Pacific. Besides the Philippines, the strategically situated island of Guam changed colonial masters from the Spanish to the Americans. But the United States showed little interest in the rest of the Spanish Marianas, end even less in Spain's recently acquired Carolines. Instead, Spain sold these islands to Germany in 1899, whose New Guinea Colony was thus extended far north of the equator to encompass almost all of Micronesia.[97] Besides the USA, the only other European settler state in the Americas that ventured into Pacific imperialism was Chile, which claimed Rapa Nui (Easter Island) in 1888, based on a controversial bilingual document similar to the treaty of Waitangi. This arrangement was not actually implemented until 1896, with colonization outsourced to a Chilean and later a Scottish company, making Latin America's only Oceanian colony look more like a company state.[98]

Establishment of Creole Societies

At the margins of the complex political developments hitherto described, Oceania's three creole societies were born.[99] Unlike the ethnically and culturally mixed strata of society that developed in and around the main port cities in the larger archipelagoes, but remained attached and connected to the less mixed native communities in the hinterlands, the three creole societies consisted of ethnically mixed people in their entirety, and their mixed languages swiftly developed from pidgins (contact languages used for communication only) to creoles (mixed languages as mother tongues).

---

[96] Beamer, *No Mākou ka Mana*, 196; Sai, *Ua Mau ke Ea*.
[97] F.X. Hezel, *Strangers in Their Own Land: A Century of Colonial Rule in the Caroline and Marshall Islands* (Honolulu: University of Hawai'i Press, 2003).
[98] G. McCall, 'Riro, Rapu and Rapanui: Refoundations in Easter Island Colonial History', *Rapa Nui Journal* 11, 3 (1996), 112–22; S.R. Fischer, *Island as the End of the World: The Turbulent History of Easter Island* (London: Reaktion Books, 2005).
[99] These societies are included here because they deserve more attention from historians. It is ignorance of their history that enables the current colonialist encroachment by Australia against Norfolk Islanders to remain virtually unchallenged by both Island nations' governments and activist communities that would normally be up in arms against such treatment of Indigenous communities.

The oldest and best known of these communities was founded in 1790 on the then-uninhabited island of Pitcairn, east of Mangareva, by the participants in the famous mutiny on the British ship *Bounty* and their Tahitian partners. This unique mixed society became formally a British colony in 1838, but less than two decades later its entire population was resettled on Norfolk Island in 1856, after the former British penal colony there had been closed down. Eventually two small groups of Islanders moved back to Pitcairn in the 1850s and 1860s. While Pitcairn remained an internally self-governing Crown colony attached to the Western Pacific High Commission, Norfolk Island lost its self-governing status in 1896 and was made a dependency of New South Wales, later to become an external territory of Australia.[100]

The second creole society was established on the then-uninhabited Bonin Islands in northwestern Micronesia in 1830 by a group of Hawaiians and British and American settlers on the initiative of the British Consul in Honolulu. Since London did not follow through, the settlement remained a de facto self-governing independent community until it was annexed by Japan in 1875; in consequence its population became further mixed with the arrival of Japanese settlers, and the language switched from a Hawaiian-English creole to a Hawaiian-English-Japanese one.[101] The third Oceanian creole community was founded on the then-uninhabited atoll of Palmerston, northwest of Aitutaki in the Cook Islands, by a British adventurer and his three Cook Islander partners in 1863. Great Britain annexed the atoll in 1891 and it became subsequently attached to the Cook Islands colony in 1901.[102]

Despite their small size, the three creole communities held significance for the political history of nineteenth-century Oceania, as they represent yet another hybrid form of community, containing characteristics of both a native Islander and a European settler society. Similarly their political systems (before definitive annexation as non-self-governing colonies towards the end of the century) held elements of both independent Islander-ruled states and European colonies.

---

[100] M. Hoare, *Norfolk Island: A Revised and Enlarged History, 1774–1998* (Rockhampton: Central Queensland University Press, 1999); R. Nobbs, *Norfolk Island and Its Third Settlement, The First Hundred Years: The Pitcairn Era, 1856–1956, and the Melanesian Mission, 1866–1920* (Sydney: Library of Australian History, 2006).

[101] D. Chapman, *The Bonin Islanders, 1830 to the Present: Narrating Japanese Nationality* (London: Lexington Books, 2016); S. Kramer and H.K. Kramer, 'The other islands of Aloha', *Hawaiian Journal of History* 47 (2013), 1–26.

[102] R. Hendery, *One Man Is an Island: The Speech Community William Marsters Begat on Palmerston Island* (London: Battlebridge, 2015).

Conclusion

Nineteenth-century political developments were of central importance for the history of Oceania. Rather than merely a prelude to colonialism, they sowed the seeds of most of what currently matters in the politics of the region. The creation of literary languages established the units of national consciousness in Polynesia and Micronesia as we know them today, along with the small unique creole societies, such as the Norfolk Islanders, that are now struggling for recognition as distinct Indigenous societies. In terms of constitutional development, the nineteenth century saw a slow democratization of stratified societies as well as the rise of hybrid systems of government combining traditional with Western elements. All of this was most evident in the Hawaiian Kingdom, but similar trajectories could be observed in many other archipelagoes. Towards the end of the century, a long interlude of colonial rule interrupted these processes, but the same features can be found in post-colonial constitutionalism as well; Sāmoa's post-independence constitution is remarkably similar to the one created under Hawaiian influence in the 1870s.[103] Furthermore, the current debate on the development of Pacific regionalism has its origins in the nineteenth century. There has been a cyclical reassertion of regional Oceanian identity by more independent-minded island leaders, first in the 1970s and 1980s, and now again in the twenty-first century.[104] We are familiar with the inclusive vision formulated by Epeli Hau'ofa in 'Our Sea of Islands',[105] but it should not be forgotten that this vision first arose a century earlier, when King Kalākaua initially promoted the idea of an Oceanian confederation.

---

[103] Davidson, *Samoa mo Samoa*; Larmour, *Foreign Flowers*, 67.

[104] G. Fry, *Recapturing the Spirit of 1971: Towards a New Regional Political Settlement in the Pacific*, State, Society & Governance in Melanesia Discussion Paper 2015/3 (Canberra: Australia National University, 2015).

[105] E. Hau'ofa, 'Our Sea of Islands', in E. Hau'ofa, V. Naidu, and E. Waddell (eds.), *A New Oceania: Rediscovering our Sea of Islands* (Suva: School of Social and Economic Development, University of the South Pacific in association with Beake House, 1993), 2–16.

50

Timorese Islanders and the Portuguese Empire in the Indonesian Archipelago

RICARDO ROQUE

This chapter approaches the long history of the Portuguese Empire in the Asia-Pacific world through a micro-history of a paradigmatic colonial object: national flags.[1] It analyses the 'fantastic stories' told by the nineteenth- and twentieth-century Europeans about the Indigenous cultural appropriations of Portuguese flags in East Timor – the eastern half of Timor island, a small but durable Portuguese establishment from the 1500s until 1974 – with a view to discussing the complex exchanges between Indigenous people and European objects from overseas. From the outset of Portuguese imperial expansionism in the 1500s, flags accompanied Portugal's ambitions and became an ubiquitous presence throughout the Portuguese imperial world for centuries. They were handed over to the rulers of Indigenous polities as tokens of Portuguese kingship power, as vassalage gifts in exchange for allegiance and obedience to the Crown of Portugal. This was initiated by early modern strategies of conquest and vassalage expansionism that in some settings seem to have persisted until the 1910s. It was the case of East Timor. In this remote but lasting Portuguese colony in the Asia-Pacific region, flags of Portuguese origin became significant not only in the practices and imaginaries of Europeans, but also in the Indigenous societies that, at some point in the past, had forged ties with the Portuguese – and in this process came into possession of Portuguese flags.

---

[1] Earlier versions of this chapter were presented at seminars and workshops in Cambridge, Lisbon, and Paris, since 2008. I thank the audiences and organizers for important input. Special thanks are due to the volume editors Jane Samson, Anne Perez Hattori, and Paul D'Arcy for their insightful suggestions and critiques; and to Ângela Barreto Xavier and Miguel Metelo de Seixas for important comments and clarifications regarding the early modern period. I have translated into English all passages originally in Portuguese. Research for this chapter was funded through national funds by a grant from the Foundation for Science and Technology (FCT), Portugal, through the project *Indigenous Colonial Archives: Micro-histories and Comparisons* (PTDC/HAR- HIS/28577/2017). This research also benefited from the use of the infrastructure of PRISC (Portuguese Research Infrastructure of Scientific Collections).

450

Flags as National Symbols and Beyond

Portuguese late colonial accounts recurrently point out the high value of national flags in the Timorese world. They frame this value within European nationalistic colonial ideals. From this perspective, Indigenous investment in flags is read as revelation of the virtuous expansion of a Portuguese *conscience collective* amongst the subservient natives – the manifestation of an intangible patriotic force that perpetuated the existence and the hegemony of the Portuguese Empire, from the Age of Discoveries to the twentieth century. In its nationalistic essence, this colonial viewpoint is not exclusive to the Portuguese. It resonates a wider imaginary of flags as national symbols that pervaded Western imperialisms – and which still pervades much historiography on the topic. According to an established body of literature in history and the social sciences, national flags are defined as symbolic emblems that instantiate modern national identity.[2] In accordance with the French sociologist Émile Durkheim's classic writings on flags and totems, national flags are understood as 'the emblem of the group's agreement to be a group', the group being the modern Western nation.[3] The mass-production of

---

[2] R. Firth, *Symbols: Public and Private* (London: George Allen & Unwin, 1973), chapter 10; S.R. Weitman, 'National flags: a sociological overview', *Semiotica* 8:4 (1973), 328–66. National symbolism recurs also in studies of flags as national symbols in anti- and post-colonial nation-building; see for example A. Virmani, 'National symbols under colonial domination: the nationalization of the Indian flag, March–August 1923', *Past and Present* 164 (1999), 169–97. Recent studies of East Timorese nationalism and its symbols adopt a similar viewpoint, but they tend to ignore the deeper local colonial past concerning the indigenization of Portuguese flags. See C.E. Arthur, *Political Symbols and National Identity in Timor-Leste* (New York: Palgrave Macmillan, 2019); M. Leach, *Nation-Building and National Identity in Timor-Leste* (London: Routledge, 2018). The one exception, sensitive to indigenous concepts of the Timor-Leste national flag, is E.G. Traube, 'Planting the flag', in A. McWilliam and E.G. Traube (eds.), *Land and Life in Timor-Leste: Ethnographic Essays* (Canberra: ANU Press, 2011), 117–40. See also L. Sousa, 'A bandeira portuguesa em Timor Leste: hau hanoin', in R. Fonseca (ed.), *Monumentos portugueses em Timor-Leste* (Porto: Crocodilo Azul, 2005), 36–8.

[3] C. Marvin and D.N. Ingle, *Blood Sacrifice and the Nation: Totem Rituals and the American Flag* (Cambridge: Cambridge University Press, 1999), 1. Reliance on Durkheim's work *The Elementary Forms of the Religious Life*, however, tends to miss the fact that his argument is embedded in late nineteenth-century French Republican nationalistic understandings of 'national flags'. First published in French in 1912, at the height of imperial nationalism, Durkheim's work posited that the Indigenous Australians' correspondence between totems and clans was a 'primitive' version of the modern correspondence that Europeans established between flags and nations. ('The totem *is the flag* of the clan', Durkheim famously declared.) However, Durkheim's analysis, as Anthony D. Smith observed, 'fits the case of nations and nationalism rather better'; it is possibly a theory of 'the symbolism of the nation' transposed to distinct cultural contexts – a Eurocentric application of patriotic imaginaries of national flags to a dissimilar indigenous Pacific reality. A.D. Smith, 'Nationalism and classical social theory', *British Journal of Sociology* 34:1 (1983), 19–38, at 30. Cf. Émile Durkheim, *The Elementary Forms of the Religious Life*, trans. J. Swain (London: George Allen & Unwin, 1915).

national flags in Europe in the second half of the nineteenth century is often signalled as a climactic moment of this modern process. 'The political right of nation and flag', historian Eric Hobsbawm argued, became a distinctive aspect of the late nationalist-imperialist claims of Europeans; and it was for such right that 'the term "nationalism" was actually invented in the last decade(s) of the nineteenth century'.[4] In this vein the imperialist dissemination of national flags has been interpreted as instrumental to the process through which European 'nations' and 'empires' were invented and imagined.[5] This dissemination has also been read as a straightforward tool of colonial domination, a means used by the colonizer to subjugate the colonized to the hypnotic hegemony of European national symbols. Yet, to freely paraphrase Marshall Sahlins: when European flags come into contact with different cultures, they become different flags. However, imposing nationalist symbolism as the single explanatory framework obliterates the actual significance of such differences. Indigenous agency and cultural plasticity in the face of colonial material culture must be acknowledged. In sum, the language of 'national symbolism' is a historically contingent and provincial Western idiom; it is not universal; and if applied crudely to the analysis of flags in cross-cultural colonial histories, it can lead to Eurocentric biases that one should seek to avoid.

In this chapter I reassess critically the nationalist colonial imaginary of flags as mere vehicles of Western national and imperial symbolism. I am principally interested in tracing stories and concepts of flags as agents of power relations and social formations in colonial histories. With special reference to East Timor, then, I here bring into conversation a plurality of dissonant, yet reciprocal, European and Indigenous attachments to flags as agencies imbued with special power to act in the world, rather than simply to flags as symbolic representations of nations. In the 1800s–1900s, Portuguese and Timorese cultural idioms of flags differed in important ways. However, they also intersected around one common theme. Both attributed a special agency to the materiality of flags as objects that mattered significantly for social order, authority, warfare, and governance. For Portuguese and Timorese alike, flags were no ordinary things. They carried metaphysical potency and their presence had an expected impact upon interpersonal encounters, societal order, status hierarchies, and actual

---

[4] E. Hobsbawm, *Nations and Nationalism since 1780: Programme, Myth, Reality* (Cambridge: Cambridge University Press, 1989), 102.
[5] See E. Hobsbawm and T. Ranger (eds.), *The Invention of Tradition* (Cambridge: Cambridge University Press, 1983); B. Anderson, *Imagined Communities: Reflections on the Origin and Spread of Nationalism* (London: Verso, 1991).

power relations. For those involved, as I intend to show, this impact made manifest a complex and mutual kind of flag animism that seemed to run across the colonial divide. Portuguese flags seemed as if they were animated by intangible qualities that exceeded the physicality of the objects-in-themselves. These qualities were conceived of by the Europeans as 'prestige', 'national spirit', 'patriotic affection'; they were differently conceived of by Indigenous people as ancestral *lulik* and *rota*. Such differences notwithstanding, over time the Portuguese nationalistic metaphysics somehow short-circuited and crossed paths with the Timorese *lulik* conceptions. In authority ceremonials, and in war settings in particular, as we will see, this distinct yet reciprocal animacy of flags could have significant effects. In order to consider this complex conjunction, I propose a shift of analytical perspective. I propose to follow flags as actors, rather than flags as symbols, in relational colonial histories. Hence, I ask readers to suspend national symbolism as universal idiom; to suspend a priori assumptions that national flags are no more than representations of nationhood.

I begin by tentatively tracing the origins of flags as early modern actors of imperial sovereignty in the context of the Portuguese expansion in Africa and Asia since the 1500s. I offer an interpretative overview of a process of distribution and circulation of Portuguese-origin flags as participants in the early vassalage expansionism of Portugal's empire. Over time, I suggest, a number of distinct Portuguese flags circulated to Indigenous societies as part of a set of prized insignia of power (among which also stood out sceptres and letters patent) through the mediation of which the Portuguese Crown aimed at expanding its dominion over a network of African and Asian vassals. I then briefly situate this complex long-term process of diffusion of the Portuguese material culture of kingship power in the specific history of Portuguese imperialism in Timor. I then develop my arguments from a case study set in the late nineteenth-century context of warfare and power rivalry in East Timor. I use a revealing colonial account – a parable of colonial rule based on the allegedly intangible powers of flags – as a window to explore the cross-cultural lives of flags in colonial encounters. This archival record sheds light onto the patriotic animism that pervaded the Portuguese theories of flags as agents of empire and nation in Timor. This same archival fragment, I also argue, allows me to circumvent the limitations of the colonial nationalistic viewpoint. I thus pursue the threads of this same story into Timorese conceptions of ancestor flags as *lulik* agencies, which interfere with and destabilize the notion of flags as simply national-imperial symbols.

RICARDO ROQUE

An Empire of Flags and Vassal Rulers

That he will settle and he will be obliged to serve us as our vassal and natural and loyal servant, and as sign of this he will take our flag and with it he will make those obligations and oaths in law that customarily they do and do to ourselves those who settle in our service as our vassals and servants.

King D. Manuel I of Portugal's instructions (*Ystruçam*) to his emissary, Fernão Dias, on vassalage procedures to be applied to the King of Marrakech in 1514.[6]

Since the 1980s, the indigenization of colonialism's material culture has become a fertile topic in the history and anthropology of the Pacific Ocean.[7] In this literature – dominantly concerned with British and French examples – Indigenous engagements with European flags occasionally appear. Tahitian and Māori Islanders, for instance, were quick to take notice of the British sailors' special uses of the Union Jack.[8] The locals possibly perceived the Europeans' attentions towards the flag in the light of Polynesian conceptions of *mana*-charged objects. This recognition, however, did not imply deference to the British. Flags could become a special target of Indigenous hostility towards the strangers; meanwhile, during Māori 'rebellions', the perceived potency of the outsiders' flag could be imitated and usurped for producing novel flags that were then used to fight the white foreigners.[9]

The long Portuguese presence in the region provides rich materials for further comparative reflections. In the case of Portuguese imperialism in wider Oceania, however, we need to attend to a longer chronological framework, preceding the British and French histories for almost two centuries. For by the time the British set foot in the Pacific Islands, the worlds of

---

[6] My translation. I follow the citation of this document as presented and analysed in A. Vasconcelos de Saldanha, *Iustum imperium: dos tratados como fundamento do império dos portugueses no Oriente: estudo de história do direito internacional e do direito português* (Lisbon: Instituto Português do Oriente/Fundação Oriente, 1997), 572.

[7] The seminal reference is N. Thomas, *Entangled Objects: Exchange, Material Culture and Colonialism in the Pacific* (Cambridge, MA: Harvard University Press, 1991).

[8] Greg Dening and Marshall Sahlins have arguably offered the most inspiring analytical insights into this topic. M. Sahlins, 'Other tribes, other customs: the anthropology of history', *American Anthropologist* 85:3 (1983), 529–33; G. Dening, *Mr Bligh's Bad Language: Passion, Power and Theatre on the Bounty* (Cambridge: Cambridge University Press, 1992), 253–81. See also A. Salmond, *The Trial of the Cannibal Dog: The Remarkable Story of Captain's Cook Encounters in the South Seas* (New Haven: Yale University Press, 2003).

[9] The Māori 'flag of the union of Tuhoe', for instance, displayed in the exhibition *Oceania* at London and Paris in 2018–19 exemplifies a mimetic appropriation of Europeans flags and signs as instantiations of 'power and sovereignty'; it was used in the 1860s–70s wars to fight the British. P. Brunt et al., *Oceania: Exhibition Catalogue* (London: Royal Academy of Arts, 2018). See also Sahlins, 'Other tribes, other customs'.

many Asian Islanders already had been marked deeply by exchanges with the Portuguese. Therefore, the late Portuguese colonizers' spotlight on indigenized flags in Timor must first be considered in the light of three centuries of complex intercultural exchanges in the region. This process, as we will see, will help us to frame later events concerning the agency of flags in connection to their past traces in the early modern era.

Empire as Vassalage System

Flags were one of the Portuguese power-charged items that materialized an early modern ceremonial style of Portuguese overseas expansionism based on vassal–king networks of suzerainty.[10] Alongside the expansion of the commercial empire, this ceremonial expansionism relied on imposed tokens of Portuguese kingship, circulated through rites of vassalage between the Kingdom of Portugal and the militarily defeated, or voluntarily subjected, African and Asian rulers. The early modern Portuguese overseas empire in Asia is commonly described as a maritime endeavour focused on commerce, trade, and religious conversion. Yet, simultaneously, the Portuguese empire grew into an extension of the king's sovereign body, in the form of a network of minor vassal kings who in theory paid obedience to and derived their authority from the king of Portugal. The latter was self-entitled Emperor or the 'King of kings' (rei dos reis), an expression also conveying medieval political conceptions of suzerainty (suzerania) according to which the Portuguese king was primus inter pares, the one of highest status who offered protection and granted its vassals the right to legitimate authority.[11] The circle of minor 'vassal kings' (reis vassalos) that the Portuguese king's overseas executives had been able to subject to 'obedience' through conquest and/or vassalage vows of loyalty defined the imperial dominion. The number and quality of vassal kings, in other words, was one key measure of empire.

Indeed, vital to this earliest of all European overseas empires was a hierarchical system of vassal–king rule based on ceremonials, ties of allegiance, loyalty and royal protection, tributes, and the presentation of material objects charged with the powers of Portuguese kingship. In Portugal, although the royal flag did not necessarily rank higher than other

---

[10] Yet I clarify here that my focus on Portuguese flags in intercultural imperial and colonial histories is analytical and micro-historical and it does not presume any a priori superior importance or exceptionalism to flags vis-à-vis other items of Portuguese material culture in indigenous circulation.Timorese people could also endow other objects with equal or superior lulik potency, and even early modern Portuguese could see sceptres or crowns as kingship insignia of higher significance than flags.

[11] Saldanha, Iustum imperium, 585. See also L.F. Thomaz, De Ceuta a Timor (Lisbon: Difel, 1994).

royal insignia (such as the sceptre or the crown), it was inextricably part of the performative material culture required for the coronation rites of the Portuguese king's power until the late nineteenth century.[12] In a comparable vein, as also observed below, the Crown's flag became also part of the materials implied in producing the Portuguese overseas rites of vassalage. In the early modern period, flags representing the Portuguese monarchy (including, but not exclusively, the *bandeira real*, the royal banner, bearing the dynastic coat of arms of the king of Portugal) were a constant presence in the ceremonial complex of overseas expansionism based on the institution of vassalage. Besides the king's flag, however, other flags could be used to represent the Portuguese Crown in its overseas exploits and conquests. For instance, notable among the *bandeiras* that stood for the early Portuguese Crown were flags bearing the cross of the Order of Christ (the Portuguese king was the master of this order); such flags were commonly seen as the distinctive banner of the Portuguese caravels. It seems that various Portuguese-origin flags and banners could also appear in the wars fought by Portuguese armies in Africa and Asia. The king's banner; the flag of the Order of Christ; but also a plurality of distinct Portuguese-origin flags (such as those associated, for instance, with the relatively autonomous municipal powers – the flag of Lisbon, according to one account, was among the flags hoisted by Portuguese armies in the conquest of Ceuta in 1415)[13] may have been used in this early age of Portuguese imperial expansionism. Perhaps some of this diversity could also appear in flags that became the imposed gift of the Portuguese Crown's victorious armies to those who subjected voluntarily or who had to be subdued by the force of arms to a vassal condition.

The Crown's flag embodied the Portuguese claims to lordship over foreign lands and peoples, even if the royal flag – more a dynastic sign and/or an insignia of kingship authority rather than a sign of nationhood in the modern sense – could sometimes share such claims with a variety of coexistent Portuguese-origin flags. The act of planting stone posts on shore (the *padrão*, a post bearing the royal arms and sometimes the armillary sphere) – rather than the act of planting the flag – was the characteristic Portuguese ceremony of possession of new territories adopted by the

---

[12] During the Portuguese king's coronation (*aclamação*) it was customary for the *alferes-mor* to come forward with the royal flag. M.M. de Seixas, *Heráldica, representação do poder e memória da nação: o armorial autárquico de Inácio de Vilhena Barbosa* (Lisbon: Universidade Lusíada Editora, 2011), 66, 72.

[13] Seixas, *Heráldica*, 337–8.

456

Crown's delegates.[14] However, the Crown's flag was a critical insignia of power that participated in Portugal's most important early modern ceremony of imperial expansionism in Asia and Africa: the vassalage.

The Portuguese first adapted the feudal rite of vassalage from European medieval usage to their encounters with West African rulers, and afterwards they replicated it widely in their South Asian conquests and diplomatic dealings, in the 1500s–1600s.[15] The Portuguese king's vassalage treaties with African vassal rulers first received formal acknowledgement as 'titles of territorial acquisition' by the Pope in 1497.[16] Thus, in the light of early modern legality, vassalage rites celebrated by the king of Portugal – with their accompanying paper proofs (treaties and letters) – came to constitute an important action of legitimate territorial possession in the overseas expansion.[17] In vassalage treaties, the local rulers swore loyalty, obedience, and tribute (in men, force, and military support; and in tributary taxes of some kind) to the king of Portugal, and in exchange they received the promise of the king's aid and military protection. Henceforth vassalage became a crucial institution of Portuguese early modern imperialism. In a number of historical circumstances and in certain regions, it was recurrently practised, and it remained significant. Beyond the 1500s and until the turn of the twentieth century, it seems vassalage constituted a ceremonial act of investiture and loyalty that was used to maintain and

[14] Patricia Seed notes that flag planting on land was probably secondary practice in early modern Portuguese possession approaches in America. These approaches, Seed argues, concerned mostly nautical precision on water. P. Seed, *Ceremonies of Possession: Europe's Conquest of the New World, 1492–1640* (Cambridge: Cambridge University Press, 1992).

[15] This vassalage system, however, was not reproduced, at least certainly not in equal degree, in the Portuguese imperial expansionism in Brazil, which began in the sixteenth century. Indigenous Amerindians were not systematically integrated into the empire through the same vassalage mechanisms described herein. I thank Nuno Gonçalo Monteiro and Pedro Cardim for this point.

[16] Saldanha, *Iustum imperium*, 446–7. On vassalage in the Portuguese empire, see also: for Sri Lanka, A. Strathern, *Kingship and Conversion in Sixteenth-Century Sri Lanka: Portuguese Imperialism in a Buddhist Land* (Cambridge: Cambridge University Press, 2007), 36–40; for Angola, B. Heintze, 'Luso-African feudalism in Angola? The vassal treaties of the 16th to the 18th century', *Revista Portuguesa de História* 18 (1980), 111–31; C. Madeira Santos, 'Escrever o poder: os autos de vassalagem e a vulgarização da escrita entre as elites africanas Ndembu', *Revista de História* (2006) 55, 81–95; for Timor, R. Roque, *Headhunting and Colonialism: Anthropology and the Circulation of Human Skulls in the Portuguese Empire, 1870–1930* (Basingtoke: Palgrave Macmillan, 2010).

[17] The material culture of such vassal–ruler affiliations (including flags, but also sceptres and clothing) is still underexplored in the historiography. But on diplomatic gifts in Eurasia (without reference to flags), see Z. Biedermann, A. Gerritsen, and G. Riello (eds.), *Global Gifts: The Material Culture of Diplomacy in Early Modern Eurasia* (Cambridge: Cambridge University Press, 2017).

even to expand the Portuguese power networks in relation to a number of distinct Indigenous polities and rulers, such as the *sobas* in central Angola, the *dessais* in the so-called New Conquests territories of Goa, and the *liurais* in East Timor.

Important to my concerns in this chapter, flags probably belonged to the ensemble of vassalage gifts presented by the king of Portugal to the subdued local sovereigns; they were disseminated to the Indigenous polities as part of the Portuguese ceremonial expansionism of vassalage. In effect, the early modern imperial formation of vassal kings presupposed the circulation of specific material culture. Vassal–ruler affiliations were produced and cemented through the active mediation of certain objects, which were presented on the occasion of vassalage ceremonies. Indigenous rulers typically swore fidelity in exchange for a set of material items that instantiated vassal status, the authority of Portugal, and subservience to the Portuguese king. The form of these actions also resulted in the granting of a petty kingship title to the vassal. In Asia, typically included in the material culture of vassalage were European artefacts, such as crowns (critical to vassalage rites of coronation); but also clothing; sceptres; swords; and Portuguese flags.[18] Since the early modern era Portuguese flags were among the royal gifts in exchange for political allegiance and obedience of African and Asian rulers to the Crown of Portugal. As such, the material set of vassalage gifts, along with the granted titles and papers, was probably expected to cement the native rulers' dependency upon the Portuguese Crown's insignia as necessary conditions for the exercise of legitimate authority; they conveyed the king's claim to supremacy over the native chiefdoms as his status subordinates, as satellite petty rulers, and as loyal servants within the king's sphere of symbolic power overseas. But vassalage rites and treaties also implied reciprocal acknowledgements, even if this reciprocity implied asymmetries. Thus, at the same time, the occasion also stood for the Portuguese king's acknowledgement and empowerment of the native authority as a ruler whose powers were somehow akin to his own.

Current historical evidence is still insufficient to ascertain whether or not flag giving entered all, or only some, Luso-African and Luso-Asian vassalage treaties and ceremonials. Perhaps flags were not always handed over to

---

[18] Current scholarship and documentation concerning these rites are scarce. But for an analysis of the material culture of the Portuguese early vassalage rites in Asia see Saldanha, *Iustum imperium*, 579–600; reference to flag giving appears at 582.

vassal kings. Yet, it is noteworthy that the action of 'taking the flag' figures prominently in one of the earliest and rarest of Portuguese royal documents that specify the procedures to be adopted in the vassalage ceremony of an Indigenous king. Thus in 1514, as in my epigraph above, King D. Manuel I of Portugal gave explicit instructions to his delegate, Fernão Dias, to make the king of Marrakech his vassal by ceremonially presenting the African ruler with a Crown's flag ('our flag') as 'signal' of the latter's condition as 'vassal and natural and loyal servant'; a flag which he would use to fulfil the 'obligations and oaths' to which he would be obliged thereafter. In addition to vassalage, moreover, flags could also come into Indigenous possession as part of war booty. In East Timor, for instance, one episode is documented in which flags were 'lost' or 'captured' as war booty in the 1700s.[19] Other circumstances might also be found in which Indigenous requests for flags were submitted to the Portuguese representatives, without formal vassalage rites being necessarily conducted. Nonetheless, even though vassalage may have lost much of its early imperial significance after the 1700s, one thing is clear: the Portuguese–Indigenous trade with flags did not wane after the early modern period.

Mutual desire for flags continued in West Central Africa and in the Timor region well into the 1900s. In central Angola, as in East Timor, Portuguese flags figured prominently in exchanges with local polities. From the 1500s until the 1890s flags were handed over customarily to the Angolan *sobas* as tokens of the Portuguese authority in vassalage ceremonies, which came also to be known in Angola by the term *undamentos*. There, vassalage treaties became critical authority tools both to African states and to the Portuguese administration.[20] In what suggests a close parallel to East Timor, then, it seems that in Angola Portuguese flags within the circuits of vassalage intervened as agents of mutual significance, both to European assertions of imperial expansionism and to African claims to Indigenous forms of rule on

---

[19] In November 1749, Andaya describes: 'A large number of Topasses beating drums and waving banners marched to Kupang, causing such terror among the Timorese that they fled with all their belongings to the shore.' The Topasses were eventually defeated and 'among the booty' taken from the Topasses 'were the prized 10 banners' that had terrified the enemies. L. Andaya, 'The "informal Portuguese empire" and the Topasses in the Solor archipelago and Timor in the seventeenth and eighteenth centuries', *Journal of Southeast Asian Studies* 41:3 (2010), 391–420, at 414.
[20] See Madeira-Santos, 'Escrever o poder'. See also A. Carvalho da Cruz, 'Sempre vassalo fiel de Sua Majestade Fidelíssima: os autos de vassalagem e as cartas patentes para autoridades locais africanas (Angola, segunda metade do século xviii)', *Cadernos de Estudos Africanos* 30 (2015), 61–80.

their own terms.[21] African rulers could adopt flags as tokens of war and kingship regalia to their own purposes. As African assets, flags could re-enter the Luso-African ceremonial circuits as African diplomatic gifts, for example, that helped forge or renew affiliations with the Portuguese king. In 1810, for instance, Adandozan, king of Dahomey – himself a declared consumer of Portuguese flags for his forts, armies, and parades – sent John VI, king of Portugal, a gift of sceptres and a specially made African 'wars flag' (*bandeira das guerras*).[22]

The above is suggestive of the extent to which, by the 1800s, Portuguese flags had become incorporated into Indigenous political formations. Many monarchic (and perhaps other) flags of Portuguese origins had been disseminated by force of military conquest, diplomatic gifts, and the vassalage system, for about 300 years. As vassalage gifts, the flag obliged, and simultaneously empowered, the Indigenous recipient to act under Portuguese authority, especially in war affairs. For the early flag-givers, the flag ideally served as actor that mediated a perpetual bond of loyalty and service to the Portuguese king. Yet, as the nineteenth century unfolded and modern ideas of nationality gained ground, Portuguese agents also came to see old and new flags differently. The flag as bond to the king was re-signified as a bond to Portugal as 'imperial nation'. In the nineteenth century, especially after the establishment of a Constitutional Monarchy in Portugal in 1820–2, the Portuguese monarchic flag was reconceptualized in nationalistic idioms, as a materialization of an abstract nationhood; beyond its connotations as a royal dynastic symbol, it became the 'national flag', a key piece of the imagination of Portugal as a national community.[23] Portugal remained a monarchy until 1910, when an armed revolution in

---

[21] 'A flag could be handed over to him [the *soba*]'. Heintze, 'Luso-African feudalism in Angola?', 120. Heintze mentions flags as vassalage gifts but does not develop the point further. Shana Melnysyn further underlines the continuing significance of Portuguese flags as customary presents to vassal Angolan *sobas* until at least the late nineteenth century; S. Melnysyn, 'Vagabond states: boundaries and belonging in Portuguese Angola, c. 1880–1910', PhD thesis, University of Michigan, 2017, 16, 48, 87. On the Portuguese and the Angolan *sobados*, see also the classic work: J.C. Miller, *Way of Death: Merchant Capitalism and the Angolan Slave Trade, 1730–1830* (Madison: University of Wisconsin Press, 1988).

[22] See M. de C. Soares, 'Entre Irmãos: as "Galanterias" do Rei Adandozan do Daomé ao Príncipe D. João de Portugal, 1810', in M. Cottias and H. Mattos (eds.), *Escravidão e subjetividades no Atlântico luso-brasileiro e francês (séculos XVII–XX)* (Marseilles: OpenEdition Press, 2016), https://books.openedition.org/oep/788. I thank Matheus Serva Pereira for this reference.

[23] See M.M. de Seixas, 'A emblemática oitocentista da Casa de Bragança nos tronos de Portugal e Brasil', in R. Ramos, J.M. de Carvalho, and I. Corrêa da Silva (eds.), *Dois países, um sistema: a monarquia constitucional dos Braganças em Portugal e no Brasil (1822–1910)* (Lisbon: D. Quixote, 2018), 57–84, at 84.

Lisbon installed a parliamentary Republican regime in the country. After, and even before, the advent of the Republic, Republican fervours raised the affection for the national flag to a true religious cult status.[24] With the Republic, the change of Portugal's flag colours from the traditional monarchic blue/white, to the new republican green/red colours, motivated heated and emotional public debate.[25] Afterwards, during the fascist *Estado Novo* regime (1933–74) the national flag concentrated further nationalist-imperialist devotion. At the same time, in many Indigenous societies where Portuguese traders, soldiers, missionaries, or mere travellers established contact with local chiefdoms on behalf of the Crown since the 1500s, the flags of Portugal had acquired ancient and singular local roots. They had a local antiquity that European nationalistic imaginaries in the late age of imperialism celebrated with emotional verve – but that they did not actually comprehend. In the island of Timor, in particular, the old monarchic flags handed over to vassal kings in the past had taken an independent cultural life, indifferent to the nationalist winds that changed collective existence in the Iberian metropole.

A Brief Island History

Timorese encounters with Europeans date back to the sixteenth century, when Portuguese traders and missionaries first visited the island, attracted there by the imagined wealth of its most famous local product, sandalwood. From Goa, the *Estado da Índia* (established in 1505), and from Malacca (conquered in 1511), the Portuguese expanded their military influence and trading networks throughout maritime Southeast Asia while confronting growing Dutch rivalry since the late 1500s. During that century Portugal's formal influence grew steadily through commerce, warfare, diplomacy, and conversion, to encompass Sri Lanka, Japan, Manila, Macau, the Philippines, and the Moluccas. Yet, alongside and beyond the purview of the Crown, a mobile population of Portuguese private traders, soldiers, missionaries, and adventurers freely crossed the waters of the archipelago. In many coastal areas, this dispersal resulted in the formation of Portuguese settlements, including of Portuguese identities, firmly rooted in local Indigenous structures through a wide variety of ties, including intermarriage and cultural

---

[24] See R. Ramos, *A segunda fundação (1890–1926)* (Lisbon: Círculo de Leitores, 1994).
[25] N.S. Teixeira, 'Do azul e branco ao verde-rubro. A simbólica da bandeira nacional', in F. Bethencourt and D.R. Curto (eds.), *A memória da Nação* (Lisbon: Livraria Sá da Costa, 1991), 319–37.

mixing.[26] This organic and informal process of settlement characterized in particular the Lesser Sunda Islands – Solor, Flores, and Timor. There, from around the early 1500s, a singularly local 'Portuguese' world, deeply entangled with the Islanders' existing systems, came into being.

Portuguese traders and soldiers based at Solor and then at Larantuka in eastern Flores gave rise to a powerful mestizo ruling and warlike class, the so-called *Topasses* (also known as 'Black Portuguese'). The Topasse lineages embraced Christianity and a Portuguese identity, and simultaneously adopted Indigenous traditions, concepts, and social norms. The Topasses dominated the early Portuguese settlements in Solor and Flores, either independently or on behalf of the Portuguese Crown, from which they received authority, titles, and honours.[27] In the 1600s the Topasses expanded their influence to the island of Timor. They settled in Lifau, from where they expanded their power by military means over most of the western part of Timor island. Meanwhile, Catholic Dominican friars followed in the wake of Topasses. The friars created ties with Topasses and successfully Christianized Timorese rulers, who saw in their alliance with the white foreigners, and with Portuguese kingship (*El-Rei*), and in their conversion to Christianity, an opportunity to increase their powers. Following the Portuguese-Topasse victory over the prestigious Indigenous realm of Wehali in 1642, Portuguese influence increased in the island. In contrast, however, elsewhere in the Asian world, the Portuguese were losing most of their strongholds to the Dutch. The Portuguese definitively lost Malacca to the Dutch in 1641, and in 1653, after a longstanding military dispute, the Portuguese stronghold of Kupang in West Timor came into Dutch hands for good.

In effect, Portuguese royal expansionism in the Sunda Islands was limited by intense competition with the Dutch as well as by the ambivalent Topasse claims to de facto overlordship in the island. War and military confrontations involving the Dutch, the Portuguese, the Topasses, and their networks of

---

[26] Compare, on the formation and dispersal of Portuguese identities and informal communities as imperial agents in this period, L. Andaya, 'The Portuguese tribe in the Malay-Indonesian Archipelago in the seventeenth and eighteenth centuries', in F. Dutra and J.C. dos Santos (eds.), *The Portuguese and the Pacific* (Santa Barbara: Center for Portuguese Studies, 1995), 129–48; S. Halikowski-Smith, 'No obvious home. The Flight of the Portuguese "tribe" from Makassar to Ayuttahaya and Cambodia during the 1660s', *International Journal of Asian Studies* 7:1 (2010), 1–28; and A.M. Hespanha, *Filhos da terra: identidades mestiças nos confins da expansão portuguesa* (Lisbon: Tinta-da-China, 2019).

[27] On the early history of Timor and Topass influence see Andaya, 'The "informal Portuguese empire" and the Topasses'; C.R. Boxer, *The Topasses of Timor* (Amsterdam: Koninklijke Vereeniging Indisch Instituut, 1947); H. Hägerdal, *Lords of the Land, Lords of the Sea: Conflict and Adaption in Early Colonial Timor, 1600–1800* (Leiden: Brill, 2012).

local allies were constant. For long, although invested by authority in the name of Portugal and using the Portuguese Crown's flag, the Topasses were unwilling to accept external orders from Goa or from Lisbon over their realm. It was only in 1701–2 that Goa was able effectively to appoint the first governor, António Coelho Guerreiro, to Lifau. In 1769, however, pressed by both Dutch and Topasses, the Portuguese governor was forced to abandon Lifau and retreat to Dili, in eastern Timor. Through contracts of vassalage with the eastern Timorese rulers, the governor established there a small but durable Portuguese stronghold. By then, however, the Portuguese position in the region had steadily deteriorated; in the Lesser Sunda Islands it had also contracted dramatically. Dutch hegemony prevailed across the archipelago; the British and French empires expanded their maritime influence and powers across the Pacific; the golden days of Portugal's Asian empire had definitively come to an end. In the 1800s Portugal's domains in Asia were reduced to Goa and Macau and to a handful of scattered settlements in Solor, Flores, Oecussi, and East Timor. In 1851, in an act seen by many as an ultimate marker of imperial decay, Solor and Flores were sold to Holland. Thereafter, based in Dili, the Portuguese laid their territorial claims over East Timor and the last refuge of the Topasses, the Oecussi enclave. The western part of the island became a Dutch-controlled territory.

Portuguese colonial authority was extended and consolidated over the late nineteenth century through a series of violent military campaigns led by the governor Celestino da Silva, a hard-line army colonel whose unique writings on flags and power will form the main case-study of this chapter. In 1912–13, the Kingdom of Manufahi and its allies led the largest and most devastating anti-Portuguese uprising in East Timor. Portuguese military victory was followed by a series of important changes in the ceremonial structure of colonial administration and its relations with Indigenous polities – including the aboli-tion of vassalage and the structure of *reinos* (kingdoms). In 1941–2 the country was invaded by Allied and then Japanese forces, and only in 1945, following the Japanese defeat, was Portuguese administration resumed. After the war the Portuguese *Estado Novo* nationalist-imperialist dictatorship invested in the 'reconstruction' of the country. It also gave former nationalistic ideologies of imperial grandeur a new impetus, and continued to claim East Timor – then renamed *Timor Português* (Portuguese Timor) – as an integral part of Portugal's national empire. Decolonization came slowly, when, after a brief bout of civil fighting in 1975, the Portuguese colonial administration abandoned the pro-vince, only to be replaced by a militarized Indonesian occupation that lasted until 1999, finally followed by a much desired national independence.

By the twentieth century, the eastern half of the island of Timor was a small and remote possession of Portugal since some 250 years; a Portuguese colony it would remain until 1975. This fragment of the golden days of the Portuguese maritime empire in Asia proved remarkably resilient to the regional changes and inter-imperial rivalries that ultimately determined the decline of Iberian supremacy in the region. Furthermore, this island's unusually long and in some ways unique colonial history offers a compelling case for exploring the lasting intercultural significance of flags as actors.

Vassalage in the Island

Portuguese flags had been distributed to the Timorese traditional jural-political lords (the so-called *liurais*, Tetum term for 'lord of the land') since the early period of Portuguese presence and until the 1910s. When vassalage was discontinued, the ancient flags continued to be preserved by the Timorese as valuable collections. The local origins of the custom are difficult to determine but it seems plausible that Portuguese flags were already widely disseminated as token of authority in association with vassalage ties in Timor in the early 1700s. By 1701, in order to keep the Timorese authorities under the government's ceremonial sphere, the first formally appointed Portuguese governor, Coelho Guerreiro, reinforced the vassalage as a state rite of investiture of Portuguese authority upon Timorese *liurais*. Guerreiro also allegedly started the practice of granting the title of kings (*reis*), the noble title of *Dom*, and high military ranks (*patentes*), to the loyal or vassal chiefs.[28] Archival evidence is fragile concerning the exact chronology of these Portuguese ceremonial activities. Yet some pieces suggest the hypothesis that the vassalage and the distribution of Portuguese insignia as tokens of power bestowed by the Portuguese Crown on Timorese vassal kings and nobles may have preceded the actions of this governor. As Governor Afonso de Castro, a keen observer of local history, wrote in 1867: 'When the temporal power [the Estado da Índia government] first sent there [Timor] its delegate [c. 1701], *he found the peoples already linked to Portugal through contracts, made vassals [avassalados] and compromised with certain obligations*'.[29] In 1645, a so-called *termo de sujeição* (letter

[28] A main historical source on Guerreiro's action (the Instructions of Count Sarzedas) seems to express some uncertainty about the chronology and originality of such actions ('isto parece que teve o seu principio no anno de 1701'); it is yet to be determined whether or not Guerreiro's initiatives implied changes in the material culture of vassalage. See 'Instrucções do Conde de Sarzedas', in A. de Castro, *As possessões portuguezas na Oceania* (Lisbon: Imprensa Nacional, 1867), 198–9; C.R. Boxer, *António Coelho Guerreiro e as relações entre Macao e Timor no começo do século xviii* (Macau: Escola Tipográfica da Imaculada Conceição de Macau, 1940), 10.
[29] My emphasis. Castro, *As possessões portuguezas na Oceânia*, 53.

464

of subjection) was celebrated between the king of Kupang (as vassal) and the king of Portugal (as sovereign). This letter reads as a vassalage treaty and it is an early record of the Portuguese empire expanding through vassal–ruler ties on the island of Timor.[30] Flags may have been part of these processes. In the 1690s, for instance, native rulers in Larantuka (Flores) were distributing Portuguese flags, apparently in order to expand their independent power, thus forging local versions of king–vassal affiliations where they played the superior king's position as donors of insignia of authority.[31]

A few other seventeenth-century war accounts provide brief glimpses of what seems already a disseminated presence of Portuguese flags in the battlefield – one sees Portuguese flags intervening in the Topasse-led wars of conquest in Timor, for instance, a kind of war agency to which I return below. In any case, it is certain that the practice of vassalage as a formal act of the governor's administration, and as a follow-up to victorious Portuguese wars, was systematically continued by Guerreiro's successors after 1701 and until the early twentieth century. Then, the nineteenth-century vassalage ceremonial and contract implied an exchange of gifts. The Timorese *liurai* swore obedience to the government while presenting the governor with buffaloes, horses, and other valuables. In exchange, the governor reciprocated to the vassal with the royal title, a military rank, a certificate attesting to the titles, and, principally, the tokens of office – the sceptre and the national flag. 'At the end' of the vassalage ceremony, Governor Celestino da Silva described in 1901 in an official letter to Lisbon, 'the 'oath certificate' [*termo de juramento*] is signed' and 'the governor hands over to the *régulo* [petty king] the sceptre and the national flag'; a shared meal with port wine and sweets follows; the governor receives 'a horse' and a tribute (*serpina*) and in return the government gives presents of 'equal value' to the enthroned Timorese 'vassal' king.[32]

This practice of vassalage investiture through the bestowment of authority-charged objects was not exclusive to the Portuguese. In effect, it seems, in the image of their European rivals, the Dutch representatives

---

[30] See Saldanha, *Iustum imperium*, 606–7.
[31] In 1692, writes historian Hans Hägerdal, the rajah of Larantuka 'tried to expand his power via Portuguese symbols, bestowing a Portuguese flag on the Watan Lema-affiliated princedom of Labala ... with unknown results'; Hägerdal, *Lords of the Land, Lords of the Sea*, 178; see also H. Hägerdal, 'Rebellions or factionalism? Timorese forms of resistance in an early colonial context, 1650–1769', *Bijdragen tot de Taal-, Land- en Volkenkunde* 163:1 (2007), 1–33, at 20.
[32] José Celestino da Silva to Minister and Secretary of Navy and Overseas Affairs, 25 January 1901. Lisbon: Arquivo Histórico Ultramarino (hereafter AHU), Macau e Timor, ACL_SEMU_DGU_1 Reparticao_002_Cx 11. 1901–4.

followed the same custom with a view to competing with the Portuguese and extending the Dutch East Indies Company's influence in the region. The distribution of Portuguese insignia (including sceptres, paper titles, and flags) to the Timorese aristocracy in the course of vassalage contracts established a set of reciprocal obligations between the outsiders and the kingdoms. These obligations were critical to ensure the Portuguese establishment the position of a kind of ceremonial centre of symbolic power – a centrality the Dutch tried to rival by following similar processes until a late period.[33] Since at least the mid-1600s, in what reads perhaps as an imitation of the Portuguese ceremonial style, the Dutch started handing over flags, drums, cloths, weapons, and sceptres (or staffs as insignia of rule, which came to be known in West Timor by the name of *tongkat*) to the local rulers.[34] Henceforth, as historian Hans Hägerdal documents, Dutch flags went through a process of indigenization homologous to the Portuguese flags, a process that was still active in the late nineteenth and early twentieth centuries. Similarly, Dutch flags would also turn into sacred ancestral heirlooms of West Timorese princedoms, a patrimony referred to by the Indonesian term, *pusaka*.[35]

The above overview reveals Portuguese flags were not a modern 'invention' of nineteenth-century imperialists in Timor. The early modern world left many and varied profound traces in both colonial and Indigenous structures – one trace of which was the resilient presence of Portuguese-origin flags. Their physical presence had roots in early modern interactions between the white Portuguese, the Dutch, the Topasses, and the Timorese *liurais* or 'kings'. These interactions resulted in a plural material world of European (Portuguese and Dutch) flags with distinct physical, graphic and visual qualities, and to which a changing complex of human meanings and practices would be attached over time. Their presence was complementary to other insignia of power, sometimes deemed of higher value, such as the sceptre. But their careful preservation over the decades and across generations, as we will see, suggests their local significance was not negligible.

I have traced the significance of flags as actors of Portuguese imperial expansionism within a wide vassalage phenomenon that ranged from West Africa to the remote Sunda Islands in the Indonesian Archipelago. The material culture of vassalage remained active and significant in late

---

[33] On Portuguese ceremonial government in Timor, see Roque, *Headhunting and Colonialism*, chapter 2.
[34] Dutch flags could be given following the local rulers' request. Hägerdal, *Lords of the Land, Lords of the Sea*, 235, 260–1, 352–3.
[35] Hägerdal, *Lords of the Land, Lords of the Sea*, 410–11, 139.

Portuguese imperial structures; it remained active and significant in Timorese societies as well. I now turn attention to some active aspects of this resilience. I discuss engagements with the 'national flag' as an actor in the late period of Portuguese colonialism in Timor. I start with a war story recounted by a Portuguese officer that suggests flags could intervene as mediators of relations of distance and respect in warfare. I then frame the story according to two nationalistic variants of a colonial metaphysics of the powers of national flags: a variant centred on the notion of 'prestige' as intangible force; and another on the idea of an invisible affective patriotism.

The Colonial Metaphysics of National Flags

In 1894, the governor of Timor, Colonel José Celestino da Silva (1849–1911), reported to his superiors, the governor of Macau and the minister of navy and overseas in Lisbon, on the difficult conditions of government in the remote district under his charge. Wars between kingdoms, and wars between the kingdoms and the Dili government were constant. Limited to a handful of European officers and soldiers, the Portuguese governor was forced to resort to Timorese irregulars (so-called *moradores*) and to Indigenous warriors (so-called *arraiais*) supplied to the government by vassal Timorese authorities, as a customary tribute of vassalage. Under these circumstances, the governor felt powerless to develop plantation agriculture, extend administration to the inland districts, and supervise trade and taxes. Above all, he saw himself as powerless to crash the threatening 'independence', he complained, of 'many of the so-called *reinos* [kingdoms] that not only do not pay any tax (the *finta*), as they do not show obedience to the government's instructions'.[36]

Imperial anxiety and vulnerability over the independency, and latent, or manifest, hostility of the Indigenous authorities was a common motif in the writings of colonial administrators. The chronic shortage of European armed forces – soldiers, officers, weaponry – made the white Portuguese in Dili vulnerable to the many power-hungry Timorese kingdoms that composed the political landscape of the colony. Nineteenth-century colonial maps usually portray East Timor as a patchwork of small *reinos* (kingdoms).

---

[36] Celestino da Silva to Governor of Macao and Timor, 1 Sept. 1894, Lisbon, AHU, Macao and Timor, ACL_SEMU_DGU_RM_003_Cx 7, 1890–1895.

In that historical period the acknowledged kingdoms numbered between forty-seven and fifty-four; and the number changed at rapid rate according to the moving state of alliances and the outcome of wars. Yet, the governor and many of his contemporaries were also aware that the Portuguese were not external to this state of affairs. To an important extent, as we have seen, the landscape of Timorese kingship polities in the 1890s had been shaped by Portuguese intervention since the sixteenth century. The authority of *liurais* as 'kings' was grounded (importantly though not exclusively) on 'vassalage', tribute ties, warfare, and insignia of power granted by the Portuguese. This system could give certain hierarchical precedence to the Portuguese. But over time, it kept the Portuguese government hostage to their vassals' tributes and recognition. By the late nineteenth century, the volatility and aggressiveness of this 'pulsating' vassal system – a kind of 'galactic polity', to use Stanley Tambiah's insightful expression, within which the Portuguese in Dili struggled to achieve centrality – had turned into a dramatic source of distress for the Portuguese.[37]

Isolated; unequipped; dependent on deceitful vassals; confined to the coastal city of Dili. Under these circumstances, Portuguese authority was without objective explanation. 'It is hard to understand how the natives still have some sort of respect for us', Governor Celestino remarked; 'because they know we have no [armed] force to compel them and that we cannot do anything against some [enemy kingdoms] without the help of others [vassal kingdoms]'.[38] He was concerned with the need to increase metropolitan officers and soldiers. But ultimately he did not perceive colonial authority as grounded on disciplined armies and apparatuses made of men, nor on solid fortresses made of stone. In fact, the same governor felt safe for distinct reasons. For he also had a clear theory of how Portuguese authority in Timor was actually maintained – a theory he expressed in his official letter in the form of a story, a moral tale, a kind of parable of colonial rule. Besides all constraints, the Portuguese in Timor had a 'force' on their side – of which they should take advantage. This force was 'prestige', a kind of immaterial quality that came especially into existence through the presence and action of a certain material object: the Portuguese national flag. It mattered little that colonial rulers were deprived of troops and surrounded by hordes of Timorese warriors. Portuguese flags made the difference.

---

[37] S. Tambiah, 'The galactic polity: the structure of traditional kingdoms in Southeast Asia', *Annals of the New York Academy of Sciences* 293 (1977), 69–97.
[38] Celestino da Silva to Governor of Macau and Timor, 1 September 1894.

The Parable of the Mighty Flag

'This admirable fact [Timorese respect for the Portuguese]', the governor explained in his letter, 'is the indisputable result of the prestige of our flag, the only one they [natives] respect, which they name *bandeira* [flag], because all other [flags] they call by the mere name of *'panno'* [cloth]'.[39] The governor's suggestion was that the Timorese Tetum term *bandera* (from the Portuguese *bandeira*) was distinctly used to name the Portuguese national flag. This selective use of the word indicated its higher place in Timorese conceptions, as compared to other European national flags. In Timor, the governor would conclude, the Portuguese empire was made possible through the intercession of a single material item: the *bandeira*. In order to persuade his readers of this extraordinary fact, the governor told a 'factual' story. The story referred to an event experienced directly by the former chief medical officer, Dr José Gomes da Silva (1853–1905), at an unknown date, but in recent years.[40] The governor narrated thus:

> Not long ago, Dr Gomes da Silva, head of the provincial Health Services, was in this colony and found himself in one of the south coast districts at the moment when the commander had put a native *maioral* [noble] under arrest for disobedience; in the garrison were only Dr Gomes da Silva, the officer, one soldier, and the prisoner; a great number of natives put the garrison under siege with a view to set the prisoner free, but seeing our flag, they sent an emissary requesting us to lower the flag, because otherwise they could not attack; it is obvious that the flag was not lowered, and it is certain that the attack did not occur.
>
> Nothing is truer than this, nothing is more signifying.
>
> Under these circumstances we just have to regret that we do not take useful advantage of the prestige that our flag has here, and that we do not put in the shadow of the flag officers who care for the observance of the government's commands and incite the natives to work, here a source of wealth that is far from having been properly explored.

Thus in this vivid episode, the flag of Portugal was alone capable of bringing on 'admirable' changes in the otherwise unequal balance of forces between the small Portuguese establishment in Dili and the numerous Timorese kingdoms. The governor wrote about a national flag that shifted the course of events in colonial relationships, by means of the distance effects that it brought

---

[39] Celestino da Silva to Governor of Macau and Timor, 1 September 1894.
[40] José Gomes da Silva served as medical doctor in Timor between 1881 and 1894. His published writings do not mention this episode.

into existence. In that it elicited in the Timorese attackers gestures of avoidance and 'respect', the hoisted flag made possible a differential of power that was advantageous to the colonizers inside the fort. 'Respected', the flag inverted relations of force; it transformed a vulnerable garrison into an unconquerable fortress; it turned threatening hordes of warriors into docile natives. As above noted, in late nineteenth-century Portugal (as elsewhere in Europe), the national flag had become a critical symbol for imagining Portugal as a national community of imperialist ambitions. However, it was not as a symbol that the Portuguese flag was evoked in the governor's narrative – but as an actor. This was a performative story of agency, in which national flags behave as 'mediators': '*any thing* that modifies a state of affairs by making a difference', suggested Bruno Latour, 'is an actor', or a 'mediator'.[41]

In Timor, this capacity of flags to act as mediators of distance and protection was put to its most dramatic test in the battlefield. The 1890s were marked by violent punitive campaigns led by the same governor. In this extremely bellicose context the account compared to references made by other contemporary Portuguese officers to the aura of sacredness with which the Timorese seemed to surround the Portuguese flag during actual battles. In 1896, for instance, Captain Francisco Elvaim reported that the Timorese irregulars under his command left the dead and wounded to rest 'under the shadow of the flag', believing the flag's shadow would alone protect their companions from being attacked and decapitated by their enemies.[42] Rather than symbols, flags were presented in these nineteenth-century accounts as actors that could interfere with, and potentially transform, power imbalances, especially in warfare. Earlier evidence of flags (alongside drums) called to play the role of war actors in Portuguese or Topasse armies may be discerned in a few eighteenth-century documents. In 1788, for instance, the kings of Senobai and Amanaban and their neighbours asked the Portuguese governor Vieira Godinho for military support in the form of 'guns, powers, bullets and flags of Portugal, [and they were] given upon request;' and in 1779–82, virtually unarmed parties of Timorese 'rebels' reportedly marched against the Portuguese forces holding simply flags and Catholic items.[43]

---

[41] Emphasis in the original. B. Latour, *Reassembling the Social: An Introduction to Actor-Network Theory* (Oxford: Oxford University Press, 2005), 71.

[42] F. Elvaim, 'Relatório', in J.C. da Silva, *Relatório das operações de guerra no Districto Autónomo de Timor no anno de 1896* (Lisbon: Imprensa Nacional, 1897), 50–67, at 139.

[43] Cited in F. Figueiredo, 'Timor. A presença portuguesa (1769–1945)', PhD thesis, University of Porto, 2004, 124; see also 125.

The governor and his contemporaries may have been unaware of the deeper historical echoes of the events they experienced in the 1890s. Informed by nationalistic imageries, they also did not make an effort to interpret such events in Timorese cultural terms. In the 1890s the governor's concern with storytelling was allegorical rather than historiographical. The tale served a moral purpose; it acted as a parable of colonial rule. Thus, the governor's moral story implied, if left in the hands of a few white people the Portuguese empire in Timor would die; but if human colonizers relied on the action of a particular material object – the national flag – the empire would prosper. Remarkable in this colonial parable is also the acknowledged fact that the Portuguese flag in colonial Timor held more than just European value; it held an extra Indigenous significance too. The providential flag that helped the miserable garrison was not simply a Portuguese possession; it was a Timorese possession as well, something with which the Timorese warriors appeared to establish a special relationship that could not be broken. It was if the colonial officer suggested the flag only made a convenient colonialist difference on condition of being an integral part of a world that cut across the colonial divide. The story thus referred to an agency that came into being because the object that made the difference was of mutual significance, and only such shared significance could put the flag into a position of admirable arbitrator of Portuguese prestige, distance, and respect.

By telling his compatriots at Lisbon a story about the valour of Portuguese flags in Portugal's most distant colony, the governor satisfied the prevailing European imageries of national flags and the imperialist fantasies of power over 'primitive' and 'superstitious' natives. Through the lens of patriotic ideologies, then, the Portuguese saw reflected in Timorese behaviours the coeval significance that the Europeans at home attributed to flags as active entities in the fabrication of 'nations' and 'empires'. For it was the nineteenth-century Portuguese storyteller first of all who endowed flags with a potency beyond the objects-in-themselves. Nevertheless, fantastic as they might seem, such colonial stories of flags are to be counted as real. In many instances, they speak about events that really happened; events to which we gain access in the archives through written accounts embedded in colonial animistic imaginaries about flags as agencies of national imperial power. In addition, though distorted, accounts such as Celestino da Silva's also speak to the existence of parallel Indigenous conceptions of flags. Finally they point to a complex common ground that enabled different Portuguese and Timorese flag animisms, as it were, to coexist and prosper.

To begin, the governor's fantastic account is suggestive of a twofold flag-centred metaphysics of the Portuguese empire in Timor. First, it reveals a colonial understanding of flags as agents animated by metaphysical qualities that caused the Portuguese empire to exist in Timor. This colonial theory of flags as imperial agents is entailed in the governor's interpretation that the relations of distance that protected the fortress were a factual instantiation of an intangible Portuguese power that caused Timorese deference – an active potency of 'prestige' immanent in the flag, acknowledged as such by the Indigenous. Second, it suggests an interconnected, though analytically distinct, idea of flags as imperial agents that instantiated affects and sentiments of patriotism. Here, less than carriers of a prestige-potency, flags were addressed as agents of metaphysical qualities of affective patriotism. This latter view would dominate Portuguese writings on Timorese flag cults in the twentieth century. It supposed the Portuguese and the Timorese formed a common 'nation' by force of common feelings of attachment to the national flag. Here, it was as if shared patriotic affect towards the object-flag made a national society under Portuguese hegemony possible.

'Prestige'

According to the governor's parable of colonial rule, national flags were almighty things, capable of an extraordinary feat. By inducing the Timorese Islanders to show 'respect' and keep distance, they could transfigure Portuguese colonialism from weak into strong. This governor's parable expressed a wider theory of the religious intangibility of Portuguese colonial power manifested tangibly in the national flag. It was in line with a pervasive nineteenth-century imaginary of Portuguese domination in Timor as grounded upon spiritual forces and, specifically, on the existence of a so-called Timorese 'religion' or 'cult' centred on the Portuguese flag.

Timorese 'respect towards the Portuguese', the same governor wrote in 1897, 'is with rare exceptions a kind of religion'.[44] 'Portuguese domination', another officer explained in 1903, resulted from a 'moral force'; from 'respect' showed by Timorese for 'the prestige of Portuguese name' and – above all – the Portuguese flag.[45] 'The Portuguese establishment in Timor', governor Afonso de Castro remarked in 1864, is 'benevolently and solidly established' because it is grounded on 'unanimous consent'; because, he continued, 'the sovereignty of Portugal became for all people a sacred thing; respect for the

---

[44] Silva, *Relatório das operações de guerra*, 38.
[45] R. das Dores, 'Apontamentos para um diccionario chorographico de Timor', *Boletim da Sociedade de Geografia de Lisboa* 7:12 (1903), 763–826, at 766.

Portuguese flag is a religious feeling, the love for Portugal is a cult and a necessity'.[46] In this view, the flag's capacity to transform and sustain the colonial empire derived from a metaphysical quality that the object itself seemed to possess and enact. This almost religious power was described as 'prestige': an invisible force that seemed to emanate from certain Portuguese bodies and materials in their interactions with Timorese people, and through the filter of Timorese conceptions. This 'force' was discernible in the relations of awe and distance – relations conveyed by the governor's term 'respect' – that the Timorese established especially with flags. Hence empire was conceived of as enmeshed in a spiritual, religious, or metaphysical potency (designated 'prestige') that ultimately materialized in, and was activated by, one kind of object-agent: the flag; or, more specifically, each one of the many national flags that had circulated in Timor since ancient times. Therefore, the flag was the tangible actor through which the immateriality of colonial rule was believed to intervene in the Indigenous world, to Portuguese advantage.

Portuguese accounts of flags as agents of 'prestige' seem to express a kind of colonial animism of the flag that, in some ways, as we shall see, may have been growing locally over time, in connection with and/or parallel to Timorese conceptions of *lulik* powers. Conversely, *lulik* conceptions may have gained force from the fact that successive Portuguese officers in Timor treated flags as if possessed by extraordinary and intangible special qualities. This is in line with Chris Shepherd's argument that Timorese 'animism changed through the colonial encounter'.[47] Yet, this argument can be extended to the Portuguese nationalistic animisms of flags as imperial agents. For, as much as Timorese animism changed, Portuguese colonial animism also changed and gained new force through its encounter with Timorese notions and practices. Interactions, such as the one narrated by Governor Celestino da Silva in 1894, may have mutually reinforced, and mutually transformed, colonial and Indigenous forms of flag animism. Flag-raising ceremonies, martial parades of Timorese irregulars (so-called *moradores*), and the ritual display of ancient Portuguese flags by the Timorese *liurais* and nobles on the occasion of the Portuguese officers' or governors' visits to

---

[46] My translation. A. de Castro, 'Une rébellion à Timor en 1861', *Tijdschrift voor Indische Taal-, Land- en Volkenkunde* 13 (1864), 389–409, at 391.
[47] Shepherd's original argument also elaborates upon my earlier work. C.J. Shepherd, *Haunted Houses and Ghostly Encounters: Ethnography and Animism in East Timor, 1860–1975* (Singapore: NUS Press, 2019), 41.

villages, reiterated in the colonial observers the impression of the superior importance of flags, since at least the mid-nineteenth century.[48]

Colonial readings of animistic potencies in these public events tend to change throughout the twentieth century. They shift focus from notions of a religious prestige to ideas of an affective patriotism, with growing emphasis on Timorese subordination to Portuguese patriotism. The idea of a Timorese religion gives way to the notion of an indigenous version of Portuguese nationalism. From the 1920s–1930s until at least the 1970s, the Timorese indigenization of flags is thus dominantly portrayed as a patriotic cult that spontaneously integrates the Timorese into the Portuguese nation.

Patriotism

Flag-raising occasions and parades of Timorese *moradores* displaying their ancient *lulik* and war flags before the colonial authorities were then framed as the ultimate demonstration of indigenous patriotic rites. The flags here allegedly mediated sentiments and affects that united the Timorese to the metropolitan Portuguese. Thus emotional colonizers felt as if an invisible flow of common affectivity held together 'the natives' and 'the Portuguese' as one and the same spiritual community of national grandeur. Colonel Leite de Magalhães, a colonial army officer in Timor in 1908–12, described this vividly in a text of 1937. He celebrated his virtually religious experience of shared patriotism with the Timorese, during the raising of the flag in Timor:

> As a Portuguese, I could only be intensely commoved – yes! – when, for the first time, on the side of stiff and half-naked natives, I attended to the hoisting of a flag coloured with the national arms of Portugal, proudly raising up to the sky, blown by the wind and kissed by the sunlight, as if crying out to the ears of human perfidy, in a hosanna of glory: – It is here at the end of the world that the Empire of Portugal stops![49]

In the 1930s–1940s, the *Estado Novo* regime stimulated ideologies of imperial nationalism and paved the way for a pervasive imagery of Timorese patriotic flag cults as evidence of Portuguese colonial exceptionalism. During World War II, East Timor suffered Japanese military occupation. Stories of Timorese sacrifices for their old *lulik* flags during this period were

---

[48] See R. Roque, 'The colonial command of ceremonial language: etiquette and custom-imitation in nineteenth century East Timor', in L. Jarnagin (ed.), *Culture and Identity in the Luso-Asian World: Tenacities and Plasticities* (Singapore: ISEAS, 2012), 67–87.

[49] A.L. de Magalhães, 'Timor, a desventurada', *O Mundo Português* 45:4 (1937), 391–5, at 395.

disseminated widely by the regime, as revelations of indigenous patriotism and spiritual subordination to Portugal. Timorese deference to the flag then achieved exponential visibility and diffusion in popular imagination and propaganda. Literature, cinema, photography, and varied imagery, often sponsored by the regime, presented Timorese 'devotion' to the flag as proof of the Portuguese unique type of colonization – mild, spiritual, and benign. It stood for the uniqueness and non-violent nature of Portuguese colonization as single-handedly capable of awakening 'spontaneous' patriotism in the hearts of the so-called primitive *indigenas*. Even after the demise of Portuguese rule, such fantasies reverberate in post-colonial understandings of flag cults as markers of *lusophone* affective identity and community. In 1994, for example, historian Luis Filipe Thomaz (also a former colonial officer in Timor in the 1970s) echoed such nationalist fantasies in suggesting the Timorese 'cult of the flag' expressed Timorese integration into a wider 'lusophone civilization'.[50] With the end of Indonesian occupation in 1999 and even today, ideas of an affect-based post-colonial lusophone community between Portugal and Timor continue to be fed by stories and images of the Timorese attachment to olden Portuguese flags.

Reframing the Timorese 'Flag Cult'

Framed by imaginaries of 'prestige' and 'patriotism' the above accounts misunderstood Timorese actions and conceptions as if determined by and orientated towards the national symbolism supposedly contained in Portuguese flags. In many Timorese eyes, as it were, flags are unlikely to have been national emblems in that sense. To begin, the kind of indigenous 'societies' attached to those flags that become endowed with *lulik* qualities were not 'nations'.[51] As Timorese possessions, instead, Portuguese flags helped to activate a distinct kind of social group: Timorese descent groups or 'houses'. Additionally, perhaps, in the Portuguese colonial period, they helped to activate 'kingdoms' as well. Paradoxically, flags could only realize colonial nationalist-imperialist fantasies through the filter of Timorese self-interested actions and conceptions about 'flags' that, I argue, aimed primarily at selfishly producing power and authority for specific lineages and descent groups.

---

[50] Thomaz, *De Ceuta a Timor*, 652.
[51] The literature is extensive but see, for example, J.J. Fox (ed.), *The Flow of Life: Essays on Eastern Indonesia* (Cambridge, MA: Harvard University Press, 1980).

Portuguese flags (often in connection with drums) did figure prominently in East Timorese origin-myths in the late colonial period, and were of critical significance to many descent groups in the region.[52] Among the Mambai in the 1970s, as Elizabeth G. Traube revealed, the Portuguese national flag was the object of mythic narratives about worldly powers that originated outside of the realm and in the wild and mysterious sea. The flag, Traube then recorded, was the mythic token of jural power brought by the 'outsider' ancestors, the Portuguese, for bringing order and exercising rule over worldly affairs, and thereafter passed on to the indigenous delegates of jural power for sustaining order in the kingdoms. 'In mythological tradition', writes Traube, '[the sea] is the source of a strange, new, and "heavy" law, embodied in the Portuguese flag.'[53] Hence, by the end of the Portuguese colonial period, the long-standing circulation of national flags by the European strangers could appear already integrated into cosmology. Then, flags, on account of their condition as outsider objects of ocean-origin, had turned into sources of autochthonous forms of sovereignty.

In this vein, my intention now is to reassess the colonial metaphysics of flags in the light of Timorese conceptions. In the Timorese world, Portuguese flags became possessed as *lulik* ancestral heirlooms and/or as *rota* tokens of authority. As such, they were meant to bring about ancestral links without which indigenous groupings could not exist; at the same time, they helped to sustain the noble houses' claims for status distinction and political authority – including, importantly, the claims of *liurais* as kings at the head of kingdoms. Moreover, as we shall see, by analysing these conceptions we can reframe from a Timorese perspective the fantastic story told above by Governor Celestino da Silva. By crossing the archival registers and the ethnographic record, one may be able to reinterpret the colonial story in the light of parallel indigenous constructs of flag agencies that implied relations of distance to be made manifest.

Banderas, Lulik Agencies and *Rota* Authority

In East Timor, the traditional elementary social unit was the house and its defining element was claim to common ancestry. Attachment to a common patrimony of material objects deemed to have been inherited from the

---

[52] E.G. Traube, *Cosmology and Social Life: Ritual Exchange among the Mambai of East Timor* (Chicago: University of Chicago Press, 1986).
[53] Traube, *Cosmology and Social Life*, 234.

ancestors was critical to define house membership and social standing. This ancestral heirloom was considered *luli* or *lulik* (Tetum term for sacred or prohibited, more below on this term) and was kept separately from other valuables inside the ritual house of each descent group, the *uma lulik*.[54] The Tetum term *lulik* was widely used in East Timor with reference to people, landscape, and also objects, and conveyed a double meaning of 'prohibition' and 'sacredness'. In the Portuguese colonial period, and still today, *lulik* was also applied to inherited ancestral objects without which the unity and the rank of every type of Timorese collective unit – whether at the level of clans, of houses, of communities, or even of kingdoms – could not be maintained. Although some objects may typically be identical to all houses within one community, the significance of other objects relied on their capacity to *differentiate* and hierarchize houses between themselves – flags possibly being one example of items that contributed to the latter function. Ancestral *lulik* heirlooms created status, political authority, and a sense of nobility. They helped create what sociologist Pierre Bourdieu would call a sense of *distinction*.[55] In particular, the possession of ancestral *lulik* collections of objects as insignia of office was the basis upon which the status of noble and royal houses, as well as their claims to legitimate authority, were displayed and exercised – especially during the colonial period.

Flags and Kingdoms

In fact, it was as *lulik* ancestral heirlooms of some descent groups that national flags had apparently turned into a Timorese possession. They were objects around which ancestry and status could be arranged. Various colonial accounts emphasize the presence of flags as sacred objects in the cult houses of *reinos* (kingdoms) and the fact that they were especially prized for their antiquity, as inheritance from the ancestors. In particular, flags were enshrined in the *uma luliks* of the royal or noble lineages whose members, at some point in the historical past, had established a vassal–ruler affiliation with the Portuguese government. Inside the cult houses, *lulik* flags came to be perceived not as a stranger object of colonial domination or national identity but as an indigenized Timorese possession related to ancestral kin – even if the ancestors were imagined as 'Portuguese' from overseas. As such, they were objects around which genetic linkages and differences of ancestry

---

[54] D. Hicks, *Tetum Ghosts and Kin: Fertility and Gender in East Timor*, 2nd edn (Long Grove: Waveland Press, 2004), 26.
[55] P. Bourdieu, *La distinction* (Paris: Minuit, 1979).

RICARDO ROQUE

and status could be arranged. In the 1890s, flags were widely disseminated in East Timorese *lulik* ancestral collections, especially in the houses of descent groups that claimed royalty, nobility and *liurai* authority, or who, at some point in the historical past, had possibly established a vassal–ruler affiliation with the Portuguese government. Uniforms, flags, sceptres, paper certificates of honour and titles, and other materials of European make (such as flintlock guns) received by former holders of royal or noble office could qualify as *lulik* heirlooms of lineages and kingdoms. In 1891, for instance, Lieutenant Acácio Flores, who served under Governor Celestino da Silva, defined *uma lulik* as: 'House where they keep the flag and all the objects that the kingdom possesses as sacred and where the *estylos* [rites] are performed.'[56] 'Every kingdom', another colonial officer claimed in 1883, possessed Portuguese flags with 'great veneration'.[57] Nationalist obsession possibly prevented colonial observers from looking at these heirlooms beyond the fixation on flags alone. In fact, the latter were related to other Timorese heirlooms in *lulik* collections according to Timorese dualisms of power (and often, moreover, flags were not the most crucial sacred objects). In any case, although they tended to fail to see flags in Timorese terms, various colonial accounts emphasized the presence of flags inside the cult houses of most Timorese kingdoms, and the fact that they were prized as a sacred and potent legacy from the ancestors.

This repossessing of flags as agencies of ancestry, sovereignty, and rank of indigenous lineages and kingdoms helps to explain why old flags (and other insignia) were removed temporarily from the *lulik* houses to be exhibited to Portuguese authorities in the nineteenth and twentieth centuries (see Figure 50.1[58]). Then, *lulik* flags and other insignia were ritually presented to assert the high authority and status of the *liurais* as kings before the Portuguese presence. Such actions were ceremonial occasions in their own right; ceremonial demonstrations of allegiance – and simultaneously manifestations of Timorese independent sovereignty. Therefore, as *lulik* ancestral heirlooms

---

[56] A.F. [Acácio Flores], *Uma guerra no districto de Timor* (Macau: Typographia Commercial, [1891]), 30. See also J. dos Santos Vaquinhas, 'Timor. Usos – superstições de guerra', *Boletim da Sociedade de Geografia de Lisboa* 4 série, 8 (1884), 476–92, at 488; A.P. Correia, *Gentio de Timor* (Lisbon: Lucas & Ca., 1935), 59.

[57] J. dos Santos Vaquinhas, 'Timor. I', *Boletim da Sociedade de Geografia de Lisboa* 4 série, 7 (1883), 307–28, at 328.

[58] This ancestral flag was named *bandera monarkia* and it was (and still is) considered to be *rota*. See R. Roque and L. Sousa, 'The stones of Afaloicai: colonial archaeology and the authority of ancient objects', in R. Roque and E.G. Traube (eds.), *Crossing Histories and Ethnographies: Following Colonial Historicities in Timor-Leste* (Oxford: Berghahn, 2019), 203–38, for a detailed analysis of the contemporary resonances of this episode as an instance of demonstration to Portuguese officials of high status and a kind of Timorese Indigenous sovereignty.

Figure 50.1 Exhibition of a deteriorated ancient *lulik* monarchic flag by ritual keepers from the sacred houses of Afaloicai to Portuguese colonial authorities in 1957. Photographer Victor Santa. IICT Photography Collection. ULisboa-IICT-MAT26678. Courtesy of Museu Nacional de História Natural e da Ciência, Lisbon.

and/or as *rota* tokens of authority, Portuguese flags were meant to bring about ancestral links without which indigenous groupings could not exist; at the same time, they helped to sustain the noble houses' claims for status distinction, sovereignty, and political authority – including, importantly, the kingship claims of *liurais* as heads of 'kingdoms' on behalf of the king of Portugal.

In the past, as we have seen, flags were distributed to Timorese vassals as a way of expressing subordination to the Portuguese Crown, the King, or the Portuguese nation and empowering indigenous *liurais* as vassal kings to exercise authority in their own domains. But flags and vassals proliferated in a diffuse political landscape of competing indigenous kingdoms and kings. By the time Celestino da Silva narrated his fantastic story, however, this world of flags and vassals had taken a dynamic of its own.

The Indigenous Desire for Outsider Flags

Since their introduction in the 1500s, Portuguese-origin flags were captured by the Timorese appetite for foreign objects as indigenized agents and insignia of power and status. The creation and circulation of sceptres and Portuguese flags became embedded in Timorese disputes between elite lineages for superiority and independent ritual-political authority and centrality. Such disputes often concerned complex local ties of allegiance and opposition between minor and major 'kingdoms' that sometimes had less to do with the Portuguese colonizers than with alternative regional claims for hegemonic ritual and political centrality. In effect, over time, the regular flow of Portuguese flags became critical to the competing claims of Timorese aristocratic houses, allowing the latter to fashion themselves as persons of rank and holders of authority over worldly affairs in their communities. 'The *régulos*, *datós* and *principais* use very pompous names', explained an official in 1897, 'and they are very proud of their ranks (*patentes*): they talk a lot about the King of Portugal and one cannot give them a better present than a national flag.'[59] Portuguese flags added to the Timorese dynamic of status distinction and authority building by means of the accumulation and display of *lulik* objects. Instead of unity, the circulation of Portuguese flags multiplied the Timorese lineages' voracious desire for distinction and social distance. It was a centrifugal force of which the Portuguese had long lost control.

This situation, as I observed at the beginning of this chapter, is not exceptional to Timor, or even to the wider Portuguese empire. Comparative historical cases abound of European flags, bibles, and other objects made iconic for indigenous reasons in other imperial histories – in particular as extensions of autonomous indigenous sovereignty.[60] Moreover, the East Timorese Islanders'

---

[59] B. da França, *Macau e os seus habitantes: relações entre Macau e Timor* (Lisbon: Imprensa Nacional, 1897), 235.

[60] 'A phial of oil, a code of laws, a Bible, a crown, and a sceptre', Greg Dening wrote about the investiture ceremonies of the Tahitian king Pomare III in which the British participated in the 1820s; 'these were the sacred things that made Pomare III king; they were the cargo that made him "king". These were the cultural artefacts of the strangers from across the beach ... the personifications of his "kingdom" and the extensions of his sovereignty.' Dening, *Mr. Bligh's Bad Language*, 237.

interest in possessing Portuguese flags was part of a wider stranger–kingship pattern of formation of political authority from outsider sources.

Indigenous interest in absorbing foreign power through possession of foreign objects anteceded European arrival and, as Janet Hoskins observed, was reflected in the potency attributed to regalia of office; throughout maritime Southeast Asia a variety of imported objects became inextricably entangled with local claims to rule.[61] While such evidence suggests the category of regalia of rule originally encompassed a wide array of objects associated with sovereignty, the Europeans' practice of distribution of sceptres and flags interfered with existing structures and may have partly displaced former traditional heirlooms with new symbols. Portuguese strategies of ceremonial power and vassalage also became meaningful within these indigenous conceptions. In fact, it was in this context that Portuguese flags may have been re-signified in at least some East Timorese kingdoms as *rota*, a Timorese concept that eventually accompanied the classification and storage of national flags as *lulik* ancestral heirlooms.[62] *Rotas* were foundational tokens of superior (especially, but not exclusively) sociopolitical authority in the Timorese realms during the colonial period. As such, flags were inseparable from other heirlooms (e.g. stones) that typically stood for ritual or spiritual authority. They were understood in accordance with indigenous diarchic theories of power and authority (often disregarded by colonial writers) that positioned old *banderas* as tokens of sociopolitical authority that could, or could not, have a Portuguese origin. In fact, in some instances, flags bearing the Portuguese coat of arms were not perceived as bestowments from the Portuguese government in the past. Over time, they could acquire distinct significance as ancestral heirlooms from different origins. Moreover, some Timorese polities, in seeking to assert their powers as parallel or alternative to the Portuguese in Dili, could also put flags in circulation as *rota* tokens of authority. Flags were strategic to creating alternative power sources and symbolic centres that could compete with the processes adopted by the foreigners, by the Portuguese as well as the Dutch.

---

[61] J. Hoskins, *The Play of Time: Kodi Perspectives on Calendars, History and Exchange* (Berkeley: University of California Press, 1997). See also E.G. Traube, 'Outside-in: Mambai expectations of returning outsiders', in R. Roque and E.G. Traube (eds.), *Crossing Histories and Ethnographies: Following Colonial Historicities in Timor-Leste* (Oxford: Berghahn Books, 2019), 49–75.

[62] Compare J. Gunter, 'Kabita-Kakurai, de cada dia: indigenous hierarchies and the Portuguese in Timor', *Portuguese Literary and Cultural Studies* 17/18 (2010), 281–301; Roque, *Headhunting and Colonialism*, 44; Roque and Sousa, 'The stones of Afaloicai', 203–40.

A Multitude of Indigenized Flags

Twentieth-century Portuguese observers often realized that the Timorese were especially attached not to flags as an abstract sign, but to specific and concrete physical flags – usually the old and sometimes physically deteriorated flags that had belonged to their lineage ancestors. As observed above, a plurality of Portuguese-origin flags – the different flags representing the Portuguese monarchy but also a variety of other flags used in naval affairs and in warfare – had been used by Portuguese agents in their dealings with African and Asian societies since the 1500s. By the early twentieth century, this plural world of flags with different patterns and formats (some of them out of date in European usages) surprised the colonizers. Many colonial observers wondered why the Timorese still exhibited with great pomp the old monarchic flags from one or two centuries ago, while expressing lesser consideration for the Portuguese Republican flag or even to any other that was not part of their ancestral belongings.[63] In effect, a supposed Timorese predilection for monarchic flags was one of the reasons put forward by some Portuguese observers in their attempts to explain the great anti-Portuguese Manufahi revolt of 1912, which followed the replacement of the blue/white monarchic flag by the red/green Republican flag of Portugal, in 1911.[64]

Yet the colonizers' self-centred nationalistic obsession could overlook the fact that some Timorese lineages were not so interested in Portuguese national flags as such; they could also safeguard as *lulik* a variety of other old flags of outsider origin. Dutch national flags, for example, could appear in the *lulik* heritage of certain houses and kingdoms in East Timor. This was the case especially in the kingdoms whose traditional holders of office once paid obedience to the Dutch government. In 1897, perhaps aware of this circumstance, Governor Celestino suggested the Timorese aura of 'respect' for the Portuguese flag 'excludes the kingdoms near the Dutch border'.[65] Maubara, a kingdom that only became a formal Portuguese domain after a Luso-Dutch diplomatic agreement in the late 1850s, still preserved *lulik* Dutch flags and displayed them proudly to the Portuguese authorities until at least 1909.[66] Changes in the *régulos'* colours – especially in replacing Dutch with Portuguese – could occur coercively in the course of the 1890s. Defeated

---

[63] See Correia, *Gentio de Timor*, 59.   [64] See J. Inso, *Timor – 1912* (Lisbon: Cosmos, 1939).
[65] Silva, *Relatório das operações de guerra*, 38.
[66] At Maubara, complex ceremonials of change of Dutch for Portuguese flags occurred, involving Timorese nobles; see D. Kammen, *Three Centuries of Conflict in East Timor* (New Brunswick: Rutgers University Press, 2015), 57–9. A.O. de Castro, *A ilha verde e vermelha de Timor* (Lisbon: Cotovia, 1996 [1943]), 48.

Timorese Islanders and the Portuguese Empire

by the armies of Governor Celestino, Timorese authorities who hoisted Dutch flags in wars against the Portuguese government had to pay vassalage to Portugal, receiving new Portuguese flags, and eventually giving up the old ones.[67]

The consequences of the century-old practice of diffusing European flags throughout the Timorese world were manifold – and on no account always convenient for the colonial government. For the same kinds of objects that were supposed to instantiate symbolic dependence on Portuguese authority could also serve to empower autonomous political authority against the colonial government. Whether or not 'Portuguese' in origin, ancient flags associated with (real or imagined) outsider origin could become a potent object in the arrangement of ancestry, social hierarchy, and power. In order to establish an alternative source of outsider power that countered the Portuguese, the Dutch, as observed above, had followed a strategy of sceptres and flags gifting that mirrored the Portuguese actions, since some-time in the 1600s. Perhaps Timorese rulers themselves could also copy and usurp the same method to their own purposes; they could start chains of vassal–ruler affiliation, acting as givers of Portuguese-like insignia of power to subordinate Timorese realms. Hence some Timorese rulers could repli-cate sceptres (wooden staffs), military ranks, and other Portuguese-origin tokens of status and authority (including perhaps the flag) for the sake of producing ancestry and authority differences, which lay beyond Portuguese colonial control.[68]

Portuguese and Dutch practices of circulating miscellaneous flags since the early modern period were thus further augmented and multiplied by certain Indigenous mimetic practices. This resulted in a multitude of Portuguese and other flags, bearing many distinct patterns, and the sight of which could puzzle late colonial observers. In 1883, Major José dos Santos Vaquinhas took note of such proliferation of flags. He described a number of distinct flags possessed by East Timorese kings as *lulik*, but whose designs exceeded the monarchic and national heraldic:

> At Diribate I saw that the flag was white, with the red royal arms in the centre; at Ossuquele I noticed they used the imperial flag of Portugal and

---

[67] Flores, *Uma guerra no districto de Timor*, 36–7.
[68] Janet Gunter's fieldwork in the Baguia and Viqueque regions, for instance, suggested that, especially prior to the 1920s–30s, 'the "legitimacy" of [the Indigenous] hierarchies was located in a mimetic appropriation of what were believed to be Portuguese symbols', the monarchic flag, military ranks, and – in particular – the sceptres (wooden staffs); Gunter, 'Kabita-Kakurai', 282.

483

Brazil; at Reimean a white flag with a black cross close to the staff and the royal arms in the centre; Ossuala has one with green squares with an allegoric figure of wings in the centre and a small black cross close to the staff.[69]

Eventually, at Diribate, Vaquinhas saw the ancient Portuguese Crown flag, used between c. 1640 and 1816; at Ossuquele, he saw the flag created to represent the United Kingdom of Portugal, Brazil, and the Algarves, and used between 1815 and 1822. However, at Reimean and Ossuala, the officer witnessed the Timorese use of (possibly) two Portuguese naval flags (not the royal flag): the first bearing the royal arms in connection with a black cross; and the second combining a set of colours and figures that may, or may not, have been used by Portuguese ships in the region.[70] Thus it seems Vaquinhas had before him a variety of outsider-origin flags, most likely Portuguese, but not all of which were necessarily associated with the Portuguese Crown and less so the nation. Hence flags that became *lulik* could embody a plurality of insignias and patterns that exceeded national symbolism or even the symbolism of the Portuguese Crown. As Timorese possessions, rather than signifying the expansion of colonial authority, let alone of Portuguese national identity, such flags enabled indigenous kin and linkage to common indigenous ancestry to become manifest; at the same time they authorized the members of certain houses to exercise power as legitimate holders of status and authority. A crucial characteristic of *lulik* collections of flags in the past, therefore, was their potential to orchestrate social and political differences and hierarchies.

The Lulik *Agency of Flags*

This sociological potential was further enhanced by Timorese procedures and concepts that endowed such *lulik* flags with special potencies, with a specific capacity to act in the world. Classified as *lulik*, flags were treated by their indigenous holders as actors that possessed spiritual forces that could make a real difference in the world of the living. The Timorese notion of *lulik* as a realm of the sacred contains considerable complexity. It implies an indigenous ontology of flags as agencies that stand ambivalently between the human, or living, and the non-human or spiritual worlds. '*Lulik* has agency: it can be angry or hungry and even "jump away"', anthropologist

---

[69] Vaquinhas, 'Timor. I', 328.
[70] I am grateful to Miguel Metelo de Seixas for this interpretation of Vaquinhas's passage.

Judith Bovensiepen observed, and, like Polynesian *mana*, it 'inspires reverence and awe, but also intense fear and anxiety'.[71] The management of distance and proximity to *lulik* is key to the reproduction of power relations and to the establishment of authority by some groups over others. In this regard, a crucial characteristic of *lulik* flags was their potential to orchestrate power differentials through actual, physical, relations of distance and respect. According to Traube, *lulik* potency is above all relational. What defines something as *lulik* is a 'relation of distance' of varying degrees of respect. 'An object that is called *luli* [*sic*] possesses no inherent quality or intrinsic force', Traube insightfully observed. 'In all its contexts, *luli* signifies a *relation of distance*, a boundary between things, created out of gestures of avoidance. This structural relation subsumes a set of disparate attitudes which range from mild respect to awe.'[72]

Thus incorporated into *lulik* collections, Portuguese flags were cared for as active group members of the descent group. They received personal names. They were the object of specific personal origin stories and narratives. They enabled ancestry, status, and authority to be presented and perpetuated within the lineage. In addition, they could be called to intervene as power-charged devices in the making of war and peace. For *lulik* flags were conceived of as an active potency that could generate *distance effects* in situations of armed conflicts. In Timorese uses, it seems it was most notably on occasions of war that the *lulik* agency of flags was expected to come into being. We saw above that, in European eyes, wars were the critical trial for the so-called 'prestige' of Portuguese power. But in Timorese eyes, wars also were the arena of *lulik* flag agency, and it was also for the ritual purpose of acting as war agents that flags came out of the *lulik* houses.

In this light, then, the above colonial story narrated by Governor Celestino da Silva in 1894 reads as a record of a situation in which Timorese actions made manifest a *lulik* mode of relating to Portuguese flags. It is thus now opportune to return to the kind of confrontational contexts that configured the fantastic contours of the governor's account of 1894. Rather than relating flags to European 'nations' and Timorese 'houses', I intend now to consider briefly their active part in the turbulence of war and peace that, as indicated above, characterized the vassals–rulers polity in Timor.

---

[71] J. Bovensiepen, '*Lulik*: taboo, animism, or transgressive sacred? An exploration of identity, morality and power in Timor-Leste', *Oceania* 84:2 (2014), 122–3.
[72] Traube, *Cosmology and Social Life*, 143; emphasis original.

War and Peace of Flags

Timorese kings, according to the same officer Vaquinhas in 1883, credited flags in their possession 'with many virtues, and tell fabulous stories with reference to the times when they received the same flags, and the wars in which the flags have intervened'.[73] 'Fabulous stories', then, this officer claimed in 1883, the Timorese nobility told about the agency of flags in battles. This passage suggests the Timorese (similarly to the Portuguese governor in 1894) had also certain fantastic stories to tell about mighty flags in wars. For it seems *lulik* flags were called to play a role either as protective devices or as makers of loyalty in armed conflicts in the late colonial past. They were mobilized to try to shift relations of force in two main circumstances: as agents aimed at protecting or pacifying situations of hostility or as agents called to produce bonds of affiliation and loyalty.

In both instances, however, their *lulik* effectiveness was not always guaranteed; the norms and precepts associated with flag agencies could be disrespected and transgressed. Thus, for example, to swear on the flag was a gesture of obedience and social affiliation that followed conquest by the force of arms: 'the *régulo* Bey-Cina', reported officer Flores in 1891, 'received the Portuguese flag and swore on the flag an oath of fidelity, and afterwards he hoisted it in front of the *casa do Pomal* [sacred house]'.[74] In the early 1860s, the former 'rebel' *régulo* of Ulmera voluntarily expressed their submission to Portugal by coming to the presence of the governor covered with the national flag, which he then 'kissed'.[75] Similarly, Timorese nobles who sought government's 'forgiveness' for previous misbehaviours would come to the presence of Portuguese officers with their Portuguese flags hoisted, as proof of the truthfulness of their vow of obedience.[76] Thus, in a context characterized by recurrent wars, both Timorese and Portuguese could appeal to flags in order to pacify states of hostility, to stabilize associations, or to dramatically achieve political advantage in the battlefield. However, flags were not always as 'miraculously' effective in engendering peace and protection, as Celestino da Silva claimed in 1894. Timorese nobles on the warpath typically took actions of disrespect for flags hoisted in Portuguese fortresses, which counted as declaration of war. Moreover, in many instances flags could simply fail to become fabulous actors of

---

[73] Vaquinhas, 'Timor. I', 328.   [74] Flores, *Uma guerra no districto de Timor*, 36–7.
[75] Flores, *Uma guerra no districto de Timor*, 36–7; França, *Macau e os seus habitantes*, 276.
[76] F. Duarte, 'Documento B. Commando militar de Thiarlelo', in J. Celestino da Silva, *Relatório das operações de guerra no Districto Autónomo de Timor no anno de 1896*, 67–106, at 75–6.

distance, despite the aspirations of their Timorese and Portuguese human companions. A dramatic episode of the so-called Laleia war of 1878–80 illustrates this point and offers further contrast with Celestino's parable of colonial rule.

A Failed Actor

In 1878, an armed party headed by Portuguese Lieutenant Cândido da Silva was put in charge of escorting two Timorese nobles, Major Pedro and Don João of Cairuy, to the small garrison of Tui. They were under death threat from their Timorese enemies. In passing through the kingdom of Vemasse, the officer requested the king of Vemasse – who, however, was secretly allied to the enemies of Pedro and João – to give military protection to the party on its march to the garrison. The Vemasse king swore on the flag that he would take responsibility for the two men and escort them safely to Tui. Fearing betrayal, during the march to Tui the two nobles and the Portuguese officer remained 'close to the flag'. All of a sudden, the king of Vemasse and his people treacherously attacked the Portuguese group, intending to kill and decapitate Pedro and João.[77] In despair, Lieutenant Cândido, according to one report, 'nevertheless covered the two chased men with the flag', 'in the hope that at least on this account they would be respected'.[78] This was of no avail: 'even though D. João of Cairuy and the major of his kingdom, loyal to the government, were covered with the flag they were murdered'.[79]

Archival documentation is obscure about the reasons that may have led to the failed intervention of the flag in these events. Clear opposition and detachment from the Portuguese outsider power, along with complex rivalries between Timorese royal and noble lineages, and/or belief in or adherence to other superior protective forces, probably explain the attackers' defiant act of transgressive desecration of the distance that ought to be owed to the flag's *lulik*. The story made clear to the Portuguese that Timorese vassals could deceive. It revealed, simultaneously, that Portuguese flags could deceive. Their *lulik* agencies of distance and protection, which left such an impression on Governor Celestino da Silva in the 1890s, could be transgressed; and they were not always active on the Portuguese side.

---

[77] Cândido da Silva to Governor of Timor, 11 December 1878, AHU, Macau e Timor, ACL_SEMU_DGU_1R_002_Cx 1, 1879–80.
[78] Father João Gomes Ferreira to Minister of Navu and Overseas, 1 July 1881, AHU, Macau e Timor, 1R ACL_SEMU_DGU_1R_002_Cx 2, 1881.
[79] Governor de Timor, Hugo Lacerda, to Minister of Overseas, 9 June 1879, AHU, Macau e Timor. ACL_SEMU_DGU_1R_002_Cx 1, 1879–80.

'Objects, by the very nature of their connections with humans', observed Bruno Latour, 'quickly shift from being mediators to being intermediaries, counting for one or nothing, no matter how internally complicated they might be.'[80] Similarly, *lulik* flags could quickly shift from being fabulous mediators charged with invisible potencies of unstoppable might to being useless 'intermediaries'. Instead of counting for a powerful one, they could count for nothing – and then the flag's magic of distance could be broken.

Conclusion

The imaginary of flags as emblems of nationality dominated the age of national imperialism to the age of decolonization in the twentieth century. This nationalistic imaginary, I suggest, resonates in historical scholarship that tends to conceptualize the overseas histories of European national flags as – almost exclusively – symbolic representations of the nation. This idiom, however, is not universal. I argued that it fails to capture the ways in which flags could take part effectively as actors of relations of hierarchy, ancestry, loyalty, or protective distance in many accounts – indigenous, European, chronologically 'early modern', or even 'modern'. From this perspective, flags appeared, even in a number of Portuguese nationalist-imperialist stories, as prestige-charged actors that brought forth the metaphysical forces of empire and that made a pragmatic difference in concrete colonial interactions. Hence, national symbolism is a limited explanatory framework even to explain certain forms of flag animism that emerge in the European archival record. I have proposed to circumvent these limitations, and I have developed an analysis sensitive to the differences and transits between colonial and indigenous animistic stories of the agency of flags.

I have traced these transits in the early modern imperial past, when Portuguese flags became an active part of an imagined empire of vassal kings; and in the modern colonial past, where flags emerged as imperial agents of distance, 'prestige', and patriotic affect. Finally I have crossed these European constructs and actions with indigenous appropriations of outsider flags as ancestral *lulik* and *rota* insignia of authority. Portuguese Crown flags crossed the seas with a view to glorify and affirm the Portuguese Empire as a global dominion in the small and remote colony of Timor. The Portuguese relied on vassalage materiality – including the flags and other tokens of

---

[80] Latour, *Reassembling the Social*, 79.

power – to establish the king's higher authority. Yet this materiality found a fertile cultural ground for creative appropriations in the Indonesian Archipelago. The proliferation of flags as vassalage tokens stimulated difference and independent rule among the autochthonous communities eager to absorb foreign objects as stranger–king sources of power. Portuguese flags, alongside other external objects, thus fed on a state of growing individuation of 'kingdoms' and lineages that both depended upon and threatened the Portuguese claims to colonial rule. Yet the multitude of flags in the country was caught into a ceaseless animistic game of Portuguese–Timorese reciprocal possession. The usurping *lulik* indigenization of flags by vassal rulers would provide fertile local foundations for the development of European flag animisms of a nationalistic kind. Since the nineteenth century, diffuse but pervasive nationalistic animisms of flags as agents of imperial-national hegemony grew and prospered in parallel to Timorese *lulik* animisms.

In the war theatres, as the story of Governor Celestino illuminates, these two worlds dramatically intersected, and were partially juxtaposed. Hence Portuguese flags could be *lulik* and national simultaneously; they could coexist in distinct ontological planes. Conceived of as colonial actors of relations of distance, flags could hold the promise of a Portuguese empire based on intangible energies of prestige or patriotism; at the same time, they supported contrasting local claims for Timorese lineage power based on ancestry and the spiritual potency of sacred heirlooms. Distinct idioms of object-animism made it possible for national flags to become a potential (though not obligatory) actor in the arrangement of differentials of status and power in Timorese social units; in military conflicts; in structures of authority; in group genealogies; and in imageries and in the local efficacy of Portuguese imperialism itself. The flag agencies were most dramatically tested in situations of war, a 'fantastic' atmosphere that fascinated the governor in 1894. Then, flags could instantiate a sociological paradox. They could bring the Timorese Islanders and the Portuguese empire together, not by means of shared representations or beliefs, but instead by force of the relations of distance they brought into existence.

51

Pacific Bodies and Personal Space Redefined, 1850–1960

JACQUELINE LECKIE

The violence of this form of colonization entailed, as Talal Asad expressed it, monumental destruction at every level, precisely because it attempted to reorganize not only the polity, but social relations, economic structures, and values. It was not just the violence of pillage, but the violence of self conscious and self righteous transformation of social life. And its destructiveness was not just a question of conquest but of law: an attempt to redefine norms as well as practices.[1]

This bold statement about the pervasive penetration of colonialism, into the most intimate spaces of life, challenges narratives of the colonial project being imposed through brute violence, and then the word of God, colonial pacification and commercial development, or 'saving' Indigenous societies. Post-colonial deconstruction has considered how colonialism pervaded the lives, bodies, and spaces of Pacific peoples. The 'fatal impact' of exogenous diseases on the Pacific has been intensely debated,[2] but health history monographs tended to focus on specific islands and colonial administrations.[3] Yet commonalities within and between far-flung islands reveal how colonialism introduced and imposed medical and associated regimes (such as in education and labour) and infrastructure that redefined bodies and spaces across the ocean. Discourse, power, and practices in relation to health, that aimed to 'save the race', mapped, classified, legislated, incarcerated,

---

[1] F. Cooper and A.L. Stoler, 'Introduction. Tensions of empire: colonial control and visions of rule', *American Ethnologist* 16 (1989), 609–21, at 618.
[2] See D. Igler, 'Diseased goods: global exchanges in the eastern Pacific Basin, 1770–1850', *American Historical Review* 109:3 (2004), 693–719, at 694 n.3.
[3] E.g. D. Denoon, *Public Health in Papua New Guinea: Medical Possibility and Social Constraint, 1884–1984* (Cambridge: Cambridge University Press, 2002); A.P. Hattori, *Colonial Dis-ease: US Navy Health Policies and the Chamorros of Guam, 1898–1941* (Honolulu: University of Hawai'i Press, 2004); K. Inglis, *Mai Lepera: Disease and Displacement in Nineteenth-Century Hawaii* (Honolulu: University of Hawai'i Press, 2013); J. Leckie, *Colonizing Madness: Asylum and Community in Fiji* (Honolulu: University of Hawai'i Press, 2020).

Pacific Bodies and Personal Space Redefined

separated, excluded, nurtured, treated, vaccinated, educated, trained, and employed Pacific bodies and minds. These patterns applied throughout the tropical Pacific Islands. This chapter focuses on the British colonies (especially Fiji), and on American (mainly Guam and Hawai'i) and New Zealand territories, and refers to some Australian and French colonies.

The vast and encompassing areas where the net of colonialism was cast, through embodiment, medicine, and redefined spaces, is suggestive of medicine being a 'tool' of empire – a sometimes subtle but powerful means to convince indigenous peoples of the wisdom of pacification, colonial rule, and the 'magic of modernity'.[4] Medically trained missionaries had a proactive role in early efforts to replace indigenous medical systems with what they considered to be superior Western practices.[5] Leading pioneers of colonial and tropical medicine in the Pacific, such as Dr Raphael Cilento and Dr Sylvester Lambert, were convinced that their projects would not only rectify depopulation within Pacific societies during the nineteenth and early twentieth centuries, but also impart civilization.[6]

Michel Foucault did not address colonialism, let alone the Pacific, but his concept of biopower is pertinent to this chapter.[7] Biopower has been cast as lying at the crux of modern medicine and the modern state, whereby state hegemony is exercised through the control of bodies and minds. Bodies are controlled and governed, demarcated as diseased or healthy, abnormal or normal, not necessarily via raw coercion but through the power of discourse and the inculcation, internalization, and performance of – in the Pacific – colonized and racialized bodies.[8] Biopower operated through managing and

---

[4] E. LiPuma, *Encompassing Others: The Magic of Modernity in Melanesia* (Ann Arbor: University of Michigan Press, 2000). Also D. Arnold, *Imperial Medicine and Indigenous Societies* (Manchester: Manchester University Press, 1988).

[5] K.A. Inglis, 'Disease and the "other": the role of medical imperialism in Oceania', in G.D. Smithers and B.N. Newman (eds.), *Native Diasporas: Indigenous Identities and Settler Colonialism in the Americas* (Lincoln: University of Nebraska Press, 2014), 385–410, at 387. Also, for example, S. Archer, *Sharks upon the Land: Colonialism, Indigenous Health, and Culture in Hawai'i, 1778–1855* (Cambridge: Cambridge University Press, 2018); E. Kettle, *That They Might Live* (Sydney: F.P. Leonard, 1979); R. Lange 'European medicine in the Cook Islands', in R. MacLeod and M. Lewis (eds.), *Disease, Medicine, and Empire: Perspectives on Western Medicine and the Experience of European Expansion* (London: Routledge, 1988), 61–79.

[6] A. Cameron-Smith, 'Raphael Cilento's empire: diet, health and government between Australia and the colonial Pacific', *Journal of Australian Studies* 38:1 (2014), 103–18, at 110; A. Stuart, 'We are all hybrid here: the Rockefeller Foundation, Sylvester Lambert, and health work in the colonial South Pacific', *Health and History* 8:1 (2006), 56–79.

[7] M. Foucault, *The History of Sexuality*, vol. 1, *An Introduction*, trans. R. Hurley (New York: Random House, 1978), 140–4.

[8] See Denoon, *Public Health in Papua New Guinea*, 44–52; R. MacLeod, 'Introduction', in R. MacLeod and M.J. Lewis (eds.), *Disease, Medicine, and Empire: Perspectives on Western*

491

regulating cultures both directly, through coercive means such as the imposition of Western medical infrastructure, or indirectly, via entanglements with chiefly authority and indigenous customs.

Despite the semblance of order and control, colonial administrations were riddled with contradictions. In Fiji there was tension between non-intervention and informal rule, sustaining customary hierarchies and intervention to subordinate indigenous structures and power to the state.[9] When the New Zealand administration in Western Sāmoa recognized the Fono of Faipule in 1923, a 'militaristic structure' strengthened public health enforcement.[10] Indirect rule did not feature everywhere in the Pacific. In Guam between 1899 and 1950 (except for Japanese occupation during World War II), martial law under the American naval governor dominated. From 1887 to 1946, Kanaks in New Caledonia were subjected to the *Code de l'indigénat*. The uneven impact of colonial rule throughout the Pacific partly reflected limited funding and resources from the metropole. British Pacific colonies were hardly regarded as the 'jewel in the crown', and were more often represented as 'islands in a far sea'[11] where peoples lived in paradise. Even once colonial centres became aware of the devastating impact of outside forces, evident in population decline, health expenditure was a low priority within colonial budgets. The difficulty in recruiting physicians was a compelling reason for investment in indigenous and locally trained personnel, such as native medical practitioners (NMPs) and nurses. Meanwhile, during the early colonial years, missions provided much of the health care that redefined Pacific bodies and spaces. This role persisted into the twentieth century in weak or divided colonies such as the New Hebrides (now Vanuatu).[12]

Medicine and the Experience of European Expansion (London: Routledge, 1988), 1–18, at 6–7; D. Arnold, *Colonizing the Body: State Medicine and Epidemic Disease in Nineteenth Century India* (Berkeley: University of California Press, 1993); W. Anderson, *Colonial Pathologies: American Tropical Medicine, Race, and Hygiene in the Philippines* (Durham, NC: Duke University Press, 2006).

[9] N. Thomas, 'Sanitation and seeing: the creation of state power in early colonial Fiji', *Comparative Studies in Society and History* 32 (1990), 149–70, at 170.

[10] S. Firth, 'The agencies and ideologies of colonialism', in D. Denoon, S. Firth, J. Linnekin, M. Meleisea, and K. Nero (eds.), *The Cambridge History of the Pacific Islanders* (Cambridge: Cambridge University Press, 1997), 253–60, at 258.

[11] E. Hau'ofa, 'Our Sea of Islands', in E. Waddell, V. Naidu, and E. Hau'ofa (eds.), *A New Oceania: Rediscovering Our Sea of Islands* (Suva: University of the South Pacific in association with Beake House, 1993), 2–16, at 7.

[12] M. Jolly, 'Other mothers: maternal "insouciance" and the depopulation debate in Fiji and Vanuatu, 1890–1930', in K. Ram and M. Jolly (eds.), *Maternities and Modernities: Colonial and Postcolonial Experiences in Asia and the Pacific* (Cambridge: Cambridge University Press, 1998), 177–212, at 182–97; Lange, 'European medicine in the Cook Islands'.

The contradictions and uneven impact of colonialism on Pacific bodies and spaces also lies with Pacific peoples who were hardly passive victims of bodily, biological, and spatial restructuring. This chapter emphasizes the entanglement between colonial administrations, missions, philanthropic bodies, migrant communities, and indigenous cultures, in the redefinition of Pacific bodies and personal spaces. Entanglement was not merely hybridity, plurality, or the intermeshing of cultures, ontologies, and health systems, or even a more nuanced and uneven process than hegemonic top-down colonialism. Indeed, it actively entailed agency, ranging from hidden or subtle forms, to evasion, rejection, and resistance, as well as incorporation of the external world into Oceanic cultures and modes of power.

Spaces and Bodies

This chapter locates bodies within environmental, social, and spiritual spaces. Epeli Hau'ofa has stressed the vast and interconnected spaces inherent in Oceania but there were also many isolated spaces. Despite distance there had always been mobility and cultural interaction, which intensified after colonization. As Pacific bodies were redefined, so too were spaces eliminated, restricted, or redefined, while sites such as plantations, mines, and urban settlements emerged. New spaces and mobility were facilitated by new modes of travel and communication.[13] Steamships were a conduit in the transmission of disease, but other technology, such as the trans-Pacific cable, enabled Western medicine, personnel, and knowledge, especially from the late nineteenth century with the growth of tropical medicine, to spread. The flow of ideas and practice was not always unidirectional. Nineteenth-century social reformist projects that aimed to uplift the working classes of industrial Britain were instrumental in the reconstruction of the maternal body,[14] but ideas about public health could also be shaped by colonial experience, as when Cilento transferred his concepts of public health from the Territory of Papua New Guinea to Australia.[15]

New medical spaces were created where bodies were examined, treated, and confined, in 'controlling and disaggregating forms of spatiality suggested by such recurring terms as "isolation", "confinement", "segregation", and

---

[13] D. Arnold, 'Leprosy: from "imperial danger" to postcolonial history – an afterword', *Journal of Pacific History* 52:3 (2017), 407–19, at 409–10.

[14] M. Jolly, 'Introduction. Colonial and postcolonial plots in histories of maternities and modernities', in Ram and Jolly (eds.), *Maternities and Modernities*, 1–25, at 9–11.

[15] Cameron-Smith, 'Raphael Cilento's empire'.

"exclusion"'.[16] Health programmes sought to probe and restructure intimate personal spaces.[17] The 'clinic' might be a tent in the bush, a Fijian *bure* (house), an imposing edifice such as Fiji's Colonial War Memorial Hospital completed in 1923, or a site of fear and separation like a leprosarium or a mental hospital. New clinical spaces, such as the Susana Hospital for women that opened in Guam in 1905, could be a fearful and radical departure from familiar spaces filled with family where indigenous Chamorro medical practitioners, such as *pattera* (midwife) or *suruhana* and *suruhanu* (female and male traditional healers) were called upon. The Susana Hospital was a new gendered space with a male medical corps where childbirth was treated as a private matter within a private space.[18] Although Chamorros, like other colonized Pacific peoples, may have eventually accommodated to change, they also negotiated and resisted bodily interventions and spatial transformations.[19] Communities hid and cared for Hawaiians with leprosy or were *kōkua* (helpers) for those banished to the Kaulaupapa leprosy settlement.[20] New communities were also constituted within sites of bodily confinement, such as the multicultural, pan-Pacific community at the Central Lepers' Hospital at Makogai in Fiji.[21]

Perceptive health practitioners sought to bridge the spaces of indigenous and colonial medical care. In the Cook Islands after World War II, the New Zealand government adopted 'open-air' treatment, whereby tuberculosis patients convalesced on the veranda of the local public hospital. Patients might be treated close to family in 'native structure huts', somewhat like the provisions introduced for Māori tuberculosis patients in New Zealand.[22] Community interaction within state medical provision in the Cook Islands

---

[16] Arnold, 'Leprosy', 409–10.

[17] See J. Comaroff and J. Comaroff, *Ethnography and the Historical Imagination* (Boulder, CO: Westview Press, 1992); Jolly, 'Other mothers'; A.L. Stoler, 'Making empire respectable: the politics of race and sexual morality in twentieth-century colonial cultures', in L. Lamphere, H. Ragone, and P. Zavella (eds.), *Situated Lives: Gender and Culture in Everyday Life* (New York: Routledge, 1997), 374–99.

[18] A.P. Hattori, '"The cry of the little people of Guam": American colonialism, medical philanthropy, and the Susana Hospital for Chamorro women, 1898–1941', *Health and History* 8:1 (2006), 1–23.

[19] See also, for example, Ram and Jolly (eds.), *Maternities and Modernities*; Leckie, *Colonizing Madness*; I. Sykes, 'Disability, leprosy, and Kanak identity in twentieth-century New Caledonia', *Journal of Literary and Cultural Disability Studies* 10:2 (2016), 173–89.

[20] Inglis, *Mai Lepera*, 78–108.

[21] J. Buckingham, 'The inclusivity of exclusion: isolation and community among leprosy-affected people in the South Pacific', *Health and History* 13:2 (2011), 65–83.

[22] D. Futter-Puati, L. Bryder, J.K. Park, J. Littleton, and P. Herda, 'Partnerships for health: decimating tuberculosis in the Cook Islands, 1920–1975', *Health and Place* 25 (2014), 10–18, at 12.

was influenced by Chief Medical Officers, Dr Pohau Ellison and Dr Tom Davis, respectively Māori and Cook Islands Māori, who had trained in New Zealand. The early provision of local medical training at the Fiji Native Medical School from 1885 and from 1908 at Suva Colonial Hospital focused on training Native Medical Practitioners (NMPs) as vaccinators and Native Obstetric Nurses (NONs) as midwives, but they came to have a significant role in merging traditional and colonial medicine in the Pacific.[23] This was one reason why Lambert advocated more professional training of indigenous Pacific Islanders at the Central Medical School during the 1920s.

Gathering and Mapping Bodies

Knowledge about people and places was a foundation of colonial governmentality. Population and medical censuses counted, classified, and reordered bodies into new definitions and categories.[24] 'Races' were defined and measured, and sociobiological difference was assigned into categories within colonial engagements.[25] The colonizers believed they knew Pacific bodies, presuming not just expertise in tropical medicine, and the anthropology of 'primitive' cultures, but also social power over subjects through governing bodies.

Documentation of colonial subjects extended far beyond the basic population census. In New Guinea during the 1920s health patrols gathered a wide range of data, providing a 'perfect graphic record of the health state of the whole area'.[26] The introduction of the census by Dr Rayner Bellamy, the first Australian resident government officer in the Trobriand Islands, represented a 'hallmark of modem governmentality: an individual relationship between each person in a population and the state'.[27] Knowledge gathering penetrated

---

[23] V. Luker, 'Native obstetric nursing in Fiji', in V. Luker and M. Jolly (eds.), *Birthing in the Pacific: Beyond Tradition and Modernity?* (Honolulu: University of Hawai'i Press, 2002), 100–24; Stuart, 'We are all hybrid here'.

[24] See A. Appadurai, 'Number in the colonial imagination', in C.A. Breckenridge and P. van der Veer (eds.), *Orientalism and the Post-Colonial Predicament* (Philadelphia: University of Pennsylvania Press, 1993), 314–39; A. Widmer, 'The effects of elusive knowledge: census, health laws and inconsistently modern subjects in early colonial Vanuatu', *Journal of Legal Anthropology* 1:1 (2008), 92–116.

[25] B. Douglas and C. Ballard (eds.), *Foreign Bodies: Oceania and the Science of Race 1750– 1940* (Canberra: ANU Press, 2008); A. Widmer and V. Lipphardt (eds.), *Health and Difference: Rendering Human Variation in Colonial Engagements* (New York: Berghahn Books, 2016).

[26] 'Report of the International Pacific Health Conference', *Commonwealth Parliamentary Papers* 5, 1926, 834. Cited in Cameron-Smith, 'Raphael Cilento's empire', 110.

[27] A. Connelly, 'Ambivalent empires: historicising the Trobriand Islands, 1830–1945', PhD thesis, Australian National University, Canberra, 2014, 135.

into the most intimate bodily spaces when European officials inspected the genitalia of Trobriand Islanders aged over eight years on the grounds of treating venereal disease. While contemporary anthropologists such as Bronislaw Malinowski offered rich ethnographic data on Trobriand sexuality, the quantitative census also contributed to knowledge about Trobriand bodies and culture in an accessible format, so that officials could measure and monitor health indices. Moreover, the state had the power of punishment to enforce the gathering and mapping of bodies, although Bellamy pointed out that people complied once they knew that they would be punished if they avoided examination.

Several medical censuses and surveys were conducted during the interwar years throughout the Pacific by Lambert, the Rockefeller Foundation's regional director, at the invitation of colonial administrations and under the auspices of the Western Pacific Health Service. Such censuses not only mapped bodies and villages, but were also entwined with public health projects aiming to reverse depopulation and to ensure that populations were productive and healthy. Inspections were carried out with militaristic efficiency, as when Lambert and his team proudly recorded impressive tallies of the bodies counted and treated. For example, in a survey on Rotuma in 1928, 2,020 out of 2,040 bodies were inspected, many of which were tested and treated for yaws and hookworm.[28] Lambert's bodily census was achieved by requiring villagers, including some women, to strip to the waist, with one health official inspecting the head, upper limbs and trunk, while another surveyed the lower limbs, feet, and genitalia. Counting did not end with humans – pigs were also counted and inspected, as were latrines, water tanks, dwellings, and even the density of fly infestation. During World War II, the counting of mosquitoes on indigenous bodies and in dwelling spaces became imperative in the fight against malaria.[29] As will be outlined below, sanitation projects were fundamental to the redefinition of Pacific bodies and spaces.

In Fiji there was even a census of minds conducted by four general censuses between 1911 and 1946. Respondents were asked to 'State the name of any person in this dwelling or establishment who is . . . "Lunatic, imbecile, or feeble-minded".'[30] The published results provided evidence of the

---

[28] S.M. Lambert, 'Health Survey of Rotuma', Rockefeller Archive Center (RAC), Record Group (RG) 5, Series 3/419, Box 161, Folder 1977.

[29] J.A. Bennett, *Natives and Exotics: World War II and Environment in the Southern Pacific* (Honolulu: University of Hawai'i Press, 2009), 54–60.

[30] E. Berne, 'Difficulties of comparative psychiatry: the Fiji Islands', *American Journal of Psychiatry* 116:2 (1959), 104–9, at 105.

distribution of disordered minds, within Fiji's racial categories (Fijians, Indians, Europeans, Half-castes and Polynesians), but methods of gathering such data were dubious and the numbers were probably under-reported. The prevalence of disabilities may have been hidden from census-takers because of the shame associated with disability within some communities in Fiji. It is not known how easily English terms for mental disability were translated into other languages. More precision can be accorded to statistics for subjects certified under the 1884 'Ordinance to Provide for the Care and Maintenance of Lunatics and Idiots', in which a lunatic was 'every person of unsound mind and every person being an idiot'. This documentation was part of a process whereby madness was constituted by the state.[31] The paper trail began with certification papers, by which individuals became a case: 'an object like a branch of knowledge and a hold for a branch of power'.[32] Once certified insane and committed to Fiji's asylum, mad subjects became patients. Case notes produced lunatic patient identity, as well as knowledge about colonial populations, and constructions of human difference.[33] Patient details were entered on registers, which also recorded if minds were cured and the bodily outcome: discharge or death. Doctors assigned patients into modern Western categories of mental illness that were neither objective nor static. Case records formed only one part of knowledge about lunacy within the Pacific. In Fiji the medical superintendent also logged asylum observations, such as an entry by Dr Lynch in 1903: 'Natives as usual.' Boards of Visitors reported to government on the asylum, the Medical Superintendent submitted an annual report to government, and statistical details were submitted to the British Colonial Office in the Blue Books.[34] Order was brought to the management of Fiji's insane through quantifying asylum details, including the cubic and window space per patient, type and duration of restraints, diet, and tallies of specific mental disorders. Statistical documentation presented a semblance of pervasive efficiency, order, and control,

---

[31] J. Leckie, 'Modernity and the management of madness in colonial Fiji', *Paideuma* 50 (2004), 551–74.
[32] A. Suzuki, 'Framing psychiatric subjectivity: doctor, patient and record-keeping at Bethlem in the nineteenth century', in J. Melling and B. Forsythe (eds.), *Insanity, Institutions and Society, 1800–1914: A Social History of Madness in Comparative Perspective* (London: Routledge, 1999), 115–36, at 116–17.
[33] C. Coleborne, *Insanity, Identity and Empire: Immigrants and Institutional Confinement in Australia and New Zealand, 1873–1910* (Manchester: Manchester University Press, 2015).
[34] British colonies had to submit annual Blue Books of statistical and other information to the Colonial Office. The books also had sections on the colony's finances, population, education, imports and exports, agriculture, land, prisons, hospitals, charitable institutions, banks, transportation, and government employees.

and accorded legitimacy to the colonial management of disordered minds. Fiji's lunacy documentation was far more detailed than in other island colonies, but similar processes of documenting bodies and spaces within closed institutions such as leprosariums, prisons, and some schools were followed to varying degrees in and beyond the British Empire. Precision about knowledge of categories of normal and abnormal colonial bodies and minds and the constitution of colonial subjects enabled management and administration.

Communities, Self, and Health

Colonialism did not redefine only bodies and spaces, but also personal space and relationships with others, with profound implications for Pacific concepts of community, family, and ancestors. Christian conversion stressed the self through a personal relationship with God, one that often was accompanied by economic change, at the heart of which was individualism and private property. Missionary influence was a form of a biopolitics with 'power over individual bodies and populations through the moral control of personal conducts and the embodiment of new disciplines of the self'.[35] Pacific ontologies of being, personhood, and existence, that defined the self through relationships with ancestors, kin, and the environment, were in tension with new individualistic concepts.[36]

Western medicine sought to restructure bodies, health, and Pacific beliefs of illness, causation, health, wellness, and healing. Common assumptions about illness extended across most Pacific cultures.[37] Diagnosis depended upon assessing social, spiritual, and ancestral worlds to restore individual and community wellness.[38] Illness could lie within a disturbance among ancestral spirits that had been caused by failure to fulfil social obligations or conform to cultural norms. The roots of illness and healing lay within the community, with the supernatural, or in sorcery. In Kanak society, disease and disability

---

[35] Y. Fer, 'Introduction. Missions, politics and biopolitics in the Pacific Island societies', *Social Sciences and Missions* 31 (2018), 3–5, at 3; R. Eves, 'Colonialism, corporeality and character: Methodist missions and the refashioning of bodies in the Pacific', *History and Anthropology* 10:1 (1996), 85–138.

[36] See U.L. Vaai and U. Nabobo-Baba, *The Relational Self: Decolonising Personhood in the Pacific* (Suva: University of the South Pacific Press; Pacific Theological College, 2017).

[37] See for example, C.D.F. Parsons (ed.), *Healing Practices in the South Pacific* (Laie: Institute for Polynesian Studies, Brigham Young University, 1985).

[38] See for example, D. Spencer, *Disease, Religion and Society in the Fiji Islands* (New York: J.J. Augustin, 1941).

were rarely isolated or separated from social life.[39] In Hawai'i disease was considered to emanate from losing *mana*, possibly from offending an *amakua* (ancestral god), or breaking a *kapu* (tabu). Only the restoration of *mana* would restore wellness.[40] 'Doing sickness' among Samoans aimed to re-establish spiritual wholeness, for the sick person and the social group, through the processes of care and cure. In Sāmoa and in some other Pacific territories, indigenous medical systems also expanded through the assimilation of foreign medical perspectives and practices.[41]

New personal spaces emerged as notions of the self and the other became more sharply defined. Historian Kerri Inglis argues that the colonial demar-cation of healthy and contagious bodies was pivotal in the self/other dichot-omy, whereby the healthy indigenous population came to regard their own people who had disease as a cultural 'other'. Indigenous health practitioners were trained not only to treat disease but also to identify diseased and otherwise different bodies in their own societies. Yet these practitioners could also be important intermediaries between indigenous and Western concepts and practices of health and healing.[42] Although colonialism redefined Pacific bodies and spaces there was extensive persistence of trad-itional healing rituals and medical remedies, as well as resistance to coercion and the negotiation of Western medical systems. Pacific peoples frequently shunned medical centres or hid when villages were surveyed.[43]

Reproductive Bodies

Imperial projects tried to reshape reproduction and sexuality.[44] Just as working-class mothers in late nineteenth- and early twentieth-century Britain were blamed for 'population problems, racial degeneration and imper-ial decline', mothers within several British Pacific colonies were blamed for depopulation. Surveillance and intervention policed 'maternal incompetence' or 'insouciance' and instructed women to be 'better' mothers.[45] Not only were

---

[39] Y. Mouchenik, 'The elder's child of Maré Island, New Caledonia', *Transcultural Psychiatry* 44 (2007), 136–56, at 137.

[40] Inglis, 'Disease and the "other"', 402.

[41] P. Kinloch, *Talking Health but Doing Sickness: Studies in Samoan Health* (Wellington: Victoria University Press, 1985); C. Macpherson and L. Macpherson, *Samoan Medical Beliefs and Practice* (Auckland: Auckland University Press, 1990).

[42] Luker, 'Native obstetric nursing in Fiji', 112–13.

[43] E.g., B. Quain, *Fijian Village* (Chicago: University of Chicago Press, 1948), 69–70.

[44] Ram and Jolly, *Maternities and Modernities*; Luker and Jolly (eds.), *Birthing in the Pacific*.

[45] Jolly, 'Other mothers', 178.

reproductive practices targeted, but sexuality, gender roles, and identities were profoundly affected. Fiji's Decrease Report became the Pacific's foremost treatise on bad mothering.[46] The report attributed depopulation to the 'General insouciance of the native mind, heedlessness of mothers, and weakness of maternal instinct'. Gendered practices considered to affect the unborn child, such as arduous work during pregnancy, and even fishing by child-bearing women, were condemned. Indirect rule and native regulations provided an ideal means for the state to implement the Commission's recommendations. Women-centred and indigenous childbirthing practices within 'dirty' spaces such as *bures* (houses) were criticized.[47] Efforts were made to reform and scrutinize indigenous childrearing practices, especially in relation to diet and sanitation. Mothers were to cease pre-masticating infant food and urged to introduce cow's or goat's milk rather than prolong breast-feeding. Restrictions on women's work included a prohibition on fishing at night. But women's agency was not quashed and, although the role of traditional midwives (*buinigone*) was diminished, Native Obstetric Nurses amalgamated some aspects of indigenous reproductive practice with Western midwifery and nursing.[48]

Throughout the Pacific, missionaries and colonial officials became 'committed to a new model of the bourgeois family, with the domesticated woman, the mother, at its moral and religious core'.[49] Village women's committees, such as *Au Vaine* in the Cook Islands, *Langa Fonua* in Tonga, and *Komiti Tumana* in Sāmoa, often based upon customary roles and headed by elite women, were bolstered by the state and the church to play a key role in the redefinition of gendered roles, strengthening of feminine crafts, and surveillance of reproductive and sanitation practices.[50] Women's Committees in Fiji were 'expected to watch expectant mothers' and encourage regular infant feeding at set times.[51] Mothers were required to attend

---

[46] *Report of the Commission Appointed to Inquire into the Decrease of the Native Population 1893–1896* (Suva: Government Printer, 1896), 6–7.

[47] Jolly, 'Other mothers', 201.   [48] Luker, 'Native obstetric nursing in Fiji'.

[49] Jolly, 'Other mothers', 200. Also, for example, M. Jolly and M. Macintyre, *Family and Gender in the Pacific: Domestic Contradictions and Colonial Impact* (Cambridge: Cambridge University Press, 1988); C. Ralston, 'Women workers in Samoa and Tonga in the early twentieth century', in C. Moore, J. Leckie, and D. Munro (eds.), *Labour in the South Pacific* (Townsville: James Cook University Press, 1990), 67–77; R. Eves, 'Race rescue. Methodist mission and the population question in Papua, 1890–1910', *Social Sciences and Missions* 31 (2018), 34–68.

[50] E.g., P. Schoeffel, 'The origins and development of women's associations in Western Samoa, 1830–1977', *Journal of Pacific Studies* 3 (1977), 1–21.

[51] R. Flood-Keyes Roberts, 'Routine of child-welfare work', *Native Medical Practitioner* 2 (1931), 40–3, at 42.

Pacific Bodies and Personal Space Redefined

baby and welfare clinics that were established in some colonies during the inter war years. In the Cook Islands these clinics were based on the New Zealand Plunket Society and closely monitored the development of infant bodies. The clinics could be somewhat authoritarian, but compliance was entangled with cultural practices of obedience to superiors.[52]

As in colonies worldwide, Pacific societies were subjected to regulations and moral codes that condemned sexual relations outside heterosexual monogamous marriage, in the name of reversing depopulation and controlling venereal disease.[53] During the 1840s and 1850s, missionaries, supported by Hawaiian ruling chiefs, had pushed for reglementation or 'sex laws', banning adultery, prostitution, and *moe kolohe* ('mischievous sleeping').[54] In Fiji polygamy and consanguineous marriage were banned. In all Pacific colonies the transmission of venereal disease was surveilled – a gendered and racialized process – as non-European women, and especially those considered prostitutes or promiscuous, were prone to inspection and marked as having diseased bodies.[55] Women's bodies, mobility, and above all their sexuality came under even stricter control when foreign troops were stationed on the islands during the Pacific War, although women frequently flouted these restrictions.[56]

Legislation

Health and sanitary legislation gave an authoritative basis for the restructuring of bodies and spaces in colonies in the Pacific. Those 'who carried diseases with marked physical manifestations, such as leprosy, were treated like criminals to be hunted and confined, closely surveyed and excised from the public view'.[57] Legislation was also introduced in some colonies to confine people with mental abnormalities when lunacy was classified as a disease. To enforce the wide range of sanitary legislation, indigenous authorities were often enlisted.

[52] Futter-Puati et al., 'Partnerships for health', 13.   [53] Fer, 'Introduction'.
[54] Archer, *Sharks upon the Land*, 222–3.
[55] D. Walther, *Sex and Control: Venereal Disease, Colonial Physicians, and Indigenous Agency in German Colonialism, 1884–1914* (Oxford: Berghahn Books, 2015), 99–100.
[56] J.A. Bennett and A. Wanhalla (eds.), *Mothers' Darlings of the South Pacific: The Children of Indigenous Women and US Servicemen, World War Two* (Honolulu: University of Hawai'i Press, 2016).
[57] W. Cavert, 'At the edge of an empire: plague, state, and identity in New Caledonia 1899–1900', *Journal of Pacific History* 51:1 (2016), 1–20, at 2.

Colonial legislation also regulated indigenous health, hygiene, and reproductive practices that officials considered to be contributing to depopulation and the spread of disease. Infringements could result in punishments varying from imprisonment or fines to enforcing customary gender-based labour. In 1927 the Fijian court could order women found guilty of an offence to make mats or *masi* (cloth).[58] Indigenous health practices were frequently banned in the name of public health and sanitation, but this also exerted colonial control and cultural assimilation.[59] Anthropologist Margaret Jolly suggests that the concern about high infant mortality and indigenous mothering in the Pacific was intrinsic to the broader shift towards governmentality concerned with overseeing and intervening in populations, justified as 'improvement'.[60] In the Trobriand Islands, for example, a 'British/Australian colonial "paradigm of order" in which geometry, hygiene and openness to surveillance were commingled' pervaded native regulations. Bellamy's insistence upon clearing native bush within fifty yards of a village was warranted by more than just maintaining village hygiene.[61]

Bodies in Segregated Spaces

Legislation was considered by Europeans to be humane, instilling civilization and order, but it defined, banned, and separated Pacific bodies and spaces. Regulations, in fact, created racialized spaces by stipulating where indigenous people and non-white migrants could move, reside, and work. Colonial limitations on mobility became entwined with tradition and were especially restrictive for women. In Fiji in 1912, women could be fined if they were absent from their villages for over sixty days.[62] State control of infectious diseases provided a convincing rationale to curtail mobility. Immigration restrictions, such as the Cook Islands 1898 Asiatic Restriction Act, targeted racial groups, such as Chinese, who were essentialized as leprosy carriers. Health and mobility laws were mutually reinforcing, especially in colonies with strict controls on indigenous residence and movement. Under the *indigénat*, Kanaks had to obtain permission to leave the reservations that most were confined on, and if living in town, they faced curfews. In contrast, Samoans had much greater freedom of mobility, although during the 1920s

---

[58] G. Powles and M. Pulea, *Pacific Courts and Legal Systems* (Suva: Institute of Pacific Studies, University of the South Pacific, 1988), 80.
[59] E.g., Thomas, 'Sanitation and seeing'.   [60] Jolly, 'Other mothers', 182.
[61] Connelly, 'Ambivalent empires', 141–2.   [62] Jolly, 'Other mothers', 195–6.

children suffering from yaws were forbidden to leave their home villages unless visiting a doctor.

Quarantines at ports were among the first public health laws in the Pacific to control the spread of infectious diseases. These measures began under the Hawaiian Kingdom in 1836 with the inspection and quarantine of ships entering Honolulu harbour.[63] The quarantine of and strict controls over non-white people that accompanied the outbreak of bubonic plague at the nineteenth century's end reinforced links between infectious disease, race, and colonial hegemony. Martial law was introduced by physicians of Hawai'i's Board of Health when the plague epidemic coursed through Honolulu during 1898–1900.[64] In New Caledonia, non-whites had to carry health passports and were subjected to strict medical surveillance for signs of plague. Employers were responsible for the control and social behaviour of *indigènes* or *engagés* (Asian workers).[65] *Indigènes* who violated government *arrêtés* (legal declarations) were quarantined on the island of St Marie. The chequered history of quarantine in the Pacific revealed the unevenness of colonial rule in controlling bodies, spaces, and disease: devastatingly so during the 1918–19 influenza pandemic. In Western Sāmoa mortality rates were around 26 per cent, compared to zero deaths in American Sāmoa.[66] The New Zealand administration failed to secure quarantine, in contrast to a two-year quarantine imposed through a naval blockade in American Sāmoa.

Leprosaria and mental asylums were the most feared spaces in which Pacific bodies were separated and confined. Both institutions were instrumental in associating stigma with leprosy or mental illness. Physical sites could be forbidding, even if located in environments of tropical beauty. Islands offered ideal spaces for separating diseased bodies. From 1890 until 1925, leprosy sufferers in the Cook Islands were isolated on *motu* (small reef islets). In 1902 Martin Nagle, the Resident Agent on Penrhyn, forbade visits to Matunga except under police supervision, prohibited leprosy sufferers from having canoes, and required pastors to conduct religious services from a boat if possible.[67] Matunga became known as Molokai or Morokai – after Hawai'i's leprosarium. According to a health official, Penrhyn Islanders 'recognized the infectivity of the disease, and without any prompting from

---

[63] Archer, *Sharks upon the Land*, 208.   [64] Inglis, 'Disease and the "other"', 391.
[65] Cavert, 'At the edge of an empire'.
[66] J.R. McLane, 'Paradise locked: the 1918 influenza pandemic in American Samoa', *Sites: A Journal of Anthropology and Cultural Studies* 10:2 (2013), 30–51.
[67] R. Lange, 'Leprosy in the Cook Islands, 1890–1925', *Journal of Pacific History* 52:3 (2017), 302–24, at 313.

the white man insisted upon strict isolation'.[68] It is difficult to know if such acceptance reflected a redefinition of bodies and personal spaces, or simply an acquiescence to colonial and customary authority.

Both leprosaria and asylums were associated with prisons, metaphorically as well as by location. On islands that lacked mental health facilities, mentally ill people were often confined in gaol. A leprosy colony was established on the site of a former penitentiary in the remote Belép Islands in New Caledonia in 1892 before sufferers were transferred to Île aux Chèvres near Nouméa, and in 1918 to Ducos, a former high-security penitentiary.[69] No one was discharged from Ducos until 1976. The tiny lunatic asylum that operated from around 1933 to 1942 at Tulagi, the capital of the British Solomon Islands Protectorate, was located beside the prison. Until 1959, when the Laloki psychiatric centre opened near Port Moresby, people certified as insane were confined at Bomana gaol. Fiji's lunatic asylum, founded in 1884, was built next to Suva's gaol and cemetery, and known within the community as a 'prison' rather than as a hospital. It signified the exercise of colonial power over bodies and minds by invoking a space of incarceration. Locals referred to it as *vale ni mate* (place of death) or *bakava* (tin shack) – from the fencing that replaced the hospital's forbidding concrete walls during the 1960s. *Bakava* also became an adjective meaning a crazy, silly person.[70] Similar linguistic shifts emerged within communities where leprosy was prevalent. *Ma'i ho'oka'awale 'ohana* – 'the disease that separates families' – is a poignant reminder of the time when approximately 5,000 Hawaiians were diagnosed with leprosy and separated from their families between 1865 and 1900 to the 'natural prison' on Kalaupapa peninsula on Molokai Island.[71] Although the disease of leprosy – *atektok* (to hug each other) – was not shameful, Chamorros experienced *mamahlao* (shame and embarrassment) when they were unable to care for loved ones who had been exiled to the Culion leper colony in the Philippines.[72] Pacific Islanders from Cook Islands, Tonga, Niue, and Sāmoa also were separated great distances when sent to Makogai Island in Fiji between 1911 to 1969. 'The dread was not primarily over what the disease did to one's body, but rather over how government policies relating to the disease separated sufferers

---

[68] Lange, 'Leprosy in the Cook Islands', 311.
[69] Sykes, 'Disability, leprosy, and Kanak identity'.
[70] R. Gatty, *Fijian–English Dictionary: With Notes on Fijian Culture and Natural History* (Suva: Southeast Asia Program, Cornell University, 2010), 11.
[71] Inglis, 'Disease and the "other"', 400; Inglis, *Mai Lepera*.
[72] Hattori, *Colonial Dis-ease*, 61–90.

Pacific Bodies and Personal Space Redefined

from their loved ones'.[73] The separation of leprosy sufferers in Sāmoa from 'aiga (family) under the Isolation of Leprosy Regulation 1896 was associated with Samoan understandings of shame, banishment, and punishment.[74]

The separation and incarceration of leprosy sufferers had much in common with state provisions for those with severe mental illness. Policies towards both groups were underlaid with negative connotations of danger, pollution, and contagion, but also overlaid with humane and civilizing discourses of care, cure, and compassion. For Pacific peoples redefined by diseased and abnormal bodies, and confined within isolated spaces, the resulting identities were similar for leprosy and mental health patients. Leprosy patients were 'totally out of sight from their families which made them feel equally out of mind and forgotten'.[75] On the eve of Fiji's political independence, Dr David Sell observed: 'The mental hospital has stood for too long in isolation with its inhabitants out of sight, out of mind and socially stigmatized.'[76]

Drugs and Technology

Drugs and medical technologies were powerful weapons of Western medicine, but before the advent of sulfa drugs and antibiotics during the 1930s–1940s medication had limited efficacy in curing disease. Quinine may have eased malarial symptoms but was mainly used by Europeans and was poorly tolerated. Vaccinations such as that for smallpox, introduced as early as 1841 by missionaries in the Cook Islands,[77] prevented the transmission of some deadly diseases, but the causation was still not understood. The impact of quarantine and new sanitary measures on health was also not obvious. Hookworms were eradicated from bodies, initially with the toxic oil of chenopodium, then with carbon tetrachloride, pioneered by Lambert, and later tetrachloroethylene, but the connection between hookworm infestation, nutritional deficiencies, and disease (such as anaemia) could not yet be seen. In contrast, the curative properties of anti-yaws drugs had a visibly

---

[73] K.A. Inglis, 'Nā hoa o ka pilikia (friends of affliction): a sense of community in the Molokai leprosy settlement of 19th century Hawai'i', *Journal of Pacific History* 52:3 (2017), 287–301, at 289.
[74] S. Akeli Amaama, 'Cleansing Western Samoa: leprosy control during New Zealand administration, 1914–1922', *Journal of Pacific History* 52:3 (2017), 360–73, at 364.
[75] D. McMenamin, 'Out of sight and out of mind: the ongoing problem of treating leprosy', *Journal of Pacific History* 52:3 (2017), 343–59, at 347.
[76] Fiji Government, Council Paper 39/69, *Medical Department: Annual Report for 1968* (Suva: Government Printer, 1969), 10.
[77] Lange 'European medicine in the Cook Islands', 6.

dramatic impact on the body. Yaws caused widespread suffering and morbidity, including bone, tissue, and organ disease, and physical deformities. Lambert argued that yaws was implicated in miscarriage, lowered birth rates, and infant mortality among the 'Pacific Races'.[78] Dr Duncan Macpherson described yaws in the Ellice Islands as 'debilitating, so unsightly, and frequently so productive of deformity', that some patients were hospitalized for up to four years. The economic impact of yaws probably offered the most convincing rationale for colonial governments and employers to support yaws work in Pacific territories. Lambert reported in 1925, that yaws was the most prevalent disease in the New Hebrides after malaria and hookworm disease, being 'the greatest apparent cause of economic loss ... A big percentage of the labor forces hobble out to the fields, crippled by yaws of the feet and yaws' ulcer of the legs, or are so bad that they must be kept near the quarters, cutting copra, so that they do not have to walk' (Figure 51.1).[79]

Treatment of deformed and diseased bodies, initially with salvarsan, followed by improved arsenicals, impressed not only doctors but also Pacific communities. Yaws programmes were endorsed by colonial governments and at the forefront of the Rockefeller's Pacific campaigns. Lambert observed that yaws treatment 'in Pacific islanders is probably the finest demonstration to them of the value of Western Medicine'.[80] The needle delivered this 'magic': 'the natives in the Ellice have no fear of the "needle" and great faith in its efficacy'.[81] Between 1923 and 1926, 75,000 yaws injections were administered to Western Sāmoa's population of around 38,003.[82] Samoans appeared so enthusiastic about the injections that the Faipule introduced very stringent yaws regulations. Drug compliance could also reflect cultural structures of obedience, duty, and respect. Compliance with tuberculosis treatment in the Cook Islands was partly because of cultural norms of obedience to traditional leaders, the church, and government departments.[83]

Far more embodied coercion was applied when doctors altered Pacific minds with psychotropic drugs and new technologies after World War II.

---

[78] S.M. Lambert, 'Health Survey of Western Samoa', 1924, RAC, RG 5, Series 2/245, Box 22, Folder 134.

[79] S.M. Lambert, 'Health Survey of the New Hebrides with Special Reference to Hookworm Disease', RAC, RG 5, Series 2/419, Box 40, Folder 241, 1925, p.26.

[80] Lambert, 'Health Survey of Western Samoa', 1924.

[81] Dr Macpherson to Heiser, 'Soil sanitation, hookworm and yaws', 9 October 1933, RAC, 1.1, Series 417, Box 1, Folder 4.

[82] Lambert to Heiser, 28 July 1932. RAC, RG 1.1, RG 1.1, Series 417, Box 1.

[83] Futter-Puati et al., 'Partnerships for health'.

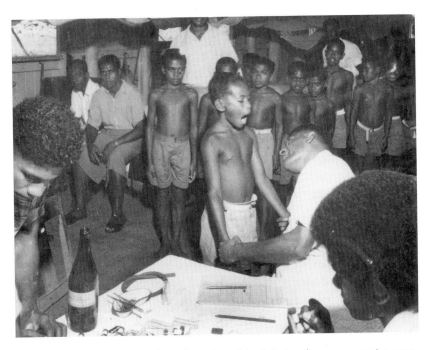

Figure 51.1 Examining a schoolboy of Bucalevu School during the yaws campaign, 1955.

Highly experimental shock and coma therapies were transferred to some Pacific hospitals, where doctors had a relatively open field for experimentation. Fiji led the foray in 1947 when Cardiazol (Metrazol) shock therapy was introduced, followed soon by modified insulin coma therapy and electroconvulsive therapy (ECT).[84] Even during the 1950s a doctor on Niue tried to treat a patient with insulin shock therapy. Renowned Canadian-born psychiatrist Eric Berne instructed Papeete physicians in Cardiazol therapy during the late 1950s. Cardiozol and insulin were soon discarded in Pacific institutions, because of dangerous side effects and patient resistance, but not ECT. New drugs offered the promise that those with severe mental illness could be treated not only within but outside coercive spaces, in order to become productive bodies. Largactil (chlorpromazine), a major sedative and antipsychotic drug, was introduced in Fiji in 1955 and by the following decade was stocked in most major hospitals and many nursing stations in the Pacific.

[84] J. Leckie, 'Discourses and technologies of mental health in post-war Fiji', in B.V. Lal (ed.), *The Defining Years: Pacific Islands, 1945–65* (Canberra: Australian National University, 2005), 151–73.

Medical testing and investigation became another 'scientific' means to define and order Pacific bodies. Hookworm treatment usually involved stool testing, although Chamorro children in Guam were routinely 'dosed' for worms without tests. Lambert encountered difficulties in obtaining stool specimens within Melanesian and Micronesian societies where bodily substances could be used for sorcery. He finally extracted a tiny sample on Bellona after offering fishhooks in exchange.[85] During the late 1920s Wasserman, and, by the 1940s, Kahn blood tests were administered to an increasing number of Pacific bodies, to test blood or cerebrospinal fluid to detect the pathogens that caused syphilis and yaws. The tests were not conclusive in identifying these diseases.

Sanitation

Discourse and practices in the name of sanitation were pervasive in the colonial redefinition of Pacific bodies and spaces. Scattered hamlets might be amalgamated or villages relocated, ostensibly for hygienic reasons, as in the Gilbert and Ellice Islands when government tried to regroup villages to areas where tides flowed in and out of lagoons.[86] The early nineteenth-century relocation of the Colo people in Fiji's highlands was driven by the imposition of colonial order, and was a discursive motif inscribed on bodies as well as communal spaces.[87] By the second half of the century medical reformers were convinced that many diseases were caused by miasmatic effluvia that bred within insanitary environments. While knowledge from the emerging discipline of tropical medicine and acceptance of germ theory eventually superseded miasmatic theory, colonial regulations still tried to redefine Pacific bodies in relation to the environment. Sanitation reform was to be all-encompassing.

Soil sanitation was synonymous with the extensive hookworm campaigns launched by colonial governments and the Rockefeller Foundation in the Pacific. It was also a polite euphemism for the 'hygienic' containment and disposal of human and animal faeces to eradicate not only intestinal worms, but also pests, such as flies, linked to the spread of infectious diseases. The separation of drinking water from human and animal excreta was pivotal to

---

[85] S.M Lambert, 'Health survey of Rennell and Bellona Islands', *Oceania* 2:2 (1931), 136–73, at 170.
[86] Lambert, 'Health Survey of the Gilbert and Ellice Islands, with special reference to hookworm infection', RAC, RG 5, Series 2/419, Box 40, Folder 241. p. 7.
[87] Thomas, 'Sanitation and seeing', 167.

the colonial compulsion to build latrines and to insist – under threat of fines or imprisonment – that people used them.[88] Pigs had to be enclosed and separated from villages: as far away as 100 metres in Fiji.[89] When the New Zealand government introduced extensive health restructuring in Sāmoa during the early 1920s, sanitary regulations prohibited dead animals and refuse from polluting not only drinking water supplies but also latrines and bathing pools. Even rotten breadfruit came under scrutiny and villagers could be fined if they allowed fruit to rot on the ground. The New Zealand regime was intent on showing that it was serious about health improvement, after being held culpable for the disaster of the 1918–19 influenza pandemic.

The brunt of sanitation projects fell upon villagers, especially with new punishable proscriptions about cleaning and the disposal of rubbish. Definitions of dirt and rubbish included leaves and matter left by the tide on the foreshore. Personal and communal labour expectations widened along gendered lines, and women's workload increased.[90] Regulations in the Gilbert and Ellice Islands stipulated that under a policeman's supervision women must clean leaves and rubbish in and around their houses between 5 and 6 p.m. The lagoon foreshore also had to be cleared. In Sāmoa *matai* were responsible for ensuring village and domestic cleaning, and villagers who infringed this would be fined 40 shillings. Chamorros were scrutinized by navy personnel to ensure that women did not dry clothes on bushes and that they maintained regulation-mowed lawns.[91] Mosquito breeding sites were also targeted in Pacific-wide village cleaning, especially after links were proven between the *Anopheles* mosquito and malaria, and to control other mosquito-borne diseases such as filariasis and dengue.[92]

Domestic spaces in the Pacific underwent even deeper changes than just sanitation surveillance. Social and spatial restructuring followed metropolitan norms governing the separate spaces that adults, children, married couples, and animals should occupy.[93] Extended families crowded together in dwellings were considered both unsanitary and immoral, and attempts were made

---

[88] R. Taylor, 'History of public health in Pacific Island countries', in M.J. Lewis and K.L. MacPherson (eds.), *Public Health in Asia and the Pacific: Historical and Comparative Perspectives* (London: Routledge, 2008), 276–306, at 286.
[89] Colo North Provincial Council, 1913 minutes, resolution VII (National Archives of Fiji).
[90] Ralston, 'Women workers'.   [91] Hattori, *Colonial Dis-ease*, 197.
[92] Bennett, *Natives and Exotics*, 49–71.
[93] J. Samson, *Race and Redemption: British Missionaries Encounter Pacific Peoples, 1797–1920* (Grand Rapids, MI: Eerdmans, 2017), 195.

in some colonies to prohibit people from asking friends and kin if they could share houses.[94] In 1901 the Anglican New Guinea Mission complained of several families cohabiting, 'where the sexes are not divided nor the married separated from the unmarried, not to mention a plentiful supply of pigs'.[95] Yet also in Papua and New Guinea attempts were made to prevent men from sleeping in separate houses because this was associated with ritual and cult activities. Women's domestic space throughout the region became increasingly linked to private space, although missionary, colonial, and native regulations were often ignored.

Regulations tried to enforce where and how houses should be constructed and furnished. For example, in Fiji sleeping places were to be raised at least 45 centimetres above the floors.[96] The insistence that each house had sufficient clean mats, spread on floors and beds, overlooked customary exchange and ceremonial uses. Regulations throughout the region insisted upon separate kitchens and sleeping spaces. Domestic spaces were closely defined, with the location of agriculture away from villages. Colonial authorities prohibited customary burial of the dead within domestic spaces. The Fiji Cemeteries Act of 1871 and native regulations prohibited burial within 'the limits of a town' or 'near a sea beach'.[97]

Sanitation was so much more than instilling cleanliness and saving lives. In Guam, 'Practices such as washing hands and faces before eating, and wearing shoes, became emblems of progress and evolution, rather than neutral indicators of better sanitary practices.'[98] Insanitary bodies and spaces not only spread disease but were seen to signal ignorance: primitive bodies and minds. The Rockefeller Foundation's worldwide hookworm eradication campaigns were based upon soil sanitation, as well as chemical treatments, that were pioneered in the southern United States, where they tackled ill health, especially among children. The programme laid the ground for a healthy productive workforce but also inculcated invasive public health measures. Lambert wanted that outcome in the Pacific. Sanitation may have denoted 'progress' and saved lives, but it could also be a form of cultural imperialism and assimilation, as when naval authorities tried to insist children wore shoes in pre-World War II Guam. During the previous century the British had insisted that Fijians abandon hairstyles considered

---

[94] Thomas, 'Sanitation and seeing', 162.   [95] Cited in Samson, *Race and Redemption*, 196–7.
[96] Colo North Provincial Council, 1913 minutes.
[97] Native Regulations Board, Regulation no. 14 of 1877, cited in Thomas, 'Sanitation and seeing', 159.
[98] Hattori, *Colonial Dis-ease*, 192.

Cooperative Bodies

to be evidence of heathenism, although some tribes refused.[99] Papuans were forbidden, except under special circumstances, to wear clothes on their upper bodies because this was considered a danger to health.[100]

Cooperative Bodies

The inculcation and acceptance of state authority and medicine that redefined bodies and spaces could not have been sustained if reliance was only upon quarantine, exile, separation, legislation, imprisonment, and fines. Sanitation and health projects were also rooted within the Western education that had been spearheaded by missionaries throughout the Pacific. Christian education was not only a transformation of the soul but was also embodied through, for example, dress, comportment, hygiene, and labour.[101] White women often taught these practices, as they did the literacy that was instrumental in health education. Medical officers were also teachers at many levels. Patrols and census expeditions provided opportunities to educate people about sanitation. A 'captive audience' assembled when bodies were compulsorily inspected and treated for hookworm, yaws, tuberculosis, or other diseases. Curious villagers might find white visitors amusing, and their technology interesting, as when the hidden secrets of a microscope were shared, large jars of hookworms were displayed, or educational films were screened. Nurse Geeves in Fiji took a doll, Adi Beti, on her village rounds to demonstrate efficient bathing of babies to mothers and to educate children about 'the need of cleansing every part of the body thoroughly'.[102] The Rockefeller Foundation considered that education and health missions were inseparable. Lambert was a proactive educator in the field and in the 1920s at the regional level pushed for the establishment of the Central Medical School in Suva.[103] Children were forged as 'compliant colonial subjects', with 'clean' bodies, when educated under hegemonic systems such as Guam's naval administration.[104]

---

[99] B.V. Lal, 'The passage out', in K.R. Howe, R.C. Kiste, and B.V. Lal, *Tides of History: The Pacific Islands in the Twentieth Century* (Honolulu: University of Hawai'i Press, 1994), 435–61, at 445.
[100] Samson, *Race and Redemption*, 206.
[101] E.g., Archer, *Sharks upon the Land*, 46–7, 208; Samson, *Race and Redemption*, 194–244.
[102] E.B. Geeves, 'Child welfare work in Nadroga and Colo West, Fiji', *Native Medical Practitioner* 3:2 (1940), 473–7, at 473.
[103] A. Stuart, 'Parasites lost? The Rockefeller Foundation and the expansion of health services in the colonial South Pacific, 1913–1939', PhD thesis, University of Canterbury, 2002.
[104] Hattori, *Colonial Dis-ease*, 158.

Health educational endeavours would have had little impact if they were not taken up by indigenous and women's groups in cooperation with medical authorities, and these groups often assumed responsibility for bodily and spatial inspections, and compliance with sanitation regulations. In Cook Islands, for example, the state worked with island councils, village health committees, and *Au Vaine* to enforce and promote personal and village sanitation, and health and reproductive education. Although instigated by missionaries and the Resident Commissioner, *tutaka*, when houses and villages were inspected by a travelling group of government officials including the Chief Medical Officer, became an important annual event that enlisted the support of local leaders and *Au Vaine*.[105] Similarly in Western Sāmoa, the annual *malaga* when officials toured villages was a grand occasion when sports and dancing showcased healthy bodies, but also when education and thousands of health inspections were carried out. In the Cook Islands, Davis also secured cooperation for Western medicine by working with *ta'unga* (indigenous healers), who often became health intermediaries between the state and villagers.[106]

Conclusion: Bodies and Spaces Redefined

The chapter's opening quotation stressed how the restructuring and redefinition of bodies and spaces were central to the colonization of the Pacific. This process could be highly coercive and overt, notably through the separation and confinement of bodies and minds deemed to be diseased. Legislation and regulations, whether enacted and enforced by the state or through custom, shaped parameters and codes for bodies and spaces. Race and gender permeated health and sanitation projects. Colonization was embodied as individuals inculcated new ways of thinking that became normative within Pacific cultures. While there was a shift from communal to individuated spaces, this process was never complete and it affected Pacific cultures unevenly at different times. Health colonization was a paradoxical process whereby external institutions (the state, the church, the Rockefeller Foundation) and professionals assumed a coercive and educative mass authority over bodies, but the individual body was acted upon, and individuals and communities were still expected to be actively responsible for health.

[105] Lange, 'European medicine in the Cook Islands', 68; Futter-Puati et al., 'Partnerships for health', 12.
[106] T. Davis and L. Davis, *Doctor to the Islands* (London: Michael Joseph, 1955); J. Baddeley, 'Traditional healing practices of Rarotonga, Cook Islands', in C.D. Parsons (ed.), *Healing Practices in the South Pacific* (Honolulu: The Institute of Polynesian Studies, 1995), 129–243.

Embodied colonization was never monolithic, neither within territories nor throughout the Pacific. The process of colonization, and the reach of health and sanitation projects within this chapter's timeframe, was uneven, with vast regions, as in Papua New Guinea, barely touched by public health.[107] Pacific peoples sometimes overtly resisted and, in more nuanced ways, negotiated the unacceptable or irritating practices that health practitioners tried to impose. There was also agency in the acquiescence to new spaces. For many reasons, it could suit villagers and their leaders to relocate or amalgamate villages, or for women to give birth in new spaces.[108] Even the fear of handing over one's faeces to a stranger could be overcome, when exchanged for useful goods such as fishhooks. Lambert realized that Samoan children were more willing to be lined up and stripped for bodily inspections if bribed with lollies.[109]

Health missions in the Pacific may have had humane objectives, but they were embedded within a colonialism whose control over indigenous bodies and reordering of spaces became an end in itself. This raises questions about the embodied legacy of health restructuring. Negative consequences endure that still impede contemporary health provision, such as the stigma associated with bodies in spaces like psychiatric asylums. But initially alien understandings and practices of health and caring were nevertheless incorporated and, it could be argued, indigenized within Pacific cultures.

---

[107] V. Luker, 'Papua New Guinea: epidemiological transition, public health and the Pacific', in Lewis and MacPherson (eds.), *Public Health in Asia and the Pacific*, 250–74.
[108] R. Nicole, *Disturbing History: Resistance in Early Colonial Fiji* (Honolulu: University of Hawai'i Press, 2011), 153–4; Ram and Jolly (eds.), *Maternities and Modernities*.
[109] Lambert, 'Health Survey of Western Samoa', 5.

52

The Pacific in the Age of Steam, Undersea Cables, and Wireless Telegraphy, 1860–1930

FRANCES STEEL

At the heart of this chapter lies a set of interdependent technologies whose development and application had remarkable global resonance and reach. Steamships, undersea cables, and wireless telegraphy rose to prominence during an era of heightened imperial expansion and rivalry from the second half of the nineteenth century. These industrial technologies of transport and communications that developed in distant metropoles are generally argued to have 'globalized' the Pacific, hooking this vast ocean into worldwide circuits of exchange. Yet it was only with the advent of a Pacific world networked through steam and electricity that such circuits were in effect global for the first time. The world's largest ocean was fundamental to any such claims of world-spanning, earth-girding effects.

Steamship and telegraph networks also reveal histories that were contained by and particular to the Pacific because geography mattered. Trans-oceanic movement and exchange long shaped this ocean basin; steam and electricity did not herald a newly interconnected Pacific. Yet they would soon alter the nature, range, and speed of regional linkages and the wider territorialization of the ocean. The communities and people they came to connect, and the understandings of the Pacific that emerged as a result, can be approached at different scales, both in their long-distance reach from 'coast to coast' and in their operation within many regional seas. Islands, while frequently cast as peripheral or marginal to 'big-power' geopolitics, were central to these connections, supporting and sustaining new forms of rim state interaction across the Pacific.

Ships and cables were a means to various ends, enabling the long-distance movement of people, goods, and ideas to advance a range of itineraries and projects. In this respect they have often slipped to the background of historical inquiry, as functional yet largely unremarkable infrastructure.

Shipping and telegraphy also tend to be studied separately. This mirrors the growing distance between transportation and communications following the laying of undersea cables, with information now able to move faster than people or goods. Yet steamships, cables, and wireless were each discussed in remarkably similar ways, celebrated as annihilating time and space, accelerating exchange, and binding distant peoples and places more tightly together. Nor did one technology displace another, as if to mark a rupture or radical break. Rather, they were interdependent and entangled, and, together with existing modes of mobility, these technologies fashioned a Pacific networked at many scales and to different speeds and rhythms. Accordingly, this chapter examines ships, cables, and wireless together, albeit sequentially. It outlines some predominant ways in which they were envisaged, sketches their introduction, and examines the consequences of their use, including in the collective disruption and reconfiguration of the Pacific in an industrial age.

The Age of Steam

From the perspective of ocean-spanning connections, the Pacific is often perceived as a 'slow' or belated ocean, the last to be criss-crossed routinely by steamship networks.[1] With steam so closely tied to the extension and consolidation of imperial power overseas, its application and impact were highly uneven. Steam was first trialled in the Pacific from the 1820s along the South American coastline, at roughly the same time it was introduced in northern hemisphere river, lake, and coastal trades. In the wake of the Spanish-American wars of independence, British and American merchants and officials hoped to counter political instability by strengthening lines of communication with Atlantic centres of power. After early failures due to expense and technical problems, William Wheelwright, a merchant-mariner and American consul at Guayaquil in the 1820s, proposed regular connections from Peru to both Chile and Panama. He recruited local support and eventually secured backers in London to establish the Pacific Steam Navigation Company in 1838.[2] The launch of its first vessel was rhetorically tied to the restoration of good government and the 'civilizing' of native

---

[1] 'The Atlantic is crossed daily by steamers, the Pacific not once a year', M.F. Maury, 1861, cited in D. Armitage, 'The Atlantic Ocean', in D. Armitage, A. Bashford, and S. Sivasundaram (eds.), *Oceanic Histories* (Cambridge: Cambridge University Press, 2018), 85–110, at 90.

[2] R.E. Duncan, 'William Wheelwright and early steam navigation in the Pacific 1820–1840', *The Americas* 32 (1975), 257–81. See also *Documents Relating to Steam Navigation in the Pacific* (Lima: Joseph M. Masias, 1836).

peoples.[3] This conflation of steam with Western-initiated progress, order, and superiority would reverberate down the decades.

Steam's imagined progressive influence sat alongside its demonstrative utility as a symbol of force. Its early uses in the Pacific included military campaigns, such as the New Zealand Wars from the 1840s. At mid-century the head of the British Naval hydrographical survey of New Zealand equated one steamship with one regiment of troops, asserting that steam power would communicate to native peoples the 'futility' of uprising or resistance.[4]

Steam promised to surmount the winds and ocean currents that had long battered the age of sail, and in doing so enhance the stability, speed, and regularity of sea transport. Heightened confidence in connectivity promoted the reach of the state over new territories, linking centres of administrative power and distant territories. Such aspirations were reflected in the establishment of the Pacific Mail Steamship Company in 1848 in New York. After securing a Congressional subsidy for a mail route to the newly acquired Oregon Territory, the company opened a coastal service between Panama and Astoria via Mexican ports and San Francisco.[5] This route foreshadowed later American advocacy for a canal at Panama, with naval strategist Alfred Mahan arguing that such a project would tie the 'exposed pioneers of European civilisation' on the Pacific coast back to the 'European family . . . the main body'.[6]

The application of steam to deep-ocean crossings took more work. It was an enormously expensive proposition to run a scheduled trans-oceanic service compared to shorter coastal routes. Early steamship propulsion mechanisms were inefficient, and ships were too small to carry the passengers and freight required to offset higher fuel consumption and running costs. Ongoing innovations over the second half of the nineteenth century, including iron and steel hull construction and high-pressure expansion engines, as well as more complex administrative coordination, greatly improved the efficiency and range of steam.

---

[3] C. Smith, *Coal, Steam and Ships: Engineering, Enterprise and Empire on the Nineteenth Century Seas* (Cambridge: Cambridge University Press, 2018), 215.
[4] F. Steel, 'Cruises and the making of Greater New Zealand', in F. Steel (ed.), *New Zealand and the Sea: Historical Perspectives* (Wellington: Bridget Williams Books, 2018), 251–73.
[5] J.H. Kemble, 'Pacific Mail service between Panama and San Francisco, 1849–1851', *Pacific Historical Review* 2 (1933), 405–17; J.H. Kemble, 'The genesis of the Pacific Mail Steamship Company', *California Historical Society Quarterly* 13 (1934), 386–406; R.M. López, 'From sail to steam: coastal Mexico and the reconfiguration of the Pacific in the nineteenth century', *International Journal of Maritime History* 22 (2010), 247–75.
[6] A.T. Mahan, *The Interests of America in Sea Power, Present and Future* (Boston: Little, Brown and Company, 1898), 260.

In reducing time in transit, steam would also come to alter the course of ocean routes, directing new attention to the Pacific as a realm of imperial connections. Steam first entered trans-Pacific trades during attempts to improve communications between Britain and its colonies in Australia and New Zealand. Initial proposals at mid-century included services around the Cape of Good Hope, 'overland' across the Mediterranean and through Suez, as well as via Panama and across the Pacific to Sydney.[7] Britain discounted the Pacific route because coaling would entail reliance on foreign possessions. Yet its appeal, particularly to aspiring political leaders and commercial interests in the Australasian colonies, endured, for branch connections from Panama promised access to a range of economic exchanges throughout the Americas – alternatives to their existing reliance on imperial networks via Asia, places with which they had 'very little of social affinity'. A trans-Pacific service, by contrast, spoke to Australia's position in 'the new empire' being founded around the Pacific based on the heritage of 'English civilisation'.[8]

The discovery of gold in California and Australia further elevated Panama as an international crossroads, attracting record numbers of people from the Atlantic coast to San Francisco (expedited by the isthmus railway completed in 1855). This crossing eventually displaced the traditional sailing route around Cape Horn into the Pacific. A regular Sydney–Panama connection opened in the mid-1860s, but was soon abandoned after problems with coaling and quarantine delays, and a shortage of passengers and freight, along with a reliance on inefficient and unsuitable ships.

Steam may have been a boon to empire, but it also facilitated connections that decentred Britain in global affairs, a prospect that steam and cable connections in the Pacific repeatedly posed. The principal interchange point of trans-Pacific shipping shifted north from Panama to San Francisco after the completion of the railroad to that port in 1869. In the Pacific, unlike other oceans, the construction of railroads repeatedly provided impetus for the introduction of steamship routes.[9] On their completion to west coast ports, North American railroad companies reached across the sea to recruit traffic to their lines. But as some observers seem to have feared:

---

[7] *The Routes to Australia, Considered in Reference to Commercial and Postal Interests by the Directors of the Australian Direct Steam Navigation Company, via Panama, in a Letter to the Right Hon. Viscount Canning, her Majesty's PM General* (London: Edward Stanford, 1854).

[8] H. Parkes, 6 August 1858, in Parkes, *Fifty Years in the Making of Australian History* (London: Longmans, Green, & Co., 1892), 122.

[9] J.C. Perry, *Facing West: Americans and the Opening of the Pacific* (Westport, CT: Praeger, 1994), 145.

When all nations had to round the Cape of Good Hope, England started fair, and could beat all Europe. When the passage across the Isthmus of Suez became the route, she was at the keel of the hunt, liable to have her passage disputed by lower European nations nearer to the Isthmus. Now that the Pacific Railway is complete America and Russia can join hands behind the back of England in the Pacific and Chinese Seas, and her Empire in India will be dissolved in one night.[10]

In a quest for new markets, the US directed its gaze first to Asia, rather than the white settlements in Australia and New Zealand. Pacific Mail opened services to Yokohama and Hong Kong in 1867 (building on earlier trans-Pacific traffic under sail). The company's failure to trans-ship cargo and passengers at San Francisco for the US east coast, favouring instead its own branch services to Panama, encouraged the Central Pacific and Union Pacific railroads to combine in competition. They established the Occidental and Oriental Steamship Company (O&O) in 1874, chartering ships from Britain to enter the run to Asia.[11]

New connections across the Pacific would soon demand the reshaping of island environments. In 1870 Pacific Mail looked to establish a mid-ocean coaling station to avoid high port taxes imposed at Honolulu. It initiated 'improvements' at Midway Island, situated roughly halfway between Japan and North America, which the USA had claimed three years earlier. Supported by a Congress appropriation, Pacific Mail commenced blasting a channel through the reef, but was forced to abandon the project as it proved too costly and difficult.[12]

In the southwest Pacific the Australasian colonies continued to view trans-Pacific connections to Britain as useful alternatives to those via Suez. British metropolitan firms did not engage directly in Pacific shipping, which opened up space for American and settler entrepreneurs. Early steamship operations between Sydney and San Francisco (c. 1870–5) were, however, unstable and short-lived, as neither the individual governments nor businessmen-financiers were willing to make long-term commitments or investments. Crossing times

---

[10] Irish historian John Patrick Prendergast to George Grey, 26 May 1869, GL P30.1 (Grey Letters), Sir George Grey Special Collections, Auckland City Library.
[11] Pacific Mail and O&O would eventually work under the same management, with O&O selling its ships to Pacific Mail in 1906. Perry, *Facing West*, 146; J.G.B. Hutchins, *The American Maritime Industries and Public Policy, 1789–1914* (Cambridge, MA: Harvard University Press, 1941), 529.
[12] 'Midway Islands', *Hawaiian Gazette* [reprinted from *Washington Daily Globe*] (7 April 1869), 4; 'The Midway Island Speculation, and what came of it', *Pacific Commercial Advertiser* (28 January 1871), 2.

The Age of Steam, Undersea Cables, and Wireless Telegraphy

Fig 52.1 Stranding of the steamship *Macgregor* in Kadavu Passage, Fiji, 18 May 1874.

varied enormously, and unsuitable ships chartered from other trades often met with difficulties, as seen in the stranding of the ship *Macgregor* at Kadavu in Fiji in 1874 (note the rigging, as early steam vessels still relied heavily on sail) (Figure 52.1). This incident was later immortalized to exemplify rim state beneficence, rather than epitomize the challenges and frictions of early steam. Islands appeared as the passive recipients of steam-age abundance: 'a very cornucopia was poured upon Kadavu', as fruit and tins of salmon were off-loaded to refloat the vessel, replaced with 70,000 coconuts as ballast to Sydney. This was recalled as 'America's last act of benediction' in Fiji, with the British annexation of the islands formalized later that year.[13]

In 1875 the Sydney–San Francisco service was put on a more secure footing through a ten-year contract with Pacific Mail, whose route network now stretched from New York to Oregon and San Francisco to Asia. This trans-Pacific connection was pitched as the best way to voyage 'Home' to Britain, for passengers would cross the tropics almost at 'right angles' and as rapidly

---

[13] *Daily Alta California* (1 January 1885).

as possible, fostering perceptions of an annihilated ocean.[14] The appeal lay not with the sea crossing but with a rail journey across the United States, where British settlers could observe what 'new world' development might promise for their own futures. Even a 'hurriedly made' trip across the USA would have a 'good educative effect' on the colonial traveller.[15] This pitch endured, with route advertisements in the 1930s extolling 'America: The world between two seas'.[16] In encouraging such encounters, this route seemingly affirmed ideals of an emergent Anglo-Saxon 'brotherhood' around the Pacific and, in its trans-Atlantic extension to Britain, it would further unite the 'English-speaking peoples of the world'.[17]

Ocean-spanning connections largely privileged rim state goals and priorities, yet in doing so placed new pressures on islands, as indicated again in Fiji. The Pacific Mail route forked at Kadavu to ports in Australia and New Zealand. A medical officer, a magistrate, police, customs, and quarantine were all required to be stationed at Kadavu, yet being so distant from the seat of government at Levuka, and thus from more stringent supervision, steamer visits were 'a constant source of anxiety' to colonial officials, while the transshipment of people and cargo was attended with great difficulty.[18] The Fiji call was subsequently dropped.

Pacific Mail did not re-tender when contracts came up for renewal in 1885. The American interest persisted in the form of the Oceanic Steamship Company of San Francisco, this time in partnership with British settler interests in New Zealand, represented by the Union Steam Ship Company of New Zealand (USSCo.) Oceanic's origins lie with the Hawaiian sugar 'empire' of German-born plantation owner Claus Spreckels and the traffic between Honolulu and San Francisco, before its shipping network was extended to Australia.[19]

Political realignments would soon undermine cross-imperial collaboration in trans-Pacific shipping. Following the American annexation of Hawai'i in 1898, the islands were incorporated by the terms of the Organic Act 1900 and

[14] Pacific Mail Steamship Company, *The American Route to Europe, and How to Travel By It* (1877), ephemera, National Library of Australia.
[15] *The Australian Handbook (incorporating NZ, Fiji and New Guinea) and Shippers' and Importers' Directory* (London: Gordon and Gotch, 1881), 517.
[16] *Sydney Morning Herald* (11 February 1932), 13.
[17] F. Steel, 'Re-routing empire? Steam age circulations and the making of an Anglo Pacific, c.1850–90', *Australian Historical Studies* 46 (2015), 356–73.
[18] A. Gordon to Colonial Office, 6 April 1877, no. 56, Fiji Despatches, National Archives of Fiji (hereafter NAF).
[19] J. Adler, 'The Oceanic Steamship Company: a link in Claus Spreckels' Hawaiian sugar empire', *Pacific Historical Review* 29:3 (1960), 257–69, at 267.

Honolulu was deemed a coastal port of the USA. Foreign shipping, including the USSCo., was barred from trading between the Hawaiian archipelago and the US mainland, the most remunerative leg of Pacific trade. Oceanic alone continued the trans-Pacific service. British settlers could choose to cross the Pacific in American ships, but the USSCo. eventually circumvented the US coastal restrictions to open an alternative pathway, steaming from Australia and New Zealand to the United States via Rarotonga and Tahiti (instead of Pago Pago and Honolulu).

If the forging of tighter 'Anglo bonds' centred the United States in trans-Pacific exchange, it also came to be seen as a competitive force and a rival pole of attraction to British imperial hubs. Hence the promotion of an alternative trans-Pacific bridge from Sydney to London via Canada, known as the 'All Red Route'. This was the 'missing link' in a globe-girding system to join British settlements exclusively through British enterprise. It also rested on prior rail networks, with the Canadian Pacific Railroad completed to Vancouver in 1885. From 1893 steamships linked Sydney, Brisbane, Suva, Honolulu, Victoria, and Vancouver, restoring Fiji's position as a South Pacific crossroads (now centred on its new colonial capital). Proposals initially included New Zealand, yet its omission (until 1911) spoke to the ways in which ambitions for steam were frequently at odds and difficult to reconcile. Australia valued speed over the rhetoric of imperial kinship. New Zealand's inclusion would entail significant delays for the carriage of passengers and mails to and from Australian ports. New Zealand continued to support the alternative network to San Francisco, for access to reliable shipping ultimately exceeded the national or imperial identity of any particular route.[20]

Steam transformed Vancouver as a Pacific gateway. Again, connections with Asia pre-dated those to the white settler colonies. The Canadian Pacific Railroad hoped to compete with Pacific Mail and O&O. Unlike the 'all red' service to Australasia, Britain saw strategic value in an alternative route across the Pacific to Asia, and British and Canadian subsidies supported the construction of a fleet of 'Empress' ships to call at Japan, Shanghai, Hong Kong, and Manila. North American railroads continued to express Pacific Slope rivalries, when in 1896 the Great Northern Railway, in consort with Japan's Nippon Yusen Kaisha (NYK), opened a monthly service from Seattle to Nagasaki, Yokohama, and Hong Kong. Its Seattle promoters aimed to siphon traffic away from Vancouver and Canadian Pacific. Japan's leaders

---

[20] F. Steel, '"The missing link": space, race and transoceanic ties in the settler-colonial Pacific', *Transfers: Interdisciplinary Journal of Mobility Studies* 5 (2015), 49–67.

recognized maritime developments as central to its emergence as a modern power and subsidized shipping as a key strategic industry. British shipbuilding yards supplied the fleets of commercial operators, including NYK. In turn, Toyo Kisen Kaisha (TKK) entered service between Japan and San Francisco in 1899.

In all of these ways, steam shaped new geographies of power, marking a notable Pacific turn in the USA and Canada and centring the North American continent between two oceans. Political and commercial leaders in the Pacific embraced steam's potential to free them from European dominance in an 'old' Atlantic world. Cast in this geopolitical light, the Pacific was 'the ocean of the future'.[21] However, this North American emphasis should not overshadow connections newly binding South America and Asia. Pacific Mail's coastal network between Panama and Oregon had long hooked Mexico into trans-Pacific exchange, but Mexico, China, and Japan eventually sought to break the company's monopoly along with San Francisco's intermediary port status. In the early twentieth century, the China Commercial Steamship Company (from 1903) and TKK (from 1910) established regular direct services between Asian and Mexican ports.[22]

Trans-Pacific routes were, in effect, narrow pathways across the sea. In adhering to strict timetables, they bypassed most islands and spent only a handful of hours in the small number of ports en route. Most major routes crossed the Pacific once every four weeks (the passage between Sydney and San Francisco took twenty-one days). Ports might easily be omitted if they proved detrimental to the timetable or state subsidies were not forthcoming. The advent of ocean-spanning networks charts a somewhat paradoxical separation between islands and rim in a period of heightened mobility and integration.[23] Yet attending to inter-island services can also illuminate steam's importance in shaping a set of new constellations of inter-regional exchange.

Steam entered coastal trades in Australia and New Zealand from the mid-nineteenth century and by the 1870s these services extended to neighbouring island groups. This 'second tier' of Pacific shipping encompassed the larger islands in the southwest, grouped broadly as Melanesia, which trans-Pacific

---

[21] G.E. Foster (Canada) in *Report by the Right Hon. the Earl of Jersey, G.C.M.G., on the colonial conference at Ottawa, with the proceedings of the conference and certain correspondence, 1894*. C7553, 272, House of Commons Parliamentary Papers Online (Proquest).
[22] R. López, 'Transpacific Mexico: encounters with China and Japan in the age of steam (1867–1914)', PhD thesis, University of British Colombia, 2012.
[23] A. McKeown, 'Movement', in D. Armitage and A. Bashford (eds.), *Pacific Histories: Ocean, Land, People* (Basingstoke: Palgrave Macmillan, 2014), 143–65, at 151.

services bypassed. Such operations also reveal the close connections between steam shipping and the commercial exploitation of island resources. The Sydney-based Burns Philp & Company (BP), established in 1883, extended its northern Australian interests in stores and coastal shipping further north into Papua and New Guinea, the New Hebrides, and the Solomon Islands, as well as the Gilbert, Ellice, and Marshall Islands. It invested in plantations and copra production to secure cargo for its vessels.[24] Across the Pacific, like the Oceanic Company which it would eventually absorb, the Matson Steam Navigation Company, founded in 1882, invested in sugar and pineapple plantations in Hawai'i as well as oil fields in California. It was described as 'a seafarer that has dug itself in on the land, intermingling with the sources of the commodities that keep its ships breathing'.[25]

Steamship operations were central to the expansive colonial nationalism and imperial aspirations of both Australia and New Zealand in the Pacific. BP represented the practical and recognizable form of Australian engagement in the region for many decades. Political leaders typically learned about their island neighbours through BP, and as commercial and territorial rivalries in the Pacific intensified in the early twentieth century, company officials often felt they were left at the front line in conflicts with Germany, France, and Japan.[26] New Zealand used shipping to assert and promote its authority throughout Polynesia, including through cruises by government officials, scientists, journalists, and tourists, as well as the promise of improved regional connections. Yet Niue, annexed by New Zealand in 1901, did not see a promised timetabled shipping service with the 'metropole' for over two decades.[27]

Routes shaped, and were shaped by, political ideologies and cultural sensibilities. This is apparent not only at the level of strategic power, but also in everyday labour relations. Britain's settler colonies waged battles from the 1870s to uphold white labour supremacy in the mercantile marine, notably to oust Chinese and Pacific Islander crews from the fleets of local companies trading between Australasia and the Islands. By the time the USSCo. entered trans-Pacific shipping in 1885 it had conceded to union agitation and employed only British and white colonial crews. Chinese

---

[24] K. Buckley and K. Klugman, *The History of Burns Philp: The Australian Company in the South Pacific* (Sydney: Burns Philp and Company, 1981).

[25] 'With Matson down to Melbourne', *Fortune* 16:3 (1937).

[26] These points were previously made in F. Steel, 'Shipping, imperial', in J. MacKenzie (ed.), *Encyclopedia of Empire*, vol. IV (Oxford: Wiley-Blackwell, 2016).

[27] Steel, 'Cruises and the making of Greater New Zealand', 251–73.

employment in American trans-Pacific shipping to Australasia (but not Asia) was curtailed as labour union agitation in Australia and New Zealand folded into wider political battles against 'Asiatic' mobility around the Pacific, culminating in the enactment of immigration restrictions. US legislation in 1915 attempted to reduce Asian crews through English-language requirements, but many Chinese were retained by allowing sign language and 'pidgin' English.[28]

White settler states excluded non-white labour from contact with trans-Pacific shipping, yet they were highly dependent on Islander labourers at the lower tiers of extraction and transportation in ports of call, including coaling, cargo handling, lightering, pilotage, and laundry work. These intensive yet casual and cyclical labour demands brought shipping companies into contact with a host of other intermediaries in port. At times this generated conflict, as the shipping industry enticed young men away from outlying regions and the oversight of traditional structures of authority, and as colonial officials sought to police their patterns of sociability and modes of residence in port towns.[29]

Greater centralized control over maritime industry could also diminish Island livelihoods. In 1901 Hawaiian vessels were subject to new US regulations, which stipulated carrying licensed officers. Schools were established to train crew to pass US examinations, yet most Hawaiians were unable to attend classes and licensed crew from the mainland filled their positions. Their unfamiliarity with coastal conditions in Hawai'i led to accidents. Rising costs, including higher wages and the refitting of ships to meet new specifications, were passed on to local passengers and traders.[30]

Everyday engagements offer other perspectives on the reshaping of the Pacific under steam. Intergenerational aspirations for wealth and prosperity motivated many men to cross the ocean from China to North America. The imprint of what has come to be termed the 'Cantonese Pacific' was most legible around the rim and in the two-way flows of letters, money, and goods, as well as the repatriation of the bones of dead emigrants. It was also felt in the Islands as Cantonese merchants and small business operators spread throughout the Pacific, as well as Southeast Asia.[31] In this respect,

---

[28] J. Martinez, C. Lowrie, F. Steel, and V. Haskins, *Colonialism and Male Domestic Service across the Asia Pacific* (London: Bloomsbury, 2019), 151.
[29] F. Steel, *Oceania under Steam: Sea Transport and the Cultures of Colonialism, c.1870–1914* (Manchester: Manchester University Press, 2011), 171–92.
[30] M. Thomas, *Schooner from Windward: Two Centuries of Hawaiian Interisland Shipping* (Honolulu: University of Hawai'i Press, 1983), 96.
[31] E. Sinn, *Pacific Crossing: California Gold, Chinese Migration, and the Making of Hong Kong* (Hong Kong: Hong Kong University Press, 2013), esp. chapter 3; H. Yu, 'Unbound space: migration,

North America's developing 'west' was not simply the product of a settler colonial march overland from 'sea to shining sea', but also emerged through a series of multi-ethnic and trans-oceanic conjunctions.[32] The fundamental tension between steam-age expansion and containment was most pronounced here, as rising white settler nationalism cemented border controls and regimes of racial exclusion. This transformed the nature of mass voluntary migration across the Pacific, particularly in the first decades of the twentieth century.

These border controls did not curtail all movement, and short-term and cyclical itineraries, including for leisure and education, persisted and in many instances found room for expansion. Route networks also orientated Islanders towards one another. It was not uncommon for Māori in New Zealand to expect the arrival of Hawaiians to their shores, with Auckland newly linked to Honolulu by trans-Pacific steam. Their journeys could attest to and reassert deep genealogical ties across Polynesia, dramatically different ocean-spanning affinities than those recently set in motion by Anglo imperial expansion.[33] Throughout the Islands, non-elites routinely boarded steamships to sustain kindship bonds, travelling to participate in feasting and other rituals of exchange. This was perhaps most notable between Fiji, Tonga, and Sāmoa, the encompassing 'native sea' of Vasa Loloa.[34] Island communities also engaged with new circuitries, for example exploring markets for their produce in New Zealand, Australia, and Canada.

The age of steam inaugurated mass tourism and with it new forms of textual and visual representation of the Pacific. Shipping companies became publicists and tour operators, and, in the key hubs of Suva and Honolulu, hotel proprietors. Guidebooks and magazines combined with published travel narratives and advertising fashioned shipping as pleasurable and educational.[35] This shaped new worlds of encounter and contact, while also promoting rim state trade and investment opportunities in the islands.

---

aspiration and the making of time in the Cantonese Pacific', in W. Anderson, M. Johnson, and B. Brookes (eds.), *Pacific Futures: Past and Present* (Honolulu: University of Hawai'i Press, 2018), 178–204.

[32] K.S. Chang, *Pacific Connections: The Making of the US–Canadian Borderlands* (Berkeley: University of California Press, 2012).

[33] For instance the travel accounts of J.T. Baker in K. Cook, *Return to Kahiki: Native Hawaiians in Oceania* (Cambridge: Cambridge University Press, 2018). See also H. Moanau to Collector of Customs, 28 December 1878, 1878/918, Box 181, A78 5544, BBAO, National Archives of New Zealand.

[34] D. Salesa, 'The Pacific in indigenous time', in Armitage and Bashford (eds.), *Pacific Histories*, 31–52; Steel, *Oceania under Steam*, 193–214.

[35] V. Kuttainen, S. Liebich, and S. Galletly, *The Transported Imagination: Australian Interwar Magazines and the Geographical Imaginaries of Colonial Modernity* (Amherst, NY: Cambria Press, 2018).

Still, many island communities, such as the Marquesas and across the Cook, Society, Gilbert, and Ellice Islands groups, had little or nothing to do with steam-age maritime industry, and were orientated to the world beyond their native seas only through intermittent visits by trading, missionary, or naval vessels. Colonial governments concentrated calls of foreign ships to specific ports in order to collect dues and streamline quarantine and immigration procedures, which further diminished visits to outlying islands. Relative inaccessibility beyond the main routes could also render island places and peoples more susceptible to exoticization and recuperation as authentic and 'untouched'. In this respect, steam-age 'civilizing' might be cast as a corrupting intrusion, rather than beneficent and progressive.

Undersea Telegraph Cables

We have left America. Our ship is British, of the White Star line, but hired by an American Company [O&O]. We were an hour late in starting, because we were required to carry despatches to Hawaii to announce the Annexation which Congress decreed and the President ratified yesterday. With the despatches have come on board four correspondents from San Francisco papers, full of the importance of their mission – for there is no cable to Honolulu and we shall be the first to announce to the first American colony that Uncle Sam is going to imitate Brother Bull.[36]

Written at sea between San Francisco and Honolulu in 1898, this British traveller's account illuminates the ubiquity of technology in executing imperial goals, as well as the entanglement of British and American industry in making Pacific connections. It also speaks to the long standing maritime conflation of transportation and communication. People and news travelled together in the same ships at the same speed across oceans. Yet this was a moment on the cusp of change; within five years the laying of undersea cables would effect a dramatic transformation. Electric current 'far outstripped' steam, able to transmit information in minutes that otherwise took ships days or weeks.[37]

---

[36] C.P. Trevelyan, Letter to father, Sir G.O. Trevelyan, per steamship *Coptic*, 7 July 1898. Reproduced in C.P. Trevelyan, *Letters from North America and the Pacific* (London: Chatto & Windus, 1969), 117.
[37] G.O. Squier, 'An American Pacific cable', *Transactions of the American Institute of Electrical Engineers* 16 (1899), 662–3.

The Age of Steam, Undersea Cables, and Wireless Telegraphy

Submarine cables were developed in the mid-nineteenth century following the discovery of the insulating properties of gutta percha, a rubber-like gum. Cables were about 2.5 centimetres in diameter, comprising a core copper wire, insulating layer, and hemp covering. Like the steamship, the cable annihilated distance, yet the sea itself provided a form of insulation, more effective than land in that it was less vulnerable to routine human interference.[38] Ocean surveys were required before cables could be laid, revealing new insights into ocean depths and the sea floor. This displaced popular perceptions of wild, even hostile ocean worlds to invite more benign, even inviting associations.[39] In the Pacific, imagined 'insuperable physical difficulties' for cable-laying, including unfathomable depths, jagged coral precipices and subterranean fires, delayed comprehensive surveys, as did the British Admiralty's reluctance to conduct or support them.[40] However, by the mid-1880s there was increasing confidence that trans-Pacific cables could be laid, and surveys soon indicated that the greatest depths were located closer to land.[41] Nearly 600 samples of the sea bottom were obtained during a survey for the British 'all red' cable, revealing also that in the tropics the richer surface marine life, once decayed, provided a bed of dust on the ocean floor in which cables could rest, thereby extending their lifespan compared to colder ocean regions.[42] The greatest ocean depths known until then, the Nero Deep southeast of Guam, was named after the US naval vessel *Nero*, which recorded them during its 1899 cable survey between Hawai'i, the Philippines, and Japan.[43]

Trans-Pacific cables were proposed from the mid-1860s, about the same time trans-Pacific steamship routes were opening up. Both systems demanded intermediate stops. The telegraph signal in long sections became weaker, affecting transmission speeds along the whole network. Just as Pacific Mail sought to construct a coaling station at Midway Island in 1870, its appeal as a cable station was also apparent. In some instances, cable

---

[38] N. Starosielski, *The Undersea Network* (Durham, NC: Duke University Press, 2015), 30.
[39] H.M. Rozwadowski, *Fathoming the Ocean: The Discovery and Exploration of the Deep Sea* (Cambridge, MA: Belknap Press), 2005.
[40] G. Johnson, *The All Red Line: The Annals and Aims of the Pacific Cable Project* (Ottawa: James Hope & Sons, 1903), 384.
[41] Johnson, *The All Red Line*, 299–300.
[42] O. Klotz, 'Transpacific longitudes', *Transactions and Proceedings of the Royal Society of New Zealand* 39 (1906), 49–70, at 50, 51.
[43] J.M. Flint, 'A contribution to the oceanography of the Pacific, compiled from data collected by the United States steamer *Nero* while engaged in the survey of a route for a trans-Pacific cable', *Bulletin of the United States National Museum* 55 (1905), 1–2.

stations mapped onto steamer ports, but they were also needed in places where routine shipping did not call. This provided further insulation, with less danger of cable interruption in areas of limited shipping.

Two trans-Pacific cables, one British and the other American, opened in 1902 and 1904 respectively. The British 'all red' cable connected Vancouver (Bamfield), Fanning Island, Suva, and Norfolk Island, where it bifurcated to Auckland (Doubtless Bay) and Queensland (Southport). The Vancouver–Fanning leg would be the longest section of any cable yet laid. The American cable linked San Francisco, Honolulu, Midway, and Guam, with branch extensions to Manila and Shanghai, and to the Bonin Islands and Yokohama. Both cables were intended as strategic alternatives if global tensions disrupted cables laid in the Indian or Atlantic oceans. They were expected to stimulate new demand for communication rather than rely on the existing demand.

Just as the steamer route between Sydney and Vancouver was described as the 'missing link' in an imperial chain, so too was the British trans-Pacific cable. Canadian interests inspired this project, notably the Scottish inventor and railroad pioneer Sir Sandford Fleming. He was one of a number of promoters bent on the reform of imperial and international communications, seeking to wrest control from commercial monopolies – notably the Eastern Extension Telegraph Company, whose cable web stretched across Asia and encompassed Australia via a connection between Darwin and Java (and from there to Singapore and London).[44] The Pacific Cable would be the first state-run cable, envisaged as a 'public service oriented' network with Britain, Canada, Australia, and New Zealand sharing its costs and operation.[45]

Despite the 'all red' rhetoric, the Pacific cable was less of a British strategic priority. Britain was wary of new centres of influence displacing or marginalizing London as a global communications hub. This slowed its commitment to the project, as did Eastern Extension's commercial objections to route diversity.[46] The company mounted 'rear guard' action, including lowering cable rates to Australia and opening a new Indian Ocean line between Perth and Cape of Good Hope. Some Australian stakeholders were

[44] S. Müller-Pohl, 'Wiring the Pacific: North American perspectives on a (de)colonial project', in E. Bischoff, N. Finzsch, and U. Lehmkuhl (eds.), *Provincializing the United States: Colonialism, Decolonization, and (Post)colonial Governance in Transnational Perspective* (Heidelberg: Winter, 2014), 155–80, at 163.

[45] D. Winseck and R. Pike, *Communication and Empire: Media, Markets and Globalization* (Durham, NC: Duke University Press, 2007), 150–67.

[46] R.W.D. Boyce, 'Imperial dreams and national realities: Britain, Canada and the struggle for a Pacific telegraph cable, 1879–1902', *English Historical Review* 115 (2000), 39–70, at 50–1.

also threatened by the Pacific project, even as existing cables were often interrupted or out of service, leaving the colonies cut off for days.[47]

Meanwhile, French interests (the Société Française des Télégraphes Sous-Marins) opened a cable from Queensland to New Caledonia in 1893. Designed to stimulate trade and potentially develop into a trans-Pacific service, controversially both New South Wales and Queensland offered subsidies. Celebrated as the first step in breaking the Eastern Extension monopoly, French initiative only showed up British inaction.[48] Despite various colonial conventions and committees in the 1890s, the political tide in Britain only decisively turned to the Pacific as US officials endorsed the urgency of a cable of their own after seizing Guam and the Philippines in 1898.[49] In 1901 a Pacific Cable Board was formed with members from Britain, Canada, Australia, and New Zealand, and the cable opened in 1902.

In strategizing for greater control in the Pacific and in building commercial relations with Asia, America recognized the cable as a powerful adjunct to the trans-Pacific steamship lines. Many cable bills were brought before Congress, with members divided over whether to pursue state ownership or leave it to private enterprise.[50] The Commercial Pacific Cable Company eventually managed the American cable project, which opened in 1904. Presumed to be an American enterprise, Eastern (British) and Northern (Danish) cable interests in fact held 75 per cent of Commercial's stock, although this was not made public until 1921.[51] Such agreements were deemed necessary as, unlike the British 'all red' route, these existing operators already served many landing points, and Britain remained apprehensive about America's future influence in Asia. Historians have emphasized Commercial's 'strategic nationalism', in that its all-American image was mobilized at particular times, but set aside in negotiations for access to Asian markets.[52]

---

[47] Winseck and Pike, *Communication and Empire*, 161–2; 'The All-British trans-Pacific Cable', *Blackwoods Edinburgh Magazine* 161:876 (1897), 269–79.
[48] *Daily Telegraph* [Sydney] (18 October 1893), 5; *The Telegraph* [Brisbane] (26 October 1893), 4; D.R. Headrick, *The Tentacles of Progress: Technology Transfer in the Age of Imperialism, 1850–1940* (Oxford: Oxford University Press, 1988), 122. Thanks to Alexis Bergantz for correspondence on this topic.
[49] Squier, 'An American Pacific cable'. Such rivalry would also manifest over a disagreement about cable landing rights at Necker Island, an outlying island in the Hawaiian archipelago.
[50] L.B. Tribolet, *The International Aspects of Electrical Communications in the Pacific Area* (Baltimore: Johns Hopkins University Press, 1929), 181; Winseck and Pike, *Communication and Empire*, 168.
[51] Tribolet, *International Aspects*, 155.
[52] S. Müller, *Wiring the World: The Social and Cultural Creation of Global Telegraph Networks* (New York: Columbia University Press, 2016), 247; Winseck and Pike, *Communication and Empire*, 170, 268.

Regardless, this cable held more immediate significance for military and defence, particularly for US naval priorities in Guam, which as Commercial's vice-president asserted to the Secretary of the Navy, was a 'valueless' atoll now elevated to 'one of the most important islands in the Pacific Ocean'.[53] In 1905 three Dutch-German cables were laid from Yap (an island positioned roughly midway between Guam and Manila) to the Dutch East Indies (Menado), Shanghai, and Guam. Cables fashioned new hubs that were often not visible in the existing trans-Pacific steamship route systems. German ownership of Yap troubled the USA as it provided an alternative telegraph route to Commercial Pacific's network, while Japan's seizure of the island in World War I raised new fears about interference in both shipping and telegraphy between the USA and the Philippines. A dispute during 1920–1 was resolved when the Yap–Guam cable went to the USA, Yap–Manado to the Dutch, and Yap–Shanghai to Japan.[54]

Interactions at specific sites can offer different angles of vision on these large-scale projects and their geopolitical extensions. The 'all red' cable, praised for binding white settler societies across the Pacific, depended on the labour of racially diverse, 'pre-fabricated' communities at the cable stations, the route's 'core geography'.[55] During the nineteenth century, various groups intermittently inhabited Fanning Island (Tabuaeran) and claimed it for Britain. With the cable's advent, about twenty Europeans employed by the cable board lived there on two-year shifts, many recruited from Australia or New Zealand. Colonial cultural hierarchies more familiar to British India heavily imprinted domestic life, with Indian men recruited from Suva to Fanning Island to work for single European men as servants and cooks.[56] About thirty Gilbertese Islanders also worked at the station, some in domestic service (for European families), others as carpenters and general labourers. Attempts to fashion a sense of 'cable community' through leisure activities, including sports days, expressed ideas about bodily discipline and the civilizing project that cable stations liked to promote (Figure 52.2). Gilbertese who worked for the cable station often competed with those indentured to the island's copra plantation, which employed up to 150 men.[57]

---

[53] 10 November 1903, cited in Tribolet, *International Aspects*, 188.
[54] Starosielski, *Undersea Network*, 189.   [55] Starosielski, *Undersea Network*, 87.
[56] Pacific Cable Board to Agent General Immigration, 20 March 1920, 20.1673, CSO, NAF. See also J. Martínez, 'Asian servants for the imperial telegraph: Imagining North Australia as an Indian Ocean colony before 1914', *Australian Historical Studies* 48 (2017), 227–43; Martínez et al, *Colonialism and Male Domestic Service*, esp. chapter 2.
[57] E.K. Edie, 'Fanning Island: an outpost of the empire', *Otago Daily Times* (22 March 1926), 7; see also Starosielski, *Undersea Network*, 99–111.

The Age of Steam, Undersea Cables, and Wireless Telegraphy

Fig 52.2 Fanning Island – sports day 1926 [at the Pacific Cable Board Cable station].

Ships remained vectors and spaces of communication, vital for the movement and exchange of people and goods. They continued to carry mails that followed up on communications first sent in shorthand via the cable. The telegraph also benefited the commercial operation and safety of shipping, with merchants able to calculate more accurately when to expect steamers (which was crucial for trade in perishables such as fruit), and to obtain more up-to-date market information to inform the timing and volume of shipments.

While the cable did more than shipping to free communication from geographical constraints, there were still material constraints, including cost, as telegrams were charged by the word.[58] There were also environmental constraints, as cables were vulnerable to breakages caused by subterranean earthquakes and volcanic activity. The greatest stresses occurred close to islands, through the effects of strong currents and sharp coral rock. In the 1920s and 1930s, reports of cable breakages were most common near Norfolk Island, the Philippines, and Japan, while during 1918 alone there were at least eight breaks in the American trans-Pacific cable, mostly near Guam.[59]

---

[58] J.D. Peters, 'Technology and ideology: the case of the telegraph revisited', in J. Packer and J. Robertson (eds.), *Thinking with James Carey: Essays on Communications, Transportation, History* (New York: Peter Lang, 2006), 137–55, at 148.
[59] See *Burlington Free Press* (22 December 1919); *New Zealand Herald* (13 March 1920); *Otago Daily Times* (20 September 1929).

In any case, and as elsewhere in the world, high tariff rates limited the cable's utility. The telegram was best suited to brief and urgent communications, and, combined with the expense, it served colonial administrators and commercial interests better than the press. Neither trans-Pacific cable became a means of mass communication, and both lay idle for significant periods.[60] Cable rates across the North Pacific were significantly higher than the 'all red' service – so high, in fact, that press messages between China and the USA were sent via London. Even the British cable earned well below the projected traffic, and ran annual deficits prior to World War I.[61] Cheaper 'social' rates were introduced from 1913, and cable receipts increased substantially. With these reduced rates it became an important tool for the diaspora, with Indian settlers in Fiji turning to the Pacific Cable for communications with India and to advance their commercial and social networks, again pointing to emergent and highly networked worlds of Asia in/and the Pacific.[62] The 'all red' cable accumulated sufficient reserves to duplicate the network. By contrast, US officials were dissatisfied with the operation of the North Pacific cable and sought to wrest control from commercial enterprise.[63]

The differential and limited impact of the cable has been described in terms of 'lumps', or 'institutional agglomerations of power' that produced rigid and channelled connections, rather than more diverse and open-ended flows.[64] The undersea cable network was controlled by a limited number of agencies, 'surfaced' only at a very small number of islands, and cost so much to use that it benefited only a self-selecting few. New communications technology in the form of wireless telegraphy promised to counter or offset these 'lumps' of power in the Pacific.

Wireless and the 'Pacific Silence'

Radiotelegraphy inaugurated the modern era of wireless communication. Wireless installations required transmission and relay towers but otherwise dispensed with connecting wires and fixed routes. (This chapter does not consider telephony, i.e. voice broadcasting.) They were cheaper than laying

---

[60] Squier, 'An American Pacific cable', 662; Winseck and Pike, *Communication and Empire*, 150.
[61] Tribolet, *International Aspects*, 84; Winseck and Pike, *Communication and Empire*, 179–80.
[62] Winseck and Pike, *Communication and Empire*, 193. See also T. Ballantyne, 'Imperial futures and India's Pacifics: space, temporality and the textures of empire', in *Pacific Futures*, 157–77.
[63] Winseck and Pike, *Communication and Empire*, 268.
[64] S.J. Potter, 'Webs, networks, and systems: globalization and the mass media in the nineteenth- and twentieth-century British empire', *Journal of British Studies* 46 (2007), 621–46, at 634.

undersea cables, could not be cut or destroyed, and were considerably faster. Despite a key limitation in its susceptibility to interception and breaches of secrecy, wireless telegraphy promised to enhance long-distance communications very greatly. It also enabled communication between ship and shore and enhanced that between ships at sea. Vessels could now be plotted against one another at sea. Relaying information about weather conditions and hazards, as well as ships in distress, it promised a safer, more informationally dense ocean. The British Marconi Wireless Telegraph Company, established in 1900, dominated early radiotelegraphy. Shipping companies were soon compelled by law to install wireless sets, rented from Marconi and operated by its own personnel. Shipboard wireless quickly became so routine that a steamer 'without wireless' was like a steamer 'without a captain'.[65]

Wireless offered connections to islands either off the main shipping routes or omitted from the trans-Pacific cable networks. This appealed especially to Europeans who had established themselves in comparatively remote sites, notably missionaries, traders, and those with interests in plantation and mining ventures.

In 1909 a Pacific Radio Telegraph Company was formed in London, aiming to introduce wireless throughout the islands. Its board included steamship company directors and the head of the Pacific Islands Phosphate Company. Needing to recruit state subsidies, its prospectus specifically targeted Australia. It pitched wireless as central to Australia's identity as an emergent Pacific power. It referred to the 'familiar' story of Britain's failure to annex islands, leaving Australia surrounded by rival imperial powers. If most Australians perceived islands 'merely as the outposts of naval power – mere ports of refuge, or (at best) inferior coaling-stations', the prospectus sought to stimulate interest in their untapped commercial prospects that only needed wireless telegraphy to be brought within reach. It held out the potential of wireless telegraphy transforming Australia into a 'great Continental emporium' for island trade, with the term 'emporium' possibly meant to evoke associations with London's role as the world's emporium. It argued that many regional actors struggled with the 'Pacific silence'. The tourist, even when following a 'recognised and stereotyped route, wanders out of touch with his friends in Australia'; so too did naval cruisers 'plunge for a while into the unknown'. Yet the trader 'who roams further afield,

---

[65] 'Through California and the East: impressions by the way', *Kai Tiaki: The Journal of the Nurses of New Zealand* (1 July 1912), 12. An international convention of 1906 prevented Marconi from refusing to communicate with ships fitted with rival systems.

vanishes from ken altogether for weeks or months at a time'. Rapid wireless communication was essential for trade, for it 'suffers most from the Pacific silence'.[66]

Pacific Radio hoped to install high-powered wireless stations at Suva and Ocean Island (Banaba) and from there to 'chief islands' – in the first instance to Papua, New Hebrides, Solomon Islands, Tonga, Rarotonga, Tahiti, Nauru, and Sāmoa, so as to 'thoroughly cover the Pacific in overlapping circles'.[67] Figure 52.3 depicts the estimated range of each station. In such a 'spacious' scheme, Australia and New Zealand would be in touch with every island where ships loaded phosphate, copra, bêche-de-mer, and tropical fruits. The prospectus stressed a complementary relationship with the Pacific Cable, in that long-distance wireless stations erected at Southport and Doubtless Bay would supplement the undersea cable service in the event of breakdown or interference. Cable traffic would also increase, as most of the wireless business had to pass over the cable.

A Radio Telegraphic Conference in Melbourne considered these proposals in 1909.[68] It looked favourably on wireless to connect islands that lay within 'the sphere of British influence' and bring them into contact with Australia and New Zealand, 'to which they naturally belong'. However, it insisted that services should be under state rather than private control, effectively scuppering the company's prospects, although its director was briefly contracted to work for Marconi in Australia. The 1911 Imperial Conference endorsed the principle of state-owned wireless. Its extension into the Pacific would await the results of radio experiments from stations erected at Fiji that year. British authorities were slow to embrace wireless, however, and its extension throughout the southwest Pacific, particularly in the Solomons, the New Hebrides, and Ocean Island, was largely due to World War I.[69]

Ultimately, commercial concerns, rather than the state, drove further wireless development in the British Pacific. In 1913 Amalgamated Wireless (Australasia) Limited (AWA), was established in Sydney, a merger of two

---

[66] Enclosed in 'Wireless in Pacific. Proposals of Conference of Dec. 1909', 1911/14178, A1, Department of External Affairs, National Archives of Australia. The director, J.W. Hamilton, had proposed an earlier scheme, 'Wireless telegraphy. An Australian scheme. Looping islands and mainland', *Age* (26 May 1905), 5.
[67] 'Pacific Wireless Telegraph', *Otago Witness* (23 March 1910), 14.
[68] 'Wireless in Pacific. Proposals of Conference of Dec. 1909', *Otago Witness* (23 March 1910), 14.
[69] M.L. Hadlow, 'Wireless and empire ambition: wireless telegraphy/telephony and radio broadcasting in the British Solomon Islands Protectorate, South-West Pacific (1914–1947): political, social and developmental perspectives', PhD thesis, University of Queensland, 2016, chapter 5.

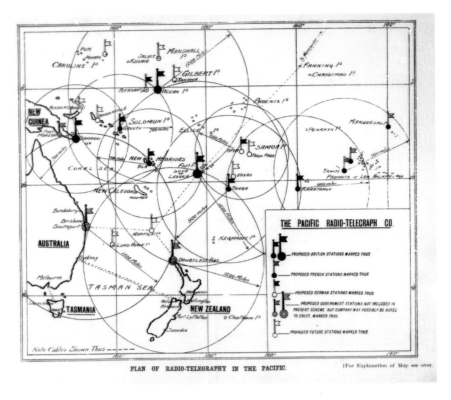

Fig 52.3 'Plan of Radiotelegraphy in the Pacific' in *Linking Australia and New Zealand with the Pacific Islands by Radiotelegraphy* (Melbourne: Pacific Radiotelegraphy Company, 1909).

rival international wireless companies active in Australia – Marconi and Telefunken – who both opposed state involvement in wireless development.[70] In 1922 AWA negotiated with government to assume control of all wireless stations in the British Pacific. It aimed to replace an inefficient system of isolated stations with limited range, and link them directly with Australia and the wider world. AWA took control of services in New Guinea and Papua in 1922 and Fiji in 1928, with the latter soon described as the 'nerve-centre of the South Seas'. Not only was the Fiji station in touch with every ship in the southern Pacific, it served as an interconnection point at the

---

[70] J. Given, 'Not being ernest: uncovering competitors in the foundation of Australian wireless', *Historical Records of Australian Science* 18 (2007), 159–76; J. Given, 'Born global, made local: multinational enterprise and Australia's early wireless industry', *Australian Economic History Review* 57 (2017), 158–93.

heart of a nest of subsidiary wireless stations, linking them to the trans-Pacific cable.[71] Beyond the AWA network, Christian missions and trading and plantation concerns, including BP, operated island wireless stations, as did the governments of France, New Zealand, and Japan in their own Pacific territories.[72] By 1930 newspapers celebrated the fact that a resident of almost any island could send a message to Europe, or America or Australia, 'and receive a reply within twelve hours'.[73] Network gaps still posed challenges in everyday use, as seen in 1932, for instance, when a trans-Pacific steamer struck Kings Wharf at Suva. The ship wanted to signal for a pilot at 6 a.m. to guide it into harbour, yet Suva's wireless station did not open until 8 a.m.[74]

The US Navy was the first agency to open an effective trans-Pacific system of radio communication. From 1913 it established stations at Pearl Harbor, American Sāmoa, Guam, and the Philippines, as well as at Beijing to connect with its ships in Asiatic waters. This network far surpassed British services in its 'continuous operation and technical efficiency'.[75] The establishment of the Radio Corporation of America (RCA) in 1919 soon facilitated a commercial service. By 1922, RCA handled 50 per cent of international traffic across the Pacific; the rest went to the undersea cables.[76] America's swift embrace of wireless appeared to signal a shift in the balance of power in the Pacific and beyond. RCA's Pacific divisional manager celebrated that America achieved with wireless in six years what took the British cable system 'a half century or more of constant effort'.[77] These impressions underpinned claims that as London was the 'cable centre' of the world, New York was the centre of wireless – also paving the way to America's 'probable future leadership in aviation'.[78]

Cable companies were able to operate effectively with wireless until the 1920s, arguing the latter could only ever be a supplementary technology. Increased traffic afforded cable duplication, with new cables laid between Australia, New Zealand, and Fiji in 1923. The development of cables with a new alloy coating allowed the transmission of ten times more words per minute. The Pacific Cable Board aimed to harness this innovation as a tool of mass communications. Yet Canada, which used the Pacific Cable far less than

---

[71] *New Zealand Herald* (12 December 1929), 7; 'Radio links the Pacific', *Pacific Islands Monthly* 1 (16 August 1930), 1–2.
[72] D. Yang, 'Crossing the Pacific: wireless telegraphy and spatial practices in early twentieth-century Japan', *Pacific Historical Review* 88 (2019), 524–53.
[73] 'Radio links the Pacific', 1.   [74] 41/51 Marine, CSO, NAF.
[75] Winseck and Pike, *Communication and Empire*, 236.   [76] Tribolet, *International Aspects*, 215.
[77] Harold Porter, quoted in *Newcastle Morning Herald and Miners' Advocate* (28 September 1927), 9.
[78] Tribolet, *International Aspects*, 2–3.

Australia, New Zealand, or Britain, resisted the huge expense of cable duplication in the long northern section between Fanning and Bamfield. It believed priority should now be given to shortwave or 'beam', a new-generation wireless. Unlike longwave, it did not curve around the Earth but bounced off the atmosphere.[79] Five times as fast, it was more reliable and harder to intercept, although new submarine cables were faster still and always more secure, a key strategic consideration for Britain. In a context of rising Dominion nationalism, Canada resented what it regarded as British attempts to dictate its interests. The duplicate northern cable segment opened in 1926, yet competition from cheaper beam rates soon threatened the cable's commercial viability both in the Pacific and worldwide, as Canada predicted. In the United States these technologies were more complementary, for American cable interests had already ceded cheaper 'social communication' in the Pacific to the wireless.[80]

This tension between an imperial outlook and colonial interests underlined both a commercial as well as a political challenge to Britain's dominance. In order to consolidate its global position and to forestall cable's massive losses, in 1929 British imperial wireless and cable communications were amalgamated. A privately owned company, but under significant government oversight, it would come to be known as Cable and Wireless, Ltd. This entity shored up cable on the grounds of empire security, now subsidized by wireless profits.[81] From Canada's perspective, the merger released it from the growing burdens of the Pacific Cable Board and thereby marked the end of an integrated imperial service.[82]

Conclusion

Imperial encroachment in the Pacific can be approached as a series of territorial projects that partitioned islands, exploited resources, and transformed modes of production. Imperial control also entailed forging new connections between islands, with rim states, and the world beyond,

---

[79] D. Headrick, 'Shortwave radio and its impact on international telecommunications between the wars', *History and Technology* 11 (1994), 21–32, at 22–3.
[80] Winseck and Pike, *Communication and Empire*, 321–2. In Australia cable rates (in US cents) before and after beam were 62c and 50c respectively, compared to the beam start-up rate of 41c.
[81] Winseck and Pike, *Communication and Empire*, 319–28.
[82] R.W.D. Boyce, 'Canada and the Pacific cable controversy, 1923–28: forgotten source of imperial alienation', *Journal of Imperial and Commonwealth History* 26 (1998), 72–92. Canada was equally resistant in the same period to supporting British Imperial Airways' ambitions for a global route network.

restricting and regulating movement and exchange, while encouraging and channelling them in new directions. As this overview of the Pacific in the age of steam, undersea cables, and wireless has demonstrated, political tensions, commercial conflicts, and uneven technical advances marked the deployment of these technologies. Their impact within the Pacific was also uneven and differentiated, and Islanders' engagements with them, whether as traders, workers, or passengers, varied widely. Steamships, cables, and wireless were frequently extolled for their imagined universalizing and progressive benefits. They reinforced the centrality of island 'crossroads' such as Hawai'i and Fiji, while other islands, including Yap, Guam, and Fanning Island, came to new prominence. Yet places not strategically vital to Western imperial interests remained poorly connected by these industrial technologies.

The changing structures of political and social life in the Pacific may also be viewed in relationship to these new modes of transport and communications. From the perspective of British imperial interests, the Pacific Ocean was framed as the 'missing link', vital to achieving a global imperial communications web – a refrain repeated for shipping, cables, and wireless. In the face of rising white settler nationalism and the growing regional ambitions of the United States, a Pacific networked by steam and cables also had the potential to unsettle British claims to global hegemony. This era of industrial connectivity might instead herald a new set of geopolitical affinities and priorities, and foster the emergence of metropolitan hubs of power and influence at a distance from an Atlantic-centred global power base. Seen in this light, space was not annihilated but reconfigured, regulating, directing, and selectively intensifying activity within and across the Pacific and in ways that shaped wider global connections.

53

Latin America's Pacific Ambitions,
1571–2022

EDWARD MELILLO

In Chile, a common expression for something absurd is *loco como un pirata Boliviano* (crazy as a Bolivian pirate). While amusing to a Chilean, this adage is a bitter pill for a Bolivian to swallow. Since the late nineteenth century, landlocked Bolivia has been forced to rely on the good graces of its neighbours for access to Pacific harbours.

This was not always the case. The history of Bolivia's alienation from its western ocean began with the War of the Pacific (1879–84). During this prolonged conflict, Chile's military defeated the allied forces of Peru and Bolivia. Naval confrontations augured this victory. Among the most decisive of these encounters was the Battle of Angamos in the Pacific waters off the Mejillones Peninsula (22°S, 70°W). On 8 October 1879, two armoured Chilean frigates bombarded and captured Peru's ironclad, steam-propelled warship *Huáscar*. This victory – along with the Chilean navy's successful blockade of Callao, in which the Chileans set the Peruvian fleet on fire and shattered the defences of the Peruvian port – marked a turning point in the war.

Even before hostilities had formally concluded, Chile's military ascendancy in the Pacific had troubled rival Latin American powers. In 1881, Colombian writer Adriano Páez warned, 'Chile ... will have a coastline more extensive than that of Brazil on the Atlantic. And since neither Ecuador nor Colombia has a fleet, Chile will dominate from the Strait [of Magellan] to the Panamanian Isthmus.' Páez continued, '[Chile] will dominate commerce in the Pacific with the largest naval fleet in the Americas, with the exception of the United States.'[1] These concerns were shared by other regional commentators who derided Chile as 'the Prussia of the Pacific'.[2]

---

[1] A. Páez, *La Guerra del Pacífico y deberes de la América* (Colón, Panama: Oficina del Canal, 1881), 9–10.
[2] W.F. Sater and H.H. Herwig, *The Grand Illusion: The Prussianization of the Chilean Army* (Lincoln: University of Nebraska Press, 1999), 31.

Such apprehensions were not unfounded. With the 1883 Treaty of Ancón, Chile acquired the provinces of Tarapacá, Tacna, and Arica. Additionally, Bolivia forfeited its coastal access when it ceded the Pacific seaport of Antofagasta to Chile in 1884.[3] Thus, Chile secured dominion over a 644-kilometres expanse of *salitre* (sodium nitrate) mines in the Atacama Desert. Between 1875 and 1929, Chile exported nearly 80 million metric tons of this prized, nitrogen-rich substance to distant lands. For nearly half a century, a relentless procession of clippers and steamships docked at Chile's northern ports, filled their holds with burlap bags of the powdery fertilizer, and conveyed these sacks from Latin America's Pacific coast to North American and European ports. As I have argued elsewhere, Chilean sodium nitrate – along with nutrient-dense Peruvian guano – was a fundamental component of 'The First Green Revolution' in global agricultural history.[4]

The transnational connections that structured the nitrogen fertilizer commodity chain followed well-established patterns of other commercial exchanges throughout the modern world. Far more often than not, Latin America has been a net exporter of raw materials and a net importer of value-added products from Europe and North America. The persistence of these asymmetrical relations validates the central assertion of dependency theory, namely that, across the capitalist world system, resources tend to flow from an underdeveloped 'periphery' to a 'core' of wealthier states, enriching the latter at the expense of the former. Critics of such debilitating imbalances have often turned to maritime metaphors. In the evocative words of the late Uruguayan writer Eduardo Galeano, 'Development is a voyage with more shipwrecks than navigators.'[5]

As both a literal ocean and an allegorical realm, the Pacific occupies a distinctive place in Latin America's voyages of development. This chapter

---

[3] In 2018, judges at the International Criminal Court in the Hague handed down a 12–3 verdict, affirming that Chile did not have to grant Bolivia access to the Pacific Ocean. Chile's President Sebastián Piñera welcomed the rejection, declaring, 'The court has done justice and has put things in their place, establishing clearly and categorically that Chile has never had any obligation to negotiate an exit to the sea.' Agence France-Presse, '"Justice done" by ICJ on Bolivia claim: Chile president', *Agence France-Presse* (1 October 2018): https://au.news.yahoo .com/justice-done-icj-bolivia-claim-chile-president-165217068-spt.html.

[4] E.D. Melillo, 'The First Green Revolution', *American Historical Review* 117:4 (2012), 1028–60; E.D. Melillo, *Strangers on Familiar Soil: Rediscovering the Chile–California Connection* (New Haven: Yale University Press, 2015), 92–112. For more on the twentieth-century history of Peruvian guano, see G.T. Cushman, *Guano and the Opening of the Pacific World: A Global Ecological History* (Cambridge: Cambridge University Press, 2013).

[5] E. Galeano, *Open Veins of Latin America: Five Centuries of the Pillage of a Continent* (New York: Monthly Review Press, 1973), 171.

demonstrates that the planet's largest body of water has simultaneously functioned as a conduit for material exchanges and as a laboratory for ideological experiments. On the one hand, Latin America's western ocean served as an aquatic corridor for the long-distance transfers of commodities, labourers, and technocrats. On the other hand, dictators, revolutionaries, pundits, and policymakers throughout the Americas have anchored their aspirations to diverse trans-Pacific visions. Much like the currents on which they depend, these material and ideological flows have mingled in the tides of history, shaping the possibilities and constraints of the human and non-human communities that comprise the Pacific World.[6]

Trade networks connecting Latin America's Pacific ports to distant parts of the world long pre-dated the 1800s. Centuries before Chilean and Peruvian fertilizers provided a vital influx of nutrients to the impoverished soils of North America and Europe, Spanish colonists and unfree Native labourers in the Bolivian Andes developed durable trans-Pacific relations with civilizations across the world's largest ocean. Following Spain's successful conquest of Manila in 1571, the Pacific served as a watery thoroughfare for the lucrative trade voyages of Spanish galleons that carried cargoes of American silver to Asian entrepôts. Disturbed only by the sporadic raids of privateers like the British 'Master Thief' Sir Francis Drake (c. 1540–96) and the Dutch freebooter Piet Heyn (1577–1629), Spanish merchants and their Asian counterparts developed the world's first truly global trade circuit. Social, economic, and biological exchanges enlivened this network, and for the first time in history, people, commodities, and organisms circulated among Asia, Europe, the Americas, and Africa. The focal point of this worldwide web of bullion was a seemingly bottomless trove of silver in the 5,000-metres Cerro Rico (Rich Mountain) of Potosí, Bolivia, located in the immense Viceroyalty of Peru.[7]

In the 1570s, the Spanish viceroy of this region, Don Francisco de Toledo, organized a brutal corvée system, forcing hundreds of thousands of Quechua Indians to trek across the *Altiplano* (high plateau) of the Andes to mine silver

---

[6] The question of historical agency is a profoundly political one. The eminent Brazilian historian Emília Viotti da Costa was fond of reminding her Yale University graduate students to maintain an unwavering focus on the interplay of freedom and necessity and the pursuit of those fleeting moments when this tension resolves itself in historical upheavals.

[7] The Viceroyalty of Peru (*Virreinato del Perú*) was an administrative district that encompassed the entire territory of Spanish South America, with the exception of the Venezuelan coast. Spain's colonial agents ruled this sprawling viceroyalty from their capital at Lima. The Spanish also mined silver from the region north and west of Mexico City, centered on the provinces of Zacatecas and Guanajuato. See P.J. Bakewell, *Silver Mining and Society in Colonial Mexico, Zacatecas, 1546–1700* (Cambridge: Cambridge University Press, 1971).

from the Cerro Rico. Toledo's draconian labour regime, known as the *mita*, required each of sixteen Indian provinces to send an annual contingent of one-seventh of their adult male population to work in the dank, disease-infested mines.[8] The *mita* lasted from 1575 to 1825, eventually accommodating forms of wage labour for skilled mineworkers.[9] In 1669, the Peruvian viceroy, Count Lemos, wrote to his king about the Indian miners, known as *mitayos*, who carved a labyrinth of tunnels into the mountain and heaved ungainly sacks of silver-laden ore up wooden ladders to the surface: "There is no people in the world so exhausted. I unburden my conscience to inform your Majesty with due clarity. It is not silver that is brought to Spain, but the blood and sweat of Indians."[10] The Spanish Crown did, at times, acknowledge the grisly connotations of the expression *plata es sangre* (silver is blood), but Iberian officials made few efforts to interfere with the brutal labour system. Royal inaction stemmed from the apprehension that the silver trade's astronomical revenues would falter in the absence of the *mita*.[11]

[8] J.A. Cole, 'An abolition born of frustration: the Conde de Lemos and the Potosi mita, 1667–73', *Hispanic American Historical Review* 63:2 (1983), 307–33, at 307. The *mita* system was known as the *repartimiento* in Spanish Mexico (New Spain), where this rotational labour draft predominately supplied agricultural workers.

[9] P.J. Bakewell, *Miners of the Red Mountain: Indian Labor in Potosi, 1545–1650* (Albuquerque: University New Mexico Press, 1984); E. Tandeter, 'Forced and free labour in late colonial Potosí', *Past and Present* 93 (1981), 98–136; T. Saignes, 'Indian migration and social change in seventeenth-century Charcas', in B. Larson and O. Harris with E. Tandenter (eds.), *Ethnicity, Markets, and Migration in the Andes: At the Crossroads of History and Anthropology* (Durham, NC: Duke University Press, 1995), 167–95. Important early histories of Potosí and the *mita* include L. Hanke, *The Imperial City of Potosí: An Unwritten Chapter in the History of Spanish America* (The Hague: Martinus Nijhoff, 1956); G. René Moreno, *La mita de Potosí en 1795* (Potosí: Universidad Tomás Frías, 1959). Bartolomé Arzáns de Orsúa y Vela's chronicle of life in Potosí, originally written in the early 1700s, was published in English as L. Hanke and G. Mendoza (eds.), *Tales of Potosí: Bartolomé Arzáns de Orsúa y Vela*, 3 vols. (Providence, RI: Brown University Press, 1965). It provides a fascinating account of life in the world's highest mining city by a young, first-generation Creole. Jeffrey Cole has written an institutional history of the forced labour system in Potosí from its founding in 1573 to 1700 in which he discusses Indian resistance to the *mita* and the debates that evolved among colonial officials over whether to reform, abolish, or retain its basic parameters; J.A. Cole, *The Potosí Mita, 1573–1700: Compulsory Indian Labor in the Andes* (Stanford: Stanford University Press, 1985). J.E. Mangan's social history of Potosí, *Trading Roles: Gender, Ethnicity, and the Urban Economy in Colonial Potosí* (Durham, NC: Duke University Press, 2005) traces the commercial and cultural development of this multi-ethnic urban centre from the silver strikes of 1545 to Potosí's decline as a mining zone in the 1700s.

[10] Count Lemos, as quoted in E. Galeano, *Memory of Fire*, vol. I, *Genesis*, 2nd edn (New York: W.W. Norton, 1998), 248.

[11] This phrase was originally coined by missionary Sebastiao Manrique, who recalled that during the 1600s the Chinese in Manila saw silver as the lifeblood of their profession. C.R. Boxer, 'Plata es sangre: sidelights on the drain of Spanish-American silver in the Far East, 1550–1700', *Philippine Studies* 18:3 (1970), 457–78, at 463.

Although colonial officials shipped sizeable quantities of bullion back to Spain, much of the silver travelled by donkey trains and cabotage vessels to coastal Acapulco, Mexico, where West African slaves minted it into pesos and loaded chests of the coins onto galleons for passage across the Pacific Ocean to the Philippines. Once these colossal Spanish ships – which frequently exceeded 1,000 tons and took as many as 2,000 trees to build – docked at the bustling port city of Manila, Chinese merchants traded silk, jade, tea, porcelain, and lacquerware for the precious South American metal.[12] Such cross-cultural commodity exchanges indulged the European demand for Chinese material culture and precipitously enlarged the treasury of the Ming Dynasty (1368–1644). Many generations of *mitayos* who mined Potosí's silver were essential to building the world's first truly global trade network, which spanned an ocean that most of them would never see.

After the Manila Galleons had completed their lengthy return trip to Acapulco, the Chinese luxury goods they carried fetched high prices in Mexico City and Potosí. Local shopkeepers often found themselves overwhelmed with a glut of stylish alternatives from afar.[13] In the words of nineteenth-century Mexican writer Juan Niceto de Zamacois y Urrutia, 'there was nothing less pleasing to the merchants of the capital than the arrival of the Manila galleon at the port of Acapulco'.[14]

Transformations in the Chinese economy were the driving forces behind this lucrative trade route. Between 1520 and 1619, Ming officials shifted units of tax collection from rice to silver throughout the empire, paying administrative salaries, conducting inter-regional commerce, and collecting duties in the precious metal.[15] Chinese administrators and merchants preferred

[12] On the size of the galleons, see A.Giráldez, *The Age of Trade: The Manila Galleons and the Dawn of the Global Economy* (Lanham: Rowman & Littlefield, 2015), 123.
[13] The most influential work on the Manila Galleon Trade remains W.L. Schurz, *The Manila Galleon: The Romantic History of the Spanish Galleons Trading between Manila and Acapulco* (New York: E.P. Dutton, 1939). Sailing with the trade winds, the journey from Acapulco to Manila often took eight to ten weeks, while the far more dangerous eastward trip could occupy four to seven months. J.H. Parry, *The Spanish Seaborne Empire* (New York: Alfred A. Knopf, 1966), 132.
[14] J. Niceto de Zamacois y Urrutia, *Historia de Méjico*, 22 vols. (Barcelona, Mexico: J.F. Párres y compañia, 1878–1902), vol. v, 550. For a comprehensive overview of European contact with Asian cultures in the Indian Ocean and the Pacific during the Manila Galleon period, see J.E. Wills Jr, 'Maritime Asia, 1500–1800: the interactive emergence of European domination', *American Historical Review* 98:1 (1993), 83–105. Katharine Bjork has critiqued the way in which world systems theorists marginalize the role of Latin American merchants in the Manila Galleon trade; K. Bjork, 'The link that kept the Philippines Spanish: Mexican merchant interests and the Manila Trade, 1571–1815', *Journal of World History* 9:1 (1998), 25–50.
[15] See M. Wan, 'The monetization of silver in China: Ming China and its global interactions', in M.D. Elizalde and Wang Jianlang (eds.), *China's Development from a Global Perspective* (Newcastle-upon-Tyne: Cambridge Scholars Publisher, 2017), 274–96.

Mexican pesos, since each coin contained an unwaveringly reliable quantity of silver. They were not alone in this numismatic judgement. As historian William Schell Jr pointed out, 'the peso was the most widely circulated coin in history'.[16] In 1593, Spain's King Philip II attempted to limit the Manila Galleons to an annual trading ceiling of 250,000 pesos, but this strategy failed. By the end of the sixteenth century, Spanish ships were smuggling an annual average of 5 million pesos from Mexico to the Philippines.[17]

Throughout the seventeenth century, the amount of silver being trafficked across the Pacific Ocean grew exponentially, reaching an annual average of 50 tons of Spanish-American specie entering the Chinese economy via Manila.[18] The half-century reign of China's Emperor Wanli, which lasted from 1572 until his death in 1620, relied rather precariously on the shifting fortunes of the Spanish silver trade.[19] Enough silver from Mexico and Japan eventually flooded the Chinese economy to diminish the metal's buying power. This caused an episode of uncontrollable inflation, which hastened the downfall of the Ming Dynasty in 1644.[20]

The Manila Galleon Trade lasted from 1571 to 1815, making it one of the world's longest-lived, continuous trade routes. Among the most durable legacies of this trans-Pacific exchange was a trio of botanical gifts to Chinese society. The introduction of three cultivars from the Americas – the peanut (*Arachis hypogaea*), maize (*Zea mays*), and the sweet potato (*Ipomoea batatas*) – transformed China's agricultural landscapes and its

---

[16] William Schell Jr, 'Silver symbiosis: reOrienting Mexican economic history', *Hispanic American Historical Review* 81:1 (2001), 89–133, at 89.

[17] J. TePaske, 'New World silver, Castile, and the Philippines, 1598–1800', in J.F. Richards (ed.), *Precious Metals in the Later Medieval and Early Modern Worlds* (Durham, NC: Carolina Academic Press, 1983), 425–45, at 433–8.

[18] This figure does not include the 55-year-period from 1633 to 1688, for which there is a shortage of reliable data; R. von Glahn, 'Myth and reality of China's seventeenth-century monetary crisis', *Journal of Economic History* 56:2 (1996), 429–54, at 443–4. Vast quantities of silver also entered China from Japan and from Europe via sea and overland routes.

[19] D.O. Flynn and A. Giráldez, 'Born with a "silver spoon": the origin of world trade in 1571', *Journal of World History* 6:2 (1995), 201–21; F. Wakeman, 'China and the seventeenth-century crisis', *Late Imperial China* 7:1 (1986), 1–26; W.S. Atwell, 'International bullion flows and the Chinese economy circa 1530–1650', *Past and Present* 95 (1982), 68–90. Despite criticisms of his claims about the role of silver in the collapse of the Ming Dynasty, Atwell has maintained that his conclusions in 1982 were largely sound. For his revisions, see W.S. Atwell, 'Another look at silver imports into China, ca. 1635–1644', *Journal of World History* 16 (2005), 467–89.

[20] R.B. Marks, *Tigers, Rice, Silk, & Silt: Environment and Economy in Late Imperial South China* (Cambridge: Cambridge University Press, 1998), 141–2. An opposing viewpoint to this argument appears in von Glahn, 'Myth and reality of China's seventeenth-century monetary crisis', 429–54.

foodways in far-reaching ways. These three plants also shaped the demographic revolutions that characterized the Ming and Qing (1644–1911) dynasties.[21]

Here, as in so many other historical cases, the non-human passengers who travelled on long-distance shipping routes profoundly altered the civilizations and environments of their new destinations. The Manila Galleons, along with Portuguese ships trading at Macau, served as vectors for the introduction of all three American cultivars to China. As environmental historian Alfred Crosby depicted this biotic transfer in his 1972 masterwork, *The Columbian Exchange*, 'No large group of the human race in the Old World was quicker to adopt American food plants than the Chinese. While men who stormed Tenochtitlán with Cortés still lived, peanuts were swelling in the sandy loams near Shanghai; maize was turning fields green in south China and the sweet potato was on its way to becoming the poor man's staple in [Fujian].'[22] Peanuts are nitrogen-fixing legumes that provide farmers with protein and oil, while helping to restore soil fertility; maize is an anchor starch that matures quickly, thriving in marginal landscapes; and sweet potatoes, which are able to tolerate nutrient-poor soils, deliver essential beta carotene and tremendous caloric value for the minimal labour time required for their cultivation. This trio of plants, originally domesticated by sophisticated pre-Columbian societies in the Americas, provided a 'portmanteau biota' to Chinese settlers as they moved westward, out of the well-watered rice paddies of the southeast and into less fertile terrain. Unlike their Ming predecessors, who discouraged migration, Qing officials promoted resettlement, using tax subsidies and promises of cheap land to entice immigrants into territories historically inhabited by Tibetans, Uighurs, and Miao people. Peanuts, maize, and sweet potatoes from the Americas became staples of settler colonial agriculture in western China.[23]

While Han peasants were pushing westward, droves of other Chinese migrants travelled eastward during the later decades of the Qing Dynasty, thereby amplifying trans-Pacific connections between China and Latin America. From 1847 to 1874, upwards of 100,000 'coolies' from China came to Peru aboard an estimated 276 ships. Often, these passengers were

---

[21] The first English-language article to make these connections was Ho Ping-Ti, 'The introduction of American food plants into China', *American Anthropologist* 57:2 (1955), 191–201.

[22] A.W. Crosby Jr, *The Columbian Exchange: The Biological Consequences of 1492* (Westport, CT: Greenwood, 1972), 199.

[23] C. Mann, *1493: Uncovering the New World Columbus Created* (New York: Alfred A. Knopf, 2011), 174–5.

unwilling itinerants, conscripted to the sprawling army of labourers that built the material foundations of the capitalist world system. Just as the trans-Atlantic slave trade was losing its battle with trans-Atlantic Abolitionism, a new trans-Pacific trade in unfree labour arose. 'Vessels, it appears, are equipped for the business upon the model of slave ships', explained a *New York Daily Times* correspondent in 1853 when describing the ships transporting Chinese workers to Peru: 'The victims – men, and even children – are kidnapped. They are crowded down between low decks, where any other than a prone or sitting posture is out of the question.'[24]

Mutinies were frequent. As maritime writer Basil Lubbock remarked, 'a rising of the coolies was the one terror that ever stalked behind the captain of a Chinese coolie ship. In order to prevent the ships from being captured by their passengers, the decks and hatchway openings were barred and barricaded like the old convict ships.'[25] No fewer than sixty-eight 'coolie ships' experienced some sort of uprising during their trans-Pacific passage.[26]

If these vessels managed to reach Peru, the Chinese labourers who had been aboard began their terms of indenture. These bondage arrangements demanded years of toil on coastal cotton and sugar plantations, domestic servitude for Peru's elites, backbreaking railroad construction in the Andes, or the arduous task of digging seabird faeces on the Chincha Islands, three granite outcroppings located 21 kilometres off Peru's southwest coast.[27] Although employers promised to free coolies after three to five years, such timely terminations of bondage contracts were rare. The Peruvian government had outlawed slavery in 1854, but it willingly offset potential labour shortages with *la trata amarilla*, the so-called 'yellow trade' in coerced Chinese workers.[28]

---

[24] 'The Asiatic slave trade', *New York Daily Times* (22 July 1853), 4.

[25] B. Lubbock, *Coolie Ships and Oil Sailers* (Glasgow: Brown, Son & Ferguson, 1935), 33.

[26] Melillo, 'The First Green Revolution', 1029; A.J. Meagher, *The Coolie Trade: The Traffic in Chinese Laborers to Latin America, 1847–1874* (Philadelphia: Xlibris, 2008), 191.

[27] See E. Hu-Dehart, 'Coolies, shopkeepers, pioneers: the Chinese of Mexico and Peru (1849–1930)', *Amerasia* 15:2 (1989), 91–116.

[28] Watt Stewart claims that 90,000 Chinese arrived in Peru during this period: W. Stewart, *Chinese Bondage in Peru: A History of the Chinese Coolie in Peru, 1849–1874* (Durham, NC: Duke University Press, 1951), 74. Arnold J. Meagher puts the number at 109,146: Meagher, *The Coolie Trade*, 222 n.142. For ship numbers, see W.L. Lai, 'Chinese indentured labor: migrations to the British West Indies in the nineteenth century', *Amerasia* 15:2 (1989), 117–38, at 120. The term 'coolie' may have originated as a derivation of the Tamil word for wages, *kūli*; see H. Yule and A.C. Burnell, *Hobson-Jobson: A Glossary of Colloquial Anglo-Indian Words and Phrases, and of Kindred Terms, Etymological, Historical, Geographical and Discursive*, new edn, ed. W. Crooke (London: J. Murray, 1903), 250. In South America, the Caribbean, and the North American

Global shipping firms like W.R. Grace and Company made sizeable fortunes through the trans-Pacific trade in Chinese indentured workers to Latin America, but international outrage over the horrifying conditions that plagued such ventures eventually pushed the governments of Peru and China to shut down this brutal labour trade.[29] On 26 July 1874, representatives of the Qing government and Peruvian officials signed the *Tratado de paz, amistad, comercio y navegación* (Treaty of Peace, Friendship, Commerce and Navigation), which formally ended the coolie trade.[30]

As indenture contracts expired and the trans-Pacific trade in coolie labour came to its formal end, many Chinese workers settled in Lima. A few city blocks from the Plaza de Armas (the city's main square), they established a thriving Chinatown that became known as the Barrio Chino (利马唐人街).[31] On 19 October 1873, Peru's most prominent nineteenth-century newspaper, *El Commercio*, noted, 'Nearly all settlers who have finished their contracts are in Chinatown and work as cooks, which is what they really like to do.' It was on the cutting boards and in the cooking pots of these kitchens that a spontaneous fusion of Peruvian and Cantonese food traditions, the *chifa*, first transpired. The term *chifa*, which also came to mean 'Chinese-Peruvian restaurant', derives from a Hispanicization of the Cantonese pronunciation of chī fàn (吃饭) 'to eat'.[32] By the 1920s, this savory gastronomic hybrid had become the most popular cultural expression of Peru's large Chinese population. Dishes like *arroz chaufa* (Cantonese-Peruvian fried rice), *tallarines saltado* (Peruvian chow mein), and *wantán frito* (fried wonton) remain staples in this inimitable cuisine.[33] As a street vendor declared to me in 2005, 'No hay

---

West, 'coolie' was a derogatory term for cheap, servile labourers. In 1821, there were at least 41,228 slaves of African descent in Peru; M.E. del Río, *La inmigración y su desarrollo en el Perú* (Lima: Sanmartí y cía., 1929), 38. On Peruvian abolition, see C. Aguirre, *Agentes de su propia libertad: los esclavos de Lima y la desintegración de la esclavitud, 1821–1854* (Lima: Pontificia Universidad Católica del Perú, 1993).

[29] On the Grace Company's involvement in the coolie trade, see C.A.G. de Secada, 'Arms, guano, and shipping: the W.R. Grace interests in Peru, 1865–1885', *Business History Review* 59:4 (1985), 597–621; and Melillo, 'The First Green Revolution', 1040–1.

[30] The text of the treaty appears in Ministerio de Relaciones Exteriores, *Coleccion de los tratados del Perú* (Lima: Imprenta del Estado Calle de la Rifa 58, 1876), 159–65. Such trans-Pacific diplomatic arrangements occurred elsewhere in Latin America. Mexico and China signed a similar treaty (*Tratado de Amistad, Comercio y Navegación entre China y México*) on 14 December 1899.

[31] I. Lausent-Herrera, 'The Chinatown in Peru and the changing Peruvian Chinese community (ies)', *Journal of Chinese Overseas* 7:1 (2011), 69–113.

[32] H. Capellà Miternique, 'Fusion in multicultural societies: chifa food as a means of spreading Chinese culture in the Hispanic world', *Asian Journal of Humanities and Social Studies* 2:5 (2014), 648–56, at 650.

[33] M. Balbi, *Los chifas en Perú: historias y recetas* (Lima: Universidad San Martín de Porres, 1999).

Figure 53.1 A chifa (Chinese-Peruvian restaurant) in Lima's Barrio Chino (photograph by author).

nada más peruano que la sopa wantán' ('Nothing is more Peruvian than wonton soup').[34]

As the twentieth century unfolded, the trans-Pacific links between Peru and China were as much ideological as alimentary. Abimael Guzmán Reynoso, the founder and leader of Peru's Maoist guerilla movement – the *Sendero Luminoso* (Shining Path) – made several extended visits to China in the 1960s, just prior to and during China's Cultural Revolution (1966–76). In 2002, he recalled the itinerary of his first trip across the Pacific in 1965:

> I went to a cadre school, a school that had two parts, the first was political, it started with the study of the international situation and ended with Marxist philosophy; there were various courses and a second part which was

[34] Alejandra Espinosa, interview with author on Jirón Ucayali in Lima, Peru (16 February 2005).

military, held at a military school in Nanjing, where I studied theory and practice in a deeper way.[35]

Guzmán's fraternal relations with the Chinese Communist Party enhanced his prestige among his comrades back in Peru. As the influence of the Shining Path grew, Guzmán's followers came to regard the former philosophy professor as the 'Fourth Sword' of communist thought, after Marx, Lenin, and Mao. In April 1980, the Fourth Sword proclaimed to his supporters, 'The trumpets begin to sound, the roar of the masses grows, and will continue to grow, it will deafen us, it will take us into a powerful vortex' of revolution.[36]

During the decade that followed, such ideological platitudes manifested themselves in a far-reaching guerrilla war that engulfed the Andean highland regions of Ayacucho, Huancavelica, and Apurímac. Building on rural discontent with centuries of widespread poverty, the Shining Path trained and armed peasants for an insurgency against government forces. This conflict ended up costing 20,000 lives and plunged the country into a chaotic period of political and social upheaval. In September 1992, military police captured Guzmán and fourteen other top Shining Path commanders. A military court wasted no time sentencing the leadership of the *Sendero Luminoso* to life in prison.[37]

The incarceration of Guzmán and his comrades marked the culmination of an aggressive anti-insurgency campaign orchestrated by another Peruvian with strong trans-Pacific ties to Asia. Alberto Fujimori was born in 1938 to parents who had immigrated from Kumamoto, Japan, four years earlier. After receiving an undergraduate degree in agricultural engineering, Fujimori left for Strasbourg, France to study physics. He subsequently attended the University of Wisconsin-Milwaukee where he earned a master's degree in mathematics in 1969. Fujimori, whom the media dubbed *El Chino* (the Chinaman), orchestrated an electoral upset in the 1990 presidential election, defeating distinguished writer Mario Vargas Llosa. Fujimori's authoritarian regime wasted no time imposing a neoliberal austerity programme known as 'Fujishock'. The removal of subsidies and the defunding of entitlement programmes sent food prices soaring by 500 per cent, while

---

[35] Guzmán, as quoted in M.D. Rothwell, *Transpacific Revolutionaries: The Chinese Revolution in Latin America* (New York: Routledge, 2013), 56.
[36] Guzmán, as quoted in G. Gorriti, *The Shining Path: A History of the Millenarian War in Peru*, trans. R. Kirk (Chapel Hill: University of North Carolina Press, 1999), 35.
[37] On the long-term consequences of the Shining Path's guerilla war and the government's counterinsurgency campaign, see the chapters in D.H. Soifer and A. Vergara (eds.), *Politics after Violence: Legacies of the Shining Path Conflict in Peru* (Austin: University of Texas Press, 2019).

gasoline prices skyrocketed by 3,000 per cent.[38] The regime also dissolved Peru's congress in an *autogolpe* (self-coup) and called for a new constitution (promulgated in 1993). Fujimori mercilessly repressed all forms of opposition until his political downfall in 2000. That year, following a corrupt political campaign and a tainted election, he fled Peru for Japan prior to his indictment for moral incapacity.

Fujumori attempted to mount several more electoral comebacks from across the Pacific, eventually returning to Peru via extradition from Chile. Once he was back in Lima, Fujimori faced multiple court trials for human rights violations, money laundering, wiretapping, and bribery, resulting in several prison sentences, which he is still serving. The peculiar trans-Pacific career of a man who variously dressed up as a samurai and an Inca during his political campaigns thus came to an inglorious end behind bars.[39]

While daily life in Peru was being reshaped by fast-moving ideological battles with trans-Pacific valences, a durable element of the Atacama Desert was buttressing Chile's links to Asia. For most of the twentieth century, Chile was the world's leading copper exporter. Copper deposits at Chuquicamata, Escondida, Collahuasi, and El Teniente rank among the planet's most extensive reserves of the red metal. Because copper exhibits unusually high thermal and electrical conductivity, malleability, and resistance to corrosion, it has long been crucial for electrical wiring, plumbing, and industrial applications. For Chileans, copper has also been among the foremost raw materials that kept their nation's economic engine running; many refer to it as *el sueldo de Chile* ('Chile's salary') or *oro rojo* ('red gold').[40]

After World War II, China emerged as a major destination for Chile's copper exports. This link encouraged an array of other exchanges between the pair of Pacific powers. In 1952, just three years after China's Communist Revolution, Chile became the first Latin American nation to sign a trade agreement with the People's Republic of China (PRC). That year, the two countries also inaugurated the Instituto Chileno Chino de Cultura (Chilean-Chinese Cultural Institute), which arranged diplomatic and scholarly exchanges between the PRC and Chile, published articles on Sino-Chilean

---

[38] A.B. Stensrud, 'Safe milk and risky quinoa: the lottery and precarity of farming in Peru', *Focaal: Journal of Global and Historical Anthropology* 83 (2019), 72–84, at 76.
[39] J. Lesser, *Immigration, Ethnicity, and National Identity in Brazil, 1808 to the Present* (Cambridge: Cambridge University Press, 2013), 161.
[40] M. Radetzki, 'Seven thousand years in the service of humanity: the history of copper, the red metal', *Resources Policy* 34:4 (2009), 176–84; N. Arndt and C. Ganino, *Metals and Society: An Introduction to Economic Geology* (New York: Springer, 2012), 92–3.

relations, and sponsored lectures and films about China.[41] In 2006, a half-century after the emergence of these groundbreaking trade and cultural accords, China concluded a free-trade agreement with Chile, the first such agreement it forged with a Latin American nation. Six years later, China was consuming 80 per cent (US$ 14 billion) of Chile's copper exports.[42]

The future of Chile's copper output and its relationship to Chinese demand remains unclear. China's own expansion of smelting and refining capacity, declining ore grades at many Chilean mining sites, clashes between extractive operations and local communities over finite water supplies in Chile's Atacama region, doubts about the solvency of Chile's state-owned National Copper Corporation of Chile (Corporación Nacional del Cobre de Chile, or CODELCO), and the strength of the Chilean labour movement in the twenty-first century will all factor into the future of this relationship.[43] What is beyond question is that the post-war decades of the 1950s and 1960s comprised a new phase of westward, trans-oceanic trade expansion for the Chilean economy.

Chile's relations with China and the world took a dramatic turn on 11 September 1973, when a US-backed military coup d'état – or *el golpe de Estado* to Chileans – overthrew the democratically elected socialist government of President Salvador Allende. Allende, who won a three-way election in 1970, had immediately instituted a suite of policies known as *la vía chilena al socialismo* (the Chilean path to socialism). This agenda of land reforms, industrial nationalizations, literacy campaigns, minimum wage increases, low-income housing initiatives, expansions of workers' rights, and the

---

[41] D. de la Fuente, *Instituto Chileno Chino de Cultura, cuarenta años* (Santiago: Instituto Chileno Chino de Cultura, 1992), 40.

[42] C. Labarca, 'Identidad e institucionalización como estrategias de construcción de confianza: el caso sino-chileno', *Revista de Ciencia Política* 33:2 (2013), 489–511; A.E. Fernández Jilberto, 'Neoliberalised South–South relations: free trade between Chile and China', in A.E. Fernández Jilberto and B. Hogenboom (eds.), *Latin America Facing China: South–South Relations beyond the Washington Consensus* (New York: Berghahn Books, 2012), 77–98; D. Lin Chou, *Chile y China: inmigración y relaciones bilaterales, 1845–1970* (Santiago: Pontificia Universidad Católica de Chile, Instituto de Historia: Centro de Investigaciones Diego Barrios Arana, 2004), 332. The 2012 statistic is from P. Rey Mallén, 'Trade between Chile and China grew 22 percent in 7 years as China became Chile's biggest trading partner', *International Business Times* (6 September 2013), www.ibtimes.com/trade-between-chile-china-grew-22-percent-7-years-china-became-chiles-biggest-trading-partner.

[43] L. Ebert and T. La Menza, 'Chile, copper and resource revenue: a holistic approach to assessing commodity dependence', *Resources Policy* 43 (2015), 101–11. On the lives of workers in the Chilean copper mining sector, see J.L. Finn, *Tracing the Veins: Of Copper, Culture, and Community from Butte to Chuquicamata* (Berkeley: University of California Press, 1998), and T.M. Klubock, *Contested Communities: Class, Gender and Politics in Chile's El Teniente Copper Mine, 1904–1951* (Durham, NC: Duke University Press, 1998).

establishment of a government-administered health care system had raised the ire of domestic elites and foreign opponents, alike. US President Richard Nixon and his national security advisor Henry Kissinger were among those most opposed to the Allende government's progressive policies. From 1970 to 1973, the US Central Intelligence Agency spent US$ 8 million funding covert action campaigns to undermine Allende's social and economic programmes.[44]

The 1973 coup terminated civilian rule and swept General Augusto Pinochet to power. Pinochet and his henchmen wasted no time enacting retribution against their opponents, murdering thousands of dissidents, and jailing and torturing tens of thousands of others. The dictatorship 'disappeared' several hundred opponents in the Pacific Ocean, which became a watery grave for dissenters.[45] In response to these blatant displays of brutality, the exiled Chilean folk group Inti-Illimani composed a tribute song, 'Vino del mar' ('She Came from the Sea'). The anthem was dedicated to Marta Ugarte Román, a leftist professor who was murdered by the dictatorship's secret police and whose body they dumped into the waters off Valparaíso.[46]

Meanwhile, with heavy-handed mentoring from neoliberal economists in North America, a group of technocrats from the University of Chicago returned to Chile in 1975 and implemented a comprehensive regimen of far-right economic and social programmes. This cohort of Chilean graduate students, known as the 'Chicago Boys', replaced Allende's social democratic institutions with sweeping tariff reductions, unbridled austerity measures, and the mass privatization of state-run industries.

Such policies were part of an ideological formula known as 'neoliberalism'. As geographer and social theorist David Harvey put it, 'Neoliberalism is in the first instance a theory of political economic practices that proposes that human well-being can best be advanced by liberating individual entrepreneurial freedoms and skills within an institutional framework characterized by strong private property rights, free markets, and free trade.'[47] The rise of neoliberalism in Chile was part of a global trend in the 1970s and 1980s.

---

[44] United States Congress, *Covert Action in Chile, 1963–1973: Staff Report of the Select Committee to Study Governmental Operations with Respect to Intelligence Activities, United States Senate* (Washington, DC: US Government Printing Office, 1975), 148.

[45] M.H. Spooner, *The General's Slow Retreat: Chile after Pinochet* (Berkeley: University of California Press, 2011), 189–90. The *Rettig Report* (published in 1991) and the *Valech Report* (originally published in 2004 and revised in 2005) established the bases for these numbers.

[46] For a performance of the song by Inti-Illimani, see www.youtube.com/watch?v= qBMJdAKIoX4

[47] D. Harvey, *A Brief History of Neoliberalism* (Oxford: Oxford University Press, 2005), 2.

During those decades, the right-wing governments of Ronald Reagan (United States), Margaret Thatcher (Great Britain), Helmut Kohl (Germany), and Brian Mulroney (Canada) enacted policies to privatize public goods and services and shift the management of social functions to free-market mechanisms. The Chilean rendering of neoliberal ideology was a partner in crime with the repressive tactics of the military dictatorship. Pablo Barahona, one of Friedman's students who eventually served as minister of the economy under Pinochet, remarked in 1980: 'I have no doubts that as of 1973 and for many years before in Chile an authoritarian government – absolutely authoritarian – that could implement reform despite the interests of any group, no matter how important it was, was needed.'[48] Friedman concurred with his former student. In a 1982 *Newsweek* editorial, the economics professor contended that Pinochet's junta 'has supported a fully free-market economy as a matter of principle. Chile is an economic miracle.'[49] For most Chileans, the miracle was a chimera, tethered to extreme poverty, violent suppression of dissent, and the commonplace use of torture by the regime.[50]

Decades of popular resistance from exiles abroad and social movements within Chile finally pushed the dictatorship over a precipice. An alliance of left and centre parties known as the Concertación de Partidos por la Democracia (Alliance of Parties for Democracy) – or simply the Concertación – defeated Pinochet in a popular referendum in February 1988. Two years after the plebiscite, Christian Democrat Patricio Aylwin Azócar became Chile's first post-dictatorship president, formally ending nearly seventeen years of autocratic rule. The four sequential Concertación governments of Aylwin, Eduardo Frei Ruiz-Tagle, Ricardo Lagos Escobar, and Verónica Michelle Bachelet Jeria instituted a truth-and-reconciliation process and administered significant civil liberties reforms, yet none of these governments posed major challenges to the neoliberal economic policies that had been hallmarks of the Pinochet era.[51]

---

[48] Pablo Barahona, quoted by G. Arriagada Herrera and C. Graham, 'Chile: sustaining adjustment during democratic transition', in S. Haggard and S.B. Webb (eds.), *Voting for Reform: Democracy, Political Liberalization, and Economic Adjustment* (Oxford: Oxford University Press for the World Bank, 1994), 242–89, at 245.

[49] M. Friedman, 'Free markets and the Generals', *Newsweek* (25 January 1982), 59.

[50] For more on the extreme poverty in Santiago's urban shantytowns under Pinochet, see A. Bruey, *Bread, Justice, and Liberty: Grassroots Activism and Human Rights in Pinochet's Chile* (Madison: University of Wisconsin Press, 2018).

[51] On the continuation of neoliberal policies under the Concertación governments, see A. Solimano, *Chile and the Neoliberal Trap: The Post-Pinochet Era* (Cambridge: Cambridge University Press, 2012); and M. Antonio Garretón, *Neoliberalismo corregido y progresismo limitado: los gobiernos de la Concertación en Chile, 1990–2010* (Santiago: ARCIS-CLACSO, 2012).

During the 1980s and 1990s, neoliberal advocates contended that the Pacific region was the geographic stage on which their emerging success story of social marketization would be performed. As Ronald Reagan remarked on 9 May 1984, 'But you cannot help but feel that the great Pacific Basin, with all its nations and all its potential for growth and development – that is the future.'[52] Six months later, Japanese prime minister Yasuhiro Nakasone, another avowed neoliberal champion, announced during a radio broadcast, 'The Pacific era is a historical inevitability.'[53] Scholars also commented on this triumphalist trend. In the words of Felipe Fernández-Armesto, 'That the world was entering a "Pacific Age" became conventional wisdom in the early 1980s, as dwellers on its shores exchanged admiring glances across "the ocean of the future".'[54]

Chile's admission to this trans-Pacific laissez-faire fantasy club was not a foregone conclusion. Historian Arif Dirlik and cultural studies theorist Rob Wilson noted 'the glibly economistic habit by which Latin America is reified as an impoverished "South" and thus excluded from contemporary Pacific Rim Discourse, even though Chile has the longest coastline of any country in the Pacific'.[55] Chilean elites were undeterred by such exclusionary narratives, stubbornly asserting their right to a central role in this emerging ideological drama. During the late 1980s, the Chilean press routinely featured cameos of a cartoon kangaroo wearing a cowboy hat with dollars and financial documents in its pouch. As a reporter noted in the *New York Times*, 'The kangaroo is a sign of the times as Chile's fast-growing, free-market economy increasingly looks across the Pacific – to Asia, Australia, and New Zealand – for trade and investments.'[56]

A menagerie of aggressive predators soon supplanted amicable kangaroos in the zoo of neoliberal metaphors. Beginning in the 1990s, Chilean political pundits began referring to the country as a 'jaguar', South America's feline counterpart to the 'Asian Tiger Economies' of South Korea, Malaysia,

---

[52] R. Reagan, 'Written responses to questions submitted by the *Far Eastern Economic Review*' (9 May 1984), Ronald Reagan Presidential Library Archives, www.reagan.utexas.edu/archives/speeches/1984/50984i.htm.
[53] Yasuhiro Nakasone, as quoted in L. Xing, J. Hersh, and J. Dragsbœk Schmidt, 'The new "Asian drama": catching-up at the crossroads of neoliberalism', in P.P. Masina (ed.), *Rethinking Development in East Asia: From Illusory Miracle to Economic Crisis* (New York: Routledge, 2001), 29.
[54] F. Fernández-Armesto, *Civilizations: Culture, Ambition, and the Transformation of Nature* (New York: The Free Press, 2001), 463.
[55] R. Wilson and A. Dirlik, 'Introduction: Asia/Pacific as space of cultural production', *Boundary 2* 21:1 (1994), 14–16.
[56] S. Christian, 'Chile's growing trans-Pacific ties', *New York Times* (28 March 1988), D10.

Singapore, the Philippines, and Hong Kong.[57] In 1995, a reporter for the *Boston Globe* channelled this narrative: 'Stretched along the Pacific Ocean on an area roughly twice the size of California, Chile has become the Latin American jaguar, an economic powerhouse that in the past decade has recorded the world's fourth-fastest growth rate.'[58] A Pacific-centred taxonomic order had emerged, and Chile was playing its part.

Not all was well in the world of neoliberal 'big cats', however. In July 1997, the inexorable Pacific Century hit an impasse when the world awoke to the Asian Financial Crisis. Investor panic, currency depreciations, and widespread bank insolvencies engulfed economies across Southeast Asia, igniting accusations of 'crony capitalism' and causing extreme economic downturns for many of the region's economies. The financial crisis 'zapped the once buoyant confidence of Asian tigers who boasted of a coming "Pacific Century", plunging these nations into uncharted waters, with little more than the International Monetary Fund as a compass', wrote Robert A. Manning in the *Los Angeles Times*.[59] Diplomat and former State Department official Morton Abramowitz concurred. As he remarked in the *Washington Post*, 'Asia's economies ran ahead of their political and institutional growth, and aspirations to regionalism ran ahead of their development as nation states.'[60] Pacific rhetoric had also outpaced practical reality in Chile; according to economist José Cademartori, 'There has been a loss of confidence in the free market because the benefits of "modernity" have been concentrated in a small minority who enjoy First World standards of living while the general population remains firmly ensconced in the Third World.'[61]

Even though its neoliberal variant ran aground at the end of the twentieth century, the concept of a 'Pacific Age' has proved extraordinarily seaworthy.[62]

---

[57] M. Sznajder, 'The Chilean jaguar as a symbol of a new identity', in L. Roniger and T. Herzog (eds.), *The Collective and the Public in Latin America* (Portland, OR: Sussex Academic Press, 2000), 285–98; C. Pietrobelli, *Industry, Competitiveness and Technological Capabilities in Chile: A New Tiger from Latin America?* (New York: St. Martin's Press, 1998); M. Sznajder, 'Dilemmas of economic and political modernization in Chile: a jaguar that wants to be a puma', *Third World Quarterly* 17:4 (1996), 725–36; R. Riva Palacio, 'Chile: la otra cara del jaguar: la ilusion neoliberal', *El Norte* (Monterrey, Mexico) (13 October 1996), 14; R.A. Baeza-Yates et al., 'Computing in Chile: the jaguar of the Pacific Rim?' *Communications of the ACM* 38:9 (1995), 23–8.
[58] D. Ribadeneira, 'A jewel in an economic rough: revitalized Chile looks to join NAFTA', *Boston Globe* (18 January 1995), 39.
[59] R.A. Manning, 'Asia crisis: now for the hard part', *Los Angeles Times* (4 January 1998), 2.
[60] M.I. Abramowitz, 'Asia: look out for more surprises', *Washington Post* (4 January 1998), C7.
[61] J. Cademartori, 'The Chilean neoliberal model enters into crisis', *Latin American Perspectives* 30:5 (2003), 79–88, at 79.
[62] P. Korhonen, 'The Pacific Age in world history', *Journal of World History* 7:1 (1996), 41–70.

This durability was on display in Chile's twenty-first-century campaign to join the Asia-Pacific Economic Cooperation (APEC) forum, a free-trade bloc of twenty-one Pacific Rim nations. When the Sixteenth APEC Economic Leaders' Meeting occurred in 2004, Chile became the first Latin American nation to host this summit.[63] Chilean political scientist and politician Ignacio Walker reflected on these linkages when he wrote in 2006, 'We have discovered a new neighbourhood. Our natural neighbourhood is Latin America. But, Asia, the Asia-Pacific basin, and what it represents in world economics and in politics today is a very promising region ... Chile, with 4,000 miles of coasts, looks face to face with Asia and the Asia-Pacific.'[64]

This outward-facing strategic pose has undergone many revisions. During the first two decades of the twenty-first century, the Chilean government began reminding its citizens and its continental neighbours that Chile is *un país tricontinental* (a tricontinental country), with a conical expanse of territory spanning the regions of South America, Oceania, and Antarctica. Hernán Santis Arenas, the founder of the Institute of Geography at the Pontificia Universidad Católica de Chile, first conceived of this in 1990, but the notion has gained new currency in recent years. Maps representing the doctrine of *Chile tricontinetal* now appear in official government publications and have been fully incorporated into grade-school curricula (Figure 53.2).[65]

These cartographic projections are based on territorial claims to Chile's west and south that parallel the nation's far-reaching northward expansion into the Atacama Desert during the War of the Pacific. Chile asserts its Antarctic identity through its Provincia de la Antártica Chilena (Antártica Chilena Province), which encompasses the southern part of Isla Grande de Tierra del Fuego, the islands south and west of Isla Grande, and Chile's Antarctic zone. The Main Antarctic Treaty of 23 June 1961 registered Chile's claim to this zone, which stretches from 53°W to 90°W.[66] Such claims

---

[63] Founded in 1989, the Asian Pacific Economic Community (APEC) initially brought together member nations, including Australia, Brunei, Canada, China, Hong Kong, Indonesia, Japan, South Korea, Malaysia, New Zealand, the Philippines, Singapore, Taiwan, Thailand, and the United States.

[64] I. Walker, *Chile and Latin America in a Globalized World* (Singapore: Institute of Southeast Asian Studies, 2006), 25.

[65] H. Santis Arenas, 'Significado y contenido de Chile: país marítimo y tricontinental', *Revista Chilena de Geopolítica* (Santiago, Chile) 6:3 (1990), 81–92.

[66] Ó. Pinochet de la Barra, *La Antártica chilena* (Santiago: Editorial Andrés Bello, 1976).

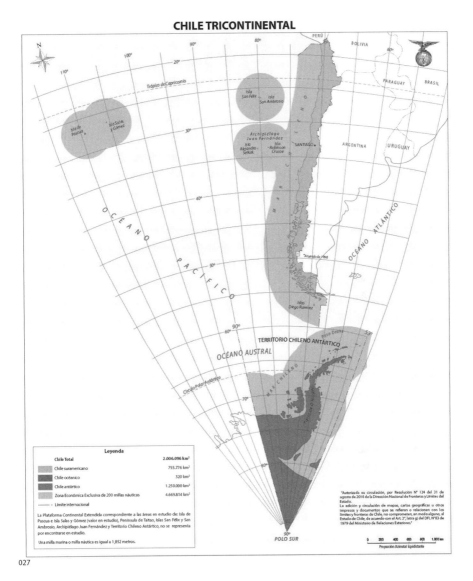

Figure 53.2 A map published by Chile's Ministry of Education showing a depiction of *Chile tricontinental* (Tricontinental Chile), which is used as part of the basic history, geography, and social sciences curriculum in Chilean high schools.

matured from deep roots in conquistador mythology. In the opening stanzas of his sixteenth-century epic poem *La Araucana* (1556), the Spanish nobleman Alonso de Ercilla y Zúñiga rendered Chile as 'fértil provincia y señalada de la

Figure 53.3 Rano Raraku *mo'ai* on the lower slopes of Rapa Nui's Terevaka Volcano.

región antártica famosa' ('a notable and fertile province of the famous Antarctic region').[67]

Chile's westward expansion into Oceania – among the most prominent sites where the histories of Latin America and Polynesia converge – has a more recent provenance.[68] In 1888, Chile annexed the 170-square-kilometre island of Rapa Nui. Located 3,600 kilometres west of Chile's mainland port of Caldera, just below the Tropic of Capricorn, Rapa Nui is the world's most remote, continuously inhabited island.[69] The Polynesian canoe voyagers who settled there around 1200 CE are best known for having used a compressed volcanic ash called tuff to create more than 900 extant monumental statues, called *mo'ai*. These enormous figures, the largest of which may have weighed as much as 165 tons, featured the living faces of deified ancestors (Figure 53.3).[70]

---

[67] A. de Ercilla y Zúñiga, *La Araucana* (1556), canto 1, www.memoriachilena.gob.cl/602/w3-article-3286.html.

[68] The Polynesian Triangle – one representation of Polynesian civilization in the Pacific – is formed by Hawai'i to the north, Aotearoa (New Zealand) to the west, and Rapa Nui to the east.

[69] S.R. Fischer, *The Island at the End of the World: The Turbulent History of Easter Island* (London: Reaktion Books, 2005).

[70] Europeans rendered the name of these statues as 'moai'. More recently, linguists have reintroduced the glottal stop, thus offering a more authentic version of the term. See Fischer, *The Island at the End of the World*, 31.

On Easter Sunday (5 April 1888), Dutch explorer Jacob Roggeveen became the first European to land at Rapa Nui. Roggeveen dubbed Rapa Nui *Paasch-Eyland*, an eighteenth-century Dutch term meaning 'Easter Island'. The island's official name in Spanish, Isla de Pascua, also carries this meaning. A series of eighteenth-century visits by Spanish, British, and French explorers preceded a spate of horrific abductions of Islanders in the late 1800s by Peruvian slave raiders. These kidnappings, along with devastating outbreaks of smallpox and tuberculosis, reduced the Native population of the island from over 6,000 in 1862 to approximately 600 by 1869.[71]

Following its annexation of the island on 9 September 1888, the Chilean government confined the surviving Rapa Nui to the town of Hanga Roa on the island's southwest side and rented the rest of the island to the Anglo-Chilean Williamson-Balfour Company for use as a sheep farm. This oppressive arrangement lasted for more than half a century. In the words of anthropologist Grant McCall, 'What fell into oblivion were the Rapa Nui themselves, as sheep roamed and the Islanders were confined to pens.'[72] When the wool company's lease expired in 1953, the Chilean Navy assumed control of Isla de Pascua and managed the island as a military outpost.

Everything changed in 1964 when a popular 22-year-old schoolteacher named Alfonso Rapu led an uprising that forced the Chilean government to return land rights and cultural patrimony to the Rapa Nui. Rapu subsequently became the first Rapa Nui person to be elected mayor of the island. On 22 February 1966, Chilean president Eduardo Frei signed the 'Easter Island Law', creating the Departamento de Isla de Pascua, a commune in the Valparaíso Administrative Region. Military rule officially ended a few months later, in June, when the Rapa Nui won full Chilean citizenship.[73]

While such gains gave the Rapa Nui crucial footholds in their uphill struggle against colonialism, the political and cultural sovereignty that their community seeks has proven elusive.[74] Since 2010, recurring bouts of dengue fever, the absence of a decent hospital, a ceaseless accumulation of garbage

---

[71] E. Teave and L. Cloud, 'Rapa Nui National Park, Cultural World Heritage: the struggle of the Rapa Nui people for their ancestral territory and heritage, for environmental protection, and for cultural integrity', in S. Disko and H. Tugendhat (eds.), *World Heritage Sites and Indigenous Peoples' Rights* (Copenhagen: International Working Group for Indigenous Affairs, 2014), 403–21, at 406.

[72] Grant McCall, as quoted in Fischer, *The Island at the End of the World*, 197.

[73] G. McCall, 'Riro, Rapu and Rapanui: refoundations in Easter Island colonial history', *Rapa Nui Journal: Journal of the Easter Island Foundation* 11:3 (1997), 112–22.

[74] For an extensive account of Rapanui resistance to Chilean colonialism, see R. Delsing, *Articulating Rapa Nui: Polynesian Cultural Politics in a Latin American Nation-State* (Honolulu: University of Hawai'i Press, 2015); S. Romero, 'Slow burning challenge to Chile on Easter

from the tourism industry, clashes over the management of local fisheries, and ongoing disputes with Chilean authorities over land rights have continued to plague the Rapa Nui.[75] Likewise, their language – part of the East Polynesian language family and closely related to Māori – is endangered. At the dawn of the twenty-first century, Rapanui was spoken by fewer than 2,000 people.[76]

The contested role that Rapa Nui plays at the crossroads of Oceania and Latin America is a microcosm of larger issues that resonate throughout the Pacific World. Across this vast region, the attempts of Islanders to maintain their heritage and assert their political sovereignty have faced profound challenges, ranging from political repression and the privatization of increasingly scarce resources to watershed degradation and rising sea levels. Many of these ongoing struggles also characterize the daily lives of Native peoples along the Pacific coastline of the Americas – stretching from the Mapuche in Patagonia to the Makahs in the Pacific Northwest.[77]

This chapter makes the case for understanding Latin America's relationship with the Pacific as the dialectical outcome of material and imaginative processes. From the Quechua Indian *mitayos* who mined Potosí's silver to the Chinese cooks who invented chifas, ordinary people have done as much as tyrants, traders, and technocrats to create the Pacific World. A more democratic and capacious understanding of trans-Pacific history – one capable of reading the history of this vast oceanic region 'from the bottom up' – will illuminate myriad human experiences that occur beyond the confines of nation-states and more traditional political frameworks. Such an approach is not just a convenient heuristic device. It is a lived notion with deep historical value for accessing how people in other times and places have understood their relationship to the human and non-human communities around them. At some junctures, it has involved the production or reproduction of colonial and neoliberal geographies, while, in other cases, it signifies acts of resistance against oppressive regimes.

Island', *The New York Times* (6 October 2012), www.nytimes.com/2012/10/07/world/americas/slow-burning-rebellion-against-chile-on-easter-island.html.

[75] For example, see *BBC News*, 'Easter Island land dispute clashes leave dozens injured', (4 December 2010), www.bbc.com/news/world-latin-america-11917511.

[76] V. du Feu, *Rapanui: A Descriptive Grammar* (New York: Routledge, 1996), ii.

[77] The most comprehensive history of the Mapuche is J. Bengoa, *Historia del pueblo mapuche: (sigo XIX y XX)* (Santiago: Ediciones Sur, 1985). On the Makah, see J.L. Reid, *The Sea Is My Country: The Maritime World of the Makahs* (New Haven: Yale University Press, 2015).

PART XI

*

THE PACIFIC CENTURY?

54

The USA and the Pacific since 1800

Manifestly Facing West

DAVID HANLON

On 11 October 2011, then Secretary of State Hillary Clinton announced a major shift in United States foreign policy.[1] Anticipating a reduction in American forces in Iraq and Afghanistan, major battlegrounds of the war on terror, Clinton pointed to the Asia-Pacific region as the 'driver of global politics'. Defining the region broadly as spanning both the Indian and the Pacific oceans and including such rising powers as China, India, and Indonesia, Clinton noted that the region held half the world's population, figured prominently in the global economy, and was the source of major environmental problems confronting the globe. Given these facts, the United States now needed to make substantial diplomatic, strategic, and economic investments in the region. Coming to be called the 'Pacific pivot', Clinton's pronouncement was only the most recent reiteration of a long standing history of American interest and activity in the larger region. While there are those who argue that American interests have often been both subservient to and informed by priorities elsewhere in the world, most notably Europe, the region has been a consistent theatre of American desire, ambition, profit, and power. This chapter offers an overview of the United States' historical presence on the ocean, islands, and bordering lands of the region conventionally labelled the 'Pacific', a term that, as Clinton's policy pronouncement indicates, is fluid, amorphous, and subject to the changing times and contexts in which it is deployed.[2]

In the Pacific, early American motivations proved varied, complex, changing, and even contradictory, and would continue to be so into the start of the twentieth century. According to Donald Johnson, these motivations

---

[1] H. Clinton, 'America's Pacific century', *Foreign Policy*, online edition, 11 October 2011, http://foreignpolicy.com/2011/10/11/americas-pacific-century (accessed 6 February 2018).
[2] On the politics of naming in the 'Asia-Pacific' region, see A. Dirlik, 'The Asia-Pacific idea: reality and representation in the invention of a regional structure', *Journal of World History* 3:1 (1992), 55–79.

included personal ambition, missionary zeal, and nationalist goals, either in concert with or against the aims of the investors and merchants whose focus was the economic exploitation of China.[3] The one constant over time, however, was a fairly steady expansion and broadening of American interests in the region, an extension of activities that were initially economic in character and capitalist in nature. Over time, these became intertwined with strategic and security concerns, and took on the features of empire.

Unlike Johnson, who writes of the United States as having no coherent Pacific policy from its inception as a nation to 1898, Michael Green argues for an early and growing American presence that developed into a strategic policy towards the Asia-Pacific region.[4] Though not always efficient or effective, this varied presence resulted over time in the application of military, diplomatic, economic, and ideational tools to promote, expand, and formalize an American governmental policy. An insistence on American pre-eminence in the region has remained a constant that goes back two centuries and can be seen in John Quincy Adams's assertion of the continental Northwest as America's gateway to the Pacific, John Tyler's application of the Monroe Doctrine to include Hawai'i, and William McKinley's acquisition of Hawai'i, and his decision to hold on to the Philippines.[5] America's Pacific expansion was linked to a preceding westward, cross-continental movement explained by a belief in manifest destiny, the nineteenth-century doctrine that God himself had blessed and directed this expansion.

Arguing along similar lines, Thomas Paterson has written that Americans crafted from a consciousness of their historical experience a national ideology that integrated political and economic tenets into a 'peace and prosperity' view of life.[6] By the Cold War period, Americans came to believe they were prosperous because they were democratic, and democratic because they were prosperous. In an extension of this view, American ideology held that peace and prosperity in the larger world were dependent upon economic prosperity and political democracy for all. Despite the harsh counter-realities that disturbed the equation in terms of race, class, and gender relations, this dominant

---

[3] D.D. Johnson (with G.D. Best), *The United States in the Pacific: Private Interests and Public Policy, 1784–1899* (Westport, CT: Praeger, 1995), xii.

[4] M.J. Green, *By More than Providence: Grand Strategy and American Power in the Asia Pacific Since 1783* (New York: Columbia University Press, 2019).

[5] Green, *By More Than Providence*, p. 5. See also B. Cumings, *Dominion from Sea to Sea: Pacific Ascendancy and American Power* (New Haven: Yale University Press, 2009).

[6] T.G. Paterson, *American Foreign Policy: A History* (Lexington: D.C. Heath, 1977), 346. Cited in D. Hanlon, *Remaking Micronesia: Discourses over Development in a Pacific Territory, 1844–1982* (Honolulu: University of Hawai'i Press, 1989), 5.

ideology, and the sense of virtuous exceptionalism that underlay it, was used to justify American expansion in the larger world, including the Pacific.[7]

An analysis of the deep, layered, and complex histories of the United States in the Pacific lies beyond the scope of this chapter. Nonetheless, there are several prominent themes that emerge: expansion, territorial acquisition, the rise of an imperial presidency, the building of empire, the deep denial of the colonization that accompanied that building of empire, and a turn to militarization. These are processes grounded in privilege and patriarchy, and that were racialized, gendered, and sexualized. They affected the domestic as well as the foreign realms. At the same time, the responses of people subsumed by the extension of this American empire have had profound effects on the homeland itself. Indeed, a strict focus on the history of United States activities in the Pacific risks the omission of counter and alternative histories in the region, an issue taken up in the last section of this chapter.

The Reach of Early Empire

The desire to profit from trade with China initially brought American merchants west across the Pacific Ocean.[8] In 1784, the *Empress of China* was the first American flag vessel to dock at a Chinese port, an event promoted by John Ledyard who had been with Captain James Cook on his third Pacific voyage. Like European merchants, American traders found it difficult to balance their desire for tea, silk, and other Chinese commodities with the Qing government's disdain for Western goods. Hard currency was required to trade with China – a fact that limited profits and caused a drain on the national treasuries of Western nations. Between 1805 and 1808, America's trade with China had a total value of between \$10 and \$15 million dollars, and accounted for 15 per cent of the country's foreign trade, though this

---

[7] For an extended analysis of the ways in which American exceptionalism and liberalism mask the fact of empire, see C. Julien, *America's Empire*, trans. R. Bruce (New York: Pantheon Books, 1971). There is also H. Zinn, *A People's History of the United States* (New York: Harper Perennial American Classics, 2003).

[8] I rely on Johnson's *The United States and the Pacific* to provide a summary of American interests and activities in the Pacific from 1784 to 1899. Other general histories include S. Banner, *Possessing the Pacific: Land, Settlers, and Indigenous People from Australia to Alaska* (Cambridge, MA: Harvard University Press, 2007); A.P. Dudden, *The American Pacific: From the Old China Trade to the Present* (Oxford: Oxford University Press, 1992); W.A. McDougall, *Let the Sea Make a Noise: A History of the North Pacific from Magellan to MacArthur* (New York: Basic Books, 1993); W.P. Strauss, *Americans in Polynesia, 1783–1842* (East Lansing: Michigan State University Press, 1963).

percentage would later drop.[9] In the 1820s and 1830s, thirty to forty American ships dropped anchor at Canton or Guangzhou, the only Chinese port open to foreign trade before 1842. American vessels were also involved in the illegal smuggling of opium into China, and the country benefited significantly, along with European nations, from the liberalized trade treaties and opening of additional Chinese ports that followed the Opium Wars of 1839–42. In 1844, the Treaty of Wangxia granted the United States most-favoured-nation status with China.

The Northwest fur trade brought Americans to the eastern edge of the Pacific, and provided an important supplement to the nation's commerce with China. The United States came to dominate the fur trade, and from 1787 into the 1830s exported 15 to 20 million dollars' worth of furs and pelts to China.[10] The trade with China also drove the exploitation of sandalwood forests in Fiji, Hawai'i, and the Marquesas Islands, and the harvesting of other Pacific Islands products such as pearl shell, tortoise shell, and bêche-de-mer or sea cucumber, all of which possessed considerable value in the Chinese market.

Whaling and sealing were two other commercial industries that increased the American presence in the Pacific.[11] While British ships controlled the early trade, the shift in whaling grounds from the East Asian and South American coasts to eastern Polynesia and along the equator led to American domination from the 1820s to mid-century. Sealing was initially done along the southern latitudes of the Juan Fernandez Islands off Chile and off New Zealand. Later, the hunt for seals moved to waters off California and the Northwest Coast. Between 1829 and 1845, American whaling in the Pacific accounted for 10–20 per cent of the country's total foreign commerce tonnage.[12] As with the Northwest fur trade, the business of whaling and sealing had devastating consequences on the populations of these two mammalian groups.

The crews that sailed these vessels became increasingly multi-ethnic in composition over time. The names of Afro-American, Bengali, Chinese, Filipino, Native American, and Pacific Islander men filled ships' rolls. Their labour proved crucial to the development of capitalism and empire, and

---

[9] Johnson, *The United States in the Pacific*, 19.
[10] Johnson, *The United States in the Pacific*, 33, citing T. Dennett's *Americans in Eastern Asia: A Critical Study of the Policy of the United States with Reference to China, Japan, and Korea in the 19th Century* (New York: Octagon Books, 1979).
[11] For a general history of the American whaling industry, see H. Morton, *The Whale's Wake* (Honolulu: University of Hawai'i Press, 1982); E. Stackpole, *The Sea Hunters: The New England Whalemen during Two Centuries, 1635–1835* (Philadelphia: Lippincott, 1953); A. Starbuck, *History of the American Whale Fishery* (Secaucus, NJ: Castle, 1989).
[12] Johnson, *The United States in the Pacific*, 51.

challenged the narrative of American expansionism as singularly and simply national.[13] These American commercial and shipping interests also resulted in temporary communities of beachcombers and castaways on Pacific Islands whose members, despite the disruption their presence sometimes caused, also offered instruction to island populations in the ways of the intruding modern world.[14] These early beach communities were small, ramshackle, racially mixed, and socially relaxed places where island women held a prominent role. Their egalitarian features disappeared with the influx of more foreigners and their commercial priorities. Beach communities became port towns over time, and, like the diverse crews aboard American whaling and sealing ships, evidenced the cross-cultural and transnational dynamics that were a part of the rise of empire.

While ships were almost exclusively the domain of men, women at home and in Pacific ports provided critical labour and support services that enabled American voyaging and commercial enterprise in the region.[15] The absence of women aboard sailing vessels did create problems and drove the sexual commerce between ship and shore that was a part of the economy of developing empire in the Pacific. In Honolulu, American sailors rioted on three separate occasions between 1825 and 1827 against the prohibition on prostitution declared by Hawaiian chiefs.[16] The desire and demand of Euro-American men for island women was fuelled in part by the perceived exotic primitivism of the Pacific muse. This stereotype lay deeply embedded in the intellectual and literary history of the West, and portrayed Pacific women as simple, sensual, available, and willing. The large number of ships' crews coming into the Pacific during the first half of the nineteenth century greatly exacerbated the conditions that enticed or forced women into the sale of their sexual favours. Pacific women were reduced to the status of a natural resource in the economy of empire.[17] At the same time, such stereotyping ignored or sought to subvert the very prominent role of women in Pacific societies.

[13] D.A. Chappell, *Double Ghosts: Oceanian Voyagers and Euro-American Ships* (New York: M.E. Sharpe, 1997), 41.
[14] C. Ralston, 'The beachcombers', in *Grass Huts and Warehouses: Pacific Beach Communities in the Nineteenth Century* (Canberra: ANU Press, 1977), 20–43. See also H.E. Maude, 'Beachcombers and castaways', *Journal of the Polynesian Society* 73:3 (1964), 254–93.
[15] L. Norling, 'Ahab's wife: women and the American whaling industry', in M. Creighton and L. Norling (eds.), *Iron Men and Wooden Women: Gender and Seafaring in the Atlantic World* (Baltimore: Johns Hopkins University Press, 1996), 70–91.
[16] N. Arista, *The Kingdom and the Republic: Sovereign Hawai'i and the Early United States* (Philadelphia: University of Pennsylvania Press, 2019), 168, 178.
[17] P. O'Brien, *The Pacific Muse: Exotic Femininity and the Colonial Pacific* (Seattle: University of Washington Press, 2006), 15–16.

Missionaries increased the American presence in the Pacific region. The Boston-based American Board of Commissioners for Foreign Missions sent missionaries to Hawai'i in 1820, and later to the Marquesas and eastern Micronesia.[18] Territorial interests showed themselves earlier and elsewhere in the island Pacific. David Porter, commander of the USS *Essex*, engaged in a battle with a British warship near the Marquesas Islands as part of the War of 1812. Porter saw strategic advantage to the Marquesas and claimed the island of Nukuhiva. American naval ships later made regular visits to South American ports, and the creation of the Pacific squadron in 1822 only added to a small but growing American naval presence in the region.[19]

The decision of the American government to fund what came to be called the United States Exploring Expedition (1838–42) also reflected increasing American interest in the Pacific region.[20] Commissioned to extend the bounds of science and promote the acquisition of knowledge, the expedition, under the command of Lieutenant Charles Wilkes, visited numerous Pacific Islands and bordering continental lands, intervened forcefully at times in defence of American merchants and missionaries, built two meteorological observatories at Ovalau in Fiji and Honolulu, claimed the continent of Antarctica, advocated for the value of the harbour at Pago Pago in Sāmoa as a naval base, and ended its four-year voyage at New York City. Though considered to be of limited success by its sponsors, the expedition did amass a great deal of scientific, linguistic, and ethnographic data that would prove useful to future generations.

The competing territorial and commercial claims of Spain, Russia, Mexico, and Great Britain limited for a time the United States' westward continental expansion and the further expansion of its oceanic initiatives. Fur trading companies and governmental officials with strong Western interests pressed the United States government to be more aggressive in the settlement of these disputes. Following a series of complicated, often confounding agreements, the United States government signed a treaty with Great Britain that recognized as American territory all land south of the 49th parallel and

---

[18] Arista, *The Kingdom and the Republic*, 100. See also J. Osorio, *Dismembering Lāhui: A History of the Hawaiian Nation to 1867* (Honolulu: University of Hawai'i Press, 2002), 9; K.R. Howe, *Where the Waves Fall: A New South Sea Islands History from First Settlement to Colonial Rule*, Pacific Islands Monograph Series 2 (Honolulu: University of Hawai'i Press, 1984), 120.

[19] W.P. Strauss, 'Policemen in Polynesia: the American Navy', in *Americans in Polynesia, 1783–1842*, 83–5; also Johnson, *The United States in the Pacific*, 41–42.

[20] N. Philbrick, *Sea of Glory: America's Voyage of Discovery: The U.S. Exploring Expedition, 1838–1842* (New York: Viking, 2003); also W.R. Stanton, *The Great United States Exploring Expedition of 1838–1842* (Berkeley: University of California Press, 1975).

extending east to the Rocky Mountains, an area more commonly known as the Oregon Territory. The lure of profits in the Northwest also brought Americans to California. A tumultuous and violent course of events ended in the 1847 Treaty of Guadalupe Hidalgo that ceded California to the United States. As a result of the acquisition of California and the Oregon Territory, the United States now had 2,400 kilometres of Pacific coastline. The later purchase of Alaska from Russia in 1867, and the turn-of-the-century settlement with Great Britain over the border between Canada and Alaska, would add to that coastline and the maritime access it provided.

As noted earlier, the whaling industry provided the preface to an expanded American presence in the Hawaiian islands. By 1820, there had developed a maritime commerce managed almost exclusively by Americans. The unification of the islands under Kamehameha, and the establishment of an islands-wide government at Honolulu, could not hold in check foreign influences and the destructive pressures they brought to bear on the islands and their people. Disease, death, missionary teachings, and the rise of a market economy severely harmed Hawaiian culture.[21] Hawaiian chiefs, seeking to counter the foreign influences flooding their islands, enlisted the help of American nationals; this strategy worked only for a time. Fears of foreign interference from France, Great Britain, and Russia led American interests to lobby for annexation, a move strongly opposed at the time by the Hawaiian monarch Liholiho, or Kamehameha II, and his successor Kauikeaouli.

What would come to make a difference in US–Hawaiian relations was the growing sugar industry in the islands that relied on imported labour largely from Japan and later the Philippines.[22] As whaling declined, sugar rose. Exports of sugar increased dramatically from 289,908 pounds in 1855 to 23,129,101 pounds by 1873.[23] To insure against the price declines that came with economic depressions, Hawai'i's sugar planters sought a reciprocity treaty with its principal market, the United States. Following two failed attempts, a treaty was signed in 1875, and renewed two years later with provisions that granted the United States Navy exclusive rights to Pearl Harbor. The revision and amendments reflected a growing awareness of Hawai'i's strategic value in an area of the world marked by increasing imperial rivalries. The reciprocity treaty looked to some like a preface to

---

[21] For an extremely sophisticated cross-cultural analysis of Hawaiians' engagement with commerce, Christianity, and Western law, see Arista, *The Kingdom and the Republic*.
[22] C.A. MacLennon, *Sovereign Sugar: Industry and Environment in Hawai'i* (Honolulu: University of Hawai'i Press, 2017).
[23] Johnson, *The United States in the Pacific*, 104.

annexation. In 1867, US Minister to Hawai'i Edward McCook wrote to Secretary of State William Steward: 'When the Pacific railroad is complete and the commerce of Asia directed to our Pacific ports, then these islands will be needed as a rendezvous for our Pacific navy, and a resort for merchant ships, and this [reciprocity] treaty will have prepared the way for their quiet absorption.'[24] Years later, in 1881, Secretary of State James G. Blaine identified Hawai'i as 'key to the American dominion of the Pacific'.[25]

Compared to the country's domestic and trans-Atlantic trade, the value of America's Pacific maritime commerce decreased in the period 1865–70. Events elsewhere would revive and expand America's Pacific presence, however. The earlier forced opening of Japan by Commodore Matthew Perry, the development of the steamship, the consequent increase in shipping along the western coasts of North, Central, and South America, and the 1847 Clayton-Bulwer Treaty that made possible the later construction of the Panama Canal, all enabled the expansion of American commercial activity. American contact with Australia and New Zealand in this period proved limited due to their colonial relations with Great Britain.

United States trade with the Pacific Islands beyond Hawai'i proved minor. Salem merchants did hold the Fijian chief Cakobau responsible for the burning of their ships and trade goods, and presented him with a bill for US$ 43,000.00 through John Williams, the American consular agent in Fiji. William Steinberger, with close ties to the San Francisco-based Central Polynesian Land and Commercial Company, was sent by President Ulysses Grant to represent the United States in Sāmoa.[26] He came to serve as an advisor to the forces of self-government, but in the end proposed annexation to the United States as a solution to the internal and foreign pressures undermining local efforts at self-government. The 1874 establishment of the Office of the High Commissioner for the Western Pacific, in response to the abuses of British nationals in the Melanesian labour trade tied to sugar plantations in northeastern Australia, Fiji, and Sāmoa, gave the British dominance in the southwest Pacific. American participation in this labour trade proved minimal but did reflect the racism that was such a prominent feature of Americans' relations with Native Americans, Asian immigrants

---

[24] Johnson, *The United States in the Pacific*, 104–5.
[25] Johnson, *The United States in the Pacific*, 106.
[26] For a history of the imperial rivalry and eventual partition of Sāmoa, see P. Kennedy, *The Samoan Tangle: A Study in Anglo-German-American Relations, 1878–1900* (St Lucia: Queensland University Press, 1974).

from China and Japan, and those brought over from Africa to work as slaves on the plantations of the South.[27]

American acquisition of territory preceded 1898, the date most often cited as the beginning of its Pacific empire. Captain William Reynolds of the USS *Lakawanna* claimed Midway Island in 1867. Reynolds's action was actually the second American claim to the island, the first being in 1859 by Captain N.C. Brooks and under the terms of the Guano Act of 1856. The Guano Act was an effort by the United States Congress to aid the country's agricultural industry through the identification and exploitation of deposits of guano fertilizer.[28] The act allowed American citizens to take possession of and occupy any unclaimed islands on which were found deposits of guano. It led to multiple and sometimes duplicate claims by American citizens that caused confusion over actual ownership and later created diplomatic conflicts with foreign nations that were euphemistically referred to as the 'guano wars'. In 1872, Commander Richard W. Meade of the USS *Narragansett* signed a treaty with the chiefs of Tutuila that gave the United States the right to build a coaling and naval base at Pago Pago. It wasn't until 1899, however, that the United States Congress funded construction of that base in the wake of the partition of Sāmoa by Great Britain, Germany, and the United States. By the terms of that partition, the United States received jurisdiction over eastern Sāmoa, including Tutuila and its harbour.

The acquisition of territory could involve more than simple claims or diplomatic negotiations. A perfect storm of events and crises coalesced to bring about the American-sponsored overthrow of the Hawaiian monarchy in 1893, and the annexation of the islands in 1898. The imposition of a tariff on Hawaiian sugar by the United States Congress, and Queen Lili'uokalani's stated intention to promulgate a new constitution that restored the powers of the monarchy compromised by an earlier 1887 version, worried commercial and plantation interests.[29] American minister John L. Stevens responded to the urgings of the local Annexation Club and requested the landing of marines from the USS *Boston*, ostensibly to protect American lives and property. Lili'uokalani surrendered her authority with the hope of restoration even as

---

[27] G. Horne, *The White Pacific: U.S. Imperialism and Black Slavery in the South Seas after the Civil War* (Honolulu: University of Hawai'i Press, 2007).

[28] For a broader global history of the trade in Pacific fertilizers, see G.T. Cushman, *Guano and the Opening of the Pacific World: A Global Ecological History* (Cambridge: Cambridge University Press, 2014).

[29] For an account of the imposed 1887 constitution, see J.K.K Osorio, 'Bayonet', in *Dismembering Lāhui*, 193–249.

Stevens proceeded with the recognition of the provisional government. The Blount Report, commissioned by President Grover Cleveland, recommended the restoration of the monarchy. Restoration didn't happen. American President William McKinley proclaimed: 'We need Hawaii just as much and a good deal more than we did California. It is manifest destiny.'[30] War with Spain reinforced the Hawaiian islands' strategic importance in the minds of American military and governmental personnel. In 1898, both houses of Congress set aside the issue of a formal treaty and voted instead to approve a joint resolution annexing the Hawaiian islands. Against the protests of Native Hawaiians, the American flag was raised over 'Iolani Palace on 12 August 1898.[31] Wake Island was claimed the following year by Commander Edward D. Taussig, thus providing the USA with a geographic link between Hawai'i and the continental West Coast. Commercial expansion, the acquisition of territory, and the growth of empire thus marked America's first century in the Pacific. The heavy costs of these developments were paid for by others, a pattern that would continue well into the next century.

1898 and the Creation of an American Lake

The war with Spain in 1898 marked not so much the inauguration of an American empire in the Pacific as a more formal government policy of support for a process already in place.[32] Promoted by imperial advocates such as Theodore Roosevelt, Henry Cabot Lodge, and Admiral Alfred Thayer Mahan, war with Spain added Guam and the Philippines to the United States. Following the defeat of the Spanish fleet at Manila, Commodore George Dewey had no clear orders as to what to do next. Emilio Aguinaldo, the Filipino nationalist leader, claimed to have received assurances of independence for his country in return for aid against Spain. Reluctant though it may have been, the acquisition and administration of the Philippines proved bloody and brutal in its first years as Filipinos resisted the imposition of an American colonial regime. That war would last three years, and was driven by a mix of racism, paternalism, and capitalist desire.[33] In the

[30] W. LaFeber, *The American Age: United States Foreign Policy at Home and Abroad since 1750* (New York: W.W. Norton, 1989), 193.
[31] N.K. Silva, *Aloha Betrayed: Native Hawaiian Resistance to American Colonialism* (Durham, NC: Duke University Press, 2004).
[32] This summary of US foreign policy in the Pacific from 1898 to the end of the twentieth century draws on LaFeber, *The American Age*.
[33] Zinn, *A People's History of the United States*, 313–14.

treaty negotiations ending the Spanish-American war, the United States also secured Guam, where a naval administration was established much like that in eastern Sāmoa.

The early American colonial administration of the Philippines, led from Manila by future president William Howard Taft, sought to cover the violence and racism of conquest with the cloak of benevolence and development. It was a cloak whose colours were ultimately self-serving. Hygiene was one of the disciplinary structures established to transform Filipinos into a more sanitary and civilized race. In the words of Warwick Anderson, the new colony became a 'laboratory of hygiene and modernity' where the actual priorities were the welfare of resident American troops and the advantages to metropolitan populations and international health organizations gained from local medical research and testing.[34] The rhetoric of development in the field of health elided the turmoil created among the Filipino public. Whiteness and masculinity were also at stake in a tropical environment deemed threatening and dangerous to its latest colonizers.

The assassination of President McKinley, one of the prime architects of US imperial expansion, brought Theodore Roosevelt to power. Like McKinley, Roosevelt was an ardent believer in the idea of the imperial presidency that drove much of the expansion of 1898 and after. Roosevelt won from Colombia through the Hay-Pauncefote Treaty the right to fortify as well as build the Panama Canal. By 1900, the United States held or laid claim to Alaska, the Philippines, the Aleutians, and the islands of Midway, Wake, Kingman Reef, Howland, Baker, and Guam. These holdings created a veritable bridge or set of stepping-stones to the other side of the Pacific, where China was being carved up like a melon by European imperial powers.

The East Asian border, more particularly China and Japan, became the prime focus of America's Pacific policy. Americans had long had an interest in Chinese markets and Chinese souls, but little actual power in the region. The Open Door Notes were an attempt to secure for the United States more political clout and economic leverage there. As promulgated by Theodore Roosevelt's Secretary of State John Hay, signatories to the notes agreed to fair and equitable shipping and railway charges for all foreigners in their respective spheres of influence. Chinese tariffs were to be applied to all, and duties on imported goods were to be collected by the Chinese themselves. The agreement had the avowed advantage of preserving Chinese territorial

---

[34] W. Anderson, *Colonial Pathologies: American Tropical Medicine, Race, and Hygiene in the Philippines* (Durham, NC: Duke University Press, 2006), 5.

integrity while, at the same time, enhancing the American profile in the region. Hay's Open Door Notes would find reinforcement in the Dollar Diplomacy of the succeeding William Taft administration.

Missionaries complemented this growing American influence. By the end of the nineteenth century, there were over 1,000 American Protestant missionaries in China; that number would grow to 3,000 by 1920.[35] Their presence, and consequent requests for support and assistance from the government, facilitated greater American involvement in China. Undermining the credibility of this larger American presence, however, was the US Congress's passage of the 1882 Chinese Exclusion Act that placed a ten-year moratorium on Chinese immigration.[36] This piece of congressional legislation did nothing to stop the anti-Chinese violence on the West Coast of the United States that continued well into the next century. The racism that was a part of America's own continental expansion was inextricably linked to and affected its empire building in the Pacific.[37]

One impediment to the realization of the Open Door policy was Japan, itself an emerging imperial power. Japan's decision to close off Korea to United States interests and to expand its activities in Manchuria on the East Asian continent proved troublesome. Equally threatening to the diplomatic status quo in East Asia was increased Japanese immigration into California. By 1900, there were 24,000 Japanese citizens in the state; their presence sparked riots and ugly, racist forms of discrimination.[38] The 1908 Root-Takahira Agreement sought to address the tensions between the two countries by recognizing Japan's pre-eminence in southern Manchuria in return for a pledge to uphold the Open Door and the independence of China. Roosevelt, however, believed that the only way to maintain the Open Door in East Asia was through war with Japan. In 1911, the United States military drafted a document called Plan Orange that outlined the American response to an anticipated future war with Japan.

American policymakers increasingly viewed Japan as a threat to the stability of Asia and to the normalcy of a world order. Charles Evans Hughes, Warren G. Harding's Secretary of State, believed he had reached an understanding with Japan that would allow for the joint and mutually

---

[35] LaFeber, *The American Age*, 205, 335.
[36] G.Y. Okihiro, *American History Unbound: Asians and Pacific Islanders* (Oakland: University of California Press, 2015).
[37] R. Drinnon, *Facing West: The Metaphysics of Indian-Hating and Empire-Building* (Minneapolis: University of Minnesota Press, 1980).
[38] LaFeber, *The American Age*, 239.

The USA and the Pacific since 1800

profitable development of China and other areas of Asia. The 1924 US Immigration Law gave the lie to Hughes's vision of progress. The law sought to reduce the entry into the country of those considered undesirable. It completely shut out Asians, in large part because of the pressure from California where anti-Japanese sentiment was exceptionally strong.

Tensions between the two Pacific powers persisted into the 1930s. President Franklin Roosevelt sought to constrain Japan in China by arranging for the termination of European loans extended by the Harding administration; he also persuaded Congress to extend credit to Chiang Kai-shek's struggling nationalist government. Japan's response was the Amau Statement that asserted its right to act alone to preserve peace and order in Asia. Bad feelings escalated exponentially when Japan in 1937 declared all-out war on China to protect its interests in Manchuria, stop Chinese discriminatory actions against Japanese goods, and insure its own self-sufficiency by securing sustained access to continental resources and markets. Japan later announced the formulation of the Greater East Asian Co-Prosperity Sphere that, despite its anti-colonial rhetoric, was designed to place much of Asia and the western Pacific under Japanese control.

As Germany advanced on eastern Europe and Russia in 1941, Japan seized France's colonial holdings in Southeast Asia. Roosevelt's response was to freeze all Japanese assets in the United States and to pressure Great Britain to do the same. An American-imposed oil embargo, and military aid to Chinese forces fighting Japan, only hardened the lines. There followed the attack on Pearl Harbor, war between Japan and the United States, and the internment of Americans of Japanese ancestry on the West Coast and to a lesser extent in Hawai'i. Already in possession of much of Micronesia through the 1919 League of Nations award of a mandate over the Caroline, Marshall, and Northern Mariana Islands, Japan moved quickly to capture Guam, Wake Island, and the Philippines. The United States responded with successful naval engagements off Midway Island and in the Coral Sea. American military forces embarked upon an island-hopping strategy that included some of World War II's bloodiest fighting. In Micronesia, there were the battles on Tarawa, Kwajalein, Angaur, Peleliu, Guam, and Saipan, and the bombing of the Truk or Chuuk lagoon. The former Japanese Mandate Islands later became a strategic trust territory awarded to the United States in 1947 by the United Nations.

In the southwestern Pacific, successful campaigns for the Solomon Islands, the Philippines, and Okinawa preceded a final assault on the Japanese home islands that was rendered unnecessary by the firebombing of Tokyo and the dropping of atomic devices on Hiroshima and Nagasaki. While much of the history of the Pacific War centres on the military campaigns, what is often ignored is the disruption, dislocation, and suffering of island populations caught in the crossfire of a war that was not theirs.[39] Notable also was the destruction caused to island environments and island ways by the markedly racist character of the violence that the combatants delivered upon each other. John Dower termed the conflict a 'war without mercy'.[40] On Peleliu in the Palau group of western Micronesia, for example, fighting between Japanese and American forces resulted in horrific casualties on both sides, and left the island permanently scarred and its inhabitants displaced for years following the end of hostilities.[41]

Both Presidents Roosevelt and Harry Truman had wanted a democratic, open, liberal post-war world along the lines envisioned in the Atlantic Charter. Stalin's determination to dominate eastern and central Europe complicated that vision, as did the rise of the Chinese Communist Party, and Britain's and France's reclaiming of their former colonies in Africa, the Pacific, and Southeast Asia. The United States had more success managing the rebuilding of Japan, where their occupation spared the emperor, and brought about the gradual revitalization of the economy.

In the still-lingering spirit of the Open Door, Truman's Secretary of State Dean Acheson believed that foreign policy was ultimately about business transactions, credit through international banking institutions, and assistance in the general area of economic development. The Truman Doctrine sought to secure the American version of the free world against hostile forces, the most notable being the Soviet Union. In this post-war environment, the United States promoted the construction and maintenance of a sphere of influence within the western hemisphere, the domination of the Atlantic and

---

[39] L. Poyer, S. Falgout, and L.M. Carucci, *The Typhoon of War: Micronesian Experiences of the Pacific War* (Honolulu: University of Hawai'i Press, 2002); G.M. White, D. Gegeo, D. Akin, and K. Watson-Gegeo (eds.), *The Big Death: Solomon Islanders Remember World War II* (Suva: Institute of Pacific Studies, 1991); G.M. White and L. Lindstrom (eds.), *The Pacific Theater: Island Representations of World War II*, Pacific Islands Monograph Series 8 (Honolulu: University of Hawai'i Press, 1989). See also J.A. Bennett and A. Wanhalla (eds.), *Mothers' Darlings of the South Pacific: The Children of Indigenous Women and U.S. Servicemen, World War II* (Honolulu: University of Hawai'i Press, 2016); S. Falgout, L. Poyer, and L.M. Carucci, *Memories of War: Micronesians in the Pacific War* (Honolulu: University of Hawai'i Press, 2008).
[40] J.W. Dower, *War without Mercy: Race and Power in the Pacific War* (New York: Pantheon Books, 1986); J.A. Bennett, *Natives and Exotics: World War II and Environment in the Southern Pacific* (Honolulu: University of Hawai'i Press, 2009).
[41] S.C. Murray, *The Battle over Peleliu: Islander, Japanese, and American Memories of War* (Tuscaloosa: University of Alabama Press, 2016), 1–4.

Pacific oceans, an extensive system of bases in both oceans to project American power, access to the markets and natural resources of Eurasia, and global nuclear superiority. To many, the Pacific now took on the features of an American lake. The Communists' seizure of power in China, war in Korea, and the Soviet Union's detonation of a nuclear warhead, however, threatened American pre-eminence in the region.

A string of military installations came to dot the seascape of the Pacific in the post-war period; these included bases in Hawai'i, Guam, the Philippines, Okinawa, Australia, Japan, and South Korea. These militarized spaces were gendered male in their practices, policies, and priorities.[42] For local and native women, they were places that represented employment opportunities but also presented considerable danger and exploitation. As Cynthia Enloe has observed, military bases and prostitution were assumed to be a natural twosome by military planners.[43] This sexual commerce was racialized in these environments, and included the military-condoned creation of separate brothels for Afro-American troops, a practice that continued into the Vietnam War era and beyond. Violence and sexual assault on host country women by American servicemen proved particularly pronounced and drew strong protests in Okinawa, Korea, and the Philippines.[44]

With its emphasis on access to feminized, passive, and alluring landscapes, tourism developed as a complement to the military's concern for security, and enhanced the American presence in the region.[45] In Hawai'i and the Philippines, prostitution also became a metaphor for the gross commodification of culture and the displacement of local histories in favour of narratives that extolled the courage and sacrifice of the American war effort.[46] This aspect of modernization depended heavily on the exploitation of women and land, and required the collusion of local elites. The expansion of the global

---

[42] C. Enloe, *Bananas, Beaches, and Bases: Making Feminist Sense of International Politics*, rev. edn (Berkeley: University of Californai Press, 2014), 128–39.

[43] Enloe, *Bananas, Beaches, and Bases*, 157.

[44] The literature on this topic is large and growing. See for example K.H. Moon, *Sex among Allies: Prostitution in U.S.–Korea Relations* (New York: Columbia University Press, 1997); M. Koikari, *Cold War Encounters in U.S.-Occupied Okinawa: Women, Militarized Domesticity, and Transnationalism in East Asia* (Cambridge: Cambridge University Press, 2015).

[45] V.V. Gonzalez, *Securing Paradise: Tourism and Militarism in Hawai'i and the Philippines* (Durham, NC: Duke University Press, 2013), 7.

[46] On this point, see H.-K. Trask, 'Lovely hula hands: corporate tourism and the prostitution of Hawaiian culture', in *From a Native Daughter: Colonialism and Sovereignty in Hawai'i*, rev. edn (Honolulu: University of Hawai'i Press, 1999 [1993]), 136–50. On the politics of war memory and commemoration, see G.M. White, *Memorializing Pearl Harbor: Unfinished Histories and the Work of Resistance* (Durham, NC: Duke University Press, 2016).

economy has also witnessed a massive migration of labour both from and to the Pacific region. In 2013, a million Filipinos, many of them women, were working abroad, including in America's Pacific territories and under conditions that could best be described as abusive.[47] In short, the expansion of empire has required the exploitation of human and cultural resources as well as those of the natural world.

Nuclearization has been an integral part of militarization in the post-war and more recent Pacific. The assumed need to develop enhanced nuclear capabilities drove the United States, Great Britain, and France into testing programmes in the Pacific. In the Marshall Islands, the United States exploded sixty-four nuclear devices between 1946 and 1954.[48] This testing destroyed island environments, disrupted lives, necessitated the relocation of island people, and caused cancers and illnesses that brought death to the living and the unborn.[49] Eisenhower saw nuclear weapons as a necessary part of a conventional weapons inventory while others thought the United States needed to prepare itself for only limited wars in the Pacific and elsewhere. War in Vietnam underscored this later view in revealing the limits to the deployment of nuclear weapons.

The Cold War dominated American foreign policy in the Pacific. Vietnam and the perceived threat of communist insurgencies and revolutions elsewhere in the world challenged the global order and stability sought by the administrations of Presidents John F. Kennedy and Lyndon B. Johnson. Following Johnson, Richard Nixon and his Secretary of State, Henry Kissinger, felt that the long-term protection of American interests in the world required the reduction of overseas obligations. The two sought a global partnership in which the established powers of China, Japan, the Soviet Union, and the United States would work to quell revolutionary unrest and instability in the undeveloped world. The answer to the problems in Vietnam was 'Vietnamization'. Nixon announced his intention to withdraw American troops and have them replaced with qualified Vietnamese forces. On Guam, in 1968, he formally proclaimed what came to be called the

---

[47] Enloe, *Banana, Beaches, and Bases*, 302.

[48] P. Boyer, *By the Bomb's Early Light: American Thought and Culture at the Dawn of the Atomic Age* (Chapel Hill: University of North Carolina Press, 1994); J. Dibblin, *Day of Two Suns: US Nuclear Testing and the Pacific Islanders* (New York: New Amsterdam Books, 1990); S. Firth, *Nuclear Playground* (Honolulu: University of Hawai'i Press, 1987).

[49] H.M. Barker, *Bravo for the Marshallese: Regaining Control in a Post-Nuclear, Post-Colonial World* (Belmont, CA: Wadsworth/Thomson Learning, 2004); J.H. Genz et al., *Militarism and Nuclear Testing in the Pacific*, Teaching Oceania Series 1, Interactive I-Book, Center for Pacific Islands Studies, University of Hawai'i, Mānoa, 2018, http://hdl.handle.net.10125/42430., accessed 11 July 2018.

Nixon Doctrine; the United States would continue to help defend and develop its allies, 'but cannot – and will not – conceive all the plans, design all the programs, execute all the decisions and undertake all the defence of the free nations of the world'.[50] Relations with China improved and there were efforts at detente with the Soviet Union in the form of a Strategic Arms Limitation Treaty and Anti-Ballistic Munitions Agreement. This stunning, unexpected initiative opened up Chinese markets to American goods, changed the dynamics of major power relations, and created serious tensions in Washington's relationship with the Taiwan-based Republic of China.

Succeeding Nixon, Gerald Ford proclaimed his own Pacific Doctrine. Ford believed the centre of political power in the world had shifted towards Asia; as a result, American Pacific interests and concerns had increased. This shift demanded a more equitably distributed exercise of US power in the world. Announced in Hawai'i, Ford's Pacific Doctrine focused on American commercial involvement in Asia and an increased commitment to Pacific markets. For the first time in the history of the nation, US economic interests in Asia were becoming greater than those in Europe.

Jimmy Carter struggled to find a foreign policy consensus in a world where American power now sagged. Under Ronald Reagan, however, spending on the military increased by 40 per cent between 1980 and 1984, and with emphasis on more sophisticated military technology such as the Strategic Defense Initiative (SDI), dubbed the 'Star Wars' defense plan by its critics. In contrast to Carter's emphasis on human rights, Reagan distinguished between totalitarian and authoritarian governments, the latter being supportable and sometimes preferable. Foreign policy became more ideological, with support for anti-communist forces, called 'freedom fighters', in places such as Afghanistan, Angola, Kampuchea, and Nicaragua. His successor George H.W. Bush proved a somewhat more flexible cold warrior; among other things, he pushed for free trade in the form of the North American Free Trade Agreement (NAFTA) with Canada and Mexico, improved relations with China, and signed the most comprehensive nuclear disarmament agreement to date.

William J. Clinton proved an advocate of the global economy, seeing democracy as an instrument of American foreign policy in an increasingly globalizing world. Tensions persisted in Asia, however. China's build-up in its military forces worried its neighbours. Environmental problems resulting from expanding populations and economies also added tension to the larger Asian environment. Meanwhile, the United States abandoned its military and

---

[50] Quoted in LaFeber, *The American Age*, 605.

air bases in the Philippines because of domestic cuts in military spending and strong local protests against the American presence there. Guam became the new defence perimeter for American interests in Asia. Barack Obama's focus on the Pacific region led to the decision to expand the military presence on Guam, making the western Pacific a militarized border for the United States and a fortified platform in the war against terror. There was a similar military expansion in the Philippines. Ten years after the 1991 closing of its two major bases, the United States military reopened both Subic Naval Station and Clark Air Force Base.

Environmental concerns in the Pacific took on increasing prominence by the end of the twentieth century and have only intensified of late.[51] While the industrialized nations of the world debate the reality of climate change, the necessity of developing alternative energy sources, and the level at which to reduce greenhouse gas emissions, islands in the Pacific have begun to disappear under the rising sea levels caused by global warming. Representatives of these island nations have been quite vocal in their criticisms of the United States's refusal to sign the Kyoto Protocol, withdrawal from the Paris Climate Change Agreement (later accepted by the Biden administration in early 2021), and a general ignoring when convenient of the United Nations Convention on Climate Change.[52]

The new century has also witnessed America's return to a preoccupation with China. The Pacific is no longer an American lake, claims Eric Margolis.[53] As evidence, he points to the challenge posed by China's growing naval power in the region. Expanding on Margolis's argument, Robert Underwood sees China's increased economic assistance to the Pacific region, more particularly its island states, as a vehicle for political penetration.[54] Whatever China's intentions and the possibilities for leverage they offer Pacific Islands nations in their negotiations with the United States, there

---

[51] J. Dobbins et al., *Choices for America in a Turbulent World* (Santa Monica, CA: Rand Corporation, 2015), www.jstor.org/stable/10.7249/j.ett17mvhfj.13.
[52] G. Carter, 'Establishing a Pacific voice in climate change negotiations', in G. Fry and S. Tarte (eds.), *The New Pacific Diplomacy* (Canberra: ANU Press, 2015), 205–20. See also J. Barnett and J. Campbell, *Climate Change and Small Island States: Power, Knowledge, and the South Pacific* (Washington, DC: Earthscan, 2010).
[53] E. Margolis, 'The North Pacific is no longer an American lake', *The Blog, Huffpost*, 11 January 2011, www.huffingtonpost.com/eric-margolis/the-north-pacific-is-no-l_b_806885.html., accessed 23 May 2018.
[54] See also R. Underwood, 'The changing American lake in the middle of the Pacific', a talk at the Center for Australian, New Zealand, and Pacific Studies, School of Foreign Service, Georgetown University, Washington, DC, 16 November 2017, www.uog.edu/_resources/files/news-and-announcements/robert-underwood_changing_american_lake., accessed 13 March 2018.

remains the question of America's perceptions of China's increased activity in the region.[55] The concept of strategic denial continues to shape United States policy in the Pacific, and is complemented by humanitarian initiatives, educational exchanges, and other soft-power projects such as the Peace Corps that promote a world order dependent on American power and influenced by American values.

In the Trump era, the advocacy of democracy and human rights was put aside, as were multilateral approaches to trade issues. The TransPacific Trade Pact (TTP), thought by some to be an antidote to growing Chinese economic activity in the region, was abandoned in favour of bilateral deals.[56] This flexing of national muscle is in stark contrast to the Asia rebalance and Pacific pivot of the Obama administration and is especially problematic for US allies such as Australia.[57] The Australia, New Zealand and United States Treaty Alliance (ANZUS) has been an essential element of Australian defence policy since 1951. China, however, is Australia's biggest trading partner while the United States is the country's biggest investor. The challenge for Australia, then, as for much of the region, will be adjusting to the often unpredictable, confusing, and even conflicting policy pronouncements coming out of Washington, DC. In addition, the rise of a more public and pronounced white nationalism during the Trump administration has reverberated across the globe, including the Pacific. Though focused on the Mexican border, Trump's war against immigrants has had unsettling and even intimidating effects on the movement of Filipinos and other groups of people from the greater Asia-Pacific region into the United States and its Pacific territories.

'The Anarchy of Empire'

Understanding America's rise to empire in the Pacific is about much more than a chronology of events. The phrase 'the anarchy of empire' is from a poem by W.E.B. DuBois entitled 'A Hymn to the People' that addresses the sufferings of those under colonial domination. It is also part of the title of Amy Kaplan's *The Anarchy of Empire in the Making of U.S. Culture*. For Kaplan,

---

[55] On the question of what China's increased presence in the Pacific might mean for Pacific Islands states, see T. Wesley-Smith and E.A. Porter (eds.), *China in Oceania: Reshaping the Pacific?* (New York: Berghahn Books, 2010).

[56] J. McBride, 'The trans-Pacific partnership and U.S. trade policy', *Backgrounder*, Council on Foreign Relations, 31 January 2017, www.cfr.org/backgrounder/state-us-trade-policy, accessed 3 April 2018.

[57] C. Mills, 'The United States' Asia-Pacific policy and the rise of the dragon', Indo-Pacific Strategic Papers, Centre for Defence and Strategic Studies, Australian Defence College, August 2015, www.defence.gov.au/ADC/Publications/IndoPac/R23177605-1.pdf. Accessed 3 April 2018.

the domestic and the foreign are inextricably linked.[58] Drawing on the work of Frederick Cooper and Ann Stoler, she challenges the traditional understanding of imperialism as a one-way imposition of power on distant colonies and calls attention instead to the role of imperial relations in the formation of a national culture.[59] She is concerned with how international struggles for domination abroad profoundly shape representations of American national identity at home and how, in turn, cultural attributes thought of as domestic or particularly national are forged from the engagements with others. Mark Twain's writings on Hawai'i, for example, evidence a strong tension between his benign preconceptions about colonialism and race in a plantation society derived from his boyhood experiences in Missouri, and the political and social displacement he witnessed while in the islands. This tension led him in later life to be an ardent if conflicted critic of American imperialism.

Similarly, Paul Lyons's *American Pacificism* examines the ways in which two fundamental conceptions regarding the Pacific are entwined in the American literary imagination. First, there are the islands envisioned as economic and geopolitical stepping-stones to larger places; secondly, they are imagined as pristine, available places unencumbered by notions of sin, and the antithesis to the economic and political modernity of the industrial world.[60] Empire in the Pacific was thus imagined before it actually occurred. Textual productions are linked to imperial enterprise in a given historical period. At different times, the islands have been described as places for scientific self-discovery, soul-saving and civilizing missions, Western masculine adventure, and eroticized furlough from the work of empire building. From the confluence of commerce, mission, discovery, and travel emerges a literary form Lyons terms 'histourism'. This histourism shows itself in the work of canonical American writers from Herman Melville to James Michener and in more ethnographic work such as that of Margaret Mead.[61]

Empire can also be seen in American popular culture's representation of current and former colonies in the Pacific. As Camilla Fojas has noted, the major storylines and narratives of empire in popular films both reflect and help determine the fantasies, desires, and emotions of their audiences.[62]

---

[58] A. Kaplan, *The Anarchy of Empire in the Making of U.S. Culture* (Cambridge, MA: Harvard University Press, 2002), 12.

[59] Kaplan, *The Anarchy of Empire*, 14.

[60] P. Lyons, *American Pacificism: Oceania in the U.S. Imagination* (New York: Routledge, 2006), 24.

[61] Lyons, *American Pacificism*, 21.

[62] C. Fojas, *Islands of Empire: Pop Culture and U.S. Power* (Austin: University of Texas Press, 2014), 4. On the related topic of early American cinematic representations of Polynesia, see

The cinematic representations of Guam, Hawai'i, the Philippines, and other Pacific places often reflect a particular moment in time that explains and justifies their place and purpose in the American empire. In these films, different islands or island groups come across as at once unique, homogenous, and interchangeable. In effect, they normalize and make acceptable the projection of American power abroad. Historian Andrew Bacevich believes that romanticized versions of war, promoted through such popular media as film and video games, give the American public an unrealistic view of the nature and effectiveness of military action.[63] Other earlier and current forms of popular culture, including music, newsreels, postcards, tourist brochures, television shows, Broadway musicals, commercials, fashion styles, restaurants, and children's books, also become imperially tinged and complicit. As William Appleman Williams put it, empire becomes a way of life for domestic populations that knowingly or unknowingly benefit from it.[64]

The focus on the dynamics that have driven the rise and spread of the American empire often neglects the histories of local responses to imperial intrusions. DuBois's phrase, 'anarchy of empire', is about not just the violence imposed on colonized peoples but also the subversive threat that their presence within imperial and domestic boundaries poses to empire. In the accounting of empire, there needs to be much more attention to the histories of those upon whom empire was imposed, the forms of historical expression that they employed to record these colonial encounters, and how those histories engage their descendants today. Reflective of these local histories, David Chang's *The World and the Things Upon It* asks us to understand indigenous people as active travellers and explorers rather than the passive objects of Western imagination.[65] Chang traces how Native Hawaiians or Kānaka Maoli in the nineteenth century explored the outside world, generated their own understandings of it, and placed themselves strategically in the global geography they created.

Writing on a later period in Hawaiian history, Adria Imada links American imperialism and Hawaiian culture through the practice of hula, and within

---

J. Geiger, *Facing the Pacific: Polynesia and the U.S. Imperial Imagination* (Honolulu: University of Hawai'i Press, 2007).

[63] A. Bacevich, *The New American Militarism: How Americans Are Seduced by War* (New York: Oxford University Press, 2005).

[64] W.A. Williams, *Empire as a Way of Life: An Essay on the Causes and Character of America's Present Predicament, along with a Few Thoughts about an Alternative* (Oxford: Oxford University Press, 1980).

[65] D.A. Chang, *The World and All the Things upon It: Native Hawaiian Geographies of Exploration* (Minneapolis: University of Minnesota Press, 2016), xiv.

the larger political and economic contests that led to the annexation and incorporation of Hawai'i. As elsewhere in the Pacific Islands, the colonial imagination subjected Hawai'i to gendered and sexualized forms of conquest. Representations of Hawaiian women as simple, sexual, and available reinforced the logic and necessity of imperial rule.[66] Redefined and commodified by the forces of empire, hula became cover for the colonization of the Hawaiian islands. Hawaiian women, however, had their own voices and motivations, and did not always transmit the messages intended.[67] Their performances could be disruptive, even counter-colonial. Dancing in a variety of venues on the North American continent in the first half of the twentieth century, these women unsettled preconceptions of Hawaiians as pre-modern. Their dances evoked an earlier Hawaiian past not gone or forgotten despite the colonization of the islands.

The histories of the people of the greater Pacific region are closely intertwined. That connection is denied, however, by the contemporary discourses of national security that blanket independence and self-government movements, and that dissociate military bases on foreign soil from the colonial histories that enable them. Important to recognize too are the gendered and sexualized nature of empires and its effects on indigenous and local populations. In recent decades, the American empire in the Pacific has taken on a more militarized character. As Keith Camacho and Setsu Shigemitsu note in the introduction to their edited volume, *Militarized Currents: Toward a Decolonized Future in Asia and the Pacific*, the American empire is both expansive and pervasive, dynamic and changing, and not limited to continental spaces. It is also more androgynous, more fluid and permeable, in its effects on civilian populations. A critique of militarism and the history that precedes it brings into question the meanings of liberation, and how the discourses of gender and race have been altered, transformed, and more generally affected.[68]

Empire buries and paves over that which it seeks to eliminate, as Jon Osorio (author of Chapter 40 in this volume) reminds us in his account of how the United States reinscribed a sacred Hawaiian site, Pu'uola, as national cemetery to honour its war dead.[69] An essay by the late Teresia Teaiwa

---

[66] A.L. Imada, *Aloha America: Hula Circuits through U.S. Empire* (Durham, NC: Duke University Press, 2012), 11.
[67] Imada, *Aloha America*, 17.
[68] S. Shigematsu and K.L. Camacho, *Militarized Currents: Toward a Decolonized Future in Asia and the Pacific* (Minneapolis: University of Minnesota Press, 2010), xxvi.
[69] J.K.K. Osorio, 'Memorializing Pu'uola and remembering Pearl Harbor', in Shigematsu and Camacho (eds.), *Militarized Currents*, 3–14.

The USA and the Pacific since 1800

analyses how the nuclear testing in the Marshalls was normalized by a Western, heteronormative discourse of femininity that hides the horrors of that testing behind the Bikini bathing suit.[70] Tourism, militarism, and colonialism intertwine in local Pacific economies such as those in Hawai'i, Guam, and the Philippines. As noted earlier, a critical examination of the American empire in the Pacific also necessitates an awareness of the sexualized economies produced and regulated by military practices, and the sexual exploitation of specific classes and groups of people in the region, including Okinawa and the Philippines.[71] Militarization can also affect desire and helps explain the recruitment of Chamorros, Hawaiians, Micronesians, and Samoans to the United States armed forces. Involved here is a complex process that is as much about local obligations, responsibilities, and cultural values, as it is about masculinity and the remaking of those recruits into American soldiers.[72]

As is painfully clear, racism has accompanied the expansion of empire in the Pacific; its roots run deep in American history. Gary Okahiro observes that the earliest definitions of American citizenship were understood in terms of race. When the framers of the constitution wrote of Americans as 'one people with common ancestors, language, religion, and culture', they meant whites and free people. In the words of US Supreme Court Justice Roger Taney, non-whites were 'another and different class of people'.[73] Native people occupying lands on the North American continent were regarded as savages and impediments to the westward expansion of the American nation-state. Moving beyond the continental frontier, the United States, in the words of Richard Drinnon, exported its metaphysics of Indian-hating and empire-building to the Pacific.[74]

Empire was also rife with contradictions and inconsistencies. In *Pacific Connections*, Kornel Chang focuses on the US–Canadian borderlands.[75] These borderlands were part of the expansion of empire in the Pacific; their

---

[70] T.K. Teaiwa, 'Bikinis and other s/pacific n/oceans', *Contemporary Pacific* 6:1 (1994): 87–109; repr. in Shigematsu and Camacho (eds.), *Militarized Currents*, 15–31.

[71] See especially the chapters by K.H. Moon, 'South Korean movements against militarized sexual labor', 125–45, and N. Sakai, 'On romantic love and military violence: transpacific imperialism and U.S.–Japan Complicity', 205–21, in Shigematsu and Camacho (eds.), *Militarized Currents*. Also Enloe, *Bananas, Beaches, and Bases*; and Gonzalez, *Securing Paradise*.

[72] K.L. Camacho and L.A. Monnig, 'Uncomfortable fatigues: Chamorro soldiers, gendered identities, and the question of decolonization in Guam', in Shigematsu and Camacho (eds.), *Militarized Currents*, 147–79.

[73] Quoted in Okihiro, *American History Unbound*, 3.   [74] Drinnon, *Facing West*.

[75] K.S. Chang, *Pacific Connections: The Making of the Western US–Canadian Borderlands* (Berkeley: University of California Press, 2012).

histories reflect the complex and entangled interplay of local and global histories. The migration of peoples and capital gave rise to a fluid world of shifting boundaries, even as the USA, Canada, and Great Britain sought to police and restrict such movement. The global intrusion of capitalism and its need for labour required the manipulation of racial prejudices; decisions on the inclusion or exclusion of colonized or affected people often shifted to respond to the expansionist needs of global capitalism. At the same time, these immigrant labourers – Chinese, Japanese, and South Asians – employed their own strategies of manipulation, adaptation, acquiescence, and resistance in this diverse and conflicted world whose inhabitants came from multiple locations in the Pacific. The reality of empire was far more complex, entangled, and messier than its advocates ever envisioned.

There have also been more overt forms of resistance to the intrusion of empire in the Pacific. Violent, widespread revolt marked the first years of the American occupation of the Philippines. Hawaiians reacted with petitions, protests, and rebellion to the 1893 overthrow of their monarchy. In 1937, members of the Guam Congress led a drive for American citizenship that began a critical examination of naval rule there. Beginning in 1975, different groups of people from within the Trust Territory of the Pacific Islands engaged in intense negotiations over the right of self-government. Protests against nuclear testing in the Pacific have come from within the Marshall Islands and more regionally through the drafting and advocacy of the South Pacific Nuclear Free Zone Treaty, or the Treaty of Rarotonga as it is more officially known. Pacific Island nations have engaged in vigorous, often heated negotiations with the United States over fishing rights and revenues, maritime borders and economic resource zones, and the Law of the Sea. Pacific Island nations have proven particularly vigorous and prominent in their advocacy of international agreements to combat global warming and climate change. Sovereignty movements have emerged in Hawai'i and on Guam while indigenous scholars throughout the region are challenging the conventional scholarship on the history of empire.[76] The rise of Chamorro, Filipino, Hawaiian, Micronesian, and Samoan communities on the American

---

[76] On the issue of Hawaiian sovereignty, there is N. Goodyear-Ka'ōpua, I. Hussey, and E. Kahunawaika'ala (eds.), *A Nation Rising: Hawaiian Movements for Life, Land, and Sovereignty* (Durham, NC: Duke University Press, 2014). For recent histories of Guam by Indigenous and local scholars, see K.L. Camacho, *Cultures of Commemoration: The Politics of War Memory, and History in the Mariana Islands*, Pacific Islands Monograph Series 25 (Honolulu: University of Hawai'i Press, 2011); V.M. Diaz, *Repositioning the Missionary: Rewriting the Histories of Colonialism, Native Catholicism, and Indigeneity in Guam*, Pacific Islands Monograph Series 24 (Honolulu: University of Hawai'i Press, 2010); A.P. Hattori, *Colonial Dis-ease: US Navy Health*

The USA and the Pacific since 1800

continent as well as the continuing presence of communities created by earlier Asian migrants demonstrate how fluid imperial boundaries have become and how deeply the homeland is being affected by the consequences of imperial reach.

The historian Paul Kennedy offers a sobering analysis of nations obsessed with national security and committed to military build-up as a way to insure that security: 'Great powers in relative decline instinctively respond by spending more on security, thereby diverting potential resources from investment and compounding this long-term dilemma.'[77] We may be witnessing the disappearance of the nation-state as a form of government and the redefinition of empire. Walter LaFeber writes of a revolution in technology, communication, and commerce, led by global corporations, that over-rides national boundaries and renders irrelevant current forms of government.[78] The future of the United States in the Pacific may well be about transformation by the counter forces and discourses it has unleashed abroad and at home, and within the borders of its fading empire.[79]

Policies and the Chamorros of Guam, 1898–1941, Pacific Islands Monograph Series 19 (Honolulu: University of Hawai'i Press, 2004). For a critique of American environmental policy, see A.T.P. Somerville, 'The great Pacific garbage patch as metaphor: the (American) Pacific you can't see', in B.R. Roberts and M.A. Stephens (eds.), *Archipelagic American Studies* (Durham, NC: Duke University Press, 2017), 320–340.

[77] Quoted in LaFeber, *The American Age*, 675.

[78] W. LaFeber, *Michael Jordan and the New Global Capitalism*, rev. edn (New York: W.W. Norton, 2002).

[79] L. Kurashige (ed.), *Pacific America: Histories of Transoceanic Crossings* (Honolulu: University of Hawai'i Press, 2017); also Roberts and Stephens (eds.), *Archipelagic American Studies*.

55

World War II and the Pacific

JUDITH A. BENNETT AND LIN POYER

The Pacific War of 1942–5 was no 'Fatal Impact' on Pacific peoples and cultures but, like first contact with foreigners from the eighteenth century, it was fatal to many individual Indigenous people and, unsurprisingly, to thousands of the belligerents.[1] The war's effects differed greatly, depending on whether islands became sites of combat or of rear-line support. Almost all of Polynesia remained behind the front lines, where islands hosting military installations experienced a few giddy years of unparalleled prosperity, a marked contrast to the battlegrounds of much of Micronesia and western Melanesia, where people suffered deprivation, fear, and loss. Lasting impacts of the war have been varied, subtle, and less susceptible to quantification.

Outline of the War's Strategy and Chronology

The spheres of influence of Japan, Great Britain, France, the Netherlands, Australia, New Zealand, and the United States set the parameters within which war in the Pacific Islands was fought and experienced. On 7/8 December 1941, Japan launched attacks (some originating in Micronesian bases) against US holdings in Hawai'i, Wake Island, Guam, and the Philippines, and against British, Dutch, Portuguese, and Australian territory. Allied response was slowed by demands of war in Europe and by the speed and efficacy of Japan's advance in the first months of 1942. At its greatest reach, Japanese occupation extended from islands in the Aleutian chain to the north coast of New Guinea.

War was experienced very differently in different command areas. In what Allies called the Central Pacific theatre, Japan governed the peoples of

---

[1] A. Moorehead, *The Fatal Impact: An Account of the the Invasion of the South Pacific, 1767–1840* (London: Hamish Hamilton, 1966).

588

Micronesia – from the Northern Marianas, Palau, and Yap in the west, through the Caroline Islands, to the atolls of the Marshall Islands in the east – as a League of Nations Mandate. (Guam, however, had been a US territory since 1898.) By the mid to late 1930s, international tensions shifted Japan's focus from economic development of the islands to fortifying them as an outer line of defence for the empire. The Imperial Japanese Navy base at Chuuk was strengthened; Marshall Islanders' land was confiscated and communities were relocated to make way for airbases; Saipan's and Tinian's military infrastructure was developed. Most Islanders began the war confident in Japanese military superiority and willing to support the war effort.[2]

In the southwest Pacific theatre, war had a different chronology. As Japan began fortifying Micronesia, European and American territories in the central and southwest Pacific saw little military preparation. Great Britain and its Pacific allies were focused on the European conflict, with Australian and New Zealand forces serving in European, Mediterranean, and North African theatres. French Pacific Islands were initially caught in internal Vichy–Free French contests, but the Free prevailed.[3] Believing Japanese invasion of the Philippines likely, the USA in October 1941 began to construct a new 'ferry route' of airfields across the Pacific for its B-17 bombers, but maintained formal neutrality, until it entered the war after Japanese planes bombed Pearl Harbor.[4] The Allies' decision to prioritize war in Europe, and to put overall direction of the Pacific in American hands, shaped strategy in this region.

At the start of 1942, Japan quickly occupied New Britain, New Ireland, Bougainville, parts of the Solomon Islands, and northern New Guinea, and bombed Darwin in Australia, meeting little opposition. The delayed Allied response gained momentum as the USA poured troops and material into bases bridging the ocean, from Bora Bora to the New Hebrides and New Zealand. Despite British pleas, Australia in May recalled most of its infantry from the Middle East. The Japanese advance was stymied after the naval battles of the Coral Sea and Midway, and in mid-1942 the Allied

---

[2] F.X. Hezel, *Strangers in Their Own Land: A Century of Colonial Rule in the Caroline and Marshall Islands* (Honolulu: University of Hawai'i Press, 1995); M. Peattie, *Nan'yō: The Rise and Fall of the Japanese in Micronesia, 1885–1945* (Honolulu: University of Hawai'i Press, 1988); L. Poyer, S. Falgout, and L.M. Carucci, *The Typhoon of War: Micronesian Experiences in the Pacific War* (Honolulu: University of Hawai'i Press, 2001), 1–72.

[3] J.-M. Regnault and I. Kurtovitch, 'Les ralliements du Pacifique en 1940. Entre légende gaulliste, enjeux stratégiques mondiaux et rivalités Londres/Vichy', *Revue d'Histoire Moderne & Contemporaine* 49:4 (2002), 71–90.

[4] D.T. Fitzgerald, 'Air Ferry Routes across the South Pacific', in B.W. Fowle (ed.), *Builders and Fighters: US Army Corps of Engineers* (Fort Belvoir: Office of History, US Army Corps of Engineers, 1992), 47–64.

counteroffensive was underway with the Australians repulsing the Japanese at Milne Bay and US forces invading Guadalcanal in August. Allied forces continued to push back and neutralize Japanese power in the southwest Pacific through to the end of the war. The Allies' Central Pacific campaign began with attacks on the Japanese-occupied Gilbert Islands in November 1943, then to the Marshall Islands at the start of 1944. Islanders' lives in Japanese Micronesia changed dramatically in 1943 with the imposition of military rule, increasing labour demands, and strict controls on movement and food production. Through mid-1944 and 1945, the USA gained control of western Micronesia (Guam, Saipan, Tinian, Peleliu), proceeding towards Japan. American forces played the major role in attacking Japanese Micronesia. Australian troops were the major force in Papua and New Guinea, with US bases along the coast of other Melanesian islands.

The Southwest Pacific War Zone

Japan's rapid advance at the start of 1942 had met little resistance in Papua and New Guinea. European settlers and colonial officials fled ahead of the Japanese, leaving local people to face the new occupation force. The abandonment made a lasting impression, cemented when incoming Japanese emphasized their own power by humiliating or executing POWs and other remaining whites. Japanese authorities appointed new village leaders and organized labour and food supplies for their military. Commanders at first insisted on troop discipline, paying for goods and labour, implemented pro-Japanese schooling and propaganda, and dismantled colonial and Christian authority. In many places, the policy was initially successful, building good relations with villagers. But by September 1942 the Japanese were in retreat. In all, more than 300,000 Japanese troops served in New Guinea, where more than half eventually died of sickness and starvation, as did many of the tens of thousands of conscripted labourers and POWs (Chinese, Malayan, Indian, Indonesian, Taiwanese, and others) sent to support the Japanese advance.[5]

---

[5] K.S. Inglis, 'War, race, and loyalty in New Guinea, 1939–1945', in *The History of Melanesia: Papers Delivered at a Seminar Sponsored by the University of Papua and New Guinea [et al.] and Held at Port Moresby* (Port Moresby: University of Papua and New Guinea, 1969), 503–29; H. Nelson, '"Taim Bilong Fait": the impact of the Second World War on Papua New Guinea', in A.W. McCoy (ed.), *Southeast Asia under Japanese Occupation*, Monograph Series 22 (New Haven: Yale University Press, 1980), 246–66; N.K. Robinson, *Villagers at War: Some Papua New Guinea Experiences in World War II* (Canberra: ANU Press, 1981).

Figure 55.1 World War II, the Pacific War 1937–42. [Artist: Les O'Neill]

In Allied-held areas of Papua and New Guinea, Australian military rule replaced colonial civil administration. Papua (an Australian territory) and New Guinea (an Australian League of Nations Mandate) were amalgamated into Papua and New Guinea in 1942. (Western New Guinea, formerly a Dutch colonial possession, was under Japanese occupation from late March 1942.) ANGAU (Australia New Guinea Administrative Unit) was established in March 1942, an uneasy military–civilian mix that managed labour, refugees, economic activity such as plantations, and police and medical matters.[6] Allied forces in the Melanesian region numbered at least a million Americans, nearly half a million Australians, and smaller numbers from New Zealand, Fiji, Tonga, and other Pacific Islands, supported by tens of thousands of civilian Indigenous labourers. As the Allied counteroffensive got underway, people living between the lines found themselves in perilous positions. Here and in Micronesia, those living near invasion sites or military bases suffered most intensely from bombing and ground combat, forced labour, and destruction and confiscation of property and gardens. On the high islands, including the Solomon Islands, many could flee into the hinterland, but faced famine and illness. War made some people into refugees for years, as in New Guinea, where Japanese and then Allied operations caused numerous village relocations, with thousands of people moving from combat zones or base construction areas.[7]

As war in the southwest Pacific went on, the Allied supply situation constantly improved, but the situation for Japanese troops steadily worsened. As Japan's military situation deteriorated, so did relations with villagers, with confiscations, forced labour, and reprisals against any sign of aiding the enemy. American and Australian shipments of goods allowed Allies to maintain local support in a way that the Japanese, once their supply lines were cut, could not. Japanese soldiers who had begun by purchasing goods and food eventually seized them from villagers. Allied actions also disrupted local food supplies, though less drastically. ANGAU's intense recruitment (sometimes conscription) of military labour, based on the colonial plantation system, drew thousands of workers from their homes, decreasing food production. New Guinea, Bougainville, New Britain, New Ireland, and parts of the Solomon Islands saw significant population drops, as the vulnerable

---

[6] A. Powell, *The Third Force: ANGAU's New Guinea War, 1942–46* (South Melbourne: Oxford University Press, 2003).
[7] Powell, *Third Force*, 92–139; A.I.K. Kituai, *My Gun, My Brother: The World of the Papua New Guinea Colonial Police, 1920–1960* (Honolulu: University of Hawai'i Press, 1998), 168–71.

died from malnutrition and disease, and fewer children were born; food supplies were reduced for years after the war.[8]

The Central Pacific

Allied strategy called for a US Navy-led 'second road to Tokyo' through the central and northwestern Pacific, starting with the November 1943 Battle of Tarawa to retake the Gilbert Islands, which Japanese forces had occupied at the start of the Pacific War. Tarawa then became a base for the next Allied invasion targets in the Marshall Islands, Kwajalein, Eniwetok, and Majuro (1 January to 4 February 1944). Nearly 200 Marshallese died at Kwajalein, where some who had been employed by the Japanese military fought alongside them. As in the southwest Pacific, the Allies' Central Pacific strategy was 'island-hopping' – avoiding some Japanese-held areas, invading other islands to set up bases from which to prosecute the war, rebuilding former Japanese bases (e.g. Kwajalein) or establishing new ones (e.g. Ulithi). Planes from US bases on Guam, Saipan, and Tinian facilitated bombing runs on Japan, including the August 1945 atomic bombings of Hiroshima and Nagasaki, launched from Tinian. Islands not invaded – especially those holding Japanese bases, such as Truk/Chuuk Lagoon, Maloelap and Mili Atolls in the Marshalls, and Babelthuap in the Palaus – were heavily bombed and blockaded into starvation, conditions that in some places lasted for the eighteen months until the end of war (Figures 55.2 and 55.3).[9]

By the time of US invasion (or, in the case of bypassed islands, after Japanese surrender), near-starvation and harsh military discipline had alienated Islanders from any previous sense of loyalty to Japan. The American military decided to treat Islanders as neutral civilians rather than as enemies, opening a new era – though a difficult one, as Americans were unfamiliar and many islands were devastated by war. Micronesians especially in the western islands had long and close relationships with the Japanese and Okinawan immigrants who far outnumbered Indigenous people. The post-war decision to repatriate all foreigners – not just POWs, but also thousands of civilian settlers – left some islands eerily empty, as small businesses and skilled workers were gone and intermarried families separated.[10]

Unlike other Micronesians, the people of Guam, the only pre-war US territory in Micronesia, were familiar with Americans and welcomed their

---

[8] Powell, *Third Force*, 191–240.   [9] Poyer et al., *Typhoon of War*, 117–229.
[10] Poyer et al., *Typhoon of War*, 230–314.

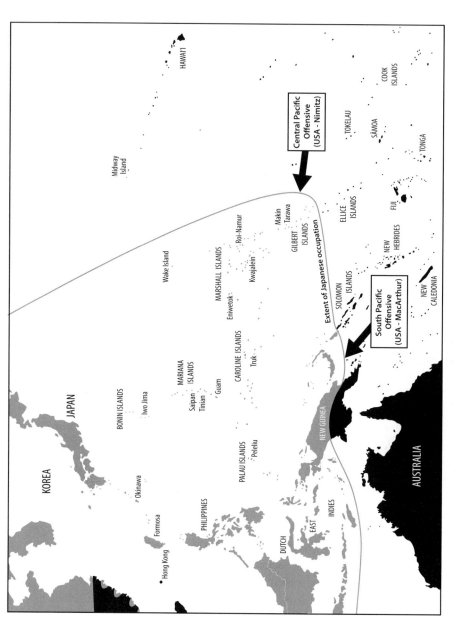

Figure 55.2 Two-pronged offensives by the Allies. [Artist: Les O'Neill]

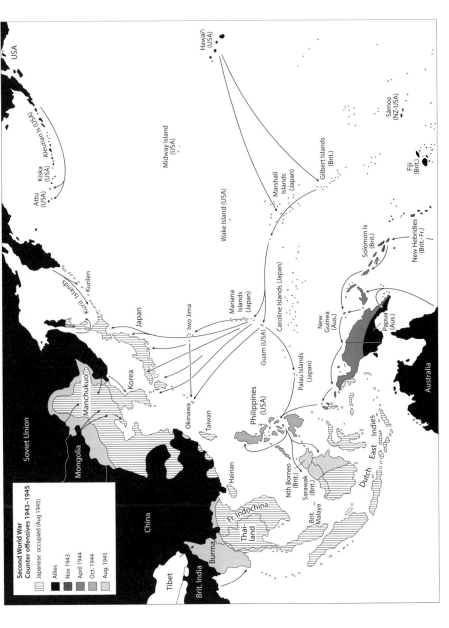

Figure 55.3 World War II counter offensives, 1943–5. [Artist: Les O'Neill]

invasion in July 1944. Guam's Chamorro people had maintained strong passive resistance during the occupation, despite an intensive Japanization programme introduced after occupation in December 1941.[11] Chamorros from Saipan and Rota interpreted and assisted Japanese police and administrators on Guam, creating long-term repercussions for post-war politics.[12] Guam's people were tasked to labour on military defences and agriculture, experiencing increasing abuse as US forces neared, with killings, rapes, and several massacres on the eve of invasion. Chamorro men guided and fought alongside invading US troops. Immediately after Guam was retaken, it became a US stronghold for continuing the war on Japan. Rapid development of airfields, harbours, and other infrastructure signalled a change in Guam's relationship with the USA, as military landholdings, employment, and governance dominated civilian life.

What affected most Micronesians in Japanese-held areas more than direct combat was the militarization of daily life, confiscation of land and goods, relocations, and military labour; and, during the worst of the war, long months of bombing and starvation. The numbers of troops far exceeded what local resources could support, and shelling, bombing, and combat destroyed military stores and local food production. In Palau, for example, some 5,700 Micronesians lived under siege with about 29,700 Japanese Army and Navy personnel and 14,300 foreign civilians (immigrants and conscript labourers). They lived from Japanese stockpiles and local resources, but under constant threat of starvation along with continual bombing.[13] After a large Japanese garrison occupied the British island of Nauru in August 1942, authorities moved 1,200 Nauruans to Chuuk Lagoon in 1943, where they suffered extreme privation; Chuuk was already experiencing food shortages, Nauruans had no access to local gardens, and the Japanese regarded them as enemies.[14] The Japanese military made efforts to evacuate civilians from battle zones, but especially on small islands and atolls, and in the face of massive daily air raids, that was not always feasible. In 1944, with shipping cut

[11] P.C. Sanchez, *Uncle Sam, Please Come Back to Guam* (Agaña: Star Press, 1979); R.F. Rogers, *Destiny's Landfall: A History of Guam*, rev. edn (Honolulu: University of Hawai'i Press, 2011); W. Higuchi, *The Japanese Administration of Guam, 1941–1944: A Study of Occupation and Integration Policies, with Japanese Oral Histories* (Jefferson, NC: McFarland, 2013).
[12] K.L. Camacho, 'The politics of indigenous collaboration: the role of Chamorro interpreters in Japan's Pacific empire, 1914–1945', *Journal of Pacific History* 43 (2008), 207–22.
[13] S.C. Murray, *The Battle over Peleliu: Islander, Japanese and American Memories of War* (Tuscaloosa: University of Alabama Press, 2016), 98–117.
[14] L. Poyer, 'Dimensions of hunger in wartime: Chuuk Lagoon, 1943–1945', *Food and Foodways* 12 (2004), 137–64; P. McQuarrie, *Conflict in Kiribati: A History of the Second World War* (Christchurch: Macmillan Brown Centre, 2000), 41–8, 119–20, 163, 166–7.

off and Allied bombs destroying stores, military authorities on garrison islands confiscated Islanders' food sources and forced men, women, and even children into exhausting labour. As conditions grew desperate, so did military supervision, suspicion, and mistreatment, eroding any previous sense of loyalty to the empire.

The Central and South Pacific: Island Bases Supporting the Front Lines

While places that experienced combat suffered the most direct impacts, war's global infrastructure dominated and sometimes overwhelmed island communities as US industrial strength, manpower, and shipping capacity transformed the region. Hawai'i, placed under martial law after the Pearl Harbor attack, became a massive military base. US bases were built across the region, with large installations in New Zealand, New Caledonia, Fiji, and American Sāmoa, and smaller units in many other islands, combining to ferry men and supplies from Hawai'i or the US mainland to the front lines. These bases served as defensive deterrents, transit points, refuelling and repair ports, hospitals, and rest and recreation sites; by the end of 1942, over 200,000 US troops were in place across the region. Local governments formed their own responses to the invasion threat. For example, Tonga, an independent Kingdom with British protection, acted quickly under Queen Sālote to mobilize home defences and soon hosted a US base. Even in islands away from the front lines – like Aitutaki in the Cook Islands, Funafuti in the Ellice Islands, Ulithi in the western Carolines – the presence of a military base and large numbers of American troops, sometimes for years, had a significant impact on the local economy and social life, introducing new tastes and leaving several thousand part-American children.[15]

Islanders' Experiences with Labour

The aspect of war that affected the largest number of Islanders was military labour. Combatant forces needed local labour to build and maintain bases and infrastructure, to provide food and building supplies, to handle massive amounts of imported materiel, and to carry supplies to troops, guide them

---

[15] Chapters in J.A. Bennett and A. Wanhalla (eds.), *Mothers' Darlings of the South Pacific: The Children of Indigenous Women and U.S. Servicemen, World War II* (Honolulu: University of Hawai'i Press, 2016).

through unfamiliar territory, and gather information on the enemy. During the New Guinea campaigns of 1943–5, the labour demand was all-consuming. At its peak, ANGAU employed more than 45,000 workers. Despite official limits on Allied conscription, in some villages 80 per cent or more of the men were taken.[16] Away from the combat zones, on Allied-controlled islands from the Gilberts to the New Hebrides and the Sāmoas, island people were keen to work for the generous Americans.

In some Japanese-occupied areas, especially in the latter part of the war, work was forced, unpaid, and abusive. At times, Islanders' work for the Allies, too, was coerced and oppressive, but for the most part Allied workers had adequate or even good conditions and pay – sometimes, as in New Caledonia and American Sāmoa, exceeding peacetime standards. The war gave some women a chance of employment, but for many, war's main impact was that the absence of able-bodied men increased their workload at home. Regardless of the attractions and pressures to work for Allied or Japanese militaries, Islanders exercised their own options when they could. Kanaks in New Caledonia protested poor conditions and Solomon Islands Labour Corps men organized strikes in response to combat conditions and low wages; some conscripted labourers ran away or changed sides. In combat areas of western Melanesia, there was little civilian loyalty to the colonial power, but often to individual whites or to the more powerful military of whichever side.[17]

Japanese and Allied armies competed for local labour, recognizing it as key to operations in difficult terrain. Military historians note the crucial role of carriers in Papua and New Guinea in enabling Allied troops to move and fight with adequate supplies, while Japanese movements were limited by scarcity of carriers, especially in later phases of the war when their relationships with local people deteriorated.[18] The arduous work of carrying supplies and ammunition to the front and manoeuvring the wounded out on stretchers was exacerbated by overwork, lack of food, exposure to the elements, and disease. Dozens were killed or wounded by enemy fire; hundreds of others died of disease, accident, or other causes.[19] Carriers who evacuated and cared for wounded

---

[16] J.A. Bennett, *Natives and Exotics: World War II and Environment in the Southern Pacific* (Honolulu: University of Hawai'i Press, 2009), 139–48.

[17] Bennett, *Natives and Exotics*, 148–54.

[18] P. Bradley, *The Battle for Wau: New Guinea's Frontline 1942–1943* (Cambridge: Cambridge University Press, 2008), 7, 240–1.

[19] N. Riseman, *Defending Whose Country? Indigenous Soldiers in the Pacific War* (Lincoln: University of Nebraska Press, 2012).

Australian soldiers on the Kokoda Track campaign became part of the lore of the war in Papua and New Guinea.

In addition to civilian labour, men also served in combat on the Allied side. (The Japanese military less often recruited Islanders as soldiers though Micronesian men served in police and military labour corps, and civilians were used extensively for military and subsistence labour.) The Fiji Defence Force, including Tongan volunteers, and Solomon Islands Defence Force troops served in the Solomon Islands in 1942 and 1943. Papua and New Guinea men volunteered in the Royal Papuan Constabulary, the Papuan Infantry Battalion (PIB), and the New Guinea Infantry Battalion (the latter two combined as the Pacific Islands Regiment). During the Kokoda Track campaign, Papuan and New Guinea men served as both carriers and PIB soldiers. These groups received praise for service as fighters, guides, and spies but also experienced discrimination in conditions and pay.

Allied military records and war journalism record many accounts of enlisted and civilian Islanders serving with notable courage in combat and in intelligence work.[20] Perhaps the best-known military work of Islanders in the southwest Pacific was their participation in coastwatching groups along the coast of New Guinea and in New Georgia, New Britain, and the Solomon Islands. As many as a thousand Islanders trained and operated under European officers, gathering intelligence of Japanese numbers, and ship and plane movements, and performing other tasks such as rescuing downed airmen and capturing Japanese. After the Allied invasion of Guadalcanal in August 1942, they joined US Marines in guerrilla operations.[21]

Combatants' Attitudes to 'Natives' and Vice Versa

The presence of large numbers of foreign troops on small islands had a transformative, if sometimes temporary, effect on Pacific communities. Some Islanders, too, spent the war years fighting or working far from home. Japan recruited small military labour units from Palau and Pohnpei to serve in the southwest Pacific, where many of the enlistees died. The Allies recruited efficient Gilbertese to work the wharves on Guadalcanal, after Samoans

---

[20] For examples, see Colonial Office, Great Britain, [H. Cooper], *Among Those Present: The Official Story of the Pacific Islands at War* (London: HMSO, 1946); Powell, *Third Force*, 206–40; Bennett, *Natives and Exotics*, 134–8. Official military websites of Allied nations hold details of commendations and awards.
[21] A.A. Kwai, *Solomon Islanders in World War II: An Indigenous Perspective* (Canberra: ANU Press, 2017).

refused to travel for the work because it did not pay enough.[22] British and French Pacific territories raised military and labour units for service abroad. The Free French formed a Pacific Battalion to fight in Africa and Europe; by the end of 1943 it totalled 1,200 Europeans, nearly 1,600 Melanesians, and 300 Tahitians.[23] New Zealanders fought with British forces from the Battle of Britain through the Middle East, the Mediterranean, Southeast Asia, North Africa, and the Solomon Islands. The best-known Pacific Islander military unit was the 28th (Māori) Battalion, formed October 1939 at the request of Māori leaders. The Māori Battalion remained all-volunteer throughout the war and was never short of recruits, some coming from other Pacific Islands.[24] Fighting in Europe and North Africa, the unit completed the war as New Zealand's most-decorated battalion, including the first Māori Victoria Cross awarded posthumously to 2nd Lt. Moana-Nui-a-Kiwa Ngarimu for bravery against German forces in Tunisia.[25] Such heroism was not his alone. Fijian Sefanaia Sukanaivalu also won a posthumous VC fighting with the Fijian Infantry on Bougainville.[26]

Islanders serving in the military gained new skills, a wider experience of the world, local pride, and increased self-confidence. Ravuvu comments that the service of more than 8,500 Fijian men in the Fiji Force helped Fiji emerge from colonial subordination.[27]

The arrival in the islands of hundreds of thousands of foreign troops offered even more opportunities for new perspectives on economic, political, and racial realities. Indigenous views of colonial rulers changed as Japanese invaders humiliated previously powerful whites, or US soldiers took Japanese prisoners in Micronesia. The inverse point was made where foreign troops were stationed. Wartime employment and interactions with Australian and white and black American servicemen shook up pre-war patterns of labour and race relations. Soldiers and sailors were more casual and friendly,

[22] Bennett, *Natives and Exotics*, 146–8.
[23] K. Munholland, *Rock of Contention: Free French and Americans at War in New Caledonia* (New York: Berghahn Books, 2005), 61–83.
[24] L.M.T. Mataia, '"Odd men from the Pacific": the participation of Pacific Island men in the 28 (Maori) Battalion in the Second World War', MA thesis, University of Otago, 2007.
[25] I. McGibbon, *New Zealand and the Second World War: The People, the Battles and the Legacy* (Auckland: Hodder Moa Beckett, 2004), 153–4; W. Gardiner, *Te Mura O Te Ahi: The Story of the Maori Battalion* (Auckland: Reed, 1992); J.F. Cody, *28 (Maori) Battalion, Official History of New Zealand in the Second World War*, vol. xvi (Wellington: War History Branch, Department of Internal Affairs, 1956).
[26] Bennett, *Natives and Exotics*, 137.
[27] A. Ravuvu, *Fijians at War, 1939–1945* (Suva: Institute of Pacific Studies, University of the South Pacific, 1974), 13.

World War II and the Pacific

uninterested in shoring up white prestige (despite some efforts by the military and ANGAU to maintain it). The segregated US military had its own racism, but still, meeting black Americans as wealthy and skilled as whites offered Islanders a view of a future in which skin colour did not determine the limits of occupation, wages, or status. Colonial authorities worried that the friendly and generous Americans would cause discontent and pressure for political change after the war, all the more so when some groups in the British Solomon Islands and the Gilberts expressed a desire to have the USA as the government. The Japanese, too, disturbed the pre-war racial order. Initial Japanese military successes, the flight of colonial authorities in the face of invasion, and efforts to build good relations with local people and promote anti-colonial ideas began to dissolve ideas of white superiority. In Micronesia, though, Japanese racial hierarchies were well established, with Islanders ranked below both Japanese, and Okinawan and Korean immigrants; here, it was post-war familiarity with American rulers that introduced new experiences and views.[28]

Studies of sexual activity during the Pacific War deal mostly with the conscription of 'comfort women' by the Japanese military. Information about Pacific Islander women's experiences is scarcer, a lack significantly addressed by Bennett and Wanhalla, who point out the difficulties of such research.[29] In at least Guam and New Guinea, local women were drawn into Japanese military sex work.[30] Allied militaries handled sexual relations by controlling soldiers' movements and in some places the establishment or monitoring of brothels.[31] Wherever troops were stationed, interactions included voluntary relationships, both transactional and romantic. Local attitudes towards these varied, as did military regulations and soldiers' cultural ideas – for example in the way white and African American US troops' attitudes towards island women were shaped by Hollywood stereotypes of Polynesia as 'paradise'.[32]

---

[28] Bennett, *Natives and Exotics*, 28–30

[29] J. Bennett and A. Wanhalla, 'Introduction: a new net goes fishing', in Bennett and Wanhalla (eds.), *Mothers' Darlings*, 1–30.

[30] On Guam, K.L. Camacho, *Cultures of Commemoration: The Politics of War, Memory, and History in the Mariana Islands* (Honolulu: University of Hawai'i Press, 2011), 44; in New Guinea, Sekiguchi Yuka (Noriko), *Senso Daughters* (Canberra: Ronin Films; 55 min. film, 1990; English version, 1991).

[31] E.g. in New Caledonia, Munholland, *Rock of Contention*, 142–72; in Hawai'i, B. Bailey and D. Farber, *The First Strange Place: The Alchemy of Race and Sex in World War II Hawaii* (New York: The Free Press, 1992).

[32] R.T. Stella, *Imagining the Other: The Representation of the Papua New Guinea Subject* (Honolulu: University of Hawai'i Press, 2007); S. Brawley and C. Dixon, *Hollywood's South Seas and the Pacific War: Searching for Dorothy Lamour* (New York: Palgrave Macmillan, 2012).

601

Chapters in Bennett and Wanhalla's *Mothers' Darlings* describe not only the wartime circumstances of these relationships, but also the impact on the generation of children born to such unions.

Conditions at End of War

The impacts of war's social changes and physical destruction were distributed unequally. On islands not in the line of fire, much of the impact was temporary. US bases across the Pacific closed, often so abruptly as to be disruptive. On French colonial Bora Bora, the June 1946 shuttering of the base of 4,000 US servicemen (on an island of 1,300 Polynesians) meant loss of food, medical care, PX supplies, and money, causing a spike in infant deaths.[33] The physical imprint of military sites was more permanent, with some serving as the foundation for post-war infrastructure. A wartime airstrip became Sāmoa international airport, and US marines built Opolu's first cross-island road and upgraded Tutuila's infrastructure.[34] On Tonga, American occupation left behind new crops and agricultural techniques, roads, water systems, piers, and what is now Fua'amotu International Airport.[35]

Much of the Pacific War was fought on small islands with limited subsistence resources. Bennett's *Natives and Exotics* inventories the damage in devastating detail. Repeated bombing, base construction, and ground combat destroyed tree crops, gardens, taro pits, and fishing areas, the bases of island subsistence. Harbour, airfield, and road construction meant dredging, borrow pits, and blasting out live coral from reefs and lagoons to surface runways. Such work meant the permanent loss of land, especially atoll taro pits – losses seldom compensated for in operational zones. The military's need for timber decimated some coastal forests, not only for logs but for thatch for building, bamboo, and bark for camouflage netting. Furthermore, roadbuilding, wartime inventories, the use of and compensation for natural resources, and wage labour all accelerated monetization of local economies. Other long-lasting problems have been the spread of intrusive or harmful plants, animals, and diseases into new areas.[36]

---

[33] J. Bennett, 'Bora Bora: "Like a dream"', in Bennett and Wanhalla (eds.), *Mothers' Darlings*, 31–41.

[34] S.L.M.T. Mataia-Milo, '"There are no commoners in Samoa"', in Bennett and Wanhalla (eds.), *Mothers' Darlings*, 42–82.

[35] C.J. Weeks, 'The United States occupation of Tonga, 1942–1945: the social and economic impact', *Pacific Historical Review* 56 (1987), 399–426.

[36] Bennett, *Natives and Exotics*, 99, 198–240.

Combat left battle zones devastated. Major battlefields in Micronesia never recovered. Saipan's Japanese-built urban centre of Garapan was levelled, and much of the countryside destroyed. Unlike Saipan, Peleliu's civilians were evacuated before the US invasion, but the damage to their home island was severe and irrecoverable, after construction of Japanese defences, more than two months of intense yard-by-yard combat, then US construction of a military base along the invasion beaches. Residents returned to a barren landscape made dangerous by unexploded ordnance, with nothing left of the five villages, the community houses, piers, boathouses, and cemeteries they had known, and no way even to determine landownership boundaries.[37]

The end of war brought material gains and losses, as demobilizing armies quickly sold, gave away, or simply dumped machinery and stores in the ocean. Some communities gained valuable medical or industrial equipment, and individuals gathered what they could as gifts from departing soldiers or scavenging. Clearing scrap from the islands went on for decades, even serving as an export commodity. While some infrastructure such as roads, bridges, or wharves remained, money to maintain them was seldom forth-coming. Today, war debris on land and under sea remains as a source of tourist value, but also as potential environmental dangers.

Munitions were not so easily 'mopped up', especially unexploded bombs or ordnance simply left in place or dumped at sea, with little provision for civilian safety. Bomb disposal units have visited the islands repeatedly in the decades since, but damage and deaths from leftover munitions continue, despite pleas by island leaders for the former combatant powers to complete a clean-up.[38] As late as 2009, President Toribiong of Palau requested help from the United Nations, and Canada, Germany, Australia, and New Zealand provided over US$ 2 million for clearing dangerous World War II ordnance on Peleliu carried out by the Cleared Ground Demining NGO.[39]

Recolonization and Decolonization – the Beginnings

Historians often point to World War II as the transition from the era of empires and colonialism to the modern world of independent nation-states.

---

[37] N. Price et al., 'After the typhoon: multicultural archaeologies of World War II on Peleliu, Palau, Micronesia', *Journal of Conflict Archaeology* 8 (2013), 193–248; Murray, *Battle over Peleliu*.
[38] Bennett, *Natives and Exotics*, 198–210
[39] D.R. Shuster, 'Political reviews: Republic of Palau', *Contemporary Pacific* 15 (2013), 142–9.

British, Australian, French, Dutch, and American claims to protect their subjects failed the crucial test in the face of Japanese invasion. The evacuation of Europeans from New Guinea and the Solomon Islands looked like abandonment to local residents, and Japanese victory dissolved the myth of white superiority. After the war, colonies moved in different directions. Most British Pacific Islands moved towards independence. French holdings became more fully integrated into the metropole and gained some degree of self-governance. The former Japanese mandate of Micronesia first came under US military governance, then over the post-war decades developed different levels of autonomy and affiliation with the USA.

Islanders' own wartime efforts also pushed change. In New Zealand, the Māori Battalion and homefront coordination of war support by the Māori War Effort Organization – both notably successful – demonstrated Māori leadership and the efficacy of traditional political organization. Policy discussions produced the Māori Social and Economic Development Act of 1945, the outcome of a contest between Māori leaders seeking to maintain and extend the autonomy they had gained during wartime, and Native Department officials' efforts to constrain such autonomy along pre-war lines.[40] On New Caledonia, the good wages, new experiences, and new ideas Kanaks gained from working for the US military forced colonial authorities to alter restrictive policies. Kanaks received French citizenship in 1946.[41] While the end of war pulled the rug of material supply out from under the islands, the area's human capital had been permanently enriched. In Papua and New Guinea, thousands of war workers had learned skilled trades and served in army, police, or medical units. Their increased skills and self-confidence precluded any return to pre-war race relations, yet their new capabilities were stymied by lack of immediate material support. Veterans returned to villages but had no way to turn their ambitions into reality. The post-war years saw some in Papua and New Guinea, the Solomon Islands, and the New Hebrides turning to cargo cults or other unproductive activity. When major political change came to these islands in the 1960s and 1970s, it was led by a new generation, though in independent Papua New Guinea (PNG) its leading

---

[40] R.N. Love, 'Policies of frustration: the growth of Maori politics – the Ratana-labour era', PhD thesis, Victoria University of Wellington, 1977; C. Orange, 'The price of citizenship? The Maori war effort', in J. Crawford (ed.), *Kia Kaha: New Zealand in the Second World War* (Oxford: Oxford University Press, 2000), 236–51; R.S. Hill, *State Authority, Indigenous Autonomy: Crown–Maori Relations in New Zealand/Aotearoa 1900–1950* (Wellington: Victoria University Press, 2004).
[41] Munholland, *Rock of Contention*; D.A. Chappell, 'Ethnogenesis and frontiers', *Journal of World History* 4 (1993), 267–75.

politician, Michael Somare, recalled with fondness the Japanese school he attended as a child.[42]

The Territory of Papua and New Guinea (TPNG) did benefit from an improved relationship with the Australian public. The trope of the 'Fuzzy Wuzzy Angel' – a sentimental and patronizing image of New Guinea stretcher-bearers that nonetheless acknowledged their skill and caring – gained public visibility in Australia.[43] The public was now more familiar with the island and appreciative of the Islanders' war service – and of how New Guinea had shielded Australia from the Japanese advance. Given this much more sympathetic view than it had held before the war, the Australian public was willing to support more generous post-war aid. Yet despite praise of Islanders' wartime efforts, the victors' goal was to reinstate colonialism and racial hierarchy, albeit with improved conditions (such as an end to indentured labour, and greater funding). There was some war damage compensation, humanitarian aid, and economic development, but colonial structures remained strong until PNG independence in 1975.

Whereas colonial territories occupied by Japan during wartime reverted to their victorious 'owners', Japan's colonial possessions in Micronesia became a United Nations Trust Territory, a 'strategic trust' assigned to US control.[44] The US Navy Military Government took on administration of this vast, war-destroyed region, whose people and culture were almost completely unfamiliar to the new rulers. The American focus was strategic, with military government in place until 1951.[45] Cold War concerns led the US military to continue or even accelerate its use of the islands. On Guam, 1,350 families lost their land and homes to military use by 1947.[46] Bikini and Enewetak became sites of nuclear weapons testing (1946–58) with damaging and virtually eternal harm to the people, lands, and seas, sending those populations into

---

[42] Powell, *Third Force*, 213, 202–6, 241–56; Nelson, '"Taem Bilong Faet"', 255–61; M. Somare, *Sana: An Autobiography of Michael Somare* (Port Moresby: Niuguinea Press, 1975). On the role of wartime events in the development of Maasina Rule, see D.W. Akin, *Colonialism, Maasina Rule, and the Origins of Malaitan Kastom* (Honolulu: University of Hawai'i Press, 2013).
[43] Inglis, 'War, race'; Stella, *Imagining the Other*, 110–11; E. Rogerson, 'The "Fuzzy Wuzzy Angels": looking beyond the myth', SVSS paper (Canberra: Australian War Memorial, 2012).
[44] H.M. Friedman, *Creating an American Lake: United States Imperialism and Strategic Security in the Pacific Basin, 1945–1947* (Westport, CT: Greenwood, 2001).
[45] Poyer et al., *Typhoon of War*, 276–314.
[46] A.P. Hattori, 'Guardians of our soil: indigenous responses to post-World War II military land appropriations on Guam', in L.E.A. Ma (ed.), *Farms, Firms, and Runways: Perspectives on U.S. Military Bases in the Western Pacific* (Chicago: Imprint Publications, 2001), 186–202; F. Quimby, 'Fortress Guåhån: Chamorro nationalism, regional economic integration and U.S. defense interests shape Guam's recent history', *Journal of Pacific History* 46 (2011), 357–80.

permanent refugee status and an endless series of compensation negotiations.[47] (Great Britain and France have also conducted nuclear tests in Pacific territories.) Military installations on Guam, the Northern Marianas, and Kwajalein Atoll sequestered scarce land. The Department of the Interior took over administration through the end of the Trust Territory of the Pacific Islands after 1978, when the island groups variously moved towards independence or some form of affiliation with the USA. While basic education, healthcare, policing, and political representation were put in place, the USA, unlike the Japanese empire, saw no economic benefit in the islands and made no serious effort to rebuild local economies.[48]

New Zealand, Britain, and Australia, however, were less determined to hang on to their territories, including United Nations Trust Territories of Western Sāmoa, Nauru, and New Guinea. Western Sāmoa's emergence as a state in 1962 was a product of post-war cooperation, as New Zealand rapidly expanded formal education, localized public services, and increased Samoan participation in regional organizations. Australia did the same, more hastily, later in the 1960s in TPNG, including establishing the first western Pacific university in Port Moresby in 1965, of enormous benefit to the country and region.[49] Nauru gained its independence in 1968, sued for compensation for environmental damage in the 1990s, but invested compensation funds and phosphate earnings in a succession of grandiose schemes and ended up in debt and at the mercy of others.[50]

The United Nations' ethos of 'development' and independence made colonies increasingly costly to administer. Britain withdrew from Fiji in 1970, and rushed Solomon Islands into independence in 1978. Kiribati (Gilbert) and Tuvalu (Ellice) soon followed, separating because of their perceived differences in cultural and colonial trajectories.[51] France funnelled some colonial discontent into representation in the French parliament, and

---

[47] M. Smith-Norris, *Domination and Resistance: The United States and the Marshall Islands during the Cold War* (Honolulu: University of Hawai'i Press, 2016).
[48] D. Hanlon, *Remaking Micronesia: Discourses over Development in a Pacific Territory, 1944–1982* (Honolulu: University of Hawai'i Press, 1998).
[49] M. Boyd, 'The record in Western Samoa since 1945', in A. Ross, *New Zealand's Record in the Pacific Islands in the Twentieth Century* (Auckland: Longman Paul, 1968), 189–27; I. Downs, *The Australian Trusteeship in Papua New Guinea, 1945–75* (Canberra: Australian Government Publishing Service, 1980).
[50] C. Weeramantry, *Nauru: Environmental Damage under International Trusteeship* (Oxford: Oxford University Press, 1992); J. Connell, 'Nauru: the first failed Pacific state?', *Round Table: Commonwealth Journal of International. Affairs* 95:383 (2006), 47–63.
[51] W.D. McIntyre, *Winding up the British Empire in the Pacific Islands* (Oxford: Oxford University Press, 2014).

when President de Gaulle offered full independence in 1958, it was declined. The sterile hybrid, the Condominium of the New Hebrides, despite official French resistance, finally became independent in 1980. In all this, Christian churches, always a potent Pacific force and, by the 1960s, a crucible for trans-island exchange, largely championed self-government and local control in both ecclesiastical and secular spheres.[52] Their voices are raised currently against another manifestation of imperialism, the systematic exploitation by Indonesia of the Melanesians of West Papua, absorbed by a rigged 'act of free choice' in 1969, with the tacit assent of Australia and the United States.[53]

The same strategic importance that brought war to the islands in the mid-twentieth century continues to shape their internal economy and international relations. Micronesians are aware of their islands' strategic value – indeed, it is their sole essential bargaining chip in dealing with powerful nations eyeing the Pacific world.[54] US military activities continue to affect the islands, from continued litigation over nuclear testing harm to Bikini and Enewetak Marshallese to current protests against live-fire training on Pagan and Tinian in the Commonwealth of the North Mariana Islands. Guam's politics is continually engaged with issues of the military's dominant role in the island's physical territory and economy.

The war confirmed Australia's fear of the north, an enduring strategic imperative that spurred it to develop the TPNG towards independence in 1975, a card the independent PNG government is not hesitant to play. Annual aid for PNG's stability thus has been forthcoming. In the mid-1970s, Tonga had its airfield extension funded by Australia to over-ride an offer from the USSR. Similarly, Australia's concern for stability in the region led to the spending of millions of dollars to resolve Solomon Islands' 'Tensions' of the early 2000s – a small but painful civil war. More recently, Chinese 'investment'

---

[52] H. Gardner, 'Praying for independence', *Journal of Pacific History* 48:2 (2013), 122–43; C. Weir, 'The opening of the coconut curtain: Pacific influence on the World Council of Churches through the Campaign for a Nuclear-Free Pacific, 1961 to 2000', *Journal of Pacific History* 54:1 (2019), 116–38.

[53] J. Pouwer, 'The colonisation, decolonisation and recolonisation of West New Guinea', *Journal of Pacific History* 34:2 (1999), 157–79.

[54] G. Petersen, 'The Micronesians', in J.M. Fitzpatrick (ed.), *Endangered Peoples of Oceania: Struggles to Survive and Thrive* (Westport, CT: Greenwood Press, 2001), 93–105; L. Poyer, S. Falgout, and L.M. Carucci, 'The impact of the Pacific War on modern Micronesian identity', in V.S. Lockwood (ed.), *Globalization and Culture Change in the Pacific Islands* (Upper Saddle River, NJ: Pearson Prentice Hall, 2004), 307–23; L.B. Wilson, *Speaking to Power: Gender and Politics in the Western Pacific* (New York: Routledge, 1995); G. Puas, *The Federated States of Micronesia's Engagement with the Outside World: Control, Self-Preservation, and Continuity* (Canberra: ANU Press, 2021).

JUDITH A. BENNETT AND LIN POYER

and soft loans in Pacific states have become the concern of the USA, Australia, and New Zealand, but, given these countries' considerable export dependence on China, they publicly welcome 'development partners'.[55]

As to the war's impact on Indigenous politics, the only substantial change was the hunger for more material progress in much of the western Pacific. Aspirations were raised but the immediate wherewithal was largely absent. Education and more diversified economies were the keys. Without strong economic bases some island peoples such as the Cook Islanders and Niueans opted for forms of independence but retained New Zealand citizenship and aid grants, similar to some of the Micronesian states.

Memory Work and Forgetting

Changes in the global order continue, even as World War II recedes on the horizon of public memory. The major combatants, victors and losers, victims and heroes, are commemorated at battlefields, cemeteries, and war memorials, as well as in literature, history books, songs, dances, and family stories.[56] Major combatants and Indigenous peoples on whose lands the war was fought differ in how they memorialize the war, though the connections through the physical remains of war, the bodies of the honoured dead, and the echo of war in modern geopolitics keep them linked in perpetuity.

Cemeteries are a physical link between combatant nations and their wars fought far from home. Soldiers were often buried at or near the site of battle, meaning that Islanders often dealt with the war dead. Americans, British, and Australians built and maintained cemeteries in the region, or moved bodies

---

[55] Australian Department of Foreign Affairs, 'The South Pacific', Submission to the Senate Standing Committee on Foreign Affairs and Defence Inquiry into 'The Need for an Increased Australian Commitment to the South Pacific', Canberra: AGPS, March 1977, 21; 'Roubles for Tonga from Russia with Love', *Pacific Islands Monthly*, August 1976, 14–15; I. Webley, 'Tonga and the Soviet Union: problems in New Zealand–Tonga relationships', *New Zealand International Review* 1:5 (1976), 11–15; R.A. Herr, 'Regionalism, strategic denial and South Pacific security', *Journal of Pacific History* 21:4 (1986), 170–82; C.A. Wilson, *New Zealand and the Soviet Union: A Brittle Relationship* (Wellington: Victoria University Press, 2004), 94; S. Firth, 'New developments in the international relations of the Pacific Islands', *Journal of Pacific History* 48:3 (2013), 286–93.

[56] S. Falgout, L. Poyer, and L.M. Carucci, *Memories of War: Micronesians in the Pacific War* (Honolulu: University of Hawai'i Press, 2007). Pacific Islands literature on World War II deserves its own discussion, which we cannot address here. Patricia Grace's *Tu*, for example, draws on personal stories to bring to life the experience of Māori Battalion men in Europe; Chris Perez Howard's *Mariquita: A Tragedy of Guam* evokes the stress of wartime for Chamorro people; Vincent Eri's *The Crocodile*, set during the war, was the first English-language novel by a New Guinea writer.

after the war as cemeteries were consolidated. The bodies of most Americans who died in the Pacific War were sent to hometown cemeteries or reinterred in national cemeteries, such as the National Memorial Cemetery of the Pacific ('Punchbowl Cemetery') in Hawai'i. (That effort continues, with recent new efforts to retrieve and identify the remains of Americans who died on Tarawa.)

Japanese cremated their dead where possible and sent ashes home, but conditions of war left tens of thousands unburied. Japanese bone-collecting expeditions to conduct funeral rituals have gone on throughout the islands since the 1950s, continuing into the present. The first missions to find Japanese war dead in the Solomons, TPNG, and the Gilbert Islands met resistance from colonial authorities and local people. This resistance eventually succumbed to peacetime political courtesy. In the Northern Mariana Islands, Japanese came to commemorate war dead as soon as the US military lifted travel restrictions in 1962. Until protections were put in place, 'bone-collecting' was uncontrolled, resulting in indiscriminate collection of any human remains, including destruction of Chamorro archaeological sites.[57]

Indigenous people also cared for and dealt with those who died on their lands. Gilbert Islanders helped clear the battlefields of bodies and bury Japanese dead on Tarawa. In Papua and New Guinea, people used their knowledge of the landscape to help recover bodies lost in jungle. At a temporary US cemetery in Tonga, Queen Sālote had each grave covered in flowers.[58] American remains have been removed from Peleliu, but residents sense a link with the war dead.

> Older locals on the island described how, in the years immediately after the battle, all of Peleliu was visibly full of the foreign dead. They could be seen in their hundreds, everywhere, shadowy figures in uniforms standing silently either alone or in groups, on the beaches, in the forest and hills, on the roads and in the buildings, even right next to you in the store.[59]

Where the bodies of foreign war dead remain in island cemeteries, they become symbols of sentiment and history, subject to reinterpretation as political relationships shift. Also, the remains of Indigenous people who died in foreign wars remain in foreign cemeteries – Māori leaders have called for

---

[57] Bennett, *Natives and Exotics*, 279–80; Camacho, *Cultures of Commemoration*, 116–23. On Japanese memorial activity in the islands, B. Trefalt, 'Collecting bones: Japanese missions for the repatriation of war remains and the unfinished business of the Asia-Pacific War', *Australian Humanities Review* 61 (2016), 145–59; Bennett, *Natives and Exotics*, 279–80.
[58] Bennett, *Natives and Exotics*, 268–78.   [59] Price et al., 'After the typhoon', 226.

repatriation of bodies of Māori war dead buried overseas, after attacks on the graves of New Zealand soldiers in military cemeteries in Libya.[60]

Public memorials reflect shifts in how the Pacific War is perceived in terms of current political concerns. World War II commemorations globally are primarily organized by and conducted for the major combatant nations. Until recently, the only statue of an Indigenous person in a public space in Solomon Islands was a memorial to World War II hero Jacob Vouza, but in 2011 one titled 'The Pride of Our Nation' was erected to the coastwatchers, Solomon Islanders and Australians.[61] While this may have contributed to nation-building after the 'tensions' of localized civil war, it also points to increased Indigenous participation as more inclusive histories and more political awareness have drawn attention to their role, and as war tourism gains economic valence. In Pacific Islands, commemorations are relatively few, seldom well attended, and limited in public scope. As years pass, new generations have less contact, less knowledge, and usually less interest in wartime experiences. Historical research and official archives remain, but public memories will change.

Most Micronesians see the war as a foreign conflict. 'Liberation Day' is a national or local holiday in many islands, but it is marked by community events, athletic competitions, dances, and feasts that do not necessarily reference the war.[62] In the Northern Mariana Islands, which was a part of the Japanese Empire, commemorating the war has been problematic. People appreciated relief from the trauma of war, but invading US forces interned Chamorro and Refaluwasch (Carolinians in the NMI) in camps for two years, releasing them on 4 July 1946 – a date chosen by the US military government and named Liberation Day to craft a narrative of loyalty to the USA. The islands became a US commonwealth in 1978, and by the 1990s and the fiftieth anniversary war commemorations, public memories began to speak more clearly in 'the language of American loyalty'. Issues of collaboration – the Chamorro interpreters who worked for Japanese on Guam, and 'women of war' who served in brothels or had relations with Japanese men – are not yet dealt with in official narratives or public commemorations: making

---

[60] 'Iwi leaders call for repatriation', *The Northern Advocate* (Whangarei, New Zealand) (16 March 2012), B:11.
[61] G.M. White, 'Remembering Guadalcanal: national identity and transnational memory-making', *Public Culture* 7 (1995), 529–55; Kwai, *Solomon Islanders*, 93–111.
[62] E.g., W. Turner and S. Falgout, 'Time traces: cultural memory and World War II in Pohnpei', *Contemporary Pacific* 14 (2002), 101–31; but note Enewetak's elaborate memorialization of wartime and post-war events, L.M. Carucci, *Nuclear Nativity: Rituals of Renewal and Empowerment in the Marshall Islands* (DeKalb: Northern Illinois University Press, 1997).

history 'as much about forgetting as it is about remembering'.[63] In contrast, Liberation Day on Guam displays a clear sense of US patriotism in parades, religious services, and other activities.[64]

Physical memorials are sites of public memory, sometimes of reverence, sometimes of contention, as we see in conflicts over historical displays about Pearl Harbor or the Hiroshima bombing. Japanese bone-collecting missions can ride roughshod over local land and historical sites, and also reflect ongoing intergenerational and nationalist political factions at home.[65] Allied memorials similarly may ignore local concerns and use Pacific War history as a proxy for modern international issues. In Solomon Islands, Australians and Americans competed with Japanese in constructing memorials, seeking 'to dominate the landscape, not with guns but with their definitive texts'.[66] Americans have shown much less interest than Australians in erecting memorials in Melanesia, reflecting relative lack of US strategic interest in the area.

Guam's War in the Pacific National Historical Park, too, is a contested site of historical memory. In 1967, a Japanese war memorial association dedicated a site for a peace memorial, raising criticism – especially since there was not yet a major US war memorial on Guam. The Japanese move spurred development of the already-proposed War in the Pacific park. While it celebrates the American story of Guam's liberation from Japanese occupation and the strong patriotism of Guam's people (true enough), the park also brings to mind the way the US military has occupied the island ever since, with increasing resistance from each generation of Chamorros. Only in 1996 was a marker added to commemorate Chamorros' war experience. In the Northern Mariana Islands, Japanese, Korean, and Okinawan memorials far outnumber the few monuments to US military actions. Not until the war's fiftieth anniversary was American Memorial Park, a small park in Garapan, expanded as a monument to the Americans, with a memorial to Islanders who died in the war added later.[67]

Local people's relative lack of interest in foreigners' memorials, leaving them in many cases to be damaged or overgrown, shows vividly the sense

---

[63] Camacho, *Cultures of Commemoration*, 131, 160.
[64] But see discussion in V. Diaz, 'Deliberating "Liberation Day": identity, history, memory, and war in Guam', in T. Fujitani, L. Yoneyama, and G. White (eds.), *Perilous Memories: The Asia-Pacific War(s)* (Durham, NC: Duke University Press, 2001), 155–80.
[65] Murray, *Battle over Peleliu*, 191–222.
[66] Bennett, *Natives and Exotics*, 283–7; Kwai, *Solomon Islanders*.
[67] Camacho, *Cultures of Commemoration*; R.D.K. Herman, 'Inscribing empire: Guam and the War in the Pacific National Park', *Political Geography* 27 (2008), 630–51.

that, for Islanders, this was 'someone else's war'.[68] Still, local people must deal with foreigners' war memories. In some places, those memories have actually become valuable resources. Fascination with sites of war and other horrors has gained commercial attention and a name, 'dark tourism'.[69] After the US lifted travel restrictions on the Mariana Islands in 1962, Guam's tourist economy began to develop, with Japanese as the largest and most lucrative tourist market. On Saipan, the proliferation of Japanese, Korean, and Okinawan memorials at Marpi Point brought Asian war tourism – and here, personal relationships and familiarity with Japanese language and culture promoted a warmer welcome to those visitors.[70] Solomon Islands' war-related tourism, at first linked to US and Japanese veterans, is now shifting to new generations.[71]

The Kokoda Trail, site of early battles in the Japanese invasion of New Guinea, is a tourist trek as well as 'sacred ground' to Australians, whose interests shape land use along the trail. Tourism and related fees have proved profitable to those in communities bordering the Kokoda Trail, despite the fact that the wartime carriers came from more distant regions. But how should PNG people balance Australians' historical and tourism interests against other options, such as mining or other uses of the land along the track?[72] The Federated States of Micronesia includes Chuuk (Truk) Lagoon, an important cultural heritage site marking the destruction of the Japanese naval base there. It is now a world-famous diving site for shipwrecks and downed aircraft.[73] The Marshall Islands Bikini Atoll nuclear test range is now a UN World Heritage Site. On Peleliu, people must negotiate Japanese and US tourists' political sensibilities – especially since both countries provide Palau with foreign aid.[74] For their part, Islanders' own ideas about what

---

[68] J.A. Bennett, '"Inevitable erosion of heroes and landmarks": an end to the politics of Allied war memorials in Tarawa', in M. Gegner and B. Ziino (eds.), *The Heritage of War* (New York: Routledge, 2012), 88–107.

[69] J. Lennon and M. Foley, *Dark Tourism: The Attraction of Death and Disasters* (London: Thomson, 2000).

[70] Camacho, *Cultures of Commemoration*, 120–3.

[71] C. Panakera, 'World War II and tourism development in Solomon Islands', in C. Ryan (ed.), *Battlefield Tourism: History, Place and Interpretation* (Amsterdam: Elsevier, 2007), 125–41.

[72] S. Brawley and C. Dixon, 'Who owns the Kokoda Trail? Australian mythologies, colonial legacies and mining in Papua New Guinea', *Social Alternatives* 28:4 (2009), 24–9; Bennett, *Natives and Exotics*, 286–7; H. Nelson, 'Kokoda: and two national histories', *Journal of Pacific History* 42 (2007), 73–88.

[73] B. Jeffery, 'World War II underwater cultural heritage sites in Truk Lagoon: considering a case for World Heritage listing', *International Journal of Nautical Archaeology* 33 (2004), 106–21; D.M. Strong, *Witness to War: Truk Lagoon's Master Diver Kimiuo Aisek* ([s.l: s.n], 2013).

[74] Murray, *Battle over Peleliu*.

aspects of their history are most precious focus on Indigenous history and legend, not on foreigners' colonial sites and battlegrounds.[75] Yet for some nations, such as Solomon Islands, memorials to local heroes signifying national cohesion are seen as a partial cure for longstanding divisions.[76]

Memorials are in a sense an aid to memories of war, but war's lessons are more pertinent. Aside from tragic personal loss and the tsunami of incoming troops and materiel, the most prominent wartime imprint on the Pacific Islands has been the lesson to their peoples of their strategic value within the wide Pacific Ocean. Certainly, while some island groups have resources of timber and minerals, and all have a stake in fisheries and tourism, today's governing reality is their role in global geopolitics. Relations with Australia, New Zealand, Japan, Taiwan, China, Russia, and the USA – and other nations as well – phrased as development aid, international friendship, or economic partnerships – are also, inevitably, strategic. That can include access to trade, to safe passage by sea and air, and to sites for military bases and testing weapons, as well as security in a general sense. It is no small irony that the island states' diplomatic and economic trump card in this ocean of 'peace' has been and remains their potential value in other nations' wars and preparations for war.

---

[75] L. Poyer, 'Defining history across cultures: insider and outsider contrasts', *Isla: A Journal of Micronesian Studies* 1 (1992), 73–89; Murray, *Battle over Peleliu*; Bennett, *Natives and Exotics*, 283–7.
[76] Kwai, *Solomon Islanders*, 93–111

56

The Nuclear Pacific

From Hiroshima to Fukushima, 1945–2018

BARBARA ROSE JOHNSTON

The Nuclear Pacific is a term born from a uniquely resonant pairing of a science and technology that made its historical appearance as an expression of military power in an Oceanian and archipelagic world – and has legacies that extend thousands of years into the future. From the atomic bombings of Hiroshima and Nagasaki in 1945, to years of the Pacific being utilized as an experiment site for America, British, and French nuclear testing, to renewed concerns about environmental and global public health issuing from the breach of a reactor in Fukushima, Japan as a consequence of a devastating 2011 tsunami, the Pacific has been a figurative and literal ground zero for nuclear diplomacy, popular resistance, and continuing debates about human rights, international law, economic and political power, and the environment (Figure 56.1).

The atomic bombings of Japan loom large as cautionary tales of the destructive and radiological warfare that world powers have claimed to try to avoid since 1945 with a 'balance of terror' strategy, sanguine about mutually assured destruction, and the terrifying and generations-long effects on human populations. These histories, arguably, began in August 1945 with the destruction of Hiroshima and Nagasaki. Months later the balance of terror strategy was deployed again, with the July 1946 Operation Crossroads detonation of two atomic bombs in Bikini Lagoon. This time the power of the atom was displayed before an audience of tens of thousands, including representatives of the world's nations brought to the Marshall Islands to witness the power of the atomic bomb.[1] Thus, with the Pacific War concluded, the Cold War began with military activities shifting from the battlefield to the proving grounds. In relatively distant deserts,

---

[1] J.M. Weisgall, *Operation Crossroads: The Atomic Tests at Bikini Atoll* (Annapolis: Naval Institute Press, 1994). Additional research, collaboration, and editorial assistance by Matt Matsuda and Paul D'Arcy.

614

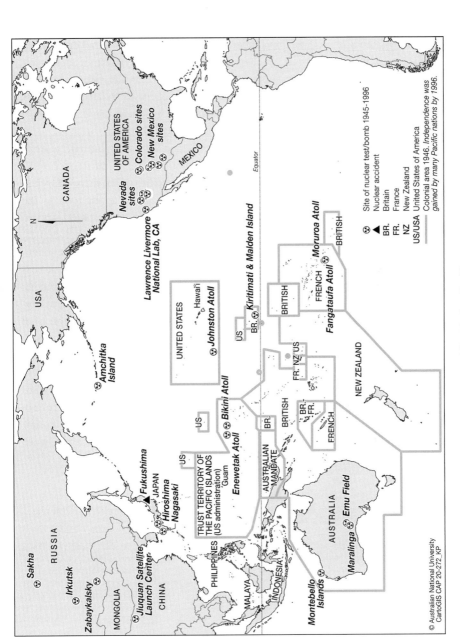

Figure 56.1 The Nuclear Pacific.

mountains, and oceans of the world where weapons of mass destruction were tested, new threats and dangers enveloped local communities and the environments on which they depended.[2] Important to remember, nuclear history is, in many ways, a never-ending story given the nature of radioactive half-life and related environmental health threats. It is critically a story of militarism, colonialism, and the disproportionate burden borne by Indigenous peoples and ethnic minorities whose traditional ways of life make them immensely vulnerable to radiation in the environment and the food chain.

The scope of nuclear colonialism, testing, and threats to human, animal, and plant life, and the environment – in additional to political, economic, social, and cultural fallout – is staggering when examined in historical relief. The USA, the UK, and France all conducted nuclear weapons tests in the Pacific resulting in widespread and severe contamination, devastation, and, in a number of instances, complete atomization of long-inhabited homelands. China conducted its nuclear tests in the remote western section of the inland province of Gansu, while the Russians tested in a number of locations across their vast Central Asian, Arctic, and Siberian territories.[3] Marshall Islanders, Aleut who seasonally visited Amchitka Island in the far west of the Aleutians, southern Tuamotu Islanders in French Polynesia, I Kiribati from the Line Islands, and Australian desert Aborigines from South Australia – all suffered the experience of host nuclear militarism. Some were evacuated prior to detonation with minimalist information and false promises of a healthy return. Yet, in other well-documented instances, nuclear weapons were detonated without notifying and relocating communities living in the immediate region.[4] Lives were lost, ancestral homelands were severely contaminated, and measures to provide redress to affected communities were woefully inadequate.

---

[2] A. Smith, 'Colonialism and the bomb in the Pacific', in J. Schofield and W. Cocroft (eds.), *A Fearsome Heritage: Diverse Legacies of the Cold War* (Walnut Creek, CA: Left Coast Press, 2007), 51–72.

[3] J. Eichelberger et al., 'Nuclear stewardship: lessons from a not-so-remote island', *GeoTimes* 47:3 (2002), 20–3; P. Miller, *Nuclear flashback: report of a Greenpeace scientific expedition to Amchitka Island, Alaska – site of the largest underground nuclear test in U.S. history* (Washington, DC: Greenpeace USA, 1996); D. Perlman, 'Blast from the past: researchers worry that radiation from nuclear test decades ago may be damaging marine life today', *San Francisco Chronicle* (17 December 2001), www.sfgate.com/news/article/BLAST-FROM-THE-PAST-Researchers-worry-that-2839679.php; R.T. Jones, 'The environment', in D. Armitage and A. Bashford (eds.), *Pacific Histories: Ocean, Land, People* (Basingstoke: Palgrave Macmillan, 2014), 121–42, at 137.

[4] B. Johnston and H. Barker, *Consequential Damages of Nuclear War: The Rongelap Report* (Walnut Creek, CA: Left Coast Press, 2008).

At the dawn of the nuclear age much was unknown about the nature and behaviour of unstable isotopes and the consequences of acute or persistent exposure. In the event of individual or community-wide, high-level exposure to radiation, opportunistic research was conducted on humans and the environments in which they lived, with the aim to establish relatively safe, dangerous, or deadly human exposure levels. In many instances, research occurred with knowledge or informed consent. Research involving Indigenous and ethnic communities was especially valuable, as traditional lifeways reflected dependence upon and deep immersion in the local environment. Some of the most extensive studies involved the 1954 Bravo hydrogen bomb and related exposure and study of Marshall Island Rongelap and Utrik Atoll communities.[5]

National allied servicemen served as workers during nuclear tests, and some served as human subjects in studies establishing safety thresholds in war and radiation health effects in the aftermath of exposure. This service often generated adverse health effects, with little or no government acknowledgement or assistance in addressing such adverse outcomes. For example, Aotearoa New Zealand soldiers were exposed to radiation as occupying troops following the atomic bombing of Hiroshima; they were deployed as support troops for British atomic tests in Australia and Kiribati and as protest witnesses to French tests at Mururoa Atoll.

In some cases, different registers of both the Pacific War and the post-war period are present in the same landscapes and local histories. Kwajalein Atoll in the Marshall Islands is a powerful reminder of the links and unfinished grieving that surrounded the Pacific War and its nuclear aftermath. Almost 8,000 Japanese soldiers and civilians, Korean labourers, Marshallese, and American servicemen died during the brutal battle to retake Kwajalein. Only the American dead were repatriated. The remainder were buried anonymously in mass graves all over the island, and remained there as part of the sand, soil, and unclosed sorrow of grieving relatives when the Americans rebuilt the atoll to house part of their nuclear testing programme. Memorials have since been collected, but the memory and pain remain, etched in and imperceptible from the landscape. The dominant theme in Japanese national collective memory of the Pacific War is that it was akin to a natural disaster, in which

---

[5] Cf. B.R. Johnston, '"More like us than mice": radiation experiments with indigenous peoples', in B.R. Johnston (ed.), *Half-lives and Half-truths: Confronting the Radioactive Legacies of the Cold War* (Santa Fe, NM: School for Advanced Research Press, 2007), 25–54; Johnston and Barker, *Consequential Damages of Nuclear War*.

the emperor and his subjects were all victims of the military elite.[6] For the Americans, Kwajalein with its central Pacific location became a strategic point literally to project power while testing new technologies.

The vast and relatively underpopulated expanses of Oceania proved ideal for nuclear testing by the Americans, British, and French, especially as Islanders were politically marginal in essentially colonial relationships in American Micronesia, the British Gilbert Islands, and French Polynesia. The nuclear weapons exploded in this period increased in magnitude to be many hundreds of times more powerful than those dropped on Hiroshima and Nagasaki. Atmospheric testing of nuclear warheads was eventually replaced, first by underground testing and then by computer simulations and delivery system testing as protests mounted within the region and around the world.

In some cases, the logic of such displays of nuclear weapons testing power followed a familiar post-war scenario – that of national gamesmanship in an arriving Cold War era. The United Kingdom, for example, asserted its continuing sense of imperial grandeur in the face of a crumbling global empire by brandishing its thermonuclear credentials as a major power – suitably far from the British Isles in the Pacific. In this, Britain found a willing partner in the Australian government – Prime Minister Robert Menzies declaring as an alliance of honour that Australia would assist Britain by offering the Monte Bello Islands, and then the western lands of South Australia, in particular Maralinga.

In a remarkable perpetuation of the *terra nullius* doctrine by which the British Crown had appropriated lands for settler colonialism in the eighteenth century, government scientists decided the arid western lands of South Australia were empty, and therefore suitable for nuclear weapons testing. As Stewart Firth and Karin von Strokirch point out, this was far from true. Rather, 'The Yankunytjatjara and Pitjantjatjara were continuing to move over the desert country which became the Maralinga Prohibited Area, in search of hunting grounds, food and water, to reassert social connections and for ceremonial purposes. Groups of people were constantly forming and re-forming, splitting and recombining.'[7] Officials who did

---

[6] S. Falgout, L. Poyer, and L.M. Carucci, *Memories of War: Micronesians in the Pacific War* (Honolulu: University of Hawai'i Press, 2007); S. Firth, *Nuclear Playground* (Honolulu: University of Hawai'i Press, 1987); G. Dvorak, 'Who closed the sea? Archipelagoes of amnesia between the United States and Japan', *Pacific Historical Review* 83:2 (2014), 350–72.

[7] S. Firth and K. von Strokirch, 'A nuclear Pacific', in D. Denoon, S. Firth, J. Linnekin, M. Meleisea, and K. Nero (eds.), *The Cambridge History of the Pacific Islanders* (Cambridge: Cambridge University Press, 1997), 324–58.

directly engage with the Aboriginal peoples like the Pitjantjatjara warned them of dangerous spiritual forces and poisons in the air as a means to limit the loss of human life. But when the British bombs were detonated, only cursory aerial checks were employed to determine that the region was, if not uninhabited, at least cleared of local communities. Researchers from the Australian Royal Commission would later hear of illness and death from interviews with the Yankunytjatjara and Pitjantjatjara, as a result both of fallout and also of measles from exposure to outsiders in the territory. Just as with the declaration of empty territory, an epidemic scourge of British intrusion in the eighteenth century was grafted onto an unknown sickness of the twentieth.

As compared to Britain, the United States was not only defending historical prerogatives, but asserting its growing might as a global political, military, and economic giant of the post-war era. Strategically, this meant demonstrating continuing technological prowess for destructive capabilities in displays of atomic firepower. Within one year of the atomic bombing of Japan, in 1946, the US Navy was already mounting Operation Crossroads to test the parameters of the new atomic bombs, displacing local peoples in the Bikini Atoll of the Marshall Islands and exploding atmospheric atomic weapons. This was only the beginning. In 1954, the USA tested a newer weapon, the hydrogen bomb, known as the Bravo test, which rained down radioactive fallout across multiple island chains, with immediate – and continuing – consequences for the inhabitants.

It is important to keep in mind that the American nuclear and military impact was not limited to high-profile events like the Crossroads or Bravo tests. Between 1946 and 1958, the United States conducted a total of twenty-three nuclear bomb tests around Bikini Atoll, and an additional forty-four around Enewetak and in the region. These explosions vaporized reefs, atomized islands, and produced both regional and global fallout with heaviest deposition in the Marshall Islands.

The role of nuclear militarism in shaping and contorting Pacific life has been examined from historical, human rights, scientific, and avowedly political perspectives for decades. An increasingly salient perspective is that of understanding cases like the Marshall Islands through the lens of global ecologies, as forwarded by environmental anthropologist Barbara Rose Johnston. Here, the focus is not only on overviewing events and responses, but on considering meanings and value systems, and the ways they can 'both shape and contort biophysical ecosystems with anthropogenic consequence on local and global scales', leading to consequences that put forward not only strategic or political objectives, but 'the ethical imperative for greater social and environmental justice'.[8]

More, Barbara Rose Johnston points out the uniqueness of this phenomenon and analysis historically. In effect, the rise of atomic science and militarism not only grew hand in hand, but quickly established themselves as progenitors of completely unique and novel ecologies – which themselves artificially created new elements with radiogenic and mutagenic properties. As such, this new era heralded the possibility of fundamental alteration to local and planetary systems themselves – as well as to all of the living organisms they supported.

The intersection of science and militarism heralded a history whose challenges were unique to the twentieth century – the possibilities of physically and environmentally changing the entire globe through the deployment of a new technology. What was not new was the pairing of this with a continuing struggle: that of Western empire and colonialism in the Pacific Islands. In this, the subjugated are an Indigenous nation whose atolls and islands have been altered or destroyed, while generations struggle to recognize radiogenic threats and address harm. As claimants and survivors their knowledge and advocacy has demonstrably shaped both local and global efforts to secure nuclear justice. The testimonies of Lijon Eknilang, a Marshallese nuclear survivor, have become signal evidence of these claims, following the massive American test code-named Bravo.

> The fall-out that our bodies were exposed to caused the blisters and other sores we experienced over the weeks that followed. Many of us lost our hair, too. The fall-out was in the air we breathed, in the fresh water we drank, and in the food we ate during the days after Bravo. This caused internal exposure and sickness. We remained on Rongelap for two and one-half days after the fall-out came. The serious internal and external exposure we received caused long-term health problems that affected my parents' generation, my generation, and the generation of my children.[9]

Notably, Eknilang makes the point that nuclear histories are critical not only for their effects on the human survivors, but for their central shaping of

---

[8] B.R. Johnston, 'Nuclear disaster: the Marshall Islands experiences and lessons for a post-Fukushima world', in E. DeLoughery, J. Didur, and A. Carrigan (eds.), *Global Ecologies and the Environmental Humanities: Postcolonial Approaches* (London: Routledge, 2016), 140–61.
[9] Johnston, 'Nuclear disaster', 141.

global ecologies – the alteration of entire environments. She points out that essential food crops such as arrowroot would no longer grow, tapioca would not bear fruit, and 'what we did eat gave us blisters on our lips and in our mouths and we suffered terrible stomach problems and nausea. Some of the fish we caught caused the same problems.'[10] Even more, this nuclear colonialism became the foundation not only for suffering, but for extended chronicles of affliction across generations, in terms of toxic exposure and congenital disease.

> Many of my friends keep quiet about the strange births they had. In privacy, they give birth, not to children as we like to think of them, but to things we could only describe as 'octopuses', 'apples', 'turtles', and other things in our experience. We do not have Marshallese words for these kinds of babies because they were never born before the radiation came.[11]

Important to remember, the histories of nuclear colonialism in the Pacific are not only of victims, but are bound together with anti-colonial resistance. Eknilang's words were not only testimonies, but political advocacy and a claim to human rights and redress, denied to her community, and presented before the World Court. She testified before and asked the court to address and provide, through global justice, the experience of the Marshallese people and to provide security for health, and also 'the safety of the environment upon which their survival depends'.[12]

Eknilang's work unified the claims of Indigenous peoples around the world who have been dispossessed, have been experimented upon, and have suffered from nuclear colonialism and militarism. Drawing on these testimonies illustrates the ways that these voices like Eknilang's were not singular cases of victimization or misfortune, but responses to an intentional and highly institutionalized system for drawing upon the lives and health of Pacific Islands for colonial and scientific purposes. American support was available, yet far from responding to the consequences of unintentional human experiment due to dangerous exposure, US medical teams travelled regularly to the Marshall Islands to collect information on radiogenic

---

[10] Johnston, 'Nuclear disaster', 141.
[11] Johnston, 'Nuclear disaster', 142; Z. dé Ishtar (ed.), *Pacific Women Speak Out for Independence and Denuclearisation* (Christchurch: Raven Press, 1998).
[12] Johnston, 'Nuclear disaster', 143; M. Silk, interviewer, 'Interview of Lijon Eknilang', Marshall Islands Story Project, http://mistories.org/nuclear-Eknilang-text.php; M. Todeschini, 'The bomb's womb? Women and the atom bomb', in V. Das, A. Kleinman, M. Lock, M. Ramphele, and P. Reynolds (eds.), *Remaking a World: Violence, Social Suffering, and Recovery* (Berkeley: University of California Press, 2001), 102–56.

health – human subjects for radiation exposure from weapons testing. Indeed, the cycles of data collection continued for decades.

In 1954, the US detonated the first hydrogen bomb at Bikini Atoll. Downwind, extremely high fallout prompted evacuation of military personnel on Rongerik. Rongelap, Ailinginae, and Utrik Atolls received heavier fallout and in subsequent days they were evacuated and examined. Rongelap community displayed severe signs of radiation poisoning. The entire population was retained for further study. In 1957, Rongelap community was shipped back to their heavily contaminated home islands where they began an unwitting servitude as subjects in a 'living laboratory'. Periodic exams and biosamples taken by US scientists generated evidence of the presence, movement, accumulation, and consequential damages of radiation in the environment, food chain, and human body. This classified research documented a wide array of individual and intergenerational health effects from living in a highly radioactive environment. Twenty years passed before the US government acknowledged a continuing obligation to assess and address environmental damages. In 1977, 'cleanup' efforts began on Enewetak where a military base was demolished, soil scraped, and highly radioactive debris dumped into an unlined pit created by earlier detonation of an atomic bomb on Runit Island. The resulting dome was capped by 4 inches of cement. Radioactive bulldozers, cranes, boats, and other large objects were dumped into the lagoon. In 1980, some forty islets were declared clean enough to support human life, assuming that Islanders would not eat produce, drink water, or breathe air from those islets too contaminated to support 'cleanup' efforts.[13]

Notably, the ability to live from the land and sea – the foundations of local culture – was replaced by heavy reliance on food supplements provided by the USDA, and whatever safe fishing might be allowed. But who or what defined 'safe'?[14] By and large, Islander populations were not part of that administrative and military decision-making process. Even the local handicraft and local coconut industry were directly impacted. Whereas some island societies could traditionally earn a small income from copra and oil from these atolls, fear of radioactive contamination prevented the products from being accepted by distributors and processors for wider markets.

As a result, in spite of remediation efforts, the consequential damages remain. Prior to the nuclear testing and American military presence, the

---

[13] B.R. Johnston and B.T. Abraham, 'Environmental disaster and resilience: the Marshall Islands experience continues to unfold', *Indigenous Policy Journal* 28:3 (2017), www.culturalsurvival.org.
[14] Johnson, 'Nuclear disaster', 152.

Marshalls were self-sustaining in terms of resources and local farming, harvesting, and fishing. Since the testing, the legacies of radioactive fallout, and 'bioaccumulation in the environment and human body', have directly contributed to cultural depredations, serious public health challenges, and social and economic stigma against entire communities and island nations.[15]

Nuclear testing began in 1946 and continued through 1958. Some 67 nuclear bombs were detonated in, on, and over the Marshall Islands with heaviest fallout in the Northern Atolls. Traditional landowners filed lawsuits in US courts for property and other damages and, with no final judgment in those cases, in 1988, the two nations agreed to terms in a Compact of Free Association that included a promise by the United States government to repair damages. A Marshall Islands Nuclear Claims Tribunal, intended to operate in perpetuity, brought in independent experts to evaluate the extent of damage and develop remediation recommendations. A 2012 United Nations Human Rights Council report framed the continuing challenges and consequences in terms of human rights violations – the loss of a healthy environment from nuclear contamination, a fundamental contravention of a culturally distinctive and viable Pacific Island way of life. The evidence was clear, from destroyed island homelands, deadly nuclear waste dumps, and chronic health impacts on local peoples. The United Nations Human Rights Commission weighed in directly, declaring the Marshall Islands had suffered from 'violations of humanitarian law resulting from the development, testing, and use of weapons of mass destruction'.[16]

This challenge for historical justice was not a simple matter of compensation and, once again, the impacts become clearer from a global ecological as well as a juridical perspective. Bodies like the Tribunal and the Commission deliberated thoughtfully but already faced internal and problematic questions based not only upon harm, but upon cultural frameworks. A notable example would be property claims in Enewetak and Bikini. The

---

[15] Johnston, 'Nuclear disaster', 152–3; B.C. Hacker, *Elements of Controversy: The Atomic Energy Commission and Radiation Safety in Nuclear Weapons Testing 1947–1974* (Berkeley: University of California Press, 1994).

[16] United Nations Human Rights Commission, A/HRC/21/48/Add.1); G.H. Alcalay, 'Utrik Atoll: the sociocultural impact of living in a radioactive environment. An anthropological assessment of the consequential damages from Bravo', 28 June 2002, 1–43; prepared for Utrik Atoll Local Government and the Office of the Public Advocate of the Nuclear Claims Tribunal, Majuro, Republic of the Marshall Islands; H.M. Barker, *Bravo for the Marshallese: Regaining Control in a Post-Nuclear, Post-Colonial World* (Belmont, CA: Wadsworth/Thomson Learning, 2004); Barker and Johnston, *Consequential Damages of Nuclear War*.

framework for settling claims was developed utilizing Western legal concepts of individual ownership and fair market value cash compensation. Yet, culturally and historically, land is not bought and sold in the Marshalls. Land and resources are held in a common rights system, with use rights inherited through female descendants, and access granted through family networks – to those who demonstrate social and environmental responsibility and stewardship.

More, the 'boundaries' of property claims were fixed not by surveyors, but by custom and practice. Contamination of terrestrial surfaces meant extended harm also to marine environments. Therefore, redress required accounting for both land- and seascapes, and features not always easily defined, including underwater reefs, seamounts, and ridges, and the places both in and around lagoons.[17] Likewise, physiological and biological damages to Rongelap and Marshallese people themselves were not limited to what medical personnel and researchers catalogued – radiation burns, cancers, abnormal blood counts, immune deficiency, loss of hair, and malformed infants. In addition, fear and cultural stigma marginalized entire communities. As Alimira Matayoshi expressed in a 2001 interview: 'People didn't want to shake our hands for fear we would contaminate them.'[18] Bias in education, courtship, and employment opportunities developed – and could persist across generations.

As such, major issues remain unaddressed even by legal and material efforts towards redress by failures to engage broader environmental, cultural, and human rights questions. Notably and consistently with the American colonial perspective, the USA framed questions of claims within a framework of continuing support, aid, and national strategic prerogatives, and rejected approaches fundamentally based on rights violations, focusing almost uniquely on soil remediation and belated medical treatments.

Even here, much of the work was framed around the importance of the testing for military reasons and the medical and data collection for scientific purposes. Both scientific as well as strategic and military rationales were also cited by the French government, which continued its own nuclear testing programme in Mururoa, Tahiti into the late twentieth century. The French programme is notable for its longevity, as well as the global anti-colonial sentiment it raised. France carried out 210 nuclear tests between 1960 and 1996; 193 were carried out in French Polynesia on the atolls of Mururoa

---

[17] B.R. Johnston, 'Atomic times in the Pacific', *Anthropology Now* 1:2 (2009), 1–9, at 5.
[18] Johnston, 'Atomic times in the Pacific', 5.

and Fangataufa in the Tuamotu Archipelago. In 2013, the French newspaper *Le Parisien* revealed the content of newly declassified French Ministry of Defence papers concerning the French atmospheric nuclear testing programme in French Polynesia in the 1960s and 1970s.

Of the 2,050 pages declassified, 114 remained redacted. The documents especially caused concern over the revelation that French authorities knew 'that plutonium fallout hit the whole of French Polynesia, a much broader area than France had previously admitted. Tahiti, [above,] the most populated island, was exposed to 500 times the maximum accepted levels of radiation' over a two-day period in July 1974 after a test explosion at Mururoa.[19] Around 150,000 military and civilian personnel were potentially exposed to nuclear fallout in this period, including 127,000 inhabitants of French Polynesia. At the time of *Le Parisien* article, only eleven had received compensation for nuclear exposure. Nuclear programme workers were given limited protection during testing, with a number reporting observing atmospheric detonations within fallout zones in the open in only shorts and T-shirts, without even eye protection.

Such exposures and hazards took place within a framework of unconcern dictated by hegemonic political, military – and economic – authority. Military veteran and then activist Pouvanaa a Oopa had joined the Pacific Batallion in World War I and supported Charles de Gaulle's Free French in World War II, yet when he agitated for social reform as a Tahitian nationalist in the postwar, he was arrested and exiled by the government. He sought expanded autonomy for Tahitians, becoming a major political figure. Eventually, he campaigned for independence and became president of the Territorial Assembly in 1972. The French government, however, continued to weaken local political authority, and anti-nuclear protests became a key issue involving the peace movement, trade union leaders, and politicians between Papeete and Paris. By 1984, the French state devolved some powers to Tahitian control, but not over foreign relations, immigration, or judicial, defence, or public services. Representative Oscar Temaru ridiculed the supposed concessions as the islands continuing to be seen as 'a rubbish bin where one can put anything one wants'.[20]

The issues were geostrategic, yet framed within what by that time had become French Polynesia's economic reliance on support from Paris.

---

[19] A. Chrisafis, 'French nuclear tests "showered vast area of Polynesia with radioactivity"', *Guardian* (4 July 2013), www.theguardian.com/world/2013/jul/03/french-nuclear-tests-polynesia-declassified.
[20] Firth and von Strokirch, 'A nuclear Pacific'.

Through the period of the Pacific War, the local economy had been reasonably stable and localized, dominated by copra, coffee, pearl shell, vanilla, and mining. Yet in a developing world-market trading system dominated by giant industrial economies, prices for local goods and manufactures declined. Mines were exhausted, agricultural crops were seasonally unreliable, and pearl shell was out-competed by plastics and synthetic substitutes. In 1963, de Gaulle announced a significant investment in French Polynesia, heavily based on establishing a Centre d'Expérimentation du Pacifique (CEP) to advance France's nuclear testing ambitions. This was a local economic benefit – with a price. At its peak four years later, the infrastructure development and support of the CEP was employing about 5,400 local workers and provided an economic basis for local jobs and continued government support – all dependent upon nuclear testing, and for as long as strategic and scientific interests dictated from Paris were the priority.[21]

The outcomes were reasonably predictable. With so much investment in building jobs around the nuclear infrastructure, other sectors lagged. Farming and fishing trades were depopulated in favour of government wages. Food self-sufficiency in the 1950s evolved into import dependence in the 1960s, and by the 1990s three-quarters of all food had to be brought in. The growth period of the 1960s and 1970s, abetted by French spending on public works and administration, belied the stagnation of local production and opportunities taking place. As the testing programmes were scaled back in the following decades, the territorial government was in debt, producing only one-quarter of its own revenues, the other 75 per cent issuing from France and almost half of that from military expenditures. The largely colonial framework remained.

The French Polynesian example is just one case. But a clear legacy there, and in much of the Nuclear Pacific, is the complex, conflicting, or mutually supportive and dependent interaction of multiple parties and actors, from policymakers to military personnel to workers, often local, hired to transport materials, build facilities, or support operations on the ground or at sea. Addressing such issues historically has required methodologies and voices not traditionally part of such accounts – which are generally dominated by scientific reports, military briefs, or governmental statements. Historian Nic Maclellan has focused on the hydrogen bomb test series, Operation Grapple, conducted by the British government between spring 1957 and autumn 1958

---

[21] Firth and von Strokirch, 'A nuclear Pacific'.

The Nuclear Pacific

around Malden and Christmas (Kirimati) Islands, to examine local complexities through oral histories.[22]

The Grapple tests were overseen by the British Army with the cooperation of both New Zealand and Fiji. The island test sites were part of the Gilbert Islands, to become the Republic of Kiribati in 1979. As with the American testing, both Islanders and service personnel reported harmful health consequences including birth defects, lingering illnesses, and unexpected early death – and were largely ignored or discounted. As with the testimonies of Lijon Eknilang in the Marshall Islands, Maclellan captures the voices and experiences of the British nuclear colonialism through interviews and statements, including stories 'beyond victimhood' and where both the resistances to and collusions with the testing took place. These include – familiarly – political figures, but also Fijian veterans, a continuing emphasis on women's voices as those who both suffer and demand recognition and redress, and key figures, like the Fijian High Chief Ratu Penaia Ganilau. Ratu Penaia's biographer notes:

> In 1957, forty Fijian naval ratings were invited by the Royal Navy to travel to Christmas Island to show the Navy 'how to live on a small Pacific Island' while atomic bomb tests were carried out. It was deemed appropriate that a Fijian chief should also be present on this momentous occasion in Pacific history, so Ratu Penaia was invited . . . Later [Commander Stan] Brown and Ratu Penaia were taken ashore to Malden Island to check the radioactivity. They were given rubber boots to protect their feet but the Navy couldn't find a pair large enough for Ratu Penaia's feet. So he went without. 'It was rather frightening as bushes were still smouldering', Brown comments.[23]

Such portraits frame the very localized complexities of the major geopolitical issues in that the chief remained deeply committed to British interests, which he aligned with his own, even through the development of autoimmune diseases, to the moment of his death from leukemia and sepsis. His family maintains that his cancer resulted from the fallout exposure, and have noted that swelling, skin diseases – like those suffered by veterans of the test sites – and inability to have children have afflicted Ratu Penaia's own sons who were born after the tests.[24]

---

[22] N. Maclellan, *Grappling with the Bomb: Britain's Pacific H-Bomb Tests* (Canberra: ANU Press, 2017).
[23] D. Tarte, 'Turaga: the life and times and chiefly authority of Ratu Sir Penaia Ganilau (GCMG, KCVO, KBE, DSO, KStJ, ED) in Fiji', *Fiji Times*, 1993; also collected in Maclellan, *Grappling with the Bomb*, 149–50.
[24] Firth and von Strokirch, 'A nuclear Pacific'.

Though the lines of cooperation, shared elite interest, or outright political and economic dependence continued to complicate the picture of the actors in the Nuclear Pacific, over decades the employment of Pacific Islands sites to test weapons of unprecedented destructive and contaminating power raised alarms across Oceania. The South Pacific Forum of island leaders took action by appealing for an end to the tests, and the governments of Australia and New Zealand became concerned about both radioactive and political fallout as urban middle-class and unionist agitation grew in their nations. Protests marked the 1970s and led to a proposal for a South Pacific Nuclear Free Zone in 1975, paralleled by a Niuklia Fri Pasifik in 1981 led by Islanders in Papua New Guinea and Vanuatu. Building on these, the People's Charter for a Nuclear Free and Independent Pacific in 1983 linked opposition to testing with sovereignty questions, and drew on broad-based support for clearly anti-colonial sentiments and activism.

These statements were backed by mass protests in Australia, New Zealand, the Philippines, Tahiti, and Hawai'i, and across the Pacific Islands. A treaty signed in Rarotonga in 1985 was a first step towards a formalized agreement, but it was only partially supported – and was declined by Vanuatu, the Solomon Islands, Tonga, Nauru, and Papua New Guinea. None of the nuclear powers – the United States, Great Britain, or France – supported the agreement at all, and the Marshall Islands, under American jurisdiction, were completely excluded from consideration.

Anti-nuclear tactics were not only diplomatic but directly activist. Individuals and groups sailed into test waters, challenging the Western powers, opposing visits of nuclear warships to local harbours, and rallying and protesting in national capitals. In 1985 a ship of the environmental Greenpeace organization, the *Rainbow Warrior*, harassed French testing efforts in Tahiti and was mined and sunk by French military saboteurs in Auckland harbour, an incident that attracted the attention of the world. Criticism of France mounted diplomatically, as well as in popular protests and economic boycotts that threatened French exports and business.

A South Pacific Nuclear Free Zone (SPNFZ) was declared in 1985 by island nations, with only Australia qualifying its support out of concern for its military alliance with the United States which used nuclear powered and nuclear armed vessels. SPNFZ bordered the South American nuclear free zone making it the largest contiguous nuclear free zone in the world covering well over half of the southern hemisphere.[25] Still, it was not until 1996 that the South Pacific Nuclear Free Zone was fully established, formalized by signatories that also included the American and European nuclear powers, and a United Nations Comprehensive Test Ban Treaty.[26]

Yet just as the formal diplomatic end of the Pacific War did not end the death and destructiveness of nuclear colonialism, the Test Ban Treaty did not mean the end of nuclear contamination and politics. As noted, between 1946 and 1958 the United States alone had tested sixty-six nuclear weapons on or near Bikini and Enewetak atolls, atomizing entire islands and, according to records declassified in 1994, blanketing the entire Marshallese nation with measurable levels of radioactive fallout from twenty of these tests – more than 7,000 Hiroshima bombs equivalent. The hydrogen bomb tests were especially destructive, generating intense fallout which included radioactive iodine, which concentrates in the thyroid and can cause cancer. It is estimated that 150 times more Iodine-131 was released into the atmosphere from Marshall Islands tests than the amount released by the Chernobyl nuclear disaster.

The data from Bikini Lagoon is the most detailed on the effect of nuclear testing on marine ecosystems, while a study of Amchitka neritic biota is also important as the only temperate sea site for nuclear fallout when a 5-megaton bomb was exploded underground there in 1971.[27] This bomb was 400 times more powerful than the Hiroshima bomb and registered as a magnitude 7 earthquake on seismographs. Surveys of marine ecosystems exposed to nuclear testing consistently reveal massive amounts of iodine, cesium, strontium, and other radioactive isotopes moved through the marine and terrestrial food chain and the human body, in well-documented ways, with degenerative and at times deadly outcomes. For example, dangerous radioactive material has been found throughout the food chain in terrestrial and marine environments, including lagoon sediments, coral reefs, and reef fish, of Marshall Islands atolls subject to nuclear testing.[28]

---

[25] Firth, *Nuclear Playground*, 128–31, 137–43.
[26] Overview, M.K. Matsuda, *Pacific Worlds: A History of Seas, Peoples, Cultures* (Cambridge: Cambridge University Press, 2012), 315–34.
[27] Perlman, 'Blast from the past'.
[28] Z.T. Richards et al., 'Bikini Atoll coral biodiversity resilience five decades after nuclear testing', *Marine Pollution Bulletin* 56 (2008), 503–15; M. Merlin and R. Gonzalez, 'Environmental impacts of nuclear testing in Remote Oceania', in J.R. McNeill and Corinna Unger (eds.), *Environmental Histories of the Cold War* (Cambridge: Cambridge University Press, 2010), 167–202; Johnston and Barker, *Consequential Damages of Nuclear War*; A. Smith and K.L. Jones, *Cultural Landscapes of the Pacific Islands* (Paris: ICOMOS (International Council on Monuments and Sites) Thematic Study, 2007).

In French Polynesia, nuclear contamination of atolls remains a serious issue, with tests of Mururoa subsoils in 1998 finding nuclear waste radioactivity at 371 times the safety threshold for French nuclear power plants. Cracking of base rock from underground testing on Mururoa has also raised the spectre of a possible collapse of part of the atoll which would spill radioactive rock into the surrounding sea. In addition, French authorities disposed of more than 3,200 tons of radioactive waste into deep ocean off Mururoa and Hao Island.[29]

Yet even the consequences of generations of contamination are challenging to assess – not for scientific but for geopolitical reasons. As was the case with American researchers reaching critical conclusions from working with Japanese atomic bombing survivors, research findings from nuclear testing were framed to adhere to official government narratives of strategic necessity and generous medical support for affected populations. Contradictory findings were censored and silenced. Johnston notes how the military-industrial biases were easily built into the research efforts themselves. For example, the 'assumption that radiogenic health effects must be demonstrated through direct causality (one isotope, one outcome) meant that science on cumulative and synergistic effects was not pursued'.[30] It was this unique pairing of scientific research and military imperatives that shaped the post-war Nuclear Pacific – and continues to do so through delimited criteria of what constitutes health threats or can be clearly traced to weapons testing contamination.

Public health risks to humans are largely suppressed, classified, or simply and persistently denied. Greenpeace testing of waters around the Amchitka blast site in the Aleutian Islands off Alaska (1965–71) found plutonium and americium. American officials concluded radioactive pollution must have come from fallout from Chinese nuclear weapons tests in the atmosphere and that the island blast crater had not been breached and leaked. However, the Federal agency in charge of environmental monitoring around test sites never monitored the waters off Amchitka, or tested coastal rocks, kelp beds, or marine animals for radiation. Decades later, construction workers who had helped build infrastructure for the Amchitka tests remember wearing typical rain gear while researchers wore full protective suits. Workers developed bone lesions, leukemia, and lymphatic disease. Some 'wondered why

---

[29] www.theguardian.com/world/2012/feb/07/france-polynesia-atolls-nuclear-tests.
[30] Johnston, 'Nuclear disaster', 151.

The Nuclear Pacific

government supervisors wore dosimeters while they were given no equipment or warnings. They talked about it among themselves but did nothing.'[31]

Environmental historians have an important opportunity and an as yet unfulfilled role to play in analysing this era. Most histories of the nuclear era in the Pacific have been either anthropological studies of communities displaced by nuclear testing or largely focused on the region-wide political machinations and implications of the nuclear Cold War. Smith has noted the unique but relatively unexplored landscapes of infrastructure and abandonment that resulted.[32] Detailed environmental histories are beginning to emerge for affected atolls, using the vast array of ethnographic data on marine and land tenure and subsistence prior to evacuation for testing, and scientific data on environmental degradation and recovery due to nuclear contamination, human resilience, and ecosystem tolerance and adaptation of nuclear fallout as Islanders now move towards recolonizing the atolls of their parents and grandparents. These islands are now also landscapes of harm and neglect, with a culture of fear and enduring sense of place for the dispossessed.[33]

In the face of such exploitation of entire communities and ecosystems by nuclear colonialism, local peoples continue to agitate for global justice, and also – as evidenced by activists in the Marshalls, French Polynesia, and the many coalitions leading to the Nuclear Free Pacific agreements – to control their own stories and narratives. In the first half of the twenty-first century, Marshallese Islander communities continue to rebuild their lives and livelihoods alongside localized practices and environmentally sustainable projects, such as commercial capacities with fish hatcheries and farming. This has led to greater expansion of both educational and scientific training for local people, as well as employment – all promising developments.[34]

The twenty-first century has also brought other challenges, not all of them related to Cold War geopolitics, but still framed by struggles over recognition, restoration, and redress along with rebuilding lives and communities. The reminders of what a Nuclear Pacific can mean in these cases are easily experienced through the reactor breach of the Fukushima Daiichi power plant in

---

[31] C. Wohlforth, 'Why a bomb test in the Aleutians still strikes fear in workers 46 years later', *Anchorage Daily News* (28 January 2017).

[32] Merlin and Gonzalez, 'Environmental impacts of nuclear testing in Remote Oceania'; Johnston and Barker, *Consequential Damages of Nuclear War*; Smith and Jones, *Cultural Landscapes of the Pacific Islands*.

[33] F.R. Fosberg, *Vegetation of Bikini Atoll, 1985*, Atoll Research Bulletin 315, National Museum of Natural History (Washington, DC: Smithsonian Institution, 1988); Richards et al., 'Bikini Atoll coral biodiversity resilience'.

[34] Johnston and Abraham, 'Environmental disaster and resilience'.

Japan, struck by an earthquake and tsunami in 2011. Sensors and power grid problems shut down the reactor's electricity supplies while waves flooding over the plant's seawall led to failure of circulating pumps to cool the reactor. The resulting hydrogen explosions released radioactive contamination into the atmosphere, resulting in a 20-kilometre-radius evacuation zone.

Though a case of contamination not from military testing, but rather from domestic power generation, the Fukushima crisis still laid bare questions of hegemonic political and economic power, expendable peoples, government opaqueness, environmental and health depredations, and cultural and personal marginalization of victims. As in French Polynesia, large capital and commercial interests came to dominate the economy of Japan in the 1950s along with, in this case, cheap American food imports. Farming towns and fishing villages faced tough conditions for their livelihoods and many villagers depopulated their local regions in search of work in construction and other large-scale investment projects. Some of these were displaced into a permanent workforce for the power plants. As Adam Broinowski reports, 'by the early 1980s, irregular workers came to compromise nearly 90 per cent of all nuclear workers'.

As in the test site islands, these vulnerable populations were not always properly informed of the consequences of exposure to radiation and nuclear debris. During maintenance protocols and crises, the workers are paid more – not having insurance deductions. 'Sworn to secrecy, after a superficial safety education drill, they are sent into highly contaminated, hot and wet labyrinthine areas', to do cleaning and deal with problem areas and materials. Health surveys of residents in the exposure areas after the Fukushima breach also determined, as in nuclear test fallout zones, that particular maladies increased. A Fukushima Health Management Survey estimated that, after the containment unit explosions, 'paediatric thyroid cancers were "several tens of times larger"' than would be otherwise estimated.[35]

Also as elsewhere, the social impacts of questioning official narratives about safety and information transparency were met with resistance. Bloggers like Nishiyama Chikako or Takenouchi Mari found their websites critical of official action shut down by hackers and their Internet accounts suspended, and became the subject of anonymous threats and insults; TV

---

[35] A. Broinowski, 'Informal labour, local citizens and the Tokyo Electric Fukushima Daiichi nuclear crisis: responses to neoliberal disaster management', in T. Morris-Suzuki and Eun Jeong Soh (eds.), *New Worlds from Below: Informal Life Politics and Grassroots Action in Twenty-First-Century Northeast Asia* (Canberra: ANU Press, 2017), 131–66, at 135–6, 147.

The Nuclear Pacific

journalist Iwaji Masaki filed investigative stories and died under mysterious circumstances by a reported suicide; politicians and writers who published stories were cut off from news outlets and editors for 'spreading rumours'; demonstrators were charged by police for trespassing violations; citizens' claims for loss and redress against the power plant management – especially recognition of wrong – were brought to court but then dismissed; small business owners like Yokota Asami and her family 'found themselves the victims of bullying when they called attention to radiation dangers'. Yokota's son was told by his principal he had failed the high school entrance exam, whereas an examination of his actual paper showed he had easily passed. As in other irradiated communities around the Pacific, social stigmas developed, and doctors attending patients facing paediatric thyroid issues issued advice not to speak of the cancer, 'to enhance their employment or marriage prospects'.[36]

As research and reporting of the disaster spread widely, differing conclusions spread conflicting information. In May 2012 a World Health Organization report concluded that Fukushima radiation emissions posed minimal health risk. However, the United States National Academy of Sciences demonstrated that by late 2011 cesium-134 and cesium-137 from Fukushima was present in Pacific blue fin tuna taken off San Diego. Surveys of marine ecosystems exposed to nuclear testing consistently reveal that massive amounts of iodine, cesium, strontium, and other radioactive isotopes moved through the marine and terrestrial food chain and the human body. Public health risks to humans – in a familiar narrative – were often suppressed, classified, attributed to other causes than nuclear contamination, or persistently denied.

For too long, 'science' and strategic imperatives decided from centres of political and economic authority have meant the imposition of external regimes upon subjects of study, and victims of war, negligence, and disaster, whose struggles continue biologically, environmentally, socially, and culturally. This persistence means that nuclear colonialism is not a history that exists only in a defined period. Impacts that damage health and environment are not overcome, but expand over time and can be passed on to future generations. Political remedies based on addressing economic liability are inseparable from historical justice and restoration of cultures and livelihoods. Otherwise, they continue to ignore the true legacies of the Nuclear Pacific.

---

[36] Broinowski, 'Informal labour, local citizens', 157.

57

Shrinking the Pacific since 1945

Containerships, Jets, and Internet

PETER J. RIMMER AND HOWARD W. DICK

Over recent decades the global economy has tilted from a trans-Atlantic Euro-American economy towards an Asia-Pacific one, a shift encapsulated by the term Pacific Century. Nine Group of Twenty (G20) nations – Australia, Canada China, Indonesia, Japan, Mexico, Russia, South Korea, and the USA – are contiguous with the Pacific Rim. Yet despite common use of the adjectives Pacific, trans-Pacific, and Asia-Pacific, the boundaries and structure of this notional economy are still vague. This chapter maps the articulation of a Pacific economy since 1945 through geologistics as a two-stage process, first reformation and densification of pre-war networks until the end of the 1960s, then transformation through the new technologies of container shipping, jet aircraft, and the Internet. It becomes apparent that this transformation had had much greater impact upon adjacent continental economies than upon the vast coastal and almost hollow archipelagic region that may be denoted as Pacifica.

So rapid has been the pace of change, especially in East Asia, and so dramatic its results, as seen most noticeably in the rise of China, that the narrative of transformation almost overwhelms history. Yet the seven decades of increasing trans-Pacific integration since the end of the Pacific War are no new phenomenon but a sequel to rapid changes since the mid-nineteenth century. US annexation of California in 1846 and the subsequent gold rush, Britain's imposition of the treaty port system upon China in the early 1840s, the American-led opening of Japan to foreign trade in the 1850s, and the US purchase of Alaska from the Russian Empire in 1867 marked the beginnings of a new trans-oceanic order. As European colonialism encroached upon the Asia-Pacific from the west, American colonialism

Assistance is appreciated from: Jennings Bae; Jeremy Chow, OAG Aviation Worldwide Limited; Kay Dancey and Jenny Sheehan, CartoGIS Service, ANU College of Asia and the Pacific; Stephen Kentwell; Christopher Kissling; Markus Krisetya, TeleGeography; Kevin O'Connor; Rachel Rimmer; the National Library of Australia; and the Korea Maritime Institute Library.

634

Shrinking the Pacific since 1945

encroached upon Hawai'i, the Philippines, and sundry Pacific islands from the east. These imperial conquests were facilitated by the new technologies of steamships, railways, undersea cables, and telegraphic communication. Steamships reduced trans-Pacific voyages from months to weeks while telegraphs cut communication time from months by sea to a matter of hours. Railways linked gateway ports to the interior. Those changes also assisted the rise of imperial Japan, culminating in its conquest of all the western Pacific except for Australia and New Zealand by early 1942.

At 1945, however, there is a marked discontinuity, the end, or at least the beginning of the end, of the imperial era. Japan's cities were in ruins, its infrastructure wrecked, its economy collapsing, and its people starving. In China and Korea the situation was not much better. Southeast Asia had suffered three-and-a-half years of increasingly autarkic Japanese occupation and would be beset by further violence and turmoil in a long and painful process of decolonization. No engine of growth was apparent and the paradigm of underdevelopment would soon be invoked to explain vicious cycles of stagnation in East Asia, as also in the Pacific Islands, Mexico, and Central and South America. As late as the 1970s, this paradigm still prevailed, even though the high-speed growth of Japan and then Taiwan and South Korea along the same path was already enlivening Northeast Asia.

The early post-1945 narrative is therefore one less of transformation than of partial reformation. The revival of the Asian Rim of the Pacific began in the 1950s with the US-backed recovery and expansion of the Japanese economy, then still reliant on pre-war technologies of transport and communications. The watershed dates to around 1970 when the new technologies of container shipping and wide-bodied jet aircraft triggered a new phase of transformation. Both dramatically reduced the unit cost of freight by sea and air and gave rise to a global relocation of manufacturing from Europe and North America to East Asia. The first economies to benefit were South Korea, Taiwan, Hong Kong, and Singapore, then the new 'tiger' economies of Indonesia, Malaysia, the Philippines, and Thailand. China was held back by its internal politics and lack of infrastructure until the 1990s but thereafter reaped all the advantages of being a late starter.

Contemporary Pacific transport and communications networks are therefore now in marked contrast with those on the eve of World War II. Pre-war networks were organized on imperial principles. Subsidized mail and passenger steamship lines connected the imperial centres of Britain, France, the Netherlands, USA, and Japan with their dominions and colonies and, in turn, on a much smaller scale, from their respective gateway ports even to remote

635

Table 57.1 *Moving goods, people, and information.*

Item	Dimensions	Characteristics
Goods	Commodity classification	Movement slower
		Requires handling
People	Business	Transfers between modes
	Personal	self-motivated
		Movement requires
		preparation – not instant
Information/	Produced (flow)	Changing mode alters mass
Capital	Economic (demand)	Virtually instant
	Social (interaction)	Easily transformed
	Institutional (exchange)	

districts and islands. This well-articulated system, complemented by overland and undersea cables, pulsed to the monthly or fortnightly tempo of the steamship mails; colonial cities and towns throbbed to the faster beat of the daily newspaper with the latest cable news. In the twenty-first century not only have air transport and Internet communications increased the tempo to daily international traffic and almost instantaneous global news flashes but the network itself has transcended old imperial structures and their successor nations. The new underlying logic is not so much geopolitical as geo-economic and is best described by the term, 'geologistics', originally coined by the US military in the identification, storage, and movement of resources.[1]

Geologistics is used here in a broader sense to encompass all flows within the Pacific economy. These are represented as occurring within spatial networks comprising hubs and spokes that correspond to the modes for moving goods, people, and information. Attention is focused on three networks: containers for the movement of commodities, jet air transport for the transfer of people, and telecommunications for the transmission of information. Each mode has its own dimensions and characteristics (Table 57.1). Together they constitute a 'network of networks'.

This chapter begins with a brief review of the last phase of conventional sea and air transport from the early post-war years to about 1969. The second part charts the introduction of the new technologies of container shipping, jet aircraft, and the Internet and shows how they have re-articulated trans-Pacific networks. The final part goes behind these narratives to propose how a

[1] H.A. Sachaklian, 'Geopolitics versus geologistics', *Air University Quarterly Review* 1 (1947), 53–63.

notional Pacific economy can be disaggregated and reconstructed to distinguish more sharply its continental, coastal, and archipelagic parts, each with its own characteristics, potentials, and challenges.

Reformation: The Early Post-war Years, 1945–1969

Pacific shipping and communications networks were restored within about two years from the end of the Pacific War in August 1945. In the case of shipping, American and European lines were able to draw upon surplus war-built tonnage to replace war losses and resume normal frequencies for cargo-passenger lines within the familiar framework of liner conferences (cartels). The obvious difference from the pre-war situation was the absence of Japanese-flag shipping. Allied submarine warfare had almost completely destroyed the ocean-going Japanese merchant fleet and those ships that did survive were restricted to coastal and shortsea trades under the Shipping Control Authority for the Japanese Merchant Marine (SCAJAP).[2] Japan did not regain sovereignty and commercial autonomy until the peace treaty came into effect in April 1952. As the Japanese economy got into its stride during the 1950s, Japanese shipping companies rebuilt their fleets with new and faster ships and re-entered their former liner trades.

Three other changes marked the early post-war period. One was the marginalization of the China trade. Until the outbreak of the Sino-Japanese War in mid-1937, Shanghai had been the great Northeast Asian entrepôt. Trans-Pacific liner services were restored from 1946 but shut down again after the Communist capture of Shanghai in May 1949. The new People's Republic allowed limited access from August 1949 but normalization was hampered by US trade sanctions and the US-backed Nationalist blockade of the Taiwan Straits, even after the end of the Korean War in 1953. In response, China's more modest foreign trade was reorientated from the North Pacific to Communist-bloc countries, while the once sleepy British colony of Hong Kong became the prime entrepôt for trade with Western nations.

The second change was the rapid decolonization of Southeast Asia: Indonesia (1945–9), the Philippines (1946), Burma (1947), Indo-China (1954), Malaya/Malaysia (1957–63), and Singapore (1963–5). Independence was accompanied by political instability, sporadic warfare, and economic stagnation. Foreign trade and the demand for shipping therefore lagged,

---

[2] S. Kizu, *Nihon Yūsen Senpaku 100-nenshi (A 100 Years' History of the Ships of Nippon Yusen Kaisha)* (Tokyo: Kaijinsha, 1984).

notwithstanding America's insatiable demand for rubber to supply its booming automobile and aviation industries, and Japan's increasing demand for Indonesian oil. Despite Indonesia's blockade from 1963 to 1966, Singapore retained its role as their Southeast Asian entrepôt, a node in round-the-world freight lines and a terminus for trans-Pacific lines. However, prosperity would come only after lifting of the blockade in 1966 and the formation of the Association of Southeast Asian Nations (ASEAN) in the following year. Once political stability was assured, the newly independent city-state of Singapore was able to begin investing in state-of-the-art sea- and airports and to encourage supporting financial and managerial services. The benefits would flow in the 1970s.[3]

The third notable change was the marginalization of deep-sea passenger shipping as air travel became both faster and cheaper. In hindsight, the apogee of trans-Pacific liner shipping had been around 1930. During the 1920s American, Canadian, British, and Japanese lines had all commissioned luxurious passenger liners of around 20,000 gross tons and capable of about 20 knots in speed. Most of these became troopships during World War II and many were sunk. Only one of the survivors was refitted for trans-Pacific service and then lasted just five years. In 1947 subsidized American President Lines commissioned two smaller 15,000-ton liners for the California–Japan–HK–Manila route. Impressive superliners were mooted, but when large public subsidies were not forthcoming, they came to nothing.[4] During the 1950s Japan's OSK reintroduced several emigrant ships to its Brazil/Argentina line via Honolulu and the Panama Canal, but Japan's NYK concentrated upon cargo liners and Canadian-Pacific withdrew from the North Pacific. From 1956 Matson's provided monthly passenger sailings between San Francisco and Sydney via Pacific Island ports with two converted freighters, but, despite a crew of 286, *Mariposa* and *Monterey* each carried only 365 passengers, equivalent to twelve per day, much less than an aeroplane. The line was sustainable only because of freight and US subsidies.

Trans-Pacific passenger shipping became uneconomic not only because of high crew costs and port congestion but also because time was becoming more highly valued. By the mid-1930s it was possible by Cunard Line's 28.5-knot *Queen Mary* to cross the Atlantic from Southampton to New York in just four days. In the Pacific in the mid-1950s four days at sea would still be no

---

[3] W.G. Huff, *The Economic Growth of Singapore* (Cambridge, Cambridge University Press, 1984).
[4] D. Williams and R.P. De Kerbrech, *Damned by Destiny*, 1st edn (Brighton: Terado Books, 1982).

Shrinking the Pacific since 1945

further than San Francisco to Honolulu. The voyage from San Francisco to Tokyo by one of the 20-knot American 'President' liners took ten days, from San Francisco to Sydney by 20-knot Matson liner three weeks. Such long voyages would become popular as cruises for well-off American tourists but were impractical for business travellers or government officials.

The aerial conquest of distance in the Pacific began in November 1935 with the first trans-Pacific flight from San Francisco to Manila by Pan Am flying boat.[5] With four refuelling stops and mostly daytime flying, it took six days. In mid-1940 Pan Am also introduced a route through to Auckland via Honolulu and Pago Pago by Boeing-314 flying boat with connection through to Sydney. According to a 1941 survey by Sydney Smith of Lockheed Aircraft Corporation, an international air network linked most colonies in the Pacific (Figure 57.1).[6] British, French, and Dutch airlines operated scheduled flights between Europe and their Asian colonies, and at their farthest extent inter-meshed with Chinese, Japanese, and Soviet airline services. In the western hemisphere Pan Am linked with Mexican and Canadian domestic services to forge an unbroken line of air connections from the Arctic Circle as far as Singapore, Auckland, and Santiago.

Most commercial airline flights were suspended during the Pacific War, but the Allied powers recognized the need to cooperate in the reconstruction of war-torn China and the opening up of the more remote areas in Indonesia, Malaysia, and the Pacific Islands. *The International Air Transport Agreement 1944*, signed in Chicago, adopted a bilateral rather than a multilateral approach, which allowed each contracting state to determine with the other contracting party the airlines that would be granted landing rights to fly a particular route, the capacity of each airline, and the access of third-country airlines. As former colonies gained independence, this IATA agreement gave them powerful leverage and encouraged the formation of many new national airlines. Nevertheless, Pacific air networks developed around a small number of prominent hubs, notably Bangkok, Hong Kong, Los Angeles, Manila, San Francisco, Singapore, Sydney, and Tokyo.[7]

Wartime improvements in aircraft technology and airfield construction rendered trans-oceanic seaplanes all but obsolete. The most readily available

[5] Pan Am Clipper Flying Boats, 'Pan Am across the Pacific', no date, accessed 14 December 2018.
[6] S.B. Smith, *Air Transport in the Pacific Area* (New York: International Institute of Pacific Relations, 1942).
[7] K. O'Connor and A. Scott, 'Airline services and metropolitan areas in the Asia-Pacific region 1970–1990', *Review of Urban and Regional Development Studies* 4:2 (2007), 240–53.

639

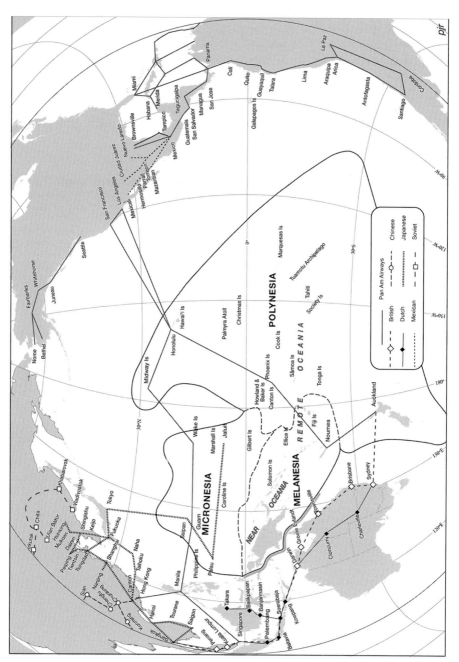

Figure 57.1 Principal international airlines in the Pacific, June 1941.

aircraft was the ex-military DC-4 Skymaster, with long-haul capacity for around forty passengers.[8] In 1946 Pan Am began flying them from San Francisco to Auckland for transfer on to Sydney, while British Commonwealth Pacific Airways (BCPA) flew via Auckland, Fiji, Canton Island, and Honolulu to San Francisco and Vancouver. By 1949 Qantas was flying DC-4s to Hong Kong and Japan as well as flying boats to Fiji. During the 1950s, larger propeller-driven aircraft with longer range were introduced to international service such as the DC-7 and Lockheed Super Constellation, which Northwest Orient operated between Seattle and Tokyo and Qantas from 1954 on the former BCPA route. Recently established Japan Airlines (JAL) commenced trans-Pacific flights from Tokyo to San Francisco via Wake Island and Honolulu in 1954. Thus, even before the jet era began in 1960, a trans-Pacific air passenger network had already been established. The routes were slow and island-hopping, with only modest frequency, but the flights were regular and much safer than pre-war. This network sufficed for the limited passenger traffic of the 1950s, saved weeks on the sea voyage, and speeded the conveyance of mails from weeks to a few days. What awaited the jet age was high-capacity aircraft capable of non-stop trans-Pacific flights that were quicker and less expensive than sea transport.

Transformation: post-1970

Container Shipping

Trans-Pacific liner shipping networks remained fairly stable until the late 1960s. Despite some mergers and new entrants, the principals remained much the same and there was only a marginal increase in the size and speed of new ships. The most notable change in the 1960s was the increasing differentiation between liner and bulk shipping. Hitherto 'bulk' shipments had tended to be by older and slower vessels, often war-built tonnage, and were fairly standard at around 10,000 tons per shipment with much of that cargo still carried in bagged form. The 1960s saw purpose-built bulk carriers of increasing size, often without cargo gear and having wide hatches and clear holds suitable for loose loading and grab discharge. Such ships would serve the voracious demands of the Japanese iron and steel industry for coal and iron ore and new 10-million-tonne mills would be built with deep-water access to accommodate them. South Korea would do likewise. These mills would source

---

[8] 'Douglas DC-4', *Airliners*, www.airliners.net/aircraft-data/douglas-dc-4/189.

from Australia and from as far away as Brazil with giant 'Cape-size' ships that by the mid-1970s could load more than 100,000 tonnes of iron ore or coal.

Economies of scale were much more difficult to achieve in break-bulk liner shipping. Main ports employed thousands of dock workers in the piece-by-piece loading, stowing, and discharge of the diverse shapes, weights, and sizes of the general cargo that made up thousands of lines on a ship's manifest. These items were subject to delays, pilfering, damage, and leakages, especially in transfer between sea and land transport. Stacking bags or sacks on forklift pallets was an early, practical form of unitization but port bottlenecks persisted. Cargo liners could take four to five months to complete one roundtrip between the west coast of America and Australia. Archipelagoes were highly exposed to the consequent high freight rates and poor services.[9]

In 1956 Malcolm McLean's Sea-Land organization demonstrated the feasibility of putting general cargo into steel boxes and shipping them by converted tanker along the US Atlantic coast. In 1958 Matson Navigation Company sought to break the bottleneck of slow cargo handling in west coast US ports by carrying 24-foot containers on deck from San Francisco to Honolulu.[10] It then began converting freighters to carry containers in cell guides in the hold. In 1961 America President Lines (APL) introduced two new trans-Pacific ships with cell guides for containers in one hold and a self-handling crane.[11] By 1966, when containerization was adopted by consortia in the trans-Atlantic trade, 22 per cent of APL's cargo volume was already being shipped in containers. Japanese lines struggled to find consensus on the way ahead because Japanese ports were relatively efficient. However, by 1967 when Matson introduced a truly containerized services from San Francisco to Yokohama, the Japanese lines had also committed to containerization. NYK's *Hakone Maru* entered trans-Pacific service in August 1968. In US ports containerized operations allowed 40-foot containers of 20–25 tons to be handled in 2.5 minutes instead of using 18–20 man-hours when handled as break bulk.[12] In 1968 a fast 40-hour

---

[9] A.D. Couper, 'The island trade: an analysis of the environment and operation of seaborne trade among three island groups in the Pacific', PhD thesis, Australian National University, Canberra, 1967; H.C. Brookfield with D. Hart, *Melanesia: A Geographical Interpretation of an Island World* (London: Methuen, 1971); P.J. Rimmer, *Freight Forwarding in the Australia–Papua New Guinea Trade*, New Guinea Research Bulletin 48 (Canberra: New Guinea Research Unit, Australian National University, 1972).
[10] F.A. Stindt, *Matson's Century of Ships* (Modesto, CA: privately published, 1982).
[11] MDS, 'Industry leaders discuss containerization in Japan', *Maritime Day Supplement*, 20 July 1966 (Tokyo: Shipping and Trade News).
[12] J.J. Goldberg, 'Containerization as a force for change on the waterfront', *Monthly Labor Review* 91:1 (1968), 8–13.

Shrinking the Pacific since 1945

rail service was initiated between Los Angeles and Chicago so that packed containers could be transferred smoothly between ship and rail.

In 1970 the International Organization for Standardization (ISO) designated a container standard of 8 feet wide, 8 feet high and 10, 20, 30, or 40 feet long. Henceforth the capacity of container vessels would be measured in terms of 20-foot equivalent units (TEUs). There was also a rapid increase in scale. On the Atlantic early containerships were around 1,000 TEUs, from 1969 on the Europe–Australia route, then 1,200 TEUs, and from 1972 on the Europe–Asia route 2,000 TEUs. Singapore and Hong Kong entered the container era at this highest scale while Yokohama, Kobe, and Busan moved up to this size. Taiwan sought to develop Kaohsiung as a trans-shipment port between Southeast Asia and the USA. The rest of the region was served by small feeders from these hubs. Other adaptations during the 1970s included multipurpose and roll-on/roll off (ro-ro) ships deemed more flexible for some trades, notably from Australia to the US west coast, Northeast Asia, and Southeast Asia. Small multipurpose ships proved well suited to the small, diverse trade of the Pacific Islands and had less need of expensive port facilities. Worldwide in 1980 cellular container ships accounted for 52 per cent of container carrying capacity, multipurpose ships 31.5 per cent, and ro-ro 12 per cent.

During the 1970s, container movements within the Pacific were dominated by bilateral trade between North America and Japan (Table 57.2). Nevertheless, containerization diffused quite rapidly to other Pacific nations. The benefit was not so much reduced ocean shipping rates, which actually increased because of escalating fuel prices, but reduced door-to-door transit time and also insurance and inventory costs through more efficient intermodal transportation.[13] By 1983 another twenty-six Pacific countries had adopted containerization.[14] Nevertheless, the increasing size of container vessels meant that ports with draught restrictions or modest volumes of cargo were bypassed and had to rely on feeder services from an adjacent 'hub' port. Some island nations, especially the more remote, thereby struggled to maintain their traditional agricultural exports and had to look more to fishing and the mineral resources of their Exclusive Economic Zones (EEZ).[15]

[13] D. Hummels, 'Transportation costs and international trade in the second era of globalization', *Journal of Economic Perspectives* 21:3 (2007), 131–54.
[14] D.N. Bernhofen, Z. El Sahli, and R. Kneller, 'Estimating the effects of the container revolution on international trade', *Journal of International Economics* 98:C (2016), 36–50.
[15] R.G. Ward, 'Earth's empty quarter? The Pacific Islands in a Pacific Century', *Geographical Journal* 155 (1989), 235–46.

Table 57.2 *Throughput of the Pacific's major container port ranges, 1975, 1990, and 2010.*

Port range	1975 Mn TEUs	1990 Mn TEUs	2010 Mn TEUs
Japan	1.90	8.00	17.73
West Coast North America	1.72	7.70	19.83
China and Hong Kong	0.80	6.30	148.80
Australia	0.75	1.64	6.65
Taiwan	0.47	5.45	12.50
Southeast Asia (ASEAN)	0.29	9.94	69.91
Southwest Pacific	0.07	0.59	2.34
South Korea	0	2.35	18.95
West Coast Central and South America	0	1.25	27.33
Sub-total	6.00	43.22	324.04
World total	17.00	85.60	503.51
Percentage	35.3	50.5	64.4

Containerisation International Yearbook (London: National Magazine Co., 1967–2012).

By 1990 container flows had grown rapidly from ports within ASEAN, notably in Malaysia, Indonesia, the Philippines, and Thailand (Table 57.2). Reliable door-to-door container logistics allowed hitherto vertically integrated manufacturing corporations in industries such as garments, footwear, motor vehicles, and electronics to unbundle their production system and relocate the making of parts and their assembly to lower-cost countries around the Pacific Rim and create global supply chains.[16]

By 1995 trans-Pacific and trans-Suez container traffic had surpassed the trans-Atlantic (Table 57.3). The gap further widened as East Asia unleashed its economic potential on course to become the global centre of manufacturing. By 2015 two-way traffic was 24 million and 22 million TEUs respectively compared with only 7 million for the North Atlantic.

Within East Asia the dynamic effects of containerization were much smaller than in North America or Australasia because rail had little part in a poorly connected intermodal transport system and roads were heavily congested. This has not prevented China moving ahead of the USA as the world's leading generator of container traffic since the mid-1990s (Table 57.4).

[16] R. Baldwin, *Global Supply Chains: Why They Emerged, Why They Matter and Where They Are Going*, Working Paper FG-2012-1 (Hong Kong: Fung Global Institute, 2012).

Table 57.3 *Containerized trade on major east–west trade routes 1995, 2005 and 2015 (millions 20-foot equivalent units)*

	Trans-Pacific		Trans-Suez		Trans-Atlantic	
	East Asia– North America	North America– East Asia	East Asia– Europe	Europe– East Asia	North America– Europe	Europe– North America
	m TEUs	m TEUs	m TEUs	m TEUs	m TEUs	m TEUs
1995	4.0	3.5	2.4	2.0	1.7	1.7
2005	11.9	4.5	9.3	4.4	2.0	3.7
2015	16.8	7.2	14.9	6.8	2.7	4.1

UNCTAD, *Review of Maritime Transport: Report by the UNCTAD Secretariat* (New York: United Nations, 1997–2016).

Table 57.4 *Top-three countries in the world container port traffic league at five-yearly intervals, 1995–2010*

1995		2000		2005		2010	
Country	Mn TEUs	Country	Mn TEUs	Country	Mn TEUs	Country	MnTEUs
USA	19.5	China	35.5	China	88.5	China	148.8
China	17.1	USA	27.3	USA	38.5	USA	35.6
Singapore	10.8	Singapore	17.1	Singapore	23.1	Singapore	29.18

Note: China includes Hong Kong. Figures for countries are no longer published. *Containerisation International,* 1997, 2002, 2005, 2012.

In the mid-1990s mainland China still lacked the port facilities and rail and road infrastructure to cope with the rapid increase in container trade. Hong Kong was able to take advantage of this situation and supersede Singapore as the world's leading container port. As China invested heavily in building its own deep-sea container ports, Hong Kong's potential traffic growth drained away and Singapore was able to re-establish its position in the mid-2000s. By 2015 the construction of Yangshan deep-water port from 2004 onwards had enabled Shanghai to supplant Singapore as the world's leading container port while Hong Kong had slipped to fifth position (Table 57.5).

In 2015 no fewer than twenty-one of the world's top-100 container ports were in mainland China (Figure 57.2). Another nine of the fifty-two container ports within the Pacific were located in Southeast Asia: five in Japan and

Table 57.5 *World's top-five container ports, 1995, 2005, and 2015*

Rank	1995		2005		2015	
	Port	Mn TEUs	Port	Mn TEUs	Port	Mn TEUs
1	Hong Kong	12.55	Singapore	23.16	Shanghai	36.54
2	Singapore	10.80	Hong Kong	22.43	Singapore	30.92
3	Kaohsiung	5.23	Shanghai	18.08	Shenzhen	24.20
4	Rotterdam	4.79	Shenzhen	16.20	Ningbo-Zhoushan	20.60
5	Busan	4.50	Busan	11.84	Hong Kong	20.11

Containerisation International, 1997, 2007. Lloyd's List, 'The top 100 ports in 2015' (London: Lloyd's List, 2016).

three each in Korea and Taiwan. There were only five on the west coast of North America, four on the west coast of Central and South America, and two in Australia. None was in the Russian Far East. Although by now China's coastal regions are regarded as mature container markets, other opportunities have emerged within the Pacific, notably in Vietnam and west coast South America.

Analysis of the top global container terminal operators underpinning this port pattern, led by China's Cosco Shipping, Hong Kong's Hutchison Ports, and fourth-ranking Singapore's PSA International, showed that they had pre-packaged their expertise and exported it around the Pacific.[17] These operators are now facing challenges from the deployment of ever-larger container ships. The size of container ships has increased remarkably. In 1972 the maximum size was 2,000 TEUs, by 2006 it was over 10,000 TEUs, and by 2017 it had exceeded 20,000 TEUs. Such giant ships are too large to transit the widened Panama Canal and few ports in the Pacific are deep enough to allow them to berth.

The need to fill these larger ships has required the top-25 container liner operators going between Europe, Asia, and North America to form alliances and share vessels (Table 57.6). Twelve of the top-25 global liner operators, which collectively controlled over 40 per cent of the group's total capacity, are based in East Asia, including China's fourth-ranking COSCO and Taiwan's fifth-ranking Evergreen.[18] Along with their leading European-based counterparts – Maersk, MSC, and CMA CGM – these East Asian companies

[17] Drewry, *Global Container Terminal Operators: Annual Review and Forecast: Annual Report 2017* (London: Drewry Maritime Research, 2017).
[18] D. Morgan, *The Top 25 Container Liner Operators Trading Profiles: November 2014* (Alkmaar: Dynamar B.V., 2014).

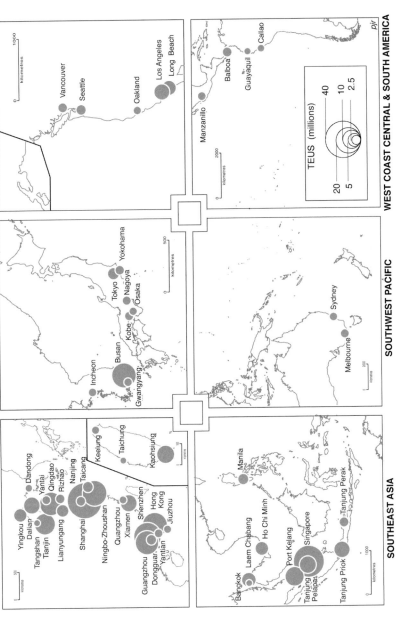

Figure 57.2 Container ports with the world's top-100 located in the Pacific, 2015. Lloyd's List, 'The top 100 ports in 2015' (London: Lloyd's List, 2016).

Table 57.6 *Main and feeder services offered by the top-twenty-five container liner operators between East Asia and other trade zones, 2014.*

East–west axis (main)		North–south axis (feeder)	
East Asia–North America west coast	68	East Asia–West Coast Central and South America	26
East Asia–North America east Coast	46	East Asia–Australia/New Zealand	5
East Asia–North Europe	48	East Asia–Middle East/Indian Subcontinent	87
East Asia–Mediterranean	37	East Asia–Africa	33

D. Morgan, *The Top 25 Container Liner Operators Trading Profiles: November 2014* (Alkmaar: Dynamar B.V., 2014).

must provide connecting feeder services to move containers to and from their hub ports, including from ports south of the equator in Indonesia, Australasia, and South America. As yet, no southern Pacific route can sustain ships of even 10,000 TEU and the usual size is much smaller, with alliances of the leading containership operators providing what is now a quite dense web of intersecting lines and loops ('strings of ports') that with adequate frequency connect the main ports of even small island nations back to Asia, North America, and Europe.

The shipping container has therefore been instrumental in shrinking the Pacific and increasing the size of its trans-oceanic economy. Nevertheless, in terms of port-to-port speed, containerships are little faster or even a bit slower than the best trans-Pacific passenger liners of the 1930s. To economize on fuel costs and emissions, a service speed of around 20 knots is still about the norm. Multi-port voyage time, however, is greatly reduced by much quicker port turnaround, so the timeliness, cost, and security of the door-to-door shipment of their cargo boxes is very much faster.

Jets

Jet aircraft had the potential to carry 50 per cent more passengers at twice the speed than propeller-driven aircraft such as the Lockheed L1049 Super Constellation (Table 57.7). The first civil aviation jet was Britain's de Havilland Comet which entered commercial service in 1952, but several fatal crashes led to Pan Am, Japan Airlines, and Qantas turning to the American manufacturers Boeing and Macdonald Douglass to provide jet aircraft for their trans-Pacific routes and around-the-world services. In 1959 the

Table 57.7 *Aircraft operated by Qantas Empire Airways Ltd and Qantas Airways Ltd on the Australia–North America route, 1954–2008.*

Aircraft	First commercial service	Speed (km/hr)	Maximum range at full payload (km)	Seating capacity
Lockheed L1049 Super Constellation	1954	511	5,920	78
Boeing 707-138B	1959	897	6,820	120
Boeing 747-238B	1972	907	9,045	385
Boeing 747SP-38	1984	1,004	10,800	400
Boeing 747-438	1989	1,004	13,490	416
Airbus A380	2008	950	14,186	501

Note: Cruising speeds, range, and seats vary according to source.
Annual Report and Financial Accounts (Sydney: Qantas Empire Airways Ltd, 1956–66); *Annual Report* (Sydney: Qantas Airways Ltd, 1967–2006); P.J. Rimmer, 'Australia through the prism of Qantas: distance makes a comeback', *Otemon Journal of Australian Studies* 31 (2005), 135–57.

introduction of the Boeing 707 by Qantas – a year later than Pan Am – reduced flying time between Sydney and San Francisco from 27.30 hours to 16.10 hours, though still with stopovers in Honolulu and Fiji. Introduction of the 707 made jet aircraft unambiguously better than passenger ships in both time and cost and brought selected Pacific cities much closer to each other. Tokyo's Narita Airport (1978) developed as the dominant trans-Pacific airport hub, because it was within range of the USA for the first generation of transcontinental jets and was supported by a strong local market.

Since the introduction by Qantas of Boeing 707s there has been no significant improvement in speed of flight, but subsequent wide-bodied aircraft with a longer flying range, more fuel-efficient engines, and larger passenger capacity have dramatically reduced unit costs and fares. The 385-seat Boeing 747s could carry as many passengers as a medium-size liner with a much smaller crew and thereby opened air travel to a mass market of tours and excursions. By 1984 the Boeing 747 Special Performance (SP) aircraft commenced non-stop operations between Sydney and Los Angeles with a flying time of 16 hours. Then in 1989 the longer range B747–400, commissioned by both Qantas and many Asian carriers, was dubbed 'the Pacific Airliner' because it drew a wider range of airports on the Pacific Rim closer to each other and the rest of the world. Nevertheless Tokyo Narita remained dominant because US airlines enjoyed generous landing rights to access third countries in Asia.[19] Since 2008 the larger Airbus-A380 has reduced the slower westbound flying time between Los Angeles and Sydney to just over 15 hours. In Asia, these larger, long-distance aircraft led to the commissioning and rapid expansion of new 'super-hub' airports: Singapore Changi (1981), Kansai (1994), Hong Kong Lantau (1998), Shanghai Pudong (1999), and Seoul-Incheon (2001).

Regulatory changes accelerated these technological trends. The US Civil Aeronautics Board allowed direct international flights to route through inland hubs such as Chicago, Denver, and Atlanta. Its demise in 1978 ended the restrictive practices among US airlines to maintain high fares, low frequencies, and high-load factors. Canada, Australia, and New Zealand then also gradually deregulated their airspace with new opportunities for Asian airlines and budget carriers. In consequence, the inflation-adjusted price of air transport began to decline, and halved between 1995 and 2015.[20]

Cheaper airfares saw the emergence of international holiday destinations. Hawai'i had long been a popular choice for American tourists. After April 1964, when Japan began to issue its citizens with passports for holiday travel, Japanese tourists also chose to go there as well as to Guam and Saipan. South Korea (ROK) followed suit in 1971. New Zealand, Fiji, and Tahiti ceased to be stopovers on flights between Australia and the USA but became holiday destinations in their own right, while Bali emerged as a prime destination for tourists from both Australia and Asia. To reduce their dependence upon foreign airlines, promote tourism, provide employment, and earn foreign currency, Pacific Islands nations started up their own airlines, either singly or jointly, often with unanticipated budget distortions from aircraft financing.[21] Nevertheless, interconnectivity between the main island groups was still inadequate and outer islands were usually poorly served.

Between 1995 and 2015 the number of non-stop unique city-pair connections between airports within the Pacific had more than doubled, not least from cities within China. Since 2010 when air traffic growth resumed after the Global Financial Crisis, it has been led by China, which rebounded to the benefit of increased international traffic through Hong Kong and, to a lesser

---

[19] M. Hansen and A. Kanafani, 'Airline hubbing and airport economics in the Pacific market', Transportation Research Part A, 24:3 (1990), 217–30.

[20] IATA, WATS 2016 – World Air Transport Statistics (Montreal: International Air Transport Association, 2016).

[21] C.C. Kissling, 'Networks enabling air transport services in the South Pacific: 40 years of change', in D.T. Duvall (ed.), Air Transport in the Asia Pacific (New York: Routledge, 2016), 33–51.

extent, Shanghai. By 2015, data on top passenger airport pairs for international and regional traffic within the Pacific showed that the busiest movements were within Asia. Hong Kong served as the main Asian hub together with Singapore and Tokyo and these flows incorporated the holiday resorts of Guam and Honolulu. Such was the intensity of traffic between Asian airports that neither Beijing nor Manila featured among the top-10 city-pairs in Asia. The second busiest traffic flows were between an array of airports in Northeast Asia that were concentrated on Los Angeles in North America. The third-busiest set of passenger movements focused on reciprocal connections between Singapore and Bali (Denpasar) in Southeast Asia and a range of airports in Australia; there was also an assortment of trans-Tasman flows between Australia and New Zealand. The lightest bi-directional traffic was from Los Angeles and Vancouver in North America and the Southwest Pacific. Apart from strong connection between Los Angeles and Mexico City on the west coast of Central America, the only link of significance was the isolated one between Lima and Santiago due to the dominance of stronger links in South America with east coast North America airports (Figure 57.3).

Since 2015 an array of airports in China have been connected with airports on the west coast of the USA. There are now direct flights from Changsha, Chengdu, Fuzhou, Guangzhou, Kunming, Nanjing, Wuhan, and Xi'an to either Los Angles or San Francisco, but COVID-19 has affected their frequency.[22] Tokyo Narita has become much less of a hub, a trend compounded by the introduction of extended long-range aircraft that can fly more than 13,000 kilometres and 15 hours.[23] The new Boeing B787–900 series with a range of 14,140 kilometres now flies direct on the 13,580-kilometre route from Singapore to San Francisco westbound in 16.20 hours by United Airlines. Other city-pair connections now extend beyond Pacific Rim airports, such as the 16,700-kilometre non-stop link by the Airbus A-380-900 ULR (ultra-long-range) flown by Singapore Airlines between Singapore and New York in 19 hours. The South Pacific and the Atlantic have been bridged.

Internet

The watershed in information technology (IT) came much later than in shipping and air transport. Until the mid-1990s telecommunications systems were still

[22] OAG, *The Future of Transpacific-Services – United's Longest Route Gives a Taste of Things to Come* (Luton: OAG Aviation Worldwide Ltd, 2016).
[23] G. Baxter and N.S. Bardell, 'Can the renewed interest in ultra-long-range passenger flights be satisfied by the current generation of civil aircraft?', *Aviation* 21:2 (2017), 42–54.

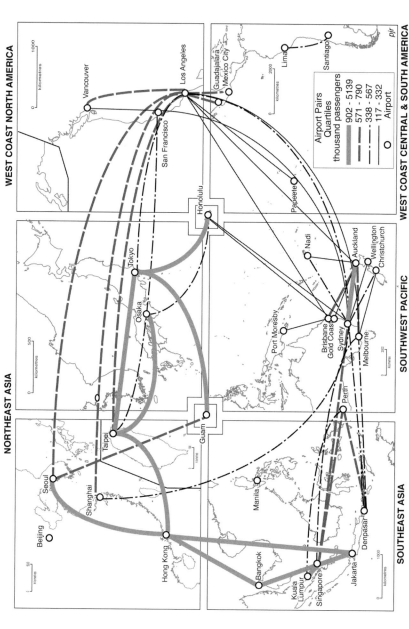

Figure 57.3 Top passenger airport pairs in international traffic, 2015, based on designated route areas: Asia–North America, Asia–Southwest Pacific, Latin America/Caribbean–North America, North America–Southwest Pacific, and within Asia, Latin America, and Southwest Pacific. *WATS* 2016, 69–71.

Shrinking the Pacific since 1945

characterized by undersea cables, satellites, state monopolies and regulation, the International Telecommunication Union (ITU), television, and teleconferencing.[24] Users were still reliant upon fixed-voice communications systems wired to homes and offices: people travelled but their telephones remained stationary. Within the Pacific most telephones were installed in the USA, Japan, Australia, and Canada.[25] Connectivity throughout the Pacific was rudimentary.

International direct dialling had been introduced by the 1950s but trans-oceanic calls were far from routine. Even the largest trans-Pacific cable could handle only a few thousand calls simultaneously at a price that exceeded $3 per minute.[26] For business firms, telex and fax became cheaper substitutes. A handful of international communication satellites were added, including in 1967 Intelstat II to cover the Pacific Ocean, but in island nations reception was often poor and intermittent. Eventually market deregulation, liberalization, and privatization opened national markets to competition, restructured telecommunications operators, and accelerated growth in the number of telephone subscribers.

Reviews of the Pacific telecommunications sector in the mid-1990s, however, made little reference to the Internet; its revolutionary potential remained undetected.[27] Since then the Internet has so transformed international long-distance communications that not only has the network for data transmission been more profitable than the international movement of freight and passengers but also the operations of container shipping and air transport have become dependent upon its increased speed, volume, and density. Although the Arpanet had been a means of exchanging data between military establishments and universities since 1971, the advent of the World Wide Web (1989) reincarnated it as the Internet for worldwide interactive information exchange. Then it became a disruptive force in telecommunications by replacing telephony by Voice-over-the-Internet (VoIP) and its offspring Skype. The Pacific telecommunications market became much more dynamic through competition, rapid expansion of international fibre-optic bandwidth, and broadband and, in response to ever-cheaper Internet access, the recruitment of billions of users of personalized mobile (wireless) services.[28]

---

[24] Y. Kwon and J. Kwon, 'An overview of *Telecommunications Policy*'s 40–year research history: text and bibliographic analyses', *Telecommunications Policy* 41 (2017), 878–90.
[25] *ITU Historical Statistics (1849–1967)* (Geneva: International Telecommunication Union, 2018).
[26] G. Staple, 'Mapping tomorrow: 25 years of *TeleGeography*', *Medium.com* (23 November 2014).
[27] E. Noam, S. Komatsuzaki, and D.A. Conn (eds.), *Telecommunications in the Pacific Basin: An Evolutionary Approach* (Oxford: Oxford University Press, 1994); J. Ure, *Telecommunication in Asia: Policy, Planning and Development* (Hong Kong: Hong Kong University Press, 1995).
[28] A.A. Huurdeman, *The Worldwide History of Telecommunications* (New York: Wiley, 2003).

653

By the new millennium, data centre hubs around the edge of the Pacific and their spokes provided the transmission links to the global Internet network. Since then the Internet has become the largest consumer of the region's international submarine cable capacity that carries 99 per cent of all trans-oceanic data traffic.[29] As early narrowband Internet services migrated to broadband, East Asian economies, notably South Korea, Taiwan, and China, became prominent in both fixed and mobile broadband Internet services and also in cell phone services. The next generation of undersea cables increased capacity by another order of magnitude and reduced the cost per minute of simultaneous international phone calls to almost zero.[30] Consumers in more remote parts of the Pacific have enjoyed some benefit from this trend but, as reflected in Papua New Guinea's low 15 per cent Internet penetration in 2021, the overall growth of telecommunications has been mainly in mobile cellular subscriptions.[31] Internet penetration has generated innovation in financial services in Hong Kong and Singapore, encouraged the outsourcing of phone calls to the Philippines, and boosted the migration of highly skilled professionals around the region. The Internet has also allowed some of the more agile telecommunications companies from the monopoly era such as AT&T in the USA to take on a new lease on life as international carriers.

Notwithstanding that much Internet traffic originates in Asia, the bulk of information movements are still routed, by the cheapest path, through the world's telecommunications backbone in the USA, reflecting the trans-Atlantic's greater share of trade in services than Eurasia and the Pacific. Most trans-Pacific traffic from Los Angeles and San Francisco passes through the hubs of Hong Kong, Singapore, Sydney, and Tokyo. Traffic from west coast Latin America is a notable exception because, apart from the connection between Los Angeles and Mexico City, most traffic on the west coast of Latin America involves linkages with centres outside the Pacific, especially Miami.[32] Elsewhere a newer and less US-centric World Wide Web has been created by the spread of ever-cheaper Internet bandwidth capacity within

---

[29] N. Starosielski, *The Undersea Network (Sign, Storage, Transmission)* (Durham, NC: Duke University Press, 2015).

[30] C.M. Risotto, B. Wellenius, A. Lewin, and C.R. Gomez, *Competition in International Voice Communications*, World Bank Working Paper 42 (Washington, DC: The World Bank, 2004).

[31] M.I. Franklin, *Postcolonial Politics, the Internet and Everyday Life: Pacific Traversals Online* (New York: Routledge, 2004); R.J. Foster and H.A. Horst (eds.), *The Moral Economy of Mobile Phones: Pacific Islands Perspectives* (Canberra: ANU Press, 2018); ITU, 'Percentage of individuals using the Internet' (Geneva: International Telecommunication Union, 2018).

[32] T. Stronge, 'The future of submarine networks in South America', 2012, www.slideshare .net/CienaCorp/the-future-of-submarine-networks-in-latin-america.

Asia and the rest of the Pacific. Most new international bandwidth within the Pacific is now being located within Asia, where most usage occurs.

In 2015 this transition away from the USA could be seen in capacity usage within the Pacific as measured by minutes of telecommunication traffic (MiTT) over common bandwidth (Figure 57.4). China recorded the largest outgoing traffic, with 59 per cent connecting to Hong Kong, Macau, and Taiwan, 26 per cent with other Asian economies, and 11 per cent with the USA. Nevertheless, the USA along with Hong Kong, Singapore, Australia, and Canada were net generators of traffic within the Pacific. China along with the Philippines, Indonesia, Thailand, and Vietnam had net inflows. Reflecting the diaspora of over 7 million overseas Filipinos, the Philippines had the greatest net inflow, suggesting that the pattern of flows reflects human as much as economic geography.[33]

The Internet has also changed the ranks of international carriers in the Pacific. During the mid-1990s the largest carriers were based in the USA and Japan. These carriers, typified by Japan's NTT Cable, were also owners of the Pacific's main undersea cables. The ranking of these carriers has been surpassed by new companies such as India's Tata Communications and has, in turn, been challenged by new voice and messaging applications such as Skype (Microsoft) and WhatsApp (Facebook) that run over the top of existing telecommunications services.

International content providers such as Facebook and Google have themselves invested in cable construction and their share of the growth is outpacing the rate of additions to the Internet bandwidth in the Pacific. Google, for example, has joined consortia constructing a submarine cable between Southeast Asia and Japan, and both the 'Unity' and 'Faster' cables between Japan and the USA that have strengthened intra-Asian and trans-Pacific bandwidth respectively. As reflected in the weighted median lease price of 10Gbps wavelength MRC (month recurring charge), there are still marked geographical variations with the Pacific: the Los Angeles–Sydney price of US\$ 29,000 in 2017 was four times greater than the US\$ 7,190 between Singapore and Tokyo and US\$ 7,087 between Los Angeles and Tokyo.[34]

---

[33] Commission on Filipinos Overseas [CFO], *Global Mapping of Filipinos Overseas* (Manila: CFO, 2019).
[34] P. Brodsky, 'Global enterprise networks and submarine cable capacity: coverage, pricing and traffic trends', *TeleGeography* (2017), www2.telegeography.com/hubfs/2017/wan-summit/Presentations/WSS/SubCables.pdf?t=1509031204960.

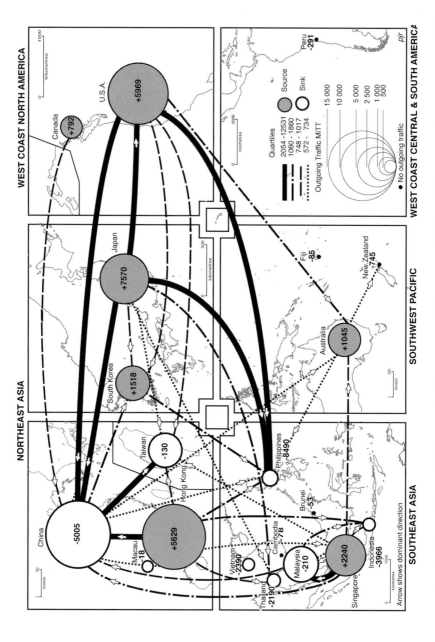

Figure 57.4 Outgoing flows and strength of connections between countries in terms of Millions of Telecommunications Minutes (MiTT), 2015.

Internet exchanges have emerged to accommodate the need for strong peer-to-peer relationships involving shared information between carriers in response to dispersed Cloud-based and storage services across borders and the rapid rise in the consumption of Internet television and data services. As measured by the co-location floor space among carriers in 2017, the primary hubs for carriers linking content and applications within the Pacific were Tokyo, Seoul, Hong Kong, Los Angeles, Singapore, San Francisco, Sydney, Seattle, Shanghai, and Beijing.[35] These centres have attracted Cloud providers with global profiles such as Amazon Web Service, Global Facebook, and Microsoft, but also regional providers in China's Alibaba and Tencent (the parent company of WeChat).[36]

Network of Networks

The Internet foreshadowed a Pan-Pacific society in which all things would be interconnected (the Internet of Things) without need for older forms of integration (Figure 57.5). Total displacement, however, is not to be expected. The outcome is a network of networks in which container shipping, jet aircraft, and the Internet constitute three complementary networks with similar traffic patterns across all three modes. The common features are intense intra-Asian activity; a strong bridge between Asia and west coast North America; durable links between the west coasts of North America and Central and South America; strengthening connections between the Southwest Pacific and Asia; and the absence of any representation in the Russian Far East.

These trends have reinforced the importance of strategic gateways within the Pacific favoured by power, connectivity, population, and business climate. From the Pacific representatives among the top-100 container ports,[37] the top airport-hubs distinguished by Airbus,[38] and the top Internet hubs identified by TeleGeography,[39] ten gateways stand out by their presence across all three modes: Los Angeles, San Francisco, and Seattle on the west

---

[35] Brodsky, 'Global enterprise networks and submarine cable capacity'.
[36] 'TeleGeography analyst Jonathan Hjembo shares insights on Internet development trends in Asia', China Cache (2 May 2018), https://en.chinacache.com/telegeography-analyst-jonathan-hjembo-shares-insights-internet-development-trends-asia/.
[37] Lloyd's List, 2016.
[38] Airbus, Global Market Forecast 2018–2037: Global Networks Global Citizens (Leiden: Airbus Group, 2018).
[39] TeleGeography: Global Internet Map, 2018 (Washington, DC: PriMetrica Inc., 2018).

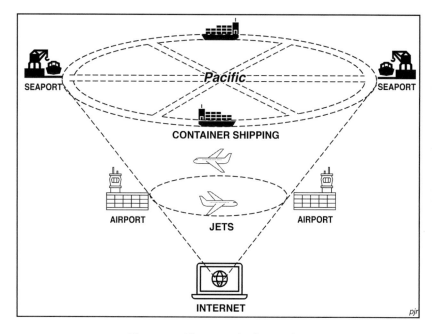

Figure 57.5 The network of networks.

coast of North America; Hong Kong, Seoul, Shanghai, Singapore, Taipei, and Tokyo in East Asia; and Sydney in the southwest Pacific (Figure 57.6). A second group of sub-gateways have presence in two modes: an airport-Internet hub combination comprising the inland centres of Beijing and Kuala Lumpur in Asia, and Lima and Santiago in South America whose container ports of Callao and Valparaiso did not make the top-100; and airport-container port combinations typified by Bangkok, Guangzhou, Ho Chi Minh City, Jakarta, Manila, Osaka, Melbourne, Panama, and Vancouver that do not rank as major Internet hubs. Finally, there is a third group of eight specialist airport cities that include national or state capitals, and tourist destinations such as Bali, Honolulu, and Phuket, and twenty-nine specialist container ports of which sixteen are based in mainland China and two in Taiwan. Within China, clustering has given rise to three gateway regions – Bohai Rim, Lower Yangtze, and the Pearl River Delta – linked by land-based corridors that may be seen as counterparts to the corridors linking gateway regions on west coast North America centred on the Pacific Northwest and southern California. These gateway regions are pivotal to comprehending geologistics within the Pacific.

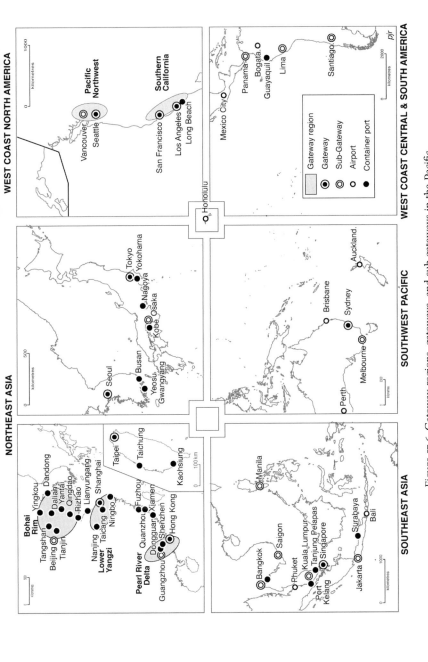

Figure 57.6 Gateway regions, gateways, and sub-gateways in the Pacific.

Table 57.8 *Time taken to traverse the Pacific by mode, 1900–30 and 2015.*

Item	1900–30	2015
Goods	Months	Weeks
Person/person	Weeks	Hours
Information/ capital	Hours	Milliseconds/minutes

Continents, Coasts and Archipelagoes

The perception of a shrinking Pacific is valid but the process has by no means been uniform. The extent of shrinkage differs by orders of magnitude according to mode (Table 57.8). Containerization has cut weeks from the door-to-door transit time for goods but, except in the case of airfreight, it still takes weeks. Until the 1930s travellers took weeks even by fast mail steamer on trans-Pacific voyages. Propeller-driven aircraft reduced this to days and jets to a matter of hours. Until airmail became feasible in the 1930s, mails took weeks to cross the Pacific by sea, though cable traffic took no longer than hours from sender to receiver. Modern information technology allows massive amounts of data to be transmitted point-to-point across the Pacific within minutes or milliseconds. This mode has annihilated distance and time.

Because of the nexus between trade volume and economies of scale, shrinkage has also been uneven across space. The greatest shrinkage can be seen across the narrow neck of the North Pacific, a route that in the 1850s scarcely existed yet is now the world's leading trade route in terms of value and frequency in all three modes. The southern hemisphere has no equivalent sub-Antarctic link and neither Australia nor the west coast of South America sustains a north–south link of comparable scale. Terms such as 'Pacific Century' therefore conflate too much of the vast Pacific into a single proposition.

A conceptual geologistics map of the Pacific that does not foreground nation-states and does not scale by distance may better reveal the impact over recent decades of advances in shipping, aviation, and IT (Figure 57.7). The fundamental Mackinder-like distinction is between contiguous land-based economies or continents, and fragmented economies or archipelagoes.[40] In the latter half of the nineteenth century North America (USA and Canada) began to emerge as a continental economy when it was

---

[40] H.J. Mackinder, 'The geographical pivot of history', *Geographical Journal* 2:4 (1904), 421–44.

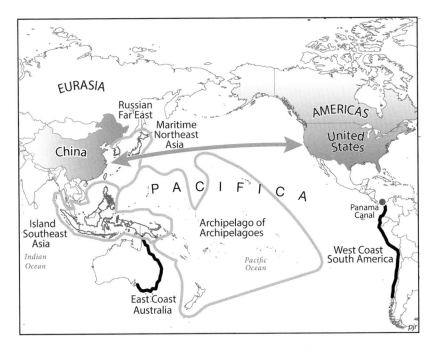

Figure 57.7 Geologistics map of the Pacific.

connected coast to coast by trans-continental railways, thereby obviating the almost 25,000-kilometre steamship voyage from New York to San Francisco via Cape Horn and opening west coast gateways to Asia and Australasia. On the other side of the Pacific, Japan was quick to integrate its small island economy by rail and from the 1960s by high-speed rail. After decades of extra-territoriality, warfare, and political turmoil, China was much slower to integrate as a land-based economy but since the 1990s has done so with remarkable speed and may now also be regarded as a continental economy. Yet despite the century-old rail connection between Moscow and Vladivostok, Russia's remote Far East is still a backward dependency rather than an economic entity is its own right.

Most of the rest of the Pacific, including Japan and South Korea, may be reclassified as either coasts or archipelagoes. Geographically Australia is a continent but Australia's cities struggle along a narrow east/southeast coast corridor. Its slow-speed railway system connects south–north with only one east–west rail link. The long coastline of South America to the west of the Andes range from Punta Arenas to the Panama Canal is not yet joined by a continuous coastal highway, while illegal migration into the USA from its southern G-20 neighbour Mexico became a divisive political issue in the USA after the election of President Trump in 2016.

Island Southeast Asia – the Philippines and Indonesia – merges into the peninsulas and as yet a poorly articulated mainland as one vast archipelago. The islands constellations of the Pacific from northernmost Hawai'i, Guam, and Saipan southwards through Micronesia, Melanesia, and Polynesia to New Zealand constitute a more obvious set of archipelagoes.

Such conceptual reconfiguration of the Pacific allows a sharper focus upon the region's underlying geopolitics. Historically, except for whalers, traders, and missionaries, America has remained orientated towards its origins on the other side of the Atlantic. In the twentieth century America fought two world wars in western Europe and each time brokered the peace. The European Union was formed under benign US protection mediated though NATO. In the twenty-first century a more confident China has begun to look west to build land-bridges with Europe and the southeast to link by rail and road into mainland Southeast Asia and Pakistan with beachheads to the India Ocean.[41] Russia has accommodated President Xi Jinping's Belt and Road Initiative and, like the rest of Europe, stands to benefit from a more integrated Eurasia. Southeast Asian nations and Australia are more ambivalent, but realize they have no better economic destiny. The USA, along with India, is opposed. Although the continental economies of China and North America are joined at the neck by flows of goods, people, information, and money/debt that in principle are regulated by a rules-based international order, the reality is more complex.

For all its economic importance the North Pacific has become a geopolitical contest between two continental powers with seemingly incompatible aspirations and predilections. China no longer accepts US hegemony under a nominally benign open-door policy backed by a military presence. Conversely the USA, and perhaps Canada, perceive no direct benefit from the Belt and Road Initiative and feel threatened by trade deficits and Chinese IT systems and protocols. Japan and South Korea are looking both ways, investing in some of China's Belt and Road projects while continuing to host the US defence shield. The technological advances over recent decades and the consequent shift in economic activity and population, especially rural–urban population migration, have opened new opportunities and raised

---

[41] P.J. Rimmer, 'China's Belt and Road Initiative: underlying economic and international relations dimensions', *Asian Pacific Economic Literature* 32:2 (2018), 3–26.

living standards for many hundreds of millions of people, while arguably foreclosing upon other opportunities. North America has experienced rapid structural change but without much growth in welfare for the lower and middle classes. The future peace and prosperity of the Pacific will depend upon how new opportunities and old resentments are negotiated between China and the USA.

The Pacific economy is therefore an awkward aggregation. It includes too much of China, North America, and Russia beyond their seaboards. America's Pacific economy is really California, the Pacific Northwest (Cascadia and British Columbia), Alaska, and Hawai'i. China's Pacific seaboard includes the Bohai Rim, the Yangtze Basin flowing through to Shanghai, and the Pearl River Delta. The Chinese economy is therefore more weighted to the Pacific than those of the USA or Canada or Russia. The vast Russian Far East has a population of only 6 million and is barely 5 per cent of the Russian economy.[42]

Overweighting the size of the Pacific economy has the unfortunate effect of downgrading the relative importance of the rest of the region. If the continental economies are separated out, what remains is a substantial Pacific archipelagic/coastal economy, including Japan, Korea, Taiwan, Southeast Asia, Australia, New Zealand, Chile, and Peru, that may be denoted as Pacifica. Whereas the technological advances of containerization, jet aircraft, and IT have wrought a total logistics revolution in the continental economies, there has been only a partial revolution in Pacifica. The Internet has annihilated time and distance, jet aircraft have collapsed time, but goods movement is still time-consuming and expensive beyond island gateways. Japan is the only island economy in which goods movement has moderated distance by means of very expensive bridges and tunnels. Elsewhere sophisticated information technology and air travel have raised aspirations, but slow and costly inter-island logistics continue to be stubborn obstacles to raising common welfare. Without continental economies of scale, island peripheries across the Pacific face an as yet intractable challenge of development that decades of foreign aid and loans, migration and remittances have failed to overcome. Logistics have reconfigured Pacifica's vast oceanic space of scattered archipelagoes and its rim of coastlines, cities, and hinterlands but its political institutions are still rudimentary.

---

[42] J. Min and B. Kang, 'Promoting new growth: "Advanced Special Economic Zones" in the Russian Far East', in H. Blakkisrud and E.W. Rowe (eds.), *Russia's Turn to the East: Domestic Policy-Making and Regional Cooperation* (Cham: Palgrave Pivot, 2018), 51–74.

58

China and the Pacific since 1949

FEI SHENG AND PAUL D'ARCY

This chapter outlines the evolution of the People's Republic of China's (China) interactions with the Pacific Ocean since its formation in 1949. China inherited a long history of engagement with Pacific oceanic environments and other nations that inhabit its shores. After briefly outlining the post-war legacy of these interactions through maritime trade, fishing, diplomacy, and migration, the chapter details the history of China in the Pacific since 1949. It is a story of two distinct eras. Until 1978, China focused inwards to repair and restructure a nation torn apart by war, disunity, and neglect of the majority of the population. Its Pacific interactions focused largely on defending its sovereign waters and harvesting its coastal fishery, while its diplomatic stance further afield espoused solidarity for the decolonization and sovereignty of fellow developing nations. From 1978, China increasingly focused on economic reform, involving greater engagement with the overseas economy as it rapidly rose to become a global powerhouse of manufacturing. Two engagements with the Pacific are explored for this period. The first is China's engagement with the Pacific Ocean as an environmental space, and especially a fishery and sea lane resource. The second is the expansion of China's diplomatic and strategic engagement with the wider Pacific community from the 1970s. The final section looks at present and future engagements with Pacific Island nations in particular, as the nations that are under the most immediate threat of climate change damage. China has competitive advantages in skills and technologies vital to its Pacific allies and a long history of productive partnerships with them.

Introduction: The Post-1949 Political and Economic Transformation of China

It took almost twenty years to repair war damage across East Asia. This rebuilding involved modernizing industry to innovate and experiment in a

664

nurturing domestic setting before becoming globally competitive exporters. Japan sustained greater infrastructure destruction than South Korea and Taiwan during World War II, largely due to aerial bombardment. Broadly similar reconstruction processes occurred in the post-war economies of Japan, South Korea, and Taiwan. Building momentum in the 1950s, their surging economies took off in the 1960s and 1970s as so-called Asian (Little) Dragons (Hong Kong, Singapore, Taiwan, and South Korea) economies. A second group of Asia-Pacific economies known as the Asian (Little) Tigers followed and were boosted by the freeing up of global capital from the 1970s to relocate industry in their more competitive labour markets as wages grew in response to the economic success of the original Asian Dragon economies. These economies were all in Southeast Asia, such as Thailand, Malaysia, the Philippines, and Indonesia. They continue to grow today as international regulations and conditions promote private sector mobility in pursuit of cost savings on labour, taxation, infrastructure, and resource access. The People's Republic of China (PRC) has been the exception, rising recently to become the second largest economy in the world after the United States through strong state control of its economic modernization under the policy of reform and opening up by Deng Xiaoping from 1978. The rise of East Asia since World War II led to the centre of global trade and commerce moving from the Atlantic world to the Pacific world.

Although propelled by Utopian social engineering projects, food security in the face of widespread famines and public health measures to counter epidemics like plague for China's predominantly rural population occupied the attention of the state in the first decades of the PRC's history. This was gradually supplemented by rapid industrialization utilizing China's vast coal resources, especially in the era of Mao Zedong's successor, Deng Xiaoping, from the late 1970s. Environmental conservation was not a key consideration in these initial years, apart from attention paid to rectifying water shortages and soil erosion in pursuit of food security.[1] Similarly, the inshore fishery remained healthy and productive in this period and was not considered in need of government attention.

The 1972 United Nations Conference on the Human Environment in Stockholm signalled a crucial watershed in the Chinese government's environmental thinking. China sent a large delegation to showcase its considerable

---

[1] M. Bao, 'Environmentalism and environmental movements in China since 1949', in J.R. McNeill and E. Stewart Mauldin (eds.), *A Companion to Global Environmental History* (Chichester: Wiley-Blackwell, 2012), 474–92, at 474–9).

successes in improving water and soil management and to use this international forum to articulate its stand against United States aggression and exploitation of the Third World. The conference also exposed Chinese delegates to the fact that pollution was a widespread side effect of all modernization and industrialization and not solely a feature of capitalism. This did not lead to a more environmentally conscious campaign of modernization under Deng, as China industrialized in only thirty years in a process that had taken Europe 200 years.[2] By the first decade of the twenty-first century, however, surveys showed that both policymakers and members of the public believed pollution posed a serious threat to China's environmental and government policies and development plans began to include more measures to restrict pollution.[3] Another response has been to expand China's resource base through trade partnerships since 1978. This has led to the expansion of China's Pacific interactions and interests to almost every corner of this vast oceanic area.

China's Long Pacific Maritime Engagement

Chinese civilization, especially that of coastal southeast China, has a long and deep engagement with its coastal oceans and the seas beyond. Preceding chapters by Hsiao-chun Hung, Kent Deng, Ronald Po, Daria Dahpon Ho, and Xing Hang (Chapters 17, 23, 24, 29 and 30 respectively) demonstrate the extensive and profound engagement Chinese peoples have had with the sea from the first maritime colonization of the Pacific Ocean from southern China to the Austronesian diaspora throughout the Pacific Islands, to the extensive trade networks between China, island Southeast Asia, and the Indian Ocean in the early modern era, which continued beyond the establishment of European empires in the region from the 1500s.[4] The South Pacific remained largely unexplored and was rarely crossed by Chinese vessels until the post-World War II period discussed in this chapter. Most Chinese fishing, trading, and transport vessels kept to China's sovereign waters in the Yellow Sea, East China Sea, and South China Sea, or travelled south and west

---

[2] Bao, 'Environmentalism and environmental movements', 479–81.
[3] J.Y. Liu, 'Status of marine biodiversity of the China Seas', *PLoS ONE* 8:1 (2013), e50719, 79–80.
[4] R.J. Antony, *Like Froth Floating on the Sea: The World of Pirates and Seafarers in Late Imperial China* (Berkeley, CA: Institute of East Asian Studies, 2003). For general histories of maritime China see G. Deng, *Chinese Maritime Activities and Socioeconomic Development, ca. 2100 BCE–1900 CE* (Westport, CT: Greenwood, 1997), and *Maritime Sector, Institutions, and Sea Power of Premodern China* (Westport, CT: Greenwood, 1999). For the voyages of Zheng He see Deng, Chapter 23 in this collection.

beyond these waters for trade.[5] When China endeavoured to become a modern industrial nation in the 1980s, there was a strong sense that China is a civilization distinguished not simply by loess culture, but also by a marine tradition. This transition soon heightened the importance of sea transport to import raw materials and export manufactured products around the globe, including across the Pacific to North America and beyond via the Panama Canal. At the same time, China's rising prosperity increased demand for seafood to the point China now has the largest fishing fleet in the world.

Southeast China's maritime trade links with Southeast Asia resulted in a large Chinese diaspora in this region. A smaller number of coastal peoples predominantly from the southern Fujian province also moved into the Pacific Islands, Australia, and New Zealand, seeking trade goods and commercial opportunities. Gold was also a motive for Cantonese arriving in Australia and New Zealand in the second half of the nineteenth century. Professor Wang Gungwu distinguishes three categories of overseas Chinese: *huashang*, traders who went abroad in search of commercial opportunities; *huagong*, overseas labourers from the late nineteenth century; and *huaqiao*, sojourners who established communities in the early twentieth century but remained connected to the motherland and included both *huashang* and *huagong*. A new phenomenon has emerged since 1980, that of the *huayi* who no longer hold Chinese nationality. This category consists of Chinese who are globally mobile in pursuit of economic success.[6]

Ethnic Chinese are now the largest non-Western population in Australia and New Zealand.[7] They are the third-largest non-Indigenous group in the

[5] The most comprehensive review of the evidence for Chinese trans-Pacific voyaging is J. Needham and G.-D.Lu, *Trans-Pacific Echoes and Resonances: Listening Once Again* (Singapore: World Scientific Publishing, 1985). See also C.-m. Hsieh, 'Geographical exploration by the Chinese', in H. Friis (ed.), *The Pacific Basin: A History of Its Geographical Exploration* (New York: Geographical Society, 1967), 87–95.

[6] G. Wang, 'The study of Chinese identities in Southeast Asia', in J.W. Cushman and G. Wang (eds.), *Changing Identities of the Southeast Asian Chinese since World War II* (Hong Kong: Hong Kong University Press, 1988), 1–21, at 11–16; B. Willmott, 'The overseas Chinese experience in the Pacific', in T. Wesley-Smith and E.A. Porter (eds.), *China in Oceania: Reshaping the Pacific?* (New York: Berghahn Books, 2010), 93–103; R. Crocombe, *Asia in the Pacific Islands: Replacing the West* (Suva: University of the South Pacific for the Institute of Pacific Studies, 2007).

[7] Chinese are now the second-largest immigrant group in Australia, comprising 8.9 per cent of the overseas-born population and 2.6 per cent of the total population. The number of Chinese residents has doubled since 2008; see Department of Home Affairs, Australia, Country Profiles – China, www.homeaffairs.gov.au/research-and-statistics/statistics/country-profiles/profiles/china. Chinese also figure prominently in Aotearoa New Zealand's immigration statistics; see Statistics New Zealand, New Zealand's Population Reflects Growing Diversity, 23 September 2019. www.stats.govt.nz/news/new-zealands-population-reflects-growing-diversity

Pacific Islands behind Indo-Fijians and Filipinos.[8] One of the more insightful recent studies of Chinese migrant communities in the Pacific comes in Graeme Smith's detailed study of New Chinese in Papua New Guinea. Smith found that most came from the city of Fuqing in Fujian province, which has a long history of out-migration. For Papua New Guinea's Fuqing migrants, the central and the local Chinese state were effectively absent from their daily lives. These business migrants have little contact with the embassy in Port Moresby beyond when they need to renew their passports. As relatively recently arrivals, they had little accumulated capital and therefore tended to set up small retail businesses supplied by predominantly longer-established 'old Chinese' wholesalers originally from Southeast Asia. The diminishing number of old Chinese might disrupt this arrangement unless more prosperous Fuqing Chinese were able to fill the gap. However, Smith found that most Fuqing settlers in Papua New Guinea intended to settle in Fuqing after making their money in Papua New Guinea.[9] Persons of Chinese or part-Chinese ancestry do not seem as likely disproportionately to occupy as many important political and economic roles as did the long-established old Chinese in the first decades of Pacific Island independence in the 1970s and 1980s. Reflecting on this past era, Crocombe noted how 'Sir Julius Chan was twice prime minister of PNG, Anote Tong is the current president of Kiribati, Gaston Tong Sang is president of French Polynesia, Jim Ah Koy was minister of finance in Fiji and at least two other heads of Pacific Islands' governments do not discuss their Chinese heritage.'[10]

China and the Pacific Ocean since 1949

China's territorial waters encompass almost 5 million square kilometres, while its 32,000 kilometre coastline extends from the temperate Yellow and

---

[8] See, for example, Crocombe, *Asia in the Pacific Islands*, 93; B.N.K. Ali, *Chinese in Fiji* (Suva: Institute of Pacific Studies, 2002); P. D'Arcy, 'The Chinese Pacifics: a brief historical review', *Journal of Pacific History* 49:4 (2014), 396–420.

[9] G. Smith 'Fuqing dreaming: "New" Chinese communities in Papua New Guinea', in P. D'Arcy, P. Matbob, and L. Crowl (eds.), *Pacific Asian Partnerships in Resource Development* (Madang: Divine Word University Press, 2014), 126–40.

[10] Crocombe, *Asia in the Pacific Islands*, 90. A recent work by Dr Fei Sheng investigates how Vanuatu Chinese have built and kept their network among China, Australia, and the Pacific Islands since the 1920s. It shows how significant it is that the small island communities can benefit a China which is integrated into but not isolated from the South Pacific. See F. Sheng and G. Smith, 'The shifting fates of China's Pacific diaspora' in G. Smith and T. Wesley-Smith (eds.), *The China Alternative: Changing Regional Order in the Pacific Islands* (Canberra: ANU Press, 2021), 427–50.

East China seas in the north to the tropical South China Sea in the south. Ongoing and extensive surveys of marine biota in this vast area since the 1950s have recorded high biodiversity, with 22,629 species spanning forty-six phyla being identified. China's extensive continental shelf and the sedimentary discharge of many large rivers produces rich shallow-water fisheries in many coastal areas. Offshore, currents such as the Kuroshio Current and areas of frontal convergence and interaction such as where the warm, northward-flowing Kuroshio meets the shallow brackish Yangtze discharge enhance productivity and form spawning grounds for species such as the large and small yellow croaker, and cuttlefish.[11]

China's rich coastal fisheries have sustained considerable fishing industries throughout its history that have progressively expanded to keep pace with the expanding population. The three notable expansions in China's early modern and modern history took place in periods of mounting commercial imperatives and state policies promoting fisheries' expansion. These expansions occurred during the Ming Dynasty (1368–1644 CE), the latter part of the Qing Dynasty (1644–1911), and the recent period (2000–20). In the last two centuries of the Qing Dynasty especially, mounting land pressure due to population growth combined with better integration of transport and marketing systems to supply expanding urban markets to spur many small holders to 'farm the sea' by cultivating clams, oysters, and seaweed near to shore. Improved storage facilities using ice and salt allowed fisherfolk to increase their offshore catch as the harvest of fresh water fish failed to keep up with demand. This placed pressure on the marine fishery. Demand for high-priced marine goods such as trepang (sea cucumbers), sandalwood, seal furs, and shark fins saw Chinese and Euro-American merchants extend their purchase networks for these products into island Southeast Asia and the Pacific Islands.[12]

China's offshore fishery was placed under more pressure in the first forty years of the twentieth century as Japan's modernization of its naval, military, and industrial infrastructure extended to its fishing fleet. By 1910 the Japanese catch equalled that of the world's largest fishing nation, Great Britain. In 1938 Japan was the leading fishing nation of the world, landing three times as much fish as the second nation, Great Britain. Japan's fishing expansion mirrored its increasing imperial ambitions so that by the 1930s Japanese tuna

---

[11] Liu, 'Marine biodiversity'.
[12] M.S. Muscolino, 'Fishing and whaling', in J.R. McNeill and E.S. Mauldin (eds.), *A Companion to Global Environmental History* (Oxford: Blackwell, 2012), 279–96, at 284.

fleets were harvesting the tuna-rich waters of Japanese Micronesia while its modern trawlers were competing with Chinese fishermen for harvests in the Yellow, East China, and South China seas. After almost exhausting stock of high-value species such as sea bream in the 1920s, Japanese fleets moved to exploit yellow croaker fish off southeast China in the 1930s. Tensions mounted between Chinese and Japanese fishers as each rushed to exploit the fishery before other nations' fleets exhausted it. Japanese vessels' superior technology and better state support won out, and yellow croaker stocks went the same way as sea bream by the end of the 1930s.[13] This lesson on the consequences of not controlling one's coastal waters profoundly influenced post-war modern Chinese strategic and fishery policy.

The pressures on China's nearshore fisheries prior to World War II were noticeable in declining catches per unit effort (CPUE) over time. This decline escalated after the war and became Pacific-wide as China and many other Pacific Rim nations modernized and fishing came to be conducted by huge industrial fishing fleets. Japan took the lead in the 1950s and 1960s after its post-war reconstruction. Chinese fishing fleets also steadily rose in numbers over time, but only became the dominant fleet as well as the dominant national seafood market after 2000.[14] From the 1950s onwards, fishing has increasingly been dominated by large multinational fishing enterprises ranging the globe in large fleets harvesting the world's oceans through increasingly mechanized, industrial production. These vessels utilize onboard processing and refrigeration to minimize port visits for the offloading of catch as much as possible. High-tech fishing on this scale was expensive, and the profits were vast, so that by 1995 government subsidies to the fishing industry reached an estimated US$ 50 billion per annum globally as global fishing vessel tonnage doubled between 1970 and 1995. The North Pacific and North Atlantic were the main focus of the 1950s and 1960s as the nearest waters for the industrializing nations that the fleets came from bordering their shores in North America, East Asia, and Europe. By the 1970s these fleets were increasingly moving into the South Pacific and South Atlantic as catches increased and indiscriminate techniques such as fine-mesh driftnets increased catch and bycatch, with much of the latter jettisoned during onboard processing. The decline of high-value species made less-desired species more

[13] Muscolino, 'Fishing and whaling', 285–6. See also M.S. Muscolino, 'A forest of sails and masts: environment and economy in an early twentieth-century Chinese fishery', *Twentieth-Century China* 31:1 (2005), 3–32, and 'The yellow croaker war: fishery disputes between China and Japan, 1925–1935', *Environmental History* 13 (2008), 305–24.
[14] Muscolino 'Fishing and whaling', 286–7.

attractive. In response, driftnets were banned in the late 1980s and increasing attempts were made to set up regional agreements based on voluntary principles of sustainable fishing. By the late 1980s all the world's major fisheries were being targeted.[15]

The rise of China to be the dominant fishing nation on Earth dates to this post-1980s period. When there were no new reasonably intact fisheries left to move on to, catches began to decrease globally from the early 1990s, although large-scale illegal and unreported fishing makes accurate data hard to compile. It is estimated that all major marine fisheries will have collapsed by 2050 if current rates of declared fish take continue.[16] The 1990s also saw the final ratification of the United Nations Convention on the Law of the Sea (UNCLOS), which extended maritime sovereignty through Exclusive Economic Zones (EEZ).

China's fishing industry experienced phenomenal growth after the implementation of the open door and other economic reforms in 1978. The combined fresh water and marine catch went from 4.7 million metric tonnes in 1978 to 67 million in 2015, which represented one third of the total declared global catch.[17] By 2015, China had the largest fishing fleet in the world, with over 672,416 motorized fishing vessels, including 2,512 distant-water fishing vessels capable of operating for long periods of time beyond China's coastal fisheries around the globe. In 1985, an estimated 90 per cent of China's fish production came from inshore waters. However, the period since 1978 has been notable for the dramatic decline of annual catches in most coastal fisheries, prompting a shift to fish farming and offshore fishing as the two major sources of fish. By 2015, aquaculture accounted for around 75 per cent of the total fish catch, while the catch from distant-water vessels working on the high seas and in other nations' EEZs overtook that of coastal fishery vessels in 2002. Over time, Chinese vessels have increasingly moved away from traditionally targeted species such as anchovy and shrimp to high-value species such as red coral, sea turtles, and giant clams. Most of these high-value species attain their value because of their scarcity, and some are endangered.[18]

Aquaculture output has increased as ocean ecosystem biota have declined under pressure from overfishing. Aquaculture-based output increased fivefold

---

[15] Muscolino, 'Fishing and whaling', 287–9. For yearly overviews of the decline of fish stock see the Food and Agriculture Organisation of the United Nations (FAO) annual *The State of World Fisheries and Aquaculture* (SOFIA) reports, www.fao.org/publications/sofia/2020/en/.

[16] Muscolino, 'Fishing and whaling', 290.

[17] Bureau of Fisheries of China, 2016, cited in H. Zhang and F. Wu, 'China's marine fishery and global ocean governance', *Global Policy* 8:2 (2017), 216–26.

[18] Zhang and Wu, 'China's marine fishery'.

between between 1980 and 2000, with China contributing approximately 60 per cent of the world aquaculture production in fresh water and salt water farms. Most production is centred on fresh water carp, with the majority of salt water production dedicated to shrimp, prawns, and salmon. Aquaculture can generate considerable pollution from the concentrations of nutrients and antibiotics used to feed and protect fish.[19] Another form of aquaculture China has expertise in is seaweed farming. Blessed with a long coastline stretching from temperate zones in the north to tropical seas in the south, China has the ability to boost production of a great variety of seaweed as long as the damaging effects of pollution and sea temperature rises associated with climate change can be kept in check.[20]

China's coastal fishery has not been threatened only by overfishing. Pollution and climate change also pose serious challenges. Coastal urban development and its associated increase in human and industrial waste discharge have caused high levels of toxic matter in a number of fishery ecosystems. Rapid intensification of coastal agriculture through the application of nitrogen and phosphate additives has also led to eutrophication and harmful algal blooms in a number of areas, which result in mass mortalities in marine ecosystem food webs as well as fish farms. Increasing numbers of China's fish species are being added to its Red List of endangered species.[21]

Since 2011, President Xi's administration has given added emphasis to marine fisheries as a key component of China's food security and committed added resources to the fishing industry and China's blue-water naval capacity. This money was used largely to subsidize boat fuel and constructing or refurbishing fishing vessels.[22] The marine fishery was designated as a state strategic industry in China's 12th National Five-Year Plan in 2011, as well as a key area for international cooperation in the Belt and Road initiative. China's preferred cooperation involves bilateral relationships rather than dealing with regional institutions such as the Pacific Islands' collective voice in the form of the Forum Fishery Agency.

---

[19] Muscolino, 'Fishing and whaling', 291.

[20] X. Li et al., 'Aquaculture industry in China: current state, challenges, and outlook, July 2011', *Reviews in Fisheries Science* 19:3 (2012), 187–200.

[21] See, for example, M.J. Zhou, Z.L. Shen, and R.C. Yu, 'Responses of a coastal phytoplankton community to increased nutrient input from the Changjiang (Yangtze) River', *Continental Shelf Research* 28 (2008), 1483–9, and Y. Qi, J. Zou, and S. Liang (eds.), *Red Tides along Chinese Coast* (Beijing: Science Press, 2003).

[22] T.G. Mallory, 'Fisheries subsidies in China: quantitative and qualitative assessment of policy coherence and effectiveness', *Marine Policy* 68 (2016), 74–82.

China and the Pacific since 1949

China's Post-War Diplomatic Relations
with the South Pacific

The People's Republic of China was largely concerned with rectifying serious legacies and problems at home for the early decades of its existence. By 1980, however, China was rapidly modernizing under the economic reforms of Deng Xiaoping and increasing its external relations. This coincided with the recent decolonization of most Pacific Island nations in the 1970s. Most Pacific Island nations remained closely linked to their former colonial rulers and their ongoing financial commitments to development aid to create modern nation-state infrastructure lacking in independence. China commenced diplomatic relations with New Zealand and Australia in 1972. In 1975 Premier Zhou Enlai formally opened relations with newly independent Fiji, and Western Sāmoa, which had been independent since 1960. Premier Zhou also announced China's intention of recognizing Papua New Guinea, which also gained independence in late 1975, before his untimely death in January 1976. PNG's first prime minster, Sir Michael Somare, developed particularly close relations with China. Recognition of Kiribati followed in 1980 and of Vanuatu in 1982. From the outset of relations, China has always emphasized its respect for the sovereignty of Pacific states and their EEZs, and a policy of non-interference. It has also emphasized its common ground as a similar developing nation to Pacific Island states and a policy of partnership as equals.[23]

Fears of economic viability as micro-economies in a global world and political coherence as colonial boundaries united diverse peoples delayed independence until the mid to late 1970s for most Pacific nations. Questions about sustainable futures for island states have dominated environmental and economic literature on Pacific Island nations since independence.[24] Independent Pacific Island states vary considerably in size, from 10,847 in Nauru to just under 9 million in Papua New Guinea. A variety of languages are spoken within larger states like Papua New Guinea and the Solomon Islands, most of whose citizens retain a primarily kin-based way of life. Most people in the region still practise highly localized subsistence lifestyles supplemented by cash crops. While a new class-based urban identity is discernible in

---

[23] M. Godley, 'China: the waking giant', in A. Ali and R. Crocombe (eds.), *Foreign Forces in Pacific Politics* (Suva: Institute for Pacific Studies, University of the South Pacific, 1983), 130–42, at 130–2, 136

[24] See for example, G. Bertram, 'The MIRAB Model twenty years on', *Contemporary Pacific* 11:1 (1999), 105–38.

673

cities such as Suva in Fiji, most people of rural origin living in cities rely upon wantoks – networks who speak the same language and share cultural origins.[25]

China has increased its commitments in the Pacific Islands since 2000. China is now the second-largest aid donor to the Pacific Islands after Australia and has the largest distant-water fishing fleet in the world.[26] Its environmental footprint in the Pacific extends beyond fishing, however. China has embarked on numerous large infrastructure projects in response to Pacific Island needs. The large size of certain Chinese projects has particularly raised concerns about their environmental and social impact on relatively poorly developed localities such as the Ramu mine site in inland Madang province in Papua New Guinea. The Ramu mine has faced community opposition to labour conditions at the mine site and inadequate environmental safeguards along the pipeline transferring mined slurry from the mine to port facilities in Basamuk Bay, and slurry dumping provisions into the bay.[27]

China announced a major increase in its aid package to Pacific Island nations when Premier Wen Jiabao visited Fiji in April 2006. It was valued at 3 billion yuan or US$ 484 million, and most was in the form of low-interest preferential loans favouring primary industries such as fishing and agriculture. These loans will be typically set at interest rates of around 2 per cent for terms up to twenty years. Generous grace periods are also provided for, with the additional possibility that loans extended in this way could also be turned into grants on a case-by-case basis. Other aid donors have expressed mounting concern that these loans will cause problems for Pacific nations as repayment draws near because their generous terms have perhaps encouraged these small-nation economic entities to take on too much debt. Other measures announced then included establishing a fund to encourage Chinese companies to invest in the region, the cancellation of debts maturing at the end of 2005, and removal of tariffs on exports to the PRC from the least-developed Pacific nations. Arrangements to provide free anti-malarial

---

[25] See P. Thomas and M. Keen (eds.), *Urban Development in the Pacific*, special issue of *Development Bulletin* 78 (2017), and C. Moore, 'Honiara: arrival city and Pacific hybrid living space', *Journal of Pacific History* 50:4 (2015), 419–36.

[26] H. Zhao, 'China's overseas resource investment: myths and realities', in P. D'Arcy, P. Matbob, and L. Crowl (eds.), *Pacific Asian Partnerships in Resource Development* (Madang: Divine Word University Press, 2014), 110–21; Zhang and Wu, 'China's marine fishery and global ocean governance'; J.S.A. Leong, 'China's growing tuna fleet in the Pacific Ocean: a Samoan fisheries perspective', in M. Powles (ed.), *China and the Pacific: The View from Oceania* (Wellington: Victoria University Press, 2016), 244–7; P. D'Arcy, 'China and the sea: potential for Pacific partnerships?', in Powles (ed.), *China and the Pacific*, 248–55.

[27] G. Smith, 'Nupela Masta? Local and expatriate labour in a Chinese-run nickel mine in Papua New Guinea', *Asian Studies Review* 7:2 (2013), 178–95.

China and the Pacific since 1949

medicines and training for 2,000 government officials and technicians were also put in place. Additional bilateral arrangements were signed with the eight Pacific Island nations diplomatically aligned with China.[28] Perhaps more influential in the long term will be the Chinese policy of broadcasting CCTV Channel 9 in English to countries with which it has relations, providing Pacific peoples with daily Chinese perspectives in their homes.[29] This aid package prompted a step up in aid packages by other major aid donors to the Pacific, such as Australia, Japan, and the United States.

Most concerns expressed by other aid donors about Chinese aid being used to buy influence couch it in terms of future possibilities rather than a tangible reality. In 2016, Changsen Yu, executive director of Sun Yat-sen University's National Centre for Oceania Studies, presented a comprehensive overview of China's interests in the Pacific Islands at the National University of Sāmoa. It remains one of the few statements by a Chinese academic in an increasingly crowded field of largely Western scholars commenting on China's interests and priorities in the region. Yu noted that Pacific Island nations are small, are 4,000 to 10,000 kilometres from China with no direct flights, and do not figure prominently in the maritime dimension of the Belt and Road Initiative, commonly termed the maritime silk road. Relations with newly independent Pacific Island nations began in 1975 largely in pursuit of principles of developing nation solidarity and were not seen as central to China's geopolitical strategic priorities which focused on the potential threats from the Soviet Union and the United States.[30]

Yu noted that China's engagement with the Pacific had stepped up since 2000 as its economic engagement with the global economy and strategic reach increased. The Pacific is now increasingly important for four areas of China's national interests. The first is that many of the sea lanes transporting China's imports and exports run through or near to Pacific islands; 90 per cent of China's imports and exports and 40 per cent of its petrol and oil travel by sea, especially through the western Pacific and Southeast Asia to the Indian Ocean and the Middle East, across the North Pacific to North America and the Panama Canal, and to a lesser extent south to mineral-rich Australia,

---

[28] J. Wen, 'Speech at the opening of the first ministerial conference of the China-Pacific Island countries', Fiji, 5 April 2006, available at http://english.gov.cn/2006-04/05/content_245681.htm. In 2019, Solomon Islands and Kiribati, again, turned to China and abandoned their official relationship with Taiwan.
[29] Crocombe, *Asia in the Pacific Islands*.
[30] C. Yu, 'The Pacific Islands in China's geo-strategic thinking', in Powles (ed.), *China and the Pacific*, 89–97, at 89.

primary product exporter New Zealand, the Antarctic where China has four bases, and mineral-rich Chile and around Cape Horn into the South Atlantic. Seabed mineral discoveries in the Pacific Islands and eastern Pacific have increased the economic value of this region.[31]

The second area of enhanced interest involving the Pacific Islands is marine defence strategy.[32] China's marine strategy involves protecting China's national maritime territorial sovereignty, maintaining the security of sea lanes vital to its imports and exports, and 'establishing a stable relationship of great powers supporting maritime order'.[33] Since 2000, China has increasingly seen that it was vital to develop blue-water naval capacity, including aircraft carriers, to be able to operate beyond the range of land-based air and missile defence systems in what had been until then a territorial waters defence force.[34] China's main naval focus remains coastal defence centred on the first island chain of the Ryukyu, Senkaku, and Paracel and Spratly Islands among others, controlling the Yellow, East China, and South China seas which are all within reach of land-based air and missile assets. However, China increasingly believes its global interests require developing a blue-water fleet capable of breaking through the second island chain controlled by the United States and its allies, stretching through the Mariana Islands to Guam, and on to Micronesia, New Zealand, and Australia.[35] The United States' recent upgraded redevelopment of Guam as a base and recent re-engagement with Micronesian states in free association with the United States destined to end in 2023 is a direct result of concerns that the old policy of containing China was under threat. For its part, China has sought to avoid direct confrontation with the United States, preferring soft-power influence in the Pacific Islands through economic development projects to military bases.

The first comprehensive analysis of China's motivations in the Pacific Islands was not published until 2011 when Auckland University international relations expert Jian Yang published *The Pacific Islands in China's Grand Strategy*.[36] Born and raised in China, Yang completed his PhD in Australia before joining Auckland University in 1999 as an

---

[31] Yu, 'The Pacific Islands', 90–1.   [32] Yu, 'The Pacific Islands', 91–3.
[33] Yu, 'The Pacific Islands', 92.
[34] Yu, 'The Pacific Islands', endnotes 6 and 7. See also A.S. Erikson, L.J. Goldstein, and N. Li (eds.), *China, the United States, and 21st Century Sea Power: Defining a Maritime Security Partnership* (Annapolis, MD: Naval Institute Press, 2010).
[35] D. Bennett, 'China's offshore active defense and the People's Liberation Army Navy', *Global Security Studies* 1:1 (2010), 126–41.
[36] J. Yang, *The Pacific Islands in China's Grand Strategy: Small States, Big Games* (New York: Palgrave Macmillan, 2011).

international relations expert.[37] Yang argued that Beijing's strategy in the South Pacific centred around maintaining a form of international peace that allowed China to focus on developing the domestic economic and technological foundations at the heart of modern national power in the global world. Yang believed China lacked both the means and the desire to challenge Western powers in the Pacific Islands, and that it was also not in China's interests to do so.

Terence Wesley-Smith and Ed Porter's edited collection *China in Oceania* was published around the same time. It was more a Pacific Island focused book that also argued against China as a threat to existing dominant external donors such as Australia and the United States, a discourse prevalent among think tanks in these two donor nations. Wesley-Smith and most Pacific Island specialists writing on Pacific Island–China relations argue that China has allowed Pacific Islanders a greater degree of freedom of choice over aid donors than at any other time since independence by being the one significant contributor not to push for compliance with free market principles as a requirement of development aid and loans. This so-called Washington Consensus is portrayed more often as compliance with good governance requirements such as accountability and transparency and less with adherence to free market ideas hostile to 'excessive' government control of development agendas, national expenditure, and business legal frameworks.[38]

China also largely avoided involvement in Pacific nuclear Cold War politics which lasted from 1945 until the fall of the Berlin Wall in 1989. The Pacific continued to be a focus for nuclear weapons after nuclear bombing of Hiroshima and Nagasaki ended World War II. The vast and relatively underpopulated expanses of Oceania proved ideal for nuclear testing by the Americans, British, and French, especially as Islanders were politically marginal in essentially colonial relationships in American Micronesia, the British Gilbert Islands, and French Polynesia. Marshall Islanders from Bikini, Enewetak, and other northern atolls, Aleut in the far west of the Aleutians, southern Tuamotu Islanders in French Polynesia, I Kiribati from the Line Islands, and Australian desert Aborigines from South Australia all lost their ancestral homelands in the Cold War era. China conducted its nuclear tests

---

[37] Yang left academia in 2011 to become a National Party politician in the New Zealand House of Representatives. The National Party is the right-of-centre party in government which advocates smaller government and more privatization of public assets.

[38] T. Wesley-Smith, *China in Oceania: New Forces in Pacific Politics*, Pacific Islands Policy 2 (Honolulu: East-West Center, 2007), and T. Wesley-Smith and E.A. Porter (eds.), *China in Oceania: Reshaping the Pacific?* (New York: Berghahn Books, 2010).

in the remote western section of the inland province of Gansu, while the Russians tested in a number of locations across their vast Central Asian, Arctic, and Siberian territories.

Atmospheric testing of nuclear warheads was eventually replaced by first underground testing and then computer simulations and delivery system testing as protests mounted within the region. The bombs exploded in this period increased in magnitude to be many hundreds of times more powerful than those dropped on Hiroshima and Nagasaki. The South Pacific Nuclear Free Zone (SPNFZ) was declared in 1985, with only Australia qualifying its support out of concern for its military alliance with the United States which used nuclear-powered and nuclear-armed vessels. SPNFZ bordered the South American nuclear-free zone, making it the largest contiguous nuclear-free zone in the world covering well over half of the southern hemisphere.[39]

It was only in May 1980 that China conducted its first Inter-Continental Ballistic Missile (ICBM) test. The missile landed in open ocean 1,200 kilometres northwest of Fiji and 10,000 kilometres from its PRC launch site.[40] At the time, Vice Premier Li Xiannian was on a friendship tour of Pacific Island nations and noted China had no intention of conducting nuclear bomb tests in the Pacific.[41] While the other major world nuclear powers, the United States, Great Britain, and France have all conducted nuclear bomb tests in the Pacific, China has always tested nuclear warheads within its metropolitan terrestrial territory. A number of Pacific Island nations expressed concern about the missile testing.[42] Chinese naval capacity and actions remained essentially limited to coastal defence at this time, and Chinese media and government spokesmen indicated China was happy with the role Australia, New Zealand, and the United States played in the region as a counter to Soviet attempts to expand their influence into the region.[43]

The third area where Yu noted that the Pacific Islands are important for China's national interest is in seeking diplomatic recognition of its One China policy by recognizing China rather than Taiwan. Four of Taiwan's fifteen diplomatic allies are in the Pacific – Palau, the Marshall Islands, Nauru, and Tuvalu – as China's increasing prosperity has allowed it to increase its aid significantly since 2000 to become the second-largest Pacific Island donor after Australia. All of Taiwan's remaining allies are small nations allowing

[39] S. Firth, *Nuclear Playground* (Honolulu: University of Hawai'i Press, 1987), esp. 128–31, 137–43.
[40] Godley, 'China: the waking giant', 130.   [41] Godley, 'China: the waking giant', 132.
[42] Godley, 'China: the waking giant', 133.   [43] Godley, 'China: the waking giant', 134–5.

Taiwan to deliver a high level of aid per capita, although Taiwan's total aid budget is dwarfed by that of China. In September 2019, Taiwan's two largest Pacific Island nation allies, the Solomon Islands and Kiribati, switched their diplomatic recognition from Taiwan to China.[44]

Aid to promote peaceful Chinese reunification also overlaps with the fourth and final area where the Pacific figures in China's national interests – economic aid and access to the Chinese market to Pacific Island nations to promote sustainable development and economic independence. This continues the long-term foreign policy stance of China in promoting China as a fellow developing nation willing to be a responsible international partner for developing nations. While China seeks recognition of itself over Taiwan, it still maintains amicable, informal relations with Taiwan's Pacific allies, and imposes no conditions on internal government policy as a condition of its aid.[45] The United States and Australia drew criticism in some quarters in the early 2000s for seeking to link aid to government policy based on the so-called Washington Consensus of cutting government spending and promoting private sector led growth and development.[46]

Future Relations in the Era of Climate Change

This final section examines how climate change may affect China's economic development priorities and relations with Pacific Islands nations and potential future directions that might occur in response to changing Pacific Island needs and requirements. Within the Pacific Islands, increasing emphasis is being placed on lessening dependence on aid and the price that goes along with this, and especially developing the blue (i.e. maritime) economy as Big Ocean nations rather than small island nations. This idea is particularly relevant to smaller island nations in Micronesia and eastern Polynesia who are small population, Big Ocean nations. All are also at the forefront of climate change as the first to go underwater as archipelagoes of atolls with few or no high islands. The imminent danger of inundation they face due to failure to reach global CO_2 lower emission standards has resulted in a more assertive diplomatic stance towards aid and development. China has competitive advantages in skills and technologies vital to its Pacific allies. The small island nations of the Pacific are also potential stages to explore more effective cooperation with other aid donors in the future at a time when

[44] Yu, 'The Pacific Islands', 93.   [45] Yu, 'The Pacific Islands', 94–5.
[46] Wesley-Smith, *China in Oceania: New Forces in Pacific Politics*.

discoveries of vast amounts of seabed minerals raise the possibility of global rivalry to control this new frontier of resources. Ultimately however, future aid will only succeed if it is in true partnership with Pacific nations.

A new phase of globalization is now underway, led by the Asia-Pacific world rather than the Atlantic world. China's Belt and Road initiatives are taking place at a time of unprecedented human damage to the natural environment of the Asia Pacific Region. The Belt and Road Initiative interconnects China and the rest of the world by land and sea. It signals the rising centrality of the Chinese economy in the world. The detrimental outcomes noted above are not an inevitable consequence of global integration, however. Ten years ago, inclusive development, green growth, and sustainable development were not mainstream concepts as they increasingly are now. Thirty years ago, few would have believed the world's fastest growing economy, China, would commit to reforesting almost 10 per cent of its land in a Green Wall to hold back and reverse the southward advance of the Gobi Desert. It was no surprise therefore that green, sustainable development initiatives figured prominently at the Second Belt and Road Forum for International Cooperation in Beijing in April 2019.[47]

In a 2014 visit to Fiji, President Xi Jinping also promised support for climate change issues which have become a prime concern for the majority of Pacific Island nation leaders.[48] China is taking action on this prime concern of Pacific Island nations in two ways: by committing to reduced domestic emissions as a leading global carbon emitter, and by funding climate change mitigation projects in Pacific Island nations. China has adopted the CBDR (Common But Differential Responsibility) principle to carbon reduction targets. China's Pacific climate-related aid focuses on enhanced food security and sustainable energy through providing biogas equipment and solar power generators.[49] In the same forum in which Professor Yu spoke, Dame Meg Taylor, Secretary General of the Pacific Islands Forum Secretariat, noted China had established its first embassy in the region in 1976, and had developed mutually beneficial

---

[47] See Belt and Road Forum, 'The Second Belt and Road Forum for International Cooperation' at www.beltandroadforum.org/english/. See also President Xi Jinping, 'Working together for a green and better future for all', President of the People's Republic of China's Opening Address at the Opening Ceremony of the International Horticultural Exhibition 2019 Beijing China, Beijing, 28 April 2019, www.bjreview.com/Beijing_Review_and_Kings_College_London_Joint_Translation_Project/2019/201909/t20190903_800177587.html, and Y. Lyu et al., 'Desertification control practices in China', *Sustainability* 12 (2020), 1–15.
[48] Yu, 'The Pacific Islands', 95.
[49] X. Wang, 'Non-traditional security and global governance: China's participation in climate adaptation in Oceania', in Powles (ed.), *China and the Pacific*, 154–8, at 155.

economically focused partnerships with many Pacific nations. She noted China's support for Pacific Island nation concerns over climate change, natural disaster, and food security.[50]

Pacific Island nations strongly support global frameworks for climate change mitigation such as the Paris Agreement and the Sustainable Development Goals adopted in 2015. The IPCC and other international scientific bodies consider a 3.7 to 4.0 degree increase in global temperatures as the tipping point for irreversible environmental damage. The general failure of most nations to achieve the carbon emission reduction targets necessary to avoid this tipping point has serious implications for Pacific Island nations. Pacific Island nations are at the frontline of global warming because of their high proportion of low-lying atoll islands in the face of record warming of both polar caps and as a global climate hot spot where the impact of climate change is three times the global average. Ocean acidification levels in the Pacific are already 52 parts per million (ppt) beyond the maximum safe limit of 350 ppm, while Pacific fisheries are shifting in response to changes in water temperature. Warmer temperatures are also affecting food and water security on land because of variable rainfall and the intensification of natural hazards.[51]

China has stepped up its climate change aid in response to Pacific Island leaders' universal prioritizing of climate change mitigation as their greatest priority. However, China's investment in this area still remains marginal compared to other major Pacific donors such as Australia, the EU, and the Green Climate Fund. Like Australia, it also remains opposed to the 1.5 degrees temperature rise limit preferred by Pacific Island nations. China's climate change aid to the Pacific is divided between donations of funds and provision of materials in response to appeals, especially in the wake of natural disasters, assistance in constructing climate-related infrastructure such as hydro-electric dams, and capacity training in climate mitigation through scholarships and short-term training programmes. During Solomon Islands Prime Minister Sogavare's visit to Beijing in September 2019 following his nation's transfer of diplomatic recognition from Taiwan to China the previous month, President Xi emphasized that China and Pacific

---

[50] M. Taylor, 'China's growing impact on the regional political order', in Powles (ed.), *China and the Pacific*, 41–5, at 45.

[51] See, for example, G. Fry and S. Tarte (eds.), *The New Pacific Diplomacy* (Canberra: ANU Press, 2015) and IPCC (Intergovernmental Panel on Climate Change), 'AR6 climate change 2021: impacts, adaptation and vulnerability', www.ipcc.ch/report/sixth-assessment-report-working-group-ii/.

Island nations shared a common concern over climate change as developing nations. In September 2019, President Taneti Maamau of Kiribati transferred his nation's diplomatic recognition from Taiwan to China. President Maamau is holding discussions with Chinese officials about using Chinese expertise to build up, extend, and consolidate the nations' vulnerable low-lying atolls from sea erosion and sea level rise.

Climate change poses further challenges to food security and residential security for many Pacific nations such as China which are at the frontline of climate change induced degradation. It is a challenge they are determined to beat, and one in which China has much to offer its Pacific allies and others, in both the green economy of land and the blue economy of sea. Three thousand years of 'unsustainable growth' by China to be the centre of the world economy suggest this is another challenge China will rise to overcome.[52]

[52] M. Elvin, 'Three thousand years of unsustainable development: China's environment from archaic times to the present', *East Asian History* 6 (1993), 7–46.

59

Pacific Island Nations since Independence

STEPHANIE LAWSON

Introduction

In the wake of World War II European colonial powers, considerably weakened by six years of devastating warfare, found it increasingly difficult to impose their will on populations inspired at least partly by their own (i.e. European) doctrines of nationalism, self-determination, and popular sovereignty. The experience of the World War II had also given rise to a widespread conviction, at least among Western nations, that democratic institutions and practices were vastly superior to those of the defeated fascists and, by implication, to virtually all other forms of authoritarianism. And if democracy was good for the nations of Europe, it must be equally good for those emerging from colonialism.

The principles of liberal democracy promoted by Western nations were, of course, challenged by the Soviet Union's alternative interpretation of democracy – a challenge underpinning key aspects of the Cold War which, in turn, provided the principal dynamic of world politics for over four decades. Given the dominance of Western colonial powers in the Pacific, however, the impact of the Cold War was not felt quite as keenly in the island countries there as it was in Africa and Asia. A largely successful policy of 'strategic denial' meant, for the most part, that Soviet political influence in the newly independent Pacific Island countries was restricted. China, also a communist state, did have a political presence in the region through a number of resident missions, but was not regarded as posing any real threat to Western interests at the time. Indeed, it used whatever influence it had to decry the threat of 'Soviet hegemonism' in the region.[1] Times have changed, and Chinese activity in the Pacific Islands now provokes much more concern than does a still quite minimal Russian presence.

---

[1] R.A. Herr, 'Regionalism, strategic denial and South Pacific security', *Journal of Pacific History* 21:4 (1986), 170–82, at 175.

In the meantime, the phenomenon of decolonization had gathered considerable momentum from around the late 1940s. The Declaration on the Granting of Independence to Colonial Countries and Peoples, promulgated by the UN in 1960, formally delegitimized imperialism, proclaiming 'the necessity of bringing to a speedy and unconditional end colonialism in all its forms and manifestations'.[2] By the end of the 1960s, most former colonies on the African and Asian continents had achieved independence in the form of sovereign statehood and with constitutions that reflected basic principles of democratic government. Independence for most of the Pacific Islands lagged behind Africa and Asia and it took until the 1990s for some Pacific Island nations to achieve independent status. Even now, a significant number of countries remain in arrangements with colonial powers which fall short of full sovereign status while West Papua's 'independence' from the Netherlands amounts to forcible incorporation within the state of Indonesia.

In considering 'the Pacific Islands since independence', it is therefore instructive to provide first a brief survey of the political status of Pacific Island countries in the three sub-regions of Polynesia, Melanesia, and Micronesia. The classification and naming of these sub-regions as geocultural entities is, incidentally, itself a legacy of Western imperialism, and objections by historians and anthropologists have been made on the grounds that they lack integrity as ethnic, cultural, or geographical categories. But they have acquired an ongoing salience in regional politics, not least among the island elites themselves, and are now firmly embedded in the language of regionalism within the islands.

Dependence and Independence in the Pacific Islands

From the 1960s, Britain, along with Australia and New Zealand, had developed more enthusiasm for decolonization, although more so under leftist Labour governments than Conservative ones. Of the other major colonial powers, the USA was in no hurry to decolonize while France remained intensely resistant to change. The first Pacific Islands to achieve independence were mainly those located in western Polynesia, starting with Western Sāmoa (now Sāmoa) in 1962. A German colony until 1914 when New Zealand became an occupying wartime power, Western Sāmoa

---

[2] United Nations, 'Declaration on the Granting of Independence to Colonial Countries and Peoples', GA 1514 (xv), 14 December 1960.

continued as a League of Nations mandate from 1920, and then a UN Trust Territory under New Zealand control. The Cook Islands entered into a novel arrangement in 1965, becoming self-governing in 'free association' with New Zealand, an arrangement also made with Niue in 1974. This means that they remain part of the 'realm of New Zealand', giving the people of both island groups New Zealand citizenship while New Zealand retains formal responsibility for foreign affairs and defence, although both island countries do conduct relatively independent foreign relations. In 1968, Nauru, a Micronesian island, became fully independent and is now the smallest sovereign state in the world after Monaco and the Vatican. Nauru had also been annexed by Germany in the late nineteenth century, becoming a League of Nations mandate, and subsequently a UN trust territory under Australian administration. It now hosts a notorious detention facility for asylum seekers on behalf of the Australian government.

Fiji, a British Crown Colony from 1874, was the next to move to full sovereign statehood in 1970, although its conservative chiefly leaders had initially resisted decolonization, reflecting perhaps a close identity of interests with the highly paternalistic British colonial regime there. Fiji's leading political figure in the pre- and post-independence period, Ratu Sir Kamisese Mara, had shown a certain antipathy to the forces pushing for decolonization during the 1960s. But Britain's determination to divest itself of most colonial possessions and the liabilities these entailed saw its departure from Fiji in 1970. Tonga, the only surviving monarchy in the Pacific Islands, had been a British protected state under a Treaty of Friendship from 1900, and its status also shifted to full sovereignty in 1970.

Among the last of the western Polynesian countries to achieve independence was Tuvalu, formerly the Ellice Islands, in 1976. Along with the Gilbert Islands, it had become a British protectorate in 1892, and then the joint Crown Colony of the Gilbert and Ellice Islands in 1916. Tokelau, initially part of the Gilbert Islands protectorate but administered by New Zealand from 1926, became incorporated into New Zealand in 1949 and remains a dependent territory, although a 2006 referendum to change its political status to one of free association with New Zealand on a basis similar to the Cook Islands and Niue failed only by the narrowest of margins, making a further referendum some time in the future likely.

The Micronesian island group of Kiribati, formerly the Gilbert Islands, also became independent in 1979. American Sāmoa is, as its name suggests, an unincorporated territory of the United States, a status maintained under various constitutional arrangements since 1900. The last of the western

Polynesian island groups, Wallis and Futuna, remains French, having become first a protectorate in 1887–8, and then a colony from 1917, in both periods under administration by New Caledonia. It became a French overseas territory from 1961 and a French overseas collectivity with self-government in 2003. Here we may note that the French empire 'decolonized' at a semantic level in 1946, when colonies were renamed *Départements d'outre-mer* (Overseas Departments or DOMs) or *Territoires* (TOMs) in a Union, and later a Community.[3]

Independence for Melanesian states, apart from Fiji,[4] came a little later than most of the western Polynesian states. Papua New Guinea, following a complex colonial history involving German, British, and Australian administrations, became fully independent in 1975. Solomon Islands, a British protectorate from 1893, followed in 1978. Vanuatu, formerly the New Hebrides, had been an Anglo-French condominium since 1906, an awkward arrangement that made the road to independence in 1980 more complicated and protracted. While Britain had maintained a proactive decolonization strategy, France was less than cooperative – an important factor in a local rebellion followed by a regional intervention as Vanuatu crossed the threshold into independent statehood.[5] New Caledonia became a French colony in 1854, and a French overseas territory in 1946, and is presently a 'sui generis collectivity'. A referendum on independence in November 2018 saw just over 56 per cent of voters opt to remain with France. Further referenda in 2020 and 2021 maintained the status quo, but pro-independence activism continues.

The Dutch colonization of Netherlands New Guinea (commonly referred to as West Papua[6]) dates from the establishment of coastal administrative posts from 1898. When Indonesia emerged as an independent nation in 1949, it also laid claim to Netherlands New Guinea, effectively annexing it in 1962. An 'Act of Free Choice' on the part of the Papuan people in 1969, supervised by Indonesian authorities albeit with (largely incompetent) oversight by the

---

[3] D.A. Chappell, 'The Nouméa Accord: decolonization without independence in New Caledonia?', *Pacific Affairs* 72: 3 (1999), 373–91, at 374.
[4] Although Fiji is often classed as Melanesian it has a mixture of Melanesian and Polynesian ethnic groups and its chiefs at independence were largely orientated to the Polynesian culture area.
[5] See N. McQueen, 'Beyond Tok Win: the Papua New Guinea intervention in Vanuatu', *Pacific Affairs* 61:2 (1980), 235–52.
[6] Technically, the western part of the island of New Guinea as a whole now consists of two Indonesian provinces – Papua and West Papua – but the latter term is still commonly used to refer to both. This territory generally has had more names applied to it than almost any other entity in the Pacific region. These include Netherlands (or Dutch) New Guinea, West New Guinea, Irian Barat, Irian Jaya Barat, Irian Jaya, Papua Barat, and West Papua.

UN, is widely considered to have been a complete farce, but was nonetheless endorsed by the UN General Assembly. Writing in 1997, one commentator noted the tendency to marginalize West Papua in the story of Pacific Islands independence, due to a prevailing 'rhetoric of region' that saw the Pacific Islands region end at the Papua New Guinea/Indonesian border.[7] In recent years, however, activism on the part of West Papuans (especially those in exile) and their supporters has seen its 'return' to the regional agenda.

Also at least partially included in the region is Timor Leste, a Portuguese colony from 1702 to 1975, and then occupied by Indonesia until 1999 when it became independent. As with West Papua, Indonesia set up a farcical Popular Assembly in an attempt to legitimate incorporation into the Indonesian state, but the UN and most of the international community declined to recognize it. Australia stood out as the only country to endorse Indonesia's claims to sovereignty officially, despite evidence of mass atrocities. In the context of the Cold War, however, Indonesia once again had at least tacit support from the USA as well as Canada, the UK, and Japan. East Timor has participated marginally in Pacific Island politics. It has observer status at the Pacific Islands Forum, and has joined the Fiji-sponsored Pacific Islands Development Forum (PIDF), as discussed below.

In eastern Polynesia, French Polynesia also remains a French overseas collectivity. Colonization of the widely dispersed islands began with a protectorate in Tahiti and Tahuata in 1842, gradually becoming established over the whole group by 1889. It became a French overseas territory in 1946 and then a French overseas collectivity in 2003. French Polynesia was re-listed for decolonization by the UN in 2013 after a campaign by pro-independence activists. Hawai'i, annexed by the United States in 1898 following the overthrow of the native monarchy in 1893, became its fiftieth state in 1959 but a sovereignty movement there remains active. Rapa Nui (Easter Island) was annexed by Chile in 1888 and there is also an active movement for self-government. Britain maintains one very small dependency in the eastern Polynesia region – Pitcairn. Its population of around fifty, descended mainly from the mutineers of HMS *Bounty* and their Tahitian partners, makes it the smallest country in the world. It is noteworthy that around 170 Pitcairners relocated permanently to Norfolk Island off the coast of Australia in the 1850s. The decision by Australia to end a measure of self-government on

---

[7] S. Firth, 'The rise and fall of decolonisation', in D. Denoon (ed.), *Emerging from Empire? Decolonisation in the Pacific*, Proceedings of Workshop, Australian National University, Canberra, July 1997, 13.

Norfolk Island in 2016 has prompted a nationalist movement there to call on the UN to list it for decolonization.

The sub-region of Micronesia (excluding Nauru and Kiribati) presents another complex picture with a colonial history involving Spain, Germany, and Japan. The USA took control of the Trust Territory of the Pacific Islands (TPPI) in 1947, which included Japan's former League of Nations South Pacific Mandate. These territories now comprise the Republic of the Marshall Islands, the Republic of Palau, and the Federated States of Micronesia (FSM), all in a Compact of Free Association with the USA which came into effect in 1986. Each Compact arrangement, which is subject to periodic renewal, provides for a significant US military presence in the islands in return for certain benefits. The Commonwealth of the Northern Mariana Islands became a self-governing territory of the United States in 1986. Guam, ceded to the USA by Spain in 1898 (but occupied by the Japanese during World War II), is also a non-self-governing territory and hosts significant US military bases.

The limited extent of decolonization in the Pacific is further underscored by the fact that the UN Committee on Decolonization lists six Pacific Island countries (out of a total of seventeen around the world) as non-self-governing. In addition to French Polynesia, New Caledonia, and Tokelau, noted above, American Sāmoa and Pitcairn are also listed, even though both do have some form of self-government and are not seeking independence. The Cook Islands and Niue are not listed, but this accords with the UN's position of recognizing that genuine acts of self-determination may opt for something short of full sovereignty. The UN's list of those that 'remain to be decolonized' assumes that their populations, or at least a majority of them, do actually want independence.[8] Significant movements for independence, however, are largely absent except in the case of New Caledonia and French Polynesia. There is also increasing pro-independence activity on Guam. But West Papua, which has had a significant self-determination movement for decades, is not listed at all.

Neocolonialism and Aid Dependency

A further point to be considered in relation to independence is the extent to which the Pacific Islands are aid dependent. Indeed, the region as a whole has

---

[8] UN, 'The United Nations and decolonization: non-self-governing territories', www.un.org/en/decolonization/nonselfgovterritories.shtml.

the highest level of official development assistance (ODA) per capita in the world. Australia is the largest provider, although its distribution varies given that the Micronesian countries and American Sāmoa are generally more reliant on funding from the United States, while the French territories are obviously supported by France.[9] The EU is also a major donor, partly a reflection of the fact that there are significant numbers of EU citizens in the region by virtue of the French connection. Thus aid patterns tend to reflect colonial ties and may be seen as perpetuating neocolonial relations.

The steadily increasing aid from China, however, may also be seen as creating neocolonial relations, although China does not impose any form of aid conditionality, and funding through its overall aid programme is still well behind the major donors. But China is now the third most important source of ODA, much of it taking the form of concessional loans.[10] A significant problem for a number of countries – Sāmoa, Vanuatu, and Tonga in particular – is that their level of external debt is unsustainably high.[11] Although often seen as designed to enhance its status vis-à-vis Western powers, China's strategy has also been driven by competition with Taiwan, noting that until recently six Pacific Island countries – Palau, Marshall Islands, Solomon Islands, Tuvalu, Kiribati, and Nauru – gave Taiwan diplomatic recognition. Solomon Islands and Kiribati switched to recognizing China in 2019. These issues aside, some popular resentment among Chinese working or doing business in the region has been manifest in anti-Chinese riots in Papua New Guinea and Solomon Islands in particular, although the causes are complex and cannot be explained by any single factor.[12]

Aid is sometimes seen as creating a form of welfare dependence which inhibits entrepreneurial activity and economic development.[13] This means that although all countries are economically *inter*dependent, the sovereignty of those relying substantially on foreign aid remains significantly compromised. To push the concept of neocolonialism too far, however, is to run the risk of portraying Pacific Island governments and people as passive victims of

---

[9] M. Dornan and J. Pryke, 'Foreign aid to the Pacific: trends and developments in the twenty-first century', *Asia and the Pacific Policy Studies* 4:3 (2017), 386–404.
[10] Dornan and Pryke, 'Foreign aid to the Pacific', 394.
[11] G. Smith, 'PRC aid to the Pacific?', *China Matters* (April 2018), 1, http://chinamatters.org.au/wp-content/uploads/2018/04/China-Matters-Recommends-04-April-2018-PRC-Aid-Pacific.pdf.
[12] See G. Smith, 'Chinese reactions to Anti-Asian riots in the Pacific', *Journal of Pacific History* 47:1 (2012), 93–109.
[13] R. Duncan, 'Sources of growth spurts in Pacific Island economies', *Asia and the Pacific Policy Studies* 3:2 (2016), 351–65. See also the influential and controversial paper by Helen Hughes, 'Aid has failed the Pacific', Centre for Independent Studies, Issue Analysis 33, May 2003, www.cis.org.au/publications/issue-analysis/aid-has-failed-the-pacific/.

completely self-interested external actors, and lacking any agency in determining their own futures.[14] One commentator notes that the dynamics of the Cold War, which provided an opportunity for former colonies to play one side off against the other, tended to maximize access to aid funds while minimizing control over their expenditure or other aspects of their internal affairs. This changed with the end of the Cold War, the rise of neoliberal economic doctrines, and the implementation of 'good governance' agendas accompanied by aid conditionality, reminiscent in some ways of the preconditions for independence.[15] Even so, Pacific Island governments and other actors (such as NGOs) now have considerable experience and a certain leverage in managing aid diplomacy in a competitive regional environment.

In recent years, the magnitude of security threats arising from climate change has also seen Pacific Island countries adopt a proactive stance on the international stage, particularly at the UN level where the Pacific small island developing states (PSIDS) group, representing twelve island states, lobbies hard on issues concerning climate change and sustainable development in particular. Such coalition strategies enable small island states to engage in effective diplomacy and maximize their agency in global politics.[16] It is also worth noting that Fiji's regional and international activism in the wake of the 2006 coup and its subsequent suspension from the Pacific Islands Forum in 2009, as well as a (relatively mild) sanctions regime, demonstrates that small countries can exercise genuine agency in international politics and are by no means powerless in the face of pressures from larger and ostensibly more influential actors.[17]

Political Developments since Independence

Decolonization in the Pacific Islands, as elsewhere, brought much optimism about the future, and the first generation of leaders are still valorized today as heroic figures ushering in a new era. Contemporary politicians, however, are often held in low esteem.[18] Writing in the mid-1990s, one prominent literary

---

[14] P. Phipps, 'Neocolonialism', in H.K. Anheier and M. Juergensmeyer (eds.), *Encyclopedia of Global Studies* (Thousand Oaks, CA: Sage, 2012), 1232–5.
[15] B. Macdonald, 'Decolonisation and "good" governance: precedents and continuities', in D. Denoon (ed.), *Emerging from Empire? Decolonisation in the Pacific*, Proceedings of Workshop, Australian National University, Canberra, July 1997, 1–9.
[16] G. Carter, 'Establishing a Pacific voice in climate change negotiations', in G. Fry and S. Tarte (eds.), *The New Pacific Diplomacy* (Canberra: ANU Press, 2015), 205–22.
[17] S. Lawson, 'Fiji's foreign relations: retrospect and prospect', *Round Table* 104:2 (2015), 209–20.
[18] J. Corbett, *Being Political: Leadership and Democracy in the Pacific Islands* (Honolulu: University of Hawai'i Press, 2015).

Pacific Island Nations since Independence

figure noted that he had 'watched the euphoria of independence throughout the Pacific degenerate after ten years into political corruption', with the new elites of the islands carrying on 'a form of colonialism which may be even worse than what we got rid of'.[19] If there are widespread perceptions of a deep malaise, however, specific explanations of its root causes are difficult to come by. Is it to be found in the adoption of alien systems of rule and the abandonment of traditional forms? In the nature of continuing aid dependency? In the more general social transformations taking place with urbanization and migration? Or in the pressures to 'develop' and to participate in the wider global economy? The overarching theme in almost all these factors is an implicit dichotomy between 'tradition and modernity'. Here we consider aspects of the national political institutions that emerged at independence in the context of assumptions about the tensions between modern representative democracy and traditional political and social practices.

Tradition, Modernity, and Democracy

There is no one-size-fits-all model of democracy, and if this is true for the countries of Europe and the West more generally, it is even more so for the hugely diverse sovereign entities that emerged in the former colonial world. As these gained independence, most adopted constitutions reflecting basic principles of representative democracy. Constitutional development usually took place with the participation of departing colonial powers whose own institutions left their distinctive imprint. Even so, the new arrangements were also tailored to the specific circumstances of each colony, with local elites very much engaged in the process, although the extent to which they did so varied from extensive consultation in Papua New Guinea to very little in Solomon Islands.[20]

In Fiji, a system of communal representation had been introduced in the early colonial period with separate representation for the three major ethnic communities (European, Indo-Fijian, and Indigenous Fijian) as well as special provision for a Great Council of Chiefs (GCC). Indigenous Fijian 'commoners' and women from all ethnic groups, however, were not enfranchised until the 1960s, less than a decade before independence. At independence, the communal electoral system as well as a prominent role for traditional chiefly figures was retained largely on the insistence of Indigenous leaders.

[19] Albert Wendt quoted in Corbett, *Being Political.*
[20] See H. Gardner and C. Waters, 'Decolonisation in Melanesia', *Journal of Pacific History* 48:2 (2013), 113–21.

691

Today, this system has been demolished by former military coup leader, and now prime minister, Voreqe (Frank) Bainimarama. The communal system has given way to a single national electorate with no regional or ethnic elements while the GCC has been abolished and chiefly figures are relegated to the margins of national politics.

In (Western) Sāmoa, eligibility to both vote and stand for office was restricted to the chiefly *matai* class – again very male dominated – and this remained so at independence. Universal suffrage was not introduced until 1990 but it remains the case that only *matai* can stand for office. Although enjoying relative stability, Sāmoa's democratic credentials are tarnished by the continuing exclusion of non-*matai* from political office. It had also become, at least until a new party gained office in 2021, akin to a one-party state with power increasingly vested in the executive. This was reinforced by the continuing promotion of *fa'a Sāmoa* (the Sāmoan Way) and thus of traditional leaders at the village level who generally benefited under the former ruling party's patronage system. According to one observer, these constraints meant that Sāmoa could not be considered a 'functioning democracy'.[21]

Tongan political institutions were, from the nineteenth century, heavily influenced by models derived from Hawai'i and the UK, and the constitution adopted in 1875 established the monarch and a small group of 'nobles' in control of government. The relative stability of Tongan politics over the ensuing century or so has been attributed to a 'unique amalgam of Tongan chiefly authority and British forms of government and law'.[22] From the early 1990s, however, a pro-democracy movement demanded reforms to allow for more effective participation of 'commoners' and to hold political leaders to account for what were increasingly seen as corrupt practices. Reforms in 2010 gave popularly elected representatives a majority in the legislature over the nobles' representatives. Even so, the monarch retains certain executive powers and in 2017 exercised these unilaterally by dismissing parliament and calling for fresh elections. Critical perspectives see the Tongan concept of *faka'apa'apa* (respect) as constituting a form of social control that has long underscored dominance and manipulation by the traditional ruling class.[23]

---

[21] A. Toleafoa, 'One party state: the Samoan experience', in D. Hegarty and D. Tryon (eds.), *Politics, Development and Security in the Pacific* (Canberra: ANU Press, 2013), 69–76, at 76.
[22] Guy Powles quoted in M. Tupou, 'Constitutional development in Tonga: Tonga's idea of responsible executive', Presented at the Law and Culture Conference, Port Vila, Vanuatu, 9 September 2013.
[23] Finau Kolo quoted in *Loop Pacific News*, www.looptonga.com/tonga-news/respect-obstacle-tongan-democracy-researcher-66521.

In the Cook Islands, under its self-governing arrangements, a House of Ariki was modelled partly on the House of Lords. Although this was designed to accommodate traditional leaders in the parliamentary system, they have no legislative power and elected leaders have generally ensured that their own agendas prevail – as they do in the UK.

The nature of traditional leadership and political relations have always been more difficult to define in the Melanesian sub-region. It was once commonly assumed that Melanesian societies had no 'real chiefs', or at least nothing like the hereditary chiefs that populated the relatively rigid Polynesian hierarchies, but instead had 'big men' whose status was achieved rather than ascribed.[24] Matters are actually more complex and, like the Melanesia/Polynesia/Micronesia divide itself, the distinctions can be rather crude.[25] In Vanuatu, a National Council of Chiefs was founded in the lead-up to independence in a country where 'chiefship' as such was a fairly novel institution.[26] Papua New Guinea and the Solomon Islands have no special provisions for traditional rulers at the national level, but they are active at the local level and Solomon Islands has District Houses of Chiefs. In New Caledonia, recognition of Kanak identity has seen the transformation of the New Caledonian Customary Council into a Customary Senate with certain administrative, consultative, propositional and legislative functions in matters concerning Kanak identity, although it remains subordinate to the New Caledonian government.[27]

Chiefs continue to play a key role in local communities throughout Micronesia, although they generally have less visibility at the national level. There was considerable debate about the status of chiefs in the FSM during constitutional deliberations and negotiations. Interestingly, the incorporation of traditional leaders in the new, national system was seen as endangering,

---

[24] This assumption was based largely on Marshall Sahlins's influential article, 'Poor man, rich man, big-man, chief: political types in Melanesia and Polynesia', *Comparative Studies in Society and History* 5:3 (1963), 285–303.

[25] L. Lindstrom and G.M. White, 'Introduction: chiefs today', in G.M. White and L. Lindstrom (eds.), *Chiefs Today: Traditional Pacific Leadership and the Postcolonial State* (Stanford: Stanford University Press, 1997), 1–18, at 9.

[26] See L. Bolton, 'Chief Willie Bongmatur Maldo and the role of chiefs in Vanuatu', *Journal of Pacific History* 33:2 (1998), 179–95. Bolton (p. 179) writes that missionaries and officials of the Anglo-French condominium government introduced the concept of 'chief' which became a title used to designate men who represented their communities in the non-traditional contexts of church and state.

[27] R.D. Morrison, 'The institutionalisation of "Kanak identity" in the New Caledonian Customary Senate and Kanak customary law', http://caepr.cass.anu.edu.au/events/institution alisation-kanak-identity-new-caledonian-customary-senate-and-kanak-customary-law.

rather than protecting, their vital role. One argument was that 'the institution of chieftainship itself would be threatened if chiefly roles were made subject to western legal precepts', while another held that the 'codification of chieftainship would be likely to freeze the relative rankings of titles, lineages, and clans in place and thus destroy the fluidity that characterizes the entire system'.[28] In both the Marshall Islands and Palau, provision has been made for chiefly councils with advisory functions only.

The overall picture shows that on entering the independence era, many Pacific Island countries did so with systems of government which fused some aspects of traditional (or, perhaps more accurately, neotraditional) forms with aspects of Western parliamentary democracy, if not at the national level then certainly at the local level. While this might seem to have provided a fortuitous blend of modern state forms with Indigenous structures, none has proved unproblematic. It soon became evident that some traditional leaders, on the one hand, were adept at manipulating the new systems to their own advantage or, on the other, proved ill-equipped by education or training to work effectively in modern governance. Even so, it was seen that traditional leadership at least at the local level was an essential complement to more formal, modern bureaucratic governance at the national level.[29]

The emergence of representative politics also saw the development of less formal political institutions, including political parties. Although these may suggest simple imitation of Western political practices, they have also incorporated much in the way of local practices, values, and traditions.[30] Having said that, some of the smaller nations lack anything that might resemble a regular ensemble of political parties organized to contest elections with an agreed platform. In the Micronesian sub-region, Palau, FSM, and Marshall Islands have virtually no political parties. Kiribati and Nauru have had some loose, unstable groupings, while Tuvalu has barely any. Even so, political rivalries can be intense, and Nauru has evinced a degree of instability with motions of no-confidence resulting in some very short-lived governments although until recently there had been rather more concerns about heavy-handed authoritarianism.

---

[28] G. Petersen, 'At the intersection of chieftainship and constitutional government: some comparisons from Micronesia', *Journal de la Société des Océanistes* 141 (2015), 255–65, at 264.
[29] N. Meller, 'Traditional leaders and modern Pacific Island governance', *Asian Survey* 24:7 (1984), 759–72, at 772.
[30] S. Ratuva, 'Primordial politics? Political parties and tradition in Melanesia', in R. Rich, L. Hambly, and M.G. Moran (eds.), *Political Parties in the Pacific Islands* (Canberra: ANU Press, 2008), 27–42.

But Nauru is not the only country to experience such difficulties and political stability has been in short supply in the Melanesian sub-region in particular. Political parties abound, but party allegiances are fluid, to say the least, leading in some cases to chronic regime instability.[31] Parliamentary politics in Vanuatu has been plagued by frequent changes of government. Similar problems have occurred in Papua New Guinea – and worse. Between 1988 and 1998 the country experienced a prolonged civil war in what is now its autonomous Bougainville region. A referendum on independence took place in 2019 with around 98 per cent voting in favour of independence, but the process still has a long way to go. In New Caledonia, violence on the part of both pro-French and anti-colonial forces as well as French security forces eventually gave way to accords in 1988 and 1998 pending the 2018 referendum. In the Solomon Islands the near collapse of the state was precipitated by ongoing ethnic strife and a coup in 2000 followed by a long-term regional intervention led by Australia. Fiji has had four coups since May 1987 and its current government approximates an elected dictatorship.

Such developments have led to the Melanesian states, in particular, being described in terms of an 'arc of instability' comprised of fragile states plagued by violence, corruption, highly personalized politics, and social fragmentation. The latter is reflected in significant levels of ethnic and linguistic diversity as well as small-scale, localized polities with largely non-hierarchical structures. All this suggests that the modern centralized state is a poor fit in the Melanesian sub-region.[32] However, it is always instructive to put aspects of these cases in a wider comparative perspective. As one commentator has observed, 'a PNG prime minister over the past two decades has spent – on average – more than 40 per cent more time in the top job than their Australian counterpart'.[33]

Turning to the independent countries of the Polynesian sub-region, this may appear to be a sea of relative tranquillity although in the case of Sāmoa this was perhaps due largely to a long period as a one-party state. Tonga enjoyed a long period of stability under the monarchy but discontent with the lack of democratic opportunity saw the situation deteriorate, leading to

---

[31] M.G. Morgan, L. Baker, and L. Hambly, *Political Parties, Parliamentary Governance and Party Strengthening in Melanesia: Issues and Challenges* (Canberra: Centre for Democratic Institutions, Australian National University, 2005), 6.

[32] See G.M. White, *Indigenous Governance in Melanesia*, SSGM Discussion Paper, Canberra, Australian National University, February 2006.

[33] S. McLeod, 'Prime Ministerial persistence: Australia vs PNG', *The Interpreter* (21 August 2018), www.lowyinstitute.org/the-interpreter/prime-ministerial-persistence-australia-vs-png.

deadly riots in 2006 followed eventually by the reforms of 2010. Although opening up much greater space for political participation, the reforms have brought their own challenges to a country unaccustomed to the dynamics of democratic politics. Cook Islands, Niue, Tuvalu, Wallis and Futuna, American Sāmoa, and French Polynesia have all had political dramas of one kind or another, including serious riots in Tahiti in 1995 protesting French nuclear tests, but there have been few to cause concerns with the ultimate viability of the polity.

Gender and Politics

A further aspect of politics and society in the region that bears scrutiny concerns the participation of women, given that the Pacific Islands generally have the lowest proportion of female political representation of any region in the world. In the Papua New Guinean general elections of 2017, not a single woman was elected to any of the 111 seats.[34] As of 2018 there were no women holding national elected office in Vanuatu and only two in Solomon Islands. Fiji, with ten women in a parliament of fifty after the elections of 2018, has fared somewhat better. In Sāmoa, where eligibility to stand for elected office is restricted to *matai*, the fact that only around 10 per cent of *matai* are women, and that some villages ban women outright from holding *matai* titles, is clearly a major problem. Special measures which guarantee a minimum of five seats for women in the Samoan parliament were implemented in 2013. Among the arguments against the introduction of special measures were that they would discriminate against men, that women holding reserved seats would face ridicule, and that the election of women to parliament in any case 'contradicted women's traditional role in Samoan culture to *fa'amaepaepa* (sit aside); to be the peace-keeper and peace-maker (*pae ma le auli*); and not be *fa'aeleelea* (tainted) with political discussions'.[35]

In Tonga, all nobles are by definition male, once again restricting opportunities for women. Before pro-democracy campaigner Akilisi Pohiva became prime minister, a woman had been appointed to Cabinet from outside parliament to provide at least one female voice in government. But when elections in 2014 delivered Pohiva the prime ministership in an all-male parliament, he

---

[34] K. Baker, 'Experiences of female candidates in the 2017 Papua New Guinea General Election', *In Brief* 2017/38, Canberra, Department of Pacific Affairs, Australian National University, 1.

[35] UNDP, *Temporary Special Measures to Increase Women's Political Participation in the Pacific*, 2015, 15, www.pacific.undp.org/content/dam/fiji/docs/UNDP%20PO%20TSM_Womens%20Political%20Participation.pdf.

Pacific Island Nations since Independence

declined to follow suit, although he acknowledged that non-representation of women in the legislature was an issue.[36] In 2017, however, two women were elected without any special provisions. Cook Islands has done better with four women elected in 2018, again without special provisions.

Women in Micronesian countries have generally fared no better, with Palau, Nauru, and FSM standing out as having especially poor records, although Palau, after electing its first women ever in 2008, now has four in the legislature, as does Kiribati. The Marshall Islands has three, and its current president is a woman. Nauru has two while the FSM has zero.[37] The Northern Marianas has never elected a women as a delegate to the US House of Representatives, and only three to its own legislature. In contrast, following the 2018 elections, women in Guam now hold the governorship, the Speaker's position and a majority in the legislature (incidentally, making it the first US state or territory to have a female majority). In the case of the French territories, French parity laws mandating equal numbers of male and female candidates on party lists have applied since 1999, a practice that has seen a significant increase in representation in French Polynesia and New Caledonia, although the lack of political parties in Wallis and Futuna means that female representation there follows the general Pacific pattern more closely.[38] In New Caledonia, opposition to the parity provisions was some-times expressed in terms suggesting that 'women, and particularly Kanak [Indigenous] women, were not "ready" to enter parliament'.[39] Given the generally poor record of women's participation in the Pacific Islands sketched here, it is interesting to note that the very first country in the world in which women were awarded the constitutional right to vote was Pitcairn in 1838, although that particular polity was, and remains, unique in many respects.[40]

The relatively low level of representation of women in politics is, not surprisingly, partly attributable to wider issues of gender disparity linked in turn to 'tradition' or 'custom'. The implications of the retention of traditional status in formal politics in Sāmoa and Tonga have been noted above, but in most of Melanesia, where hierarchies are more fluid, the barriers are still

---

[36] K. Baker, 'Women's under-representation and special measures in the Tongan parliament', *In Brief*, 2015/33, Canberra, Department of Pacific Affairs, Australian National University, 1.
[37] For a table showing the level of representation as of 2018 in fifteen Pacific Island countries see www.pacwip.org/women-mps/national-women-mps/.
[38] See, generally, K. Baker, 'Great expectations: gender and political representation in the Pacific Islands', *Government and Opposition* 53:3 (2018), 542–68.
[39] UNDP, *Temporary Special Measures*, 16.
[40] International Business Publications, *Pitcairn Islands Business Law Handbook: Strategic Information and Basic Laws* (Washington, DC: IBP, 2013).

formidable. Traditional leaders in Melanesia are overwhelmingly male, even where matrilineal practices prevail. Tradition in this context can become 'a rigid ideology' deployed against women interested in taking on a more active political role.[41] Then there is the related problem of domestic violence which is also relatively high across the Pacific region as a whole. Once again, the ideology of tradition can and has been used to justify acts of violence, as reflected in the fact that national and regional leaders have found it necessary to declare formally that 'culture, religion and tradition can never be an "excuse for abuse"'.[42] Yet again, it is instructive to look to wider comparisons. One news report in early 2019, prompted by a particular problem within Australia's then governing conservative coalition, noted the more general paucity of women among conservative parties in Western countries compared to centre-left and green parties.[43] This further suggests that social and political conservatism shares at least some important cross-cultural elements.

Regional Politics

Pacific Island nations moved to independence in a broad global context which had seen the regeneration and expansion of international institutions. In the early post-war period, security concerns prompted Australia and New Zealand to canvas the idea of a broad-based regional organization. This led to the establishment of the South Pacific Commission (SPC) in 1947 with the principal colonial powers – Australia, New Zealand, the USA, the UK, France, and the Netherlands – all joining in. But French concerns about maintaining their status as a colonizing power ensured that all matters considered to be political – which included security, independence, and trade – were firmly excluded from the SPC's remit. The organization's functions were therefore restricted to development-orientated and welfare programmes. By the early 1960s, however, the predominance of the colonial powers in the SPC had become anachronistic. Various reforms were instituted and Indigenous leaders eventually came to control the agenda, despite continuing resistance on the part of the French. But these reforms would not lead to an expansion of the SPC's agenda to encompass political concerns. To this day, the organization (since renamed the Pacific Community) remains strictly apolitical.

[41] White, *Indigenous Governance*, 12.
[42] Pacific Islands Forum, Communiqué, Koror, Republic of Palau, 29–31 July 2014, 4.
[43] J. Baird and S. Bold, 'Conservative parties around the world have a problem – and women are losing patience', ABC News, 8 February 2019, www.abc.net.au/news/2019-02-07/women-in-parliament-labor-liberal/10783234.

Frustrations with lack of a venue for political discussions led in due course to the formation in 1971 of the South Pacific Forum. Its membership was open to Pacific Island countries which had achieved independence – at that stage (Western) Sāmoa, Nauru, Cook Islands, Tonga, and Fiji. As decolonization proceeded, the Forum's membership grew and by the beginning of the twenty-first century it had sixteen member states and had changed its name to the Pacific Islands Forum in 2000 in recognition of its geographic scope. Its founding members, however, also included Australia and New Zealand, both of which had been strongly supportive of a new institution capable of dealing with political concerns. But they have always occupied a rather ambiguous position, being both former colonies themselves as well as colonial powers in their own right. Analyses of regional politics – and Forum politics in particular – have often tended to depict relations in terms of a simple binary, with Australia and New Zealand on one side and the island countries on the other, underpinned by neocolonial attitudes on the part of the former, although this approach tends to treat the island countries as a single undifferentiated entity and also fails to take account of other dynamics at work.[44]

In the meantime, the Forum certainly facilitated discussion of the most vexed political concerns which, in addition to decolonization issues, included nuclear testing, although these issues were intertwined in the case of French Polynesia. The USA had ceased testing in the Marshall Islands in 1962 but France had shifted its own testing programme from North Africa to French Polynesia in 1966 and continued, with some pauses, until 1996. The sinking by French operatives of the Greenpeace protest vessel, the *Rainbow Warrior*, in Auckland Harbour in 1985, combined with earlier attempts to sabotage Vanuatu's independence and the violence in New Caledonia, saw France's relations with all Pacific countries sink to an all-time low. These improved with the visit by moderate French prime minister Michel Rocard to the region in 1988 and the signing of the first Accord in New Caledonia,[45] but there was still a very long way to go.

Over the next decade or so, France was to moderate its position further, albeit in response to ongoing regional activism and international criticism.[46] Continuing devolution of power to New Caledonia and French Polynesia means that both territories are now virtually self-governing although

---

[44] See S. Lawson, 'Australia, New Zealand and the Pacific Islands Forum: a critical review', *Commonwealth and Comparative Politics* 55:2 (2017), 214–35.

[45] S. Henningham, 'France and the South Pacific in the 1980s: an Australian perspective', *Journal de la Société des Océanistes* 92–3 (1991), 21–45, at 21.

[46] D. Fisher, *France in the South Pacific: Power and Politics* (Canberra: ANU E-Press, 2013), 2.

responsibility for defence, security, and the administration of justice remains with France. In 2006, New Caledonia and French Polynesia were admitted as associate members of the Forum. The governments of both territories then worked assiduously, as did France, to demonstrate that their degree of autonomy was sufficient to allow for full membership. This campaign proved ultimately successful and both were admitted as full members at the Forum's 2016 summit.

It was noted above that there has been a tendency to treat the Pacific Islands as a single entity without due regard to differing identities and interests. While this may appear an error most likely to be committed by external actors, it was in fact implicit in the idea of the 'Pacific Way' nurtured by Pacific Island leaders themselves, or at least some of them. Foremost among these was Fiji's Ratu Sir Kamisese Mara, who introduced the term during his first speech to the UN General Assembly in October 1970.[47] The Pacific Way was to become an expansive idea, embracing elements relating to almost every aspect of life in the Pacific Islands. But it has been most commonly associated with a distinctive style of Pacific Island politics and governance at both national and regional levels. This style, not surprisingly, is closely associated with traditional values and practices which have been set in opposition to, or at least in contrast with, 'Western' values and practices. In its initial formulation, however, the Pacific Way appeared to reflect the worldview of a rather limited set of Indigenous elites in the Southwest Pacific. Ron Crocombe's influential analysis, published in 1976, suggested that it applied primarily 'to an inner group of English-speaking, tropical islands of the *south* Pacific'.[48] Thus, although purporting to embrace the entire island Pacific, the Pacific Way appeared to be an expression of identity drawing much of its inspiration from a chiefly Polynesian model, noting that Mara was himself a paramount chief in the Polynesian tradition, and did not regard himself as Melanesian.[49]

The Pacific Way's distinctive Polynesian character, and the rather condescending attitude that some Polynesian leaders had to their Melanesian counterparts, is perhaps one reason that a discourse of 'Melanesianism' emerged from the mid-1970s as most Melanesian countries moved to

---

[47] Text of 'Address to the United Nations', Appendix 4 in K. Mara, *The Pacific Way: A Memoir* (Honolulu: University of Hawai'i Press, 1997), 238.

[48] R. Crocombe, *The Pacific Way: An Emerging Identity* (Suva: Lotu Pasifika Productions, 1976), 9.

[49] See S. Lawson, '"Melanesia": the history and politics of an idea', *Journal of Pacific History* 48:1 (2013), 1–22, at 10.

independence, although it certainly had strong anti-colonial overtones as well. A series of newspaper articles by PNG intellectual Bernard Narokobi, published between 1976 and 1978 just after PNG gained independence from Australia, were subsequently published in book form under the title *The Melanesian Way*.[50] A similarly titled volume, produced by Kanak leader Jean-Marie Tjibaou not long after, focused primarily on issues of Melanesian identity and culture under French colonialism in New Caledonia.[51] These and other developments supporting ideas about *kastom* in Vanuatu and the Solomon Islands were associated not only with a strong anti-colonial sentiment but also with the rise of more critical attitudes towards the conservative Pacific Way discourse and its close association with Polynesian interests.[52]

Despite the Forum's engagement with political issues, Melanesian members saw it as taking too soft a line, especially with respect to the position of Kanaks in New Caledonia. This was a factor behind the formation of a Melanesian sub-regional grouping designed to give Melanesian countries more clout in the Forum generally.[53] By 1988, the prime ministers of PNG, Vanuatu, and the Solomon Islands had signed up to a set of Agreed Principles under the banner of the Melanesian Spearhead Group (MSG) to facilitate cooperation on regional and international issues. The formal agreement under which the MSG now operates was signed in March 2007. The Front de Libération Nationale Kanak et Socialiste (FLNKS) of New Caledonia was admitted to full membership in 1991, boosting its political profile and giving it a regional voice. Fiji did not join the MSG until 1996, indicating its lesser identification with Melanesia to that time. Fiji's generation of prominent chiefly leaders with close Polynesian connections has passed, and a new generation with a different power base has emerged. Even so, Fiji will always have the potential to play either side of the Polynesia/Melanesia divide in regional politics.

Despite the MSG's founding ideology of anti-colonialism and commitment to the 'Melanesian brotherhood', the issue of West Papua has seen divisions within the group. While Vanuatu, the Solomon Islands, and the FLNKS have generally been strong supporters of West Papuan activists, and have spoken

---

[50] B. Narokobi, *The Melanesian Way*, rev. edn (Port Moresby: Institute of Papua New Guinea Studies, 1983).

[51] J.-M. Tjibaou and C. Missotte, *Kanaké: The Melanesian Way*, trans. C. Plant (Papeete: Les Éditions du Pacifique, 1978).

[52] M. Howard, 'Vanuatu: the myth of Melanesian socialism', *Labour, Capital and Society* 16:2 (1983), 176–203, at 184.

[53] See R. May, *The Melanesian Spearhead Group: Testing Pacific Island Solidarity*, ASPI Policy Analysis 74 (Canberra: ASPI, 2011).

up about human rights abuses, Papua New Guinea and Fiji have shown themselves more willing to cater to Indonesian interests. Indonesia, along with Timor Leste, was granted observer status at the MSG in 2012, followed by associate membership in 2015, while the United Liberation Movement for West Papua (ULMWP) – akin to the FLNKS – was given only observer status. The ULMWP has continued to lobby for full membership status but wariness of Indonesian sensitivities is likely to continue to prove a stumbling block.

Other developments in sub-regionalism include the establishment of the Micronesian Presidents' Summit (MPS) in 2001, while the Micronesian Chief Executives' Summit (MCES), established in 2003, meets biennially. In 2014, a treaty establishing the Micronesian Trade and Economic Community (MTEC) was signed by the FSM, the Marshall Islands, and Palau, designating the MPS as its supreme constituent body.[54] Micronesian sub-regionalism has been a largely pragmatic exercise, as reflected in successive agendas of both the MPS and the MCES which have focused on issues of mutual concern such as fisheries management, trade and investment, sustainable development, aviation and shipping facilities, education, energy, climate change, and cooperation with the wider regional bodies, especially the SPC and the Forum. Thus, while sub-regional governance has become reasonably well established, a common Micronesian identity, especially in contradistinction to Melanesia and/or Polynesia, has not been articulated in anything but the mildest terms. This confirms earlier findings that, despite efforts by some politicians and writers to promote a 'Micronesian Way' or a pan-Micronesian identity, it simply has not taken root, with localized identities retaining much greater salience.[55] This is especially so among the Chamorro people of Guam and the Northern Marianas who generally do not consider themselves 'Micronesian' in any ethnic sense.

Although Polynesian leaders were the first to forge a presence in regional politics, a Polynesian sub-regional organization was the last to make an appearance on the scene. This was due, perhaps, to a certain level of satisfaction with the status quo. But with both the MSG and the Micronesian groups becoming well established, it seemed inevitable that a Polynesian group would eventually form. The establishment of the Polynesian Leaders' Group (PLG) was finally achieved in November 2011 when a meeting of

[54] See www.mtec-northpacific.com/the-micronesian-presidents-summit-mps/.
[55] L. Poyer, 'Ethnicity and identity in Micronesia', in R.C. Kiste and M. Marshall (eds.), *American Anthropology in Micronesia: An Assessment* (Honolulu: University of Hawai'i Press, 1999), 197–223, at 213.

leaders from French Polynesia, Niue, Tokelau, the Cook Islands, Tonga, Tuvalu, and American Sāmoa gathered in Apia at the invitation of Samoan prime minister Tuilaepa Sailele, and agreed a set of principles to provide 'a systematic approach to cooperation among Polynesian countries'.[56] A further declared purpose was 'the continued preservation of Polynesian culture, traditions and languages as the common uniting foundation of the PLG'.[57] The latter statement reflects an emphasis on identity which contrasts with their Micronesian counterparts but is comparable to the underpinnings of the MSG.

What the PLG will actually contribute to regional politics remains to be seen. One observer has suggested that the PLG could help stabilize Pacific regionalism by counterbalancing the influence of the MSG and providing support to Australia and New Zealand vis-à-vis 'belligerent MSG members'.[58] The reference here is almost certainly to Fiji. When it was suspended from the Forum in 2009 following the failure of 2006 coup leader Bainimarama to follow a timely roadmap for a return to electoral democracy, Fiji appeared to be embraced by the MSG. The complicating factor here, however, is that, with the exception of the FLNKS, MSG members are all Forum members as well. Yet all Forum members supported Fiji's suspension. There is a temptation to view this as a result of Australia's and New Zealand's disproportionate influence in the Forum. To take this view, however, once again suggests a lack of agency on the part of island leaders and certainly ignores the fact that the Samoan prime minister, in particular, was proactive in pressing for Fiji's suspension at the time.[59]

None of the three sub-regional organizations based on the Melanesia/Micronesia/Polynesia division include any former (or current) colonial power, indicating that island leaders have perhaps moved further along the pathway to autonomy. This is further reinforced by the fact that, as another result of Fiji's suspension from the Forum, coup leader Bainimarama established a rival pan-regional organization in 2013 – the Pacific Island Development Forum (PIDF). The latter, however, appears to have presented no real threat to the now long-established Forum which, despite all the problems and shortcomings one might expect of such a body, remains the premier regional organization.

---

[56] M. Ilalio, 'Polynesian leaders groups formed in Samoa', *Samoa Observer* (2011) http://archives.pireport.org/archive/2011/November/11-21-01.htm.
[57] Polynesian Leaders' Group, *Communiqué from Third Meeting*, Auckland, 30 August 2013, 1.
[58] I. Iati, 'Pacific regionalism and the Polynesian Leaders' Group', *Round Table* 106:2 (2017), 175–85, at 185.
[59] See Lawson, 'Australia, New Zealand and the Pacific Islands Forum'.

Conclusion

Given the vastness and diversity of the Pacific Islands region, it is difficult to generalize about the experience of Pacific Island countries except to say that all the Pacific Islands have been transformed by imperialism – mainly, but not exclusively, of the modern European kind. The independence era has seen many acquire full sovereign statehood, although a significant number fall short of this status. In most cases, however, the present status quo reflects an arrangement that more or less fulfils criteria for self-determination, and shows that political autonomy can work in a variety of forms tailored to circumstances. There is also scope for further acts of self-determination depending on the wishes of island people, although this could well compromise aid funding and other forms of support. In the case of West Papua, however, the aspirations of the Melanesian population for greater political autonomy, or even freedom of expression, are unlikely to be realized in the foreseeable future, given Indonesia's rather pugnacious nationalism and invocations of its right to non-interference, combined with a strategy that simply denies human rights abuses or other problems.

Governance arrangements in the Pacific Islands, as elsewhere, are also highly diverse, although they have all been expected to meet basic criteria for representative democracy. This expectation, however, is not just what the 'international community' (however defined) has placed on Pacific Islands. It is now also a product of local demands. The Tongan pro-democracy movement, for example, which agitated for democratization for many years, was entirely home-grown and locally led. Similarly, the various campaigns to improve representation for women, while obviously supported by wider international bodies, have also been driven largely by local actors. As for regional organization, this is still characterized by a sense of partnership with former colonial powers, or at least some of them, although a more recent phase has seen the assertion of alternative forms of regionalism or sub-regionalism which exclude former colonial powers. These and other examples, including the extent to which island leaders are playing a proactive role in climate change diplomacy and in other arenas, again emphasizes the fact that Pacific Islanders are active agents in shaping their own lives and futures.

PART XII

★

PACIFIC FUTURES

60

Ancestral Voices of the Sea

Hearing the Past to Lead the Future

TĒVITA O. KAʿILI

Moana ko e Tupuʿangá

Moana ko e tupuʿangá
Limu mo Kele ko e mātuʿá
Tētēkina ʿi he Vahanoá
ʿO fatu ai siʿi ʿuluaki tangatá

Tangaloa vaka mai he manu muʿá
Siutaka he vaha ʿo kumi fonuá
Toki ʿafio siʿi hakau tupuʿá
Fakakelea ʿe Tangaloa Tufungá

Māui e mo e Mātaʿu Manuká
Fusifonua ʿo Tokelau mo Tongá
Fānifo ai ʿa Hina mo ʿene ʿangá
ʿI he peautā ʿo e Halakakalá

Hauʿofa ko e tufunga Moaná
Moʿui manatu ki he Vahanoá
Mo hotau fatongia tapuá
Ko e tauhi ʿa tahi ke tuʿuloá

Ocean, the Ancestor

The Ocean is our original ancestor
Seaweed and Sea Sediment, our
    progenitors
Floating continually in the Open
    Seawater
In the procreation of our first
    predecessor

Tangaloa incarnates as the first avian
    man
Flew around the ocean searching for
    land
Finally found the first coral sand
Transformed by Tangaloa Tufunga to
    a homeland

Māui and his Manuʿa Fishhook
Fished up the islands north and south
Where Hina, the shark goddess, surfs
In the breaking waves of Halakakala

Hauʿofa, the Oceanian artisan
Who remembered our Open Sea
And our sacred responsibility
To keep our sea in sustainability

Tēvita O. Kaʿili

TĒVITA O. KAʻILI

Ancestors of Moana Nui, Oceania

The people of Moana Nui, Oceania, abound with historico-cultural accounts, in stories, songs, chants, incantations, poems, proverbs, dances, and symbols, about the ancestors who emerged and resided in the seascapes, landscapes, and skyscapes of the Indigenous world.[1] These ocean-land-cosmic ancestors were not limited to humans; they were also natural beings and elements of the *fonua*, socio-ecology, namely stars, birds, fishes, reptiles, animals, plants, waters, soils, rocks, and mountains.[2] They were relatives who were nurtured and venerated by all. At death, certain human ancestors were divinized and returned as avian life, marine life, floral, fauna, or other elements to care for and protect their descendants. In mutual dependence, the descendants safeguard and venerate their ancestors in all their multiplicity of forms. Consulting the ancestors and their wisdom in all matters relating to life and death was a common Indigenous practice in Moana Nui. This cultural practice was philosophically grounded on the Moana Nui arrangement of *tā* and *vā*, time and space.[3] In Tongan, tā is an expression of time. It means to mark time with beats, rhythms, and actions. Vā, on the other hand, means space between time-markers, tā. It is relational space. Tā and vā, or time and space, are inseparable. Time is spatially constituted while space is temporally marked. For example, in Moana Nui cultures, the temporal past, present, and future are spatially located in front, middle, and back.[4] 'In historical ways, however, it logically follows that the past, which has stood the test of time-space, is placed in front of people in the present as guidance, and the unknown future is located in their back in the present, informed by past experiences, with the past and future permanently negotiated in the conflicting present.'[5] Ancestral knowledge and skills were placed in front as the guide

---

[1] Moana Nui literally means great ocean. It is an Indigenous Polynesian name for the Pacific Ocean and Oceania. I use the name Moana Nui to highlight the Indigenous knowledge and history that are associated with Oceania.

[2] Fonua is the Tongan cognate for the pan-Austronesian term for land or earth. It is known in other Moana Nui cultures as honua (Hawaiian), vanua (Fijian), whenua (Māori), fenua (Tahitian), and fanua (Samoan).

[3] ʻO. Māhina, 'Tā, vā, and moana: temporality, spatiality, and indigeneity', *Genealogies: Articulating Indigenous Anthropology in/of Oceania*, special issue of *Pacific Studies* 33:2/3 (2010), 168–202; T.O. Kaʻili, *Marking Indigeneity: The Tongan Art of Sociospatial Relations* (Tucson: University of Arizon Press, 2017).

[4] T.O. Kaʻili, 'Tāvani: intertwining tā and vā in Tongan reality and philology', *Pacific Studies* 40:1/2 (2017): 62–78.

[5] T.O. Kaʻili, ʻO. Māhina, and P.-A. Addo. 'Introduction: tā–vā (time–space): the birth of an indigenous Moana theory', *Pacific Studies* 40:1/2 (2017), 1–15.

for the present and future. This is one of the reasons ancestors, elders, grandparents, parents, and elder siblings are endowed with the roles of leaders in many Moana Nui societies. They are the repositories and custodians of knowledge and skills. Ancestors, however, are placed at the highest level as the holders of deep knowledge and refined skills. They are the libraries of Indigenous Moana Nui historical knowledge and information. Certain ancestors were deified due to their extraordinary knowledge and skills. In this chapter, I will discuss three of the significant deified ancestors of Moana Nui, namely, Tangaloa, Māui, and Hina. Furthermore, I will discuss these ancestors within the seminal works of Epeli Hau'ofa.

Although ancestors are found in all the scapes of Moana Nui, I will primarily focus this chapter on the ancestors that are associated with the oceanscape, particularly Tongan ancestors from my corner of the sea. To get a fuller account of the *mana* (power, potency, authority) and might of these ancestors, I will also discuss their works outside the realm of the ocean. I will also focus specifically on the late Epeli Hau'ofa and his urging for all of us to hear the voices of our ocean ancestors and to let them lead us to a better future in caring for our environment, particularly the ocean. Part of our histories is preserved in the voices of our ancestors. Hau'ofa is significant because he is a prominent Oceanian scholar who is now an ancestor in front guiding and leading us in the present to the future.

Emerging from the Sea: The Tongan Creation Story

In the beginning there existed only the Open Sea, *Vahanoa*, and the ancestral homeland of Pulotu, which is generally considered by Indigenous scholars to be an island in Fiji.[6] Within the depths of the sea emerged the two primordial forebears of all Tongans, namely Limu, Seaweed, and Kele, Sea Sediment. Waves and wind brought Limu and Kele together. They floated for eons in the sea until they finally landed in Pulotu (Fiji) where they gave birth to the forebears of all Tongans. Tongan cosmogony is based on *hoa*, pairs of beings, emerging from the sea. *Hoa*, pairs of opposites or pairs of similarities, are

---

[6] 'O. Māhina, 'The Tongan traditional history tala-ē-fonua: a vernacular ecology-centred historico-cultural concept', PhD thesis, Australian National University, Canberra, 1992), 59.

fundamental to Moana Nui ontology and epistemology. Reality is constituted of pairs and reality is known through pairs.

The first line of the Tongan creation story is profoundly powerful. It is also a story of the migration history of Tongans from the west to Fiji. It identifies Vahanoa, the Open Sea, as the original ancestor of the Tongans, the people from the sea, *ko e kakai mei tahi*.[7] Like many creation stories from Oceania, the sea is the earliest home and primordial ancestor for the peoples of Moana Nui. Tongans, like many of their cousins in Oceania, are autochthonous to the ocean.[8] In the Tongan version, from the ocean arise two life-giving entities, Limu (Seaweed) and Kele (Sea Sediment), who are the ancient parents of the Tongan people.[9] Thus, the eminent Moana Nui anthropologist Epeli Hauʻofa's concept of Oceania resurrected Indigenous ideas firmly anchored in Tongan cosmogony. The story of Moana Nui characterizes the ocean as *tupu ʻanga* – the ancestor who provided the source of sustenance and growth for the people who began from the sea. Tupuʻanga is the source of emanation. As a Tongan anthropologist, my reading of Epeli Hauʻofa, a fellow Tongan anthropologist of an older generation, is that Tonga's cosmo-gonic story of ocean roots deeply impacted his consciousness of Oceania as home and mother. In his words, 'conquerors come, conquerors go, the ocean remains, mother only to her children. The mother has a big heart though; she adopts anyone who loves her.'[10]

In addition to the creation story from Tonga, other historical narratives shaped Hauʻofa's 'vision of Oceania' as a vast, boundless, salt water continent that allowed its peoples a high level of mobility in travelling unrestricted from place to place[11]. One such folktale passed down in storytelling from generation to generation is that of the deity Tangaloa ʻAtulongolongo transforming into *kiu*, a Pacific golden plover bird, which is the *vaka* (vessel) he used to fly and search above the ocean for an island to settle. Another tale is of the demi-gods Māui ʻAtalanga and Māui Kisikisi voyaging to Manuka, Manuʻa Island in Sāmoa, to procure the supernatural Mātuʻa Fusifonua, the land-fishing hook from the Tuʻi Manuʻa, Tongamatamoana (which literally means Tonga with Oceanic eyes).[12] Tongamatamoana is also known as

---

[7] E. Hauʻofa, *We Are the Ocean: Selected Works* (Honolulu: University of Hawaiʻi Press, 2008).
[8] M. Jolly, 'On the edge? Deserts, oceans, islands', *Contemporary Pacific* 13:2 (2001), 417–66. I am fully aware that not everyone from Oceania identifies with the ocean.
[9] In this chapter, I have capitalized the nouns Open Sea, Seaweed, and Sea Sediment because when Tongans retell traditional history in their mother tongue, they are the names of our ancestors.
[10] Hauʻofa, *We Are the Ocean*, 34–5.   [11] Hauʻofa, *We Are the Ocean*, 27–8.
[12] J. Martin, 'Origin of the name Tonga Island', *Journal of the Polynesian Society* 20:4 (1911), 165–9.

Tonga Fusifonua, or Tonga-the-Fisher-of-Islands. Both names denote the significance of the ocean as well as the significant role of Manuʻa, Sāmoa in the settlement of Tonga. The extraordinary fishhook of Tonga-the-Fisher-of-Islands was used to pull up numerous islands throughout Oceania, including the North and South Islands of Aotearoa New Zealand, where Māui Kisikisi was known as Māui Tikitiki, and Hawaiʻi, where he was known as Māui Kiʻikiʻi. My village of Kolonga in Tonga, where I trace my paternal ancestry, lays claim to the place Haʻa Māui, the Māui Clan, where members of the Māui clan resided in ancient days and established their first astronomical observatory known as Haʻamonga ʻa Māui, the Burden of Māui.[13] The magical fishhook is a poetic reference to the historical role of the Scorpio constellation, which is shaped like a fishhook, as a group of stars for navigating to Tonga, Hawaiʻi, and Aotearoa New Zealand. My home village Kolonga is also associated with the story of Hina, the shark goddess that is also associated with Māui in some traditions. It was said that Hina, a young Tongan woman, metamorphosed into a shark goddess where still, to this day, she surfs the waves of the Oceanic waterway named *Halakakala*, the fragrant flower road, near the island of ʻEua in Tonga.[14]

These heritage stories make sense of where the ancient Tongans came from and are sources of history and identity for the descendants of Tangaloa ʻAtulongolongo, Māui ʻAtalanga, Māui Kisikisi, and Hina, who are living in the present. Based on my interpretation of Hauʻofa's scholarly works, it appears that Hauʻofa was listening to the voices of his ancestors that were emanating from the stories of deified ancestors. To some, these stories may have been myths and legends from the past, but Hauʻofa listened and then connected how Moana Nui was conceived in days gone by to the present-day voyages of a Moana diaspora migrating from islands to lands in search for new places to settle, as did their ancient ancestors. This diaspora began in southeast China to Taiwan, and from Taiwan to the Philippines. From the Philippines, one group voyaged to northern Oceania to form Micronesia, and another migrated to southern Oceania, and then to eastern Oceania to form Polynesia. Today, Indigenous peoples of Taiwan, the Philippines, Micronesia, and Polynesia all belong to the cultural group known as

---

[13] Tēvita Fale, personal communication, 7 August 2015.
[14] T.J.B. Pulu, 'Ko e Kakai Tonga ʻo Nuʻu Sila. Tongan generations in Auckland New Zealand', PhD thesis, University of Waikato, Hamilton, 2007.

Austronesia. This was not to say that the world of Oceania is tiny or deficient in resources, he wrote.[15] Instead, it was Oceania as the genesis of life, the connector of lands and peoples, the salt water highway that allowed for the exchange of ideas, material goods, and relationship ties that stayed with him in his intellectual thought and heartfelt sentiments that he put in writing, urging us all to care for the ocean. These connections were fruitful for both the ancient diaspora and the contemporary diaspora of Hauʻofa.

Deep History and Hauʻofa

In his writings, Hauʻofa did not retell in specific detail stories of the sea. He did, however, nod to the significance that 'kakai mei tahi', people from the sea, played in the Oceanian psyche, noting 'that the sea is home to such people'.[16] From closely reading his work I conclude that Oceanic deep history in the form of myths, legends, and oral traditions, linked to the broader narrative of Moana Nui cosmology, was in the foreground of his thinking, expressly in his groundbreaking essay, 'Our Sea of Islands'.[17] Hauʻofa argued that 'if we look at the myths, legends, and oral traditions, indeed the cosmologies of the peoples of Oceania, it becomes evident' that '[t]heir world was anything but tiny' because '[t]heir universe comprised not only land surfaces but the surrounding ocean as far as they could traverse'.[18] I would add that it also included the skyscape where celestial bodies were known as ancestors or objects of the ancestors, such as the Fishhook of Māui, the Scorpio constellation. Hauʻofa's view that 'Oceania is vast, Oceania is expanding', therefore came from his deep understanding of oral histories and the importance of retelling stories to bind people and places to the Pacific Ocean as home and mother, and guide people in the present to the future.[19] As he illuminated in 'Our Sea of Islands', Oceanians 'thought big and recounted their [ancestors'] deeds in epic proportions' because stories were their source of historical memory and guidance.[20] The voices of the ancestors lived on in our stories that are integrally linked to the skyscapes, landscapes, and seascapes of Moana Nui.

Hauʻofa furthered this line of reasoning in his essay, 'The ocean in us', where he asserted that Oceanians 'must tie history and culture to empirical

---

[15] Hauʻofa, *We Are the Ocean*, 35. [16] Hauʻofa, *We Are the Ocean*, 32.
[17] Hauʻofa, *We Are the Ocean*, 27–40. [18] Hauʻofa, *We Are the Ocean*, 31.
[19] Hauʻofa, *We Are the Ocean*, 39. [20] Hauʻofa, *We Are the Ocean*, 31.

Ancestral Voices of the Sea

reality and practical action'.[21] He was referring to 'a common regional identity', one that united the islands and peoples from the sea to take back ownership and representation of history as 'ecologically based oral narratives'.[22] This was to be a system of knowledge grounded in the ecology of the region's islands, but particularly Oceania. They were the histories of our forebears written 'on the landscape and seascape; [histories that] carved, stenciled, and wove our metaphors on objects of utility; and [histories that were] sang and danced in rituals and ceremonies for the propitiation of the awesome forces of nature and society'.[23]

Histories were also identified and drawn on the skyscapes in a grid system such as the *Kohi 'a Velenga*, the Intersecting Star Lines of the goddess Velenga, in Tonga.[24] The Intersecting Star Lines of Velenga was used as a compass in deep-sea voyaging as well as for determining the appropriate time to cultivate, harvest, and perform rituals. In his essay 'Pasts to remember', Hau'ofa acknowledged the work of historian-anthropologist 'Okusitino Māhina, who argued very strongly that ecologically based oral traditions should be treated as valid sources for academic history, equal to written documents.[25] Māhina wrote 'an entire history based largely on oral traditions [and] backed wherever possible with the findings of archaeology and related disciplines'.[26] For Hau'ofa, Māhina was fashioning a new Pacific historiography of interweaving oral and written texts, one that was relevant for advancing Oceanian histories in public and academic media in the terms of Indigenous peoples and their ancestral origins.

Responsibilities to the Ocean

Importantly, Hau'ofa used 'ecologically based oral traditions' to support a 'vision of Oceania' that advocated for Oceanians to hear the voices of their ancestors and take up their custodian responsibilities to the ocean, their home and mother.[27] He understood that the Pacific Ocean, the largest salt

---

[21] Hau'ofa, *We Are the Ocean*, 55.   [22] Hau'ofa, *We Are the Ocean*, 55, 64.
[23] Hau'ofa, *We Are the Ocean*, 55.
[24] 'O. Māhina, *Reed Book of Tongan Proverbs: Ko e Tohi 'a e Reed ki he Lea Tonga Heliaki* (Auckland: Reed Publishing, 2004), 107.
[25] Hau'ofa, *We Are the Ocean*, 64; Māhina, 'The Tongan traditional history'.
[26] Hau'ofa, *We Are the Ocean*, 64; Māhina, 'The Tongan traditional history'.
[27] Hau'ofa, *We Are the Ocean*, 64, 27–8.

water terrain in the world, was essential not only to the peoples who lived there but also to peoples who lived outside of the region because the sea purified the Earth's air, stabilizing 'the global environment'.[28] Inspired by oceanographer Sylvia Earle's scientific view of the sea, he cited her discussion in 'The ocean in us'.

> The sea shapes the character of this planet, governs weather and climate, stabilizes moisture that falls back on the land, replenishing Earth's fresh water to rivers, lakes, streams – and us. Every breath we take is possible because of the life-filled life-giving sea; oxygen is generated there, carbon dioxide absorbed. Both in terms of the sheer mass of living things and genetic diversity, that's where the action is.[29]

Hauʻofa was born on the brink of World War II, and died at the end of the first decade of the twenty-first century, a lifetime of seventy or so years allowing him to see increasing amounts of Oceania's destruction through nuclear testing, toxic waste disposal, 'wall-of-death fishing methods', over-fishing, and the pollution by industrialized countries.[30] He was, in many ways, one of the few academics writing from Oceania during his thirty-year career who anticipated that leaders of Pacific Islands governments would take up the narrow-minded view that the region's prosperity could be commercially exploited through fisheries and seabed mining.[31] Hauʻofa's far-sightedness has come true in the sense that never in modern history have the Pacific Islands states converged as much as they do in the present day around the very idea that the ocean is an object of potential wealth to be commodified and exploited for economic gain. From hearing voices within Oceania's traditional narratives, Hauʻofa came to an understanding that scientific and economic views of the Pacific restricted and controlled ordinary people from thinking outside the bounds of hegemonic capitalist perspectives.[32]

> When our leaders and planners say that our future lies in the sea, they are thinking only in economic terms; about marine and seabed resources and their development. When people talk of the importance of the oceans for the continuity of life on Earth, they are making scientific statements. But for us in Oceania, the sea defines us, what we are and have always been.

---

[28] Hauʻofa, *We Are the Ocean*, 37.   [29] Hauʻofa, *We Are the Ocean*, 52.
[30] Hauʻofa, *We Are the Ocean*, 37.   [31] Hauʻofa, *We Are the Ocean*, 54.
[32] Hauʻofa, *We Are the Ocean*, 27, 54.

Hau'ofa knew that '[o]ur roots, our origins, are embedded in the sea', and that it is something we all share in common wherever we are in Oceania.[33] He affirmed that *ko e kakai mei tahi*, the people from the sea, have responsibilities to the sea as its caretaker, defender, and protector.[34] Therefore, 'ecologically based oral traditions' had taught him to appreciate the Pacific Ocean as the first ancestor, home, and an elder – indeed as a mother and provider for her peoples – the most central figure of the Oceanian family.[35]

Cosmogony, Responsibility, and Poetry

'No people on earth are more suited to be guardians of the world's largest ocean than those for whom it has been home for generations', according to Hau'ofa.[36] Hau'ofa was resolute that the present-day descendants of *ko e kakai mei tahi*, the people from the sea, were the rightful guardians of Oceania.[37] This chapter began with a *maau*, a poem, grounded in cosmogonic stories about the Tongans of Oceania and their spiritual, ancestral, historical, and cultural relationship to Vahanoa, the Open Sea. The stories to which my introductory poem allude remind Oceanians of *fatongia*, their reciprocal responsibility to the ocean. The poem is written in Tongan *heliaki*, a figurative and formal language, the actual function of which is to provide a creative strategy in which *mālie*, beauty, can be created by expressing the unity of two things that are similar. *Heliaki* is also used in a poetic account of history. Māhina identifies *heliaki* as one of the 'artistic and literary devices' used in the Tongan performing arts.[38] It is similar to other artistic devices, such as *kupesi* (geometric designs), *haka* (choreographic motif), and *fatongia* (mutual responsibility). *Heliaki* in the Tongan language can be distinguished as two types; Māhina has identified *heliaki* as a qualitative technique called epiphoric, as well as being associative, or metaphoric.[39] In my work, I have classified *heliaki* as metonymic (or synecdochic) and metaphoric. By this, I mean that metonymic *heliaki* signifies the unity between two things, whereas metaphoric *heliaki* connotes that a similarity exists.[40] The poems that I have composed at the opening and closing of this chapter pay tribute to Hau'ofa's cosmogonic stories about the sea and their relationship to contemporary environmentalism and they use both forms of *heliaki*, metonymic

---

[33] Hau'ofa, *We Are the Ocean*, 57–58.   [34] Hau'ofa. *We Are the Ocean*, 32.
[35] Hau'ofa, *We Are the Ocean*, 64.   [36] Hau'ofa, *We Are the Ocean*, 37.
[37] Hau'ofa, *We Are the Ocean*, 32.   [38] Māhina, 'Tā, vā, and moana'.
[39] Māhina, 'Tā, vā, and moana'.   [40] Ka'ili, *Marking Indigeneity*, 61.

and metaphoric. I now offer an explanation of the meanings that my first poem conveys and also a detailed explanation of the ancestors, particularly Tangaloa, Māui, and Hina, that are mentioned in the poem.

The Ocean as an Ancestor

The first stanza of the poem prompts Tongans specifically and Oceanians generally to remember that the sea is an ancient ancestor, as well as an original homeland.[41] Highlighting marine life, such as *Limu*, Seaweed, and *Kele*, Sea Sediment, as relatives and family members, it implores Tongans, as well as Oceanians, to take into account our Indigenous cosmology and worldview of ocean resources. It calls on Pacific peoples to unite against economic pressures to mine our seabeds for minerals. *Kele*, Sea Sediments, are kin, and not merely objects or commodities for commercial extraction and exploitation, as some seabed acts have prescribed. To contextualize some of the Tongan language terms used in the introductory poem, *Tupu'anga* is the Tongan cognate for *tupuna, tupuga, kupuna* – words meaning 'ancestor' in a variety of Moana Nui languages.[42] The piece is comprised of four Tongan verses – focusing specifically on ancestors Tangaloa, Māui, and Hina – and an English translation of those verses, which makes a total of eight verses. In Moana Nui numerology, the number eight signifies power and might.[43] Eight was the number of men who manned a fishing vessel taken out to Vahanoa (the Open Sea), to search for Hina (the shark goddess). Eight therefore symbolizes perfect symmetry in the Tongan performing arts.[44] My poetic reference to the god Tangaloa 'Atulongolongo transforming into Kiu or Tuli'one – a plover bird indigenous to the Tonga Islands – emphasizes his flight over the sea in search of the first land. According to Tongan deep history, from the deeds of Tangaloa 'Atulongolongo came 'Ata, the first island in the Tonga Group. Lastly, my recollection of the Tongan oral tradition of Māui 'Atalanga and Māui Kisikisi who sailed to Manuka – Manu'a in Sāmoa – illustrates how they obtained Māta'u Fusifonua – the

---

[41] I am aware that the sea is an original homeland to some Oceanians, not all.

[42] *Tupuna* is ancestor in Māori, *tupuga* is ancestor in Samoan, and *kupuna* is ancestor in Hawaiian.

[43] T.O. Ka'ili, 'Hoa patterns: binary, repetition, symmetry, kupesi, and mana', keynote address during the Pacific Patterns Session of the Interstices Under Construction Symposium (Auckland University of Technology, 4 June 2017).

[44] Ka'ili, 'Hoa patterns'.

Land Fishing Hook, from the Tu'i Manu'a. Tongamatamoana, as mentioned above, was also known by the name Tonga Fusifonua – Tonga, the Land Fisher and Hauler. The island of Tonga, which is the main atoll in the Tonga Group, is named after Tongamatamoana, otherwise known as Tonga Fusifonua.[45]

Tangaloa: Creation God Manifested in Winged Creatures, Marine Life, and Ocean

The second verse recalls the story of Tangaloa 'Atulongolongo, the ancient Tongan deified ancestor who metaphorically transformed into a Pacific golden plover searching for an island to settle. Tangaloa 'Atulongolongo combed the ocean far and wide, sighting a coral reef rising from out of the sea. He asked his divinized brother Tangaloa Tufunga (Tangaloa the Artisan) to pour down shavings and wood chips from his workshop in *Langi*, Skyworld, to help the coral reef grow into an island. This part of the poem is a poetic reference to the history of settlement of Tonga by the Tangaloa clan. The poem also appeals to Tongan people to care for their corals, which are an integral natural resource named in the origin story of our islands. My views of Oceania are those at the level of ordinary people, urging Tongans to dispute all human activity that leads to coral bleaching and work towards the conservation of this natural resource, especially considering that Tonga has 7 per cent of the world's coral reefs and 6 per cent of the world's sea mountains.[46] My words appeal to Tongan sensitivities in the hope that people will embrace their spiritual and cultural connection to migratory shore birds, like Kiu – the Pacific golden plover – along with their responsibilities to conserve all Tongan avian species, whether they be shore birds, sea birds, or land birds.[47] Tongan deep history points to the Kiu as a significant bird in the deep-sea migration of Tongans. Protecting avian habitats is crucial to the twenty-first century survival of birds that are indigenous to the Tonga Islands. Tangaloa, in many eastern Moana Nui traditions, is also associated with the ocean.

Within the Moana Nui region, there is an annihilation of both environmental and ancestral seascapes. This is a cataclysm ushered in at the advent

---

[45] Martin, 'Origin of the name Tonga Island'.   [46] Hau'ofa, *We Are the Ocean*, 27

[47] M. Moala, *'Efinangá: Ko e Ngaahi Tala mo e Anga Fakafonua 'o Tongá* (Nuku'alofa, Tonga: Lali, 1994), 220–2; D. Watling, *Tohi Talateu ki he Manupuna 'o Tonga. Guide to the Birds of the Kingdom of Tonga* (privately published, 2006).

of European colonization and perpetuated today within the 'logic of erasure' and practice of denying history, two core features of settler colonialism.[48] In spite of this onslaught, there is a hint of hope on the horizon with the re-emergence of Tangaloa in Oceania.

This section floats on the sea of Tangaloa while firmly anchored on the Indigenous-based tā–vā (time–space) philosophy of reality;[49] specifically, the Moana Nui configuration of time–space to honour the deep history and ancestral geography of foremothers and forefathers. This tā–vā, time–space, orientation is at the heart of the contemporary rising of the ancestor Tangaloa. Ancestors are at the core of Moana Nui Indigenous spirituality because they are temporospatially located at the front as leaders to guide the present and future.[50] They are also the origin of *mana*, spiritual power, and the creators of deep genealogical ties to all elements of the ecosystem. These extensive kinship ties give rise to sacred responsibility, *fatongia*, to care for and protect all elements of the *fonua* (ecology); particularly, elements that are ancestral, like Tangaloa and his ocean.[51]

For the Moana Nui region, a place where many diverse cultures have intimate relationships with the ocean, it makes sense that the ocean would give rise to sea deities such as Tangaloa, Hina, Māui, and a concourse of others. As mentioned above, Tangaloa, in Moana Nui, emerged as the god of creation and the ocean. He is widely regarded throughout Moana Nui as one of the primordial gods of the ancient religion. He is venerated through-out the region by the divine title of Tangaloa, Tangaroa, Tagaloa, Ta'aroa, Tana'oa, Tanaloa, and Kanaloa. Even in places such as the Philippines, it is believed that Tangaloa was worshipped as Angaro.[52] The expansive scope of the spread of Tangaloa points to him as one of the founding ancestors, at least in Moana Nui. His Highness Tui Atua Tupua Tamasese Ta'isi Efi refers to Tangaloa as 'a very important founding ancestor' who is mythology,

---

[48] H.-K. Trask, 'Settlers of color and "immigrant" hegemony: "locals" in Hawai'i', *Amerasia Journal* 26:2 (2000), 1–24; P. Wolfe, 'Settler colonialism and the elimination of the native', *Journal of Genocide Research* 8:4 (2006), 387–409.

[49] Māhina, 'Tā, vā, and moana'; 'O. Māhina, 'Time, space, and culture: a new tā–vā theory of Moana anthropology', *Pacific Studies* 40:1/2 (2017), 105–32; Ka'ili et al., 'Introduction: tā–vā (time–space)'.

[50] L. Kame'eleihiwa, *Native Land and Foreign Desires: Ko Hawai'i Āina a me Nā Koi Pu'umake a ka Po'e Haole* (Honolulu: Bishop Museum Press, 1992).

[51] S.F.P. Lafitani, 'Moanan-Tongan fatongia and deontic of Greco-Rome: *fiefia*, happiness, of *tauēlangi*, climactic euphoria, and *'alaha kakala*, permeating fragrance – *Mālie! Bravo!*', PhD thesis, Australian Catholic University, 2011.

[52] Lane Wilcken, personal communication, 15 March 2017.

history, culture, and heritage; all lands and chiefly titles link back to him.[53]. Fundamentally, Tangaloa and other deified ancestors are the origin of chiefly lineages, and in Tonga the current king, Tupou VI, and all the chiefs, *hou'eiki*, are descendants of Tangaloa. In certain parts of Moana Nui, Tangaloa is the creation god, who brought forth the ocean and the islands, and in other parts, he is the god of the ocean, the master navigator-astronomer of long-distant voyaging. He is also the avatar of all forms of marine life and migratory winged creatures. In Tonga and Sāmoa he is linked to the Pacific golden plover bird (Kiu, Tulī, Tuli'one), and in Hawai'i he is the embodiment of the Hawaiian hoary bats ('Ōpe'ape'a) and marine life, such as octopuses, whales, dolphins, corals (also an incarnation of the goddess Hina), and other oceanic creatures. In some islands, Tangaloa is multiplied into several deities who are responsible for different divine realms. Tonga, for example, has at least seven Tangaloa deities. They are Tangaloa 'Eiki (ruler of Langi-Skyworld), Tangaloa Tufunga (deity of material arts), Tangaloa 'Atulongolongo (divine messenger), Tangaloa Tamapo'ulialamafoa, Tangaloa 'Eitumatupu'a (divine father of the First King of Tonga), Tangaloa Langi (ruler of natural forces), and Tangaloa Mana. It is Tangaloa Mana, or Powerful Tangaloa, who is the specific god of the ocean in Tongan lore.[54] By naming the god of the ocean Tangaloa Mana, it points to the *mana*, spiritual power/potency, of the sea. Although there are various aspects of Tangaloa, such as his important link to *kava*, I will limit my focus in this section to Tangaloa Mana and his ocean sphere since I have focused on Tangaloa 'Atulongolongo and Tangaloa Tufunga in the above section.

In reality, Tangaloa is an actual ancestor who was divinized as a result of his vast knowledge and profound relationship to the ocean. He was a leading Indigenous scientist of ancient times and spaces who gained empirical knowledge after generations of empirical observations of the ocean; hence, he became legendary and mythical. Today, most Islanders from Moana Nui trace their genealogy to Tangaloa. As for me, Tangaloa is my 36th great-grandfather.

---

[53] Tupua Tamasese Ta'isi Tui Atua Efi, *Su'esu'e Manogi: In Search of Fragrance* (Lepapaigalagala, Sāmoa: The Centre for Samoan Studies, National University of Sāmoa, 2009), 191; Tupua Tamasese Ta'isi Tui Atua Efi, 'Whispers and vanities in Samoan Indigenous religious culture', in T.M. Suaalii-Sauni et al. (eds.), *Whispers and Vanities: Samoan Indigenous Knowledge and Religion* (Wellington: Huia, 2014), 42–4.
[54] Moala, *'Efinangá*, 4.

Eradication of Tangaloa and His Ocean Realm

The eradication of Tangaloa and his oceanic realm began with European imperialism; particularly, the pernicious extraction of resources from the ocean for the sole benefit of the imperial centre. European whaling, for example, hunted and killed whales to near extinction to obtain meat, oil, and blubber for Europe. While resources were being squeezed out at an alarming rate from the sea of Tangaloa, some of the Christian missionaries mounted a frontal attack on Tangaloa and the Indigenous Moana Nui deities and labelled them as 'paganism'. In Tonga and Sāmoa, Tangaloa was de-divinized and relegated to superstition. In Hawai'i, Kanaloa was recast by Christian missionaries as Satan. This dethroning of Tangaloa led to all forms of desecration by colonizers and settlers, from demolishing sacred Tangaloa stones to the defilement of carved images of Tangaloa. This iconoclastic ideology led not only to the loss of beautiful arts but also Indigenous scientific knowledge. Today, in Tonga, not a single carved image or even a replica of a carved image of Tangaloa survived the onslaught of colonization. Other places, such as Hawai'i, Tahiti, Cook Islands, Niue, and Aotearoa, were more successful in protecting their carved images of Tangaroa from overzealous missionaries, both foreign and local.

Once Tangaloa was weakened, it was just a matter of time before other forms of debasement followed. As Tangaloa waned into obscurity, the ocean was viewed no longer as an ancestor, a spiritual place, or a source of *mana*, but rather as a raw material to be extracted for colonial and corporate greed. Over the years of intense colonization, the ocean began to suffer immensely from the pathologies of modernity. These extend to the devastation from nuclear testing (Marshall Islands, Christmas Island, Johnston Atoll, Muroroa, Fangataufa), military weapons testing (Kanaloa-Kaho'olawe, Pōhakuloa, Mākua, Hawai'i, Gåni, Guåhan), and the corporate drilling for oil. Oceania's desecration continues in forms such as pollution from the ubiquitous plastics of modernity and noise from industrial and military ships. Single-use plastics and discarded nets/ropes choke the life out of Tangaloa's marine environment. Noise from seismic surveying for oil and military sonar testing (i.e. the US Navy's sonar testing in Hawai'i) deafens and disorientates ocean life, which has led to numerous whale beachings and other problems. In addition, Oceania suffers from the depletion of fish stocks, particularly tuna, due to overfishing; deep-sea trawling nets that 'bulldoze' the seabed have destroyed the ocean floor and killed nearly all its living creatures. Deep-sea bottom trawling is oceanocide. Acidification of the ocean due to high concentrations of carbon dioxide in the atmosphere from the over-consumption of fossil fuel, the killing of sharks for their fins (shark-finning), the killing of turtles for their shells, the over-harvesting of sea cucumbers, the bleaching of corals as a result of the high usage of oxybenzone sunscreen products, and the depletion of sea sand because of sand mining to feed the voracious appetites of concrete construction (i.e. mining of sand from Māui for constructions on Oʻahu) continue the threats. Now, the world is on the brink of yet another marine life decimation with the beginning of seabed mining (in Papua New Guinea) for the purpose of attaining minerals to keep up with the demands of modern technology. This is a result of nations and corporations nearly exhausting the minerals on land in their unsustainable development projects.

This depressing story only accounts for the oceanic realm of Tangaloa. On land, Tangaloa is also under attack. Two examples will suffice. First is the slaughtering of ʻŌpeʻapeʻa (Hawaiian hoary bats), a symbolization of Tangaloa,[55] by the operation of industrial wind turbines throughout Hawaiʻi in the march for renewable clean energy. Industrial wind turbines are destructive to all bats and birds, supposedly to save the world in the twisted logic of settler colonialism. Second is the demolishing of historical sites associated with the chiefly descendants of Tangaloa for modern development. Case in point, the destruction of the historically culturally significant *sia*, mounds, in Tonga for a modern eighteen-hole golf course.

Re-emergence of Tangaloa and His Ocean Sphere

The heartbreaking account of the colonial destruction and settler denial and erasure of Tangaloa is not the end of the story. Fortunately, certain groups within Oceania and their allies are mounting an ambitious effort to listen to and revive ancestor Tangaloa and his creation. His Highness Tui Atua Tupua Tamasese Taʻisi Efi and others are at the forefront of resuscitating Tangaloa and the Indigenous religion of Sāmoa.[56] Whether or not you agree with Tui Atua and his approach to reconcile Tangaloa and the Christian God, his work is noteworthy in raising awareness of Tangaloa and the Indigenous spirituality of kinship with all living things. Tui Atua maintains that Tangaloa is the ʻprogenitor of all living things on earth (humans, animals, plants, cosmos,

---

[55] R.K.K. Johnson, *The Kumulipo Mind: A Global Heritage in the Polynesian Creation Myth* (Honolulu: University of Hawaiʻi Press, 2000), 78.

[56] Tupua Tamasese Taʻisi Tui Atua, ʻWhispers and vanities in Samoan Indigenous religious culture'; D. Pouesi (dir.), *The Search for Tagaloa*, YouTube video, 2017, https://youtube/NAUJvKTipCQ.

sea, land, etc.) and that as such all relationships between these living things are governed by the imperatives of being kin'.[57] This Indigenous cosmology (worldview) of being kin with all living things is now advanced by several groups in Oceania. These groups are also listening to the symphony of voices for guidance that are singing from the multiple Oceanic avatars of Tangaloa.

Māui: An Oceanian Deity Fishing Up Islands

The third verse of my introductory poem evokes the ocean deities, Māui and Hina. These salt water divinities are common throughout certain areas of Moana Nui. In Tonga, Māui Kisikisi or Māui Fusifonua acquired the magical fishhook from the Tuʻi Manuʻa to fish up the island archipelago. Therefore, I call to Tongan fishers – men and women – to use their collective power to uplift the Tonga Islands, in the same manner in which Māui Kisikisi elevated the islands from out of the sea. Urging local fishers to be good stewards by fishing sustainably in Tongan waters, I point to destructive methods such as the 'wall-of-death' technique that Hauʻofa mentioned, where outsized nets haphazardly slay not only the catch being fished for, but also threatened species. For inshore fisheries, the over-harvesting of *mokohunu*, sea cucumber, for sale on the Asian market has depleted Tonga's stock to the point where state moratoriums have been enforced on the gathering and selling of this marine species.

Besides fishing up islands, Māui is also known for snaring the sun and slaying ferocious monsters. Māui also seized fire from the gods. He surfed and battled monsters simultaneously. Deep history points to Māui as the one who invented surfing. Māui also originated tattooing and created the first dog in some of the traditions. He was an accomplished agriculturist. In my homeland of Tonga, he was the first person to plant and harvest sweet potatoes, taros, breadfruits, and yams. As a farmer, he was also skilled in cooking his food in an ʻumu, an underground oven. He was probably the inventor of the ʻumu technology in Moana Nui. Māui used his trickery to outsmart his oppressors; hence the nickname, 'Māui, the trickster'. Finally, Māui was a great leader, a liberator and freedom fighter; he always fought for the underdog and liberated the oppressed.

The grand messages of Māui's stories are to advocate for justice by transforming society. Māui's feats are actually heliaki, beautiful poetic

---

[57] Tupua Tamasese Taʻisi Tui Atua, 'Whispers and vanities in Samoan Indigenous religious culture', 43.

Ancestral Voices of the Sea

expressions, of resisting oppression and fighting injustice for the benefit of humanity.[58]

As a devout student of Moana Nui traditions, a voracious reader of Māui stories, and a direct descendant of Māui who feasted upon the tales of Māui from a young age, there are lessons I hear and learn from Māui's legacy.

Let me explain: In Moana Nui traditions, Māui the landfisher was the youngest child, the one with the least status. He had older brothers who took pride in taking advantage of him, particularly making fun of his skill as a fisherman. However, despite his status as the youngest, Māui acquired the most potent *mana*, or supernatural power, from his ancestors. His position gave him insights into sibling rivalries, power relations, and the unfairness of certain cultural rules, particularly the automatic granting of prestige and wealth to the people who did not work for and sometimes abused their power. The dualistic tension between older siblings and younger siblings, between the powered and the less powered, is a central motif in the Māui saga.

In Moana Nui culture generally and Tongan specifically, the sun is a symbol for paramount chiefs. The legendary act of snaring and slowing down the sun to give Māui's mother, Hina, time to make tapa cloths and Māui's relatives time to plant and fish, points to Māui freeing society from its oppressive rulers. These rulers oppressed people by giving them little time to complete demanding tasks. The impressive feat of lifting up the sky so that humans could stop crawling and start walking upright denotes Māui liberating the masses from the taxing burdens of the oppressive class. In a similar fashion, the epic task of fishing up islands signifies Māui searching and locating islands for those without lands, exiles, and refugees.

Fire, another Oceanic symbol, signifies knowledge and technology.[59] Māui seized fire from the hoarding hands of the gods and shared it with the rest of humanity. In this way, Māui democratized knowledge and shared technology freely with the world. It can be seen as an ancient version of open-source. Māui was the champion of the underclass, the dispossessed, and the marginalized. Finally, the courageous deed of slaying man-eating monsters symbolizes Māui dismantling of monstrous institutions of domination that were devouring humanity. In all the accounts of Māui, he refused to accept his

---

[58] Māhina, 'The Tongan traditional history'; 'O. Māhina, 'Oceanic mythology', in J. Parker and J. Stanton (eds.), *Mythology: Myths, Legends, & Fantasies* (Australia: Global Book Publishing, 2003), 374–81.

[59] I.F. Helu, *Critical Essays: Cultural Perspectives from the South Seas* (Canberra: Journal of Pacific History, 1999).

marginalized lot in society. He resisted and fought against all forms of injustice, from ageism to xenophobia. Through his wisdom as a grand-master trickster of Oceania, he transformed society from inequality to equality. Māui is the leader and culture hero who is the embodiment of fairness, justice, and equity. His power is said to emanate from the goddess Hina, who is often described in mythologies as Māui's grandmother, mother, wife, or sister. The feminine is the true source of Māui's *mana*, the power that he exercised in transforming the impossibility to the possibility.

Hina: Goddess of the Moon, Tapa, and Sharks

Again in verse three, the two lines about Hina advise the Tongan people to remember and hearken to her as the shark goddess of ancient times, suggesting that shark fishing must be carried out in a sustainable way with respect to the same fashion in which the legendary Sinilau and the shark-hunters of old venerated Hina, the shark, by throwing fragrant flowers into the ocean as an offering before taking their catch. These lines pay homage to Halakakala, the fragrant garland pathway of the ocean, which lay beyond the island of 'Eueiki in the Tongan archipelago in a sacred sea area where the old shark-hunters would offer flowers to Hina to attract their catch.[60] The reference to Hina, the shark goddess, beseeches Tongans to protect sharks by discontinuing the inhumane practice of shark-finning, which is increasing in Tonga due to the high demand for shark fins from certain Asian markets.

Hina is the archetypal goddess while Māui is the archetypal god. This duality of female and male deities appears in various forms in Moana Nui legends as Hina and Sinilau, Hine and Tinirau, Sina and Tuna, Hina and Rū, or Hina and Kū. At times the duality is complementary, and at other times it is rife with tensions. In Moana Nui lores, the association of a powerful goddess with a mighty god creates symmetry which gives rise to harmony, and, above all, beauty in the stories. This symmetrical configuration is a common motif.

Within the indigenous-based tā–vā (time–space) philosophy of reality, symmetry, or rhythmicity lies a coexisting harmony and beauty.[61] This is

---

[60] T.J. Brown Pulu, 'Kakai Tonga 'i Okalani Nu'u Sila: Tongan generations in Auckland New Zealand', PhD thesis, University of Waikato, Hamilton, 2007, xxi; K. Velt and T. Helu, *Langi Tau'olunga & Hiva Kakala: A Collection of Currently Popular Tau'olunga Dance Songs in Tonga, with Some Translations, History, Music Sheets and Video Recordings* (Nuku'alofa: Tau'olunga Komipiuta, 2001), 17.

[61] Māhina, 'Tā, vā, and moana'; Ka'ili et al., 'Introduction: tā–vā (time–space)'.

vividly displayed in many of the Oceanian art forms: in myths, proverbs, chants, incantations, fine mats, *tā tatau* (tattoos), tapa cloths, performances, and drummings. In the exquisite decorative-binding lashing known as Tongan *lalava*, the black coconut-sennit cord signifies female, and the red/brown coconut-sennit cord denotes male.[62]

The symmetrical interweaving of these two sennit cords creates *kupesi*, intricate-complex geometrical designs, like the patterns in Moana Nui tattoos. Similarly, in Moana Nui myths, the symmetrical juxtaposition within the same mythological narrative of a powerful god, like Māui, and an equally *mana*-ful goddess, like Hina, constitutes harmony, and of course, *mālie* (beauty).

Hina, as the archetypal goddess, is one of the oldest matriarchal deities in Polynesia. She is the goddess that is most widely known throughout Moana Nui, referred to regionally by the names of as Hina, Sina, Hine, and Ina. In fact, many of the Moana Nui goddesses have names with the prefix Hina, Hine, Sina, or Ina. Traditionally, Hina is closely linked to the moon, ocean, sea creatures (particularly sharks, corals, and spiny creatures), tapa making, mat weaving, coconut, breadfruit, and beauty. In most Māui accounts, Hina is the supreme source of Māui's *mana*, supernatural power.

Depending on the version, the goddess Hina (or Hina-like goddess) is Māui's grandmother, mother, wife, or sister. In one Māori version, Hina is the oldest sister of Māui. She taught Māui how to use her hair to plait a supernatural rope for snaring the sun and lengthening the days.

By using her hair, Hina infused *mana* into Māui's sun-snaring lasso. In one legend, Māui attempted seven times to capture the sun and failed. He finally succeeded on the eighth try when he used a rope made from Hina's hair. In Hawai'i, Hina is a central goddess in Māui's land fishing expeditions. In one version, Māui threw his fishhook to the ocean and called upon Hina for help. Hina took Māui's fishhook and carried it deep into the moana (ocean). She fastened it to the mouth of the protector one-tooth shark, Ka'unihokahi, who was responsible for holding down the islands. In this version, it is both Hina and Māui who fished up the Hawaiian islands. Like Māui, Hina is a land-fisher.

---

[62] Filipe Tohi, *Filipe Tohi: Genealogy of Lines: Hohoko e Tohitohi* (New Plymouth: Govett-Brester Art Gallery, 2002); S.F. Potauaine and 'O. Māhina, 'Kula and 'uli: red and black in Tongan thinking and practice', in T.M. Steen and N.L. Drescher (eds.), *Tonga: Land, Sea and People* (Nuku'alofa: Vava'u Press, 2011), 194–216.

Here in Kahuku where I live, Hina secured and fastened the floating island of Kahuku to Oʻahu with two mighty fishhooks, known as Pōlou and Kalou (in another version, this feat was accomplished by Māui).[63] The close relationship between Hina and sharks appears in Tongan legends in which Hina shape-shifts into a shark. Yes, Hina can shape-shift like Māui. In Tonga, shark-hunters recite a chant, in chiefly language, to the shark goddess Hina for success in their shark fishing expeditions. This is why in some stories Hina resides undersea.

In another Hawaiian legend, Hina is the mother of Māui. She bestowed upon Māui the magical rope and adze to snare the sun. It was also Hina, in the form of an ʻalaeʻula, mudhen bird, who taught Māui the secret of firemaking in Hawaiʻi. Māui, in one Hawaiian account, used the ʻalaeʻula bird as bait for fishing up islands. In one Samoan tale, Māui obtained his powerful fishhook from Sina.[64] Several of the legends give credit to Hina or a Hina-like figure (Muri-ranga-whenua in Aotearoa or Tavatava-i-manuka in Tonga) for granting Māui his fishhook. Other tales say that Māui fashioned his fishhook from a shell from Hina's reef. Hina and Māui are also memorialized in the landscapes of the same locality. In my ancestral home island of Koloa, Vavaʻu, Hina's Cave (ʻAna ʻo Hina) and ʻAtalanga (Māui's residence) are located in the same island. Finally, the complementary roles of Hina and Māui are manifested in their respective links to the moon and the sun.

Mythologically, Hina is the lunar goddess while Māui is the solar god. During the day Māui guides voyagers with the sun, and at night Hina directs them with the moon. In Tahiti, Hawaiʻi, and Tonga, Hina is seen sitting in the moon beating tapa under a tree (breadfruit or banyan tree). Like Māui, Hina is intimately connected to navigation. According to Tahitians, Hina is the guardian and protector of travellers at night. In one Hawaiian tale, the moon and the stars escaped to the heavens from Hina's food calabash. All of these complementary roles of Hina and Māui are revealed in the foundational colours of dark and light in Moana Nui intricate and elaborate geometrical designs, kupesi. Again, the symmetrical intertwining of dark/Hina and light/Māui creates beautiful intricate-complex geometrical patterns.

Hina, the shark and coral goddess in Moana Nui cosmology, is speaking to us that the ocean is a feminine place of power that we need to nurture and safeguard.

---

[63] Hina is known as Waka in the Kahuku story. Waka is another name for Hina-i-ke-kā.

[64] J. Fitisemanu, 'Maui is more than a vacation destination', 19 November 2016, www.facebook.com/notes/jacob-fitisemanu-jr/maui-is-more-than-a-vacation-destination/10155588051978521/.

Ancestral Voices of the Sea

Paying Homage to Epeli Hau'ofa, an Ancestor

In the final stanza of my introductory poem, I pay my respects to the late Epeli Hau'ofa for sharing and spreading his vision as *tufunga Moana*, the Oceanian artisan, who remembered and revered our spiritual and cultural links to the Pacific Ocean, and our ancestral duty to safeguard, nurture, and sustain ocean life, which in turn sustains us, the people from the sea, *ko e kakai mei tahi*.[65] The writings of Hau'ofa raised global awareness of climate change in the Pacific Ocean – the plastic pollution, the acidification of the sea, and the rising salt water levels affecting fresh water reserves on small low-lying islands. These were just some, not all, of the multiple stressors that can have a lethal and lasting effect on our ocean, our ancestor, our home. Thus, Hau'ofa is calling us from Pulotu, the ancestral world of spirits, to rise to the challenge of performing our vā'ifaiva, tempo-spatial role, as the 'guardians of the largest ocean'.[66]

On that note, I conclude my chapter with another poem of mine to encourage the descendants of the people from the sea who are living today, to listen to their ancestors Tangaloa, Māui, and Hina.

Fanongo kia Tangaloa, Māui, mo Hiná

Listen to Tangaloa, Māui, and Hina

Tulou atu ki he Moaná
'O Tangaloa, Māui, mo Hiná
Kae 'atā pea ngofua e vahá
Ketau folau mo tuli kaveingá
He kuo langitamaki e taulangá

My deepest reverence to the Ocean
Of ancestors Tangaloa, Māui, and
  Hina
So that we may be granted permission
To voyage and follow the
  constellations
Away from the Climate Crisis of our
  situation

Tala tokua ko e fakalakalaká
Hono ta'angaloa e vaotā tupu'á
Mo e keli lotomoana mo e
  lolofonuá
Isa, ta koa ko si'ono tāpalasiá
Si'i Ta'ahine ko Langi, Moana, mo
  Fonuá

They tell us it was progress
To cut and clear our ancient forests
And mine our seas and underground
  fortress
But in reality it was all to oppress
Our Heaven, Sea, and Land Empress

'E Tangaloa ko e 'uluaki tufungá

Oh Tangaloa the first artisan
Formed and laid us a foundation

---

[65] Hau'ofa, *We Are the Ocean*, 32.   [66] Hau'ofa, *We Are the Ocean*, 37.

727

Tā mo fakatoka mai ha makatuʻungá Ke tuʻu ai e ʻotu motu fonuá ʻO talia e ngalu mo e peau fakaʻauhá	To establish our island nations And weather the waves of devastation
Māui ko e ʻiloa he fusifonuá Fakatele mai hoʻo mātaʻu maná Ke keina ia e matafonuá Pea maʻanu ai he tahi kaifonuá	Oh Māui the legendary fisher of land Throw us your magical hook and hand To catch our coastal sea and land Keeping us afloat the rising sea at hand
ʻE Hina e ko e ʻanga mei muʻá Maʻanuʻanu ketau kamatá Potanga ika mo luki tenifá ʻI he tahi ʻo e kau fakakovifonuá	Oh Hina our ancestral shark Surface that we may embark On ways to unite and fight The slayers of our Earth's rights
Siʻi kāinga ʻo e Moana-Nui-a-Kivá Fanongo kia Tangaloa, Māui, mo Hiná Pea mo e ui mei hotau Tahi Tuʻufonuá Ko e hūfanga ia hotau kuongá	My dear kin of the Great Sea of Kiwa Listen to our ancestors Tangaloa, Māui, and Hina And hear the call of our Indigenous Oceania There, you will find the sanctuary for our Era

61

Defining the Contours of the Lagoon

*Political Strategies towards Post-Nouméa Accord Political Futures
in New Caledonia*

ANTHONY TUTUGORO

Introduction

If, for most of the states of the Pacific region, the question of political
sovereignty is now an old subject, it remains the keystone of all struggles
in New Caledonia. Since the end of the sixties, with the return of young
Kanak[1] and non-Kanak people who had gone to train in French universities,
and particularly later at the University of the South Pacific, the idea of
restoring the archipelago's lost sovereignty has been a constant source of
debate. The 'Pacific Way' so much advocated by Fiji's first post-
independence leader, Prime Minister Ratu Sir Kamisese Mara, has found
attentive ears on these South Pacific islands and the Kanak have not ceased
since then to overturn the stigmas of the past, assert themselves, and influence the future of their ancestral space.[2] The question of these islands'
accession to the rank of state is an ongoing process which still prompts
frequent, lively public debate. This makes it a special territory in a geographical area where the sovereignty of the Indigenous inhabitants of most of the
neighbouring countries has been recovered.

This chapter examines these issues as they have played out in New
Caledonia since the implementation of the Nouméa Accord signed on
5 May 1998.[3] Under the terms of the Accord, the French Republic committed
to increasing the political and economic power of the Indigenous inhabitants,

---

[1] Kanak is the term for the Indigenous inhabitants of New Caledonia whose ancestors first
arrived on the shores of the archipelago 3,000 years ago, around 1000 BCE.
[2] Ratu Sir Kamesese Mara, *The Pacific Way: A Memoir* (Honolulu: University of Hawai'i
Press, 1997).
[3] An English translation of the Nouméa Accord can be found in the *Australian Indigenous Law
Reporter*, 'Nouméa Accord', www.austlii.edu.au/au/journals/AILR/2002/17.html.

729

the Kanak, over a twenty-year period in response to their marginalization as a demographic minority in their own land. At the end of this period, three referenda would be held in 2018, 2020, and 2022 (later changed to 2021) respectively on whether the residents of New Caledonia wished to remain as part of France or to become an independent nation.[4] On a macro-political level, the debate concerns three main actors: the French state which colonized this space, the pro-independence groups who wish to achieve full sovereignty, and the non-independence groups who wish to remain within the French Republic. On a micro-political level, the situation is much more complex than it seems. Like Foucault, we need to look behind the surface to understand the micro-fights that are taking place on different terrains to conquer various legitimacies.[5] Behind the stakes of a favourable or unfavourable plebiscite on the country's self-determination, there are also multitudes of fierce battles to convince others that a shared future is achievable according to a number of arrangements that differ in their conceptions.

French settlement and conquest began in 1853 and was a slow and bloody process in which Indigenous resistance was never broken despite massive land confiscation and displacement onto reserves, a process, in part, enabled by the ravages of introduced disease. The Kanak population reached its lowest level in the 1890s as a result of introduced pathogens which spread over the archipelago as soon as the first ships arrived in the eighteenth century. Kanak population numbers began to slowly rise after this nadir. However, just as in other settler colonies such as Australia and Aotearoa New Zealand, connection to land and sea was never lost.[6] Farming, the service economy for a significant French government and military presence, and especially nickel have formed the backbone of the modern economy.[7] Economic opportunities

---

[4] N. MacLellan, 'The Nouméa Accord and decolonisation in New Caledonia', *Journal of Pacific History* 34:3 (1999), 245–52.

[5] See for example, M. Foucault, *L'archéologie du savoir* (Paris: Gallimard, 1969), and *Security, Territory, Population: Lectures at the Collège de France, 1977–78* (Basingstoke: Palgrave Macmillan, 2007).

[6] See for example C. Sand, J. Bolé, and A. Ouétcho, 'Prehistory and its perception in a Melanesian archipelago: the New Caledonia example', *Antiquity* 77:297 (2003), 505–19; C. Sand, J. Bolé, and A. Ouétcho, 'Les sociétés pré-européennes de Nouvelle-Calédonie et leur transformation historique: l'apport de l'archéologie', in A. Bensa and I. Leblic (eds.), *En pays kanak: ethnologie, linguistique, archéologie, histoire de la Nouvelle-Calédonie* (Paris: Éditions de la Maison des Sciences de l'Homme, 2000), 171–94; J. Guiart, *Structure de la chefferie en Mélanésie du sud*, vol. 1 (Paris: Institut d'Ethnologie, 1992); R. Ramsey, *Nights of Storytelling: A Cultural History of Kanaky-New Caledonia* (Honolulu: University of Hawai'i Press, 2011).

[7] For the modern history of New Caledonia, see J. Connell, *New Caledonia of Kanaky: The Political History of a French Colony* (Canberra: Development Studies Centre, Research School of Pacfic Studies, The Australian National University, 1987); D. Chappell, *Le réveil kanak: la montée*

Defining the Contours of the Lagoon

have drawn thousands of migrants to New Caledonia from other parts of the French Pacific, Asia, and metropolitan France, so that Kanak remain a minority in their own land. However, Kanak are the majority in two of the three provinces New Caledonia is divided into, with most non-Kanak concentrated in the South Province where the capital Nouméa is situated.[8]

'Nations are artefacts produced by the convictions, solidarity and loyalty of men', wrote philosopher and anthropologist Ernest Gellner in 1983.[9] According to this outlook, national outcomes therefore depend on which convictions are placed in which path forward, and solidarity and loyalty in whom to place one's faith. New Caledonia is a perfect example to illustrate these kinds of antagonisms.

The question of defining a flag is, for example, an efficient measurement tool to estimate the convictions, the solidarity, and the political loyalties during national constructions. On 6 March 2020, a curious debate occurred at the most representative assembly of New Caledonia's diversity, the Congress.[10] The high commissioner Laurent Prévost, highest representative of the French state in New Caledonia, who took up his post in July 2019 convened the Congress in an extraordinary session in order to discuss a decree concerning the use of the French flag during the campaign of the second referendum scheduled for 4 October 2020. An intense political debate ensued because this proposal had not been raised during the first consultation on 4 November 2018 in which New Caledonia's body of voters were asked 'Do you want New Caledonia to attain full sovereignty and become independent?'[11] The result was that the 'No' vote obtained a majority of 56.7 per cent and the 'Yes' 43.3 per cent. In 2020, the French state decided to put a juridical innovation into the second referendum in which only the French flag associated with the non-independence movement was to be flown. This would have overturned the 2010 vote by the Congress of New Caledonia in favour of flying the Kanak flag of the independence party FLNKS alongside the French tricolor.

---

du nationalisme en Nouvelle-Calédonie [French translation of *The Kanak Awakening*] (Noumea: Éditions Madrépores et l'Université de la Nouvelle-Calédonie, 2017).

[8] According to 2019 data, Kanak comprise 41.2 per cent of the population, Europeans 24.1 per cent, while the remaining 34.7 per cent are made up of a host of diverse groups, most notably Wallis and Futunan Islanders (8.3 per cent), and those defined as 'mixed' (11.3 per cent).

[9] E. Gellner, *Nations et nationalisme* (Paris: Bibliothèque Historique Puyot, 1989), 19.

[10] Congrès de la Nouvelle-Calédonie, Séance publique – vendredi 06 mars 2020 – 9h, public audience, 6 March 2020, www.youtube.com/watch?v=ulyydbzQKuA&t=7928s.

[11] In public law, the voting is not technically a 'referendum' but a 'consultation'. It means that the French parliament has to vote for a constitutional law after the consultation to enact New Caledonia's independence.

The Front de Libération Nationale Kanak et Socialiste (FLNKS) flag is rich in symbols of Kanak peoples' attachment to place and ancestry. Its three horizonal stripes represent the blue of the sky and especially the ocean symbols of sovereignty, the red of the blood spilt in the struggle for independence and the uterine blood which unites every Kanak, and the green of the nourishing land. A large yellow disc on the left-hand side representing the rising sun, in contrast to the West, frames a black *flèche faîtière*, the carved symbol representing the protecting ancestor at the top of houses, and crowned by the conch shell which is blown into in order to gather the clans for various occasions. The *flèche faîtière* connects Kanak to their ancestral spirits.

The high commissioner's proposal caused an uproar. Each 'non-independence' group argued in favour of this decree while all independence group representatives were against. Only a young party, the Eveil Océanien ('Oceanian Rising') composed of both independence and non-independence supporters didn't want to take part in the vote. The intensity of this public debate is apparent in the following statements made by the different political groups at the Congress. For some non-independence parties, the decree was considered as positive. Here is the position of the Avenir en Confiance (Confident Future) given among others by Sonia Backès:

> And so, I think that the fact that we are defending the maintenance of Caledonia in France is that we want to maintain the French flag in opposition to the independentists who no longer want to maintain the French flag. Simply so that there is no ambiguity! ... If you want independence, you don't want to be French any more, so I think that at some point you have to say things anyway. It seems obvious, but I think it's better to say it anyway.[12]

For another young party, Generation NC, which emerged from a fission within Calédonie Ensemble (Caledonia Together), the position of its leader Nicolas Metzdorf is even stronger:

> What country do you want to build? Because you're not sending us good signs! When we disagree with you, you change the rules. You support changing the rules. So the independent country you're carrying, what's behind it? Is it a tie between the two of us, or when we disagree, we're pushed aside? Where we do not defend the same rights. This debate is absurd! This debate is absurd! Preventing the supporters of maintaining

---

[12] Congrès de la Nouvelle-Calédonie, public audience, 6 March 2020.

Defining the Contours of the Lagoon

French New Caledonia from using the French flag? In a referendum for or against independence? Are we serious here?[13]

His former party, Calédonie Ensemble, seemed more reserved and open to discussions. For example, Philippe Michel, the president of the group, stated:

> I am very sad and concerned about what is happening today in the debate ... There is no doubt in the mind of any New Caledonian called upon to speak on 6 September ... that the FLNKS flag is indeed the flag of those who support access to full sovereignty and there is no doubt opposite that the 'blue white red' flag is indeed that of those who support maintaining New Caledonia in France! ... If we are in the first case, risk of confusion, we discuss seriously and we can move forward. If we are in the second case, it is insoluble. Let's vote right away and we know what the result of the vote will be. Voilà![14]

In contrast, the independence movement in the Congress of New Caledonia is composed of two political groups. Here was the position of the Union Calédonienne – Front de Libération Nationale Kanak et Socialiste given by Caroline Machoro:

> Mr State representative. All of us, the State and the Caledonians, were pleased with the smooth running of the 2018 consultation. Today, we have the right to question the behaviour of the State which unilaterally, I say unilaterally, and arbitrarily modifies the organisation of the next consultation. Introducing here doubt, confusion, suspicion, could set the country on a path and behaviour that we do not want to relive! We appeal to the responsibility of the State for the process of decolonization and emancipation for which it pledged its word in the Nouméa agreement to guarantee the peaceful conduct of the elections and to enable Caledonians to continue building their common destiny. Thank you.[15]

The Union Nationale pour l'Indépendance's position has yet to be given around this question. This group's chief, Louis Mapou, however, voiced strong disapproval of the decree:

> I find that you have the art of proposing conditions to set things in motion! And that, I denounce this attitude of the State! We don't agree! I'm telling you that with force here! We still have the fact that all the national parties

---

[13] Congrès de la Nouvelle-Calédonie, public audience, 6 March 2020.
[14] Congrès de la Nouvelle-Calédonie, public audience, 6 March 2020.
[15] Congrès de la Nouvelle-Calédonie, public audience, 6 March 2020.

that have succeeded the French government since 1988 have been careful not to interfere in the debate here. We are saying that the State, by displaying, by deciding to derogate from Article 27,[16] is taking a stand. I say this with great serenity. Takes position with all due respect to the representative of the State who has intervened in the commissions. Takes position in favour of maintaining within the Republic.[17]

Straight after this debate, a group of non-independence militants flew the French flag in the village of La Foa supporting their political parties. One day a month,[18] the independence militants fly the Kanak flag, in preparation for the next referendum which was scheduled for 6 September 2020. These scattered and frequent demonstrations show how divisive the issue of the flag can be, as it is representative of the current cleavage in New Caledonia between independence and non-independence proponents.[19] The second referendum occurred on 4 October 2020 and resulted in a slightly reduced vote against independence of 53.26 per cent as opposed to 56.7 per cent in 2018. Voter turnout was high at 85.69 per cent, meaning that New Caledonia remains deeply divided on this issue.

However, the end of the Nouméa Accord was supposed to be, from a juridical point of view, relatively simple. Indeed, many competences have already been transferred from the French state to New Caledonia's Congress, Government, and Provinces. At the end of the accord, a provision is in place that a consultation will occur asking New Caledonia's citizens only if they agree or not with 'the transfer to New Caledonia of the reserved powers, its achievement of full international responsibility status and the conversion of citizenship into nationality. Their approval would mean full sovereignty for New Caledonia.'[20] And in the case of a second majority of 'No' vote, a third consultation can occur later. In the case of three 'No' votes, the Nouméa Accord provides that, 'Should no majority in favour again be recorded, the

---

[16] This mention refers to Article R-27 of the French Electoral Code which prohibits 'the use of the national emblem as well as the juxtaposition of the three colours: blue, white and red as long as it is likely to cause confusion with the national emblem'. This article should not be confused with Article 27 of the 1999 Organic Law on New Caledonia, the implications of which will be explained later.

[17] Congrès de la Nouvelle-Calédonie, public audience, 6 March 2020.

[18] The second referendum was supposed to stand on 6 September 2020 but was postponed to 4 October 2020 because of the Covid-19 pandemic.

[19] Ideas developed in previous research in A. Tutugoro, 'The invention of a flag in New Caledonia. The beginnings of a common identity under construction', Master's 1 thesis, University of Rennes 1, 2014.

[20] *Australian Indigenous Law Reporter.*

political partners would meet to consider the situation thus arising.'[21] As we know, juridical solutions are always easier to find than political consensus. Even the question at the first consultation of 4 November 2018 wasn't asked in such a way as to raise both the terms of independence and full sovereignty in the same question.

These different positions just outlined through the flag debate reveal much about New Caledonia's political complexity. The different arguments exposed envisage different conceptions of the present and the future. During a conference held at the Jean Marie Tjibaou Cultural Center, anthropologist research fellow at the Centre de Recherche et de Documentation sur l'Océanie (CNRS) Benoît Trépied introduced his subject by noting that in New Caledonia 'everyone pretends to be claiming they favour decolonization but none of them puts the same concepts behind it'.[22] He outlined three tendencies among those favouring decolonization: those who conceptualize decolonization as independence, those who militate for decolonization inside another state, in this case France, which leads to more autonomy, and finally, those who see decolonization as the emergence of Indigenous rights defining a Kanak sovereignty.

The remainder of this chapter seeks to throw light on these different positions in order to give a broadened view of the different political strategies around the concept of sovereignty in New Caledonia. It details the complexity with which strategies are carried out on the spot with a view to achieving a multi-conceptual means of living together for New Caledonia's different communities of interest. It is transdisciplinary, borrowing tools from different branches of the political sciences such as history, sociology, and anthropology, and also uses reading grids utilized in public law. Multiple sources are included: scientific publications, the news media, personal notes, observation, and interviews with political actors conducted in New Caledonia during the author's PhD research.[23]

The different positions and political strategies of both sides are reviewed to give a cartography of the political landscape and multiple strategies used by the 'yes camp' and the 'no camp'. The complexity and diversity of

---

[21] *Australian Indigenous Law Reporter.*
[22] Caledonia Conference: 'Qu'est-ce que "décoloniser" veut dire?', 10 October 2018, .www .youtube.com/watch?v=EMGDZ2HrvqE&t=543s
[23] Anthony Tutugoro's thesis in process about the reclaiming strategies in use by the independence movement in New Caledonia and its conceptualization of sovereignty, provisionally entitled '(Re)thinking sovereignty. Reclaiming strategies by the independence movement in New Caledonia', L'université de la Polynésie française, Puna'aui'a/Université de la Nouvelle-Calédonie, Nouméa.

circumstances in New Caledonia mean we cannot deal with all the collective organizations campaigning for different outcomes in the territory. Rather it is intended to outline the most representative of them to get a picture of the political landscape in New Caledonia. We first illuminate the complexity of the different reactions and proposals around the question of New Caledonia's political future by asking the 'people concerned' and seeking their strategies to convince others, before then investigating the different possibilities envisaged for ending the Nouméa Accord for each side should they secure a majority vote.

Consider the 'Lagoon': New Caledonia's Diverse Political Strategies

This section will first present a holistic vision of the different tendencies within the political landscape of New Caledonia. We will first examine the Indigenous rights proponents militating for a Kanak sovereignty, before having a look at the classical duality between the pro-independence and non-independence political strategies.

Militating for a Kanak Sovereignty: 'A Narrow Path'?

Kanak groups have struggled to have their customary legitimacy recognized according to principles outlined in United Nations Indigenous rights statements.[24] The CNDPA, for example, is an organization composed of representatives of the Indigenous people of New Caledonia.[25] It has struggled to have Kanak rights to their territory recognized, regardless of the statutory evolution of the archipelago. In a 2012 interview, Dick Saihu, the CNDPA president, noted:

> The CNDPA in Kanaky works alongside the country's customary authorities. The Council's central post is still the customary ones. And the other non-governmental association works alongside the Customary Senate of New Caledonia. We are associated with different problems that are raised by the customary authorities of New Caledonia. We are a bit like the arms and feet of the Customary Senate in the field.[26]

---

[24] In reference to Isabelle Leblic's famous study, *Les Kanak face au développement: la voie étroite* (Grenoble: Presses Universitaires de Grenoble, 1993).

[25] Conseil National du Peuple Autochtone de Kanaky Nouvelle-Calédonie, see www.facebook .com/CNDPAKNC/.

[26] Nouvelle-Calédonie la Première [TV show], 'Interview with Dick Saihu, Président of the CNDPA', 2012, www.dailymotion.com/video/xsp86t.

In fact, the Nouméa agreement was supposed to place 'the Kanak at the centre of the system'.[27] However, it only gave an advisory role to the Customary Senate, the body that was supposed to embody the Kanak identity. The Customary Senate must be consulted for its opinion on any draft or proposed *loi de pays*[28] relating to Kanak identity and may optionally be consulted on any other matter. This has led the customary representatives to campaign in other forms to gain recognition for their proposals. Let us take up again the text of the agreement here:

> Colonisation harmed the dignity of the Kanak people and deprived them of their identity. In this confrontation, some men and women lost their lives or their reasons for living. Much suffering resulted from it. These difficult times need to be remembered, the mistakes recognized and the Kanak people's confiscated identity restored, which equates in its mind with a recognition of its sovereignty, prior to the forging of a new sovereignty, shared in a common destiny.[29]

For a researcher like New Caledonian educator and scholar Hamid Mokaddem, this section of the agreement constitutionally endorses any possibility of Kanak or Kanaky's sovereignty.[30] The new sovereignty is to be built only with all the components of the population of New Caledonia. However, the CNDPA in particular is positioning itself in a complementary manner to the Customary Senate in order to make its own contribution to this reflective debate. As the organization confided during an interview with Raphael Mapou and as Dick Saihu also reminded it during a conference commemorating the fiftieth anniversary of the distribution of the leaflet giving birth to the Foulards Rouges (Red Scarves), the CNDPA proposes asking about the restitution of sovereignty only to the Kanak people during the remaining referendum.[31] The thought behind this idea is to give visibility to who wishes to become independent among the Kanak people. The idea behind this proposal is not to militate against an internal sovereignty, as some New Caledonia French researchers have suggested.[32] Such an internal

---

[27] This formula is a common way of describing the Nouméa Accord's finality.
[28] A law which is applicable only in New Caledonia.
[29] Preamble of Nouméa Accord, see *Australian Indigenous Law Reporter*.
[30] H. Mokaddem, 'L'accord de Nouméa. Pratique de discours et forclusion de la souveraineté de Kanaky', *Journal de la Société des Océanistes*, 2018/2:147 (2018) 319–328. https://www.cairn.info/revue-journal-de-la-societe-des-oceanistes-2018-2-page-319.htm.
[31] The event took place at the Customary Senate on 4 Septembre 2019. Personal notes from the meeting.
[32] See the interview with Patrice Godin and Jone Passa, 'The anthropological basis of custom', intervention during a colloquium entitled 'Custom in Caledonian law' which took place on 27 May 2017 in Nouméa, www.youtube.com/watch?v=ocCbn1-gYtU&t=1634s.

sovereignty would mean a decolonization within the supervisory power. Rather, the aim is to try to demonstrate electorally to the French state that the majority of Kanak remain attached to their self-determination which would give it a strong legitimacy. For the time being, it seems that no consideration has been made by the High Commission regarding this request. One can anticipate such a move's effects on the social climate of New Caledonia if it were to be done. New Caledonia as a French colony is strongly imbued with a form of republican universalism inherited from the spirit of Les Lumières (The Enlightenment) in which its citizens (essentially non-Kanak) have a sacrosanct abhorrence of any form of positive discrimination or displayed ethnicity.

On the question of the referendum, for the time being there is no merger between these representatives of the Kanak people and the pro-independence leaders. We will immediately see why this is the case and will return to this issue later when we discuss possible future convergences.

Militating for a 'Sovereign Kanaky-New Caledonia': The Independence Movement Strategy to Get to Full Sovereignty

The independence movement here can only be understood through a holistic approach. Although the FLNKS used a 2019 press release to position itself as the 'sole representative of the independence movement',[33] the reality is that four political parties make up the liberation front, and have not been able to integrate their diverse components for the full sovereignty of Kanaky and/or New Caledonia: political parties such as the Parti Travailliste (Labour Party), the Libération Kanak Socialiste (Socialist Kanak Liberation), the very young Mouvement Nationaliste Indépendantiste Souverainiste (Sovereignist, Nationalist and Pro-Independence Movement), the Mouvement des Océaniens Indépendantistes (Independence Oceanian Movement), or Dynamik Unitaire Sud (Unitary Dynamic South). Trade unions such as USTKE, which emerged from the Front in 1989, the Confédération Nationale des Travailleurs du Pacifique (National Confederation of Pacific Workers), and the Front de Luttes Sociales (Social Struggle Front) also take an active part in the struggle to achieve full sovereignty for Kanaky and/or New Caledonia.

The FLNKS published a brochure in 2018 aimed at drawing up a portrait of what a 'Kanaky-New Caledonia sovereign', secular, and multicultural

---

[33] Front de Libération Nationale Kanak et Socialiste, press release, 17 December 2019.

Defining the Contours of the Lagoon

solidarity might consist of.[34] Their ideal multiculturalism would be one of integration in which all the components of New Caledonian society could find their place. If the idea of a Westphalian type nation-state is in the offing, the FLNKS has made an effort to think about the architecture of its institutions in the image of the population by, for example, opening up representation in the Customary Senate to the other communities inhabiting the archipelago. The global must be conceived here in multiple manifestations. For example, there would be no antagonism, as Paul Néaoutyine likes to remind us in his speeches during political meetings, to being 'citizens of New Caledonia (and/or Kanaky) of Javanese, Walisian, and Vanuatuan etc. origin'.[35] This position is easily understood by the position of the majority independentist fringe embodied by the Front Indépendantiste in 1983 when it was going to sign the declaration of Nainville les Roches recognizing the 'victims of history's' right to self-determination in New Caledonia alongside the Kanak.

Despite occasional nuanced differences between its component groups, it seems that the FLNKS coalition is positioning itself within the framework of future independence for a partnership with France and with any other state wishing to enter into competence-sharing agreements. As a priority, it appears that the Front wishes to establish strong links with its old partners from the Melanesian Spearhead Group (MSG) countries. But, according to the different positions taken by the Front, multiple future choices remain on the table and could concern the entire international community which will keep a watchful eye on possible exchanges with the new independent country. Roch Wamytan, one of the Union Calédonienne leaders, started his speeches during the first consultation campaign by claiming: 'We must turn the page on colonialism.' During these meetings, the different speakers were also presenting the possibilities of a partnership with other states. The FLNKS is aware that some of its governing competencies will have to be shared and sometimes even delegated to external entities. However, in order to have the legal and political capacity to do so, it is first necessary for it to pass through the course of having sovereignty conferred.

---

[34] Front de Libération Nationale Kanak et Socialiste, 'The FLNKS project for a sovereign Kanaky-New Caledonia', FLNKS self-publishing, 2018.
[35] Speech delivered at a closing meeting of the UNI for the 2019 provincial campaign, at the Poindimié town hall square, 9 May 2019, personal notes. See also his reflections about New Caledonia's citizenship in P. Néaoutyine, *L'indépendance au présent: identité kanak et destin commun* (Paris: Éditions Syllepse, 2006).

However, to the Parti Travailliste (Labour Party) led by Louis Kotra Uregei, the very signing of the Nouméa Accords was a mistake because the colonized people were made a minority.[36] That is why his party had positioned itself in favour of not taking part in the referendum of 4 November 2018. In the 2020 referendum, riding the wave of a new coalition with the young MNIS party, through the Mouvement National pour la Souveraineté de Kanaky (National Movement for the Sovereignty of Kanaky), the Labour Party was campaigning with its new brother party. The only pro-independence party that would not be campaigning this time for the 'Yes' was the Libération Kanak Socialiste, also called Dynamique Autochtone (Indigenous Dynamic). Believing that it did not have sufficient guarantees that the legitimacy of the customary authorities would be taken into account in the organization of a sovereign country, it preferred to wait for the third referendum to keep on working on this objective.

A More or Less Enlarged Autonomy: The Position of Non-independence Groups

On the other side of the political divide, the non-independence parties trend is towards autonomy, sometimes within the same status as now and sometimes with a more reinforced autonomy. For a political group like L'Avenir en Confiance (The Future in Confidence), 'France gives in the best possible way.'[37] In a debate held on Radio Rythme Bleu, Pierre Bretegnier was speaking on behalf of a non-Kanak electorate in New Caledonia, referring to decisions taken by customary authorities that should only concern those affected by custom.[38] By this he meant persons under customary civil law. The idea here is not of multiculturalism but rather of peaceful coexistence where each person should be governed by his or her own authorities.

Philipe Gomès of Calédonie Ensemble had the opportunity to present his party's position on the vision that independence proponents can have on the issue of sovereignty during a colloquium held at the University of New Caledonia. He spoke about what he calls a second of sovereignty:

[36] Y. Mainguet, 'The Labour Party will not participate in the referendum', *Les Nouvelles Calédoniennes* (16 July 2018).
[37] Nouvelle-Calédonie la Première (TV show), 'La preuve par quatre', theme 'Peut-on se passer de l'argent de la France?' ('Can we do without France's money?'), interview with Sonia Backès, November 2013, www.youtube.com/watch?v=H1zbLqi9IIY.
[38] P. Bretegnier, 'Interview with Pierre Bretegnier', *Le club politique*, Radio Rythme Bleu, April 2020.

Defining the Contours of the Lagoon

Finally, give me my sovereignty for a second. There, you give it back to me, because you took it from me in 1853, you stole that sovereignty from me, I did not give you my consent for that sovereignty. You occupied my country, give me back my sovereignty, give it back to me for a second, I give it back to you and I give it back to you right now, in the second that follows. And we will thus pass from a French sovereignty that has been suffered to a French sovereignty that has been consented to. We will thus pass from a territory of the Republic to an associated state or a territory in free association with France, whatever the words.[39]

This argument developed by Philippe Gomès is not very far from the theory of the delegation of sovereignty developed previously by Guy Agniel[40]. It would consist in defining the contours of this partnership with the French state beforehand, rather than going to a consultation that is divisive and frustrating for part of the population and leads to a harmful social climate.

Moreover, it seems that the idea of a departmentalization of New Caledonia has been definitively buried. Indeed, it is agreed that the non-independence parties remain autonomist and do not question the various transfers of powers issued by the French state to New Caledonia. However, a local fringe is campaigning for a requalification of the relations that animate France and New Caledonia from a federal state to a federated state, as can be the case in the United States, for example.[41] Another debate that has come more frequently to the forefront in recent years is the partition of New Caledonia. The Nouméa Accord outlaws it, but we shall see later on the reasoning that this debate is once again becoming topical for certain militants who prefer to partition New Caledonia in a more radical way: the South within the French Republic, and the North and the Loyalty Islands as one sovereign country. As this hypothesis remains outlawed under the Nouméa Accord and is defended by only a tiny branch of the Caledonian population, we will not deal with it here.

Nevertheless, it is clear that there are still divisions over how to view the near future of New Caledonia. There are points of convergence and divergence, which we shall now try to show.

[39] P. Gomès, 'Interview with Philippe Gomès', Université de la Nouvelle-Calédonie Colloquium, n.d. or colloquium topic.
[40] G. Agniel, 'Le Parlement et la Nouvelle-Calédonie: du "droit à la bouderie" ... à la délégation de souveraineté?', *Revue Française de Droit Constitutionnel* 90:2 (2012), 227–38.
[41] See the works of Jean-Yves and Florence Faberon, for example in J.-Y. Faberon and F. Faberon (eds.), *Les fédéralismes* (Clermont-Ferrand: Éditions Recherches sur la Cohésion Sociale, 2020).

ANTHONY TUTUGORO

Imagining the 'Lagoon': Different Approaches
to New Caledonia's Near Future

So how can New Caledonia combine or reconcile all these visions of the period 'after' the final referendum is decided? It is clear that in the near future the essential solution lies in the hands of the next referendum. These different approaches to try and perceive the potential links and the possible convergences will now be discussed. We will try to consider three hypotheses: first, a majority of three 'No' votes, then, second, a majority 'Yes' vote in the third election, before finally identifying the major challenges that will remain to be taken up by the citizens of Kanaky and/or New Caledonia regardless of the referendum outcomes.

The Hypothesis of Three 'No' Votes Answering Nouméa's Accord Consultation: Multiple Scenarios

As mentioned, on 4 November 2018, 57 per cent of the voters on the list provided for this purpose gave a negative answer to the question of their support for independence. At present, even beyond the question of the referendum, the question of Article 27 of the organic law of 27 March 1999 remains an open debate.[42] This article provides for a final transfer to New Caledonia of competences which at present still reside in the French state, namely audiovisual communication, the free administration of local authorities, and higher education including the University of New Caledonia (UNC). These competences can be transferred to New Caledonia by a three-fifths majority vote of its Congress. For the time being, no political group has yet tabled a country bill to put this vote on the agenda. The transfer of these powers would take New Caledonia to a further level of autonomy. It remains to be seen when the political groups in Congress will take up this issue and demand this transfer.

With regard to the transfer of competences, it is constitutionally guaranteed as irreversible. In other words, the state cannot take back a transferred competence. As Jean-Jacques Urvoas recalled during a colloquium held at the UNC in 2017, borrowing an old adage noting 'what the law can do, it can

---

[42] Article 27 of the Organic Law No. 99-209 of 19 March 1999 on New Caledonia states 'The Congress may, as from the beginning of its term of office starting in 2009, adopt a resolution to transfer to it, by a subsequent organic law, the following powers: rules relating to the administration of the provinces, communes and their public establishments, control of the legality of the provinces, communes and their public establishments, accounting and financial regime of public authorities and their public establishments; higher education; audiovisual communication.'

Defining the Contours of the Lagoon

undo', and that while changes could occur in the context of an amendment to the current French Constitution, or a change in its constitution in the hypothetical framework of a 6th Republic, the transfer of competences is still guaranteed as irreversible.[43] The institutional history of New Caledonia shows that each time the state withdraws a competence granted to New Caledonia, the political and social climate is strongly affected. The disruptive and divisive 'events' of the 1980s, for example, were rooted in the new status proposed by Georges Lemoine in 1984, to which the independence fighters were ardently opposed.

Current voting trends after the first two referenda suggest that a non-majority vote for the third 'Yes' vote in 2022 is possible, especially as parties such as Calédonie Ensemble have conceptualized it together with the need to approach the issue from the angle of a shared referendum to prevent any sense of frustration. Indeed, the hypothesis of three successive 'No' votes would suggest that a discussion between the different partners of the agreement was needed to plan the road or roads ahead. But what would they talk about? For Jean-Louis D'Anglebermes, a Union Calédonienne militant and also 'Minister' in New Caledonia's government, it will be a question of 'talking about independence', as he announced during a political speech delivered in Païta in 2018.[44] For the non-independence proponents, who consider themselves to be in the majority, this hypothesis is essentially not conceivable. Several factors suggest that this hypothetical and probable situation will occur. However, in recent years the leaders of the majority pro-independence parties, namely Palika and the Union Calédonienne, have opened loopholes, giving rise to the idea of a bilateral discussion with the state. Between whom and whom though? This discussion would take place between the colonizing state and the Kanak people. This hypothesis for the time being is a fiction because the state is constantly taking refuge behind its position as arbitrator in the Nouméa Accord by referring the responsibility to the independence and non-independence partners. However, many pro-independence political leaders no longer skimp on claiming in speeches or interviews that the state is responsible for colonization. And, therefore, by implication it is also responsible for decolonization. Proposing exit formulas would therefore be its responsibility. For the time being, the state does not

---

[43] Université de la Nouvelle-Calédonie, 'Interview with Jean-Jacques Urvoas' during the 'État associé ou État fédéré, des pistes pour l'avenir institutionnel de la Nouvelle-Calédonie' colloquium (Associated State or Federated State, avenues for the institutional future of New Caledonia colloquium).
[44] Consultation campaign meeting which took place in Païta, October 2018.

seem ready to assume this role and sticks to its so-called neutral position. However, echoing the introductory remarks to this chapter, when the state itself asks to review the rules of the first referendum for the second and to integrate the French tricolor flag into the campaign for the second referendum, one is entitled to question this claim of state neutrality.

What future should be envisaged for New Caledonia in the event of three successive majority 'No' votes in the consultations provided for in the Nouméa Accord for the pro-independence supporters? As noted in a previous study, the independence movement could turn a corner. Indeed, the hypothesis that the colonized people decide to discuss directly with their main interlocutor, namely the colonizer, is not to be excluded, deciding no longer to invite the non-independence proponents around the table. But according to what strategy? The various analyses suggest the hypothesis of the 'Kanak people' rather than the 'independence' banner being carried. It is therefore no longer a given ideology that would be carried to discuss with the state but simply that of a population whose sovereignty was taken away on 24 September 1853 by the French state under Napoleon III.

This negotiating strategy would reflect a significant shift in the political and institutional history of New Caledonia, since parties or groups that are pro-independence or that claim to have acquired rights relating to Indigenous peoples' rights as provided for by the United Nations and that have not taken part in the various referenda could now join the negotiating table alongside the elected pro-independence Kanak representatives. This fictitious scenario cannot inform us about the reactions that non-independence groups in the Territory might have, but it is clear that the social climate would be disrupted. The Kanak people have since 1983 opted for involving all the victims of history in New Caledonia's emancipation process. There is a well-known saying that 'no one can claim his own turpitude'. It remains to be seen whether the Kanak people will not derogate from this.

Before proceeding further on the possibility of these different hypotheses and their consequences on the social level, we must first observe the current strategy of the majority of the independence movement, after considering the consequences of the three successive 'No' votes, to win one of the consultations provided for in the Nouméa Accord.

Implications of a 'Yes' Vote: Opening Up a Field of Possibilities?

The hypothesis of a 'Yes' majority vote in the final referendum would give New Caledonia full and complete access to its sovereignty. The FLNKS in its communications and through its working groups frequently evokes the so-called transition period where the French state would accompany the various services of the territory to ensure the handover. One often hears remarks on this subject from non-independent groups that there is a 'black hole' regarding the 'Yes' day. Activists in discussion forums like to say with humour that on the day of the Yes 'I will continue to go and buy my bread as I do every morning.' Or this joke launched by Mathias Chauchat during 2019's Pacific Islands Political Science Association (PIPSA) conference: 'we must stop saying the day after the yes the sun stops rising, our crops will be swept away by hail, nothing will happen'.[45] This period would make it possible to draw up new relations that could establish the new state with the former guardian power, especially concerning the management of sovereign competences such as defence. The FLNKS says it is ready to negotiate such partnerships, aware that the number of trained personnel is not for the moment likely to cover all New Caledonia's needs such as, for example, its exclusive economic zone.

This period would also be the first time New Caledonia has had a constituent assembly. It remains to be seen what the contours would be. An elected assembly, an assembly made up of the elected representatives in place, assemblies drawn by lot and a project adopted by referendum – in short, the options and their degree of involvement of the population of the archipelago are multiple. This new population would, in any case, be interesting to observe. Since the state would become sovereign, the citizenship criterion of twenty years of residence in the territory could be modified through these new provisions. Determining who will be the nationals and citizens of this state would be fundamental since this would determine the political majorities. The entire institutional architecture undertaken by the Nouméa Accord was built around proportional representation to guarantee political representation for each tendency and the obligation of collegiality at the governmental level.

It now remains to be seen how the citizens and technicians who would make up this constituent assembly would arrange this institutional architecture. The current institutions are built so that one ethnic group does not gain the upper hand over the other. That is why the Nouméa Accord established, for example, a Customary Senate to ensure customary representation.

---

[45] M. Chauchat, 'Quel avenir institutionnel partagé pour la Nouvelle-Calédonie?', Pacific Islands Political Science Association (PIPSA) Conference, 'Democracy, Sovereignty and Self-Determination in the Pacific Islands', Nouméa, 2019.

However the use of these institutions is made by two or even three major ideologies, that of independence, that of a maintenance in the Republic, and that of claiming to be neutral as announced by the new Eveil Océanien (Oceanian Awakening). This duality within the new state will no longer be necessary. Indeed, given the current vision of the management of Covid-19, for example, or the use of resources, everything suggests that the confrontation in the new political arena would be fairly classic between the supporters of an exacerbated, uncomplicated, or moderate liberalism and the defenders of a collective vision of the institutions where who owns contributes for who does not. These crucial issues, whatever the outcome of the consultations, will in any case have to be put on the table, debated, and decided.

A Possible New Way of Managing Power in Kanaky and/or New Caledonia?

The global Covid-19 crisis hit New Caledonia, like the rest of the world, at the beginning of 2020. This period was an opportunity to shed light on certain latent antagonisms. On the side of the Kanak people, the threat of the virus made its constituent groups appear united in the fight against its spreading. Independence political actors and customary authorities have worked together to propose convergent lines and instructions. These instructions have sometimes been in opposition to directives imposed by the state or by the majority holding the presidency of New Caledonia's collegial government. A press release first issued by the Customary Senate and then a second co-signed[46] by all the elected independence representatives opposed the arrival of a military aircraft loaded with 180 soldiers. The reasons given were not of course against the arrival of more troops but against the fact that they represented a serious and imminent threat of importing the virus into New Caledonia. The 'Pweyta chieftaincy' mobilized itself on the day the plane was due to land on New Caledonian soil to bring together all the clans making up the customary sector in order to demonstrate their opposition to this flight. And this position was approved by the Customary Senate and by all pro-independence ministers of New Caledonia's government through different press releases, which has never happened before.

On the other side of the Caledonian political spectrum, L'Avenir en Confiance sees these various interventions by the customary sector in a very

[46] Jean-Louis D'Anglebermes, Jean-Pierre Djaïwé, Valentine Eurisouké, Didier Poidyaliwane, and Gilbert Tyuienon, Communiqué, 22 April 2020.

Defining the Contours of the Lagoon

negative light. The following example of a communiqué issued by Sonia Backès, president of the South Province, exemplifies their tone: 'everyone must stay in their place'.[47] In the Nouvelle-Calédonie la Première news on television the next day, she reiterated her position: 'We must let those who have to make the decisions make them.' The idea that the customary authorities are influential in the Islands Province because 99 per cent of the province is made up of customary land seems to this political fringe to legitimize the subordination of decisions by the customary authorities to political decision-makers. On the other hand, this is not the case in the anti-independence majority South Province where the political authorities for them must keep a tight rein. This deliberate antagonism on the part of the president of South Province is very interesting to observe for the future.

In an article written prior to the second referendum, the author noted a possible bridge between customary authorities and independent political representatives in the event of a second and third 'No' in the next referendum.[48] The proposed solution involved reading grids outlining all parties' positions. This display could simply appear under the banner of the 'Kanak people'. The observable facts during the Covid-19 crisis reaffirm, today more than ever, that when they wished to do so and when circumstances do not offer alternatives, these different political and customary authorities are able to speak with one voice when it comes to the survival of their people. Perhaps such reading grids will be used in the future, should New Caledonia face a similar need to improve communication between customary authorities and independent political representatives. Looking at what we can describe here as a 'war of press releases' fought by the non-independence and independence parties during this crisis confirms that this trend is being reinforced. In the press release we mentioned previously issued on 23 April 2020, Sonia Backès was criticizing the opposition of the customary senators and members of the government: 'In this particular context, I firmly condemn the remarks of the Customary Senate, the members of the pro-independence government, and the president of the Caledonian Union. First of all, because everyone must stay in their place. If the authorities of the Islands Province accept that it is the customary authorities who decide on

[47] S. Backès, 'Communiqué de Sonia Backès, présidente de la province Sud: chacun doit rester à sa place!', 23 April 2020, www.ncpresse.nc/Communique-de-Sonia-Backes-presidente-de-la-province-Sud-Chacun-doit-rester-a-sa-place-_a8167.html.
[48] A. Tutugoro, 'Incompatible struggles? Reclaiming indigenous sovereignty and political sovereignty in Kanaky and/or New Caledonia', Department of Pacific Affairs, Discussion Paper 2020/5.

their own soil, it is their choice, it is not ours in South Province.' These press releases carry within them the seeds of a territorial duality, raising the spectre of a separatist tendency among a certain branch of the New Caledonian political class.

While differences may be observed within the Kanak world concerning strategies for achieving sovereignty, as we have tried to show earlier, the results of the first two referenda have shown, however, that the Kanak people are nevertheless unanimous in their desire to see their sovereignty restored. It would be damaging for the future of the 'will to live together' approach according to Ernest Renan[49] if these communiqués and positions were to be repeated, at the risk of truly observing Carl Schmitt's vision of society, or rather of the societies of New Caledonia.[50] Bloc opposing against bloc and returning to the criterion of legitimacy as the first to arrive rather than the one who wishes to make a workable society that accommodates all concerns. The friend–enemy duality conceptualized by Carl Schmitt could take place. The 'we' would exist no longer as the vision of a desire to live together but rather in opposition to an enemy that does not resemble us. The idea of a strategy of a Kanak people, a colonized people, acting bilaterally with the colonizing state, would change 180 degrees and would turn its back on a will of 'co-construction' driven by the Kanak people itself.

Conclusion: From Autonomy to Sovereignty, How to Move from a Divided Society to a Fully Fledged People?

Kanak people are a minority in their own archipelago. Since recapturing and reasserting their identity and land in the political process, Kanak have resorted to multiple strategies to succeed in regaining the sovereignty of New Caledonia. It is obvious that the empowerment logic that local elected representatives can protect themselves allows them to establish a certain legitimacy on the spot. However, these legitimacies are given by an electorate which, for the moment, is rather unfavourable to seeing the French Republic do without New Caledonia. The president of the French Republic Emmanuel Macron,

---

[49] E. Renan, 'Qu'est-ce qu'une nation?', lecture given at the Sorbonne on 11 March 1982 (Paris: Bulletin de l'Association scientifique de France, 26 March 1882).
[50] C. Schmitt, *The Nomos of the Earth in the International Law of Jus Publicum Europaeum*, translated and annotated G.L. Ulmen (New York: Telos Press, 2003).

Defining the Contours of the Lagoon

commenting on the results of the 4 November 2018 elections, declared: 'France would be less beautiful without New Caledonia.'[51]

In view of the results of these first two referenda, it is clear that the majority of Kanak people are still in favour of this idea and that the concept of full sovereignty has the potential to progress favourably among non-Kanak people. The campaign for the second referendum, like the debate presented in the introduction, has hardened semantically. The 'No' camp is trying to comfort its electorate to establish a second victory by playing on arguments that are favourable to it: the fear of the unknown in the face of the certainty of the security of remaining French. However, all the political parties, all sides combined, never ceased during this campaign to claim to be 'Oceanians'. Perhaps the key against the demographic barrier and the phobia of the unknown lies in this commonly perceived identity.

The Covid-19 crisis as it presented in Nouméa has frightened the crowds, in an island that imports a large majority of its consumption. However, the populations of the Grande Terre and the islands not living in the capital did not necessarily have to rush to the shops to stock up. The practice of the existing coastal reserves has, for example, enabled them to have a daily supply of fish. Food crops that have been cultivated in these islands for thousands of years[52] through sophisticated land and water management systems have provided the population with taro, yams, bananas, kumara, and manioc.[53] Young people, who are often blamed for not having a job and not being able to run the economy of their archipelago, have been able to go hunting and, for example, send meat to their relatives. On the island of Maré,

---

[51] Emmanuel Macron, Transcription of the speech of the president of the French Republic on New Caledonia in Nouméa, 5 May 2018, www.elysee.fr/emmanuel-macron/2018/05/05/dis cours-du-president-de-la-republique-emmanuel-macron-sur-la-nouvelle-caledonie-a-noumea.

[52] See the study conducted by the Institut Agronomique Néo-Calédonien which has shown that this informal economy, in tribal space, including gifts, exchanges during customary ceremonies, and self-consumption, would represent a total of 12.5 billion cfp in monetary terms. (around 94 million pounds sterling). In Stéphane Guyard, Leïla Apithy, Séverine Bouard, Jean-Michel Sourisseau, Michel Passouant, Pierre-Marie Bosc, and Jean-François Bélières, 'L'agriculture en tribu. Poids et fonctions des activités agricoles et de prélèvement' (Païta, enquête Institut Agronomique Néo-calédonien (IAC), 2013).

[53] C. Gaillard and H.I. Manner, 'Yam cultivation on the east coast of New Caledonia: adaptation of agriculture to social and economic changes', *Australian Geographer* 41:4 (2010), 485–505; J.L. Barrau, *L'agriculture vivrière autochtone de la Nouvelle-Calédonie* (Nouméa: Commission du Pacifique Sud, 1956); S. Cornier and I. Leblic, 'Kanak coastal communities and fisheries meeting new governance challenges and marine issues in New Caledonia', in S. Pauwels and E. Fache (eds.), *Fisheries in the Pacific: The Challenges of Governance and Sustainability* (Marseilles: Pacific Credo Publications, 2016), 119–74. See also Chapter 64 of this volume.

harvests were collectively made and sent by boat to their families living in the capital.

Like other Pacific Islands such as Nauru, which have experienced prodigious economic upheavals in proportion to an unprecedented recession, it is perhaps up to the current political leaders not to be trapped by the mirage of development.[54] At a time when everything is coming to a halt, primary needs are paramount. Covid-19 is an opportunity for many to open their eyes to the fact that entire families and clans are living almost in self-sufficiency in a country with one of the highest GDPs in the area. More than opening their eyes to political solutions to New Caledonia's political problems, they needed these local producers to meet their food needs. Cutting out the middlemen, going back to more direct circuits for accessing food and other needs, and encouraging people to (re)connect to the land according to age-old Oceanian practices will undoubtedly create this social link that the archipelago lacks. It is only to be hoped that the state of ambient reflexivity surrounding this crisis is not just temporary and will lead to a real awareness of the population. From this deeply rooted social bond can be born the will for all to assert sovereignty, not imposed by the power of the ballot box. For the moment, fear of the unknown is sclerosing the situation and opposing this logic of 'one bloc against the other', which leads the non-independence parties to be satisfied with internal decolonization. For all that, it is unlikely that the independence movement will one day renounce its recapture of full sovereignty.

If the situation seems difficult to reconcile on a macro-political level, we must rely on the micro-fights and micro-solidarities created by the individuals making up the archipelago to succeed perhaps in this external decolonization. During the pandemic crisis, the political majority in power once again sought the solution outside the coral reef. The government of New Caledonia, supported by the Congress of New Caledonia, urgently contracted an interest-bearing loan (1.48 per cent interest rate) of 28.5 billion CFP francs (217,005,829 pounds) repayable by New Caledonia over twenty-five years (until 2045). While the argument of urgency is obviously not called into question, it is clear that such a substantial loan, contracted the same year as the consultation on New Caledonia's self-determination, can only raise

---

[54] On the Pacific-wide issue of striking a balance between political sovereignty and the economic advantages of retaining close links with former colonial powers, see S. Firth, 'Contemporary politics of the Pacific Islands' and 'Security in the Pacific Islands', in J. Love (ed.), *The Far East and Australasia 2017* (Abingdon: Routledge, 2017); G. Bertram, 'The MIRAB model twelve years on', *Contemporary Pacific* 11:1 (1999), 105–38, and Chapter 59 of this volume.

Defining the Contours of the Lagoon

questions about France's position on the future of this archipelago. The argument put forward, the legitimacy of which is not disputed here, consists of the need to preserve the Caledonian economy and to limit the damage. For a country that could potentially accede to full sovereignty in the same year, taking out a twenty-five-year loan can only be perplexing. It is thus future generations who are committed to repaying a debt to their guardianship and ex-colonial power. Given the size of the archipelago in proportion to its population, there are many alternative solutions to make up for what is considered to be a shortfall in the economy. Few Pacific islands can boast of having so much space. The logic of the sharing of competences between New Caledonia and the French state in such emergency situations does not allow the archipelago to act in accordance with in its soul and conscience and simply to decide what is good or bad for it. The future will tell whether Kanaky and/or New Caledonia will be able to have all the levers and skills to rebuild its image in a Pacific space that is watching it and waiting for its entry into the concert of Oceanian nations.

The lagoon encircling this South Pacific archipelago did not need humanity to stand on the horizon and protect its coasts. However, humanity can influence the lagoon, either to strengthen it or to destroy it. It will be up to the men and women who live and wish to remain on this archipelago to find the appropriate solutions together to make this lagoon last in the best possible way and to return it to their image at the risk of being permanently affected. A Pacific island without a solid coral reef is an exposed and vulnerable island, particularly in cyclonic periods.

62

New Pacific Voyages since Independence

1960 Onwards

ROANNIE NG SHIU AND ROCHELLE BAILEY

The new economic reality made nonsense of artificial boundaries, enabling people to shake off their confinement and they have since moved, by the tens of thousands, doing what their ancestors had done before them: enlarging their world as they go, but on a scale not possible before.[1]

In this chapter we discuss new contemporary voyages Pacific people have embarked upon since the independence period of the 1960s. In doing so we adopt Epeli Hauʻofaʻs view of contemporary Pacific migration and transnationalism as a process of world enlargement. Pacific migration has often been viewed in limited terms such as outward migration and one-directional flows. The migration patterns and experiences of the region are varied and complex, and current economic theories of migration are inadequate in capturing the nuances of the Pacific region and fail to recognize migration, mobility, and movement as a social and cultural act and not merely economically motivated; they are culturally specific, grounded in social ontologies and historical encounters. In this chapter we argue for a transnational approach in thinking about and understanding Pacific contemporary migration since the 1960s. Pacific migration, mobility, and movement is not simply about individuals themselves but rather about complex networks and flows of people, families, organizations, ideas, and goods, creating communities that expand across multiple nation-states. The chapter begins with a discussion on what is Pacific transnational flow and how this differs to dominate discourses on international migration and movement. We then describe different types of flows beginning with where people have moved to and explore the main drivers of migration: money and remittances. We then outline the different types of migration and mobility pathways that Pacific

---

[1] E. Hauʻofa, ʻOur Sea of Islandsʻ, in E. Waddell, V. Naidu, and E. Hauʻofa (eds.), *A New Oceania: Rediscovering Our Sea of Islands* (Suva: School of Social and Economic Development, University of the South Pacific, 1994), 2–16, at 10.

people have undertaken since the 1960s, with a particular focus on educational opportunities and employment opportunities such as seasonal labour migration schemes and sports migration. We conclude the chapter by considering the impact of climate change and migration for future generations of Pacific people.

Pacific Transnational Flows

Hau'ofa's analysis of Pacific migration and transnational flows is akin to Arjun Appadurai's concept of ethnoscapes which he defines as:

> the landscape of persons who make up the shifting world in which we live: tourists, immigrants, refugees, exiles, guest workers, and other moving groups and persons constitute an essential feature of the world and appear to affect the politics of and between nations to a hitherto unprecedented degree.[2]

Ethnoscapes and indeed Hau'ofa's vision of Pacific migration and transnationalism acknowledge that contemporary notions of people, place, and community have become much more complex, where a 'single community' may now expand across various boundaries. Further Macpherson contends that to understand the real impact of emigration and change in contemporary Oceania we may need to reconceptualize Pacific societies.[3] One possible reconceptualization is a Pacific ethnoscape given that the lived realities of Pacific transnational communities across the globe are having a political impact between and within nations. This is most evident when looking at political elections and the inclusion of overseas constituencies to represent significant populations living abroad. In the Pacific the Cook Islands had an overseas seat that was created in 1981 and then abolished in 2003. More recently the Kingdom of Tonga began floating the idea of an overseas seat in 2017, given the large numbers of Tongans living abroad.[4]

Transnationalism is the sustained and meaningful flows, networks, and relations connecting individuals and social groups across the borders of nation-states. It highlights the complex and complicated network of ties between Pacific individuals, groups, and institutions by including an analysis

---

[2] A. Appadurai, 'Global ethnospaces: notes and queries for a transnational anthropology', in R. Fox (ed.), *Recapturing Anthropology* (Santa Fe, NM: School of American Research Press, 1991), 191–210, 192.

[3] C. Macpherson, 'Migration and transformation in the contemporary Pacific', *New Zealand Sociology* 23:1 (2008), 30–40.

[4] B. Hill, 'Seats in parliament for overseas Tongans seen as problematic', *ABC Radio Australia*, 1 June 2017, www.abc.net.au/radio-australia/programs/pacificbeat/seats-in-parliament-for-overseas-tongans-seen-as/8580498.

of the positive and negative outcomes of migration. Migration and the term diaspora tend to be narrow in focus and often exclude circular or return migration, an important feature of Pacific migration as Pacific peoples abroad still maintain strong links and connections back to the Pacific.[5] These connections are highlighted through this chapter. Migrants are not individual movers. There is no detachment from their families and communities. Furthermore, Pacific cross-border movement is associated with supporting families and communities in their respective localities. Even while abroad, migrants experience an attachment to place – a homeland where identity and being 'of place' is often the source of inspiration and wellbeing while absent from familial surroundings and members.

Such mobility and interconnectedness have a long history. The settlement and colonization of the Pacific Islands by Austronesian-speaking peoples was the greatest nautical diaspora in world history in the pre-modern era, stretching from Madagascar in the west to Rapa Nui in the southeast Pacific in the east. Long-distance voyaging and regular inter-island contacts continued until European conquest in a number of Pacific societies, with all economic exchanges tied to social and political interactions that enhanced community interactions and extended resource bases through intermarriage between kin groups involving mutual obligations. European discovery, exploration, and trade created opportunities for Pacific Islanders to ship out as crew and return with enhanced status through European goods as payment as crew and experiences of the outside world. After European colonial rule, hundreds of thousands of Pacific Islanders from Melanesia in particular worked in commercial plantations in other Pacific Island locations, or in Queensland.[6]

---

[5] A. Liki, 'Moving and rootedness: the paradox of brain drain among Samoan professionals', *Asia-Pacific Population Journal* 16:1 (2001), 67–84. S. Lilomaiava-Doktor, 'Beyond "migration": Samoan population movement (malaga) and the geography of social space (vā)', *Contemporary Pacific* 21:1 (2009), 1–32; F.A.L. Uperesa, 'Fabled futures: migration and mobility for Samoans in American football', *Contemporary Pacific* 26:2 (2014), 281–301.

[6] On pre-colonial inter-island exchanges see N. Gunson, 'Two indigenous chiefly systems, title and trade', in B.V. Lal and K. Fortune (eds.), *The Pacific Islands: An Encyclopedia* (Honolulu: University of Hawai'i Press, 2000), 132–5, and P. D'Arcy, *The People of the Sea: Environment, Identity and History in Oceania* (Honolulu: University of Hawai'i Press, 2006). On shipping out on Western vessels, see D.A. Chappell, *Double Ghosts: Oceanic Voyagers on Euroamerican Ships* (Armonk, NY: M.E. Sharpe, 1997), and on the Pacific labour trade in the colonial era, see P. Corris, *Passage, Port and Plantation: A History of Solomon Islands Labour Migration, 1870–1914* (Melbourne: Melbourne University Press, 1973).

New Pacific Voyages since Independence

The fact that the Pacific region is often left out from international theories of migration is conspicuous. Rather, theories of migration for the Pacific have been based loosely on regional geography. For example, small island-states in Polynesia are characterized by over-reliance on international migration and remittances as outlined by Bertram and Watters.[7] Melanesia is characterized by intraregional migration and Micronesia is a hybrid of both international and intraregional migration.[8]

The MIRAB model refers to the geographical realities and colonial legacies of small Pacific Island nation-states. Most achieved independence only in the 1970s and inherited limited infrastructure from their colonial rulers. The majority of their populations practise largely subsistence lifestyles occasionally supplemented by cash crops. A significant proportion of the population now travel beyond their place of birth to work in the modern economy, especially in national capitals.[9] The MIRAB model designates the majority of Pacific nations as small, non-viable economies dependent on aid from former colonial powers. As most aid is absorbed in civil service bureaucracy salaries, remittances sent from labour markets in former colonial power nations become the main income source for those outside of government. Such economies predominate in Polynesia and Micronesia, whereas the larger Melanesian states of the southwest Pacific, until very recently, exhibited much less out-migration and considerable resource bases in the mining, forestry, and agricultural sectors. Hauʻofa argued that the MIRAB 'basket cases' were the result of barriers created by colonial boundaries and policies that imposed an artificial sense of isolation and separation upon Islanders. They must now decolonize their minds, and recast their sense of identity by rediscovering the vision of their ancestors for whom the Pacific was a boundless sea of possibilities and opportunities.[10] Numerous chapters in this collection show that Hauʻofa's vision was grounded in fact rather than a mythical vision of the past. While colonial rule opened new opportunities for movement such as travelling overseas to work, it also artificially restricted many social and other ties which expanded the worlds and opportunities open to Pacific Islanders. The flows discussed in this chapter are the latest manifestation of a long

---

[7] I.G. Bertram and R.F. Watters, 'The MIRAB economy in South Pacific microstates', *Pacific Viewpoint* 26:3 (1985), 497–519.

[8] J. Goss and B. Lindquist, 'Placing movers: an overview of the Asian-Pacific migration system', *Contemporary Pacific* 12:2 (2000), 385–414.

[9] K. Nero, 'The material world unmade', in D. Denoon (ed.), *The Cambridge History of the Pacific Islander* (Cambridge: Cambridge University Press, 1997), 359–96.

[10] Bertram and Watters 'The Mirab economy in the south Pacific microstates', and Hauʻofa, 'Our Sea of Islands'.

history of expanding resource bases by means of forging social, political, and economic links. Our chapter is anthropological or, perhaps more correctly, more Pacific-orientated than most migration analysis in that its themes are woven together through the strands of community, family, and personal ties which lie at the heart of Pacific identity and action.

From a regional geography analysis, the majority of international migration comes from Polynesian small island state MIRAB economies such as Niue, Wallis and Futuna, the Cook Islands, and Tokelau, all of which have a majority of their populations living overseas. International migration from Melanesia is mostly from Fiji, with increased migration of skilled and semi-skilled Indo-Fijians as the result of political unrest marked by the first of three military coups in 1987. Micronesians' migration flows from Guam and the Northern Marianas to Hawai'i and the US mainland.[11] This focus on out-migration does provide some useful insights into sociocultural change, economic aid and development, and immigration and migration. As Chappell argues, this 'analysis might also benefit from a *transnational* perspective that gets beyond the mental straitjacket of bounded nation-states'[12] as national economic development perspectives are mostly concerned with the international core–periphery relations between nations that supply raw materials and those that manufacture these materials into high-value exports. This narrow focus distorts Indigenous meanings and expanded notions of Pacific movement.[13] Although transnational communities are an outcome of international labour migration, international labour migration is necessary but not sufficient to understand the motivations, processes, and outcomes of Pacific transnational communities.

Islands, Spaces, and Flow

Since independence the main destination countries for Pacific people have been Australia, New Zealand, the United States, and France.[14] These destinations are unsurprising considering the colonial histories and remaining legacies of Western imperialism. New Zealand, the United States, and France have permanent pathways of inward migration for former territories. New Zealand

---

[11] Goss and Lindquist, 'Placing movers'.
[12] D.A. Chappell, 'Transnationalism in central Oceanian politics: a dialectic of diasporas and nationhood?', *Journal of the Polynesian Society* 108:3 (1999), 277–303, at 2.
[13] Liki, 'Moving and rootedness'.
[14] See H. Lee and S. Francis (eds.), *Migration and Transnationalism: Pacific Perspectives* (Canberra: ANU Press, 2009) for a history of Pacific movement to New Zealand, Australia, and North America.

New Pacific Voyages since Independence

introduced the Samoan Quota in 1970, allowing 1,100 Samoan nationals who meet the criteria to become a permanent resident under a ballot system to ensure fairness.[15] The United States enacted the Compact of Free Association, or the compact, in 1986, allowing free association between the United States and the Federated States of Micronesia (FSM), Palau, and the Marshall Islands. Australia does not have any Pacific-specific permanent migration pathway for former territories, including Papua New Guinea, Australia's closest neighbour.

In 1997 Gerard Ward estimated that over 400,000 Pacific people lived overseas, including 170,000 in New Zealand and 150,000 in the United States. Since then this number has increased significantly, with over 1.2 million Pacific people living in the United States alone.[16] The figures in Table 62.1 represent approximately 13 per cent of the total Pacific Islander (PI) population. This number would be significantly higher if we also included European destination countries. The table provides an overview of the census data of populations both at home and in the three main destination countries of Australia, New Zealand, and the United States of selected Pacific Islands and Territories.

The table provides a useful illustration of how migration patterns are affected by colonial pasts, with significant numbers of Pacific people living in former colonial administrative countries. For example, the data from the New Zealand Pacific realm countries of the Cook Islands, Niue, and Tokelau show that there are significantly more Cook Islanders, Niueans, and Tokelauans living in New Zealand than back in their home islands. However, these colonial links differ, as is evident in their immigration policy settings. Polynesian countries have a number of avenues for migration to New Zealand, whereas, as mentioned above, Australia provides limited immigration opportunities to countries such as PNG. This is in part due to Australia's historical race-based immigration policies.

Mass migration to cities in destination countries was also enabled by chain migration, where once one or two Pacific households have established themselves with secure housing and employment new family members from the Pacific would then migrate and the chain or cycle begins again.[17] This is

---

[15] C.W. Stahl and R. Appleyard, 'Migration and development in the Pacific Islands: lessons from the New Zealand experience', Report for the Australian Agency for Development (AusAid), Canberra, April 2007.
[16] Asian Americans Advancing Justice (AAAJ), *A Community of Contrasts: Native Hawaiians and Pacific Islanders in the West*, (Washington, DC: AAAJ, 2015), 2.
[17] C. Macpherson. 'Transnationalism and transformation in Samoan society', in V. Lockwood, *Globalisation and Culture Change in the Pacific Islands* (Upper Saddle River, NJ: Pearson/Prentice Hall 2004), 165–81, at 167–8.

Table 62.1 *Selected Pacific Islands and Territories population census data at home and abroad.*

Country	Census year	Population	Population in Australia (2017)	Population in New Zealand (2013)	Population in United States (2010)
American Sāmoa	2012	55,519	–	–	184,440*
Cook Islands	2016	17,434	22,228	62,631	–
Federated States of Micronesia	2017	104,590	–	–	9,226
Fiji	2017	884,887	37,003	14,445	32,304
Guam	2018	165,768	–	–	147,798
Hawai'i	2019	1.43 million	473	336	527,077^
Kiribati	2015	110,110		2,115	401
Marshall Islands	2011	53,158	871	–	22,434
Nauru	2015	11,288	512	129	–
New Caledonia	2014	269,000	270		–
Niue	2011	1,611	4,958	23,883	–
Palau	2015	17,661			7,450
Papua New Guinea	2011	7,275,324	18,802	807	416
Pitcairn	2008	66	741	177	–
Sāmoa	2016	195,979	75,753	144,138	*
Solomon Islands	2009	515,870	1,883	603	122
Tahiti	2017	189,517		1,407	5,062
Tokelau	2016	1,285	2,329	7,176	925
Tonga	2016	100,745	32,695	60,336	57,183
Tuvalu	2017	10,645		3,537	–
Vanuatu	2016	272,459	956	492	91

Note: Census data for Pacific Countries and Territories and New Zealand from Statistics New Zealand. Australian figures compiled from the Australian Bureau of Statistics census 2016 using the Australian classification of Cultural and Ethnic groups, and the data for the United States from EPIC and AAAJ, 'A community of contrasts' (2014). *Both American Samoans and Samoans were classified as one category with a majority from American Samoa. ^This is the number of Native Hawaiians in the United States.

demonstrated in the clustering of Pacific transnational communities in certain cities. In the United States for example, the majority of Pacific communities on the mainland are located in California (24 per cent). Further demographic analysis reveals enclaves of Pacific groups across the United States, with one in four Tongans living in Salt Lake City, Utah, while over half of the Pacific community in Arkansas are from the Marshall Islands.[18]

However, recent examination of the experiences of Pacific transnational communities has highlighted that the idea of migration leading to better socio-economic positions in most cases has been fantasy rather than reality. Research has shown that many Pacific transnational communities in urban cities have experienced significant educational and social inequalities and inequities[19] particularly as their vulnerabilities are often linked to their visa status like other migrant groups.

Migrant groups are susceptible to domestic immigration, economic, and welfare policy. In New Zealand, Pacific communities are arguably adversely impacted the most by economic policy changes than any other group.[20] This highlights how migration, which until recently was the exclusive domain of domestic immigration policy for wealthy countries, has now become central to the debate on international development and poverty alleviation.[21]

For Pacific countries, issues of 'brain drain', that is the loss of highly qualified and productive workers, have arisen time and time again in reference to processes of international labour migration. This is a valid argument, however, as a key feature of Pacific migration is that it is often circular in nature. Therefore, rather than viewing the upskilling of Pacific migrants overseas as a brain drain a more apt description would be a brain exchange as Pacific people return home. As Liki argues in her research based on the migration of Samoan professionals, for Pacific people and Samoans, 'mobility spans geographic and social spaces yet is firmly anchored in the 'aiga (family)'.[22] Inevitably there will always be some professionals who will remain overseas; however, it is in the best economic and sociocultural interests of Pacific families, communities, and nations to continue to support brain exchanges.

[18] AAAJ, 'A community of contrasts', 67.
[19] AAAJ, 'A community of contrasts'; Macpherson, 'Transnationalism and transformation in Samoan Society'.
[20] Stahl and Appleyard, 'Migration and development in the Pacific Islands'.
[21] M. Luthria, 'Seasonal migration for development? Evaluating New Zealand's RSE Program overview', *Pacific Economic Bulletin* 3:3 (2008), 165–70.
[22] Liki, 'Moving and rootedness', 80.

Money Flows

The role of remittances in the Pacific has been researched extensively, though much is reliant on financial money transfers. An important motivator for movement is obtaining incomes to send home to families and communities. Most migration in the Pacific is based on household and community decisions. There is also individual choice, however, with the reasons given based around family and community needs and obligations. The act of migration to access further education or obtain incomes often comes with an expectation of reciprocity through remittances, whether it be economic, social, or material.

Many Pacific Island countries are reliant on remittances and for some it is their highest source of income. Sāmoa and Tonga are the highest remittances receivers in the Pacific and are high on the list globally by GDP.[23] Since the Covid-19 pandemic, where many have lost jobs, remittances from overseas-based citizens have become crucial, even in countries that prior to temporary labour schemes were not reliant on remittances such as Vanuatu. Access to overseas temporary labour programmes has provided many ni-Vanuatu with incomes not available at home and are seen as better than aid provided by donor countries: 'We would rather work for our money than be given aid. To do it for ourselves and not be dependent on aid, yes that is why we are here' (Ron an RSE worker).[24]

In recent times the MIRAB model has come under scrutiny specifically due to how remittances are conceptualized and how small island states have been able to diversify national economies.[25] The MIRAB model and other remittance theories have argued that over time there will be a change in generational attitudes and the willingness to continue to remit otherwise known as 'remittance decay'. However, remittances continue to feature strongly in small island economies with many Pacific countries reporting larger remittance contributions compared to aid. This was evident in a recent comparative analysis of remittances from Tongans participating in Australia's Seasonal Worker Program versus total of received Australian aid.[26]

---

[23] T.K. Jayaraman, C.K. Choong, and R. Kumar, 'Role of remittances in economic growth in Pacific Island countries: a study of Samoa', *Perspectives on Global Development and Technology* 8:4 (2009), 611–27, at 618.

[24] R. Bailey, 'Unfree labour: ni-Vanuatu workers in New Zealand's Recognised Seasonal Employer Scheme', Master's thesis, University of Canterbury, Christchurch, 2009, 58.

[25] C. Tisdell, 'The MIRAB model of small island economies in the Pacific and their security issues: revised version', Social Economics, Policy and Development Working Papers 165087, University of Queensland, School of Economics, 2014.

[26] S. Howes and B. Orton, 'For Tonga, Australian labour mobility more important than aid and trade combined', 2020, https://devpolicy.org/for-tonga-australian-labour-mobility-more-important-than-aid-and-trade-combined-20200121/.

The continuity of significant remittance contributions is based not on economics but rather on the deeply embedded sociocultural nature of migration and the subsequent networks of flows of people, labour, and goods and this is highlighted in research from traditional MIRAB economies such as the Cook Islands.[27]

Knowledge Flows

Pacific people have been migrating for further educational opportunities and scholarships since at least 1885 when the Suva Medical School was established. The first Pacific university established was the University of Hawai'i, founded in 1907. It took more than fifty years before the next Pacific university was established when from 1965 all independent Pacific countries began establishing their own national universities in earnest. The University of the South Pacific (USP) was established in 1968 and became one of only two multinational, regional universities in the world.[28] USP has campuses in twelve different Pacific countries, with the main campus based in Suva, Fiji. Table 62.2 outlines national universities established across the region in chronological order.

The need to attain post-secondary education and formal qualifications as a pathway for social mobility became a prominent feature of Pacific migration post-independence. This process was facilitated not only by Pacific countries encouraged by Christian ideals but also by former and current colonial powers who were keen to build capacity in a public service sector. This was evident in the number of tertiary training facilities across the region that initially focused on training pathways for teachers, healthcare workers, clerical workers, and agricultural workers. Prior to the establishment of these universities in the Pacific, most students would relocate to New Zealand for their university education as well as for their senior secondary schooling. By the early 1970s, for example, the majority of Samoan migrant families in New Zealand were there for educational opportunities.[29]

Australia introduced the flagship programme the Australia-Pacific Technical Coalition (APTC) in 2007. The main purpose of the programme

---

[27] E. Marsters, N. Lewis., and W. Friesen, 'Pacific flows: the fluidity of remittances in the Cook Islands', *Asia Pacific Viewpoint* 47:1 (2006), 31–44.
[28] The University of the West Indies was the first regional university established in 1948.
[29] C. Macpherson, R. Bedford, and P. Spoonley, 'Fact or fable? The consequences of migration for educational achievement and labour market participation', *Contemporary Pacific* 12:1 (2000), 57–82, at 65.

Table 62.2 *Pacific national university institutions.*

Year	Institution	Location
1907	University of Hawai'i	Various campuses. Main campus Mānoa, Hawai'i
1965	University of Guam	Mangilao, Guam
1965	Papua New Guinea University of Technology	Lae, Papua New Guinea
1965	University of Goroka	Goroka, Papua New Guinea
1966	University of Papua New Guinea	Port Moresby, Papua New Guinea
1968	University of the South Pacific	Various campuses. Main campus Suva, Fiji
1975	'Atenisi Institute	Nuku'alofa, Tonga
1980	Divine Word University	Madang, Papua New Guinea
1984	National University of Sāmoa	Apia, Sāmoa
1984	Pacific Adventist University	Port Moresby, Papua New Guinea
1987	University of French Polynesia	Papeete, French Polynesia
1999	University of New Caledonia	Nouméa, New Caledonia
2004	University of Fiji	Lautoka, Fiji
2009	Papua New Guinea University of Natural Resources and Environment	East New Britain, Papua New Guinea
2010	Fiji National University	Suva, Fiji
2013	Solomon Islands National University	Honiara, Solomon Islands

is to promote economic development and growth across the region through skills training and employment. Building skills and trades capacity in the region through APTC can provide development gains for the region as well as in developed Pacific Rim countries as APTC offers Australian qualifications. These training schemes can therefore address the issues of high youth unemployment throughout the region and governments can provide training for skills needed both in the region and further abroad. APTC provides a comparative advantage over Pacific-based institutions with Australian qualifications, thereby providing a potential pathway for labour migration for Pacific graduates as skilled workers into Australia and further abroad.[30]

Today there is much discussion regarding gender inequalities and migration as recent educational opportunities have now expanded both in sector

---

[30] S. Chand and H. Dempster, 'A Pacific skills partnership: improving the APTC to meet skills needed in the region', Center for Global Development, 2 August 2009, www.cgdev.org/blog/pacific-skills-partnership-improving-aptc-meet-skills-needed-in-region.

and in region. Historical notions of specified gender roles[31] have clearly been re-defined over the years, but their legacy remains in scholarship policy and decision-making where women are over-represented in vocational training such as teaching and nursing. Scholarships have broadened to Europe and Asia and now include student athlete scholarships targeted towards Pacific males to play rugby union from Japan to the United Kingdom and New Zealand, or American football in the United States. Sports migration is discussed in more detail later in the chapter.

Scholarships have always been based on meeting the occupational and skills needs of Pacific countries and therefore governments have flexibility over determining in which subject areas to allocate scholarship funding. In recent times there has been a focus on environmental sciences and policy, given the climate crisis facing the region. Scholarships are important for soft-power diplomacy where the provision of benefits seeks to develop empathy for the donor nation.[32] For the recipients they provide an opportunity to increase social mobility for themselves and their families but these recipients are also seen as ambassadors in their respective host countries.

People Flow

This next section provides a brief overview of the main labour and employ-ment migrations that have taken place since independence, including Kiribati seafarers; Pacific healthcare workers; peacekeepers, military and security; labour mobility schemes; and Pacific sports migration. With limited oppor-tunities for formal-sector employment, labour migration is reflective of ambitions and government needs, and is often linked to family and commu-nity motivations.

Kiribati Seafarers

The opportunity for Kiribati seafarers to train as crew for international shipping began in the late 1960s. Borovnik credits the 'development of training and recruitment facilities' as the key entry point for opportunities in shipping, further describing seafarer migration as 'transversal' temporary

---

[31] K. Mahina-Tuai, 'A land of milk and honey? Education and employment migration schemes in the postwar era', in S. Mallon, K. Māhina-Tuai, and D. Salesa (eds.), *Tangata O Le Moana* (Wellington: Te Papa Press, 2012), 161–77.
[32] D. Zhang, S. Hogg, and S. Gessler, 'Pacific Island countries, China & sustainable develop-ment goals part 3: Chinese scholarships in the Pacific', DPA, *In Brief* 2017/22, Canberra, ANU, 2017.

contract labour circulation and, unlike other migrations situated in land-based communities, creating possible links and roots. This type of migration is multisited in a number of locations. As Borovnik noted:

> Seafarers cannot be immediately recognised as contributing to the transnationalism of their home countries. Criss-crossing internationalised and national waters during their employment of merchant vessels and living with multi-national crews, seafarers could rather be seen in many ways as pioneers of global citizenship.[33]

Understanding how and if seafarers contribute to diaspora links is still in question, when migrating from ship to ship and port to port. It has been an important source of labour migration for Kiribati and Tuvalu since the 1970s.

Pacific Healthcare Workers

Globally, healthcare professionals make up a large proportion of international migrants. Pacific health workers often seek to access initial or continued training in their field conducted overseas. According to Connell, 'By the 1980s it was evident that becoming a [skilled health worker] ... not only provided an income and upward social mobility, especially for many women, who might otherwise be unemployed, but that nursing offered job opportunities outside the Pacific.'[34] Some go on to become qualified in various aspects of their chosen fields and for others this move is primarily to further their knowledge and use their skills abroad. Nonetheless, there is concern that this can result in brain drain.[35] Connell and Brown's analysis of Samoan and Tongan nurses in Australia further contributes to the discussion of remittances for Pacific peoples and counters the remittance decay argument often related to migration and diasporic studies.[36] As this chapter highlights, Pacific people's experiences show evidence there is a need to reframe and rethink the MIRAB paradigm.

In regard to scholarships, Connell highlights that Pacific scholarships offered were not necessarily in people's preferred interests.[37] However, they

---

[33] M. Borovnik, 'Transnationalism of merchant seafarers and their communities in Kiribati and Tuvalu', in H. Lee and S. Francis (eds.), *Migration and Transformation: Pacific Perspectives* (Canberra: ANU Press, 2009), 143–57.
[34] J. Connell, 'The two cultures of health worker migration: a Pacific perspective', *Social Science Medicine* 116 (2014), 73–81, at 75.
[35] Connell. 'The two cultures of health worker migration'.
[36] J. Connell and R.P. Brown, 'The remittances of migrant Tongan and Samoan nurses from Australia', *Human Resources for Health* 2:2 (2004), 1–21.
[37] Connell, 'The two cultures of health worker migration'.

provided overseas educational opportunities. For example, 'Many people, and especially the more skilled, only became health workers because scholarships were available.'[38] Pacific migrants in health sectors often hope to gain the education and skills and use them in their respective countries. However, returned healthcare workers are often frustrated due to the lack of infrastructure or resources they became accustomed to in their countries of training, which results in many returning to these destinations. This can have a negative impact on the already limited numbers of skilled healthcare workers within the Pacific.[39] Healthcare workers are not necessarily migrating to the metropolitan Pacific Rim countries. Increasingly, healthcare workers are participating in intraregional migration, often assisting with shortages of skilled labour in neighbouring countries. For example, a number of Solomon Island nurses work in neighbouring Vanuatu.[40]

Peacekeepers, Military and Security

Service in the armed forces has been one of the main pathways for migration to the United States for compact Pacific countries and United States Pacific territories, as well as for social upward mobility.[41] Elsewhere in the Pacific, military service provides transnational movement further afield, including twinning training programmes between former British Pacific colonies Fiji and Papua New Guinea and the United Kingdom. The Fiji military are well known for their different roles as UN peacekeepers and as private security guards, particularly in the Middle East, with more than 800 Fijian personnel actively involved in peacekeeping duties during the 1990s.[42] However, there are risks of income insecurity from pay disputes, as highlighted by Maclellan: 'The boom for recruiting in Iraq and Kuwait has raised many issues for the Government of Fiji: the unregulated role of private recruitment contractors, the social impacts on family life, and the capacity of government to support workers with pay disputes or post-deployment health problems.'[43] Apart from these risks the most obvious risk is of course the loss of life during

---

[38] Connell, 'The two cultures of health worker migration', 78.
[39] T.S. Yamamoto et al., 'Migration of health workers in the Pacific Islands: a bottleneck to health development', *Asia Pacific Journal of Public Health* 24:4 (2012), 697–709.
[40] https://dailypost.vu/news/vanuatu-needs-800-nurses-director/article_fc466a75–1086-5589-9563-9c5e9e6f091c.html.
[41] T. Fa'aleava, 'Fitafita: Samoan landsmen in the United States Navy, 1900–1951', PhD thesis, University of California, Berkeley, 2003; Uperesa, 'Fabled futures'.
[42] T.K. Teaiwa, 'Articulated cultures: militarism and masculinities in Fiji during the mid 1990s', *Fijian Studies: A Journal of Contemporary Fiji* 3:2 (2005), 201–22.
[43] N. Maclellan, 'Fiji, the war in Iraq, and the privatisation of Pacific Island security', APSNet Policy Forum, 6 April 2006, 3, https://nautilus.org/apsnet/0611a-maclellan-html/.

warfare. An argument used when New Zealand announced the Recognised Seasonal Employment Scheme (RSE) was that it was a labour mobility alternative to people from the Pacific entering war-torn countries and risking their lives for the sake of employment.

South Pacific Work Schemes 1960s–1980s

Temporary work visas have been made available to a number of Pacific Island nations since the initiation of New Zealand's South Pacific Work schemes in the 1960s, and the Fijian Rural Work Permit Scheme. All involved short-term migration only. Nonetheless, many immigration policies, restrictions, and opportunities are reflective of the migrant-receiving country's needs.

New Zealand's South Pacific Work schemes were initiated in the mid-1960s and ended twenty years later. At the time, there was a need for labour in specific locations either that New Zealander citizens would not work in or that had low unemployment rates. Stahl and Appleyard noted, 'By responding to short-term labour requirements immigration intakes basically reflected contemporary economic conditions.'[44] These work schemes had limited capacities for the Pacific labour force to source permanent migration. They were essentially temporary schemes with varying governance mechanisms for particular countries and communities. Fiji was the biggest winner in this scheme. Levick provides in-depth analysis of the evolution of these schemes and Pacific Islander engagement.[45]

During the first ten to fifteen years of this period, Australia and the USA did not have any specific work schemes available to Pacific Island nations. Nonetheless, as this chapter demonstrates, this evolved over time. As with other host nations already discussed, their own labour needs were the prime catalyst for change.

The South Pacific Work schemes continued until 'a decision by the New Zealand Labour Government in October 1987 to restrict Fijian workers to employment opportunities in New Zealand effectively puts an end to the reality of temporary labour migration under the terms of the South Pacific Work scheme as it was developed in 1976'.[46] Levick and Bedford suggested 'The *coups d'état* in Fiji provided a convenient excuse to put an end to the

[44] Stahl and Appleyard 'Migration and development in the Pacific Islands', 19.
[45] W. Levick, 'Contract labour migration between Fiji and New Zealand: a case study of a South Pacific work permit scheme', MSc thesis, University of Canterbury, Christchurch, 1988.
[46] W. Levick and R. Bedford, 'Fiji labour migration to New Zealand in the 1980s', *New Zealand Geographer* 44:1 (1988),14–21, at 14.

most successful work permit scheme that had evolved between New Zealand and a Pacific country.'[47] This demonstrates that the sustainability of labour schemes is dependent on the economic and political climates in which they exist, as was notable with Fiji's initial exclusion from Australia and New Zealand seasonal workers programmes.

Seasonal Worker Programmes from the 2000s

Since 2007, new temporary labour mobility programmes have been established that favour citizens of Pacific Island Forum (PIF) nations, with the exclusion of the French territories of New Caledonia and French Polynesia, who were not full members of the PIF at the time of establishing the temporary labour programmes.[48] Australia's labour mobility schemes also include Timor-Leste. The chronology of recent labour schemes is:

2007 New Zealand's Recognised Employer Scheme (RSE)
2008 Pacific Seasonal Worker Pilot Scheme (PSWPS)
2011 Added to H-2A and H-2B visa programmes in the United States[49]
2012 Australia's Seasonal Worker Program (SWP)[50]
2018 Australia's Pacific Labour Scheme (PLS).

Recognised Seasonal Employer Scheme (RSE)

In 2005, industry growth and the reduction of available seasonal labour in New Zealand's horticulture and viticulture industries led to a collaboration with the government and the formation of a seasonal labour strategy for the future. As a result, in 2007 the Recognised Seasonal Employer Scheme was established.[51] The RSE scheme was a grower-initiated policy to provide New Zealand growers with reliable labour in the horticulture and viticulture sectors. The objectives of this policy are twofold: first, to fill labour gaps of

---

[47] Levick and Bedford, 'Fiji labour migration to New Zealand', 21.
[48] The Pacific Islands Forum consists of eighteen Pacific Island member nations: Australia, Cook Islands, Federated States of Micronesia, Fiji, French Polynesia, Kiribati, Nauru, New Zealand, Niue, New Caledonia, Palau, Papua New Guinea, Republic of the Marshall Islands, Sāmoa, Solomon Islands, Tonga, Tuvalu, and Vanuatu.
[49] www.uscis.gov/archive/archive-news/new-countries-eligible-participate-h-2a-and-h-2b-programs.
[50] Prior to SWP Australia piloted the Pacific Seasonal Workers Program (PSWP), 2008–12.
[51] Bailey, 'Unfree labour'; C. Bedford, 'Picking winners? New Zealand's Recognised Seasonal Employer (RSE) policy and its impacts on employers, Pacific workers and the island-based communities', PhD thesis, University of Adelaide, 2013; S. Ramasamy, V. Krishnan, R. Bedford, and C. Bedford, 'The Recognised Seasonal Employer policy: seeking the elusive triple wins for development through international migration', *Pacific Economic Bulletin* 23:3 (2008), 171–86.

the horticulture and viticulture industries, and second, to encourage economic development in Pacific Island states by prioritizing workers from the region. Historical temporary labour schemes with the Pacific discussed above 'had a significant influence on the design of the RSE policy'.[52]

Participation in the RSE has resulted in positive individual and community developments. In 2007, the Lolihor Development Council (LDC) from North Ambrym, Vanuatu, selected twenty-two men to participate in the RSE. The objectives were to earn money for the 'good of the community'. During 2007–11 there was much success. RSE incomes contributed to a market house, community wells for twelve villages, scholarships for education, and two boat motors to continue generating income for the communities; they paid a salary to a nurse to reside at and run the local medical clinic, built a kindergarten, made renovations to three local churches, established a micro-credit scheme, and purchased water tanks for villages.[53] Bedford et al. record the range of RSE community projects in Tonga, Sāmoa, and Vanuatu.[54]

Although some RSE workers have participated for many years, permanent migration is not a goal for all. Their relationship with their families, home communities, and land is embedded in their personhood and identity.[55] Even those who migrate permanently often have goals of returning to their homelands. Temporary labour schemes provide the option of obtaining overseas incomes. Due to the circular nature of the schemes, people return home and can apply for successive seasons, without the need to migrate permanently. These incomes are an additional source of resources that are often used for the purposes of school fees, building homes and purchasing land, community development, customary practices, and, for some, small business enterprises. Nonetheless, there are positive and negative unintended consequences that are related to temporary labour schemes. Because of this, the schemes require constant monitoring and management in order to ensure that potential benefits continue to flow for Pacific Island families and communities.

The PSWPS and SWP

In 2008, Australia introduced the Pacific Seasonal Worker Pilot Scheme (PSWPS). Although this was small in scope, PSWPS ceased in June 2012 and

---

[52] Bedford. 'Picking winners?', 57.   [53] Bailey, 'Unfree labour', 102–3.
[54] C. Bedford, R. Bedford, and H. Nunns, 'RSE impact study: Pacific stream report', 2020, www.immigration.govt.nz/documents/statistics/rse-impact-study-pacific-stream report.pdf
[55] J. Bonnemaison, 'The tree and the canoe: roots and mobility in Vanuatu societies', in M. Chapman and S. Morrison (eds.), *Mobility and Identity in the Island Pacific* (Wellington: Victoria University Press, 1985), 30–62.

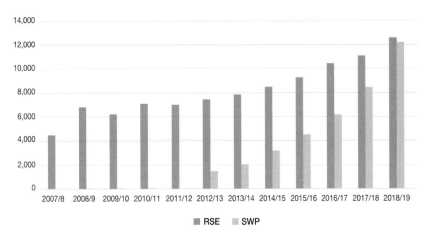

Figure 62.1 Participation rates of RSE and SWP 2007–2019.

was replaced by the Seasonal Worker Program (SWP) on 1 July 2012. SWP is open to nine Pacific countries and Timor-Leste. One significant difference from SWP is that it is part of Australia's aid programme, whereas the RSE scheme was industry driven. These schemes fill a void in industries that have low uptake by domestic citizens, due to the rurality and seasonal nature of these often temporary occupations. The largest labour contributing country for both the RSE and SWP is Vanuatu, followed by Tonga.

Prior to these temporary work schemes, citizens from Melanesian countries have had limited access to visas in Pacific Rim countries. In the case of New Zealand, a number of visas have been available, mainly for Polynesian countries, especially those with historical colonial links. Yet the links with Australia and Papua New Guinea have never developed into similar access avenues. There has been extensive growth in both RSE and SWP as shown in Figure 62.1.

Australia's Pacific Labour Scheme (PLS)

In July 2018, Australia's Pacific Labour Scheme commenced. Like SWP, PLS is open to Pacific Island nations and Timor-Leste; it allows not only for low-skilled workers but also for semi-skilled workers for a period of up to three years in rural and regional Australia. Like the SWP, it does include accommodation and tourism sectors, but this scheme also includes aged care, non-seasonal agriculture work, forestry, and fishing. This visa offering of up to three years is significantly higher than RSE's seven months (except Kiribati and Tuvalu, nine months) and SWP, which increased to nine months in 2018. Visas for PLS and SWP are multi-entry, giving employers and workers greater flexibility in immigration processing. Australia's establishment of temporary labour schemes shows changes within Australia's immigration policies. However, these changes also reflect labour needs in both Australia and New Zealand.

Australia's and New Zealand's temporary seasonal worker schemes have no potential pathways for permanent migration. Given the new longer-term visa for workers it will only be a matter of time before there needs to be more consideration of pathways to permanent residency. This transition will be vital, especially for workers from countries suffering climate and environmental degradation. Labour migration is not necessarily the answer to these problems. It can, however, assist financial needs, population pressure, and possible connections to set up a new transnational diaspora.

The New Zealand government is exploring new industries for Pacific Island countries, such as construction and fisheries, while other industries such as forestry and dairy have also been lobbying for an overseas workforce similar to that of the RSE.[56] The recent Pacific Trades Partnership (PTP) recruiting Pacific workers for the Canterbury rebuild after the devastating 2011 Christchurch earthquake has made positive achievements so far, and demonstrated potential for further expansion.[57] The government of New Zealand is working with Pacific nations, taking stock of the impacts associated with labour mobility programmes in an attempt to understand the unintended and intended consequences resulting from participation to engage in future pathways. Australia and New Zealand have greatly benefited from these labour schemes, and for the Pacific the main benefits of participating in these programmes are the financial, social, and material remittances. However, unintended negative outcomes need further examination. As Macpherson observed:

> there is a significant literature which documents the history of Pacific migration to the Rim countries and analyses the social, economic, demographic and political ramifications of movement for the 'receiving' countries.

[56] R. Tipples and P. Rawlinson, 'The RSE, a tool for dairying? Understanding the Recognised Seasonal Employer policy and its potential application to the dairy industry', Working Paper 16, Lincoln University NZ Faculty of Agribusiness and Commerce, 2014.
[57] www.scoop.co.nz/stories/ED1806/S00077/mbie-contracts-ara-to-assess-pacific-island-labourers.htm, accessed 13 May 2019.

There is a very much smaller literature on the history and ramifications of that movement for the labour-supplying economies.[58]

The United States Agricultural Programmes

The United States offers the H-2A and H-2B Agricultural Visa Programs for citizens from the independent Pacific nations of Fiji, Kiribati, Nauru, Papua New Guinea, Sāmoa, Solomon Islands, Tonga, Tuvalu, and Vanuatu. Yet the uptake of this opportunity has never been realized. Like RSE and SWP, this programme is driven by employer demand and there is no pathway to permanent residency. Advocates have promoted these programmes in places like Vanuatu, and also brought farmers from the United States to visit the country.[59] This visa is similar to PLS in that it is for up to three years. However, as Hay noted, the cost of this visa is between five to ten times that of RSE and SWP.[60] The significant associated costs, distance from home islands, and the lack of information in the region explains why the uptake of this by Pacific people has not been noticeable.

Pacific Sports Migration

A new Pacific migration phenomenon has recently begun in which two distinct gendered pathways to social mobility have emerged. While Pacific women are still encouraged into the education pathway, Pacific men are increasingly looking to sports as an avenue to improve their social status through semi-professional and professional pathways, particularly in the sporting codes of American football, rugby union, and rugby league. This trend has largely been facilitated by the increasing visibility of Pacific male athletes in American football in the USA, and rugby union and rugby league in New Zealand, Australia, and France. This sport-related migration reflects sports' preferences promoted by the former colonial powers that now benefit from these flows.[61] The rising presence of Pacific athletes has received much media attention since the 1980s, as typified by rugby union journalist Spiro Zavos in his now infamous 1987 sports article on 'the browning of

---

[58] Macpherson, 'Migration and transformation in the contemporary Pacific', 34.
[59] www.pidcsec.org/news/united-states-interested-in-vanuatu-seasonal-workers/.
[60] www.devpolicy.org/new-pacific-seasonal-workers-scheme20110131/.
[61] S. Zavos, 'The browning of the Wallabies', *The Roar*, 31 May 2007, www.theroar.com.au/2007/06/01/the-browning-of-the-wallabies/.

the All Blacks', noting the over-representation of Pacific athletes in New Zealand's national rugby team. Twenty years on Zavos reused 'the browning' term, this time in relation to the Wallabies, the Australian national rugby union team, when four Pasifika athletes played in an international test match.[62] Today, it would be of interest to see what catchphrase Zavos would use to describe the National Rugby League (NRL) competition in Australasia where almost half of all players in the competition are of Pacific heritage.

Professional sports have become a widely accepted vehicle for social mobility, particularly for men. While sports migration is often described as a type of 'muscle trade'[63] or 'brawn drain',[64] commentary is mostly focused on the spatial movements of athletes and the economic push and pull factors for migrating, and an increasing number of scholars contend that Pacific sports migration is enmeshed within the broader arena of sports politics. These scholars argue that the participation and over-representation of Pacific males in sports reveal deeper identity, citizenship, and mobility complexities for Pacific migrants in their respective nations.[65] The life of former National Rugby League star Leaupepe Nigel Vagana epitomizes this transnational existence. Nigel is a dual rugby league international and captained both New Zealand and Sāmoa national rugby league teams over the fourteen years of his professional rugby league career. He retired in 2008 as New Zealand's all-time leading try scorer at international level. Nigel is the only player in the history of the game to have topped the try-scoring charts in both the southern hemisphere (NRL) and the northern hemisphere (Super League) elite rugby league competitions.[66]

Nigel was born in New Zealand in 1975 to Samoan parents who had both migrated to New Zealand in the early 1970s. In 1995 Nigel was selected for a

---

[62] Uperesa. 'Fabled futures'; L. Panapa and M. Phillips, 'Ethnic persistence: towards understanding the lived experiences of Pacific Island athletes in the National Rugby League', *International Journal of the History of Sport* 31:11 (2014), 1374–88.

[63] W. Andreff, 'Sport in developing countries', in W. Andreff and S. Szymanski (eds.), *Handbook on the Economics of Sport* (Cheltenham: Edward Elgar, 2006), 8–15.

[64] J. Bale, *The Brawn Drain: Foreign Student-Athletes in American Universities* (Urbana: University of Illinois Press, 1991).

[65] A. Grainger, 'From immigrant to overstayer: Samoan identity, rugby, and cultural politics of race and nation in Aotearoa/New Zealand', *Journal of Sport and Social Issues* 30:1 (2006), 45–61; B. Hokowhitu, 'Tackling Māori masculinity: genealogy of savagery and sport', *Contemporary Pacific* 16:2 (2004), 259–84; Y. Kanemasu and G. Molnar, 'Pride of the people: Fijian rugby labour migration and collective identity', *International Review for the Sociology of Sport* 48:6 (2013), 720–35.

[66] Co-author of this chapter Ng Shiu (ANU) and Nigel Vagana have worked extensively together on intercultural sports education in a partnership between the Australian National Rugby League and Pacific Studies at the ANU.

wider squad for the newly established franchise, then the Auckland Warriors, in the National Ruby League competition. In 1996 at the age of 21 he debuted for the Auckland Warriors in the NRL competition. At the end of 1996 Nigel was recruited to play in the United Kingdom's Super League competition commencing in 1996. Nigel was part of the first wave of rugby league players who were recruited straight out of high school into a professional sporting team environment. Out of the twelve players for this first wave, eight were of Pacific heritage.

Nigel continued to play in the Super Leagues during the 1997 season, when he was recruited again by the Auckland Warriors for the following 1998 season. He continues to play in the NRL competition for the next ten years. Towards the end of his playing career Nigel was offered contracts to play in the United Kingdom again or play rugby union in either France or Japan.

Rather than continuing his professional athletic career he decided to retire in 2008 and remain in Australia for family reasons. Nigel became the first Pacific Wellbeing and Education Manager for the NRL. In 2019 Nigel's sports migration story came full circle when he returned to New Zealand to become the General Manager Football and Wellbeing for New Zealand rugby league.

In reflecting on his migration story he recounts how often Pacific male athletes do not have the luxury of choosing where they play or who they play for, as playing professional sports provides a kick start in life for families who are often struggling out of poverty. Of the first wave of high school players who moved to the United Kingdom, all but one player have returned to New Zealand since then. Most returned via Auckland and the NRL.

Having played professional sport and now working as a sports administrator focusing on Pacific athletes, Nigel has observed that more Pacific families are relocating from New Zealand to Australia to pursue the NRL dream for their sons, some as young as 14 years old. Parents and families are now more aware of how sport can lead to social and upward mobility, adding further pressure on young boys to succeed. Unfortunately, this pressure mounts the more successful a player becomes.

Nigel's story exemplifies the transnational nature of Pacific sports migration, where the drive is financial but the motivation is family. The network of flows not only is limited to athletes themselves but involves a complex network of people, families, organizations, media, and ideas moving across multiple boundaries, and sometimes the same boundaries multiple times. In the end, the majority return home.

Future Flows

Internationally, a number of reports and researchers have suggested international migration will become a major adaptation strategy for those experiencing detrimental climate change impacts. There is therefore a pressing need for countries across the globe to begin to develop and implement climate migration policies.[67] There is concern that climate migration will become a reality sooner rather than later for significant populations due to climate change impacts and responses associated with sea level rise; water insecurity from lack of access to safe drinking water and sanitation; coral reef degradation; and further food insecurity from reduced agricultural productivity.[68] Environmental migration is not a new phenomenon in the Pacific. People have relocated and resettled for generations due to climatic conditions and changing environments across the region. The majority of these relocations have been internal. For example, a series of volcanic eruptions between 1905 and 1911 on the island of Savai'i in Sāmoa forced the relocation of several villages to the island of Upolu in Sāmoa.[69] In more recent times the people of the Carteret Islands in Papua New Guinea have risen to global prominence after being labelled as 'the world's first environmental refugees' in international media.[70] They have been involved in a number of formal relocation programmes since the 1980s to the island of Bougainville, with limited success due to resettlement issues and Carteret Islanders preferring to remain on the island, a sentiment shared with Tuvaluans. A widely cited study investigating climate migration for people living on Funafuti, the main island of Tuvalu, has shown that Tuvaluans are less concerned with climate migration and would prefer to remain on the island.[71] Adapting to climatic variation was part of the reason for of Pacific Island peoples' social and political alliances across large areas throughout their history, as noted in the opening quote from Hauʻofa.

International migration is becoming increasingly popular as an adaptation strategy globally, even with resistance and reluctance from people living in

---

[67] R. Black, S. Bennett, and S. Thomas, 'Migration as adaptation', *Nature* 478 (2011), 447–9.

[68] J.R. Campbell, 'Climate-change migration in the Pacific', *Contemporary Pacific* 26:1 (2014), 1–28.

[69] A. Fepuleai, E. Weber, K. Németh, T. Muliaina, and V. Iese, 'Eruption styles of Samoan volcanoes represented in tattooing, language and cultural activities of the indigenous people', *Geoheritage* 9:3 (2017), 395–411.

[70] J.M. Luetz, 'Over-researching migration "hotspots"? Ethical issues from the Carteret Islands', *Forced Migration Review* 61 (2019), 20–2.

[71] C. Mortreux and J. Barnett, 'Climate change, migration and adaptation in Funafuti, Tuvalu', *Global Environmental Change* 19:1 (2009), 105–12.

the Pacific. The irony is that the migration opportunities that do exist are least available to those who live in the most vulnerable locations and circumstances. Opportunities for migration overseas are limited for those without the requisite qualifications.[72] The World Bank Pacific Possible report, for instance, recommended that there should be open-access migration from Tuvalu and Kiribati for work and permanent settlement in Australia and New Zealand.[73] This is an important start in acknowledging the peculiar environmental vulnerabilities that small island atoll nations such as Tuvalu and Kiribati face. However, it is also worth noting that all the detrimental influences of climate change will affect all Pacific Island nations.

A Pacific Ethnoscape? Reconceptualizing Pacific Flows

Pacific migration, mobility, and movement is best described by Epeli Hauʻofaʻs process of world enlargement. This perspective is shared by many Pacific scholars whose research and case studies have shown that current labour migration theories cannot fully encapsulate the Pacific experience. The economic drive for migration and movement is real; however, the underpinning motivation is family.

Rather than limiting migration to outward flows and emigration that is economically driven at both micro and macro levels, Pacific migration must be viewed as an enterprise involving a broad and complex network of various actors and agencies. Flows must be multidirectional, expanding across multiple nation-states and involving multiple generations. This argument is not new, and the various case studies in this chapter highlight how the notion of a Pacific ethnoscape of transnational communities is not merely an abstract reconceptualization but an actualization of the lived experiences of Pacific communities across the globe. As we have highlighted, this Pacific ethnoscape is not without its problems, issues, and limitations. This latest Pacific ethnoscape provides just as many opportunities as challenges for Pacific peoples who are now making new voyages across the globe as humanity faces the existential threat of global warming.

---

[72] R. Curtain and M. Dornan, 'A pressure release valve? Migration and climate change in Kiribati, Nauru and Tuvalu', Canberra: Development Policy Centre, ANU, 2019.
[73] http://pubdocs.worldbank.org/en/555421468204932199/pdf/labour-mobility-pacific-possible.pdf.

63

Creating Sustainable Pacific Environments during the Anthropocene

The Lessons of Pacific History

TAMATOA BAMBRIDGE AND GONZAGA PUAS

Pacific Island nations are some of the most vulnerable nations on Earth to the negative consequences of global warming. Low-lying atoll nations in the Pacific are already experiencing climate change in terms of the threat of sea level rise, ocean warming, and the intensification of tropical storms. Island nations are increasingly asserting their perspectives on global warming on the world stage as commitments made at international forums consistently fall short of the scientifically agreed minimum reduction of anthropogenic carbon emissions needed to avoid irreversible damage to planetary ecosystems. Less well documented, however, are moves domestically to climate-proof food security and enhance social resilience in island communities. After briefly outlining common threats faced by the majority of Pacific Island communities, this chapter focuses on avenues that are being explored in Federated States of Micronesia (Puas) and French Polynesia (Bambridge) to enhance climate resilience and create sustainable terrestrial and marine ecosystems. Both regions emphasize successful ancestral ways of resource management in partnership with Western science and technology. Colonial rule was more disruptive to these cultural institutions in French Polynesia than in Micronesia, but these institutions persisted in local practice in both locations to enable their recent revival. Both utilize culturally distinct ways of understanding the natural environments and humans' place in them. Huge challenges remain. Results have been promising, however, and make a strong argument that humans need to respond quickly and flexibly to these latest environmental challenges, drawing inspiration from past generations of Pacific Islanders who colonized and enhanced some of the most challenging ecosystems on Earth.

Introduction

Pacific Island nations strongly support global frameworks for climate change mitigation such as the 2015 Paris Agreement and the Sustainable Development Goals adopted in that year. The general failure of most nations to achieve the carbon emission reduction targets set out at Paris and other international meetings focused on climate change mitigation has serious implications for Pacific Island nations. Pacific Island nations are at the frontline of global warming because of their high proportion of low-lying atoll islands in the face of record warming of both polar caps and as a global climate hotspot where the impact of climate change is three times the global average. Ocean acidification levels in the Pacific are already 52 parts per thousand beyond the maximum safe limit of 350 parts per miliion, while Pacific fisheries are shifting in response to changes in water temperature. Warmer temperatures are also affecting food and water security on land because of variable rainfall and the intensification of natural hazards.

The majority of Pacific Island nations are generally politically stable nations accommodating diversity. Their chief problems are economic and environmental. Smaller, more coherent post-colonial nation-states in the central and eastern Pacific face problems of economic viability in an ever-increasing global economy dependent on economies of scale on the one hand, and geographical proximity and access to large markets with disposable income on the other. Larger, resource-rich Pacific Island nations concentrated in the southwest Pacific export minerals, fish, timber, and agricultural produce largely unprocessed through multinational companies. In such relations, much of the profit goes offshore rather than benefiting locals. In recent years, the ongoing search for economic solutions to overcome too much reliance on aid monies has increasingly been linked to environmental factors.[1]

Faced with rising population pressure and variable migration options, Pacific Island nations are increasingly championing the development of sustainable, low-energy-emitting ocean and land economies. Atoll nations such as Kiribati, Marshall Islands, and Tuvalu face inundation but still consider mass relocation as the last resort. Even the largest island nations with substantial mountainous interiors such as Papua New Guinea, Solomon

---

[1] See G. Bertram, 'The MIRAB model twelve years on', *Contemporary Pacific* 11:1 (1999), 105–8; H. Lee, and S.T. Francis (eds.), *Migration and Transnationalism: Pacific Perspectives* (Camberra : ANU Press, 2009), and especially Ng Shiu and Bailey, Chapter 62 of this collection.

Islands, and Fiji face mounting population pressure and climatic threats to crop production and the health of marine ecosystems. Fish such as tuna and corals are sensitive to even one degree of variation in average water temperature, while crop production tends to diminish with each rise in average annual temperature and reduction in annual average rainfall.[2] This chapter examines the development of sustainable blue and green economies throughout the history of the area encompassed by Federated States of Micronesia (FSM) and French Polynesia respectively. These two case studies make particular reference to how past practices are informing and enhancing this contemporary response to the existential threat of climate change.

The FSM and Its Environment in Historical Perspective

The Federated States of Micronesia (FSM) lies immediately above the equator between Papua New Guinea to the south, Guam to the north, Palau to the west, and the Marshall Islands to the east. It has more than 600 islands dispersed in a vast oceanic space in the northwest Pacific. The islands range from low-lying atolls that barely exceed 4 metres above sea level to many mountainous islands across the four states. The total land area of FSM is approximately 702 square kilometres.[3] It has 2,978,000 square kilometres of economic exclusive zone (EEZ).[4] The climate is tropical and the temperature is usually around 80 degrees F with two seasons: the dry months, which are generally from May to September, and the windy months from October to April. In Chuukese-Mortlockese[5] the dry months are called *lerak* (bountiful season), and the lean months *lefang*. The FSM is situated within what many have called typhoon alley where typhoons usually generate strong winds,

---

[2] See J. Bell, M. Taylor, M. Amos, and N. Andrew, *Climate Change and Pacific Island Food Systems: The Future of Food, Farming and Fishing in the Pacific Islands under a Changing Climate* (Copenhagen and Wageningen: CCAFS and CTA, 2016); IPCC (Intergovernmental Panel on Climate Change), AR6 climate change 2021: impacts, adaptation and vulnerability, www.ipcc .ch/report/sixth-assessment-report-working-group-ii.
[3] G. Puas, *The Impact of Climate Change on Health in the Federated States of Micronesia: The Case of the Low-lying Islands of the Mortlocks* (Palikir, Report for Pohnpei State, Federated States of Micronesia, June 2016), 7–8.
[4] G. Puas, *Federated States of Micronesia's Engagement with the Outside World: Control, Self-preservation and Continuity* (Canberra: Australian National University Press, 2021).
[5] Chuukese-Mortlockese refers to the Indigenous people of the State of Chuuk. The Mortlock Islands are an archipelago of atolls within Chuuk State. Mortlockese are considered as a distinct group because of their language and cultures. The first author of this chapter, Puas, is an Indigenous person of Lukunor Island in the Mortlocks.

especially in the southern part of Chuuk, and intensify as they travel to Yap, Guam, and the Philippines, or alternatively to Japan and Taiwan.[6]

Climate change is leaving devastating scars on the nation's environment. Local fishermen observe that tropical depressions and sea surges are more frequent and more intense than before.[7] Sea grass and the reef ecosystems are on the brink of collapse due to rising temperatures. Catches are getting fewer and smaller in size because of lack of sustenance in the food chain system. Today species are threatened because of the changes in their natural habitat due to human-induced climate change, and also overfishing activities by fishing fleets from Asia.[8] Studies on climate change[9] have confirmed the fishermen's observation and the rise in the sea level which is slowly hindering the island inhabitants' economic production, as their livelihoods depend on the sea and small-scale farming to meet their daily survival.[10]

Naturally, the ocean with the many tiny islands upon it presents a unique set of environmental circumstances for the Micronesian Islanders. Unlike continental people, the people of FSM are closely connected to the sea, upon which many of their livelihoods depend. This dependency on the ocean means that the inhabitants are acutely aware of their susceptibility to the changes in the environment. The island dwellers have developed a system of integrating the *leset–lemal* (terrestrial–marine environment) and became the custodians of such since time immemorial. Self-preservation, control, and continuity are therefore at the heart of Indigenous environmental preservation practices.[11] Fundamental responsibility for the preservation of the environment rests with the Indigenous community-based approaches which are inherently connected to traditional and customary practices to ensure the long-term continuity of the people. The oceanic environment is deeply

---

[6] Puas, *Federated States of Micronesia's Engagement with the Outside World*; P. D'Arcy, *The People of the Sea: Environment, Identity, and History of Oceania* (Honolulu: University of Hawai'i Press, 2006), 2. See Figure 9.1 in Volume I for typhoon paths.

[7] Personal interviews with elders from the many islands within the Mortlocks.

[8] Asian fishing fleets such as those from Taiwan and China are often the culprit regarding illegal fishing. They have been practising fishing methods that are destructive to the oceanic environment. Also interview with Sirel James, executive officer of surveillance ship *Micronesia-02*, during visits to the northwest islands in Chuuk, 21–6 February 2020.

[9] R. Henry, W. Jeffery, and C. Pam, *Heritage and Climate Change in Micronesia: A Report on a Pilot Study Conducted on Moch Island, Mortlocks Islands, Chuuk, Federated States of Micronesia* (Townsville: James Cook University, 2008), 5–10; C.H. Fletcher and B.M. Richmond, *Climate Change in the Federated States of Micronesia: Food and Water Security, Climate Risk Management, and Adaptive Strategies* (Honolulu: US Department of Agriculture Forest Service and the State and Federal Government of FSM, 2010), 17.

[10] Puas grew up in the Mortlocks and travelled to the islands in March 2020. Indigenous conservation practices remain the source of environment preservation.

[11] Puas, *Federated States of Micronesia's Engagement with the Outside World*, chapter 2.

embedded in Micronesian historical consciousness, yet it is dynamically challenging, with its own subtleties. The oceanic islands have nurtured and prepared the *shon matau*[12] (the people of the deep seas) to adapt continually to both natural and human-induced circumstances for many centuries. *Shon matau* remain the custodians of their islands and the surrounding seas despite the destructive nature of modern forces imposed by the external world. Inherently so, Micronesian Islanders must fight environmental threats to safeguard their home islands, just like their progenitors did in the past.

Continuity of human–environmental relations is at the heart of Micronesian centuries of adaptation, and this is more transparent today in light of the islands under threat because of climate change. To the Islanders, long-term sustainability rests fundamentally upon three epistemological doctrines of universal realism which are integral to the island environment.[13] They include all the natural elements associated with *lang*,[14] *fanou*,[15] and *saat*,[16] or alternatively the doctrine of *nonon aramas*.[17] These elements influence nature and the manner in which the inhabitants behave towards the environment. They all simultaneously work in sync to provide stability, identity, and continuity for the Indigenous population. *Lang* provides a compass on how the weather system functions by the celestial movements of the wind, stars, moon, and sun. *Fanou* is the physical soil which produces (*mongo*) and controls agricultural activities, while *saat* is the sea which provides the watery highway for movement between islands and fishing activities. *Saat* gains its character and personality by interacting with both *fanou* and *lang*. *Saat* is the provider of protein sustenance (*salei*) while *fanou* complements *salei* with its vegetative produce – *mongo*. A meal must have both *mongo* and *salei*, otherwise it would be considered not a complete meal. An incomplete meal can be seen as lacking knowledge of the environment on the part of the family who provided the meal.

Lang dictates and shapes how the inhabitants conduct their daily activities such as fishing, sailing, or alternatively agricultural activities, for example, planting taros and coconuts. The interaction between *lang, saat,* and *fanou* influences how *nonon aramas* treat the environment in which they have lived

---

[12] *Shon matau* refers to the Islanders of the low-lying Mortlocks where the deep blue sea occupies most of their life.
[13] Jack Fritz, personal interview, Palikir, Pohnpei, 3 April 2020.
[14] *Lang* is the heaven and all the things within in its universe.
[15] *Fanou* refers to any island even if it is few inches above the water with only handful of shrubs or trees.
[16] *Saat* is defined as whereever one can see or feel the sea.
[17] *Nonon aramas* is in reference to how people live with the environment historically.

Creating Sustainable Pacific Environments

for millennia. Environmental care is essentially about the total knowledge of the unity between *lang, fanou*, and *saat* working together in harmony. Micronesians, for many centuries, have studied and respected such interaction. It has enabled them, for instance, to predict or anticipate changes in the weather pattern, allowing them to organize their weekly activities structurally. Western science has also acknowledged the conservation value of *nonon aramas*, and has sought to learn the system from the Islanders.[18]

Historically the Indigenous people divided their atoll islands into common zones, from the ocean side to the middle of the lagoon or vice versa. The zones, however, differ slightly from the volcanic islands because of their topography, as Table 63.1 demonstrates.[19]

The purpose of these zones is for cultural maintenance, conservation, and communication. The zones are vital for everyday communication between the residents of each island because they pinpoint space, events, and time; that is, zones specify where people are during the day in terms of work and leisure activities. For example, a person may be working at the *lepwel* (taro farms) or fishing in the *lenomw* (lagoon centre) and remain there until the sun reaches the height of *lenunu* (i.e. tall coconut trees). Communication with the ancestral gods is an important part of island life as it provides spiritual healing to resolve problems, or predict likely future events. As Victor Puas, former mayor of Lekinioch municipality stated, 'environmental zones are like our traditional library as they provide useful information about nature and our relationship with it'.[20]

Moreover, the zones are crucial environmental references to those who have specialized skills, such as *sou safei* (traditional doctors), *sou set* (fishermen), or *sou fal wa* (canoe builders), to locate the resources that their professions

---

[18] T. Gladwin, 'Canoe travel in the Truk area: technology and its psychological correlates', *American Anthropologist* 60:5 (1958), 893–9.

[19] This was taught to me (Puas) on the atoll where I grew up and learned about the zones and their relationship within the ecosystems from my uncles. I also learned from my elders the importance of knowing the zones. For fishing zones in the low-lying islands in Pohnpei State see M. Lieber, *More Than a Living: Fishing and Social Order on a Polynesian Atoll* (Boulder, CO: Westview Press, 1994), 51–9. For Yap State see W. Alkire, *Lamotrek Atoll and Inter Island Socio-Economic Ties* (Urbana: University of Illinois Press, 1965), 19–22. For the high island of Yap see S.T. Price, 'The transformation of Yap: causes and consequences of socio-economic change in Micronesia', PhD thesis, Washington State University, Pullman, 1975, 54 and 57–60. For a general outline of the Pacific Islands see D'Arcy, *The People of the Sea*, 21–3.

[20] Victor Puas, pers. comm., 2 July 2013, Palikir, Pohnpei. See H. Segal, *Kosrae: The Sleeping Lady Awakens* (Kosrae: Kosrae Tourist Division, Department of Conservation and Development, Kosrae State Government, Federated States of Micronesia, 1989), 212–15 and 218–20; A.L. Debuce, *Cultural Change in Horticultural Practices on the High Island of Kosrae, Micronesia* (Eugene: University of Oregon Press, 1996), 58–9.

Table 63.1 *Environmental zones in the Mortlock Islands, FSM.*

Name of zone	The environmental part	Usual activities
Lematau	The deep ocean near the horizon	Deep-water fishing, trawling
On mong	Behind the crashing waves	Underwater big-fish spear fishing
Likin ounou	The exposed reef system	Reef fish food source
Fan ounou	Where the waves crash	Pole and net fishing
On alang	Shellfish area	Shell fish and sea crab gathering
Fan net	Beach at the ocean side	Plants for medicines and leisure activities like picnics
Ilik	Inland breadfruit trees	Breadfruit farms
Lenunu	Where tall coconuts grow	Garden areas
Lepwel	Taro farms	Taro farming
Imor	The edges of taro farms	Coconut planting and gardening
Leal	The lagoon-side road system	Inter-village road system
Roro	The foreshore	Small-scale gardening
Leppei	The beach	Canoes for the lagoon and leisure activities
Lemoshiset	Swimming zone for children	Spear throw fishing
Lein imwmwimw	The sea grass zone	Line throw fishing
Wenen	The exposed lagoon side	Pathway for canoe transportation
Lepweshepwesh	Swimming zone for adults	Spear fishing for amateurs
Mesenpal	The sloping part of the lagoon	Underwater spear fishing
Lelol	The first deep part of the lagoon floor	Bottom line-fishing and turtle hunting
Lekung	Invisible depth of the lagoon	Deep bottom line-fishing
Lenomw	The centre of the lagoon	Big fish trapping

require. For example, *sou safei* only need to locate specific zones to collect the ingredients for medical remedies, or to train students as to what particular fauna or flora grow in each zone to treat specific ailments. Island priests also rely on the zones to determine which ancestral gods to pray to or where to direct their *waitawa*[21] when the need arises.

---

[21] This is according to the oral history of Lekinioch Island. *Waitawa* means channelling in order to communicate with the ancestors. See J. Peter, 'Chuukese travellers and the idea of horizon', *Asia Pacific Viewpoint* 41:3 (2000), 253–67, at 264.

Islanders have developed deep knowledge of the zones and an understanding of the interdependency between the species in the food chain hierarchy. Changes in any of the zones are warning signs of a threat to certain species, which would mean a likely impact on the food chain system, or certain parts of environment. It would therefore require Islanders to react quickly and implement remedies to curtail such a threat. The zones provide information regarding the habitual behaviour of species, allowing the Indigenous population to locate them easily for food sources.[22] Likewise, knowledge of the thirty stages of the moon such as *sikauru or wereian anu* (visible to ghosts), *eling* (visible to humans), and *meseling* (all can see)[23] is also crucial to the ecosystem as they influence the behaviour of species. For example, during a full moon in the Mortlocks, land crabs migrate en masse to the beach to lay their eggs. The Islanders only need to go to the beach at midnight when the tide is high to capture them for food. Certain schools of fish like *momishik* (island sardines, *Clupeidia*) and *kish* (squirrel fish, *Holocentridae (Beryciformes)*) are caught only at certain time during *lefang* and *lerak*.

Moreover, *sou set* have developed a sophisticated regime in calculating when and how to harvest certain fish. Other fishing techniques are used at specific times of the month or season to lure other types of fish like *angerap* (skipjack tuna, *Katsuwonus pelamis*) close to the beach into *lalo* (encircled traps made from coconut fronds) or *maaii* (fish weirs). *Ngorongor* (ritual chants) are used before, during, and after the fishing activities to pay respect to the ancestral gods. Each clan has a specific system of *ngorongor*, which is passed down from one generation to the next for the purposes of continuing the clan's history as well as safeguarding its reputation as protector of the intricacies of the environment.[24]

---

[22] This is based on my own personal experience (Puas). For zones in the volcanic islands such as Yap see M.V.C Falanruw, 'Food production and ecosystem management in Yap', *ISLA: A Journal of Micronesian Studies* 2:1 (1994), 2–22. For low-lying atolls see D.I. Nason, 'Clan and copra: modernization of Etal, Eastern Caroline Islands', PhD thesis, University of Michigan, Ann Arbor, 1971), 28–33. For specific fauna and flora see K. Marshall, 'The structure of solidarity and alliance on Namoluk Atoll', PhD thesis University of Washington, 16–19.

[23] Kamilo Likichimus, master canoe carver and oral historian from Lekinioch Island. See also O. Uman, F. Saladier, and A. Chipen, *Uruon Chuuk: A Resource of Oral Legends, Traditions, and History of Truk*, vol. 1 (Moen, Truk: ESEA Title IV Omibus Program for Social Studies-Cultural Heritage Trust Territory of the Pacific Islands, 1979), 359–61.

[24] Being a member of an *ainang* means you are permanently locked into it and it demands your total loyalty. Emotional attachment to one's *ainang* is as strong as it is about personal identity and history.

Social Environmental Care

In pre-colonial Micronesia, economic resources were community owned and jointly managed by members of the extended *ainang*,[25] *mwalo*,[26] or *inepwine*.[27] Two customary principles of social relations, *alilis fengen* (caring for each other) and *eaea fengen* (sharing resources) are the fabrics of human relations. The strength of such relations depends heavily on what the environment provides economically. The social order is economically based, whereby the extended family system is grouped into different units, *inepwine*, *mwalo*, and *ainang*, and is assigned certain parts of the environment as custodians. *Inepwine* is at the bottom of the social hierarchy, followed by *mwalo*, and then *ainang* which occupies the apex of the social order. *Ainang* is therefore the total collection of *inepwine* and *mwalo* combined. It has its own diaspora throughout the island archipelagoes. It is the biggest form of the extended family system, with its members, *shon ainang*,[28] numbering in the thousands. *Ainang* are headed by many *samol*[29] and their status is ranked according to the pattern of settlement of each particular island or along the hierarchical order of the family tree. The paramount *samol* exercised power over resources, and the manner in which resources from the land and sea should be distributed and preserved. The clan's intricate knowledge of the environment is shared with individual members based on their ascribed status; they are the transmitters and guardians of clan history. Food production has always been a collective enterprise[30] that connects the *mwalo* and *ainang* who control particular areas of the integrated surrounding land and the sea environment.

Traditional methods of environmental management are still in practice today. They include *pwau*,[31] *otoul*, *oneisat*, *mwenmei*, and *unupwel* (restrictions from harvesting the land and sea) until they are lifted by the offerings of the

---

[25] *Ainang* is the largest form of the extended family system which included *inepwine* and *mwalo*. This is more so in the State of Chuuk and other parts of the outer islands of Yap.
[26] *Mwalo* is usually the extended family on the maternal side which includes the grandma, her siblings, and their offspring. I have not come across any literature speaking of *mwalo*.
[27] *Inepwine* is equivalent to the concept of immediate family.
[28] *Shon ainang* is a member of a clan from the mother's side; however, in many islands of Yap it is the father's side.
[29] *Samol* is the chief, ranked in relation to the unit or sub-unit of the extended family system.
[30] Food production brought many members of the clan together, especially during feasts where historical speeches to strengthen connection are told and retold.
[31] *Pwau* involves extensive restriction of access to a particular area or part of an area depending on specific circumstances. Extensive restriction relates to death of a *samol* of a clan, for example, or on the alternative to allow the land or a given reef to reproduce. Limited restriction is by *inepwine*'s own decision as custodians of small parcels of land or the reef. Puas's own experience as an Islander from the Mortlocks and also interview with elders from the Mortlocks.

first harvest of: coconuts (*otoul, Cocos nucifera*), fish (*oneiset*), breadfruit (*mwenmai, Artocarpus altilis*), and taro (*unupwel, Colocasia esculenta*) to the *samol*. These actions are considered as thanksgiving to honour their ancestral gods who continue safeguarding the environment they depend upon both economically and socially. The opening season for each of the crops is blessed and directed by the *samol*. *Samol* could also put restrictions to ban harvesting particular traditional crops by rationing their consumption for conservation purposes. Fishing and agricultural restrictive practices are common in the low-lying islands where customs and traditions remain the essence of life. Many of these practises are also common throughout Micronesia. Micronesians therefore have lived perpetually in close harmony and conformity with *lang, fanou*, and *saat* for many centuries while managing their resources to ensure their continuity. Disharmony arose when recalcitrant clans sought to reorder control of resources in the environment that they were not historically entitled to. This can cause long conflict and destruction in the environment when conflict arises, which can lead to destruction of food crops or the reef system, for example, or the killing of any *samol* who is responsible for maintaining order in the environment.

In the low-lying islands *pwau* is one of the most effective methods of conservation where it restricts human activities from degrading fragile parts of the coral reef, seashores, and also the land. It also restricts the harvesting of certain fish in some areas during reproduction season on the reef or island shores. *Pwau* serves two purposes: first, to honour the death of an important person in the clan, and second, to conserve resources by public announcement following the pattern of the yearly seasons to allow replenishment or restocking of resources. For example, when an important member of a clan who owns the reef dies, a *pwau* is automatically imposed. Publicly announced *pwau* are also imposed when the clan decides to close the reef during the windy season. A big tree branch called *shell*[32] is planted in the designated area to warn the public to stay away from the reef or part of an island or the entire island. The restriction is ended when the branch is removed upon the decision of the *samol* as advised by his clan's best fishermen and farmers. The public respects this form of conservation method as it benefits the whole island community.

Any violation of the *pwau* system could lead to severe consequences, including violence or even death. Oral history details violence between members of the clan who imposed the *pwau* and the opposing side who

---

[32] *Shell* is a large coconut leaf or branch of a tree used to signify a designated area where people are not allowed access.

fought a bloody conflict for many years. The dispute ended when the heads of the fighting clans came together for settlement, as to continue the fight will not resolve the pressure on the environment they relied upon. *Pwau* is also practised on the land by *sou fanou* (landowners). For instance, coconut fronds are tied around important trees such as breadfruit or coconuts to warn people off from particular land areas. Uninhabited islands, or parts thereof, are subject to the same restrictive measures by the clan who has the traditional rights and as guardians of the land. These methods are examples of traditional laws of the land which today are recognized by the national and state constitutions.

During the summer season called *lerak*,[33] usually from May to September, restrictions on taro consumption might be imposed on members of a clan or sub-clan by its *samol*. Such restrictions allowed taro to mature fully as they take three years to harvest. Also, during *lerak*, when breadfruits are in abundance, members of each *mwalo* would band together to harvest the fruits, and store them in underground storage (*maar*). This is a method of preservation for later consumption during the lean *lefang* season,[34] the lean season. Restriction of movement between villages was another way to ensure maintenance of a clan's resources. For example, members of village A may not enter village B without prior permission. This is to prevent wanderers from damaging the land or helping themselves to the resources on someone else's land.

Marine and coastal management took many forms. For instance, coral and rocks were arranged in a particular way to facilitate the natural flow of currents and patterns of waves to minimize shoreline erosion. Fish weirs are constructed and reconstructed along the pattern of the migratory movement of specific schools of fish by using traditional system of tides and currents during the harvesting season. *Maii*[35] or *laleo* are also used for safekeeping of schools of fish and shellfish such as octopuses and clams to shelter from the windy season.

---

[33] *Lerak* is referred to when breadfruit trees are off season from October to May – the windy months.
[34] *Lefang* is when breadfruits are harvested abundantly during the summer months from May to September. Fish are easy to catch on and near the reef system.
[35] *Maii* are fish weirs constructed along the reef system used to catch schools of fish. The event is called *peo* and often involved the whole community as invited by the clan's chief who controlled the reef. A large fleet of canoes would come together, using coconut fronds to chase the school of fish into the weir. An alternative to this is called *laleo* where, for example, bonito are chased to the beach to be trapped in a series of coconut fronds tied together. Certain fish are owned by different clans. The catch is distributed by the owner of the fish or the clan or sub-clan which owns the weir. Distribution is based on the ranks of the sub-clan system.

Creating Sustainable Pacific Environments

Planting of native plants such as *rakish* (sea oaks, *Casuarina equisetifoli*), *fash* (pandanus, *Pandanaceae*), *mosor* (*Guettarda speciosa*), and *shia* (mangrove, *Rhizophora*) a few feet from the shorelines was a method of protecting foreshores. Rocks and solid heavy debris fill the gap between the shoreline and the native plants, often by natural process. This was a form of local adaptation and mitigation strategy to strengthen the beaches where they were most susceptible to currents and strong waves which caused erosion.

Alteration of the Environment

Successive waves of imperial colonizers permanently altered the land- and seascape. Colonists built foreign-style buildings, docks for their ships, and sea walls supposedly to strengthen shoreline protection, and dug trenches wherever they desired for security reasons. They also built big houses with their own designs, used fertilizers not suitable to the island soil to maintain big gardens, and introduced a restrictive regime contrary to the traditional conservation system.[36] New problems arose because of their ignorance of the environment. Such practices affected land and near-shore use for conserving crops and fish resources which Islanders had depended upon throughout history. Many of these problems remained into the post-colonial period. A consultative approach with the Indigenous experts was not part of the colonial environmental policy. Any opposition to the colonial system that contradicted traditional methods of environmental conservation was met with punishments.[37] These legacies have been under re-evaluation for the purposes of adapting to a new environmental threat – climate change. Climate change is caused by the external industrialized countries and yet impacts tremendously on the island environment. It is altering the integrity of the fragile ecosystem, especially in the low-lying atolls. To this end, re-imagining the past traditional methods has been re-invited into the present to strengthen adaptation strategies to mitigate the impact of climate change on the environment.

There are layers of responsibilities for adapting to environment damage in the FSM. At the national level, legal instruments such as the Constitution,

---

[36] Oral testimony revealed the activities of outsiders that were implemented without local consultation. This foreign attitude became destructive to the environment. However, there were some activities borrowed by the locals as they fitted into the preservation of the environment.

[37] Oral history by those who lived during the Japanese era, for example, testified about severe punishment if the Indigenous people opposed Japanese environmental practices. Some showed body scars left by Japanese punishment.

787

statutory laws, and the common law system are employed. For example, the Constitution allocates environmental responsibilities between the municipality, the state, and the national governments, mirroring the common law system. For instance, marine space between these respective jurisdictions is clearly defined. Ownership of reefs by different clans and villages is acknowledged in the Constitutions of the states of Yap and Chuuk, for example. Municipalities control the areas around the reefs, often using the traditional methods of *pwau* to encourage good practices conducive to the long-term resiliency of the environment. The states are responsible for conservation outside the municipal border at the drop of the barrier reef on the oceanside of the lagoon to the outer 12 mile limit from the reef.[38] The national government has conservation jurisdiction from the 12 mile zone to the 200 mile Exclusive Economic Zone (EEZ).[39]

The Importance of Historical Continuity in FSM

As history is about continuity, identity, maintenance of resources, and the relationship between humans and the environment, *allikin fanou*[40] were and remain also needed to govern the island communities. *Allikin fanou* were expressed and supported by environmental rituals as reinforced by the island social system. Rituals are embedded in traditions as defined by the *sou uruo*[41] of the different clans. Contests over ownership of resources are often scrutinized by clan leaders. Historical evidence relates to how a clan fits into the overall sociopolitical structure of an island, or group of islands. *Sou uruo* positions are often accepted as the best mechanism of settling environmental disputes concerning the land and the sea. Collective social identity is connected to honouring the sacredness of the environment as transmitted through the generations. Respecting the sanctity of nature requires collective effort – to abandon such would mean disappearance of their identities and connection to history. Everything in the environment corresponds to the order of both living and non-living things created by nature, and that is the basis of equilibrium and harmonious coexistence between people and the environment. Naturally, the people of the Federated States of Micronesia, like their

---

[38] The Constitution of the Federated States of Micronesia (Palikir, Pohnpei, Federated States of Micronesia Government, 2000), Article 1.
[39] Constitution of the Federated States of Micronesia, Article 1
[40] *Alliken fonou* is the common law system of the FSM Islanders as handed down to them through the generations from their ancestors who first settled the islands and became the custodians of the integrated environment of the islands in the sea.
[41] *Sou uruo* are traditional historians.

ancestors have done in the past, will keep adapting to new environmental threats and continue to survive on their own terms.

French Polynesia and Its Environment in Historical Perspective

Situated at the opposite end of the Pacific Islands to FSM in the southeast Pacific, French Polynesia's EEZ extends over approximately 5,000,000 square kilometres of ocean. It consists of 120 islands located in five distinct archipelagoes. Most islands are volcanic, but there are also many atolls, especially in the Tuamotu archipelago, which contains 25 per cent of all atolls worldwide. These islands comprise about 3,500 square kilometres of land surrounded by 15,000 square kilometres of lagoon. The population numbers 278,400, with 75 per cent of them concentrated on the island of Tahiti.[42] The distant ancestors of the inhabitants of French Polynesia migrated via Southeast Asia across the western Pacific as part of the Austronesian expansion, settling in present-day West Polynesia around 900 BCE. It was from this region, and more exactly from the group formed by the Sāmoa, 'Uvea (Wallis), and Futuna Islands, that much later, during the first millennium CE, groups who became Polynesians resumed their movement of colonization towards the east.[43]

Like FSM, French Polynesia has two main seasons: the dry season (from May to October) and the humid season (from November to April). *Matari'i-i-ni'a* is the Mā'ohi[44] name of our Polynesian spring which carries powerful natural energies of renewal and regeneration. Its arrival, which is around 20 November, marks the return of abundance and is signalled by the reappearance of the constellation of the Pleiades in the Polynesian skies. *Matari'i-i-ni'a* opens the season of natural abundance. This prosperous period is known as *tau 'auhune* (whether it concerns harvests or fishing), follows the period of shortage known as *tau o'e* which begins around 20 May, and is signalled by the disappearance of the constellation Pleiades, it is the *matari'i-i-raro*. The rising of the Pleiades in November coincides with the return of the rains. It is from *matari'ini'a* that nature becomes generous in providing fruits, vegetables, and

---

[42] ISPF (Institut de la Statistique de la Polynésie Française), *Recensement de la population 2017* (Papeete : ISPF, 2018).
[43] E.N. Conte, G. Mole, and E. Nolet E., 'Des atolls et des hommes', in T. Bambridge and J.-P. Latouche (eds.), *Les atolls du Pacifique face au changement climatique: une comparaison Tuamotu-Kiribati* (Paris: Éditions Karthala, 2016). Bambridge is the author of this section of the chapter. On origin migrations, see also Chapters 16, 17, and especially 19 in Volume I.
[44] Mā'ohi is the Tahitian Indigenous name for themselves.

tubers. Tuberous plants such as taro are still the dietary base of the populations of these islands. It is also the time of abundance of reef or lagoon fish, most of which breed during this time.

Archaeological reconstructions of the environment of the low islands such as the atolls of the Tuamotu two centuries ago, prior to European colonial rule, reveal a self -sustaining ecosystem. Atoll islands were covered in extensive forests of large trees, the *Pisonia grandis*. Remnant stands still impress with their stature. Their thick foliage sheltered important bird colonies, while their leaf fall formed a humus enriched with bird droppings containing fertilizing phosphate. The shade of the high *Pisonia* permanently retains humidity. There was, no doubt, a plant cover and animal life far richer than under the current coconut groves on more arid ground exposed by the multiple fires now associated with copra exploitation. One of the most common plants in the atolls, and the most used by the inhabitants, was the pandanus (*Pandanus tectorius*). Each of its elements was exploited. Children gnawed on the fruits at the sweet end of the drupes. These drupes also provided seeds which, when dried and crushed, gave flour. The trunk was used for construction, while its roots contained fibres which were pulled to make ropes and fishing lines. The leaves were used to make covers for houses, mats, baskets, etc. The roots of purslane (*Potulaca lutca/pokea*) were also consumed after baking. On some atolls, fields of this plant were planted using a hardwood dibble, utilizing transplanted cuttings chosen from perennial plants with large roots.

Pre-European atoll vegetation cover was more resilient to climatic variation than the current cover, as well as providing shelter and multiple uses for life adapted to atolls. The cultivation of taro pits was particularly widespread in the Tuamotu. These pits, which were also used on Micronesian atolls, provided very effective adaptation to the ecological conditions of the atolls. On some atolls, as in Rēao, pits over 100 metres long were excavated several metres deep, sometimes into hard layers using picks made from *miki miki* (*Pemphis acidula*) to reach the underlying atoll fresh water lens.[45] At the bottom of the pit where the water was flush, compost was created from humus enriched with droppings of birds and mixed with various plants (*Pisonia* leaves, etc.). A variety of hardy food plants were cultivated for their resilience: taro (*Colocasia esculenta*), bananas (*Musa paradisiaca*), ti (*Cordyline terminalis*), but also kape (*Alocasia macrorrhiza*) and maota (*Cyrtosperma chamissonis*). By this means, the

---

[45] J.-M. Chazine, 'Du présent au passé: questions d'ethnoarchéologie, les fosses de culture des Tuamotu', *Techniques et Culture* 6 (1985), 85–99.

Paʻumotu (as the inhabitants of the Tuamotu refer to themselves) were able to cultivate and water a varied range of plants and develop relative self-sufficiency in food which they lost with the establishment of the coconut monoculture. The collection of traditional knowledge related to biodiversity today in the Tuamotu demonstrates that atoll societies knew how to take advantage of their marine and terrestrial biodiversity to adapt to withstand significant climate change.[46] Forests enhanced the underground water table, as well as providing shelter for the population in case of strong swells.

Māʻohi usually consider land and sea, island and lagoon, as a continuity. A good illustration of this principle in eastern Polynesia is the *rāhui*, an institution organizing and regulating access rights to lands, lagoons, and resources in the context of this continuity.[47] *Rāhui* were applied to all marine and terrestrial ecosystems. Strictly speaking, *rāhui* is defined as a temporary restriction in time or space, over a resource or a territory. The Polynesian Lexicon (Pollex) proposes the protoform *raafui* for East Polynesia and gives the restrictive definition 'prohibit'. According to the Pollex, *rāhui* is variously defined as 'prohibit' (Easter Island), 'prohibition or restriction laid on hogs, fruit ... by the chief', 'to lay on such a rāhui' (Tahiti), or 'a restriction' (Manihiki–Rakahanga). These definitions are applicable to the whole geographical area of eastern Polynesia.[48]

The *rāhui* on land and at sea gave rise to several kinds of rights and duties according to the status of the chief. The decision of a chief to set down a *rāhui* on resources reflected local social organization. The chief was rarely the sole decision-maker. Cultural norms meant that extended family members and other leaders should be included in the many debates involved in *rāhui* decisions.[49] The literature regarding *rāhui* in the Society Islands suggests

---

[46] G. Camus, *Tabiteuea Kiribati* (Paris: Hazan-Fondation Culturelle Musée Barbier-Mueller, 2014); E. Worliczek, 'La vision de l'espace littoral sur l'île Wallis et l'atoll Rangiroa dans le contexte du changement climatique. Une analyse anthropologique de la perception des populations locales', thèse de doctorat, Universités de Vienne et de Nouvelle-Calédonie, Nouméa, 2013.
[47] With the *rāhui*, we are dealing with a concept as important as *tapu* and *mana*. D. Oliver, *Ancient Tahitian Society*, 3 vols. (Honolulu: University of Hawaiʻi Press, 1974; T. Bambridge (ed.), *The Rāhui: Legal Pluralism in Polynesian Traditional Management of Resources and Territories* (Canberra: ANU Press, 2016); T. Hoffmann, 'The reimplementation of the raʻui: coral reef management in Rarotonga, Cook Islands', *Coastal Management* 30 (2002), 401–18.
[48] E. Dieffenbach, 'Dictionary, part III: grammar and dictionary', in E. Dieffenbach, *Travels in New Zealand with Contributions to the Geography, Geology, Botany, and Natural History of that Country*, vol. II (London: John Murray, 1843); J. Davies, *A Tahitian and English Dictionary with Introductory Remarks on the Polynesian Language and a Short Grammar of the Tahitian Dialect* (London: London Missionary Society's Press, 1851).
[49] Oliver, *Ancient Tahitian Society*.

the *rāhui* of the lagoon was not so different from the *rāhui* on the land in terms of usages associated with duties and rights: access rights, extractive rights, penalties for violations, and relevant jurisdictions.[50] This localized resource management regime has endured until the present day and has proved highly effective.

As in many island societies of the Pacific, the political economy of Tahiti was based on a ramified organization that anthropologist Raymond Firth referred to as a ramage.[51] A chiefdom grouped one or more ramages. The eldest member of a ramage is normally the chief, not only of his extended family group but of the whole chiefdom. But the ramage was a multibranched organization, in which every senior member of each ramage was recognized as the head of his own extended family on its own territory. This implies recognition of the ramage's specific rights to control the land and lagoon attached to its territory. Among these rights, we must emphasize the power to implement a *rāhui* on land and marine territory of its ramage. The use rights associated with these *rāhui* held by the ramage were more relative than absolute. On some occasions and in different contexts, the *ari'i* (chief of the ramage) could benefit from solemn *rāhui* rights on a territory that he did not directly control (in terms of the first fruits or the first fish given to him). On other occasions, the right to implement a *rāhui* by a smaller extended family leader was independent of the privilege of the main leader. These rights not only concern the right to land but also address the lagoon territories as part of the territory controlled by the extended family in a context of overlapping functions and responsibilities.

Another social aspect of the resilience of societies on the atolls and islands related to their mobility. Because the land and marine tenure was based on a collective ownership, members had claims to many land and lagoon spaces as they belonged to several ramages. Basic dwellings made of materials available on most atolls or islands allowed their rapid dismantling and human groups to change residences when a coast was too exposed to repetitive and regular environmental hazards. The matrimonial networks and the mobility of the societies of the atolls and islands allowed groups to settle more or less temporarily in other atolls and islands when famines and climatic hazards threatened.[52]

---

[50] Bambridge, *The Rāhui*.

[51] R. Firth, *We the Tikopia: A Sociological Study of Kinship in Primitive Polynesia*, 2nd edn (London: George Allen & Unwin, 1967).

[52] K.P. Emory, *Material Culture of the Tuamotu Archipelago*, Pacific Anthropological Records 22 (Honolulu: Bernice P. Bishop Museum, 1975); P. Ottino, *Rangiroa: parenté étendue, résidence et terres dans un atoll polynésien* (Paris: Éditions Cujas, 1972); T. Bambridge, *La terre dans l'archipel des îles Australes: étude du pluralisme juridique et culturel en matière foncière* (Paris: Institut de Recherche pour le Développement (IRD) and Aux Vents des Îles, 2009).

Historical Changes under Colonial Rule

Prolonged contact with Europeans and subsequent colonial rule not only transformed the social organization of the inhabitants, but also modified radically the ecology of atolls and some islands, reducing their resilience in the case of extreme climate change. Christianization and political centralization favoured the fixing of populations in a few villages and encouraged copra plantations. These changes profoundly transformed local society. The monoculture of coconut palms, in addition to contributing to the disappearance of large forests, made the soils of atolls bare, much less fertile and resilient. The now transformed atoll ecosystem no longer allowed, as in the past, good management of duckweed water,[53] and soft humus sheltered by tall *miki miki* (*Coprosma linariifolia*) trees. Vegetative protections against strong swells and cyclonic events had already disappeared by the end of the nineteenth century, causing hundreds of deaths in some atolls.

The recognition of customary use rights on the lagoon and on the land remained intact during the missionary period prior to French colonization, despite efforts to erode its usual form.[54] In the first period of the centralization of Indigenous state power, the central ruler Pomare II's Code of 1824 instructed that the *rāhui* would become the monopoly of the *ari'i nui* (great chief), with the other chiefs of ramages becoming the *tāvana* (translated from the English word for governor) rather than *ari'i*. From this period, the ancient *ari'i* came under the control of Pomare II. In the years 1820–30, Pomare II did use the *rāhui* extensively for his own benefit to control the trade of the Tuamotu black pearls, the pigs and the starch of the Society Islands and the Leeward Islands. All specified lagoon or land resources could not be consumed and were ordered to be given to Pomare.

The pre-colonial independent era of Tahitian history witnessed a variable geometry of power and resource control according to islands and archipelagoes. For religious rather than economic reasons, missionaries tried and succeeded in abolishing the *rāhui*, which they associated with a form of maintaining links with the ancestors and old deities. The conservation of such an institution seemed inconceivable at a time when the political objective was to impose a new Judeo-Christian god excluding Tahitian gods and deified ancestors. As regards to the user rights on the lagoon, French scholar

---

[53] Duckweed refers to a kind of subterranean water that is too salty to drink, but perfectly suitable to use on certain crops.

[54] T. Bambridge, 'Généalogie des droits autochtones en Nouvelle-Zélande (Aotearoa) et à Tahiti (1840–2005)', *Droits et Sociétés* 22:1 (2007), 153–82.

René Cochin notes that under the Protectorate, Act XXIV of the Tahitian Code in its revised versions of 1842 and 1848, provides that portions of the lagoon (the 'fish holes', the 'lakes', passes, shorelines) can be an object of priority, absolute, or relative control.[55]

The use of the term owner was a delicate issue, even in the 1840s. As already noted, the pre-European period was characterized less by concern with property rights than with different types of access rights, relative or absolute exclusion, and priority controls, according to the statuses of the individuals and the family group considered. However, the issue of land and marine tenure, if recognized, will never be addressed by a state authority in terms other than that of ownership in the Western sense.

Soon afterwards, the new Polynesian state, under the French Protectorate, organized a procedural claim of title. The Tahitian Act of 1852, as the codified law of the Leeward Islands in 1898, organized a land claim procedure. Even if the designers of these laws did not necessarily plan to include marine territories in property claims, many marine territories were claimed in Tahiti and in the Leeward Islands.[56] These claims were in line with the Polynesian vision of the territory, appropriating both terrestrial and marine areas adjoining it.

The *rāhui*, abolished by missionaries, was paradoxically reintroduced into the legal order by the colonial state in the Leeward Islands, whose main town was on the island of Raiatea, after the annexation in 1897, and continued until its repeal in 1917. But the reintroduced *rāhui* in this context no longer concerned lagoon resources, but only land resources (coconut, harvest); the *rāhui* was now introduced or removed by the district chief, and was incorporated into the coercive state apparatus and did not refer to any land and marine use rights. This new reality raised at least three important issues. First, the institution of *rāhui* which regulates the right of access on land as well as the lagoon disappeared, or at the very least changed profoundly when it was 'incorporated' into state law. Second, it was phrased in terms of ownership rather than in terms of praxis. Finally, the incorporation of marine territories into titles led to several disputed claims in court to address the situation of these lagoon territories.[57]

---

[55] R. Cochin, 'L'application du droit civil et du droit pénal français aux autochtones des Établissements Français de l'Océanie', thèse de doctorat, University of Paris, 1949, 31.

[56] For Tahiti, see E. Vaimeho-Peua, 'La toponymie des terres de Faaa et les représentations foncières tahitiennes', thèse de civilisation polynésienne, Université de la Polynésie Française, 2008; and for the Leeward Islands, see R.L. Calinaud, 'La situation juridique des lagons polynésiens', *Bulletin de la Société des Études Océaniennes* 22:12 (1993), 47–53; P. Huguenin, *Raiatea la sacrée* (Papeete: Edition Haere Po, 2005; reprint of 1st edn, 1902).

[57] Calinaud 'La situation juridique des lagons polynésiens' 51–2.

French Polynesia's regime of property rights is based on the application of the French Civil Code introduced to the Polynesian legal order in 1866.[58] On non-urban land this has led to a situation of generalized joint ownership in the islands of French Polynesia.[59] During the French nineteenth-century annexation, Mā'ohi were urged to accept a private property regime under the 1887 land tenure decree. Under this decree, land not claimed by anyone would become a public domain. This prompted around 60,000 land claims that also encompassed large areas of reef, lagoons, and fish holes. Mā'ohi also resisted this land tenure reform by not dividing most land and lagoon areas among them since the claim. Thus, most of the land in French Polynesia remains undivided land between groups that vary from four to seven generations.

This new form of socio-ecological organization in the high and low islands implied new consequences in terms of environmental resilience. First, land tenure reform combined with religious influence has therefore entailed a social organization now less mobile and instead fixed in a few villages. Faced with coastal erosion and great swells, these villages proved to be less resistant to climatic hazards and, in recent history, have had to be moved several times. Second, societies have become much more dependent on external resources, particularly important foodstuffs requiring storage and preservation in metal boxes and the like. With less self-sufficiency, community resilience and daily life of the inhabitants of the atolls is also now increasingly tied to wider communication links via boats and sometimes planes, coming from the capital (Papeete) and the main production centres of consumer commodities (for the Pacific, New Zealand, Australia, China, and the United States of America).

All these issues would have been considered crucial, were it not for the impact of the nuclear economy developed from the 1960s onwards. From this date, French Polynesian development was structured around the French nuclear experimentation centre in the Pacific, inducing profound transformations. These included: significant exodus from outer islands to the main island, Tahiti; a severe increase in land prices in the capital, Papeete, as land became transferable; and a rapid increase of local wealth artificially maintained by France's financial transfer for the nuclear programme. Even since the end of nuclear testing in 1996, the political elite, whether autonomist or pro-independence, has monopolized the discourse on the Mā'ohi identity and has benefited from massive public transfers. They have regularly negotiated

---

[58] Except for the island of Rapa.   [59] Bambridge, *La terre dans l'archipel des îles Australes.*

statutory changes, supposed to put an end to independence tendencies or economic problems. In doing so, this 'race for political competences' has obliterated any other economic or social policy. Instead of laying the foundations for locally sustainable economic development, the transfer policy has increased the weight of the public sector in the economy. Public resources represent up to 71 per cent of GDP in 2015. This political strategy has generated an economic model unsuited to development challenges and has increased French Polynesian's socio-economic dependency on France.[60]

Recent Resistance and Empowerment

Surveys of low and high island populations reveal a paradoxical response to climate change. On the one hand, the Māʻohi populations surveyed are aware of the phenomena of climate change conditions in various forms (temperature rise, rising sea level, drought). In practice, these changes appear in several forms: salinization of the fresh water duckweed (Tuamotu), retreat of the coast (Tuamotu and Society Islands), death of trees due to the combined salinization and drought, and loss of agricultural yields for growing. A decrease in the abundance of marine resources has also been observed as increased water temperature leads to the massive mortality of bivalves and certain species of fish. On the other hand, this local experience of climate change in environments exposed to risks seems insensitive to the scientific discourse conveyed by the media or in a Western format. Little attention is paid to it in everyday life on atolls or higher islands. Paradoxically, it is likely that this indifference of the populations is also a form of resilience in the face of scientific discourse, especially after the silence that dominated the nuclear era.

The answer to this paradox may hinge on the praxis of the Māʻohi. Bambridge prefers the term 'habitus Māʻohi', in Bourdieu's sense of habitus – deep-seated and socially ingrained habits, skills, and dispositions towards our environs and others. Bourdieu's notion of practices 'collectively orchestrated without being the product of the orchestrating action of a conductor' allows for shared social structures that are embodied, perpetuated, and embedded in everyday practice.[61] For generations, Māʻohi habitus has helped Islanders

---

[60] See B. Danielsson and M.-T. Danielsson, *Poisoned Reign: French Nuclear Colonialism in the Pacific* (New York: Penguin Books, 1986); S. Firth, *Nuclear Playground* (Honolulu: University of Hawaiʻi Press, 1987); B. Johnston in Chapter 56 of this volume. For recent events in French Polynesia see L. Gonschor, 'French Polynesia', *Contemporary Pacific* 32:1 (2020), 232–9.

[61] P. Bourdieu, *Outline of a Theory of Practice* (Cambridge : Cambridge University Press, 1977), 72. Bourdieu developed a theory of action, around the concept of habitus. This theory seeks to show that social agents develop strategies, based on a small number of dispositions acquired by

Creating Sustainable Pacific Environments

transmit their identity and unique relationships to each other and their environment. Ever emergent, it takes on a variety of forms and is not always directly tied to nature. Rooted in the relational, reciprocal bonds that link Islanders to resources and each other, Māʻohi habitus dissolves classic Western distinctions between human and non-human, nature and culture, as objects, environment, and individuals respond to the continual flow of life and materials.

Fifty-six-year-old fisherman Patrick Rochette from Teahupoo illustrates the Māʻohi habitus: a standardized improvisation based on, not just skills and activities, but a spiritual connection to one's environment.[62] Fishing activity reveals Māʻohi habitus's intimate relationship with both natural and cultural resources. In historic seascapes that contain taro plantations, fish nurseries, and coral historic sites, ancestral spirits make themselves felt and heard through strange animal calls, goosebumps, or a tingling of the feet. Most Islanders who sense these disgruntled spirits respond by demonstrating what Māʻohi call *faʻatura* (respect): either withdrawing from that place or following certain behaviours like asking permission, speaking to the spirits; not going into or playing on historic structures or trees; not disturbing the stones of historic ruins; not spitting on *marae* stones or objects; and not urinating, defecating, or lighting fires on or around historic ruins or sacred trees.

At the end of his village, far away in a dense purau (*Hibiscus tiliaceus*) forest that borders the shore of the lagoon, Patrick noted a testimony to his ancestor's *puna iʻa* (stone fish): a large stone that has the shape of a big fish orientated towards the mountain. 'Many people think it is a stone', he noted, 'but it is alive.' A hundred years before religious and French colonization, the *puna iʻa* was already used by Patrick's ancestors as a means to ask favours and generously give back to the spirit of nature dedicated to the fishers and their resources. In Teahupoo, the Māʻohi habitus emerges not only from Indigenous traditions, but from a troubled history of internal conflicts between chiefs from Taiarapu, along with Western colonization, religious changes, and depopulation. The present generations in Teahupoo are the

---

socialization which, although unconscious, are adapted to the necessities of the social world; see P. Bourdieu, *Le sens pratique* (Paris: Minuit, 1980).

[62] Patrick Rochette pers. comm. with Tamatoa Bambridge. The author has been involved with the Teahupoo MPA since its inception. See for example T. Bambridge, 'Le foncier terrestre et marin en Polynésie française. L'étude de cas de Teahupoo', *Revue des Questions Foncières* 2:12 (2013), 118–43.

descendants of the people who lived these historical events, still remembered and recorded in Patrick's *puta tupuna* (book of the ancestors).

The past is not only embodied by traumatic historic events, as habitus also emerges from 'the historically and socially situated conditions of its production'.[63] Past history also refers to heroic stories and history of skilled and fishing activities. Patrick recalls that 'the first *rāhui* ever known in Taiarapu date back from the thirteenth century and a more recent one put in place by the *ari'i* Teauroa at the end of the nineteenth century'. This memory is recalled with deep respect as part of today's identity.

Often associated with resistance, the Mā'ohi habitus can also reveal itself in a more positive way. In Teahupoo, some local fishers decided to protect their fish and lagoon by placing a *rāhui* to close off the lagoon. As the *tāvana* (mayor) recalled during a meeting with the fishers: 'this place is *rāhui* meaning not only fishing is forbidden but also passing along, stopping by, etc'. Since 2010, the Teahupoo *rāhui* has been kept alive by discussions, exchanges, and surveillance by the fishers of Teahupoo and all the population living nearby. The incredible biomass increase that resulted from this careful upholding of the *rāhui* is interpreted in terms of *tupuna*'s (ancestor's) satisfaction testified by some unusual apparition of the family *taura'a* (a totem animal that personified an extended family group) such as apparitions of turtles, whales in the lagoon where the *rāhui* were installed, or simply a sensation of happiness felt during a walk near the *rāhui* place. Conversely, everyone is aware that breaking the *rāhui* rule would mean offending spirits and may induce illness, bad luck, and even death.

A common socialization mechanism in Polynesia is Islanders' attention to the birds, wind, currents, and tides, and the carefully guarded secret knowledge has served to transmit ancestral knowledge across generations. As one elder explained, these behavioural rules come from Mā'ohi 'origins' from the 'ancient *tapu*' that once structured Tahitian society around *mana*.

In fact, certain types of transmission have continued through praxis, embedded in a Mā'ohi habitus based on the observation, practice, and perpetuation of a uniquely Tahitian, post-settler, and embodied cultural capital. This transmission is also rooted in social and moral expectations that perpetuate an active Indigenous relationship with history, the land, the lagoon, and each other. Such transmitted patterns of resource use and relations both respond to, and resist, ongoing colonial processes, including French land tenure, Christianity, commodification, and, most recently, the

---

[63] Bourdieu, *Outline of a Theory of Practice*, 95.

advance of conservation initiatives. Yet Māʻohi habitus emerges directly from local histories and knowledge of family lands and seascape according to ancestral, rather than legal, ownership.

Dissonance and the Reassertion of Māʻohi Habitus

This relationship has recently come under scrutiny from international conservation initiatives. Settled over a thousand years ago by highly adept voyagers and settlers in giant outrigger canoes, the Māʻohi are now subject to the scrutiny of such global institutions as UNESCO, scientific research centres, National Geographic, the World Wildlife Fund, and BirdLife International. Current international projects in French Polynesia include the Marquesas Protected Marine and Terrestrial Area, a UNESCO World Heritage designation for Taputapuatea Marae in 2019, the world's largest Ocean MPA, and various lagoon reef management projects since 1990.[64]

Money and political power, rather than ancestral respect, are increasingly driving the local treatment of resources, even as Islanders continue to grapple with the notion of respect and the lingering spiritual power, the *mana* and *tapu*, of certain places and things. The resulting battle, embodied by Māʻohi habitus, highlights colonial against Indigenous, rationalization against enchantment, orthodoxy against heterodoxy, even as it questions and ultimately dissolves each of these binary categories. Generated through a traumatic history of religious and political colonization, depopulation, and religious conversion, the ongoing practice of the Māʻohi habitus reflects the fragmented sacred, or *tapu*, structures of the past as well as externally derived institutionalized environmental management structures of the present.

Global conservation projects from private foundations, research centres, and the French Polynesian government also drive environmental management, alongside the Polynesian custom of *rāhui*. On the surface, it appears that a magic formula is in place where cultural identity could be reconciled with modern ecological science and the conservation of endangered species. But this approach contains a fundamental dissonance. *Rāhui* rules expressed by a set of Māʻohi habitus conflict with the top-down governance culture of Polynesian administrations in charge of marine protected areas. Certain tutelar spirits personifying particular extended families become symbols of

---

[64] See for example UNESCO World Heritage Centre – Taputapuātea, https://whc.unesco .org/en/list/1529/, and J. Petit and D. Tanret of the Pew Charitable Trust comment on the Marquesan MPA, 'In French Polynesia, a chance to protect ocean and culture', article on the Pew Charitable Trust website, 27 March 2019, www.pewtrusts.org/en/research-and-analysis/ articles/2019/03/27/in-french-polynesia-a-chance-to-protect-ocean-and-culture.

endangered species for humankind. Land- and seascape associated with families whose *mana* and ancestors' remains are still known, whereas the Christian religion tends to erase the knowledge and praxis associated with ancient spirits. The official land and maritime law supported by the French Polynesian and French governments, separates the sea from the land whereas Mā'ohi habitus tends to integrate them into a meaningful, holistic appreciation of the relation between nature and culture. Privatization of land law conflicts with extended families' lands still apprehended as a common heritage.

To rethink this Oceanian habitus in relation to the colonial, religious, and capitalist influences which have crossed the Pacific for at least a century, the Tongan sociologist Epeli Hau'ofa initiated a reflection on the Oceanian identity. He noted, 'our diversity is necessary for the struggle against the homogenizing forces of the global juggernaut. It is even more necessary for those of us who must focus on strengthening their ancestral cultures against seemingly overwhelming forces, to regain their lost sovereignty.'[65] It is notable that Hau'ofa focuses on individuals and their affinities rather than on the legally constituted state as the source of sovereign rights. He suggests that the state as traditionally defined in Westphalian terms is not sufficiently positioned to cope with contemporary issues, underlining the geographical and institutional limitation of the concept of state-based sovereignty in Oceania. Hau'ofa scrutinizes the cognitive dilemma faced by Islander habitus: 'It is one of the great ironies of the Law of the Sea Convention, which enlarged our national boundaries, that it also extended the territorial instinct to where there was none before.'[66] As a result, unlike a sovereignty delimited by state borders or an 'indigenous community', Hau'ofa discuss a new paradigm of an open sovereignty whose nature is fundamentally relational. He labels this relationship Oceanian, noting that the alternative term for the Pacific Islands, Oceania, 'refers to a world of people connected to each other'.[67] In line with local ways of managing resources through *rāhui* mechanism, Hau'ofa suggests at a regional scale that 'Our most important role should be that of custodians of the ocean, and as such we must reach out to similar people elsewhere for the common task of protecting the seas for the general welfare of all living things.'[68]

---

[65] E. Hau'ofa, 'The ocean in us', in A. Hooper (ed.), *Culture and Sustainable Development in the Pacific* (Canberra: ANU Press, 2000), 32–43, at 33–4. The content was first published in E. Waddell, V. Naidu, and E. Hau'ofa (eds.), *A New Oceania: Rediscovering Our Sea of Islands* (Suva: School of Social and Economic Development, University of the South Pacific,1993).
[66] Hau'ofa, 'The ocean in us', 39.   [67] Hau'ofa, 'The ocean in us', 36.
[68] Hau'ofa, 'The ocean in us', 40.

Conclusion

Coastal tropical communities around the Pacific now face a rising wave of coral bleaching as the Anthropocene takes hold. The ultimate deciding factor on the continuation of the practices outlined in this chapter may be their ability to ameliorate the consequences of the Anthropocene rather than their cultural value. These practices arose to manage one of the most resource-poor environments on Earth where colonists literally had to bring most of their food crops with them and practise sophisticated agriculture, making extensive use of irrigation, mulching, and complementary farming, as well as fish farming, and covering risk through propagating and planting a wide variety of food crops. Landscapes and even nearshore seascapes such as those in Hawai'i contain predominantly introduced dietary flora and fauna. Cultural practices that have endured, nurtured, and enriched resource-poor environments over millennia of varied conditions deserve respect.

Despite the mounting international interest in successful community-based conservation practices just noted for French Polynesia, Pacific Indigenous voices remain marginal to most global discussions on solutions. They remain largely portrayed as reluctant victims rather than as proactive and successful climate mitigators as this chapter has shown. Dame Meg Taylor, Secretary General of the Pacific Islands Forum from 2014 to 2021, was the world's first Ocean Commissioner. Healthy marine ecosystems are not only crucial to Pacific Islander nutritional and cultural health, but also vital if the Pacific is to continue its vital global role as a carbon sink and major component of the planet's thermal regulation. Pacific peoples' proactive responses to the more destructive aspects of climate change point the way towards more sustainable development that embraces and directly benefits a larger proportion of the world's population than is currently the case, and in a manner that is both sustainable and beneficial for ecological restoration of Earth's ecosystems.

64

Concluding Reflection

'Choppy Waters'

ANNE PEREZ HATTORI

Pacific. Peaceful. Placid. Pacifying. Magellan named our Ocean in 1519 because of the calm waters he encountered, then unaware of its life-threatening typhoons and hurricanes, tsunamis and tidal waves, undertows and rip currents. Those of us who make the Pacific our home know it to be an ocean of vivid contrasts, an ocean whose spirits and power one never takes lightly, regardless of how 'pacific' the waters might appear. These conflicting understandings of the ocean have likewise informed our lives as Pacific peoples for centuries as these contrary understandings of the ocean are indeed mirrored more broadly in our daily realities. The world at large may think of Pacific Islanders as beach-going, hula-dancing, laughter-filled peoples for whom there is not a care in the world, yet that superficial stereotype works mainly to feed the self-interests of those swimming in the warm waters of tourism, colonialism, and militarism. The reality is infinitely more complex, not only today in the face of global warming, overfishing, and oceanic pollution, but also in the past when Islanders faced the daunting challenges of their eras. Coping and thriving in the face of natural disasters, diseases, and invasions of all sorts are stories not new to Oceania. In this placid Pacific, we live a life of contrasts. Always have.

When I was invited to be part of this project, I initially cringed at the entire concept. For too long, Pacific History has struggled to dissociate itself from the 'Asia-Pacific' categorization, one in which 'small' Pacific places become dwarfed by entities that are larger both in land mass and in population size. Despite sharing Pacific Ocean boundaries, Pacific Historians have fought for more than a half-century now to distance the Oceanic Islands intellectually from their Asian and American neighbours. I feared that histories of California and China, Indonesia and Canada would shroud Oceania's stories. Yet I also know Paul D'Arcy, both personally and from his impressive publication history. I know Paul and his almost obsessive dedication to honouring the Islands and paying homage to the Islanders. As I learned more about the project, I understood that he would not tolerate the marginalization

Concluding Reflection: 'Choppy Waters'

of Oceania, but that he would instead pull together a lineup to showcase the depths and widths of its proportions. In this project, the Pacific is big not just because of its square footage or the amount of water it holds. Rather, the expansiveness of the Pacific extends to its rich history, and to its dynamic interplay between peoples and cultures, humans and animals, nature and the supernatural, and colonizers and colonized. I came to this project ultimately because I understood that Cambridge University Press's ambitious Oceans Series represented an incomparable opportunity to collaborate with a large group of scholars who span the globe and the disciplines, yet who unify in their dedication to our Pacific World.

My initial reticence related also to the relative smallness of Guam, my island home – only 48 kilometres long and its width ranging from 6 to 12 kilometres – and our uncomfortable sense that, contrary to the popular cliché, size does matter. Colonizers and those who continue to espouse the colonial discourse have inculcated us for centuries to believe and even proclaim our inadequacies, in particular our smallness, poverty, and helplessness. As a child growing up on Guam, I was indoctrinated to be ashamed of my indigeneity and grateful to the USA for supposedly rescuing us from backwardness and poverty. This belittling discourse, so trenchantly critiqued more than two decades ago by Epeli Hauʻofa in his still-imperative essay 'Our Sea of Islands', is not unique to Guam. It has left scars that are still healing in many islands, while on others the scars have yet even to form due to ongoing invasions. Yet despite Oceania's very real challenges, in both the historic and the contemporary Pacific, the field of Pacific History has inched forward over more than seventy years of existence as an academic field of study to locate Islanders properly at the front lines of encounter. No longer represented as silent puppets with hands extended to grab the colonizers' handouts, Pacific peoples are acknowledged for tapping into their deep reserves of creativity, diligence, and intelligence to face the challenges before their villages and islands.

These volumes, moreover, dare to position Oceania's past well outside the bounds of the typical geopolitical, military stories of colonial conquest that predominate in early versions of Pacific History. Those stories proliferate across the ocean, emphasizing the deeds of powerful men, often non-Indigenous, who perchance happened upon our Islands. But those one-dimensional stories do not feature in these volumes. History is, after all, about not simply politics and leadership, but the totality of life in the past. It includes Islanders' relationships with the ocean and the land, art and architecture, song and dance, religion and politics and economics, as well as with foreigners who entered our seascapes and landscapes. Pacific History includes women and men, navigators and warriors, commoners and chiefs. The broad approach taken in these volumes, in fact, reflects the complexity and heterogeneity of life in this great Ocean. Pacific History transcends any disciplinary boundaries, and these volumes boldly showcase this density of life.

Like these volumes, the robust health and eclectic composition of organizations such as the Pacific History Association speak to the wide-ranging interests of Oceania's scholarly community. The organization's biennial conference features panels on art, dance, gender, race, religion, archival practices, museum collections, land rights, decolonization, film, and teaching, to highlight just a few. In addition, the vitality of major publications such as the *Journal of Pacific History* and *The Contemporary Pacific* testify to this fervent understanding and appreciation of our history as expansive, not only because of the Pacific Ocean's size but because of the complexity and diversity of experiences in the Islands.

Today, Pacific Islanders fill the frontlines of battles against global issues including climate change, decolonization, overfishing, and industrial pollution, and these volumes speak to this active, highly self-aware agenda to protect our region and our planet. Pacific peoples, unified with scholars dedicated to the region, can no longer be made invisible in Oceania's histories. I hope that you, like me, will consume these volumes, whether in their entirety or even in small bites, and witness for yourself the Pacific as a place of rich diversity and creativity and sometimes competing and colliding interests. Pacific peoples feature as the ever-vigilant guardians of their seas and soil, whether swimming, sailing, or surfing through sometimes choppy waters. Pacific History here serves as the vehicle through which their voices and experiences are heard.

References to Volume II

Abramowitz, M.I. 'Asia: look out for more surprises', *Washington Post* (4 January 1998), C7.

Adler, J. 'The Oceanic Steamship Company: a link in Claus Spreckels' Hawaiian sugar empire', *Pacific Historical Review* 29:3 (1960), 257–69.

Agence France-Presse. 'Bikini Atoll nuclear test: 60 years later and islands still unliveable', *The Guardian* (2 March 2014), www.theguardian.com/world/2014/mar/02/bikini-atoll-nuclear-test-60-years.

'"Justice done" by ICJ on Bolivia claim: Chile president', Agence France-Presse (1 October 2018), https://au.news.yahoo.com/justice-done-icj-bolivia-claim-chile-president-165217068-spt.html.

Agniel, G. 'Le Parlement et la Nouvelle-Calédonie: du "droit à la bouderie" ... à la délégation de souveraineté?', *Revue Française de Droit Constitutionnel* 90:2 (2012), 227–38.

Aguirre, C. *Agentes de su propia libertad: los esclavos de Lima y la desintegración de la esclavitud, 1821–1854.* Lima: Pontificia Universidad Católica del Perú, 1993.

Aichuan, N. (ed.). *Jinping linkuang lunwenji.* Lianyungang: Lianyungang shi Jinping jinkuang, 1999.

Airbus. *Global Market Forecast 2018–2037: Global Networks Global Citizens.* Leiden: Airbus Group, 2018, www.airbus.com/aircraft/market/global-market-forecast.html.

Akami, T. *Internationalizing the Pacific: The US, Japan and the Institute of Pacific Relations in War and Peace, 1919–1945.* London: Routledge, 2002.

Akeli Amaama, S. 'A goodwill mission? Revisiting Samoa–New Zealand relations in 1936', *New Zealand Journal of History* 53:2 (2019), 65–82.

'Cleansing Western Samoa: leprosy control during New Zealand Administration, 1914–1922', *Journal of Pacific History* 52:3 (2017), 360–73.

Akimichi, T. 'Japanese views on Oceania in modernist images of Paradise', in Kenji Yoshida and J. Mack (eds.), *Images of Other Cultures: Re-viewing Ethnographic Collections of the British Museum and the National Museum of Ethnology, Osaka.* Tokyo: NHK Service Center, 1997.

Akin, D.W. *Colonialism, Maasina Rule and the Origins of Malaitan Kastom.* Honolulu: University of Hawai'i Press, 2013.

Akutagawa, M., L. Han, E. Noordhoek, and H. Williams. 'Molokai Agriculture Needs Assessment: a Molokai-Pedia project of Sust 'āina Ble Molokai'. Unpublished, 2011.

Alafurai, L. *Beyond the Reef: The Records of the Conference of Churches and Missions in the Pacific.* Apia: Malua Theological College, Western Samoa, 1961.

Alcalay, G.H. 'Utrik Atoll: the sociocultural impact of living in a radioactive environment. An anthropological assessment of the consequential damages from Bravo', 28 June 2002, 1–43; prepared for Utrik Atoll Local Government and the Office of the Public Advocate of the Nuclear Claims Tribunal, Majuro, Republic of the Marshall Islands.

Alefaio, O. 'Aim high: look past our problems to get past our problems', 2018 Asia-Pacific Library and Information Conference (APLIC), keynote address (Gold Coast, Australia, 30 July–2 August 2018).

'Archival revival, heritage and social media: the example of the National Archives of Fiji', Oceanic Knowledges, conference paper (Canberra, Australian National University, 27–8 July 2017).

'Archives connecting with the community', paper presented at IFLA WLIC 2016, Columbus, OH: Connections, Collaboration, Community in Session 96, Asia and Oceania.

Alessio, D., and A. Kelen. 'Waan Aelōñ in Majōl: canoes of the Marshall Islands', in A.L. Loeak, V.C. Kiluwe, and L. Crowl (eds.), *Life in the Republic of the Marshall Islands*. Suva: Institute of Pacific Studies, University of the South Pacific, 2004, 192–225.

Ali, B.N.K. *Chinese in Fiji*. Suva: Institute of Pacific Studies, 2002.

Alkire, W. *Lamotrek Atoll and Inter Island Socio-Economic Ties*. Urbana: University of Illinois Press, 1965.

Allen, R. *Missionary Methods: St Paul's or Ours*. London: Robert Scott, 1912.

Andaya, L.Y. *The Heritage of Arung Palakka: A History of South Sulawesi (Celebes) in the Seventeenth Century*. The Hague: Nijhoff, 1981.

'The "informal Portuguese Empire" and the Topasses in the Solor archipelago and Timor in the seventeenth and eighteenth centuries', *Journal of Southeast Asian Studies* 41:3 (2010), 391–420.

'The Portuguese tribe in the Malay-Indonesian Archipelago in the seventeenth and eighteenth centuries', in F.A. Dutra and J.C. dos Santos (eds.), *The Portuguese and the Pacific*. Santa Barbara: Center for Portuguese Studies, 1995, 129–48.

The World of Maluku: Eastern Indonesia in the Early Modern Period. Honolulu: University of Hawai'i Press, 1993.

Anderson, A. 'Alternative perspectives upon Tupaia's mapmaking', *Journal of Pacific History* 54:4 (2019), 537–43.

Race against Time: The Early Maori-Pakeha Families and the Development of the Mixed-Race Population in Southern New Zealand. Dunedin: Hocken Library, 1990.

The First Migration: Māori Origins 3000BC–AD1450. Auckland: Bridget Williams Books, 2016.

'The prehistory of south Polynesia', in E.E. Cochrane and T.L. Hunt (eds.), *The Oxford Handbook of Prehistoric Oceania*. Oxford: Oxford University Press, 2018, 396–415.

Anderson, B. *Imagined Communities: Reflections on the Origin and the Spread of Nationalism*. London: Verso, 1991.

Anderson, C. 'Multiple border crossings: convicts and other persons escaped from Botany Bay and residing in Calcutta', *Journal of Australian Colonial History* 3:2 (2001), 1–22.

Anderson, M.K., *Tending the Wild: Native American Knowledge and the Management of California's Natural Resources*. Berkeley: University of California Press, 2005.

References to Volume II

Anderson, W. 'Ambiguities of race: science on the reproductive frontier of Australia and the Pacific between the Wars', *Australian Historical Studies* 40:2 (2009), 143–60.
Colonial Pathologies: American Tropical Medicine, Race, and Hygiene in the Philippines. Durham, NC: Duke University Press, 2006.
'Racial conceptions in the Global South', *Isis* 105 (2014), 782–92.

Anderson, W., M. Johnson, and B. Brookes (eds.). *Pacific Futures: Past and Present.* Honolulu: University of Hawai'i Press, 2018.

Andrade, T. *Commerce, Culture, and Conflict: Taiwan under European Rule, 1624–1662.* New Haven: Yale University Press, 2000.
How Taiwan Became Chinese: Dutch, Spanish, and Han Colonization in the Seventeenth Century. New York: Columbia University Press, 2008.

Andreff, W. 'Sport in developing countries', in W. Andreff and S. Szymanski (eds.), *Handbook on the Economics of Sport.* Cheltenham: Edward Elgar, 2006, 308–15.
'14th Annual Native Hawaiian Convention, September 22–24, 2015'. Conference programme, www.nhec.org/event/14th-annual-native-hawaiian-convention/.

Anon. 'Programme des prix mis au concours dans la première assemblée générale annuelle de l'an 1822', *Bulletin de la Societé de Géographie* 1 (1822), 65–6.
Recordkeeping for Good Governance Toolkit. Australia: PARBICA, 2007.
'The Asiatic slave trade', *New York Daily Times* (22 July 1853), 4.

Anon., [Sino-Spanish (Boxer) Codex], [c. 1590], LMC 2444, Lilly Library, Indiana University, Bloomington, IN.

Antonio Garretón, M. *Neoliberalismo corregido y progresismo limitado: los gobiernos de la Concertación en Chile, 1990–2010.* Santiago: ARCIS-CLACSO, 2012.

Antony, R.J. *Like Froth Floating on the Sea: The World of Pirates and Seafarers in Late Imperial China.* Berkeley, CA: Institute of East Asian Studies, 2003.

Appadurai, A. 'Global ethnospaces: notes and queries for a transnational anthropology', in R. Fox (ed.), *Recapturing Anthropology.* Santa Fe, NM: School of American Research Press, 1991, 191–210.
'Number in the colonial imagination', in C.A. Breckenridge and P. van der Veer (eds.), *Orientalism and the Post-Colonial Predicament.* Philadelphia: University of Pennsylvania Press, 1993, 314–39.

Archer, S. *Sharks upon the Land: Colonialism, Indigenous Health, and Culture in Hawai'i, 1778–1855.* Cambridge: Cambridge University Press, 2018.

Ardern, J. 74th United Nations General Assembly: New York, USA, www.stuff.co.nz/national/politics/opinion/116076101/jacinda-ardern-is-smashing-it-on-the-world-stage-right-now.

Arista, N. 'Ka Waihoma Palapala Manaleo: research in a time of plenty: colonialism and ignoring the Hawaiian language archive', in T. Ballantyne, L. Paterson, and A. Wanhalla (eds.), *Indigenous Textual Cultures: Reading and Writing in the Age of Global Empire.* Durham, NC: Duke University Press, 2019, 31–59.
The Kingdom and the Republic: Sovereign Hawai'i and the Early United States. Philadelphia: University of Pennsylvania Press, 2019.

Armitage, D. 'The Atlantic Ocean', in D. Armitage, A. Bashford, and S. Sivasundaram (eds.), *Oceanic Histories.* Cambridge: Cambridge University Press, 2018, 85–110.
'The Red Atlantic', *Reviews in American History* 29:4 (2001), 479–86.

REFERENCES TO VOLUME II

Armitage, D., and A. Bashford (eds.). *Pacific Histories: Ocean, Land, People*. Basingstoke: Palgrave Macmillan, 2014.

Armitage, D., A. Bashford, and S. Sivasundaram (eds.). *Oceanic Histories*. Cambridge: Cambridge University Press, 2018.

Arndt, N., and C. Ganino. *Metals and Society: An Introduction to Economic Geology*. New York: Springer, 2012.

Arnold, D. *Colonizing the Body: State Medicine and Epidemic Disease in Nineteenth Century India*. Berkeley: University of California Press, 1993.

Imperial Medicine and Indigenous Societies. Manchester: Manchester University Press, 1988.

'Leprosy: from "imperial danger" to postcolonial history – an afterword', *Journal of Pacific History* 52:3 (2017), 407–19.

Arnold, J. (ed.). *The Origins of a Pacific Coast Chiefdom: The Chumash of the Channel Islands*. Salt Lake City: University of Utah Press, 2001.

Arosemena Garland, G. *El Almirante Miguel Grau*. Lima: Banco de Crédito del Perú, 1979.

Arriagada Herrera, G., and C. Graham. 'Chile: sustaining adjustment during democratic transition', in S. Haggard and S.B. Webb (eds.), *Voting for Reform: Democracy, Political Liberalization, and Economic Adjustment*. Oxford: Oxford University Press for the World Bank, 1994, 242–89.

Arthur, C.E. *Political Symbols and National Identity in Timor-Leste*. New York: Palgrave Macmillan, 2019.

Arvin, M.R. *Possessing Polynesians: The Science of Settler Colonial Whiteness in Hawaii and Oceania*. Durham, NC: Duke University Press, 2019.

Asian Americans Advancing Justice (AAAJ). *A Community of Contrasts: Native Hawaiians and Pacific Islanders in the West*. Washington, DC: AAAJ, 2015.

Atkinson, A. *The Europeans in Australia*, vol. 1, The Beginning. Oxford: Oxford University Press, 1997.

Atwell, W.S. 'Another look at silver imports into China, ca. 1635–1644', *Journal of World History* 16:4 (2005), 467–89.

'International bullion flows and the Chinese economy circa 1530–1650', *Past and Present* 95 (1982), 68–90.

Atwill, D.G. *Chinese Sultanate: Islam, Ethnicity, and the Panthay Rebellion in Southwest China, 1856–1873*. Stanford: Stanford University Press, 2005.

Australian Department of Foreign Affairs. 'The South Pacific', Submission to the Senate Standing Committee on Foreign Affairs and Defence Inquiry into 'The Need for an Increased Australian Commitment to the South Pacific', Canberra: AGPS, March 1977.

Australian Indigenous Law Reporter. 'Nouméa Accord' (2002), www.austlii.edu.au/au/journals/AILR/2002/17.html.

Avia, T. *Wild Dogs under my Skirt*. Wellington: Victoria University Press, 2004.

Aydın, C. *The Politics of Anti-Westernism in Asia: Visions of World Order in Pan-Islamic and Pan-Asian Thought*. New York: Columbia University Press, 2007.

Bacevich, A. *The New American Militarism: How Americans Are Seduced by War*. Oxford: Oxford University Press, 2005.

Backes, S. 'Communiqué de Sonia Backes, présidente de la province Sud: chacun doit rester à sa place!' (Communiqué from Sonia Backes, President of South Province: Everyone must stay in their place!) 23 April 2020, www.ncpresse.nc/Communique-

808

References to Volume II

de-Sonia-Backes-presidente-de-la-province-Sud-Chacun-doit-rester-a-sa-place-_a8167 .html.

Baddeley, J. 'Traditional healing practices of Rarotonga, Cook Islands', in C.D. Parsons (ed.), *Healing Practices in the South Pacific*. Honolulu: The Institute of Polynesian Studies, 1995, 129–243.

Baeza-Yates, R.A., D.A. Fuller, J.A. Pino, and S.E. Goodman. 'Computing in Chile: the jaguar of the Pacific Rim?' *Communications of the ACM* 38:9 (1995), 23–8.

Bagnall, K. 'Rewriting the history of Chinese families in nineteenth-century Australia', *Australian Historical Studies* 42:1 (2011), 62–77.

Baigent, E. 'Dillon, Peter (1788–1847)', in *Oxford Dictionary of National Biography* (Oxford: Oxford University Press, 2004); online edn, October 2008.

Bailey, B.L., and D. Farber. *The First Strange Place: The Alchemy of Race and Sex in World War II Hawaii*. New York: The Free Press, 1992.

Bailey, R. *Health Care Management in Australia's and New Zealand's Seasonal Workers Schemes*. DPA Working Paper Series 2020/2. Canberra: ANU, 2020.

'*New Zealand's Recognised Employer Scheme (RSE): 10 year longitudinal case study'*. Department of Pacific Affairs, The Australian National University. Canberra: ANU, 2019.

Health Care Management in Australia's and New Zealand's Seasonal Workers Schemes. DPA Working Paper Series 2020/22, ANU, Canberra, 2020.

Bailleul, M. *Les Îles Marquises: histoire de la terre des hommes du XVIIIème siècle à nos jours*. Papeete: Ministère de la Culture de Polynésie Française, 2001.

Baird, J., and S. Bold. 'Conservative parties around the world have a problem – and women are losing patience', *ABC News*, 8 February 2019, www.abc.net.au/news/2019-02-07/women-in-parliament-labor-liberal/10783234.

Baker, K. 'Experiences of female candidates in the 2017 Papua New Guinea'. *In Brief* 2017/38, http://dpa.bellschool.anu.edu.au/sites/default/files/publications/attachments/2017-12/ib-2017-38_baker.pdf.

'Great expectations: gender and political representation in the Pacific Islands', *Government and Opposition* 53:3 (2018), 542–68.

'Women's under-representation and special measures in the Tongan parliament'. *In Brief*, 2015/33, Canberra, Department of Pacific Affairs, Australian National University, 1.

Bakewell, P.J. *Miners of the Red Mountain: Indian Labor in Potosi, 1545–1650*. Albuquerque: University New Mexico Press, 1984.

Silver Mining and Society in Colonial Mexico, Zacatecas, 1546–1700. Cambridge: Cambridge University Press, 1971.

Balbi, M. *Los chifas en Perú: historias y recetas*. Lima: Universidad San Martín de Porres, 1999.

Baldwin, R. *Global Supply Chains: Why They Emerged, Why They Matter and Where They Are Going*. Working Paper FG-2012-1. Hong Kong: Fung Global Institute, 2012.

Bale, J. *The Brawn Drain: Foreign Student-Athletes in American Universities*. Urbana: University of Illinois Press, 1991.

Balenaivalu, T. 'Designing how Pacific archives are perceived: using empathy and experimentation to make archives more "relevant" in a resource poor environment',

Joint International Council on Archives (ICA), Australian Society of Archives (ASA), Archivists and Records Managers Association of New Zealand (ARANZ), Pacific Regional Branch of the International Council on Archives (PARBICA) Conference, conference paper (Adelaide, 21–5 October 2019).

Balint, R. 'Aboriginal women and Asian men: a maritime history of color in white Australia', *Signs: Journal of Women in Culture and Society* 37:3 (2012), 544–54.

Ballantyne, T. 'Imperial futures and India's Pacifics: space, temporality and the textures of empire', in W. Anderson, M. Johnson, and B. Brookes (eds.), *Pacific Futures: Past and Present*. Honolulu: University of Hawai'i Press, 2018, 157–77.

Orientalism and Race: Aryanism and the British Empire. Basingstoke: Palgrave, 2002.

Webs of Empire: Rethinking New Zealand's Colonial Past. Wellington: Bridget Williams Books, 2012.

Ballantyne, T., and A. Burton. 'Introduction: the politics of intimacy in an age of empire', in T. Ballantyne and A. Burton (eds.), *Moving Subjects: Gender, Mobility, and Intimacy in an Age of Global Empire*. Chicago: University of Chicago Press, 2009, 1–28.

Bambridge, T. 'Généalogie des droits autochtones en Nouvelle-Zélande (Aotearoa) et à Tahiti (1840–2005)', *Droits et Sociétés* 22:1 (2007), 153–82.

La terre dans l'archipel des îles australes: étude du pluralisme juridique et culturel en matière foncière. Paris: Institut de Recherche pour le Développement (IRD) and Aux Vents des Îles, 2009.

'Le foncier terrestre et marin en Polynésie française. L'étude de cas de Teahupoo', *Revue des Questions Foncières* 2:12 (2013), 118–43.

(ed.). *The Rāhui: Legal Pluralism in Polynesian Traditional Management of Resources and Territories*. Canberra: ANU Press, 2016.

Bambridge, T., and J.-P. Latouche (eds.). *Les atolls du Pacifique face au changement climatique: une comparaison Tuamotu-Kiribati*. Paris, Editions Karthala, 2016.

Banivanua-Mar, T. *Decolonisation and the Pacific: Indigenous Globalisation and the Ends of Empire*. Cambridge: Cambridge University Press, 2016.

Violence and Colonial Dialogue: The Australian-Pacific Indentured Labor Trade. Honolulu: University of Hawai'i Press, 2006.

Banner, S. *Possessing the Pacific: Land, Settlers, and Indigenous People from Australia to Alaska*. Cambridge, MA: Harvard University Press, 2007.

Bao, M. 'Environmentalism and environmental movements in China since 1949', in J.R. McNeill and E. Stewart Mauldin (eds.), *A Companion to Global Environmental History*. Chichester: Wiley-Blackwell, 2012, 474–92.

Barclay, B. *Our Own Image*. Auckland: Longman Paul, 1990.

Barker, H. *Bravo for the Marshallese: Regaining Control in a Post-Nuclear, Post-Colonial World*. Belmont, CA: Wadsworth/Thomson Learning, 2004.

'Religion', in M. Rapaport (ed.), *The Pacific Islands: Environment and Society*. Honolulu: University of Hawai'i Press, 2013, 214–24.

Barman, J. *French Canadians, Furs, and Indigenous Women in the Making of the Pacific Northwest*. Vancouver: UBC Press, 2014.

'New land, new lives: Hawaiian settlement in British Columbia', *Hawaiian Journal of History* 29 (1995), 1–32.

References to Volume II

'Taming aboriginal sexuality: gender, power and race in British Columbia, 1850–1900', *BC Studies* 115/16 (1997/8), 237–66.

Barman, J., and B.M. Watson. *Leaving Paradise: Indigenous Hawaiians in the Pacific Northwest, 1787–1898.* Honolulu: University of Hawai'i Press, 2006.

Barnett, J., and J. Campbell. *Climate Change and Small Island States: Power, Knowledge, and the South Pacific.* Washington, DC: Earthscan, 2010.

Barratt, G. *Russia and the South Pacific 1696–1840, vol. II, Southern and Eastern Polynesia.* Vancouver: UBC Press, 1988.

'Russian activity among the Cook Islands, to 1820', *New Zealand Slavonic Journal* (1998), 34–98.

Barrau, J. *L'agriculture vivrière autochtone de la Nouvelle-Calédonie.* Nouméa: Commission du Pacifique Sud, 1956.

Bastian, J. 'Records, memory and space: locating archives in the landscape', *Public History Review* 21 (2014), 45–69.

Bateson, C. *Dire Strait: A History of Bass Strait.* Sydney: Angus Reed, 1973.

Bauer, B.S., and R.A. Covey. 'Processes of state formation in the Inca heartland (Cuzco, Peru)', *American Anthropologist* 104:3 (2002), 846–64.

Baxter, G., and N.S. Bardell. 'Can the renewed interest in ultra-long-range passenger flights be satisfied by the current generation of civil aircraft?', *Aviation* 21:2 (2017), 42–54.

Bayliss-Smith, T. 'Colonialism as shell shock: W.H.R. Rivers's explanations for depopulation in Melanesia', in E. Hviding and C. Berg (eds.), *The Ethnographic Experiment: A.M. Hocart and W.H.R. Rivers in Island Melanesia, 1908.* New York: Berghahn Books, 2014, 179–213.

Bayly, C., and T. Harper. *Forgotten Wars: Freedom and Revolution in Southeast Asia.* Cambridge, MA: Belknap Press, 2007.

Bayly, G., P. Statham-Drew, and R. Erickson (eds.). *A Life on the Ocean Wave: The Journals of Captain George Bayly.* Melbourne: Miegunyah Press, 1998.

BBC News, 'Easter Island land dispute clashes leave dozens injured', 4 December 2010, www.bbc.com/news/world-latin-america-11917511.

Beaglehole, J.C. (ed.). *The Journals of Captain James Cook on His Voyages of Discovery*, 4 vols. Cambridge: Hakluyt Society, 1955–74.

The 'Endeavour' Journal of Joseph Banks 1768–1771. 2nd edn. Sydney: Public Library of New South Wales with Angus and Robertson, 1963.

Beamer, B.K. '*Na wai ka Mana?* 'Ōiwi agency and European imperialism in the Hawaiian Kingdom'. PhD thesis, University of Hawai'i, 2008.

No Mākou ka Mana: Liberating the Nation. Honolulu: Kamehameha Schools Press, 2014.

Beasley, W.G. *Japanese Imperialism 1894–1945.* Oxford: Clarendon Press, 1987.

Beckman, E. 'The creolization of imperial reason: Chilean state racism in the War of the Pacific', *Journal of Latin American Cultural Studies* 18:1 (2009), 73–90.

Bedford, C. 'Picking winners? New Zealand's Recognised Seasonal Employer (RSE) policy and its impacts on employers, Pacific workers and their island-based communities'. PhD thesis, University of Adelaide, 2013.

Bedford, C., R. Bedford, and H. Nunns. 'RSE impact study: Pacific stream report', 2020, www.immigration.govt.nz/documents/statistics/rse-impact-study-pacific-stream%20report.pdf.

REFERENCES TO VOLUME II

Behlmer, G.K. *Risky Shores: Savagery and Colonialism in the Western Pacific*. Stanford: Stanford University Press, 2018.

Beier, U. *Decolonising the Mind: The Impact of the University on Culture and Identity in Papua New Guinea, 1971–74*. Canberra: Pandanus Books, 2005.

Niugini Lives. Milton, QLD: Jacaranda Press, 1974.

Belich, J. *Making Peoples: A History of the New Zealanders, from Polynesian Settlement to the End of the Nineteenth Century*. Honolulu: University of Hawai'i Press, 1996.

Replenishing the Earth: The Settler Revolution and the Rise of the Anglo-World. Oxford: Oxford University Press, 2009.

Bell, J.A. 'Sugar plant hunting by airplane in New Guinea: a cinematic narrative of scientific triumph and discovery in the "remote jungles"', *Journal of Pacific History* 45:1 (2010), 37–56.

Bell, J., M. Taylor, M. Amos, and N. Andrew. *Climate Change and Pacific Island Food Systems: The Future of Food, Farming and Fishing in the Pacific Islands under a Changing Climate*. Copenhagen and Wageningen: CCAFS and CTA, 2016.

Belogurova, A. *The Nanyang Revolution: The Comintern and Chinese Networks in Southeast Asia 1890–1957*. Cambridge: Cambridge University Press, 2018.

Belshaw, C.S. *Island Administration in the Southwest Pacific*. Oxford: Oxford University Press, 1950.

Bengoa, J. *Historia del pueblo mapuche: (siglo XIX y XX)*. Santiago: Ediciones Sur, 1985.

Bennett, D. 'China's offshore active defense and the People's Liberation Army Navy', *Global Security Studies* 1:1 (2010), 126–41.

Bennett, J.A. 'A vanishing race or a vanishing discourse? W.H.R. Rivers's "psychological factor" and the depopulation in the Solomon Islands and the New Hebrides', in E. Hviding and C. Berg (eds.), *The Ethnographic Experiment: A.M. Hocart and W.H.R. Rivers in Island Melanesia, 1908*. New York: Berghahn Books, 2014, 214–51.

'Bora Bora: "Like a dream"', in J.A. Bennett and A. Wanhalla (eds.), *Mothers' Darlings of the South Pacific: The Children of Indigenous Women and U.S. Servicemen, World War II*. Honolulu: University of Hawai'i Press, 2016, 31–41.

'"Inevitable erosion of heroes and landmarks": an end to the politics of Allied war memorials in Tarawa', in M. Gegner and B. Ziino (eds.), *The Heritage of War*. New York: Routledge, 2012, 88–107.

'Malaria, medicine, and Melanesians: contested hybrid spaces in World War II', *Health and History* 8:9 (2006), 27–55.

Natives and Exotics: World War II and Environment in the Southern Pacific. Honolulu: University of Hawai'i Press, 2009.

Wealth of the Solomons: A History of a Pacific Archipelago, 1800–1978. Honolulu: University of Hawai'i Press, 1987.

Bennett, J.A., and A. Wanhalla (eds.). *Mothers' Darlings of the South Pacific: The Children of Indigenous Women and U.S. Servicemen, World War II*. Honolulu: University of Hawai'i Press, 2016.

'Introduction: a new net goes fishing,' in Bennett and Wanhalla (eds.), *Mothers' Darlings of the South Pacific: The Children of Indigenous Women and U.S. Servicemen, World War II*. Honolulu: University of Hawai'i Press, 2016, 1–30.

Bennion, T. 'Treaty-making in the Pacific in the nineteenth century and the Treaty of Waitangi', *Victoria University of Wellington Law Review* 35:1 (2004), 165–205.

References to Volume II

Bentley, T. *Pakeha-Maori: The Extraordinary Story of the Europeans Who Lived as Maori in Early New Zealand*. Auckland: Penguin, 1999.

Berdan, F. *The Aztecs of Central Mexico: An Imperial Society*, 2nd edn. Belmont, CA: Wadsworth Cengage, 2005.

Berne, E. 'Difficulties of comparative psychiatry: the Fiji Islands', *American Journal of Psychiatry* 116:2 (1959), 104–9.

Bernhofen, D.N., Z. El Sahl, and R. Kneller. 'Estimating the effects of the container revolution on international trade', *Journal of International Economics* 98:c (2016), 36–50.

Bertram, G. 'The MIRAB model twelve years on', *Contemporary Pacific* 11:1 (1999), 105–38.

Bertram, I.G., and R.F. Watters. 'The MIRAB economy in South Pacific microstates', *Pacific Viewpoint* 26:3 (1985), 497–519.

Biedermann, Z., A. Gerritsen, and G. Riello (eds.). *Global Gifts: The Material Culture of Diplomacy in Early Modern Eurasia*. Cambridge: Cambridge University Press, 2017.

Biggs, B. 'What is oral tradition', in S. Vatu (ed.), *Na Veitalanoa me baleta na i tukutuku maroroi = Talking about Oral Traditions. Proceedings of a Workshop on Fijian Oral Traditions Held at the Fiji Museum, August 16th–August 21st, 1976*. Suva: Fiji Museum, 1977, 1–12.

Billé, F., and S. Urbansky (eds.). *Yellow Perils: China Narratives in the Contemporary World*. Honolulu: University of Hawai'i Press, 2018.

Binney, J. '"In-between" lives: studies from within a colonial society', in T. Ballantyne and B. Moloughney (eds.), *Disputed Histories: Imagining New Zealand's Pasts*. Dunedin: Otago University Press, 2006, 93–118.

Birrell, K. '"An essential ghost": indigeneity within the legal archive', *Australian Feminist Law Journal* 22 (2010), 81–99.

Bjork, K. 'The link that kept the Philippines Spanish: Mexican merchant interests and the Manila Trade, 1571–1815', *Journal of World History* 9:1 (1998), 25–50.

Black, R., S. Bennett, and S. Thomas. 'Migration as adaptation', *Nature* 478 (2011), 447–9.

Black, R.H. 'The epidemiology of malaria in the Southwest Pacific: changes associated with increasing European contact', *Oceania* 27:2 (1956), 136–42.

Blanchard, E. *Anthropologie, Voyage au pôle sud et dans l'Océanie sur les corvettes l'Astrolabe et la Zélée; exécuté . . . pendant les années 1837–1838–1839–1840 . . .* Paris: Gide et J. Baudry, 1854.

Blanckaert, C. 'Of monstrous métis? Hybridity, fear of miscegenation, and patriotism from Buffon to Paul Broca', in S. Peabody and T. Stovall (eds.), *The Color of Liberty: Histories of Race in France*. Durham, NC: Duke University Press, 2003, 42–70.

Blumenbach, J.F. *Beyträge zur Naturgeschichte*, 2nd edn, 2 vols. Göttingen: H. Dieterich, 1806–11.
  De Generis Humani Varietate Nativa, 2nd edn. Göttingen: A. Vandenhoek, 1781.
  De Generis Humani Varietate Nativa, 3rd edn. Göttingen: Vandenhoek & Ruprecht, 1795.
  Handbuch der Naturgeschichte, 5th edn. Göttingen, J.C. Dieterich, 1797.

Blythe, M. *Naming the Other: Images of the Māori in New Zealand Film and Television*. London: Metuchen, 1994.

Bolton, L. 'Chief Willie Bongmatur Maldo and the role of chiefs in Vanuatu', *Journal of Pacific History* 33:2 (1998), 179–95.

Bonnemaison, J. 'The tree and the canoe: roots and mobility in Vanuatu societies', in M. Chapman and S. Morrison (eds.), *Mobility and Identity in the Island Pacific*. Wellington: Victoria University Press,1985, 30–62.

813

REFERENCES TO VOLUME II

Borovnik, M. 'Transnationalism of merchant seafarers and their communities in Kiribati and Tuvalu', in H. Lee and S. Francis (eds.), *Migration and Transformation: Pacific Perspectives*. Canberra: ANU Press, 2009, 143–57.

Bourdaghs, M. *The Dawn that Never Comes: Shimazaki Tōson and Japanese Nationalism*. New York: Columbia University Press, 2003.

Bourdieu, P. *La distinction*. Paris: Minuit, 1979.

Le sens pratique. Paris: Minuit, 1980.

Outline of a Theory of Practice. Cambridge: Cambridge University Press, 1977.

Bovensiepen, J. 'Lulik: taboo, animism, or transgressive sacred? An exploration of identity, morality and power in Timor-Leste', *Oceania* 84:2 (2014), 121–37.

Bowen, H.V. 'Britain in the Indian Ocean region and beyond: contours, connections, and the creation of a global maritime empire', in H.V. Bowen, E. Mancke, and J.G. Reid (eds.), *Britain's Oceanic Empire: Atlantic and Indian Ocean Worlds, c.1550–1850*. Cambridge: Cambridge University Press, 2012, 45–65.

Bower, P. 'The state of the National Archives: Fiji', UNESCO Assignment Report RP/ 1990-1991/11.C(i) (1992).

Bowes, J. 'The Australian Aborigine' in J. Colwell (ed.), *A Century in the Pacific*. Sydney: William H. Beale 1914, 153–4.

Boxer, C.R. 'A late sixteenth century Manila MS', *Journal of the Royal Asiatic Society of Great Britain and Ireland* 1/2 (1950), 37–49.

António Coelho Guerreiro e as relações entre Macao e Timor no começo do século XVIII. Macau: Escola Tipográfica da Imaculada Conceição de Macau, 1940.

'Plata es sangre: sidelights on the drain of Spanish-American silver in the Far East, 1550–1700', *Philippine Studies* 18:3 (1970), 457–78.

The Topasses of Timor. Amsterdam: Koninklijke Vereeniging Indisch Instituut, 1947.

Boyce, J. *Van Diemen's Land: A History*. Melbourne: Black, 2008.

Boyce, R.W.D. 'Canada and the Pacific cable controversy, 1923–28: forgotten source of imperial alienation', *Journal of Imperial and Commonwealth History* 26 (1998), 72–92.

'Imperial dreams and national realities: Britain, Canada and the struggle for a Pacific telegraph cable, 1879–1902', *English Historical Review* 115 (2000), 39–70.

Boyd, M. 'The record in Western Samoa since 1945', in A. Ross (ed.), *New Zealand's Record in the Pacific Islands in the Twentieth Century*. Auckland: Longman Paul, 1968, 189–27.

'The Southwest Pacific in the 1970s', in B. Brown (ed.), *Asia and the Pacific in the 1970s: The Roles of the United States, Australia, and New Zealand*. Canberra: ANU Press, 1971, 61–88.

Boyer, P. *By the Bomb's Early Light: American Thought and Culture at the Dawn of the Atomic Age*. Chapel Hill: University of North Carolina Press, 1994.

Bozic-Vrbancic, S. *Tarara: Croats and Maori in New Zealand, Memory, Belonging, Identity*. Dunedin: University of Otago Press, 2008.

Bradley, P. *The Battle for Wau: New Guinea's Frontline 1942–1943*. Cambridge: Cambridge University Press, 2008.

Brantlinger, P. *Dark Vanishings: Discourse on the Extinction of Primitive Races, 1800–1930*. Ithaca, NY: Cornell University Press 2003.

Brathwaite, E.K. *Rights of Passage*. Oxford: Oxford University Press, 1967.

814

References to Volume II

Brawley, S., and C. Dixon. *Hollywood's South Seas and the Pacific War: Searching for Dorothy Lamour*. New York: Palgrave Macmillan, 2012.

'Who owns the Kokoda Trail? Australian mythologies, colonial legacies and mining in Papua New Guinea', *Social Alternatives* 28:4 (2009), 24–9.

Bretegnier, P. 'Interview with Pierre Bretegnier', *Le club politique*, Radio Rythme Bleu, April 2020.

Brett, J. *Australian Liberals and the Moral Middle Class: From Alfred Deakin to John Howard*. Cambridge: Cambridge University Press, 2003.

Breward, I. 'Christianity in Polynesia', in C.E. Farhadian (ed.), *Introducing World Christianity*. Malden, MA: Wiley-Blackwell, 2012, 218–29.

Brison, K.J. 'Constructing identity through ceremonial language in rural Fiji', *Ethnology* 40:4 (2001), 309–26.

Brodsky, P. 'Global enterprise networks and submarine cable capacity: coverage, pricing and traffic trends', *TeleGeography* (2017), www2.telegeography.com/hubfs/2017/wan-summit/Presentations/WSS/SubCables.pdf?t=1509031204960.

Broinowski, A. 'Informal labour, local citizens and the Tokyo Electric Fukushima Daiichi nuclear crisis: responses to neoliberal disaster management', in T. Morris-Suzuki and Eun Jeong Soh (eds.), *New Worlds from Below: Informal Life Politics and Grassroots Action in Twenty-First-Century Northeast Asia*. Canberra: ANU Press, 2017, 131–66.

Brookfield, H.C., with D. Hart. *Melanesia: A Geographical Interpretation of an Island World*. London: Methuen, 1971.

Brosses, C. de. *Histoire des navigations aux terres australes, contenant ce que l'on sçait des mœurs & des productions des contrées découvertes jusqu'à ce jour; & où il est traité de l'utilité d'y faire de plus amples découvertes, & des moyens d'y former un établissement*, 2 vols. Paris: Durand, 1756.

[Brosses, C. de], *Terra Australis Cognita, or, Voyages to the Terra Australis, or Southern Hemisphere, during the Sixteenth, Seventeenth, and Eighteenth Centuries: Containing an Account of the Manners of the People, and the Productions of the Countries, Hitherto Found in the Southern Latitudes; the Advantages that may Result from Further Discoveries on this Great Continent, and the Methods of Establishing Colonies there, to the Advantage of Great Britain*, trans. and ed. J. Callander, 3 vols. Edinburgh: A. Donaldson, 1766–8.

Brown, B. (ed.). *Asia and the Pacific in the 1970s: The Roles of the United States, Australia, and New Zealand*. Canberra: ANU Press, 1971.

Brown, J.S.H. *Strangers in Blood: Fur Trade Company Families in Indian Country*. Vancouver: UBC Press, 1980.

Brown Pulu, T.J. '*Kakai Tonga 'i Okalani Nu'u Sila*: Tongan generations in Auckland New Zealand'. PhD thesis, University of Waikato, Hamilton, 2007.

Brué, A.-H. *Grand atlas universel, ou collection de cartes encyprotypes, générales, particulières et détaillées, des cinq parties du monde*. Paris: Desray, 1815.

Bruey, A. *Bread, Justice, and Liberty: Grassroots Activism and Human Rights in Pinochet's Chile*. Madison: University of Wisconsin Press, 2018.

Brunt, P., et al. *Oceania: Exhibition Catalogue*. London: Royal Academy of Arts, 2018.

Buck, E.M. *Island of Angels: The Growth of the Church on Kosrae, Kapkapak lun Church fin acn Kosrae, 1858–2002*. Honolulu: Watermark, 2005.

REFERENCES TO VOLUME II

Buckingham, J. 'The inclusivity of exclusion: isolation and community among leprosy-affected people in the South Pacific', *Health and History* 13:2 (2011), 65–83.

Buckley, K., and K. Klugman. *The History of Burns Philp: The Australian Company in the South Pacific*. Sydney: Burns Philp and Company, 1981.

Buffon, G.-L. Leclerc, comte de. *Histoire naturelle, générale et particulière, avec la description du cabinet du roi*, 15 vols. Paris: Imprimerie Royale, 1749–67.

Servant de suite à l'histoire naturelle de l'homme, in *Histoire naturelle, générale et particulière: Supplément*, 7 vols. Paris: Imprimerie Royale, 1777–89.

Bulbeck, C. *Australian Women in Papua New Guinea: Colonial Passages 1920–1960*. Cambridge: Cambridge University Press, 1992.

Burkinshaw, R.K. *Pilgrims in Lotus Land: Conservative Protestantism in British Columbia, 1917–1981*. Montreal: McGill-Queen's University Press, 1995.

Burney, J. *A Memoir on the Voyage of d'Entrecasteaux in Search of La Pérouse*. London: Luke Hansard, 1820.

Burton, J., and O.A. Burton, 'Some reflections on anthropology's missionary positions', *Journal of the Royal Anthropological Institute* 13 (2007), 209–17.

Bushnell, A.F. '"The Horror" reconsidered: an evaluation of the historical evidence for population decline in Hawai'i, 1778–1803', *Pacific Studies* 16:3 (1993), 115–62.

Bushnell. O.A. *The Gifts of Civilization: Germs and Genocide in Hawai'i*. Honolulu: University of Hawai'i Press, 1993.

Cachola-Abad, C.K. 'The evolution of Hawaiian socio-political complexity: an analysis of Hawaiian oral traditions'. PhD thesis, University of Hawai'i, 2000.

Cadematori, J. 'The Chilean neoliberal model enters into crisis', *Latin American Perspectives* 30:5 (2003), 79–88.

Caledonia Conference. 'Qu'est-ce que "décoloniser" veut dire?', 10 October 2018, www .youtube.com/watch?v=EMGDZ2HrvqE&t=543s.

Calinaud, R.L. 'La situation juridique des lagons polynésiens', *Bulletin de la Société des Études Océaniennes* 22:12 (1993), 47–53.

Camacho, K. *Cultures of Commemoration: The Politics of War, Memory, and History in the Mariana Islands*. Honolulu: University of Hawai'i Press, 2011.

'The politics of indigenous collaboration: the role of Chamorro interpreters in Japan's Pacific empire, 1914–1945', *Journal of Pacific History* 43 (2008), 207–22.

Camacho, K.L., and L. Monnig. 'Uncomfortable fatigues: Chamorro soldiers, gendered identities, and the question of decolonization in Guam', in S. Shigematsu and K.L. Camacho (eds.), *Militarized Currents: Toward a Decolonized Future in Asia and the Pacific*. Minneapolis: University of Minnesota Press, 2010, 147–79.

Cameron, P. *Grease and Ochre: The Blending of Two Cultures at the Colonial Sea Frontier*. Launceston: Fuller's Bookshop, 2011.

Cameron-Smith, A. 'Raphael Cilento's empire: diet, health and government between Australia and the colonial Pacific', *Journal of Australian Studies* 38:1 (2014), 103–18.

Campbell, I.C. *Classical Tongan Kingship*. Nuku'alofa: 'Atenisi University, 1989.

Island Kingdom: Tonga Ancient and Modern, 2nd edn. Christchurch: Canterbury University Press, 2001.

'More celebrated than read: the work of Norma McArthur', in D. Munro and B.V. Lal (eds.), *Texts and Contexts: Reflections in Pacific Islands Historiography*. Honolulu: University of Hawai'i Press 2006, 98–110.

816

References to Volume II

'The demise of the Tuʻi Kanokupolu: Tonga 1799–1827', *Journal of Pacific History* 24:2 (1989), 150–63.

Worlds Apart: A History of the Pacific Islands. Christchurch: Canterbury University Press, 2003.

Campbell, J.R. 'Climate-change migration in the Pacific', *Contemporary Pacific* 26:1 (2014), 1–28.

Camus, G. *Tabiteuea Kiribati*. Paris: Hazan-Fondation Culturelle Musée Barbier-Mueller, 2014.

Capellà Miternique, H. 'Fusion in multicultural societies: chifa food as a means of spreading Chinese culture in the Hispanic world', *Asian Journal of Humanities and Social Studies* 2:5 (2014), 648–56.

Carey, J., and J. Lydon (eds.). *Indigenous Networks: Mobility, Connections and Exchange*. New York: Routledge, 2014.

Carter, G. 'Establishing a Pacific voice in climate change negotiations', in G. Fry and S. Tarte (eds.), *The New Pacific Diplomacy*. Canberra: ANU Press, 2015, 205–22.

Carucci, L.M. *Nuclear Nativity: Rituals of Renewal and Empowerment in the Marshall Islands*. DeKalb: Northern Illinois University Press, 1997.

Castro, A.O. de. *A ilha verde e vermelha de Timor*. Lisbon: Cotovia, 1996 [1943].

As possessões portuguezas na Oceania. Lisbon: Imprensa Nacional, 1867.

'Une rébellion à Timor en 1861', *Tijdschrift voor Indische Taal-, Land- en Volkenkunde* 13 (1864), 389–409.

Cattani, J.A. 'The epidemiology of malaria in Papua New Guinea', in R.D. Attenborough and M.P. Alpers (eds.), *Human Biology in Papua New Guinea: The Small Cosmos*. Oxford Oxford University Press, 1992, 302–12.

Cavert, W. 'At the edge of an empire: plague, state, and identity in New Caledonia 1899–1900', *Journal of Pacific History* 51:1 (2016), 1–20.

Cawsey, K.S.K. *The Making of a Rebel: Captain Donald Macleod of the New Hebrides*. Suva: Institute of Pacific Studies, University of the South Pacific, 1988.

CFO. *Global Mapping of Filipinos Overseas*. Manila: Commission on Filipinos Overseas, 2013, www.cfo.gov.ph/downloads/statistics/global-mapping-of-overseas-filipinos.html.

Chambers, N., et al. *Endeavouring Banks: Exploring Collections from the 'Endeavour' Voyage 1768–1771*. Sydney: Paul Holberton, University of Washington Press, 2016.

Chamisso, A. *A Voyage around the World with the Romanzov Expedition in the Years 1815–1818 in the Brig Rurik, Captain Otto von Kotzebue*, ed. and trans. H. Kratz. Honolulu: University of Hawaiʻi Press, 1986 [1836].

Chand, S., and H. Dempster. 'A Pacific skills partnership: improving the APTC to meet skills needed in the region'. Center for Global Development, 2 August 2019, www.cgdev .org/blog/pacific-skills-partnership-improving-aptc-meet-skills-needed-in-region.

Chang, D.A. *The World and All the Things upon It: Native Hawaiian Geographies of Exploration*. Minneapolis: University of Minnesota Press, 2016.

Chang, K.S. *Pacific Connections: The Making of the Western U.S.–Canadian Borderlands*. Berkeley: University of California Press, 2012.

Chapin, H.G. 'Newspapers of Hawaiʻi 1834 to 1903: from "He Liona" to the *Pacific Cable*', *Hawaiian Journal of History* 18 (1984), 47–86.

Chapman, D. *The Bonin Islanders, 1830 to the Present: Narrating Japanese Nationality*. London: Lexington Books, 2016.

REFERENCES TO VOLUME II

Chappell, D.A. 'Active agents versus passive victims: decolonized historiography or problematic paradism?' *The Contemporary Pacific* 7:2 (1995), 303–26.

Double Ghosts: Oceanian Voyagers on Euroamerican Ships. Armonk, NY: M.E. Sharpe, 1997.

'Ethnogenesis and frontiers', *Journal of World History* 4 (1993), 267–75.

Le réveil kanak: la montée du nationalisme en Nouvelle-Calédonie [French translation of The Kanak Awakening]. Nouméa: Éditions Madrépores et l'Université de la Nouvelle-Calédonie, 2017.

'The forgotten Mau: anti-navy protests in American Samoa, 1920–1935', *Pacific Historical Review* 69 (2000), 217–60.

'The Nouméa Accord: decolonization without independence in New Caledonia?', *Pacific Affairs* 72:3 (1999), 373–91.

'Transnationalism in central Oceanian politics: a dialectic of diasporas and nationhood?', *Journal of the Polynesian Society* 108:3 (1999), 277–303.

Chauchat, M. 'What shared institutional future for New Caledonia?'. Pacific Islands Political Science Association (PIPSA) Conference, 'Democracy, Sovereignty and Self-Determination in the Pacific Islands', Nouméa, 2019.

Chazine, J.-M. 'Du présent au passé: questions d'ethnoarchéologie, les fosses de culture des Tuamotu', *Techniques et Culture* 6 (1985), 85–99.

Cheng, W. *War, Trade, and Piracy in the China Seas, 1622, 1683.* Leiden: Brill, 2013.

Ching, L.T.S. *Becoming 'Japanese': Colonial Taiwan and the Politics of Identity Formation.* Berkeley: University of California Press, 2001.

Choris, L. *Voyage pittoresque autour du Monde: avec des portraits de sauvages d'Américque, d'Asie, d'Afrique.* Paris: Fermin Didot, 1822.

Chou, D.L. *Chile y China: inmigración y relaciones bilaterales, 1845–1970.* Santiago: Pontificia Universidad Católica de Chile y Instituto de Historia: Centro de Investigaciones Diego Barrios Arana, 2004.

Choy, C.C., and J.T.-C. Wu (eds.). *Gendering the Trans-Pacific World: Diaspora, Gender and Race.* Leiden: Brill, 2017.

Chrisafis, A. 'French nuclear tests "showered vast area of Polynesia with radioactivity"', *Guardian* (4 July 2013), www.theguardian.com/world/2013/jul/03/french-nuclear-tests-polynesia-declassified.

Christen, K. 'Tribal archives, traditional knowledge, and local contexts: why the "s" matters', *Journal of Western Archives* 6:1 (2015), 1–19.

Christian, S. 'Chile's growing trans-Pacific ties', *New York Times* (28 March 1988), D10.

Christie, C. *Ideology and Revolution in Southeast Asia 1900–1980.* Richmond: Curzon, 2001.

Christophe, A. 'What's in a map? Remapping Oceania in Taiwan museums through exhibitions', *Pacific Arts* 15:1–2 (2016), 8–20.

Cleave, P. 'Tribal and state-like political formations in New Zealand Maori society 1750–1900', *Journal of the Polynesian Society* 92:1 (1983), 51–92.

Clery, T., and R. Metcalfe. 'Activist archives and feminist fragments: claiming space in the archives for the voices of Pacific women and girls', *Education as Change* 22:2 (2018), 1–29.

Clifford, J. 'Reciprocity and the making of ethnographic texts. The example of Maurice Leenhardt', *Man* 15 (1980), 518–32.

Clinton, H. 'America's Pacific Century', *Foreign Policy*, online edition, 11 October 2011, http://foreignpolicy.com/2011/10/11/americas-pacific century.

818

References to Volume II

Close Barry, K. *A Mission Divided: Race, Culture and Colonialism in Fiji's Methodist Mission.* Canberra: ANU Press, 2015.

'The Reverend Setareki Tuilovoni: mobile Pacific leader in the decolonisation era', *Journal of Pacific History* 50 (2015), 149–67.

Cochin, R. '*L'application du droit civil et du droit pénal français aux autochtones des Établissements Français de l'Océani'.* Thèse de doctorat, Univerity of Paris, 1949.

Cody, J.F. *28 (Maori) Battalion: Official History of New Zealand in the Second World War 1939–1945,* vol. XVI. Wellington: War History Branch, Department of Internal Affairs, 1956.

Coffman, T. *Nation Within: The History of the American Occupation of Hawai'i,* 3rd edn. Durham, NC: Duke University Press, 2016.

(dir.). *The First Battle: The Battle for Equality in War-Time Hawaii.* San Francisco: Center for Asian American Media, 2006. DVD.

Cole, J.A. 'An abolition born of frustration: the Conde de Lemos and the Potosi mita, 1667–73', *Hispanic American Historical Review* 63:2 (1983), 307–33.

The Potosí Mita, 1573–1700: Compulsory Indian Labor in the Andes. Stanford: Stanford University Press, 1985.

Coleborne, C. *Insanity, Identity and Empire: Immigrants and Institutional Confinement in Australia and New Zealand, 1873–1910,* Manchester: Manchester University Press, 2015.

Colonial Office, Great Britain, [Cooper, H.]. *Among Those Present: The Official Story of the Pacific Islands at War.* London: HMSO, 1946.

Comaroff, J., and J. Comaroff. *Ethnography and the Historical Imagination.* Boulder, CO: Westview Press, 1992.

Connell, J. 'Nauru: The first failed Pacific State?', *The Round Table: Commonwealth Journal of International. Affairs* 95:383 (2006), 47–63.

New Caledonia of Kanaky: The Political History of a French Colony. Canberra: Development Studies Centre, Research School of Pacific Studies, The Australian National University, 1987.

'The two cultures of health worker migration: a Pacific perspective', *Social Science Medicine* 116 (2014), 73–81.

Connell, J., and R.P. Brown. 'The remittances of migrant Tongan and Samoan nurses from Australia', *Human Resources for Health* 2:2 (2004), 1–21.

Connelly, A. 'Ambivalent empires: historicising the Trobriand Islands, 1830–1945'. PhD thesis, Australian National University, Canberra, 2014.

Connery, C.L. 'Pacific Rim discourse: the U.S. global imaginary in the late Cold War years', *boundary 2* 21:1 (1994), 30–56.

Conrad, G.W., and A.A. Demarest. *Religion and Empire: The Dynamics of Aztec and Inca Expansionism.* Cambridge: Cambridge University Press, 1984.

Constitution of the Federated States of Micronesia. Palikir, Pohnpei: Federated States of Micronesia Government, 2000.

Containerisation International Yearbook. London: National Magazine Co., 1967–2012.

Conte, E.N., G. Mole, and E. Nolet. 'Des atolls et des hommes', in T. Bambridge and J.-P. Latouche (eds.), *Les atolls du Pacifique face au changement climatique: une comparaison Tuamotu-Kiribati.* Paris: Éditions Karthala, 2016.

REFERENCES TO VOLUME II

Cook, J. *A Voyage towards the South Pole and Round the World Performed in His Majesty's Ships the Resolution and Adventure in the Years 1772, 1773, 1774, and 1775* ..., 2 vols. London: W. Strahan and T. Cadell, 1777.

Cook, J. *Charts and Views: Drawn by Cook and His Officers and Reproduced from the Original Manuscripts*, ed. R.A. Skelton. Cambridge: Hakluyt Society and Cambridge University Press, 1955.

Cook, K.R. *Return to Kahiki: Native Hawaiians in Oceania*. Cambridge: Cambridge University Press, 2017.

Cook, T. 'Evidence, memory, identity, and community: four shifting archival paradigms', *Archival Science* 13:2–3 (2013), 95–120.

Coombes, A.E. *Rethinking Settler Colonialism: History and Memory in Australia, Canada, Aotearoa New Zealand and South Africa*. Manchester: Manchester University Press, 2006.

Cooper, F., and A.L. Stoler. 'Introduction. Tensions of empire: colonial control and visions of rule', *American Ethnologist* 16 (1989), 609–21.

Corbett, J. *Being Political: Leadership and Democracy in the Pacific Islands*. Honolulu: University of Hawai'i Press, 2015.

Cordy, R. *Exalted Sits the Chief: The Ancient History of Hawai'i Island*. Honolulu: Mutual Publishing, 2000.

Cordy, R., and T. Ueki. 'The development of complex societies on Kosrae', unpublished paper presented at the 48th Annual Meeting of the Society for American Archaeology, 1983.

Cornier, S., and I. Leblic. 'Kanak coastal communities and fisheries meeting new governance challenges and marine issues in New Caledonia', in S. Pauwels and E. Fache (eds.), *Fisheries in the Pacific: The Challenges of Governance and Sustainability*. Marseilles: Pacific Credo Publications, 2016, 119–74.

Correia, A.P. *Gentio de Timor*. Lisbon: Lucas & Ca., 1935.

Corris, P. *Passage, Port and Plantation: A History of Solomon Islands Labour Migration, 1870–1914*. Melbourne: Melbourne University Press, 1973.

Cortesão, A. 'António Pereira and his map of circa 1545: an unknown Portuguese cartographer and the early representation of Newfoundland, Lower California, the Amazon, and the Ladrones', *Geographical Review* 29 (1939), 205–55

Cortesão, A., and A. Teixeira da Mota (eds.). *Portugaliae Monumenta Cartographica*, 6 vols. Lisbon: Comemorações do V Centenário da Morte do Infante D. Henrique, 1960–2.

Couper, A. *Sailors and Traders: A Maritime History of the Pacific Peoples*. Honolulu: University of Hawai'i Press, 2009.

'The island trade: an analysis of the environment and operation of seaborne trade among three island groups in the Pacific'. PhD thesis, Australian National University, Canberra, 1967.

Crane, E. 'King Cakobau's government or, an experiment in government in Fiji: 1871–1874'. MA thesis, University of Auckland, 1938.

Creed, B., and J. Hoorn (eds.). *Body Trade: Captivity, Cannibalism and Colonialism in the Pacific*. New York: Routledge, 2001.

Crocombe, M. *Two Hundred Changing Years: A Story of New Zealand's Little Sisters in the Pacific – the Cook Islands, the Tokelau Islands, and Niue Island*. Wellington: Islands

820

References to Volume II

Education Division of the New Zealand Department of Education for the Department of Island Territories, 1962.

Crocombe, R. *Asia in the Pacific Islands: Replacing the West.* Suva: University of the South Pacific for the Institute of Pacific Studies, 2007.

'Latin America and the Pacific Islands', *Contemporary Pacific* 3:1 (1991), 115–44.

The Pacific Way: An Emerging Identity. Suva: Lotu Pasifika Productions, 1976.

Crocombe, R., and M. Crocombe. 'Early Polynesian authors – the example of Ta'unga', *Historical Studies: Australia and New Zealand* 10:37 (1961), 92–3.

(eds.) *The Works of Ta'unga: Records of a Polynesian Traveller in the South Seas, 1833–1896.* Canberra: ANU Press, 1968.

Crookston, M. 'Record keeping for good governance in the Pacific: the work of the Pacific regional branch of the International Council on Archives. *Archifacts* (2011), 73–83.

Crosby, A. *Ecological Imperialism: The Biological Expansion of Europe, 900–1900.* Cambridge: Cambridge University Press, 1986.

'Hawaiian depopulation as a model for the Amerindian experience', in T. Ranger and P. Slack (eds.), *Epidemics and Ideas: Essays on the Historical Perception of Pestilence.* Cambridge: Cambridge University Press, 1992, 175–201.

'Interview', *Environmental History* 14:3 (2009), 562.

The Columbian Exchange: Biological and Cultural Consequences of 1492. Westport, CT: Greenwood, 1972.

'Virgin soil epidemics as a factor in the aboriginal depopulation in America', *William and Mary Quarterly* 33:2 (1976), 289–99.

Crossley, P. *The Manchus.* Cambridge, MA: Blackwell, 1997.

Crow, J. *The Mapuche in Modern Chile: A Cultural History.* Gainesville: University Press of Florida, 2013.

Cruz, A.C. da. 'Sempre vassalo fiel de Sua Majestade Fidelíssima: os autos de vassalagem e as cartas patentes para autoridades locais africanas (Angola, segunda metade do século XVIII)', *Cadernos de Estudos Africanos* 30 (2015), 61–80.

Cumings, B. *Dominion from Sea to Sea: Pacific Ascendancy and American Power.* New Haven: Yale University Press, 2009.

Parallax Visions: Making Sense of American–East Asian Relations. Durham, NC: Duke University Press, 2002.

Cunningham, A, 'Archival institutions', in S. McKemmish, M. Piggott, B. Reed, and F. Upward (eds.), *Archives: Recordkeeping in Society.* Wagga Wagga: Charles Sturt University, 2005, 21–50.

Curnow, J., N. Hopa, and J. McRae (eds.). *Rere atu, taku manu! Discovering History, Language and Politics in the Maori-language Newspapers.* Auckland: Auckland University Press, 2002.

Curtain, R., and M. Dornan. 'A pressure release valve? Migration and climate change in Kiribati, Nauru and Tuvalu'. Canberra: Development Policy Centre, ANU, 2019.

Curtin, P. *Disease and Empire: The Health of European Troops in the Conquest of Africa.* Cambridge: Cambridge University Press 1998.

Cushman, G.T. *Guano and the Opening of the Pacific World: A Global Ecological History.* Cambridge: Cambridge University Press, 2014.

Cuvier, G. *Leçons d'anatomie comparée,* 5 vols. Paris: Crochard, Fantin, 1800–5.

REFERENCES TO VOLUME II

(ed.). 'Rapport sur un ouvrage manuscrit de M. André, ci-devant connu sous le nom de P. Chrysologue de Gy, lequel ouvrage est intitulé *Théorie de la surface actuelle de la terre*', *Mémoires de la classe des sciences mathématiques et physiques de l'Institut national de France*, premier semestre (1807), 128–45.

Le règne animal distribué d'après son organisation, pour servir de base à l'histoire naturelle des animaux et d'introduction à l'anatomie comparée, 4 vols. Paris: Deterville, 1817.

Cvetkovich, A. *An Archive of Feelings: Trauma, Sexuality, and Lesbian Public Cultures*. Durham, NC: Duke University Press, 2003.

D'Altroy, T.N. *The Incas*. Oxford: Blackwell, 2002.

D'Arcy, P. 'China and the sea: potential for Pacific partnerships?', in M. Powles (ed.), *China and the Pacific: the View from Oceania*. Wellington: Victoria University Press, 2016, 248–55.

'Cultural divisions and island environments since the time of Dumont d'Urville', *Journal of Pacific History* 38:2 (2003), 217–35.

'Forum introduction: women and the sea in the Pacific: a neglected dimension', *International Journal of Maritime History* 20:2 (2008), 259–64.

'Lessons for humanity from the ocean of ancestors', in S. Hessler (ed.), *Tidalectics: Imagining an Oceanic Worldview through Art and Science*. Cambridge, MA: MIT Press, 2018, 117–26.

'The Chinese Pacifics: a brief historical review', *Journal of Pacific History* 49:4 (2014), 396–420.

The People of the Sea: Environment, Identity, and History in Oceania. Honolulu: University of Hawai'i Press, 2006.

'The Philippines as a Pacific nation: a brief history of interaction between Filipinos and Pacific Islanders', *Journal of Pacific History* 53 (2018), 1–23.

Transforming Hawai'i: Balancing Coercion and Consent in Eighteenth-Century Kānaka Maoli Statecraft. Canberra: ANU Press, 2018.

D'Entrecasteaux, B. *Voyage to Australia and the Pacific 1791*, trans. E. Duyker and M. Duyker. Carlton: Melbourne University Press, 2001.

Dalrymple, A. *An Historical Collection of the Several Voyages and Discoveries in the South Pacific Ocean*, 2 vols. London: The Author, 1770–1.

Dampier, W. *A Continuation of a Voyage to New-Holland, &c. in the Year 1699*. London: James Knapton, 1709.

A New Voyage Round the World . . . London: James Knapton, 1697.

Danielsson, B., and M.-T. Danielsson. *Poisoned Reign: French Nuclear Colonialism in the Pacific*. New York: Penguin Books, 1986.

Davidson, J.W. *Peter Dillon of Vanikoro: Chevalier of the South Seas*. Oxford: Oxford University Press, 1975.

'Problems of Pacific history', *Journal of Pacific History* 1:1 (1966), 5–21.

Samoa mo Samoa: The Emergence of the Independent State of Western Samoa. Oxford: Oxford University Press, 1967.

Davies, J. *A Tahitian and English Dictionary with Introductory Remarks on the Polynesian Language and a Short Grammar of the Tahitian Dialect*. London: London Missionary Society's Press, 1851.

Davis, T., and L. Davis. *Doctor to the Islands*. London: Michael Joseph, 1955.

References to Volume II

Dawson, C. *Religion and Culture: Gifford Lectures*. Washington, DC: Catholic University of America Press 1948.

de Bruce, L. 'A tartan clan in Fiji: narrating the coloniser "within" the colonised', in B.V. Lal and V. Luker (eds.), *Telling Pacific Lives: Prisms of Process*. Canberra: ANU Press, 2008, 93–105.

'Histories of diversity: Kailoma testimonies and "part-European" tales from colonial Fiji (1920–1970)', *Journal of Intercultural Studies* 28:1 (2007), 113–27.

de Galaup, J.-F., Comte de La Pérouse. *The Voyage of La Pérouse Round the World, in the Years 1785, 1786, 1787 and 1788*, ed. and trans. M.L.A. Milet Mureau. London: John Stockdale, 1798.

dé Ishtar, Z. (ed.). *Pacific Women Speak Out for Independence and Denuclearisation*. Christchurch: Raven Press, 1998.

de la Fuente, D. *Instituto Chileno Chino de Cultura, cuarenta años*. Santiago: Instituto Chileno Chino de Cultura, 1992.

Debuce, A.L. *Cultural Change in Horticultural Practices on the High Island of Kosrae, Micronesia*. Eugene: University of Oregon Press, 1996.

DeLoughrey, E. 'Globalizing the routes of breadfruit and other bounties', *Journal of Colonialism and Colonial History* 8 (2007), https://muse.jhu.edu/.

Delsing, R. *Articulating Rapa Nui: Polynesian Cultural Politics in a Latin American Nation-State*. Honolulu: University of Hawai'i Press, 2015.

Denfeld, D.C. 'Korean laborers in Micronesia during World War II', *Korea Observer* 15:1 (1984), 3–17.

Deng, G. *Chinese Maritime Activities and Socioeconomic Development, ca. 2100 BCE–1900 CE*. Westport, CT: Greenwood, 1997.

Maritime Sector, Institutions, and Sea Power of Pre-modern China. Westport, CT: Greenwood, 1999.

Dening, D. *Beach Crossings: Voyaging across Times, Cultures and Self*. Carlton: Miegunyah Press, 2004.

Islands and Beaches: Discourse on a Silent Land, Marquesas 1774–1880. Chicago: The Dorsey Press, 1980.

Mr Bligh's Bad Language: Passion, Power and Theatre on the Bounty. Cambridge: Cambridge University Press, 1992.

Performances. Carlton: Melbourne University Press, 1996.

Dennett, T. *Americans in East Asia: A Critical Study of the Policy of the United States with Reference to China, Japan, and Korea in the 19th Century*. New York: Octagon Books, 1979.

Denoon, D. *A Trial Separation: Australia and the Decolonisation of Papua New Guinea*. Canberra: ANU Press, 2012.

'Davidson, James Wightman (Jim) (1915–1973)', in *Australian Dictionary of Biography*, vol. XIII. Melbourne: Melbourne University Press, 1993.

'Pacific Island depopulation, natural or unnatural history?', in L. Bryder and D.A. Dow (eds.), *New Countries and Old Medicine, Proceedings of an International Conference on the History of Medicine and Health*. Auckland: Pyramid Press, 1995, 324–39.

Public Health in Papua New Guinea: Medical Possibility and Social Constraint, 1884–1984. Cambridge: Cambridge University Press, 2002.

Denoon, D., S. Firth, J. Linnekin, M. Meleisea, and K. Nero (eds.). *The Cambridge History of the Pacific Islanders*. Cambridge: Cambridge University Press, 1997.

Derrick, R.A. *A History of Fiji*. Suva: Government Press, 1950.

DeSilva, K. 'Iwikuamo'o o ka Lāhui: Nā Mana'o Aloha 'Āina i nā Mele Nahenahe'. PhD thesis, University of Hawai'i, Mānoa. 2018.

Dezaki, M. *Shusenjo: The Main Battleground of the Comfort Women Issue*. USA: No Man Productions, 2018. 122 min. film.

Di Piazza, A., and E. Pearthree. 'A new reading of Tupaia's chart', *Journal of the Polynesian Society* 116:3 (2007), 321–40.

'Does the avatea system offer a new key for reading Tupaia's maps?', *Journal of Pacific History* 54:4 (2019), 543–9.

Diamond, A.I. 'The Central Archives of Fiji and the Western Pacific High Commission', *Journal of Pacific History* 1:1 (1966), 204–11.

Diamond, J. *Collapse: How Societies Choose to Fail or Succeed*. New York: Viking, 2005.

Diamond, M. *Creative Meddler: The Life and Fantasies of Charles St Julian*. Melbourne: Melbourne University Press, 1990.

Diaz, V. 'Deliberating "Liberation Day": identity, history, memory, and war in Guam', in T. Fujitani, L. Yoneyama, and G. White (eds.), *Perilous Memories: The Asia-Pacific War(s)*. Durham, NC: Duke University Press, 2001, 155–80.

Repositioning the Missionary: Rewriting the Histories of Colonialism, Native Catholicism, and Indigeneity in Guam. Pacific Islands Monograph Series 24. Honolulu: University of Hawai'i Press, 2010.

Dibblin, J. *Day of Two Suns: US Nuclear Testing and the Pacific Islanders*. New York: New Amsterdam, 1990.

Dickson-Waiko, A. 'Women, nation and decolonisation in Papua New Guinea', *Journal of Pacific History* 48:2 (2013), 177–93.

Dieffenbach, E. 'Dictionary, part III: grammar and dictionary', in E. Dieffenbach, *Travels in New Zealand with Contributions to the Geography, Geology, Botany, and Natural History of that Country*, vol. II. London: John Murray, 1843.

Dillon, P. *Narrative and Successful Result of a Voyage in the South Seas: Performed by the Order of the Government of British India, to Ascertain the Actual Fate of La Pérouse's expedition*, 2 vols. London: Hurst, Chance & Co. 1829.

Dirlik, A. 'The Asia-Pacific idea: reality and representation of a regional structure', *Journal of World History* 3:1 (1992), 55–79.

Dobbins, J., et al. *Choices for America in a Turbulent World*. Santa Monica: Rand Corporation, 2015.

Dobyns, H.F. 'Estimating aboriginal American population: an appraisal of techniques with a new hemispheric population estimate', *Current Anthropology* 7 (1966), 395–416.

Their Number Become Thinned: Native American Population Dynamics in Eastern North America. Knoxville: University of Tennessee Press, 1983.

Dores, R. das. 'Apontamentos para um diccionario chorographico de Timor', *Boletim da Sociedade de Geografia de Lisboa* 7:12 (1903), 763–826.

Dornan, M., and J. Pryke. 'Foreign aid to the Pacific: trends and developments in the twenty-first century', *Asia and the Pacific Policy Studies*, 4:3 (2017), 386–404.

References to Volume II

Douglas, B. 'Christianity, tradition and everyday modernity: towards an anatomy of women's groupings in Melanesia', *Oceania* 74:1/2 (2003), 6–23.

'Climate to crania: science and the racialization of human difference', in B. Douglas and C. Ballard (eds.), *Foreign Bodies: Oceania and the Science of Race 1750–1940*. Canberra: ANU Press, 2008, 33–96.

'In the event: indigenous countersigns and the ethnohistory of voyaging', in M. Jolly, S. Tcherkezoff, and D. Tryon (eds.), *Oceanic Encounters: Exchange, Desire, Violence*. Canberra: ANU Press, 2009, 175–98.

'Naming places: voyagers, toponyms, and local presence in the fifth part of the world, 1500–1700', *Journal of Historical Geography* 45 (2014), 12–24.

'"Novus Orbis Australis": Oceania in the science of race, 1750–1850', in B. Douglas and C. Ballard (eds.), *Foreign Bodies: Oceania and the Science of Race 1750–1940*. Canberra: ANU Press, 2008, 99–155.

'Pasts, presents and possibilities of Pacific history and Pacific studies: as seen by a historian from Canberra', *Journal of Pacific History* 50:2 (2015), 224–8.

Science, Voyages, and Encounters in Oceania, 1511–1850. New York: Palgrave Macmillan, 2014.

'Seaborne ethnography and the natural history of man', *Journal of Pacific History* 38 (2003), 3–27.

'Tupaia's map', *Journal of Pacific History* 54:4 (2019), 529–30.

Douglas, B., and C. Ballard (eds.). *Foreign Bodies: Oceania and the Science of Race 1750–1940*. Canberra: ANU Press, 2008.

'Douglas DC-4'. *Airliners*. 2019. www.airliners.net/aircraft-data/douglas-dc-4/189.

Dower, J.W. *War without Mercy: Race and Power in the Pacific War*. New York: Pantheon Books, 1986.

Downs, I. *The Australian Trusteeship in Papua New Guinea, 1945–75*. Canberra: Australian Government Publishing Service, 1980.

Drayton, R. *Nature's Government: Science, Imperial Britain, and the 'Improvement' of the World*. New Haven: Yale University Press, 2000.

Drewry. *Global Container Terminal Operators: Annual Review and Forecast: Annual Report 2017*. London: Drewry Maritime Research, 2017.

Drinnon, R. *Facing West: The Metaphysics of Indian-Hating and Empire-Building*. Minneapolis: University of Minnesota Press, 1980.

Driver, F., and L. Jones. *Hidden Histories of Exploration: Researching the RGS-IBG Collections*. London: Royal Holloway, University of London, in association with the Royal Geographical Society (with IBG), 2009.

du Feu, V. *Rapanui: A Descriptive Grammar*. New York: Routledge, 1996.

Duarte, F. 'Documento B. Comando militar de Thiarlelo', in J. Celestino da Silva, *Relatório das operações de guerra no Districto Autónomo de Timor no anno de 1896*. Lisbon: Imprensa Nacional, 1897, 67–106.

Dudden, A.P. *The American Pacific: From the Old China Trade to the Present*. Oxford: Oxford University Press, 1992.

Dumont d'Urville, J. *Histoire du voyage, 5 vols., Voyage de la corvette l'Astrolabe exécuté . . . pendant les années 1826–1827–1828–1829 . . .* Paris: J. Tastu, 1830–3.

Histoire du voyage, 10 vols., Voyage au pôle sud et dans l'Océanie sur les corvettes l'Astrolabe et la Zélée; exécuté . . . pendant les années 1837–1838–1839–1840 . . . Paris: Gide, 1841–6.

'Sur les îles du grand Océan', *Bulletin de la Société de Géographie* 17 (1832), 1–21; trans. I. Ollivier, A. de Biran, and G. Clarke as 'On the islands of the Great Ocean', *Journal of Pacific History* 38:2 (2003), 163–74.

[Dumoutier, P.-M. A.], *Atlas anthropologique, Voyage au pôle sud et dans l'Océanie sur les corvettes l'Astrolabe et la Zélée; exécuté ... pendant les années 1837–1838–1839–1840 ...* Paris: Gide, 1846.

Duncan, R. 'Sources of growth spurts in Pacific Island economies', *Asia and the Pacific Policy Studies* 3:2 (2016), 351–65.

Duncan, R.E. 'William Wheelwright and early steam navigation in the Pacific 1820–1840', *The Americas* 32 (1975), 257–81.

Dundon, G. '"Walking the road" from colonial to post-colonial mission: the life, work and thought of the Reverend Dr Alan Richard Tippett, Methodist missionary in Fiji, anthropologist and missiologist, 1911–1988', PhD thesis, University of New South Wales, 2000.

Dunmore, J. *French Explorers in the Pacific.* Oxford: Clarendon Press, 1965.

Pacific Explorer: The Life of Jean-François de La Pérouse, 1741–1788. Palmerston North: Dunmore Press, 1985.

(ed.). *The Journal of Jean-François de Galaup de la Pérouse, 1785–1788.* London: Hakluyt Society, 1994.

Visions and Realities: France in the Pacific, 1695–1995. Waikanae: Heritage Press, 1997.

Durkheim, É. *The Elementary Forms of the Religious Life*, trans. J. Swain. London: George Allen & Unwin, 1915.

Duus, P. *The Abacus and the Sword: The Japanese Penetration of Korea, 1895–1910.* Berkeley: University of California Press, 1995.

Dvorak, G. *Coral and Concrete: Remembering Kwajalein Atoll between Japan, America, and the Marshall Islands.* Honolulu: University of Hawai'i Press, 2018.

'Who closed the sea? Archipelagoes of amnesia between the United States and Japan', *Pacific Historical Review* 83:2 (2014), 350–72.

'Who closed the sea? Postwar amnesia and the Pacific Islands', in Lon Kurashige (ed.), *Pacific America.* Honolulu: University of Hawai'i Press, 2017, 229–46.

Ebert, L., and T. La Menza. 'Chile, copper and resource revenue: a holistic approach to assessing commodity dependence', *Resources Policy* 43 (2015), 101–11.

Eckstein, L., and A. Schwarz. 'Authors' response: the making of Tupaia's map revisited', *Journal of Pacific History* 54:4 (2019), 549–56.

'The making of Tupaia's map: a story of the extent and mastery of Polynesian navigation, competing systems of wayfinding on James Cook's *Endeavour*, and the invention of an ingenious cartographic system', *Journal of Pacific History* 54:1 (2019), 1–95.

Edmond, R. *Representing the South Pacific: Colonial Discourse from Cook to Gauguin.* Cambridge: Cambridge University Press, 1997.

Edmonds, P. 'Collecting Looerryminer's "testimony": Aboriginal women, sealers, and Quaker humanitarian anti-slavery thought and action in the Bass Strait Islands', *Australian Historical Studies* 45 (2014), 13–33.

Edwards, J.B. 'Phosphate mining and the relocation of the Banabans to northern Fiji in 1945: lessons for climate change-forced displacement', *Journal de la Société des Océanistes* 138–9 (2014), 121–36.

References to Volume II

Efi, Tupua Tamasese Ta'isi Tui Atua. *Su'esu'e Manogi: In Search of Fragrance.* Lepapaigalagala, Samoa: The Centre for Samoan Studies, National University of Samoa, 2009.

Whispers and Vanities: Samoan Indigenous Knowledge and Religion. Wellington: Huia 2014.

Eichelberger, J., J. Freymueller, G. Hill, and M. Patrick. 'Nuclear stewardship: lessons from a not-so-remote island', *GeoTimes* 47:3 (2002), 20–3, www.geotimes.org/mar02/feature_amchitka.html.

Elbourne, E. 'Indigenous peoples and imperial networks in the early nineteenth century: the politics of knowledge', in P. Buckner and R.D. Francis (eds.), *Rediscovering the British World.* Calgary: University of Calgary Press, 2005, 59–85.

Elegant, R.S. *Pacific Destiny: Inside Asia Today.* New York: Crown, 1990.

Elias, A. *Coral Empire: Underwater Oceans, Colonial Tropics, Visual Modernity.* Durham, NC: Duke University Press, 2019.

Ellerman, E. 'The Literature Bureau: African influence in Papua New Guinea', *Research in African Literatures* 26:4 (1995), 206–15.

Ellis, A.F. *Ocean Island and Nauru.* Sydney: Angus and Robertson, 1936.

Elsmore, B. *Mana from Heaven: A Century of Maori Prophets in New Zealand.* Tauranga: Moana Press, 1989.

Elvaim, F. 'Relatório', in J.C. da Silva, *Relatório das operações de guerra no Districto Autónomo de Timor no anno de 1896.* Lisbon: Imprensa Nacional, 1897, 50–67.

Elvin, M. 'Three thousand years of unsustainable development: China's environment from archaic times to the present', *East Asian History* 6 (1993), 7–46.

Emory, K.P. *Material Culture of the Tuamotu Archipelago.* Pacific Anthropological Records 22. Honolulu: Bernice P. Bishop Museum, 1975.

Enetama, M. 'Cyclone Heta: disaster preparedness and response. A brief report on actions taken by Pacific archives following recent disaster', *PARBICA 14: Evidence and Memory in the Digital Age*, conference paper, Samoa, 2011.

Enloe, C. *Bananas, Beaches, and Bases: Making Feminist Sense of International Politics*, rev. edn. Berkeley: University of California Press, 2014.

Ercilla y Zúñiga, A. de. *La Araucana* (1556), Canto 1, www.memoriachilena.gob.cl/602/w3-article-3286.html.

Eri, V. *The Crocodile.* Milton, Queensland: Jacaranda Press, 1970.

Erikson, A.S., L.J. Goldstein, and N. Li (eds.). *China, the United States, and 21st Century Sea Power: Defining a Maritime Security Partnership.* Annapolis, MD: Naval Institute Press, 2010.

Erlandson, J.M., M.H. Graham, B.J. Bourque, and D. Corbett. 'The Kelp Highway Hypothesis: marine ecology, the coastal migration theory, and the peopling of the Americas', *Journal of Island and Coastal Archaeology* 2 (2007), 161–74.

Eves, R. 'Colonialism, corporeality and character: Methodist missions and the refashioning of bodies in the Pacific', *History and Anthropology* 10:1 (1996), 85–138.

'Race rescue. Methodist mission and the population question in Papua, 1890–1910', *Social Sciences and Missions* 31 (2018), 34–68.

Fa'aleava, T. '*Fitafita*: Samoan landsmen in the United States Navy, 1900–1951', PhD thesis, University of California, Berkeley, 2003.

REFERENCES TO VOLUME II

Faberon, J.-Y., and F. Faberon (eds.). *Les fédéralismes*. Clermont-Ferrand: Éditions Recherches sur la Cohésion Sociale, 2020.

Fairbank, J.K. 'Maritime and continental in China's history', in J.K. Fairbank (ed.), *The Cambridge History of China, vol. XII, Republican China, 1912–1949*, part 1. Cambridge: Cambridge University Press, 1983, 1–27.

The Great Chinese Revolution, 1800–1985. New York: HarperPerennial, 1987.

Falanruw, M.V.C. 'Food production and ecosystem management in Yap', *ISLA: A Journal of Micronesian Studies* 2:1 (1994), 2–22.

Falgout, S., L. Poyer, and L.M. Carucci. *Memories of War: Micronesians in the Pacific War*. Honolulu: University of Hawai'i Press, 2007.

Fara, P. *Sex, Botany and Empire: The Story of Carl Linnaeus and Joseph Banks*. New York: Columbia University Press, 2003.

Farcau, B. *The Ten Cents War: Chile, Peru, and Bolivia in the War of the Pacific, 1879–1884*. London: Praeger, 2000.

Farmer, J. *Trees in Paradise: The Botanical Conquest of California*. Berkeley, CA: Heyday, 2017.

Fenton, S. (ed.). *For Better or for Worse: Translation as a Tool for Change in the South Pacific*. Manchester: St Jerome, 2004.

Fepuleai, A., E. Weber, K. Németh, T. Muliaina, and V. Iese. 'Eruption styles of Samoan volcanoes represented in tattooing, language and cultural activities of the indigenous people', *Geoheritage* 9:3 (2017), 395–411.

Fer, Y. 'Introduction. Missions, politics and biopolitics in the Pacific Island societies', *Social Sciences and Missions* 31 (2018), 3–5.

Fernández-Armesto, F. *Civilizations: Culture, Ambition, and the Transformation of Nature*. New York: The Free Press, 2001.

Fernández Jilberto, A.E. 'Neoliberalised South–South relations: free trade between Chile and China', in A.E. Fernández Jilberto and B. Hogenboom (eds.), *Latin America Facing China: South–South Relations beyond the Washington Consensus*. Oxford: Berghahn Books, 2012, 77–98.

Figueiredo, F. 'Timor. A presença portuguesa (1769–1945)'. PhD thesis, University of Porto, 2004.

Fiji Government. Council Paper 39/69, *Medical Department: Annual Report for 1968*. Suva: Government Printer, 1969.

Report of the Commission Appointed to Inquire into the Decrease of the Native Population 1893–1896. Suva: Government Printer, 1896.

Finn, J.L. *Tracing the Veins: Of Copper, Culture, and Community from Butte to Chuquicamata*. Berkeley: University of California Press, 1998.

Finney, B. 'Myth, experiment, and the reinvention of Polynesian voyaging', *American Anthropologist* 93:2 (1991), 383–404.

Finney, B., et al. 'Hawaiian historians and the first Pacific History Seminar', in N. Gunson (ed.), *The Changing Pacific: Essays in Honour of H.E. Maude*. Oxford: Oxford University Press, 1978, 308–16.

Firpo, C., and M. Jacobs. 'Taking children, ruling colonies: child removal and colonial subjugation in Australia, Canada, French Indochina, and the United States, 1870–1950s', *Journal of World History* 29:4 (2018), 529–62.

Firth, R. *Symbols: Public and Private*. London: George Allen & Unwin, 1973.

References to Volume II

We the Tikopia: A Sociological Study of Kinship in Primitive Polynesia, 2nd edn. London: George Allen & Unwin, 1967.

Firth, S. 'Contemporary politics of the Pacific Islands', in J. Love (ed.), *The Far East and Australasia 2017*. Abingdon: Routledge, 2017, 756–62.

'New developments in the international relations of the Pacific Islands', *Journal of Pacific History* 48:3 (2013), 286–93.

New Guinea under the Germans. Melbourne: Melbourne University Press, 1984.

Nuclear Playground. Honolulu: University of Hawai'i Press, 1987.

'Security in the Pacific Islands', in J. Love (ed.), *The Far East and Australasia 2017*. Abingdon: Routledge, 2017, 770–6.

'The agencies and ideologies of colonialism', in D. Denoon, S. Firth, J. Linnekin, M. Meleisea, and K. Nero (eds.), *The Cambridge History of the Pacific Islanders*. Cambridge: Cambridge University Press, 1997, 253–60.

'The rise and fall of decolonisation', in D. Denoon (ed.), *Emerging from Empire? Decolonisation in the Pacific*, Proceedings of Workshop, Australian National University, Canberra, July 1997, 10–21.

Firth, S., and K. von Strokirch. 'A nuclear Pacific', in D. Denoon, S. Firth, J. Linnekin, M. Meleisea, and K. Nero (eds.), *The Cambridge History of the Pacific Islanders*. Cambridge: Cambridge University Press, 1997, 324–58.

Fischer, J.R. *Cattle Colonialism: An Environmental History of the Conquest of California and Hawai'i*. Chapel Hill: University of North Carolina Press, 2015.

Fischer, S.R. *The Island at the End of the World: The Turbulent History of Easter Island*. London: Reaktion Books, 2005.

Fisher, D. *France in the South Pacific: Power and Politics*, Canberra: ANU Press, 2013.

Fison, L. 'Address of the president to Section G Anthropology', in A. Morton (ed.), *Report of the Australasian Association for the Advancement of Science* (1892), 144–53.

Fitisemanu, J. 'Maui is more than a vacation destination', 19 November 2019, www .facebook.com/notes/jacob-fitisemanu-jr/maui-is-more-than-a-vacation-destination/ 10155588051978521/.

Fitzgerald, D.T. 'Air ferry routes across the South Pacific', in B.W. Fowle (ed.), *Builders and Fighters: US Army Corps of Engineers*. Fort Belvoir: Office of History, US Army Corps of Engineers, 1992.

Fitzpatrick, G.L., and R.M. Moffat. *Mapping the Lands and Waters of Hawai'i: The Hawaiian Government Survey*. Honolulu: Editions Limited, 2004.

Flanary, L.M. *Tokyo Hula*. Honolulu: Lehua Films, 2019; 72 min. film.

Fletcher, C.H., and B.M. Richmond. *Climate Change in the Federated States of Micronesia: Food and Water Security, Climate Risk Management, and Adaptive Strategies*. Honolulu: US Department of Agriculture Forest Service and the State and Federal Government of FSM, 2010.

Fleurieu, C.P.C., *Voyage autour du Monde: pendant les années 1790, 1791 et 1792*. Paris: De l'Imprimerie de la République, 1798–1800.

Flint, J.M. 'A contribution to the oceanography of the Pacific, compiled from data collected by the United States steamer *Nero* while engaged in the survey of a route for a trans-Pacific cable', *Bulletin of the United States National Museum* 55 (1905), 1–2.

REFERENCES TO VOLUME II

Flood-Keyes Roberts, R. 'Routine of child-welfare work', *Native Medical Practitioner* 2 (1931), 40–3.

Flores, A. [A.F.]. *Uma guerra no districto de Timor*. Macau: Typographia Commercial, [1891].

Flynn, D.O., and A. Giraldez. 'Born again: globalization's sixteenth century origins', *Pacific Economic Review* 13:3 (2008), 359–87.

'Born with a "silver spoon": the origin of world trade in 1571', *Journal of World History* 6:2 (1995), 201–21.

Fojas, C. *Islands of Empire: Pop Culture and U.S. Power*. Austin: University of Texas Press, 2014.

Fornasiero, J., and J. West-Sooty (eds.). *French Designs on Colonial New South Wales*. Adelaide: State Library of South Australia, 2014.

Forster, G. *A Voyage Round the World in His Britannic Majesty's Sloop, Resolution, Commanded by Capt. James Cook, during the Years 1772, 3, 4, and 5*, 2 vols. London: B. White, J. Robson, P. Elmsly, and G. Robinson, 1777.

'Cook, der Entdecker', in *Geschichte der See-Reisen und Entdeckungen im Süd-Meer* . . ., 7 vols. Berlin: Haude und Spener, 1787, vol. vi, 1–106.

'Noch etwas über die Menschenrassen', *Teutsche Merkur* (October–November 1786), 57–86, 150–66.

Forster, J.R., *Observations Made during a Voyage Round the World, on Physical Geography, Natural History, and Ethic Philosophy*. London: G. Robinson, 1778.

Fosberg, F.R. *Vegetation of Bikini Atoll, 1985*. Atoll Research Bulletin 315, National Museum of Natural History. Washington, DC: Smithsonian Institution, 1988.

Foster, R.J., and H.A. Horst (eds.). *The Moral Economy of Mobile Phones: Pacific Islands Perspectives*. Canberra: ANU Press, 2018.

Foucault, M. *L'archéologie du savoir*. Paris: Gallimard, 1969.

Security, Territory, Population: Lectures at the Collège de France, 1977–78. Basingstoke: Palgrave Macmillan, 2007.

The History of Sexuality, vol. 1, An Introduction, trans. R. Hurley. New York: Random House, 1978.

Foucault, M., and J. Miskowiec. 'Of other spaces', *Diacritics* 16:1 (1986), 22–7.

Fox, J.J. (ed.). *The Flow of Life: Essays on Eastern Indonesia*. Cambridge, MA: Harvard University Press, 1980.

Fozdar, F., and K. McGavin (eds.). *Mixed Race Identities in Australia, New Zealand and the Pacific*. London: Routledge, 2017.

França, B. da. *Macau e os seus habitantes: relações entre Macau e Timor*. Lisbon: Imprensa Nacional, 1897.

France, P. *The Charter of the Land: Custom and Colonization in Fiji*. Oxford: Oxford University Press, 1969.

'The Kaunitoni migration: notes in the genesis of a Fijian tradition', *Journal of Pacific History* 1 (1966), 107–13.

Franke, H. 'The Chin Dynasty', in H. Franke and D. Twitchett (eds.), *The Cambridge History of China*, vol. vi, *Alien Regimes and Border States*. Cambridge: Cambridge University Press, 1994, 215–320.

Franklin, M.I. *Postcolonial Politics, the Internet and Everyday Life: Pacific Traversals Online*. London: Routledge, 2004.

830

References to Volume II

Frazer, J. 'Preface', in B. Malinowski, *Argonauts of the Western Pacific: An Account of Native Enterprise and Adventure in the Archipelagoes of Melanesian New Guinea*. London: Routledge & Keegan Paul, 1922), i–xxi.

Freeman, D. *The Pacific*. London: Routledge, 2010.

Friedman, H.M. *Creating an American Lake: United States Imperialism and Strategic Security in the Pacific Basin, 1945–1947*. Westport, CT: Greenwood, 2001.

Friedman, M. 'Free markets and the generals', *Newsweek* (25 January 1982), 59.

Front de Libération Nationale Kanak et Socialiste. Press release, 17 December 2019. 'The FLNKS project for a sovereign Kanaky-New Caledonia'. FLNKS self-publishing, 2018.

Fry, G. *Recapturing the Spirit of 1971: Towards a New Regional Political Settlement in the Pacific*. State, Society & Governance in Melanesia Discussion Paper 2015/3. Canberra: Australia National University, 2015.

Fry, G., and S. Tarte (eds.). *The New Pacific Diplomacy*. Canberra: ANU Press, 2015.

Fujikane, C., and J. Okamura. *Asian Settler Colonialism: From Local Governance to the Habits of Everyday Life in Hawai'i*. Honolulu: University of Hawai'i Press, 2008.

Fujitani, T., G.M. White, and L. Yoneyama (eds.). *Perilous Memories: The Asia-Pacific War(s)*. Durham, NC: Duke University Press, 2001.

Fullagar, K. *The Savage Visit*. Berkeley: University of California Press, 2012.

Fullagar, K., and M.A. McDonnell (eds.). *Facing Empire: Indigenous Experiences in a Revolutionary Age*. Baltimore: Johns Hopkins University Press, 2018.

Funaki, K.P., and Y. Satō. 'Wanted: a strategic dialogue with Pacific Island countries', *The Japan Times* (28 January 2019).

Futter-Puati, D., L. Bryder, J.K. Park, J. Littleton, and P. Herda. 'Partnerships for health: decimating tuberculosis in the Cook Islands, 1920–1975', *Health and Place* 25 (2014), 10–18.

Gaillard, C., and H.I. Manner. 'Yam cultivation on the east coast of New Caledonia: adaptation of agriculture to social and economic changes', *Australian Geographer* 41:4 (2010), 485–505.

Galeano, E. *Memory of Fire*, vol. 1, *Genesis*, 2nd edn. New York: W.W. Norton, 1998. *Open Veins of Latin America: Five Centuries of the Pillage of a Continent*. New York: Monthly Review Press, 1973.

Galvão, A. *Tratado . . . dos diuersos & desuayrados caminhos, por onde nos tempos passados a pimenta & especearia veyo da India ás nossas partes, & assi de todos os descobrimentos antigos & modernos, que são feitos ate a era de mil & quinhentos & cincoenta . . .* Lisbon: Ioam de Barreira, 1563.

Gamble, L. *The Chumash World at European Contact: Power, Trade, and Feasting among Complex Hunter-Gatherers*. Berkeley: University of California Press, 2008.

Gammage, B. 'The Rabaul Strike, 1929', *Journal of Pacific History* 10:3 (1975), 3–29.

García-Bryce, I. *Haya de la Torre and the Pursuit of Power in Twentieth-Century Peru and Latin America*. Chapel Hill: University of North Carolina Press, 2018.

Garden, D.S. *Australia, New Zealand, and the Pacific: An Environmental History*. Santa Barbara, CA: ABC-CLIO, 2005.

Gardiner, C.H. *The Japanese and Peru, 1873–1973*. Albuquerque: University of New Mexico Press, 1975.

REFERENCES TO VOLUME II

Gardiner, W. *Te Mura O Te Ahi: The Story of the Maori Battalion*. Auckland: Reed, 1992.

Gardner, H. 'New heaven and new earth: translation and conversion on Aneityum', *Journal of Pacific History* 41:3 (2006), 293–311.

'Praying for independence: the Presbyterian Church in the decolonisation of Vanuatu', *Journal of Pacific History* 48:2 (2013), 122–43.

Gardner, H., and C. Waters. 'Decolonisation in Melanesia', *Journal of Pacific History* 48:2 (2013), 113–21.

Garrett, J. *Where Nets Were Cast: Christianity in Oceania since World War II*. Suva: Institute of Pacific Studies, 1997.

Gasch-Tomás, J.L. *The Atlantic World and the Manila Galleons: Circulation, Market, and Consumption of Asian Goods in the Spanish Empire, 1565–1650*. Leiden: Brill, 2019.

Gascoigne, J. 'Cross-cultural knowledge exchange in the Age of the Enlightenment', in S. Konishi, M. Nugent, and T. Shellam (eds.), *Indigenous Intermediaries: New Perspectives on Exploration Archives*. Canberra: ANU Press, 2015, 131–46.

Encountering the Pacific in the Age of Enlightenment. Cambridge: Cambridge University Press, 2014.

Joseph Banks and the English Enlightenment: Useful Knowledge and Polite Culture. Cambridge: Cambridge University Press, 1995.

Science in the Service of Empire: Joseph Banks, the British State, and the Uses of Science in the Age of Revolution. Cambridge: Cambridge University Press, 1998.

Gatty, R. *Fijian–English Dictionary: With Notes on Fijian Culture and Natural History*. Suva: Southeast Asia Program, Cornell University, 2010.

Gaynor, J.L. *Intertidal History in Island Southeast Asia: Submerged Genealogy and the Legacy of Coastal Capture*. Ithaca, NY: Cornell University Press, 2016.

Geeves, E.B. 'Child welfare work in Nadroga and Colo West, Fiji', *Native Medical Practitioner* 3:2 (1940), 473–7.

Gegeo, D.W. 'Cultural rupture and indigeneity: the challenge of (re)visioning "place" in the Pacific', *Contemporary Pacific* 13:2 (2001), 467–507.

Geiger, J. *Facing the Pacific: Polynesia and the U.S. Imperial Imagination*. Honolulu: University of Hawai'i Press, 2007.

'Imagined islands: white shadows in the South Seas and cultural ambivalence', *Cinema Journal* 41:3 (2002), 98–121.

Gellner, E. *Nations et nationalisme*. Paris: Bibliothèque Historique Puyot, 1989.

Gelpke, J.H.F.S. 'On the origin of the name Papua', *Bijdragen tot de Taal-, Land- en Volkenkunde* 149 (1993), 318–32.

General Election, In Brief 2017/38. Canberra: Department of Pacific Affairs, Australian National University.

Genz, J.H., et al. *Militarism and Nuclear Testing in the Pacific*. Teaching Oceania Series 1. Interactive I-book. Center for Pacific Islands Studies. Honolulu: University of Hawai'i at Mānoa, 2018, http://hdl.handle.net,10125/42430.

Gibson, W.M. (ed.). *King Kalakaua's Tour round the World: A Sketch of Incidents of Travel, with a Map of the Hawaiian Islands*. Honolulu: P.C. Advertiser Co., 1881.

Gille, B. *Histoire des institutions politiques à Tahiti du XVIIe siècle à nos jours*. Papeete: Ministère de l'Éducation de la Polynésie Française, 2006.

832

References to Volume II

Gilroy, P. *The Black Atlantic: Modernity and Double Consciousness*. Cambridge, MA: Harvard University Press, 1993.

Gilson, R.P. *Samoa 1830–1900: The Politics of a Multi-Cultural Community*. Oxford: Oxford University Press, 1970.

The Cook Islands 1820–1950. Wellington: Victoria University Press, 1980.

Giráldez, A. *The Age of Trade: The Manila Galleons and the Dawn of the Global Economy*. Lanham: Rowman & Littlefield, 2015.

Given, J. 'Born global, made local: multinational enterprise and Australia's early wireless industry', *Australian Economic History Review* 57 (2017), 158–93.

'Not being ernest: uncovering competitors in the foundation of Australian wireless', *Historical Records of Australian Science* 18 (2007), 159–76.

Gladwin, T. 'Canoe travel in the Truk area: technology and its psychological correlates', *American Anthropologist* 60:5 (1958), 893–9.

Goddard, M. 'A categorical failure: "mixed race" in colonial Papua New Guinea', in F. Fozdar and K. McGavin (eds.), *Mixed Race Identities in Australia, New Zealand and the Pacific*. London: Routledge, 2017), 133–46.

Godley, M. 'China: the waking giant', in A. Ali and R. Crocombe (eds.), *Foreign Forces in Pacific Politics*. Suva: Institute for Pacific Studies, University of the South Pacific, 1983, 130–42.

Goldberg, J.J. 'Containerization as a force for change on the waterfront', *Monthly Labor Review* 91:1 (1968), 8–13.

Gonschor, L. 'A power in the world: the Hawaiian Kingdom as a model of hybrid statecraft in Oceania and a progenitor of pan-Oceanianism', PhD thesis, University of Hawai'i, 2016.

A Power in the World: The Hawaiian Kingdom in Oceania. Honolulu: University of Hawai'i Press, 2019.

'French Polynesia', *Contemporary Pacific* 32:1 (2020), 232–9.

'Revisiting the Hawaiian influence on the political thought of Sun Yat-sen', *Journal of Pacific History* 52:1 (2017), 52–67.

Gonzalez, V.V. *Securing Paradise: Tourism and Militarism in Hawai'i and the Philippines*. Durham, NC: Duke University Press, 2013.

González Pizarro, J.A. *La pampa salitrera en Antofagasta: la vida cotidiana durante los ciclos Shanks y Guggenheim en el desierto de Atacama*. Antofagasta: Corporación Pro Antofagasta, 2003.

Goodyear-Ka'ōpua, N. *The Seeds We Planted: Portraits of a Native Hawaiian Charter School*. Minneapolis: University of Minnesota Press. 2013.

Goodyear-Ka'ōpua, N., I. Hussey, and E. Kahunawaika'ala (eds.). *A Nation Rising: Hawaiian Movements for Life, Land, and Sovereignty*. Durham, NC: Duke University Press, 2014.

Gordon-Chipembere, N. (ed.). *Representation and Black Womanhood: The Legacy of Sarah Baartman*. New York: Palgrave Macmillan, 2011.

Gorriti, G. *The Shining Path: A History of the Millenarian War in Peru*, trans. R. Kirk. Chapel Hill: University of North Carolina Press, 1999.

Goss, J., and B. Lindquist. 'Placing movers: an overview of the Asian-Pacific migration system', *Contemporary Pacific* 12:2 (2017), 385–414.

REFERENCES TO VOLUME II

Gotō, K. *Tensions of Empire: Japan and Southeast Asia in the Colonial and Postcolonial World*, ed. and with an intro. by P.H. Kratoska. Athens: Ohio University Press, 2003.

Grace, P. *Chappy*. Auckland: Penguin, 2015.

Tu. Honolulu: University of Hawai'i Press, 2004.

Graham, R. *Independence in Latin America: Contrasts and Comparisons*, 3rd edn. Austin: University of Texas Press, 2013.

Grainger, A. 'From immigrant to overstayer: Samoan identity, rugby, and cultural politics of race and nation in Aotearoa/New Zealand', *Journal of Sport and Social Issues* 30:1 (2006), 45–61.

Great Britain Parliament. *Journals of the House of Commons from November the 16th 1699, in the eleventh year of the reign of King William the Third, to May the 25th 1702, in the first year of the reign of Queen Anne*, reprinted. s.l.: s.n., 1803.

Green, M.J. *By More Than Providence: Grand Strategy and American Power in the Asia Pacific Since 1783*. New York: Columbia University Press, 2017.

Green, R.C. 'Protohistoric Samoan population', in P.V. Kirch and J.-L. Rallu (eds.), *The Growth and Collapse of Pacific Island Societies*. Honolulu: University of Hawai'i Press, 2007, 203–31.

Grimshaw, P. 'Interracial marriages and colonial regimes in Victoria and Aotearoa/New Zealand', *Frontiers* 23:3 (2002), 12–28.

Paths of Duty: American Missionary Wives in Nineteenth-Century Hawaii. Honolulu: University of Hawai'i Press, 1989.

Grove, R.H. *Green Imperialism: Colonial Expansion, Tropical Island Edens, and the Origins of Environmentalism, 1600–1860*. Cambridge: Cambridge University Press, 1995.

Guan, A.C. *Southeast Asia's Cold War: An Interpretative History*. Honolulu: University of Hawai'i Press, 2018.

Guiart, J. *Structure de la chefferie en Mélanésie du sud*, vol. 1. Paris: Institut d'Ethnologie, 1992.

Gunson, N. (ed.). *Australian Reminiscences & Papers of L.E. Threlkeld: Missionary to the Aborigines 1824–1859*, vol. 1. Australian Aboriginal Studies 40. Canberra: Australian Institute of Aboriginal Studies, 1974.

Messengers of Grace: Evangelical Missionaries in the South Pacific 1796–1860. Oxford: Oxford University Press, 1978.

(ed.). *The Changing Pacific: Essays in Honour of H.E. Maude*. Oxford: Oxford University Press, 1978.

'Two indigenous chiefly systems, title and trade', in B.V. Lal and K. Fortune (eds.), *The Pacific Islands: An Encyclopedia*. Honolulu: University of Hawai'i Press, 2000, 132–5.

Gunter, J. 'Kabita-Kakurai, de cada dia: indigenous hierarchies and the Portuguese in Timor', *Portuguese Literary and Cultural Studies* 17/18 (2010), 281–301.

Haberkorn, G. 'Pacific Islands' population and development: facts, fictions and follies', *New Zealand Population Review*, 33/4 (2008), 95–127.

Hackel, S. *Children of Coyote, Missionaries of Saint Francis: Indian–Spanish Relations in Colonial California*. Chapel Hill: University of North Carolina Press, 2005.

Hacker, B.C. *Elements of Controversy: The Atomic Energy Commission and Radiation Safety in Nuclear Weapons Testing 1947–1974*. Berkeley: University of California Press, 1994.

834

References to Volume II

Hadlow, M.L. 'Wireless and empire ambition: wireless telegraphy / telephony and radio broadcasting in the British Solomon Islands Protectorate, South-West Pacific (1914–1947): political, social and developmental perspectives'. PhD thesis, University of Queensland, 2016.

Hägerdal, H. *Lords of the Land, Lords of the Sea: Conflict and Adaptation in Early Colonial Timor, 1600–1800*. Leiden: Brill, 2012.

'Rebellions or factionalism? Timorese forms of resistance in an early colonial context, 1650–1769', *Bijdragen tot de Taal-, Land- en Volkenkunde* 163:1 (2007), 1–33.

Haines, D. 'In search of the "whaheen": Ngai Tahu women, shore whalers, and the meaning of sex in early New Zealand', in T. Ballantyne and A. Burton (eds.), *Moving Subjects: Gender, Mobility, and Intimacy in an Age of Global Empire*. Urbana: University of Illinois Press, 2009, 49–66.

Haines, D., and J. West. 'Crew cultures in the Tasman world', in F. Steel (ed.), *New Zealand and the Sea: Historical Perspectives*. Wellington: Bridget Williams Books, 2018, 181–200.

Halikowski-Smith, S. 'No obvious home. The flight of the Portuguese "tribe" from Makassar to Ayuttahaya and Cambodia during the 1660s', *International Journal of Asian Studies* 7:1 (2010), 1–28.

Hamilton, A. 'The French Catholic Mission to Samoa 1845–1914'. PhD thesis, Australian National University, Canberra, 1997.

Hanazaki, K. 'Ainu Moshir and Yaponesia: Ainu and Okinawan identities in contemporary Japan', in D. Denoon, M. Hudson, and G. McCormack (eds.), *Multicultural Japan: Paleolithic to Postmodern*. Cambridge: Cambridge University Press, 2001, 117–31.

Hanke, L. *The Imperial City of Potosí: An Unwritten Chapter in the History of Spanish America*. The Hague: Martinus Nijhoff, 1956.

Hanke, L., and G. Mendoza (eds.). *Tales of Potosí: Bartolomé Arzáns de Orsúa y Vela*, 3 vols. Providence, RI: Brown University Press, 1965.

Hanlon, D. 'A different historiography for "a handful of chickpeas flung over the sea": approaching the Federated States of Micronesia's deeper past', in W. Anderson et al. (eds.), *Pacific Futures: Past and Present* (Honolulu: University of the Hawai'i Press, 2018), 81–104.

'Another side of Henry Nanpei', *Journal of Pacific History* 23:1 (1988), 36–51.

'Histories of the before: Lelu, Nan Madol, and deep time', in E. Hermann (ed.), *Changing Contexts, Shifting Meanings: Transformations of Cultural Traditions in Oceania*. Honolulu: University of Hawai'i Press in association with the Honolulu Academy of Arts, 2011, 41–55.

Making Micronesia: A Political Biography of Tosiwo Nakayama. Honolulu: University of Hawai'i Press, 2014.

Remaking Micronesia: Discourses over Development in a Pacific Territory, 1944–1982. Honolulu: University of Hawai'i Press, 1998.

Upon a Stone Altar: A History of the Island of Pohnpei to 1890. Honolulu: University of Hawai'i Press, 1988.

Hansen, M., and A. Kanafani. 'Airline hubbing and airport economics in the Pacific market', *Transportation Research Part A*, 24:3 (1990), 217–30.

Hara, K. *Cold War Frontiers in the Asia-Pacific: Divided Territories in the San Francisco System*. New York: Routledge, 2007.

REFERENCES TO VOLUME II

Harkin, N. 'The poetics of (re)mapping archives: memory in the blood', *Journal of the Association for the Study of Australian Literature* 14:3 (2014), 1–15.

Harris, J. *Navigantium atque Itinerantium Bibliotheca: or, a Compleat Collection of Voyages and Travels: Consisting of above Four Hundred of the most Authentick Writers* ... [ed J. Campbell], 2nd edn, 2 vols. London: T. Woodward et al., 1744–8.

Harvey, D. *A Brief History of Neoliberalism.* Oxford: Oxford University Press, 2005.

Hasebe, K. 'Nanyō Guntō-jin no Kao Rinkaku-gata' (The facial shapes of South Sea Islanders), *Jinruigaku Zasshi (Anthropology Magazine)* 56:1, Bulletin Edition 639, January 1942.

Hasegawa, R. *Chizu kara Kieta Shimajima: Maboroshi no Nihon-ryō to Nanyō Tankenka-tachi (The Islands that Disappeared from the Map: Phantom Japanese Territories and Japanese Southern Explorers).* Tokyo: Yoshikawa Kōbunkan, 2011.

Hasteen, J.C. *Americanos: Latin America's Struggle for Independence.* Oxford: Oxford University Press, 2008.

Hattori, A.P. *Colonial Dis-ease: US Navy Health Policies and the Chamorros of Guam.* Honolulu: University of Hawai'i Press, 2004.

'Guardians of our soil: indigenous responses to post-World War II military land appropriations on Guam', in L.E.A. Ma (ed.), *Farms, Firms, and Runways: Perspectives on U.S. Military Bases in the Western Pacific.* Chicago: Imprint Publications, 2001, 106–202.

'Textbook tells: gender, race, and decolonizing Guam history textbooks in the 21st century', *AlterNative* 14:2 (2018), 173–84.

'"The cry of the little people of Guam": American colonialism, medical philanthropy, and the Susana Hospital for Chamorro women, 1898–1941', *Health and History* 8:1 (2006), 1–23.

Hau'ofa, E. 'A new Oceania: an interview with Epeli Hau'ofa by Juniper Ellis', *Antipodes* 15:1 (2001), 22–5.

'Epilogue, pasts to remember', in R. Borofsky (ed.), *Remembrance of Pacific Pasts: An Invitation to Remake History.* Honolulu: University of Hawai'i Press, 2000, 453–71.

Kisses in the Nederends. Auckland: Penguin, 1987.

'Our Sea of Islands', in E. Waddell, V. Naidu, and E. Hau'ofa (eds.), *A New Oceania: Rediscovering Our Sea of Islands.* Suva: School of Social and Economic Development, University of the South Pacific in association with Beake House, 1993, 2–16.

'Our Sea of Islands', *Contemporary Pacific* 6:1 (1994), 147–61.

Tales of the Tikongs. Auckland: Penguin, 1983.

'The ocean in us', in A. Hooper (ed.), *Culture and Sustainable Development in the Pacific.* Canberra: ANU Press and Asia Pacific Press, 2005, 32–43.

'We are the ocean', in *We Are The Ocean: Selected Works.* Honolulu: University of Hawai'i Press, 2008, 41–59.

Hau'ofa, E., and N. Thomas. '"We were still Papuans": a 2006 interview with Epeli Hau'ofa', *Contemporary Pacific* 24:1 (2012), 120–32.

Hawaiian Kingdom Government. *Treaties and Conventions Concluded between the Hawaiian Kingdom and Other Powers since 1825.* Honolulu: Elele Book, Card and Job Print, 1887.

Hawkesworth, J. *An Account of the Voyages Undertaken by the Order of His Present Majesty, for Making Discoveries in the Southern Hemisphere*, 3 vols. Dublin: James Williams, 1775.

836

References to Volume II

Headrick, D. 'Shortwave radio and its impact on international telecommunications between the wars', *History and Technology* 11 (1994), 21–32.

The Tentacles of Progress: Technology Transfer in the Age of Imperialism, 1850–1940. Oxford: Oxford University Press, 1988.

Hedrich, D.J. 'Towards an understanding of Samoan star mounds', *Journal of the Polynesian Society* 100:4 (1991), 381–435.

Hegel, G.W.F. *The Philosophy of Right*, trans. A. White. Indianapolis: Hackett, 2015.

Heintze, B. 'Luso-African feudalism in Angola? the vassal treaties of the 16th to the 18th century', *Revista Portuguesa de História* 18 (1980), 111–31.

Helu, 'I.F. *Critical Essays: Cultural Perspectives from the South Seas.* Canberra: Journal of Pacific History, 1999.

Hempenstall, P.J. *Pacific Islanders under German Rule: A Study in the Meaning of Colonial Resistance.* Canberra: ANU Press, 1978.

Hendery, R. *One Man Is an Island: The Speech Community William Marsters Begat on Palmerston Island.* London: Battlebridge, 2015.

Henige, D. *Numbers from Nowhere: The American Indian Contact Population Debate.* Norman: University of Oklahoma Press, 1998.

Henningham, S. 'France and the South Pacific in the 1980s: an Australian perspective', *Journal de la Société des Océanistes* 92–3 (1991), 21–45.

Henry, R., W. Jeffery, and C. Pam. *Heritage and Climate Change in Micronesia: A Report on a Pilot Study Conducted on Moch Island, Mortlocks Islands, Chuuk, Federated States of Micronesia.* Townsville: James Cook University, 2008.

Herbert, C. *Culture and Anomie: Ethnographic Imagination in the Nineteenth Century.* Chicago: University of Chicago Press, 1991.

Herda, P. 'Introduction: writing the lives of some extraordinary Polynesian women', *Journal of the Polynesian Society* 123:2 (2014), 113–28.

Hereniko, V. 'Representations of cultural identities', in K.R. Howe, R.C. Kiste, and B.V. Lal (eds.), *Tides of History.* Honolulu: University of Hawai'i Press, 1994, 406–34.

'Representations of Pacific Islanders in film and video', *Documentary Box* 14 (1999), 18–20.

Herman, R.D.K. 'Inscribing empire: Guam and the War in the Pacific National Park', *Political Geography* 27 (2008), 630–51.

Hermann, E. 'Emotions and the relevance of the past: historicity and ethnicity among the Banabans of Fiji', *History and Anthropology* 16:3 (2005), 275–91.

Herr, R.A. 'Regionalism, strategic denial and South Pacific security', *Journal of Pacific History* 21:4 (1986), 170–82.

Herrera y Tordesillas, A. de. *Historia general de los hechos de los Castellanos en las Islas i Tierra firme del mar Oceano . . .*, 4 vols. Madrid: Iuan Flamenco and Iuan de la Cuesta, 1601–15.

Hespanha, A.M. *Filhos da terra: identidades mestiças nos confins da expansão portuguesa.* Lisbon: Tinta-da-China, 2019.

Hessler, S. (ed.). *Tidalectics: Imagining an Oceanic Worldview through Art and Science.* Cambridge, MA: MIT Press, 2018.

Hezel, F.X. 'Christianity in Micronesia', in C.E. Farhadian (ed.), *Introducing World Christianity.* Malden, MA: Wiley-Blackwell, 2012, 230–43.

'From conversion to conquest: the early Spanish mission in the Marianas', *Journal of Pacific History* 17:3 (1982), 115–37.

Strangers in Their Own Land: A Century of Colonial Rule in the Caroline and Marshall Islands. Honolulu: University of Hawai'i Press, 1995.

The First Taint of Civilization: A History of the Caroline and Marshall Islands in Pre-Colonial Days, 1521–1885. Honolulu: University of Hawai'i Press, 1983.

Hicks, D. *Tetum Ghosts and Kin: Fertility and Gender in East Timor.* 2nd edn. Long Grove: Waveland Press, 2004.

Hiery, H.J. (ed.). *Die Deutsche Südsee 1884–1914: Ein Handbuch.* Paderborn: Ferdinand Schöningh, 2001.

Higuchi, W. *Islanders' Japanese Assimilation and Their Sense of Discrimination.* Mangilao: University of Guam Micronesian Area Research Center, 1993.

'Japan and War reparations in Micronesia', *Journal of Pacific History* 30:1 (1995), 87–98.

The Japanese Administration of Guam, 1941–1944: A Study of Occupation and Integration Policies, with Japanese Oral Histories. Jefferson, NC: McFarland, 2013.

Hill, B. 'Seats in parliament for overseas Tongans seen as problematic'. *ABC Radio Australia*, 1 June 2017, www.abc.net.au/radio-australia/programs/pacificbeat/seats-in-parliament-for-overseas-tongans-seen-as/8580498.

Hill, R.S. *State Authority, Indigenous Autonomy: Crown–Maori Relations in New Zealand/ Aotearoa 1900–1950.* Wellington: Victoria University Press, 2004.

Hindmarsh, B. 'Patterns of conversion in early Evangelical history', in B. Stanley (ed.), *Christian Missions and the Enlightenment.* Grand Rapids, MI: Eerdmans, 2001, 71–98.

Ho, D. 'The burning shore: Fujian and the coastal depopulation, 1661–1683', in T. Andrade and Xing Hang (eds.), *Sea Rovers, Silver, and Samurai: Maritime East Asia in Global History, 1550–1700.* Honolulu: University of Hawai'i Press, 2016.

Ho, P.T. 'The introduction of American food plants into China', *American Anthropologist* 57:2 (1955), 191–201.

Hoare, M. *Norfolk Island: A Revised and Enlarged History, 1774–1998.* Rockhampton: Central Queensland University Press, 1999.

Hobsbawm, E. *Nations and Nationalism since 1780: Programme, Myth, Reality.* Cambridge: Cambridge University Press, 1989.

Hobsbawm, E., and T. Ranger (eds.). *The Invention of Tradition.* Cambridge: Cambridge University Press, 1983.

Hodge, M. 'Archaeological views of Aztec culture', *Journal of Archaeological Research* 6:3 (1998), 195–238.

Hoffenberg, P.H. 'Displaying an oceanic nation and society: the Kingdom of Hawai'i at nineteenth-century international exhibitions', in R. Fulton and P.H. Hoffenberg (eds.), *Oceania and the Victorian Imagination: Where All Things Are Possible.* Aldershot: Ashgate, 2013, 59–76.

Hoffmann, T. 'The reimplementation of the ra'ui: coral reef management in Rarotonga, Cook Islands', *Coastal Management* 30 (2002), 401–18.

Hofmeyr, I., U. Dhupelia-Mesthrie, and P. Kaarsholm. 'Durban and Cape Town as port cities: reconsidering Southern African Studies from the Indian Ocean', *Journal of Southern African Studies* 42:3 (2016), 375–87.

References to Volume II

Hokowhitu, B. 'Tackling Māori masculinity: genealogy of savagery and sport', *Contemporary Pacific* 16:2 (2004), 259–84.

Hombron, J.-B. 'Aperçu sur la côte nord de l'Australie et sur la côte sud de la Nouvelle-Guinée; description de leurs habitants', *Comptes rendus hebdomadaires des séances de l'Académie des Sciences* 20 (1845), 1568–73.

De l'homme dans ses rapports avec la création, vol. 1 in J.-B. Hombron and H. Jacquinot, Zoologie, 5 vols., Voyage au pôle sud et dans l'Océanie sur les corvettes l'Astrolabe et la Zélée ... pendant les années 1837–1838–1839–1840. Paris: Gide, 1846.

Hommon, R.J. *The Ancient Hawaiian State: Origins of a Political Society*. Oxford: Oxford University Press, 2013.

Hooker, J.D. (ed.). *Journal of the Right Hon. Sir Joseph Banks* ... London: Macmillan, 1896.

Horn, J. 'Primacy of the Pacific under the Hawaiian Kingdom'. MA thesis, University of Hawai'i, 1951.

Horne, G. *The White Pacific: U.S. Imperialism and Black Slavery in the South Seas after the Civil War*. Honolulu: University of Hawai'i Press, 2007.

Horowitz, A.J. *Nuclear Savage*. Santa Fe: Primordial Soup Company and Adam Jonas Horowitz, 2011.

Hoshino, N. 'Racial contacts across the Pacific and the creation of *minzoku* in the Japanese empire', *Inter-Asia Cultural Studies* 17:2 (2016), 186–205.

Hoskins, J. *The Play of Time: Kodi Perspectives on Calendars, History and Exchange*. Berkeley: University of California Press, 1997.

Hoston, G.A. 'The state, modernity, and the fate of liberalism in prewar Japan', *Journal of Asian Studies* 51:2 (1992), 287–316.

Howard, C.P. *Mariquita: A Tragedy of Guam*. Suva: Institute of Pacific Studies of the University of the South Pacific, 1986.

Howard, M. 'Vanuatu: the myth of Melanesian socialism', *Labour, Capital and Society* 16:2 (1983), 176–203.

Howe, K.R. *Nature, Culture, and History: The 'Knowing' of Oceania*. Honolulu: University of Hawai'i Press, 2000.

'Recalling the Coombs – Pacific History 1970–73', in B.V. Lal and A. Ley (eds.), *The Coombs, House of Memories*? Canberra: Pandanus Press, 2006, 265–8.

'The fate of the "savage" in Pacific historiography', *New Zealand Journal of History* 11:2 (1977), 137–54.

'The fortunes of the Naisilines: portrait of a chieftainship', in D. Scarr (ed.), *More Pacific Islands Portraits*. Canberra: ANU Press, 1978, 1–18.

(ed.). *Vaka Moana: Voyages of the Ancestors: The Discovery and Settlement of the Pacific*. Auckland: David Bateman, 2006.

Where the Waves Fall: A New South Sea Islands History from First Settlement to Colonial Rule. Honolulu: University of Hawai'i Press, 1984.

Howes, S., and B. Orton. 'For Tonga, Australian labour mobility more important than aid and trade combined', 2020, https://devpolicy.org/for-tonga-australian-labour-mobility-more-important-than-aid-and-trade-combined-20200121/.

Hoyle, M., and L. Millar. 'The challenge of records and archives education and training in the Pacific', *Archives & Manuscripts* 32:2 (2004), 114–41.

Hsieh, C.-m. 'Geographical exploration by the Chinese', in H. Friis (ed.), *The Pacific Basin: A History of Its Geographical Exploration*. New York: Geographical Society, 1967, 87–95.

Hu-Dehart, E. 'Coolies, shopkeepers, pioneers: the Chinese of Mexico and Peru (1849–1930)', *Amerasia* 15:2 (1989), 91–116.

Huff, W.G. *The Economic Growth of Singapore*. Cambridge: Cambridge University Press, 1994.

Hughes, H. 'Aid has failed the Pacific', Centre for Independent Studies, Issue Analysis 33, May 2003, www.cis.org.au/publications/issue-analysis/aid-has-failed-the-pacific/.

Huguenin, P. *Raiatea la sacrée*. Papeete: Edition Haere Po, 2005; reprint of 1st edn, 1902.

Hummels, D. 'Transportation costs and international trade in the second era of globalization', *Journal of Economic Perspectives* 21:3 (2007), 131–54.

Hunt, T.L., F. Black, et al. Book review forum, *Pacific Studies* 13:3 (1990), 255–301.

Hunt, T., and C. Lipo. 'Ecological catastrophe, collapse, and the myth of "ecocide" on Rapa Nui (Easter Island)', in P. McAnany and N. Yoffee (eds.), *Questioning Collapse: Human Resilience, Ecological Vulnerability, and the Aftermath of Empire*. Cambridge: Cambridge University Press, 2010, 21–44.

'The archaeology of Rapa Nui (Easter Island)', in E.E. Cochrane and T.L. Hunt (eds.), *The Oxford Handbook of Prehistoric Oceania*. Oxford: Oxford University Press, 2018, 416–49.

Hutchins, J.G.B. *The American Maritime Industries and Public Policy, 1789–1914*. Cambridge, MA: Harvard University Press, 1941.

Huurdeman, A.A. *The Worldwide History of Telecommunications*. New York: Wiley, 2003.

IATA. *WATS 2016 – World Air Transport Statistics*. Montreal: International Air Transport Association, 2016.

Iati, I. 'Pacific regionalism and the Polynesian leaders' group', *Round Table* 106:2 (2017), 175–85.

Igarashi, Y. 'Mothra's gigantic egg: consuming the South Pacific in 1960s Japan', in W. Tsutsui and M. Ito (eds.), *In Godzilla's Footsteps: Japanese Pop Culture Icons on the Global Stage*. New York: Palgrave Macmillan, 2006, 83–102.

Igler, D. 'Diseased goods: global exchanges in the eastern Pacific Basin, 1770–1850', *American Historical Review* 109:3 (2004), 693–719.

The Great Ocean: Pacific Worlds from Captain Cook to the Gold Rush. Oxford: Oxford University Press, 2013.

Iitaka, S. 'Appropriating successive colonial experiences to represent national culture: a case analysis of the revival of war canoes in Palau, Micronesia', *People and Culture in Oceania* 24 (2009), 1–29.

Ilalio, M. 'Polynesian leaders groups formed in Samoa', *Samoa Observer*, http://archives.pireport.org/archive/2011/November/11-21-01.htm.

Imada, A.L. *Aloha America: Hula Circuits through U.S. Empire*. Durham, NC: Duke University Press, 2012.

Imafuku, R. 'Noah's stories in shaky archipelagos: Martinique, Haiti, Fukushima', *Open Democracy*, 8 June, 2012.

Imaizumi, Y. *Nihon Teikoku Hōkaiki 'Hikiage' no Hikaku Kenkyū (Comparative Studies of 'Returnees' during the Fall of the Japanese Empire)*. Tokyo: Nihon Keizai Hyōronsha, 2016.

References to Volume II

Ing, T. *Reclaiming Kalākaua: Nineteenth Century Perspectives on a Hawaiian Sovereign.* Honolulu: University of Hawai'i Press. 2019.

Inglis, A. *'Not a White Woman Safe': Sexual Anxiety and Politics in Port Moresby, 1920–1934.* Canberra: ANU Press, 1974.

Inglis, K.A. 'Disease and the "other": the role of medical imperialism in Oceania', in G.D. Smithers and B.N. Newman (eds.), *Native Diasporas: Indigenous Identities and Settler Colonialism in the Americas.* Lincoln: University of Nebraska Press, 2014, 385–410.

Mai Lepera: Disease and Displacement in Nineteenth-Century Hawaii. Honolulu: University of Hawai'i Press, 2013.

'Nā hoa o ka pilikia (friends of affliction): a sense of community in the Molokai leprosy settlement of 19th century Hawai'i', *Journal of Pacific History* 52:3 (2017), 287–301.

Inglis, K.S. 'War, race, and loyalty in New Guinea, 1939–1945', in *The History of Melanesia: Papers Delivered at a Seminar Sponsored by the University of Papua and New Guinea [et al.] and held at Port Moresby.* Port Moresby: University of Papua and New Guinea, 1969, 503–29.

Inoue, M. *Wasurerareta Shimajima: 'Nanyō Guntō' no Gendai-shi (Forgotten Islands: A Modern History of the South Sea Islands of Japan).* Tokyo: Heibonsha Shinsho, 2015.

Inso, J. *Timor – 1912.* Lisbon: Cosmos, 1939.

International Business Publications. *Pitcairn Islands Business Law Handbook: Strategic Information and Basic Laws.* Washington, DC: IBP, 2013.

Inti-Illimani. 'Vino del Mar', www.youtube.com/watch?v=qBMJdAKI0X4.

Ip, M. *Being Maori Chinese: Mixed Identities.* Auckland: Auckland University Press, 2008.

'Maori–Chinese encounters: indigine–immigrant interaction in New Zealand', *Asian Studies Review* 2:2 (2003), 227–52.

'Redefining Chinese female migration: from exclusion to transnationalism', in L. Fraser and K. Pickles (eds.), *Shifting Centres: Women and Migration in New Zealand History.* Dunedin: University of Otago Press, 2002, 149–66.

(ed.). *The Dragon and the Taniwha: Maori and Chinese in New Zealand.* Auckland: Auckland University Press, 2009.

IPCC (Intergovernmental Panel on Climate Change). 'AR6 climate change 2021: impacts, adaptation and vulnerability', www.ipcc.ch/report/sixth-assessment-report-working-group-ii.

ISPF (Institut de la Statistique de la Polynésie Française). *Recensement de la population 2017.* Papeete: ISPF, 2018.

ITU. *ITU Historical Statistics (1849–1967).* Geneva: International Telecommunication Union, 2018, www.itu.int/en/history/Pages/HistoricalStatistics.aspx.

'*Percentage of individuals using the Internet*'. Geneva: International Telecommunication Union, 2018, www.itu.int/en/ITU-D/Statistics/Pages/stat/default.asp.

'Iwi leaders call for repatriation', *The Northern Advocate* (Whangarei, New Zealand), 16 March 2012, B:11.

Jaffer, A. *Lascars and Indian Ocean Seafaring, 1780–1860.* Rochester: Boydell and Brewer, 2015.

Jayaraman, T.K., C.K. Choong, and R. Kumar. 'Role of remittances in economic growth in Pacific Island countries: a study of Samoa', *Perspectives on Global Development and Technology* 8:4 (2009), 611–27.

Jeffery, B. 'World War II underwater cultural heritage sites in Truk Lagoon: considering a case for World Heritage listing', *International Journal of Nautical Archaeology* 33 (2004), 106–21.

Jenkinson, H. 'The English archivist: a new profession', in R.H. Ellis and P. Walne (eds.), *Selected Writings of Hilary Jenkinson*. Chicago: Society of American Archivists, 2003, 236–59.

Jetñil-Kijiner, K. *Iep jāltok*. Tucson: University of Arizona Press, 2017.

Johnson, D. *Bruny D'Entrecasteaux and His Encounter with Tasmanian Aborigines: From Provence to Recherche Bay*. Lawson, NSW: Blue Mountain, 2012.

Johnson, D.D., with G.D. Best. *The United States in the Pacific: Private Interests and Public Policy, 1784–1899*. Westport, CT: Praeger, 1995.

Johnson, G. *The All Red Line: The Annals and Aims of the Pacific Cable Project*. Ottawa: James Hope & Sons, 1903.

Johnson, R.K.K. *The Kumulipo Mind: A Global Heritage in the Polynesian Creation Myth*. Honolulu: University of Hawai'i Press, 2000.

Johnston, A. 'Australian travel writing', in N. Das and T. Youngs (eds.), *The Cambridge History of Travel Writing*. Cambridge: Cambridge University Press, 2019, 267–82.

'Exhibiting the Enlightenment: Joseph Banks's *Florilegium* and colonial knowledge production', *Journal of Australian Studies* 43:1 (2019), 118–32.

Missionary Writing and Empire, 1800–1860. Cambridge: Cambridge University Press, 2003.

Johnston, A., and M. Rolls (eds.). *Reading Robinson: Companion Essays to Friendly Mission*. Clayton: Monash University Press, 2012 [2008].

Johnston, B.R. 'Atomic times in the Pacific', *Anthropology Now* 1:2 (2009), 1–9.

'"More like us than mice": radiation experiments with indigenous peoples', in B.R. Johnston (ed.), *Half-lives and Half-truths: Confronting the Radioactive Legacies of the Cold War*. Santa Fe, NM: School for Advanced Research Press, 2007, 25–54.

'Nuclear disaster: the Marshall Islands experiences and lessons for a post-Fukushima world', in E. DeLoughery, J. Didur, and A. Carrigan (eds.), *Global Ecologies and the Environmental Humanities: Postcolonial Approaches*. London: Routledge, 2016, 140–61.

Johnston, B.R., and B.T. Abraham. 'Environmental disaster and resilience: the Marshall Islands experience continues to unfold', *Indigenous Policy Journal* 28:3 (2017), www .culturalsurvival.org.

Johnston, B.R., and H. Barker. *Consequential Damages of Nuclear War: The Rongelap Report*. Walnut Creek, CA: Left Coast Press, 2008.

Johnston, H. *Ho'oulu Hawai'i: The King Kalākaua Era*. Honolulu: Honolulu Museum of Art, 2018.

Jolly, M. 'Imagining Oceania: indigenous and foreign representations of a Sea of Islands', *Contemporary Pacific* 19:2 (2007), 508–45.

'Introduction. Colonial and postcolonial plots in histories of maternities and modernities', in K. Ram and M. Jolly (eds.), *Maternities and Modernities: Colonial and Postcolonial Experiences in Asia and the Pacific*. Cambridge: Cambridge University Press, 1998, 1–25.

'Moving objects: reflections on Oceanic collections', in E. Gnecchi-Ruscone and A. Paini (eds.), *Tides of Innovation in Oceania: Value, Materiality and Place*. Canberra: ANU Press, 2017, 77–114.

'Oceanic hauntings? Race–culture–place between Vanuatu and Hawai'i', *Journal of Intercultural Studies* 28:1 (2007), 99–112.

'On the edge? Deserts, oceans, islands', *Contemporary Pacific* 13:2 (2001), 417–66.

References to Volume II

'Other mothers: maternal "insouciance" and the depopulation debate in Fiji and Vanuatu, 1890–1930', in K. Ram and M. Jolly (eds.), *Maternities and Modernities: Colonial and Postcolonial Experiences in Asia and the Pacific*. Cambridge: Cambridge University Press, 1998, 177–212.

Women of the Place: Kastom, Colonialism and Gender in Vanuatu. Philadelphia: Harwood, 1994.

Jolly, M., and M. Macintyre. *Family and Gender in the Pacific: Domestic Contradictions and Colonial Impact*. Cambridge: Cambridge University Press, 1988.

Jones, A., and P. Herda (eds.). *Bitter Sweet: Indigenous Women in the Pacific*. Dunedin: Otago University Press, 2000.

Jones, A., and K. Jenkins. *He Kōrero, Words between Us: First Maori–Pakeha Conversations on Paper*. Wellington: Huia, 2011.

Jones, D.S. 'Virgin soils revisited', *William and Mary Quarterly* 60:4 (2003), 703–42.

Jones, E., L. Frost, and C. White. *Coming Full Circle: An Economic History of the Pacific Rim*. Oxford: Oxford University Press, 1993.

Jones, R.T. *Empire of Extinction: Russians and the North Pacific's Strange Beasts of the Sea, 1741–1867*. Oxford: Oxford University Press, 2014.

'Kelp highways, Siberian girls in Maui, and nuclear walruses: the North Pacific in a Sea of Islands', *Journal of Pacific History* 49:4 (2014), 373–95.

'The environment', in D. Armitage and A. Bashford (eds.), *Pacific Histories: Ocean, Land, People*. Basingstoke: Palgrave Macmillan, 2014, 121–42.

Joppien, R., and B. Smith. *The Art of Captain Smith's Voyages*, 4 vols. Oxford: Oxford University Press, 1985–7.

Julien, C. *America's Empire*, trans. R. Bruce. New York: Pantheon Books, 1971.

Jun, H.H. *Race for Citizenship: Black Orientalism and Asian Uplife from Pre-Emancipation to Neoliberal America*. New York: New York University Press, 2011.

Kaeppler, A.L. *'Artificial Curiosities': Being an Exposition of Native Manufactures Collected on the Three Pacific Voyages of Captain James Cook, R.N., at the Bernice Pauahi Bishop Museum, January 18, 1978–August 31, 1978*. Honolulu: Bishop Museum Press, 1978.

The Pacific Arts of Polynesia and Micronesia. Oxford: Oxford University Press, 2008.

Kaeppler, A.L., C. Kaufman, and D. Newton. *L'art océanien*. Paris: Citadelles & Mazenod, 1993.

Kaeppler, A.L., and J.W. Love. *Australia and the Pacific Islands*. New York: Garland, 1998.

Ka'ili, T.O. *'Hoa patterns: binary, repetition, symmetry, kupesi, and mana'*, keynote address during the Pacific Patterns session of the Interstices Under Construction Symposium, Auckland University of Technology, 4 June 2017.

Marking indigeneity: the Tongan art of sociospatial relations. Tucson: University of Arizona Press, 2017.

'Tāvani: intertwining tā and vā in Tongan reality and philology', *Pacific Studies* 40:1/2 (2017): 62–78.

Ka'ili, T.O., O. Māhina, and P.-A. Addo. 'Introduction: tā–vā (time–space): the birth of an indigenous Moana theory', *Pacific Studies* 40:1/2 (2017), 1–17.

Kaima, S. 'Education and training for archivists and record keepers in the Pacific', *Information Development* 15:1 (1999), 51–5.

REFERENCES TO VOLUME II

Kamakau, S.M. *Ke Aupuni Mōʻī: Ka Moʻolelo Hawaiʻi no Kauikeaouli Keiki Hoʻoilina a Kamehameha a me ke Aupuni āna i Noho Mōʻī ai.* Honolulu: Kamehameha Schools Press, 2001.

Ke Kumu Aupuni: Ka Moʻolelo Hawaiʻi no Kamehameha Ka Naʻi Aupuni a me kāna Aupuni i Hoʻokumu ai. Honolulu: ʻAhahui ʻŌlelo Hawaiʻi, 1996.

Kameʻeleihiwa, L. ʻHawaiʻi-nui-akea cousins: ancestral gods and bodies of knowledge are treasures for the descendants', *Te Kaharoa* 2:1 (2009), 42–63.

Native Land and Foreign Desires: Ko Hawaiʻi Āina a me Nā Koi Puʻumake a ka Poʻe Haole. Honolulu: Bishop Museum Press, 1992.

Kamehiro, S.L. *The Arts of Kingship: Hawaiian Art and National Culture of the Kalākaua Era.* Honolulu: University of Hawaiʻi Press, 2009.

Kammen, D. *Three Centuries of Conflict in East Timor.* New Brunswick: Rutgers University Press, 2015.

Kanahele, P.K. *Ka Honua Ola: ʻeliʻeli Kau Mai (The Living Earth: Descend, Deepen the Revelation).* Honolulu: Kamehameha Publishing, 2011.

Kanemasu, Y., and G. Molnar. ʻPride of the people: Fijian rugby labour migration and collective identity', *International Review for the Sociology of Sport* 48:6 (2013), 720–35.

Kant, I. ʻBestimmung des Begriffs einer Menschenrace', *Berlinische Monatsschrift* 6 (1785), 390–417.

ʻUeber den Gebrauch teleologischer Principien in der Philosophie', *Teutsche Merkur* (January–February 1788), 36–52, 107–36.

Kaplan, A. *The Anarchy of Empire in the Making of U.S. Culture.* Cambridge, MA: Harvard University Press, 2002.

Kaplan, M., and J.D. Kelly. ʻRethinking resistance: dialogics of "disaffection" in colonial Fiji', *American Ethnologist* 21 (1994), 123–51.

Kauanui, J.K. *Hawaiian Blood: Colonialism and the Politics of Sovereignty and Indigeneity.* Durham, NC: Duke University Press, 2008.

Kawamura, M. *Nanyō-Karafuto no Nihon Bungaku (Japanese Literature of the South Seas and Sakhalin).* Tokyo: Chikuma Shobō, 1994.

Keesing, R.M. ʻCreating the past: custom and identity in the Pacific', *Contemporary Pacific* 1:1–2 (1989), 19–42.

Kelon, P. *Epidemics and Enslavement: Biological Catastrophe in the Native Southeast.* Lincoln: University of Nebraska Press, 2007.

Kemble, J.H. ʻPacific Mail service between Panama and San Francisco, 1849–1851', *Pacific Historical Review* 2 (1933), 405–17.

ʻThe genesis of the Pacific Mail Steamship Company', *California Historical Society Quarterly* 13 (1934), 386–406.

Kempf, W. ʻ"Songs cannot die": ritual composing and the politics of emplacement among the Banabans resettled on Rabi Island in Fiji', *Journal of the Polynesian Society* 112:1 (2003), 33–64.

Kempf, W., and E. Hermann. ʻReconfigurations of place and ethnicity: positionings, performances and politics of relocated Banabans in Fiji', *Oceania* 75:4 (2005), 368–86.

Kennedy, P.M. *The Samoan Tangle: A Study in Anglo-German-American Relations, 1878–1900.* St Lucia: Queensland University Press, 1974.

Keown, M. *Pacific Islands Writing: The Postcolonial Literatures of Aotearoa/New Zealand and the Pacific.* Oxford: Oxford University Press, 2007.

References to Volume II

Ketelaar, E. 'Access: the democratic imperative', *Archives and Manuscripts* 34:2 (2006), 62–81.

'Archives as spaces of memory', *Journal of the Society of Archivists* 29:1 (2008), 9–27.

Kettle, E. *That They Might Live.* Sydney: F.P. Leonard, 1979.

Kim, H. *Holy War in China: The Muslim Rebellion and State in Chinese Central Asia, 1864–1877.* Stanford: Stanford University Press, 2004.

Kimberley Declaration. International Indigenous Peoples Summit on Sustainable Development, Khoi-San Territory, Kimberley, South Africa, 20–23 August 2002, https://digitallibrary.un.org/record/499219?ln=en.

Kinloch, P. *Talking Health but Doing Sickness: Studies in Samoan Health.* Wellington: Victoria University Press, 1985.

Kirch, P.V. *A Shark Going Inland Is My Chief: The Island Civilization of Ancient Hawai'i.* Berkeley: University of California Press, 2012.

'Concluding remarks', in P.V. Kirch and J.-L. Rallu (eds.), *The Growth and Collapse of Pacific Island Societies: Archaelogical and Demographic Perspectives.* Honolulu: University of Hawai'i Press, 2007, 326–38.

How Chiefs Became Kings: Divine Kingship and the Rise of Archaic States in Ancient Hawai'i. Berkeley: University of California Press, 2010.

'"Like shoals of fish": archaelogy and population in pre-contact Hawai'i', in P.V. Kirch and J.-L. Rallu (eds.), *The Growth and Collapse of Pacific Island Societies: Archaelogical and Demographic Perspectives.* Honolulu: University of Hawai'i Press, 2007, 52–69.

'Peopling of the Pacific: a holistic anthropological perspective', *Annual Review of Anthropology* 39 (2010), 131–48.

Review of 'The Horror', *Contemporary Pacific* 2:2 (1990), 394–6.

Kirch, P.V., and J.-L. Rallu. 'Long-term demographic evolution in the Pacific Islands', in P.V. Kirch and J.-L. Rallu (eds.), *The Growth and Collapse of Pacific Island Societies: Archaelogical and Demographic Perspectives.* Honolulu: University of Hawai'i Press, 2007, 1–14.

(eds.). *The Growth and Collapse of Pacific Island Societies: Archaelogical and Demographic Perspectives.* Honolulu: University of Hawai'i Press, 2007.

Kisō, T. *Uta no Furusato to Kikō (The Birthplace and Environment of Songs).* Tokyo: Tokyo Hōsō Shuppan Kyōkai, 1986.

Kissling, C.C. 'Networks enabling air transport services in the South Pacific: 40 years of change', in D.T. Duvall (ed.), *Air Transport in the Asia Pacific.* New York: Routledge, 2016, 33–51.

Kiste, R.C., and M. Marshall (eds.). *Anthropology in Micronesia: Assessing Fifty Years of American Involvement.* Honolulu: University of Hawai'i Press, 1999.

Kituai, A.I.K. *My Gun, My Brother: The World of the Papua New Guinea Colonial Police, 1920–1960.* Honolulu: University of Hawai'i Press, 1998.

Kizu, S. *Nihon Yūsen senpaku 100-nenshi (A 100 Years' History of the Ships of Nippon Yusen Kaisha).* Tokyo: Kaijinsha, 1984.

Klieger, P.C. *Kamehameha III: He Mo'olelo no ka Mo'i Lokomaika'i, King of the Hawaiian Islands, 1824–1854.* San Francisco: Green Arrow Press, 2015.

Klotz, O. 'Transpacific longitudes', *Transactions and Proceedings of the Royal Society of New Zealand* 39 (1906), 49–70.

REFERENCES TO VOLUME II

Klubock, T.M. *Contested Communities: Class, Gender and Politics in Chile's El Teniente Copper Mine, 1904–1951.* Durham, NC: Duke University Press, 1998.

Knapman, C. *White Women in Fiji, 1835–1930: The Ruin of Empire?* Sydney: Allen & Unwin, 1986.

Kneubuhl, L.M. *The Smell of the Moon.* Wellington: Huia, 2006.

Knight, A. *The Mexican Revolution.* Cambridge: Cambridge University Press, 1986.

Kobayashi, I. 'Japan's diplomacy towards member countries of Pacific Islands Forum: significance of Pacific Islands Leaders Meeting (PALM)', *Asia-Pacific Review* 25:2 (2018), 89–103.
   Minami no Shima no Nihonjin (The Japanese of the Southern Islands). Tokyo: Sankei Shimbun Shuppan, 2010.

Koikari, M. *Cold War Encounters in U.S.-Occupied Okinawa: Women, Militarized Domesticity, and Transnationalism in East Asia.* Cambridge: Cambridge University Press, 2015.

Konishi, S. 'François Péron's meditation on death, humanity and savage society', in A. Cook, N. Curthoys, and S. Konishi (eds.), *Representing Humanity in the Age of Enlightenment.* London: Pickering and Chatto, 2013, 109–122.

Konishi, S., M. Nugent, and T. Shellam (eds.). *Indigenous Intermediaries: New Perspectives on Exploration Archives.* Canberra: ANU Press, 2015.

Korhonen, P. 'The Pacific Age in world history', *Journal of World History* 7:1 (1996), 41–70.

Kramer, A. *Salamasina: Scenes from Ancient Samoan Culture and History*, trans. Brother Herman. Pago Pago, American Samoa: Association of the Marist Brothers' Old Boys, 1949.

Kramer, P.A. *The Blood of Government: Race, Empire, the United States, & the Philippines.* Chapel Hill: University of North Carolina Press, 2006.

Kramer, S., and H.K. Kramer. 'The other islands of Aloha', *Hawaiian Journal of History* 47 (2013), 1–26.

Kroeber, A.L. 'Review *Patterns of Culture*, Ruth Benedict', *American Anthropologist* 37 (1934), 689.

Kurashige, L. (ed.). *Pacific America: Histories of Transoceanic Crossings.* Honolulu: University of Hawai'i Press, 2017.

Kurchanski, A. *The Rules of Contagion.* London: Profile Books, 2020.

Kuttainen, V., S. Liebich, and S. Galletly. *The Transported Imagination: Australian Interwar Magazines and the Geographical Imaginaries of Colonial Modernity.* Amherst, NY: Cambria Press, 2018.

Kuwada, B.K. 'How blue is his beard? An examination of the 1862 Hawaiian language translation of "Bluebeard"', *Marvels & Tales* 23:1 (2009), 17–39.

Kuykendall, R. *The Hawaiian Kingdom*, vol. II, *1854–1874: Twenty Critical Years.* Honolulu: University of Hawai'i Press, 1953.

Kwai, A.A. *Solomon Islanders in World War II: An Indigenous Perspective.* Canberra: ANU Press, 2017.

Kwon, Y., and J. Kwon. 'An overview of *Telecommunications Policy*'s 40-year research history: text and bibliographic analyses', *Telecommunications Policy* 41 (2017), 878–90.

Labarca, C. 'Identidad e institucionalización como estrategias de construcción de confianza: el caso sino-chileno', *Revista de Ciencia Política* 33:2 (2013), 489–511.

References to Volume II

Labillardière, M. *An Account of a Voyage in Search of La Perouse, Undertaken by Order of the Constituent Assembly of France and Performed in the Years 1791, 1792 and 1793 Translated from the French*. 2 vols. London: J. Debrett, 1800.

LaBriola, M.C. 'Planting islands: Marshall Islanders shaping land, power, and history', *Journal of Pacific History* 54:2 (2019), 182–98.

Ladds, C. 'Eurasians in treaty-port China: journeys across racial and imperial frontiers', in J. Leckie, A. McCarthy, and A. Wanhalla (eds.), *Migrant Cross-Cultural Encounters in Asia and the Pacific*. New York: Routledge, 2016, 19–35.

LaFeber, W. *Michael Jordan and the New Global Capitalism*, rev. edn. New York: W.W. Norton, 2002.

  The American Age: United States Foreign Policy at Home and Abroad since 1750. New York; W.W. Norton, 1989.

Lafitani, S.F.P. 'Moanan-Tongan *fatongia* and deontic of Greco-Rome: *fiefia*, happiness, of *tauēlangi*, climactic euphoria, and *'alaha kakala*, permeating fragrance - *Mālie! Bravo!'* PhD thesis, Australian Catholic University, 2011.

Lai, W.L. 'Chinese indentured labor: migrations to the British West Indies in the nineteenth century', *Amerasia* 15:2 (1989), 117–38.

Lake, M. *Progressive New World: How Settler Colonialism and Transpacific Exchange Shaped American Reform*. Cambridge, MA: Harvard University Press, 2019.

Lal, B.V. *Girmitiyas: The Origins of the Fiji Indians*. Lautoka: Fiji Institute of Applied Studies, 2004.

  Islands of Turmoil: Elections and Politics in Fiji. Canberra: ANU Press, 2006.

  'The passage out', in K.R. Howe, R.C. Kiste, and B.V. Lal (eds.), *Tides of History: The Pacific Islands in the Twentieth Century*. Honolulu: University of Hawai'i Press, 1994, 435–61.

Lal, B.V., D. Munro, and E,D. Beechert (eds.). *Plantation Workers: Resistance and Accommodation*. Honolulu: University of Hawai'i Press, 1993.

Lamb, J., V. Smith, and N. Thomas (eds.). *Exploration and Exchange: A South Seas Anthology*. Chicago: University of Chicago Press, 2000.

Lambert, S.M. 'Health survey of Rennell and Bellona Islands', *Oceania* 2:2 (1931), 136–73.

Lange, R. 'European medicine in the Cook Islands', in R. MacLeod and M. Lewis (eds.), *Disease, Medicine, and Empire: Perspectives on Western Medicine and the Experience of European Expansion*. London: Routledge, 1988, 61–79.

  'Leprosy in the Cook Islands, 1890–1925', *Journal of Pacific History* 52:3 (2017), 302–24.

Larmour, P. *Foreign Flowers: Institutional Transfer and Good Governance in the Pacific Islands*. Honolulu: University of Hawai'i Press, 2005.

Larson, B. *Trials of Nation Making: Liberalism, Race, and Ethnicity in the Andes, 1810–1910*. Cambridge: Cambridge University Press, 2004.

Lary, D. *China's Republic*. Cambridge: Cambridge University Press, 2007.

Lasaqa, I.Q. *The Fijian People before and after Independence*. Canberra: ANU Press, 1984.

Latour, B. *Reassembling the Social: An Introduction to Actor-Network Theory*. Oxford: Oxford University Press, 2005.

Lātūkefu, S. *Church and State in Tonga: The Wesleyan Methodist Missionaries and Political Development, 1822–1875*. Honolulu: University of Hawai'i Press, 1974.

'Oral traditions: an appraisal of their value in historical research in Tonga', *Journal of Pacific History* 3 (1968), 135–43.

Lausent-Herrera, I. 'The Chinatown in Peru and the changing Peruvian Chinese community(ies)', *Journal of Chinese Overseas* 7:1 (2011), 69–113.

Laux, C. *Les théocraties missionnaires en Polynésie au XIXe siècle: des cités de Dieu dans les Mers du Sud ?* Paris: L'Harmattan, 2000.

Laval, H. *Mémoires pour servir à l'histoire de Mangareva, ère chrétienne 1834–1871*, ed. C.W. Newbury and P. O'Reilly. Paris: Musée de l'Homme, 1968.

Lawson, S. 'Australia, New Zealand and the Pacific Islands Forum: a critical review', *Commonwealth and Comparative Politics* 55:2 (2017), 214–35.

'Fiji's foreign relations: retrospect and prospect', *Round Table* 104:2 (2015), 209–20.

'"Melanesia": the history and politics of an idea', *Journal of Pacific History* 48:1 (2013), 1–22.

Tradition versus Democracy in the South Pacific: Fiji, Tonga and Western Samoa. Cambridge: Cambridge University Press, 1996.

Layton, S. 'Discourses of piracy in an age of revolutions', *Itinerario* 35 (2011), 81–97.

Leach, M. *Nation-Building and National Identity in Timor-Leste.* London: Routledge, 2018.

Leacock, E. 'Anthropologists in search of a culture: Margaret Mead, Derek Freeman, and all the rest of us', in L. Foerstel and A. Gilliam (eds.), *Confronting Margaret Mead: Scholarship, Empire and the South Pacific.* Philadelphia: Temple University Press 1992, 3–30.

Leblic, I. *Les Kanak face au développement: la voie étroite.* Grenoble: Presses Universitaires de Grenoble, 1993.

Leckie, J. *Colonizing Madness: Asylum and Community in Fiji.* Honolulu: University of Hawai'i Press, 2020.

'Discourses and technologies of mental health in post-war Fiji', in B.V. Lal (ed.), *The Defining Years: Pacific Islands, 1945–65.* Canberra: ANU Press, 2005, 151–73.

'Modernity and the management of madness in colonial Fiji', *Paideuma* 50 (2004), 551–74.

Lee, E. 'Hemispheric Orientalism and the 1907 Pacific Coast race riots', *Amerasia Journal* 33:2 (2007), 19–47

Lee, H., and S. Francis (eds.). *Migration and Transnationalism: Pacific Perspectives.* Canberra: ANU Press, 2009.

Lennon, J., and M. Foley. *Dark Tourism: The Attraction of Death and Disasters.* London: Continuum, 2000.

Leong, J.S.A. 'China's growing tuna fleet in the Pacific Ocean: a Samoan fisheries perspective', in M. Powles (ed.), *China and the Pacific: The View from Oceania.* Wellington: Victoria University Press, 2016, 244–7.

Leong, K.J. 'The many labors of the gendered trans-Pacific world', in C.C. Choy and J.T.-C Wu (eds.), *Gendering the Trans-Pacific World.* Leiden: Brill, 2017, 20–38.

Lesser, J. *Immigration, Ethnicity, and National Identity in Brazil, 1808 to the Present.* Cambridge: Cambridge University Press, 2013.

Lesson, R.-P. 'Considérations générales sur les îles du Grand-Océan, et sur les variétés de l'espèce humaine qui les habitent', in R.-P. Lesson and P. Garnot, *Zoologie,* 2 vols.,

References to Volume II

Voyage autour du monde . . . pendant les années 1822, 1823, 1824 et 1825 . . . Paris: Arthus Bertrand, 1826–30, vol. 1, 36–113.

Description de mammifères et d'oiseaux récemment découverts, précédée d'un tableau sur les races humaines. Paris: Lévêque, 1847.

Manuel de mammalogie, ou histoire naturelle des mammifères. Paris: Roret, 1827.

[*Manuscrit d'une partie du voyage de la Coquille*], [1823–4], 2 vols. MS 1793, Muséum national d'Histoire naturelle, Paris.

Voyage autour du monde entrepris par ordre du gouvernement sur la corvette la Coquille, 2 vols. Paris: R. Pourrat frères, 1839.

Lester, A. *Imperial Networks: Creating Identities in Nineteenth-Century South Africa and Britain.* London: Routledge, 2001.

Leupp, G.L. *Interracial Intimacy in Japan: Western Men and Japanese Women, 1543–1900.* London: Continuum, 2003.

Levick, W. 'Contract labour migration between Fiji and New Zealand: a case study of a South Pacific work permit scheme'. MSc thesis, University of Canterbury, Christchurch, 1988.

Levick, W., and R. Bedford. 'Fiji labour migration to New Zealand in the 1980s', *New Zealand Geographer* 44:1 (1988), 14–21.

Lewis, D. *Belonging on an Island: Birds, Extinction, and Evolution in Hawai'i.* New Haven: Yale University Press, 2018.

Li, K. *The Ming Maritime Trade Policy in Transition.* Wiesbaden: Harrassowitz, 2010.

Li, X., et al. 'Aquaculture industry in China: current state, challenges, and outlook, July 2011', *Reviews in Fisheries Science* 19:3 (2012), 187–200.

Lieber, M. *More Than a Living: Fishing and Social Order on a Polynesian Atoll.* Boulder, CO: Westview Press, 1994.

Ligeremaluoga. *The Erstwhile Savage: An Account of the Life of Ligeremaluoga (Osea) – An Autobiography.* Melbourne: Cheshire, 1932; repr. Port Moresby: UPNG Press, 2016.

Lightfoot, K., and O. Parrish. *California Indians and Their Environment.* Berkeley: University of California Press, 2009.

Liki, A. 'Moving and rootedness: the paradox of brain drain among Samoan professionals', *Asia-Pacific Population Journal* 16:1 (2001), 67–84.

Lilomaiava-Doktor, S. 'Beyond "migration": Samoan population movement (malaga) and the geography of social space (vā)', *Contemporary Pacific* 21:1 (2009), 1–32.

Lindstrom, L., and G.M. White. 'Introduction: chiefs today', in G.M. White and L. Lindstrom (eds.), *Chiefs Today: Traditional Pacific Leadership and the Postcolonial State.* Stanford: Stanford University Press, 1997, 1–18.

Lingenfelter, R.E. *Presses of the Pacific Islands 1817–1867: A History of the First Half Century of Printing in the Pacific Islands.* Los Angeles: The Plantin Press, 1967.

Linnekin, J. *Sacred Queens and Women of Consequence: Rank, Gender, and Colonialism in the Hawaiian Islands.* Ann Arbor: University of Michigan Press, 1990.

LiPuma, E. *Encompassing Others: The Magic of Modernity in Melanesia.* Ann Arbor: University of Michigan Press, 2000.

Little, S., and P. Ruthenberg (eds.). *Life in the Pacific of the 1700s: The Cook/Forster Collection of the Georg August University of Gottingen*, 3 vols. Honolulu: Honolulu Academy of Arts, 2006.

REFERENCES TO VOLUME II

Liu, J.Y. 'Status of marine biodiversity of the China Seas', *PLoS ONE* 8:1 (2013), e50719, 79–80.

Liua'ana, B.F. 'Dragons in little paradise: Chinese (mis-)fortune in Samoa, 1900–1950', *Journal of Pacific History* 32:1 (1997), 29–48.

Llanos Mansilla, R. 'La mediterraneidad de Bolivia', *Agenda Internacional* 11:21 (2004), 11–26.

Lloyd's List. *'The top 100 ports in 2015'*. London: Lloyd's List, 2016, https://lloydslist.maritimeintelligence.informa.com/one-hundred-container-ports-2016.

Lo, J.-P. *China as a Sea Power, 1127–1368: A Preliminary Survey of the Maritime Expansion and Naval Exploits of the Chinese People during the Southern Song and Yuan Periods*, ed. B.A. Elleman. Hong Kong: Hong Kong University Press, 2012.

Long, D., and K. Imamura. *The Japanese Language in Palau*. Tokyo: National Institute for Language and Linguistics, 2013.

Loop Pacific News, www.looptonga.com/tonga-news/respect-obstacle-tongan-democracy-researcher-66521.

López, R. 'From sail to steam: coastal Mexico and the reconfiguration of the Pacific in the nineteenth century', *International Journal of Maritime History* 22 (2010), 247–75.

'Transpacific Mexico: encounters with China and Japan in the age of steam (1867–1914)'. PhD thesis, University of British Colombia, 2012.

Love, H. *'Nga Korero E Pa Ana Ki Nga Wahine Māori*: a guide to manuscripts and archives on Māori women held at the Alexander Turnbull Library', Master of Library and Information Studies thesis, School of Communications and Information Management, Victoria University of Wellington, 2000.

Love, R.N. 'Policies of frustration: the growth of Maori politics – the Ratana-labour era', PhD thesis, Victoria University of Wellington, 1977.

Lu, S.X. *The Making of Japanese Settler Colonialism: Malthusianism and Trans-Pacific Migration, 1868–1961*. Cambridge: Cambridge University Press, 2019.

Lubbock, B. *Coolie Ships and Oil Sailers*. Glasgow: Brown, Son & Ferguson, 1935.

Luetz, J.M. 'Over-researching migration "hotspots"? Ethical issues from the Carteret Islands', *Forced Migration Review* 61 (2019), 20–2.

Luker, T. 'Decolonising archives: indigenous challenges to record keeping in "reconciling" settler colonial states', *Australian Feminist Studies* 32:91–2 (2017), 108–25.

Luker, V. 'Native obstetric nursing in Fiji', in V. Luker and M. Jolly (eds.), *Birthing in the Pacific: Beyond Tradition and Modernity?* Honolulu: University of Hawai'i Press, 2002, 100–24.

'Papua New Guinea: epidemiological transition, public health and the Pacific', in M.J. Lewis and K.L. MacPherson (eds.), *Public Health in Asia and the Pacific: Historical and Comparative Perspectives*. London: Routledge, 2008, 250–74.

'The half-caste in Australia, New Zealand, and Western Samoa between the wars: different problem, different places?', in B. Douglas and C. Ballard (eds.), *Foreign Bodies: Oceania and the Science of Race, 1750–1840*. Canberra: ANU Press, 2008, 307–35.

'The lessons of leprosy? Reflections on Hansen's Disease in the response to HIV and Aids in the Pacific', *Journal of Pacific History* 52:3 (2017), 388–90.

850

References to Volume II

Luker, V., and M. Jolly (eds.). *Birthing in the Pacific: Beyond Tradition and Modernity?* Honolulu: University of Hawai'i Press, 2002.

Luthria, M. 'Seasonal migration for development? Evaluating New Zealand's RSE Program overview', *Pacific Economic Bulletin* 3:3 (2008), 165–70.

Lynch, J. *The Spanish American Revolutions, 1808–1826*, 2nd edn. New York: Norton, 1986.

Lyons, P. *American Pacificism: Oceania in the U.S. Imagination.* New York: Routledge, 2006.

Lyu, Y., et al. 'Desertification control practices in China', *Sustainability* 12 (2020), 1–15.

Macdonald, B. 'Decolonisation and "good" governance: precedents and continuities', in D. Denoon (ed.), *Emerging from Empire? Decolonisation in the Pacific.* Proceedings of Workshop, Australian National University, Canberra, July 1997, 1–9.

MacDonald, K. *Placing Empire: Travel and the Social Imagination in Imperial Japan.* Oakland: University of California Press, 2017.

MacKenzie, M.K., S.K. Serrano, D.K. Sproat, A.K. Obrey, and A.K. Poai. *Native Hawaiian Law: A Treatise.* Honolulu: Kamehameha Publishing, 2015.

Mackinder, H.J. 'The geographical pivot of history', *Geographical Journal* 2:4 (1904), 421–44.

Maclellan, N. 'Fiji, the war in Iraq, and the privatisation of Pacific island security', APSNet Policy Forum, 6 April 2006, https://nautilus.org/apsnet/0611a-maclellan-html/.

Grappling with the Bomb: Britain's Pacific H-Bomb Tests. Canberra: ANU Press, 2017.

'The Nouméa Accord and decolonisation in New Caledonia', *Journal of Pacific History* 34:3 (1999), 245–52.

'The nuclear age in the Pacific Islands', *Contemporary Pacific* 17:2 (2005), 363–72.

MacLennan, C.A. *Sovereign Sugar: Industry and Environment in Hawai'i.* Honolulu: University of Hawai'i Press, 2014.

MacLeod, R. 'Introduction', in R. MacLeod and M.J. Lewis (eds.), *Disease, Medicine, and Empire: Perspectives on Western Medicine and the Experience of European Expansion.* London: Routledge, 1988), 1–18.

Macpherson, C. 'Migration and transformation in the contemporary Pacific', *New Zealand Sociology* 23:1 (2008), 30–40.

'Transnationalism and transformation in Samoan society', in V. Lockwood (ed.), *Globalisation and Culture Change in the Pacific Islands.* Upper Saddle River, NJ: Pearson/Prentice Hall, 2004, 165–81.

Macpherson, C., R. Bedford, and P. Spoonley. 'Fact or fable? The consequences of migration for educational achievement and labour market participation', *Contemporary Pacific* 12:1 (2000), 57–82.

Macpherson, C., and L. Macpherson. *Samoan Medical Beliefs and Practice.* Auckland: Auckland University Press, 1990.

Madeira Santos, C. 'Escrever o poder: os autos de vassalagem e a vulgarização da escrita entre as elites africanas Ndembu', *Revista de História* (2006) 55, 81–95.

Magalhães, A.L. de. 'Timor, a desventurada', *O Mundo Português* 45:4 (1937), 391–5.

Mahan, A.T. *The Interests of America in Sea Power, Present and Future.* Boston: Little, Brown and Company, 1898.

Māhina, 'O. 'Oceanic mythology', in J. Parker and J. Stanton (eds.), *Mythology: Myths, Legends, & Fantasies.* Sydney: Global Book Publishing, 2003, 374–81.

Reed Book of Tongan Proverbs: Ko e Tohi 'a e Reed ki he Lea Tonga Heliaki. Auckland: Reed Publishing, 2004.

'Tā, vā, and moana: temporality, spatiality, and indigeneity', *Pacific Studies* 33:2/3 (2010), 168–202.

'The Tongan traditional history tala-e-fonua: a vernacular ecology-centred historico-cultural concept', PhD thesis, Australian National University, Canberra, 1992.

'Time, space, and culture: a new tā–vā theory of Moana anthropology', *Pacific Studies* 40:1/2 (2017), 105–32.

Māhina-Tuai, K. 'A land of milk and honey? Education and employment migration schemes in the postwar era', in S. Mallon, K. Māhina-Tuai, and D. Salesa (eds.), *Tangata O Le Moana*. Wellington: Te Papa Press, 2012, 161–77.

Mainguet, Y. 'The Labour Party will not participate in the referendum', *Les Nouvelles Calédoniennes* (16 July 2018).

Makihara, M. 'Linguistic syncretism and language ideologies: transforming sociolinguistic hierarchy on Rapa Nui (Easter Island)', *American Anthropologist* 106:3 (2004), 529–40.

Malinowski, B. *A Diary in the Strict Sense of the Term*. London: Athlone Press, 1967.

Argonauts of the Western Pacific: An Account of Native Enterprise and Adventure in the Archipelagoes of Melanesian New Guinea. London: Routledge & Keegan Paul, 1922.

Mallory, T.G. 'Fisheries subsidies in China: quantitative and qualitative assessment of policy coherence and effectiveness', *Marine Policy* 68 (2016), 74–82.

Mangan, J.E. *Trading Roles: Gender, Ethnicity, and the Urban Economy in Colonial Potosí*. Durham, NC: Duke University Press, 2005.

Mann, C. *1493: Uncovering the New World Columbus Created*. New York: Alfred A. Knopf, 2011.

Manning, P., and D. Rood. *Global Scientific Practice in the Age of Revolutions*. Pittsburgh: University of Pittsburgh Press, 2016.

Manning, R.A. 'Asia crisis: now for the hard part', *Los Angeles Times* (4 January 1998), 2.

Maohong, B. 'Environmentalism and environmental movements in China since 1949', in J.R. McNeill and E. Stewart Mauldin (eds.), *A Companion to Global Environmental History*. Chichester: Wiley-Blackwell, 2012, 474–92.

Mara, K. *The Pacific Way: A Memoir*. Honolulu: University of Hawai'i Press, 1997.

Marchant, L.R. 'La Pérouse, Jean-François de Galaup (1741–1788)', in *Australian Dictionary of Biography*, National Centre of Biography, Australian National University, http://adb.anu.edu.au/biography/la-perouse-jean-francois-de-galaup-2329/text3029.

Maretu. *Cannibals and Converts: Radical Change in the Cook Islands*, trans. and ed. T. Crocombe. Suva: Institute of Pacific Studies, University of the South Pacific, 1983.

Margolis, E. 'The North Pacific is no longer an American lake', *The Blog, Huffpost*. 11 January 2011, https://huffingtonpost.com/eric-margolis/the-north-pacific-is-no-l_b_806885.html.

Marks, R.B. *Tigers, Rice, Silk, & Silt: Environment and Economy in Late Imperial South China*. Cambridge: Cambridge University Press, 1998.

Marshall, K. 'The structure of solidarity and alliance on Namoluk Atoll', PhD thesis, University of Washington, 1972.

Marsters, E., N. Lewis, and W. Friesen. 'Pacific flows: the fluidity of remittances in the Cook Islands', *Asia Pacific Viewpoint* 47:1 (2006), 31–44.

References to Volume II

Martin, J. 'Origin of the name Tonga Island', *Journal of the Polynesian Society* 20:4 (1911), 165–6.

Martínez, J. 'Asian servants for the imperial telegraph: imagining North Australia as an Indian Ocean colony before 1914', *Australian Historical Studies* 48 (2017), 227–43.

'Indigenous Australian–Indonesian intermarriage: negotiating citizenship rights in twentieth-century Australia', *Aboriginal History* 35 (2011), 177–95.

Martire d'Anghiera, P. *De Orbe Novo*. Compluti: Michaelé de Eguia, 1530.

Martínez, J., C. Lowrie, F. Steel, and V. Haskins. *Colonialism and Male Domestic Service across the Asia Pacific*. London: Bloomsbury, 2019.

Marvin, C., and D.N. Ingle. *Blood Sacrifice and the Nation: Totem Rituals and the American Flag*. Cambridge: Cambridge University Press, 1999.

Mataia, L.M.T. '"Odd men from the Pacific": the participation of Pacific Island men in the 28 (Maori) Battalion in the Second World War', MA thesis, University of Otago, 2007.

Mataia-Milo, S.L.M.T. '"There are no commoners in Samoa"', in J.A. Bennett and A. Wanhalla (eds.), *Mothers' Darlings of the South Pacific: The Children of Indigenous Women and U.S. Servicemen, World War II*. Honolulu: University of Hawai'i Press, 2016, 42–82.

Matsuda, M.K. *Pacific Worlds: A History of Seas, Peoples and Cultures*. Cambridge: Cambridge University Press, 2012.

'The Pacific', *American Historical Review* 111:3 (2006), 758–80.

Maude, H.E. 'Baiteke and Binoka of Abemama: arbiters of change in the Gilbert Islands', in J.W. Davidson and D. Scarr (eds.), *Pacific Islands Portraits*. Canberra: ANU Press, 1976, 201–24.

'Beachcombers and castaways', *Journal of the Polynesian Society* 73:3 (1964), 254–93.

Maupertuis, P.L. Moreau de. *Lettre sur le progrès des sciences*. S.l.: s.n., 1752.

Mawyer, A. 'Video irradient: Micronesia and monsters in post-war Japanese film', MA thesis, University of Chicago, 1998.

May, R. *The Melanesian Spearhead Group: Testing Pacific Island Solidarity*. ASPI Policy Analysis 74. Canberra: ASPI, 2011.

'Weak states, collapsed states, broken backed states, kleptocracies: general concepts and Pacific realities', *New Pacific Review* 2:1 (2003), 35–58.

May, T. *The Mongol Conquests in World History*. London: Reaktion, 2012.

McArthur, N. *Island Populations of the Pacific*. Canberra: ANU Press, 1967.

'Population and prehistory, the late phase on Aneityum', PhD thesis, Australian National University, Canberra, 1974.

McBride, J. 'The trans-Pacific partnership and U.S. trade policy', Backgrounder, Council on Foreign Relations, 31 January 2017, www.cfr.org/backgrounder/state-us-trade-policy.

McCabe, J. *Race, Tea and Colonial Resettlement: Imperial Families, Interrupted*. London: Bloomsbury, 2017.

McCall, G. 'Japan, Rapanui and Chile's uncertain sovereignty', *Rapa Nui Journal: Journal of the Easter Island Foundation* 9:1 (1995), 1–7.

'Riro, Rapu and Rapanui: refoundations in Easter Island colonial history', *Rapa Nui Journal* 11:3 (1997), 112–22.

McClintock, A. *Imperial Leather: Race, Gender and Sexuality in the Colonial Conquest*. London: Routledge, 1995.

McCormack, T. 'The Niue Archives Project', *Panorama* 2 (2008), 7.

McDougall, W.A. *Let the Sea Make a Noise: A History of the North Pacific from Magellan to MacArthur*. New York: Basic Books, 1993.

McGibbon, I. *New Zealand and the Second World War: The People, the Battles and the Legacy*. Auckland: Hodder Moa Beckett, 2004.

McGonigal, D., and L. Woodworth. *Antarctica: The Blue Continent*. Noble Park: The Five Mile Press, 2002.

McGregor, D.P., *Nā Kua'Āina: Living Hawaiian Culture*. Honolulu: University of Hawai'i Press, 2006.

McIntyre, D.W. *Winding Up the British Empire in the Pacific Islands*. Oxford: Oxford University Press, 2014.

McKemmish, S. 'The smoking gun: recordkeeping and accountability', 22nd Annual Conference of the Archives and Records Association of New Zealand, 'Records and Archives Now – Who Cares?', keynote address (Dunedin, September 1998).

McKeown, A.M. *Melancholy Order: Asian Migration and the Globalization of Borders*. New York: Columbia University Press, 2008.

'Movement', in D. Armitage and A. Bashford (eds.), *Pacific Histories: Ocean, Land, People*. Basingstoke: Palgrave Macmillan, 2014, 143–65.

McLane, J.R. 'Paradise locked: the 1918 influenza pandemic in American Samoa', *Sites: A Journal of Anthropology and Cultural Studies* 10:2 (2013), 30–51.

McLeod, S. 'Prime ministerial persistence: Australia vs PNG', *The Interpreter* (21 August 2018), www.lowyinstitute.org/the-interpreter/prime-ministerial-persistence-austra lia-vs-png.

McMenamin, D. 'Out of sight and out of mind: the ongoing problem of treating leprosy', *Journal of Pacific History* 52:3 (2017), 343–59.

McNeill, J.R., 'Of rats and men: a synoptic environmental history of the Island Pacific', *Journal of World History* 5:3 (1994), 299–349.

McNeill, W.H. *Plagues and Peoples*. Garden City, NY: Anchor Press, 1976; repr. Harmondsworth: Penguin, 1979.

McQuarrie, P. *Conflict in Kiribati: A History of the Second World War*. Christchurch: Macmillan Brown Centre, 2000.

McQueen, N. 'Beyond Tok Win: the Papua New Guinea intervention in Vanuatu', *Pacific Affairs* 61:2 (1980), 235–52.

MDS 'Industry leaders discuss containerization in Japan', *Maritime Day Supplement*, 20 July 1966. Tokyo: Shipping and Trade News.

Mead, M. *Coming of Age in Samoa: A Psychological Study of Primitive Youth for Western Civilization*. New York: William Morrow 1928.

Meagher, A.J. *The Coolie Trade: The Traffic in Chinese Laborers to Latin America, 1847–1874*. Philadelphia: Xlibris, 2008.

Meleisea, M. *The Making of Modern Samoa: Traditional Authority and Colonial Authority in the Modern History of Western Samoa*. Suva: Institute of Pacific Studies of the University of the South Pacific, 1987.

Meleisea, M., and P. Schoeffel. 'Forty-five years of Pacific Island studies: some reflections', *Oceania* 87:3 (2017), 337–43.

References to Volume II

Melillo, E.D. *Strangers on Familiar Soil: Rediscovering the Chile–California Connection*. New Haven: Yale University Press, 2015.

'The First Green Revolution: debt peonage and the making of the nitrogen fertilizer trade, 1840–1930', *American Historical Review* 117:4 (2012), 1028–60.

Meller, N. 'Traditional leaders and modern Pacific Island governance', *Asian Survey* 24:7 (1984), 759–72.

Melnysyn, S. 'Vagabond states: boundaries and belonging in Portuguese Angola, *c. 1880–1910*', PhD thesis, University of Michigan, 2017.

Merchant, C. *Ecological Revolutions: Nature, Gender, and Science in New England*. Chapel Hill: University of North Carolina Press, 1989.

Merleau-Ponty, M. *Phenomenology of Perception*. London: Routledge, 1986.

Merlin, M., and R. Gonzalez. 'Environmental impacts of nuclear testing in Remote Oceania', in J.R. McNeill and C. Unger (eds.), *Environmental Histories of the Cold War*. Cambridge: Cambridge University Press, 2010, 167–202.

Merry, S.E. *Colonizing Hawai'i: The Cultural Power of Law*. Princeton: Princeton University Press, 2000.

Meskin, K. 'Navigating *Moananuiākea*, the vast expanse of ocean', *Ka'Elele* (Fall 2013), 10.

Micco, H.M. (ed.). *King Island and the Sealing Trade, 1802*. Canberra: Roebuck Society, 1971.

Mikaere, A. *Colonising Myths: Māori Realities*. Wellington: Huia, 2011.

Milcairns, S.M. *Native Strangers: Beachcombers, Renegades and Castaways in the South Seas*. Auckland: Penguin, 2006.

Miles, J. *Infectious Diseases: Colonising the Pacific?* Dunedin: University of Otago Press, 1997.

Miller, J.C. *Way of Death: Merchant Capitalism and the Angolan Slave Trade, 1730–1830*. Madison: University of Wisconsin Press, 1988.

Miller, P. *Nuclear Flashback: Report of a Greenpeace Scientific Expedition to Amchitka Island, Alaska – Site of the Largest Underground Nuclear Test in U.S. History*. Washington, DC: Greenpeace USA, 1996.

Millet, M. *1878, carnets de campagne en Nouvelle-Calédonie: précédé de la guerre d'Ataï, récit Kanak*, ed. A. Bensa. Toulouse: Anacharsis, 2013.

Mills, C. 'The United States' Asia-Pacific policy and the rise of the dragon', Indo-Pacific Strategic Papers. Centre for Defence and Strategic Studies, Australian Defence College, August 2015, www.defence.gov.au/ADC/Publications/IndoPac/R23177605-1.pdf.

Min, J., and B. Kang. 'Promoting new growth: "Advanced Special Economic Zones" in the Russian Far East', in H. Blakkisrud and E. Wilson Rowe (eds.), *Russia's Turn to the East: Domestic Policy-Making and Regional Cooperation*. Cham: Palgrave Pivot, 2018, 51–74.

Ministerio de Educación, Gobierno de Chile. 'Unidad de currículum y evaluación: Chile tricontinental', https://curriculumnacional.mineduc.cl/614/articles-29379_recurso_jpg.jpg.

Ministerio de Relaciones Exteriores. *Coleccion de los tratados del Perú*. Lima: Imprenta del Estado Calle de la Rifa 58, 1876.

Mita, M. *Palauan Children under Japanese Rule: Their Oral Histories*. Osaka: National Museum of Ethnology, 2009.

'The soul and the image', in J. Dennis and J. Bieringa (eds.), *Film in Aotearoa New Zealand*. Wellington: Victoria University Press, 1992, 36–54.

Moala, M. *'Efinangá: Ko e Ngaahi Tala mo e Anga Fakafonua 'o Tongá*. Nuku'alofa, Tonga: Lali, 1994.

Mokaddem, H. 'L'accord de Nouméa. Pratique de discours et forclusion de la souveraineté de Kanaky', *Journal de la Société des Océanistes* 147 (2018), 319–28.

Molisa, G.M. *Black Stone: Poems*. Suva: Mana Publications, 1983.

Moon, K.H. *Sex among Allies: Prostitution in U.S.–Korea Relations*. New York: Columbia University Press, 1997.

'South Korean movements against militarized sexual labor', in S. Shigematsu and K.L. Camacho (eds.), *Militarized Currents: Toward a Decolonized Future in Asia and the Pacific*. Minneapolis: University of Minnesota Press, 2010, 125–45.

Moon, P. *Fatal Frontiers: A New History of New Zealand in the Decade before the Treaty*. Auckland: Penguin Books, 2006.

Moore, C. 'Honiara: arrival city and Pacific hybrid living space', *Journal of Pacific History* 50:4 (2015), 419–36.

Making Mala: Malaita in Solomon Islands, 1870s–1930s. Canberra: ANU Press, 2017.

(ed.) *Solomon Islands Historical Encyclopaedia 1893–1978*, www.solomonencyclopaedia .net/.

Moorehead, A. *The Fatal Impact: An Account of the Invasion of the South Pacific, 1767–1840*. London: Hamish Hamilton, 1966.

Morgan, D. *The Top 25 Container Liner Operators Trading Profiles: November 2014*. Alkmaar: Dynamar B.V., 2014.

Morgan, M.G., L. Baker, and L. Hambly. *Political Parties, Parliamentary Governance and Party Strengthening in Melanesia: Issues and Challenges*. Canberra: Centre for Democratic Institutions, Australian National University, 2005.

Morris, N.J. 'Hawaiian missionaries abroad, 1852–1909', PhD thesis, University of Hawai'i, 1987.

Morris-Suzuki, T. 'Debating racial science in wartime Japan', *Osiris* 13 (1998), 354–75.

The Past within Us: Media, Memory, History. New York: Verso, 2005.

Morrison, R.D. 'The institutionalisation of "Kanak identity" in the New Caledonian Customary Senate and Kanak customary law', http://caepr.cass.anu.edu.au/events/ institutionalisation-kanak-identity-new-caledonian-customary-senate-and-kanak-custom ary-law.

Morton, H. *The Whale's Wake*. Honolulu: University of Hawai'i Press, 1982.

Mortreux, C., and J. Barnett. 'Climate change, migration and adaptation in Funafuti, Tuvalu', *Global Environmental Change* 19:1 (2009), 105–12.

Mote, F.W. *Imperial China, 900–1800*. Cambridge, MA: Harvard University Press, 1999.

Motonicocoka, I. 'The story of the "lila balavu" (wasting sickness) and of the cokadra (dysentery); and the meke (ballads) relating to those events', in *Report of the Commission Appointed to Inquire into the Decrease of the Native Population*. Suva: Edward John Marsh, Government Printer, 1896, appendix 1.

Mouchenik, Y. 'The elder's child of Maré Island, New Caledonia', *Transcultural Psychiatry* 44 (2007), 136–56.

Mowhee and B. Woodd. 'Memoir of Mowhee, a New Zealander who died at Paddington, December 28, 1816', *Missionary Papers* 10 (1818), n.p.

References to Volume II

Muckle, A., and B. Trépied. 'The transformation of the "métis question" in New Caledonia, 1853–2009', in F. Fozdar and K. McGavin (eds.), *Mixed Race Identities in Australia, New Zealand and the Pacific Islands*. London: Routledge, 2017, 116–32.

Müller, S. *Wiring the World: The Social and Cultural Creation of Global Telegraph Networks*. New York: Columbia University Press, 2016.

Müller-Pohl, S. 'Wiring the Pacific: North American perspectives on a (de)colonial project', in E. Bischoff, N. Finzsch, and U. Lehmkuhl (eds.), *Provincializing the United States: Colonialism, Decolonization, and (Post)colonial Governance in Transnational Perspective*. Heidelberg: Winter, 2014, 155–80.

Mullins, S., and D. Wetherell. 'LMS teachers and colonialism in Torres Strait and New Guinea, 1871–1915', in D. Munro and A. Thornley (eds.), *The Covenant Makers: Islander Missionaries in the Pacific*. Suva: Pacific Theological College and Institute of Pacific Studies, University of the South Pacific 1996, 196–209.

Munholland, K. *Rock of Contention: Free French and Americans at War in New Caledonia, 1940–1945*. New York: Berghahn Books, 2005.

Munro, D., I. Campbell, J. Osorio, J. Samson, and N. Thomas. 'Islanders: the Pacific in the age of empire', *Journal of Pacific History* 47:3 (2012), 421–32.

Munro, D., and G. Gray. '"We haven't abandoned the project": the founding of the *Journal of Pacific History*', *Journal of Pacific History* 48:1 (2013), 63–77.

Murray, S.C. *The Battle over Peleliu: Islander, Japanese, and American Memories of War*. Tuscaloosa: University of Alabama Press, 2016.

Murton, J. *Creating a Modern Countryside: Liberalism and Land Resettlement in British Columbia*. Vancouver: UBC Press, 2007.

Muscolino, M.S. 'A forest of sails and masts: environment and economy in an early twentieth-century Chinese fishery', *Twentieth-Century China* 31:1 (2005), 3–32.

'Fishing and whaling', in J.R. McNeill and E.S. Mauldin (eds.), *A Companion to Global Environmental History*. Oxford: Blackwell, 2012, 279–96.

'The yellow croaker war: fishery disputes between China and Japan, 1925–1935', *Environmental History* 13 (2008), 305–24.

Myers, R.H., and M.R. Peattie (eds.). *The Japanese Colonial Empire, 1895–1945*. Princeton: Princeton University Press, 1984.

Nabobo-Baba, U. *Knowing and Learning an Indigenous Fijian Approach*. Suva: Institute of Pacific Studies, University of the South Pacific, 2006.

'Vanua Research Framework', in *Sustainable Livelihood and Education in the Pacific Project (SLEP)*. Suva: Institute of Education, University of the South Pacific, 2007.

Nagakuni, J. and J. Kitadai. *Drifting toward the Southeast: The Story of Five Japanese Castaways Told in 1852 by John Manjiro*. New Bedford: Spinner Publications. 2003.

Nagata, K. 'Early plant introductions in Hawai'i', *Hawaiian Journal of History* 19 (1985), 35–61.

Najita, S. *Decolonising Cultures in the Pacific: Reading History and Trauma in Contemporary Fiction*. New York: Routledge, 2006.

Nakajima, A. *Nanyō Tsūshin (Nanyō Communiqué)*. Tokyo: Chūō Kōron Shinsha, 2001 [1941–2].

Narokobi, B., *The Melanesian Way*. Port Moresby: Institute of Papua New Guinea Studies, 1980; rev. edn 1983.

Nason, D.J. 'Clan and copra: modernization of Etal, Eastern Caroline Islands', PhD thesis, University of Michigan, Ann Arbor, 1971.

National Biodiversity Team of the Republic of the Marshall Islands. *The Marshall Islands: Living Atolls amidst the Living Sea.* Santa Clarita, CA: St. Hildegard Publishing Company, 2000.

National Library of New Zealand. *Pacific Virtual Museum,* https://natlib.govt.nz/about-us/collaborative-projects/pacific-virtual-museum.

Navarro-Génie, M.A. *Augusto 'César' Sandino: Messiah of Light and Truth.* Syracuse: Syracuse University Press, 2002.

Néaoutyine, P. *L'indépendance au présent: identité kanak et destin commun.* Paris: Éditions Syllepse, 2006.

Needham, J., and G.-D. Lu. *Trans-Pacific Echoes and Resonances: Listening Once Again.* Singapore: World Scientific Publishing, 1985.

Neich, R. *Carved Histories: Rotorua Ngati Tarawhai.* Auckland: Auckland University Press, 2001.

Painted Histories: Early Figurative Painting. Auckland: Auckland University Press, 1994.

Nelson, H. 'Kokoda: and two national histories', *Journal of Pacific History* 42 (2007), 73–88.

'"Taim Bilong Fait": the impact of the Second World War on Papua New Guinea', in A.W. McCoy (ed.), *Southeast Asia under Japanese Occupation.* Monograph Series 22. New Haven: Yale University Press, 1980, 246–66.

Nero, K. 'The material world unmade', in D. Denoon (ed.), *The Cambridge History of the Pacific Islanders.* Cambridge: Cambridge University Press, 1997, 359–96.

Nery, J. *Revolutionary Spirit: José Rizal in Southeast Asia.* Singapore: Institute of Southeast Asian Studies, 2011.

Newbury, C. *Tahiti Nui: Change and Survival in French Polynesia 1767–1945.* Honolulu: University of Hawai'i Press, 1980.

Newell, J. *Trading Nature: Tahitians, Europeans, and Ecological Exchange.* Honolulu: University of Hawai'i Press, 2010.

Ng, C.-k. *Trade and Society: The Amoy Network on the China Coast 1683–1735,* 2nd edn. Singapore: NUS Press, 2015.

Ngũgĩ wa Thiong'o. *Decolonising the Mind: The Politics of Language in African Literature.* Portsmouth: Heinemann, 1986.

Ni, A. (ed.). *Jinping linkuang lunwenji.* Lianyungang: Lianyungang shi Jinping linkuang, 1999.

Niceto de Zamacois y Urrutia, J. *Historia de Méjico,* 22 vols. Barcelona, Mexico: J.F. Párres y Compañia, 1878–1902.

Nicole, R. *Disturbing History: Resistance in Early Colonial Fiji.* Honolulu: University of Hawai'i Press, 2011.

Niebuhr, H.R. *Christ and Culture.* New York: Harper & Row, 1956.

Nishino, R. 'The awakening of a journalist's historical consciousness: Sasa Yukie's Pacific Island journeys of 2005–2006', *Japanese Studies* 37:1 (2017), 71–88.

'The self-promotion of a maverick travel-writer: Suzuki Tsunenori and his southern Pacific Islands travelogue', *Nanyō Tanken Jikki: Studies in Travel Writing* 20:4 (2016), 1–14.

Niumeitolu, L. 'when we tell', in *Whetū Moana: Contemporary Polynesian Poems in English.* Auckland: Auckland University Press, 2003, 167.

References to Volume II

Noam, E., S. Komatsuzaki, and D.A. Conn (eds.). *Telecommunications in the Pacific Basin: An Evolutionary Approach.* Oxford: Oxford University Press, 1994.

Nobbs, R. *Norfolk Island and Its Third Settlement, the First Hundred Years: The Pitcairn Era, 1856–1956, and the Melanesian Mission, 1866–1920.* Sydney: Library of Australian History, 2006.

Nogelmeier, M.P. *Mai Pa'a I Ka Leo: Historical Voice in Hawaiian Primary Materials, Looking Forward and Listening Back.* Honolulu: Bishop Museum Press, 2010.

Norling, L. 'Ahab's wife: women and the American whaling industry', in M. Creighton and L. Norling (eds.), *Iron Men and Wooden Women: Gender and Seafaring in the Atlantic Word.* Baltimore: Johns Hopkins University Press, 1996, 70–91.

Nouvelle-Calédonie la Première [TV show]. 'Interview with Dick Saihu, Président of the CNDPA', 2012, www.dailymotion.com/video/xsp86t.

'La preuve par quatre', theme 'Peut-on se passer de l'argent de la France?' ('Can we do without France's money?'), interview with Sonia Backès, November 2013, www.youtube.com/watch?v=H1zbLqi9lIY.

O'Brien, P. 'Bridging the Pacific: Ta'isi O.F. Nelson, Australia and the Sāmoan Mau', *History Australia* 14 (2017), 1–19.

'Gender', in D. Armitage and A. Bashford (eds.), *Pacific Histories: Ocean, Land, People.* Basingstoke: Palgrave Macmillan, 2014, 238–304.

Tautai: World History and the Life of Ta'isi Olaf Nelson. Wellington: Huia Publishers and University of Hawai'i Press, 2017.

The Pacific Muse: Exotic Femininity and the Colonial Pacific. Seattle: University of Washington Press, 2006.

O'Connor, K., and A. Scott. 'Airline services and metropolitan areas in the Asia-Pacific region 1970–1990', *Review of Urban and Regional Development Studies* 4:2 (2007), 240–53.

O'Malley, V. *Haerenga: Early Māori Journeys across the Globe.* Wellington: Bridget Williams Books, 2015.

O'Neal, J.R. '"The right to know": decolonizing Native American archives', *Journal of Western Archives* 6:1 (2015), article 2.

OAG. *The Future of Transpacific-Services – United's Longest Route Gives a Taste of Things to Come.* Luton: OAG Aviation Worldwide Limited, 2016, www.oag.com/future-of-transpacific-services.

Obeyesekere, G. *Cannibal Talk: The Man-Eating Myth and Human Sacrifice in the South Seas.* Berkeley: University of California Press, 2005.

Oguma, E. *A Genealogy of 'Japanese' Self-Images.* Melbourne: Trans Pacific Press, 2002.

Ojinmah, U. *Witi Ihimaera: A Changing Vision.* Dunedin: Otago University Press, 1993.

Okihiro, G.Y. *American History Unbound: Asians and Pacific Islanders.* Oakland: University of California Press, 2015.

Olhausen, M. 'The archival challenges and choices of a small non-profit organization attempting to preserve its unique past', *Journal of Western Archives* 10:2 (2019), 1–14.

Oliver, D. *Ancient Tahitian Society,* 3 vols. Honolulu: University of Hawai'i Press, 1974.

Olmsted, K.S. *Right Out of California: The 1930s and the Big Business Roots of Modern Conservatism.* New York: The New Press, 2015.

Orange, C. *An Illustrated History of the Treaty of Waitangi.* Auckland: Bridget Williams Books, 2004.

REFERENCES TO VOLUME II

'The price of citizenship? The Maori war effort', in J. Crawford (ed.), *Kia Kaha: New Zealand in the Second World War*. Oxford: Oxford University Press, 2000, 236–51.

Orbell, M. '*Directions in Pacific Traditional Literature: Essays in Honor of Katharine Luomala* [review]', *Journal of the Polynesian Society* 88:1 (1979), 106–9.

Osorio, J.H. '(Re)membering '*Upena* of Intimacies: a *Kanaka Maoli Mo'olelo* beyond queer theory', PhD thesis, University of Hawai'i, Mānoa. 2018.

Osorio, J.K.K. *Dismembering Lāhui: A History of the Hawaiian Nation to 1887*. Honolulu: University of Hawai'i Press, 2002.

'Memorializing Pu'uola and remembering Pearl Harbor', in S. Shigematsu and K.L. Camacho (eds.), *Militarized Currents: Toward a Decolonized Future in Asia and the Pacific*. Minneapolis: University of Minnesota Press, 2010, 3–14.

Otero, J.L., and P.R. Pardo. 'El imaginario social marítimo Boliviano: una explicación social de la política exterior de Bolivia hacia Chile', *Diálogo Andino* 57 (2018), 111–20.

Ottino, P. *Rangiroa: Parenté étendue, résidence et terres dans un atoll polynésien*. Paris: Éditions Cujas, 1972.

PACFB. 'Pan Am across the Pacific', *Pan Am Clipper Flying Boats* (n.d.), www.clipperflyingboats.com/transpacific-airline-service.

Pacific Islands Forum. Communiqué, Koror, Republic of Palau, 29–31 July 2014.

Pacific Islands Forum Secretariat. 'The framework for Pacific regionalism', www.forumsec.org/wp-content/uploads/2017/09/Framework-for-Pacific-Regionalism.pdf.

'Opening address by Prime Minister Tuilaepa Sailele Mailelegaoi of Samoa to open the 48th Pacific Islands Forum 2017', www.forumsec.org/opening-address-prime-minister-tuilaepa-sailele-mailelegaoi-samoa-open-48th-pacific-islands-forum-2017/.

Padrón, R. *The Indies of the Setting Sun: How Early Modern Spain Mapped the Far East as the Transpacific West*. Chicago: University of Chicago Press, 2020.

Páez, A. *La Guerra del Pacífico y deberes de la América*. Colón, Panama: Oficina del Canal, 1881.

Panadés Vargas, J.L., and J.A. González Pizarro. *Antofagasta, historia de mi ciudad*. Antofagasta: Corporación Pro Antofagasta, 1998.

Panakera, C. 'World War II and tourism development in Solomon Islands', in C. Ryan (ed.), *Battlefield Tourism: History, Place and Interpretation*. Amsterdam: Elsevier, 2007, 125–41.

Panapa, L., and M. Phillips. 'Ethnic persistence: towards understanding the lived experiences of Pacific Island athletes in the National Rugby League', *International Journal of the History of Sport* 31:11 (2014), 1374–88.

Panitch, J.M. 'Liberty, equality, posterity? Some archival lessons from the case of the French Revolution', *American Archivist* 59:1 (1996), 30–47.

Pantsov, A. *The Bolsheviks and the Chinese Revolution 1919–1927*. Honolulu: University of Hawai'i Press, 2000.

Parham, V. '"All go to the hop fields": the role of migratory and wage labor in the preservation of indigenous Pacific Northwest Culture', in G.D. Smithers and B.N. Newman (eds.), *Native Diasporas: Indigenous Identities and Settler Colonialism in the Americas*. Lincoln: University of Nebraska Press, 2014, 317–46.

Parke, A. *Degei's Descendants: Spirits, Place and People in Pre-cession Fiji*, edited by M. Spriggs and D. Scarr. Canberra: ANU Press, 2014.

Parkes, H. *Fifty Years in the Making of Australian History*. London: Longmans, Green, & Co., 1892).

Parry, J.H. *The Spanish Seaborne Empire*. New York: Alfred A. Knopf, 1966.

References to Volume II

Parry, J.T. *Ring Ditch Fortifications in the Rewa Delta, Fiji, Air Photo Interpretation and Analysis.* Bulletin of the Fiji Museum 3 (1977).

Parsons, C.D.F. (ed.). *Healing Practices in the South Pacific.* Laie: Institute for Polynesian Studies, Brigham Young University, 1985.

Parsons, H. 'British and Tahitian collaborative drawing strategies on Cook's Endeavour voyage', in S. Konishi, M. Nugent, and T. Shellam (eds.), *Indigenous Intermediaries: New Perspectives on Exploration Archives.* Canberra: ANU Press, 2015, 147–68.

Parsonson, G.S. 'The literate revolution in Polynesia', *Journal of Pacific History* 2 (1967), 39–57.

Pascoe, P. *What Comes Naturally: Miscegenation Law and the Making of Race in America.* Oxford: Oxford University Press, 2009.

Paterson, L. 'Hāwhekaihe: Māori voices on the position of "half-castes" within Māori society', *Journal of New Zealand Studies* 9 (2010), 135–56.

'Print culture and the collective Māori consciousness', *Journal of New Zealand Literature* 18:2 (2010), 105–29.

Paterson, T.G. *American Foreign Policy: A History.* Lexington: D.C. Heath, 1977.

Peattie, M. *Nan'yō: The Rise and Fall of the Japanese in Micronesia, 1885–1945.* Honolulu: University of Hawai'i Press, 1988.

Pellion, A. 'Îles des Papous: Divers portraits de naturels vus sur l'île Rawak', engraving, in J. Arago, A. Pellion et al., *Atlas historique, Voyage autour du monde . . .* (1825), plate 43, NGA 2016.497, National Gallery of Australia, Canberra.

Peltier, P. 'Men's houses, other people's houses', in S. Tcherkézoff and F. Douaire-Marsaudon (eds.), *The Changing South Pacific: Identities and Transformations.* Canberra: ANU Press, 2008, 63–84.

Peralto, N. '*Kokolo Mai Ka Mole Uaua O 'Ī*: the resilience and resurgence of *Aloha 'Āina* in Hāmākua Hikina, Hawai'i', PhD thesis, University of Hawai'i, Mānoa, 2018.

Perlman, D. 'Blast from the past: researchers worry that radiation from nuclear test decades ago may be damaging marine life today', *San Francisco Chronicle* (17 December 2001), www.sfgate.com/news/article/BLAST-FROM-THE-PAST-Researchers-worry-that-2839679.php.

Perrier Bruslé, L. 'La Bolivie, sa mer perdue et la construction nationale', *Annales de Géographie* 689:1 (2013), 47–72; trans as 'Bolivia: its lost coastline and nation-building', www.cairn-int.info/article-E_AG_689_0047–bolivia-its-lost-coastline-and-nation-bu.htm.

Perry, A. *Colonial Relations: The Douglas-Connolly Family and the Nineteenth-Century Imperial World.* Cambridge: Cambridge University Press, 2015.

On the Edge of Empire: Gender, Race and the Making of British Columbia. Toronto: University of Toronto Press, 2001.

Perry, J.C. *Facing West: Americans and the Opening of the Pacific.* Westport, CT: Praeger, 1994.

Peter, J. 'Chuukese travellers and the idea of horizon', *Asia Pacific Viewpoint* 41:3 (2000), 253–67.

Peters, J.D. 'Technology and ideology: the case of the telegraph revisited', in J. Packer and J. Robertson (eds.), *Thinking with James Carey: Essays on Communications, Transportation, History.* New York: Peter Lang, 2006, 137–55.

REFERENCES TO VOLUME II

Petersen, G. 'At the intersection of chieftainship and constitutional government: some comparisons from Micronesia', *Journal de la Société des Océanistes* 141 (2015), 255–65.

'The Micronesians', in J.M. Fitzpatrick (ed.), *Endangered Peoples of Oceania: Struggles to Survive and Thrive*. Westport, CT: Greenwood, 2001.

Peterson-del Mar, D. 'Intermarriage and agency: a Chinookan case study', *Ethnohistory* 42:1 (1995), 1–30.

Peteru, C. 'Protection of indigenous knowledge', Preservation of Local and Indigenous Knowledge Workshop, conference paper (Suva, World Wide Fund for Nature and Department of Environment, 16–17 November 1999).

Petit, J., and D. Tanret. Comment on the Marquesan MPA, 'In French Polynesia, a chance to protect ocean and culture', article on the Pew Charitable Trust website, 27 March 2019, www.pewtrusts.org/en/research-and-analysis/articles/2019/03/27/in-french-polynesia-a-chance-to-protect-ocean-and-culture.

Philbrick, N. *Sea of Glory: America's Voyage of Discovery: The U.S. Exploring Expedition, 1838–1842*. New York: Viking, 2003.

Phipps, P. 'Neocolonialism', in H.K. Anheier and M. Juergensmeyer (eds.), *Encyclopedia of Global Studies*. Thousand Oaks, CA: Sage, 2012, 1232–5.

Pietrobelli, C. *Industry, Competitiveness and Technological Capabilities in Chile: A New Tiger from Latin America?* New York: St. Martin's Press, 1998.

[Pigafetta, A.], *Le voyage et navigation, faict par les Espaignolz es Isles de Mollucques, des isles quilz ont trouve audict voyage, des roys dicelles, de leur gouvernement & maniere de vivre, avec plusieurs austres choses*. Paris: Simon de Colines, [1525].

Pinochet de la Barra, Ó. *La Antártica chilena*. Santiago: Editorial Andrés Bello, 1976.

Pirie, P. 'The effects of treponematosis and gonorrhoea on the populations of the Pacific', *Human Biology in Oceania* 1:3 (1972), 187–206.

Plancius, P. *Insulae Moluccae celeberrimæ sunt ob maximam aromatum copiam quam per totum terrarum orbem mittunt* . . . [Amsterdam: Cornelis Claesz], 1592–4.

Plomley, B., and K.A. Henley. *The Sealers of Bass Strait and the Cape Barren Island Community*. Hobart: Blubber Head Press, 1990.

Pocock, J.G.A. *The Machiavellian Moment: Florentine Thought and the Atlantic Republican Tradition*. Princeton: Princeton University Press, 2003.

Polynesian Leaders' Group. Communiqué from Third Meeting, Auckland, 30 August 2013.

Pomfret, D. 'Raising Eurasia: race, class and age in French and British colonies', *Comparative Studies in Societies and History* 51:2 (2009), 314–43.

Potauaine, S.F., and 'O. Māhina. *'Efinanga: Ko e Ngaahi Tala mo e Anga Fakafonua 'o Tonga*. Kolomotu'a: Lali, 1994.

'Kula and 'uli: red and black in Tongan thinking and practice', in T.M. Steen and N.L. Drescher (eds.), *Tonga: Its Land, Sea, and People*. Nuku'alofa: Vava'u Press, 2011, 194–216.

Potter, S.J. 'Webs, networks, and systems: globalization and the mass media in the nineteenth- and twentieth-century British empire', *Journal of British Studies* 46 (2007), 621–46.

Pouesi, D. (dir.). *The Search for Tagaloa*, YouTube video, 2017, www.youtube.com/watch?v=NAUJvKTipCQ&feature=youtube.

Pouwer, J. 'The colonisation, decolonisation and recolonisation of West New Guinea', *Journal of Pacific History* 34:2 (1999), 157–79.

References to Volume II

Powell, A. *The Third Force: ANGAU's New Guinea War, 1942–46*. Oxford: Oxford University Press, 2003.

Powles, C.G. 'The persistence of chiefly power and its implications for law and political organisation in Western Polynesia', PhD thesis, Australian National University, Canberra, 1979.

Powles, G., and M. Pulea. *Pacific Courts and Legal Systems*. Suva: Institute of Pacific Studies, University of the South Pacific, 1988.

Poyer, L. 'Defining history across cultures: insider and outsider contrasts', *Isla: A Journal of Micronesian Studies* 1 (1992), 73–89.

'Dimensions of hunger in wartime: Chuuk Lagoon, 1943–1945', *Food and Foodways* 12 (2004), 137–64.

'Ethnicity and identity in Micronesia', in R.C. Kiste and M. Marshall (eds.), *American Anthropology in Micronesia: An Assessment*. Honolulu: University of Hawai'i Press, 1999, 197–223.

Poyer, L., S. Falgout, and L.M. Carucci. 'The impact of the Pacific War on modern Micronesian identity', in V.S. Lockwood (ed.), *Globalization and Culture Change in the Pacific Islands*. Upper Saddle River, NJ: Pearson Prentice Hall, 2004, 307–23.

The Typhoon of War: Micronesian Experiences of the Pacific War. Honolulu: University of Hawai'i Press, 2001.

Pratt, M.L. *Imperial Eyes: Travel Writing and Transculturation*. New York: Routledge, 1992.

Prebble, M., A. Anderson, and D.J. Kennett. 'Forest clearance and agricultural expansion on Rapa, Austral Archipelago, French Polynesia', *Holocene* 23 (2013), 179–96.

Prestholdt, J. 'Similitude and empire: on Comorian strategies of Englishness', *Journal of World History* 18:2 (2007), 113–38.

Price, J. *Orienting Canada: Race, Empire, and the Transpacific*. Vancouver: UBC Press, 2011.

Price, N., et al. 'After the typhoon: multicultural archaeologies of World War II on Peleliu, Palau, Micronesia', *Journal of Conflict Archaeology* 8 (2013), 193–248.

Price, S.T. 'The transformation of Yap: causes and consequences of socio-economic change in Micronesia', PhD thesis, Washington State University, Pullman, 1975.

Prichard, J.C. *Researches into the Physical History of Man*. London: J. and A. Arch, 1813.

Researches into the Physical History of Mankind, 2nd edn, 2 vols., London J. and A. Arch, 1826; 3rd edn, 5 vols., London: Sherwood, Gilbert, and Piper, 1836–47.

Ptolemy, C. *Geographia universalis, vetus et nova, complectens*, ed. S. Münster. Basel: Henricum Petrum, 1540.

Puas, G., *The Federated States of Micronesia's Engagement with the Outside World: Control, Self-Preservation, and Continuity*. Canberra: ANU Press, 2021. Canberra: ANU Press, 2021.

The Impact of Climate Change on Health in the Federated States of Micronesia: The Case of the Low-Lying Islands of the Mortlocks. Palikir, Report for Pohnpei State, Federated States of Micronesia, June 2016.

Pulu, T.J.B. 'Ko e Kakai Tonga 'o Nu'u Sila. Tongan generations in Auckland New Zealand', PhD thesis, University of Waikato, Hamilton, 2007.

Puputauki, M. *E mau atoga magareva akataito*. Honolulu: Imprimerie Catholique, 1852.

Pybus, C. *Truganini: Journey through the Apocalypse*. Sydney: Allen & Unwin, 2020.

QAL. *Annual Report*. Sydney: Qantas Airways Ltd, 1967–2006,

Annual Report and Financial Accounts. Sydney: Qantas Empire Airways Ltd, 1956–66.

REFERENCES TO VOLUME II

Quain, B. *Fijian Village*. Chicago: University of Chicago Press, 1948.

Qi, Y., J. Zou, and S. Liang (eds.). *Red Tides along Chinese Coast*. Beijing: Science Press, 2003.

Quilici, F. *The Blue Continent*. New York: Rinehart & Co., 1954.

Quimby, F. 'Fortress Guåhån: Chamorro nationalism, regional economic integration and U.S. defense interests shape Guam's recent history', *Journal of Pacific History* 46 (2011), 357–80.

Quirós, P.F. de. *Memoriales de las Indias Australes*, ed. O. Pinochet. Madrid: Historia 16, 1990.

Quoy, J.-R.C. [Autobiographie], 1864–8, Papiers Quoy, MS 2507, Médiathèque Michel-Crépeau, La Rochelle, France.

'De l'homme', in J.-R.C. Quoy and J.-P. Gaimard, *Zoologie*, 4 vols., *Voyage de découvertes de l'Astrolabe exécuté . . . pendant les années 1826–1827–1828–1829* (Paris : J. Tastu, 1830–5), vol. I, 15–59.

'Voyage autour du monde, pendant les années 1817, 1818, 1819, & 1820: Journal', 1817–20, R-2520-11702, Archives centrales de la Marine, Service historique de la Défense, Rochefort, France.

Quoy, J.-R.C., and J.-P. Gaimard. *Zoologie*, 4 vols., *Voyage de découvertes de l'Astrolabe exécuté . . . pendant les années 1826–1827–1828–1829*. Paris: J. Tastu, 1830–5.

Zoologie, Voyage autour du monde . . . exécuté sur les corvettes de S.M. l'Uranie et la Physicienne, pendant les années 1817, 1818, 1819 et 1820 . . . Paris: Pillet aîné, 1824.

Radetzki, M. 'Seven thousand years in the service of humanity: the history of copper, the red metal', *Resources Policy* 34:4 (2009), 176–84.

Rallu, J.-L. 'Pre- and post-contact population in island Melanesia: can projections meet retrodictions?', in P.V. Kirch and J.-L. Rallu (eds.), *The Growth and Collapse of Pacific Island Societies: Archaeological and Demographic Perspectives*. Honolulu: University of Hawai'i Press, 2007, 15–34.

Ralston, C. *Grass Huts and Warehouses: Pacific Beach Communities of the Nineteenth Century*. Canberra: ANU Press, 1977.

'The study of women in the Pacific', *Contemporary Pacific* 4:1 (1992), 162–75.

'Women workers in Samoa and Tonga in the early twentieth century', in C. Moore, J. Leckie, and D. Munro (eds.), *Labour in the South Pacific*. Townsville: James Cook University Press, 1990, 67–77.

Ralston, C., and N. Thomas (eds.). *Sanctity and Power: Gender in Polynesian History,* special issue of *Journal of Pacific History* 22 (1987).

Ram, K., and M. Jolly (eds.). *Maternities and Modernities: Colonial and Postcolonial Experiences in Asia and the Pacific*. Cambridge: Cambridge University Press, 1997.

Ramasamy, S., V. Krishnan, R. Bedford, and C. Bedford. 'The Recognised Seasonal Employer policy: seeking the elusive triple wins for development through international migration', *Pacific Economic Bulletin* 23:3 (2008), 171–86.

Ramos, R. *A segunda fundação (1890–1926)* (Lisbon: Círculo de Leitores, 1994).

Ramsey, R. *Nights of Storytelling: A Cultural History of Kanaky-New Caledonia*. Honolulu: University of Hawai'i Press, 2011.

Ratuva, S. 'Primordial politics? Political parties and tradition in Melanesia', in R. Rich, L. Hambly, and M.G. Moran (eds.), *Political Parties in the Pacific Islands*. Canberra: ANU Press, 2008, 27–42.

'Reconceptualising contemporary Pacific Island states: towards a syncretic approach', *New Pacific Review* 2:1 (2003), 246–62.

864

References to Volume II

Ravuvu, A. *Fijians at War, 1939–1945*. Suva: Institute of Pacific Studies, University of the South Pacific, 1974.

The Fijian Ethos. Suva: Institute of Pacific Studies, University of the South Pacific, 1987.

Vaka i Taukei: The Fijian Way of Life. Suva: Institute of Pacific Studies, University of the South Pacific, 1983.

Reagan, R. 'Written responses to questions submitted by the *Far Eastern Economic Review*' (9 May 1984), Ronald Reagan Presidential Library Archives, www.reagan.utexas.edu/archives/speeches/1984/50984i.htm.

Reclaiming the Ocean Collective. 'The rush for Oceania: critical perspectives on contemporary oceans governance and stewardship', http://repository.usp.ac.fj/11405/1/SGDIA_WORKING_PAPER_SERIES_-_No._9_-_Rush_for_Oceania.pdf.

Regnault, J.-M., and I. Kurtovitch. 'Les ralliements du Pacifique en 1940. Entre légende gaulliste, enjeux stratégiques mondiaux et rivalités Londres/Vichy', *Revue d'Histoire Moderne & Contemporaine* 49:4 (2002), 71–90.

Reid, A. *A History of Southeast Asia: Critical Crossroads*. Chichester: Wiley-Blackwell, 2015.

Imperial Alchemy: Nationalism and Political Identity in Southeast Asia. Cambridge: Cambridge University Press, 2010.

Southeast Asia in the Age of Commerce, 1450–1680, 2 vols. New Haven: Yale University Press, 1988–93.

Reid, J.L. *The Sea Is My Country: The Maritime World of the Makahs*. New Haven: Yale University Press, 2015.

Reilly, T.H. *The Taiping Heavenly Kingdom: Rebellion and the Blasphemy of Empire*. Seattle: University of Washington Press, 2004.

René Moreno, G. *La mita de Potosí en 1795*. Potosí: Universidad Tomás Frías, 1959.

Rey Mallén, P. 'Trade between Chile and China grew 22 percent in 7 years as China became Chile's biggest trading partner', *International Business Times* (6 September 2013), www.ibtimes.com/trade-between-chile-china-grew-22-percent-7-years-china-became-chiles-biggest-trading-partner.

Reynolds, H. *Nowhere People*. Camberwell: Penguin, 2005.

Ribadeneira, D. 'A jewel in an economic rough: revitalized Chile looks to join NAFTA', *Boston Globe* (18 January 1995), 39.

[Ribeiro, D.], [Carta Castiglioni], 1525, Biblioteca estense universitaria, Modena https://edl.beniculturali.it/beu/850013656.

Richards, Z.T., et al. 'Bikini Atoll coral biodiversity resilience five decades after nuclear testing', *Marine Pollution Bulletin* 56 (2008), 503–15.

Rimmer, P.J. 'Australia through the prism of Qantas: distance makes a comeback', *Otemon Journal of Australian Studies* 31 (2005), 135–57.

'China's Belt and Road Initiative: underlying economic and international relations dimensions', *Asian Pacific Economic Literature* 32:2 (2018), 3–26.

Freight Forwarding in the Australia—Papua New Guinea Trade. New Guinea Research Bulletin 48. Canberra: New Guinea Research Unit, Australian National University, 1972.

Río, M.E. del. *La inmigración y su desarrollo en el Perú*. Lima: Sanmartí y cía., 1929.

Riseman, N. *Defending Whose Country? Indigenous Soldiers in the Pacific War*. Lincoln: University of Nebraska Press, 2012.

REFERENCES TO VOLUME II

Risotto, C.M., B. Wellenius, A. Lewin, and C.R. Gomez. *Competition in International Voice Communications*. World Bank Working Paper 42. Washington, DC: The World Bank, 2004.

Riva Palacio, R. 'Chile: la otra cara del jaguar: la ilusion neoliberal', *El Norte* (Monterrey, Mexico) (13 October 1996), 14.

Rivers, W.H.R. 'The psychological factor', in W.H.R. Rivers (ed.), *Essays on the Depopulation of Melanesia*. Cambridge: Cambridge University Press, 1922, 84–113.

Roberts, B.R., and M.A. Stephens (eds.). *Archipelagic American Studies*. Durham, NC: Duke University Press, 2017.

Robin, L. 'Australia in global environmental history', in J.R. McNeill and E.S. Mauldin (eds.), *A Companion to Global Environmental History*. Chichester: Wiley-Blackwell, 2012, 182–95.

Robineau, C. 'La construction du premier État tahitien moderne', in P. de Dekker and P. Lagayette (eds.), *États et pouvoirs dans les territoires français du Pacifique*. Paris: L'Harmattan, 1987, 28–43.

Robinson, N.K. *Villagers at War: Some Papua New Guinean Experiences in World War II*. Pacific Research Monograph 2. Canberra: ANU Press, 1981.

Robson, A.E. *Prelude to Empire: Consuls, Missionary Kingdoms and the Pre-colonial South Seas Seen through the Life of William Thomas Pritchard*. Vienna: Lit Verlag, 2004.

Rocha, Z.L. 'Re-viewing race and mixedness: mixed race in Asia and the Pacific', *Journal of Intercultural Studies* 39:4 (2018), 510–26.

Rocha, Z.L., and M. Webber (eds.). *Mana Tangatarua: Mixed Heritages, Ethnic Identity and Biculturalism in Aotearoa/New Zealand*. London: Routledge, 2018.

Rodman, M.C. *Far from Home: British Colonial Space in the New Hebrides*. Honolulu: University of Hawai'i Press, 2001.

Rodríguez O., J.E. *The Independence of Spanish America*. Cambridge: Cambridge University Press, 1998.

Rogers, R.F. *Destiny's Landfall: A History of Guam*, rev. edn. Honolulu: University of Hawai'i Press, 2011.

Rogerson, E. 'The "Fuzzy Wuzzy Angels": looking beyond the myth', Australian War Memorial SVSS Paper, www.awm.gov.au/sites/default/files/svss_2012_rogerson_paper.pdf.

Rokowaqa, E. *Ai Tukutuku Kei Viti: sa vola ko Rev. Epeli Rokowaqa*. Suva: [Methodist Missionary Magazine], 1926.

Romero, S. 'Slow burning challenge to Chile on Easter Island', *The New York Times* (6 October 2012), www.nytimes.com/2012/10/07/world/americas/slow-burning-rebellion-against-chile-on-easter-island.html.

Ropeti, M. 'One Gospel: Pacific Island women's perspective and response to Rev. Marie Ropeti', *Pacific Journal of Theology* 17 (1997), 31–53.

Roque, R. *Headhunting and Colonialism: Anthropology and the Circulation of Human Skulls in the Portuguese Empire, 1870–1930*. Basingstoke: Palgrave Macmillan, 2010.

'The colonial command of ceremonial language: etiquette and custom-imitation in nineteenth-century East Timor', in L. Jarnagin (ed.), *Culture and Identity in the Luso-Asian World: Tenacities and Plasticities*. Singapore: ISEAS, 2012, 67–87.

866

References to Volume II

Roque, R., and L. Sousa. 'The stones of Afaloicai: colonial archaeology and the authority of ancient objects', in R. Roque and E.G. Traube (eds.), *Crossing Histories and Ethnographies: Following Colonial Historicities in Timor-Leste*. New York: Berghahn Books, 2019, 203–40.

Ross, F., S. McKemmish, and S. Faulkhead. 'Indigenous knowledge and the archives: designing trusted archival systems for Koorie communities', *Archives and Manuscripts* 34:2 (2006), 112–40.

Rostworowski de Diez Canseco, M. *History of the Inca Realm*. Cambridge: Cambridge University Press, 1999.

Rothwell, M.D. *Transpacific Revolutionaries: The Chinese Revolution in Latin America*. New York: Routledge, 2013.

'Roubles for Tonga from Russia with Love', *Pacific Islands Monthly*, August 1976, 14–16.

Rountree, K. 'Re-making the Maori female body: Marianne Williams's Mission in the Bay of Islands', *Journal of Pacific History* 35:1 (2000), 49–66.

Rousseau, J.-J. *On the Social Contract (1762)*, ed. and intro. David Wootton, 2nd edn (Indianapolis: Hackett, 2019).

Routledge, D. *Matanitū: The Struggle for Power in Early Fiji*. Suva: University of the South Pacific, 1985.

Roy, A.G. *Imperialism and Sikh Migration: The Komagata Maru Incident*. London: Routledge, 2017.

Rozwadowski, H.M. *Fathoming the Ocean: The Discovery and Exploration of the Deep Sea*. Cambridge MA: Belknap Press, 2005.

Rüegg, J. 'Mapping the forgotten colony: the Ogasawara Islands and the Tokugawa pivot to the Pacific', *Cross-Currents: East Asian History and Culture Review E-Journal* 23 (2017).

Russell, L. *A Little Bird Told Me: Family Secrets, Necessary Lies*. Crows Nest, NSW: Allen & Unwin, 2012.

Roving Mariners: Australian Aboriginal Whalers and Sealers in the Southern Oceans, 1790–1870. Albany: State University of New York Press, 2012.

Rutherford, N. *Shirley Baker and the King of Tonga*, 2nd edn. Honolulu: University of Hawai'i Press, 1996.

Ryan, L. *Tasmanian Aborigines: A History since 1803*. Sydney: Allen & Unwin, 2012.

Saada, E. *Empire's Children: Race, Filiation and Citizenship in the French Colonies*, trans. A. Goldhammer. Chicago: University of Chicago Press, 2012.

Sachaklian, H.A. 'Geopolitics versus geologistics', *Air University Quarterly Review* 1:2 (1947), 53–63.

Saeki, E. *Umi no Seimeisen: Waga Nanyō Shotō (Lifeline of the Sea: Our South Southern Islands)*. Yokohama: Yokohama Cinema Shōkai, 1932. 35 mm, 16 mm; 72 min. film, 'talkie' version (archived by Mainichi Films Company, Tokyo and Japan National Film Center, Tokyo).

Sahlins, M. *Moala: Culture and Nature on a Fijian Island*. Ann Arbor: University of Michigan Press, 1962.

'Other tribes, other customs: the anthropology of history', *American Anthropologist* 85:3 (1983), 529–33.

'Poor man, rich man, big-man, chief: political types in Melanesia and Polynesia', *Comparative Studies in Society and History* 5:3 (1963), 285–303.

REFERENCES TO VOLUME II

Sai, D.K. *Ua Mau ke Ea, Sovereignty Endures: An Overview of the Political and Legal History of the Hawaiian Islands*. Honolulu: Pūʻā Foundation, 2011.

Said, E.W. *Orientalism*. New York: Vintage, 1979.

Saignes, T. 'Indian migration and social change in seventeenth-century Charcas', in B. Larson and O. Harris with E. Tandenter (eds.), *Ethnicity, Markets, and Migration in the Andes: At the Crossroads of History and Anthropology*. Durham, NC: Duke University Press, 1995, 167–95.

Sakai, N. 'On romantic love and military violence: transpacific imperialism and U.S. –Japan complicity', in K. Camacho and S. Shigematsu (eds.), *Militarized Currents: Toward a Decolonized Future in Asia and the Pacific*. Minneapolis: University of Minnesota Press, 2010, 206–16.

Saldanha, A.V. de. *Iustum imperium: dos tratados como fundamento do império dos portugueses no Oriente: estudo de história do direito internacional e do direito português*. Lisbon: Instituto Português do Oriente / Fundação Oriente, 1997.

Salesa, D. 'A Pacific destiny: New Zealand's overseas empire, 1840–1945', in S. Mallon, K. Mahina-Tuai, and D. Salesa (eds.), *Tangata o le Moana: New Zealand and the People of the Pacific*. Wellington: Te Papa Press, 2012, 97–122.

'Emma and Phebe: "weavers of the border"', *Journal of the Polynesian Society* 123:2 (2014), 145–67.

Racial Crossings: Race, Intermarriage, and the Victorian British Empire. Oxford: Oxford University Press, 2011.

'Samoa's half-castes and some frontiers of comparison', in A.L. Stoler (ed.), *Haunted by Empire: Geographies of Intimacy in North American History*. Durham, NC: Duke University Press, 2006, 71–93.

'The Pacific in indigenous time', in D. Armitage and A. Bashford (eds.), *Pacific Histories: Ocean, Land, People*. Basingstoke: Palgrave Macmillan, 2014, 31–52.

'"Troublesome half-castes": tales of a Samoan borderland', MA thesis, University of Auckland, 1997.

Salmond, A. *Aphrodite's Island: The European Discovery of Tahiti*. Auckland: Viking and Berkeley: University of California Press, 2009.

Bligh: William Bligh in the South Seas. Berkeley: University of California Press, 2011.

'Hidden hazards: reconstructing Tupaia's chart', *Journal of Pacific History* 54:4 (2019), 534–37.

The Trial of the Cannibal Dog: The Remarkable Story of Captain's Cook Encounters in the South Seas. New Haven: Yale University Press, 2003.

'Their body is different, our body is different: European and Tahitian navigators in the 18th century', *History and Anthropology* 16:2 (2005), 167–86.

Sampson, C.A. 'Tahiti, George Pritchard et le "mythe" du "royaume missionnaire"', *Journal de la Société des Océanistes* 29:38 (1973), 57–68.

Samson, J. 'Exploring the Pacific World', in D. Kennedy (ed.), *Reinterpreting Exploration: The West in the World*. Oxford: Oxford University Press, 2014, 154–71.

Race and Redemption: British Missionaries Encounter Pacific Peoples, 1797–1920. Grand Rapids, MI: Eerdmans, 2017.

'Rescuing Fijian women? The British Anti-Slavery Proclamation of 1852', *Journal of Pacific History* 30:1 (1995), 22–38.

References to Volume II

'The sleepiness of George Sarawia: the impact of disease on the Melanesian Mission at Mota, c. 1870–1900', *Journal of Pacific History* 52:2 (2017), 156–71.

San Juan, E., Jr. *U.S. Imperialism and Revolution in the Philippines*. New York: Palgrave Macmillan, 2007.

Sanchez, P.C. *Uncle Sam, Please Come Back to Guam*. Agaña: Star Press, 1979.

Sand, C., J. Bolé, and A. Ouétcho. 'Les sociétés pré-européennes de Nouvelle-Calédonie et leur transformation historique: l'apport de l'archéologie', in A. Bensa and I. Leblic (eds.), *En pays kanak: ethnologie, linguistique, archéologie, histoire de la Nouvelle-Calédonie*. Paris: Éditions de la Maison des Sciences de l'Homme, 2000, 171–94.

'Prehistory and its perception in a Melanesian archipelago: the New Caledonia example', *Antiquity* 77:297 (2003), 505–19.

'What were the real numbers? The question of pre-contact population densities in New Caledonia', in P.V. Kirch and J.-L. Rallu (eds.), *The Growth and Collapse of Pacific Island Societies*. Honolulu: University of Hawai'i Press, 2007, 306–25.

Santis Arenas, H. 'Significado y contenido de Chile: país marítimo y tricontinental', *Revista Chilena de Geopolítica* 6:3 (1990), 81–92.

Sanz, C. *Australia su descubrimiento y denominación: con la reproducción facsimil del memorial número 8 de Quirós en español original, y en las diversas traducciones contemporáneas*. Madrid: Ministerio de Asuntos Exteriores, 1973.

Sater, W.F. *Andean Tragedy: Fighting the War of the Pacific, 1879–1884*. Lincoln: University of Nebraska Press, 2007.

The Heroic Image in Chile: Arturo Prat, Secular Saint. Berkeley: University of California Press, 1973.

Sater, W.F., and H.H. Herwig. *The Grand Illusion: The Prussianization of the Chilean Army*. Lincoln: University of Nebraska Press, 1999.

Saura, B. *Histoire et mémoire des temps coloniaux en Polynésie française*. Papeete: Éditions au Vent des Îles, 2015.

(ed.). *La lignée royale des Tama-toa de Ra'iātea (Îles-sous-le Vent): Puta 'ā'amu nō te 'ōpū hui ari'i Tama-toa nō Ra'iātea*. Papeete: Service de la Culture et du Patrimoine de Polynésie Française, 2003.

Saveliev, I. 'Migrants and borderland identity: a comparative study of Japanese communities in British Columbia and the Priamur region in the 1870s–1900s', *Forum of International Development Studies* 40 (2011), 79–94.

Scarr, D. *Fragments of Empire: A History of the Western Pacific High Commission, 1877–1914*. Canberra: ANU Press, 1967.

The Majesty of Colour: A Life of Sir John Bates Thurston, 2 vols. Canberra: ANU Press, 1973.

Schell, W., Jr. 'Silver symbiosis: reOrienting Mexican economic history', *Hispanic American Historical Review* 81:1 (2001), 89–133.

Schmitt, C. *The Nomos of the Earth in the International Law of Jus Publicum Europaeum*, trans. and annotated G.L. Ulmen. New York: Telos Press, 2003.

Schmitt, R.C. *Hawaii in the Movies 1998–1959*. Honolulu: Hawaiian Historical Society, 1988.

Schoeffel, P. 'The origins and development of women's associations in Western Samoa, 1830–1977', *Journal of Pacific Studies* 3 (1977), 1–21.

Schottenhammer, A. 'China's emergence as a maritime power', in J.W. Chaffee and D. Twitchett (eds.), *The Cambridge History of China*, vol. v, part 2, *Sung China, 960–1279*. Cambridge: Cambridge University Press, 2015, 437–525.

Schroeder, S. *Tlacaelel Remembered: Mastermind of the Aztec Empire*. Norman: University of Oklahoma Press, 2016.

Schurz, W.L. *The Manila Galleon: The Romantic History of the Spanish Galleons Trading between Manila and Acapulco*. New York: E.P. Dutton, 1939.

Schweizer, N.R. *Turning Tide: The Ebb and Flow of Hawaiian Nationality*, 3rd edn. Berne: Lang, 2005.

Scott, J.S. *The Common Wind: Afro-American Currents in the Age of the Haitian Revolution*. London: Verso, 2018.

Scott, J.W. *Gender and the Politics of History*. New York: Columbia University Press, 1988.

Secada, C.A.G. de. 'Arms, guano, and shipping: the W.R. Grace interests in Peru, 1865–1885', *Business History Review* 59:4 (1985), 597–621.

Seed, P. *Ceremonies of Possession: Europe's Conquest of the New World, 1492–1640*. Cambridge: Cambridge University Press, 1992.

Segal, H. *Kosrae: The Sleeping Lady Awakens*. Kosrae: Kosrae Tourist Division, Department of Conservation and Development, Kosrae State Government, Federated States of Micronesia, 1989.

Seijas, T. *Asian Slaves in Colonial Mexico: From Chinos to Indians*. Cambridge: Cambridge University Press, 2014.

Seixas, M.M. de. 'A emblemática oitocentista da Casa de Bragança nos tronos de Portugal e Brasil', in R. Ramos, J.M. de Carvalho, and I. Corrêa da Silva (eds.), *Dois países, um sistema: a monarquia constitucional dos Braganças em Portugal e no Brasil (1822–1910)*. Lisbon: D. Quixote, 2018, 57–84.

Heráldica, representação do poder e memória da Nação: o armorial autárquico de Inácio de Vilhena Barbosa. Lisbon: Universidade Lusíada Editora, 2011.

Sekiguchi, Y. *Senso Daughters*. Canberra: Ronin Films; 55 min. film, 1990; English version, 1991.

Shankman, P. 'Interethnic unions and the regulation of sex in colonial Samoa, 1839–1945', *Journal of the Polynesian Society* 110:2 (2001), 119–48.

The Trashing of Margaret Mead: Anatomy of an Anthropological Controversy. Madison: University of Wisconsin Press, 2009.

Sharrad, P. *Albert Wendt and Pacific Literature: Circling the Void*. Auckland: Auckland University Press, 2003.

Shellam, T., M. Nugent, S. Konishi, and A. Cadzow. *Brokers and Boundaries: Colonial Exploration in Indigenous Territory*. Canberra: ANU Press, 2016.

Shen, S., and T. Binns. 'Pathways, motivations and challenges: contemporary Tuvaluan migration to New Zealand', *GeoJournal* 77:1 (2012), 63–82.

Sheng, F., and G. Smith, 'The shifting fates of China's Pacific diaspora', in G. Smith and T. Wesley-Smith (eds.), *The China Alternative: Changing Regional Order in the Pacific Islands*. Canberra: ANU Press, 2021, 427–50.

Shennan, J., and M.C. Tekenimatang (eds.). *One and a Half Pacific Islands/Teuana ao Teiterana n aba n te Betebeke: Stories the Banaban People Tell of Themselves/I-Banaba aika a Karakin oin Rongorongoia*. Wellington: Victoria University Press, 2005.

References to Volume II

Shepherd, C.J. *Haunted Houses and Ghostly Encounters: Ethnography and Animism in East Timor, 1860–1975*. Singapore: NUS Press, 2019.

Shepherd, J.R. *Statecraft and Political Economy on the Taiwan Frontier, 1600–1800*. Stanford: Stanford University Press, 1993.

Shigematsu, S., and K.L. Camacho (eds.). *Militarized Currents: Toward a Decolonized Future in Asia and the Pacific*. Minneapolis: University of Minnesota Press, 2010.

Shilliam, R. *The Black Pacific: Anti-Colonial Struggles and Oceanic Connections*. London: Bloomsbury, 2015.

Shimada, K. *Bōken Dankichi Manga Zenshū (Compiled Collection of 'Dankichi the Adventurous')*. Tokyo: Kōdansha, 1976 [1939].

Shimazaki, T. *Shimazaki Tōson Zenshū II (Collected Works of Shimazaki Tōson, II)*. Tokyo: Shinchōsha, 1949 [1901].

Shineberg, D. *The People Trade: Pacific Island Laborers and New Caledonia, 1865–1930*. Honolulu: University of Hawai'i Press, 1999.

Shuster, D.R. 'Political reviews: Republic of Palau', *Contemporary Pacific* 15 (2013), 142–9.

Sigrah, R.K., and S.M. King. *Te Rii ni Banaba*. Suva: Institute of Pacific Studies, University of the South Pacific, 2001.

Silva, J.C. da. *Relatório das operações de guerra no Districto Autónomo de Timor no anno de 1896*. Lisbon: Imprensa Nacional, 1897.

Silva, N.K. *Aloha Betrayed: Native Hawaiian Resistance to American Colonialism*. Durham, NC: Duke University Press, 2004.

The Power of the Steel Tipped Pen: Reconstructing Native Hawaiian Intellectual History. Durham, NC: Duke University Press, 2017.

Silva, N., and I. Badlis. 'Early Hawaiian newspapers and Kanaka Maoli intellectual history, 1834–1855', *Hawaiian Journal of History* 42 (2008), 105–34.

Simpson, G. *An Overland Journey round the World during the years 1841 and 1842*, vol. II. Philadelphia: Lea and Blanchard, 1847.

Sinn, E. *Pacific Crossing: California Gold, Chinese Migration, and the Making of Hong Kong*. Hong Kong: Hong Kong University Press, 2013.

Sissons, J. *The Polynesian Iconoclasm: Religious Revolution and the Seasonality of Power*. New York: Berghahn Books, 2014.

Sivasundaram, S. *Islanded: Britain, Sri Lanka, and the Bounds of an Indian Ocean Colony*. Chicago: University of Chicago Press, 2013.

Nature and Godly Empire: Science and Evangelical Mission in the Pacific, 1795–1850. Cambridge: Cambridge University Press, 2005.

Waves across the South: A New History of Revolution and Empire. Chicago: University of Chicago Press, 2020.

Sivasundaram, S., A. Bashford, and D. Armitage. 'Introduction: writing world oceanic histories', in D. Armitage, A. Bashford, and S. Sivasundaram (eds.), *Oceanic Histories*. Cambridge: Cambridge University Press, 2018, 1–28.

Siwatibau, S. 'Traditional environment practices in the South Pacific: a case study in Fiji', *Ambio* 13:5–6 (1984), 365–8.

Smethurst, P. *Travel Writing and the Natural World, 1768–1840*. Basingstoke: Palgrave, 2013.

Smith, A. 'Colonialism and the bomb in the Pacific', in J. Schofield and W. Cocroft (eds.), *A Fearsome Heritage: Diverse Legacies of the Cold War*. Walnut Creek, CA: Left Coast Press, 2007, 51–72.

Smith, A., and K.L. Jones. *Cultural Landscapes of the Pacific Islands*. Paris: ICOMOS (International Council on Monuments and Sites) Thematic Study, 2007.

Smith, A.D. 'Nationalism and classical social theory', *British Journal of Sociology* 34:1 (1983), 19–38.

Smith, B. 'Captain Cook's artists and the portrayal of Pacific peoples', *Art History* 7:3 (1984), 295–312.

European Vision and the South Pacific, 3rd edn. Oxford: Oxford University Press, 1989.

Smith, C. *Coal, Steam and Ships: Engineering, Enterprise and Empire on the Nineteenth Century Seas*. Cambridge: Cambridge University Press, 2018.

Smith, G. 'Chinese reactions to anti-Asian riots in the Pacific', *Journal of Pacific History* 47:1 (2012), 93–109.

'Fuqing dreaming: "New" Chinese communities in Papua New Guinea', in P. D'Arcy, P. Matbob, and L. Crowl (eds.), *Pacific Asian Partnerships in Resource Development*. Madang: Divine Word University Press, 2014, 126–40.

'Nupela Masta? Local and expatriate labour in a Chinese-run nickel mine in Papua New Guinea', *Asian Studies Review* 7:2 (2013), 178–95.

'PRC aid to the Pacific?', *China Matters* (April 2018), 1, http://chinamatters.org.au/wp-content/uploads/2018/04/China-Matters-Recommends-04-April-2018-PRC-Aid-Pacific.pdf.

Smith, L.T. *Decolonizing Methodologies: Research and Indigenous Peoples*, 2nd edn. London: Zed Books, 2012.

Smith, S.B. *Air Transport in the Pacific Area*. New York: International Institute of Pacific Relations, 1942.

Smith, V. 'Banks, Tupaia, and Mai: cross-cultural exchanges and friendship in the Pacific', *Parergon* 26:2 (2009), 139–60.

Intimate Strangers: Friendship, Exchange, and Pacific Encounters. Cambridge: Cambridge University Press, 2010.

'Joseph Banks's intermediaries: rethinking global cultural exchange', in S. Moyn and A. Sartori (eds.), *Global Intellectual History*. New York: Columbia University Press, 2013, 66–86.

Smith-Norris, M. *Domination and Resistance: The United States and the Marshall Islands during the Cold War*. Honolulu: University of Hawai'i Press, 2016.

Smyth, R. 'Reel Pacific history: the Pacific Islands on Film', video, and in B.V. Lal (ed.), *Pacific Islands History: Journeys and Transformations*. Canberra: Journal of Pacific History, 1992, 203–24.

So, B.K.L. *Prosperity, Region and Institutions in Maritime China: The South Fukien Pattern, 946–1368*. Cambridge, MA: Harvard University Press, 2001.

Soares, M. de C. 'Entre Irmãos: as "Galanterias" do Rei Adandozan do Daomé ao Príncipe D. João de Portugal, 1810', in M. Cottias and H. Mattos (eds.), *Escravidão e subjetividades no Atlântico Luso-brasileiro e Francês (séculos XVII–XX)*. Marseilles: OpenEdition Press, 2016, https://books.openedition.org/oep/788.

Soifer, D.H., and A. Vergara (eds.). *Politics after Violence: Legacies of the Shining Path Conflict in Peru*. Austin: University of Texas Press, 2019.

References to Volume II

Solimano, A. *Chile and the Neoliberal Trap: The Post-Pinochet Era.* Cambridge: Cambridge University Press, 2012.

Solnit, R. 'Notes on California as an island: there's truth in old maps', *Boom: A Journal of California* 4 (2014), 36–45.

Somare, M. *Sana: An Autobiography of Michael Somare.* Port Moresby: Niugini Press, 1975.

Sorrenson, R. 'The ship as a scientific instrument in the eighteenth century', in T. Ballantyne (ed.), *Science, Empire and the European Exploration of the Pacific.* Aldershot: Ashgate, 2004 [1996], 123–236.

Sousa, L. 'A bandeira portuguesa em Timor Leste: *hau hanoin*', in R. Fonseca (ed.), *Monumentos portugueses em Timor-Leste.* Porto: Crocodilo Azul, 2005, 36–8.

Spate, O.H.K. *The Spanish Lake.* Canberra: ANU Press, 2004 [1979].

Spence, J.D. *Gate of Heavenly Peace: The Chinese and Their Revolution, 1895–1980.* New York: Viking, 1981.

  God's Chinese Son: The Chinese Heavenly Kingdom of Hong Xiuquan. Hammersmith: Flamingo, 1997.

Spencer, D. *Disease, Religion and Society in the Fiji Islands.* New York: J.J. Augustin, 1941.

Spennemann, D.H.R. *Gifts from the Waves: A Case of Marine Transport of Obsidian to Nadikdik Atoll and the Occurrence of Other Drift Materials in the Marshall Islands.* Albury: Charles Sturt University, The Johnstone Centre of Parks, Recreation and Heritage, 1995.

Spiller, C., H. Barclay-Kerr, and J. Panoho. *Wayfinding Leadership: Groundbreaking Wisdom for Developing Leaders.* Wellington: Huia Publishers, 2015.

Spitz, C. *Island of Shattered Dreams.* Wellington: Huia Publishers, 2007.

Splinder, M.R. 'The legacy of Maurice Leenhardt', *International Bulletin of Missionary Research* 13:4 (1989), 170–4.

Spooner, M.H. *The General's Slow Retreat: Chile after Pinochet.* Berkeley: University of California Press, 2011.

Spriggs, M. 'Aubrey Parke, an enthusiastic amateur in Fiji?', in A. Parke, *Degei's Descendants: Spirits, Place and People in Pre-cession Fiji,* edited by M. Spriggs and D. Scarr. Canberra: ANU Press, 2014.

  'Landscape catastrophe and landscape enhancement: are either or both true in the Pacific?', in P.V. Kirch and T. Hunt (eds.), *Historical Ecology in the Pacific Islands: Prehistoric and Environmental Landscape Change.* New Haven: Yale University Press, 1997, 80–104.

  'Vegetable kingdoms: taro irrigation and Pacific prehistory', PhD thesis, Australian National University, Canberra, 1981.

Spurway, J. *Ma'afu, Prince of Tonga, Chief of Fiji: The Life and Times of Fiji's First Tui Lau.* Canberra: ANU Press, 2015.

Squier, G.O. 'An American Pacific cable', *Transactions of the American Institute of Electrical Engineers* 16 (1899), 662–3.

St. Julian, C. *Official Report on Central Polynesia: With a Gazetteer of Central Polynesia by Edward Reeve.* Sydney: John Fairfax & Sons, 1857.

Stackpole, E. *The Sea Hunters: The New England Whalemen during Two Centuries, 1635–1835.* Philadelphia: Lippincott, 2003.

REFERENCES TO VOLUME II

Stahl, C.W., and R. Appleyard. 'Migration and development in the Pacific Islands: lessons from the New Zealand experience'. Report for the Australian Agency for Development (AusAid), Canberra, April 2007.

Standfield, R. (ed.). *Indigenous Mobilities: Across and Beyond the Antipodes*. Canberra: ANU Press, 2018.

Stanley, B. 'The church of the three selves: a perspective from the World Missionary Conference, Edinburgh, 1910', *Journal of Imperial and Commonwealth History* 36 (2008), 435–51.

The World Mission Conference Edinburgh 1910. Grand Rapids, MI: Eerdmans, 2009.

Stannard, D.E. *Before the Horror: The Population of Hawaii on the Eve of Western Contact*. Honolulu: University of Hawai'i Press, 1989.

'Disease and infertility: a new look at the demographic collapse of native populations in the wake of Western contact', *Journal of American Studies* 24:23 (1990), 325–50.

'Recounting fables of savagery: native infanticide and the functions of political myths', *Journal of American Studies* 25:3 (1991), 381–418.

Stanton, W.R. *The Great United States Exploring Expedition of 1838–1842*. Berkeley: University of California Press, 1975.

Staple, G. 'Mapping tomorrow: 25 years of *TeleGeography*', *Medium.com* (23 November 2014), https://medium.com/@gregstaple/mapping-tomorrow-c340d7dcc03f.

Starbuck, A. *History of the American Whale Fishery*. Seacausus, NJ: Castle, 1989.

Starbuck, N. *Baudin, Napoleon and the Exploration of Australia*. London: Pickering and Chatto, 2013.

Starosielski, N. *The Undersea Network (Sign, Storage, Transmission)*. Durham, NC: Duke University Press, 2015.

Starr, K. *Americans and the California Dream, 1850–1915*. Oxford: Oxford University Press, 1973.

State of Queensland. 'The prickly pear story', State of Queensland, Department of Agriculture and Fisheries, 2016, 1–3, www.daf.qld.gov.au/__data/assets/pdf_file/0014/55301/IPA-Prickly-Pear-Story-PP62.pdf.

Steel, F. 'Cruises and the making of Greater New Zealand', in F. Steel (ed.), *New Zealand and the Sea: Historical Perspectives*. Wellington: Bridget Williams Books, 2018, 251–73.

Oceania under Steam: Sea Transport and the Cultures of Colonialism, c.1870–1914. Manchester: Manchester University Press, 2011.

'Re-routing empire? Steam age circulations and the making of an Anglo Pacific, c.1850–90', *Australian Historical Studies* 46 (2015), 356–73.

'Shipping, imperial', in J. MacKenzie (ed.), *Encyclopedia of Empire*, vol. IV. Oxford: Wiley-Blackwell, 2016.

'"The missing link": space, race and transoceanic ties in the settler-colonial Pacific', *Transfers: Interdisciplinary Journal of Mobility Studies* 5 (2015), 49–67.

Steen, T.M., and N.L. Drescher (eds.). *Tonga: Land, Sea and People*. Nuku'alofa: Vava'u Press, 2011.

Stella, R.T. *Imagining the Other: The Representation of the Papua New Guinean Subject*. Honolulu: University of Hawai'i Press, 2007.

References to Volume II

Stensrud, A.B. 'Safe milk and risky quinoa: the lottery and precarity of farming in Peru', *Focaal: Journal of Global and Historical Anthropology* 83 (2019), 72–84.

Stepan, N. *Picturing Tropical Nature*. Ithaca, NY: Cornell University Press, 2001.

Stevens, K. '"Every comfort of a civilized life": interracial marriage and mixed race respectability in southern New Zealand', *Journal of New Zealand Studies* 14 (2014), 87–105.

'"Gathering places": the mixed descent families of Foveaux Strait and Rakiura/Stewart Island, 1824–1864', BA research essay, University of Otago, 2008.

Stevens, K., and A. Wanhalla. 'Intimate relations: kinship and the economics of shore whaling in southern New Zealand', *Journal of Pacific History* 52:2 (2017), 135–55.

Stevens, M.J. 'An intimate knowledge of "Maori and mutton-bird": Big Nana's story', *Journal of New Zealand Studies* 14 (2014), 106–21.

Stewart, W. *Chinese Bondage in Peru: A History of the Chinese Coolie in Peru, 1849–1874*. Durham, NC: Duke University Press, 1951.

Stindt, F.A. *Matson's Century of Ships*. Modesto, CA: privately published, 1982.

Stocking, G.W., 'Boas and the culture concept in historical perspective', *American Anthropologist* 68 (1966), 867–82.

'Introduction: the basic assumptions of Boasian anthropology', in G. Stocking (ed.), *A Franz Boas Reader: The Shaping of American Anthropology 1883–1911*. Chicago: University of Chicago Press, 1982, 1–20.

'Matthew Arnold, E.B. Tylor and the uses of invention', *American Anthropologist* 32 (1963), 784–5.

Stoler, A.L. *Carnal Knowledge and Imperial Power: Race and the Intimate in Colonial Rule*. Berkeley: University of California Press, 2002.

(ed.). *Haunted by Empire: Geographies of Intimacy in North American History*. Durham, NC: Duke University Press, 2006.

'Making empire respectable: the politics of race and sexual morality in twentieth-century colonial cultures', in A. McClintock, A. Mufti, and E. Shoat (eds.), *Dangerous Liaisons: Gender, Nation, and Postcolonial Perspectives*. Minneapolis: University of Minneapolis Press, 1997, 344–73; also in L. Lamphere, H. Ragone, and P. Zavella (eds.), *Situated Lives: Gender and Culture in Everyday Life*. New York: Routledge, 1997, 374–99.

'Sexual affronts and racial frontiers: European identities and the cultural politics of exclusion in colonial Southeast Asia', in F. Cooper and A.L. Stoler (eds.), *Tensions of Empire: Colonial Cultures in a Bourgeois World*. Berkeley: University of California Press, 1997, 198–237.

Stopp, M. 'Eighteenth century Labrador Inuit in England', *Arctic* 62:1 (2009), 45–64.

Stopp, M., and G. Mitchell. '"Our amazing visitors": Catherine Cartwright's account of Labrador Inuit in England', *Arctic* 63:4 (2010), 399–413.

Strathern, A. *Kingship and Conversion in Sixteenth-Century Sri Lanka: Portuguese Imperialism in a Buddhist Land*. Cambridge: Cambridge University Press, 2007.

et al. *Oceania: An Introduction to the Cultures and Identities of Pacific Islanders*, 2nd edn. Durham: Carolina Academic Press, 2017.

REFERENCES TO VOLUME II

Strauss, W.P. *Americans in Polynesia, 1783–1842*. East Lansing: Michigan State University Press, 1963.

'Policemen in Polynesia: the American Navy', in W.P. Strauss, *Americans in Polynesia, 1783–1842*. East Lansing: Michigan State University Press, 1963, 83–5.

Strong, D.M. *Witness to War: Truk Lagoon's Master Diver Kimiuo Aisek*. [s.l: s.n], 2013.

Stronge, T. 'The future of submarine networks in South America', 2012, www.slideshare .net/CienaCorp/the-future-of-submarine-networks-in-latin-america.

Struve, L.A. *The Qing Formation in World-Historical Time*. Cambridge, MA: Harvard University Asia Center, 2004.

The Southern Ming, 1644–1662. New Haven, Yale University Press, 1984.

Stuart, A. 'Parasites lost? The Rockefeller Foundation and the expansion of health services in the colonial South Pacific, 1913–1939', PhD thesis, University of Canterbury, 2002.

'We are all hybrid here: the Rockefeller Foundation, Sylvester Lambert, and health work in the colonial South Pacific', *Health and History* 8:1 (2006), 56–79.

Suaali-Sauni, T., et al. *Whispers and Vanities: Samoan Indigenous Knowledge and Religion*. Wellington: Huia, 2014.

Suárez, T. *Early Mapping of the Pacific*. Singapore: Periplus, 2004.

Subramani. *South Pacific Literature: From Myth to Fabulation*. Suva: University of the South Pacific, 1985.

Sudō, N. *Nanyō Orientalism: Japanese Representations of the Pacific*. Amherst: Cambria Press, 2010.

Sugihara, K. 'The economy since 1800', in D. Armitage and A. Bashford (eds.), *Pacific Histories: Ocean, Land, People*. Basingstoke: Palgrave Macmillan, 2014, 166–90.

Suzuki, A. 'Framing psychiatric subjectivity: doctor, patient and record-keeping at Bethlem in the nineteenth century', in J. Melling and B. Forsythe (eds.), *Insanity, Institutions and Society, 1800–1914: A Social History of Madness in Comparative Perspective*. London: Routledge, 1999, 115–36.

Sykes, I. 'Disability, leprosy, and Kanak identity in twentieth-century New Caledonia', *Journal of Literary and Cultural Disability Studies* 10:2 (2016), 173–89.

Sznaider, M. 'Dilemmas of economic and political modernization in Chile: a jaguar that wants to be a puma', *Third World Quarterly* 17:4 (1996), 725–36.

'The Chilean jaguar as a symbol of a new identity', in L. Roniger and T. Herzog (eds.), *The Collective and the Public in Latin America*. Portland, OR: Sussex Academic Press, 2000, 285–98.

Szpilman, C.W.A. 'Conservatism and conservative reaction', in S. Saaler and C.W.A. Szpilman (eds.), *Routledge Handbook of Modern Japanese History*. London: Routledge, 2017.

Takaki, R. *Pau Hana: Plantation Life and Labor in Hawaii, 1835–1920*. Honolulu: University of Hawai'i Press, 1983.

Takayama, J. *Nankai no Daitankenka Suzuki Tsunenori (Suzuki Tsunenori, the Great Adventurer of the Southern Seas)*. Tokyo: Sanichi Shobō, 1995.

Taketani, E. *The Black Pacific Narrative: Geographic Imaginings of Race and Empire between the World Wars*. Hanover, NH: Dartmouth College Press, 2014.

References to Volume II

Tale, S., and O. Alefaio. 'We are our memories: community and records in Fiji', in J.A. Bastian and B. Alexander (eds.), *Community Archives: The Shaping of Memory*. London: Facet Publishing, 2009, 87–94.

Tambiah, S. 'The galactic polity: the structure of traditional kingdoms in Southeast Asia', *Annals of the New York Academy of Sciences* 293 (1977), 69–97.

Tandeter, E. 'Forced and free labour in late colonial Potosí', *Past and Present* 93 (1981), 98–136.

Tarte, S. *Japan and the Pacific Islands: The Politics of Fisheries, Access, Aid and Regionalism*. Uppsala: Life and Peace Institute, 1995.

Taum, R. 'Ancient wisdom, future thinking: raising the Blue Continent', TEDx. Richardson Law School, University of Hawai'i, 29 September 2011, http://youtu .be/RjIWKfofRMM.

Taylor, M. 'China's growing impact on the regional political order', in M. Powles (ed.), *China and the Pacific: The View from Oceania*. Wellington: Victoria University Press, 2016, 41–5,

  'Opening remarks to the 2017 Pacific Update', Pacific Islands Forum Secretariat, 20 June 2017, www.forumsec.org/secretary-general-dame-meg-taylors-opening-remarks-to-the-2017-pacific-update/.

Taylor, R. 'History of public health in Pacific Island countries', in M.J. Lewis and K.L. MacPherson (eds.), *Public Health in Asia and the Pacific: Historical and Comparative Perspectives*. London: Routledge, 2008, 276–306.

Tcherkézoff, S. 'Multiculturalism and construction of a national identity: the historical case of Samoan/European relations', *New Pacific Review* 1:1 (2000), 168–86.

Te Awekotuku, N. *Mana Wahine Maori: Selected Writings on Maori Women's Art, Culture and Politics*. Auckland: New Woman's Press, 1991.

Te Punga Somerville, A. *Once Were Pacific: Māori Connections to Oceania*. Minneapolis: University of Minnesota Press, 2012.

  'The great Pacific garbage patch as metaphor: the (American) Pacific you can't see', in B.R. Roberts and M.A. Stephens (eds.), *American Archipelagic Studies*. Durham, NC: Duke University Press, 2017, 320–40.

Teaiwa, K. 'Banaban Island: paying the price for other peoples' development', *Indigenous Affairs* 1 (2000), 38–45.

  Consuming Ocean Island: Stories of People and Phosphate from Banaba. Bloomington: Indiana University Press, 2014.

Teaiwa, K., A. Henderson, and T. Wesley-Smith. 'Teresia K. Teaiwa: a bibliography', *Journal of Pacific History* 53:1 (2018), 103–7.

Teaiwa, T.K. 'Articulated cultures: militarism and masculinities in Fiji during the mid 1990s', *Fijian Studies: A Journal of Contemporary Fiji* 3:2 (2005), 201–22.

  'Bikinis and other s/pacific n/oceans', *Contemporary Pacific* 6:1 (1994): 87–109; repr. in S. Shigematsu and K.L. Camacho (eds.), *Militarized Currents: Toward a Decolonized Future in Asia and the Pacific*. Minneapolis: University of Minnesota Press, 2010, 15–31.

  'On analogies: rethinking the Pacific in a global context', *Contemporary Pacific* 18:1 (2006), 71–87.

  'Review of *A New Oceania: Rediscovering Our Sea of Islands*, edited by Eric Waddell, Vijay Naidu, and Epeli Hau'ofa', *Contemporary Pacific* 8 (1996), 214–17.

Teave, E., and L. Cloud. 'Rapa Nui National Park, Cultural World Heritage: the struggle of the Rapa Nui people for their ancestral territory and heritage, for environmental protection, and for cultural integrity', in S. Disko and H. Tugendhat (eds.), *World Heritage Sites and Indigenous Peoples' Rights*. Copenhagen: International Working Group for Indigenous Affairs, 2014, 403–21.

Teixeira, N.S. 'Do azul e branco ao verde-rubro. A simbólica da bandeira nacional', in F. Bethencourt and D.R. Curto (eds.), *A Memória da Nação*. Lisbon: Livraria Sá da Costa, 1991, 319–37.

TeleGeography. *TeleGeography: Global Internet Map, 2018*. Washington, DC: PriMetrica Inc., 2018, https://global-internet-map-2018.telegeography.com/.

Teng, E.J. *Eurasian: Mixed Identities in the United States, China and Hong Kong, 1842–1943*. Berkeley: University of California Press, 2013.

'The Asian turn in mixed race studies: retrospects and prospects', *Asia Pacific Perspectives* 14:2 (2017), 80–5.

TePaske, J. 'New World silver, Castile, and the Philippines, 1598–1800', in J.F. Richards (ed.), *Precious Metals in the Later Medieval and Early Modern Worlds*. Durham: Carolina Academic Press, 1983, 425–45.

Theological Education in the Pacific. London: Theological Education Fund Committee of the International Missionary Council, 1961, 17.

Thomas, M. *Schooner from Windward: Two Centuries of Hawaiian Interisland Shipping*. Honolulu: University of Hawai'i Press, 1983.

Thomas, N. *Colonialism's Culture: Anthropology, Travel and Government*. Carlton: Melbourne University Press, 1994.

Entangled Objects: Exchange, Material Culture and Colonialism in the Pacific. Cambridge, MA: Harvard University Press, 1991.

Islanders: The Age of Empire in the Pacific. New Haven: Yale University Press, 2010.

'Lisa Reihana: encounters in Oceania', *Artlink* 37:2 (2017), 22–6.

'Sanitation and seeing: the creation of state power in early colonial Fiji', *Comparative Studies in Society and History* 32 (1990), 149–70.

Thomas, N., J. Adams, B. Lythberg, M. Nuku, and A. Salmond (eds.). *Artefacts of Encounter: Cook's Voyages, Colonial Collecting, and Museum Histories*. Dunedin: Otago University Press, 2016.

Thomas, P., and M. Keen (eds.). *Urban Development in the Pacific, special issue of Development Bulletin* 78 (2017).

Thomaz, L.F. *De Ceuta a Timor*. Lisbon: Difel, 1994.

Thompson, A. *Culture in a Post-Secular Context: Theological Possibilities in Milbank, Barth and Bediako*. Eugene: Pickwick Publications, 2014.

Thompson, C. *Sea People: The Puzzle of Polynesia*. New York: HarperCollins, 2019.

Thompson, L. *Imperial Archipelago: Representation and Rule in the Insular Territories under U.S. Dominion after 1898*. Honolulu: University of Hawai'i Press, 2010.

Thrush, C. *Indigenous London: Native Travelers at the Heart of Empire*. New Haven: Yale University Press, 2016.

Tierney, R.T. *Tropics of Savagery: The Culture of Japanese Empire in Comparative Frame*. Berkeley: University of California Press, 2010.

References to Volume II

Tipples, R., and P. Rawlinson. 'The RSE, a tool for dairying? Understanding the Recognised Seasonal Employer policy and its potential application to the dairy industry'. Working Paper 16. Lincoln University NZ Faculty of Agribusiness and Commerce, 2014.

Tisdell, C. 'The MIRAB model of small island economies in the Pacific and their security issues: revised version', Social Economics, Policy and Development Working Papers 165087, University of Queensland, School of Economics, 2014.

Tjibaou, J.-M, and P. Missotte. *Kanaké: The Melanesian Way*, trans. C. Plant. Papeete: Les Éditions du Pacifique, 1978.

Todeschini, M. 'The bomb's womb? Women and the atom bomb', in V. Das, A. Kleinman, M. Lock, M. Ramphele, and P. Reynolds (eds.), *Remaking a World: Violence, Social Suffering, and Recovery*. Berkeley: University of California Press, 2001, 102–56.

Todorov, T. *Nous et les autres: la réflexion française sur la diversité humaine*. Paris: Seuil, 1989.

Tohi, F. *Filipe Tohi: Genealogy of Lines: Hohoko ē Tohitohi*. New Plymouth: Govett-Brewster Art Gallery, 2002.

Toleafoa, A. 'One party state: the Samoan experience', in D. Hegarty and D. Tryon (eds.), *Politics, Development and Security in the Pacific*. Canberra: ANU Press, 2013, 69–76.

Tomiyama, I. 'The "Japanese" of Micronesia: Okinawans in the Nan'yō Islands', in R.Y. Nakasone (ed.), *Okinawan Diaspora*. Honolulu: University of Hawai'i Press, 2002, 57–70.

Tongan Constitution: A Brief History to Celebrate its Centenary. Nuku'alofa: Tonga Traditions Committee, 1975.

Torodash, M. 'Steinberger of Samoa: some biographical notes', *Pacific Northwest Quarterly* 68:2 (1977), 49–59.

Totman, C. *Early Modern Japan*. Berkeley: University of California Press, 1993.

Tough, A. 'Good government and good governance: record keeping in a contested arena', *Journal of the Eastern and Southern Africa Regional Branch of the International Council on Archives* 38 (2017), 108–15.

Townsend, S. *Yanaihara Tadao and Japanese Colonial Policy: Redeeming Empire*. Richmond: Curzon Press, 2000.

Trask, H.-K. 'Coalition building between natives and non-natives', *Stanford Law Review* 43:6 (1991), 1197–1213.

From a Native Daughter: Colonialism and Sovereignty in Hawai'i, rev. edn. Honolulu: University of Hawai'i Press, 1999 [1993].

'Hawaii, colonization and decolonization', in A. Hooper, S. Britton, R. Crocombe, J. Huntsman, and C. Macpherson (eds.), *Class and Culture in the South Pacific*. Suva: Institute of Pacific Studies, 1987, 157–75.

'Lovely hula hands: corporate tourism and the prostitution of Hawaiian culture', in *From a Native Daughter: Colonialism and Sovereignty in Hawai'i*, rev. edn. Honolulu: University of Hawai'i Press, 1999 [1993]), 136–50.

'Natives and anthropologists: the colonial struggle', *Contemporary Pacific* 3:1 (1991), 159–67.

'Politics in the Pacific Islands: imperialism and native self-determination', *Amerasia Journal* 16:1 (1990), 1–19

'Settlers of color and "immigrant" hegemony: "locals" in Hawai'i', *Amerasia Journal* 26:2 (2000), 1–24.

Traube, E.G. *Cosmology and Social Life: Ritual Exchange among the Mambai of East Timor*. Chicago: University of Chicago Press, 1986.

'Outside-in: Mambai expectations of returning outsiders', in R. Roque and E.G. Traube (eds.), *Crossing Histories and Ethnographies: Following Colonial Historicities in Timor-Leste*. Oxford: Berghahn Books, 2019, 49–75.

'Planting the flag', in A. McWilliam and E.G. Traube (eds.), *Land and Life in Timor-Leste: Ethnographic Essays*. Canberra: ANU Press, 2011, 117–40.

Trefalt, B. 'Collecting bones: Japanese missions for the repatriation of war remains and the unfinished business of the Asia-Pacific War', *Australian Humanities Review* 61 (2016), 145–59.

Trevelyan, C.P. *Letters from North America and the Pacific*. London: Chatto & Windus, 1969.

Tribolet, L.B. *The International Aspects of Electrical Communications in the Pacific Area*. Baltimore: Johns Hopkins University Press, 1929.

Tuimaleali'ifano, A.M. *O Tama a 'Āiga: The Politics of Succession to Sāmoa's Paramount Titles*. Suva: Institute of Pacific Studies, University of the South Pacific, 2006.

Tumbe, C. *India Moving: A History of Migration*. Gurgaon: Penguin Random House, 2018.

Tupou, M. 'Constitutional development in Tonga: Tonga's idea of responsible executive', presented at the Law and Culture Conference, Port Vila, Vanuatu, 9 September 2013, www.usp.ac.fj/index.php?id=13024.

Turnbull, D. 'Eckstein and Schwarz's translation of Tupaia's chart: the Rosetta Stone of Polynesian navigation?', *Journal of Pacific History* 54:4 (2019), 530–4.

'(En)-countering knowledge traditions: the story of Cook and Tupaia', in T. Ballantyne (ed.), *Science, Empire and the European Exploration of the Pacific*. Aldershot: Ashgate, 2004, 225–46.

Masons, Tricksters and Cartographers: Comparative Studies in the Sociology of Scientific and Indigenous Knowledge. Amsterdam: Harwood Academic, 2000.

Turner, J. '"The water of life": kava ritual and the logic of sacrifice', *Ethnology* 25:3 (1986), 203–14.

Turner, J.W., and S. Falgout. 'Time traces: cultural memory and World War II in Pohnpei', *Contemporary Pacific* 14 (2002), 101–31.

Tutugoro, A. 'Incompatible struggles? Reclaiming indigenous sovereignty and political sovereignty in Kanaky and/or New Caledonia', Department of Pacific Affairs, Discussion Paper 2020/5, http://dpa.bellschool.anu.edu.au/sites/default/files/pub lications/attachments/2021-01/dpa_discussion_paper_anthony_tutugoro_2020_05_ incompatible_struggles_reclaiming_indigenous_sovereignty_and_political_sover eignty_in_kanaky_and_or_new_caledonia.pdf.

'The invention of a flag in New Caledonia. The beginnings of a common identity under construction', Master's thesis, University of Rennes 1, 2014.

Tylor, E.B. *Primitive Culture: Researches into the Development of Mythology, Philosophy, Religion, Art, and Custom*. London: John Murray 1871.

Uman, O., F. Saladier, and A. Chipen. *Uruon Chuuk: A Resource of Oral Legends, Traditions, and History of Truk*, vol. 1. Moen, Truk: ESEA Title IV Omibus Program for Social Studies-Cultural Heritage Trust Territory of the Pacific Islands, 1979.

UNCTAD. *Review of Maritime Transport: Report by the UNCTAD Secretariat*. New York: United Nations 1997–2016.

Underwood, R. 'The changing American lake in the middle of the Pacific', a talk at the Center for Australian, New Zealand, and Pacific Studies, School of Foreign Service, Georgetown

References to Volume II

University, Washington, DC, 16 November 2017, www.uog.edu/_resources/files/news-and-announcements/robert_underwood_changing_american_lake.

UNDP (United Nations Development Program). *Temporary Special Measures to Increase Women's Political Participation in the Pacific*, 2015, www.pacific.undp.org/content/dam/fiji/docs/UNDP%20PO%20TSM_Womens%20Political%20Participation.pdf.

UNESCO. *Museums, Libraries and Cultural Heritage: Democratising Culture, Creating Knowledge and Building Bridges*. Hamburg: Druckerei Semann, 1999.

United Nations. Declaration on the Granting of Independence to Colonial Countries and Peoples, GA 1514 (XV), 14 December 1960.

'The United Nations and decolonization: non-self-governing territories', www.un.org/en/decolonization/nonselfgovterritories.

United States Congress. *Covert Action in Chile, 1963–1973: Staff Report of the Select Committee to Study Governmental Operations with Respect to Intelligence Activities, United States Senate*. Washington, DC: US Government Printing Office, 1975.

Université de la Nouvelle-Calédonie. 'Interview with Jean-Jacques Urvoas' during the 'État associé ou État fédéré, des pistes pour l'avenir institutionnel de la Nouvelle-Calédonie' colloquium (Associated State or Federated State, avenues for the institutional future of New Caledonia colloquium).

Uperesa, F.A.L. 'Fabled futures: migration and mobility for Samoans in American football', *Contemporary Pacific* 26:2 (2014), 281–301.

Ure, J. *Telecommunication in Asia: Policy, Planning and Development*. Hong Kong: Hong Kong University Press, 1995.

Uriam, K.K. *In Their Own Words: History and Society in Gilbertese Oral Tradition*. Canberra: Journal of Pacific History, 1995.

Vaai, U.L., and U. Nabobo-Baba. *The Relational Self: Decolonising Personhood in the Pacific*. Suva: University of the South Pacific Press; Pacific Theological College, 2017.

Vaimeho-Peua, E. 'La toponymie des terres de Faaa et les représentations foncières tahitiennes', thèse de civilisation polynésienne, Université de la Polynésie Française, 2008.

van Dijk, K. *Pacific Strife: The Great Powers and Their Political and Economic Rivalries in Asia and the Western Pacific 1870–1914*. Amsterdam: Amsterdam University Press, 2015.

Van Kirk, S. *Many Tender Ties: Women in Fur-Trade Society, 1670–1870*. Norman: University of Oklahoma Press, 1980).

'Tracing the fortunes of five founding families of Victoria', *BC Studies* 115/16 (1997/8), 149–79.

van Toorn, P. *Writing Never Arrives Naked: Early Aboriginal Cultures of Writing in Australia*. Canberra: Aboriginal Studies Press, 2006.

Vancouver, G. *A Voyage of Discovery to the North Pacific Ocean and Round the World, 1791–1795*, ed. W.K. Lamb. London: Hakluyt Society, 1984.

Vaquinhas, J. dos Santos. 'Timor. I', *Boletim da Sociedade de Geografia de Lisboa* 4 série, 7 (1883), 307–28.

'Timor. Usos – superstições de guerra', *Boletim da Sociedade de Geografia de Lisboa* 4 série, 8 (1884), 476–92.

Velt, K., and T. Helu. *Langi Tau'olunga & Hiva Kakala: A Collection of Currently Popular Tau'olunga Dance Songs in Tonga, with Some Translations, History, Music Sheets and Video Recordings*. Nuku'alofa: Tau'olunga Komipiuta, 2001.

REFERENCES TO VOLUME II

Veracini, L. *Settler Colonialism: A Theoretical Overview*. Basingstoke: Palgrave Macmillan, 2010.

Viney, K. 'Problems and prospects for tuberculosis prevention and care in the Pacific Islands', PhD thesis, Australian National University, Canberra, 2015.

Virmani, A. 'National symbols under colonial domination: the nationalization of the Indian flag, March–August 1923', *Past and Present* 164 (1999), 169–97.

von Glahn, R. 'Myth and reality of China's seventeenth-century monetary crisis', *Journal of Economic History* 56:2 (1996), 429–54.

Waddell, E., V. Naidu, and E. Hau'ofa (eds.). *A New Oceania: Rediscovering Our Sea of Islands*. Suva: School of Social and Economic Development, University of the South Pacific in association with Beake House, 1993.

Wagner, R.G. *Reenacting the Heavenly Vision: The Role of Religion in the Taiping Rebellion*. Berkeley: University of California, 1982.

Wakeman, F. 'China and the seventeenth-century crisis', *Late Imperial China* 7:1 (1986), 1–26.

The Great Enterprise: The Manchu Reconstruction of Imperial Order in Seventeenth-Century China. Berkeley: University of California Press, 1985.

Walker, I. *Chile and Latin America in a Globalized World*. Singapore: Institute of Southeast Asian Studies, 2006.

Walker, R. *Ka Whafai Tonu Matou: Struggle without End*. Auckland: Penguin Books, 2004.

Wallace, L. *Sexual Encounters: Pacific Texts, Modern Sexualities*. Ithaca, NY: Cornell University Press, 2003.

Walther, D.J. *Sex and Control: Venereal Disease, Colonial Physicians, and Indigenous Agency in German Colonialism, 1884–1914*. Oxford: Berghahn Books, 2015.

'Sex, race and empire: white male sexuality and the "other" in Germany's colonies, 1894–1914', *German Studies Review* 33:1 (2010), 45–71.

Wan, M. 'The monetization of silver in China: Ming China and its global interactions', in M.D. Elizalde and Wang Jianlang (eds.), *China's Development from a Global Perspective*. Newcastle-upon-Tyne: Cambridge Scholars, 2017, 274–96.

Wang, G. 'The study of Chinese identities in Southeast Asia', in J.W. Cushman and G. Wang (eds.), *Changing Identities of the Southeast Asian Chinese since World War II*. Hong Kong: Hong Kong University Press, 1988, 11–16.

Wang, X. 'Non-traditional security and global governance: China's participation in climate adaptation in Oceania', in M. Powles (ed.), *China and the Pacific: The View from Oceania*. Wellington: Victoria University Press, 2016, 154–8.

Wanhalla, A. *In/visible Sight: The Mixed-Descent Families of Southern New Zealand*. Wellington: Bridget Williams Books, 2009.

Matters of the Heart: A History of Interracial Marriage in New Zealand. Auckland: Auckland University Press, 2013.

'"The natives uncivilize me": missionaries and interracial intimacy in early New Zealand', in P. Grimshaw and A. May (eds.), *Missions, Indigenous Peoples and Cultural Exchange*. Brighton: Sussex Academic Press, 2010, 24–36.

Wanhalla, A., and L. Paterson, '"Tangled up": intimacy, emotion, and dispossession in colonial New Zealand', in P. Edmonds and A. Nettelbeck (eds.), *Intimacies of Violence in the Settler Colony: Economies of Dispossession around the Pacific Rim*. Basingstoke: Palgrave Macmillan, 2018, 179–200.

References to Volume II

Wanhalla, A., and K. Stevens. '"A class of no political weight": interracial marriage, mixed-race children, and land rights in southern New Zealand, 1840s–1880s', *History of the Family*, published online, 23 May 2019.

Ward, R.G. 'Earth's empty quarter? The Pacific Islands in a Pacific Century', *Geographical Journal* 155:2 (1989), 235–46.

Wareham, E., 'From explorers to evangelists: archivists, recordkeeping, and remembering in the Pacific Islands', *Archival Science* 2:3–4 (2002), 187–207.

Watling, D. *Tohi Talateu ki he Manupuna 'o Tonga: Guide to the Birds of the Kingdom of Tonga*. Privately published, 2006.

Watson, R. 'HBC in the Hawaiian Islands', *The Beaver* (June 1930), 7–8.

Weaver, F.S. 'Reform and (counter)revolution in post-independence Guatemala: liberalism, conservatism, and postmodem controversies', *Latin American Perspectives* 26:2 (1999), 129–58.

Weaver, Jace. *The Red Atlantic: American Indigenes and the Making of the Modern World, 1000–1927*. Chapel Hill: University of North Carolina Press, 2014.

Weaver, John. *The Great Land Rush and the Making of the Modern World, 1650–1900*. Montréal: McGill-Queen's University Press, 2003.

Weber, T., and J. Watson (eds.). *Cook's Pacific Encounters: The Cook-Forster Collection of the Georg-August University of Göttingen*. Canberra: National Museum of Australia, 2006.

Webley, I. 'Tonga and the Soviet Union: problems in New Zealand–Tonga relationships', *New Zealand International Review* 1:5 (1976), 11–15.

Weeks, C.J. 'The United States occupation of Tonga, 1942–1945: the social and economic impact', *Pacific Historical Review* 56 (1987), 399–426.

Weeramantry, C. *Nauru: Environmental Damage under International Trusteeship*. Oxford: Oxford University Press, 1992.

Wehner, M., and E. Maidment. 'Ancestral voices: aspects of archives administration in Oceania', *Archives and Manuscripts* 27:1 (1999), 23–41.

Weir, C. 'An accidental biographer? On encountering, yet again, the ideas and actions of J.W. Burton', in B.V. Lal and V. Luker (eds.), *Telling Pacific Lives: Prisms of Process*. Canberra, ANU Press 2008, 215–66.

'The opening of the coconut curtain: Pacific influence on the World Council of Churches through the Campaign for a Nuclear-Free Pacific, 1961 to 2000', *Journal of Pacific History* 54:1 (2019), 116–38.

Weisgall, J. *Operation Crossroads: The Atomic Tests at Bikini Atoll*. Annapolis: Naval Institute Press, 1994.

Weitman, S.R. 'National flags: a sociological overview', *Semiotica* 8:4 (1973), 328–66.

Wen, J. 'Speech at the opening of the first ministerial conference of the China-Pacific Island countries', Fiji, 5 April 2006, available at www.chinadaily.com.cn/china/2006-04/05/content_560573.htm.

Wendt, A. *The Mango's Kiss*. Auckland: Vintage, 2003.

'Towards a new Oceania', *Mana Review: A South Pacific Journal of Language and Literature* 1:1 (1976), 49–60.

Werrett, S. 'Introduction: rethinking Joseph Banks', *Notes and Records: The Royal Society Journal of the History of Science* 73:4 (2019), 1–5.

REFERENCES TO VOLUME II

Wesley-Smith, T. *China in Oceania: New Forces in Pacific Politics*. Pacific Islands Policy 2. Honolulu: East-West Center, 2007.

Wesley-Smith, T., and E.A. Porter (eds.). *China in Oceania: Reshaping the Pacific?* New York: Berghahn Books, 2010.

Westney, D.E. *Imitation and Innovation: The Transfer of Western Organizational Patterns to Meiji Japan*. Cambridge, MA: Harvard University Press, 1987.

Whimp, G. 'A search for the new Oceania', *Contemporary Pacific*. 22:2 (2010), 382–8.

White, G.M. *Indigenous Governance in Melanesia*. SSGM Discussion Paper, Canberra, Australian National University, February 2006.

Memorializing Pearl Harbor: Unfinished Histories and the Work of Resistance. Durham, NC: Duke University Press, 2016.

'Remembering Guadalcanal: national identity and transnational memory-making', *Public Culture* 7 (1995), 529–55.

(ed.). *Remembering the Pacific War*. Occasional Paper 36, Center for Pacific Islands Studies School of Hawaiian, Asian & Pacific Studies. Honolulu: University of Hawai'i, 1991.

White, G.M., D. Gegeo, D. Akin, and K. Watson-Gegeo (eds.). *The Big Death: Solomon Islanders Remember World War II [Bikfala Faet: Olketa Solomon Aelanda Rimembarem Wol Wo Tu]*. Solomon Islands College of Higher Education, Honiara, and the University of the South Pacific. Suva: Institute of Pacific Studies, 1988.

White, G.M., and L. Lindstrom (eds.). *The Pacific Theater: Island Representations of World War II*. Pacific Islands Monograph Series 8. Honolulu: University of Hawai'i Press, 1989.

Wickman, D. 'Recordkeeping legislation and its impacts: the PARBICA recordkeeping for good governance toolkit', *Comma: The International Journal on Archives* 2011(1), 51–9.

Widmer, A. 'The effects of elusive knowledge: census, health laws and inconsistently modern subjects in early colonial Vanuatu', *Journal of Legal Anthropology* 1:1 (2008), 92–116.

Widmer, A., and V. Lipphardt (eds.). *Health and Difference: Rendering Human Variation in Colonial Engagements*. New York: Berghahn Books, 2016.

Williams, D., and R.P. De Kerbrech *Damned by Destiny*. Brighton: Terado Books, 1982.

Williams, E.B. *Information Needs in the Pacific Islands: Needs Assessment for Libraries, Archives, Audio Visual Collection and ICT Development in the Pacific Islands*. Samoa: UNESCO, 1998.

Williams, G. *The Great South Sea: English Voyages and Encounters, 1570-1750*. New Haven: Yale University Press, 1997.

Williams, J. *A Narrative of Missionary Enterprises in the South Sea Islands: With Remarks upon the Natural History of the Islands, Origin, Languages, Traditions, and Usages of the Inhabitants*, 7th edn. London: J. Snow, 1838 [1837].

Williams, R. *French Botany in the Enlightenment: The Ill-Fated Voyages of La Pérouse and His Rescuers*. Dordrecht: Kluwer Academic, 2003.

Williams, W.A. *Empire as a Way of Life: An Essay on the Causes and Character of America's Present Predicament, along with a Few Thoughts about an Alternative*. Oxford: Oxford University Press, 1980.

References to Volume II

Willmott, B. 'The overseas Chinese experience in the Pacific', in T. Wesley-Smith and E.A. Porter (eds.), *China in Oceania: Reshaping the Pacific?* New York: Berghahn Books, 2010, 93–103.

Wills, J.E., Jr. 'Maritime Asia, 1500–1800: the interactive emergence of European domination', *American Historical Review* 98 (1993), 83–105.

Wilson, A.C. *New Zealand and the Soviet Union: A Brittle Relationship.* Wellington: Victoria University Press, 2004.

Wilson, E.O. *Half-Earth: Our Planet's Fight for Life.* New York: Norton, 2016.

Wilson, L.B. *Speaking to Power: Gender and Politics in the Western Pacific.* New York: Routledge, 1995.

Wilson, R. *Reimagining the American Pacific: From South Pacific to Bamboo Ridge and Beyond.* Durham, NC: Duke University Press, 2000.

Wilson, R., and A. Dirlik. 'Introduction: Asia/Pacific as space of cultural production', *Boundary 2* 21:1 (1994), 1–14.

Winchester, S. *Pacific Rising: The Emergence of a New World Culture.* New York: Prentice Hall, 1991.

Wineera, V. *Into the Luminous Tide: Pacific Poems.* Provo: Centre for the Study of Christian Values in Literature/BYU, 2009.

Winseck D., and R. Pike. *Communication and Empire: Media, Markets and Globalization.* Durham, NC: Duke University Press, 2007.

Wise, T. *The Self-Made Anthropologist: A Life of A.P. Elkin.* Sydney: George Allen & Unwin, 1985.

Wohlforth, C. 'Why a bomb test in the Aleutians still strikes fear in workers 46 years later', *Anchorage Daily News* (28 January 2017).

Wolfe, P. 'Settler colonialism and the elimination of the native', *Journal of Genocide Research* 8:4 (2006), 387–409.
    Settler Colonialism and the Transformation of Anthropology: The Politics and Poetics of an Ethnographic Event. London: Cassell, 1999.

Wolters, O.W. *Early Indonesian Commerce: A Study of the Origins of Srivijaya.* Ithaca, NY: Cornell University Press, 1967.
    The Fall of Srivijaya in Malay History. Ithaca, NY: Cornell University Press, 1970.

Woodd, B. 'Memoir and obituary of Mowhee, a young New Zealander, who died at Paddington, December 28, 1816', *CMS (Church Missionary Society) Missionary Register* (February 1817), 71–9.

Woodside, A. 'The Asia-Pacific idea as a mobilization myth', in A. Dirlik (ed.), *What Is in a Rim? Critical Perspectives on the Pacific Region Idea*, 2nd edn. Lanham: Rowman & Littlefield, 1998, 37–52.
    Lost Modernities: China, Vietnam, Korea, and the Hazards of World History. Cambridge, MA: Harvard University Press, 2006.

Worden, N. 'Writing the global Indian Ocean', *Journal of Global History* 12:1 (2017), 145–54.

Worliczek, E. 'La vision de l'espace littoral sur l'île Wallis et l'atoll Rangiroa dans le contexte du changement climatique. Une analyse anthropologique de la perception des populations locales', thèse de doctorat, Universités de Vienne et de Nouvelle-Calédonie, Nouméa, 2013.

REFERENCES TO VOLUME II

Xi, J., President. 'Working together for a green and better future for all.' President of the People's Republic of China's Opening Address at the Opening Ceremony of the International Horticultural Exhibition 2019, Beijing China, Beijing, 28 April 2019. www.bjreview.com/Beijing_Review_and_Kings_College_London_Joint_Translation_Project/2019/201909/t20190903_800177587.html.

Xing, L., J. Hersh, and J. Dragsbœk Schmidt. 'The new "Asian drama": catching-up at the crossroads of neoliberalism', in P.P. Masina (ed.), *Rethinking Development in East Asia: From Illusory Miracle to Economic Crisis.* New York: Routledge, 2001, 29–52.

Yaguchi, Y. *Akogare no Hawai: Nihonjin no Hawai-kan (Hawaiian Yearning: Japanese Perspectives on Hawai'i).* Tokyo: Chūo Kōron Shinsha, 2011.

'Longing for Paradise through "authentic" hula performance in contemporary Japan', *Japanese Studies* 35:3 (2015), 303–15.

Yamamoto, T.S et al. 'Migration of health workers in the Pacific Islands: a bottleneck to health development', *Asia Pacific Journal of Public Health* 24:4 (2012), 697–709.

Yanagita, K. 'Kaijō no Michi' (Passage on the sea), in *Yanagita Kunio Zenshū 1. (The Complete Works of Yanagita Kunio Vol. 1).* Tokyo: Chikuma Shobō, 1968 [1961], 1–216.

Yang, D. 'Crossing the Pacific: wireless telegraphy and spatial practices in early twentieth-century Japan', *Pacific Historical Review* 88 (2019), 524–53.

Yang, J. *The Pacific Islands in China's Grand Strategy: Small States, Big Games.* New York: Palgrave Macmillan, 2011.

Yano, T. *Nanshin no Keifu: Nihon no Nanyō Shikan (The History of 'Southbound Expansion of Japan': Historical Patterns of Japanese Views on Southeast Asia).* Tokyo: Chikura Shobō, 2009.

Young, F.W. '"I Hē Koe? Placing Rapa Nui', *Contemporary Pacific* 24:1 (2012), 1–30.

'Unsettling the boundaries of Latin America: Rapa Nui and the refusal of Chilean settler colonialism', *Settler Colonial Studies* (2020), doi:10.1080/2201473X.2020.1823751.

Young, K.G.T. *Rethinking the Native Hawaiian Past.* New York: Garland, 1998.

Young, M.J. *Malinowski: Odyssey of an Anthropologist 1884–1920.* New Haven: Yale University Press, 2004.

Yu, C. 'The Pacific Islands in China's geo-strategic thinking', in M. Powles (ed.), *China and the Pacific: The View from Oceania.* Wellington: Victoria University Press, 2016, 89–97.

Yu, H. 'Mixing bodies and cultures: the meaning of America's fascination with sex between "Orientals" and "Whites"', in E. Reis (ed.), *American Sexual Histories.* Oxford: Blackwell, 2000, 446–58.

'Unbound space: migration, aspiration and the making of time in the Cantonese Pacific', in W. Anderson, M. Johnson, and B. Brookes (eds.), *Pacific Futures: Past and Present.* Honolulu: University of Hawai'i Press, 2018, 178–204.

Yule, H., and A.C. Burnell. *Hobson-Jobson: A Glossary of Colloquial Anglo-Indian Words and Phrases, and of Kindred Terms, Etymological, Historical, Geographical and Discursive,* new edn, ed. W. Crooke. London: J. Murray, 1903.

Zarrow, P. *China in War and Revolution 1895–1949.* New York: RoutledgeCurzon, 2005.

Zavos, S. 'The browning of the Wallabies'. *The Roar,* 31 May 2007, www.theroar.com.au/2007/06/01/the-browning-of-the-wallabies/.

Zhang, H., and F. Wu. 'China's marine fishery and global ocean governance', *Global Policy* 8:2 (2017), 216–26.

886

References to Volume II

Zhang, X. 'Jiyi zhong de Jinping linkuang', *Lianyunggang shi zhi* 1 (2014), 41–3.

Zhang, D., S. Hogg, and S. Gessler. 'Pacific Island countries, China & sustainable development goals part 3: Chinese scholarships in the Pacific'. DPA, *In Brief* 2017/22, Canberra, ANU.

Zhao, G. *The Qing Opening to the Ocean: Chinese Maritime Policy, 1684–1757*. Honolulu: University of Hawai'i Press, 2013.

Zhao, H. 'China's overseas resource investment: myths and realities', in P. D'Arcy, P. Matbob, and L. Crowl (eds.), *Pacific Asian Partnerships in Resource Development*. Madang: Divine Word University Press, 2014, 110–21

Zhou, M.J., Z.L. Shen, and R.C. Yu, 'Responses of a coastal phytoplankton community to increased nutrient input from the Changjiang (Yangtze) River', *Continental Shelf Research* 28 (2008), 1483–9.

Zinn, H. *A People's History of America*. New York: Harper Perennial American Classics, 2003.

Index

Page numbers in italics and bold indicate figures and tables respectively.

Abel, Charles, missionary 357
Aboriginal Australians
  and archives 191
  and nuclear testing 158
  relationships with migrant workers 215
  and Stolen Generation 197, 226
Abramowitz, M. I. 555
Abu'ofa, Peter 355
academic studies
  of art and artefacts 289, 291
  film 279
  Hawai'i 233–45
  in Hawaiian language 235
  Hawaiian research in nupepa archive 238
  Native Hawaiian 239, 243–4
  need for research on disease 345
  of 'Pacificism' (nineteenth-century)
    80–5
  twentieth-century 85–91
  see also archives; histories and
    historiography
Acapulco, Mexico, Manila galleons 543
Acheson, Dean, US Secretary of State 576
acidification, of oceans 681, 720, 777
Adams, John Quincy 564
Admiralty Islands, sighting of La Pérouse in
  326
Adventure (film) 273
Africa, ancestral origins and links with
  Pacific 139
African Americans
  and civil rights alliance with Japan
    142
  in Pacific ('Black Pacific') 139–43
  as servicemen World War II 143
Africans, as sailors 140

agency
  and Fatal Impact 339, 342, 347
  and foreign aid 689
  Hau'ofa on 348
  and health projects 513
  Indigenous 89–91, 156, 348, 395
  of women 207, 213, 331, 500
Agniel, G., New Caledonia 741
Aguinaldo, Emilio 572
Ainu, recognition as indigenous by Japan 130
air networks
  city-pairs 650–1, *652*
  first transpacific flight 639
  holiday destinations 650
  hubs 639
  post-war 639–41
  regulatory changes 650
  routes 641, 649, 651
aircraft
  Airbus-A380 650
  Boeing 707 648
  Boeing 747 649
  Boeing 787 651
  DC-4 Skymaster 641
  DC-7 641
  flying boats 639, 641
  jets 648–51
  Lockheed Super Constellation 641, 648
  operated by Qantas **649**
aircraft manufacturers
  Boeing 648
  Lockheed 639
  Macdonald Douglas 648
airlines *640*
  British Commonwealth Pacific Airways 641
  Japan Airlines 641, 648

Index

Pacific islands national 650
Pan Am 639, 641, 648
Qantas 641, 648, **649**
Singapore Airlines 651
Aitutaki, Cook Islands 597
Akaroa Bay, New Zealand 443
Akeli, Palepa Ioane, archive memories
    (Sāmoa) 191–2
Akin, D. 363
Akutagawa, M. 240
Alafurai, Bishop Leonard 365
Alaska, US purchase from Russia 569, 634
Alegado, Rosie 241
Alexander Turnbull Library, Samoan
    archives 196
Allen, Anthony 378
Allen, Chadwick 255
Allen, R., *Missionary Methods: St Paul's or
    Ours* 354
Allende, Salvador, president of Chile 551–2
Aloha (film) 275
Aloha Oe (film) 271
Aloma of the South Seas (film) 273
The Altar Stairs (film) 273
Alvares, Francisco 76
Alvarez, Don Inigo (French spy) 325
Amalgamated Wireless (Australasia) Limited
    534
Amchitka Island, nuclear testing 616, 630
American Board of Commissioners for
    Foreign Missions 288, 568
American President Lines 638
    container ships 642
American Sāmoa 360
    unincorporated territory of US 685
    US wartime base 597
    wireless station 536
    see also Sāmoa
Americas
    Indigenous populations 340
    relationship with Pacific Ocean ('Red
        Pacific') 149–55
    Spanish empire 42, 44
    see also Canada; South America; United
        States of America
ancestry
    Ocean as an ancestor 707, 716–17
    in Timor 476–7, 481
    Tongan stories 708–9
Ancón, Treaty of (1883) 540
Andandozan, King of Dahomey 460
Anderson, A. 212, 386
Anderson, B. 429

Anderson, Jean 248–9
Anderson, M.K. 372
Anderson, W. 223, 573
Aneityum, Vanuatu
    effect of epidemic disease 340
    missionary work 351
Angamos, Battle of (1879) 539
Anglican Melanesian Mission 362
Angola, Portugal and 458–9
animals
    cattle 377, 380
    hoary bats (Hawai'i) 719, 721
    Polynesian rat 374
    rabbit (in Australia) 383
    rats 376, 386
    Steller's sea cow (extinct) 375
Antarctic
    as 'Blue Continent' 137
    Chilean claims 556
    US claims 568
anthropology 356–9, 495
    and collecting of artefacts 289
    and concept of culture 349, 361–2
    developed from missionaries'
        ethnographies 79
    view of missionaries 349, 357
    see also ethnography; science
Anti-Ballistic Munitions Agreement 579
Antofagasta, Chile 51
    ceded by Bolivia 540
Antoine, André-Paul, and Robert Lugeon,
    Chez les Mangeurs d'hommes (film) 274
Aotearoa New Zealand 44, 57, 287
    administration of Cook Islands and Niue
        446
    administration of Western Sāmoa 492
    anti-Chinese sentiment 230
    Board of Inquiry into Native Affairs (1856)
        222
    British imperial interest in 321–2
    Chinese in 667
    coastal steam routes 522
    colonization 441–2
    economic policies and migration 759
        Fijian Rural Work Permit Scheme 766
        and new industries for Pacific islands
        770
        Recognised Seasonal Employment
            Scheme 766–8, 769
        South Pacific Worker Schemes 766
    films 271–2, 275
    gold rush 45
    Goodwill Mission to Sāmoa (1936) 201

INDEX

Aotearoa New Zealand (cont.)
  greenstone sculpture 301
  health programmes 509
  Indigenous filmmaking 280
  Indigenous language literature 430
  interracial marriage 211, 228–9
    and access to land 218
    Māori-Chinese families 216
    view of mixed-race population 225
  and Māori autonomy 604
  Māori Social and Economic Development
    Act (1945) 604
  Māori wars 516
  Māui Tikitiki demi-god 711
  missionaries 213
  National Library 188, 200
  Ngāpuhi confederation project (North
    Island) 431, 441
  and nuclear weapons testing 617, 627
  Pacific islander migrants in 756, **758**
  and Pacific Studies 135
  and Pacific Trades Partnership 770
  and Polynesia 523
  and regional organizations 698
  rugby union 771
  Samoan Quota 756
  Taieri Native Reserve 229, 232
  Te Papa, National Museum 135
  tourism 650
  and trans-Pacific routes 521
  Union Steam Ship Company 520
  universities 250, 761
  US wartime bases 597
  whaling economy 209, 228
  and World War II 600
  see also Māori
Appadurai, A., ethnoscapes 753
archaeology, and population decline 343
architecture
  early illustrations of houses 292
  and household furnishings 298
archives 167–91
  affective nature of 200–1
  business records 203
  cataloguing process 198
  civil society organisations and 203
  and colonial administrations 168, 170, 177,
    196
  and communities 167, 196
  community participation 169
  conservation laboratories 173
  and cultural memory 168
  and digital security 204

digitization of 169, 175, 201–5
dynamic 167
and German Museums Association
  guidelines 199
global professionalization 170
and government recordkeeping 171, 202
and identity 169
and importance of evidence 168
incorporation of Indigenous knowledge
  193, 195
Indigenous written texts 252, 256, 261
international overview 193
judicial records 202
and lack of community trust 176, 189
literary 246, 256
online platforms 196
and oral tradition 176, 190
role of archivist 203
as source of colonial power 177, 189, 191
support resources 172, 203
traditional practice 167
tropical climate conditions 172–4, 203
and women's narratives 191, 196–200
see also Fiji, National Archives; histories
  and historiographies; Sāmoa
Ardern, Jacinda, New Zealand prime
  minister 31
Arista, N. 252
  The Kingdom and the Republic 244
Armitage, D. 156
Arning, Eduard 289
art 77
  anthropological study of 289, 291
  Anu'u Nuu' ka 'Ike (Learning step by step)
    132
  body ornamentation and personal objects
    310
  as concept 286–7
  as cultural patrimony 291
  earliest Pacific 291
  early European depictions 287
  European collectors 287–91
  exhibitions of 291
  Fijian 187
  flower ornaments 310
  household furnishings 298
  human hair, use of 310
  indirectness 286
  Japanese depictions of Micronesia 116
  Japanese manga 117
  modern Pacific 312
  objects, uses of 292
  oral music and movement 310–12

890

Index

private collections 290–1
skill 286
wallpaper design 70–2, 77, 96
see also architecture; ceremonial sites;
dance; monuments; sculpture and
carvings; settlement patterns; textiles
and fibres
Arthur, Sir George, Governor of Tasmania
330
As a Man Desires (film) 273
Asami, Yokota 633
Asia
relationship with Pacific ('Yellow Pacific')
143–9
wealthy modern elites 149, 157
Asia-Pacific Economic Cooperation forum
(APEC) 148, 556
Asian Financial Crisis (1997) 555
Asian migrants 102
social status 45
see also Japan; migration
Association of Southeast Asian Nations
(ASEAN) 638, 644
AT&T, and international communications
654
Atacama Desert
copper deposits 550
sodium nitrate deposits 540
Atai, Kanak leader 443
An Atomic Kaiju Appears (film) 278
Auckland, early cinema 268
Austral Islands 428, 444
feathered headdresses 310
Australia 44
administration of New Guinea 141
air routes 651
Australia-Pacific Technical Coalition
(2007) 761
Botany Bay convict colony 326
and British nuclear weapons testing 618
Burns Philp & Company (steamships)
523
coastal steam routes 522
Commonwealth Prickly Pear Board 384
early films 272
gold rush 45, 145, 517
immigration
Asian–Aboriginal relationships 220
Chinese in 667
Chinese-European community 230
Japanese migrants in 103
Pacific islander migrants in 756, **758**
'White Australia' policy 145, 157

imperial aspirations 523
and Indonesia 687
introduced species 383–4
judicial records 202
National Library 188
and Norfolk Island 446
overseas development assistance 689
and Pacific War (1942) 121, 590
pearl shell industry 215
and PNG 605–7
racial segregation 141
and regional organizations 698
and regional stability 607
relations with US 581
rugby union 772
and Stolen Generation 197, 226
temporary labour mobility schemes 767
Pacific Labour Scheme 769–71
Pacific Seasonal Worker Pilot Scheme
768
Seasonal Worker programme 760, 769,
769
and trans-Pacific shipping routes 517
and wireless telegraphy 533
Australia New Guinea Administrative Unit
(ANGAU) 592, 598
Australia, New Zealand and United States
Treaty Alliance (ANZUS) 581
Australian National University
Pacific Manuscripts Bureau 195
Research School of Pacific Studies 194
Australian Royal Commission, on nuclear
tests 619
Australian South Sea Islanders (Port Jackson)
(ASSIPJ), website 196
Austronesian cultural group 711
Avia, T. 'Ifoga' 252
Awabakal people, New South Wales 351
Aylwin Azócar, Patricio, president of Chile
553
Aztec Empire 42

Bacevich, A. 583
Bachelet Jeria, Verónica Michelle, president
of Chile 553
Backès, S., New Caledonia 732, 747
Backhouse, James 213
Bagnall, K. 230
Baillieu, Pierre 289
Bainimarama, Voreqe (Frank), prime
minister of Fiji 692
and Pacific Island Development Forum
703

INDEX

Baker, Shirley, Tongan adviser 433–4
Bali
  air routes 651
  tourism 650
Banaba, Kiribati (Ocean Island) 55–62
  displacement of population to Rabi, Fiji
    56
  and identity 56, 59–60
  Japanese occupation 61
  phosphate mining 55, 60–1
Bangkok, air hub 639
Banivanua-Mar, T. 90, 263
  Decolonisation and the Pacific 249
Banks, Joseph 70
  and breadfruit 381, 383
  as collector 92
  and Kew Gardens 82
  portraits 78
  and Purea 82
  at Tahiti 382
  and Tupaia 92–3
  and voyage of *Endeavour* 77
Banner, S. 157
Barahona, Pablo 553
Barclay, Barry 279
  Ngati (film) 280
  Tangata Whenua (TV series) 279
  Te Rua (film) 281
Barratt, G. 136, 152
Bass Strait, sealing community 328, 330
Bataillon, Fr Pierre 429
Baudin, Nicolas, French expedition 328
Bayard Dominick Expeditions 289
Bayly, George
  account of voyage of *St Patrick* 316, 321
  and fate of La Pérouse 318–19
beach communities 208
  'crew cultures' in 210, 567
Beachcomber (film) 271
'beachcomber communities' 209
Beaglehole, J.C., Cook's biographer 94
Beamer, B.K. 241–2, 426, 446
  No Makou Ka Mana: Liberating the Nation
    236
The Beast from 20,000 Fathoms (film) 278
Beier, U.
  Decolonising the Mind 249, 260
  Niugini Lives (anthology) 260
Beijing, US Naval wireless station 536
Belau, anti-nuclear constitution 158
Bell, J. A. 274
Bellamy, Rayner 495, 502
Bellingshausen, Fabian von 288

Belt and Road Forum for International
  Cooperation, Second (2019) 680
Benedict, Ruth, *Patterns of Culture* 362, 364
Bengal Hurkaru, Calcutta newspaper 319, 322,
  324
Bennett, J.A., *Natives and Exotics*
  602
Betty Boop: Bamboo Isle (film) 276
Between Heaven and Hell (film) 278
Bikini Atoll
  nuclear testing 29, 123, 605, 614, 629
  Operation Crossroads 619
  UN World Heritage Site 612
Binoka, ruler of Abemama atoll 439
biodiversity 30
  Chinese territorial waters 669
  Marshall Islands 27
  see also ecology
biopower 491
Bird of Paradise (film) 275
birds
  effect of wind turbines on 721
  extinctions 374
  honeycreeper feathers 309
  introduced to Tahiti 370
  Pacific Golden Plover 710, 716–17, 719
  Stumbling Moa-nalo (extinct) 374
Birrell, K. 202
Bismarck, Otto von 445
Bismarck Archipelago
  German claim to 445
  sandalwood extraction 440
  'blackbirding', labour trade 140
  Bismarck Archipelago 440
Blaine, James G., US Secretary of State 570
Blaisdell, Kekuni 234
Blanchard, É. *Anthropologie* 415, 418–19
Bligh, Captain William 75, 83
  and *Providence* 382
  and transportation of breadfruit from
    Tahiti to Caribbean 381–3
'Blue Continent'
  concept of 132–4
  as cultural entity 137–9
Blue Lagoon (film) 269
Blumenbach, J.F. 419
  and diversity of human races 401–3
Boas, Franz, critique of social evolutionism
  356–7
Bohun, strike leader 141
Bōken Dankichi, Japanese comic serial
  117–18
Boki Kamā'ule'ule, Hawaiian chief 440

892

Index

Bolivia 50–5
  identity 54
  loss of coastal territory 50–1, 54, 539
  and War of the Pacific 539
Bonin Islands, creole society 448
Bonnie, Robert 270
Bora-Bora, Leeward Islands 428, 602
  French annexation 444
Botany Bay 326
Bougainville
  civil war 695
  Japanese landings 121
Bougainville, Louis Antoine de 288
Bounty, HMS
  mutiny on 381
  at Tahiti 75
Bourdieu, P. 477, 796
Bovensiepen, J. 485
Bow, Clara 273
Bowes, Joseph, Queensland Missionary
  Conference 356
'Boxer Codex' (*c*.1590) *393*, 393
Boyd, M. 158
breadfruit 369, 381–3
Brenchley, Julius L. 288
Breteigner, Pierre, New Caledonia
  740
Brian Boroimbe, Māori seaman 319, 321
Briggs, George, sealer 332
British Columbia 157
  interracial relationships 219, 229
  Pacific Islanders and 151
British Empire 47
  and concern about race mixing 222
  expansion into Pacific 321
  and introduction of species 379
  migrants 146
British Museum, Pacific art in 288–9
Broinowski, A. 632
Brooks, Lisa 255
Brooks, Captain N.C. 571
Brosses, C. de 398, 400–1
Brown, Alohalani 238
Brown, Commander Stan 627
Brute Island (*McVeagh of the South Seas*) (film)
  272
Buchert, Martin, seaman 318
Buffon, G.-L. Leclerc, comte de 419
  on human species 398–400, 419
Burma, war in 320
Burns, James, *University of Hawai'i Law
  Review* 244
Burton, John, Methodist missionary 356

Busan, port, container shipping 643, **646**
Bush, George H.W., US President 579
Bush, John E., Hawaiian politician 435
Byron, George 288

Cable and Wireless Ltd 537
cables, undersea 526–32, 635
  alloy coating 536
  American 528–30
  breakages 531
  duplication 536
  Fanning Island 528, 530, *531*
  first British 528
  French 529
  gutta percha insulation 527
  increased capacity 654
  Indian Ocean 528
  intermediate stations 527, 530
  joint agreements on 529
  new Internet 655
  ocean surveys for 527
  Pacific Cable Board 529
  and shipping communication 531
  speed of communication 636, 660
  for telephone calls 653
  see also wireless telegraphy
Cademartori, J. 555
Cairuy, Major Pedro and Don João of,
  Timorese nobles 487
Cakobau of Bau, king of Fiji 433–4, 444, 570
Calcutta
  Dillon's Māori seaman in 319–21
  as imperial centre in East 320
  Royal Asiatic Society 319
California 569
  anti-Asian laws 219
  anti-miscegenation laws 219–20
  cannabis crop 385
  cattle 378
  gold rush 45, 145, 517, 634
  indigenous trade in species 372–3
  introduction of *Eucalyptus* from Australia
  384–5
  introduction of species by Spanish 371
  Pacific communities in 758
  seal hunting 566
  US annexation 634
Callander, J. 398
Callao, blockade of 539
Camacho, K.L. 126
  Militarized Currents 584
Cambridge Anthropological Expedition
  (1898) 270

INDEX

Cambridge University, Museum of
Archaeology and Anthropology, and
Fijian collection 187, 289, *290*
Canada
borders 569, 585
fur-trade 210, 214, 229
gold rush 45, 145
preference for wireless over cable 536
trans-continental railways 660
and trans-Pacific route to Australia 521
and undersea cables 528
see also British Columbia
Canadian Pacific Railroad 521, 638, 660
Cândido da Silva, Lieutenant 487
Cannibal Tours (film) 280
cannibalism, in film 274
canoes, Indigenous
sculpture and carving 301
significance of 138
Cantile, James, Hong Kong doctor 224
Canton (Guangzhou) 566
capitalism, transnational 157
Carey, Harry, *Brute Island* 272
cargo cults 278
post-war 604
Caribbean, and introduction of breadfruit
381, 383
Caro, Niki 282
Caroline Islands
Germany 447
origins of political structures 41
see also Federated States of Micronesia;
Palau
Carter, Jimmy, US President 579
carvings *see* sculpture and carvings
Castro, Alfonso de, governor of Timor 464,
472
Celestino da Silva, José, governor of Timor
463, 467–8, 482, 485
on flags and war 486
on vassalage ceremony 465
Central Polynesian Land and Commercial
Company 570
ceremonial sites
East Polynesia 297
Fijian godhouses 295
Nan Madol, Pohnpei 293–4
Tonga 295
Chamisso, A. 379, 419
Chamoro, Japanese racial designation of
mixed Islander and European
ancestry 111, 113, *112*

Chamorros
in Guam 393, 593
in Hawai'i 215
and leprosy 504
Chan, Sir Julius 668
Chang, Ching Yi 359
Chang, D.A. *The World and the Things Upon
It* 583
Chang, K.S., *Pacific Connections* 585
Chappell, D.A. 150, 342
Charvet, Jean Gabriel 77
Chauchat, M., New Caledonia 745
Cheng, Jingyi 354
Chiang Kai-shek 575
Chicago, University of, neoliberal school 552
children, mixed-race 207, 222–6
absent European parents 222
schools and orphanages for 222
and scientific theories on race mixing 223
Chile 539
and Antarctic claims 556
and Asia-Pacific Economic Cooperation
forum (APEC) 556
Concertación de Partidos por la
Democracia 553
copper exports 550–1
economic growth 554
military ascendancy 539–40
National Copper Corporation of Chile 551
neoliberal economic policies 552–6
and nitrates 540
overthrow of Allende 551–2
and Pacific Islanders 153
and Pacific Rim Discourse 554
and Rapa Nui 147, 447, 558–60
trade agreement with China (PRC) 550
as tricontinental country 556, *557*
under Pinochet 552
war of independence against Spain 317
and War of the Pacific 50–1, 539
China 664–82
airline city-pairs 650–1
Belt and Road Initiative 662, 672, 680
and Chilean copper 550–1
Christianity in 354, 359
coastal fisheries 669
Communist Revolution 48, 576
Cultural Revolution 548–9
and environment 665, 680
and food security 665
Fujian province 44, 667–8
gateway regions 658, 663

894

Index

and global climate change mitigation 681
and Hawaiian Kingdom 436
and Hong Kong 216
imperial 66
Internet 655
interracial relationships 216, 226
Jin dynasty 67
links with the West 662
Manchu conquest 43
and Manila galleon trade 543
marine defence strategy 676–8
  blue water naval capacity 672, 676
maritime trade 666–8
  container port traffic **645**, 645
Ming dynasty 43, 543
modern economic dominance 48, 144, 159,
  580, 634
modern industrialization 63, 635, 665–6,
  673
modern nation-state 52
Muslim rebellions 44
nationalism 64
nuclear testing in Gansu 616, 677
and Pacific 683
  aid and investment in Pacific Islands
    674–5, 677, 689
  and diaspora 143
  and environmental concerns in Pacific
    679–82
  relations with Pacific Islands 129, 580,
    607, 673–9, 681
post-dynastic structures of power 63
post-war economy 661, 664–6
post-war trade 637
Qing conquest of Taiwan 43
Qing dynasty 46, 545, 547, 565, 669
and recognition of Taiwan 675, 678–9
relationship of maritime and Eurasian
  cultures 67
steamship routes 522
territorial waters 668
treaty ports 216, 634
US trade with 565
see also Chinese
China Commercial Steamship Company 522
Chinese
in Australia 667
diaspora in Southeast Asia 667
food tradition in Peru 547–8, *548*
in Hawai'i 148
legal constraints in America 219
as migrant labour 145, 545–7

in New Zealand 667
in PNG 668
seen as threat 144–5
Chinese Exclusion Act (1882 USA) 574
Chinook people, and interracial marriage 211
Choris, L., artist 377
Christen, K. 198
Christian, Fletcher 381
Christianity
in China 354, 359
effect on political systems 427–9
and independence movements 607
Marshall Islands 31
in Micronesia 114
Pacific Islanders' enthusiasm for 352
in Tahiti 427–8
see also missionaries and missions
Christophe, A. 134
Chumash (Michumash), inhabitants of Alta
  California 372
Church Missionary Society 257
Chuuk
Japanese naval base 120–1, 589, 612
Nauruans evacuated to 596
Cilento, Dr Raphael 491, 493
cinema
and changing perceptions 266
see also film(s)
Clayton-Bulwer Treaty (1847) 570
Cleveland, Grover, US President, Blount
  Report 572
climate change
carbon reduction targets 680
and fishing 672
Hau'ofa and 727
impact of 160, 787
Japan and 128, 130
Marshall Islands and 28–9
and migration 774
as threat to Pacific Islands 679, 690, 776–7
Clinton, Hillary, US Secretary of State 563
Clinton, William J., US President 579
Cochin, R. 793
Codrington, Robert, missionary 352–3
Coe, Emma, Bismarck Archipelago 440
Coelho Guerreiro, António, governor in
  Timor 463–4
Cold War
impact in Pacific 683
and nuclear weapons 614
and US ideology 564, 578, 605
Colenso, William 214

INDEX

Collins, Ella, *The Erstwhile Savage* 260, 262
colonial administrations
  and archives 168, 170, 177
  Fiji 179
  and interracial marriages 217
  and National Archives of Fiji 171
  Portuguese in Timor 467–8
  and regulation of interracial relationships
    217–21, 223, 232
  relations with missionaries 353
colonialism
  changes to environments 787, 793–6, 801
  and ethnography 396–8
  and flags as national symbols 451
  and gender 207
  health and social regimes 490–513
  image of washing away 248
  and limitations on mobility 502
  see also decolonization; imperial expansion
Colonialism: Ogre or Angel? (film) 278
colonization 441–7
  by Asian settlers 102
  and dominance of European narrative 49
  European (English-speaking) 45
  resistance to 441, 443
  timeline **442**
colours
  'Black Pacific' 139–43
  blue 160, 162
  on maps 133
  'Red Pacific' 149–55
  thought-experiment (applied to Pacific)
    139–59
  'White Pacific' 155–9
  'Yellow Pacific' (Asia-Pacific) 143–9
Columbian Exchange 378
commemorations and war memorials 608–13
  public memorials 610
  war cemeteries 608
Commercial Pacific Cable Company 529
Commonwealth Literature Bureaus 263
Commonwealth of the Northern Mariana
  Islands
  as self-governing territory of US 688
  see also Mariana Islands
communication
  cost of cable telegrams 531
  despatches by steamship 526
  and imperial connections in Pacific 537
  satellites 653
  speed of 636
  telephones 653
  use of cable by Indian diaspora 532

Voice-over-the-Internet, and Skype 653, 655
  see also cables, undersea; Internet;
    steamships; wireless telegraphy
container shipping 641–8, **646**, 660
  development of 642
  increased size 646
  speed of ships 648
  standardization of containers 643
  throughput **644**
contamination, nuclear 29, 607
  exposure of workers to 617, 621, 625, 630,
    632
  French tests 625
  marine ecosystems 629
  Marshall Islands 619, 622–3, 629
  radioactive iodine 629
The Contemporary Pacific journal 804
Convention on Biological Diversity (2004) 30
Cook Islands 428
  archives 203
  Asiatic Restriction Act (1898) 502
  British colony 445
  constitution 693
  'free association' with New Zealand 446,
    685, 688
  histories 253
  images wrapped in barkcloth 307
  leprosy 503
  overseas parliamentary seat 753
  smallpox vaccinations 505
  tuberculosis 494
  village health committees 512
  women's village committees 500
Cook, James 70, 155
  collections 287
  at Hawai'i 424
  and introduction of diseases 339, 376
  introduction of plants and animals
    (Society Islands) 380
  La Pérouse and 325
  and North America 151
  portraits 78
  scientific information gathering 81, 87
  second voyage 404
  and Tupaia's map 91, 93
  voyage accounts 76, 292, 297, 419
Cook, T. 168
Coolidge, Calvin, US President 360
Cooper, Anna Julia, and anti-Asian prejudice
  146
Cooper, F. 582
copper, from Chile 550–1
coral reefs 159

Index

bleaching of 721, 801
Tonga 717
Coral Sea, Battle of (1942) 589
cosmogony, Indigenous Oceanian 715, 722
Costner, Kevin
Rapa Nui 281
Waterworld 281
Cousteau, Jacques 155
Covid-19 pandemic
New Caledonia 746
and remittances 760
Craig, Eric 289
creole societies, creation of 447–8
Crocombe, M. 247, 264
Two Hundred Changing Years 253
Crocombe, R. 136, 247, 700
Crocombe, R. and M.
'Early Polynesian Authors' 253
and Taʻunga 258–9
Crosby, A. 545
and Columbian Exchange 378
Ecological Imperialism 340
culture, concept of
adoption by missionaries 361–2
definitions 350, 353, 357
and local customs 357, 365
missionaries and 349
theological theories of 364, 368
see also art; traditional knowledge
Cunard Line, *Queen Mary* 638
Cuvier, G., taxonomy of race 406
Cvetkovich, A. 201

Dalrymple, A., translation of Quirós 402
Damien (film) 277
Dampier, W.
A Continuation of a Voyage to New-Holland 395
ethnographic descriptions 394–6
Guam 394–5
map of discoveries 396, 397
New Guinea 395–6
A New Voyage Round the World 394
as source for Buffon 398–400
dance
hula (Hawaiʻi) 118, 237, 242, 311, 312, 583
Japanese study of hula 124
Japanese version of South Seas 118
and poetry 311
D'Anglebermes, Jean-Louis 743
D'Arcy, P. 231
Darwin, Charles 82, 419
Davidson, J.W. 194, 209, 339
Davis, Hannah Holmes 378

Davis, Dr T. 495, 512
Daws, G., *Shoal of Time* 243
Dawson, C.
Gifford Lectures (1947) 362
Religion and Culture 364
de Bruce, L. 231
Death Drums of New Guinea (film) 276
decolonization 684
and democracy 683
and film 278
and independence movements 688
and island-centred historiography 135
Pacific churches and 367
post-war moves towards 603–8
Southeast Asia 637
Timor 463
Defoe, Daniel, *Robinson Crusoe* 271, 273
democracy
and decolonization 683
in post-colonial constitutions 449, 691
and role for traditional leaders 691–4
Deng, Xiaoping 665–6, 673
Dening, G. 82, 86–7, 382
account of Wallis at Tahiti 80
D'Entrecasteaux, B., voyage in search of La
Pérouse 326–7
DeSilva, K., *Iwikuamoʻo o ka Lāhui* 240
Dewey, Commodore George 572
Diamond, J. 386
Dias, Fernão, Portuguese envoy to
Marrakech 454, 459
Dickson, W.K.L. 268
Dickson-Waiko, A. 368
Dillon, P. 153, 288, 316
Calder voyage 317
and fate of La Pérouse 318–19, 323–4
and *Hunter* voyage 318
and Māori seamen in Calcutta 319–21
voyage of *St Patrick* from Valparaiso to
Calcutta 316–23
Dirlik, A. 554
Disaffected or Dangerous Natives Ordinance
356
disease(s) 335–48, 490
acute infections 336
blood tests 508
bubonic plague 503
chronic non-communicable 344
controls 502–5
and debate on Fatal Impact 335
dengue fever 509, 559
diabetes 345
effect on fertility 341, 343, 346–7

INDEX

disease(s) (cont.)
 endemic 346
 epidemics as cause of depopulation 346–7, 386
 gonorrhoea 336, 346
 historiography of Fatal Impact 338–44, 346–8
 hookworm 505, 508
 influenza 345
  pandemic (1918–19) 503, 509
 leprosy 337, 494, 503–5
 malaria 337–8, 496, 509
 mosquito-borne 509
 and quarantine 503
 resulting from nuclear exposure 621, 624, 627, 630, 632
 shock therapies 507
 smallpox 341
 syphilis 336–8, 346
 in Tahiti 370
 Tokelau ringworm 337
 transport (shipping) as vector 337
 tuberculosis 337, 494, 506
 venereal 495, 501
 yaws 336, 338, 346, 505, 507
 see also health
Dobyns, H.F. 340
Donaldson, Roger, *Sleeping Dogs* (film) 280
Douglass, Frederick 140
Dower, J.W. 576
Drake, Sir Francis 541
Drinnon, R. 585
drugs
 against yaws 505
 carbon tetrachloride 505
 chenopodium 505
 largactil 507
 psychotropic 506
 quinine 505
 salvarsan 506
 vaccinations 505
DuBois, W.E.B. 142, 581
Dufour, Joseph 77, 96
Dumont d'Urville, J. 288, 403, 405, 412–14
 Histoire (of voyage) 412
 map *413*, *414*
 published record of final voyage 414
 racial descriptions 412, 419
Dumoutier, P.-M. A., *Atlas anthropologique* 415, *416*, 418
Duperrey, Louis 288, 412
Durkheim, É. 451
Dutch East Indies 207–8

Earle, Sylvia 714
earthquakes, 2011 Japan 124, 127
East Asia
 and broadband Internet services 654
 economic growth 665
 global manufacturing centre 644
 East Coast District Nurse (film) 277
East Timor *see* Timor Leste
Easter Island *see* Rapa Nui
Eastern Extension Telegraph Company 528
Eastman, George 268
Eckstein, L. and A. Schwarz, and Tupaia's map 95
ecology 369–88
 and 'belonging' in ecosystems 373, 384, 388
 and early migrations 371–5
 effect of invasive species 376
 effects of nuclear testing 619–20, 622–3
 introductions intended as beneficial 379–80, 388
 and responsibilities to Oceania 713–15
 Spanish introduction of species to California 371
 and species evolution 387
 species extinctions 374–5, 387
 and species preservation 387
 transportation of biota 370, 387–8
 see also animals; birds; plants; trees
Edison, Thomas A. 268, 285
 Boys Diving HI6361 (film) 270
 Kanaka Diving for Money, No.2 (film) 270
Edmonds, P. 213
education
 and health programmes 511–12
 migration and 761–2
 scholarships 763
 and social mobility 761
 universities 761
Edwards, Bryan 382
Eisenhower, Dwight, US President 578
Eknilang, Lijon, on Bravo test 620–1
Elkin, A.P. 361
Ellice Islands (Tuvalu)
 independence 606, 685
 public health regulations 509
 relocation of villages 508
 see also Gilbert Islands; Kiribati; Tuvalu
Ellison, Dr Pohau 495
Elvaim, Captain Francisco 470
Emerson, J.S. 289
Emosi, Ratu, Fiji 363
Empress of China (US ship) 565
Encyclopaedia of Social Sciences 364

898

Index

Endeavour, HMS
  and construction of Tupaia's map 95
  as scientific laboratory 87
  voyage account 76
Endless Summer (film) 279
Enewetak (Eniwetok) Atoll 593
  nuclear testing 123, 605, 622
  Runit Dome 29
Enlightenment
  revolutionary France 77
  and view of Pacific 75
  view of religion 74
Enloe, C. 577
Ensign Pulver (film) 279
environment
  effect of nuclear testing on 631
  Hawaiian Aloha 'Āina (Loved by the
    Land) movement 239–42
  maritime 138, 159–62
  prospects for sustainable 60, 244, 776–801
  see also climate change; ecology
Ercilla y Zúñiga, A. de, *La Araucana* 557
Eri, V. *The Crocodile* 251
ethnography 389–420
  Dampier's descriptions 394–6
  early European voyages 390–8
  and film 277
  Magellan's voyage 392–4
  missionaries' 79
  monogenism 401, 405, 410, 419
  and natural history of man 398–403
  polygenism 401, 405, 411, 414–19
  taxonomies 409–14
  use of 'Indian' 396
  see also anthropology; science
ethnoscapes 753, 775
Europe
  and contact with Pacific 72–3
  and economic interests in Pacific 156
  and hierarchies of race 139, 157
  mis-reading of Pacific society 81,
    83–4
  and 'other' 80
  and view of 'yellow peril' 144–5
  visions of Pacific 73–6
  and 'White Pacific' 155–9
  see also France; Germany; Great Britain;
    Spain
European expeditions
  anthropological 254
  scientific 270
European Union 662
  development aid 689

European voyages 73, 155, 336
  and collectors 78, 92, 170, 287–91, 381
  and depictions of Pacific art 287
  and early ethnographic descriptions 390–8,
    419
  and species introductions 375–86
  violent encounters with islanders
    81
  voyage accounts 70, 76–7, 377
  see also Banks, Joseph; Bligh, Captain;
    Cook, James
Europeans, as minority racial group in
  Pacific 157
Evening Star, Dunedin newspaper 195
Extended Economic Zones 643
extractive industries 210, 212
  copper 550–1
  films about 274
  nitrates 51, 540
  phosphates 55, 63–4, 68

Fairbanks, Douglas, Sr 275
Fallen Idol (film) 272
families, cross-cultural 207, 227–32
  and identity 227–8
  Indigenous kinship models 228–9
  Māori-Chinese 216
  marginalization 229
  narratives 227, 229, 231
  and state policies 228
  and status 228
  in treaty ports 228
  see also interracial marriage; migration
Fangataufa Atoll, nuclear testing 625
Fanning Island, undersea cables 528, 530, 531
Fanon, Frantz 234
Farmer, J., *Trees in Paradise* 384
Fatal Impact 490
  and agency 339, 342, 347
  historiography 338–44, 346–8
Federated States of Micronesia (FSM) 128,
    778–89
  adaptation 780
  climate 778
  and climate change 779
  collective food production 784
  colonial changes to environment 787
  connection of islanders with sea 779
  environmental management 784
  extent 778
  importance of historical continuity 788–9
  lang, fanou, and *saat* doctrines (*nonon
    aramas*) 780, 785

899

INDEX

Federated States of Micronesia (FSM) (cont.)
 marine and coastal management 786
 and MTEC 702
 pwau conservation methods 785–6
 responsibilities for environment 787–8
 rituals 788
 social relations 784
 status of chiefs 693
 traditional environmental zones 781–3, **782**
 traditional knowledge 779
 and US Compact of Free Association 688
Fernández-Armesto, F. 554
Festival of Pacific Arts 128
Fiji
 'Back in Time' television programme of
  archive footage 185
 barkcloth presentations 308
 Beqa traditional fish drive photograph
  186–7, *187*
 colonial administration 179, 492
  Decrease Report (on maternal
   shortcomings and depopulation) 500
  Libraries Act 171
  Native Affairs Ordinance (1876) 179
  Native Lands Ordinance (1880) 179
  Public Records Act 171
 colonization 444
 foreign relations
  international treaties **437**
  and Melanesian Spearhead Group 701
  relations with China 673–4, 680
  suspension from Pacific Islands Forum
   690, 703
 Great Council of Chiefs 691
 health
  Cemeteries Act (1871) 510
  Central Lepers' Hospital, Makogai 494,
   504
  Colonial War Memorial Hospital 494
  infant mortality 346
  infectious diseases 335, 345
  lunatic asylum 504
  mental health survey 496–8
  Native Medical School 495, 511
  punishment for health contraventions
   502
  shock therapy 507
  Suva Medical School 761
  yaws campaign 507
 independence 179, 606, 685
  state-building 432
 Indian labour 147
 international migration 756

ivory artefacts 289, *290*
 sculpture 301
Japanese Official Development Assistance
 129
military and peacekeeping personnel 765
missionaries 352, 361, 363
New Zealand Worker schemes 766
and nuclear weapons testing 627
politics
 constitution 433
 instability 695, 756
 origins of political structures 41
 women in parliament 696
relocation of Colo people 508
sculptured hooks 298
society
 and ceremonial presentation of *sevusevu*
  by visitors 179–81
 communal representation 691
 interracial relationships 214
 limits on women's mobility 502
 village layouts 294
 women's village committees 500
and steamship routes 520
tales of cannibals 318
tourism 650
University of the South Pacific 250, 761
US meteorological observatory at Ovalau
 568
US wartime base 597
and wireless telegraphy 534–5
wooden sculptures *302*
see also Fiji, National Archives
Fiji Defence Force 599–600
Fiji, National Archives 167–8, 190, 194
 accessibility 177–8
 bureaucratic English of 177, 183
 climate and conservation problems
  172–4
 co-creation of archives 185–9
 collaboration with Museum of
  Archaeology and Anthropology,
  Cambridge 187
 community outreach and formal access
  179, 181–2, 188
 community participation 183–5
 and community trust 176–9
 digitization programme 185, 187, 189
 establishment and role of 170–2
 and family history 183–4
 and Fijian Art Research Project 187
 funding 188
 indentured labour records 183–4

Index

and Library Services literacy programme
182
objectives 171–2
and oral histories 187
and Pacific Virtual Museum project 188
photographic and audio-visual records
185–6
Rotuma Day Outreach (2013)
182
staffing and structural deficiencies 174–5,
189
training and capacity building 175, 178
use of social media 186–7, 187
village introductions 182–3
Filipinos, as ships' crew 144, 215
filmmakers, Indigenous 269, 279, 281, 285
film(s) 266–85
documentary 270, 274, 280
escapist romance 273, 284
ethnographic 277
feature 280
history of 268
Hollywood 275
horror 284
influence of 283
location filming 275
lost 272–3, 275
musicals and animations 276
narrative fiction 271, 273
radicalization (1960s) 278
representation of Pacific Islands 266–8,
283–5, 583
scientific expeditions 270
study of 279
surf movies 279
technical developments 268, 274
and television 279
twenty-first-century 282
underwater cinematography 274
variety of 266
World War II (Pacific War) 276, 278–9,
281
Finney, B. 94
First World War see World War I
Firth, R. 792
Fischer, J.R. 378
fish species
sensitivity to temperature 778
tuna 669
yellow croaker 669–70
fishing
Chinese coastal 669
Chinese fleet 667, 671

Chinese offshore 669–71
declining catches 670–1
driftnets 671
environmental threats to 672, 777
farmed (aquaculture) 669, 671
global tonnage 670
industrial fleets 670, 720
traditional knowledge of (FSM) 783
traditional methods 28
tuna 123
Fison, L., missionary 352–3
flags 450–89
in Africa 459
as agencies 452, 471, 478, 484–5, 489
animism of 473–4, 489
cult of 475–6
Dutch use of 466, 482
indigenization of 452, 480–1, 488
of Lisbon 456
as mediators of distance 469
as national symbols 451–3, 460, 488
New Caledonia 731–4
Order of Christ 456
and patriotism 474–5
Portuguese naval 484
Portuguese royal banner 455–6
prestige of 469–70
of Republic of Portugal 460
as royal gifts to vassals 458
Timorese preservation of ancient 464, 478,
479, 482–3
and vassalage ceremonial 465–6
and wars 459, 465, 470, 485–7, 489
see also Timor; vassalage, Portuguese
imperial system of
Flaherty, Robert, Nanook of the North (film) 274
Fleming, Sir Sandford 528
Fleming, Victor, Hula 273
Flores, Lesser Sunda Islands 462, 465
Flores, Lieutenant Acácio 478, 486
flower ornaments 310
Flynn, D., Pacific centuries 136
Flynn, D., and A. Giraldez, Pacific World 136
Foigny, Gabriel de 76
Fojas, C. 582
Ford, Gerald, US President, Pacific Doctrine
579
Ford, John 275
Wild Women (film) 272
foreign aid 32, 688–90
and agency 689
Chinese 674–5, 677, 689
conditionality 690

901

INDEX

foreign aid (cont.)
and external debt 689
and welfare dependence 689
Forster, G. 82, 379, 398, 403, 419
and Kant 404–5
Forster, J.R., ethnographic observations 398,
400–1, 411, 419
Fort Vancouver 215
Foucault, M. 87, 234, 491
France
anthropology 289, 361–2, 414
and anti-nuclear protests 625
Centre d'Expérimentation du Pacifique
626
colonizations 443–4
constitution 743
development aid 689
exploratory voyages in Pacific 325, 403
Free French Pacific Battalion 600
nuclear testing 158, 624–6, 699
Pacific islander migrants in 756
and republican universalism 738
rivalry with Britain in Pacific 323–7
rugby union 771
and sinking of *Rainbow Warrior* 628, 699
Société d'Histoire Naturelle 325
and undersea cables 529
Frank, Kiana 241
Fraser, Toa, *Dead Lands* (film) 282
Frazer, J. 357
Freeman, Derek 343
Frei Ruiz-Tagle, Eduardo, president of Chile
553, 559
French colonial empire
designation of colonies 686
Indochina 223
and mixed-race (métis) question 222–3
and New Caledonia 729, 743, 748, 750
and Pacific island colonies 604, 606, 699
resistance to decolonization 684, 686
French Polynesia 626, 789–800
changes under colonial rule 793–6
climate 789
concept of 'habitus Māʻohi' 796–8
copra plantations 793
customary use rights 793
and decolonization 687
economic effects of nuclear testing 625–6,
795
effects of climate change 796
extent 789
French overseas collectivity 687
and French property rights 795

independence movement 688
mobility of societies 792, 795
modern conservation and 'habitus Māʻohi'
799–800
nuclear contamination 630
pre-colonial ecosystem 790
rāhui system of access rights to resources
791–2
taro pits 790
and traditional knowledge 798
women in parliament 697
see also Leeward Islands; Marquesas
Islands; Tahiti; Wallis and Futuna
Freycinet, Louis de 288
Friedman, M. 553
From Here to Eternity (film) 278
Front de Libération Nationale Kanak et
Socialiste (FLNKS) (New Caledonia)
701, 738–9
flag 732
multiculturalism 738
and possible 'Yes' vote 744
Fujian province, China 44
Fujimori, Alberto, president of Peru 147, 549–50
Fukushima Daiichi power plant disaster 124,
127, 631–3
problems of official narratives and
response 632–3
Funafuti, Ellice Islands 597
Funaki, Kaituʻu 130
fur trade 566, 568
Futuna
island kingdom 428, 443
see also Wallis and Futuna

G-20 (Group of Twenty), Pacific Rim
countries 634
Galeano, E. 540
Galvão, A., chronicler 407
Garvey, Marcus 142
Gauguin, Paul, *Noa Noa* 116
Gaulle, General Charles de 607, 626
Geeves, Nurse 511
Gellner, E. 731
geo-logistics 636, 660–3
George Tupou II, king of Tonga 445
George Tupou (Tāufaʻāhau), first king of
Tonga 426, 432, 438
German Museums Association 199
Germany
acquisition of Spanish islands 447
Chinese labourers in Sāmoa 220
colonial possessions 47, 271, 445–6

902

Index

expeditions to Pacific 288
and Japan 107
law on status of mixed-race children 223
museum collections 288, 294
and Spanish possessions in Micronesia 107,
445
see also Sāmoa
Gibson, Walter, Hawaiian premier 435
Gilbert Islands
Allied invasion (1943) 590, 593
British colony 445, 685
and nuclear weapons testing 627
public health regulations 509
relocation of villages 508
and war dead 609
see also Kiribati
Gilmore, Matthew, missionary 357
Gilroy, P. 138, 140
and Atlantic World studies 137
global economy 634
and China 680
Global Financial Crisis 650
global supply chains 644
Goa, Portugal and 458, 461, 463
Godeffroy company 203, 288
Godzilla, origins of story 124
Gojira (film) 278
gold rushes 45, 517
Asian miners 145, 667
Australia 45, 145, 517
California 45, 145, 517, 634
Gomès, Philipe, New Caledonia 740
Gomes da Silva, Dr José 469
Gonschor, L. 148
Goodwin, Hannibal 268
Goodyear-Ka'ōpua, N.
A Nation Rising 236
The Seeds We Planted 236
Gordon, Sir Arthur, Governor of Fiji 179, 289
Gotō, Taketarō 103, 106
Grace, Himiona, *The Pa Boys* (film) 282
Grace, P., *Chappy* 251
Graham, Chris 282
Grant, Ulysses, US President 570
Grau Seminario, Miguel, Peruvian naval
commander 51
Great Britain
'All Red Route' to Australasia 521
and Chinese treaty ports 634
and decolonization 684
Fijians in military 765
and French rivalry in Pacific 323–7
museum collections 289

and New Zealand 441–2
nuclear weapons testing 618, 626
and Pacific steamship routes 517–18
and post-war moves towards
independence 604, 606
protectorates 445–6
and Tasmania 328
transfer of colonies to Australia and New
Zealand 446
and undersea cables 528, 537
voyage accounts 76
and wireless telegraphy 533–4, 537
see also British Empire
Greater East Asia Co-Prosperity Sphere,
Japanese 116, 119
Green, Michael 564
Green, R.C. 343
Greenpeace 630
and sinking of *Rainbow Warrior* 628, 699
Greenwood, James 140
Grey, Sir George 289
Griffith, D.W., *The Idol Dancer* 272
Guadalcanal, Solomon Islands 121, 590, 599
Guadalupe Hidalgo, Treaty (1847) 569
Guam 108, 115, 390, 803
Dampier at 394–5
early description of Chamorro inhabitants
393
hygiene 510
Japanese attack (1942) 120
Japanese war memorial 611
Liberation Day 611
non-self-governing territory of US 688
Spanish Jesuits 349
Susana Hospital for women 494
US colonization 447, 492, 586, 605, 607
US naval base 530, 580, 688
War in the Pacific National Historical
Park 611
wireless station 536
women in legislature 697
women's archival material 197
World War II 593
guano *see* nitrates
Guano Act (1856) 571
*Guinea Gold: A Romance of Australian
Enterprise* (film) 276
Guzmán Reynoso, Abimael, Shining Path
leader 548–9

Haddon, Alfred Court, Cambridge
Anthropological Expedition (1898)
270

INDEX

Hägerdal, H. 466
Haizhou, China 63–8
  history of 67–8
  Jinping mine 63–4
Hale, G.D. 419
Haley, James, *Captive Paradise*
  243
Half Life: A Parable of the Nuclear Age (film)
  280
Hall, James 275
Hamburg Scientific Foundation 288
Hanks, Tom, *Castaway* 281
Hanlon, D. 233, 235
Harding, Warren G., US President 574
Harkin, N. 191, 199
Harvard University, Peabody Museum *303*,
  303
Harvey, D. 552
Hasebe Hotondo, anthropometrist 112
Hattori, A.P. 197
Hattori, Toru 105
Hau'ofa, E. 160, 195
  and deep history 712–13
  and guardianship of Oceania 715, 800
  and Indigenous agency 348
  and Japan 131
  Kisses in the Nederends 251
  on migration 752, 769
  notion of 'sea of islands' 85–6, 449, 493
  and ocean ancestors 709, 711
  'The Ocean in Us' 712, 714
  'Our Sea of Islands' 712, 803
  'Pasts to Remember' 713
  and responsibilities to Oceania 713–15
  Tales of the Tikongs 251
  tribute to as ancestor 727
  vision of Oceania 710
Havea, Sione 364
Hawai'i 57
  academic studies 233–45
  Aloha 'Āina (Loved by the Land)
    movement 239–42
  American colonialism 234–7, 243
    as 50th US state 687
    annexation 234–7, 270, 520, 569, 571
    reaction to 586
    US maritime regulations 524
    US military operations on Kaho'olawe
      239
    and US Monroe Doctrine 564
    as US wartime base 597
    women and 583
  ancient state 424

Bernice Pauahi Bishop Museum,
  Honolulu 132, 137
bubonic plague 503
charter school movement 236
Chinese in 148
Choris's depictions 377
cultural heritage
  carved wooden bowls 298
  ceremonial sites 297–8
  feathered headdresses 310
  feathered textiles 309, *309*
  hula (dance) 118, 237, 242, 311, *312*, 583
  mele (songs) 239, 242
  music 242
  ritual objects 298
  traditional knowledge 241
  view of illness 499
  wicker sculpture 301, 304
cultural revival 233, 238
early films 268
environmental concerns 241, 244
films 271, 281
hoary bats 719, 721
identity in 232
independence 156
independence movement 687
interracial marriage with Chamorros
  215
introduction of livestock 377–8
Japanese migrant workers in 102
Japanese tourism 124, *125*, 650
Ka Lāhui Hawai'i governing initiative 235
Kapu Aloha principle 245
Kū'e and Kū'oko'a (Resistance and
  Sovereignty) 234–7
leprosy settlement (Kaulaupapa) 494, 504
Māui Ki'iki'i demi-god 711
National Memorial Cemetery of the
  Pacific 609
and North America 152
Office of Hawaiian Affairs (1978) 237
opposition to geothermal development
  241
pre-colonial population 341, 343
prostitution 577
Protest Kaho'olawe 'Ohana movement
  240
regulation of sexual relations 501, 567
resistance to Mauna Kea astronomy zone
  241–2, 245
school system 234
Senate Bill on gathering rights 242
social structure 73

Index

species introductions and extinctions 373–4
sugar plantation economy 239,
 569
Sun Yat-Sen statue in Honolulu
 148
venereal diseases in 376
whaling 569
see also Hawai'i, University of; Hawaiian
 Kingdom; Hawaiian language
 ('Olelo Hawai'i)
Hawai'i, University of 233, 250, 761
growth of Hawaiian Studies 234
Indigenous Politics 235
Ka Haka 'Ula o Ke'elikōlani College of
 Hawaiian Language 238
Kamakūokalani Center for Hawaiian
 Studies 235
Kawaihuelani Center for Hawaiian
 Language 238
Law Review 244
Hawaii 5-0 (TV series) 280
Hawaiian Holiday (film) 276
Hawaiian Kingdom 235, 244
constitution (1840) 425, 433
conversion to Christianity 425
coup d'état by American missionary
 descendants 435, 446
evolution of 424–6
global connections 436
historiography 430
influence on other constitutions 433
international treaties **437**
and Japan 436
and Kiribati 439
national culture 425
overthrown 571
political modernization 425
recognition of independence 425
regional influence 434–6, 449
and Sāmoa 435
secularization 428
and United States 434
Hawaiian language ('Olelo Hawai'i) 233,
 237–9
Kula Kaiapuni immersion schools 237
newspapers 429
and political activism 234
Pūnana Leo pre-schools 237
translation of European classics into 238
written literature 429
Hawaiians, and fur trade 215
Haweis, George, London Missionary Society
 78

Hawkesworth, J., *An Account of the Voyages*
 (1773) 77, 83
Hay, John, US Secretary of State, Open Door
 Notes 573
Hay-Pauncefote Treaty (1901)
 573
*He Murimuri Aroha ki nga Morehu o
 Maungapohatu* (film) 275
He Pito Whakaatu i te Hui i Rotorua (film)
 275
*He Pito Whakaatu i te Noho a te Māori i te Awa
 a Whanganui* (film) 275
health *see* public health
Hearts Adrift (film) 271
Hegel, G.W.F., *Philosophy of Right* 281
Heine, Dr Hilda, President of Marshall
 Islands 25
speech to SACNAS conference 25–32
Heine, Leinā'ala 242
Hereniko, V. 281
The Land Has Eyes 282
Hessler, S. 161
Heyn, Piet, Dutch freebooter 541
Higuchi, W. 113
Hijikata, Hisakatsu 116
Hina, shark goddess 711, 724–6
duality with Maui 724–5
in Hawai'i 725
as moon goddess 726
histories and historiography
and Anglophone cultural influence 48, 58
associative 39, 69
Atlantic World studies 137
of 'Blue Continent' 134–9
and challenge to imperial histories 586
disputes and struggles 34, 36
English language translations 257
of entities 34
of Fatal Impact (of disease) 338–44, 346–8
Hau'ofa's deep history 712–13
of Hawai'i 243
Hawaiian language primary sources 238
as ideological construct 35
imaginative engagement 34
Indigenous Blue Continent 133–6
Indigenous participation in 610
Indigenous traditional knowledge 58
Indigenous written texts 252, 256, 261,
 430
and institutions 34
Japanese colonialism 100, 130
Japanese contact with Pacific islanders 101
Japanese revisionism 126

905

INDEX

histories and historiography (cont.)
  literary engagement with historical texts
    252–63
  and mobility 89, 91
  and nineteenth-century divide 35, 64–5
  and oral history sources 195, 233
  origin stories 250, 476, 708–9
  of the Pacific 33–4, 39
  regional studies programmes 135
  'spatial turn' 87–9
  timeframes 41–50
  see also academic studies; archives;
    literature; traditional knowledge
Hobsbawm, E. 452
Hollywood, Pacific films 275
Holt, John Dominis 243
Holt-Takamine, Victoria 242
Hombron, J.-B. 403, 406
  De l'homme 415
Hommon, R.J. 424
Hong Kong 216
  air hub (Lantau) 639, 650–1
  container shipping 643, 645, **646**
  entrepôt trade 637
  financial services 654
  investigation into health of mixed-race
    populations 224
  Japanese attack (1942) 120
  manufacturing 635
  mixed-race children 222
Hongi Hika, Ngāpuhi paramount chief 321,
  438
Honolulu
  early cinema 268
  as US coastal port 521
  US meteorological observatory 568
hoʻomanawanui, kuʻualoha 238
Howe, K.R. 133, 137
  and Fatal Impact 339, 348
Howell, John 228
Huahine, Leeward Islands 428
  French annexation 444
Hudson's Bay Company 151
Hugel, Anatole von 289
Hughes, Charles Evans 574
Hula (film) 273
Humboldt, Alexander von 82
Hunt, T., and C. Lipo 386
Hunter, Captain John 326
Hurley, Frank
  Pearl of the South Seas (film) 274
  Pearls and Savages (film) 274
  The Hurricane (film) 275

identity
  cross-cultural families and 227–8
  and disputes 36
  effect of European colonialism on 57–9
  European view of 75
  forms of Pacific 38, 54
  language and 429–30, 449
  and race 208
ideologies
  imperialism 80–4
  liberalism 47, 64
  in nineteenth and twentieth centuries
    47
Igler, D. 153
Ihimaera, Witi 282
Ile de Paques (film) 276
Imada, A.L. 583
Imperial Conference (1911), and wireless
  telegraphy 534
imperial expansion 514
  Britain 321
  Japan 119
  Portuguese empire 461–3
  United States 157, 584
In Harm's Way (film) 279
In the Wake of the Bounty 275
Inca empire 42
India
  labourers in Fiji 147
  Tata Communications 655
India Gazette 322
Indian Ocean, undersea cable route 528
'Indians', indigenous peoples misnamed as
  149
Indonesia
  independence 686
  Japanese occupation 120
  and Melanesian Spearhead Group 701
  'tiger' economy 654
  and Timor Leste 687
  and West Papua 607, 684, 686
Industrial Revolution
  and demand for resources 53, 68
  and power imbalances 54
industrialization, global 62, 65
  and modernity 65–6
infant mortality 346, 502
infertility, resulting from nuclear exposure
  627
Ing, T. 238
Inglis, John, missionary 351
Inglis, K.S. 499
Intelsat II satellite (1967) 653

906

Index

Inter-Continental Ballistic Missile (ICBM),
  Chinese test 678
International Air Transport Agreement
  (1944) (IATA) 639
International Board of Missionaries,
  Jerusalem meeting (1928) 359
International Council on Archives 193
  Pacific Regional Branch (PARBICA) 171,
    193
International Organization for
  Standardization (ISO), container
  standards 643
International Postal Union 436
International Telecommunications Union
  (ITU) 653
Internet 651–7
  Arpanet 653
  broadband 653
  cloud providers 657
  content providers 655
  data centre hubs 654, 657
  dependence of air and sea transport on 653
  Facebook 655
  flows and connections 655, 656
  Google 655
  international carriers 655, 657
  Skype 653, 655
  transpacific traffic 654
  WhatsApp 655
  World Wide Web 653
  see also communication
interracial (cross-cultural) relationships 207,
  210
  Bass Strait sealing community 328, 330
  Chinese (in Australasia) 230
  colonial regulation of 208, 217–21
  and eugenic ideology 220
  exploitative 212, 214
  and identity of mixed-race children 208
  Indigenous view of 226
  missionaries' view of 213
  moral condemnation of 219
  World War II 601
  see also families, cross-cultural; interracial
    marriage
interracial marriage
  and access to Indigenous land 218, 226
  and Indigenous custom 211
  modern research 231
  and whaling 211, 228
Iquique, Battle of 51
Ireland, United Irishmen campaign 317
Ishida, Hitomatsu 118

Ishiwata, Tatsunosoke, in Marshall Islands
  109, 110
The Island of Dr. Moreau (film) 281, 284
Island of Lost Souls (film) 276
*Iu Mi Nao: Solomon Islands Regain
  Independence* (film) 280

Jacoulet, Paul 117
Jaluit Atoll 108
  and Greater East Asia Co-Prosperity
    Sphere 116
Japan 43, 98–131
  and African American civil rights 142
  anti-nuclear protests 124
  battlefield visits to Pacific War sites 125–7
  bone-collecting expeditions to Pacific
    islands 609, 611
  and Britain 107
  Chidorigafuchi Cemetery 126
  economy
    coal and iron ore imports 641
    modern 632
    post-war growth 635
  films 278
  fishing industry 669
  and Hawai‘i 103
  and Hawaiian Kingdom 436
  high-speed rail 661
  historical revisionism 126
  identity as island nation 127–31
  imperial expansion 101, 119
    annexation of Bonin Islands 448
    annexation of Korea (1910) 105
    annexation of Taiwan (1895) 46, 105
    move to militarism and defence (1930s)
      119
  Imperial Navy 108, 120
  and Indigenous peoples 130
  Kōchi Secondary School 118
  modern geopolitics 662
    development initiatives in Oceania 129
    and Greater East Asia Co-Prosperity
      Sphere 116, 119, 575
    and Pacific Islands Leaders Meetings
      129
  as nation-state 100
  NTT Cable 655
  and 'Oceania'
    and 'Oceanian' worldview 131
    relations with Pacific 99–104, 146–7
    and romantic view of 98
    tourism in 123–4, 650
  official emigration policy 102, 105, 116, 638

INDEX

Japan (cont.)
opening of 102, 570, 634
racialized ideology 110–13, 226, 601
and interracial relationships
216
and Rapa Nui 147
shipping
and container ships 642–3
Nippon Yusen Kaisha (NYK) steamship
line 521, 638, 642
OSK emigrant ships 638
and post-war shipping 637
Toyo Kisen Kaisha (TKK) steamship
line 522
and South Seas dancing 118
Tokyo Olympics (1964) 124
trading companies 106, 108
treaty ports 216
war with United States (1942–45) *see*
World War II (*below*)
wars with China 46, 119
invasion of Manchuria 48, 574
and Western institutions 431
World War I 107
World War II 52, 99, 119–22, 588–90, 596
and Banaba 61
nuclear bombing of Hiroshima and
Nagasaki (1945) 123, 575, 593, 614
see also Nanyō; Nanyō-chō (South Seas
Mandate)
Japan Bereaved Families Association (Nihon
Izokukai) 125
Japan International Cooperation Agency 129
Japan Overseas Cooperation Volunteers 129
Japanese, and anti-miscegenation laws in
America 220
Jenkins, Kuni 261
Jenkinson, Sir Hilary, Public Record Office
168
jet aircraft 648–51
costs and fares 649–50
de Havilland Comet 648
range 649, 651
speed 648
Jetñil-Kijiner, K. 25, 32, 130, 251
Jo-Jikum, non-profit organization 26
'Joe', lascar in Tikopia 318
John VI, king of Portugal 460
Johnson, D. 563
Johnson, Kalepa 235
Johnson, Lyndon B., US President 578
Johnson, R.K.K. 243
Johnston, B.R. 619, 630

Jolly, M. 232, 502
Jones, A. 261
Jones, R.T. 152, 375
Journal of Pacific History 194, 339, 804
study of Tupaia's map 95
Juan Fernandez Islands 566
Jun, H.H. 149
Jungle Patrol (film) 276
Jungle Woman (film) 274
Justice, Daniel Heath 255

Ka'ahumanu, of Hawai'i 428
Kadu, Caroline islander 379
Kaduva, Fiji, stranding of SS *Macgregor* 519,
519
Kaima, S. 205
Kalākaua, last king of Hawai'i 154, 425, 433,
446
circumnavigation 435
internationalism 434–5, 449
and Japan 103
Kalaunuiohua, king of Hawai'i Island 424
Kamakahi, Dennis 242
Kamakau, S.M. 430
Kamakawiwo'ole, Israel 242
Kamanā, Kauanoe 237
Kame'eleihiwa, L. 234
Native Land and Foreign Desires 234
Kamehameha dynasty 73
Kamehameha I, King of Hawai'i 151, 569
and unification 424
Kamehameha III, king of Hawai'i 428
Kanahele, Kekuhi 242
Kanahele, P.K. 241, 242, *242*
Kana'ina, Noble Charles 235
Kanak people, New Caledonia 443, 492, 604,
693
Conseil National du Peuple Autochtone
de Kanaky Nouvelle-Calédonie 736
and Covid-19 746
Customary Senate 736
demands for self-determination 736–8,
744, 748
and Nainville les Roches declaration (1983)
739
population decline 730
reservations for 502
return to New Caledonia 729
view of illness 498
see also New Caledonia
Kanaka
Japanese racial designation 111, *112*, 113
in North America 151

908

Index

Kanaka Diving for Money, No.2 (film) 270
Kanakaʻole, Edith 242
Kanepuʻu, Joseph 238
Kang, Youwei 226
Kansai airport 650
Kant, I., and theories of race 404–5
Kaohsiung, transhipment port 643
  container shipping **646**
Kaplan, Amy, *The Anarchy of Empire in the Making of U.S. Culture* 581
Kawamura, M. 116
Keate, George 292
  collection of artefacts 288
Kele, Sea Sediment 709–10
Kelly, James, role of women as sealers 332–3
Kenana, Rua, Māori leader 275
Kenilorea, Peter, prime minister of Solomon Islands 367
Kennedy, John F., US President 578
Kennedy, P. 587
Kerr, Deborah 278
Ketelaar, E. 177
Kew Gardens 82
Kimura, Kauanoe 237
King Kong (film) 276
kinship, networks 213
Kirch, P.V. 343
Kiribati (Gilbert Islands)
  and environmental change 60
  fibre armour 307
  Hawaiian envoy in 435
  Hawaiian influence 439
  independence 606, 685
  migrant seafarers 763–4
  national identity 439
  relations with China 673, 689
  women in parliament 697
  see also Banaba
Kirimati (Christmas) Island 627
Kissinger, Henry, US security adviser 552, 578
Kneubuhl, John 280
  Damien (film) 277
Kneubuhl, Lemanatele M. *The Smell of the Moon* 251
Kobayashi, I. 128
Kobayashi, Yoshinori 126
Kobe, Japan, container shipping 643
Kokoda Track campaign, PNG 598
  war tourism 612
Kokon Chomonjū (13th century) 101
Korea 43
  Japanese annexation (1910) 105, 111

litigation against Japanese corporations 129
  migrants in Japanese territories 113
  see also South Korea
Korean War (1950–3) 637
Koreans, as Japanese forced labourers 120
Korhonen, P. 154
Kosrae, Caroline Islands 114
  backstrap looms 305
  banana-fibre belts 306
  political changes 439
Kotzebue, Otto von 288, 379–80
Koy, Jim Ah 668
Krämer, Augustin 289
Kroeber, A.L. 362
Krusenstern, Admiral Adam von 288
Kupang, Timor kingdom of 464
Kuroshio (Pacific) Current 98, 101, 669
Kuwada, B.K. 238
Kuykendall, R. 243
Kwajalein Atoll 617
  Japanese naval base 120
  US invasion 593
  war graves 617
Kyoto Protocol 580

La Pérouse, Jean François de Galaup, Comte de
  fate of 318–19, 323–4
  voyage of 325–6
labour
  forced 120, 153, 545–7, 598
  indentured 183–4, 215
  mita regime for silver mines 541
  in ports 524
  post-war migrations 577, 586
  resistance to military labour 598
  ships' crews 144, 215, 337, 523, 566
  and sugar plantations 570
  wartime military 590, 592, 596–9
  see also 'blackbirding'; migrant labourers
labour schemes, temporary 760, 766–71
'*ladrones*' (thieves), use of term 392, *393*
Laenui, Pōkā 234
LaFeber, W. 587
Lagos Escobar, Ricardo, president of Chile 553
Lal, B.V. 233, 235
Lambert, S.M. 491, 510, 513
  medical censuses 496
  and medical training 495
  on yaws 506
Lancaster, Burt 278
Langsdorff, Georg von 288, 375

INDEX

languages 28
diversity of 57
and national identity 429–30, 449
pidgin and creole 447
Rapa Nui (Easter Island) 560
Tongan *heliaki* 715
see also Hawaiian language ('Olelo
Hawai'i)
Lapita culture 291, 374
Larmour, P. 431
Latin America 46
Japanese in 147
relationship to Pacific 540
trade asymmetry 540
trade networks 541
see also Bolivia; Chile; Panama; Peru
Latukefu, S. 195
Laux, C. 428
Lavachery, Henri 289
Laval, H. 429
law codes 431
French 794
Law of the Sea Convention 800
Lawes, Rev. F.G. 360
le Borg, Reginald, *Voodoo Island* (film) 284
Le Maire, Jacob 287
Le Mamea, M.K., Samoan high chief 438
League of Nations, and Japanese mandate
over Marshall Islands 107, 110
Ledyard, John, American trader 565
Lee Boo, Prince 288
Leenhardt, Maurice 361–2
Leeward Islands, Society Islands 428
French annexation 444
French land law 794
independence 443
international treaties **437**
Leipzig, museum 289
Leite de Magalhães, Colonel 474
Lemoine, Georges 743
Lemos, Count 542
Lenwood, Frank, London Missionary
Society 359
leprosy, women's archival stories 198
'Les Sauvages de la Mer Pacifique',
wallpaper 77
Lesser Sunda Islands, Portuguese in 462–3
Lesson, R.-P. 403, 406
taxonomy of human species 409–10
Lewis, A.B. 294
Lewis, D., *Belonging on an Island: Birds,
Extinction, and Evolution in Hawai'i*
373, 384

Li, Xiannian 678
Lifou island, conference of Pacific Island
Churches and Missions 365
Ligeremaluoga, account of life 260, 262
Lili'uokalani, queen of Hawai'i 446, 571
Lima, Peru, Chinese food tradition 547–8, 548
Limu, Seaweed 709–10
Lini, Walter, prime minister of Vanuatu 367
Lisiansky, Yuri 288
'Listen to Tangaloa, Maui and Hina'
(*Fanongo kia Tangaloa, Maui, mo
Hina*) (poem) 727
literacy
Fiji 182
and nation-building 429
literature
biographies and autobiographies 256
and history 246–65
inclusion of modern media 255
Indigenous written texts 252, 256, 429
literary engagement with historical texts
252–63
modern Pacific writers 251
morally improving 79
and *Nanyō* in Japanese popular culture
116–17
need for scholarly study of 255
oral 310
popular 77, 79
recorded on anthropological expeditions 254
traditional 255
voyage accounts 70, 76–7
Liua'ana, Ben Featuna'i 203
Lodge, Henry Cabot 572
Lofa, Ka 195
London
reception of Pacific Islanders 320
Royal Academy 'Oceania' exhibition 291
London, Jack 273
London Missionary Society 78, 431
collection of artefacts 288
in Tahiti 428
theological college, Sāmoa 364
Longford, Raymond, and Lottie Lyell
A Maori Maid's Love 272
Mutiny on the Bounty (film) 272
Los Angeles, air hub 639, 651
Love, H. 197
Lovers and Luggers (film) 274
Loyalty Islands 440
Lubbock, B. 546
Lucky Dragon fishing boat incident 123
and origin of Godzilla story 124

910

Index

Luker, T. 197
Lumière brothers 268
Lunalilo, king of Hawai'i 434
Lyons, P., *American Pacificism* 582

Ma'afu, Tongan chief in Fiji 432, 440
Maamau, Taneti, president of Kiribati 682
Macao, and Portugal 43
Macgregor, SS, stranding in Fiji 519, *519*
Machoro, Caroline, New Caledonia 733
Maclellan, N. 626
Macpherson, Duncan 506
Macron, Emmanuel, president of France 748
Madeira-Santos, C. 459
Madrid, Museo de América 288
Magellan, Ferdinand 390, 392–4, 802
  Pigafetta's account of voyage 391
Māhina, 'O. 713, 715
Mahan, Alfred Thayer 516, 572
Mai/Omai, Raiatean islander 78
Main Antarctic Treaty (1961) 556
Majuro island 593
Malacca (Melaka)
  Dutch in 462
  Portugal and 461
Malaita, Solomon Islands 362
Malakula, Vanuatu 412
  ethnography 404
Malaspina, Alessandro, collection of artefacts
  288
Malaya, Japanese attack (1942) 120
Malaysia, 'tiger' economy 654
Malden island 627
Malietoa Laupepa, Samoan leader 435
Malifa, Tupuola 200
Malinowski, B. 364, 496
  Argonauts of the Western Pacific 357–8
mana, spiritual power 181, 719, 723, 799
  ancestors and 718
  flags 454
  illness and 499
  pandanus mats 305
Mana Annual 264
Manchuria, Japanese in 111
Mandeville, Sir John 76
Mangareva 431
  island kingdom 428, 443
Mangareva Expedition 289
Manila, air hub 639
Manila galleons 541, 543–5
  and transfer of food crops to China 544
Manning, R.A. 555
Manuel I, king of Portugal 454, 459

manufacturing, relocation to East Asia 635,
  644
Manufahi, Timor kingdom of 463, 482
Māori
  28th (Māori) Battalion (World War II)
    600
  adoption of Christianity 352
  and assimilation policy 218
  canoes 301
  contemporary carvings 312
  creation story 299
  delegations to Britain 438
  film documentaries 271, 276
  filmmakers 279
  films 275, 277
  flax cloaks 304
  national identity 430
  and New Zealand National Museum 135
  and Ngāpuhi confederation project
    (North Island) 431, 441
  plaited mats 301
  post-war autonomy 604
  sculptured houses 298–301
  view of interracial marriage 226
  women's archival material 197
  see also Aotearoa New Zealand
The Māori: Everyone Bathes on Washing Day at
  Rotorua (film) 276
The Māori as He Was (film) 275
Māori School (film) 277
Māori Village (film) 277
Māori War Effort Organization 604
Mapou, Louis, New Caledonia 733
Mapou, Raphael, New Caledonia 737
maps
  Dampier's discoveries 396, *397*
  Dumont d'Urville's *413*, *414*
  European 76, 81, 394
  Tupaia's 88, 91–6
Maputeoa 429, 700, 729
Mara, K., Fiji 685, 700, 729
Maralinga, Monte Bello islands 618
Marconi Wireless Telegraph Company 533, 535
Margolis, E. 580
Mariana Islands 115
  American Memorial Park 611
  and commemoration of war 610
  to Germany 447
  Japanese settlers 102
  megaliths 293
  women in legislature 697
  see also Commonwealth of the Northern
    Mariana Islands

INDEX

Marin, Francisco de Paula 378
maritime environment 138, 159
  nuclear contamination 629, 633
  threats to 159–62
Marquesas Islands 287
  carved figures 302
  feathered headdresses 310
  French colonization 443–4
  and War of 1812 568
Marquesas Protected Marine and Terrestrial
  Area 799
marriage *see* interracial (cross-cultural)
  relationships; interracial marriage
Marsden, Samuel, NSW 257
Marshall Islands 27–8, 31
  and climate change 28–9
  Conservation Area Management Planning
    Framework 29
  fishing methods 28
  German claim to 445
  interracial marriage 211
    Indigenous kinship model 228
    Japanese 110
  Japanese in 103, 107–8
  naval bases 120
  kemem (celebration) 32
  land
    held in common 624
    significance of 28
  League of Nations mandate 107
  and MTEC 702
  national identity 439
  nuclear contamination and damage 619, 629
    economic effects of 622–3
  nuclear weapon testing 29, 277, 614, 629
  plaited dress mats 306
  Ri-Majol belief system 27
  role of chiefly council 694
  and South Pacific Nuclear Free Zone
    Treaty 586
  and US Compact of Free Association 688
  US invasion 121, 590, 593
  weaving 306
  see also Bikini Atoll; Enewetak (Eniwetok)
    Atoll; Kwajalein Atoll; Rongelap
    Island
Marshall Islands Nuclear Claims Tribunal 623
Martin, Liko 242
Martire, Pietro, chronicler 394
Masaki, Iwaji 632
Matayoshi, Alimira 624
Matson Steam Navigation Company 523, 638
  and container shipping 642

Matsuda, M.K. 91, 374
Mātu'a Fusifonua, land fishhook 710, 716,
  722–5
Maude, H.E. 194, 209, 262
Maudsley, Alfred 289
Maugham, W. Somerset
  'Rain' 273, 275
  The Moon and Sixpence 277
Maui, god of the sun
  advocate of justice 722
  as agriculturalist 722
  and fire 723
  and Hina 723
  see also Mātu'a Fusifonua, land fishhook
Maui 'Atalanga, demi-god 710
Maui Kisikisi, demi-god 710, 722–4
Maupertuis, P.L. Moreau de 396
McArthur, N. 339, 342–3, 346, 348
  Island Populations of the Pacific 339
McCall, G. 559
McClennan, Carol, *Sovereign Sugar* 244
McClintock, A. 207
McCook, Edward, US minister to Hawai'i
  570
McGarvie, Rev. John, on sealing community
  329
McGregor, D.P., *Na Kua'āina: Living
  Hawaiian Culture* 240
McHale's Navy (film) 281
McKinley, William, US President 564, 572–3
McLean, Malcolm, Sea-Land company 642
McNeill, J.R. 388
  'Of Rats and Men' 376
McNeill, W. 336, 340
Mead, M. 358–9
  Coming of Age in Samoa 358
Meade, Commander Richard W. 571
medicine
  community interaction 494
  data on radiation exposure 621, 630–1
  drugs and technology 505–8
  and germ theory 508
  Indigenous practitioners 499
  testing and investigation 508
  as 'tool of empire' 491
  traditional 494
  tropical 491, 493
Melaka (Malacca) 461–2
Melanesia
  constitutions and traditional leadership
    693
  dance 311
  ethnographic descriptions 414

912

Index

European view of 73
independence of states 686
international migration 756
intra-regional migration 755
linguistic diversity 440
masks 296
and 'Melanesianism' 700
missionaries 352
political development 440–1
resource bases 755
settler adventurism 440
women in 368
World War II
  Allied forces 592
  and Japanese army 592
see also Fiji; New Caledonia; Papua New
  Guinea; Solomon Islands; Vanuatu
Melanesian Spearhead Group 701
and New Caledonia 739
and West Papua 701
Melbourne, University Library, *Pacific*
  Reading 262
Meleisea, Malama 195
Méliès, Gaston
  A Ballad of the South Seas (film) 272
  Hinemoa (film) 272
  Loved by a Māori Chieftess (film) 272
  The River Whanganui (film) 272
Melville, Henry 76
Memmi, Albert 234
Mendaña, Álvaro de 287
Menzies, Robert, prime minister of Australia
  618
Meo, Kolinio Rainima 259
Merleau-Ponty, M. 99
Métraux, Alfred 276, 289
Metzdorf, Nicolas, New Caledonia 732
Mexico
  and Pacific identity 55
  revolution 46
  and steamship routes 522
Mexico City, air routes 651
Michel, Phillippe, New Caledonia 733
Micronesia
  architecture 293
  Christianity in 114
  and commemoration of war 610
  continuing role of chiefs 693
  and decolonization 688
  German claims to 445
  international and intra-regional migration
    755–6
  Japanese intermarriages 109, 119

Japanese mandated territory in 107–10,
  605, 688
loom weaving 305, 306
political developments 439
political instability 694
and promotion of Micronesian identity 702
Spain and 74
United Nations Trust Territory 605,
  688
United States administration 114, 605
women in parliament 697
World War II 575, 596
  and Japan 119–22, 588
see also Federated States of Micronesia
  (FSM); Guam; Kiribati (Gilbert
  Islands); Mariana Islands; Marshall
  Islands; Nauru; Palau
Micronesian Chief Executives' Summit 702
Micronesian Presidents' Summit 702
Micronesian Trade and Economic
  Community (MTEC) 702
Micronesian Transition Series, films 279
Midway, Battle of (1942) 52, 121, 589
Midway Island
  cable station 527
  proposed coaling station 518
  US annexation 571
migrant labourers
  Chinese 145, 215, 220
  Filipino 215, 577
  indentured 215
  Indian 147–8
  Indonesian 215
  and interracial relationships 214
  Japanese 102, 215
  post-war 577, 586
  status of non-European 230
  see also labour; labour schemes
migration 752–75, 777
  and 'brain drain' 758
  to cities in destination countries 757
  destination countries 756–9, **758**
  economic theories of 752, 755
  and education 761–2
  environmental 774
  healthcare workers 764–5
  international 755, 774
  intra-regional 765
  from islands 27
  from Japan 102, 105, 109–10, 116
  labour 763
  for military and peacekeeping
    deployment 765–6

913

INDEX

migration (cont.)
  Pacific transnational flows
    753–6
  and political inclusion of overseas
    populations 753
  and professional sports 771–3
  relationship of workers with families and
    communities 768
  and remittances 755, 760–1
  and scholarships 763
  and socio-economic hardship 759
  and temporary labour schemes 760,
    766–71
  and transnationalism 753
  US agricultural programmes 771
  see also Asian migrants
Migration, Remittances, Aid and
    Bureaucracy (MIRAB) model 755,
    760
Mikloukho-Maclay, Nicholai 289
Mili Atoll Rebellion (1943) 122
Milne Bay, Battle of (1942) 590
mineral resources 679
  see also extractive industries
Mirmont, Hortense-Louise de 272
missionaries and missions
  American 568, 574
  and anthropology 349, 361–2
  as botanical collectors 78
  Catholic Dominicans in Timor 462
  challenges to 356, 359, 362
    Indigenous 355, 360–1
  Chinese 354
  debates about methods 354
  Dissenting 75
  ethnography 79, 84
  evangelical 78
  French Catholic 429, 443
  healthcare provision 492
    medical training 491
  and independent Pacific churches 355
  and Indigenous cultures 349, 361–2, 720
  and Indigenous custom 363, 365
  interpretation of interracial relationships
    213
  and law codes 431
  and mission houses 354
  and moral regulations 501
  New Zealand/Aotearoa 213
  and notion of civilization 350
  and ordination of converts 355
  'others and brothers' paradox 84, 350

paternalism 84, 355
  and political development 439, 443
  and radical new theologies 366
  relations with colonialism 441
  and social theories 353,
    498
  Tahiti 793
  translation work 351
  and women 214, 367–8
missionary societies 78
  see also London Missionary Society
Mita, Merata
  Bastion Point (film) 280
  Mauri (film) 280
  Patu! (film) 280
Moana: A Romance of the Golden Age (film)
    274, 277
Mokil (film) 277
Mokkadem, Hamid, New Caledonia 737
Molisa, G.M. 251
Molyneux, Robert, master of Endeavour 94
Momis, John, and PNG constitution 367
Mongol conquests 41, 68
Monte Bello islands, nuclear testing 618
monuments, Marianas megaliths 293
Moore, C. 140
Moorehead, A., The Fatal Impact 338
Morgan McMurroch, Māori seaman 319–20
Mori, Koben, Japanese trader 106, 118
Mortlock Islands, Federated States of
    Micronesia, traditional
    environmental zones 781–3, 782
Morton, H. 209
Moses, John 203
Mosura (film) 278
Motonicocoka, I. 335–6
Mowhee (Maui), memoir (1817) 257–8, 260,
    262
Mr. Roberts (film) 278
Mr. Robinson Crusoe (film) 275
Munro, sealer on Preservation Island 329
Munro, D. 203
Mururoa, Tahiti, French nuclear testing 624,
    630
musical instruments 310
  drums 311
Mutiny on the Bounty (films) 272, 275, 279, 284
Muybridge, Edward 268

Nabobo-Baha, U. 181
Nagle, Martin 503
Nahale'a, Kihei 242

914

Index

Nakahama, (John) Manjiro 102
Nakajima, A. 116
Nakasone, Yasuhiro, prime minister of Japan 128, 554
Nakayama, Tosiwo, first president of FSM 128
Nanjing, Treaty of (1842) 216
Nanpei, Henry, Pohnpei leader 439
Nanyō
  Japanese concept as southern frontier 104–7, *105*
  in Japanese popular culture 116–19
Nanyō Bōeki Kaisha (NBK), South Seas Trading Company 106
Nanyō Kohatsu Kaisha (NKK), development company 108
Nanyō Takushoku Kaisha, mining company 108
Nanyō Tanken Jikki (A Record of South Seas Exploration) 103
Nanyō-chō (Japanese South Seas Mandate) 107–10, 688
  bureaucratic administration 108
  Japanese migrants 109–10, 116
  power structure 108
  schools 113
  social structure 113–15
Narokobi, B., *The Melanesian Way* 367, 701
nation-states
  and border controls 525
  modern 52
  Pacific 263
Native Hawaiian Convention, 'Blue Continent Caucus' 134
Nauru
  detention centre on 685
  German claim to 445
  independence 606, 685
  political instability 694
  women in parliament 697
  World War II 596
navigation
  gods of 726
  traditional knowledge of 74, 713
  Tupaia's map and 94–5
Nawai, Apolosi 355
Néaoutyine, P., New Caledonia 739
Nelson, Olive Virginia Malienafau 198
neoliberalism, Chile 552–6
Netherlands
  rivalry with Portugal 461–3
  and Southeast Asia 43

and use of flags in ceremonies 466, 482
and West Papua 684
network of networks **636**, 657–8, *658*
  strategic gateways 657, *659*
Neu-Guinea (film) 271
New Caledonia 344, 604, 729–51
  aim of self-sufficiency 750
  Avenir en Confiance (Confident Future) party 732
  bubonic plague 503
  Calédonie Ensemble (Caledonia Together) party 732, 740, 743
  call for greater (non-independent) autonomy 740–1
  citizenship criterion 745
  Confédération Nationale des Travailleurs du Pacifique union 738
  Congress of New Caledonia 733–4
  constitution 693
  Covid-19 pandemic 746, 749
  Customary Senate 736, 745
  debate on flag 731–4
  debate on independence 729
  Dynamik Unitaire Sud (Unitary Dynamic South) party 738
  economy 730, 749
  Eveil Océanien ('Oceanian Rising') party 732, 746
  financial loan from France 750
  first referendum (2018) 730, 735, 742
  Foulards Rouges (Red Scarves) 737
  French overseas collectivity 443, 686
    transfer of competences from French State 734, 742
  French settlement and conquest 730
  Front de Libération Nationale Kanak et Socialiste (FLNKS) 701, 732, 738–9, 744
  Front de Luttes Sociales (Social Struggle Front) union 738
  Generation NC party 732
  immigration 730
  indentured labour 215
  independence movement 688, 738–40
  Jean Marie Tjibaou Cultural Center 735
  Kanak demands for self-determination 736–8
  l'Avenir en Confiance (The Future in Confidence) group 740, 746
  leprosy colony 504
  Libération Kanak Socialiste (Dynamique Autochtone) 738

915

New Caledonia (cont.)
Mouvement des Océaniens
Independantistes party 738
Mouvement National pour la
Souveraineté de Kanaky (National
Movement for the Sovereignty of
Kanaky) 740
Mouvement Nationaliste Indépendantiste
Souverainiste party 738
and Nainville les Roches declaration (1983)
739
Nouméa Accord (1998) 729, 734, 741, 745
Palika party 743
Parti Travailliste (Labour Party) 738, 740
political complexity on decolonization 735
political instability 695
proposal for federated state 741
proposed reading grids for political parties
747
provision for constituent assembly 745
second referendum (2020) 730–1, 749,
734
South Province 731
third referendum 734, 740, 742–8
implications of 'Yes' vote 744–6
three 'No' vote hypothesis 742–4
Union Calédonienne 733, 739, 743
Union Nationale pour l'Indépendance
party 733
US wartime base 597
USTKE trade union 738
and Wallis and Futuna 685
women in parliament 697
see also Kanak people
New Guinea 407
Anglican Mission 510
artefacts 290
buildings 292, 294, 296
ceremonial spaces 294
and challenge to missionaries 361
Dampier at 395–6
exploration 289
films 274
German-occupied 271, 445, 447
health census 495
Japanese occupation 590
masks 294, 295
Triton Bay 417
under Australian control 141, 592, 606–7
wartime labour 598
wireless telegraphy 535
see also Papua New Guinea; West Papua
New Guinea Infantry Battalion 599

New Hebrides 440
cargo cults 604
Condominium of 607
see also Vanuatu
New York
Museum of Modern Art, 'Art of the South
Seas' exhibition 291
Museum of Natural History 299, 300
New Zealand Plunket Society 501
New Zealand, see Aotearoa New Zealand
Newell, J., Trading Nature 369–70
Ngarimu, 2nd Lt Moana-Nui-a-Kiwa, VC 600
Ngũgĩ wa Thiong'o, 234
Decolonising the Mind 249
Niceto de Zamacois y Urrutia, J. 543
Niebuhr, H.R. Christ and Culture 364
Nishiyama Chikako 632
nitrates
Chile 540
guano 540
nineteenth-century demand for 51
Niue
cyclone damage to archives 172
'free association' with New Zealand 446,
685, 688
and steamships 523
Niugini see Papua New Guinea
Niumeitolu, Loa, 'when we tell' 252
Nixon, Richard, US President 552, 578
Doctrine 578
Nogelmeier, M.P., Mai Pa'a I ka Leo:
Historical Voices in Hawaiian Primary
Materials 238
noise, effect on marine life 720
Nordoff, Charles 275
Nordyke, Eleanor 341
Norfolk Island 449
to Australia 446, 687
population of Pitcairn moved to 448
North American Free Trade Agreement
(NAFTA) 579
Nuclear Pacific 615, 677
and anti-nuclear protests 625, 628, 631
conflicting policies 626
ethnographic studies 631
nuclear power, Fukushima Daiichi power
plant disaster 631–3
nuclear waste 128, 623, 630
nuclear weapon testing 29, 53, 123, 157, 578,
605, 720
atmospheric 618
Castle Bravo explosion (1954) 29, 123, 277, 619
claims for redress 623–4

Index

'clean-up' operations 622
and contamination 29, 607, 616, 625, 629
ecological effects of 619–20, 622–3
employment of servicemen 617
France 158, 624–6
geological threats 630
as human rights violation 623
Operation Crossroads 614, 619
Operation Grapple (UK) 626
physical effects of exposure 617, 621, 625, 630
and regional organizations 699
relocation of inhabitants 622
South Australia 618
underground 618, 678
see also contamination
nuclear weapons
atomic bombings of Hiroshima and
Nagasaki 123, 575, 593, 614
hydrogen bomb 619, 629
ICBMs 678
magnitude 618
see also nuclear weapon testing
Nukuhiva Island, claimed by US
568

Obama, Barack, US President 143, 580
O'Brien, P. 198
Occidental and Oriental Steamship
Company (O&O) 518
'Ocean, the Ancestor' (*Moana ko e
Tupu'angá*) (poem) 707, 715
ocean warming 681, 776
'Oceania'
as genesis of life 712
'Moana Nui' 708–9
responsibilities to 713–15
tupu'anga 710
use of term 85
Oceanic Steamship Company, San Francisco
520, 523
Oecussi, Timor 463
Ogasawara Islands 102, 105
oil
drilling for 720
Indonesia 638
Okihiro, G.Y. 585
Okinawa 101, 113
emigrants from 102, 108
'Olelo Hawai'i *see* Hawaiian language
Oliveira, Kapā 238
Ōnaka, Toraji 98
opium, smuggling trade 566

Opium Wars (1839-42) 566
Orbell, M., review of *Directions in Pacific
Traditional Literature* (festschrift)
253–5
Oregon, United States 569
anti-miscegenation law (1866) 218–19
O'Rourke, Dennis, *Ileksen: Politics in Papua
New Guinea* (film) 280
Osorio, Jamaica 240
Osorio, J.K.K. 234, 584
Dismembering Lāhui 235
Oswald, Richard, *Die Blume von Hawaii/
Flower of Hawaii* (film) 272
Otago Daily Times 221
Owen, Chris, *Jakupa* (film) 280
Oxford, Pitt Rivers Museum 288

'Pacific Age', concept of 554–5
The Pacific Arts Association 292
Pacific Cable 528
Pacific Cable Board 529, 536
Pacific Community 26, 698
Pacific Conference of Churches 365, 367
Pacific History Association 804
Pacific Island Churches and Missions 364
Pacific Islanders
agency of 89–91, 156, 348, 395
with Allied forces in World War II 599
and British Columbia 151
challenges 560, 803
connections by steamship routes 525
contact with Americas 149–55
early descriptions of 392, *393*
early encounters with Europeans 81
inter-island mobility 264, 345, 374, 493,
754
in London 78
and maritime environment 160
and nuclear testing 616, 618, 620–2
reaction to introduced species 380, 385
relations with foreign troops 599–602
response to American imperialism 583–4,
586
and transfer of species 371–5, 382
World War II
memory of Japanese occupation 99
relations with Japanese army 592–3,
598–9
relations with US military 593
and war dead 609
and wartime military labour 590, 592,
596–9
see also ethnography

917

INDEX

Pacific Islands
in American popular culture 582
atoll nations 777
and China
Chinese diaspora 667
economic aid 674–5, 677, 679
loans and debt 674, 689
trade with 679
commemorations and war memorials
608–13
and communications connections 537
depopulation 339, 342, 345–6, 386
diaspora populations 757, **758**
economic viability 673, 679, 777
extent and population 194
and freight shipping 643
and global climate change mitigation 681
independence movements 128, 168, 688
international treaties **437**
and Japan 128
limited post-colonial infrastructure 755
links with colonial powers 684
modern nation-state identities 51
and official traditional cultures 58
population pressure 777
post-colonial political developments 690
post-war moves towards independence
603–8, 684
pre-colonial populations 338, 345, 347
and species preservation 387
subordination to European and American
power 45
and traditional–modern asymmetries 53–4
World War II 575
battlefields 603
effect on 602–3, 608
war debris 603
wartime infrastructure 602–3
see also histories and historiography;
Melanesia; Micronesia; Pacific
Ocean; Pacific Rim; Polynesia
Pacific Islands Association of Libraries,
Archives and Museums (PIALA) 193
Pacific Islands Development Forum (PIDF)
687, 703
Pacific Islands Forum 30, 159, 161, 687, 699
and China 672
Melanesia and 701
National Adaptation Plan 30
suspension of Fiji 690, 703
and temporary labour mobility
programmes 767
see also South Pacific Forum

Pacific Islands Leaders Meetings (PALM) 129
Pacific Islands Monthly 264
Pacific Islands Phosphate Company 533
Pacific Islands Political Science Association
conference (2019) 745
Pacific Journal of Theological Studies 365
Pacific Mail Steamship Company 516, 518
Pacific Northwest
interracial marriage 228
see also British Columbia; Canada; Oregon
Pacific Ocean 778
acidification levels 681, 720, 777
American domination (twentieth-century)
572–81, 584
archipelagoes 662
coastal economies 661
as contact zone 72–3
earliest migrations across 133, 390, 711,
754
exploitation of resources 714, 720
geo-logistics 636, 660–3, 661
geopolitics 158–9, 662–3
histories 33–4
and identity 54
as ideological construct 35
Nero Deep 527
as 'sea of islands' 85
strategic significance 158–9, 584, 607, 613
tourism 155
travel times **660**, 660
water temperatures 681, 776
see also 'Blue Continent'; histories and
historiography; Pacific Islands
Pacific Radio Telegraph Company 533–4
Pacific Reading (magazine) 262
Pacific Regional Branch of the International
Council on Archives (PARBICA) 171,
193
Pacific Rim 134, 802
continental economies 660
global industrial nations 52, 634
and maritime environment 159
risk of exploitation by 160
and wealthy Asian elites 149, 157
Pacific Steam Navigation Company (1838) 515
Pacific Theological College 366
Pacific Trades Partnership 770
Pacific Virtual Museum project 188
Pacific War *see* World War II in the Pacific
'Pacific Way'
concept of 700, 729
Polynesian character of 700
'Pacificism', in academic discourse 80–5

918

Index

Páez, A. 539
The Pagan (film) 274
Palau
  canoe races 128
  houses 292
  Japanese imperial visit (2005) 99
  and MTEC 702
  role of chiefly council 694
  and US Compact of Free Association 688
  women in parliament 697
  World War II 596
Palmerston atoll, creole society 448
Pan Pacific Theological College, Suva, Fiji
  365
Panama
  proposed canal 516
  US rights over 573
Papua New Guinea (PNG)
  buildings 294, 296
  campaign for Niuklia Fri Pasifik 628
  Carteret Island 774
  civil war in Bougainville 695
  constitution 367
  contemporary writing 260, 262
  films 274, 276, 280
  history of arts in 249
  independence 686
  influenza 345
  and Internet 654
  Japanese migrants in 103
  Japanese occupation 590
  Kokoda Track campaign 598, 612
  local role of traditional rulers 693
  masks 295
  missionaries 361
  National Archives 194
  portraits of Papuans 408, 408
  post-war 604
  Ramu mine site 674
  relations with Australia 605–6
  relations with China 673, 689
  University 250, 260, 606
  and war dead 609
  wartime labour 598
  wireless telegraphy 535
  see also New Guinea; West Papua
'Papuan', as racial description 407, 410
Papuan Infantry Battalion 599
Paris, Quay Branly, 'Oceania' exhibition 291
Paris Agreement 580
  Sustainable Development Goals (2015)
    681, 777
Le Parisien 625

Parke, Aubrey 336
Parkinson, Sydney 70
Pascoe, P. 218
Paterson, L. 226
Paterson, T.G. 564
patriotism 474–5
Pauli, Gustav, *The Romance of Hine-Moa*
  (film) 275
Pearl Harbor (Pu'uloa, Hawai'i)
  Japanese bombardment 120, 575
  US Navy rights 569
  wireless station 536
pearl divers 103
  films 274, 270
pearl shell industry 566
  Australia 215
Peattie, M. 104
  Nan'yō: The Rise and Fall of the Japanese in
    Micronesia 100
Peleliu island 603, 609, 612
Pellion, A., portraits of Papuans 408, 408
People's Charter for a Nuclear Free and
  Independent Pacific (1983) 628
Peralto, N. 240
Péron, François, on seals 328
Perry, Commodore Matthew 102, 570
Peru
  Chinese forced labour in 545–7
  and Fujimori 549–50
  ideological links with China 548–9
  and Pacific Islanders 153
  Shining Path guerrilla movement 548–9
  Treaty of Peace, Friendship, Commerce
    and Navigation with China 547
  and War of the Pacific 50–1, 539
Philip II, king of Spain 544
Philippines
  Culion leper colony 504
  Japanese attack (1942) and occupation 120
  migrant labour from 215, 577
  migration across Pacific 144
  modern nation state 52
  prostitution 577
  and Spain 42
    revolution against 46
  telecommunications 654–5
  'tiger' economy 655
  US colonization 447, 572–3
  wireless station 536
  withdrawal of US military 579
phosphates, mining of 63, 68
  Banaba 55
  Jinping, Haizhou 63–4

919

INDEX

photographs
 of architecture 293
 archive 185–6, 200, 294
 see also film(s)
phrenology 408, 415, *416*, 418
Pickering, Charles 419
Pickford, Mary 271
Pigafetta, A., *Voyage* (account of Magellan's
  voyage) 391–2, 394
Pinochet, General Augusto, president of
  Chile 552–3
Pitcairn
 as British dependency 687
 creole society 448
 women's suffrage 697
Pitjanthatjara people 618
plantations 45, 570
 Caribbean 381
 French Polynesia 793
 Hawai'i 239, 569
 Sāmoa 203
plants
 breadfruit 369, 381–3
 coconuts 379
 effect of nuclear testing on 621
 introduced to Tahiti 370
 from Latin America to China 544
 maize 545
 peanuts 545
 prickly pear (in Australia) 383
 sweet potato 545
Poepoe, Joseph 238
Pohnpei
 backstrap looms 305
 banana-fibre belts 306
 Nan Dauwas islet 293
 Nan Madol ceremonial complex 293–4
 national identity 439
 and new theologies 366
 Pahn Kadira islet 293
 political developments 439
Poi Dances at Whakarewarewa (film) 271
Poindi-Poweu, New Caledonia 344
political movements
 Indigenous 90
 Solomon Islands 143, 362
political parties 694–5
 see also New Caledonia
political structures
 and concepts of parity, similitude and
  hybridity 425
 early 41
 regional Pacific 698–703

political systems 423–49,
  704
 creole societies 447–8
 and democratisation 449, 691–4
 effect of Christianity on development of
  427–9
 and idea of pan-Oceanian confederation
  434–6
 Indigenous 423–4
 and international treaties **437**
 and law codes 431
 limited participation of women 696–8
 'missionary kingdoms' ('Christian
  theocracies') 428
 networks of institutional transfer 430–4,
  432
 Oceanian constitutions **427**
 post-independence constitutions 691–6
 role of traditional leaders in 691–4
pollution 666
 and fishing 672
 noise 720
 plastics 720
Polo, Marco 76
Polynesia
 collections of art 290
 cultural commonality 36
 dance 311
 international migration 755–6
 landscape management 373
 limit of migrations (13th century) 41
 and 'Pacific Way' 700
 politics 695–6
 and regional politics 702
 social structure 73
 spatial organization 294–7
 see also Aotearoa New Zealand; Sāmoa;
  Solomon Islands; Tonga; Tuvalu;
  Vanuatu
The Polynesians of Kapingamarangi (film) 277
Polynesian Leaders' Group 702
Pomare dynasty, Tahiti 73, 443–4
Pomare II, of Tahiti 428, 793
 conversion to Christianity 428, 431
Pomare IV, queen of Tahiti 428
popular culture
 American 582
 Japanese 116–19
population decline 339, 342, 345
 archaeology and 343
 epidemic disease and 346–7, 386
 health policies and 492
 and women's reproductive health 499

920

Index

Port Moresby, Laloki psychiatric centre 504
Porter, David 568
Porter, E.A., *China in Oceania* 677
ports
  Asian treaty 216, 228–9, 634
  container port rankings **646**, *647*
  and container ships 642–3, **645**, *645*
  dock workers 642
  mixed-race communities 208–9, 228
  railways to 635, 642
  Southern Pacific 648
  and transmission of disease 338
Portugal
  as constitutional monarchy 460
  fascist *Estado Novo* regime 461, 463, 474
  and Macao 43
  as republic 460
Portuguese empire
  and colonial authority 467–8
  expansion in Asia 461–3
  rivalry with Dutch 461–3
  stone posts planted on shores 456
  as vassalage system 455–61, 488
  see also Timor
Pōtatau Te Wherowhero, Māori King 442
Potosí, Bolivia, silver mines 541
pottery, Lapita earthenware 291, 298
Pouvanaa a Oopa, nuclear activist 625
Prat, Arturo, Chilean naval officer 51
Prestholdt, J. 426
prestige 453, 472–4
  and colonial authority 468, 472
  of flags 469–70
Prevost, Laurent, high commissioner of
    New Caledonia 731
Prichard, J.C. 419
prisons, mentally ill confined in 504
prostitution 577
  American imperialism and 567
  Japanese and 119, 601
  US military brothels 577, 601
PT-109 (film) 279
Puas, Victor, FSM 781
public health 490–513
  anti-mosquito campaigns 509
  and birthing practices 500
  censuses and surveys 495–8
  compliance with treatments 506, 511–12
  construction of housing 510
  and education 511
  female reproductive 499–501
  and hygiene 510
  and Indigenous attitude to illness 498–9

  and infant mortality 346, 502
  legislation on 501–2, 512
  leprosy colonies 503–5
  mental health asylums 503–5
  mental health surveys 496–8
  mixed-race populations 224
  native medical practitioners 492, 495,
    499
  native obstetric nurses 495, 500
  and overcrowding 509
  public health and sanitation projects 496,
    502, 508–11
  relocation of villages 508
  US policy in Philippines 573
  yaws campaigns 506, *507*
  see also disease(s); medicine
Pukui, Mary Kawena 311
'Puloto', ancestral homeland 709
Puniwai, Noelani 241
Puputauki, M. 430
Purea, 'Queen' of Tahiti 82

quarantines, for disease 503
Quirós, P.F. de 391, 400, 402
Quoy, J.-R.C. 403
  ethnography of 'Papuans' 405–10
Quoy, J.-R.C. and J.P. Gaimard, *Zoologie* 407,
  411

Rabaul
  Japanese base 121
  strike (1929) 141
Rabi, Fiji, Banabans relocated to 56
race
  and American imperialism 574, 585
  categorised 223, 495
  classification of mixed-race children 223
  and eugenic ideology 220, 226
  European superiority 157, 220
  hierarchies of 139, 157, 356, 401, 414, 418
  and 'hybrids' 415
  and identity 208
  investigations into health of mixed-race
    populations 224
  and moral character 225
  and problem of 'race mixing' 222–6
  theories of 401–5
  use of term 401, 404
  and World War II 576, 601
  see also interracial relationships; science of
    race
Radcliffe-Brown, Alfred 361
Radio Corporation of America (RCA) 536

INDEX

Radio Telegraphic Conference, Melbourne
(1909) 534
Raiatea, Leeward Islands 428
French annexation 444
railways, to ports 635
Rain (film) 284
Raione, Taito 182
Rallu, J.L. 343
Ralston, C. 209
Rapa Nui (Easter Island)
artefacts from 289
barkcloth cloaks 307
as Chilean colony 147, 447, 558–60, 687
dengue fever 559
and European diseases 386, 559
film 276
first European landing 287, 292, 559
Hanga Roa town 559
and introduced species 385–6
Japan and 147
language 560
Lavachery and Métraux expedition 289
law code 431
and Mapuche people 38
Peruvian slave traders at 559
rats 386
Rongorongo script 246
sculpture 301
sheep farming 559
stone statues 292, 302, 558, *558*
uprising (1964) 559
Rapa Nui (film) 281
Rapu, Alfonso, Rapa Nui uprising 559
Rarotonga, staff god from 307
Rarotonga, Treaty of 586, 628
Ratu Penaia Ganilau, Fijian High Chief
627
Reagan, Ronald, US President 553–4, 579
Reeve, Edward, Hawaiian envoy 433–4
Reichel, Keali'i 242
Reihana, Lisa, *Pursuit of Venus (Infected)*
(digital video) 70–2, *71*, 77, 87, 96
Reinhold, Johann 82
religion
'arioi elites 75
Enlightenment view of 74
see also Christianity; missions and
missionaries
remittances 755, 760–1
see also Migration, Remittances, Aid and
Bureaucracy (MIRAB) model
Remote Oceania
chronology 36–8

cultural commonality 36
see also Hawai'i; Aotearoa New Zealand;
Rapa Nui (Easter Island)
Renan, Ernest 748
revolutions 48, 315–16, 333–4
China 48, 576, 548–9
Mexico 46
Philippines 46
Russian 46
Reynolds, Joshua, painter 78
Reynolds, Captain William 571
Ribeiro, Diogo, cartographer 394
Robinson Crusoe (films) 271, 273, 275
Robinson, George Augustus
and removal of Tasmanians to Bass Strait
330–2
and rescue of Aboriginal women 330–2
Robson, A.E. 423
Rocard, Michel, French prime minister
699
Rochette, Patrick 797
Rockefeller Foundation in the Pacific 510
and education 511
health campaigns 506, 508
Rodan (film) 278
Roggeveen, Jacob 287, 292
at Rapa Nui 386, 559
Rokowaqa, E. (Mokunitulevu na Rai), *Ai
Tukutuku Kei Viti* 259
The Romance of Hine-Moa (film) 275
Romanticism, view of exotic 75
Rongelap Island, radiation contamination
622
Rongorongo, Rapanui script 246
Roosevelt, Franklin, US President
and China 575
and World War II 575
Roosevelt, Theodore, US President 572
and US policy in Pacific 573–4
Root-Takahira Agreement (1908) 574
Rotorua N.Z. (film) 276
Rotterdam, container shipping **646**
Rotuma island, health survey 496
Rousseau, J.-J., *The Social Contract* 75
Routledge, Katherine 289
Royal Navy
African sailors 140
hydrographical survey 516
Royal Papuan Constabulary 599
Ruapuke, New Zealand, interracial
relationships 214
rubber, US demand 637
Russia 212

922

Index

Bolshevik revolution
46
and China 662
and Cold War 683
Far East 646, 661, 663
nuclear testing 616, 678
relationship with Pacific 152, 375, 683
Russian Pacific history 136
Ryūkyū Kingdom
Japanese conquest 116
see also Okinawa
Ryūkyūans, recognition as indigenous by
Japan 130

Saada, E. 222
Sadie Grey (film) 284
Sadie Thompson (film) 273
Sahlins, M. 452
on Fiji 294
Sai, D.K. 236
Ua Mau Ke Ea: Sovereignty Endures 236
Saihu, Dick, New Caledonia 736–7
Sailele, Tiulaepa, Samoan prime minister 703
Sainson, Louis-Auguste de, 'Vanikoro: vue
du village de Nama' 412, *412*
St Julian, Charles
Chief Justice of Fiji 433
Hawaiian envoy 433
and idea of pan-Oceanian confederation
434
St Patrick (ship)
Dillon's voyage from Valparaiso to
Calcutta 316–23
multi-cultural crew 317–18
St Petersburg, Pacific art in 288
Saipan 115, 603
Japanese imperial visit (2005) 99
war memorials 612
Sakai, N. 123
Salesa, D. 217–18
Salmond, A. 383
Bligh: William Bligh in the South Seas 381
Sālote, queen of Tonga 597, 609
Sāmoa
archives
German 199, 205
Goddefroy und Sohn Company records
203
Mau rebellion (1926–36) 192, 198,
201–2
memories of Palepa Ioane Akeli 191–2
National Archives Records Authority
(NARA) 205

transferred to Alexander Turnbull
Library 196
women's material 197
Chan Mow Supermarket Chain 203
Christianity in 358
feathered headdresses 310
German invasion (1887) 435, 445
and Hawai'i 435, 449
health
leprosy 505
public health regulations 509
view of illness 499
indentured labour 215, 220
international treaties **437**
and interracial marriage 211, 220
Japanese Official Development Assistance
129
law code 431
Manu'a Island 710, 716
Margaret Mead on culture of 358
Mau rebellion (1926–36) 360
in archives 192, 198, 201–2
mixed-race children 223
Pacific Island Churches and Missions
conference 364
Pago Pago harbour 568, 571
partition of 571
photographic exhibition in New Zealand
National Library 200
pigeon snaring mounds 297
politics
constitution 433
one-party state 695
origins of political structures 41
women in parliament 696
presentation of fine mats 305, *305*
Public Records Act (2011) 205
Tongan influence 432
treaty with United States (1879) 438
US wartime infrastructure 602
village layouts 295
volcanoes (1905-11) 774
women's village committees 500
see also American Sāmoa; Western
Sāmoa
Sāmoa, National University of
Centre for Samoan Studies 200
National Digital Library 203
Samson, J. 84
San Francisco
air hub 639
'Art of the South Pacific Islands'
exhibition 291

923

INDEX

San Francisco (cont.)
  steamship route to Sydney 518
  and trans-Pacific routes 517
Sanadhya, Pandit Totaram 356
Sand, C. 344
sand mining 721
sandalwood 440
  Timor 461
  trade in 566
Santis Arenas, H. 556
Santos, Jerry 242
Sapir, Edward 364
Sasa, Yukie 126
Sau Deleur dynasty, Pohnpei 293
Sauer, Martin 375
Schell, W., Jr. 544
Schmitt, C. 748
Schmitt, Robert 341
scholarships 763
  for health care 764
Schouten, Willem 287
Schweizer, N. 425
science
  and body of knowledge from Pacific 79,
    81, 87, 96
  deductive (systems) 389, 405
  inductive (facts) 389, 405, 411
  and militarism (nuclear testing) 620, 624,
    630–1
  and Pacific species of flora and fauna 74
  popular 79
  and traditional knowledge 27, 30, 32
  see also anthropology; ethnography
science of man, and theories of human
    diversity 389, 398–403, 419
science of race (raciology) 390, 398, 403–20
  and phrenology 408, 415, *416*, 418
scientific classification (taxonomies) 74, 79
Scorpio constellation, and magical fishhook
    711–12
Scott, J.S., *The Common Wind* 140
sculpture and carvings
  barkcloth-covered 301, *303*, 303
  canoes 301
  human figures 298, 302
  ivory 301
  Māori houses 298–301
  Māori storage house (*pataka*) 299, *300*
  tools 298
  traditions 301–3
  wicker 301, 304
  wooden *302*, 302
  wooden bowls 298

sea cucumber, over-fishing of 722
sea levels, risk of rise to islands 28–9, 679,
    681, 690, 776–7
seal hunting (sealing)
  America and 566
  Tasmania 328–33
Seattle, steamship route to Nagasaki 521
Second World War *see* World War II in
    Europe and World War II in the
    Pacific
Sell, Dr David 505
sennit cords, coconut 304, 725
Seoul, Incheon airport 650
settlement patterns, Fiji 294
settler populations, and interracial
    relationships 217
sevusevu, Fijian ceremonial presentation
    179–81
sexuality
  European view of Pacific islanders' 75, 82,
    155, 220–1
  and male–male relationships 83
Shanghai
  Pudong airport 650
  treaty port 216
Shanley, John Patrick, *Joe vs. the Volcano*
    (film) 281
The Shark God (film) 271
Shepherd, C.J. 473
Shiga, Shigetaka 104–5
Shigemitsu, S., *Militarized Currents* 584
Shilliam, R. 140
Shimada, K. 117
Shimao, Toshio 101
Shimazaki, Tōson, 'Yashinomi' (Coconut) 98
Shintōism 114
Shipping Control Authority for the Japanese
    Merchant Marine (SCAJAP) 637
shipping lines
  CMA CGM 646
  container operator cooperation 646
  Cosco Shipping (China) 646
  Cunard 638
  Evergreen (Taiwan) 646
  Hutchison Ports (Hong Kong) 646
  Japanese 521, 638, 642
  Maersk 646
  MSC 646
  PSA International (Singapore) 646
  Sea-Land company 642
ships
  bulk carriers 641
  and cable communications 531

924

Index

Chinese 'coolie' 545
encounters in Pacific 322–3
freight costs 642
and Indigenous seafaring 337
Islanders as crew 337, 754, 763–4
as metaphor 138
multi-ethnic crews 144, 215, 317–18, 523, 566
multipurpose 643
passenger liners 638–9
post-war cargo-passenger lines 637
roll-on/roll-off (ro-ro) 643
and spatial thinking 87
and transmission of disease 345
and wireless telegraphy 533
see also container shipping; shipping lines;
   steamships
Silent Death (film) 284
Silva, N.K. 234
   Aloha Betrayed 236
   The Power of the Steel Tipped Pen 238
silver trade 541–4
   as globalized system 150
   minting of Mexican pesos 543–4
   and *mita* labour regime 541
Simpson, Sir George, Hudson's Bay
   Company 156
Singapore
   air hub (Changi) 639, 650–1
   container port traffic **645**
   container shipping 643, **646**
   entrepôt trade 638
   financial services 654
   Japanese attack (1942) 120
   manufacturing 635
Sino-Japanese war, (from 1937) 46, 119
Sione's Wedding (film) 282
skyscapes, Intersecting Star Lines of the
   goddess Velenga 713
Smith, G. 668
Smith, S.B. 639
Smith, Terence Wesley, *China in Oceania* 677
social evolution
   criticism of 356–7
   theories of 352
social mobility
   and education 761
   professional sports and 772
social reform 493
social structure, European view of Pacific
   islanders 73, 75
Société de Géographie, Paris 409
Société Française des Télégraphes Sous-
   Marins 529

Society for Advancement of Chicanos/
   Hispanics & Native Americans in
   Science (SACNAS), 2019 conference 25
Society Islands 287
   canoes 301
   coconut fibre images 304
   feathered headdresses 310
   houses 292
   introduced plants and animals 380
   mourning dress *304*, 304
   Tupaia's map chart *88*, 91–6
   see also Tahiti
Sogavare, prime minister of Solomon Islands
   681
Solander, Daniel 82
Solomon Islands 287
   cargo cults 604
   film 280
   German claim to 445
   independence 606, 686
   Japanese landings 121
   local role of traditional rulers 693
   lunatic asylum 504
   Maasina Rule movement 143, 362
   Malaita revolt 362
   political instability 695
   relations with China 681, 689
   and South Seas Evangelical Mission 355
   state formation 440
   statue of Jacob Vouza 610
   war memorials 611
   World War II 592
Solomon Islands Defence Force 599
Solor, Lesser Sunda Islands 462
Somare, Sir Michael, PNG
   673
South America
   coastal economies 661
   container ports 646
   steamship routes 515, 522
   trade with Pacific Islanders 151
   use of Pacific Islanders as forced labour 153
   see also Bolivia; Chile; Peru
South American nuclear free zone 628
South Korea
   manufacturing 635
   modern geopolitics 662
   post-war economic growth 635
South Pacific (film) 277
South Pacific Commission (SPC) 262, 698
South Pacific Forum 158, 699
   and nuclear testing 628
South Pacific Literature Bureau (SPLB) 262

INDEX

South Pacific Nuclear Free Zone Treaty 586, 628, 678
South Seas Evangelical Mission 355, 363
Southeast Asia
 Chinese diaspora 667
 economic growth 665
 Islam in 42–3
 trade network 67
 see also Indonesia; Malaya, Japanese attack; Singapore
Soviet Union *see* Russia
Spain
 American empire 42, 44, 67
 cession of possessions to US 447
 and Micronesia 74
 north Pacific islands 390
 and Philippines 42
 sale of Micronesian possessions to Germany 107, 445
 trans-Pacific trade 150, 541
Spanish American War 446, 515, 572
Spanish Jesuits, Guam 349
Spate, O.H.K. 86
Spitz, C. 247
 L'Île des rêves écrasés (*Island of Shattered Dreams*) 248–9
Spreckels, Claus 520
Spriggs, M. 347, 373
Sproat, D.K. 240
Stanley, B. 354
Stannard, D.E. 342
 Before the Horror: Hawaiian Population... 341
steamships 515–26, 635, 660
 coaling stations 517–18
 and continued isolation of islands 526
 crews 523
 deep-ocean crossings 516
 'Empress' fleet 521
 imperial network 635
 innovations 516
 and inter-island services 522
 and migration 524
 military use of 516
 shipbuilding yards 522
 timetables 522
 and tourism 525
Steinberger, Albert 289
 and Sāmoan constitution 433, 435
Steinberger, William 570
Stevens, John L. 571
Stevens, M.J. 228
Stevenson, Robert Louis, *Treasure Island* 116
Steward, William, US Secretary of State 570

Stocking, G. 353
Stoler, A.L. 207–8, 582
Strategic Arms Limitation Treaty 579
Sudō, N. 116
Sugar Cane Hunting (film) 274
Sukanaivalu, Sefanaia, VC 600
Sulawesi (Celebes) 417
Sun Yat-Sen
 education in Hawai'i 436
 statue in Honolulu 148
Sunda islands, Indonesia 417
Suva, Fiji
 Medical School 761
 wireless station 536
Suzuki, Keikun 103
Sydney
 air hub 639
 steamship route to San Francisco 518

tā and *vā*, time and space 708, 718, 724
Tabu: A Story of the South Seas (film) 275
Taft, William Howard, US President 573
Taguchi, Ukichi 105
Tahiti
 anti-nuclear riots 696
 barkcloth presentations 308
 Bligh on 75, 83, 369
 breadfruit from 369, 381–3
 claimed by Wallis for George III 80, 369–70
 Cook and 369
 films 274
 French annexation 444
  claimed by Bougainville 288, 369
 French overseas collectivity 687
 French protectorate 443, 625
 Indigenous histories 430
 international treaties **437**
 introduced species 369–70
 law code 431
 nuclear testing 625
 political economy 792
 Pomare dynasty 73
 public sexual performances 82
 regional influence 431
 role of Christianity in establishment of kingdom 427–8
 tourism 650
Tahitians, physical diversity 402
Ta'imua (principal chiefs) of Sāmoa 433, 435
Taipei, Japan and 104
Taiping uprising (1850–64) 44

Index

Taiwan
annexed by Japan 46, 111
Austronesian-speaking migration from 133
container shipping 643
Kaohsiung Museum of Fine Arts, 'The Great Journey' exhibition 133
post-war economic growth 635
manufacturing 635
Qing conquest 43
recognition of 678–9, 681, 689
and trade network 43
US relations with 579
Takahashi, Yoshio 226
Takenouchi, Mari, 632
Tamahori, Lee 280
Once Were Warriors 281
Tamasese, Tusi, *The Orator: O Le Tulafale* (film) 282
Tambiah, S. 468
Tamuera Terei, author 253
Taney, Roger, US Justice 585
Tangaloa 'Atulongolongo, deity 710, 716
different deities of 719
eradication by Western imperialism 720–1
as god of creation 717–19
and Pacific Golden Plover 710, 716–17, 719
re-emergence of 721–2
Taputapuatea Marae, UNESCO World Heritage site 799
Tarawa, Battle of (1943) 61, 593
Tardieu, A. 413
Tarerenorer, Aboriginal Tasmanian woman 332
Tarr, George, *Hinemoa* (film) 272
Tasman, Abel Janszoon 287
Tasmania 287, 327–33
colonial settlers 329
regulation of shipping 330
reserve for Aboriginals 330
seal hunting 328–33
Tasmanian wars 329, 333
tattooing and body painting 310, 722, 725
Taum, R. 133, 162
Ta'unga, early Cook Island writer 253, 258–9
Tāwhiao, Māori king 438
Taylor, Dame Meg, Pacific Islands Forum 161, 680, 801
Te Hui Aroha ki Turanga/Gisborn Hui Aroha (film) 271
Teaiwa, T.K. 584
Teariki Taraare, author 253
Teavai-Murphy, Hinano 95

Telefunken wireless company 535
telegraph *see* cables, undersea
telephones 653
personal mobile 653
Teng, E. 225, 227
Terra Australis 396
textiles and fibres 303–9
barkcloth 301, 303–4, *303*, 307–9, *308*
basketry 307
clothing 304
coconut sennit 304, 725
colours and dyes 306
decorations 306
flax 304
loom weaving (Micronesia) 305, *306*
pandanus mats 305–6
plaited mats 301, 306
and red feathers 304–5, 309–10
Thailand, 'tiger' economy 665
Thilenius, Georg Christian 288
Thomas, N. 78, 83
Islanders 244
Thomaz, L.F. 475
Thompson, Gordon Augustus 288
Thomson, W.J. 289
Thor: Ragnarok (film) 282
Threlkeld, Lancelot, missionary 351
Thurston, John Bates, Governor of Fiji 179, 444
Tikopia island 318
Timor 450–89
Catholic Dominicans in 462
eastern, as Portuguese colony 463–4
flags
adoption of foreign flags and insignia 480–1
cult of 475–6
and Dutch flags 482
origin-myths and Portuguese flag 476
preservation of ancient 464, 478, 479, 482–3
and prestige of Portuguese flag 469, 471–2
use of by *liurai* houses 477–80, 485, 489
flags as war booty 459
history of 461–4
importance of ancestry in 476–7
independence 463
Indonesian occupation (1975–99) 463, 475
influence of Topasses 462–3
Japanese occupation 463, 474
Laleia war (1878-80) 487–8
liurais, traditional jural-political lords 464, 468

INDEX

Timor (cont.)
lulik
  agency of flags 484–5
  ancestral *lulik* heirlooms 477–8, 481
  concept 453, 473, 475–6, 484
  uma lulik cult houses 477
Manufahi revolt (1912) 482
patriotic parades of *moradores* 474
Portuguese vassalage in 464–7
replica insignia 483
and *rota* (tokens of authority) 453, 476, 478,
  481
wars between kingdoms 467
Timor Leste
  independence 687
  and Melanesian Spearhead Group 702
Tippett, Allan, missionary to Fiji 363
Tjibaou, J.-M., *The Melanesian Way* 701
Tokelau
  British colony 445
  dependent territory of New Zealand
    685
Tokyo, air hub (Narita airport) 639, 649, 651
Toledo, Don Francisco de 541
Tong, Anote 668
Tong Sang, Gaston 668
Tonga, Kingdom of 426–33
  'Ata island 716
  and Australian Seasonal Worker
    Programme 769
  British protectorate 445
  chiefly lineages 719
  Christianity in 358
    Methodist mission 426
  constitution 433, 692
  constitutional monarchy 426, 685, 692
  coral reefs 717
  creation story 709–12
    ancestor stories 708–9
  cultural heritage
    barkcloth *308*, 308
    destruction of historical sites 721
    early canoe 287
    feathered headdresses 310
    ivory sculpture 301
    sculptured hooks 298
    stone tombs 295
  houses of chiefs 295, *297*
  independence 685
  international treaties **437**
  law code 431
  politics
    origins of political structures 41

proposed overseas parliamentary seat
  753
reforms 695, 704
women in parliament 696
remittances 760
state-building 432
US wartime base 597
US wartime infrastructure 602
and war dead 609
women's village committees 500
Tongamatamoana, Tonga the Fisher of
  Lands 710
Topasses ('Black Portuguese' mestizo class),
  and Timor 462–3
Toribiong, Johnson, President of Palau 603
Toro, Albert, *Tukuna* (film) 280
Torres Strait, Cambridge Anthropological
  Expedition (1898) 270
tourism 155, 585
  cruise liners 639
  Japanese 123–4, *125*
  jet aircraft 649–50
  and prostitution 577
  and steamships 525
  war 609–12
trade networks 634
  China 675
  container main and feeder services **648**
  east–west containerized trade **645**
  Japan and Micronesia 105
  Latin America 541
  multiracial 141
  North America-Japan container routes 643
  Southeast Asia 67, 144
  and wireless telegraphy 533
traders, relations with colonialism 441
trading companies, Japan 106, 108
traditional knowledge 29, 58
  ancestral (Moana Nui) 708
  and archives 193, 195
  environmental zones in Mortlock Islands,
    FSM 781–3, **782**
  Federated States of Micronesia 779, 784
  French Polynesia 798
  Hawai'i 241
  Hawai'i, revival 237
  Japan and 130
  loss of 27
  and modern science 27, 30, 32
  navigation 74
  of resource management 776
  value of 176
Trans-Pacific Partnership 159

928

Index

transnationalism 753
TransPacific Trade Pact (TTP) 581
transport
  Chinese seaborne 667
  freight costs 635
  see also container shipping; ships
Trask, H.-K. 234, 239, 341
  From A Native Daughter 234
Trask, Mililani 234
Traube, E.G. 476, 485
trees
  breadfruit 369, 381–3
  coconuts 379
  Eucalyptus (from Australia to California)
    384–5
  see also plants; textiles and fibres
Trépied, Benoît, New Caledonia 735
Tripp, Captain Alfred, Hawaiian envoy
    441
Trobriand Islands
  culture of 357–8
  health surveys 495, 502
tropical medicine 491, 493
Truman, Harry, US President, Doctrine 576
Trump, Donald, US President 581
Tucker, Thomas, sealer 331
Tui Atua Tupua Tamasese Ta'isi Efi, His
    Highness 718, 721
Tuilaepa Lupesoliai Sailele Malielegaoi,
    Prime Minister of Sāmoa
    160–1
Tuilovoni, Setereki 364
Tully, Richard, *Birds of Paradise* 271
Tupaia, navigator 70
  map *88*, 91–6
  watercolour drawings 92, 293
Tupou, George *see* George Tupou
Tupou VI, king of Tonga 719
Tuvalu
  and climate migration 774
  independence 606, 685
  see also Ellice Islands
Twain, Mark 582
Tyler, John 564
Tylor, E.B., *Primitive Culture* (1871) 352
Typhoon Treasure 275

Ugarte Román, Marta 552
Ulithi, Caroline Islands 597
Umi no Seimeisen (Lifeline of the Sea),
    Japanese propaganda film (1933) 120
Unalaska Island 379
Underwood, R. 580

UNESCO
  International Council on Archives 193
  and Pacific Islands archives 173–4
Union Steam Ship Company, New Zealand
    520, 523
United Nations
  Climate Change Conference, Paris
    Agreement (2015) 30
  Climate Summit (New York 2014) 26
  Committee on Decolonization 688
  Comprehensive Test Ban Treaty (1996) 629
  Conference on the Human Environment,
    Stockholm (1972) 665
  Convention on Climate Change 580
  Declaration on the Granting of
    Independence to Colonial Countries
    and Peoples (1960) 684
  and 'development' ethos 606
  Development Programme (UNDP) 203
  Human Rights Commission 623
  Intergovernmental Oceanic Commission
    161
  Pacific small island developing states
    group (PSID) 690
  Trust Territory, former Japanese colonies
    605–6, 688
United States of America 563–87
  Agricultural Visa Programs 771
  airlines 650
  American football 771–2
  annexation of Spanish possessions 107, 572
  and China 662
    and Chinese defence strategy 676
    economic interests in 564, 573–4
    post-war relations with 579–81
  and Cold War 564, 578–9, 605
  Compact of Free Association 757
  conflicting views of Pacific 581–7
  container port traffic **645**
  cross-cultural relationships in West 218
  and decolonization 684
  development aid 689
  early interests in Pacific 563–72
  and environmental concerns in Pacific 580
  foreign policy 563
    reduction of overseas obligations 578
    relations with Britain 568, 570
  and geopolitics of Pacific 158–9, 584, 607
  Great Northern Railway 521
  and Hawai'i
    imperial interests in 434, 446–7, 564, 569,
      634
    occupation of 234–7, 270, 521

929

INDEX

United States of America (cont.)
Immigration Law (1924) 575
imperialism
acquisition of territory 571
in Pacific 45, 565, 568, 573
westward expansion 157
and Indonesia 687
and Japan 147, 574–6
and administration of Japanese
Micronesia 114, 605, 688
invasion of Japanese mandated islands
121, 593
and island bases 593, 597
and Japanese attack on Pearl Harbor
and other possessions 120, 589
post-war take over of Japanese empire
123, 604
war with (1942–45) 52, 575, 589
Monroe Doctrine 564
museum collections 288, 294
nuclear contamination remediation 621,
624
nuclear weapon testing 29, 619, 629
and overthrow of Allende of Chile 551–2
and Pacific coast mail service 516
Pacific economy 663
Pacific islander migrants in 756, **758**
and Philippines 447, 564
racism 574, 585
anti-Asian 146, 574
anti-miscegenation laws 218
sociological investigations into race
mixing 225
railroads 517–18, 520, 642
restrictions on immigration 220
and steamship routes 521
and telecommunications 654
trade with Pacific Islands 570
trans-continental railways 660
and trans-Pacific routes to Asia 518
Truman Doctrine (anti-communism) 576
and undersea cables 528–30
preference for wireless over cable
537
and Vietnam war 48
and war dead 609
see also California
United States Exploring Expedition (1838–42)
288, 380, 568
United States National Academy of Sciences,
on Fukushima contamination 633
universities 761, **762**

Aotearoa New Zealand 250, 761
see also Australian National University;
Hawai'i, University of; Sāmoa,
National University of
University of Papua New Guinea 250, 260, 606
University of the South Pacific, Suva, Fiji
250, 761
Up Periscope (film) 281
Urale, Sima, O Tamaiti (film) 281
Uregei, Kotra, New Caledonia 740
Urvoas, Jean Jacques 742
US Navy
and administration of UN Trust Territory
605
Pacific squadron 568
and Pacific War 593
wartime island bases 593, 597
and wireless telegraphy 536
US Trust Territory of the Pacific Islands
(1947) 123, 688
'Uvea, island kingdom 428, 443

Vagana, Leaupepe Nigel, rugby player 772–3
Vahanoa, Open Sea 709
Vaimua Lavelua 429
Van Kirk, S. 229
Vancouver, George 288
at Hawai'i 377
Vancouver, and trans-Pacific routes 521
Vancouver Island, First Nations 151
Vanikoro, Santa Cruz islands 324, 411, 412
Vanuatu (New Hebrides)
and Australian Seasonal Worker
Programme 769
campaign for Niuklia Fri Pasifik 628
independence 367, 686
National Council of Chiefs 693
and NZ Recognised Seasonal
Employment scheme 768
political instability 695
relations with China 673
Vanuatu Cultural Centre 367
Vaquinhas, Major José dos Santos 483, 486
Vargas Llosa, Mario 549
vassalage, Portuguese imperial system of
455–61
abolition (1913) 463
ceremonies of 458, 465–6
and colonial authority 467–8
in east Timor 464–7
and grant of titles and ranks 464
material culture of 466

Index

network of minor vassal kings 455
rites of 457–8
royal gifts 458, 488
treaties of 457, 459, 464
see also flags
Vaughan, Mehana Blaich 241
Veiera Godinho, João Baptista, governor of
Timor 470
Velenga, goddess 713
Vemasse, Timor kingdom 487
Vengeance of the Deep (film) 274
Venn, Henry, missionary 354
Vidor, King, *Bird of Paradise* (film) 275
Vienna, Reishek collection of Māori artefacts
289
Vietnam war 48, 578
*Voelkenkunliche Filmodokumente Aus Der
Sudsee* (film) 271
volcano sacrifice trope 271, 275
Voodoo Island (film) 284
Vouza, Jacob, war hero 610
Vowell, Sarah, *Unfamiliar Fishes* 243

Waddell, E. 86
Waigeo, Papuan islands 407, 417
Waitangi, Treaty of (1840) 441
Waititi, Taika
Boy (film) 282
Hunt for the Wilderpeople (film) 282
What We Do in the Shadows (film) 282
Wake Island
Japanese attack (1942) 120
US annexation 572
Wake Island (film) 276
Wakefield, Edward Gibbon 218
Walker, George Washington 213
Walker, I. 556
Wallace, L. 83
Wallis, Captain Samuel 288
Dolphin voyage 80, 92
Wallis and Futuna
French overseas collectivity 685
Futuna island kingdom 428, 443
women in parliament 697
Wamytan, Roch, New Caledonia 739
Wang, G. 667
Wangxia, Treaty of (1844) 566
Wanli, emperor of China 544
War of 1812 568
War of the Pacific (1879-84) 50–1, 539
Ward, R.G. and Webb, J.W., *The Settlement
of Polynesia* (1973) 86

Wareham, E. 170, 178, 194–5
warfare, modern industrial 48, 61
Warrior, Robert 255
Washington, Booker 142
Washington, DC
National Gallery of Art, 'The Art of the
Pacific Islands' exhibition 291
Smithsonian Institution 289
Washington Consensus 677
Washington State, United States, anti-
miscegenation law 219
water supplies, Marshall Islands 31
Waterhouse, John, missionary 352
Waterworld (film) 281
Weaver, Jace 152
Webber, John 325
Wells, H.G. 276
Wen, Jiabao 674
Wendt, A. 195
The Mango's Kiss 250
'Towards a new Oceania' 246
West, Benjamin, painter 78
West Africa, Portugal and 457, 459
West Papua
constitutional status 704
incorporation within Indonesia 607, 684
resistance to Indonesian rule 686, 688
United Liberation Movement for West
Papua 702
see also New Guinea; Papua New Guinea
Western Pacific High Commission 171
Western Sāmoa
decolonization 684
New Zealand/Aotearoa 492, 606
relations with China 673
restriction of franchise to *matai* class 692,
696
yaws campaign 506
Westney, D.E. 431
Whale Rider (film) 282
whaling 566, 569, 720
and collection of artefacts 288
and interracial marriage 211,
228
and kinship networks 213
multicultural workforce 214
social dimensions 209
see also seal hunting
Wheelwright, William, and Pacific Steam
Navigation Company 515
White Shadows in the South Seas (film)
274

Whitehouse, Alfred, *The Departure of the Second Contingent for the Boer War* (film, 1900) 271
Wilhelm II, German Kaiser 144
Wilkes, Charles, United States Exploring Expedition 288, 568
Williams, E.B. 173
Williams, F.E. 294
Williams, J.
  A Narrative of Missionary Enterprises in the South Sea Islands (1837) 79
Williams, John, US consular agent in Fiji 570
Williams, W.A. 583
Williamson-Balfour Company 559
Wilson, E.O. 387
Wilson, Henry, collection of artefacts 288
Wilson, Pila 237
Wilson, R. 161, 554
wind turbines 721
Wineera, V. 247, 264–5
  'Heritage' 264
  'Walking on Water' 264
Wings over New Guinea (film) 276
wireless telegraphy 532–7, 635
  island stations 536
  and remote islands 533
  state ownership 534
  transmission and relay stations 532, 534, 535
  US Navy transpacific operation 536
  see also cables, undersea
Wohlers, Johannes 214
Womack, Craig 255
women
  Aboriginal Tasmanian 330–2
  agency of Indigenous 207, 213, 331, 500
  American Pacific ports 567
  and archive materials 191, 196–200
  and civil society organisations 203
  and colonial health projects 499–501
  colonial limitations on mobility 502
  and cooperation with health authorities 512
  and domestic space 510
  and domestic violence 698
  and educational opportunities 762
  effect of disease on fertility 341, 343, 346–7
  and extractive industries 210
  as forced labour in South America 153
  and gender relations 206
  Hawaiian 584

as healthcare workers 764
  imperial representations of 82, 567
  and infant mortality 346, 502
  and interracial marriage 211, 214
  limited political participation 696–8
  and making of textiles 303, 307
  regulation of domestic life 500
  role in Christian missions 367–8
  in Samoan plantation economy 203
  as sealers 332–3
  Tahitian 70, 81
  and traditional gender disparity 697
  and US military installations 577
  view of Micronesian in Japanese popular culture 119
  and village committees 500
  wartime employment 598
  see also interracial (cross-cultural) relationships; interracial marriage
women, European
  and education 511
  marriage to Indigenous men 220–1
  as missionary wives 207
  role of 207
Woodd, B.
  Missionary Register 258
  and Mowhee 257, 260
Worethmaleyerpodyer, Aboriginal Tasmanian woman 331
World War I 47, 107, 446
  and extension of wireless telegraphy 271
  and film 271
World Bank, Pacific Possible report 775
World War II in Europe 589
  Allied offensives 594
  coastwatching groups 599
  counter-offensives 595
  Pacific Islanders service in 600
World War II in the Pacific 48, 52, 61, 575, 590
  casualties 122, 590
  Central Pacific zone 593–7
  and collaboration 610
  commemorations and war memorials 608–13
  and democracy 683
  effect on Japanese-occupied islands 121–3
  films 276, 278–9, 281
  Japan and 99, 119–22, 575
  Micronesia 575
  and Pearl Harbor 120
  post-war economy 635
  post-war transport and communications 637–41

Index

and race 576
sexual activity 601
Southwest Pacific zone 590–3
strategy and chronology 588–90
US island bases 593, 597, 602
World Council of Churches 365
World Health Organization, report on
Fukushima 633
World Missionary Conference, Edinburgh
(1910) 354
World Wide Web 653
W.R. Grace and Company, Chinese
indentured workers trade 547

X, Malcolm 142
Xi, Jinping 680–1
and Belt and Road Initiative 662
and marine fisheries 672

Yanagita, K. 98
Yanaihara, Tadao 113
Yang, J. 676
Yankunytjatjara people 618
Yap: How Did You Know We'd Like TV? (film)
280
Yap island, undersea cables 530
Yokohama, container shipping 643
Young, Florence, Evangelical 355
Young, K.G.T, 234
Rethinking the Native Hawaiian Past 235
Young, John L. 289
Yu, C. 675, 680

Zavos, S. 771
Zheng He, voyages of 68
Zheng organization, Qing and 43
Zhou, Enlai 673